American Music Recordings

A DISCOGRAPHY OF
20TH-CENTURY U. S. COMPOSERS

A Project of the Institute for Studies in American Music
for the Koussevitzky Music Foundation, Inc.

CAROL J. OJA, Editor

Foreword by William Schuman

American Music Recordings

A DISCOGRAPHY OF
20TH-CENTURY U. S. COMPOSERS

A Project of the Institute for Studies in American Music
for the Koussevitzky Music Foundation, Inc.

CAROL J. OJA, Editor

Foreword by William Schuman

Institute for Studies in American Music
Conservatory of Music
Brooklyn College
of the City University of New York

Assistant Editor: R. Allen Lott
Researchers: Bruce MacIntyre
                    Terry Pierce
                    Judy Sachinis

Copyright © 1982 by Koussevitzky Music Foundation, Inc.
Library of Congress Catalog Card No. 82-083008
ISBN 0-914678-19-1

Published by Institute for Studies in American Music
Conservatory of Music
Brooklyn College of the City University of New York
Brooklyn, New York 11210

DEDICATION

The Directors of the Koussevitzky Music Foundation, Inc., dedicate
this work to the memory of Olga Koussevitzky, the widow of Dr. Serge
Koussevitzky, the founder of the Foundation. For more than twenty-
five years after his death she was the guiding spirit of the Foundation,
working untiringly to serve the ideals of Dr. Koussevitzky and the
Foundation. Her indomitable devotion and gracious charm were a
symbol and an inspiration to all of us.

Foreword

There are four ways in which a completed composition goes from the privacy of the composer's studio to the ears of his listeners: live performance, broadcast, printed music, and recording. In our contemporary society the most far-reaching and important of these for the public at large is recording. The reasons are many.

When a new work is performed by a symphony orchestra, chamber music group, or any other performing medium, its exposure is limited to those who attend the concert. If the work is broadcast, the potential audience is, of course, vast. But after either the concert performance or the broadcast, the work no longer exists as a living organism until its next performance. This means that in a given city the average contemporary work—even one of proven acceptability—often goes for years without a performance.

The role of printed music, while still very important, has greatly changed in this technological age. Gone are the days when four-hand piano versions of symphonies found their way into the homes of cultivated amateurs. Even if contemporary scores were to be published in this manner, the vocabulary of music and its instrumental investiture have so increased in complexity that such substitute versions would be meaningful only to the most skilled professional. In art music, then, with the exception of songs and simpler instrumental works, printed music is primarily a vehicle for performance by professionals and others who sing in choruses or perform in bands.

Printed music is not to be downgraded; it remains essential in supplying the basic ingredient of performance. But, for the listening public at large, concerned solely with hearing rather than performing, the recording is the thing. Indeed, a contemporary composer cannot really be considered "published" unless his music is recorded. There is ample evidence to show that there are thousands upon thousands of listeners whose entire familiarity with contemporary music (or standard-repertory music, for that matter) comes from listening to records.

If recording is of such primary importance, does it not follow that the composer of recognized attainment should as a matter of course have his music available directly to the public through recordings? This is

logical, but there is an obstacle—one which can be described in a single, non-esoteric term: money.

Recording companies exist to make money. While it is true that, occasionally, enlightened leaders of the industry have believed that part of their profit should be used to promote worthy artistic enterprises of dubious commercial worth, such leadership has always been rare and in the United States today would seem to be virtually non-existent. In this year of 1982, I know of no major commercial recording companies with an ongoing commitment to record serious American music. The few works that do get recorded are the occasional popular successes, or ones that reach the market through subsidy or as a result of some special celebration. The situation is dismal, and recognition of this lies behind the decision to undertake the present discography.

In order to know what we need in the way of recordings of contemporary American music, the Koussevitzky Music Foundation first had to find out what had been recorded in the past and how many of those recordings are still available for purchase. As late as the mid-1930's, there were few recordings of contemporary American music. Over the years, however, as this discography attests, some 13,000 record releases of nearly 8,000 works by 1,300 composers have been issued. Of these releases, 9,000 (8,500 33's and 500 78's) were issued by small commercial firms and by non-profit organizations, often subsidized by the composers themselves. Of these, some 4,300—approximately 47%—are currently extant. The other 4,000 releases (3,000 33's and 1,000 78's) were recorded by major commercial manufacturers (EMI, CBS/Columbia, RCA/Victor, Philips/Mercury, Deutsche Grammophon Gesellschaft) and their subsidiaries. Unfortunately, only 750 of these 4,000 recordings—approximately 18%—are now available. And this points to one of the most serious problems facing recordings of contemporary American music.

Commercial companies do not keep records in their catalogues unless they maintain a specified sales level. Since the measure used is fiscal and not artistic, contemporary American music recordings do not, as a rule, last long in the catalogues. Even subsidy does not guarantee permanence.

There are numerous examples of performances recorded commercially with the aid of contributed money which were nevertheless dropped from catalogues after a year or two. Commercial companies, even after dropping such works, are hesitant (and often immovable) in granting rights to non-profit organizations to re-issue them, even though this in no way subjects the original recording company to financial loss (rather the contrary, since a consideration is usually demanded). To exacerbate the problem further, few stores keep in stock a full range of recordings of contemporary American music. Those who would purchase such records must be determined searchers, not casual shoppers.

Without recordings, the extraordinary development of our native creative musical art remains inaccessible both to present and succeeding generations. The true measure of a nation's achievements in music is not fully to be found in its wonderful performers and institutions of education but in the literature of music created by its own citizens. We have American music in abundance. Some of it is of peripheral value, some of it merely of professional competence; but the best American composers take second place to no other national school.

Unless we can glory in their achievements, we are guilty, as we have been before, of that inverse chauvinism in which we think ourselves somehow inferior to our European cousins. If we do not wish to preserve and disseminate our own art, perhaps we deserve the view, which some have of us, that we are a purely materialistic people. We know that this is not true, yet even for the music of our best composers we set an example of shameful neglect and deny our listeners the opportunity made possible by modern technology.

As an important first step in reversing this unacceptable situation, the Koussevitzky Music Foundation commissioned the Institute for Studies in American Music at Brooklyn College to make the present survey, and it plans to support updating it every few years, so that there may be a historical and continually contemporary assessment of what is and what is not available on recordings. While the survey will not, of course, in itself solve the problem, it will be indispensable in providing a practical gauge to its dimensions and should prove to be a powerful tool in convincing funding sources that commercial interests cannot be relied upon.

William Schuman
Chairman
Koussevitzky Music Foundation

Contents

Introduction

American Music Recordings was compiled by the Institute for Studies in American Music at Brooklyn College under a commission from the Koussevitzky Music Foundation, Inc. It lists over 13,000 commercially distributed recordings of some 8,000 pieces by nearly 1,300 American composers from the generation of Ives and Ruggles to the present. Recordings available as of June 1980 are included, as are 78- and 45-r.p.m. discs and 33's that are out-of-print. No tapes of any sort are listed. As much as possible, the lineage of each recording is traced, from first issues through all re-releases. Performing organizations, conductors, vocalists, and instrumentalists are indexed separately in the final pages.

A discography of twentieth-century American music has long been needed by composers, musicologists, critics, librarians, radio-station personnel, and record manufacturers in the United States and abroad. As early as 1927, when the record industry was still in its infancy, the pioneering discographer Robert Donaldson Darrell had the foresight to realize that "special catalogues" of recorded American works were required before American music could be systematically and thoroughly committed to disc.[1] For nearly thirty years Darrell's plea went unheeded; information about recordings of American music could be located only within general discographies. Then, in 1956, the American Music Center compiled a 39-page, 1,000-entry catalogue of recordings of American music available for purchase in 1956.[2] No 78's or out-of-print 33's were included.

Since then, further efforts have been made. From 1955 to 1957, Sheila Keats published in *The Juilliard Review* a six-part listing of recorded American works, and in 1958 the American Music Center produced a supplement to its catalogue. Other discographies were compiled as a necessary first step in planning a recorded *Denkmäler* of American music. In the early sixties, the American Recordings Project Committee of the Music Library Association, whose members included John Edmunds, H. Wiley Hitchcock, Irving Lowens, and Victor Yellin, completed a card-file discography of American music (unpublished), and, prior to beginning its massive recording project in 1976, New World Records made a similar inventory (also unpublished). Recordings of early American music were

catalogued in I.S.A.M.'s *American Music before 1865 in Print and on Records: A Biblio-Discography,* published in 1976. But recordings of twentieth-century American music, up until now, have remained uncatalogued in any thoroughgoing fashion.

This discography, therefore, takes up where its predecessors left off. Because of the complexity of the recording industry—with its re-issues, simultaneous American and European releases, sporadic deletions, and even more unpredictable reappearances of deleted discs—no work of this sort can claim comprehensiveness. Through the efforts of a hard-working team of researchers and the editing capabilities of the computer system of the City University of New York, we have gathered as much information as possible and have attempted to organize it in a clear-cut and usable fashion.

Contents of the Discography

As stated in its title, this discography is limited to recordings of music by "20th-century U.S. composers." No jazz, folk, or popular music is included. It was often difficult to determine whether a composer spent enough of his career here to be considered "American," and equally difficult to distinguish between "serious" and "popular." Our criteria for making these decisions are outlined below.

Composers born in the United States are, obviously, included. So are naturalized citizens who spent a substantial portion of their careers here. We defined "substantial" as "having arrived in the United States by age thirty," but occasionally this definition was interpreted flexibly on the basis of the proportion of a composer's work that was produced after he immigrated. For example, Percy Grainger, who came here at age thirty-two, and Ernest Bloch, who arrived at thirty-six, are both included since so much of their work was composed in the United States. On the other hand, Stravinsky, Schoenberg, Hindemith, Milhaud, and Bartók—all of whom completed a major portion of their work before they arrived here—are excluded.

Having admitted a foreign-born composer, we list all his recorded works, whether written here or abroad. Thus a recording of two interludes from Ernest Bloch's

Macbeth, composed between 1904 and 1909 before he moved to the United States in 1916, is listed alongside entries for his "American" works. Exception to this policy is made for Percy Grainger: his newly composed pieces are cited, but his numerous folksong settings, most of which are based on English tunes, are not; the latter seem irrelevant to a discography of American music.

As regards chronological boundaries, composers born in the 1870s and thereafter are included. Occasionally the limit is stretched back to encompass slightly older persons whose work was largely produced in the twentieth century (e.g. Arthur Foote, born in 1853, and Horatio Parker, born in 1863). Again, if a composer is listed in the discography, all of his recorded pieces are included, even those written before 1900.

In determining which compositions to include, we tried to draw a line between "serious" music and pop, jazz, and folk music, fuzzy though the distinctions may be. The work of a few composers whose total output was judged as "concert pop" was ruled out (e.g. Leroy Anderson); for others, only their "serious" work was included (e.g. Leonard Bernstein, George Gershwin, Morton Gould, and Scott Joplin). With a work like *West Side Story,* recordings of the complete musical or of vocal excerpts from it are not listed, but the concert arrangement of its "Symphonic Dances" is. Film scores are excluded, but suites derived from them are included (e.g. Copland's *Red Pony Suite* and Virgil Thomson's suite from *The Plow That Broke the Plains*). Some composers—especially of church music, band marches, and turn-of-the-century salon pieces—are admitted whose works stubbornly evade clear-cut classification (e.g. Frederick Bigelow, Ernest Charles, and Walter Damrosch).

The information about recordings presented here was mostly gleaned from published record listings, a bibliography of which is appended to this introduction. If there were discrepancies between our sources, we consulted the recordings themselves (when we were able to locate copies). For 33 r.p.m. recordings, we began with the *National Union Catalogue, Music and Phonorecords* (first published in 1953) and, after combing its nineteen volumes, moved on to Kurtz Myers's *Index to Record Reviews: 1949-1977* (and his post-1977 listings in *Notes*); to *Schwann Catalogs* (published monthly since 1949); and to numerous composer, special-subject, and label discographies. For 78's, Julian Moses's *Collector's Guide to American Recordings (1895-1925), The Gramophone Shop Encyclopedia* (1936, 1942, and 1948 editions), David Hall's *The Record Book* (1946, 1948, and 1950 editions), and Clough and Cuming's *The World's Encyclopedia of Recorded Music* (published, with supplements, from

1950 to 1957) provided the nucleus of the material. Time limitations made it impossible for us to search out foreign releases other than those cited in our core sources; we were unable to consult foreign union and manufacturer's catalogues.

For Charles Ives, only recordings released after 1972, when Richard Warren's superb Ives discography was published, are listed.

User's Guide

The discography is organized systematically on several levels: alphabetically by composer; within each composer, alphabetically by title of piece; within each piece, alphabetically by the first performer's name in the entry; and within each performance group, chronologically by date of record issue (with 78's listed before 33's). Punctuation is used only to separate categories of information (seldom to terminate abbreviations). For ease in alphabetization, titles of pieces have been standardized as much as possible, and all composers' and performers' names have been listed with surname first. Entries are numbered consecutively at the performer level; those numbers are used as reference points in the page headings and as index indicators. Unfortunately, our computer system did not allow us to insert foreign accents in the text. Most umlauts have been indicated by placing an "e" after the umlauted vowel; no other accents appear.

The format model on page xiii is explained in detail below.

(1) Composer. Each composer's dates (if known) are given in parentheses after his name.

One of our biggest problems was determining nationality and date of birth for lesser-known figures. Where composers whom we believed to be American were not included in standard published reference sources (*The New Grove, Baker's Biographical Dictionary,* E. Ruth Anderson's *Contemporary American Composers: A Biographical Dictionary,* and the *ASCAP Biographical Dictionary*), we turned to the files of the American Music Center and of the Copyright Office for verification; those in the latter were especially helpful. Although the Copyright Office yielded few birth dates (only since 1978 does a copyright application form request the registrant's birth date), its files do indicate in what country the composer was living when he registered his work. Some names, however, did not even turn up there. In the discography, all composers whose American citizenship is in question have been keyed with an asterisk(*).

(2) Title of Piece. This portion of the entry includes the title of the work (together with an indication of

(1) **CARPENTER,** John Alden (1876-1951)

(2)   Adventures in a Perambulator (1914)

(3)   Minneapolis Symphony Orchestra; Ormandy, Eugene (cond)

    - Victor 8455-58 (in set M-238); 78; 4 discs; rel pre-1936

      (5a)   *(5b)*   *(5c)*   *(5d)*   *(5e)*

    - Victor 11-9231 (in set M-1063); 78; rel pre-1948 (excerpt: No 3, Hurdy Gurdy)

      (5a)   *(5b)*   *(5c)*   *(5e)*

(1) **COPLAND,** Aaron (1900-)

(2)   (Twelve) Poems of Emily Dickinson (1949-50)

(3)   Addison, Adele (sop); Copland, Aaron (pf)

(4)   Rec 11/18/64

    - CBS 32-11-0017/32-11-0018; 33m/s; rel 1967; del 1970

      (5a)   *(5b)*   *(5c)*   *(5e)*   *(5f)*

    - Columbia M-30375; 33s; rel 1970; cip

      (5a)   *(5b)*   *(5c)*   *(5e)*   *(5f)*

---

whether it is an arrangement or excerpt), the date of composition, and the opus number (if any).

Works with a generic title such as Sonata, Concerto, or Symphony are assigned standardized titles according to the Library of Congress cataloguing rules. Articles are dropped to the end of all titles, and numbers given as the first word (e.g. "Five Songs" or "Ten Poems") are placed in parentheses; the word immediately following the number is the one under which the title is alphabetized. In those few instances where the number is an integral part of the title (e.g. Steve Reich's "Four Organs"), the title is alphabetized under the number.

Often a single composition appears in this discography in several different forms—excerpts, arrangements, or alternate versions—besides the complete original. In such cases, the entries are organized with the complete work first, followed by any suite drawn from the complete work (or an abridged form of the work), individual movements from the work (with groups of multiple movements first and, descending in order of quantity, single movements last), and arrangements of the work (with those by the composer first, those by someone else following). Punctuation is used to distinguish which form or portion of the composition is being dealt with: the title of the complete work always comes first; excerpts follow a colon after the complete title; subtitles and information about arrangements are given in parentheses. Multiple movements or excerpts from larger works are cited in the order in which they appear in the complete work. If that order is not known to us or if it might make the discography difficult to use (as in the many excerpts from *Porgy and Bess,* which have been arranged for everything

from harp to harmonica), we group the excerpts alphabetically.

An example of our organizational scheme, as applied to Copland's *Billy the Kid,* is shown below:

Billy the Kid	[complete ballet score]
Billy the Kid (Suite)	[orchestral suite derived from the ballet score]
Billy the Kid: Prairie Night and Celebration	[excerpts]
Billy the Kid: Waltz	[excerpt]
Billy the Kid: Celebration, Billy's Death, and The Open Prairie Again (arr for 2 pfs by Arthur Whittemore and Jack Lowe)	[arrangement of several movements]
Billy the Kid: The Open Prairie (arr for pf by Lukas Foss)	[arrangement of one movement]

Where excerpts were issued separately but drawn from recordings of the complete work, they are grouped together with their parent releases under the performer's name. For example, an excerpt from the National Symphony Orchestra's performance of *Billy the Kid* is placed together with the orchestra's releases of the complete ballet suite. (For another example see the John Alden Carpenter entry given above as a format model.)

To the extent possible, dates of composition and opus numbers follow work titles in parentheses. These were culled from several sources, listed here in the order in which they were consulted and relied upon (meaning that if the date of a work was not contained in the first source, we went to the second, and so on): a *catalogue raisonné* of a composer's works (a list of those consulted is appended to this introduction), *The New Grove, Baker's Biographical Dictionary,* and E. Ruth Anderson's *Contemporary American Composers.* If the date of a piece did not appear in any of those sources, but did in a discography from which we obtained information about a recording, we used the date as given in the discography.

Although dates and opus numbers were seldom problematic, a few cases demanded special treatment. For Alan Hovhaness's works, many of which have been assigned two opus numbers, the numbers from his second opus ordering are cited. For Percy Grainger, many of whose works were begun, set aside, and not completed for as long as twenty years, the date in which a piece was begun is separated by a comma from the date in which it was completed. For Victor Herbert, whose works are mostly given publication dates, not dates of composition, in the catalogue by Edward Waters, dates are prefaced with "publ" in the discography.

Where an excerpt from a large work is cited, the composition date of the entire work precedes the colon (and the excerpt title). If a date is given after the excerpt title it refers to the date of composition of that particular section of the work, not of the entire piece (see, for example, the entries for some of Samuel Barber's songs).

(3) Performers. The names of all performing units, whether multi-membered organizations or individual persons, are separated by semi-colons. Abbreviations for instruments and voices appear in parentheses immediately after the performers' names. Most abbreviations are modeled on those used in the *BMI Symphonic Catalogue* (see the list appended to this introduction). If we were unable to determine the scoring of a piece, we list the performers' names alone. Works based entirely on electronically generated sound, no matter what type it is, are identified as "electronic music."

Pick-up orchestras, listed under conflicting names either in our sources or in different releases of the same performance, are consolidated as much as possible. For example, the many "Victor" orchestras—Victor Orchestra, Victor Salon Group, et al.—are subsumed under "Victor Orchestra," except for "Victor Symphony Orchestra," which is a special and distinct group. Also, the "American Recording Society Orchestra," which takes its name from the label on which it recorded, is most frequently cited in our sources as the "Vienna Symphony Orchestra," and we use that name.

All record issues of a work performed by a particular group or person(s) are placed together, unless specific, differing recording dates indicated that they should be separated.

(4) Recording Date. If known, the date of the recording session is given. It was impossible for us to consult record-company archives to determine recording dates; all those cited were drawn from secondary sources.

(5) Record Issues. Each line preceded by a hyphen describes one record issue and contains as much of the following information as we could determine: (a) record-company name, (b) disc number, (c) speed, plus mono or stereo indications, (d) number of discs and/or size of discs, (e) release date, and (f) deletion date. Following are details of each:

(5a) Record-Company Name. As much as possible, we have standardized company names. The versions most often employed are those used by Kurtz Myers in his *Index to Record Reviews.* In some special cases, outlined below, we have followed the advice of David Hall, Curator of the Rodgers and Hammerstein Archives of Recorded Sound of the New York Public Library.

- "Victor" is used for 78's and 45's produced by the company of that name.
- "RCA" (*not* "RCA Victor") is used for 33's.
- "RCA-Erato," "RCA-Italiana," and "RCA-Victrola" are occasionally given as subdivisions of "RCA."
- "Gramophone" is used for 78's issued by the company of that name, as well as for those issued as "His Master's Voice."

For several companies, we do not write out the manufacturer's name, since its acronym forms all record prefixes:

CRI = Composers Recordings, Inc.
LOU = Louisville Orchestra First Edition Records (LS is used for Louisville's stereo issues)
SPA = Society of Participating Artists
SPAMH = Society for the Preservation of the American Musical Heritage

(5b) Disc Number. In most instances, the letter prefix is joined to the record number by a hyphen (e.g. MS-6249). If a disc was issued in both mono and stereo, whether simultaneously or in different years, the record number for each version is cited, and the two are separated from one another by a slash, with the mono number first and the stereo number second. For discs that are part of larger sets (which occurs most frequently with 78's), the individual record number is followed in parentheses by the number of the album (or set) in which it is included. Matrix numbers have not been cited unless they were the only numbers we could locate for a recording.

Again, a few special cases need comment. New Music Quarterly Recordings went through two numbering systems; when known, both numbers are given here. For Yaddo Records, we worked from two lists, one compiled by Rudy Shackelford and the other given to us by Otto Luening. Although frequently the lists concurred, there are many discrepancies between them; all record numbers from those lists are cited here.[3]

(5c) Speed. Record speed, in revolutions per minute, is abbreviated as "78," "45," and "33." Immediately following "33," a designation of monaural ("m"), stereophonic ("s"), or quadraphonic ("q") is given. Mono-stereo couplings are cited as "m/s"; stereo-quad as "s/q." Where our sources were unclear as to whether a disc was mono, stereo, or quad, we simply list it as "33."

(5d) Number of Discs and Size. The number of discs has been given for record numbers encompassing two, three, or more discs. For 78's, the number of sides is cited in those instances where a work takes up 3, 5, or some other odd-numbered total of sides.

Size is given only for discs that are not 12 inches in diameter (i.e. 7 or 10 inches). If the entry includes more than one disc of less than twelve inches, the number of discs is joined to the size with a hyphen (for example, 2-10"); otherwise size is given alone.

(5e) Release Date. Dates plainly stated—without asterisks, question marks, or other qualifiers—give a fixed year of release. For the most part, these dates have been derived from *Schwann Catalogs,* where the year in which the record was first listed has been interpreted by us as the date of commercial release. *Schwann* dates are easily identifiable in this discography because they are always followed by deletion dates. If a record never appeared in *Schwann,* release dates have been culled from the *National Union Catalogue* (which frequently cites the year, taken to be the one of release, given on the record jacket) or from a date fixed by a previous researcher in one of the special-subject discographies we consulted.

Release dates for records issued in both mono and stereo are presented in several ways:

1) If both the mono and stereo versions came out in the same year, one release date is cited (e.g. Mercury MG-50420/SR-9042; 33m/s; rel 1954)

2) If mono and stereo came out in different years, both dates of release are given, separated by a slash (e.g. Golden Crest CR-4065/CRS-4065; 33m/s; rel 1963/1966)

3) If mono and stereo came out in different years but only the release date of the mono version is known, that date is cited, followed by a slash and a question mark to indicate that the stereo release date is unknown (e.g. CRI-191/CRI-SD-101; 33m/s; rel 1956/?)

If there is some question about a release date, several means are used to indicate that it is approximate or uncertain. Dates followed by an asterisk (*) are based on the date of the first review of a recording, as cited in Myers's *Index to Record Reviews.* (We allowed for a three-month lag between release and review, meaning that a review in March pushed our presumptive release date back to the previous year.) Dates preceded by "pre-" (most often appearing with 78's) indicate that the record was released during or prior to the year cited; such dates are based on the year in which the earliest source for information about the recording was published. Therefore, undated records listed in the first edition of *The Gramophone Shop Encyclopedia* (1936) are cited as "pre-1936"; those in the second edition of David Hall's *Record Book* (1948) as "pre-1948"; etc.

In a few instances, no release date is given because none was located in any of our sources. In still fewer instances, a release date is preceded by "after," meaning that the disc is a re-issue of a recording first pressed in the year specified.

(5f) Deletion Dates. Deletion dates are all based on the listings in *Schwann Catalogs* and indicate the first year in which a disc ceased to be cited there. Having computerized the discography, we were able to devise, for editing purposes, an alphanumeric index to record companies and numbers, through which we could go one step beyond *Schwann* and collate discs containing works by several different composers, making sure their release and deletion dates corresponded.

If an entry includes no deletion date, the record was not listed in *Schwann.* Recordings available in June 1980 are labeled "cip," meaning "currently in print." For mono-stereo couplings, no attempt was made to trace the deletion date of each member of a pair; rather, the year in which the longer survivor dropped from circulation is given. No deletion dates are cited for 78's or New World Records.

[1]Robert Donaldson Darrell, "A Glance at Recorded American Music," *The Music Lover's Phonograph Monthly Review* I/12 (September 1927), 495.

[2]Complete information on this and other publications cited here is given in the bibliography.

[3]Otto Luening (in a letter to me, dated 27 June 1980) has stated that no determination has yet been made as to which records included in his lists of Yaddo releases were actually pressed. For more information about the Yaddo Festivals in general, see Rudy Shackelford, "The Yaddo Festivals of American Music, 1932-1952," *Perspectives of New Music* XVII/1 (Fall-Winter, 1978), 92-125.

ACKNOWLEDGEMENTS

Research on *American Music Recordings* was begun in June 1980, and the finished book was sent to press in the spring of 1982. That this massive project could be conquered in such a short time is testimony to the extraordinary efforts of a team of researchers, typists, and computer programmers, all working under the direction of the undersigned, with guidance from H. Wiley Hitchcock. R. Allen Lott, as Assistant Editor, was incredibly meticulous in verifying record numbers, tracking down spurious entries, and general editing. He and Judy Sachinis completed the majority of the research on 33's and did most of the computer inputting. Bruce MacIntyre compiled our list of 78's; Terry Pierce assisted in the research on 33's; and Katherine Preston located composers' dates and verified their citizenship. Kathleen Mason Krotman, Nancy Pardo, and Frances Solomon, all of the regular I.S.A.M. staff, helped in typing cards, filing, entering information into the computer, and proofreading. And finally, student aides David Leibowitz, Theresa Muir, and Paul Schubert assisted in both research and clerical work.

We used a packaged computer output system called "Script" to format the discography in draft form. Type for this volume was set directly from our computer tapes by Ralph Garner Associates. Philip Drummond, programmer for *RILM Abstracts,* served as computer consultant and trouble-shooter throughout the project. The CUNY Computer Facility, through its Brooklyn College Liaison Officer Julio Berger, generously supplied us with computer time and technical advice.

Our task could never have been achieved without the aid—both through direct consultation and published record lists—of the discographers cited in our bibliography. We are indebted to each of them and to all of the consultants listed below.

Finally, special thanks for help, from each in different ways, to David Hall and to Arthur Cohn, William Curtis, Ellis J. Freedman, and William Schuman.

Carol J. Oja
May 1982

CONSULTANTS AND ADVISERS

Diette Baily, Music Librarian, Brooklyn College

Julio Berger, Director of Liaison Office, Brooklyn College Computer Facility

Arthur Cohn, Director of Serious Music, Carl Fischer, Inc.

William Curtis, discographer

Peter Dickinson, University of Keele

Charles Dodge, Brooklyn College

Philip Drummond, computer programmer for *RILM Abstracts*

Gerald Gibson, Head, Curatorial Section MBRS Division, Library of Congress

Michael Gray, Editor of *ARSC Journal* and Music Librarian at Voice of America

David Hall, Curator, Rodgers and Hammerstein Archives of Recorded Sound, New York Public Library

Ruth Henderson, Music Librarian, City College

Ruth Hilton, Music Librarian, New York University

Mary Hoos, Librarian, The Electronic Music Center of Columbia and Princeton Universities

David Horn, University of Exeter

Dorothy Klotzman, Chairperson, Conservatory of Music, Brooklyn College

Otto Luening, composer

Sherrill McConnell, Librarian, University of Louisville Archives and Record Center

Rita H. Mead, former Research Associate, I.S.A.M.

Karl F. Miller, University of Arizona

Rudy Shackelford, composer and discographer

Robert Skinner, Southern Methodist University

Dan Stehman, Executive Secretary, The Roy Harris Archive

David Walker, composer

Richard Warren, Jr., Director, Yale Record Archives

J. F. Weber, discographer

GENERAL ABBREVIATIONS

arr	arranged	q	quadraphonic
ca	circa	rel	released
cip	currently in print	rev	revised
del	deleted	s	stereophonic
m	monophonic	vol	volume
no	number	*	nationality in question
op	opus		(after a composer's name)
orchd	orchestrated		*or* date is based on a review
publ	published		(after a release date)

INSTRUMENT AND PERFORMER ABBREVIATIONS

al	alto	kbd	keyboard
acc	accordion	mand	mandolin
amplf	amplified	mrmb	marimba
b	bass	m sop	mezzo soprano
bar	baritone	nar	narrator
bcl	bass clarinet	ob	oboe
bsn	bassoon	opt	optional
bsst hn	basset horn	orch	orchestra
car	carillon	org	organ
cb	contrabass	perc	percussion
cbcl	contra bass clarinet	pic	piccolo
cbsn	contra bassoon	pf	piano
cel	celesta	qnt	quintet
cemb	cembalo	qtt	quartet
ch	chimes (bells)	rec	recorder
cimb	cimbalom	sax	saxophone
cl	clarinet	sn dr	snare drum
clav	clavichord	sop	soprano
cond	conductor	srsphn	sarrusophone
cor	cornet	str	strings
ct	contratenor	str orch	string orchestra
cym	cymbal	tbn	trombone
dr	drum	ten	tenor
E hn	English horn	timp	timpani
elec	electric	tpt	trumpet
euph	euphonium	trg	triangle
fl	flute	tu	tuba
flhn	flugelhorn	vcl	violoncello
glock	glockenspiel	vib	vibraphone
gtr	guitar	vla	viola
harm	harmonium	vln	violin
hn	horn	ww	woodwinds
hp	harp	xyl	xylophone
hpschd	harpsichord		

Bibliography

General Discographies

Clough, Francis F., and G. J. Cuming. *The World's Encyclopedia of Recorded Music.* London: Sidgwick and Jackson, 1950. First supplement, 1951. Second supplement, 1953. Third supplement, 1957.

Gramophone Shop, Inc., New York. *The Gramophone Shop Encyclopedia of Recorded Music.* New York: The Gramophone Shop, Inc., 1936. Second edition, 1942. Third edition, 1948.

Hall, David. *The Record Book, A Music Lover's Guide to the World of the Phonograph.* New York: Smith and Durrell, 1946.

_____. *The Record Book.* International Edition. New York: Durrell, 1948.

_____. *Records: 1950 Edition.* New York: Knopf, 1950.

Moses, Julian. *Collector's Guide to American Recordings, 1895-1925,* foreword by Giuseppe de Luca. New York: American Record Collectors' Exchange, 1949.

Myers, Kurtz. *Index to Record Reviews: 1949-77,* 5 vols. Boston: G. K. Hall, 1978.

Schwann Long Playing Record Catalog. Boston: W. Schwann, Inc., 1949- .

U. S. Library of Congress. *Library of Congress National Union Catalogue, Music and Phonorecords,* 19 vols. to date. Washington, DC: The Library of Congress, 1953- .

Special-Subject Discographies

American Music on Records: A Catalogue of Recorded American Music. New York: American Music Center, 1956. Supplement, 1958.

Anderson, Donna K. *Charles T. Griffes: An Annotated Bibliography-Discography.* Bibliographies in American Music No. 3. Detroit: Information Coordinators, 1977.

Berger, Arthur. *Aaron Copland.* New York: Oxford University Press, 1953. [Discography, pp. 107-112.]

_____. "An Aaron Copland Discography," *High Fidelity* V (July 1955), 64-69.

Cipolla, Wilma Reid. *A Catalogue of the Works of Arthur Foote (1853-1937).* Bibliographies in American Music No. 6. Detroit: Information Coordinators, 1980.

Cohn, Arthur. *The Collector's Twentieth-Century Music in the Western Hemisphere.* Philadelphia and New York: J. B. Lippincott, 1961.

Columbia-Princeton Electronic Music Center. "Electronic Music Discography." Typescript, 1979. Supplement, 1981.

Curtis, William D. "A Piston Discography," *American Record Guide* (June 1977), pp. 38-40.

_____. "Carl Ruggles (1876-1971)—A Comprehensive Discography," *Fanfare* IV/1 (September/October 1980), pp. 191-93.

_____. "Roy Harris." Typescript, 1980.

Darrell, Robert Donaldson. "A Glance at Recorded American Music," *The Music Lover's Phonograph Monthly Review* I/10 (July 1927), pp. 410-13; I/11 (August 1927), pp. 450-53; I/12 (September 1927), pp. 495-99.

De Lerma, Dominique-René. *Concert Music and Spirituals: A Selective Discography.* Black Music Research, Occasional Papers No. 1. Nashville: Fisk University Institute for Research in Black American Music, 1981.

Hall, David. "CRI: A Sonic Showcase for the American Composer," *Library Journal* LXXXVII (1 May 1963), pp. 1826-29.

_____. "CRI: A Sonic Showcase for the American Composer [reprint with revisions]," *American Composers Alliance Bulletin* XI/2-4 (1963), pp. 21-29.

Hamilton, David. "Aaron Copland: A Discography of the Composer's Performances," *Perspectives of New Music* IX/1 (1970), pp. 149-54.

_____. "The Recordings of Copland's Music," *High Fidelity/Musical America* XX (November 1970), pp. 64-66.

Howard, John Tasker. *Our Contemporary Composers: American Music in the Twentieth Century.* New York: Crowell, 1941; reprint, New York: Books for Libraries Press, 1975.

Jablonski, Edward and Lawrence D. Stewart. *The Gershwin Years,* rev. ed. Garden City: Doubleday, 1973. [Discography, pp. 359-387.]

Keats, Sheila. "American Music on LP Records—An Index," *The Juilliard Review* (Winter 1955), pp. 24-33; (Spring 1955), pp. 31-43; (Fall 1955), pp. 48-51. Supplement: (Fall 1956), pp. 17-20; (Winter 1956/57), pp. 33-39; (Fall 1957), pp. 36-40.

Letherer, Gary Paul. "Complete Discography of Ernest Bloch," in *Ernest Bloch Creative Spirit, A Source Book,* by Suzanne Bloch. New York: Jewish Music Council of the National Jewish Welfare Board, 1976, pp. 107-16.

Mead, Rita H. *Henry Cowell's New Music 1925-1936: The Society, the Music Editions, and the Recordings.* Ann Arbor, MI: UMI Research Press, 1981.

"Recordings of Music by Aaron Copland." Typescript in the possession of the composer.

Rouse, Christopher. *William Schuman Documentary: Biographical Essay, Catalogue of Works, Discography, and Bibliography.* New York: Theodore Presser, 1980.

Rowell, Lois. *American Organ Music on Records.* Braintree, MA: The Organ Literature Foundation, 1976.

Schwartz, Charles. *George Gershwin.* Bibliographies in American Music No. 1. Detroit: Information Coordinators, 1974.

Shackelford, Rudy. "Gordon Binkerd: Discography." Typescript, [1980].

_____. "The Yaddo Music Periods: A Catalogue of Recordings." Typescript, [1980].

Shepard, John. "An Elliott Carter Discography," in *The Music of Elliott Carter,* by David Schiff. [To be published by Eulenburg Books, London, in 1982.]

Skinner, Robert. "A Randall Thompson Discography." Typescript, 1980.

Stehman, Dan. "The Music of Roy Harris on Records: Now Available." Typescript, 1980.

Warren, Richard. *Charles E. Ives: Discography.* New Haven: Yale University Library, Historical Sound Recordings, 1972.

Weber, J. F. *Carter and Schuman.* Discography Series, XIX. Utica, NY: J. F. Weber, 1978.

_____. *Edgard Varèse.* Discography Series, XII. Utica, NY: J. F. Weber, 1975.

_____. *Leonard Bernstein,* 2nd corrected printing. Discography Series, XIII. Utica, NY: J. F. Weber, 1975.

Articles from "The Great American Composer Series" in *Hi Fi/Stereo Review:*

—"Aaron Copland: Recommended Recordings" (June 1966).

—"Babbitt on Records" (April 1969).

—"Edgard Varèse—A Discography" (June 1971).

—Goodfriend, James. "Cage on Disc" (May 1969).

—_____. "Riegger Recorded" (April 1968).

—Hall, David, "Roy Harris: The Music on Records" (December 1968).

—_____. "A Thomson Discography" (May 1965).

—"Howard Hanson on Records" (June 1968).

—Jablonski, Edward. "George Gershwin: A Selective Discography" (May 1967).

—"The Music of Cowell: A Selective Discography" (December 1974).

—Roy, Klaus George. "The Music of Walter Piston on Records" (April 1970).

—"Ruggles on Disc" (September 1966).

—Salzman, Eric, and James Goodfriend. "Samuel Barber: A Selective Discography" (October 1966).

—Trimble, Lester. "A Carter Discography" (December 1972).

Catalogues of Composers' Works

Anderson, Donna K. *The Works of Charles T. Griffes: A Descriptive Catalogue.* Ph.D. dissertation, Indiana University, 1966.

Berger, Arthur. *Aaron Copland.* New York: Oxford University Press, 1953.

Cipolla, Wilma Reid. *A Catalogue of the Works of Arthur Foote (1853-1937).* Bibliographies in American Music No. 6. Detroit: Information Coordinators, 1980.

Godwin, Joscelyn. *The Music of Henry Cowell.* Ph.D. dissertation, Cornell University, 1969.

Kostelanetz, Richard, ed. *John Cage.* New York: Praeger, 1970.

Rouse, Christopher. *William Schuman Documentary: Biographical Essay, Catalogue of Works, Discography, and Bibliography.* New York: Theodore Presser, 1980.

Waters, Edward N. *Victor Herbert: A Life in Music.* New York: Macmillan, 1955; reprint, New York: Da Capo, 1978.

General Sources

Anderson, E. Ruth. *Contemporary American Composers: A Biographical Dictionary.* Boston: G. K. Hall, 1976.

Bibliography

ASCAP Biographical Dictionary, 4th edition. New
  York: R. R. Bowker, 1981.

Baker's Biographical Dictionary of Music and Musicians,
  6th edition, rev. Nicolas Slonimsky. New York:
  Schirmer, 1978.

The New Grove Dictionary of Music and Musicians,
  ed. Stanley Sadie, 20 vols. London: Macmillan,
  1980.

DISCOGRAPHY

ABRAMSON, Robert (1928-)

Countess Kathleen, The (1957)
[1]   harp
        - Tradition TLP-501; 33m; rel
        1957; del 1968

Dance Variations (1965)
[2]   Abramson, Robert (pf); Rome
        Symphony Orchestra; Flagello,
        Nicolas (cond)
        - Serenus SRE-1014/SRS-12014;
        33m/s; rel 1966; cip

ADAM, Claus (1917-)

Concerto, Violoncello and Orchestra (1973)
[3]   Kates, Stephen (vcl); Louisville
        Orchestra; Mester, Jorge (cond)
        Rec 2/20/75
        - LS-74-5; 33s (Louisville
        Orchestra First Edition Records
        1974 No 5); rel 1975; cip

ADAMS, Alton A. (1889-)

Governor's Own, The
[4]   Goldman Band; Goldman, Richard
        Franko (cond)
        - New World NW-266; 33s; rel
        1977

ADLER, Samuel (1928-)

Canto IV
[5]   Delibero, Phil (sax)
        - Open Loop 1; 33s; rel 197?

Canto VIII
[6]   Gowen, Bradford (pf)
        - New World NW-304; 33s; rel
        1979

Capriccio
[7]   Helps, Robert (pf)
        - RCA LM-7042/LSC-7042;
        33m/s; 2 discs; rel 1966; del
        1971
        - CRI-288; 33s; 2 discs; rel 1972;
        cip

(Four) Concert Etudes for Bass Trombone: Canto II
[8]   Knaub, Donald (b tbn); Snyder,
        Barry (pf)
        - Golden Crest RE-7040; 33s; rel
        1971; cip

(Four) Dialogues (1974)
[9]   Bowman, Brian (euph); Stout,
        Gordon (mrmb)
        - Crystal S-393; 33s; rel 1978; cip

Kiss, A
[10]   King Chorale; King, Gordon (cond)
        - Orion ORS-75205; 33s; rel
        1978; cip

Mo'os tzur (Blessings for Chanukah)
[11]   Peerce, Jan (ten)
        - Vanguard VSD-79237; 33s; rel
        1967; del 1977

Quartet, Strings, No 4 (1963)
[12]   Pro Arte Quartet
        - Lyrichord LL-203/LLST-7203;
        33m/s; rel 1968; cip

Quartet, Strings, No 6 (A Whitman Serenade) (1975)
[13]   DeGaetani, Jan (m sop); Fine Arts
        Quartet
        - CRI-432; 33s; rel 1980; cip

Recitative
[14]   Noehren, Robert (org)
        - Lyrichord LL-191/LLST-7191;
        33m/s; rel 1968; cip

Sonata, Horn and Piano (1948)
[15]   Schaberg, Roy (hn); Ozanich, Lois
        (pf)
        - Coronet LPS-3039; 33s; rel
        1977; cip

Sonata breve (1963)
[16]   Gowen, Bradford (pf)
        - New World NW-304; 33s; rel
        1979

Southwestern Sketches (1961)
[17]   Cornell University Wind Ensemble;
        Stith, Marice (cond)
        - Cornell CUWE-8; 33s; rel 1971;
        cip

Strings in the Earth
[18]   King Chorale; King, Gordon (cond)
        - Orion ORS-75205; 33s; rel
        1978; cip

(Five) Vignettes (1968)
[19]   Eastman Trombone Choir
        - Mark 50500; 33s; rel 1972; del
        1975

Xenia (A Dialogue for Organ and Percussion)
[20]   Craighead, David (org)
        - Crystal S-858; 33s; rel 1977; cip

ADOLPHUS, Milton (1913-)

Elegy (1936-37)
[21]   Kiecki, H. (cl); Polish National
        Radio Orchestra; Ormicki,
        Wlodzimiertz (cond)
        - CRI-228; 33s; rel 1968; cip

AHLSTROM, David (1927-)

Scherzo for Solo Cup-Muted Trumpet, Winds, and Percussion
[22]   Logan, Jack (tpt)
        - Orion ORS-7294; 33s; rel 1972;
        cip

Sonata, Piano, No 2
[23]   Snyder, Ellsworth (pf)
        - Advance FGR-21S; 33s; rel 197?

AHROLD, Frank (1931-)

(Three) Poems of Sylvia Plath
[24]   Curry, Corrine (m sop); London
        Symphony Orchestra (members
        of); Farberman, Harold (cond)
        - CRI-380; 33s; rel 1978; cip

Second Coming
[25]   Langridge, Philip (ten); London
        Symphony Orchestra; Farberman,
        Harold (cond)
        Rec 1/21/75
        - CRI-389; 33s; rel 1978; cip

Song without Words
[26]   London Symphony Orchestra;
        Farberman, Harold (cond)
        Rec 1/21/75
        - CRI-389; 33s; rel 1978; cip

AIN, Noa (formerly known as Susan Ain)

Used to Call Me Sadness (A Portrait of Yoko Matsuda)
[27]   Matsuda, Yoko (vln); tape
        - Folkways FTS-33904; 33s; rel
        1976; cip

AITKEN, Hugh (1924-)

Cantata No 1 (on Elizabethan texts) (1958)
[28]   Bressler, Charles (ten); New York
        Chamber Soloists
        - CRI-365; 33s; rel 1977; cip

Cantata No 3 (From this White Island) (1960)
[29]   Bressler, Charles (ten); New York
        Chamber Soloists
        - CRI-365; 33s; rel 1977; cip

Cantata No 4 (on poems by Antonio Machado) (1961)
[30]   Hakes, Jean (sop); New York
        Chamber Soloists
        - CRI-365; 33s; rel 1977; cip

Fantasy, Piano (1967)
[31]   Kirkpatrick, Gary (pf)
        - CRI-365; 33s; rel 1977; cip

Montages
[32]   Grossman, Arthur (bsn)
        - Crystal S-351; 33s; rel 1975; cip

Suite, Contrabass
[33]   Peters, Lynn (cb)
        - Ubres SN-202; 33s; rel 1976;
        cip

ALBERT, Stephen (1941-)
To Wake the Dead
[34]　Allen, Sheila Marie (sop); Pro
　　　Musica Moderna; Fussell, Charles
　　　(cond)
　　　- CRI-420; 33s; rel 1980; cip

ALBRIGHT, William (1944-)
Grand Sonata in Rag (1968)
[35]　Mandel, Alan (pf)
　　　- Grenadilla GS-1020; 33s; rel
　　　1978; cip

Juba (1965)
[36]　Albright, William (org)
　　　- CRI-277; 33s; rel 1972; cip

Organbook I (1967)
[37]　Albright, William (org)
　　　- CRI-277; 33s; rel 1972; cip

Organbook II (1971)
[38]　Albright, William (org); tape
　　　- Nonesuch H-71260; 33s; rel
　　　1971; cip

Pianoagogo (1965-66)
[39]　Sanders, Dean (pf)
　　　- Trilogy CTS-1003; 33s; rel
　　　1973; del 1975

Pneuma (l966)
[40]　Mason, Marilyn (org)
　　　- CRI-277; 33s; rel 1972; cip

Take That (1972)
[41]　Blackearth Percussion Group
　　　Rec 5/27-28/74
　　　- Opus One 22; 33s; rel 1975; cip

ALBRIGHT, William and BOLCOM, William
Brass Knuckles
[42]　Bolcom, William (pf)
　　　- Nonesuch H-7l257; 33s; rel
　　　1971; cip

ALEXANDER, Josef (1907-)
Burlesque and Fugue
[43]　Ware, John (tpt); Bernstein,
　　　Seymour (pf)
　　　- Serenus SRS-12038; 33s; rel
　　　1973; cip

Incantation
[44]　Helps, Robert (pf)
　　　- RCA LM-7042/LSC-7042;
　　　33m/s; 2 discs; rel 1966; del
　　　1971
　　　- CRI-288; 33s; 2 discs; rel 1972;
　　　cip

(Three) Pieces for Eight
[45]　New York Philharmonic Chamber
　　　Ensemble; Johnson, A. Robert
　　　(cond)
　　　- Serenus SRS-12038; 33s; rel
　　　1973; cip

Songs for Eve
[46]　Mandac, Evelyn (sop); Brenner,
　　　Englebert (E hn); Sackson, David
　　　(vln) or (vla); Bialkin, Maurice
　　　(vcl); Chertok, Pearl (hp)
　　　- Serenus SRS-12038; 33s; rel
　　　1973; cip

ALFORD, Harry L. (1883-1939)
Purple Carnival
[47]　Incredible Columbia All-Star Band;
　　　Schuller, Gunther (cond)
　　　- Columbia M-33513/MQ-33513;
　　　33s/q; rel 1975; cip

ALLAN, Douglas R.
Conflict (Approach! Battle! Retreat!)
[48]　Percussion Ensemble, The; Kraus,
　　　Phil (cond)
　　　- Golden Crest
　　　CR-4004/CRS-4004; 33m/s; rel
　　　1957/1979; cip

ALLEN, T. S.
Whip and Spur (1902)
[49]　Eastman Symphonic Wind
　　　Ensemble; Fennell, Frederick
　　　(cond)
　　　- Mercury MG-50314/SR-90314;
　　　33m/s; rel 1963; del 1976
　　　- Mercury SRI-75087; 33s; rel
　　　1977; cip

ALLING, John*
Afro Fuga
[50]　Ithaca Percussion Ensemble;
　　　Benson, Warren (cond)
　　　- Golden Crest
　　　CR-4016/CRS-4016; 33m/s; rel
　　　1960/1961; cip

ALLING, Vernon*
Overture de ballet
[51]　Ithaca Percussion Ensemble;
　　　Benson, Warren (cond)
　　　- Golden Crest
　　　CR-4016/CRS-4016; 33m/s; rel
　　　1960/1961; cip

ALMAND, Claude (1915-57)
John Gilbert (A Steamboat Overture)
[52]　Louisville Orchestra; Whitney,
　　　Robert (cond)
　　　- LOU-60-5; 33m (Louisville
　　　Orchestra First Edition Records
　　　1960 No 5); rel 1961; del 1978

ALTER, Louis (1902-1980)
American Serenade
[53]　Meredith Willson Orchestra;
　　　Willson, Meredith (cond)
　　　- Decca 29104 (in set A-219); 78;
　　　rel pre-1956

AMIRKHANIAN, Charles (1945-)
Dutiful Ducks (1977)
[54]　Electronic music
　　　- 1750 Arch S-1779; 33s; rel
　　　1980; cip

Heavy Aspirations (Portrait of Nicolas Slonimsky) (1973)
[55]　Electronic music
　　　- 1750 Arch S-1752; 33s; rel
　　　1975*

Just (1972)
[56]　Electronic music
　　　- 1750 Arch S-1752; 33s; rel
　　　1975*

Mahogany Ballpark (1976)
[57]　Electronic music
　　　- 1750 Arch S-1779; 33s; rel
　　　1980; cip

Muchrooms (1974)
[58]　Electronic music
　　　- 1750 Arch S-1779; 33s; rel
　　　1980; cip

MUGIC (1973)
[59]　Electronic music
　　　- 1750 Arch S-1779; 33s; rel
　　　1980; cip

Seatbelt Seatbelt (1973)
[60]　Electronic music
　　　- 1750 Arch S-1779; 33s; rel
　　　1980; cip

She, She, and She (1974)
[61]　Electronic music
　　　- 1750 Arch S-1779; 33s; rel
　　　1980; cip

AMRAM, David (1930-)
After the Fall: Waltz
[62]　orchestra; Amram, David (cond)
　　　- RCA VCS-7089; 33s; 2 discs; rel
　　　1971; del 1975

Allegro for Strings (Sonata allegro)
[63]　Washington Square Chamber
　　　Orchestra; Peress, Maurice (cond)
　　　- Audiosonic Stereo Studios; 33; rel
　　　1963

Autobiography (1959)
[64]　strings; Amram, David (cond)
　　　- RCA VCS-7089; 33s; 2 discs; rel
　　　1971; del 1975

Brazilian Memories
[65]　soloists; orchestra; Amram, David
　　　(cond)
　　　- RCA VCS-7089; 33s; 2 discs; rel
　　　1971; del 1975

Concerto, Triple, Woodwinds, Brass, Jazz Quintet, and Orchestra (1970)
[66]   David Amram Quintet; Rochester Philharmonic Orchestra; Zinman, David (cond)
- RCA ARL-1-0459; 33s; rel 1974; del 1975
- Flying Fish GRO-751; 33s; rel 1979; cip

Dirge and Variations (1962)
[67]   Marlboro Trio
- DV-200; 33m; rel 1965
- Washington 469/9469; 33m/s; rel 1966; del 1968

Elegy (1970)
[68]   Weiss, Howard (vln); Rochester Philharmonic Orchestra; Zinman, David (cond)
- RCA ARL-1-0459; 33s; rel 1974; del 1975
- Flying Fish GRO-751; 33s; rel 1979; cip

Final Ingredient, The
[69]   vocalists; ABC Symphony Orchestra; Amram, David (cond) Rec 4/11/65
- FI-200; 33m; rel 1965

Friday Evening Service (Shir l'erer shabat) (1960)
[70]   Shirley, George (ten); chorus; organ; Peress, Maurice (cond) Rec 2/20/62
- SS-1000; 33m; rel 1962

Going North
[71]   soloists; orchestra; Amram, David (cond)
- RCA VCS-7089; 33s; 2 discs; rel 1971; del 1975

King Lear Variations (1965)
[72]   orchestra; Amram, David (cond)
- RCA VCS-7089; 33s; 2 discs; rel 1971; del 1975

Lysistrata (1960)
[73]   Perras, John (fl)
- M-100; 33m; rel 1961*

Portraits
[74]   Cantilena Chamber Players
- Grenadilla GS-1029-30; 33s; 2 discs

Pull My Daisy
[75]   soloists; orchestra; Amram, David (cond)
- RCA VCS-7089; 33s; 2 discs; rel 1971; del 1975

Quintet, Winds (1968)
[76]   Clarion Wind Quintet
- Golden Crest CRS-4125; 33s; rel 1974; cip

Rivalry, The
[77]   instrumental ensemble
- Audiosonic Stereo Studios; 33; rel 1963

Sao Paulo
[78]   soloists; orchestra; Amram, David (cond)
- RCA VCS-7089; 33s; 2 discs; rel 1971; del 1975

Shakespearean Concerto (1959)
[79]   Serbage, Midhat (vln); Roseman, Ronald (ob); Barrows, John (hn); Cowan, Daniel (hn); orchestra; Peress, Maurice (cond)
- M-100; 33m; rel 1961*
- Washington 470/9470; 33m/s; rel 1966; del 1968

[80]   soloists; orchestra; Amram, David (cond)
- RCA VCS-7089; 33s; 2 discs; rel 1971; del 1975

Sonata, Piano
[81]   Andrews, Mitchell (pf)
- DV-200; 33m; rel 1965
- Washington 470/9470; 33m/s; rel 1966; del 1968

Sonata, Violin and Piano (1960)
[82]   Wackshal, Seymour (vln); Parrott, Lalan (pf)
- M-100; 33m; rel 1961*
- Washington 469/9469; 33m/s; rel 1966; del 1968

Tompkins Square Park Consciousness Expander
[83]   soloists; orchestra; Amram, David (cond)
- RCA VCS-7089; 33s; 2 discs; rel 1971; del 1975

Trio, Tenor Saxophone, Horn, and Bassoon (1958)
[84]   Kane, Walter (sax); Cowan, Daniel (hn); Cole, Robert (bsn)
- M-100; 33m; rel 1961*

Wind from the Indies
[85]   soloists; orchestra; Amram, David (cond)
- RCA VCS-7089; 33s; 2 discs; rel 1971; del 1975

Year in Our Land, A (1965)
[86]   Interracial Chorale and Orchestra; Aks, Harold (cond)
- AY-200; 33m; rel 1965

ANDERSON, Flo

Pastiche (Improvised Encore)
[87]   Anderson, Flo (pf)
- Educo 3070; 33

ANDERSON, Laurie (1947-)

New York Social Life (1977)
[88]   Anderson, Laurie (voice); electronic music
- 1750 Arch S-1765; 33s; rel 1978; cip

Time to Go (For Diego) (1977)
[89]   Anderson, Laurie (voice); electronic music
- 1750 Arch S-1765; 33s; rel 1978; cip

ANDERSON, Robert (1934-)

Canticle of Praise
[90]   Baker, George C. (org)
- Delos DEL-FY-025; 33s; rel 1977; cip

ANDERSON, Ruth (1928-)

Points (1973-74)
[91]   Electronic music
- 1750 Arch S-1765; 33s; rel 1978; cip

ANDERSON, Thomas Jefferson (1928-)

Chamber Symphony (1968)
[92]   Royal Philharmonic Orchestra; Dixon, James (cond)
- CRI-258; 33s; rel 1970; cip

Squares (1964)
[93]   Baltimore Symphony Orchestra; Freeman, Paul (cond)
- Columbia M-33434; 33s; rel 1975; del 1979

Variations on a Theme by M. B. Tolson
[94]   DeGaetani, Jan (m sop); Contemporary Chamber Ensemble; Weisberg, Arthur (cond)
- Nonesuch H-71303; 33s; rel 1974; cip

ANDRIX, George (1932-)

Structures
[95]   Tidewater Brass Quintet
- Golden Crest CRSQ-4174; 33q; rel 1978; cip

ANTHEIL, George (1900-59)

Airplane Sonata (1922)
[96]   Hoffmann, Lydia (pf)
- New Music Quarterly Recordings 1112 (11-3); 78; rel 1935

[97]   Shields, Roger (pf)
- Vox SVBX-5303; 33s; 3 discs; rel 1977; cip

Ballet mecanique (1923-25)
[98]   New York Percussion Group; Surinach, Carlos (cond)
- Columbia ML-4956; 33m; rel 1955; cip

Ballet mecanique (1923-25)
(version for 4 pfs, perc ensemble,
recording of an airplane engine,
and 2 doorbells)
[99]   Netherlands Wind Ensemble;
        Leeuw, Reinbert de (cond)
        - Telefunken 6-42196; 33s; rel
        1977; cip

Ballet mecanique (rev 1952-53)
[100] Los Angeles Contemporary Music
        Ensemble; Craft, Robert (cond)
        - Urania UX-134; 33m; rel 1959;
        del 1969
        - Urania USD-1034; 33s; rel
        1959; del 1960
        - Urania US-5134; 33s; rel 1961;
        del 1972

Capital of the World (1953)
[101] Ballet Theatre Orchestra; Levine,
        Joseph (cond)
        - Capitol P-8278; 33m; rel 1954;
        del 1960
        - Capitol CTL-7081; 33m; rel
        pre-1956
        - Capitol SAL-9020; 33m; rel
        pre-1956 (excerpt)
        - Capitol HDR-21004; 33m; 4
        discs; rel 1966; del 1970

(Eight) Fragments from Shelley
(1951)
[102] Roger Wagner Chorale; Wagner,
        Roger (cond)
        - SPA-36; 33m; rel 1953; del
        1970

(Eight) Fragments from Shelley: To
the Moon, When the Lamp Is
Shattered, and When Soft Winds
[103] Hamline Singers; Holliday, Robert
        (cond)
        - SPAMH MIA-116; 33s; rel 1961

Jazz Symphony, A (1923-25)
[104] Niederlaendisches
        Blaeserensemble; assisting
        instrumentalists; Leeuw, Reinbert
        de (cond)
        - Telefunken 6-42196; 33s; rel
        1977; cip

McKonkey's Ferry Overture (1948)
[105] Vienna Philharmonic Orchestra;
        Adler, F. Charles (cond)
        - SPA-47; 33m; rel 1953; del
        1970

(Two) Odes of Keats (1949)
[106] Price, Vincent (speaker); Antheil,
        George (pf)
        - SPA-1; 33m; rel 1952; del 1970

Serenade No 1 (1948)
[107] MGM Orchestra; Solomon, Izler
        (cond)
        - MGM E-3422; 33m; rel 1956;
        del 1959

Serenade No 1 (1948) *(cont'd)*
[108] Oslo Philharmonic Orchestra;
        Antonini, Alfredo (cond)
        - CRI-103; 33m/s; rel 1956/?; cip

Sonata, Piano, No 4 (1948)
[109] Marvin, Frederick (pf)
        - Alco ALP-1007; 33m; 10''; rel
        1950; del 1955

Sonata, Trumpet and Piano (ca
1951)
[110] Drucker (tpt); Antheil, George (pf)
        - SPA-2; 33m; rel 1952

[111] Stith, Marice (tpt); Raleigh, Stuart
        W. (pf)
        - Redwood RRES-5; 33s; rel 1977;
        cip

Sonata, Violin and Piano, No 1
(1923)
[112] Erickson, Ronald (vln); Schwartz,
        Nathan (pf)
        - Orion ORS-73119; 33s; rel
        1973; cip

Sonata, Violin and Piano, No 1:
Finale
[113] Beths, Vera (vln); Leeuw, Reinbert
        de (pf)
        - Telefunken 6-42196; 33s; rel
        1977; cip

Sonata, Violin and Piano, No 2
(1923)
[114] Baker, Israel (vln); Menuhin, Yaltah
        (pf)
        - Music Library MLR-8-12; 78; 5
        sides
        - Music Library MLR-7006; 33m;
        rel 1952; del 1970

[115] Beths, Vera (vln); Leeuw, Reinbert
        de (pf)
        - Telefunken 6-42196; 33s; rel
        1977; cip

[116] Erickson, Ronald (vln); Schwartz,
        Nathan (pf)
        - Orion ORS-73119; 33s; rel
        1973; cip

Sonata, Violin and Piano, No 3
(1924)
[117] Erickson, Ronald (vln); Schwartz,
        Nathan (pf)
        - Orion ORS-73119; 33s; rel
        1973; cip

Sonatina, Violin and Piano (1945)
[118] Erickson, Ronald (vln); Schwartz,
        Nathan (pf)
        - Orion ORS-73119; 33s; rel
        1973; cip

(Nine) Songs of Experience (1948)
[119] Graf, Uta (sop); Antheil, George
        (pf)
        - SPA-1; 33m; rel 1952; del 1970

Symphony No 4 (1942-43)
[120] London Symphony Orchestra;
        Goossens, Eugene (cond)
        - Everest LPBR-6013/SDBR-3013;
        33m/s; rel 1959; cip

Symphony No 5 (Joyous)
(1947-48)
[121] Vienna Philharmonia Orchestra;
        Haefner, Herbert (cond)
        - SPA-16; 33m; rel 1952; del
        1970

Toccata No 2 (1948)
[122] Dubal, David (pf)
        - Musical Heritage Society
        MHS-3808; 33s; rel 1978

Valentine Waltzes (1949)
[123] Antheil, George (pf)
        - SPA-36; 33m; rel 1953; del
        1970

Wish, The (1955)
[124] Kentucky Opera Association (vocal
        soloists); Louisville Orchestra
        (members of); Bomhard, Moritz
        (cond)
        - LOU-56-4; 33m (Louisville
        Orchestra First Edition Records
        1956 No 4); rel 1959; del 1971

ANTONINI, Alfredo (1901-)
Roman Holiday
[125] Knightsbridge Symphonic Band;
        Brand, Geoffrey (cond)
        - Gallery EPG-221; 33m; rel 1965

APPLEBAUM, Edward (1937-)
Foci (1971)
[126] Mark, Peter (vla); Musgrave, Thea
        (pf)
        - Avant AV-1010; 33s; rel 1974;
        cip

Montages (1968)
[127] Montagnana Trio
        - Everest SDBR-3262; 33s; rel
        1969; cip
        - Avant AV-1010; 33s; rel 1974;
        cip

Shantih (1969)
[128] Worthington, Caroline (vcl);
        Stevenson, Doris (pf)
        - Avant AV-1010; 33s; rel 1974;
        cip

Sonata, Piano (1965)
[129] Bunger, Richard (pf)
        - Avant AV-1010; 33s; rel 1974;
        cip

Trio, Piano and Strings (1972)
[130] Fine Arts Trio
        - Avant AV-1010; 33s; rel 1974;
        cip

APPLETON, Jon H. (1939-)

Apolliana (1970)
[131] Electronic music
- Folkways FTS-33437; 33s; rel 1975; cip

C. C. C. P. (In Memorium Anatoly Kuznetsov) (1969)
[132] Electronic music
- Folkways FTS-33437; 33s; rel 1975; cip

Chef d'oeuvre (1967)
[133] Electronic music
- Flying Dutchman 103; 33s; rel 1970; del 1971
- Folkways FTS-33437; 33s; rel 1975; cip

Georganna's Fancy (1966)
[134] Electronic music
- Flying Dutchman 103; 33s; rel 1970; del 1971

Hommage to Orpheus
[135] Electronic music
- Folkways FTS-33437; 33s; rel 1975; cip

In deserto (1977)
[136] Electronic music
- Folkways FTS-33445; 33s; rel 1979; cip

Infantasy (1965)
[137] Electronic music
- Flying Dutchman 103; 33s; rel 1970; del 1971

Mussems Sang (1976)
[138] Electronic music
- Folkways FTS-33445; 33s; rel 1979; cip

Nevsehir (1971)
[139] Electronic music
- Folkways FTS-33437; 33s; rel 1975; cip

Newark Airport Rock (1969)
[140] Electronic music
- Flying Dutchman 103; 33s; rel 1970; del 1971

Nyckelharpan (1968)
[141] Electronic music
- Flying Dutchman 103; 33s; rel 1970; del 1971

'Ofa Atu Tonga
[142] Electronic music
- Folkways FTS-33437; 33s; rel 1975; cip

Second Scene Unobserved (1968)
[143] Electronic music
- Flying Dutchman 103; 33s; rel 1970; del 1971

Sones de San Blas
[144] Electronic music
- Folkways FTS-33437; 33s; rel 1975; cip

Spuyten Duyvil (1967)
[145] Electronic music
- Flying Dutchman 103; 33s; rel 1970; del 1971

Sydsing Camklang, The (1976)
[146] Electronic music
- Folkways FTS-33445; 33s; rel 1979; cip

Syntonic Menagerie
[147] Electronic music
- Flying Dutchman 103; 33s; rel 1970; del 1971

Syntonic Menagerie No 2
[148] Electronic music
- Flying Dutchman 119; 33s; rel 1970; del 1973

Syntrophia (1977)
[149] Electronic music
- Folkways FTS-33445; 33s; rel 1979; cip

Times Square Times Ten (1969)
[150] Electronic music
- Flying Dutchman 103; 33s; rel 1970; del 1971
- Folkways FTS-33437; 33s; rel 1975; cip

Visitation, The (1969)
[151] Electronic music
- Flying Dutchman 103; 33s; rel 1970; del 1971

Zeetrope (1974)
[152] Electronic music
- Folkways FTS-33445; 33s; rel 1979; cip

APPLETON, Jon H. and CHERRY, Don

Human Music
[153] Electronic music
- Flying Dutchman 121; 33s; rel 1970; del 1972

AREL, Buelent (1919-)

Electronic Music No 1 (1960)
[154] Electronic music
- Son-Nova 3/S-3; 33m/s; rel 1963; del 1970
- CRI-356; 33s; rel 1977; cip

For Violin and Piano (1966)
[155] Raimondi, Matthew (vln); Miller, Robert (pf)
- CRI-264; 33s; rel 1971; cip

Fragment (1960)
[156] Electronic music
- Son-Nova 3/S-3; 33m/s; rel 1963; del 1970

Mimiana I (Flux) (1968)
[157] Electronic music
- Finnadar SR-9020; 33s; rel 1978; cip

Mimiana II (Frieze) (1969)
[158] Electronic music
- CRI-300; 33s; rel 1974; cip
- Finnadar SR-9020; 33s; rel 1978; cip

Mimiana III (Six and Seven) (1973)
[159] Electronic music
- Finnadar SR-9020; 33s; rel 1978; cip

Sacred Service (Prelude and Postlude) (1961)
[160] Electronic music
- Son-Nova 3/S-3; 33m/s; rel 1963; del 1970
- CRI-356; 33s; rel 1977; cip

Stereo Electronic Music No 1 (1961)
[161] Electronic music
- Columbia ML-5966/MS-6566; 33m/s; rel 1964; del 1979
- J & W Chester Ltd JWC-1001; 33; rel ca 1968

Stereo Electronic Music No 2 (1970)
[162] Electronic music
- CRI-268; 33s; 2 discs; rel 1972; cip
- Finnadar QD-9010; 33q; rel 1976; cip

ARGENTO, Dominick (1927-)

(Six) Elizabethan Songs (1958) (chamber version)
[163] Martin, Barbara (sop); Palma, Susan (fl); Kaplan, Melvin (ob); Quan, Linda (vln); Wilson, Eric (vcl); Brewer, Edward (hpschd); Weisberg, Arthur (cond)
Rec 6/77
- CRI-380; 33s; rel 1978; cip

Letters from Composers (1968)
[164] Sutton, Vern (ten); Van, Jeffrey (gtr)
- CRI-291; 33s; rel 1973; cip

Postcard from Morocco (1971)
[165] Brandt, Barbara (sop); Roche, Sarita (sop); Hardy, Janis (m sop); Marshall, Yale (ten); Sutton, Vern (ten); Busse, Barry (bar); Foreman, Edward (b); Center Opera of Minnesota Instrumental Ensemble; Brunelle, Philip (cond)
- Desto DC-7137-38; 33s; 2 discs; rel 1973; cip

Royal Invitation (Homage to the Queen of Tonga) (1964)
[166]　Louisville Orchestra; Mester, Jorge
　　　(cond)
　　　- LS-76-4; 33s (Louisville
　　　Orchestra First Edition Records
　　　1976 No 4); rel 1979; cip

To Be Sung upon the Water (1972)
[167]　Stewart, John (ten); Russo, Charles
　　　(cl) (b cl); Hassard, Donald (pf)
　　　- Desto DC-6443; 33s; rel 1975;
　　　cip

ARNATT, Ronald (1930-)

**(Four) Plainsong Preludes: (No 3)
Victimae paschali**
[168]　Arnatt, Ronald (org)
　　　- Aeolian-Skinner AS-323; 33s; rel
　　　1969; del 1977

Procession
[169]　Arnatt, Ronald (org)
　　　- Aeolian-Skinner AS-323; 33s; rel
　　　1969; del 1977

ARUNDALE, Claude

Little White House, The
[170]　Coyle, Edgar (bar); piano
　　　- Columbia 2404-05; 78; 2 discs;
　　　rel pre-1925

ASHFORTH, Alden (1930-)

Aspects of Love (1977)
[171]　Blanchard, Hayden (ten); Reale,
　　　Paul (pf)
　　　- Orion ORS-78335; 33s; rel
　　　1979; cip

**Byzantia (Two Journeys after Yeats)
(1970-73)**
[172]　Bossert, James (org); Ashforth,
　　　Alden (syn)
　　　- Orion ORS-74164; 33s; rel
　　　1975; cip

Unquiet Heart, The
[173]　Beardslee, Bethany (sop); UCLA
　　　Chamber Ensemble; Dare, John
　　　(cond)
　　　- CRI-243; 33s; rel 1970; cip

ASHLEY, Robert (1930-)

Automatic Writing
[174]　Ashley, Robert (voice); Johnson,
　　　Mimi (voice); tape
　　　- Vital VR-1002; 33s; rel 1979

Backyard, The (1977)
[175]　Electronic music
　　　Rec 7/77
　　　- Lovely Music LML-1001; 33s; rel
　　　1977

**In Memoriam Crazy Horse
(Symphony) (1963)**
[176]　ONCE Festival Orchestra; Scavarda,
　　　Donald (cond)
　　　- Advance FGR-5; 33m; rel 1966;
　　　cip

**In Sara, Mencken, Christ, and
Beethoven There Were Men and
Women (1972)**
[177]　Ashley, Robert (speaker); De
　　　Marinis, Paul (syn)
　　　Rec 1973
　　　- Cramps CRSLP-6103; 33s; rel
　　　1974
　　　- 1750 Arch S-1752; 33s; rel
　　　1975* (excerpts)

Park, The (1977)
[178]　Electronic music
　　　Rec 7/77
　　　- Lovely Music LML-1001; 33s; rel
　　　1977

Purposeful Lady Slow Afternoon
[179]　Liddell, Cynthia (speaker); tape
　　　- Mainstream MS-5010; 33s; rel
　　　1972; del 1979

She Was a Visitor (1967)
[180]　Brandeis University Chamber
　　　Chorus; Lucier, Alvin (cond)
　　　- Odyssey
　　　32-16-0155/32-16-0156;
　　　33m/s; rel 1967; cip

Sonata I, II, III (1959, 1978)
[181]　multiple keyboards
　　　Rec 8-9/78
　　　- Vital VR-1062; 33s; rel 1979

ASPER, Frank Wilson (1892-1973)

Prayer
[182]　Asper, Frank (org)
　　　- Columbia ML-5615/MS-6215;
　　　33m/s; rel 1961; cip

Reflection
[183]　Asper, Frank (org)
　　　- Columbia ML-5615/MS-6215;
　　　33m/s; rel 1961; cip

AUSTIN, Larry (1930-)

Catalogo voce
[184]　Large, John (bar)
　　　- Irida 0022; 33s; rel 1980

Current (1968)
[185]　clarinet; piano
　　　- Advance FGR-9S; 33s; rel 197?

**Improvisations for Orchestra and
Jazz Soloists (1961)**
[186]　New York Philharmonic; Bernstein,
　　　Leonard (cond)
　　　- Columbia ML-6133/MS-6733;
　　　33m/s; rel 1965; del 1975

Maroon Bells
[187]　Brown, William (ten); Hunt, Jerry
　　　(pf)
　　　- Irida 0022; 33s; rel 1980

Piano Set in Open Style (1964)
[188]　Floyd, Robert (pf)
　　　- Advance FGR-10S; 33s; rel
　　　1970; cip

**Quadrants: Event/Complex No 1
(1971)**
[189]　North Texas State University
　　　Symphonic Band; Winslow, Robert
　　　(cond)
　　　- Irida 0022; 33s; rel 1980

**Second Fantasy on Ives' Universe
Symphony–The Heavens**
[190]　Diana, Mary (sop); Gibson, Lee (cl);
　　　Papich, George (vla); Mainous,
　　　Jean Harris (kbds); Schietroma,
　　　Robert (perc); Clark, Thomas
　　　(cond)
　　　- Irida 0022; 33s; rel 1980

Variations, Piano (1960)
[191]　Floyd, Robert (pf)
　　　- Advance FGR-10S; 33s; rel
　　　1970; cip

AVSHALOMOV, Aaron (1894-1965)

**Concerto, Piano, in G on Chinese
Themes and Rhythms**
[192]　Moore, Margaret (pf); Portland
　　　Junior Symphony; Avshalomov,
　　　Jacob (cond)
　　　- CRI-210; 33m/s; rel 1966; cip

[193]　Singer, Gregory (pf); Shanghai
　　　Municipal Orchestra; Avshalomov,
　　　Aaron (cond)
　　　- Columbia M-286; 78; 3 discs

Peiping Hutungs (1931-32)
[194]　Portland Junior Symphony;
　　　Avshalomov, Jacob (cond)
　　　- CRI-210; 33m/s; rel 1966; cip

[195]　Shanghai Municipal Orchestra;
　　　Paci, Mario (cond)
　　　- Columbia (Chinese) C-7016-67;
　　　78; 2-10''; rel pre-1948

AVSHALOMOV, Jacob (1919-)

How Long, O Lord (1949)
[196]　Wilson, Neil (bar); Portland
　　　Symphonic Choir; Portland Junior
　　　Symphony; Avshalomov, Jacob
　　　(cond)
　　　- CRI-210; 33m/s; rel 1966; cip

Lullaby
[197]　Dwyer, Doriot (fl); Korn, Barbara
　　　(pf)
　　　- Claremont 1205; 33m; rel
　　　1953; del 1965

Phases of the Great Land (1958)
[198] Portland Junior Symphony;
       Avshalomov, Jacob (cond)
       - CRI-194; 33m/s; rel 1964/?; cip

Prophecy (1948, rev 1952)
[199] Mid-America Chorale; Dexter, John
       (cond)
       - CRI-191; 33m/s; rel 1964/?; cip

Sinfonietta (1948)
[200] Columbia Symphony Orchestra;
       Avshalomov, Jacob (cond)
       - Columbia ML-5412/MS-6089;
       33m/s; rel 1960; del 1968
       - Columbia CML-5412/CMS-6089;
       33m/s; rel 1968; del 1973

Taking of T'ung Kuan, The (1943, rev 1953)
[201] Oslo Philharmonic Orchestra;
       Buketoff, Igor (cond)
       - CRI-117; 33m/s; rel 1957/?; cip

BABBITT, Milton (1916-)
All Set (1957)
[202] Contemporary Chamber Ensemble;
       Weisberg, Arthur (cond)
       - Nonesuch H-71303; 33s; rel
       1974; cip

[203] McKusik, Hal (sax); La Porta, John
       (sax); Mucci, Louis (tpt); Farmer,
       Art (tpt); Knepper, Jimmy (tbn);
       Di Domenico, Robert (fl); Zegler,
       Manuel (bsn); Evans, Bill (pf);
       Charles, Teddy (vib); Benjamin,
       Joe (cb); Ross, Margaret (hp);
       Buffington, James (hn); Galbraith,
       Barry (gtr); Sommer, Teddy (dr);
       Schuller, Gunther (cond) or
       Russell, George (cond)
       Rec 6/18/57
       - Columbia WL-127; 33m; rel
       1958*
       - Columbia CL-2109-10 (in set
       C2L-31)/CS-8909-10 (in set
       C2S-831); 33m/s; 2 discs; rel
       1964; del 1970

Arie da capo (1973-74)
[204] Group for Contemporary Music at
       Columbia University; Sollberger,
       Harvey (cond)
       - Nonesuch H-71372; 33s; rel
       1980; cip

Composition for Four Instruments (1948)
[205] New England Conservatory
       Chamber Ensemble; Heiss, John
       (cond)
       - Golden Crest NEC-109; 33s; rel
       1979; cip

[206] Wummer, John (fl); Drucker,
       Stanley (cl); Marsh, Peter (vln);
       McCall, Donald (vcl)
       - CRI-138; 33m/s; rel 1961/?; cip

Composition for Synthesizer (1961)
[207] Electronic music
       - Columbia ML-5966/MS-6566;
       33m/s; rel 1964; del 1979

Composition for Twelve Instruments (1948)
[208] Hartt Chamber Players; Shapey,
       Ralph (cond)
       - Son-Nova 1/S-1; 33m/s; rel
       1962; del 1967

Composition for Viola and Piano (1950)
[209] Loft, A. (vla); Weiser, Bernhard (pf)
       - New Editions 4; 33m; rel
       pre-1953

[210] Trampler, Walter (vla); Bauman,
       Alvin (pf)
       - CRI-138; 33m/s; rel 1961/?; cip

Du (1951)
[211] Beardslee, Bethany (sop); Helps,
       Robert (pf)
       - Son-Nova 1/S-1; 33m/s; rel
       1962; del 1967

Ensembles for Synthesizer (1962-64)
[212] Electronic music
       - Columbia MS-7051; 33s; rel
       1967; cip
       - Finnadar CD-4; 33q; rel 1976
       - Finnadar QD-9010; 33q; rel
       1976; cip

Ensembles for Synthesizer: Part I
[213] Electronic music
       - Time-Life TL-145/STL-145;
       33m/s; rel 1967

Partitions (1957)
[214] Helps, Robert (pf)
       - RCA LM-7042/LSC-7042;
       33m/s; 2 discs; rel 1966; del
       1971
       - CRI-288; 33s; 2 discs; rel 1972;
       cip

Philomel (1964)
[215] Beardslee, Bethany (sop); tape
       - Acoustic Research AR-0654.083;
       33s; rel 1971
       - New World NW-307; 33s; rel
       1980

Phonemena (1970)
[216] Webber, Lynn (sop); Kuderna, Jerry
       (pf)
       - New World NW-209; 33s; rel
       1977

Post-Partitions (1966)
[217] Miller, Robert (pf)
       - New World NW-209; 33s; rel
       1977

Quartet, Strings, No 2 (1954)
[218] Composers Quartet
       - Nonesuch H-71280; 33s; rel
       1973; cip

Quartet, Strings, No 3 (1969)
[219] Fine Arts Quartet
       - Turnabout TVS-34515; 33s; rel
       1973; del 1978

Reflections (1974)
[220] Miller, Robert (pf)
       - New World NW-209; 33s; rel
       1977

Sextets (1966)
[221] Zukofsky, Paul (vln); Kalish, Gilbert
       (pf)
       - Desto DC-6435-37; 33s; 3 discs;
       rel 1975; cip

Vision and Prayer (1961)
[222] Beardslee, Bethany (sop); tape
       - CRI-268; 33s; 2 discs; rel 1972;
       cip

BABER, Joseph (1937-)
Quartet, Strings (Op 30)
[223] Southern Illinois String Quartet
       - Pleiades P-102; 33s; rel 1970;
       cip

BABIN, Victor (1908-72)
David and Goliath
[224] Vronsky, Vitya (pf); Johannesen,
       Grant (pf)
       - Golden Crest GCCL-201; 33s; rel
       1976*

Russian Village
[225] Vronsky, Vitya (pf); Babin, Victor
       (pf)
       - Columbia 71672D (in set
       M-576); 78
       - Columbia ML-4157; 33m; rel
       pre-1949; del 1956

Sun Shafts
[226] Sperry, Paul (ten); McCoppin
       Ensemble
       - Golden Crest GCCL-202; 33s; rel
       1978; cip

BACON, Ernst (1898-)
Billy in the Darbies
[227] Parker, William (bar); Huckaby,
       William (pf)
       - New World NW-305; 33s; rel
       1980

Burr Frolic, The
[228] Hersh, Paul (pf); Montgomery,
       David (pf)
       - Orion ORS-76247; 33s; rel
       1977; cip

Enchanted Isle
[229] Louisville Orchestra; Whitney,
Robert (cond)
- LOU-545-11; 33m (Louisville
Orchestra First Edition Records
1955 No 11); rel 1959; del
1978

**Ford's Theatre (Easter Week 1865)
(1943)**
[230] Vienna Symphony Orchestra;
Schoenherr, Max (cond)
- American Recording Society
ARS-335; 33m; 2 discs; rel
1953
- Desto D-415/DST-6415; 33m/s;
rel 1965; cip

Friends: Grace
[231] Fuszek, Rita (pf)
- Educo 3108; 33

From Emily's Diary (1945)
[232] Gordon, Betty (voice); Peterson,
Donna (voice); Sunshine, Adrian
(pf)
- Music Library MLR-7096; 33m;
rel 1968; del 1974

(Five) Hymns
[233] San Francisco Schola Cantorum;
Camajani (cond)
- Music Library MLR-7096; 33m;
rel 1968; del 1974

Of a Feather
[234] Luening, Ethel (sop)
- Yaddo 26A; 78; 10"; rel 1937

Parting
[235] Kneubuhl, John (gtr)
- Orion ORS-78323; 33s; rel
1979; cip

Pig Town Fling, The
[236] Helps, Robert (pf)
- RCA LM-7042/LSC-7042;
33m/s; 2 discs; rel 1966; del
1971
- CRI-288; 33s; 2 discs; rel 1972;
cip

**(Four) Poems of Emily Dickinson
(1928)**
[237] Boatwright, Helen (sop); Bacon,
Ernst (pf)
- Cambridge CRM-707/CRS-1707;
33m/s; rel 1968; del 1973
[238] Steber, Eleanor (sop); Biltcliffe,
Edwin (pf)
- St/And SPL-411-12; 33m; 2
discs; rel 1963; del 1964
- Desto D-411-12/DST-6411-12;
33m/s; 2 discs; rel 1964; cip

**(Four) Poems of Emily Dickinson:
And This of All My Hopes and It's
All I Have to Bring**
[239] Hanks, John Kennedy (ten);
Friedberg, Ruth (pf)
- Duke University Press
DWR-6417-18; 33m; 2 discs; rel
1966; del 1975

Snow and the Bat, The
[240] Luening, Ethel (sop); Johansen,
Gunnar (pf)
- Yaddo M-1; 78; 10"; rel 1938

**Sonata, Violoncello and Piano
(1948)**
[241] Greenhouse, Bernard (vcl);
Pressler, Menahem (pf)
- CRI-201; 33m; rel 1965; cip

There Came a Day
[242] Luening, Ethel (sop); Nowak, Lionel
(pf)
- Yaddo IV-2; 78; 10"; rel 1940

**Tree on the Plains, A (1942):
Selections**
[243] Pazmor, Radiana (al); Converse
College Chorus and Soloists;
Bacon, Ernst (pf) (cond)
- New Music Quarterly Recordings
1613A-F; 78; rel 1942

BAILEY, Derek
(Five) Domestic Pieces
[244] Bailey, Derek (gtr)
Rec 5/22/75 and 1/76
- Quark 9999; 33m; rel 1979

BAILEY, William Horace (1910-)
Idless (1928)
[245] Siegel, Samuel (vln); Tucker,
Gregory (pf)
- New Music Quarterly Recordings
1414; 78; rel 1939

BAKER, David (1931-)
Chat qui peche, Le
[246] Anderson, Linda (sop); Aebersold,
Jamey (sax); Haerle, Dan (pf);
Clayton, John (cb); Craig, Charlie
(dr); Louisville Orchestra; Mester,
Jorge (cond)
Rec 10/10/74
- LS-75-1; 33s (Louisville
Orchestra First Edition Records
1975 No 1); rel 1976; cip

Contrasts
[247] Western Arts Trio
- Laurel LR-106; 33s; rel 1978;
cip

Dream Boogie
[248] Fisk Jubilee Singers; Kennedy,
Matthew (cond)
- NR-2597; 33s; rel 1972

Sonata, Piano and String Quartet
[249] Freire, Helena (pf); Shipps, Stephen
(vln); Gosa, Vickie Sylvester (vln);
Van Valkenberg, James (vla);
Bondi, Eugene (vcl)
- AAMOA NS-7401; 33s; rel ca
1974

**Sonata, Violoncello and Piano
(1973)**
[250] Starker, Janos (vcl); Planes, Alain
(pf)
- Columbia M-33432; 33s; rel
1975; del 1979

**Sonatina, Tuba and String Quartet
(1971)**
[251] Phillips, Harvey (tu); Composers
Quartet
- Golden Crest CRS-4122; 33q; rel
1974; cip

**(Five) Songs to the Survival of
Black Children**
[252] Fisk Jubilee Singers; Kennedy,
Matthew (cond)
- NR-2597; 33s; rel 1972

BAKER, George C.
Far-West Toccata, The
[253] Baker, George C. (org)
- Delos DEL-FY-025; 33s; rel
1977; cip

BAKER, Larry (1948-)
Before Assemblages III
[254] Indiana Chamber Orchestra;
Briccetti, Thomas (cond)
- Crystal S-532; 33s; rel 1978; cip

BAKER, Philip E.
Come Ye Faithful
[255] Washington Cathedral Choir;
Dirksen, Richard W. (org) (cond)
- Washington Cathedral Archives
CAR-009; 33s; rel 1979?

**BAKER, Robert (1925-) and
HILLER, Lejaren**
see HILLER, Lejaren and BAKER,
Robert

BALADA, Leonardo (1933-)
Cuatris (1969)
[256] Conjunto Cameristico de Barcelona
- Serenus SRS-12036; 33s; rel
1973; cip
- Serenus SRS-12064; 33s; rel
1976; cip

Cumbres (1971)
[257] Carnegie-Mellon University
Symphony Band; Strange, Richard
E. (cond)
- Serenus SRS-12036; 33s; rel
1973; cip

Geometrias No 2 (1966)
[258] Conjunto Cameristico de Barcelona
- Serenus SRS-12036; 33s; rel
1973; cip

Geometrias No 3 (1968)
[259] Chagrin Ensemble; Farberman,
Harold (cond)
- Serenus SRS-12028; 33s; rel
1972; cip

Guernica (1966)
[260] Louisville Orchestra; Mester, Jorge
(cond)
- LS-68-6; 33s (Louisville
Orchestra First Edition Records
1968 No 6); rel 1969; cip

(Two) Homages (1975): Homage to Sarasate
[261] Louisville Orchestra; Mester, Jorge
(cond)
- LS-76-5; 33s (Louisville
Orchestra First Edition Records
1976 No 5); rel 1979; cip

Maria Sabina (1969)
[262] Dunham, America (nar); University
of Louisville Choir; Louisville
Orchestra; Mester, Jorge (cond)
Rec 2/5/73
- LS-72-6; 33s (Louisville
Orchestra First Edition Records
1972 No 6); rel 1973; cip

Mosaico (1970)
[263] American Brass Quintet
- Serenus SRS-12041; 33s; rel
1972

Musica en cuatro tiempos (1959)
[264] Marshall, Elizabeth (pf)
- Serenus SRS-12064; 33s; rel
1976; cip

Sonata, Violin and Piano (1960)
[265] Harth, Sidney (vln); Franklin, Harry
(pf)
- Serenus SRS-12036; 33s; rel
1973; cip

BALAZS, Frederic (1920-)

(Two) Dances, Flute and Orchestra (1957)
[266] Pazmandy, Paul (fl); Philharmonia
Hungarica; Balazs, Frederic
(cond)
- CRI-157; 33m/s; rel 1962/?; cip

BALLANTINE, Edward (1886-1971)

Variations on Mary Had a Little Lamb (1924, 1943)
[267] Ballantine, Edward (pf)
- Technichord T-1556, T-1562 (in
set 3); 78; 2 discs; rel pre-1943
- Festival 70-201; 33m; rel 1950;
del 1956

BALLOU, Esther (1915-73)

Prelude and Allegro (1951)
[268] Vienna Orchestra; Adler, F. Charles
(cond)
- CRI-115; 33m/s; rel 1957/?; cip

BALTAN, Kid* and DISSEVELT, Tom

see DISSEVELT, Tom and BALTAN, Kid

BAMERT, Matthias (1942-)

(Five) Aphorisms
[269] Baron, Samuel (fl); Maayani, Ruth
(hp)
- Desto DC-7134; 33s; rel 1973;
cip

Mantrajana (1971)
[270] Louisville Orchestra; Bamert,
Matthias (cond)
- LS-74-1; 33s (Louisville
Orchestra First Edition Records
1974 No 1); rel 1975; cip

Septuria lunaris (1970)
[271] Louisville Orchestra; Mester, Jorge
(cond)
Rec 11/7/72
- LS-72-5; 33s (Louisville
Orchestra First Edition Records
1972 No 5); rel 1973; cip

BARAB, Seymour (1921-)

Chamber Music: Go Seek Out All Courteously, Love Came to Us in Time Gone By, and My Love Is in a Light Attire
[272] Neway, Patricia (sop); Colston,
Robert (pf)
- Lyrichord LL-83; 33m; rel 1959;
del 1978

Child's Garden of Verses, A
[273] Oberlin, Russell (ct); Weber, David
(cl); Goltzer, Harold (bsn);
Crisara, Ray (tpt); Melnick, Bertha
(pf)
- Esoteric ESJ-5; 33m; 10"; rel
1953

(Twenty-Four) Songs of Perfect Propriety
[274] Cook, Barbara (sop); Baker, Julius
(fl); Weber, David (cl); Glickman,
Loren (bsn); Glantz, Harry (tpt);
Bogin, Abba (pf) (cond)
- Urania UX-113/USD-1020;
33m/s; rel 1958; del 1960

BARATI, George (1913-)

Chamber Concerto (1952)
[275] Philadelphia Orchestra; Ormandy,
Eugene (cond)
- Columbia ML-5779/MS-6379;
33m/s; rel 1962; del 1968
- Columbia CML-5779/CMS-6379;
33m/s; rel 1968; del 1974

Chamber Concerto (1952) *(cont'd)*
- Columbia AMS-6379; 33s; rel
1974; del 1979

Concerto, Violoncello and Orchestra (1953)
[276] Michelin, Bernard (vcl); London
Philharmonic Orchestra; Barati,
George (cond)
- CRI-184; 33m/s; rel 1964/?; cip

Quartet, Flute, Oboe, Violoncello, and Harpsichord (1964)
[277] Pleasants, Virginia (hpschd);
Indiana University Baroque
Chamber Players
- CRI-226; 33s; rel 1968; cip

Quartet, Strings (1944)
[278] California String Quartet
- Contemporary CE-2001; 33m;
10"; rel 1953; del 1959

Triple Exposure
[279] Christensen, Roy (vcl)
- Gasparo GS-103; 33s; rel 1977

BARBER, Samuel (1910-81)

Adagio, Strings (Op 11) (1936)
[280] Academy of St. Martin-in-the-Fields;
Marriner, Neville (cond)
- Argo ZRG-845; 33s; rel 1976;
cip

[281] Boston Symphony Orchestra;
Munch, Charles (cond)
- RCA LM-2105/LSC-2105;
33m/s; rel 1957/1958; del
1969
- RCA ARL-2-1421; 33s; 2 discs;
rel 1976; del 1979
- RCA AGL-1-3790; 33s; rel 1980

[282] Boyd Neel String Orchestra; Neel,
Boyd (cond)
- Decca X-305; 78; rel pre-1952
- Decca LX-3042; 33m; 10"; rel
1950
- London LPS-298; 33m; 10"; rel
1951; del 1957

[283] Capitol Symphony Orchestra;
Dragon, Carmen (cond)
- Capitol P-8542/SP-8542;
33m/s; rel 1961; del 1968

[284] Chicago Symphony Orchestra;
Akos, Francis (cond)
- Pirouette JA-19024/JAS-19024;
33m/s; rel 1967; del 1972

[285] Concert Arts Orchestra;
Golschmann, Vladimir (cond)
- Capitol P-8245; 33m; rel 1954;
del 1969
- Capitol CTL-7056; 33m; rel
pre-1956

[286] Eastman-Rochester Symphony
Orchestra; Hanson, Howard
(cond)
- Mercury MG-40002; 33m; rel
1953; del 1957

Adagio, Strings (Op 11) (1936)
(cont'd)
- Mercury MG-50075; 33m; rel 1957; del 1963
- Mercury MG-50148; 33m; rel 1957; del 1969
- Mercury MG-50420/SR-90420; 33m/s; rel 1965; del 1973
- Mercury SRI-75012; 33s; rel 1974; cip

[287] Halle Orchestra; Handford, Maurice (cond)
- Classics for Pleasure (English) CFP-40320; 33s; rel 1979

[288] Hamburg Philharmonia; Walther, Hans-Jurgen (cond)
- Music Sound Books 78157; 78; 10''; rel pre-1956

[289] Hollywood Bowl Symphony Orchestra; Slatkin, Felix (cond)
- Capitol P-8444/SP-8444; 33m/s; rel 1958/1959; del 1970
- Angel S-36087; 33s; rel 1975; cip

[290] Kapp Sinfonietta; Vardi, Emanuel (cond)
- Kapp KCL-9059/KC-S-9059; 33m/s; rel 1961; del 1963

[291] Leopold Stokowski and his Orchestra; Stokowski, Leopold (cond)
- Capitol SAL-8385/SSAL-8385; 33m/s; rel 1957/1959; del 1961
- Capitol PAR-8385/SPAR-8385; 33m/s; rel 1961; del 1964
- Capitol SP-8673; 33s; rel 1968; del 1970
- Seraphim SIB-6094; 33s; 2 discs; rel 1977; cip

[292] London Symphony Orchestra; Previn, Andre (cond)
- EMI/His Master's Voice ASD-3338; 33q; rel 197?
- Angel S-37409; 33q; rel 1977; cip

[293] Musici, I
- Philips PHM-500001/PHS-900001; 33m/s; rel 1962; del 1971
- Philips 6570.181; 33s; rel 1980; cip

[294] NBC Symphony Orchestra; Toscanini, Arturo (cond)
- Victor 11-8287; 78; rel 1942
- Gramophone DB-6180; 78; rel 1945
- Gramophone ED-330; 78; rel pre-1952
- RCA LM-7032; 33m; 2 discs; rel 1964; del 1967

[295] National High School Orchestra; Wilson, George C. (cond)
- Interlochen National Music Camp NMC-1960-19; 33m; rel 1960

Adagio, Strings (Op 11) (1936)
(cont'd)
[296] New Orchestral Society of Boston; Page, Willis (cond)
- Sound Master 1068; 33m; 10''; rel 1954; del 1955
- Cook 10683; 33m/s; rel 1955/1961; del 1970
- Nixa EP-651; 45; 7''; rel pre-1956
- Rondo 502; 33s; rel 1958; del 1963

[297] New York Philharmonic; Bernstein, Leonard (cond)
- Columbia M-30573; 33s; rel 1971; cip
- Columbia MG-31155; 33s; 2 discs; rel 1972; cip

[298] New York Philharmonic; Schippers, Thomas (cond)
- CBS 32-11-0005/32-11-0006; 33m/s; rel 1966; del 1970
- Odyssey Y-33230; 33s; rel 1975; cip
- CBS (English) 61898; 33s

[299] Philadelphia Orchestra; Ormandy, Eugene (cond)
- Columbia ML-5187; 33m; rel 1957; del 1965
- Columbia ML-5624/MS-6224; 33m/s; rel 1961; cip
- Columbia M-30066; 33s; rel 1970; cip

[300] Philharmonia Orchestra; Kletzki, Paul (cond)
- Columbia LX-1595; 78; rel pre-1956

[301] Solisti di Zagreb, I; Janigro, Antonio (cond)
- Vanguard VRS-1095/VSD-2126; 33m/s; rel 1963; cip

[302] Stuttgart Chamber Orchestra; Muenchinger, Karl (cond)
- London LLP-1395; 33m; rel 1957; del 1959

[303] Tokyo String Ensemble
- Toshiba 95021; 33s; rel 1979; cip

[304] Zurich Baroque Strings
- Denon 7120; 33s; rel 1979; cip

Agnus Dei (1967)
[305] Concordia Choir
- Concordia S-6; 33s; rel 1969; del 1976

Andromache's Farewell (Op 39) (1962)
[306] Arroyo, Martina (sop); New York Philharmonic; Schippers, Thomas (cond)
- Columbia ML-5912/MS-6512; 33m/s; rel 1963; del 1970

Antony and Cleopatra (Op 40) (1965-66): Give Me Some Music, Give Me My Robe, and Put on My Crown (arr as a concert suite)
[307] Price, Leontyne (sop); New Philharmonia Orchestra; Schippers, Thomas (cond)
- RCA LSC-3062; 33s; rel 1969; cip

Beggar's Song
[308] De Loache, Benjamin (bar)
- Yaddo 8B; 78; rel 1937

Canzone (Op 38) (1962)
[309] Wilson, Ransom (fl); Villa, Joseph (pf)
- Musical Heritage Society MHS-1856; 33s; rel 1974

Capricorn Concerto (Op 2l) (1944)
[310] Baker, Julius (fl); Miller, Mitchell (ob); Freistadt, Harry (tpt); Saidenberg Symphony Orchestra; Saidenberg, Daniel (cond)
- Concert Hall A-4; 78; 2 discs; rel 1947
- Concert Hall CHS-1078; 33m; rel 1951; del 1957

[311] Mariano, Joseph (fl); Sprenkle, Robert (ob); Mear, Sidney (tpt); Eastman-Rochester Symphony Orchestra; Hanson, Howard (cond)
- Mercury MG-50224/SR-90224; 33m/s; rel 1959; del 1969
- Mercury SRI-75049; 33s; rel 1975; cip

Commando March (1943)
[312] Cornell University Wind Ensemble; Stith, Marice (cond)
- Cornell CUWE-6; 33s; rel 1971; cip

[313] Eastman Symphonic Wind Ensemble; Fennell, Frederick (cond)
- Mercury MG-40006; 33m; rel 1953; del 1957
- Mercury MG-50079; 33m; rel 1957; del 1969
- Mercury (English) MMA-11009; 33m; rel 1959
- Mercury SRI-75086; 33s; rel 1977

[314] Fredonia Concert Band; Winters, Herbert (cond)
- Fredonia State Teachers College XTV-21899; 33m; rel 1954

[315] Harvard Concert Band; Walker (cond)
- INC 7; 33s; rel 1972; del 1978

[316] U.S. Marine Band; Schoepper, Lt. Col. Albert F. (cond)
- RCA LPM-2687/LSP-2687; 33m/s; rel 1963; del 1975

Commando March (1943) *(cont'd)*
[317] U.S. Military Academy Band; Resta,
Francis E. (cond)
- ASCAP CB-177; 33m (Pittsburgh
International Contemporary Music
Festival); rel 1954

**Concerto, Piano and Orchestra (Op
38) (1962)**
[318] Browning, John (pf); Cleveland
Orchestra; Szell, George (cond)
Rec 1/3/64
- Columbia ML-6038/MS-6638;
33m/s; rel 1964; cip
- CBS (English) 61621; 33s
- Columbia (English)
33CX-1937/SAX-2575; 33m/s

[319] Ruskin, Abbott (pf); MIT Symphony
Orchestra; Epstein, David (cond)
Rec 11/76
- Turnabout QTVS-34683; 33q; rel
1977; cip

**Concerto, Violin and Orchestra (Op
14) (1939-40)**
[320] Bernard, Claire (vln); National
Opera Orchestra of Monte Carlo;
Remoortel, Edouard van (cond)
- Philips PHC-9105; 33s; rel
1968; del 1972
- Philips (French) P-35796LY; 33s

[321] Gerle, Robert (vln); Vienna State
Opera Orchestra; Zeller, Robert
(cond)
Rec 6/63
- Westminster
XWN-19045/WST-17045;
33m/s; rel 1963; del 1971
- Westminster WGS-8181; 33s; rel
1973; del 1978
- World Record Club (English)
CM-59/SCM-59; 33m/s

[322] Kaufman, Louis (vln); Concert Hall
Symphony Orchestra; Goehr,
Walter (cond)
- Concert Hall CHE-8; 33m; rel
1953*
- Musical Masterpiece Society
MMS-105; 33m; 10"; rel 1953*
- Concert Hall CHS-1253; 33m; rel
1956; del 1957
- Concert Hall H-1653; 33m; rel
1957; del 1959
- Orion ORS-79355; 33s; rel
1980; cip

[323] Stavenhagen, Wolfgang (vln);
Imperial Philharmonic Orchestra
of Tokyo; Strickland, William
(cond)
- CRI-137; 33m/s; rel 1961/?; cip

[324] Stern, Isaac (vln); New York
Philharmonic; Bernstein, Leonard
(cond)
- Columbia ML-6113/MS-6713;
33m/s; rel 1965; cip
- CBS (English) 61621; 33s
- CBS (English)
BRG-72345/SBRG-72345;
33m/s

**Concerto, Violin and Orchestra (Op
14) (1939-40)** *(cont'd)*
[325] Thomas, Ronald (vln); West
Australian Symphony Orchestra;
Measham, David (cond)
- Unicorn UNI-72016; 33s; rel
1978
- Unicorn UNS-256; 33s

[326] Zernick, Helmut (vln); Berlin Radio
Orchestra; Rother, Arthur (cond)
- Regent MG-5024; 33m; 10"; rel
1952; del 1956

**Concerto, Violoncello and Orchestra
(Op 22) (1945)**
[327] Garbousova, Raya (vcl); Musica
Aeterna Orchestra; Waldman,
Frederic (cond)
- Decca DL-10132/DL-710132;
33m/s; rel 1966; del 1975
- Varese Sarabande VC-81057;
33s; rel 1979; cip

[328] Nelsova, Zara (vcl); New Symphony
Orchestra; Barber, Samuel (cond)
Rec 12/50
- London LPS-332; 33m; 10"; rel
1951; del 1957
- Decca LX-3048; 33m; 10"; rel
pre-1952
- Decca ECS-707; 33

**Despite and Still (Op 41)
(1968-69): Solitary Hotel**
[329] Patenaude, Joan (sop); Eliasen,
Mikael (pf)
- Musical Heritage Society
MHS-3770; 33s; rel 1978

Dover Beach (Op 3) (1931)
[330] Barber, Samuel (b bar); Curtis
String Quartet
Rec 5/13/35
- Victor 8998; 78; rel pre-1936
- RCA LCT-1158; 33m; rel 1955;
del 1957
- New World NW-229; 33m; rel
1978

[331] Fischer-Dieskau, Dietrich (bar);
Juilliard String Quartet
- Columbia KS-7131; 33s; rel
1968; cip

[332] King, Paul (bar); Hartt String
Quartet
Rec 8/52-2/53
- Classic Editions CE-1011; 33m;
rel 1952; del 1958

[333] Langstaff, John (bar); Hirsch
Quartet
- Gramophone C-4201; 78; rel
pre-1953

Essay (Op 12) (1937)
[334] Eastman-Rochester Symphony
Orchestra; Hanson, Howard
(cond)
- Mercury MG-40002; 33m; rel
1953; del 1957
- Mercury MG-50075; 33m; rel
1957; del 1963

Essay (Op 12) (1937) *(cont'd)*
- Mercury MG-50148; 33m; rel
1957; del 1969

[335] London Symphony Orchestra;
Measham, David (cond)
- Unicorn RHS-342; 33s; rel
1976*
- Unicorn UNI-72010; 33s; rel
1979; cip

[336] Philadelphia Orchestra; Ormandy,
Eugene (cond)
- Victor 18062; 78; rel 1941
- Camden CAL-238; 33m; rel
1956; del 1957

Excursions (Op 20) (1944)
[337] Bates, Leon (pf)
- Orion ORS-76237; 33s; rel
1977; cip

[338] Firkusny, Rudolf (pf)
- Columbia ML-2174; 33m; 10";
rel 1951; del 1956

[339] Previn, Andre (pf)
- Columbia ML-5639/MS-6239;
33m/s; rel 1961; del 1965

[340] Shaulis, Zola (pf)
- CRI-295; 33s; rel 1973; cip

Excursions: (No 4) Allegro molto
[341] Foldes, Andor (pf)
- Vox 16068-71 (in set 174); 78;
4-10"; rel 1947

[342] Waldoff, Stanley (pf)
- Musical Heritage Society
MHS-3808; 33s; rel 1978

Hand of Bridge, A (Op 35) (1958)
[343] Neway, Patricia (sop); Alberts,
Eunice; Lewis, William (ten);
Maero, Philip (bar); Symphony of
the Air; Golschmann, Vladimir
(cond)
- Vanguard VRS-1065/VSD-2083;
33m/s; rel 1960; cip

Hermit Songs (Op 29) (1952-53)
[344] Bell, Donald (b bar); Newmark,
John (pf)
- CBC Radio Canada SM-111; 33s

[345] Browne, Sandra (m sop); Isador,
Michael (pf)
- Enigma Classics (English)
VAR-1029; 33s; rel 1977

[346] Maxwell, Joan (m sop); Duncan,
Chester (pf)
- CBC Radio Canada SM-103; 33s

[347] Price, Leontyne (sop); Barber,
Samuel (pf)
Rec 1953
- Columbia ML-4988; 33m; rel
1955; del 1968
- Columbia CML-4988; 33m; rel
1968; del 1976
- Odyssey 32-16-0230; 33s; rel
1968; cip

Hermit Songs: The Crucifixion, and The Monk and his Cat

[348] Tatum, Nancy (sop); Parsons, Geoffrey (pf)
- London OS-26053; 33s; rel 1968; del 1971

Knoxville (Summer of 1915) (Op 24) (1947)

[349] McGurk, Molly (sop); West Australian Symphony Orchestra; Measham, David (cond)
- Unicorn UNI-72016; 33s; rel 1978
- Unicorn UNS-256; 33s

[350] Price, Leontyne (sop); New Philharmonia Orchestra; Schippers, Thomas (cond)
- RCA LSC-3062; 33s; rel 1969; cip

[351] Steber, Eleanor (sop); Dumbarton Oaks Chamber Orchestra; Strickland, William (cond)
- Columbia ML-2174; 33m; 10''; rel 1951; del 1956
- Columbia ML-5843; 33m; rel 1963; del 1972
- Odyssey 32-16-0230; 33s; rel 1968; cip

[352] Steber, Eleanor (sop); Greater Trenton Symphony Orchestra; Harsanyi, Nicholas (cond)
Rec 1/13/62
- St/And SPL-420/SLS-7420; 33m/s; rel 1962; del 1964

Let Down the Bars, O Death (Op 8, No 2) (1935-36)

[353] Vienna Academy Chamber Chorus; Grossman, Ferdinand (cond)
- Vox PLP-7750; 33m; rel 1952; del 1956

[354] Washington Cathedral Choir of Men and Boys; Callaway, Paul (cond)
- Vanguard VRS-1036/VSD-2021; 33m/s; rel 1959; del 1968

Medea (Cave of the Heart) (Suite) (Op 23) (1947)

[355] Bamberg Symphony; Leitner, Ferdinand (cond)
- Decca DL-8509; 33m; rel pre-1958

[356] Eastman-Rochester Symphony Orchestra; Hanson, Howard (cond)
- Mercury MG-50224/SR-90224; 33m/s; rel 1959; del 1969
- Mercury MG-50420/SR-90420; 33m/s; rel 1965; del 1973
- Mercury SRI-75012; 33s; rel 1974; cip

[357] New Symphony Orchestra; Barber, Samuel (cond)
- Decca LX-3049; 33m; 10''; rel 1951*
- London LPS-333; 33m; 10''; rel 1951; del 1957

Medea (Cave of the Heart) (Suite) (Op 23) (1947) (cont'd)
- London LLP-1328; 33m; rel 1956; del 1960
- London CM-9145; 33m; rel 1960; del 1962
- Everest SDBR-3282; 33s; rel 1970; del 1977

Medea's Meditation and Dance of Vengeance (Op 23a) (1955)

[358] Boston Symphony Orchestra; Munch, Charles (cond)
- RCA LM-2197; 33m; rel 1958; del 1960
- RCA-Victrola VICS-1391; 33s; rel 1969; del 1976

[359] New York Philharmonic; Schippers, Thomas (cond)
- CBS 32-11-0005/32-11-0006; 33m/s; rel 1966; del 1970
- Odyssey Y-33230; 33s; rel 1975; cip
- CBS (English) 61898; 33s

Melodies passageres (Op 27) (1950-51)

[360] Bernac, Pierre (bar); Poulenc, Francis (pf)
Rec 2/15/52
- New World NW-229; 33m; rel 1978

Music for a Scene from Shelley (Op 7) (1933)

[361] Symphony of the Air; Golschmann, Vladimir (cond)
- Vanguard VRS-1065/VSD-2083; 33m/s; rel 1960; cip

[362] Vienna Symphony Orchestra; Hendl, Walter (cond)
- American Recording Society ARS-26; 33m; rel 1953
- Desto D-418/DST-6418; 33m/s; rel 1965; cip

[363] West Australian Symphony Orchestra; Measham, David (cond)
- Unicorn UNI-72016; 33s; rel 1978
- Unicorn UNS-256; 33s

Mutations from Bach (1968)

[364] Locke Brass Consort; Stobart, James (cond)
- Unicorn RHS-339; 33s; rel 1976

Natali, Die (Op 37) (1960)

[365] Louisville Orchestra; Mester, Jorge (cond)
Rec 2/20/75
- LS-74-5; 33s (Louisville Orchestra First Edition Records 1974 No 5); rel 1975; cip

Natali, Die: Chorale Prelude on Silent Night (arr for org)

[366] Hillsman, Walter (org)
Rec 5/10-11/76
- Vista VPS-1038; 33s; rel 1976

Natali, Die: Chorale Prelude on Silent Night (arr for org) (cont'd)

[367] Wichmann, Russell G. (org)
- True Image LP-125; 33m; rel 1966

Night Flight (Op 19a) (1964)

[368] London Symphony Orchestra; Measham, David (cond)
- Unicorn RHS-342; 33s; rel 1976*
- Unicorn UNI-72010; 33s; rel 1979; cip

Nocturne (Homage to John Field) (Op 33) (1959)

[369] Johannesen, Grant (pf)
- Golden Crest CR-4065/CRS-4065; 33m/s; rel 1963/1966; cip

[370] Shields, Roger (pf)
- Vox SVBX-5303; 33s; 3 discs; rel 1977; cip

Nuvoletta (Op 25) (1947)

[371] Neway, Patricia (sop); Colston, Robert (pf)
- Lyrichord LL-83; 33m; rel 1959; del 1978

[372] Steber, Eleanor (sop); Biltcliffe, Edwin (pf)
- St/And SPL-411-12; 33m; 2 discs; rel 1963; del 1964
- Desto D-411-12/DST-6411-12; 33m/s; 2 discs; rel 1964; cip

Prayers of Kierkegaard (Op 30) (1954)

[373] Capone, Gloria (sop); Southern Baptist Theological Seminary Choir; Louisville Orchestra; Mester, Jorge (cond)
Rec 3/24/77
- LS-76-3; 33s (Louisville Orchestra First Edition Records 1976 No 3); rel 1978; cip

Prayers of Kierkegaard: Lord Jesus Christ

[374] Dobbs, Battawilda (sop); Arner, Gotthard (org)
- Proprous (Swedish) 25-04-02-004; 33s; rel 1970

Quartet, Strings (Op 11) (1936)

[375] Beaux-Arts String Quartet
- Epic LC-3907/BC-1307; 33m/s; rel 1965; del 1969

[376] Borodin Quartet
- Artia/MK 1563; 33m; rel 1961; del 1971

[377] Cleveland Quartet
- RCA ARL-1-1599; 33q; rel 1976; cip

[378] Stradivari Quartet
- Stradivari STR-602; 33m; rel 1951; del 1970

Reincarnations (Op 16) (1940)
[379] C. W. Post College Chorus and
       Chamber Singers; Dashnaw,
       Alexander (cond)
       - Golden Crest CCS-8050; 33s; rel
         1978; cip

[380] Gregg Smith Singers; Smith, Gregg
       (cond)
       - Everest LPBR-6129/SDBR-3129;
         33m/s; rel 1965; cip

[381] Hufstader Singers; Hufstader,
       Robert (cond)
       - Cook 1092; 33m; 10''; rel
         1953*
       - Cook 11312; 33m/s; rel
         1957/1964; del 1970

[382] King Chorale; King, Gordon (cond)
       - Orion ORS-75205; 33s; rel
         1978; cip

**Reincarnations: (No 1) Mary Hynes
and (No 3) The Coolin**
[383] Seattle Chamber Singers;
       Shangrow, George (cond)
       Rec 8/18/76
       - Voyager VRLP-701S; 33s; rel
         1976

**School for Scandal, The (Overture)
(Op 5) (1931-33)**
[384] Eastman-Rochester Symphony
       Orchestra; Hanson, Howard
       (cond)
       - Mercury MG-40002; 33m; rel
         1953; del 1957
       - Mercury EP-1-5018; 45; 7''; rel
         pre-1956
       - Mercury MG-50075; 33m; rel
         1957; del 1963
       - Mercury MG-50148; 33m; rel
         1957; del 1969
       - Mercury MG-50420/SR-90420;
         33m/s; rel 1965; del 1973
       - Mercury SRI-75012; 33s; rel
         1974; cip

[385] Janssen Symphony Orchestra of
       Los Angeles; Janssen, Werner
       (cond)
       - Victor 11-8591; 78; rel 1944
       - Camden CAL-205; 33m; rel
         1955; del 1957

[386] New York Philharmonic; Schippers,
       Thomas (cond)
       - CBS 32-11-0005/32-11-0006;
         33m/s; rel 1966; del 1970
       - Odyssey Y-33230; 33s; rel
         1975; cip
       - CBS (English) 61898; 33s

[387] Vienna Symphony Orchestra;
       Hendl, Walter (cond)
       - American Recording Society
         ARS-26; 33m; rel 1953
       - Desto D-418/DST-6418; 33m/s;
         rel 1965; cip

Second Essay (Op 17) (1942)
[388] Hamburg Philharmonia; Korn,
       Richard (cond)
       - Allegro ALG-3148; 33m; rel
         1955?

Second Essay (Op 17) (1942)
(cont'd)
[389] London Symphony Orchestra;
       Measham, David (cond)
       - Unicorn RHS-342; 33s; rel
         1976*
       - Unicorn UNI-72010; 33s; rel
         1979; cip

[390] New York Philharmonic; Schippers,
       Thomas (cond)
       - CBS 32-11-0005/32-11-0006;
         33m/s; rel 1966; del 1970
       - Odyssey Y-33230; 33s; rel
         1975; cip
       - CBS (English) 61898; 33s

[391] Symphony of the Air; Golschmann,
       Vladimir (cond)
       - Vanguard VRS-1065/VSD-2083;
         33m/s; rel 1960; cip

Serenade (Op 1) (1929)
[392] Rome Chamber Orchestra; Flagello,
       Nicolas (cond)
       - Peters Internationale PLE-059;
         33s; rel 1978; cip

[393] Symphony of the Air; Golschmann,
       Vladimir (cond)
       - Vanguard VRS-1065/VSD-2083;
         33m/s; rel 1960; cip

Sonata, Piano (Op 26) (1949)
[394] Browning, John (pf)
       - Desto DC-7120; 33s; rel 1971;
         cip

[395] Cliburn, Van (pf)
       - RCA LSC-3229; 33s; rel 1971;
         del 1980

[396] Guralnik, Robert (pf)
       - Mace MXX-9085; 33s; rel 1970;
         del 1975

[397] Horowitz, Vladimir (pf)
       Rec 5/15/50
       - Victor DM-1466; 78; 2 discs; rel
         1950
       - RCA LM-1113; 33m; rel 1950;
         del 1956
       - RCA LD-7021; 33m; 2 discs; rel
         1963; del 1974
       - RCA ARM-1-2952; 33m; rel
         1978; cip

[398] Judd, Terence (pf)
       - Chandos (English) DBR-3001;
         33s; 3 discs; rel 1980

[399] Mitchell, Marjorie (pf)
       - Decca DL-10136/DL-710136;
         33m/s; rel 1967; del 1973

[400] Pollack, Daniel (pf)
       - Artia/MK 04318/04299; 33m;
         rel 1960; del 1963

**Sonata, Piano: Fuga (4th
Movement)**
[401] Shields, Roger (pf)
       - Vox SVBX-5303; 33s; 3 discs; rel
         1977; cip

**Sonata, Violoncello and Piano (Op
6) (1932)**
[402] Clark, Harry (vcl); Schuldmann,
       Sanda (pf)
       - Musical Heritage Society
         MHS-3378; 33s; rel 1976

[403] Epperson, Gordon (vcl); Burnett,
       Frances (pf)
       - Golden Crest RE-7026; 33m/s;
         rel 1968/1979; cip

[404] Garbousova, Raya (vcl); Kahn,
       Erich Itor (pf)
       - Concert Hall B-1; 78; 2 discs; rel
         1947
       - Concert Hall CHS-1092; 33m; rel
         1951; del 1956

[405] Greco, Lucille A. (vcl); Zeyen, Mary
       Mark (pf)
       - Orion ORS-7297; 33s; rel 1973;
         cip

[406] Piatigorsky, Gregor (vcl);
       Berkowitz, Ralph (pf)
       - RCA LM-2013; 33m; rel 1956;
         del 1961

[407] Ricci, George (Giorgio) (vcl);
       Mittman, Leopold (pf)
       - Stradivari STR-602; 33m; rel
         1951; del 1970

[408] Solow, Jeffrey (vcl); Dominguez,
       Albert (pf)
       - Pelican LP-2010; 33s; rel 1980;
         cip

**(Three) Songs (Op 2): The Daisies
(1927) and With Rue My Heart Is
Laden (1928)**
[409] Moore, Dale (bar); Tomfohrde,
       Betty Ruth (pf)
       - Cambridge CRS-2715; 33s; rel
         1973; cip

(Three) Songs (Op 2): The Daisies
[410] Gramm, Donald (b); Cumming,
       Richard (pf)
       - Music Library MLR-7033; 33m;
         rel 1954; del 1974

**(Three) Songs (Op 2): With Rue My
Heart Is Laden**
[411] Patenaude, Joan (sop); Eliasen,
       Mikael (pf)
       - Musical Heritage Society
         MHS-3770; 33s; rel 1978

**(Three) Songs (Op 2): Bessie
Bobtail (1934)**
[412] De Loache, Benjamin (bar)
       - Yaddo 8B; 78; rel 1937

[413] Hanks, John Kennedy (ten);
       Friedberg, Ruth (pf)
       - Duke University Press
         DWR-6417-18; 33m; 2 discs; rel
         1966; del 1975

(Three) Songs (Op 10) (1936)
[414] King, Paul (bar); Quincy, Samuel
       (pf)
       - Classic Editions CE-1011; 33m;
       rel 1952; del 1958

[415] Moore, Dale (bar); Tomfohrde,
       Betty Ruth (pf)
       - Cambridge CRS-2715; 33s; rel
       1973; cip

[416] Patenaude, Joan (sop); Eliasen,
       Mikael (pf)
       - Musical Heritage Society
       MHS-3770; 33s; rel 1978

**(Three) Songs (Op 10): Sleep Now
and I Hear an Army**
[417] Rideout, Patricia (al); Helmer, Paul
       (pf)
       - CBC Radio Canada SM-108; 33s

(Three) Songs (Op 10): Sleep Now
[418] Cotlow, Marilyn (sop); Stafford,
       Claire (pf)
       - Victor 10-1467; 78; 10"; rel
       1949
       - Victor 49-0679; 45; 7"; rel
       pre-1952

**(Three) Songs (Op 10): I Hear an
Army**
[419] Hanks, John Kennedy (ten);
       Friedberg, Ruth (pf)
       - Duke University Press
       DWR-6417-18; 33m; 2 discs; rel
       1966; del 1975

(Four) Songs (Op 13) (1937-40)
[420] Patenaude, Joan (sop); Eliasen,
       Mikael (pf)
       - Musical Heritage Society
       MHS-3770; 33s; rel 1978

**(Four) Songs (Op 13): Sure on this
Shining Night (1938) and
Nocturne (1940)**
[421] Hanks, John Kennedy (ten);
       Friedberg, Ruth (pf)
       - Duke University Press
       DWR-6417-18; 33m; 2 discs; rel
       1966; del 1975

[422] Moore, Dale (bar); Tomfohrde,
       Betty Ruth (pf)
       - Cambridge CRS-2715; 33s; rel
       1973; cip

**(Four) Songs (Op 13): A Nun Takes
the Veil (1937)**
[423] Lehmann, Lotte (sop)
       - Campbell 23 (in set 1-24); 33m;
       rel pre-1956

**(Four) Songs (Op 13): Sure on this
Shining Night**
[424] Amara, Lucine (sop); Benedict,
       David (pf)
       - Cambridge CRM-704/CRS-1704;
       33m/s; rel 1963; del 1975

**(Four) Songs (Op 13): Sure on this
Shining Night** *(cont'd)*
[425] Beardslee, Bethany (sop); Helps,
       Robert (pf)
       - New World NW-243; 33s; rel
       1977

[426] Yeend, Frances (sop); Benner,
       James (pf)
       - Da Vinci DRC-203; 33m; rel
       1962; del 1964

**(Two) Songs (Op 18): Monks and
Raisins (1943)**
[427] Moore, Dale (bar); Tomfohrde,
       Betty Ruth (pf)
       - Cambridge CRS-2715; 33s; rel
       1973; cip

**Souvenirs (Suite) (Op 28) (1952)
(4-hand piano version)**
[428] Gold, Arthur (pf); Fizdale, Robert
       (pf)
       Rec 8/52
       - Columbia ML-4855 (in set
       SL-198); 33m; rel 1954; del
       1958

**Souvenirs (Suite) (orchestral
version)**
[429] London Symphony Orchestra;
       Serebrier, Jose (cond)
       - Desto DC-6433; 33s; rel 1969;
       cip

[430] Philharmonia Orchestra; Kurtz,
       Efrem (cond)
       - Capitol G-7146; 33m; rel 1959;
       del 1963

**Souvenirs (Suite): Hesitation Tango
(arr for pf)**
[431] Johannesen, Grant (pf)
       - Golden Crest CRS-4132; 33s; rel
       1975; cip

**Stopwatch and an Ordnance Map, A
(Op 15) (1940)**
[432] Columbia University Men's Glee
       Club; Gottlieb, Gordon (timp);
       Smith, Gregg (cond)
       Rec 1976
       - Vox SVBX-5353; 33s; 3 discs; rel
       1979; cip

[433] Robert De Cormier Chorale;
       Symphony of the Air;
       Golschmann, Vladimir (cond)
       - Vanguard VRS-1065/VSD-2083;
       33m/s; rel 1960; cip

Summer Music (Op 31) (1956)
[434] Ayorama Woodwind Quintet
       - CBC Radio Canada SM-261; 33s

[435] Dorian Woodwind Quintet
       - Vox SVBX-5307; 33s; 3 discs; rel
       1977; cip

[436] New York Woodwind Quintet
       - Concert-Disc M-1216/CS-216;
       33m/s; rel 1960; cip

Summer Music (Op 31) (1956)
(cont'd)
[437] Philadelphia Woodwind Quintet
       - Columbia ML-5441/MS-6114;
       33m/s; rel 1960; del 1966
       - Columbia CMS-6114; 33s; rel
       1969; del 1974
       - Columbia AMS-6114; 33s; rel
       1974; del 1976

Symphony No 1 (Op 9) (1935-36)
[438] Eastman-Rochester Symphony
       Orchestra; Hanson, Howard
       (cond)
       - Mercury MG-40014; 33m; rel
       1956; del 1957
       - Mercury MG-50087; 33m; rel
       1957; del 1964
       - Mercury MG-50148; 33m; rel
       1957; del 1969
       - Mercury MG-50420/SR-90420;
       33m/s; rel 1965; del 1973
       - Mercury SRI-75012; 33s; rel
       1974; cip

[439] Japan Philharmonic Symphony
       Orchestra; Strickland, William
       (cond)
       - CRI-137; 33m/s; rel 1961/?; cip

[440] London Symphony Orchestra;
       Measham, David (cond)
       - Unicorn RHS-342; 33s; rel
       1976*
       - Unicorn UNI-72010; 33s; rel
       1979; cip

[441] Milwaukee Symphony Orchestra;
       Schermerhorn, Kenneth (cond)
       - Turnabout QTVS-34564; 33q; rel
       1974; del 1978

[442] New York Philharmonic; Walter,
       Bruno (cond)
       - Columbia 12128-29D (in set
       MX-252); 78; 2 discs; rel 1945
       - Columbia LX-1077-78; 78; 2
       discs; rel pre-1952

[443] Stockholm Symphony Orchestra;
       Lehmann, Nils (cond)
       - Classic Editions CE-1011; 33m;
       rel 1952; del 1958

**Symphony No 2 (Op 19) (1944, rev
1947)**
[444] New Symphony Orchestra; Barber,
       Samuel (cond)
       - Decca LX-3050; 33m; 10"; rel
       1951*
       - London LPS-334; 33m; 10"; rel
       1951; del 1957
       - London LLP-1328; 33m; rel
       1956; del 1960
       - London CM-9145; 33m; rel
       1960; del 1962
       - Everest SDBR-3282; 33s; rel
       1970; del 1977

Toccata festiva (Op 36) (1960)
[445] Biggs, E. Power (org); Philadelphia
       Orchestra; Ormandy, Eugene
       (cond)
       - Columbia ML-5798/MS-6398;
       33m/s; rel 1963; cip

Twelfth Night (Op 42, No 1)
[446] Capital University Chapel Choir;
Whikehart, Lewis E. (cond)
- Coronet LPS-3002; 33s

Vanessa (Op 32) (1957)
[447] Steber, Eleanor (sop); Elias,
Rosalind (m sop); Resnik, Regina
(m sop); Gedda, Nicolai (ten);
Tozzi, Giorgio (b); Metropolitan
Opera Chorus; Metropolitan
Opera Orchestra; Mitropoulos,
Dimitri (cond)
Rec 1958
- RCA LM-6138/LSC-6138;
33m/s; 3 discs; rel 1958; del
1970
- RCA LM-6062/LSC-6062;
33m/s; 2 discs; rel 1959; del
1963 (excerpts)
- RCA LM-2391/LSC-2391;
33m/s; rel 1960; del 1968
(excerpts)
- RCA ARL-2-2094; 33s; 2 discs;
rel 1977; cip (excerpts)
- RCA (English) RL-02094; 33s; 2
discs; rel 1978 (excerpts)

Vanessa: Do Not Utter a Word
[448] Price, Leontyne (sop); RCA Italiana
Opera Orchestra;
Molinari-Pradelli, Francesco
(cond)
- RCA LM-2898/LSC-2898;
33m/s; rel 1966; cip

Vanessa: Intermezzo (Act IV)
[449] Columbia Symphony Orchestra;
Schippers, Thomas (cond)
- Columbia ML-5564/MS-6164;
33m/s; rel 1960; del 1966

[450] New York Philharmonic;
Kostelanetz, Andre (cond)
- Columbia ML-5347/MS-6040;
33m/s; rel 1959; del 1965
- Columbia 91-A0-2007; 33m; rel
1972; cip
- Columbia MG-33728; 33s; 2
discs; rel 1976; del 1979

Wondrous Love (Op 34) (1958)
[451] Gehring, Philip (org)
- Valparaiso University
RR4M-6307-08 (matrix no);
33m; rel 1965

[452] Harmon, Thomas (org)
- Orion ORS-76255; 33s; rel
1977; cip

[453] Hillsman, Walter (org)
Rec 5/10-11/76
- Vista VPS-1038; 33s; rel 1976

[454] Obetz, John (org)
- Celebre/Century 36707; 33s; rel
197?

[455] Smith, Rollin (org)
Rec 8/73
- Repertoire Recording Society
RRS-12; 33s; rel 1974

BARKIN, Elaine (1932-)
Quartet, Strings (1969)
[456] American Quartet
- CRI-338; 33s; rel 1975; cip

BARLOW, Samuel (1892-)
Ballo sardo (1928): Cortege
[457] Lamoureux Concerts Orchestra;
Cornman, Robert (cond)
- CRI-178; 33m; rel 1964; cip

Circus Overture (1960)
[458] Lamoureux Concerts Orchestra;
Cornman, Robert (cond)
- CRI-178; 33m; rel 1964; cip

Mon ami Pierrot (1934): Overture
[459] Lamoureux Concerts Orchestra;
Cornman, Robert (cond)
- CRI-178; 33m; rel 1964; cip

BARLOW, Wayne (1912-)
(Three) Christmas Tunes
[460] Wichmann, Russell G. (org)
- True Image LP-125; 33m; rel
1966

**(Three) Christmas Tunes: Joseph
Dearest**
[461] Becker, C. Warren (org)
- Chapel LP-5-134/ST-134;
33m/s; rel 1968

Dynamisms (1967)
[462] Faini, Maria Luisa (pf); Yarbrough,
Joan (pf)
- MirroSound S-101; 33s; rel
1968; del 1980

Elegy (1967)
[463] Tursi, Francis (vla); Faini, Maria
Luisa (pf)
- MirroSound S-101; 33s; rel
1968; del 1980

Night Song (1957)
[464] Eastman-Rochester Symphony
Orchestra; Hanson, Howard
(cond)
Rec 5/60
- Mercury MG-50277/SR-90277;
33m/s; rel 1961; del 1964
- Eastman-Rochester Archives
ERA-1011; 33s; rel 1978; cip

Trio, Oboe, Viola, and Piano (1964)
[465] Sprenkle, Robert (ob); Tursi,
Francis (vla); Faini, Maria Luisa
(pf)
- MirroSound S-101; 33s; rel
1968; del 1980

Winter's Passed, The (1938)
[466] Eastman Philharmonia; Hanson,
Howard (cond)
Rec 1962
- Mercury MG-50299/SR-90299;
33m/s; rel 1962; del 1964

Winter's Passed, The (1938)
(cont'd)
[467] Rome Chamber Orchestra; Flagello,
Nicolas (cond)
- Peters Internationale PLE-071;
33s; rel 1978; cip

[468] Sprenkle, Robert (ob);
Eastman-Rochester Symphony
Orchestra; Hanson, Howard
(cond)
- Victor 18101 (in set M-802);
78; rel 1941
- Mercury MG-40003; 33m; rel
1953; del 1957
- Mercury EP-1-5064; 45; 7''; rel
pre-1956
- Mercury MG-50076; 33m; rel
1957; del 1963
- Eastman-Rochester Archives
ERA-1001; 33s; rel 1974; cip

**BARNES, Edward Shippen
(1887-1958)**
Prelude and Festal Hymn
[469] Barnes, William H. (org)
- HO8P-0144-45 (matrix no);
33m; rel 196?

**(Seven) Sketches (Op 34): (No 2)
Chanson**
[470] Parvin, Titus (org)
- Chime 1003; 33m; rel 1958; del
1962

BARNES, Ronald
Land of Rest
[471] Barnes, Ronald (car) or Strauss,
Richard (car)
- Washington Cathedral Archives
CAR-0002; 33s; rel 1975

Picardy
[472] Barnes, Ronald (car) or Strauss,
Richard (car)
- Washington Cathedral Archives
CAR-0002; 33s; rel 1975

Simple Gifts
[473] Barnes, Ronald (car) or Strauss,
Richard (car)
- Washington Cathedral Archives
CAR-0002; 33s; rel 1975

**BARROWS, John R., Jr.
(1913-74)**
Divertimento
[474] Porter, Lois (vln); Rood, Louise
(vla); Marsh, Douglas (vcl)
- Yaddo D-4-5; 78; rel 1938

March
[475] Fredonia Faculty Woodwind Quintet
- Fredonia State Teachers College
XTV-21902; 33m; rel 1954

[476] New York Woodwind Quintet
- Everest LPBR-6092/SDBR-3092;
33m/s; rel 1963; del 1978

Piece, Piano and Orchestra
[477] no performers given
- Yaddo 16B; 78; 10"; rel 1937

Quintet, Winds
[478] Yaddo Woodwind Quintet
- Yaddo 1A-B; 78; 1-10" and
1-12"; rel 1937 (1st and 3rd
movements)
- Yaddo 20A; 78; rel 1937 (2nd
movement)

**BARRYMORE, Lionel
(1878-1954)**
Ali Baba and the Forty Thieves
[479] Barrymore, Lionel (nar); orchestra;
Schumann, Walter (cond)
- MGM E-110; 33m; 10"; rel
1952*

BARTLES, Alfred H. (1930-)
Appalachian Portrait (1965)
[480] Marlborough Concert Band;
Cacavas, John (cond)
- Kapp KL-1455/KL-S-3455;
33m/s; rel 1966; del 1971

[481] Ohio State University Concert
Band; McGinnis, Donald E. (cond)
- Coronet S-1258; 33s; rel 1969;
del 1978

When Tubas Waltz
[482] Tennessee Tech Tuba Ensemble;
Morris, R. Winston (cond)
- Golden Crest CRSQ-4139; 33q;
rel 1977; cip

BARTLETT, Harry (1922-)
(Four) Holidays (1952)
[483] American Percussion Society; Price,
Paul (cond)
- Urania UX-106; 33m; rel 1957;
del 1969
- Urania USD-1007; 33s; rel
1958; del 1960
- Urania US-5106; 33s; rel 1961;
del 1970

BASART, Robert (1926-)
Fantasy
[484] Ketchum, Janet (fl); Schwartz,
Nathan (pf)
- CRI-371; 33s; rel 1977; cip

BASSETT, Leslie (1923-)
**Music for Saxophone and Piano
(1968)**
[485] Delibero, Phil (sax); Smellie, Mary
(pf)
- Open Loop 1; 33s; rel 197?

[486] Sinta, Donald (sax); Weckler, Ellen
(pf)
- New World NW-209; 33s; rel
1977

**Music for Saxophone and Piano
(1968)** (cont'd)
[487] Underwood, Dale (sax); Lee,
Majorie (pf)
Rec 8/15/76
- Golden Crest RE-7067; 33s; rel
1978; cip

**Music for Violoncello and Piano
(1966)**
[488] Jelinek, Jerome (vcl); Gurt, Joseph
(pf)
- CRI-311; 33s; rel 1974; cip

**(Five) Pieces, String Quartet
(1957)**
[489] Walden Quartet of the University of
Illinois
- Illini Union Bookstore CRS-7;
33m; rel 1960?

Sextet, Piano and Strings (1971)
[490] Kalish, Gilbert (pf); Concord String
Quartet; Graham, John (vla)
Rec 5/19/75
- CRI-323; 33s; rel 1975; cip

Sounds Remembered (1972)
[491] Treger, Charles (vln); Sanders,
Samuel (pf)
- Desto DC-7142; 33s; rel 1973;
cip

Suite, Trombone (1957)
[492] Sauer, Ralph (tbn)
- Crystal S-381; 33s; rel 1977; cip

**Trio, Viola, Clarinet, and Piano
(1953)**
[493] Trampler, Walter (vla); Russo,
Charles (cl); Nordli, Douglas (pf)
- CRI-148; 33m/s; rel 1962/?; cip

Variations (1963)
[494] Zurich Radio Orchestra; Sternberg,
Jonathan (cond)
- CRI-203; 33m/s; rel 1966; cip

BATSTONE, Philip (1933-)
Mother Goose Primer, A
[495] Beardslee, Bethany (sop); Bond,
Victoria (echo); UCLA Chamber
Ensemble; Dare, John (cond)
- CRI-243; 33s; rel 1970; cip

BAUER, Harold (1873-1951)
Barberini's Minuet
[496] Bauer, Harold (pf)
- Victor 1058; 78; 10"; rel 1925

Motley and Flourish
[497] Bauer, Harold (pf)
- Victor 1058; 78; 10"; rel 1925

BAUER, Marion (1887-1955)
**From New Hampshire Woods (Op
12) (1921): The White Birches**
[498] Behrend, Jeanne (pf)
- Victor 17913 (in set M-764);
78; rel 1941

**Prelude and Fugue, Flute and
Strings (Op 43)**
[499] Vienna Orchestra; Adler, F. Charles
(cond)
- CRI-101; 33m/s; rel 1956/?; cip

Symphonic Suite (Op 34) (1940)
[500] Vienna Orchestra; Adler, F. Charles
(cond)
- CRI-101; 33m/s; rel 1956/?; cip

BAUR, John (1947-)
Moon and the Yew Tree, The
[501] Anderson, Christine (sop); Baur,
Elizabeth (fl); Weirich, Robert (pf);
Burton, John (vcl)
- CRI-426; 33s; rel 1980; cip

BAVICCHI, John (1922-)
(Six) Duets, Flute and Clarinet
[502] McGinnis, Donald E. (fl) (cl)
- Coronet M-1271; 33m; rel
1969; cip

(Three) Preludes, Trombone
[503] Raph, Alan (tbn)
- Coronet S-1407; 33s; rel 1969;
cip

**Short Sonata, Violin and
Harpsichord (1959)**
[504] Brink, Robert (vln); Pinkham,
Daniel (hpschd)
- CRI-138; 33m/s; rel 1961/?; cip

**Sonata, Violin and Piano, No 1
(1965)**
[505] Kobialka, Daniel (vln); Press,
Myron (pf)
- Medea MCLP-1002; 33m/s; rel
1966; del 1971

**Trio, Clarinet, Violin, and Harp, No
4 (Op 33)**
[506] Glazer, David (cl); Raimondi,
Matthew (vln); Dell'Aquila,
Assunta (hp)
- CRI-138; 33m/s; rel 1961/?; cip

BAZELON, Irwin (1922-)
Chamber Concerto (1970)
[507] instrumental ensemble; Bazelon,
Irwin (cond)
- CRI-287; 33s; rel 1972; cip

Duo (1963)
[508] Phillips, Karen (vla); Jacobson,
Glenn (pf)
- CRI-342; 33s; rel 1975; cip

Propulsions
[509] DesRoches, Raymond (perc); Fitz, Richard (perc); Gottlieb, Gordon (perc); Harris, Herbert (perc); Land, Arnie (perc); Rosenberger, Walter (perc); Walcott, Collin (perc); Bazelon, Irwin (cond)
- CRI-327; 33s; rel 1975; cip

Quintet, Brass (1963)
[510] American Brass Quintet
- CRI-327; 33s; rel 1975; cip

Quintet, Winds
[511] Boehm Quintet
Rec 6/77
- Orion ORS-78291; 33s; rel 1978; cip

Symphony No 2 (Short Symphony, Testament to a Big City) (1962)
[512] Louisville Orchestra; Whitney, Robert (cond)
- LOU-66-4/LS-66-4; 33m/s (Louisville Orchestra First Edition Records 1966 No 4); rel 1966; cip

Symphony No 5 (1966)
[513] Indianapolis Symphony Orchestra; Solomon, Izler (cond)
- CRI-287; 33s; rel 1972; cip

BEACH, Bennie (1925-)
Lamento
[514] Le Blanc, Robert (tu); Baker, Myra (pf)
- Coronet S-1721; 33s; rel 1973; cip

Suite, Baritone Horn and Piano
[515] Young, Raymond G. (bar hn); Fraschillo, Tom (pf)
- Golden Crest RE-7025; 33m/s; rel 1968/1979; cip

BEACH, Mrs. H. H. A. (Amy Marcy Cheney) (1867-1944)
Ah, Love, But a Day
[516] Swarthout, Gladys (m sop); Hodges, Lester (pf)
- Victor 10-1050; 78; 10"; rel pre-1948

Ballad (Op 6) (1894)
[517] Eskin, Virginia (pf)
- Genesis GS-1054; 33s; rel 1974; cip

(Three) Browning Songs (Op 44) (1899): The Year's at the Spring (Pippa's Song)
[518] Eames, Emma (sop); piano
- Victor 85057; 78; 10"; rel 1905
- Victor 88008; 78
- Gramophone AGSB-22; 78

(Three) Browning Songs (Op 44) (1899): The Year's at the Spring (Pippa's Song) (cont'd)
[519] Gadski, Johanna (sop); piano
Rec 1/14/08
- Victor 87026; 78; 10"; rel 1908-10
- New World NW-247; 33m; rel 1976

[520] Souez, Ina (sop); Simpson, Loyd (pf)
- New Sound 5001; 33m; rel 1956; del 1958

Concerto, Piano and Orchestra (Op 45) (1899)
[521] Boehm-Kooper, Mary Louise (pf); Westphalian Symphony Orchestra; Landau, Siegfried (cond)
Rec 5/76
- Turnabout QTVS-34665; 33q; rel 1977; cip

Hermit Thrush at Eve (Op 92, No 1) (1922)
[522] Eskin, Virginia (pf)
- Genesis GS-1054; 33s; rel 1974; cip

Hermit Thrush at Morn (Op 92, No 2) (1922)
[523] Eskin, Virginia (pf)
- Genesis GS-1054; 33s; rel 1974; cip

(Five) Improvisations, Piano (Op 148) (1924-36)
[524] Rogers, Herbert (pf)
- Dorian 1006; 33m; rel 1962; del 1970

(Five) Improvisations, Piano: Lento molto tranquillo, Allegretto grazioso e capriccioso, and Molto lento e tranquillo
[525] Eskin, Virginia (pf)
- Genesis GS-1054; 33s; rel 1974; cip

(Five) Improvisations, Piano: Allegretto grazioso e capriccioso
[526] Behrend, Jeanne (pf)
- Victor M-764; 78; rel 1941

(Trois) Morceaux caracteristiques (Op 28) (1894)
[527] Eskin, Virginia (pf)
- Genesis GS-1054; 33s; rel 1974; cip

Nocturne (Op 107) (1924)
[528] Eskin, Virginia (pf)
- Genesis GS-1054; 33s; rel 1974; cip

(Four) Pieces, Piano (Op 15) (1892)
[529] Eskin, Virginia (pf)
- Genesis GS-1054; 33s; rel 1974; cip

Prelude and Fugue (Op 81) (1914)
[530] Eskin, Virginia (pf)
- Genesis GS-1054; 33s; rel 1974; cip

Quintet, Piano and Strings (Op 67) (1908)
[531] Boehm-Kooper, Mary Louise (pf); Kooper, Kees (vln); Rogers, Alvin (vln); Maximoff, Richard (vla); Sherry, Fred (vcl)
- Turnabout TVS-34556; 33s; rel 1974; cip

Quintet, Winds: Pastorale
[532] Lawrence, Eleanor (fl); Arrowsmith, William (ob); Neidich, Irving (cl); Vrotney, Richard (bsn); Tillotson, Brooks (hn)
- Musical Heritage Society MHS-3578; 33s; rel 1977

Scherzino
[533] Waldoff, Stanley (pf)
- Musical Heritage Society MHS-3808; 33s; rel 1978

Sonata, Violin and Piano (Op 34) (1896)
[534] Silverstein, Joseph (vln); Kalish, Gilbert (pf)
- New World NW-268; 33s; rel 1977

Symphony (Gaelic) (Op 32) (1896)
[535] Royal Philharmonic Orchestra; Krueger, Karl (cond)
- SPAMH MIA-139; 33s; rel 1968

Trio, Piano and Strings (Op 150) (1938)
[536] Clio Concert Trio
- Dorian 1007; 33m; rel 1962; del 1974

[537] Macalester Trio
- Vox SVBX-5112; 33s; 3 discs; rel 1980; cip

Valse-Caprice (Op 4) (1889)
[538] Eskin, Virginia (pf)
- Genesis GS-1054; 33s; rel 1974; cip

Variations, Flute and String Quartet (Op 80) (1920)
[539] Gold, Diane (fl); Alard Quartet
- Leonarda LPI-105; 33s; rel 1980

BEACH, Perry W. (1917-)
Then Said Isaiah
[540]　Camerata of Los Angeles Orchestra
　　　and Chorus; Mitzelfelt, H. Vincent
　　　(cond)
　　　- Crystal S-890; 33s; rel 1977; cip

BEALE, David Brooks (1945-)
Reflections on a Park Bench
[541]　Tennessee Tech Tuba Ensemble;
　　　Morris, R. Winston (cond)
　　　- Golden Crest
　　　CRS-4152/CRSQ-4152; 33s/q;
　　　rel 1977/1978; cip

BECK, John Ness (1930-)
Hymn to David, A
[542]　Capital University Chapel Choir;
　　　Snyder, Ellis Emanuel (cond)
　　　- Coronet S-1504; 33s; rel 1969;
　　　cip

BECKER, John J. (1886-1961)
Abongo (1933)
[543]　New Jersey Percussion Ensemble;
　　　DesRoches, Raymond (cond)
　　　- New World NW-285; 33s; rel
　　　1978

Concerto arabesque (1930)
[544]　Kayser, Jan Henrik (pf); Oslo
　　　Philharmonic Orchestra;
　　　Strickland, William (cond)
　　　- CRI-177; 33m; rel 1964; cip

Credo
[545]　Greek Byzantine Chorus; Vriondes,
　　　Christos (cond)
　　　- New Music Quarterly Recordings
　　　1014 (1-7); 78; rel 1934

**Symphonia brevis (Symphony No 3)
(1929)**
[546]　Louisville Orchestra; Mester, Jorge
　　　(cond)
　　　- LS-72-1; 33s (Louisville
　　　Orchestra First Edition Records
　　　1972 No 1); rel 1973; cip

BECKLER, Stanworth (1923-)
Little Suite (Op 59)
[547]　Pacific Art Woodwind Quintet
　　　- Orion ORS-79345; 33s; rel
　　　1980; cip

BEDELL, Robert L. (1909-)
Legende
[548]　Courboin, Charles (org)
　　　- Victor 15824; 78; rel 1940

Variations on a Noel
[549]　Young, Gordon (org)
　　　- Grosse Pointe 235612; 33m; rel
　　　1957

BEELER, Walter (1908-)
Blue And Gold March
[550]　Ithaca Symphonic Winds; Beeler,
　　　Walter (cond)
　　　- Golden Crest
　　　CR-4015/CRS-4015; 33m/s; rel
　　　1959/1961; cip

BEERMAN, Burton (1943-)
Sensations
[551]　Rehfeldt, Phillip (cl); tape
　　　- Advance FGR-15S; 33s; rel
　　　1973; cip

BEERS, Bob (1920-72)
Little Irish Suite, The
[552]　Beers, Bob (vln)
　　　- Amerifolk BOB-472; 33s; rel
　　　1972

BEESON, Jack (1921-)
Calvinistic Evensong (1952)
[553]　Gramm, Donald (bar); Cumming,
　　　Richard (pf)
　　　- St/And SPL-411-12; 33m; 2
　　　discs; rel 1963; del 1964
　　　- Desto D-411-12/DST-6411-12;
　　　33m/s; 2 discs; rel 1964; cip

**Captain Jinks of the Horse Marines
(1973)**
[554]　Green, Eugene (b); Jones, Robert
　　　Owen (ten); Wilcox, Carol (sop);
　　　Hook, Walter (bar); James,
　　　Carolyne (m sop); Highley, Ronald
　　　(bar); Steele, Brian (b); Kansas
　　　City Philharmonic; Patterson,
　　　Russell (cond)
　　　- RCA ARL-2-1727; 33s; 2 discs;
　　　rel 1976; cip

Dr. Heidegger's Fountain of Youth
[555]　Wilcox, Carol (sop); Christin, Judith
　　　(m sop); Hirst, Grayson (ten);
　　　Shiesley, Robert (bar); Anderson,
　　　Alfred (b bar); Beeson, Miranda
　　　(speaker); chamber orchestra;
　　　Martin, Thomas (cond)
　　　- CRI-406; 33s; rel 1979; cip

Hello Out There (1954)
[556]　Gabriele, Lenya (sop); Worden,
　　　Marvin (ten); Reardon, John (bar);
　　　Columbia Chamber Orchestra;
　　　Waldman, Frederic (cond)
　　　- Columbia ML-5265; 33m; rel
　　　1958; del 1962
　　　- Desto D-451/DST-6451; 33m/s;
　　　rel 1965; cip

Lizzie Borden (1965)
[557]　Lewis, Brenda (sop); Faull, Ellen
　　　(sop); Elgar, Anne (sop); Krause,
　　　Richard (ten); Fredericks, Richard
　　　(bar); Beattie, Herbert (b); New
　　　York City Opera Chorus and
　　　Orchestra; Coppola, Anton (cond)
　　　- Desto D-455-57/DST-6455-57;
　　　33m/s; 3 discs; rel 1966; cip

(Three) Rounds
[558]　Gregg Smith Singers; Smith, Gregg
　　　(cond)
　　　- CRI-241; 33s; rel 1970; cip

**Settings from the Bay Psalm Book:
Psalms 47 and 131**
[559]　Bushnell Choir; Dashnaw,
　　　Alexander (cond)
　　　Rec 8/22/76
　　　- Golden Crest CRS-4172; 33s; rel
　　　1979; cip

Sweet Bye and Bye, The (1956)
[560]　Rogers, Noel (sop); Anthony, Judith
　　　(sop); James, Carolyne (m sop);
　　　Seibel, Paula (sop); Green,
　　　Eugene (sop); Jones, Robert
　　　Owen (ten); Claffy, Thomas (ten);
　　　Latimer, Dennis (bar); Howell, Dennis (b
　　　bar); Hook, Walter (b); Kansas
　　　City Lyric Theatre Chorus and
　　　Orchestra; Patterson, Russell
　　　(cond)
　　　- Desto DC-7179-80; 33s; 2 discs;
　　　rel 1974; cip

Symphony No 1 (1959)
[561]　Polish National Radio Orchestra;
　　　Strickland, William (cond)
　　　- CRI-196; 33m/s; rel 1965/?; cip

BEGLARIAN, Grant (1927-)
Sinfonia, Strings (1965)
[562]　National ASTA String Orchestra;
　　　Krachmalnick, Samuel (cond)
　　　- Custom Fidelity CFS-3442; 33;
　　　rel 197?

BEHRENS, Jack (1935-)
Feast of Life, The (1975)
[563]　Behrens, Jack (pf)
　　　- Opus One 13; 33s; rel 1976; cip

BEHRMAN, David (1937-)
Runthrough (1967)
[564]　Electronic music
　　　- Mainstream MS-5010; 33s; rel
　　　1972; del 1979

BELLOW, Alexander (1912-76)
Sonata, Guitar
[565]　Provost, Richard (gtr)
　　　- Ars Nova/Ars Antiqua AN-1003;
　　　33s; rel 1969; del 1973

BELSTERLING, C.*
March of the Steel Men
[566]　University of Michigan Winds and
　　　Percussion; Lillya, Clifford P.
　　　(cond)
　　　Rec 2/18-19/75
　　　- University of Michigan SM-0002;
　　　33s; rel 1978; cip

BENARY, Barbara (1946-)
Braid
[567] Gamelan Son of Lion
- Folkways FTS-31313; 33s; rel 1980; cip

Sleeping Braid
[568] Gamelan Son of Lion
- Folkways FTS-31313; 33s; rel 1980; cip

BENCRISCUTTO, Frank (1928-)
Rondeau
[569] University of Michigan Percussion Ensemble; Owen, Charles (cond)
- Golden Crest CRSQ-4145; 33q; rel 1977; cip

BENDER, Jan (1909-)
Prelude on Lobe den Herrn
[570] Obetz, John (org)
- Celebre 8004; 33s; rel 197?

Variations on a Theme by Hugo Distler
[571] Bender, Jan (org)
- Concordia Seminary; 33; 2 discs; rel 1965

BENNETT, Frank
Song
[572] Stoltzman, Richard (cl); Douglas, Bill (pf); Serkin, Peter (pf); Koehler, David (cb); Swift, Gordon (tamboura)
- Orion ORS-73125; 33s; rel 1973; cip

BENNETT, Robert Russell (1894-1981)
Adventure in High Fidelity, An
[573] Victor Orchestra; Bennett, Robert Russell (cond)
- RCA LM-1802; 33m; rel 1954
- RCA SRL-12-1; 33m; rel 1958*

Armed Forces Suite
[574] Victor Symphony Orchestra; Victor Symphonic Band; Bennett, Robert Russell (cond)
- RCA LM-2445/LSC-2445; 33m/s; rel 1960; del 1964

Celebration
[575] Eastman Symphonic Wind Ensemble; Fennell, Frederick (cond)
- Mercury MG-50361/SR-90361; 33m/s; rel 1964; del 1966

Commemoration Symphony (1959)
[576] Pittsburgh Symphony Orchestra; Steinberg, William (cond)
- Everest LPBR-6063/SDBR-3063; 33m/s; rel 1960; del 1978

Concerto, Violin and Orchestra (1941)
[577] Kaufman, Louis (vln); London Symphony Orchestra; Herrmann, Bernard (cond)
Rec 5/20/56
- Citadel CT-6005; 33s; rel 1976; cip
- Musical Heritage Society MHS-3974; 33s; rel 1978

Hexapoda (1940)
[578] Heifetz, Jascha (vln); Bay, Emanuel (pf)
- Decca DA-23659-60 (in set DA-454); 78; 2-10"; rel pre-1948

[579] Heifetz, Jascha (vln); Kaye, Milton (pf)
- Decca DL-9760; 33m; rel 1955; del 1971

[580] Kaufman, Louis (vln); Bennett, Robert Russell (pf)
- Columbia 70727D; 78; rel pre-1942

[581] Kaufman, Louis (vln); Kaufman, Annette (pf)
- Citadel CT-6005; 33s; rel 1976; cip
- Musical Heritage Society MHS-3974; 33s; rel 1978

Rondo capriccioso
[582] Lawrence, Eleanor (fl); Heckler-Denbaum, Wendy (fl); Stewart, Susan (fl); Kahn, Sue Ann (fl)
- Musical Heritage Society MHS-3578; 33s; rel 1977

Rose Variations (1955)
[583] Hickman, David (tpt); Soderholm, Pauline (pf)
- Crystal S-363; 33s; rel 1978; cip

Sonata, Organ, in D
[584] Craighead, David (org)
Rec 7/31/57
- Mirrosonic DRE-1012; 33m; 2 discs; rel 1958; del 1965

Sonata, Organ: Allegretto grazioso
[585] Smith, Melville (org)
Rec 4/23/61
- Organ Historical Society F-MS-I-II; 33m; rel 1965

Song Sonata, A (1947)
[586] Heifetz, Jascha (vln); Smith, Brooks (pf)
- RCA LM-2382; 33m; rel 1960; cip

[587] Kaufman, Louis (vln); Kaufman, Annette (pf)
- Citadel CT-6005; 33s; rel 1976; cip
- Musical Heritage Society MHS-3974; 33s; rel 1978

Song Sonata, A (1947) *(cont'd)*
[588] Kaufman, Louis (vln); Saidenberg, Theodore (pf)
- Concert Hall CHS-1062; 33m; rel 1951; del 1952

Songs at Eventide
[589] Anderson, Marian (al); Victor Orchestra; Bennett, Robert Russell (cond)
- RCA LM-2769/LSC-2769; 33m/s; rel 1964; del 1976

Suite on Old American Dances (1949)
[590] College of the Pacific Band
- Fidelity Sound Recordings FSR-1209; 33m; rel 1958; del 1966

[591] Cornell University Wind Ensemble; Stith, Marice (cond)
- Cornell CUWE-4; 33s; rel 1971; cip

[592] Eastman Symphonic Wind Ensemble; Fennell, Frederick (cond)
- Mercury MG-40006; 33m; rel 1953; del 1957
- Mercury MG-50079; 33m; rel 1957; del 1969
- Mercury SRI-75086; 33s; rel 1977

Symphonic Picture of Porgy and Bess *see* GERSHWIN, George, Porgy and Bess (Orchestral Arrangements)

Symphonic Songs (1958)
[593] Eastman Symphonic Wind Ensemble; Fennell, Frederick (cond)
- Mercury MG-50220/SR-90220; 33m/s; rel 1960; del 1972

[594] Northwestern University Symphonic Wind Ensemble; Paynter, John P. (cond)
Rec 11/76
- New World NW-211; 33s; rel 1977

BENSON, Warren (1924-)
Aeolian Songs
[595] Hemke, Frederick (sax); Granger, Milton (pf)
- Brewster BR-1203; 33s; rel 1972; del 1978

[596] Sinta, Donald (sax); True, Nelita (pf)
- Mark MRS-22868; 33m; rel 1968; cip

Arioso
[597] Popiel, Peter J. (tu); Fuchs, Henry (pf)
- Mark MRS-28437; 33s; rel 1968; cip

Concertino, Saxophone and Winds (1967)

[598] Sinta, Donald (sax)
- Mark MRS-22868; 33m; rel 1968; cip

Farewell

[599] Hemke, Frederick (sax); Granger, Milton (pf)
- Brewster BR-1203; 33s; rel 1972; del 1978

[600] Sinta, Donald (sax); True, Nelita (pf)
- Mark MRS-22868; 33m; rel 1968; cip

Gentle Song

[601] Willett, William C. (cl); Staples, James (pf)
- Mark MRS-32638; 33s; rel 1970; del 1975

Helix (1967)

[602] Phillips, Harvey (tu); Ithaca High School Band; Battisti, Frank (cond)
- Golden Crest CR-6001/CRS-6001; 33m/s; rel 1967; cip

[603] Phillips, Harvey (tu); National High School Band; Wilson, George C. (cond)
- Golden Crest GCIN-403; 33s; rel 1975; cip

[604] tuba; Indiana University Symphonic Band; Ebbs, Frederick (cond)
- Coronet S-2736; 33s; rel 1973; cip

Leaves Are Falling, The (1965)

[605] Indiana University Symphonic Band; Ebbs, Frederick (cond)
- Coronet S-2736; 33s; rel 1973; cip

Marche

[606] American Woodwind Quintet
- Golden Crest CR-4075/CRS-4075; 33m/s; rel 1966/1967; cip

(Three) Pieces, Percussion Quartet

[607] Ithaca Percussion Ensemble; Benson, Warren (cond)
- Golden Crest CR-4016/CRS-4016; 33m/s; rel 1960/1961; cip

Polyphonies

[608] UCLA Bruin Band
- Fidelity Sound Recordings FSR-1238; 33s; rel 1968; del 1970

Prologue

[609] Levy, Robert (tpt); Levy, Amy Lou (pf)
- Golden Crest RE-7045; 33q; rel 1972; cip

Recuerdo (1967)

[610] Jaeger, Don (E hn); National High School Band; Wilson, George C. (cond)
- Golden Crest GCIN-403; 33s; rel 1975; cip

Recuerdo: Cancion de la Posadas

[611] Jaeger, Don (ob); True, Nelita (pf)
- Mark MRS-25727; 33m; rel 1968; cip

Solitary Dancer, The (1969)

[612] Indiana University Symphonic Band; Ebbs, Frederick (cond)
- Coronet S-2736; 33s; rel 1973; cip

Star Edge (1967)

[613] Sinta, Donald (sax); Ithaca High School Band; Battisti, Frank (cond)
- Golden Crest CR-6001/CRS-6001; 33m/s; rel 1967; cip

Symphony, Drums and Winds (1964)

[614] Cornell University Wind Ensemble; Stith, Marice (cond)
- Cornell CUWE-12; 33s; rel 1973; cip

Transylvania Fanfare (1953)

[615] Indiana University Symphonic Band; Ebbs, Frederick (cond)
- Coronet S-2736; 33s; rel 1973; cip

[616] Ithaca College Band; Beeler, Walter (cond)
- Golden Crest CR-4077/CRS-4077; 33m/s; rel 1967; cip

Trio, Percussion (1961)

[617] Percussion Ensemble; Price, Paul (cond)
- Period SPL-743/SPLS-743; 33m/s; rel 1958; del 1968
- Orion ORS-7276; 33s; rel 1972; cip

Variations on a Handmade Theme

[618] Ithaca Percussion Ensemble; Benson, Warren (cond)
- Golden Crest CR-4016/CRS-4016; 33m/s; rel 1960/1961; cip

BERBERIAN, Cathy (1928-)

Stripsody (1966)

[619] Berberian, Cathy (m sop); Canino, Bruno (pf) or (hpschd)
Rec 1970
- Wergo WER-60-054; 33s; rel 1977*

BERCKMAN, Evelyn (1900-)

Meavy; Washerwoman's Song

[620] Luening, Ethel (sop); Yaddo String Quartet
- Yaddo 22B; 78; rel 1937

BEREZOWSKY, Nicolai (1900-53)

Brass Suite (Op 24) (1942)

[621] brass ensemble; Voisin, Roger (cond)
- Unicorn UNLP-1031; 33m; rel 1956; del 1959
- Kapp KCL-9020; 33m; rel 1959; del 1963
- Kapp KL-1391; 33m; rel 1965; del 1971

Christmas Festival Overture (Op 30, No 2) (1943)

[622] Oslo Philharmonic Orchestra; Lipkin, Arthur Bennett (cond)
- CRI-209; 33m/s; rel 1966; cip

Fantasy, Two Pianos (Op 9) (1944)

[623] Yarbrough, Joan (pf); Cowan, Robert (pf)
- CRI-279; 33s; rel 1974; cip

Quartet, Strings (Op 16) (1933)

[624] Coolidge String Quartet
- Victor 15765-67S (in set M-624); 78; 3 discs; rel pre-1942

Quintet, Winds: 2nd and 5th Movements

[625] Barrere Woodwind Ensemble
- New Music Quarterly Recordings 1111 (11-2); 78; rel 1935

Suite, Wind Quintet (Op 11)

[626] New Art Wind Quintet
- Classic Editions CE-1003; 33m; rel 1951; del 1959

BERG, Christopher

Boyfriend (1978)

[627] Felty, Janice (m sop); Berg, Christopher (pf)
- Opus One 49; 33s; rel 1979; cip

George Hugnet (1970-71)

[628] Felty, Janice (m sop); Berg, Christopher (pf)
- Opus One 49; 33s; rel 1979; cip

Last Letter (1975-77)

[629] Felty, Janice (m sop); Berg, Christopher (pf)
- Opus One 49; 33s; rel 1979; cip

Lion in Love, The (1976)

[630] Felty, Janice (m sop); Berg, Christopher (pf)
- Opus One 49; 33s; rel 1979; cip

Selling Techniques (1978)
[631] Felty, Janice (m sop); Berg,
Christopher (pf)
- Opus One 49; 33s; rel 1979; cip

(Three) Short Piano Pieces
[632] Berg, Christopher (pf)
- Opus One 52; 33s; rel 1979; cip

Susie Asado (1970-71)
[633] Felty, Janice (m sop); Berg,
Christopher (pf)
- Opus One 49; 33s; rel 1979; cip

BERGEN, Eugene*
Quintet, Piano and Strings
[634] Johansen, Gunnar (pf); Walden
String Quartet
- Yaddo D-6; 78; rel 1938

BERGER, Arthur (1912-)
Bagatelle (1946)
[635] Marlowe, Sylvia (hpschd)
- Decca DL-10021/DL-710021;
33m/s; rel 1961; del 1971

Chamber Music, Thirteen Instruments (1956)
[636] Columbia Chamber Ensemble;
Schuller, Gunther (cond)
- Columbia ML-6359/MS-6959;
33m/s; rel 1967; del 1970
- CRI-290; 33s; rel 1972; cip

Duo, Violin and Piano (1950)
[637] Earle, R. (vln); Berger, Arthur (pf)
- New Editions 4; 33m; rel
pre-1953

[638] Zukofsky, Paul (vln); Kalish, Gilbert
(pf)
- Desto DC-6435-37; 33s; 3 discs;
rel 1975; cip

Duo, Violoncello and Piano (1951)
[639] Greenhouse, Bernard (vcl); Makas,
Anthony (pf)
- Columbia ML-4846; 33m; rel
1954; del 1968
- Columbia CML-4846; 33m; rel
1968; del 1974
- Columbia AML-4846; 33m; rel
1974; del 1976

(Three) Episodes (1933): Two Episodes
[640] Helps, Robert (pf)
- RCA LM-7042/LSC-7042;
33m/s; 2 discs; rel 1966; del
1971
- CRI-288; 33s; 2 discs; rel 1972;
cip

Intermezzo
[641] Marlowe, Sylvia (hpschd)
- Decca DL-10021/DL-710021;
33m/s; rel 1961; del 1971

Partita (1947)
[642] Weiser, Bernhard (pf)
- New Editions 1; 33m; rel 1952;
del 1959

(Five) Pieces, Piano (1968)
[643] Miller, Robert (pf)
- Acoustic Research AR-0654.088;
33s; rel 1971
- New World NW-308; 33s; rel
1980

(Three) Pieces, Two Prepared Pianos (1962)
[644] Jacobs, Paul (pf); Kalish, Gilbert
(pf)
- Columbia ML-6359/MS-6959;
33m/s; rel 1967; del 1970
- CRI-290; 33s; rel 1972; cip

Polyphony (1956)
[645] Louisville Orchestra; Whitney,
Robert (cond)
- LOU-58-4; 33m (Louisville
Orchestra First Edition Records
1958 No 4); rel 1959; del 1975

Psalm 121
[646] Mormon Tabernacle Choir; Ottley,
Jerold D. (cond)
- Columbia M-34134; 33s; rel
1976; cip

Quartet, Strings (1958)
[647] Lenox String Quartet
- CRI-161; 33m/s; rel 1963/?; cip

Quartet, Winds (1941)
[648] Dorian Woodwind Quartet
- Vox SVBX-5307; 33s; 3 discs; rel
1977; cip

[649] Fairfield Wind Ensemble
- Columbia ML-4846; 33m; rel
1954; del 1968
- Columbia CML-4846; 33m; rel
1968; del 1974
- Columbia AML-4846; 33m; rel
1974; del 1976

Septet (1956)
[650] Contemporary Chamber Ensemble;
Weisberg, Arthur (cond)
- Acoustic Research AR-0654.088;
33s; rel 1971
- New World NW-308; 33s; rel
1980

Serenade concertante (1944)
[651] Brandeis University Festival
Orchestra; Solomon, Izler (cond)
- MGM E-3245; 33m; rel 1956;
del 1959
- CRI-143; 33m/s; rel 1961/?; cip

BERGER, Jean (1909-)
Brazilian Psalm (1941)
[652] Fleet Street Choir; Lawrence, T. B.
(cond)
- Argo ARS-1003; 33m; rel
pre-1956

[653] St. Olaf Choir; Christiansen, Olaf C.
(cond)
- St. Olaf DLP-5; 33m; 10"; rel
1952; del 1953

Eyes of All Wait upon Thee, The
[654] Mormon Tabernacle Choir;
Schreiner, Alexander (org); Asper,
Frank (org); Condie, Richard P.
(cond)
- Columbia ML-6019/MS-6619;
33m/s; rel 1964; del 1966

Fandango brasileiro
[655] Adler, Larry (harmonica); Colin,
Lee (pf)
- Concert Hall CHS-1168; 33m;
10"; rel 1953; del 1957
- Mercury (French) MLP-7026;
33m; rel pre-1956
- Musical Masterpiece Society
POP-20; 33m; 7" or 8"; rel
pre-1956

Frisco Whale, The
[656] King Chorale; King, Gordon (cond)
- Orion ORS-75205; 33s; rel
1978; cip

Rose Touched by the Sun's Warm Rays, A
[657] Capital University Chapel Choir;
Snyder, Ellis Emanuel (cond)
- Coronet S-1405; 33s; rel 1969;
cip

Short Overture for Strings
[658] Rome Chamber Orchestra; Flagello,
Nicolas (cond)
- Peters Internationale PLE-071;
33s; rel 1978; cip

Snake Baked a Hoecake
[659] King Chorale; King, Gordon (cond)
- Orion ORS-75205; 33s; rel
1978; cip

Sonata da camera (arr for ob and pf)
[660] Rath, Richard (ob); Edwards, Karin
(pf)
- Golden Crest RE-7073; 33s; rel
1978; cip

They All Dance the Samba
[661] Brice, Carol (al); Brice, Jonathan
(pf)
- Columbia 17608-10D (in set
MM-910); 78; 3-10"; rel 1950
- Columbia ML-2108; 33m; 10";
rel 1950; del 1956

They All Dance the Samba *(cont'd)*
[662] Eddy, Nelson (bar); Paxson, Theodore (pf)
- Columbia ML-2130; 33m; 10"; rel 1950; del 1956

Vision of Peace (1949)
[663] St. Olaf Choir; Christiansen, Olaf C. (cond)
- St. Olaf DLP-6; 33m; 10"; rel 1952; del 1953

BERGSMA, William (1921-)

Carol on Twelfth Night, A (1954)
[664] Louisville Orchestra; Whitney, Robert (cond)
- LOU-545-10; 33m (Louisville Orchestra First Edition Records 1955 No 10); rel 1959; del 1975

Chameleon Variations (1960)
[665] Portland Junior Symphony; Avshalomov, Jacob (cond)
- CRI-140; 33m/s; rel 1961/?; cip

Concerto, Violin and Orchestra (1966)
[666] Statkiewicz, Edward (vln); Polish National Radio Orchestra; Szostak, Zdzislav (cond)
- Turnabout TVS-34428; 33s; rel 1971; del 1977

Concerto, Wind Quintet (1958)
[667] Clarion Wind Quintet
- Golden Crest CR-4076/CRS-4076; 33m/s; rel 1967; cip

Fantastic Variations on a Theme from Tristan and Isolde (1961)
[668] McInnes, Donald (vla); Hokanson, Randolph (pf)
- Musical Heritage Society MHS-3533; 33s; rel 1977

Fortunate Islands, The (1947, rev 1956)
[669] Accademia Nazionale di Santa Cecilia Orchestra, Roma; Antonini, Alfredo (cond)
- CRI-112; 33m/s; rel 1957/?; cip

Gold and the Senor Commandante (1941)
[670] Eastman-Rochester Symphony Orchestra; Hanson, Howard (cond)
- Mercury MG-50147/SR-90147; 33m/s; rel 1957/1960; del 1963
- Eastman-Rochester Archives ERA-1004; 33s; rel 1974; cip

Illegible Canons (1969)
[671] Smith, William O. (cl); Dunbar, Dan (perc)
- Musical Heritage Society MHS-3533; 33s; rel 1977

Lullee, Lullay (1948)
[672] Steber, Eleanor (sop); Biltcliffe, Edwin (pf)
- St/And SPL-411-12; 33m; 2 discs; rel 1963; del 1964
- Desto D-411-12/DST-6411-12; 33m/s; 2 discs; rel 1964; cip

March with Trumpets (1956)
[673] Cornell University Wind Ensemble; Stith, Marice (cond)
- Cornell CUWE-4; 33s; rel 1971; cip

[674] Goldman Band
- Decca DL-8633/DL-78633; 33m/s; rel 1958; del 1973

Music on a Quiet Theme (1943, rev 1946)
[675] Japan Philharmonic Symphony Orchestra; Strickland, William (cond)
- CRI-131; 33m/s; rel 1960/1971; cip

Quartet, Strings, No 2 (1944)
[676] Walden String Quartet
- American Recording Society ARS-18; 33m; rel 1953
- Desto D-425/DST-6425; 33m/s; rel 1966; del 1977

Quartet, Strings, No 3 (1953)
[677] Juilliard String Quartet
- Columbia ML-5476; 33m; rel 1960; del 1968
- Columbia CML-5476; 33m; rel 1968; del 1974
- Columbia AML-5476; 33m; rel 1974; del 1976

Quartet, Strings, No 4 (1970)
[678] Philadelphia String Quartet
- Musical Heritage Society MHS-3533; 33s; rel 1977

Riddle Me This (1957)
[679] Gregg Smith Singers; Smith, Gregg (cond)
Rec 4/76
- Vox SVBX-5354; 33s; 3 discs; rel 1979

[680] Seattle Chamber Singers; Shangrow, George (cond)
Rec 8/1-8/76
- Voyager VRLP-701S; 33s; rel 1976

Suite, Brass Quartet (1940)
[681] American Brass Quintet
- Desto DC-6474-77; 33s; 4 discs; rel 1969; cip

Tangents (1951): Book One
[682] Johannesen, Grant (pf)
- Golden Crest CRS-4111; 33q; rel 1972; cip

Wife of Martin Guerre, The (1956): Selections
[683] Judd, Mary (sop); Sarfaty, Regina (m sop); Harbachick, Stephen (bar); members of original cast; chamber orchestra; Waldman, Frederic (cond)
- CRI-105; 33m/s; rel 1956/?; cip

BERKOWITZ, Saul (1922-)

Syncopations
[684] Helps, Robert (pf)
- RCA LM-7042/LSC-7042; 33m/s; 2 discs; rel 1966; del 1971
- CRI-288; 33s; 2 discs; rel 1972; cip

BERLINSKI, Herman (1910-)

Burning Bush, The (1956)
[685] Baker, George C. (org)
- Delos DEL-FY-025; 33s; rel 1977; cip

[686] Baker, Robert (org)
Rec 7/28/57
- Mirrosonic DRE-1004; 33m; 2 discs; rel 1958; del 1965

[687] Berlinski, Herman (org)
- Musical Heritage Society MHS-3121; 33s; rel 1975

[688] Crozier, Catharine (org)
- Washington WAS-16; 33m/s; rel 1961; del 1962
- Aeolian-Skinner AS-316; 33s; rel 1963; del 1970

Elegy in Memory of Albert Einstein
[689] Berlinski, Herman (org)
- Musical Heritage Society MHS-3121; 33s; rel 1975

From the World of My Father
[690] Berlinski, Herman (org)
- Musical Heritage Society MHS-3121; 33s; rel 1975

Kol Nidre
[691] Berlinski, Herman (org)
- Musical Heritage Society MHS-3121; 33s; rel 1975

[692] David Tilman Choir; organ
- Serenus SRS-12039; 33s; rel 1976?

Sinfonia, Organ, No 2 (Symphony of Festivals)
[693] Berlinski, Herman (org)
Rec 6/71
- Musical Heritage Society MHS-1775; 33s; rel 1972
- Schwann AMS Studio 605; 33s; rel 1972

Sinfonia, Organ, No 8 (Eliyahu) (1972)
[694] Berlinski, Herman (org)
- Musical Heritage Society MHS-1965; 33s; rel 1975

Symphonic Visions (1949)
[695] Asahi Orchestra of Tokyo; Korn,
Richard (cond)
- CRI-115; 33m/s; rel 1957/?; cip

BERNSTEIN, Charles Harold (1917-)

Amphion Suite
[696] Amphion Quartet of Belgium
- Laurel LR-101-02; 33s; 2 discs;
rel 1975; cip

Cabris, A
[697] Amphion Quartet of Belgium
- Laurel LR-101-02; 33s; 2 discs;
rel 1975; cip

Duo, Flute and Viola
[698] Amphion Quartet of Belgium
- Laurel LR-101-02; 33s; 2 discs;
rel 1975; cip

Duo, Flute and Violoncello
[699] Amphion Quartet of Belgium
- Laurel LR-101-02; 33s; 2 discs;
rel 1975; cip

Elegiac Dreams and Awakening
[700] Amphion Quartet of Belgium
- Laurel LR-101-02; 33s; 2 discs;
rel 1975; cip

Interlude, Flute, Violin, and Viola
[701] Amphion Quartet of Belgium
- Laurel LR-101-02; 33s; 2 discs;
rel 1975; cip

London Flute
[702] Amphion Quartet of Belgium
- Laurel LR-101-02; 33s; 2 discs;
rel 1975; cip

Poeme transcendental
[703] Nakura, Yoshiko (vln)
- Laurel LR-105; 33s; rel 1977;
cip

Rhapsodic Outline and Drawings
[704] Brennand, Charles (vcl)
- Laurel LR-108; 33s; rel 1979;
cip

Rhapsody Israelien
[705] Nakura, Yoshiko (vln)
- Laurel LR-105; 33s; rel 1977;
cip

Trio, Strings (Nostalgic)
[706] Nakura, Yoshiko (vln); Thomas,
Milton (vla); Brennand, Charles
(vcl)
- Laurel LR-105; 33s; rel 1977;
cip

Trois Jonas, Les
[707] Brennand, Charles (vcl)
- Laurel LR-108; 33s; rel 1979;
cip

BERNSTEIN, Leonard (1918-)

Age of Anxiety, The (Symphony No 2) (1949)
[708] Entremont, Philippe (pf); New York
Philharmonic; Bernstein, Leonard
(cond)
Rec 7/19/65
- Columbia ML-6285/MS-6885;
33m/s; rel 1966; cip
- CBS (English, German, and
Italian) 72503; 33s; rel 1966*
- CBS (English) 78228; 33s; rel
1973*
- Columbia MG-32793; 33s; 2
discs; rel 1974; cip
[709] Foss, Lukas (pf); Israel
Philharmonic Orchestra;
Bernstein, Leonard (cond)
- Deutsche Grammophon
2530.968(10)-2530.970(10)
(in set 2709.077); 33s; 3 discs;
rel 1978; cip
[710] Foss, Lukas (pf); New York
Philharmonic; Bernstein, Leonard
(cond)
Rec 2/27/50
- Columbia 13121-24D (in set
MM-946); 78; 4 discs; rel 1950
- Columbia MM-931; 78; rel
pre-1952
- Columbia ML-4325; 33m; rel
1950; del 1966

(Seven) Anniversaries (1942-43): (No 1) For Aaron Copland, (No 2) For My Sister Shirley, (No 3) In Memoriam, Alfred Eisner, (No 4) For Paul Bowles, (No 5) In Memoriam, Nathalie Koussevitzky, (No 6) For Serge Koussevitzky, (No 7) For William Schuman
[711] Nos 1-7
Bernstein, Leonard (pf)
Rec ca 1949
- Camden CAL-214; 33m; rel
1955; del 1958
[712] Nos 1-3
Bernstein, Leonard (pf)
Rec ca 1949
- Victor 12-0683 (in set M-1278);
78; rel 1949-50
- Victor 12-0684-86 (in set
DM-1278); 78; 3 discs; rel
1949-50
[713] Nos 2,5,7
Bernstein, Leonard (pf)
- Hargail MW-501; 78; 2 discs; rel
1944
[714] Nos 4-7
Bernstein, Leonard (pf)
- Camden CAL-351; 33m
[715] Nos 4,5
Bernstein, Leonard (pf)
Rec 1949
- Victor 12-0228 (in set M-1209);
78; rel pre-1950
- Victor 12-0229 (in set
DM-1209); 78; rel pre-1950
- Victor 18-0114 (in set DV-15);
78; rel pre-1952

Bonne cuisine, La (1947): Rabbit at Top Speed
[716] Sanders, Felicia (sop); orchestra;
Joseph, Irving (cond)
- Decca DL-8762/DL-78762;
33m/s; rel 1958/1959; del
1971

Candide (1955-56): Overture
[717] Boston Pops Orchestra; Fiedler,
Arthur (cond)
Rec 6/12/64
- RCA LM-2789/LSC-2789;
33m/s; rel 1965; cip
- RCA (English)
RB-6629/SB-6629; 33m/s; rel
1965*
- RCA ARL-1-0108; 33s; rel 1973;
cip
- Deutsche Grammophon
2584.002; 33s; rel 1977; cip
- Deutsche Grammophon
2584.019; 33s; rel 1979; cip
[718] Cleveland Pops Orchestra; Lane,
Louis (cond)
Rec 8/21-22/58
- Epic LC-3539/BC-1013; 33m/s;
rel 1959; del 1968
- Columbia (English)
SX-1583/SCX-3503; 33m/s; rel
1963*
[719] London Symphony Orchestra;
Previn, Andre (cond)
Rec 11/30/71
- EMI/His Master's Voice
ASD-2784; 33s; rel 1971
- Angel S-37021; 33s; rel 1974;
cip
[720] Los Angeles Philharmonic
Orchestra; Mehta, Zubin (cond)
- London CSA-2246; 33s; 2 discs;
rel 1976; del 1980
- London CS-7031; 33s; rel 1977;
cip
- JBL CSL-1010; 33s; rel 1977
[721] New York Philharmonic; Bernstein,
Leonard (cond)
Rec 9/28/60, 5/16/63, and
6/18/63
- Columbia ML-6077/MS-6677;
33m/s; rel 1965; cip
- CBS (English and French)
72406; 33s; rel 1966*
- Columbia ML-6388/MS-6988;
33m/s; rel 1967; cip
- Columbia MS-7213-14 (in set
M2X-795); 33s; 2 discs; rel
1969; cip
- Columbia D3S-818; 33s; 3 discs;
rel 1970; cip
- Columbia M-30304; 33s; rel
1971; cip
- Columbia M3X-31068; 33s; 3
discs; rel 1972; cip
- Columbia MG-32174; 33s; 2
discs; rel 1973; cip
- Columbia MG-35188; 33s; 2
discs; rel 1979; cip
- CBS (Italian) 77244; 33s
- CBS (Italian) 71052; 33s
- CBS (Italian) 61199-200; 33s; 2
discs

Candide (1955-56): Overture
(cont'd)

[722] North Texas State University Symphonic Band
- Austin 6164; 33m; rel 1963; del 1971

[723] Royal Philharmonic Orchestra; Rogers, Eric (cond)
- Decca PFS-4211; 33s; rel 1971*
- London SPC-21048; 33s; rel 1972; del 1979

[724] Texas Tech Concert Band
- Austin 6240; 33m; rel 1963; del 1971

[725] Utah Symphony Orchestra; Abravanel, Maurice (cond)
- Turnabout TVS-34459; 33s; rel 1972; cip

Chichester Psalms (1965)

[726] Camerata Singers; Bogart, John (al); New York Philharmonic; Bernstein, Leonard (cond)
Rec 7/26/65
- CBS (English, German, and Italian) 72374; 33s; rel 1965
- Columbia ML-6192/MS-6792; 33m/s; rel 1966; cip

[727] Vienna Academy Chamber Choir; a Vienna choirboy; Israel Philharmonic Orchestra; Bernstein, Leonard (cond)
- Deutsche Grammophon 2530.968(10)-2530.970(10) (in set 2709.077); 33s; 3 discs; rel 1978; cip

Chichester Psalms (version for chorus, organ, and percussion)

[728] King's College Choir, Cambridge; Bowman, James (ct); Ellis, Osian (hp); Corkhill, David (perc); Lancelot, James (org); Ledger, Philip (cond)
- EMI/His Master's Voice ASD-3055; 33s; rel 1974*
- Angel S-37119; 33s; rel 1975; cip

Dybbuk (1974)

[729] Johnson, David (bar); Ostendorf, John (b); New York City Ballet Orchestra; Bernstein, Leonard (cond)
- Columbia M-33082/MQ-33082; 33s/q; rel 1974; cip

Facsimile (1946)

[730] Ballet Theatre Orchestra; Levine, Joseph (cond)
Rec 1955
- Capitol P-8320; 33m; rel 1956; del 1960
- Capitol (English) P-8320; 33m; rel 1957*
- Capitol HDR-21004; 33m; 4 discs; rel 1966; del 1970

Facsimile (1946) *(cont'd)*

[731] Concert Arts Orchestra; Irving, Robert (cond)
Rec 1967
- Capitol SP-8701; 33s; rel 1969; del 1970
- Seraphim S-60197; 33s; rel 1972; del 1976
- Time-Life SLT-159; 33s

[732] New York Philharmonic; Bernstein, Leonard (cond)
Rec 6/18/63
- CBS (English, German, and Italian) 72374; 33s; rel 1965
- Columbia ML-6192/MS-6792; 33m/s; rel 1966; cip
- Columbia MG-32174; 33s; 2 discs; rel 1973; cip

[733] Victor Orchestra; Bernstein, Leonard (cond)
Rec 1/24/47
- Victor 11-9677-78 (in set M-1142); 78; 2 discs; rel 1947
- Victor 11-9679-80 (in set DM-1142); 78; 2 discs; rel 1947
- Camden CAL-196; 33m; rel 1955; del 1960

Fancy Free (1944)

[734] Ballet Theatre Orchestra; Holliday, Billy (voice); Bernstein, Leonard (cond)
Rec 1944
- Decca 23463-66 (in set DA-406); 78; 4-10"; rel pre-1948
- Decca DL-6023; 33m; 10"; rel 1953; del 1957
- Decca DL-8701; 33m (excerpt)
- Varese Sarabande VC-81055; 33m; rel 1979; cip

[735] Ballet Theatre Orchestra; Levine, Joseph (cond)
Rec 1952
- Capitol L-8197; 33m; 10"; rel 1953; del 1957
- Capitol P-8196; 33m; rel 1953; del 1963
- Capitol (English) CCL-7517; 33m; 10"; rel 1953*
- Capitol (English) P-8196; 33m; rel 1959*
- Capitol HDR-21004; 33m; 4 discs; rel 1966; del 1970

[736] Columbia Symphony Orchestra; Bernstein, Leonard (cond)
Rec 7/13/56
- Columbia CL-920; 33m; rel 1956; del 1965

[737] Concert Arts Orchestra; Irving, Robert (cond)
Rec 1966
- Time-Life TL-145/STL-145; 33m/s; rel 1967
- Capitol SP-8701; 33s; rel 1969; del 1970
- EMI/Studio Two TWO-302; 33s; rel 1970*
- Seraphim S-60197; 33s; rel 1972; del 1976

Fancy Free (1944) *(cont'd)*

- Angel S-36084; 33s; rel 1975; del 1978 (Excerpt: Finale)

[738] Israel Philharmonic Orchestra; Bernstein, Leonard (cond)
- Deutsche Grammophon 2531.196; 33s; rel 1980; cip

[739] New York Philharmonic; Bernstein, Leonard (cond)
Rec 6/11/63
- Columbia ML-6077/MS-6677; 33m/s; rel 1965; cip
- CBS (English) 72406; 33s; rel 1966*
- Columbia ML-6271/MS-6871; 33m/s; rel 1966; del 1976 (excerpts)
- Columbia M-30304; 33s; rel 1971; cip
- Columbia MG-32174; 33s; 2 discs; rel 1973; cip

Fancy Free: Galop, Waltz, and Danzon

[740] Boston Pops Orchestra; Fiedler, Arthur (cond)
Rec 6/5/46
- Victor 11-9386; 78; rel pre-1948

[741] Boston Pops Orchestra; Fiedler, Arthur (cond)
Rec 6/25/52
- Victor 49-4003-06 (in set WDM-1726); 45; 4-7"; rel 1953?
- Victor ERA-146; 45; 7"; rel pre-1956
- RCA LM-1726; 33m; rel 1953; del 1961

[742] Boston Pops Orchestra; Fiedler, Arthur (cond)
Rec 6/18/58
- RCA LM-2294/LSC-2294; 33m/s; rel 1959; del 1964
- RCA LM-2747/LSC-2747; 33m/s; rel 1964; cip
- RCA ARL-1-0108; 33s; rel 1973; cip
- RCA CRL-3-3270; 33s; 3 discs; rel 1979; cip

[743] Philadelphia Pops Orchestra; Hilsberg, Alexander (cond)
Rec 1/3/52
- Columbia AAL-17; 33m; 10"; rel 1952; del 1957

Fancy Free: Danzon

[744] Cleveland Pops Orchestra; Lane, Louis (cond)
Rec 7/22-23/59
- Epic LC-3626/BC-1047; 33m/s; rel 1959; del 1970
- Columbia (English) SX-1583/SCX-3503; 33m/s; rel 1963*

Fancy Free: Finale

[745] Royal Philharmonic Orchestra; Rogers, Eric (cond)
- Decca (English) PFS-4211; 33s; rel 1971*
- London SPC-21048; 33s; rel 1972; del 1979

Fanfare for Bima

[746] Cambridge Brass Quintet
- Crystal S-204; 33s; rel 1977; cip

(Four) Horah Dances (1947-48): Simchu Na

[747] chorus; orchestra; Young, Victor (cond)
- Alco A-21; 78; rel 1947
- Alco ALP-1009; 33m; 10''; rel 1951; del 1955

Jeremiah Symphony (Symphony No 1) (1943)

[748] Ludwig, Christa (m sop); Israel Philharmonic Orchestra; Bernstein, Leonard (cond)
- Deutsche Grammophon 2530.968(10)-2530.970(10) (in set 2709.077); 33s; 3 discs; rel 1978; cip

[749] Merriman, Nan (m sop); St. Louis Symphony Orchestra; Bernstein, Leonard (cond)
Rec 12/1/45
- Victor 11-8971-73 (in set M-1026); 78; 3 discs; rel 1946
- Victor 11-8974-76 (in set DM-1026); 78; 3 discs; rel 1946
- Camden CAL-196; 33m; rel 1955; del 1960
- RCA (English) SMA-7002; 33s; rel 1975

[750] Tourel, Jennie (m sop); New York Philharmonic; Bernstein, Leonard (cond)
Rec 5/20/61
- Columbia ML-5703/MS-6303; 33m/s; rel 1962; cip
- CBS (English and French) 72399; 33s; rel 1966*
- CBS (English) 78228; 33s; rel 1973*
- Columbia MG-32793; 33s; 2 discs; rel 1974; cip

Jewish Holiday Songs and Dances (1947-48): Reena

[751] chorus; orchestra; Goberman, Max (cond)
- Vox 16040 (in set VX-123); 78; 10''; rel 1947

Mass (1971)

[752] Titus, Alan; Cryer, David; Ellis, Tom; Norman Scribner Choir; Berkshire Boys Choir; orchestra; Bernstein, Leonard (cond) (original cast)
Rec 8-9/71
- Columbia M2-31008/M2Q-31008; 33s/q; 2 discs; rel 1972; cip
- CBS (English) 77256; 33s; 2 discs; rel 1972*
- CBS (English) M2Q-31008; 33q; 2 discs; rel 1972*
- Columbia MQ-31960; 33q; rel 1973 (excerpts)
- Columbia MG-32174; 33s; 2 discs; rel 1973; cip (Excerpt: Two Meditations)

Mass: A Simple Song

[753] Milnes, Sherrill (b bar); New Philharmonia Orchestra; Dods, Marcus (cond)
- RCA ARL-1-0108; 33s; rel 1973; cip

Mass: Pax-Communion

[754] Philadelphia Orchestra; Ormandy, Eugene (cond)
- RCA ARL-1-0108; 33s; rel 1973; cip

Mass: Selections (arr for orch by Irwin Kostal)

[755] Boston Pops Orchestra; Fiedler, Arthur (cond)
- Deutsche Grammophon 2584.002; 33s; rel 1977; cip

Mass: Almighty Father and Meditation No 1 (arr for hps)

[756] New York Harp Ensemble; Wurtzler, Aristid von (cond)
- Musical Heritage Society MHS-3307; 33s; rel 1975

On the Town (1944): Overture

[757] orchestra; Engel, Lehman (cond)
- Columbia CL-1279/CS-8094; 33m/s; rel 1959; del 1961

On the Town: Four Dances

[758] orchestra of the original production; Bernstein, Leonard (cond)
Rec 2/3/45
- Victor 10-1158-61 (in set M-995); 78; 2-10''; rel 1945*
- Victor 10-1162-65 (in set DM-995); 78; 2-10''; rel 1945*
- Camden CAL-196; 33m; rel 1955; del 1960
- Camden CAL-336; 33m
- Camden CFL-102; 33m
- Camden CAE-203; 45; 7''

On the Town: Three Dances

[759] Cleveland Pops Orchestra; Lane, Louis (cond)
Rec 7/7/60
- Epic LC-3743/BC-1107; 33m/s; rel 1961; del 1970
- Columbia (English) SX-6048/SCX-6048; 33m/s; rel 1966*

[760] Cornell University Wind Ensemble; Stith, Marice (cond)
- Cornell CUWE-8; 33s; rel 1971; cip

[761] New York Philharmonic; Bernstein, Leonard (cond)
Rec 6/11/63
- Columbia ML-6077/MS-6677; 33m/s; rel 1965; cip
- CBS (English) 72406; 33s; rel 1966*

On the Town: Three Dances *(cont'd)*

- Columbia MS-7213-14 (in set M2X-795); 33s; 2 discs; rel 1969; cip (Excerpt: Times Square)
- Columbia M-30304; 33s; rel 1971; cip
- Columbia MG-32174; 33s; 2 discs; rel 1973; cip

On the Town: Times Square

[762] Royal Philharmonic Orchestra; Rogers, Eric (cond)
- Decca (English) PFS-4211; 33s; rel 1971*
- London SPC-21048; 33s; rel 1972; del 1979

On the Waterfront (Symphonic Suite) (1955)

[763] New York Philharmonic; Bernstein, Leonard (cond)
Rec 5/16/60
- Columbia ML-5651/MS-6251; 33m/s; rel 1961; cip
- Philips (English) BBL-7517/SBBL-652; 33m/s; rel 1961*
- CBS (English) 61096; 33s; rel 1969*
- CBS (German) 62241; 33s
- CBS (French) 72225; 33s
- Columbia M-30304; 33s; rel 1971; cip (Excerpt: Love Theme)

(Five) Pieces, Brass (1947-48): Elegy for Mippy I

[764] Eger, Joseph (hn); Menuhin, Yaltah (pf)
Rec ca 11/56
- RCA LM-2146; 33m; rel 1957; del 1960

(Five) Pieces, Brass: Elegy for Mippy II

[765] Gillespie, Robert (tbn)
- Mace MCS-9112; 33s; rel 1973

[766] Raph, Alan (tbn)
- Coronet S-1407; 33s; rel 1969; cip

Prelude, Fugue, and Riffs (1955)

[767] Goodman, Benny (cl); Columbia Jazz Combo; Bernstein, Leonard (cond)
Rec 2/20/63 and 5/6/63
- Columbia ML-6077/MS-6677; 33m/s; rel 1965; cip
- Columbia ML-6205/MS-6805; 33m/s; rel 1966; cip
- CBS (English and French) 72406; 33s; rel 1966*
- CBS (English and French) 72469; 33s; rel 1968*

Serenade (After Plato: Symposium) (1954)

[768] Francescatti, Zino (vln); New York Philharmonic; Bernstein, Leonard (cond)
Rec 7/22/65
- Columbia ML-6458/MS-7058; 33m/s; rel 1968; cip
- CBS (English) 72643; 33s; rel 1968*

[769] Kremer, Gidon (vln); Israel Philharmonic Orchestra; Bernstein, Leonard (cond)
- Deutsche Grammophon 2531.196; 33s; rel 1980; cip

[770] Stern, Isaac (vln); Symphony of the Air; Bernstein, Leonard (cond)
Rec 4/19/56
- Columbia ML-5144; 33m; rel 1956; del 1965
- Columbia CML-5144; 33m; rel 1968; del 1980
- Odyssey Y-34633; 33m; rel 1978; cip

Shivaree (1969)

[771] brass and percussion ensemble; Prausnitz, Frederik (cond)
Rec 1970
- Metropolitan Museum of Art AKS-10001; 33; rel 1970

Sonata, Clarinet and Piano (1941-42)

[772] Bunke, Jerome (cl); Hayashi, Hidemitsu (pf)
- Musical Heritage Society MHS-1887; 33s; rel 1974

[773] Drucker, Stanley (cl); Hambro, Leonid (pf)
- Odyssey Y-30492; 33s; rel 1971; cip

[774] Oppenheim, David (cl); Bernstein, Leonard (pf)
- Hargail MW-501; 78; 2 discs; rel 1944

[775] Russo, John (cl); Ignacio, Lydia Walton (pf)
- Orion ORS-79330; 33s; rel 1980; cip

[776] Snavely, Jack (cl); Hollander, Jeffrey (pf)
- Golden Crest RE-7035; 33s; rel 1972; cip

[777] Tichman, Herbert (cl); Budnevich, Ruth (pf)
- Concert Hall CHH-18; 33m; rel 1954

[778] Willett, William C. (cl); Staples, James (pf)
- Mark MRS-32638; 33s; rel 1970; del 1975

Songfest (1977)

[779] Dale, Clamma (sop); Elias, Rosalind (m sop); Williams, Nancy (m sop); Rosenshein, Neil (ten); Reardon, John (bar); Gramm, Donald (b); National Symphony Orchestra; Bernstein, Leonard (cond)
- Deutsche Grammophon 2531.044; 33s; rel 1978; cip

Symphony No 3 (Kaddish) (1961-63)

[780] Caballe, Montserrat (sop); Wager, Michael (speaker); Vienna Academy Chamber Choir; Wiener Saengerknaben; Israel Philharmonic Orchestra; Bernstein, Leonard (cond)
- Deutsche Grammophon 2530.968(10)-2530.970(10) (in set 2709.077); 33s; 3 discs; rel 1978; cip

[781] Tourel, Jennie (m sop); Montealegre, Felicia (speaker); Camerata Singers; Columbus Boychoir; Bernstein, Leonard (cond)
Rec 4/15/64
- Columbia KL-6005/KS-6605; 33m/s; rel 1964; cip
- CBS (English and French) 72265; 33s; rel 1967*
- CBS (English) 78228; 33s; rel 1973*
- Columbia MG-32793; 33s; 2 discs; rel 1974; cip

Trouble in Tahiti (1952)

[782] Williams, Nancy (m sop); Patrick, Julian (b bar); Columbia Wind Ensemble; Bernstein, Leonard (cond)
Rec 8/11-15/73
- Columbia KM-32597/KMQ-32597; 33s/q; rel 1974; cip

[783] Wolff, Beverly (sop); Atkinson, David (bar); MGM Orchestra; Winograd, Arthur (cond)
- MGM E-3646; 33m; rel 1958; del 1966
- Heliodor H-25020/HS-25020; 33m/s; rel 1966; del 1970

West Side Story: Symphonic Dances (1961)

[784] New York Philharmonic; Bernstein, Leonard (cond)
Rec 5/16/61
- Columbia ML-5651/MS-6251; 33m/s; rel 1961; cip
- Philips (English) BBL-7517/SBBL-652; 33m/s; rel 1961*
- Columbia MS-7213-14 (in set M2X-795); 33s; 2 discs; rel 1969; cip (Excerpt: Mambo)
- Columbia MS-7246; 33s; rel 1969; cip (Excerpt: Somewhere)
- CBS (English) 61096; 33s; rel 1969*

West Side Story: Symphonic Dances (1961) (cont'd)

- CBS (German) 62241; 33s
- CBS (French) 72225; 33s
- Columbia M-30304; 33s; rel 1971; cip (Excerpt: Mambo)
- Columbia M3X-31068; 33s; 3 discs; rel 1972; cip (Excerpt: Somewhere)
- Columbia MG-32174; 33s; 2 discs; rel 1973; cip

[785] Philadelphia Orchestra; Ormandy, Eugene (cond)
- RCA ARL-1-0108; 33s; rel 1973; cip (Excerpt: Somewhere)

[786] Royal Philharmonic Orchestra; Rogers, Eric (cond)
- Decca (English) PFS-4211; 33s; rel 1971*
- London SPC-21048; 33s; rel 1972; del 1979

[787] San Francisco Symphony Orchestra; Ozawa, Seiji (cond)
Rec 6/24/72
- Deutsche Grammophon 2530.309; 33s; rel 1973; cip
- Deutsche Grammophon (English) 2530.309; 33s; rel 1973*

[788] Victor Symphony Orchestra; Bennett, Robert Russell (cond)
Rec 4/8/59
- RCA LM-2340/LSC-2340; 33m/s; rel 1959; del 1963
- RCA-Victrola VICS-1491; 33s; rel 1970; del 1975
- Camden (English) CDS-1044; 33s
- Camden (Italian) KV-112/KVS-112; 33m/s

[789] orchestra; Prince, Robert (cond)
- Warner Bros B-1240/BS-1240; 33m/s; rel 1959; del 1969
- Warner Bros (English) WM-4003/WS-8003; 33m/s; rel 1960*

BERRY, Wallace (1928-)

Canto lirico (1965)

[790] Zaslav, Bernard (vla); Zaslav, Naomi (pf)
- CRI-282; 33s; rel 1973; cip

Duo, Flute and Piano (1968)

[791] Bryan, Keith (fl); Keys, Karen (pf)
- CRI-282; 33s; rel 1973; cip

Duo, Violin and Piano (1961)

[792] Loban, John (vln); Berry, Wallace (pf)
- Opus One 46; 33s; rel 1979; cip

Quartet, Strings, No 2 (1964)

[793] Composers Quartet
- CRI-282; 33s; rel 1973; cip

Sonata, Piano (1975-76)

[794] Mehta, Dady (pf)
- CRI-412; 33s; rel 1980; cip

Trio, Piano and Strings (1970)
[795] Pignotti, Alfio (vln); Moores, Margaret (vcl); Mehta, Dady (pf)
Rec 5/76
- CRI-371; 33s; rel 1977; cip

(Eight) 20th-Century Miniatures (1955): Melody
[796] Fuszek, Rita (pf)
- Educo 3107; 33

BESTOR, Charles (1924-)
Sonata, Piano (1962, rev 1974)
[797] Peltzer, Dwight (pf)
- Serenus SRS-12069; 33s; rel 1978; cip

BEVERIDGE, Thomas (1938-)
Once--In Memoriam Martin Luther King, Jr.
[798] Beveridge, Diana Pezzi (sop); Brewster, Steve (cb); Dirksen, Richard W. (org); Choral Arts Society of Washington; National Symphony Orchestra; Scribner, Norman (cond)
- Turnabout TVS-34467; 33s; rel 1972; del 1978

BEVERSDORF, Thomas (1924-81)
Sonata, Flute and Piano (1964)
[799] Pellerite, James (fl); Webb, Charles (pf)
- Golden Crest RE-7023; 33m/s; rel 1968/1979; cip

Sonata, Horn and Piano (1945)
[800] Beversdorf, Thomas (hn); Webb, Charles (pf)
- Coronet LPS-3009; 33s; rel 1975; cip

Sonata, Tuba and Piano (1956)
[801] Le Blanc, Robert (tu); Baker, Myra (pf)
- Coronet S-1721; 33s; rel 1973; cip

Sonata, Violin and Piano (1964)
[802] Israelievitch, Jacques (vln); Upper, Henry (pf)
- Orion ORS-75170; 33s; rel 1975; cip

Sonata, Violoncello and Piano (1967-69)
[803] Toth, Andor (vcl); Thompson, Marilyn (pf)
- Coronet LPS-3009; 33s; rel 1975; cip

(Three) Songs for Soprano (1955)
[804] Wrancher, Elisabeth (sop)
- Coronet LPS-3009; 33s; rel 1975; cip

BEYER, Frederick H. (1926-)
Conversations, Brass Trio
[805] Florida State University Brass Trio
- Golden Crest CRS-4081; 33s; rel 1969; cip

BEYER, Johanna Magdalena (1888-1944)
Status quo: Music of the Spheres (1938)
[806] Electric Weasel Ensemble
- 1750 Arch S-1765; 33s; rel 1978; cip

Suite, Clarinet and Bassoon
[807] Mazzeo, Rosario (cl); Allard, Raymond (bsn)
- New Music Quarterly Recordings 1413 (18-19); 78; rel 1938

BEZANSON, Philip (1916-)
Rondo-Prelude (1954)
[808] Oslo Philharmonic Orchestra; Fjeldstad, Oivin (cond)
- CRI-159; 33m; rel 1962; cip

BIALOSKY, Marshall H. (1923-)
Suite, Flute, Oboe, and Clarinet
[809] Los Angeles Philharmonic Wind Quintet
- WIM Records WIMR-9; 33s; rel 1974; cip

BIELAWA, Herbert (1930-)
Spectrum (1966)
[810] Cornell University Wind Ensemble; electronic music; Stith, Marice (cond)
- Cornell CUWE-1; 33s; rel 1971; cip

BIGELOW, Frederick
Our Director March
[811] Arthur Pryor's Band
- Victor 16795; 78; 10"

[812] Boston Pops Orchestra; Fiedler, Arthur (cond)
- Victor 49-0842; 45; 7"; rel pre-1958
- Victor WEPR-22; 45; 7"; rel pre-1958
- RCA LM-2944/LSC-2944; 33m/s; rel 1967; cip

[813] Eastman Symphonic Wind Ensemble; Fennell, Frederick (cond)
- Mercury MG-40007; 33m; rel 1955; del 1957
- Mercury MG-50113; 33m; rel 1956; del 1969

[814] Goldman Band; Cox, Ainslee (cond)
- New World NW-266; 33s; rel 1977

[815] Victor Military Band
- Victor 35024; 78

BIGGS, R. Keys (1886-1962)
Communion Processional
[816] Jesus and Mary Choral Group; Mother Marie Laetitia (cond)
- Columbia CL-2092/CS-8892; 33m/s; rel 1963

BILIK, Jerry (1933-)
American Civil War Fantasy
[817] University of Michigan Band; Revelli, William (cond)
- Vanguard VRS-9114/VSD-2124; 33m/s; rel 1963; cip

BINDER, Abraham (1895-1966)
To a Lily of Sharon
[818] Rigai, Amiram (pf) or Gold, Edward (pf)
- Musical Heritage Society MHS-1653-54; 33s; 2 discs; rel 1973

BINGHAM, Seth (1882-1972)
Baroque Suite (1943)
[819] Craighead, David (org)
Rec 7/31/57
- Mirrosonic DRE-1012; 33m; 2 discs; rel 1958; del 1965

Baroque Suite: Rhythmic Trumpet
[820] Crozier, Catharine (org)
- Kendall KRC-LP-2555; 33m; rel 1953; del 1958

Connecticut Suite (Op 56) (1954)
[821] Mason, Marilyn (org)
Rec 8/1/57
- Mirrosonic DRE-1001-03; 33m; 3 discs; rel 1958; del 1965

Harmonies of Florence (1928): Twilight at Fiesole
[822] Jones, Joyce (org)
- Word WST-8611; 33s; rel 1973

(Twelve) Hymn Preludes (Op 38, Set 1) (1942): Rise Up, O Men of God
[823] Copes, V. Earle (org)
- Graded Press SoN-3341-42, SoN-33351-52; 33m; 2 discs; rel 1959

(Twelve) Hymn Preludes: Rock of Ages
[824] Rayfield, Robert (org)
- Word W-7002-03; 33m; 2 discs; rel 196?

(Six) Pieces, Organ (Op 9) (1920-23): (No 3) Roulade
[825] Ash, Harold (org)
- WCFM-19; 33m; rel pre-1956
- McIntosh Music MC-1005; 33m; rel 1956; del 1958

[826] Fox, Virgil (org)
- Columbia ML-4401; 33m; rel 1951; del 1958

**(Six) Pieces, Organ (Op 9)
(1920-23): (No 3) Roulade** *(cont'd)*
- Columbia A-1594; 45; 7"; rel
pre-1956
- Columbia CL-813; 33m; rel
1956; del 1961
- RCA ARL-1-0666; 33s; rel 1974;
del 1979

**(Six) Pieces, Organ (Op 9): (No 4)
Chorale Prelude on St. Flavian**
[827] Bonnet, Joseph (org)
- Victor 18214 (in set M-835);
78; rel 1941
- RCA (French) 530-617; 33; rel
1966?

**(Five) Pieces, Organ (Op 36): (No
5) Bells of Riverside**
[828] Swann, Frederick (org)
- Mirrosonic CS-7230; 33s; rel
1972

BINKERD, Gordon (1916-)
Ad te levavi (1959)
[829] Mid-America Chorale; Dexter, John
(cond)
- CRI-191; 33m/s; rel 1964/?; cip

Christmas Carol, A (1970)
[830] Mid-America Chorale; Dexter, John
(cond)
- Gregorian Institute of America
EL-50; 33m

Confitebor tibi
[831] North Texas State University A
Capella Choir; McKinley, Frank A.
(cond)
- Boosey & Hawkes SNBH-5001;
33s; rel 1978

Ebb and Flow, The
[832] North Texas State University A
Capella Choir; McKinley, Frank A.
(cond)
- Boosey & Hawkes SNBH-5001;
33s; rel 1978

Jesus Weeping (1970)
[833] Mid-America Chorale; Dexter, John
(cond)
- Gregorian Institute of America
EL-50; 33m

Let Not Thy Tombstone
[834] North Texas State University A
Capella Choir; McKinley, Frank A.
(cond)
- Boosey & Hawkes SNBH-5001;
33s; rel 1978

Nativitas est hodie
[835] North Texas State University A
Capella Choir; McKinley, Frank A.
(cond)
- Boosey & Hawkes SNBH-5001;
33s; rel 1978

Omnes gentes
[836] North Texas State University A
Capella Choir; McKinley, Frank A.
(cond)
- Boosey & Hawkes SNBH-5001;
33s; rel 1978

Sonata, Piano (1955)
[837] Fletcher, Stanley (pf)
- CRI-201; 33m; rel 1965; cip

Sonata, Violin and Piano (1977)
[838] Laredo, Jaime (vln); Schein, Ann
(pf)
- Desto DC-6439; 33s; rel 1975;
cip

**Sonata, Violoncello and Piano
(1952)**
[839] Drinkall, Roger (vcl); Corbett,
Richard (pf)
- CRI-289; 33s; rel 1972; cip

Sun Singer
[840] University of Illinois Symphony
Orchestra; Goodman, Bernard
(cond)
- Illini Union Bookstore CRS-2;
33m; rel 1953*

Symphony No 1 (1955)
[841] St. Louis Symphony Orchestra;
Remoortel, Edouard van (cond)
- Columbia ML-5691/MS-6291;
33m/s; rel 1962; del 1965

Symphony No 2 (1957)
[842] Oslo Philharmonic Orchestra;
Barati, George (cond)
- CRI-139; 33m/s; rel 1961/?; cip

To Electra (1970)
[843] North Texas State University A
Capella Choir; McKinley, Frank A.
(cond)
- Boosey & Hawkes SNBH-5001;
33s; rel 1978

BIRCHALL, Steven T.
Reality Gates
[844] Electronic music
- Custom Fidelity CFS-3317; 33;
rel 1973

Reciprocals II
[845] Woodbury, Robert (tu); Trice, Jerry
(tu)
- Opus One 4; 33s; rel 1970; cip

BISCARDI, Chester (1948-)
Tenzone
[846] Dick, Robert (fl); Underwood, Keith
(fl); Weirich, Robert (pf)
- CRI-400; 33s; rel 1979; cip

BISCHOFF, John*
Rendezvous
[847] multiple keyboards
Rec 8-9/78
- Vital VR-1062; 33s; rel 1979

BITGOOD, Roberta (1908-)
Choral Prelude on Siloam
[848] Becker, C. Warren (org)
- Chapel LP-5-134/ST-134;
33m/s; rel 1968

**Offertories from Afar: Children's
Prayer from Sweden (Children of
the Heavenly Father)**
[849] Becker, C. Warren (org)
- Chapel LP-5-134/ST-134;
33m/s; rel 1968

BLACK, Frank (1894-1968)
White Cliffs of Dover, The
[850] Fontanne, Lynn (speaker); Lange,
Arthur (cond)
Rec 1941
- RCA LCT-1147; 33m; rel 1954;
del 1957

BLACKWOOD, Easley (1933-)
Chamber Symphony (Op 2) (1954)
[851] Contemporary Chamber Ensemble;
Weisberg, Arthur (cond)
- CRI-144; 33m/s; rel 1961/?; cip

**Concerto, Violin and Orchestra (Op
21) (1967)**
[852] Kling, Paul (vln); Louisville
Orchestra; Mester, Jorge (cond)
- LS-69-4; 33s (Louisville
Orchestra First Edition Records
1969 No 4); rel 1970; cip

**Sonata, Flute and Harpsichord (Op
12) (1962)**
[853] Baron, Samuel (fl); Blackwood,
Easley (hpschd)
- Desto DC-7104; 33s; rel 1970;
cip

**Sonata, Violin and Piano (Op 26)
(1973)**
[854] Zukofsky, Paul (vln); Blackwood,
Easley (pf)
Rec 5/4/76
- CP2 1; 33s; rel 1976

Symphony No 1 (Op 3) (1958)
[855] Boston Symphony Orchestra;
Munch, Charles (cond)
- RCA LM-2352/LSC-2352;
33m/s; rel 1960; del 1963

BLAND, William (1947-)
Song of David (1974)
[856] Starobin, David (gtr)
Rec 1976
- Turnabout TVS-34727; 33s; rel
1978

BLANK, Allan (1925-)

Bicinium II
[857] Smeyers, David (cl); Laskowski,
Kim (bsn)
- Advance FGR-25S; 33s; rel
1979; cip

Esther's Monologue (1970)
[858] Sabo, Marlee (sop); Colburn,
Stephen (ob); Stanick, Gerald
(vla); Peepo, Richard (vcl)
Rec 1/31/71
- Orion ORS-75169; 33s; rel
1975; cip

(Two) Ferlinghetti Songs (1964)
[859] DeGaetani, Jan (m sop); Weisberg,
Arthur (bsn)
- CRI-370; 33s; rel 1977; cip

Music for Violin (1972)
[860] Hoffman, Stanley (vln)
- Orion ORS-75169; 33s; rel
1975; cip

(Three) Novelties (1971)
[861] Delibero, Phil (al sax)
- Open Loop 1; 33s; rel 197?

**(Two) Parables by Franz Kafka
(1964)**
[862] Lamoree, Valarie (sop); Raimondi,
Matthew (vln); Dengel, Eugenie
(vla); Blank, Allan (cond)
- CRI-250; 33s; rel 1970; cip

Poem (1963)
[863] Lavanne, Antonia (sop); Sussman,
Michael (cl); Goberman, John
(vcl); Jolles, Susan (hp); Gerber,
Edward (cond)
- CRI-250; 33s; rel 1970; cip

Rotation (1959-60)
[864] Kalish, Gilbert (pf)
- CRI-329; 33s; rel 1975; cip

**(Two) Studies, Brass Quintet
(1970)**
[865] Iowa Brass Quintet
- Trilogy CTS-1001; 33s; rel
1973; del 1975

**Thirteen Ways of Looking at a
Blackbird (1964-65)**
[866] Lamoree, Valarie (sop);
Contemporary Chamber
Ensemble; Weisberg, Arthur
(cond)
- CRI-250; 33s; rel 1970; cip

BLITZSTEIN, Marc (1905-64)

Airborne, The (1944-46)
[867] Shaw, Robert (nar); Holland,
Charles (ten); Scheff, Walter (b);
Victor Chorale; New York City
Symphony Orchestra; Bernstein,
Leonard (cond)
- Victor 11-9524-30 (in set
M-1117); 78; 7 discs; rel
pre-1948
- Victor 11-9531-37 (in set
DM-1117); 78; 7 discs

[868] Welles, Orson (nar); Velis, Andrea
(ten); Watson, David (bar); Choral
Art Society; New York
Philharmonic; Bernstein, Leonard
(cond)
- Columbia M-34136; 33s; rel
1976; del 1979

(Three) Character Sketches
[869] Conway, Curt (voice); Blitzstein,
Marc (pf)
- Keynote 511 (in set 105); 78;
rel 1941

Cradle Will Rock, The (1936-37)
[870] Cast of 1964 Off-Broadway revival;
Silva, Howard da (director);
Kingsley, Gershon (pf)
- MGM
E-4289-20C/SE-4289-20C;
33m/s; 2 discs; rel 1965; del
1968
- CRI-266; 33s; 2 discs; rel 1970;
cip

Cradle Will Rock, The (Abridged)
[871] Cast of the original 1937
production; Welles, Orson
(director); Blitzstein, Marc (nar)
(pf)
Rec 1938
- Musicraft 1075-81 (in set 18);
78; 7 discs; rel 1938
- American Legacy T-1001; 33m;
rel 1965*

Cradle Will Rock, The: Excerpts
[872] Lewis, Brenda (sop); and others
- Spoken Arts 717; 33m; rel 1956

Danton's Death (1938)
[873] Smith, Muriel (sop); Blitzstein,
Marc (pf)
- Concert Hall CHC-24; 33m; 10";
rel pre-1949; del 1952

Dusty Sun
[874] Scheff, Walter (b); Bernstein,
Leonard (pf)
- Victor 11-9530 (in set M-1117);
78; rel pre-1948
- Victor DM-1117; 78

Freedom Morning (1943)
[875] Czech Radio Orchestra; Weisgall,
Hugo (cond)
- Ultraphon H-18130; 78; rel
pre-1948

Freedom Morning (1943) *(cont'd)*
- Supraphon H-18130; 78; rel
pre-1950

**Guests, The (Piano Suite) (1949):
Excerpts**
[876] Blitzstein, Marc (pf)
- Concert Hall B-9; 78; 4 discs; rel
pre-1948

Mamasha Goose
[877] Smith, Muriel (sop); Blitzstein,
Marc (pf)
- Concert Hall CHC-24; 33m; 10";
rel pre-1949; del 1952

Modest Maid (arr by John Strauss)
[878] Rae, Charlotte (voice); Baroque
Bearcats; Strauss, John (cond)
- Vanguard VRS-9004; 33m; rel
1956; del 1962

No for an Answer (1938-40)
[879] Channing, Carol; Deering, Olive;
Green, Norma; Sundergard,
Hester; Ruskin, Colby; Wolfson,
Martin; Gough, Lloyd; Conway,
Curt; Conway, Bert; Loring,
Michael; Blitzstein, Marc (pf)
- Keynote 508-12 (in set 105);
78; 3-10" and 2-12"; rel 1941
- Theme TALP-103; 33m; rel
1951*

No for an Answer: Excerpts
[880] Lewis, Brenda (sop); and others
- Spoken Arts 717; 33m; rel 1956

[881] Rae, Charlotte (voice); Baroque
Bearcats; Strauss, John (cond)
- Vanguard VRS-9004; 33m; rel
1956; del 1962 (Excerpt:
Fraught, arr by John Strauss)

[882] Robeson, Paul (b); Brown,
Lawrence (pf)
- Columbia 17357D (in set
M-534); 78; 10"; rel pre-1943
(Excerpt: The Purest Kind of a
Guy)

[883] Smith, Muriel (sop); Blitzstein,
Marc (pf)
- Concert Hall CHC-24; 33m; 10";
rel pre-1949; del 1952 (Excerpt:
In the Clear)

Orpheus with his Lute
[884] Smith, Muriel (sop); Blitzstein,
Marc (pf)
- Concert Hall CHC-24; 33m; 10";
rel pre-1949; del 1952

Regina (1946-48)
[885] Lewis, Brenda (sop); Carron,
Elizabeth (sop); Brice, Carol (al);
Hecht, Joshua (b); New York City
Opera Chorus and Orchestra;
Krachmalnick, Samuel (cond)
- Columbia OL-5361-63 (in set
03L-260)/OS-2010-12 (in set
03S-202); 33m/s; 3 discs; rel
1959; del 1973

Regina (1946-48) *(cont'd)*
- Odyssey Y3-35236; 33s; 3 discs; rel 1978; cip

Regina: Excerpts
[886]　Lewis, Brenda (sop); and others
- Spoken Arts 717; 33m; rel 1956

Show (Piano Suite) (1947): Excerpts
[887]　Blitzstein, Marc (pf)
- Concert Hall B-9; 78; 4 discs; rel pre-1948

Song of the D. P.
[888]　Smith, Muriel (sop); Blitzstein, Marc (pf)
- Concert Hall CHC-24; 33m; 10''; rel pre-1949; del 1952

BLOCH, Ernest (1880-1959)

Abodah (1929)
[889]　Bress, Hyman (vln); Reiner, Charles (pf)
- Folkways FM-3357; 33m; rel 1964; cip

[890]　Davis, Michael (vln); Harper, Nelson (pf)
- Orion ORS-79344; 33s; rel 1979; cip

[891]　Haendel, Ida (vln); Kotowska, Adela (pf)
- Decca K-1076; 78; rel pre-1948

[892]　Menuhin, Yehudi (vln); Hendrik, Endt (pf)
- Victor 15887; 78; rel pre-1942
- Gramophone DB-6139; 78; rel pre-1952
- Gramophone DB-3782; 78

America (An Epic Rhapsody) (1926)
[893]　American Concert Choir; Symphony of the Air; Stokowski, Leopold (cond)
- Vanguard VRS-1056/VSD-2065; 33m/s; rel 1960; del 1967
- Vanguard (English) VSL-11020; 33; rel pre-1976
- Vanguard SRV-346-SD; 33s; rel 1976; cip

Avodath hakodesh (Sacred Service) (1930-33)
[894]　Lawrence, Douglas (bar); Utah Chorale; Utah Symphony; Abravanel, Maurice (cond)
- Angel SQ-37305; 33q; rel 1977; cip

[895]　Merrill, Robert (bar); Metropolitan Synagogue and Community Church (New York) Choirs; New York Philharmonic; Bernstein, Leonard (cond)
- Columbia ML-5621/MS-6221; 33m/s; rel 1961; cip

Avodath hakodesh (Sacred Service) (1930-33) *(cont'd)*
[896]　Moore, Dale (bar); University of Minnesota Symphonic Chorus and Orchestra; Marsman, Richard (cond)
- ARK-3125; 33; rel pre-1976

[897]　Rothmueller, Marko (bar); Bond, Dorothy (sop); Cowan, Doris (al); London Philharmonic Choir; London Philharmonic Orchestra; Bloch, Ernest (cond)
- Decca AX-377-82; 78; 6 discs; rel pre-1952
- London LA-200; 78; 6 discs; rel pre-1952
- London LLP-123; 33m; rel 1950; del 1958
- Decca LXT-2516; 33m; rel pre-1952
- London LLP-5006; 33m; rel 1957; del 1967
- Decca ACL-278; 33m

Avodath hakodesh: Tzur Yisroel
[898]　Boothman, Donald (bar); Berlinski, Herman (org)
- Musical Heritage Society MHS-1775; 33s; rel 1972

Baal shem (Three Pictures of Chassidic Life) (1923)
[899]　Davis, Michael (vln); Harper, Nelson (pf)
- Orion ORS-79344; 33s; rel 1979; cip

[900]　Mamlock, Theodore (vln); Laugs, Richards (pf)
- Musical Heritage Society MHS-3186; 33s; rel 1975

[901]　Neaman, Yfrah (vln); Newton, Ivor (pf)
- Decca K-1192-93; 78; 2 discs; rel pre-1948

[902]　Shapiro, Eudice (vln); Berkowitz, Ralph (pf)
- Vanguard VRS-1023; 33m; rel 1958; del 1965

[903]　Stern, Isaac (vln); Zakin, Alexander (pf)
- Columbia (English) LB-84; 78; 10''; rel pre-1950 (Excerpt: Nigun)
- Columbia ML-4324; 33m; rel 1950; del 1956 (Excerpt: Nigun)
- Columbia ML-6117/MS-6717; 33m/s; rel 1965; cip
- CBS (English) SBRG-72354; 33s; rel pre-1976

[904]　Szigeti, Joseph (vln); Farkas, Andor (pf)
- Columbia (English) LX-819-22; 78; 4 discs; rel pre-1942
- Columbia 70743-44 (in set MX-188); 78; 2 discs; rel pre-1943
- Columbia (English) LOX-501-02; 78; 2 discs; rel pre-1952
- Columbia ML-2122; 33m; 10''; rel 1950; del 1956

Baal shem (Three Pictures of Chassidic Life) (1923) *(cont'd)*
- Columbia ML-4679; 33m; rel 1953; del 1957

[905]　Weiner, Stanley (vln); Capelle, Claudine (pf)
- Alpha DB-123; 33m; rel 196?

Baal shem: Yidul and Simchas torah
[906]　Bress, Hyman (vln); Reiner, Charles (pf)
- Folkways FM-3357; 33m; rel 1964; cip

Baal shem: Nigun (Improvisation)
[907]　Beilina, N. (vln); piano
- USSR HD-4272-73; 33

[908]　Besrodni, Igor (vln); Makarov, Abram (pf)
- Monitor MC-2028; 33m; rel 1959; del 1978
- USSR D-3400-01; 33; 10''

[909]　Bress, Hyman (vln); Reiner, Charles (pf)
- Folkways FM-3354; 33m; rel 1962; cip

[910]　Elman, Mischa (vln); Padwa, Vladimir (pf)
- Victor 11-8575; 78; rel pre-1948

[911]　Elman, Mischa (vln); Seiger, Joseph (pf)
- London LLP-1467; 33m; rel 1957; del 1959
- Vanguard VRS-1099/VSD-2137; 33m/s; rel 1963; del 1965

[912]　Ferras, Christian (vln); piano
- Decca M-635; 78; rel pre-1952

[913]　Fodor, Eugene (vln); Olson, Judith (pf)
- RCA ARL-1-1172; 33s; rel 1976; cip

[914]　Fourer, S. (vln); piano
- USSR D-014077-78; 33

[915]　Haendel, Ida (vln); Moore, Gerald (pf)
- Gramophone CLP-1021; 33m; rel pre-1956
- Gramophone 7EP-7011; 45; 7''; rel pre-1956
- Gramophone 7EPQ-525; 45; 7''; rel pre-1956

[916]　Harth, Sidney (vln); Anschuetz, Sonia (pf)
- Musical Heritage Society MHS-1531; 33s; rel 1973
- Iramac 6523; 33; rel pre-1976

[917]　Harth, Sidney (vln); Szperka, Hieronim (pf)
- Muza (Polish) XL-0836; 33

[918]　Heifetz, Jascha (vln); Smith, Brooks (pf)
Rec 10/23/72
- Columbia M2-33444; 33s; 2 discs; rel 1975; cip

Baal shem: Nigun (Improvisation)
(cont'd)

[919] Hidy, Marta (vln); Barkin, Leo (pf)
- CBC Radio Canada SM-135; 33

[920] Kennedy, Nigel (vln); Kin, Seow Yit (pf)
- Orion ORS-72106; 33s; rel 1973*

[921] Kogan, Leonid (vln); Mitnik, Andrei (pf)
- RCA LM-2250; 33m; rel 1959; del 1960
- USSR D-08311-12; 33

[922] Kooper, Kees (vln); piano
- Twentieth Century-Fox FX-4006/SFX-4006; 33m/s; rel 1962; del 1963

[923] Lewkowicz, H. (vln); Vallribera, P. (pf)
- Columbia (Spanish) RG-16160; 78; rel pre-1952

[924] Magyar, Thomas (vln); Hielkema, W. (pf)
- Philips N-00125R; 33m; 10''; rel pre-1953

[925] Menuhin, Yehudi (vln); Persinger, A. (pf)
- Victor 7108; 78; rel pre-1936
- Gramophone DB-1283; 78; rel pre-1936

[926] Milstein, Nathan (vln); Bussotti, Carlo (pf)
- Capitol CTL-7058; 33m; rel pre-1956
- Capitol P-8259; 33m; rel 1954; del 1959

[927] Milstein, Nathan (vln); Mittman, Leopold (pf)
- Columbia 17134D; 78; 10''; rel 1939

[928] Olof, Theo (vln); Moore, Gerald (pf)
- Gramophone B-9665; 78; 10''; rel pre-1952

[929] Peinemann, Edith (vln); Barth, Helmut (pf)
- Classic Pick 70-108; 33q; rel 1975

[930] Poulet, Gerard (vln); Blanchot, Maurice (pf)
- Deese (French) CCLX-58; 33; rel pre-1976
- Musical Heritage Society MHS-3236; 33s; rel 1976

[931] Spivakoff, Vladimir (vln); Gusak, Marina (pf)
- Melodiya (USSR) CM-03179-80; 33

[932] Spivakovsky, Tossy (vln); piano
- Parlophone R-1217; 78; 10''; rel pre-1936
- Parlophone B-12399; 78; rel pre-1936
- Decca 20020; 78; rel pre-1942
- Brunswick 12399; 78; 10''

Baal shem: Nigun (Improvisation)
(cont'd)

[933] Szigeti, Joseph (vln); Ruhrseitz, K. (pf)
- Columbia 2047M; 78; 10''; rel ca 1925-27
- Columbia (English) D-1557; 78; 10''; rel pre-1952

[934] Weiner, Stanley (vln); Demoulin, Giselle (pf)
- Musical Heritage Society MHS-3294; 33s

[935] Wicks, Camilla (vln); Ehrling, S. (pf)
- Gramophone DA-11004; 78; rel pre-1952

[936] Zhuk, V. (vln); piano
- USSR D-11019-20; 33

[937] Zighera, Leon (vln); Howard, Leslie (pf)
- Decca M-144; 78; 10''; rel pre-1936

Baal shem: Nigun (violin and orchestra version) (1939)

[938] Zukerman, Pinchas (vln); Royal Philharmonic Orchestra; Foster, Lawrence (cond)
- Columbia M-30644; 33s; rel 1971; cip

Baal shem: Nigun (arr for vcl and gtr)

[939] Vechtomov, Sasha (vcl); Vechtomov, Vladimir (gtr)
- MKCM-03161-62; 33

Baal shem: Nigun (arr for vcl and pf)

[940] Fournier, Pierre (vcl); Lush, Ernest (pf)
- Decca LXT-2766; 33m; rel pre-1956
- London LLP-700; 33m; rel 1953; del 1957
- USSR D-08379-80; 33m

Baal shem: Yidul

[941] Grumlikova, Nora (vln); Kolar, Jaroslav (pf)
- Supraphon SUA-10708/SUAST-50708; 33m/s; rel 196?

[942] Koene, Francis (vln); Van Ijzer (pf)
- Columbia D-17187; 78; rel pre-1936

Concerto, Violin and Orchestra (1937-38)

[943] Bress, Hyman (vln); Prague Symphony Orchestra; Rohan, Jindrich (cond)
- Crossroads 22-16-0212; 33s; rel 1968; del 1970
- Supraphon SUA-10881/SUAST-50881; 33m/s; rel 196?
- Supraphon 152048; 33; rel pre-1976

Concerto, Violin and Orchestra (1937-38) *(cont'd)*

[944] Menuhin, Yehudi (vln); Philharmonia Orchestra; Kletzki, Paul (cond)
- Angel 36192/S-36192; 33m/s; rel 1964; cip
- Angel 95001/S-95001; 33m/s; rel pre-1976
- EMI/His Master's Voice ASD-584; 33s; rel pre-1976

[945] Szigeti, Joseph (vln); Paris Conservatory Orchestra; Munch, Charles (cond)
Rec 1939
- Columbia M-380; 78; 4 discs; rel pre-1942
- Columbia (English) LX-819-22; 78; 4 discs; rel pre-1942
- Columbia ML-4679; 33m; rel 1953; del 1957
- Bruno Walter Society BWS-715; 33s; rel 1973*
- Turnabout THS-65007; 33m; rel 1974; cip

[946] Totenberg, Roman (vln); Vienna State Opera Orchestra; Golschmann, Vladimir (cond)
- Vanguard VRS-1083/VSD-2110; 33m/s; rel 1962; del 1975

Concerto grosso No 1, Piano Obbligato and String Orchestra (1924-25)

[947] Bailly, Louis (pf); Curtis Chamber Music Ensemble
- Victor 12438-40 (in set M-563); 78; 3 discs; rel pre-1942
- Gramophone ED-121-23; 78; 3 discs; rel pre-1952
- Victor (Japanese) JAS-236; 78; 3 discs; rel pre-1953

[948] Franklin, Harry (pf); Pittsburgh Symphony Orchestra; Steinberg, William (cond)
Rec 11/52
- Capitol CTC-7039; 33
- Capitol S-8212; 33m; rel 1953; del 1959
- Capitol CTL-7039; 33m; rel pre-1956
- ASCAP CB-153; 33m (Pittsburgh International Contemporary Music Festival); rel pre-1956
- Capitol SAL-9020; 33m; rel pre-1956 (Excerpt: 1st Movement)
- Capitol LCE-8212; 33

[949] Grier, Francis (pf); Academy of St. Martin-in-the-Fields; Marriner, Neville (cond)
- Angel S-37577; 33s; rel 1979; cip

[950] Schick, George (pf); Chicago Symphony Orchestra; Kubelik, Rafael (cond)
Rec 4/24/51
- Mercury MG-5000I; 33m; rel 1951; del 1963
- Mercury MG-50027; 33m; rel 1953; del 1960

Concerto grosso No 1, Piano Obbligato and String Orchestra (1924-25) *(cont'd)*
- Gramophone FALP-291; 33m; rel pre-1956
- Mercury MGW-14034/SRW-18034; 33m/s; rel 1963; del 1968
- Mercury SRI-75036; 33s; rel 1975; cip

[951] piano; Czech Radio Orchestra; Epstein, David (cond)
- Everest SDBR-3328; 33s; rel 1973; cip

[952] piano; Eastman-Rochester Symphony Orchestra; Hanson, Howard (cond)
Rec 5/59
- Mercury MG-50223/SR-90223; 33m/s; rel 1960; del 1973
- Mercury (English) MMA-11150/AMS-16098; 33m/s; rel 196?
- Mercury SRI-75017; 33s; rel 1973; cip

[953] piano; Philadelphia Chamber String Sinfonietta; Sevitzky, Fabien (cond)
- Victor 9596-98 (in set M-66); 78; 5 sides; rel 1930
- Victor 9599-9601 (in set AM-66); 78; 5 sides
- Gramophone DB-1987-89; 78; 5 sides; rel 1930

Concerto grosso No 2, String Quartet and String Orchestra (1952)
[954] Guilet String Quartet; MGM String Orchestra; Solomon, Izler (cond)
- MGM E-3422; 33m; rel 1956; del 1959

[955] string quartet; Eastman-Rochester Symphony Orchestra; Hanson, Howard (cond)
Rec 5/59
- Mercury MG-50223/SR-90223; 33m/s; rel 1960; del 1973
- Mercury SRI-75017; 33s; rel 1973; cip

Concerto symphonique (1947-48)
[956] Mitchell, Marjorie (pf); Vienna State Opera Orchestra; Golschmann, Vladimir (cond)
- Vanguard VRS-1078/VSD-2101; 33m/s; rel 1961; del 1965

Enfantines (1923)
[957] Ajemian, Maro (pf)
- MGM E-3445; 33m; rel 1957; del 1959

[958] Pressler, Menahem (pf)
- MGM E-3010; 33m; rel 1953; del 1959

Enfantines: With Mother, Elves, Joyous March, Melody, Teasing, and Dream
[959] Bennett, Bob L. (pf)
- Educo 3110; 33

(Four) Episodes (1926)
[960] Arizona Chamber Orchestra; Hull, Robert (cond)
Rec 9/17/78
- Laurel LR-110; 33s; rel 1979; cip

[961] Masselos, William (pf); Knickerbocker Chamber Players; Solomon, Izler (cond)
- MGM E-290; 33m; 10"; rel 1955; del 1957
- MGM E-3245; 33m; rel 1956; del 1959

[962] Smit, Leo (pf); Zurich Radio Orchestra; Scherman, Thomas (cond)
- Concert Hall CHF-4; 33m; rel 1952
- Concert Hall CHS-1238; 33m; rel 1956; del 1957
- Concert Hall H-1638; 33m; rel 1957; del 1959

Fantasie, Violin and Piano (1899)
[963] Bress, Hyman (vln); Reiner, Charles (pf)
- Folkways FM-3357; 33m; rel 1964; cip

From Jewish Life (1924)
[964] Goodman, Lillian Rehberg (vcl); Bogin, Harold (pf)
- Orion ORS-75181; 33s; rel 1975; cip

[965] Nelsova, Zara (vcl); Bloch, Ernest (pf)
- Decca M-664; 78; rel pre-1952 (Excerpts: Prayer and Jewish Song)
- London T-5698 (in set LA-226); 78; rel pre-1952 (Excerpt: Prayer)
- Decca LX-3042; 33m; 10"; rel 1950
- London LPS-298; 33m; 10"; rel 1951; del 1957

From Jewish Life: Prayer
[966] Aronson, Lev (vcl); Jones, Joyce (org)
- Word WST-8528; 33s; rel 1971; cip

[967] Janigro, Antonio (vcl); Bagnoli, Eugenio (pf)
- Westminster XWN-18004; 33m; rel 1955; del 1960

[968] Lustgarten, Edgar (vcl); Newman, Anthony (pf)
Rec 7/12/62
- La Jolla Museum of Art AC-100; 33m; rel 1963*
- Crystal S-303; 33s; rel 1967; cip

From Jewish Life: Prayer *(cont'd)*
[969] Olefsky, Paul (vcl); Silfies, George (pf)
- McIntosh Music MM-103; 33m; rel 1955; del 1958

[970] Piatigorsky, Gregor (vcl); organ
- Parlophone E-11058; 78; rel pre-1936
- Decca 25139; 78; rel pre-1942

[971] Starker, Janos (vcl); Iwasaki, Shuku (pf)
Rec 3/16-17/75
- Denon OX-7041-ND; 33s; rel 1976?; cip

From Jewish Life: Prayer (arr for cb and pf)
[972] Karr, Gary (cb); Siegel, Jeffrey (pf)
- Golden Crest RE-7012; 33m/s; rel 1962/1979; cip

Israel (1912-16)
[973] Akademie Choir (soloists); Vienna State Opera Orchestra; Litschauer, Franz (cond)
- Vanguard VRS-423; 33m; rel 1952; del 1968
- Nixa (Australian) VLP-423; 33m; rel pre-1953

[974] Christensen, Blanche (sop); Basinger, Jean (sop); Politis, Christina (al); Heder, Diane (al); Watts, Don (b); Utah Symphony Orchestra; Abravanel, Maurice (cond)
- Vanguard Cardinal VCS-10007; 33s; rel 1967; cip
- Vanguard Cardinal (Australian) VCS-10007; 33s; rel pre-1976

(Three) Jewish Poems (1913)
[975] Hartford Symphony Orchestra; Mahler, Fritz (cond)
- Vanguard VRS-1067/VSD-2085; 33m/s; rel 1961; del 1969

[976] Vienna Symphony Orchestra; Hendl, Walter (cond)
- American Recording Society ARS-24; 33m; rel 1953
- American Recording Society ARS-113; 33m; rel pre-1956
- Desto D-409/DST-6409; 33m/s; rel 1965; cip

Macbeth (1904-09): Deux interludes
[977] Orchestre du Studio de Geneve; Colombo, Pierre (cond)
- Communaute de travail pour la diffusion de la musique suisse CT-64-11; 33m; rel 1964
- Wergo CT-64-11; 33 (excerpts)

Meditation and Processional (1951)
[978] Doktor, Paul (vla); Mason, Marilyn (org)
- Mirrosonic RM-1013/RS-1013; 33m/s; rel 1961; del 1965

Meditation and Processional (1951) (cont'd)

[979] Preves, Milton (vla); Brahn, Helene (pf)
- Bloch Society 1; 33m; 10''; rel pre-1953
- Covenant 3628; 33

[980] Primrose, William (vla); Stimer, David (pf)
- Capitol P-8355; 33m; rel 1957; del 1959

[981] Toszeghi, Andras von (vla); Milne, Hamish (pf)
- Jecklin 155; 33; rel pre-1976

[982] Wallfisch, Ernst (vla); Wallfisch, Lory (pf)
- Musical Heritage Society MHS-1486; 33s; rel 1973
- Da Camera (German) SM-93806; 33s; rel 197?

Meditation hebraique (1924)

[983] Goodman, Lillian Rehberg (vcl); Bogin, Harold (pf)
- Orion ORS-75181; 33s; rel 1975; cip

[984] Joachim, Walter (vcl); Newmark, John (pf)
- CBC Transcription Programme 209; 33; rel 196?

Night (1925)

[985] Griller String Quartet
- Decca AK-1762 (in set EDA-93); 78; rel pre-1950

(Three) Nocturnes (1924)

[986] Nieuw Amsterdam Trio
- Decca DL-10126/DL-710126; 33m/s; rel 1966; del 1973

[987] Western Arts Trio
- Laurel LR-104; 33s; rel 1976; cip

Poems of the Sea (1922)

[988] Ajemian, Maro (pf)
- MGM E-3445; 33m; rel 1957; del 1959

[989] Bogas, Roy (pf)
- Fantasy 85020; 33

[990] Miller, Leroy (pf)
- Music Library MLR-7015; 33m; rel 1952; del 1974

[991] Rappaport, Jerome (pf)
- Etude ER-101; 33m; rel pre-1956

[992] Tipo, Maria (pf)
- Contrepoint MC-20020; 33m; rel pre-1956

Poems of the Sea: Waves

[993] Skipworth, George (pf)
- Educo 3097; 33

Prelude and Two Psalms (1912-14): Psalm 114

[994] Giannini, Dusolina (sop)
- International Record Collectors Club 3115; 78; rel pre-1953

Prelude and Two Psalms: Psalm 137

[995] Peerce, Jan (ten); Rogers, Allen (pf)
- United Artists UAL-3412/UAS-6412; 33m/s; rel 1965; del 1969

Proclamation (1955)

[996] Rapier, Leon (tpt); Louisville Orchestra; Whitney, Robert (cond)
- LOU-63-6/LS-63-6; 33m/s (Louisville Orchestra First Edition Records 1963 No 6); rel 1963/1965; del 1979

Quartet, Strings, No 1 (1916)

[997] Griller String Quartet
- London LLP-1125 (in set LLA-23); 33m; rel 1955; del 1957
- Decca LXT-5071; 33m; rel 1955

[998] Roth Quartet
- Mercury MG-50110; 33m; rel 1956; del 1963
- Mercury (English) MRC-2536; 33

[999] Stuyvesant String Quartet
- Columbia 69775-80 (in set M-392); 78; 6 discs; rel pre-1942
- Columbia (English) LX-934-39; 78; 6 discs; rel pre-1942
- Columbia 70320-25A; 78; 6 discs

Quartet, Strings, No 2 (1945)

[1000] Griller String Quartet
- Decca AK-1758-62 (in set EDA-93); 78; 5 discs; rel pre-1950
- London LLP-1126 (in set LLA-23); 33m; rel 1955; del 1957
- Decca LXT-5072; 33m; rel 1955

[1001] Hirsch Quartet
- Argo ARS-1011; 33m; rel pre-1956
- Argo RG-7; 33m; rel pre-1956

[1002] Musical Arts Quartet
- Vanguard VRS-437; 33m; rel 1953; del 1965

[1003] New World String Quartet
- Vox SVBX-5109; 33s; 3 discs; rel 1979; cip

[1004] Stuyvesant String Quartet
- International D-3005-08 (in set IM-302); 78; 4 discs; rel 1947*
- Concert Hall CHC-20; 33m; 10''; rel pre-1949; del 1952

Quartet, Strings, No 3 (1952)

[1005] Edinburgh Quartet
- Monitor MC-2123/MCS-2123; 33m/s; rel 1967; del 1977
- Waverly LLP-1027/SLLP-1028; 33m/s

[1006] Griller String Quartet
- Decca LM-4558; 33m; 10''; rel 1954
- London LPS-840; 33m; 10''; rel 1954; del 1957
- London LLP-1127 (in set LLA-23); 33m; rel 1955; del 1957
- Decca LXT-5073; 33m; rel 1955

Quartet, Strings, No 4 (1953)

[1007] Griller String Quartet
- London LLP-1127 (in set LLA-23); 33m; rel 1955; del 1957
- Decca LXT-5073; 33m; rel 1955

Quartet, Strings, No 5 (1956)

[1008] Fine Arts Quartet
- Concert-Disc M-1225/CS-225; 33m/s; rel 1962; cip
- Everest SDBR-3328; 33s; rel 1973; cip
- Everest (English) SDBR-4225; 33s

Quintet, Piano and Strings, No 1 (1921-23)

[1009] Casella, Alfredo (pf); Pro Arte Quartet
- Victor 7874-77 (in set 191); 78; 4 discs; rel pre-1936
- Gramophone DB-1882-85; 78; 4 discs; rel pre-1936
- Gramophone DB-5983-86; 78; 4 discs; rel pre-1952
- Gramophone ED-422-25; 78; 4 discs; rel pre-1952

[1010] Chigi Quintet
- London LLP-382; 33m; rel 1951; del 1957
- Decca LXT-2626; 33m; rel pre-1953

[1011] Glazer, Frank (pf); Fine Arts Quartet
- Concert-Disc M-1252/CS-252; 33m/s; rel 1965; cip
- Everest (English) SDBR-4252; 33s

[1012] Harris, Johana (pf); Walden String Quartet
- MGM E-3239; 33m; rel 1955; del 1959

[1013] New London Quintet
- HNH Records HNH-4063; 33s; rel 1978; del 1980

Schelomo (1915-16)

[1014] Feuermann, Emanuel (vcl); Philadelphia Orchestra; Stokowski, Leopold (cond)
- Victor 17336-38S (in set M-698); 78; 3 discs; rel pre-1942

Schelomo (1915-16) *(cont'd)*
- Gramophone DB-5816-18S; 78; 3 discs; rel pre-1948
- Gramophone DB-6055-57; 78; 3 discs; rel pre-1952
- Victor WCT-69; 45; 7''; rel 1952*
- RCA LCT-14; 33m; 10''; rel 1952; del 1953
- Camden CAL-254; 33m; rel 1956; del 1958

[1015] Fournier, Pierre (vcl); Berlin Symphony Orchestra; Wallenstein, Alfred (cond)
- Deutsche Grammophon SLPM-139128; 33s; rel 1967; del 1975
- Deutsche Grammophon 2535.201; 33s; rel 1978; cip

[1016] Janigro, Antonio (vcl); London Philharmonic Orchestra; Rodzinski, Artur (cond)
- Westminster XWN-18007; 33m; rel 1955; del 1968
- Westminster WST-14985; 33s; rel 1968; del 1970
- Westminster W-9732; 33s; rel 1970; del 1971

[1017] Machula, Tibor de (vcl); Hague Philharmonic Orchestra; Otterloo, Willem van (cond)
- Philips A-00138R; 33m; 10''; rel pre-1953
- Epic LC-3072; 33m; rel 1954; del 1961
- Philips S-06030R; 33m; rel pre-1956

[1018] Miquelle, Georges (vcl); Eastman-Rochester Symphony Orchestra; Hanson, Howard (cond)
- Mercury MG-50286/SR-90286; 33m/s; rel 1962; del 1964

[1019] Navarra, Andre (vcl); Czech Philharmonic Orchestra; Ancerl, Karel (cond)
- Epic LC-3937/BC-1337; 33m/s; rel 1967; del 1970
- Supraphon SUA-10581/SUAST-50581; 33m/s; rel 196?
- Supraphon SWP-152027; 33

[1020] Navarra, Andre (vcl); London Symphony Orchestra; Austin, Richard (cond)
- Capitol P-18012; 33m; rel 1956; del 1959
- Capitol (Italian) IGM-MM-1094; 33m; 10''; rel 195?
- Parlophone PMC-1046; 33m; rel 195?

[1021] Neikrug, George (vcl); Symphony of the Air; Stokowski, Leopold (cond)
- United Artists UAL-7005/UAS-8005; 33m/s; rel 1959; del 1969

Schelomo (1915-16) *(cont'd)*
[1022] Nelsova, Zara (vcl); London Philharmonic Orchestra; Ansermet, Ernest (cond)
- London LLP-1232; 33m; rel 1955; del 1962
- Decca LXT-5052; 33m; rel pre-1956
- Everest SDBR-3284; 33s; rel 1970; del 1977

[1023] Nelsova, Zara (vcl); London Philharmonic Orchestra; Bloch, Ernest (cond)
- London LA-226; 78; rel pre-1952
- London LPS-138; 33m; 10''; rel 1950; del 1957
- Decca LX-3016; 33m; 10''; rel pre-1952

[1024] Nelsova, Zara (vcl); Utah Symphony Orchestra; Abravanel, Maurice (cond)
- Vanguard Cardinal VCS-10007; 33s; rel 1967; cip

[1025] Piatigorsky, Gregor (vcl); Boston Symphony Orchestra; Munch, Charles (cond)
- RCA LM-2109/LSC-2109; 33m/s; rel 1958/1964; del 1975
- RCA (English) RB-6676/SB-6676; 33m/s

[1026] Rose, Leonard (vcl); New York Philharmonic; Mitropoulos, Dimitri (cond)
- Columbia ML-4425; 33m; rel 1951; del 1961
- Coronet (Australian) KLC-572; 33

[1027] Rose, Leonard (vcl); Philadelphia Orchestra; Ormandy, Eugene (cond)
- Columbia ML-5653/MS-6253; 33m/s; rel 1961; cip

[1028] Rostropovich, Mistislav (vcl); London Symphony Orchestra; Rozhdestvensky, Gennady (cond)
- Rococo 2043; 33m; rel 1974*

[1029] Rostropovich, Mistislav (vcl); Orchestre National de France; Bernstein, Leonard (cond)
- Angel SQ-37256; 33q; rel 1977; cip

[1030] Starker, Janos (vcl); Israel Philharmonic Orchestra; Mehta, Zubin (cond)
- London CS-6661; 33s; rel 1971; cip
- Decca SXL-6440; 33s; rel pre-1976

[1031] Varga, Laszlo (vcl); Westphalian Symphony Orchestra; Landau, Siegfried (cond)
  Rec 6/74
- Turnabout TVS-34622; 33s; rel 1976; cip

Schelomo (1915-16) *(cont'd)*
[1032] Walevksa, Christine (vcl); National Opera Orchestra of Monte Carlo; Inbal, Eliahu (cond)
- Philips 6500.160; 33s; rel 1972; cip

Scherzo fantasque (1948)
[1033] Hollander, Lorin (pf); Royal Philharmonic Orchestra; Previn, Andre (cond)
- RCA LM-2801/LSC-2801; 33m/s; rel 1965; del 1973

Sinfonia breve (1952)
[1034] Minneapolis Symphony Orchestra; Dorati, Antal (cond)
- Mercury MG-50288/SR-90288; 33m/s; rel 1962; del 1965
- CRI-248; 33s; rel 1970; cip
- Mercury SRI-75116; 33s; rel 1980; cip

(Five) Sketches in Sepia (1923)
[1035] Ajemian, Maro (pf)
- MGM E-3445; 33m; rel 1957; del 1959

[1036] Miller, Leroy (pf)
- Music Library MLR-7015; 33m; rel 1952; del 1974

[1037] Potter, Harrison (pf)
- Friends of Recorded Music FRM-12; 78; rel 1937

Sonata, Piano (1935)
[1038] Cumming, Richard (pf)
- Music Library MLR-7015; 33m; rel 1952; del 1974

[1039] Lev, Ray (pf)
- Concert Hall C-11; 78; 3 discs; rel pre-1950

[1040] Nadas, Istvan (pf)
- Period SPL-736; 33m; rel 1957; del 1964
- Dover HCR-5215; 33m; rel 1964; del 1976

[1041] Shaulis, Zola (pf)
- CRI-295; 33s; rel 1973; cip

Sonata, Violin and Piano, No 1 (1920)
[1042] Berkeley, Harold (vln); Berkeley, Marion (pf)
- Gamut 3; 78; 4 discs; rel pre-1943
- General 12.106-09; 78; 4 discs; rel pre-1952

[1043] Bress, Hyman (vln); Reiner, Charles (pf)
- Folkways FM-3357; 33m; rel 1964; cip

[1044] Colbertson, Oliver (vln); Appel, Erich (pf)
- PLD AC-60026; 33; rel pre-1976

Sonata, Violin and Piano, No 1 (1920) (cont'd)

[1045] Druian, Rafael (vln); Simms, John (pf)
- Mercury MG-50095; 33m; rel 1956; del 1963
- Mercury (English) MRC-2501; 33

[1046] Gingold, Joseph (vln); Rubinstein, Beryl (pf)
- Victor 12310-13S (in set M-498); 78; 4 discs; rel 1938

[1047] Goldstein, B. (vln); Selkina, E. (pf)
- USSR 025847-48; 33

[1048] Heifetz, Jascha (vln); Bay, Emanuel (pf)
- RCA LM-1861; 33m; rel 1955; del 1957
- RCA ARM-4-0947; 33m; 4 discs; rel 1975; cip

[1049] Kaufman, Louis (vln); Pozzi, Pina (pf)
- Concert Hall CHH-18; 33m; rel 1954
- Orion ORS-79355; 33s; rel 1980; cip

[1050] Stern, Isaac (vln); Zakin, Alexander (pf)
- Columbia ML-6117/MS-6717; 33m/s; rel 1965; cip
- CBS (English) SBRG-72354; 33s; rel pre-1976

Sonata, Violin and Piano, No 2 (Poeme mystique) (1924)

[1051] Davis, Michael (vln); Harper, Nelson (pf)
- Orion ORS-79344; 33s; rel 1979; cip

[1052] Druian, Rafael (vln); Simms, John (pf)
- Mercury MG-50095; 33m; rel 1956; del 1963

[1053] Heifetz, Jascha (vln); Smith, Brooks (pf)
- RCA LM-2089; 33m; rel 1957; del 1966
- RCA (English) RB-1602; 33m
- RCA ARM-4-0947; 33m; 4 discs; rel 1975; cip

Suite, Viola (1958)

[1054] Wallfisch, Ernst (vla)
- Musical Heritage Society MHS-1486; 33s; rel 1973

Suite, Viola and Orchestra (1919)

[1055] Katims, Milton (vla); Seattle Symphony Orchestra; Siegl, Henry (cond)
Rec 6/75
- Turnabout TVS-34622; 33s; rel 1976; cip

Suite, Viola and Piano (1919)

[1056] Czerny, Ladislav (vla); Palenicek, Josef (pf)
- Ultraphon H-23365-68; 78; 4 discs; rel pre-1952

Suite, Viola and Piano (1919) (cont'd)

- Supraphon SUF-20044; 33m; 10"

[1057] Gromko, William (vla); Wingreen, Harriet (pf)
- Classic Editions CE-1038; 33m; rel 1958; del 1961

[1058] Primrose, William (vla); Kitzinger, Fritz (pf)
- Victor 15475-78 (in set M-575); 78; 4 discs; rel pre-1942
- Gramophone DB-3977-80; 78; 4 discs; rel pre-1952

[1059] Primrose, William (vla); Stimer, David (pf)
- Capitol P-8355; 33m; rel 1957; del 1959

[1060] Wallfisch, Ernst (vla); Wallfisch, Lory (pf)
- Musical Heritage Society MHS-1486; 33s; rel 1973
- Da Camera (German) SM-93806; 33s; rel 197?

Suite, Viola and Piano (arr for vcl and pf)

[1061] Rejto, Gabor (vcl); Baller, Adolph (pf)
- Orion ORS-6904; 33s; rel 1969; cip

Suite, Violin, No 1 (1958)

[1062] Bress, Hyman (vln)
- Folkways FM-3357; 33m; rel 1964; cip

[1063] Gulli, Franco (vln)
- Capitol (Italian) IGM-MM-1094; 33m; 10"; rel 195?

[1064] Menuhin, Yehudi (vln)
- EMI/His Master's Voice ASD-3368; 33s; rel 1977

Suite, Violin, No 2 (1958)

[1065] Grumlikova, Nora (vln)
- Supraphon SUA-10520; 33m; rel 196?

[1066] Menuhin, Yehudi (vln)
- EMI/His Master's Voice ASD-3368; 33s; rel 1977

Suite, Violin, No 2: Andante and Allegro molto (arr for gtr)

[1067] Macaluso, Vincenzo (gtr)
- Klavier KS-508; 33s; rel 1972

Suite, Violoncello, No 1 (1956)

[1068] Hunkins, Nella (vcl)
- Golden Crest GCCL-201; 33s; rel 1976*

Suite hebraique (1951)

[1069] Bress, Hyman (vln); Prague Symphony Orchestra; Rohan, Jindrich (cond)
- Crossroads 22-16-0212; 33s; rel 1968; del 1970

Suite hebraique (1951) (cont'd)

- Supraphon SUA-10881/SUAST-50881; 33m/s; rel 196?
- Supraphon 152048; 33; rel pre-1976

[1070] Dawson, David (vla); Dawson, Zhanna (pf)
- Memorial LRS-RT-6194; 33s; rel 1976

[1071] Preves, Milton (vla); Brahn, Helene (pf)
- Bloch Society 1; 33m; 10"; rel pre-1953
- Covenant 3628; 33

[1072] Primrose, William (vla); Stimer, David (pf)
- Capitol P-8355; 33m; rel 1957; del 1959

[1073] Thompson, Marcus (vla); MIT Symphony Orchestra; Epstein, David (cond)
Rec 5/74
- Turnabout QTVS-34687; 33q; rel 1977; cip

[1074] Wallfisch, Ernst (vla); Wallfisch, Lory (pf)
- Musical Heritage Society MHS-1486; 33s; rel 1973
- Da Camera (German) SM-93806; 33s; rel 197?

Suite modale (1956)

[1075] Panitz, Murray (fl); Philadelphia Orchestra; Ormandy, Eugene (cond)
- Columbia ML-6377/MS-6977; 33m/s; rel 1967; cip

Suite symphonique (1944)

[1076] Portland Junior Symphony; Avshalomov, Jacob (cond)
- CRI-351; 33s; rel 1976; cip

Symphony, Trombone and Orchestra (1954)

[1077] Prince, Howard (tbn); Portland Junior Symphony; Avshalomov, Jacob (cond)
- CRI-351; 33s; rel 1976; cip

Visions and Prophecies (1936)

[1078] Chodos, Gabriel (pf)
- Orion ORS-73122; 33s; rel 1973; cip

Voice in the Wilderness (1936)

[1079] Nelsova, Zara (vcl); London Philharmonic Orchestra; Ansermet, Ernest (cond)
- London LLP-1232; 33m; rel 1955; del 1962
- Decca LXT-5062; 33m; rel pre-1956
- Everest SDBR-3284; 33s; rel 1970; del 1977

Voice in the Wilderness (1936)
(cont'd)
[1080] Starker, Janos (vcl); Israel
Philharmonic Orchestra; Mehta,
Zubin (cond)
- London CS-6661; 33s; rel 1971;
cip
- Decca SXL-6440; 33s; rel
pre-1976

Voice in the Wilderness (arr for vcl and pf)
[1081] Sopkin, George (vcl); Kirsch,
Florence (pf)
- Bloch Society 2; 33m; 10''; rel
1952; del 1957
- Bloch Society 5606; 33m; rel
1952*

BLUMENFELD, Harold (1923-)
Expansions (1965)
[1082] York Wind Quintet
- Washington University
TS-XM-708; 33m; rel 1968; del
1976

Rilke (1975)
[1083] Rees, Rosalind (sop); Starobin,
David (gtr)
Rec 1976
- Turnabout TVS-34727; 33s; rel
1978

(Four) Tranquil Poems (1950): Aware, Green, and Silence
[1084] Washington University Men's
Chorus; Weiss, Don (cond)
- Washington University
TS-XM-708; 33m; rel 1968; del
1976

Transformations (1963)
[1085] Peltzer, Dwight (pf)
- Washington University
TS-XM-708; 33m; rel 1968; del
1976

Voyages: Parts One and Two
[1086] Mason, Patrick (bar); Kashkashian,
Kim (vla); Starobin, David (gtr);
Gottlieb, Gordon (perc); Oddo,
Louis (perc); Weisberg, Arthur
(cond)
Rec 11/77
- CRI-387; 33s; rel 1978; cip

BODA, John (1922-)
Prelude - Scherzo - Postlude (1959-64)
[1087] Georgia State College Brass
Ensemble; Hill, William H. (cond)
- Golden Crest CRS-4084; 33s; rel
1969; cip

Sinfonia (1960)
[1088] Knoxville Symphony Orchestra; Van
Vactor, David (cond)
- CRI-155; 33m; rel 1962; cip

Sonatina, Euphonium and Synthesizer
[1089] Bowman, Brian (euph); tape
- Crystal S-393; 33s; rel 1978; cip

Sonatina, Trombone and Piano
[1090] Cramer, William F. (tbn);
Glotzbach, Robert (pf)
- Coronet S-1506; 33s; rel 1969;
cip

BODENHORN, Aaron (1898-)
Stay Oh Sweet
[1091] Luening, Ethel (sop); Yaddo String
Quartet
- Yaddo IV-2; 78; 10''; rel 1940

BOLCOM, William (1938-)
Black Host (1967)
[1092] Albright, William (org); Hodkinson,
Sydney (perc); tape
- Nonesuch H-71260; 33s; rel
1971; cip

Commedia (1972)
[1093] St. Paul Chamber Orchestra;
Davies, Dennis Russell (cond)
- Nonesuch H-71324; 33s; rel
1976; cip

(Twelve) Etudes, Piano (1959-66)
[1094] Bolcom, William (pf)
- Advance FGR-14S; 33s; rel
1972; cip

Frescoes (1971)
[1095] Mather, Bruce (pf) (harm); LePage,
Pierrete (pf) (hpschd)
- Nonesuch H-71297; 33s; rel
1974; cip

Graceful Ghost
[1096] Bolcom, William (pf)
- Nonesuch H-71257; 33s; rel
1971; cip

Open House (1975)
[1097] Sperry, Paul (ten); St. Paul
Chamber Orchestra; Davies,
Dennis Russell (cond)
Rec 11/11-12/75
- Nonesuch H-71324; 33s; rel
1976; cip

Seabiscuits
[1098] Bolcom, William (pf)
- Nonesuch H-71257; 33s; rel
1971; cip

Through Eden's Gates
[1099] Morath, Max (pf)
- Vanguard SRV-351-SD; 33s; rel
1976; cip

Whisper Moon (1973)
[1100] Aeolian Chamber Players; Kaplan,
Lewis (cond)
- Folkways FTS-33903; 33s; rel
1976; cip

BOLCOM, William and ALBRIGHT, William
see ALBRIGHT, William and
BOLCOM, William

BOLLE, James (1931-)
Oleum canis (1972)
[1101] Pilgrim, Neva (sop); Curtis, Jan (m
sop); Siena, Jerrold (ten); Miller,
Donald (b); children's chorus; The
Committee; New Hampshire
Sinfonietta; Bolle, James (cond)
- Serenus SRS-12060; 33s; rel
1976; cip

BONDS, Margaret (1913-72)
Troubled Waters (1967)
[1102] Norman, Ruth (pf)
- Opus One 39; 33s; rel 1979; cip

BORDEN, David (1938-)
(Six) Dialogues
[1103] Sauer, Ralph (tbn); Stevens,
Thomas (tpt)
- Crystal S-384; 33s; rel 1979; cip

Easter
[1104] Drews, Steve (syn); Fisher, Linda
(syn); Borden, David (syn) (elec
pf)
- Earthquack EQ-0001; 33s; rel
1974*

Variations on America by Charles Ives as Heard on the Jingle Jangle Morning in Emerson Playground by You and the Signers of the United States Constitution (And Who Knows, Maybe the FBI) (1970)
[1105] Cornell University Wind Ensemble;
Stith, Marice (cond); tape
- Cornell CUWE-7; 33s; rel 1971;
cip

BORETZ, Benjamin (1934-)
Group Variations II (1968-71)
[1106] Electronic music
- CRI-300; 33s; rel 1974; cip

BORISHANSKY, Elliot (1930-)
(Two) Pieces, Clarinet
[1107] Rehfeldt, Phillip (cl)
- Advance FGR-15S; 33s; rel
1973; cip

BORISOFF, Alexander (1902-)
Variations on a Theme of Paganini
[1108] American Chamber Virtuosi
- Crystal S-862; 33s; rel 1973; cip

BOROS, David John (1944-)
Anecdote of the Jar and Piano Interlude (The Pleasures of Merely Circulating)
[1109] Brandeis University Chamber Chorus; Boykan, Martin (pf); Nagel, Alan (cb); Satz, David (b cl); Olesen, James (cond)
Rec 5/1/77
- CRI-379; 33s; rel 1978; cip

Wedding Music
[1110] Fisher, George (pf)
Rec 5/1/77
- CRI-379; 33s; rel 1978; cip

Yet Once Again
[1111] Boykan, Constance (fl)
Rec 5/1/77
- CRI-379; 33s; rel 1978; cip

BOROWSKI, Felix (1872-1956)
Adoration
[1112] Kronold, Hans (vcl?)
- Columbia A-5222; 78

[1113] Rattay, Howard (vln); orchestra
- Victor 35024; 78; rel 1909

Madrigal to the Moon
[1114] Ohio State University Faculty Woodwind Quintet
- Coronet 543; 33m; rel 1969; cip

Mirror, The (1946)
[1115] Louisville Orchestra; Whitney, Robert (cond)
- LOU-56-2; 33m (Louisville Orchestra First Edition Records 1956 No 2); rel 1959; del 1978

Sonata, Organ, No 1: 1st Movement
[1116] Gay, Harry W. (org)
- Erico BPC-101; 33s; rel 1974

Suite, Organ, No 1: Meditation-Elegy and Solemn March
[1117] Curtis, Stanley (org)
- Apollo Sound AS-1004; 33s; rel 1968

BOWLES, Paul (1910-)
Blue Mountain Ballads
[1118] Gramm, Donald (bar); Cumming, Richard (pf)
- Music Library MLR-7033; 33m; rel 1954; del 1974
- St/And SPL-411-12; 33m; 2 discs; rel 1963; del 1964
- Desto D-411-12/DST-6411-12; 33m/s; 2 discs; rel 1964; cip

Blue Mountain Ballads: Heavenly Grass and Cabin
[1119] Hanks, John Kennedy (ten); Friedberg, Ruth (pf)
- Duke University Press DWR-6417-18; 33m; 2 discs; rel 1966; del 1975

Cafe sin nombre
[1120] Bowles, Paul (pf)
- New Music Quarterly Recordings 1414; 78; rel 1938

Concerto, Two Pianos, Winds, and Percussion (1947)
[1121] Gold, Arthur (pf); Fizdale, Robert (pf); Miller, Mitchell (ob); Kell, Reginald (cl); Schaller, L. (b cl); Freistadt, Harry (tpt); Bailey, Elden (perc); Rosenberger, Walter (perc); Saidenberg, Daniel (cond)
- Columbia MX-344; 78; 2 discs; rel pre-1952
- Columbia ML-2128; 33m; 10"; rel 1950; del 1956

Danger de mort
[1122] no performers given
- Yaddo; 78; rel pre-1952

Denmark Vesey (1938): Think of All the Hair Dressing
[1123] Spirito, Romolo de (ten); Welch, Carrington (pf)
- Disc 6017-19 (in set M-730); 78; 3-10"; rel pre-1948

Garden of Disorder, The: Song for my Sister
[1124] Spirito, Romolo de (ten); Welch, Carrington (pf)
- Disc 6017-19 (in set M-730); 78; 3-10"; rel pre-1948

Huapango No 1
[1125] Duron, Jesus (pf)
- New Music Quarterly Recordings 1414; 78; rel 1938

Huapango No 2 (El Sol)
[1126] Bowles, Paul (pf)
- New Music Quarterly Recordings 1414; 78; rel 1938

Letter to Freddy
[1127] Luening, Ethel (sop); Nowak, Lionel (pf)
- Yaddo I-2; 78; 10"; rel 1940

Mexican Dances (1943): La Cuelga, El Bejuco, and El Indio
[1128] Foldes, Andor (pf)
- Vox 16068 (in set 174); 78; 10"; rel 1947

Mexican Dances: El Bejuco and Sayula
[1129] Gold, Arthur (pf); Fizdale, Robert (pf)
- Art of this Century 803 (in set 1); 78; 10"; rel pre-1948

Music for a Farce (1938)
[1130] Glazer, David (cl); Mueller, Herbert C. (tpt); Bailey, Elden (perc); Masselos, William (pf)
- Columbia ML-4845; 33m; rel 1954; del 1968
- Columbia ML-5241; 33m; rel 1958; del 1968
- Columbia CML-4845; 33m; rel 1968; del 1974
- Columbia CML-5241; 33m; rel 1968; del 1974
- Columbia AML-4845; 33m; rel 1974; del 1976

[1131] MGM Orchestra; Surinach, Carlos (cond)
- MGM E-3549; 33m; rel 1958; del 1960

Night Waltz (1949)
[1132] Gold, Arthur (pf); Fizdale, Robert (pf)
- Columbia MM-956; 78; rel pre-1952
- Columbia ML-2147; 33m; 10"; rel 1952; del 1956
- Philips S-06614R; 33m; rel pre-1956

Night without Sleep
[1133] Spirito, Romolo de (ten); Welch, Carrington (pf)
- Disc 6017-19 (in set M-730); 78; 3-10"; rel pre-1948

Once a Lady Was Here (1946)
[1134] Gramm, Donald (bar); Hassard, Donald (pf)
- New World NW-243; 33s; rel 1977

(Three) Pastoral Songs (1945)
[1135] Hess, William (ten); Fizdale, Robert (pf)
- Hargail HN-707 (in set 0090); 78; 10"; rel 1946

Picnic Cantata, A (1952)
[1136] Davy, Gloria (sop); Flowers, Martha (sop); Gaither, Mareda (m sop); Wynder, Gloria (al); Gold, Arthur (pf); Fizdale, Robert (pf); Howard, Al (perc)
- Columbia ML-5068; 33m; rel 1955; del 1965

(Six) Preludes, Piano (1934-45)
[1137] Johannesen, Grant (pf)
- Golden Crest CR-4065/CRS-4065; 33m/s; rel 1963/1966; cip

Sailor's Song
[1138] Spirito, Romolo de (ten); Welch, Carrington (pf)
- Disc 6017-19 (in set M-730); 78; 3-10"; rel pre-1948

Scenes d'Anabase (1932)

[1139] Hess, William (ten); Marx, Josef (ob); Masselos, William (pf)
- Columbia ML-4845; 33m; rel 1954; del 1968
- Columbia CML-4845; 33m; rel 1968; del 1974
- Columbia AML-4845; 33m; rel 1974; del 1976

Sonata, Flute and Piano (1932)

[1140] LeRoy, Rene (fl); Reeves, George (pf)
- Art of this Century 801-03 (in set 1); 78; 3-10"; rel pre-1948

Sonata, Two Pianos (1945)

[1141] Gold, Arthur (pf); Fizdale, Robert (pf)
- Concert Hall 1009-12 (in set A-5); 78; 2-10"; rel pre-1948
- Concert Hall CHS-1089; 33m; 10"; rel 1951; del 1956

Song of an Old Woman (1942)

[1142] Gramm, Donald (bar); Hassard, Donald (pf)
- New World NW-243; 33s; rel 1977

(Four) Spanish Songs

[1143] Hess, William (ten); Fizdale, Robert (pf)
- Hargail HN-709 (in set 0090); 78; 10"; rel 1946

Tempest, The

[1144] Lawrence, P. (sop)
- Polymusic PR-5001-02; 33m; rel pre-1952

They Cannot Stop Death

[1145] Spirito, Romolo de (ten); Welch, Carrington (pf)
- Disc 6017-19 (in set M-730); 78; 3-10"; rel pre-1948

Three

[1146] Hess, William (ten); Fizdale, Robert (pf)
- Hargail HN-709 (in set 0090); 78; 10"; rel 1946

When Rain or Love Began

[1147] Spirito, Romolo de (ten); Welch, Carrington (pf)
- Disc 6017-19 (in set M-730); 78; 3-10"; rel pre-1948

Wind Remains, The (1941-43)

[1148] Renzi, Dorothy (sop); Driscoll, Loren (ten); MGM Orchestra; Surinach, Carlos (cond)
- MGM E-3549; 33m; rel 1958; del 1960

You Can't Trust in Love

[1149] Spirito, Romolo de (ten); Welch, Carrington (pf)
- Disc 6017-19 (in set M-730); 78; 3-10"; rel pre-1948

You're Right, the Day Ain't Mine

[1150] Spirito, Romolo de (ten); Welch, Carrington (pf)
- Disc 6017-19 (in set M-730); 78; 3-10"; rel pre-1948

BOYD, Wynn (1902-)

Petite rondo (1950)

[1151] Norman, Ruth (pf)
- Opus One 39; 33s; rel 1979; cip

BOYKAN, Martin (1931-)

Quartet, Strings, No 1 (1949)

[1152] Contemporary String Quartet
- CRI-338; 33s; rel 1975; cip

Quartet, Strings, No 2 (1967)

[1153] Pro Arte Quartet
Rec 4/78
- CRI-401; 33s; rel 1979; cip

BRAINE, Robert (1896-1940)

Choreographic Impressions: Pavane (El Greco) and Habanera (Lazy Cigarette)

[1154] Eastman-Rochester Symphony Orchestra; Hanson, Howard (cond)
- Victor 2112; 78; 10"; rel pre-1943

BRAND, Max (1896-1980)

Wonderful One-Hoss Shay, The (1950)

[1155] Philadelphia Orchestra; Ormandy, Eugene (cond)
- Columbia ML-2141; 33m; 10"; rel 1950; del 1956

BRANT, Henry (1913-)

Angels and Devils (1931, rev 1956)

[1156] New England Conservatory Chamber Ensemble; Heiss, John (cond)
- Golden Crest NEC-109; 33s; rel 1979; cip

[1157] Wilkins, Frederick (fl); flute and piccolo ensemble; Brant, Henry (cond)
- CRI-106; 33m/s; rel 1957/?; cip

Concerto, Saxophone and Nine Instruments (1941)

[1158] Rascher, Sigurd (sax); Cincinnati Symphony Orchestra; Johnson, Thor (cond)
- Remington 199-188; 33m; rel 1956; del 1959
- Varese Sarabande VC-81047; 33m; rel 1979; cip

Concerto, Trumpet and Nine Instruments (1970)

[1159] Schwarz, Gerard (tpt); ensemble; Brant, Henry (cond)
- Desto DC-7133; 33s; rel 1973; cip

Crossroads for Violins (1971)

[1160] Kobialka, Daniel (vln)
- Desto DC-7144; 33s; rel 1973; cip

Galaxy 2 (1954)

[1161] chamber ensemble; Brant, Henry (cond)
- Columbia ML-4956; 33m; rel 1955; cip

Hieroglyphics II (1966)

[1162] Kobialka, Daniel (vln); Brant, Henry (perc)
- Advance FGR-6S; 33s; rel 1970; cip

Hieroglyphics III

[1163] Satterlee, Catherine (m sop); Glick, Jacob (vla); Brant, Henry (org); Pearson, Phyllis Martin (vib) (pf); Finckel, Marianne (hpschd); Calabro, Louis (timp) (ch)
- CRI-260; 33s; rel 1971; cip

Kingdom Come (1970)

[1164] Brant, Henry (org); Oakland Symphony Orchestra; Gerhard, Samuel (cond); Oakland Youth Orchestra; Hughes, Robert (cond)
- Desto DC-7108; 33s; rel 1970; cip

Lyric Cycle

[1165] Van Loon, Helen (sop); three violas; piano
- New Music Quarterly Recordings 1311; 78; rel 1937

Machinations (1970)

[1166] Brant, Henry (ten instruments)
- Desto DC-7108; 33s; rel 1970; cip

Millennium 2 (1954)

[1167] Fenn, Louise (sop); Lehigh University Instrumental Ensembles; Brant, Henry (cond)
Rec 2/21/59
- Lehigh RINC-1103; 33m; rel 1968; del 1976

Millennium 4 (1963)

[1168] American Brass Quintet
- Nonesuch H-71222; 33s; rel 1969; cip

[1169] Modern Brass Ensemble
- Advance FGR-2; 33m; rel 1966; del 1978

A Discography

On the Nature of Things (After Lucretius) (1956)
[1170] Louisville Orchestra; Mester, Jorge (cond)
- LS-76-5; 33s (Louisville Orchestra First Edition Records 1976 No 5); rel 1979; cip

Orbits (A Spatial Symphonic Ritual)
[1171] Snyder, Amy (voice); Brant, Henry (org); Bay Bones Trombone Choir; Samuel, Gerhard (cond)
Rec 2/11/79
- CRI-422; 33s; rel 1980; cip

Quombex (1960)
[1172] Zukofsky, Paul (vla d'amore)
- Desto DC-6435-37; 33s; 3 discs; rel 1975; cip

Signs and Alarms (1953)
[1173] chamber ensemble; Brant, Henry (cond)
- Columbia ML-4956; 33m; rel 1955; cip

Symphony in B-flat (1945, rev 1950)
[1174] Vienna Symphony Orchestra; Swarowsky, Hans (cond)
- American Recording Society ARS-38; 33m; rel 1953*
- Desto D-416/DST-6416; 33m/s; rel 1965; cip

Verticals Ascending (1967)
[1175] Northwestern University Symphonic Wind Ensemble; Paynter, John P. (cond)
Rec 11/76
- New World NW-211; 33s; rel 1977

BRAXTON, Anthony (1945-)
New York, Fall 1974
[1176] Braxton, Anthony (sax) (fl) or (cl); assisting instrumentalists; Moog synthesizer
Rec 9/27/74 and 10/16/74
- Arista AL-4032; 33s; rel 1975; cip

P–JOS..4K–D–(Mix)
[1177] Rzewski, Frederic (pf)
- Finnadar SR-9011; 33s; rel 1976; cip

30–64 degrees–308M–C4DM(r)–Z
[1178] Oberlin Orchestra; Moore, John (cond); Young (cond); Baustian, Robert (cond); Gross, Murray (cond)
- Arista AL-8900; 33q; 3 discs; rel 1979; cip

BREHM, Alvin (1925-)
Colloquy and Chorale
[1179] New York Bassoon Quartet
- Leonarda LPI-102; 33s; rel 1980

Cycle of Six Songs on Poems of Garcia Lorca
[1180] DeGaetani, Jan (m sop); Composers Festival Orchestra; Brehm, Alvin (cond)
- Trilogy CTS-1002; 33s; rel 1973; del 1975

Dialogues, Bassoon and Percussion (1963)
[1181] Pachman, Maurice (bsn); Price, Paul (perc); Little, Steve (perc)
- Golden Crest RE-7019; 33m/s; rel 1967/1979; cip

Quintet, Brass (1967)
[1182] American Brass Quintet
- Nonesuch H-71222; 33s; rel 1969; cip

Theme, Syllogism, and Epilogue
[1183] Peltzer, Dwight (pf)
- Serenus SRS-12085; 33s; rel 1980; cip

Variations, Piano
[1184] Peltzer, Dwight (pf)
- Serenus SRS-12069; 33s; rel 1978; cip

BREIL, Joseph Carl (1870-1926)
Song of the Soul
[1185] Baker, Elsie (al)
- Victor 45349; 78; rel pre-1925

BRESNICK, Martin (1946-)
B's Garlands (1973)
[1186] Selmi, Giusseppe (vcl); Ravenna, Giorgio (vcl); Mascellini, Guido (vcl); Luca, Michele de (vcl); Lanzilotta, Luigi (vcl); Mastromatteo, Anamaria (vcl); Girolamo, Salvatore de (vcl); Mori, Giancarlo (vcl)
- CRI-336; 33s; rel 1977; cip

BRESS, Hyman (1931-)
Fantasy
[1187] Electronic music
- Folkways FM-3355; 33m; rel 1963; cip

BRICCETTI, Thomas (1936-)
Fountain of Youth, The (1972)
[1188] Louisville Orchestra; Briccetti, Thomas (cond)
Rec 11/7/72
- LS-73-3; 33s (Louisville Orchestra First Edition Records 1973 No 3); rel 1974; cip

BRIGHT, Houston (1916-)
I Hear a Voice a-Prayin'
[1189] Hollywood Presbyterian Church Choir; Hirt, Charles C. (cond)
- RCA LPM-1258; 33m; rel 1956; del 1958

I Hear a Voice a-Prayin' *(cont'd)*
[1190] Singing City Choir of Philadelphia; Brown, Elaine (cond)
- Fellowship FM-1/FS-1; 33m/s; rel 1961

Rainsong
[1191] Mormon Tabernacle Choir; Ottley, Jerold D. (cond)
- Columbia M-34134; 33s; rel 1976; cip

(Three) Short Dances
[1192] American Woodwind Quintet
- Golden Crest CR-4075/CRS-4075; 33m/s; rel 1966/1967; cip

BRITTENHAM, Robert
Improvisations
[1193] Brittenham, Robert (org)
- Recorded Publications Z-73001-02 (matrix no); 33s; rel 1973

BROCKWAY, Howard A. (1870-1951)
Barnyard Song
[1194] Homer, Louise (al)
- Victor 1028; 78; 10"; rel 1919-25

BROWN, Earle (1926-)
Available Forms I (1961)
[1195] Rome Symphony Orchestra; Maderna, Bruno (cond)
- RCA-Victrola VIC-1239/VICS-1239; 33m/s; rel 1967; del 1976

Corroboree (1964)
[1196] Takahashi, Yuji (pf)
- Mainstream MS-5000; 33s; rel 1970; del 1979

Folio (1952-53): December 1952
[1197] Tudor, David (pf)
- CRI-330; 33s; rel 1975; cip

Four Systems (1954)
[1198] Neuhaus, Max (cym)
- Columbia MS-7139; 33s; rel 1968; cip

Hodograph I (1959)
[1199] Hammond, Don (fl); Soyer, David (vcl); Tudor, David (pf); Kraus, Philip (perc)
- Time 58007/S-8007; 33m/s; rel 1963; del 1970
- Mainstream MS-5007; 33s; rel 1970; del 1979

Music for Violin, Violoncello, and Piano (1952)
[1200] Raimondi, Matthew (vln); Soyer, David (vcl); Tudor, David (pf)
- Time 58007/S-8007; 33m/s; rel 1963; del 1970

Music for Violin, Violoncello, and Piano (1952) *(cont'd)*
- Mainstream MS-5007; 33s; rel 1970; del 1979

Music for Violoncello and Piano (1954)
[1201] Palm, Siegfried (vcl); Kontarsky, Aloys (pf)
- Deutsche Grammophon 2530.562; 33s; rel 1975

[1202] Soyer, David (vcl); Tudor, David (pf)
- Time 58007/S-8007; 33m/s; rel 1963; del 1970
- Mainstream MS-5007; 33s; rel 1970; del 1979

Nine Rarebits (1965)
[1203] Vischer, Antoinette (hpschd); Gruntz, George (hpschd)
- Wergo WER-323; 33s; 7"; rel 196?
- Wergo WER-60-028; 33s; rel 1969?

Novara (1962)
[1204] Jurriaanse, Govert (fl); Floore, John (tpt); Sparnaay, Harry (b cl); Walta, Jaring (vln); Van Driesten, Roelof (vln); Oldeman, Gerrit (vla); Ruijsenaars, Harro (vcl); Hartsuiker, Ton (pf); Brown, Earle (cond)
- CRI-330; 33s; rel 1975; cip

Octet I (1953)
[1205] Electronic music
- CRI-330; 33s; rel 1975; cip

Quartet, Strings (1965)
[1206] Concord String Quartet
- Vox SVBX-5306; 33s; 3 discs; rel 1973; cip

[1207] La Salle Quartet
- Deutsche Grammophon 2543.002; 33s; rel 1971; del 1975

[1208] New York String Quartet
- Mainstream MS-5009; 33s; rel 1972; del 1979

[1209] no performers given
- Opus Musicum OM-116-18; 33s; 3 discs; rel 1975

Times Five (1963)
[1210] Jurriaanse, Govert (fl); Moore, Arthur (tbn); Tieu, Teresia (hp); Walta, Jaring (vln); Ruijsenaars, Harro (vcl); tape; Brown, Earle (cond)
- CRI-330; 33s; rel 1975; cip

[1211] ORTF Philharmonic Orchestra; Schaeffer (cond)
- Boite 072/5072; 33m/s; rel 1968; del 1970

BROWN, Gladys Mungen*
Black Tea
[1212] Brown, Gladys Mungen (nar)
- Opus One 53; 33s; rel 1980; cip

BROWN, J. Harold (1909-81)
Suite, Strings: Prelude
[1213] Yaddo Orchestra; Donovan, Richard (cond)
- Yaddo D-7; 78; rel 1938

BROWN, Marion (1936-) and SCHWARTZ, Elliott
Soundways
[1214] Brown, Marion (various instruments); Schwartz, Elliott (various instruments)
Rec 2/18/73
- Century (Bowdoin College Music Press) V-41746; 33s; rel 1974

BROWN, Newel Kay (1932-)
(Three) Diverse Movements
[1215] Iowa Brass Quintet
- Trilogy CTS-1001; 33s; rel 1973; del 1975

Pastorale and Dance
[1216] Brown, M.; Stone; Umiker; Levy; Evanson
- Capra 1201; 33s; rel 1969; cip

Poetics (1970)
[1217] Levy, Robert (tpt); Levy, Amy Lou (pf)
- Golden Crest RE-7045; 33q; rel 1972; cip

BROWN, Rayner (1912-)
Concertino, Harp and Brass Quintet (1962)
[1218] Chaloupka, Stanley (hp); Los Angeles Brass Quintet
- Crystal S-602; 33s; rel 1968; cip

Concertino, Piano and Band
[1219] Davis, Sharon (pf); band
- WIM Records WIMR-13; 33s; rel 1977; cip

Concerto, Two Pianos, Brass, and Percussion
[1220] Davis, Sharon (pf); Stepan, Russell (pf); Los Angeles Brass Society; Remsen, Lester (cond)
- WIM Records WIMR-8; 33s; rel 1974; cip

Fantasy-Fugue
[1221] Los Angeles Philharmonic Brass Ensemble; Remsen, Lester (cond)
- Avant AV-1005; 33s; rel 1976; cip

(Five) Pieces, Organ, Harp, Brass, and Percussion
[1222] Ladd, Thomas (org); Remsen, Dorothy (hp); Los Angeles Brass Society; Remsen, Lester (cond)
- Avant AV-1001; 33s; rel 1971; cip

Quintet, Brass, No 2 (1960)
[1223] Pacific Brass Quintet
- Avant AV-1004; 33s; rel 1972*

Sonata, Flute and Organ (1969)
[1224] Shanley, Gretel (fl); Ladd, Thomas (org)
- WIM Records WIMR-2; 33s; rel 1971; cip

Symphony, Clarinet Choir (1968)
[1225] Los Angeles Clarinet Society; Henderson, Robert (cond)
- WIM Records WIMR-8; 33s; rel 1974; cip

BROWN, Reginald Porter
Dance of the Three Old Maids
[1226] Kell, Reginald (cl); Camarata and his Orchestra; Camarata, Salvador (cond)
- Decca 16048; 78

BROZEN, Michael (1934-)
In Memoriam
[1227] Price, Janet (sop); Royal Philharmonic Orchestra; Dixon, James (cond)
- CRI-258; 33s; rel 1970; cip

BRUBECK, Dave (1920-)
Blessed Are the Poor
[1228] Dave Brubeck Trio; Mulligan, Gerry (bar sax); Cincinnati Symphony Orchestra; Kunzel, Erich (cond)
- Decca DL-710181; 33s; rel 1971; del 1974

Duke, The
[1229] Dave Brubeck Trio; Mulligan, Gerry (bar sax); Cincinnati Symphony Orchestra; Kunzel, Erich (cond)
- Decca DL-710181; 33s; rel 1971; del 1974

Elementals
[1230] Dave Brubeck Trio; Mulligan, Gerry (bar sax); Cincinnati Symphony Orchestra; Kunzel, Erich (cond)
- Decca DL-710181; 33s; rel 1971; del 1974

Forty Days
[1231] Dave Brubeck Trio; Mulligan, Gerry (bar sax); Cincinnati Symphony Orchestra; Kunzel, Erich (cond)
- Decca DL-710181; 33s; rel 1971; del 1974

Gates of Justice, The

[1232] Orbach, Harold (ten); Boatwright, McHenry (b bar); Westminster Choir; Delcamp, Robert (org); Dave Brubeck Trio; Cincinnati Brass Ensemble; Kunzel, Erich (cond)
- Decca DL-710175; 33s; rel 1971; del 1974

Happy Anniversary

[1233] Dave Brubeck Trio; Mulligan, Gerry (bar sax); Cincinnati Symphony Orchestra; Kunzel, Erich (cond)
- Decca DL-710181; 33s; rel 1971; del 1974

Light in the Wilderness, The (1961)

[1234] Justus, William (bar); University of Miami A Cappella Singers; Hancock, Gerre (org); Brubeck, Dave (pf); Cincinnati Symphony Orchestra; Kunzel, Erich (cond)
- Decca DL-740155-56 (in set DXSA-7202); 33s; 2 discs; rel 1968; del 1974

Truth Is Fallen (1971)

[1235] Peterson, Charlene (sop); St. John's Assembly Chorus; Brubeck, Dave (pf); New Heavenly Blue; Cincinnati Symphony Orchestra; Kunzel, Erich (cond)
- Atlantic SD-1606; 33s; rel 1972; del 1975

BRUNSWICK, Mark (1902-71)

(Six) Bagatelles, Piano (1958)

[1236] Helps, Robert (pf)
- RCA LM-7042/LSC-7042; 33m/s; 2 discs; rel 1966; del 1971
- CRI-288; 33s; 2 discs; rel 1972; cip

Fragment of Sappho (1932)

[1237] Hamline Singers; Holliday, Robert (cond)
- New NRLP-305; 33m; 10"; rel 1951; del 1963

Quartet, Strings (1958)

[1238] Galimir String Quartet (members of); Levine, Julius (cb)
- CRI-244; 33s; rel 1969; cip

Septet (1957)

[1239] Baker, Julius (fl); Kaplan, Melvin (ob); Listokan, Robert (cl); Froelich, Ralph (hn); Newman, Morris (bsn); Lynch, Ynez (vla); Kougell, Alexander (vcl); Jahoda, Fritz (cond)
- CRI-170; 33m; rel 1963; cip

(Seven) Trios, String Quartet (1956)

[1240] Galimir String Quartet
- CRI-244; 33s; rel 1969; cip

BRYANT, Allan (1931-)

Bouncing Little People Planet, A

[1241] Bryant, Allan (gtr)
- CRI-366; 33s; rel 1977; cip

Rocket Is a Drum, A

[1242] Bryant, Allan (gtr)
- CRI-366; 33s; rel 1977; cip

Space Guitars

[1243] Bryant, Allan (gtr)
- CRI-366; 33s; rel 1977; cip

Whirling Take-Off

[1244] Bryant, Allan (gtr)
- CRI-366; 33s; rel 1977; cip

BUBALO, Rudolph (1927-)

(Three) Pieces, Brass Quintet (1959)

[1245] Cleveland Brass Ensemble
- CRI-183; 33m/s; rel 1964/?; cip

(Five) Pieces, Brass Quintet and Percussion (1964)

[1246] Baldwin-Wallace Faculty Brass Quintet and Percussion Group
- Advent USR-5004; 33s; rel 1973; cip

BUCCI, Mark (1924-)

Concerto for a Singing Instrument: Vocalise and Tug of War (arr for voice and pf)

[1247] Addison, Adele (sop); Payne, James (pf)
- CRI-147; 33m; rel 1962; cip

Tale for a Deaf Ear (1957): Summer Aria and Spring Aria

[1248] Addison, Adele (sop); Payne, James (pf)
- CRI-147; 33m; rel 1962; cip

BUCHTEL, Forrest L. (1899-)

Polka Dots

[1249] Barron, Ronald (tbn); Bolter, Norman (tbn); Edelman, Douglas (tbn); Cooper, Kenneth (pf)
- Nonesuch H-71341; 33s; rel 1977

BUCKY, Frida Sarsen

Hear the Wind Whispering

[1250] Anderson, Marian (al); Rupp, Franz (pf)
- Victor 10-1260; 78; 10"

BUDD, Harold (1936-)

Coeur d'or (1969)

[1251] Electronic music
- Advance FGR-16S; 33s; rel 1973; cip

New Work No 1

[1252] no performers given
- Advance FGR-9S; 33s; rel 197?

New Work No 5

[1253] Stevens, Thomas (tpt); Grierson, Ralph (pf)
- Crystal S-361; 33s; rel 1976; cip

Oak of Golden Dreams (1970)

[1254] Electronic music
- Advance FGR-16S; 33s; rel 1973; cip

. . . Only Three Clouds . . . (1969)

[1255] Anderson, Miles (tbn)
- Avant AV-1006; 33s; rel 1978; cip

BUGGERT, Robert (1918-)

Introduction and Fugue (1957)

[1256] Ithaca Percussion Ensemble; Benson, Warren (cond)
- Golden Crest CR-4016/CRS-4016; 33m/s; rel 1960/1961; cip

BURGE, David (1930-)

Eclipse II (1964)

[1257] Burge, David (pf)
- Advance FGR-3; 33m; rel 1967; cip

Serenade for Musical Saw and Orchestra (1965)

[1258] Turner, Jim (musical saw); Burge, David (cond?)
- Owl QS-22; 33q; rel 1972; del 1978

Sources IV

[1259] Burge, David (pf)
Rec 10/16-17/75
- CRI-345; 33s; rel 1976; cip

BURLEIGH, Cecil (1885-1980)

Giant Hills

[1260] Heifetz, Jascha (vln); Bay, Emanuel (pf)
- Decca 24131 (in set A-592); 78; 10"; rel pre-1952
- Decca DL-9780; 33m; rel 1958; del 1971

Indian Snake Dance

[1261] Seidel, Toscha (vln)
- Columbia 33002D; 78; rel 1918-25
- Columbia 4001M; 78; rel 1918-25

Moto perpetuo

[1262] Heifetz, Jascha (vln); Bay, Emanuel (pf)
- Decca 24131 (in set A-592); 78; 10"; rel pre-1952
- Decca DL-9780; 33m; rel 1958; del 1971

BURTON, Eldin (1913-)
Fiddlestick! (1946)
[1263] Tryon, Jesse (vln); Burton, Eldin
       (pf)
       - Classic Editions CE-1006; 33m;
       rel 1952; del 1959

Nonchalance
[1264] Burton, Eldin (pf)
       - Classic Editions CE-1026; 33m;
       rel 1955; del 1958

Quintet, Piano and Strings (1945)
[1265] Burton, Eldin (pf); Contemporary
       Music Quartet
       - Classic Editions CE-1006; 33m;
       rel 1952; del 1959

Sonatina, Flute and Piano (1946)
[1266] Ben-Meir, Shaul (fl); Kilby, Muriel
       (pf)
       - Golden Crest RE-7078; 33s; rel
       1979; cip
[1267] Bryan, Keith (fl); Keys, Karen (pf)
       - Orion ORS-76242; 33s; rel
       1976; cip
[1268] Pellerite, James (fl); Webb, Charles
       (pf)
       - Coronet S-1713; 33s; rel 1972;
       cip
[1269] Wummer, John (fl); Burton, Eldin
       (pf)
       - Classic Editions CE-1006; 33m;
       rel 1952; del 1959

Sonatina, Violin and Piano (1944)
[1270] Tryon, Jesse (vln); Burton, Eldin
       (pf)
       - Classic Editions CE-1006; 33m;
       rel 1952; del 1959

BURTON, Stephen Douglas (1943-)
Songs of the Tulpehocken
[1271] Riegel, Kenneth (ten); Louisville
       Orchestra; Burton, Stephen
       Douglas (cond)
       - LS-75-7; 33s (Louisville
       Orchestra First Edition Records
       1975 No 7); rel 1977; cip

Symphony No 2 (Ariel)
[1272] Curry, Corrine (m sop); Dickson;
       Syracuse Symphony Orchestra;
       Keene, Christopher (cond)
       - Peters Internationale PLE-128;
       33s; rel 1980; cip

BUSH, Irving
Fanfares 1969 *see* **REYNOLDS,
Jeffrey, et al**

BUUCK, Paul (1911-)
Quartet, Strings
[1273] Walden String Quartet
       - Yaddo 10A-B; 78; 1-10" and
       1-12"; rel 1937 (1st and 2nd
       movements)

Quartet, Strings *(cont'd)*
       - Yaddo 107A; 78; 10"; rel 1937
       (3rd movement)
       - Yaddo 11A; 78; rel 1937 (4th
       movement)

Suite, Violin and Piano
[1274] Goodman, Bernard (vln); Johansen,
       Gunnar (pf)
       - Yaddo D-8-9; 78; rel 1938

CACAVAS, John (1930-)
Chorale and Capriccio
[1275] Marlborough Concert Band;
       Cacavas, John (cond)
       - Kapp KL-1455/KL-S-3455;
       33m/s; rel 1966; del 1971

Gallant Men, The
[1276] Knightsbridge Symphonic Band;
       Brand, Geoffrey (cond)
       - Gallery EPG-221; 33m; rel 1965

Sentry Boy, The
[1277] Marlborough Concert Band;
       Cacavas, John (cond)
       - Kapp KL-1455/KL-S-3455;
       33m/s; rel 1966; del 1971

CACIOPPO, George (1927-)
Cassiopeia (1963)
[1278] Ashley, Robert (pf); Mumma,
       Gordon (pf)
       - Advance FGR-5; 33m; rel 1966;
       cip

Time on Time in Miracles (1965)
[1279] Ashley, Robert (pf)
       - Advance FGR-5; 33m; rel 1966;
       cip

CADMAN, Charles Wakefield (1881-1946)
(Four) American Indian Songs (Op 45) (1909)
[1280] Parker, William (bar); Huckaby,
       William (pf)
       - New World NW-213; 33s; rel
       1977

**(Four) American Indian Songs:
From the Land of the Sky-Blue
Water**
[1281] Gluck, Alma (sop)
       - Victor 64190; 78; 10"; rel
       1911-15
       - Victor 659; 78; 10"; rel
       1911-15
       - Cantilena CF-6215; 33m; rel
       1969; del 1975
       - Belcantodisc BC-247; 33m; rel
       197?
[1282] Graveure, Louis (ten); piano
       - Columbia M-226; 78; rel
       pre-1936
[1283] Hinkle, Florence (sop)
       - Victor 60079; 78

**(Four) American Indian Songs:
From the Land of the Sky-Blue
Water** *(cont'd)*
[1284] Karle, Theo (ten)
       - Brunswick 13065; 78; 10"; rel
       pre-1927
[1285] Lewis, Mary (sop); orchestra
       - Victor 1140; 78; 10"; rel 1926
[1286] MacDonald, Jeanette (sop);
       Bamboschek, Giuseppe (pf)
       - Victor 2055 (in set M-642); 78;
       10"; rel pre-1948
[1287] Mason, Edith (sop)
       - Brunswick 10177; 78; 10"; rel
       1924-25
[1288] Nielsen, Alice (sop)
       - Columbia A-1732; 78; rel
       1911-15
       - Columbia A-5298; 78; rel
       1911-15
       - Columbia 39875; 78; rel
       1911-15
[1289] Nordica, Lillian (sop)
       Rec 4/29/10
       - Columbia 30486; 78; rel
       1910-11
       - Columbia 68081D; 78; rel
       1910-11
       - Acoustographic AG-4267; 33m;
       rel 1967
[1290] Williams, Evan (ten)
       - Victor 64516; 78; 10"; rel
       1911-18
       - Victor 871; 78; 10"; rel
       1911-18

**(Four) American Indian Songs:
From the Land of the Sky-Blue
Water (arr for orch)**
[1291] Albert Sandler Trio
       - Columbia DB-2129; 78; rel
       pre-1948
[1292] Andre Kostelanetz and his
       Orchestra; Kostelanetz, Andre
       (cond)
       - Columbia 7569M (in set X-284);
       78; rel pre-1948
       - Columbia MX-284; 78; rel
       pre-1952
[1293] Johnny Bothwell and his Orchestra;
       Bothwell, Johnny (cond)
       - Signature 15034; 78; 10"

**(Four) American Indian Songs:
From the Land of the Sky-Blue
Water (arr for org)**
[1294] Charles, Milton (org)
       - Columbia C-1223D; 78; rel
       pre-1936

**(Four) American Indian Songs:
From the Land of the Sky-Blue
Water (arr for vln and pf by Fritz
Kreisler)**
[1295] Kreisler, Fritz (vln); Lamson, Carl
       (pf)
       - Victor 1021; 78; 10"; rel
       1917-25

(Four) American Indian Songs: From the Land of the Sky-Blue Water (arr for vln and pf by Fritz Kreisler) *(cont'd)*
- Victor 1115; 78; 10''; rel 1926-27
- Gramophone DA-745; 78; 10''; rel 1926-27

American Suite (1936)
[1296] Philharmonia Orchestra; Walther, Hans-Jurgen (cond)
- Dorian 1008; 33m; rel 1962; del 1974

At Dawning (Op 29, No 1) (1906)
[1297] Baillie, Isobel (sop)
- EMI/His Master's Voice HLM-7063-64 (in set RLS-714); 33m; 2 discs; rel 1975

[1298] Burrows, Stuart (ten); Constable, John (pf)
- L'Oiseau-lyre SOL-324; 33s; rel 1971*

[1299] Coltham, S. (ten)
- Gramophone B-2323; 78; 10''; rel pre-1936

[1300] Eddy, Nelson (bar); Columbia Concert Orchestra and Arnaud, Leon (cond); or Paxson, Theodore (pf)
- Victor 4369 (in set C-27); 78; 10''; rel pre-1948
- Gramophone DA-1585; 78; 10''; rel pre-1948
- Columbia ML-4343; 33m; rel 1950; del 1958
- Columbia CL-812; 33m; rel 1956; del 1958

[1301] Garden, Mary (sop); Dansereau, Jean H. (pf) Rec 10/26/26
- Victor 1216; 78; 10''; rel pre-1927
- New World NW-247; 33m; rel 1976

[1302] Hislop, Joseph (ten)
- Gramophone DA-819; 78; 10''; rel pre-1936

[1303] Karle, Theo (ten)
- Brunswick 13095; 78; 10''; rel pre-1927

[1304] Kullman, Charles (ten); orchestra; Burger, Julius (cond)
- Columbia 4529M; 78; 10''

[1305] McCormack, John (ten)
- Victor 64302; 78; 10''; rel 1913-15
- Victor 742; 78; 10''; rel 1913-15

[1306] Miller, Elsie (sop)
- Decca F-3479; 78; rel pre-1936

[1307] Piccaver, Alfred (voice)
- Decca M-419; 78; rel pre-1936

[1308] Rider-Kelsey, Corinne (sop)
- Columbia M-121; 78; rel pre-1927

At Dawning (Op 29, No 1) (1906) *(cont'd)*
[1309] Robeson, Paul (b)
- Gramophone B-8731; 78; 10''; rel pre-1948

[1310] Schumann-Heink, Ernestine (al)
- Pelican LP-2008; 33m; rel 1978; cip

[1311] Stevens, Rise (m sop); orchestra; Shulman, Daniel (cond)
- Columbia M-654; 78; rel pre-1948
- Columbia ML-4179; 33m; rel pre-1949; del 1956

[1312] Stiles, Vernon (ten); orchestra
- Columbia A-2150; 78

[1313] Swarthout, Gladys (m sop); Victor Orchestra; Katims, Milton (cond)
- RCA LM-116; 33m; 10''; rel 1951; del 1953

[1314] Tauber, Richard (ten)
- Parlophone R-020524; 78; 10''; rel pre-1948

[1315] Thomas, John Charles (bar)
- Vocalion (English) B-60055; 78; rel pre-1925
- Brunswick 10167; 78; 10''; rel pre-1927

At Dawning (arr for orch)
[1316] Boston Pops Orchestra; Fiedler, Arthur (cond)
- Victor 10-1092 (in set M-968); 78; 10''; rel 1944
- Gramophone B-8599; 78; 10''; rel pre-1948

[1317] Victor Herbert's Orchestra
- Victor 45170; 78; rel pre-1927

[1318] Victor Orchestra
- Victor 20668; 78; 10''; rel pre-1927
- Gramophone B-2629; 78; 10''; rel pre-1936

At Dawning (arr for org)
[1319] Charles, Milton (org)
- Columbia 1223D; 78; rel pre-1936

[1320] Crawford, J. (org)
- Victor 20110; 78; 10''; rel pre-1936

At Dawning (arr for vln)
[1321] Lipschultz (vln)
- Columbia 904D; 78; rel pre-1936

At Dawning (arr for vln and pf by Rissand)
[1322] Kreisler, Fritz (vln); Lamson, Carl (pf)
- Victor 1165; 78; 10''; rel pre-1936
- RCA LCT-1142; 33m; rel 1954; del 1956

Call Me No More
[1323] Chamlee, Mario Archer (ten)
- Brunswick 10111; 78; 10''; rel pre-1927

[1324] De Pasquali, Berenice (sop)
- Columbia 39079; 78; rel 1912-14
- Columbia A-1446; 78; rel 1912-14

Dark Dancers of the Mardi-Gras (1933) (two-piano version)
[1325] Bitter, Marguerite (pf); Cadman, Charles Wakefield (pf)
- Co-Art 5023; 78; rel pre-1943

Far Off I Hear a Lover's Flute
[1326] Mason, Edith (sop)
- Brunswick 10215; 78; 10''; rel pre-1927

Her Shadow (Ojibway Canoe Song)
[1327] Baker, Elsie (sop)
- Victor 45495; 78; 10''; rel pre-1927

I Hear a Thrush at Eve
[1328] Hackett, Charles (ten)
- Columbia 33006D; 78; rel 1919-25
- Columbia 4017M; 78; rel 1919-25
- Columbia 1744D; 78; 10''; rel pre-1936
- Columbia 2134M; 78; 10''; rel pre-1936

[1329] Karle, Theo (ten)
- Brunswick 13073; 78; 10''; rel pre-1927

[1330] Macbeth, Florence (sop)
- Columbia 106M; 78; rel pre-1927

[1331] McCormack, John (ten)
- Victor 64340; 78; 10''; rel 1913-15
- Victor 742; 78; 10''; rel 1913-15

[1332] White, Carolina (sop)
- Columbia 39342; 78; rel 1912-14
- Columbia A-1591; 78; rel 1912-14

Legend of the Canyon
[1333] Kreisler, Fritz (vln); Lamson, Carl (pf)
- Victor 1093; 78; 10''; rel 1925

Little Firefly
[1334] Powell, Maud (vln)
- Victor 64705; 78; 10''; rel 1913-17

Love Like the Dawn Came Stealing
[1335] Maurel, Barbara (m sop)
- Columbia 52M; 78; rel pre-1927

Moon Drops Low

[1336] Branzell, Karin (al)
- Brunswick 10228; 78; 10"; rel
pre-1927

[1337] Spencer, Janet (al)
- Victor 64200; 78; 10"; rel
1911-12

[1338] Williams, Evan (ten)
- Victor 64515; 78; 10"

Moonlight Song, A

[1339] Beddoe, Dan (ten)
- Victor 64391; 78; 10"; rel
1911-14

My Desire

[1340] Chamlee, Mario Archer (ten)
- Brunswick 10188; 78; 10"; rel
pre-1927
- Brunswick 10228; 78; 10"; rel
pre-1927

Omaha Indian Tribal Song

[1341] Nordica, Lillian (sop)
- Columbia 30486; 78; rel
1907-11

**Shanewis or The Robin Woman
(1918): Spring Song of the Robin
Woman**

[1342] Baker, Elsie (sop)
- Victor 45495; 78; 10"; rel
pre-1927

[1343] Casey, Ethel (sop); orchestra and
Grieves, Wallace (concertmaster);
or Siddell, Bill (pf)
- Carolina 712C-1713; 33m; rel
1965

White Dawn Is Stealing, The

[1344] Lennox, Elizabeth (al)
- Brunswick 2575; 78; 10"; rel
pre-1927

[1345] Spencer, Janet (al)
- Victor 64249; 78; 10"; rel
1911-12
- Victor 913; 78; 10"; rel
1911-12

CAGE, John (1912-)

Amores (1943)

[1346] Blackearth Percussion Group
Rec 5/27-28/74
- Opus One 22; 33s; rel 1975; cip

[1347] Manhattan Percussion Ensemble;
Cage, John (cond); Price, Paul
(cond)
- Time 58000/S-8000; 33m/s; rel
1961; del 1970
- Mainstream MS-5011; 33s; rel
1970; del 1979

Amores: I and IV

[1348] Ajemian, Maro (pf)
- Disc 875; 78; 2 discs; rel
pre-1948
- Disc 3058 (in set 675); 78; rel
pre-1948

**And the Earth Shall Bear Again
(1942)**

[1349] Pierce, Joshua (pf)
- Tomato TOM-7016; 33s; rel
1980; cip

Aria (1958)

[1350] Berberian, Cathy (sop)
- Time 58003/S-8003; 33m/s; rel
1962; del 1970
- Mainstream MS-5005; 33s; rel
1970; del 1979

Atlas eclipticalis (1961)

[1351] Ensemble Musica Negativa; Riehn,
Rainer (cond)
- Deutsche Grammophon
SLPM-137009; 33s; rel 1970;
del 1974
- Deutsche Grammophon 643543;
33s

Bacchanale (1938)

[1352] Kirstein, Jeanne (pf)
- Columbia MS-7416 (in set
M2S-819); 33s; rel 1970; cip

Book of Music, A (1944)

[1353] Pierce, Joshua (pf); Ajemian, Maro
(pf)
Rec 2/22/76
- Labor LRS-7004-05; 33s; 2
discs; rel 1976
- Tomato TOM-1001; 33s; 2 discs;
rel 1977; cip

Cartridge Music (1960)

[1354] Cage, John (cartridge); Tudor,
David (cartridge)
- Time 58009/S-8009; 33m/s; rel
1963; del 1970
- Mainstream MS-5015; 33s; rel
1970; del 1979

[1355] Ensemble Musica Negativa; Riehn,
Rainer (cond)
- Deutsche Grammophon
SLPM-137009; 33s; rel 1970;
del 1974
- Deutsche Grammophon 643543;
33s

Cheap Imitation (1969)

[1356] Cage, John (pf)
Rec 3/7/76
- Cramps CRSLP-6117; 33s; rel
1977

**Concert, Piano and Orchestra
(1957-58)**

[1357] Tudor, David (pf); orchestra;
Cunningham, Merce (cond)
Rec 1958
- Koby 1499-1504; 33s; 3 discs;
rel 1959
- Avakian JC-1/JCS-1; 33m/s; 3
discs; rel 1960; cip

**Concerto, Prepared Piano and
Chamber Orchestra (1951)**

[1358] Takahashi, Yuji (pf); Buffalo
Philharmonic Orchestra; Foss,
Lukas (cond)
Rec 3/68
- Nonesuch H-71202; 33s; rel
1968; cip

Dance (1947)

[1359] Jacobs, Henry (pf)
- Folkways FX-6160; 33m; rel
1958; cip

[1360] Ajemian, Maro (pf); Masselos,
William (pf)
- Disc 643; 78

(Three) Dances (1945)

[1361] Ajemian, Maro (pf); Masselos,
William (pf)
- Disc 877; 78; 3 discs; rel
pre-1948

[1362] Thomas, Michael Tilson (pf);
Grierson, Ralph (pf)
- Angel S-36059; 33s; rel 1973;
cip

Dream (1948)

[1363] Kirstein, Jeanne (pf)
- Columbia MS-7417 (in set
M2S-819); 33s; rel 1970; cip

Dream (arr for vla)

[1364] Phillips, Karen (vla)
- Finnadar SR-9007; 33s; rel
1975; cip

Etudes australes (1974-75)

[1365] Sultan, Grete (pf)
- Tomato TOM-1101; 33s; 2 discs;
rel 1980; cip

**First Construction (in Metal)
(1939)**

[1366] Manhattan Percussion Ensemble
Rec 1958
- Koby 1499-1504; 33s; 3 discs;
rel 1959
- Avakian JC-1/JCS-1; 33m/s; 3
discs; rel 1960; cip

Flower, A (1950)

[1367] Berberian, Cathy (m sop); Canino,
Bruno (pf)
Rec 1970
- Wergo WER-60-054; 33s; rel
1977*

Fontana Mix (1958)

[1368] Electronic music
- Time 58003/S-8003; 33m/s; rel
1962; del 1970
- Turnabout TV-4046/TVS-34046;
33m/s; rel 1966; del 1975
- Mainstream MS-5005; 33s; rel
1970; del 1979

Fontana Mix (Feed) (1958-65)
[1369] Neuhaus, Max (perc)
- Columbia MS-7139; 33s; rel
1968; cip

[1370] Neuhaus, Max (perc) (different
performance)
- Aspen 5-6; 33s; rel 1968

[1371] Neuhaus, Max (perc) (different
performance)
- Massart M-133; 33

4'33" (1952)
[1372] Simonetti, Gianni-Emilio (pf)
- Cramps CRSLP-6101; 33s; rel
1974

(Seven) Haiku (1952)
[1373] Pierce, Joshua (pf)
- Tomato TOM-7016; 33s; rel
1980; cip

Imaginary Landscape No 1 (1939)
[1374] Cage, John; Cage, Xenia; Dennison,
Doris; Jansen, Margaret
(performing on 2 variable-speed
turntables, frequency recordings,
muted pf, and cym)
Rec 1958
- Koby 1499-1504; 33s; 3 discs;
rel 1959
- Avakian JC-1/JCS-1; 33m/s; 3
discs; rel 1960; cip

(Six) Melodies (1950)
[1375] Zukofsky, Paul (vln); Kalish, Gilbert
(pf)
- Mainstream MS-5016; 33s; rel
1974*

**(Sixty-Two) Mesostics re Merce
Cunningham (1971)**
[1376] Electronic music
- 1750 Arch S-1752; 33s; rel
1975*

[1377] Statos, Demetrio (voice)
- Cramps CRSLP-6101; 33s; rel
1974

Metamorphosis (1938)
[1378] Kirstein, Jeanne (pf)
- Columbia MS-7416 (in set
M2S-819); 33s; rel 1970; cip

**Music for Amplified Toy Pianos
(1960)**
[1379] Hidalgo, Juan (pf); Simonetti,
Gianni-Emilio (pf); Marchetti,
Walter (pf)
- Cramps CRSLP-6101; 33s; rel
1974

Music for Carillon (1952, 1954)
[1380] Tudor, David (elec car)
Rec 1958
- Koby 1499-1504; 33s; 3 discs;
rel 1959
- Avakian JC-1/JCS-1; 33m/s; 3
discs; rel 1960; cip

Music for Marcel Duchamp (1947)
[1381] Hidalgo, Juan (pf)
- Cramps CRSLP-6101; 33s; rel
1974

[1382] Kirstein, Jeanne (pf)
- Columbia MS-7417 (in set
M2S-819); 33s; rel 1970; cip

[1383] Roggenkamp, Peter (pf)
- Wergo WER-60-074; 33s; rel
1976

**Music of Changes (1951): III and
IV**
[1384] Tudor, David (pf)
Rec 3/23/53
- New World NW-214; 33m; rel
1978

Nocturne (1947)
[1385] Zukofsky, Paul (vln); Kalish, Gilbert
(pf)
- Desto DC-6435-37; 33s; 3 discs;
rel 1975; cip

(Two) Pastorales (1951)
[1386] Pierce, Joshua (pf)
- Tomato TOM-7016; 33s; rel
1980; cip

Perilous Night, The (1944)
[1387] Bunger, Richard (pf)
- Avant AV-1008; 33s; rel 1973;
del 1979

[1388] Kirstein, Jeanne (pf)
- Columbia MS-7416 (in set
M2S-819); 33s; rel 1970; cip

(Two) Pieces, Piano (ca 1935)
[1389] Kirstein, Jeanne (pf)
- Columbia MS-7416 (in set
M2S-819); 33s; rel 1970; cip

(Two) Pieces, Piano (1946)
[1390] Kirstein, Jeanne (pf)
- Columbia MS-7416 (in set
M2S-819); 33s; rel 1970; cip

Prelude for Meditation (1944)
[1391] Kirstein, Jeanne (pf)
- Columbia MS-7417 (in set
M2S-819); 33s; rel 1970; cip

**Quartet, Strings, in Four Parts
(1950)**
[1392] Concord String Quartet
- Vox SVBX-5306; 33s; 3 discs; rel
1973; cip
- Turnabout TVS-34610; 33s; rel
1976; cip

[1393] La Salle Quartet
- Deutsche Grammophon
2530.735; 33s; rel 1977; cip

[1394] New Music String Quartet
- Columbia ML-4495; 33m; rel
1952; del 1958

Radio Music (1956)
[1395] Hidalgo, Juan (radio); Simonetti,
Gianni-Emilio (radio); Marchetti,
Walter (radio)
- Cramps CRSLP-6101; 33s; rel
1974

Room, A (1943)
[1396] Pierce, Joshua (pf)
- Tomato TOM-7016; 33s; rel
1980; cip

Root of an Unfocus (1944)
[1397] Kirstein, Jeanne (pf)
- Columbia MS-7417 (in set
M2S-819); 33s; rel 1970; cip

Seasons, The (1947)
[1398] American Composers Orchestra;
Davies, Dennis Russell (cond)
- CRI-410; 33s; rel 1980; cip

She Is Asleep (1943)
[1399] Carmen, Arline (al); Cage, John
(pf); Manhattan Percussion
Ensemble; Price, Paul (cond)
Rec 1958
- Koby 1499-1504; 33s; 3 discs;
rel 1959
- Avakian JC-1/JCS-1; 33m/s; 3
discs; rel 1960; cip

[1400] Clayton, Jay (voice); Pierce, Joshua
(pf); Percussion Ensemble; Price,
Paul (cond)
- Tomato TOM-7016; 33s; rel
1980; cip

**She Is Asleep: Quartet, Twelve
Tom-toms**
[1401] Percussions-Ensemble; Fink,
Siegfried (cond)
- Thorofon MTH-149; 33s; rel
197?

(Six) Short Inventions (1933)
[1402] ensemble; Cage, John (cond)
Rec 1958
- Koby 1499-1504; 33s; 3 discs;
rel 1959
- Avakian JC-1/JCS-1; 33m/s; 3
discs; rel 1960; cip

Solo for Piano (1957-58)
[1403] Persson, Mats (pf)
- Caprice (Swedish) CAP-1071;
33s; rel 1977?

Solo for Voice 2 (1960)
[1404] Brandeis University Chamber
Chorus; Lucier, Alvin (cond)
- Odyssey
32-16-0155/32-16-0156;
33m/s; rel 1967; cip

Sonata, Clarinet (1933)
[1405] Rehfeldt, Phillip (cl)
- Advance FGR-4; 33m; rel 1966;
cip

Sonatas and Interludes, Prepared Piano (1946-48)

[1406] Ajemian, Maro (pf)
- Dial 19; 33m; 2 discs; rel 1951; del 1956
- CRI-199; 33m/s; rel 1965/?; cip

[1407] Ajemian, Maro (pf)
Rec 1958
- Koby 1499-1504; 33s; 3 discs; rel 1959
- Avakian JC-1/JCS-1; 33m/s; 3 discs; rel 1960; cip

[1408] Pierce, Joshua (pf)
Rec 7/26-27/75
- Labor LRS-7004-05; 33s; 2 discs; rel 1976
- Tomato TOM-1001; 33s; 2 discs; rel 1977; cip

[1409] Takahashi, Yuji (pf)
- Fylkingen (Swedish) FYLP-X101-2; 33

[1410] Tilbury, John (pf)
- London HEAD-9; 33s; rel 1976*

Sonatas and Interludes, Prepared Piano: Sonatas I, V, X, and XII, and Interlude II

[1411] Miller, Robert (pf)
- New World NW-203; 33s; rel 1977

Sonatas and Interludes, Prepared Piano: Sonata XIII

[1412] Roggenkamp, Peter (pf)
- Wergo WER-60-074; 33s; rel 1976

Song Books (1970): Solo for Voice 45

[1413] La Barbara, Joan (voice); Smith, Warren (timp); Ditmas, Bruce (timp)
- Chiaroscuro CR-196; 33s; rel 1978; cip

Song Books I-II/Empty Words III

[1414] Cage, John (speaker); Schola Cantorum; Gottwald, Clytus (cond); tape
Rec 6/22/75
- Wergo WER-60-074; 33s; rel 1976

(Five) Songs (1938)

[1415] Dickinson, Meriel (m sop); Dickinson, Peter (pf)
Rec 3/28/77
- Unicorn RHS-253; 33s; rel 1978*
- Unicorn RHS-353; 33s; rel 1978
- Unicorn UNI-72017; 33s; rel 1978

Suite, Toy Piano (1948)

[1416] Kirstein, Jeanne (pf)
- Columbia MS-7417 (in set M2S-819); 33s; rel 1970; cip

Tossed as It Is Untroubled (Meditation) (1943)

[1417] Kirstein, Jeanne (pf)
- Columbia MS-7417 (in set M2S-819); 33s; rel 1970; cip

Totem Ancestor (1943)

[1418] Pierce, Joshua (pf)
- Tomato TOM-7016; 33s; rel 1980; cip

TV Koeln (1958)

[1419] Bunger, Richard (pf)
- Avant AV-1008; 33s; rel 1973; del 1979

27'10.554" (1956)

[1420] Knaack, Donald (perc)
- Finnadar SR-9017; 33s; rel 1977; cip

26'1.1499" (1955)

[1421] Turetzky, Bertram (cb)
- Nonesuch H-71237; 33s; rel 1970; cip

Valentine Out of Season, A (1944)

[1422] Kirstein, Jeanne (pf)
- Columbia MS-7417 (in set M2S-819); 33s; rel 1970; cip

Variations I (1958)

[1423] Szathmary, Zsigmond (org)
- Da Camera (German) SM-93237; 33s; rel 1972

[1424] Zacher, Gerd (org)
Rec 6/67
- Wergo WER-60-033; 33s; rel 1967
- Heliodor 2549.009; 33s; rel 1970; del 1973

[1425] no performer given
- Opus Musicum OM-116-18; 33s; 3 discs; rel 1975

Variations II (1961)

[1426] Tauriello, Antonio (pf); Gandini, Gerardo (pf)
- (Argentinian) JME-ME2

[1427] Tudor, David (pf)
- Columbia MS-7051; 33s; rel 1967; cip

[1428] Vaggione, Horatio; Echarte, Pedro (tape and unusual instruments)
- (Argentinian) JME-ME2

Variations III (1963)

[1429] San Francisco Conservatory New Music Ensemble
Rec 12/70
- Wergo WER-60-057; 33s; rel 1971?

[1430] Zacher, Gerd (org)
- Heliodor 2549.009; 33s; rel 1970; del 1973

Variations III (1963) (cont'd)

[1431] Zacher, Gerd (org) (winds); Allende-Blin, Juan (org) (perc)
- Deutsche Grammophon SLPM-139442; 33s; rel 1970; del 1975

Variations IV (1963): Excerpts I

[1432] Cage, John; Tudor, David
- Everest LPBR-6132/SDBR-3132; 33m/s; rel 1966; cip

Variations IV: Excerpts II

[1433] Cage, John; Tudor, David
- Everest SDBR-3230; 33s; rel 1970; cip

Williams Mix (1952)

[1434] Electronic music
Rec 1958
- Koby 1499-1504; 33s; 3 discs; rel 1959
- Avakian JC-1/JCS-1; 33m/s; 3 discs; rel 1960; cip

Winter Music (1957)

[1435] Ensemble Musica Negativa; Riehn, Rainer (cond)
- Deutsche Grammophon SLPM-137009; 33s; rel 1970; del 1974
- Deutsche Grammophon 643543; 33s

[1436] Flynn, George (pf)
- Finnadar QD-9006; 33q; rel 1975; cip

[1437] Takahashi, Aki (pf)
- CP2 3-5; 33s; 3 discs; rel 197?

Wonderful Widow of Eighteen Springs, The (1942)

[1438] Berberian, Cathy (m sop); Canino, Bruno (pf)
Rec 1970
- Wergo WER-60-054; 33s; rel 1977*

[1439] Carmen, Arline (al); Cage, John (pf)
Rec 1958
- Koby 1499-1504; 33s; 3 discs; rel 1959
- Avakian JC-1/JCS-1; 33m/s; 3 discs; rel 1960; cip

[1440] Rees, Rosalind (sop); Starobin, David (pf)
Rec 1976
- Turnabout TVS-34727; 33s; rel 1978

CAGE, John and HARRISON, Lou (1917-)

Double Music (1941)

[1441] Manhattan Percussion Ensemble; Cage, John (cond); Price, Paul (cond)
- Time 58000/S-8000; 33m/s; rel 1961; del 1970
- Mainstream MS-5011; 33s; rel 1970; del 1979

CAGE, John and HILLER, Lejaren (1924-)

HPSCHD (1967-69)
[1442] Vischer, Antoinette (hpschd);
Bruce, Neely (hpschd); Tudor,
David (hpschd)
- Nonesuch H-71224; 33s; rel
1969; cip

CAGE, John and TUDOR, David (background music)

Indeterminacy
[1443] Cage, John (speaker); Tudor, David
- Folkways FT-3704; 33m; 2 discs;
rel 1960; cip

CAILLET, Lucien (1891-)

Birthday Fantasy, The
[1444] Boston Pops Orchestra; Fiedler,
Arthur (cond)
- RCA LM-1790; 33m; rel 1954;
del 1960

Variations on Pop Goes the Weasel (1938)
[1445] Boston Pops Orchestra; Fiedler,
Arthur (cond)
- Victor 4397; 78; 10"; rel
pre-1943

[1446] Carnegie Pops Orchestra;
O'Connell, Charles (cond)
- Columbia 4368M; 78; 10"; rel
pre-1948
- Columbia ML-4118; 33m; rel
pre-1949; del 1958

CALABRO, Louis (1926-)

Environments (1961)
[1447] Schonbeck, Gunnar (cl); Eastman
Brass Ensemble; Calabro, Louis
(cond)
- CRI-260; 33s; rel 1971; cip

CAMPBELL-TIPTON, Louis (1877-1921)

Spirit Flower, A
[1448] Albanese, Licia (sop); Trucco,
Victor (pf)
- Victor 49-0503-05 (in set
WMO-1316); 45; 3-7"

[1449] Williams, Evan (ten); orchestra
- Victor 74331; 78; rel 1911-18
- Victor 6319; 78; rel 1911-18

CAMPBELL-WATSON, Frank (1898-)

Praeludium on Puer natus est
[1450] Salvador, Mario (org)
- Technisonic Studios TMS-3-4;
33m; rel 1954

CAMPO, Frank (1927-)

Commedie (Op 42) (1971)
[1451] Anderson, Miles (tbn); Peters,
Mitchell (perc)
- Avant AV-1006; 33s; rel 1978;
cip

Commedie II
[1452] Plog, Anthony (tpt); Davis, Sharon
(pf)
- Crystal S-364; 33s; rel 1980; cip

Concertino, Three Clarinets and Piano
[1453] Los Angeles Clarinet Society; Davis,
Sharon (pf)
- WIM Records WIMR-7; 33s; rel
1973; cip

Dualidad
[1454] Spear, Julian (b cl); Peters, Mitchell
(perc)
- WIM Records WIMR-10; 33s; rel
1978; cip

Duet for Equal Trumpets
[1455] Plog, Anthony (tpt); Kid, Russell
(tpt)
- Crystal S-362; 33s; rel 1977; cip

Fanfares 1969 *see* **REYNOLDS, Jeffrey, et al**

Kinesis
[1456] Atkins, David (cl); Davis, Sharon
(pf)
- WIM Records WIMR-1; 33s; rel
1971; cip

Madrigals
[1457] Los Angeles Brass Quintet
- Crystal S-821; 33s; rel 1971; cip

(Five) Pieces for Five Winds (1958)
[1458] Los Angeles Philharmonic Wind
Quintet
- WIM Records WIMR-9; 33s; rel
1974; cip

Sonata, Violin and Piano (Op 21) (1959)
[1459] Granat, Endre (vln); Herbst, Erwin
(pf)
- Orion ORS-73128; 33s; rel
1973; cip

Times
[1460] Stevens, Thomas (tpt); Grierson,
Ralph (pf); Peters, Mitchell (perc)
- Avant AV-1003; 33s; rel 1972;
cip

CANBY, Edward Tatnall (1912-)

Interminable Farewell, The (1954)
[1461] Randolph Singers; Randolph, David
(cond)
- CRI-102; 33m/s; rel 1956/?; cip

CANFIELD, David DeBoor*

Cat Dances
[1462] Brunell, David (pf)
Rec 5/79 and 7/79
- Enharmonic EN-79-001; 33s; rel
1979

Cats
[1463] Hagerman, Karen (sop); Concentus
Felices; Fiske, Richard Allen
(cond)
Rec 5/79 and 7/79
- Enharmonic EN-79-001; 33s; rel
1979

Dog Trots
[1464] Brunell, David (pf)
Rec 5/79 and 7/79
- Enharmonic EN-79-001; 33s; rel
1979

Improvisation on the Thoughts in the Mind of a Cat
[1465] Canfield, David DeBoor (pf)
Rec 5/79 and 7/79
- Enharmonic EN-79-001; 33s; rel
1979

Sonata, Violin and Piano
[1466] Cardenes, Andres (vln); Brunell,
David (pf)
Rec 5/79 and 7/79
- Enharmonic EN-79-001; 33s; rel
1979

CANN, Richard

Bonnylee (1972)
[1467] League of Composers ISCM
International Competition
(performed at)
- Odyssey Y-34139; 33s; rel
1976; cip

CANNING, Thomas (1911-)

Fantasy on a Hymn by Justin Morgan (1944)
[1468] Eastman-Rochester Symphony
Orchestra; Hanson, Howard
(cond)
- Mercury MG-40001; 33m; rel
1953; del 1957
- Mercury MG-50074; 33m; rel
1957; del 1963

[1469] Houston Symphony Orchestra;
Stokowski, Leopold (cond)
- Everest LPBR-6070/SDBR-3070;
33m/s; rel 1962; del 1978

CAREY, Elena (1939-)

D. N. A.
[1470] Gamelan Son of Lion
- Folkways FTS-31313; 33s; rel
1980; cip

CARLOS, Walter (1939-)

Dialogues, Piano and Two Loudspeakers (1963)
[1471] Ramey, Phillip (pf); electronic
music
- Turnabout TV-4004/TVS-34004;
33m/s; rel 1965; del 1975
- Columbia M-32088; 33s; rel
1975; cip

Episodes, Piano and Electronic Sound

[1472] Ramey, Phillip (pf); tape
- Columbia M-32088; 33s; rel 1975; cip

Geodesic Dance

[1473] Electronic music
- Columbia M-32088; 33s; rel 1975; cip

Pompous Circumstances (Variations and Fantasy on a Theme by Elgar)

[1474] Electronic music
- Columbia M-32088; 33s; rel 1975; cip

Sonic Seasonings (1971-72)

[1475] Electronic music
- Columbia KG-31234; 33s; rel 1972; cip

Variations, Flute and Electronic Sound (1964)

[1476] Heiss, John (fl); tape
- Turnabout TV-4004/TVS-34004; 33m/s; rel 1965; del 1975

CARLSON, Mark (1952-)

Patchen Songs (1976)

[1477] Rohrbaugh, David (bar); Montgomery, David (pf)
- Orion ORS-78335; 33s; rel 1979; cip

CARMICHAEL, John*

Puppet Show

[1478] Smith, Cyril (pf); Sellick, Phyllis (pf)
- Polydor 2460.232; 33s; rel 1974

CARMINES, Alvin A. (1938-)

In Circles

[1479] Cast of the Judson Poets Theatre Production of 1967
- Avant Garde AV-108; 33m/s; rel 1968; del 1976

CARPENTER, John Alden (1876-1951)

Adventures in a Perambulator (1914)

[1480] Eastman-Rochester Symphony Orchestra; Hanson, Howard (cond)
Rec 10/28/56
- Mercury MG-50136/SR-90136; 33m/s; rel 1957/1959; del 1964
- Eastman-Rochester Archives ERA-1009; 33s; rel 1976; cip
- Mercury SRI-75095; 33s; rel 1977; cip

[1481] Minneapolis Symphony Orchestra; Ormandy, Eugene (cond)
- Victor 8455-58 (in set M-238); 78; 4 discs; rel pre-1936

Adventures in a Perambulator (1914) (cont'd)

- Victor 11-9231 (in set M-1063); 78; rel pre-1948 (Excerpt: (No 3) Hurdy Gurdy)

[1482] Vienna State Opera Orchestra; Swoboda, Henry (cond)
- Concert Hall CHS-1140; 33m; rel 1952; del 1957
- Concert Hall H-1640; 33m; rel 1957; del 1959

Berceuse de la guerre

[1483] Hager, Mina (m sop); Dougherty, Celius (pf)
- Musicraft 1016; 78; rel 1937

Concertino, Piano and Orchestra (1915)

[1484] Mitchell, Marjorie (pf); Goteborg Symphony Orchestra; Strickland, William (cond)
- CRI-180; 33m/s; rel 1964/1973; cip

Cryin' Blues

[1485] Vanni-Marcoux, Jean-Emile (b)
- Gramophone DA-988; 78; 10"; rel pre-1936

Day Is No More, The

[1486] Brice, Carol (al); Brice, Jonathan (pf)
- Columbia 17608-10D (in set MM-910); 78; 3-10"; rel 1950
- Columbia ML-2108; 33m; 10"; rel 1950; del 1956

Diversion

[1487] Behrend, Jeanne (pf)
- Victor 17911 (in set M-764); 78; rel 1941

Gitanjali (1914)

[1488] Hunt, Alexandra (sop); Benoit, Regis (pf)
- Orion ORS-77272; 33s; rel 1978; cip

[1489] Mock, Alice (sop); Boyes, Shibley (pf)
- Claremont 1206; 33m; rel 1952; del 1965

Gitanjali: When I Bring You Coloured Toys and Light, My Light

[1490] Bampton, Rose (al); piano
Rec 7/8/32 and 9/29/32
- Victor 1628; 78; 10"; rel pre-1936
- New World NW-247; 33m; rel 1976

Gitanjali: When I Bring You Coloured Toys and The Sleep That Flits on Baby's Eyes

[1491] Flagstad, Kirsten (sop); McArthur, Edwin (pf)
Rec 3/18/52 and 4/19/52
- RCA LM-2825; 33m; rel 1965; del 1967

Gitanjali: When I Bring You Coloured Toys

[1492] Darwin, Glenn (bar); Fiedler, Elsa (pf)
- Victor 36224; 78; rel 1939

[1493] Hanks, John Kennedy (ten); Friedberg, Ruth (pf)
- Duke University Press DWR-6417-18; 33m; 2 discs; rel 1966; del 1975

[1494] Supervia, Conchita (m sop); Newton, Ivor (pf)
Rec 3/17/32
- Historic Masters HMA-1; 33m; rel 1971?

[1495] Williams, Camilla (sop); Bazala, Borislav (pf)
- MGM E-140; 33m; 10"; rel 1952; del 1957

Gitanjali: The Sleep That Flits on Baby's Eyes

[1496] Bampton, Rose (sop); Pelletier, Wilfred (pf)
- Victor 10-1118 (in set 1607); 78; 10"; rel pre-1948
- Gramophone DA-1855; 78; 10"; rel pre-1952

Home Road, The

[1497] Crane, Ralph (bar); orchestra
- Victor 22616; 78; 10"; rel pre-1936

[1498] Schumann-Heink, Ernestine (al)
- Victor 87320; 78; 10"; rel 1917-25
- Victor 831; 78; 10"; rel 1917-25

Impromptu (1913)

[1499] Johannesen, Grant (pf)
- Golden Crest CR-4065/CRS-4065; 33m/s; rel 1963/1966; cip

[1500] Shields, Roger (pf)
- Vox SVBX-5303; 33s; 3 discs; rel 1977; cip

Krazy Kat (1921)

[1501] Los Angeles Philharmonic Orchestra; Simmons, Calvin (cond)
Rec 8/77
- New World NW-228; 33s; rel 1978

Krazy Kat: Excerpts
[1502] Hamburg Philharmonia; Korn, Richard (cond)
  - Allegro ALG-3150; 33m; rel 1955*

Little Turtle, The
[1503] Howard, Ann (sop); piano
  - Victor 36033; 78; rel pre-1936

Looking Glass River (1909)
[1504] Gramm, Donald (bar); Cumming, Richard (pf)
  - St/And SPL-411-12; 33m; 2 discs; rel 1963; del 1964
  - Desto D-411-12/DST-6411-12; 33m/s; 2 discs; rel 1964; cip

(Four) Negro Songs (1926): Jazz-Boys
[1505] Gramm, Donald (bar); Cumming, Richard (pf)
  - St/And SPL-411-12; 33m; 2 discs; rel 1963; del 1964
  - Desto D-411-12/DST-6411-12; 33m/s; 2 discs; rel 1964; cip

[1506] Vanni-Marcoux, Jean-Emile (b)
  - Gramophone DA-988; 78; 10''; rel pre-1936

(Two) Night Songs (1927): Serenade
[1507] Casey, Ethel (sop); Siddell, Bill (pf); or orchestra and Grieves, Wallace (concertmaster)
  - Carolina 712C-1713; 33m; rel 1965

[1508] Melton, James (ten); Hill, Robert (pf)
  - Victor 10-1051 (in set M-947); 78; 10''; rel pre-1948

[1509] Swarthout, Gladys (m sop); Hodges, Lester (pf)
  - Victor 16780 (in set M-679); 78; rel pre-1942

Player Queen, The
[1510] Suderburg, Elizabeth (sop); Suderburg, Robert (pf)
  - University of Washington Press OLY-104; 33q; 2 discs; rel 1976; cip

Quartet, Strings (1927)
[1511] Gordon String Quartet
  - Schirmer 2513-15 (in set 4); 78; 3 discs; rel pre-1942

Sea Drift (1933, rev 1944)
[1512] Royal Philharmonic Orchestra; Krueger, Karl (cond)
  - SPAMH MIA-142; 33s; rel 1969

Skyscrapers (1923-24)
[1513] Victor Symphony Orchestra; Shilkret, Nathaniel (cond)
  - Victor 11250-52 (in set 130); 78; 3 discs; rel 1932

Skyscrapers (1923-24) *(cont'd)*
  - Victor M-130; 78; 3 discs; rel 1932
  - Victor (Japanese) ND-313-15; 78; 3 discs; rel pre-1956

[1514] Vienna Symphony Orchestra; Zallinger, Meinhard von (cond)
  - American Recording Society ARS-37; 33m; rel 1953*
  - Desto D-407/DST-6407; 33m/s; rel 1964; del 1976

Sonata, Violin and Piano (1911)
[1515] Gratovich, Eugene (vln); Benoit, Regis (pf)
  - Orion ORS-76243; 33s; rel 1977; cip

Song of Faith (1932)
[1516] Chicago A Cappella Chorus; orchestra; Carpenter, John A. (nar); Cain, Noble (org) (cond)
  - Victor 1559-60; 78; 2-10''; rel pre-1936
  - Victor 26529-30; 78; 2-10''; rel pre-1942

Watercolors (1915)
[1517] Hager, Mina (m sop); Carpenter, John A. (pf)
  - CGS 50019P; 78; rel pre-1936

[1518] Mock, Alice (sop); Boyes, Shibley (pf)
  - Claremont 1206; 33m; rel 1952; del 1965

Watercolors: On a Screen and The Odalisque
[1519] Hager, Mina (m sop); Dougherty, Celius (pf)
  - Musicraft 1016; 78; rel 1937

CARR, Michael (pseud)
see **COHEN, Maurice**

CARTER, Charles (1926-)
Dance and Intermezzo
[1520] Ohio State University Concert Band; McGinnis, Donald E. (cond)
  - Coronet S-1503; 33s; rel 1969; del 1978

CARTER, Elliott (1908-)
Canon for Three (In Memoriam Igor Stravinsky) (1971)
[1521] Schwarz, Gerard (tpt); Ranger, Louis (tpt); Rosenzweig, Stanley (tpt)
  - Desto DC-7133; 33s; rel 1973; cip

[1522] Schwarz, Gerard (flhn); Ranger, Louis (cor); Rosenzweig, Stanley (tpt) (different performance)
  - Desto DC-7133; 33s; rel 1973; cip

[1523] Stevens, Thomas (tpt); Guarneri, Mario (tpt); Poper, Roy (tpt)
  - Crystal S-361; 33s; rel 1976; cip

Concerto, Orchestra (1969)
[1524] New York Philharmonic; Bernstein, Leonard (cond)
  Rec 2/11/70
  - Columbia M-30112; 33s; rel 1970; del 1979

Concerto, Piano and Orchestra (1964-65)
[1525] Lateiner, Jacob (pf); Boston Symphony Orchestra; Leinsdorf, Erich (cond)
  Rec 1/6-7/67
  - RCA LM-3001/LSC-3001; 33m/s; rel 1968; del 1974
  - RCA (German) LM-3001/LSC-3001; 33m/s; rel 1968
  - RCA (English) RB-6756/SB-6756; 33m/s; rel 1968*

Defense of Corinth, The (1942)
[1526] Gutheil, Thomas G. (speaker); Harvard Glee Club; Forbes, Elliot (cond)
  - Harvard Glee Club T-HGC-64; 33s; rel 1964

[1527] Opalach, Jan (speaker); Columbia University Men's Glee Club; Green, Edward (pf); Smith, Mark Sutton (pf); Smith, Gregg (cond)
  Rec 1976
  - Vox SVBX-5353; 33s; 3 discs; rel 1979; cip

Double Concerto, Harpsichord, Piano, and Two Chamber Orchestras (1961)
[1528] Jacobs, Paul (hpschd); Kalish, Gilbert (pf); Contemporary Chamber Ensemble; Weisberg, Arthur (cond)
  - Nonesuch H-71314; 33s; rel 1975; cip

[1529] Jacobs, Paul (hpschd); Rosen, Charles (pf); English Chamber Orchestra; Prausnitz, Frederik (cond)
  Rec 1/4/68
  - Columbia MS-7191; 33s; rel 1968; del 1979
  - CBS (English) 72717; 33s; rel 1969*
  - CBS (French) S-34-61093; 33s; rel 1970*

[1530] Kirkpatrick, Ralph (hpschd); Rosen, Charles (pf); orchestra; Meier, Gustav (cond)
  - Epic LC-3830/BC-1157; 33m/s; rel 1962; del 1965
  - EMI/His Master's Voice ALP-2052/ASD-601; 33m/s; rel 1965*

Duo, Violin and Piano (1973-74)
[1531] Zukofsky, Paul (vln); Kalish, Gilbert (pf)
  Rec ca 3/75
  - Nonesuch H-71314; 33s; rel 1975; cip

Elegy (string-quartet version) (1946)
[1532] Composers Quartet
- Golden Crest NEC-115; 33s/q; rel 1977; cip

(Eight) Etudes and a Fantasy (1950)
[1533] Baron, Samuel (fl); Roseman, Ronald (ob); Glazer, David (cl); Weisberg, Arthur (bsn)
- Concert-Disc M-1229/CS-229; 33m/s; rel 1963; del 1973

[1534] Dorian Woodwind Quintet
- Candide CE-31016; 33s; rel 1969; del 1977
- Candide (German) CE-31016; 33s; rel 1969
- CBS (French) S-34-61145; 33s; rel 1970*
- Vox (English) STGBY-644; 33s; rel 1971*

[1535] Panitz, Murray (fl); Roth, Jerome (ob); Glazer, David (cl); Garfield, Bernard (bsn)
- CRI-118; 33m/s; rel 1957/?; cip

(Eight) Etudes and a Fantasy: Eight Etudes
[1536] Robison, Paula (fl); Arner, Leonard (ob); De Peyer, Gervaise (cl); Glickman, Loren (bsn)
- Classics Record Library SQM-80-5731; 33s; rel 1975

Fantasy on Purcell's Fantasia on One Note (1974)
[1537] American Brass Quintet
Rec 4/1/75 and 5/31/75
- Odyssey Y-34137; 33s; rel 1976; cip

Harmony of Morning, The (1944)
[1538] Gregg Smith Singers; Orpheus Ensemble; Smith, Gregg (cond)
Rec 4/76
- Vox SVBX-5354; 33s; 3 discs; rel 1979

Heart Not so Heavy as Mine (1938)
[1539] Canby Singers; Canby, Edward Tatnall (cond)
- Nonesuch H-1115/H-71115; 33m/s; rel 1966; cip
- Nonesuch (English) H-1115/H-71115; 33m/s; rel 1967*

[1540] Hamline A Cappella Choir; Holliday, Robert (cond)
- SPAMH MIA-116; 33s; rel 1961

Minotaur, The (Suite) (1947)
[1541] Eastman-Rochester Symphony Orchestra; Hanson, Howard (cond)
Rec 1/22/56
- Mercury MG-50103; 33m; rel 1956; del 1964

Minotaur, The (Suite) (1947)
(cont'd)
- Mercury (German) MG-50103; 33m; rel 1956
- Mercury (English) MRL-2515; 33m; rel 1956*
- Mercury SRI-75111; 33s; rel 1978; cip

Mirror on Which to Dwell, A (1975)
[1542] Wyner, Susan Davenny (sop); Speculum Musicae; Fitz, Richard (cond)
- Columbia M-35171; 33s; rel 1980

Musicians Wrestle Everywhere (1945)
[1543] Canby Singers; Canby, Edward Tatnall (cond)
- Nonesuch H-1115/H-71115; 33m/s; rel 1966; cip
- Nonesuch (English) H-1115/H-71115; 33m/s; rel 1967*

[1544] Gregg Smith Singers; Smith, Gregg (cond)
Rec 1976
- Vox SVBX-5353; 33s; 3 discs; rel 1979; cip

[1545] Tanglewood Festival Chorus; Oliver, John (cond)
- Deutsche Grammophon 2530.912; 33s; rel 1979; cip

Pastorale (1940)
[1546] Ludewig-Verdehr, Elsa (cl); Liptak, David (pf);
- Grenadilla GS-1018; 33s; rel 1979; cip

[1547] Russo, John (cl); Ignacio, Lydia Walton (pf)
- Orion ORS-77275; 33s; rel 1978; cip

(Eight) Pieces, Four Timpani (One Player) (1950-66)
[1548] Lang, Morris (timp)
Rec 5/28/75 and 6/23-24/75
- Odyssey Y-34137; 33s; rel 1976; cip

(Eight) Pieces, Four Timpani: Four Pieces
[1549] Gualda, Sylvio (timp)
- Erato (French) STU-71106; 33s; rel 1978*

Pocahontas (Suite) (1939, rev 1961)
[1550] Zurich Radio Orchestra; Monod, Jacques (cond)
- Epic LC-3850/BC-1250; 33m/s; rel 1962; del 1968

(Three) Poems of Robert Frost (1943)
[1551] Dickinson, Meriel (m sop); Dickinson, Peter (pf)
Rec 3/28/77
- Unicorn RHS-353; 33s; rel 1978
- Unicorn UNI-72017; 33s; rel 1978
- Unicorn RHS-253; 33s; rel 1978*

(Three) Poems of Robert Frost: The Rose Family and Dust of Snow
[1552] Hess, William (ten); Fizdale, Robert (pf)
- Hargail HN-708 (in set 0090); 78; I0''; rel 1946

Quartet, Strings, No 1 (1950-51)
[1553] Composers Quartet
Rec 4/21-23/70
- Nonesuch H-71249; 33s; rel 1970; cip
- Nonesuch (English) H-71249; 33s; rel 1971*
- Nonesuch (French) NON-32803; 33s; rel 1975*

[1554] Walden Quartet of the University of Illinois
Rec 2/2/55
- Columbia ML-5104; 33m; rel 1956; del 1968
- Columbia CML-5104; 33m; rel 1968; del 1974
- Columbia AML-5104; 33m; rel 1974; del 1979

Quartet, Strings, No 2 (1959)
[1555] Composers Quartet
Rec 4/21-23/70
- Nonesuch H-71249; 33s; rel 1970; cip
- Nonesuch (English) H-71249; 33s; rel 1971*
- Nonesuch (French) NON-32803; 33s; rel 1975*

[1556] Juilliard String Quartet
- RCA LM-2481/LSC-2481; 33m/s; rel 1961; del 1964

[1557] Juilliard String Quartet
Rec 2/19-20/69
- Columbia M-32738/MQ-32738; 33s/q; rel 1974; cip

Quartet, Strings, No 3 (1971)
[1558] Juilliard String Quartet
Rec 11/19-21/73
- Columbia M-32738/MQ-32738; 33s/q; rel 1974; cip

Quintet, Brass (1974)
[1559] American Brass Quintet
Rec 3/31/75-4/1/75
- Odyssey Y-34137; 33s; rel 1976; cip

Quintet, Winds (1948)
[1560] Boston Symphony Chamber Players
- RCA LM-6167/LSC-6167; 33m/s; 3 discs; rel 1966; del 1976

Quintet, Winds (1948) *(cont'd)*
- RCA (English)
RB-6692/SB-6692; 33m/s; rel
1966*

[1561] Dorian Woodwind Quintet
- Candide CE-31016; 33s; rel
1969; del 1977
- Candide (German) CE-31016;
33s; rel 1969
- CBS (French) S-34-61145; 33s;
rel 1970*
- Vox (English) STGBY-644; 33s;
rel 1971*
- Vox SVBX-5307; 33s; 3 discs; rel
1977; cip

[1562] New Art Wind Quintet
- Classic Editions CE-2003; 33m;
2 discs; rel 1953; del 1961

Sonata, Flute, Oboe, Violoncello, and Harpsichord (1952)
[1563] Baron, Samuel (fl); Roseman,
Ronald (ob); Kougell, Alexander
(vcl); Marlowe, Sylvia (hpschd)
- Decca DL-10108/DL-710108;
33m/s; rel 1965; del 1973
- Serenus SRS-12056; 33s; rel
1975; cip

[1564] Brieff, Anabel (fl); Marx, Josef (ob);
Bernsohn, Lorin (vcl); Conant,
Robert (hpschd)
Rec 5/16/57
- Columbia ML-5576/MS-6176;
33m/s; rel 1960; del 1968
- Columbia CML-5576/CMS-6176;
33m/s; rel 1968; del 1974
- Columbia AMS-6176; 33s; rel
1974; cip

[1565] Dwyer, Doriot (fl); Gomberg, Ralph
(ob); Eskin, Jules (vcl); Levin,
Robert (hpschd)
- Deutsche Grammophon
2530.104; 33s; rel 1971; del
1976
- Deutsche Grammophon (English)
2530.104; 33s; rel 1971*
- Deutsche Grammophon (French)
2530.104; 33s

[1566] Sollberger, Harvey (fl); Kuskin,
Charles (ob); Sherry, Fred (vcl);
Jacobs, Paul (hpschd)
- Nonesuch H-71234; 33s; rel
1969; cip
- Nonesuch (English) H-71234;
33s; rel 1972*
- Nonesuch (French) H-71234;
33s; rel 1977*

[1567] Troob, Jolie (fl); Priebe, Cheryl
(ob); Johns, Gloria (vcl); Kies,
Christopher (hpschd)
- Golden Crest NEC-109; 33s; rel
1979; cip

Sonata, Piano (1945-46)
[1568] Lee, Noel (pf)
- Valois (French and German)
MB-755; 33; rel 1966

Sonata, Piano (1945-46) *(cont'd)*
[1569] Rosen, Charles (pf)
Rec 4/25/61
- Epic LC-3850/BC-1250; 33m/s;
rel 1962; del 1968
- EMI/His Master's Voice
ALP-2052/ASD-601; 33m/s; rel
1965*

[1570] Trenkner, Evelinde (pf)
- Orion ORS-79342; 33s; rel
1980; cip

[1571] Webster, Beveridge (pf)
- American Recording Society
ARS-25; 33m; rel 1952
- Desto D-419/DST-6419; 33m/s;
rel 1965; cip
- Dover HCR-5265/HCRST-7265;
33m/s; rel 1966/1967; del
1975
- Dover HCRST-7014; 33s; rel
1966; del 1967

Sonata, Violoncello and Piano (1948)
[1572] Greenhouse, Bernard (vcl); Makas,
Anthony (pf)
- American Recording Society
ARS-25; 33m; rel 1952
- Desto D-419/DST-6419; 33m/s;
rel 1965; cip

[1573] Krosnick, Joel (vcl); Jacobs, Paul
(pf)
- Nonesuch H-71234; 33s; rel
1969; cip
- Nonesuch (English) H-71234;
33s; rel 1972*
- Nonesuch (French) H-71234;
33s; rel 1977*

[1574] Rudiakov, Michael (vcl); Oppens,
Ursula (pf)
- Golden Crest RE-7081; 33s; rel
1979

Symphony No 1 (1942, rev 1954)
[1575] Louisville Orchestra; Whitney,
Robert (cond)
- LOU-61-1; 33m (Louisville
Orchestra First Edition Records
1961 No 1); rel 1961; del 1975

Symphony of Three Orchestras, A (1976-77)
[1576] New York Philharmonic; Boulez,
Pierre (cond)
Rec ca 2/77
- Columbia M-35171; 33s; rel
1980

Tarantella (1936)
[1577] Harvard Glee Club; Forbes, Elliot
(cond)
- Carillon 118; 33m; rel 1961; del
1970

Tell Me Where Is Fancy Bred? (1938)
[1578] Colla-Negri, Adelyn (sop); Wexler,
Julius (gtr) (from the Orson
Welles Mercury Theatre
production of The Merchant of
Venice)
- Columbia MC-6; 78; 12 discs; rel
1938
- Columbia MM-789; 78

[1579] Rees, Rosalind (sop); Starobin,
David (gtr)
Rec 1976
- Turnabout TVS-34727; 33s; rel
1978

To Music (1937)
[1580] University of Michigan Chamber
Choir; Hilbish, Thomas (cond)
- New World NW-219; 33s; rel
1978

Variations, Orchestra (1954-55)
[1581] Louisville Orchestra; Whitney,
Robert (cond)
- LOU-58-3; 33m (Louisville
Orchestra First Edition Records
1958 No 3); rel 1959; cip

[1582] New Philharmonia Orchestra;
Prausnitz, Frederik (cond)
Rec 3/67
- Columbia MS-7191; 33s; rel
1968; del 1979
- CBS (English) 72717; 33s; rel
1969*
- CBS (French) S-34-61093; 33s;
rel 1970*

Voyage (1943)
[1583] Dickinson, Meriel (m sop);
Dickinson, Peter (pf)
Rec 3/28/77
- Unicorn RHS-353; 33s; rel 1978
- Unicorn UNI-72017; 33s; rel
1978
- Unicorn RHS-253; 33s; rel
1978*

CASCARINO, Romeo (1922-)
Pygmalion
[1584] North German Symphony
Orchestra; Roehr, Wilhelm (cond)
- Somerset 2900; 33m; rel 1959;
del 1964
- Stereo-Fidelity 2900; 33s; rel
1959; del 1962

Sonata, Bassoon and Piano (1950)
[1585] Grossman, Arthur (bsn); Hokanson,
Randolph (pf)
- Coronet S-2741; 33s; rel 1973;
cip

[1586] Schoenbach, Sol (bsn); Cascarino,
Romeo (pf)
- Columbia ML-5821/MS-6421;
33m/s; rel 1963; del 1968
- Columbia CML-5821/CMS-6421;
33m/s; rel 1968; del 1974
- Columbia AMS-6421; 33s; rel
1974; cip

(Eight) Songs
[1587] Ferraro (voice)
 - Orion ORS-80367; 33s; rel
 1980; cip

CASTALDO, Joseph (1927-)
Kaleidoscope
[1588] Ignacio, Lydia Walton (pf)
 - Orion ORS-78311; 33s; rel
 1978; cip

CASTELNUOVO-TEDESCO, Mario (1895-1968)
Alt Wien (Op 30) (1923)
[1589] Castelnuovo-Tedesco, Mario (pf)
 - Polydor 516142; 78; rel
 pre-1942
 - Polydor 516781; 78; rel
 pre-1942

Alt Wien: Valse (arr for vln and pf)
[1590] Heifetz, Jascha (vln); Sandor,
 Arpad (pf)
 - Gramophone DA-1377; 78; 10";
 rel pre-1936

Aubade
[1591] vocal sextet; piano
 - Victor WE-101; 45; 7"; rel
 pre-1953
 - RCA E-101; 33m; rel pre-1953

Cancion argentina
[1592] Bitetti, Ernesto (gtr)
 - Music Guild MS-871; 33s; rel
 1969; del 1971

Capitan Fracassa (Op 16) (1920)
[1593] Abbado, M. (vln); Gavezzini (pf)
 - Gramophone GW-1062; 78; 10";
 rel pre-1936
 - EMI/His Master's Voice (Italian)
 GW-1062; 78; 10"; rel pre-1950

Capriccio diabolico (Homage to Paganini) (Op 85) (1935)
[1594] Bitetti, Ernesto (gtr)
 - Musical Heritage Society
 MHS-1428; 33

[1595] Segovia, Andres (gtr)
 - Decca DL-9733; 33m; rel 1954;
 del 1971
 - Brunswick AXTL-1070; 33m; rel
 pre-1956
 - Columbia (Spanish) San
 Sebastian CCL-35015; 33m; rel
 pre-1956
 - Festival (Australian) CFR-10-729;
 33m; rel pre-1956

Chant hebraique
[1596] Spivakovsky, Tossy (vln); piano
 - Parlophone P-9574; 78; rel
 pre-1936

Cipressi (Op 17) (1920)
[1597] Castelnuovo-Tedesco, Mario (pf)
 - Victor 16449; 78; rel pre-1942

Cipressi (Op 17) (1920) *(cont'd)*
[1598] Dominguez, Albert (pf)
 - Orion ORS-74137; 33s; rel
 1974; cip

Concertino, Harp, String Quartet, and Three Clarinets (Op 93) (1937)
[1599] Stockton, Ann Mason (hp); Arno,
 Victor (vln); Dieterle, Kurt (vln);
 Dinkin, Alvin (vla); Schnier, Harold
 (vcl); Neufeld, John (cl);
 Bambridge, John, Jr. (cl); Ulyate,
 William (b cl)
 - Crystal S-107; 33s; rel 1973; cip

Concertino, Harp, String Quartet, and Three Clarinets (Op 93) (arr for hp and chamber orch)
[1600] Chertok, Pearl (hp); Rome
 Chamber Orchestra; Flagello,
 Nicolas (cond)
 - Serenus SRS-12062; 33s; rel
 1976; cip

[1601] McDonald, Susann (hp); Arizona
 Chamber Orchestra; Hull, Robert
 (cond)
 - Klavier KS-515; 33s; rel 1973;
 cip

[1602] Michel, Catherine (hp); National
 Opera Orchestra of Monte Carlo;
 Almeida, Antonio de (cond)
 - Philips 6500.812; 33s; rel
 1976; cip

Concerto, Guitar and Orchestra, No 1 (Op 99) (1939)
[1603] Behrend, Siegfried (gtr); Berlin
 Philharmonic; Peters, Reinhard
 (cond)
 - Deutsche Grammophon
 LPM-39166/SLPM-139166;
 33m/s; rel 1967; del 1975

[1604] Bitetti, Ernesto (gtr); Orquesta de
 Conciertos de Madrid; Buenagu,
 Jose (cond)
 - Musical Heritage Society
 MHS-950-S; 33s; rel 1969

[1605] Cubedo, Manuel (gtr); Barcelona
 Symphony Orchestra; Barcons,
 Juan (cond)
 - Everest SDBR-3429; 33s; rel
 1978

[1606] Diaz, Alirio (gtr); I Solisti di Zagreb;
 Janigro, Antonio (cond)
 - Vanguard
 VRS-1152/VSD-71152; 33m/s;
 rel 1966; cip

[1607] Segovia, Andres (gtr); New London
 Orchestra; Sherman, Alec (cond)
 Rec 6-7/49
 - Columbia LX-1404-06; 78; 3
 discs; rel pre-1952
 - Columbia LVX-104-06; 78; 3
 discs; rel pre-1952
 - Columbia LFX-914-16; 78; 3
 discs; rel pre-1952
 - Columbia M-15137-39; 78; 3
 discs; rel pre-1952

Concerto, Guitar and Orchestra, No 1 (Op 99) (1939) *(cont'd)*
 - Columbia GQX-11505-7; 78; 3
 discs; rel pre-1953
 - Columbia CX-1020; 33m; rel
 pre-1953
 - Columbia FCX-127; 33m; rel
 pre-1953
 - Columbia QCX-127; 33m; rel
 pre-1953
 - Columbia ML-4732; 33m; rel
 1953; del 1957
 - EMI/Odeon QCX-127; 33m; rel
 1964; del 1971
 - EMI/His Master's Voice
 HLM-7134; 33m; rel 1978?

[1608] Williams, John (gtr); English
 Chamber Orchestra; Groves,
 Charles (cond)
 - Columbia M-35172; 33s; rel
 1979; cip

[1609] Williams, John (gtr); Philadelphia
 Orchestra; Ormandy, Eugene
 (cond)
 - Columbia ML-6234/MS-6834;
 33m/s; rel 1966; cip
 - Columbia M3X-31508; 33s; 3
 discs; rel 1972; cip

[1610] Yepes, Narciso (gtr); London
 Symphony Orchestra; Navarro,
 Garcia (cond)
 - Deutsche Grammophon
 2530.718; 33s; rel 1977; cip

Concerto, Two Guitars and Orchestra (Op 201) (1962)
[1611] Abreu, Sergio (gtr); Abreu, Eduardo
 (gtr); English Chamber Orchestra;
 Asensio, Enrique Garcia (cond)
 - Columbia M-32232/MQ-32232;
 33s/q; rel 1973; cip

Concerto, Violin and Orchestra, No 2 (I profeti) (Op 66) (1931)
[1612] Heifetz, Jascha (vln); Los Angeles
 Philharmonic Orchestra;
 Wallenstein, Alfred (cond)
 - RCA LM-2050; 33m; rel 1956;
 del 1960
 - RCA LM-2740; 33m; rel 1964;
 cip

Coplas (Op 7) (1915, orchd 1967)
[1613] Nixon, Marni (sop); Vienna
 Volksoper Orchestra; Gold, Ernest
 (cond)
 Rec 9/28-29/74
 - Crystal S-501; 33s; rel 1975; cip

Danze del re David, Le (Op 37) (1925)
[1614] Dominguez, Albert (pf)
 - Orion ORS-74137; 33s; rel
 1974; cip

[1615] Raucea, Dario (pf)
 - London LLP-1033; 33m; rel
 1955; del 1957
 - Decca LXT-2969; 33m; rel
 pre-1956

A Discography

Divan of Moses-ibn-Ezra, The (Op 207) (1966): Six Songs
[1616] Schele, Marta (sop); Holecek, Josef (gtr)
Rec 10/4-5/75
- BIS LP-31; 33s; rel 1976

Ermita de San Simon, La (Op 25b)
[1617] Farrell, Eileen (sop); Trovillo, George (pf)
- Columbia ML-5924/MS-6524; 33m/s; rel 1964; del 1966

(Deux) etudes d'ondes (Sea Murmurs)
[1618] Castelnuovo-Tedesco, Mario (pf)
- Polydor 516781; 78; rel pre-1942

(Deux) etudes d'ondes (Sea Murmurs) (arr for vln and pf by Jascha Heifetz)
[1619] Friedman, Erick (vln); Smith, Brooks (pf)
- RCA LM-2671/LSC-2671; 33m/s; rel 1963; del 1971

[1620] Heifetz, Jascha (vln); Bay, Emanuel (pf)
- Victor 10-1328; 78; 10"; rel pre-1948
- Victor 49-1294; 45; 7"; rel pre-1953
- Gramophone 7RF-191; 45; 7"; rel pre-1953
- Gramophone DA-2037; 78; 10"; rel pre-1956
- Gramophone EC-208; 78; 10"; rel pre-1956

[1621] Heifetz, Jascha (vln); Sandor, Arpad (pf)
- Victor 1645; 78; 10"; rel pre-1936

[1622] Heifetz, Jascha (vln); Smith, Brooks (pf)
Rec 10/23/72
- Columbia M2-33444; 33s; 2 discs; rel 1975; cip

[1623] Heifetz, Jascha (vln); piano
- RCA ARM-4-0946; 33m; 4 discs; rel 1975; cip
- RCA ARM-4-0943; 33m; 4 discs; rel 1975; cip

Fanfare
[1624] Ellsasser, Richard (org)
- MGM E-3585; 33m; rel 1958; del 1960

Guarda cuydadosa, La and Escarraman (Op 177) (1955)
[1625] Almeida, Laurindo (gtr)
- Capitol P-8392; 33m; rel 1957; del 1962
- Everest SDBR-3287; 33s; rel 1971; del 1972

Guarda cuydadosa, La (Op 177)
[1626] Behrend, Siegfried (gtr)
- Deutsche Grammophon 2530.561; 33s; rel 1976; cip

Lark, The (1930)
[1627] Heifetz, Jascha (vln); Bay, Emanuel (pf)
- RCA LM-2074; 33m; rel 1957; cip

Much Ado about Nothing (Overture) (Op 164) (1953)
[1628] Louisville Orchestra; Whitney, Robert (cond)
- LOU-545-4; 33m (Louisville Orchestra First Edition Records 1955 No 4); rel 1959; del 1978

Ninna-Nanna (1914)
[1629] Farrell, Eileen (sop); Trovillo, George (pf)
- Columbia ML-5924/MS-6524; 33m/s; rel 1964; del 1966

[1630] Ziliani, R. (sop); Magnetti, Ermelinda (pf)
- Parlophone TI-7053; 78; rel pre-1952

Noah's Ark (1944)
[1631] Arnold, Edward (nar); chorus; Janssen Symphony Orchestra of Los Angeles; Janssen, Werner (cond)
- Artist JS-10; 78; 5 discs; rel pre-1950
- Capitol P-8125; 33m; rel 1952; del 1957

Platero y yo (Op 190) (1960): Platero, Melancolia, Angelus, Golondrinas, and La Arrulladora
[1632] Segovia, Andres (gtr)
- Decca DL-10054/DL-710054; 33m/s; rel 1962; del 1974
- MCA 2527; 33s; rel 1974; cip
- MCA 2530; 33s; rel 1974; cip

Platero y yo: A Platero en el cielo de moquer
[1633] Mills, John (gtr)
- Discourses ABK-10; 33s; rel 1972

Platero y yo: Melancolia
[1634] Parkening, Christopher (gtr)
- Angel S-36021; 33s; rel 1969; cip

Platero y yo: Second Series
[1635] Segovia, Andres (gtr)
- Decca DL-10093/DL-710093; 33m/s; rel 1964; del 1974

Primavera, La
[1636] Bitetti, Ernesto (gtr)
- Musical Heritage Society MHS-1428; 33

Quintet, Guitar and Strings (Op 143) (1950)
[1637] Ramos, Manuel Lopez (gtr); Parrenin Quartet
- RCA-Victrola VIC-1367/VICS-1367; 33m/s; rel 1968; del 1976

[1638] Segovia, Andres (gtr); Brengola, Riccardo (vln); Benvenuti, Mario (vln); Leone, Giovanni (vla); Filippini, Lino (vcl)
- Decca DL-9832; 33m; rel 1956; del 1974

Recuerdo (1940)
[1639] Lehmann, Lotte (sop); pupils
- Campbell 8 (in set 1-24); 33m; rel pre-1956

Romancero gitano (Op 152) (1951)
[1640] Behrend, Siegfried (gtr); NCRV Vocal Ensemble; Voorberg, Marius (cond)
- Deutsche Grammophon 2530.037; 33s; rel 1971; del 1976

(Otto) Scherzi per musica (Op 35) (1924-25): La Pastorella
[1641] Farrell, Eileen (sop); Trovillo, George (pf)
- Columbia ML-5924/MS-6524; 33m/s; rel 1964; del 1966

(Twenty-Eight) Shakespeare Sonnets (Op 125) (1944-47): Sonnets 29, 31, 40, 47, 60, 64, 97, 98, 104, and 109
[1642] Brown, Gwendolyn (sop); Black, Archie (pf)
- International Castelnuovo-Tedesco Society C/T S-100; 33s; rel 1976

Sonata, Clarinet and Piano (Op 128) (1945)
[1643] Ludewig-Verdehr, Elsa (cl); Votapek, Ralph (pf)
- Grenadilla GS-1018; 33s; rel 1979; cip

Sonata, Guitar (Homage to Boccherini) (Op 77) (1934)
[1644] Holecek, Josef (gtr)
Rec 10/4-5/75
- BIS LP-31; 33s; rel 1976

[1645] Ramos, Manuel Lopez (gtr)
- Boston B-216; 33m; rel 1961; del 1967

[1646] Segovia, Andres (gtr)
- Gramophone DB-3243; 78; rel pre-1942 (Excerpt: Vivo ed energico)
- Decca DXJ-148; 33m; 3 discs; rel 1959; del 1975
- Decca DL-10034/DL-710034; 33m/s; rel 1961; del 1974
- MCA 2523; 33s; rel 1974; cip

Sonata, Guitar (Homage to Boccherini) (Op 77) (1934)
(cont'd)
- MCA 3-19000; 33m; rel 1975; cip
- Angel ZB-3896; 33m; 2 discs; rel 1980 (Excerpt: Vivo ed energico)

Sonata, Guitar (Homage to Boccherini): Vivo ed energico
[1647] Williams, John (gtr)
- Columbia ML-6096/MS-6696; 33m/s; rel 1965; cip
- Columbia M3X-32677; 33s; 3 discs; rel 1974; cip

Sonata, Violoncello and Harp (Op 208) (1967)
[1648] Stutch, Nathan (vcl); Chertok, Pearl (hp)
- Orion ORS-76227; 33s; rel 1976; cip

Sonatina, Bassoon and Piano (Op 130) (1946)
[1649] Lottridge, Richard (bsn); Chilton, Carroll (pf)
- Golden Crest RE-7055; 33s; rel 1974; cip

Sonatina, Flute and Guitar (Op 205) (1965)
[1650] Bolotowsky, Andrew (fl); Karpienia, Joseph (gtr)
- Orion ORS-78304; 33s; rel 1979; cip

[1651] Stancliff, Floyd (fl); Macaluso, Vincenzo (gtr)
- Klavier KS-537; 33s; rel 1975; cip

Sonatina canonica (Op 196) (1961)
[1652] Santos, Turibio (gtr); Caceres, Oscar (gtr)
- Musical Heritage Society MHS-1944; 33s; rel 1973*

Tango (arr for vln and pf by Jascha Heifetz)
[1653] Heifetz, Jascha (vln); Bay, Emanuel (pf)
- Victor 10-1293 (in set M-1126); 10"; rel pre-1948
- Gramophone EC-193; 78; rel pre-1956
- RCA ARM-4-0946; 33m; 4 discs; rel 1975; cip

Tarantella (Op 87a) (1936)
[1654] Almeida, Laurindo (gtr)
- Capitol P-8392; 33m; rel 1957; del 1962
- Everest SDBR-3287; 33s; rel 1971; del 1972

[1655] Aubin, Christian (gtr)
- EKO (French) LG-1; 33m; rel pre-1956

Tarantella (Op 87a) (1936) *(cont'd)*
[1656] Behrend, Siegfried (gtr)
- Deutsche Grammophon 2530.561; 33s; rel 1976; cip

[1657] Carlevaro, A. (gtr)
- Parlophone PXO-1073; 78; rel pre-1956

[1658] Ghiglia, Oscar (gtr)
- Angel S-36849; 33s; rel 1972; cip

[1659] Segovia, Andres (gtr) Rec 6-7/49
- Columbia (English) LX-1229; 78; rel pre-1950
- Columbia SCB-110; 45; 7"; rel pre-1956
- Columbia SCBQ-3016; 45; 7"; rel pre-1956
- EMI/His Master's Voice HLM-7134; 33m; rel 1978?

Tonadilla (On the Name of Andres Segovia)
[1660] Gonzalez, Jose Luis (gtr)
- Odyssey 32-16-0200; 33s; rel 1968; cip

[1661] Segovia, Andres (gtr)
- Decca DL-9795; 33m; rel 1955; del 1971
- Decca UAT-273594; 33m; rel pre-1956

Valse bluette (On the Name of Erick Friedman) (Op 170, No 24) (arr for vln)
[1662] Heifetz, Jascha (vln)
- RCA ARM-4-0943; 33m; 4 discs; rel 1975; cip

Variations plaisantes sur un petit air populaire (Op 95) (1937)
[1663] Davezac, Betho (gtr)
- Erato (French) STU-70926; 33s; rel 1976

CAZDEN, Norman (1914-80)

(Three) New Sonatas, Piano (Op 53) (1950): No 3
[1664] Helps, Robert (pf)
- RCA LM-7042/LSC-7042; 33m/s; 2 discs; rel 1966; del 1971
- CRI-288; 33s; 2 discs; rel 1972; cip

Songs from the Catskills (Op 54) (1954)
[1665] Oslo Philharmonic Orchestra; Buketoff, Igor (cond)
- CRI-117; 33m/s; rel 1957/?; cip

CEELY, Robert (1930-)
Elegia (1963)
[1666] Electronic music
- CRI-328; 33s; rel 1975; cip

Fleur, La (1972)
[1667] Electronic music
- BEEP Records 1001; 33s; rel 1976; cip

Frames
[1668] Electronic music
- BEEP Records; 33; rel 197?

Hymn (1970)
[1669] Sherry, Fred (vcl); Neidlinger, Buell (cb)
- BEEP Records 1001; 33s; rel 1976; cip

Logs (1968)
[1670] Neidlinger, Buell (cb); Palma, Donald (cb)
- BEEP Records 1001; 33s; rel 1976; cip

Lullaby
[1671] soprano; trombone
- BEEP Records; 33; rel 197?

MITSYN Music (1971)
[1672] Electronic music
- CRI-328; 33s; rel 1975; cip

Music for Brass, Copper, and Silicon
[1673] no performers given
- BEEP Records; 33; rel 197?

Music for John, Alvin, Phil, Gordon, David, La Monte, Steve, Bob, and Pauline
[1674] no performers given
- BEEP Records; 33; rel 197?

Slide Music (1975)
[1675] trombone quartet
- BEEP Records; 33; rel 197?

Stratti (1963)
[1676] Electronic music
- BEEP Records 1001; 33s; rel 1976; cip

Vonce (1967)
[1677] Electronic music
- BEEP Records 1001; 33s; rel 1976; cip

CELLA, Theodore (1897-1960)
Orchestral Rehearsal, An
[1678] Boston Pops Orchestra; Fiedler, Arthur (cond)
- Victor 4537; 78; 10"

CERVETTI, Sergio (1940-)
Aria suspendida (1974)
[1679] Hayes, Bryant (cl); tape Rec 3/76
- CRI-359; 33s; rel 1977; cip

Guitar Music (The Bottom of the Iceberg)
[1680] Fox, Stuart (gtr)
Rec 5/75
- CRI-359; 33s; rel 1977; cip

CESANA, Otto (1899-1980)

Negro Heaven
[1681] Indianapolis Symphony Orchestra; Sevitzky, Fabien (cond)
- Victor 18070; 78; rel pre-1942

CHADABE, Joel (1938-)

Daisy (1972)
[1682] Electronic music
- Opus One 16; 33s; rel 1974; cip

Echoes
[1683] Williams, Jan (perc); tape
- Folkways FTS-33904; 33s; rel 1976; cip

[1684] Zukofsky, Paul (vln)
- CP2 2; 33s; rel 197?

Flowers
[1685] Zukofsky, Paul (vln)
- CP2 2; 33s; rel 197?

Ideas of Movement at Bolton Landing (1971)
[1686] Electronic music
- Opus One 17; 33s; rel 1975; cip

Street Scene (1967)
[1687] Grignet, Patricia (E hn); tape
- Opus One 16; 33s; rel 1974; cip

CHADWICK, George W. (1854-1931)

Allah
[1688] Schumann-Heink, Ernestine (al)
- Victor 87172; 78; 10"; rel 1912-16

Euterpe (1904)
[1689] Louisville Orchestra; Mester, Jorge (cond)
Rec 10/29/75
- LS-75-3; 33s (Louisville Orchestra First Edition Records 1975 No 3); rel 1976; cip

If I Were You
[1690] Howard, Ann (sop)
- Victor 36032; 78; rel pre-1936

Lady Bird
[1691] Howard, Ann (sop)
- Victor 36032; 78; rel pre-1936

Love's Like a Summer Rose
[1692] Farrar, Geraldine (sop)
- Victor 88409; 78; rel 1912

Morning Glory, The
[1693] Howard, Ann (sop)
- Victor 22621; 78; 10"; rel pre-1936

Oh, Let the Night Speak of Me
[1694] Hanks, John Kennedy (ten); Friedberg, Ruth (pf)
- Duke University Press DWR-6417-18; 33m; 2 discs; rel 1966; del 1975

Pastorale
[1695] Beck, Janice (org)
- Musical Heritage Society OR-A-263; 33s; rel 1972

[1696] Smith, Rollin (org)
Rec 8/73
- Repertoire Recording Society RRS-12; 33s; rel 1974

Quartet, Strings, No 4 (1896)
[1697] Kohon Quartet
- Vox SVBX-5301; 33s; 3 discs; rel 1971; cip

Quartet, Strings, No 4: Andante semplice
[1698] Coolidge String Quartet
- Victor 15417 (in set M-558); 78; rel pre-1942

Sinfonietta (1904)
[1699] American Arts Orchestra; Krueger, Karl (cond)
- SPAMH MIA-104; 33s; rel 1959

(Six) Songs (Op 14) (1885): The Danza
[1700] Schumann-Heink, Ernestine (al); Victor Orchestra
- Victor 87020; 78; 10"; rel 1906-10

Suite in Variation Form (1923)
[1701] Osborne, William (org)
- Orion ORS-78317; 33s; rel 1979; cip

Symphonic Sketches (1895-1904)
[1702] Eastman-Rochester Symphony Orchestra; Hanson, Howard (cond)
- Mercury MG-50104; 33m; rel 1956; del 1964
- Mercury SR-90018; 33s; rel 1959; del 1964
- Mercury MG-50337/SR-90337; 33m/s; rel 1963; del 1967 (Excerpt: Noel)
- Mercury SRI-75050; 33s; rel 1975; cip

Symphonic Sketches: Jubilee
[1703] Eastman-Rochester Symphony Orchestra; Hanson, Howard (cond)
- Victor 15656 (in set M-608); 78; rel 1939

Symphonic Sketches: Jubilee (cont'd)
- Victor 12-0155-58 (in set DM-608); 78; 4 discs; rel pre-1942
- Gramophone DB-3999; 78; rel pre-1952

Symphonic Sketches: Noel
[1704] National Symphony Orchestra; Kindler, Hans (cond)
- Victor 18274; 78; rel pre-1942
- Gramophone ED-291; 78; rel pre-1942

Symphonic Sketches: Hobgoblin
[1705] Hamburg Philharmonia; Korn, Richard (cond)
- Allegro ALG-3150; 33m; rel 1955*
- Concord 3007; 33m; rel 1957; del 1959

Symphony No 2 (Op 21) (1883-85)
[1706] Royal Philharmonic Orchestra; Krueger, Karl (cond)
- SPAMH MIA-134; 33s; rel 1967

Symphony No 3 (1894)
[1707] Royal Philharmonic Orchestra; Krueger, Karl (cond)
- SPAMH MIA-140; 33s; rel 1968

Tabasco (ca 1899)
[1708] Goldman Band; Cox, Ainslee (cond)
- New World NW-266; 33s; rel 1977

Tam O'Shanter (1915)
[1709] Vienna Symphony Orchestra; Schoenherr, Max (cond)
- American Recording Society ARS-29; 33m; rel 1953
- Desto D-421/DST-6421; 33m/s; rel 1965; cip

Theme, Variations, and Fugue (1908)
[1710] Ellsasser, Richard (org)
Rec 2/68
- Nonesuch H-71200; 33s; rel 1968; cip

Time Enough
[1711] Howard, Ann (sop)
- Victor 36033; 78; rel pre-1936

Valentine, A
[1712] Seattle Chamber Singers; Shangrow, George (cond)
Rec 8/1-8/76
- Voyager VRLP-701S; 33s; rel 1976

CHAITKIN, David (1938-)

Etudes, Piano (1974)
[1713] Burge, David (pf)
Rec 10/16-17/75
- CRI-345; 33s; rel 1976; cip

CHAJES, Julius (1910-)

Hechassid (Op 24, No 1)
[1714] Elman, Mischa (vln); Seiger, Joseph (pf)
- Vanguard VRS-1099/VSD-2137; 33m/s; rel 1963; del 1965

[1715] Mamlock, Theodore (vln); Laugs, Richard (pf)
- Musical Heritage Society MHS-3186; 33s; rel 1975

Sonata, Piano, D Minor (1958)
[1716] Schoenfield, Paul (pf)
- VLR 1520/S-1520; 33m/s; rel 1965/?; del 1976

CHAMBERS, Joseph C. (1910-)

All-American Suite
[1717] Iturbi, Jose (pf); Iturbi, Amparo (pf)
- Victor 12-0465-66 (in set M-1246); 78; 2 discs; rel 1948*
- RCA LM-23; 33m; 10"; rel 1950; del 1956
- RCA LM-9018; 33m; rel 1953; del 1960

CHANCE, John Barnes (1932-72)

Credo (1964)
[1718] Hickman, David (tpt); Soderholm, Pauline (pf)
- Crystal S-363; 33s; rel 1978; cip

Incantation and Dance
[1719] Ithaca College Band; Beeler, Walter (cond)
- Mark MCBS-21360; 33s; rel 1968; del 1976

[1720] no performers given
- Washington Cathedral Archives CAR-004-05; 33s; 2 discs; rel 1976

Variations on a Korean Folk Song (1965)
[1721] Ohio State University Concert Band; McGinnis, Donald E. (cond)
- Coronet S-1503; 33s; rel 1969; del 1978

CHANLER, Theodore W. (1902-61)

Children, The (1945): The Children, Once Upon a Time, The Rose, and Moo Is a Cow
[1722] Gramm, Donald (bar); Hassard, Donald (pf)
- New World NW-243; 33s; rel 1977

Children, The: The Rose
[1723] McCollum, John (ten); Biltcliffe, Edwin (pf)
- St/And SPL-411-12; 33m; 2 discs; rel 1963; del 1964
- Desto D-411-12/DST-6411-12; 33m/s; 2 discs; rel 1964; cip

Doves, The (1931)
[1724] Hess, William (ten); Fizdale, Robert (pf)
- Hargail HN-708 (in set 0090); 78; 10"; rel 1946

(Eight) Epitaphs (ca 1939)
[1725] Carter, Sara (sop); Weiser, Bernhard (pf)
- New Editions 2; 33m; rel 1953; del 1959

(Eight) Epitaphs including also Four Husbands
[1726] Curtin, Phyllis (sop); Edwards, Ryan (pf)
- Columbia ML-5598/MS-6198; 33m/s; rel 1961; del 1968
- Columbia CML-5598/CMS-6198; 33m/s; rel 1968; del 1974
- Columbia AMS-6198; 33s; rel 1974; cip

(Eight) Epitaphs: Thomas Logge
[1727] Gramm, Donald (bar); Hassard, Donald (pf)
- New World NW-243; 33s; rel 1977

(Three) Epitaphs (1940)
[1728] Hess, William (ten); Fizdale, Robert (pf)
- Hargail HN-708 (in set 0090); 78; 10"; rel 1946

I Rise When You Enter (1942)
[1729] Gramm, Donald (b); Cumming, Richard (pf)
- Music Library MLR-7033; 33m; rel 1954; del 1974

[1730] McCollum, John (ten); Biltcliffe, Edwin (pf)
- St/And SPL-411-12; 33m; 2 discs; rel 1963; del 1964
- Desto D-411-12/DST-6411-12; 33m/s; 2 discs; rel 1964; cip

[1731] Uppman, Theodor (bar); Rogers, Allen (pf)
Rec 1/24/62, 2/2/62 and 2/7/62
- Internos INT-0001; 33m; rel 1962; del 1970

Policeman in the Park, The (1946)
[1732] Gramm, Donald (b); Cumming, Richard (pf)
- Music Library MLR-7033; 33m; rel 1954; del 1974

Pot of Fat, A (1955)
[1733] Stewart, Dixie (sop); Burrows, Arthur (bar); Abel, Bruce (bar); CRI Chamber Orchestra; Mester, Jorge (cond)
- CRI-162; 33m/s; rel 1963/?; cip

(Four) Rhymes from Peacock Pie (1940)
[1734] Parker, William (bar); Baldwin, Dalton (pf)
- New World NW-300; 33s; rel 1978

These, My Ophelia (1925)
[1735] Beardslee, Bethany (sop); Helps, Robert (pf)
- New World NW-243; 33s; rel 1977

[1736] Luening, Ethel (sop); Nowak, Lionel (pf)
- Yaddo I-2; 78; 10"; rel 1940

CHARLES, Ernest (1895-)

Clouds
[1737] Swarthout, Gladys (m sop); Hodges, Lester (pf)
- Victor 4318; 78; 10"; rel pre-1942

Clouds (arr by Carl Deis)
[1738] Mormon Tabernacle Choir; Schreiner, Alexander (org); Asper, Frank (org); Cornwall, J. Spencer (cond)
- Columbia ML-5203; 33m; rel 1957; del 1962

House on the Hill, The
[1739] Jagel, Frederick (ten); McArthur, Edwin (pf)
- Victor 1979; 78; 10"; rel pre-1942

Let My Song Fill Your Heart
[1740] Farrell, Eileen (sop); Trovillo, George (pf)
- Angel 35608; 33m; rel 1959; del 1966

[1741] Warenskjold, Dorothy (sop); Crossan, Jack (pf)
- Capitol P-8333; 33m; rel 1956; del 1961

My Lady Walks in Loveliness
[1742] Moore, Dale (bar); Tomfohrde, Betty Ruth (pf)
- Cambridge CRS-2715; 33s; rel 1973; cip

Spendthrift
[1743] Swarthout, Gladys (m sop); Hodges, Lester (pf)
- Victor 4318; 78; 10"; rel pre-1942

When I Have Sung My Songs (1934)
[1744] Farrell, Eileen (sop); Trovillo, George (pf)
- Angel 35608; 33m; rel 1959; del 1966

When I Have Sung My Songs (1934) *(cont'd)*
[1745] Flagstad, Kirsten (sop); McArthur, Edwin (pf)
Rec 10/27/36
- Victor 1817 (in set M-342); 78; 10''; rel 1937
- RCA LM-1738; 33m; rel 1953; del 1957
- Victor 49-4082-85 (in set WDM-1738); 45; 4-7''; rel 1953
- New World NW-247; 33m; rel 1976

[1746] McCormack, John (ten); Schneider, Edwin (pf)
- Gramophone DA-1446; 78; 10''; rel pre-1942

[1747] MacDonald, Jeanette (sop); Bamboschek, Giuseppe (pf)
- Victor 2047 (in set M-642); 78; 10''; rel pre-1942

CHASINS, Abram (1903-)

(Three) Chinese Pieces (Op 5, Nos 1 and 2; Op 7) (1928)
[1748] Chasins, Abram (pf)
- Victor 1582; 78; 10''; rel pre-1936
- Gramophone DA-1257; 78; 10''; rel pre-1936
- Master-Class 0007; 78; rel pre-1952 (Excerpt: (No 3) Shanghai Tragedy)
- Mercury MG-10025; 33m; 10''; rel 1951; del 1956

(Three) Chinese Pieces: (No 1) Flirtation in a Chinese Garden and (No 2) Rush-Hour in Hong Kong
[1749] Moiseiwitsch, Benno (pf)
- Gramophone D-1217; 78; rel pre-1952

(Three) Chinese Pieces: (No 2) Rush-Hour in Hong Kong
[1750] Hilsberg, I. (pf)
- Brunswick 4306; 78; 10''; rel pre-1952

Fairy Tale (Op 16)
[1751] Chasins, Abram (pf)
- Gramophone DA-1255; 78; 10''; rel pre-1936
- Victor 1573; 78; 10''; rel pre-1936
- Victor (Japanese) JE-22; 78; rel pre-1950
- Mercury MG-10025; 33m; 10''; rel 1951; del 1956

Parade (1930) (arr for 2 pfs)
[1752] Chasins, Abram (pf); Keene, Constance I. (pf)
- Mercury MG-10061; 33m; rel 1950; del 1956

Period Suite
[1753] Chasins, Abram (pf); Keene, Constance I. (pf)
- Mercury MG-10061; 33m; rel 1950; del 1956

Preludes, Piano (1928): (No 5) D Major (Op 10, No 5)
[1754] Chasins, Abram (pf)
- Gramophone DA-1255; 78; 10''; rel pre-1936
- Victor 1573; 78; 10''; rel pre-1936
- Mercury MG-10025; 33m; 10''; rel 1951; del 1956

[1755] Hilsberg, I. (pf)
- Brunswick 4306; 78; 10''; rel pre-1952

Preludes, Piano: (No 7) F-sharp Minor (Op 11, No 1)
[1756] Behrend, Jeanne (pf)
- Victor 17910 (in set M-764); 78; rel 1941

[1757] Chasins, Abram (pf)
- Mercury MG-10025; 33m; 10''; rel 1951; del 1956

Preludes, Piano: (No 13) G-flat (Op 12, No 1)
[1758] Chasins, Abram (pf)
- Gramophone DA-1255; 78; 10''; rel pre-1936
- Victor 1573; 78; 10''; rel pre-1936

Preludes, Piano: (No 14) E-flat Minor (Op 12, No 2)
[1759] Chasins, Abram (pf)
- Gramophone DA-1255; 78; 10''; rel pre-1936
- Victor 1573; 78; 10''; rel pre-1936
- Master-Class 0007; 78; rel pre-1952
- Mercury MG-10025; 33m; 10''; rel 1951; del 1956

Preludes, Piano: (No 23) D Minor (Op 13, No 5)
[1760] Behrend, Jeanne (pf)
- Victor 17910 (in set M-764); 78; rel 1941

CHATMAN, Stephen (1950-)

Hesitation
[1761] Loban, John (vln); Chatman, Maura (cel)
- CRI-414; 33s; rel 1980; cip

On the Contrary (1974)
[1762] Onofrey, Robert (cl); Eastman Musica Nova; Hodkinson, Sydney (cond)
- CRI-414; 33s; rel 1980; cip

Quiet Exchange (1976)
[1763] Ramsbottom, Gene (cl); Moore, Kenneth (perc)
- Opus One 46; 33s; rel 1979; cip

Whisper, Baby (1975)
[1764] Chatman, Maura (pf); University of British Columbia Chamber Singers; Hultberg, Cortland (cond)
- CRI-426; 33s; rel 1980; cip

Wild Cat (1974)
[1765] Aitken, Robert (fl)
- Opus One 52; 33s; rel 1979; cip

CHEETHAM, John (1939-)

Scherzo
[1766] Eastern Brass Quintet
- Klavier KS-561; 33s; rel 1977; cip

[1767] Los Angeles Brass Quintet
- Crystal S-602; 33s; rel 1968; cip

CHENEY, Timothy (1913-)

Rhapsody, Violin and Piano (1941)
[1768] Kobialka, Daniel (vln); Press, Myron (pf)
- Medea MCLP-1002; 33m/s; rel 1966; del 1971

CHERRY, Don (1936-) and APPLETON, Jon H.

see **APPLETON, Jon H. and CHERRY, Don**

CHERTOK, Pearl (1918-)

Around the Clock
[1769] Chertok, Pearl (hp)
- Orion ORS-76231; 33s; rel 1976; cip

Driftwood
[1770] Chertok, Pearl (hp)
- Orion ORS-76231; 33s; rel 1976; cip

Seafoam
[1771] Chertok, Pearl (hp)
- Orion ORS-76231; 33s; rel 1976; cip

CHIHARA, Paul (1938-)

Ave Maria - Scarborough Fair (1971)
[1772] UCLA Men's Glee Club; Weiss, Don (cond)
- CRI-409; 33s; rel 1979; cip

Beauty of the Rose is in its Passing
[1773] Breidenthal, David (bsn); Crystal Chamber Orchestra; Kraft, William (cond)
- Crystal S-352; 33s; rel 1978; cip

Branches (1966)
[1774] Weisberg, Arthur (bsn); MacCourt, Donald (bsn); Watson, Kenneth (perc)
- CRI-269; 33s; rel 1971; cip

Ceremony I (1971)
[1775] London Symphony Orchestra (members of); Marriner, Neville (cond)
- Turnabout QTVS-34572; 33q; rel 1975; cip

Ceremony II (1972)
[1776] Dunkel, Paul (fl); Eddy, Timothy (vcl); Sherry, Fred (vcl); Fitz, Richard (perc)
- New World NW-237; 33s; rel 1978

Ceremony III (1973)
[1777] London Symphony Orchestra; Marriner, Neville (cond)
- Turnabout QTVS-34572; 33q; rel 1975; cip

Ceremony V (Symphony in Celebration) (1975)
[1778] Houston Symphony Orchestra; Foster, Lawrence (cond)
Rec 2/9/76
- Candide QCE-31101; 33q; rel 1978; cip

Driftwood (1969)
[1779] Philadelphia String Quartet
- CRI-269; 33s; rel 1971; cip

Elegy
[1780] Mirecourt Trio
- CRI-386; 33s; rel 1978; cip

Grass (1971)
[1781] Neidlinger, Buell (cb); London Symphony Orchestra; Marriner, Neville (cond)
- Turnabout QTVS-34572; 33q; rel 1975; cip

Lie Lightly Gentle Earth (1973)
[1782] Gregg Smith Singers; Smith, Gregg (cond)
Rec 4/76
- Vox SVBX-5354; 33s; 3 discs; rel 1979

Logs (1969)
[1783] Turetzky, Bertram (cb)
- CRI-269; 33s; rel 1971; cip

Logs XVI (1970)
[1784] Turetzky, Bertram (cb); tape
- CRI-269; 33s; rel 1971; cip

Magnificat (1966)
[1785] New England Conservatory Chorus; De Varon, Lorna Cooke (cond)
- CRI-409; 33s; rel 1979; cip

Missa carminum brevis (Folk Song Mass) (1976)
[1786] New England Conservatory Chorus; De Varon, Lorna Cooke (cond)
- CRI-409; 33s; rel 1979; cip

[1787] Roger Wagner Chorale; Wagner, Roger (cond)
Rec 1/20/76
- Candide QCE-31101; 33q; rel 1978; cip

Redwood (1967)
[1788] Thomas, Milton (vla); Watson, Kenneth (perc)
- Protone 145-LP2S; 33s; rel 1972; cip

Trio, Piano and Strings (1974)
[1789] Mirecourt Trio
- CRI-386; 33s; rel 1978; cip

Willow, Willow (1968)
[1790] Sollberger, Harvey (b fl); Price, Herbert (tu); Watson, Kenneth (perc); DesRoches, Raymond (perc); Fitz, Richard (perc)
- CRI-269; 33s; rel 1971; cip

Wind Song (1972)
[1791] Solow, Jeffrey (vcl); American Symphony Orchestra; Samuel, Gerhard (cond)
- Everest SDBR-3327; 33s; rel 1973; cip

CHILDS, Barney (1926-)
Barnard I
[1792] Rehfeldt, Phillip (cl)
- Advance FGR-17S; 33s; rel 1976; cip

Duo, Flute and Bassoon (1963)
[1793] Middleton, Peter (fl); Weil, Lester (bsn)
- CRI-253; 33s; rel 1970; cip

Mr. T, His Fancy (1967)
[1794] Turetzky, Bertram (cb)
- Ars Nova/Ars Antiqua AN-1001; 33s; rel 1969; del 1973

Music, A
[1795] no performers given
- Zanja ZR-2; 33; rel 197?

Music for Two Flute Players
[1796] Sollberger, Harvey (fl); Sollberger, Sophie (fl)
- CRI-253; 33s; rel 1970; cip

Sonata, Trombone (1961)
[1797] Anderson, Miles (tbn)
- Avant AV-1006; 33s; rel 1978; cip

(Thirty-Seven) Songs (1971)
[1798] Bunger, Richard (pf)
- Avant AV-1008; 33s; rel 1973; del 1979

That It Might Be
[1799] no performers given
- Zanja ZR-2; 33; rel 197?

Trio, Clarinet, Violoncello, and Piano (1972)
[1800] Montagnana Trio
Rec 6/75
- Command COMS-9005; 33q; rel 1975; del 1977
- ABC 67103; 33q; rel 1977; del 1979
- MCA 67103; 33s; rel 1979; cip

Variations sur une chanson de Canotier (1963)
[1801] Dallas Brass Quintet
- Crystal S-203; 33s; rel 1979; cip

[1802] Modern Brass Ensemble
- Advance FGR-2; 33m; rel 1966; del 1978

CHORBAJIAN, John (1936-)
Bitter for a Sweet
[1803] King Chorale; King, Gordon (cond)
- Orion ORS-75205; 33s; rel 1978; cip

CHOU Wen-chung (1923-)
All in the Spring Wind (1952-53)
[1804] Louisville Orchestra; Whitney, Robert (cond)
- LOU-61-4; 33m (Louisville Orchestra First Edition Records 1961 No 4); rel 1961; del 1975

And the Fallen Petals (1954)
[1805] Louisville Orchestra; Whitney, Robert (cond)
- LOU-56-1; 33m (Louisville Orchestra First Edition Records 1956 No 1); rel 1959; del 1975

Cursive (1963)
[1806] Sollberger, Harvey (fl); Wuorinen, Charles (pf)
- CRI-251; 33s; rel 1970; cip

Landscapes (1949)
[1807] Peninsula Festival Orchestra; Johnson, Thor (cond)
- CRI-122; 33m; rel 1958; cip

Pien (1966)
[1808] Group for Contemporary Music at Columbia University; Sollberger, Harvey (cond)
- CRI-251; 33s; rel 1970; cip

Soliloquy of a Bhiksuni (1958)
[1809] Louisville Orchestra; Whitney, Robert (cond)
- LOU-64-1; 33m (Louisville Orchestra First Edition Records 1964 No 1); rel 1964; cip

Soliloquy of a Bhiksuni (1958)
(cont'd)
[1810] Stevens, Thomas (tpt); Los Angeles
Brass Society (members of);
Henderson, Robert (cond)
- Crystal S-361; 33s; rel 1976; cip

Suite, Harp and Wind Quintet (1950)
[1811] Otis, Cynthia (hp); Dunkel, Paul
(fl); Taylor, Stephen (ob);
Blackwell, Virgil (cl); Morelli,
Frank (bsn); Rose, Stewart (hn)
- New World NW-237; 33s; rel
1978

Willows Are New, The (1957)
[1812] Chang, Yi-an (pf)
- CRI-251; 33s; rel 1970; cip

Yu ko (1965)
[1813] Group for Contemporary Music at
Columbia University; Sollberger,
Harvey (cond)
- CRI-251; 33s; rel 1970; cip

CHRISTIANSEN, F. Melius (1871-1955)
Easter Morning (1948)
[1814] Mormon Tabernacle Choir;
Schreiner, Alexander (org); Asper,
Frank (org); Condie, Richard P.
(cond)
- Columbia ML-5302/MS-6019;
33m/s; rel 1958; cip

Lullaby on Christmas Eve
[1815] Concordia Choir; Hertsgaard, Rolf
(nar); Christiansen, Paul J. (cond)
- Concordia CDLP-5; 33m; 10"; rel
1956; del 1971

New Jerusalem, The
[1816] Concordia Choir; Hertsgaard, Rolf
(nar); flute; trumpet; Christiansen,
Paul J. (cond)
- Concordia CDLP-5; 33m; 10"; rel
1956; del 1971

CIRONE, Anthony J. (1941-)
Double Concerto
[1817] Sonic Boom Percussion Ensemble;
piano
- Crystal S-140; 33s; rel 1977; cip

4/4 for Four
[1818] Sonic Arts Symphonic Percussion
Consortium
- Sonic LS-11; 33s; rel 1979; cip

Japanese Impressions
[1819] Sonic Arts Symphonic Percussion
Consortium
- Sonic LS-11; 33s; rel 1979; cip

Overture
[1820] Sonic Arts Symphonic Percussion
Consortium
- Sonic LS-11; 33s; rel 1979; cip

Triptych
[1821] Sonic Arts Symphonic Percussion
Consortium
- Sonic LS-11; 33s; rel 1979; cip
[1822] Sonic Boom Percussion Ensemble
- Crystal S-140; 33s; rel 1977; cip

CITKOWITZ, Israel (1909-74)
(Five) Songs from Chamber Music (1930)
[1823] Beardslee, Bethany (sop); Helps,
Robert (pf)
- New World NW-243; 33s; rel
1977

(Five) Songs from Chamber Music: (No 1) Strings in the Earth and Air, (No 3) O, It Was Out in Donney-Carney, and (No 4) Bid Adieu
[1824] Carter, Sara (sop); Weiser,
Bernhard (pf)
- New Editions 2; 33m; rel 1953;
del 1959
[1825] Neway, Patricia (sop); Colston,
Robert (pf)
- Lyrichord LL-83; 33m; rel 1959;
del 1978

CLAFLIN, Avery (1898-1979)
Concerto giocoso (1957)
[1826] Magnusson, Gisli (pf); Iceland
Symphony Orchestra; Strickland,
William (cond)
- CRI-178; 33m; rel 1964; cip

Design for the Atomic Age
[1827] Randolph Singers; Randolph, David
(cond)
- CRI-102; 33m/s; rel 1956/?; cip

Fishhouse Punch (1948)
[1828] Vienna Orchestra; Adler, F. Charles
(cond)
- CRI-107; 33m/s; rel 1957/?; cip

Grande breteche, La (1947): Prologue and Two Scenes
[1829] Brinton, Patricia (sop);
Blankenship, William (ten);
Owens, Richard (bar); Gilmore,
Earl (ten); Jones, Sheila (sop);
Vienna Orchestra; Adler, F.
Charles (cond)
- CRI-108; 33m/s; rel 1957/?; cip

Lament for April 15 (1955)
[1830] Randolph Singers; Randolph, David
(cond)
- CRI-102; 33m/s; rel 1956/?; cip

Quangle Wangle's Hat, The
[1831] Randolph Singers; Randolph, David
(cond)
- CRI-102; 33m/s; rel 1956/?; cip

Teen Scenes (1955)
[1832] Accademia Nazionale di Santa
Cecilia Orchestra, Roma; Antonini,
Alfredo (cond)
- CRI-119; 33m; rel 1957; cip

CLARK, Robert Keyes (1925-)
Concerto, Clarinet and Chamber Orchestra (1971)
[1833] Bunke, Jerome (cl); Composers
Festival Orchestra; Brehm, Alvin
(cond)
- Trilogy CTS-1002; 33s; rel
1973; del 1975

CLARKE, Henry Leland (1907-)
Lark (1936)
[1834] Luening, Ethel (sop)
- Yaddo 26B; 78; 10"; rel 1937

Piece, Oboe and Piano
[1835] McBride, Robert (ob); Tucker,
Gregory (pf)
- Yaddo 33A; 78; rel 1937

CLARKE, Laurence (1920-)
Chamber Music
[1836] Renzi, Dorothy (sop); Schwartz,
Nathan (pf)
- Fantasy 5010; 33m; rel 1960;
del 1970

CLARKE, Rebecca (1886-1979)
Shy One
[1837] Frijsh, Povla (sop); Dougherty,
Celius (pf)
- Victor M-789; 78; rel 1941
- Victor 2157 (in set MO-789);
78; 10"; rel 1941

Trio, Violin, Violoncello, and Piano (1921)
[1838] Ornstein, Suzanne (vln); Kreger,
James (vcl); Eskin, Virginia (pf)
Rec 9/25/79
- Leonarda LPI-103; 33s; rel 1980

CLOUGH-LEITER, Henry (1874-1956)
My Lady Chloe
[1839] Braslau, Sophie (al)
- Victor 64742; 78; 10"; rel
1914-18
- Victor 552; 78; 10"; rel
1914-18

COBERT, Robert (1924-)
Frankie and Johnny
[1840] Mayo, Mary; Scholl, Danny;
Coburn, Joan; Frey, Nathaniel;
orchestra; Harris, Herb (cond)
- MGM E-3499; 33m; rel 1957;
del 1959

Mediterranean Suite
[1841] MGM Chamber Orchestra; Cobert, Robert (cond)
- MGM E-3497; 33m; rel 1957; del 1959

COGAN, Robert (1930-)

Phrases from "Whirl . . . As 1" (Version 2) (1967)
[1842] Heller, Joan (sop)
- Golden Crest NEC-119; 33s; rel 1979; cip

COHEN, Maurice (Michael Carr, pseud) (1905-)

Springtime Suite
[1843] Ellsasser, Richard (org)
- MGM E-3296; 33m; rel 1956; del 1959

Wintertime Suite
[1844] Ellsasser, Richard (org)
- MGM E-3284; 33m; rel 1956; del 1959

COHN, Arthur (1910-)

Kaddish (1964)
[1845] Royal Philharmonic Orchestra; Lipkin, Arthur Bennett (cond)
- CRI-259; 33s; rel 1970; cip

Quartet, Strings, No 4 (1935)
[1846] Galimir String Quartet
- Yaddo III-1; 78; 3-10"; rel 1940

COKE-JEPHCOTT, Norman (1893-1962)

Bishop's Promenade
[1847] Coke-Jephcott, Norman (org)
- Aeolian-Skinner AS-8; 33m; rel 1956; del 1958
- Washington WAS-8; 33m; rel 1958; del 1962

[1848] Matthews, Thomas (org)
- XCTV-97395-96 (matrix no); 33m; rel 1963

[1849] Pizarro, David (org)
- Grosvenor GRS-1017; 33s; rel 1973

Toccata on St. Anne
[1850] Coke-Jephcott, Norman (org)
- Aeolian-Skinner AS-8; 33m; rel 1956; del 1958
- Washington WAS-8; 33m; rel 1958; del 1962

Variation, Fugue, and Toccata on a National Air
[1851] Pizarro, David (org)
- Grosvenor GRS-1017; 33s; rel 1973

COLEMAN, Ornette (1930-)

Forms and Sounds (1965)
[1852] Philadelphia Woodwind Quintet
- RCA LM-2982/LSC-2982; 33m/s; rel 1968; del 1970

Saints and Sinners
[1853] Philadelphia String Quartet
- RCA LM-2982/LSC-2982; 33m/s; rel 1968; del 1970

Skies of America
[1854] London Symphony Orchestra; Measham, David (cond)
- Columbia L-31562; 33s; rel pre-1972
- Columbia CG-33669; 33s; 2 discs; rel 1972
- Columbia KN-31562; 33s

Space Flight
[1855] Philadelphia String Quartet
- RCA LM-2982/LSC-2982; 33m/s; rel 1968; del 1970

COLGRASS, Michael (1932-)

As Quiet As (1966)
[1856] Boston Symphony Orchestra; Leinsdorf, Erich (cond)
- RCA LM-3001/LSC-3001; 33m/s; rel 1968; del 1974

Chamber Music for Percussion Quintet (1954)
[1857] University of Illinois Percussion Ensemble; McKenzie, Jack (cond)
- Illini Union Bookstore CRS-6; 33m; rel 1960*

Concert Masters (1976)
[1858] Rudie, Robert (vln); Yanagita, Masako (vln); Oakland, Ronald (vln); American Symphony Orchestra; Akiyama, Kazuyoshi (cond)
Rec 4/18/77
- Turnabout TVS-34704; 33s; rel 1978; cip

Earth's a Baked Apple, The (1969)
[1859] New Orleans Philharmonic-Symphony Orchestra; mixed chorus; Torkanowsky, Werner (cond)
- Orion ORS-7268; 33s; rel 1972; cip

Fantasy Variations (1961)
[1860] New Jersey Percussion Ensemble; DesRoches, Raymond (cond)
- Nonesuch H-71291/HQ-1291; 33s/q; rel 1974/1976; cip

New People (1969)
[1861] Long Island Chamber Ensemble of New York
- Grenadilla GS-1010; 33s; rel 1978; cip

Percussion Music (1953)
[1862] Percussion Ensemble; Price, Paul (cond)
- Period SPL-743/SPLS-743; 33m/s; rel 1958; del 1968
- Orion ORS-7276; 33s; rel 1972; cip

Three Brothers (1951)
[1863] American Percussion Society; Price, Paul (cond)
- Urania UX-106; 33m; rel 1957; del 1969
- Urania USD-1007; 33s; rel 1958; del 1960
- Urania US-5106; 33s; rel 1961; del 1970

[1864] Percussion Ensemble; Price, Paul (cond)
- Golden Crest CR-4004/CRS-4004; 33m/s; rel 1957/1979; cip

[1865] University of Illinois Percussion Ensemble; Price, Paul (cond)
- Illini Union Bookstore CRS-3; 33m; rel 1955*

Variations, Four Drums and Viola (1956)
[1866] Boston Symphony Chamber Players
- RCA LM-6184/LSC-6184; 33m/s; 3 discs; rel 1968; del 1976

[1867] Colgrass, Michael (perc); Vardi, Emanuel (vla)
- MGM E-3714; 33m; rel 1959; del 1959

CONSOLI, Marc-Antonio (1941-)

(Tre) Canzoni
[1868] Charlston, Elsa (sop); Szlek-Consoli, Elizabeth (fl); Tsutsumi, Tsuyoshi (vcl)
Rec 11/76
- CRI-359; 33s; rel 1977; cip

Odefonia (1978)
[1869] American Composers Orchestra; Schuller, Gunther (cond)
Rec 5/24/78
- CRI-384; 33s; rel 1979; cip

Sciuri novi
[1870] Szlek-Consoli, Elizabeth (fl)
Rec 6/75
- CRI-359; 33s; rel 1977; cip

CONVERSE, Frederick Shepherd (1871-1940)

Endymion's Narrative (After Keats) (Op 10) (1901)
[1871] Louisville Orchestra; Mester, Jorge (cond)
Rec 10/29/75
- LS-75-3; 33s (Louisville Orchestra First Edition Records 1975 No 3); rel 1976; cip

Flivver Ten Million (1926)
[1872] Louisville Orchestra; Mester, Jorge
(cond)
Rec 10/29/75
- LS-75-3; 33s (Louisville
Orchestra First Edition Records
1975 No 3); rel 1976; cip

**Mystic Trumpeter, The (Fantasy
after Whitman) (Op 19) (1904)**
[1873] Vienna Symphony Orchestra;
Schoenherr, Max (cond)
- American Recording Society
ARS-29; 33m; rel 1953
- Desto D-407/DST-6407; 33m/s;
rel 1964; del 1976

**Sacrifice, The (1910): Chonita's
Prayer**
[1874] Nielsen, Alice (sop)
- Columbia A-5298; 78; rel
1911-15

COOK, John (1918-)

Fanfare
[1875] Munns, Robert (org)
- Pye TPLS-13022; 33s; rel 1970;
del 1971

[1876] Swann, Frederick (org)
Rec 4/68
- Westminster WST-17154; 33s;
rel 1969; del 1971

[1877] Teague, William (org)
- Wicks Organ Co 832W-9785;
33s; rel 1967

[1878] Thalben-Ball, George (org)
- Vista VPS-1046; 33s; rel 1977

[1878a] Whitehead, William (org)
- Cameo C-4020/SC-4020;
33m/s; rel 1963; del 1970

**Festal Voluntaries - Christmas:
Paean on Divinum mysterium**
[1879] Swann, Frederick (org)
- Mirrosonic CM-7058/CS-7058;
33m/s; rel 1964

[1880] Wichmann, Russell G. (org)
- True Image LP-125; 33m; rel
1966

Flourish and Fugue
[1881] Mason, Marilyn (org)
- Mirrosonic CM-7145/CS-7145;
33m/s; rel 1965

[1882] Swann, Frederick (org)
- Mirrosonic CS-7230; 33s; rel
1972

COOK, Will Marion (1869-1944)

Down de Lovers' Lane
[1883] Robeson, Paul (b); Brown,
Lawrence (pf)
- Victor 27430; 78; 10"

COOKE, James Francis
(1875-1960)

Ol' Car'lina
[1884] Galli-Curci, Amelita (sop);
orchestra
- Victor 628; 78; 10"; rel
1921-25
- Victor 66014; 78; 10"; rel
1921-25

COOLEY, Carlton (1898-)

Aria and Dance
[1885] Cooley, Carlton (vla); Philadelphia
Orchestra; Ormandy, Eugene
(cond)
- Columbia ML-6191/MS-6791;
33m/s; rel 1966; del 1971

COOLIDGE, Elizabeth Sprague
(1864-1953)

Quartet, Strings, E Minor
[1886] Coolidge String Quartet
- Victor M-719; 78; 3 discs; rel
pre-1942

[1887] Quartetto Poltronieri
- EMI/Odeon (Italian) GO-12895;
78; 10"; rel 193?

COOLIDGE, Peggy Stuart (1913-)

New England Autumn (1972)
[1888] Westphalian Symphony Orchestra;
Landau, Siegfried (cond)
Rec 1/75
- Turnabout
TVS-34635/QTVS-34635;
33s/q; rel 1977; del 1980

Pioneer Dances (1970)
[1889] Westphalian Symphony Orchestra;
Landau, Siegfried (cond)
Rec 1/75
- Turnabout
TVS-34635/QTVS-34635;
33s/q; rel 1977; del 1980

**Rhapsody, Harp and Orchestra
(1965)**
[1890] Wurtzler, Aristid von (hp);
Westphalian Symphony Orchestra;
Landau, Siegfried (cond)
Rec 1/75
- Turnabout
TVS-34635/QTVS-34635;
33s/q; rel 1977; del 1980

**Spirituals in Sunshine and Shadow
(1969)**
[1891] Westphalian Symphony Orchestra;
Landau, Siegfried (cond)
Rec 1/75
- Turnabout
TVS-34635/QTVS-34635;
33s/q; rel 1977; del 1980

**Spirituals in Sunshine and Shadow
(arr for hps)**
[1892] New York Harp Ensemble;
Wurtzler, Aristid von (cond)
- Musical Heritage Society
MHS-3307; 33s; rel 1975

COOPER, John (1925-)

(Three) Bagatelles (Op 13)
[1893] Carpenter, Richard (pf)
- Educo 3105; 33

COOPER, Kent (1880-1965)

Spirit of Freedom
[1894] Cities Service Band of America;
Lavalle, Paul (cond)
- Victor 547-0264-65 (in set
EPB-3120); 45; 2-7"; rel 1953?
- RCA LPM-3120; 33m; 10"; rel
1953; del 1956

COOPER, Paul (1926-)

**Quartet, Strings, No 5 (Umbrae)
(1973)**
[1895] Shepherd Quartet
Rec 3/10/77
- CRI-369; 33s; rel 1978; cip

Quartet, Strings, No 6 (1977)
[1896] Shepherd Quartet
Rec 7/78
- CRI-402; 33s; rel 1979; cip

Sonata, Flutes and Piano (1963)
[1897] Bryan, Keith (fl); Keys, Karen (pf)
- Lyrichord LL-204/LLST-7204;
33m/s; rel 1968; cip

**Symphony No 4 (Landscape)
(1973)**
[1898] Houston Symphony Orchestra;
Jones, Samuel (cond)
Rec 11/25/75
- CRI-347; 33s; rel 1976; cip

Variants (1971)
[1899] Craighead, David (org)
- Crystal S-858; 33s; rel 1977; cip

Variants II (1972)
[1900] Mark, Peter (vla); Musgrave, Thea
(pf)
- Music Now CFS-3037; 33s; rel
1974*

COPE, David (1941-)

Arena (1974)
[1901] Cope, David (vcl); tape
- Orion ORS-75169; 33s; rel
1975; cip

Bright Angel (1971)
[1902] Stith, Marice (tpt); tape
- Redwood RRES-5; 33s; rel 1977;
cip

Cycles (1969)
[1903] Martin, James (fl); Cope, David (cb)
- Opus One 14; 33s; rel 1976; cip

Glassworks (1978)
[1904] Cope, David (pf); Durling (pf); tape
- Folkways FTS-33452; 33s; rel 1980; cip

Iceberg Meadow
[1905] Cope, David (pf)
- Capra 1201; 33s; rel 1969; cip

Margins (1972)
[1906] Performance Group; Baker, Larry (cond)
- Orion ORS-75169; 33s; rel 1975; cip

(Three) Pieces, Clarinet (1972)
[1907] Russo, John (cl)
- Capra 1203; 33s; rel 1975; cip

Re-Birth
[1908] Cornell University Wind Ensemble; Stith, Marice (cond)
- Cornell CUWE-16; 33s; rel 1975; cip

Sonata, Piano, No 4 (1968)
[1909] Ignacio, Lydia Walton (pf)
- Capra 1204; 33s; rel 1976; cip

Those Years Ago Cold Mornings Held No Fears
[1910] Vance (voice?)
- Capra 1202; 33s; rel 1971; del 1973

Threshold and Visions (1978)
[1911] Santa Cruz Chamber Symphony; Cope, David (cond)
- Folkways FTS-33452; 33s; rel 1980; cip

Triplum
[1912] Di Martino, Linda (fl); Mangold, Marilyn (pf)
- Capra 1203; 33s; rel 1975; cip

Variations, Piano and Wind Orchestra (1966)
[1913] Lee, Noel (pf); Cornell University Wind Ensemble; Stith, Marice (cond)
- Cornell CUWE-13; 33s; rel 1973; cip

COPLAND, Aaron (1900-)
Agachadas, Las (1942)
[1914] New England Conservatory Chorus; Copland, Aaron (cond) Rec 3/29/65
- CBS 32-11-0017/32-11-0018; 33m/s; rel 1967; del 1970
- Columbia M-30375; 33s; rel 1970; cip

Appalachian Spring (Original Version) (1943-44)
[1915] Columbia Chamber Orchestra; Copland, Aaron (cond)
- Columbia M-32736/MQ-32736; 33s/q; rel 1974; cip (issued with Columbia BTS-34; 33s; 7": "Copland rehearses Appalachian Spring")

Appalachian Spring (Complete Ballet for Orchestra) (1945)
[1916] Philadelphia Orchestra; Ormandy, Eugene (cond)
- Columbia ML-5157; 33m; rel 1957; del 1972

Appalachian Spring (Suite) (1945)
[1917] Berlin Radio Orchestra; Rother, Arthur (cond)
- Urania URLP-7092; 33m; rel 1953; del 1960

[1918] Berlin Symphony Orchestra; Rubahn, Gerd (cond)
- Allegro-Royale 1513; 33m; rel 1954

[1919] Boston Symphony Orchestra; Copland, Aaron (cond) Rec 11/13/59
- RCA LM-2401/LSC-2401; 33m/s; rel 1960; cip
- RCA-Victrola (English) VICS-1488; 33s; rel 1970*
- RCA CRL-3-3270; 33s; 3 discs; rel 1979; cip
- Time-Life STL-570; 33s; rel 1979

[1920] Boston Symphony Orchestra; Koussevitzky, Serge (cond)
- Victor 11-9129-31 (in set DM-1046); 78; 3 discs; rel 1946
- Victor 11-9130-32; 78; 3 discs; rel 1946
- RCA LCT-1134; 33m; rel 1954; del 1960
- RCA AVM-1-1739; 33m; rel 1976; del 1980

[1921] Concert Arts Orchestra; Irving, Robert (cond)
- Time-Life TL-145/STL-145; 33m/s; rel 1967
- Capitol SP-8702; 33s; rel 1969; del 1970
- EMI/Studio Two TWO-302; 33s; rel 1969
- Seraphim S-60198; 33s; rel 1972; cip

[1922] Dallas Symphony Orchestra; Mata, Eduardo (cond)
- RCA ARL-1-2862; 33s; rel 1978; cip

[1923] Hamburg Philharmonia; Walther, Hans-Jurgen (cond)
- Music Sound Books 78-52; 78 (long-playing); rel pre-1956 (Excerpt: Simple-Gifts Variations)

Appalachian Spring (Suite) (1945)
(cont'd)
[1924] Hastings Symphony Orchestra; Bath, John (cond)
- Allegro-Elite 4056; 33m; 10"; rel 1954; del 1957

[1925] London Symphony Orchestra; Copland, Aaron (cond)
- Columbia M-30649; 33s; rel 1971; cip
- Columbia D3M-33720; 33s; 3 discs; rel 1975; cip
- Columbia (English) 72872; 33s

[1926] London Symphony Orchestra; Dorati, Antal (cond)
- Mercury MG-50246/SR-90246; 33m/s; rel 1962; del 1974

[1927] London Symphony Orchestra; Susskind, Walter (cond)
- Everest LPBR-6002/SDBR-3002; 33m/s; rel 1958; cip

[1928] Los Angeles Philharmonic Orchestra; Mehta, Zubin (cond)
- London CSA-2246; 33s; 2 discs; rel 1976; del 1980
- London CS-7031; 33s; rel 1977; cip

[1929] National Symphony Orchestra; Mitchell, Howard (cond)
- Westminster WL-5286; 33m; rel 1954; del 1956
- Nixa WLP-5286; 33m; rel pre-1956
- Westminster XWN-18284; 33m; rel 1956; del 1968
- Westminster WST-14284; 33s; rel 1968; del 1970
- Westminster W-9727; 33m; rel 1970; del 1971

[1930] New York Philharmonic; Bernstein, Leonard (cond) Rec 10/9/61
- Columbia ML-5755/MS-6355; 33m/s; rel 1962; cip
- Columbia MG-30071; 33s; 2 discs; rel 1970; cip
- Columbia MS-7521; 33s; rel 1970; cip
- Columbia MG-31155; 33s; 2 discs; rel 1972; cip
- Columbia (English) 72074; 33

[1931] Philadelphia Orchestra; Ormandy, Eugene (cond)
- RCA LSC-3184; 33s; rel 1970; cip
- RCA ARL-1-0109; 33s; rel 1973; cip
- RCA (English) LSB-4018; 33

[1932] Pittsburgh Symphony Orchestra; Steinberg, William (cond)
- Command CC33-11038/CC-SD-11038; 33m/s; rel 1968; del 1973

[1933] St. Paul Chamber Orchestra; Davies, Dennis Russell (cond)
- Sound 80 DLR-101; 33 digital; rel 1979; cip

Appalachian Spring (Suite) (1945)
(cont'd)

[1934] Vienna State Opera Orchestra;
Litschauer, Franz (cond)
- Vanguard VRS-439; 33m; rel
1953; del 1965

[1935] Vienna Symphony Orchestra;
Hendl, Walter (cond)
- American Recording Society
ARS-26; 33m; rel 1953
- Desto D-403/DST-6403; 33m/s;
rel 1964; cip

As it Fell upon a Day (1923)

[1936] Peil, Mary Beth (sop); Kraber, Karl
(fl); Kirkbride, Jerry (cl)
- Musical Heritage Society
MHS-3578; 33s; rel 1977

Billy the Kid (1938)

[1937] Ballet Theatre Orchestra; Levine,
Joseph (cond)
- Capitol P-8238; 33m; rel 1954;
del 1960
- Capitol CTL-7040; 33m; rel
pre-1956
- Capitol (Australian) CLCX-047;
33m; rel pre-1956
- Capitol LAL-9024; 33m; rel
pre-1956 (excerpts)
- Capitol HDR-21004; 33m; 4
discs; rel 1966; del 1970
(abridged)

[1938] London Symphony Orchestra;
Dorati, Antal (cond)
- Mercury MG-50246/SR-90246;
33m/s; rel 1962; del 1974

Billy the Kid (Suite)

[1939] Dallas Symphony Orchestra;
Johanos, Donald (cond)
- Turnabout TVS-34169; 33s; rel
1967; cip
- Turnabout (English) TVS-34169;
33s; rel 1967

[1940] London Symphony Orchestra;
Copland, Aaron (cond)
Rec ca 1958
- Everest LPBR-6015/SDBR-3015;
33m/s; rel 1959; cip

[1941] London Symphony Orchestra;
Copland, Aaron (cond)
Rec 11/28/69
- Columbia M-30114; 33s; rel
1970; cip
- Columbia MS-7521; 33s; rel
1970; cip (Excerpt: Celebration)
- Columbia M-30374; 33s; rel
1970; cip
- Columbia D3M-33720; 33s; 3
discs; rel 1975; cip
- Columbia (English) 72888; 33

[1942] Morton Gould and his Orchestra;
Gould, Morton (cond)
- RCA LM-2195/LSC-2195;
33m/s; rel 1958; del 1976
(Suite and Waltz)
- RCA AGL-1-1335; 33s; rel 1976;
cip
- Time-Life STL-570; 33s; rel
1979

Billy the Kid (Suite) (cont'd)

[1943] National Symphony Orchestra;
Mitchell, Howard (cond)
- Westminster WL-5286; 33m; rel
1954; del 1956
- Nixa WLP-5286; 33m; rel
pre-1956
- Westminster XWN-18284; 33m;
rel 1956; del 1968
- RCA LM-2766/LSC-2766;
33m/s; rel 1964; del 1968
(Excerpt: Street in a Frontier
Town)
- Westminster WST-14284; 33s;
rel 1968; del 1970
- Westminster W-9727; 33m; rel
1970; del 1971

[1944] New York Philharmonic; Bernstein,
Leonard (cond)
- Columbia ML-5575/MS-6175;
33m/s; rel 1960; del 1979
- Columbia MG-30071; 33s; 2
discs; rel 1970; cip
- Columbia M-31823; 33s; rel
1973; cip
- Columbia (English) 72411; 33

[1945] Philadelphia Orchestra; Ormandy,
Eugene (cond)
- Columbia ML-5157; 33m; rel
1957; del 1972 (Excerpts: The
Open Prairie and Street in a
Frontier Town)
- RCA LSC-3184; 33s; rel 1970;
cip
- RCA ARL-1-0109; 33s; rel 1973;
cip (Excerpts: Street in a Frontier
Town and Celebration)

[1946] Pittsburgh Symphony Orchestra;
Steinberg, William (cond)
- Command
CC33-11038/CC-SD-11038;
33m/s; rel 1968; del 1973

[1947] Utah Symphony Orchestra;
Abravanel, Maurice (cond)
- Westminster
XWN-18840/WST-14058;
33m/s; rel 1959; del 1967
(Suite and Waltz)
- Music Guild MS-164; 33s; rel
1970; del 1971 (Suite and
Waltz)
- Westminster WGS-8170; 33s; rel
1972; cip

[1948] Victor Symphony Orchestra;
Bernstein, Leonard (cond)
- Victor 12-1032-34 (in set
M-1333); 78; 3 discs; rel
pre-1950
- Victor DM-1333; 78; 3 discs; rel
pre-1952
- Victor WDM-1333; 45; 3-7"; rel
pre-1950
- RCA LM-1031; 33m; rel 1950;
del 1958
- Camden CAL-439; 33m; rel
1958; del 1961

Billy the Kid: Prairie Night and Celebration

[1949] New York Philharmonic; Stokowski,
Leopold (cond)
- Columbia 19011D; 78; 10"; rel
1949
- Columbia ML-2167; 33m; 10";
rel 1952; del 1956

Billy the Kid: Waltz

[1950] Dallas Symphony Orchestra; Dorati,
Antal (cond)
- Victor 12-0269 (in set
DM-1214); 78; rel 1948
- Victor 12-0270-72 (in set
M-1214); 78; 3 discs; rel 1948
- Victor WDM-1214; 45; 3-7"; rel
1950

Billy the Kid: Celebration, Billy's Death, and The Open Prairie Again (arr for 2 pfs by Arthur Whittemore and Jack Lowe)

[1951] Whittemore, Arthur (pf); Lowe,
Jack (pf)
- RCA LM-1705; 33m; rel 1952;
del 1956
- Victor WDM-1705; 45; 7"; rel
pre-1953
- RCA LM-1926; 33m; rel 1956;
del 1958 (Excerpt: Celebration)

Billy the Kid: The Open Prairie (arr for pf by Lukas Foss)

[1952] Levant, Oscar (pf)
- Columbia MM-251; 78; rel 1949
- Columbia 72873D (in set
MM-867); 78; rel 1949
- Columbia ML-2018; 33m; 10";
rel pre-1949; del 1956
- Columbia ML-2073; 33m; 10";
rel pre-1949; del 1956

Ceremonial Fanfare (1970)

[1953] brass ensemble; Prausnitz,
Frederik (cond)
Rec 1970
- Metropolitan Museum of Art
AKS-10001; 33; rel 1970

(Two) Children's Pieces (Sunday Afternoon Music and The Young Pioneers) (1935-36)

[1954] Martin, Charlotte (pf)
- Educo 3021; 33m; rel 1968; del
1972

[1955] Richter, Marga (pf)
- MGM E-3147; 33m; rel 1955;
del 1959

[1956] Singer, Joan (pf)
- Golden Age GAR-1008-09; 33s;
2 discs; rel 1977?

[1957] Smit, Leo (pf)
Rec 1/78
- Columbia M2-35901; 33s; 2
discs; rel 1979; cip

Concerto, Clarinet and String Orchestra (1947-48)

[1958] De Peyer, Gervaise (cl); London
Mozart Players; Jacob, Bernard
(cond)
- Unicorn RHS-314; 33s; rel
1973*
- Unicorn UNI-75002; 33s; rel
1978; del 1980

[1959] Goodman, Benny (cl); Columbia
Symphony Orchestra; Copland,
Aaron (cond)
Rec 11/15/50
- Columbia ML-4421; 33m; rel
1951; del 1965

[1960] Goodman, Benny (cl); Columbia
Symphony Orchestra; Copland,
Aaron (cond)
Rec 2/20/63
- Columbia ML-5897/MS-6497;
33m/s; rel 1963; cip
- Columbia ML-6205/MS-6805;
33m/s; rel 1966; cip
- Columbia (English) 72188; 33
cip
- Columbia (English) 72469; 33

Concerto, Clarinet and String Orchestra (clarinet and piano version)

[1961] Drushler, Paul (cl); Gibson, Gordon
(pf)
- Mark MC-3344; 33s; rel 1973;
del 1975 (unauthorized
recording; withdrawn by the
composer)

Concerto, Piano and Orchestra (1926)

[1962] Copland, Aaron (pf); New York
Philharmonic; Bernstein, Leonard
(cond)
Rec 1/13/64
- Columbia ML-6098/MS-6698;
33m/s; rel 1965; cip
- Columbia (English) 72352; 33

[1963] Ruskin, Abbott (pf); MIT Symphony
Orchestra; Epstein, David (cond)
Rec 11/76
- Turnabout QTVS-34683; 33q; rel
1977; cip

[1964] Smit, Leo (pf); Rome Symphony
Orchestra; Copland, Aaron (cond)
Rec ca 1951
- Concert Hall CHF-4; 33m; rel
1952
- Musical Masterpiece Society
MMS-105; 33m; 10''; rel 1952*
- Concert Hall CHS-1238; 33m; rel
1956; del 1957
- Concert Hall H-1638; 33m; rel
1957; del 1959
- Varese Sarabande VC-81098;
33s

[1965] Wild, Earl (pf); Symphony of the
Air; Copland, Aaron (cond)
Rec ca 1960
- Vanguard VRS-1070/VSD-2094;
33m/s; rel 1961; cip

Connotations (1962)

[1966] New York Philharmonic; Bernstein,
Leonard (cond)
Rec 9/23/62
- Columbia LL-1007, LL-1009 (in
set L2L-1007)/LS-1008,
LS-1010 (in set L2S-1008);
33m/s; 2 discs; rel 1962; del
1970
- Columbia MS-7431; 33s; rel
1970; cip
- CBS (English) 73198; 33s

Dance of the Adolescent

[1967] Trenkner, Evelinde (pf); Pleshakov,
Vladimir (pf)
- Orion ORS-79343; 33s; rel
1980; cip

Dance Panels (Ballet in Seven Sections) (1959, rev 1962)

[1968] London Symphony Orchestra;
Copland, Aaron (cond)
Rec 11/28/69 and 12/2/69
- Columbia M-33269; 33s; rel
1975; cip
- Columbia D3M-33720; 33s; 3
discs; rel 1975; cip

Dance Symphony (1930)

[1969] Chicago Symphony Orchestra;
Gould, Morton (cond)
- RCA LM-2850/LSC-2850;
33m/s; rel 1965; del 1970
- RCA AGL-1-1965; 33s; rel 1976;
del 1979
- Time-Life STL-570; 33s; rel
1979

[1970] Japan Philharmonic Symphony
Orchestra; Watanabe, Akeo
(cond)
- CRI-129; 33m/s; rel
1960/1970; cip

[1971] London Symphony Orchestra;
Copland, Aaron (cond)
Rec 10/2-3/67
- Columbia MS-7223; 33s; rel
1969; cip
- Columbia (English) 72731; 33

[1972] MIT Symphony Orchestra; Epstein,
David (cond)
- Turnabout QTVS-34670; 33q; rel
1977; cip

Danza de Jalisco (1963)

[1973] Pleshakov, Vladimir (pf); Trenkner,
Evelinde (pf)
- Orion ORS-79343; 33s; rel
1980; cip

Danzon cubano (1942)

[1974] Babin, Victor (pf); Vronsky, Vitya
(pf)
- RCA LM-2417/LSC-2417;
33m/s; rel 1960; del 1966
- RCA-Victrola VICS-1419; 33s; rel
1969; del 1976

[1975] Copland, Aaron (pf); Smit, Leo (pf)
Rec 1947
- Concert Hall A-1; 78; rel 1947

Danzon cubano (1942) (cont'd)
- Concert Hall CHC-51; 33m; 10'';
rel 1950; del 1953
- New World NW-277; 33m; rel
1976

Danzon cubano (orchestral version) (1944)

[1976] London Symphony Orchestra;
Copland, Aaron (cond)
- Columbia M-33269; 33s; rel
1975; cip

[1977] Minneapolis Symphony Orchestra;
Dorati, Antal (cond)
Rec 12/21/57
- Mercury MG-50172/SR-90172;
33m/s; rel 1958/1959; del
1971
- Mercury MG-50326/SR-90326;
33m/s; rel 1963; del 1966

[1978] New York Philharmonic; Bernstein,
Leonard (cond)
- Columbia ML-5914/MS-6514;
33m/s; rel 1963; cip
- Columbia ML-6271/MS-6871;
33m/s; rel 1966; del 1976
- Columbia (English) 61059; 33

Dirge in Woods (1954)

[1979] McCollum, John (ten); Biltcliffe,
Edwin (pf)
- St/And SPL-411-12; 33m; 2
discs; rel 1963; del 1964
- Desto D-411-12/DST-6411-12;
33m/s; 2 discs; rel 1964; cip

Down a Country Lane (1962)

[1980] Singer, Joan (pf)
- Golden Age GAR-1008-09; 33s;
2 discs; rel 1977?

[1981] Smit, Leo (pf)
Rec 1/78
- Columbia M2-35901; 33s; 2
discs; rel 1979; cip

Down a Country Lane (orchestral version) (1965)

[1982] London Symphony Orchestra;
Copland, Aaron (cond)
Rec 10/29/68
- Columbia M-33586; 33s; rel
1975; cip

Duo, Flute and Piano (1971)

[1983] Bryan, Keith (fl); Keys, Karen (pf)
- Orion ORS-76242; 33s; rel
1976; cip

[1984] Padorr, Laila (fl); Swearingen, Anita
(pf)
- Laurel-Protone LP-14; 33s; rel
1977; cip

[1985] Shaffer, Elaine (fl); Copland, Aaron
(pf)
Rec 1972
- Columbia M-32737; 33s; rel
1974; cip

Emblems (1964)

[1986] Cornell University Wind Ensemble;
Stith, Marice (cond)
- Cornell CUWE-1; 33s; rel 1971;
cip

[1987] Eastman Symphonic Wind
Ensemble; Hunsberger, Donald
(cond)
Rec 11/6-7/78
- Mercury SRI-75132; 33s; rel
1980; cip

[1988] Yale University Band; Wilson, Keith
(cond)
- Carillon 128; 33m; rel 1965

Episode (1940)

[1989] Ellsasser, Richard (org)
- MGM E-3064; 33m; rel 1953;
del 1959

[1990] Hillsman, Walter (org)
Rec 5/10-11/76
- Vista VPS-1038; 33s; rel 1976

[1991] Mason, Marilyn (org)
- Aeolian-Skinner AS-7; 33m; rel
1956; del 1958
- Washington WAS-7; 33m; rel
1958; del 1962

[1992] Smith, Rollin (org)
Rec 8/73
- Repertoire Recording Society
RRS-12; 33s; rel 1974

Fanfare for the Common Man (1942)

[1993] Atlanta Brass Ensemble; Morris,
Richard (cond)
- Crystal Clear CCS-7010; 33s; rel
1980; cip

[1994] Baldwin-Wallace Brass
- Mark 32565; 33s; rel 1969; del
1976

[1995] Dallas Symphony Orchestra;
Johanos, Donald (cond)
- Turnabout TVS-34169; 33s; rel
1967; cip

[1996] Hartford Symphony Orchestra;
Mahler, Fritz (cond)
- Vanguard VRS-1067/VSD-2085;
33m/s; rel 1961; del 1969

[1997] London Symphony Orchestra;
Copland, Aaron (cond)
Rec 10/29/68
- Columbia M-30649; 33s; rel
1971; cip
- Columbia D3M-33720; 33s; 3
discs; rel 1975; cip
- Columbia (English) 72872; 33s

[1998] National Symphony Orchestra;
Mitchell, Howard (cond)
- Westminster WL-5286; 33m; rel
1954; del 1956
- Nixa WLP-5286; 33m; rel
pre-1956
- Westminster XWN-18284; 33m;
rel 1956; del 1968
- Westminster WST-14284; 33s;
rel 1968; del 1970

Fanfare for the Common Man (1942) (cont'd)

- Westminster W-9727; 33m; rel
1970; del 1971

[1999] Philadelphia Orchestra; Ormandy,
Eugene (cond)
- Columbia ML-6084/MS-6684;
33m/s; rel 1965; cip
- Columbia MS-7289; 33s; rel
1969; cip
- Columbia MS-7521; 33s; rel
1970; cip
- Columbia MG-31190; 33s; 2
discs; rel 1972; cip
- Columbia (English) 72384; 33
- RCA LSC-3349; 33s; rel 1973;
del 1975
- RCA ARL-1-0109; 33s; rel 1973;
cip
- Time-Life STL-570; 33s; rel
1979

[2000] World Symphony Orchestra;
Fiedler, Arthur (cond)
- Federation of People-to-People
Programs WSO-1; 33s; rel 1973

Fantasy, Piano (1952-57)

[2001] Fierro, Charles (pf)
- Delos DEL-25436; 33s; rel
1979; cip

[2002] Lee, Noel (pf)
- Valois (French) MB-430; 33m; rel
1962

[2003] Masselos, William (pf)
- Columbia ML-5568/MS-6168;
33m/s; rel 1960; del 1965
- Odyssey
32-16-0039/32-16-0040;
33m/s; rel 1967; cip

[2004] Peebles, Antony (pf)
- Unicorn RHS-323; 33s; rel 1974

[2005] Singer, Joan (pf)
- Golden Age GAR-1008-09; 33s;
2 discs; rel 1977?

[2006] Smit, Leo (pf)
Rec 1/78
- Columbia M2-35901; 33s; 2
discs; rel 1979; cip

House on the Hill, The (1925)

[2007] Texas Boys Choir; Smith, Gregg
(cond)
Rec 1976
- Vox SVBX-5353; 33s; 3 discs; rel
1979; cip

Immorality, An (1925)

[2008] Pennsylvania College of Women
Chorus; Wichmann, Russell W.
(cond)
- ASCAP CB-161; 33m (Pittsburgh
International Contemporary Music
Festival); rel pre-1956

[2009] Treadway, Kevin (sop); Buratto,
Alan (pf)
Rec 1976
- Vox SVBX-5353; 33s; 3 discs; rel
1979; cip

Immorality, An (1925) (cont'd)

[2010] Vienna State Academy Chorus;
Grossman, Ferdinand (cond)
- Vox PLP-7750; 33m; rel 1952;
del 1956

In Evening Air (1969)

[2011] Dickinson, Peter (pf)
Rec 3/28/77
- Unicorn RHS-353; 33s; rel 1978
- Unicorn UNI-72017; 33s; rel
1978
- Unicorn RHS-253; 33s; rel
1978*

[2012] Hautzig, Walter (pf)
- Musical Heritage Society
MHS-4126; 33s; rel 197?

[2013] Singer, Joan (pf)
- Golden Age GAR-1008-09; 33s;
2 discs; rel 1977?

[2014] Smit, Leo (pf)
Rec 1/78
- Columbia M2-35901; 33s; 2
discs; rel 1979; cip

In the Beginning (1947)

[2015] McGown (voice); Pfeiffer College
Concert Choir; Brewer, Richard
(cond)
- Pfeiffer 1; 33s; rel 1966; del
1968

[2016] McKay, Marjorie (m sop); Gregg
Smith Singers; Smith, Gregg
(cond)
- Everest LPBR-6129/SDBR-3129;
33m/s; rel 1965; cip

[2017] Miller, Mildred (m sop); New
England Conservatory Chorus;
Copland, Aaron (cond)
Rec 3/29/65
- CBS 32-11-0017/32-11-0018;
33m/s; rel 1967; del 1970
- Columbia M-30375; 33s; rel
1970; cip

[2018] Morgan, Beverly (m sop);
Tanglewood Festival Chorus;
Oliver, John (cond)
- Deutsche Grammophon
2530.912; 33s; rel 1979; cip

[2019] Surian, Gloria (sop); San Jose
State College A Cappella
Chamber Chorus; Erlendson,
William (cond)
- Music Library MLR-7007; 33m;
rel 1952; del 1974

[2020] Weldon, Irene (sop); Wartburg
College Choir; Fritschell, James
(cond)
- Musical Heritage Society
MHS-3167; 33s; rel 1975

[2021] Whikehart Chorale; Whikehart,
Lewis E. (cond)
- Lyrichord LL-124/LLST-7124;
33m/s; rel 1964; cip

Inscape (1967)
[2022] New York Philharmonic; Bernstein, Leonard (cond)
- Columbia MS-7431; 33s; rel 1970; cip
- CBS (English) 73198; 33s

John Henry (1940, rev 1952)
[2023] New Philharmonia Orchestra; Copland, Aaron (cond)
Rec 10/29/68
- Columbia M-33586; 33s; rel 1975; cip

Lark (1938)
[2024] Hale, Robert (bar); New England Conservatory Chorus; Copland, Aaron (cond)
Rec 3/29/65
- CBS 32-11-0017/32-11-0018; 33m/s; rel 1967; del 1970
- Columbia M-30375; 33s; rel 1970; cip

(Three) Latin American Sketches (1972)
[2025] New Philharmonia Orchestra; Copland, Aaron (cond)
- Columbia M-33269; 33s; rel 1975; cip

Letter from Home (1944, rev 1962)
[2026] London Symphony Orchestra; Copland, Aaron (cond)
Rec 10/26/68
- Columbia M-33586; 33s; rel 1975; cip

[2027] Vienna Radio Orchestra; Eger, Joseph (cond)
Rec 6/67
- Westminster XWN-19131/WST-17131; 33m/s; rel 1968; del 1969
- Music Guild MS-858; 33s; rel 1969; del 1971

Lincoln Portrait (1942)
[2028] Douglas, Melvyn (nar); Boston Symphony Orchestra; Koussevitzky, Serge (cond)
Rec 2/7/46
- Victor 11-9389-90 (in set DM-1088); 78; 2 discs; rel 1947
- Victor 11-9391-92; 78; 2 discs; rel 1947
- RCA LCT-1152; 33m; rel 1954; del 1956
- RCA AVM-1-1739; 33m; rel 1976; del 1980

[2029] Fonda, Henry (nar); London Symphony Orchestra; Copland, Aaron (cond)
Rec 10/29/68
- Columbia M-30649; 33s; rel 1971; cip
- Columbia D3M-33720; 33s; 3 discs; rel 1975; cip
- Columbia (English) 72872; 33s

Lincoln Portrait (1942) (cont'd)
[2030] Fox (nar); Susquehanna University Symphonic Band; Steffy (cond)
- WFB 386; 33m; rel 1962; del 1963

[2031] Heston, Charlton (nar); Utah Symphony Orchestra; Abravanel, Maurice (cond)
- Vanguard VRS-1088/VSD-2115; 33m/s; rel 1963; cip
- Vanguard SRV-348-SD; 33s; rel 1976; cip

[2032] Peck, Gregory (nar); Los Angeles Philharmonic Orchestra; Mehta, Zubin (cond)
- London CS-6613; 33s; rel 1969; cip
- London (English) SXL-6388; 33s

[2033] Ragin, John (nar); Pittsburgh Symphony Orchestra; Steinberg, William (cond)
- ASCAP CB-179; 33m (Pittsburgh International Contemporary Music Festival); rel 1954

[2034] Sandburg, Carl (nar); New York Philharmonic; Kostelanetz, Andre (cond)
- Columbia ML-5347/MS-6040; 33m/s; rel 1959; del 1965
- Columbia 91-A0-2007; 33m; rel 1972; cip

[2035] Santos, Paulo (nar) (in Portuguese); Orquesta Sinfonica Brasileira; Copland, Aaron (cond)
Rec 1963
- CBS (Brazilian) 60078; 33m; rel 1963

[2036] Spencer, Kenneth (nar); New York Philharmonic; Rodzinski, Artur (cond)
- Columbia 12343-44D (in set MX-266); 78; 2 discs; rel 1946
- Columbia 12345-46D; 78; 2 discs; rel 1946
- Columbia ML-2042; 33m; 10''; rel pre-1949; del 1956

[2037] Stevenson, Adlai (nar); Philadelphia Orchestra; Ormandy, Eugene (cond)
- Columbia ML-6084/MS-6684; 33m/s; rel 1965; cip
- Columbia (English) 72384; 33

[2038] Sujo, Juana (nar) (in Spanish); Orquesta Sinfonica de Venezuela; Copland, Aaron (cond)
Rec 1957
- Sociedad Amigos de la Musica SAM-8; 33; rel 1963

Midsummer Nocturne
[2039] Smit, Leo (pf)
Rec 1/78
- Columbia M2-35901; 33s; 2 discs; rel 1979; cip

Music for a Great City (1964)
[2040] London Symphony Orchestra; Copland, Aaron (cond)
Rec 6/13-14/64
- CBS 32-11-0001/32-11-0002; 33m/s; rel 1966; del 1970
- Columbia M-30374; 33s; rel 1970; cip
- Columbia (English) 72466; 33

Music for Movies (1942)
[2041] MGM Chamber Orchestra; Winograd, Arthur (cond)
- MGM E-3334; 33m; rel 1956; del 1959
- MGM E-3367; 33m; rel 1956; del 1959

[2042] New Philharmonia Orchestra; Copland, Aaron (cond)
- Columbia M-33586; 33s; rel 1975; cip

Music for Movies: Sunday Traffic
[2043] orchestra
- Boosey & Hawkes 0-2241; 78; rel pre-1956

Music for Radio (Prairie Journal) (1937)
[2044] MGM Orchestra; Winograd, Arthur (cond)
- MGM E-3367; 33m; rel 1956; del 1959

Music for the Theatre (1925)
[2045] Eastman-Rochester Symphony Orchestra; Hanson, Howard (cond)
- Victor 17688-90 (in set DM-744); 78; 3 discs; rel 1941
- Victor 17694-96 (in set AM-744); 78; 3 discs; rel 1941

[2046] MGM Orchestra; Solomon, Izler (cond)
- MGM E-3095; 33m; rel 1954; del 1959
- MGM E-3367; 33m; rel 1956; del 1959

[2047] New York Philharmonic; Bernstein, Leonard (cond)
- Columbia ML-5755/MS-6355; 33m/s; rel 1962; cip (Excerpt: Dance)
- Columbia ML-6098/MS-6698; 33m/s; rel 1965; cip
- Columbia MG-30071; 33s; 2 discs; rel 1970; cip (Excerpt: Dance)
- Columbia (English) 72074; 33
- Columbia (English) 72352; 33

[2048] Vienna Symphony Orchestra; Hendl, Walter (cond)
- American Recording Society ARS-12; 33m; rel 1952
- American Recording Society ARS-110; 33m; rel pre-1956
- Desto D-418/DST-6418; 33m/s; rel 1965; cip

Night Thoughts (Homage to Ives) (1972)

[2049] Dickinson, Peter (pf)
Rec 3/28/77
- Unicorn RHS-353; 33s; rel 1978
- Unicorn UNI-72017; 33s; rel 1978
- Unicorn RHS-253; 33s; rel 1978*

[2050] Fierro, Charles (pf)
- Delos DEL-25436; 33s; rel 1979; cip

[2051] Singer, Joan (pf)
- Golden Age GAR-1008-09; 33s; 2 discs; rel 1977?

[2052] Smit, Leo (pf)
Rec 1/78
- Columbia M2-35901; 33s; 2 discs; rel 1979; cip

Nonet for Solo Strings (1960)

[2053] Columbia String Ensemble; Copland, Aaron (cond)
Rec 4/6/62
- Columbia M-32737; 33s; rel 1974; cip

North Star (1943): The Younger Generation

[2054] Hope, Patty; Brynner, Rocky; Martin, Michael; Baker, David (pf); Morris, John (pf)
- Walden W-300; 33m; rel 1953; del 1961

Old American Songs (1950) (voice and piano version)

[2055] Pears, Peter (ten); Britten, Benjamin (pf)
Rec 1950
- Gramophone DA-7038-39; 78; 2 discs; rel 1951

[2056] Symonette, Randolph (b bar); Harnley, Lesley (pf)
- Colosseum CLPS-1008; 33m; rel 1951; del 1958

[2057] Tear, Robert (ten); Ledger, Philip (pf)
- Argo ZRG-862; 33s; rel 1977

[2058] Warfield, William (bar); Copland, Aaron (pf)
Rec 7/10/51
- Columbia ML-2206; 33m; 10"; rel 1952; del 1956

Old American Songs (voice and piano version): Simple Gifts

[2059] Uppman, Theodor (bar); Rogers, Allen (pf)
Rec 1/24/62, 2/2/62, and 2/7/62
- Internos INT-0001; 33m; rel 1962; del 1970

Old American Songs (voice and band version)

[2060] Perez, Antonio (bar); University of Kansas Symphonic Band; Foster, Robert E. (cond)
- Golden Crest CRS-4187; 33s; rel 1979

Old American Songs (voice and orchestra version)

[2061] Warfield, William (bar); Columbia Symphony Orchestra; Copland, Aaron (cond)
Rec 5/3-4/62
- Columbia ML-5897/MS-6497; 33m/s; rel 1963; cip

Old American Songs: Long Time Ago (arr for chorus)

[2062] Seattle Chamber Singers; Shangrow, George (cond)
Rec 8/1-8/76
- Voyager VRLP-701S; 33s; rel 1976

Old American Songs: I Bought Me a Cat (arr for chorus by Fine)

[2063] Abbey Singers
- Decca DL-10073/DL-710073; 33m/s; rel 1963; del 1973

Old American Songs, Set 2 (1952) (voice and orchestra version)

[2064] Warfield, William (bar); Columbia Symphony Orchestra; Copland, Aaron (cond)
Rec 5/3-4/62
- Columbia ML-5897/MS-6497; 33m/s; rel 1963; cip
- Columbia (English) 72218; 33

Old American Songs, Set 2 (voice and piano version): Zion's Walls and At the River

[2065] Verrett, Shirley (sop); Wadsworth, Charles (pf)
Rec 1/30/65
- RCA LM-2835/LSC-2835; 33m/s; rel 1965; del 1967

Old American Songs, Set 2: Ching-a-Ring Chaw (arr for chorus)

[2066] Budapest Children's Choir; Botka, Valeria (cond); Czanyi, Laszlo (cond)
Rec 10/11/65
- RCA LM-2861/LSC-2861; 33m/s; rel 1966; del 1971

[2067] Seattle Chamber Singers; Shangrow, George (cond)
Rec 8/1-8/76
- Voyager VRLP-701S; 33s; rel 1976

Old American Songs, Set 2: At the River (arr for chorus by Raymond Wilding-White)

[2068] New England Conservatory Chorus; De Varon, Lorna Cooke (cond)
- Golden Crest NEC-111; 33s; rel 1975; cip

Our Town (piano version) (1944)

[2069] Smit, Leo (pf)
Rec ca 1946
- Concert Hall A-2; 78; 4 discs; rel 1946
- Concert Hall CHC-51; 33m; 10"; rel 1950; del 1953

Our Town (piano version): Story of Our Town

[2070] Foldes, Andor (pf)
- Vox 16069 (in set 174); 78; 10"; rel 1947

Our Town (Orchestral Suite) (1945)

[2071] Little Orchestra Society; Scherman, Thomas (cond)
- Decca DL-7527; 33m; 10"; rel 1952; del 1957
- Brunswick AXL-2006; 33m; rel pre-1956

[2072] London Symphony Orchestra; Copland, Aaron (cond)
Rec 11/8/65
- Columbia MS-7375; 33s; rel 1970; cip
- Columbia D3M-33720; 33s; 3 discs; rel 1975; cip
- Columbia (English) 72809; 33s

[2073] Utah Symphony Orchestra; Abravanel, Maurice (cond)
- Vanguard VRS-1088/VSD-2115; 33m/s; rel 1963; cip
- Vanguard SRV-348-SD; 33s; rel 1976; cip

Outdoor Overture, An (1938)

[2074] Boston Pops Orchestra; Fiedler, Arthur (cond)
- Deutsche Grammophon 2584.027; 33s; rel 1971
- Polydor 24.5006; 33s; rel 1971; del 1976

[2075] Cleveland Pops Orchestra; Lane, Louis (cond)
- Epic LC-3819/BC-1154; 33m/s; rel 1962; del 1965

[2076] London Symphony Orchestra; Copland, Aaron (cond)
Rec 11/8/65
- Columbia MS-7375; 33s; rel 1970; cip

[2077] Utah Symphony Orchestra; Abravanel, Maurice (cond)
- Vanguard VRS-1088/VSD-2115; 33m/s; rel 1963; cip
- Vanguard SRV-348-SD; 33s; rel 1976; cip

Outdoor Overture, An (band version) (1941)
[2078] Band of the Irish Guards
- Boosey & Hawkes MT-2142; 78; rel 1948

Passacaglia, Piano (1921-22)
[2079] Aitken, Webster (pf)
- Walden W-101; 33m; rel 1953; del 1961
- Lyrichord LL-104; 33m; rel 1962; cip

[2080] Chodack, Walter (pf)
- Ades (French) 14.002; 33s; rel 1976

[2081] Fierro, Charles (pf)
- Delos DEL-25436; 33s; rel 1979; cip

[2082] Silverman, Robert (pf)
- Orion ORS-7280; 33s; rel 1972; cip

[2083] Singer, Joan (pf)
- Golden Age GAR-1008-09; 33s; 2 discs; rel 1977?

[2084] Smit, Leo (pf)
Rec 1/78
- Columbia M2-35901; 33s; 2 discs; rel 1979; cip

(Four) Piano Blues (1926-48)
[2085] Copland, Aaron (pf)
Rec ca 1950
- Decca K-2372; 78; rel pre-1952
- Decca LX-3042; 33m; 10"; rel 1950
- London LPS-298; 33m; 10"; rel 1951; del 1957
- New World NW-277; 33m; rel 1976
- Decca (English) FFRR No LP-495; 33m

[2086] Silverman, Robert (pf)
- Orion ORS-7280; 33s; rel 1972; cip

[2087] Singer, Joan (pf)
- Golden Age GAR-1008-09; 33s; 2 discs; rel 1977?

[2088] Smit, Leo (pf)
- Dot DLP-3111; 33m; rel 1958; del 1966

[2089] Smit, Leo (pf)
Rec 1/78
- Columbia M2-35901; 33s; 2 discs; rel 1979; cip

[2090] Toperczer, Peter (pf)
Rec 6/72-3/73
- Supraphon 111.1721-22; 33s; 2 discs; rel 1975

(Four) Piano Blues: Nos 1 and 4
[2091] Smit, Leo (pf)
- Concert Hall CHC-51; 33m; 10"; rel 1950; del 1953

(Two) Pieces, String Quartet (1923-28)
[2092] Dorian String Quartet
- Columbia 70092D; 78; rel 1940

(Two) Pieces, String Quartet (1923-28) *(cont'd)*
[2093] Kohon Quartet
- Vox SVBX-5305; 33s; 3 discs; rel 1974; cip

(Two) Pieces, String Quartet (string-orchestra version) (1928)
[2094] London Symphony Orchestra Strings; Copland, Aaron (cond)
Rec 11/8/65
- Columbia MS-7375; 33s; rel 1970; cip
- Columbia (English) 72809; 33s

[2095] MGM String Orchestra; Izler, Solomon (cond)
- MGM E-3117; 33m; rel 1954; del 1959

(Two) Pieces, Violin and Piano (1926)
[2096] Gordon, Jacques (vln); Copland, Aaron (pf)
Rec 4/22/35
- Columbia 68321D (in set X-48); 78; rel 1935 (Excerpt: Nocturne)
- Columbia M-220; 78; 2 discs; rel 1935 (Excerpt: Nocturne)
- Columbia 68742D (in set X-68); 78; rel 1937

[2097] Novello, Franco (vln); Gachet, Maria (pf)
- Cetra (Italian) LPC-55040; 33; rel 1968

(Two) Pieces, Violin and Piano: Nocturne
[2098] Kaufman, Louis (vln); Copland, Aaron (pf)
Rec ca 1948
- Concert Hall C-10; 78; rel pre-1952

(Two) Pieces, Violin and Piano: Ukelele Serenade
[2099] Kaufman, Louis (vln); Kaufman, Annette (pf)
- Vox 627; 78; 3 discs; rel 1948
- Concert Hall CHC-58; 33m; rel 1950; del 1957
- Concert Hall CHS-1140; 33m; rel 1952; del 1957
- Concert Hall H-1640; 33m; rel 1957; del 1959

[2100] Steiner, Diana (vln); Berfield, David (pf)
- Orion ORS-74160; 33s; rel 1975; cip

(Twelve) Poems of Emily Dickinson (1949-50)
[2101] Addison, Adele (sop); Copland, Aaron (pf)
Rec 11/18/64
- CBS 32-11-0017/32-11-0018; 33m/s; rel 1967; del 1970
- Columbia M-30375; 33s; rel 1970; cip

(Twelve) Poems of Emily Dickinson (1949-50) *(cont'd)*
[2102] Browne, Sandra (m sop); Isador, Michael (pf)
- Enigma Classics (English) VAR-1029; 33s; rel 1977

[2103] Lipton, Martha (m sop); Copland, Aaron (pf)
Rec 12/22/50 and 4/4/52
- Columbia ML-5106; 33m; rel 1956; del 1967

[2104] Tear, Robert (ten); Ledger, Philip (pf)
- Argo ZRG-862; 33s; rel 1977

(Twelve) Poems of Emily Dickinson: The Chariot and When They Come Back
[2105] Hanks, John Kennedy (ten); Friedberg, Ruth (pf)
- Duke University Press DWR-6417-18; 33m; 2 discs; rel 1966; del 1975

(Twelve) Poems of Emily Dickinson: Why Do They Shut Me Out of Heaven and The World Feels Dusty
[2106] Tatum, Nancy (sop); Parsons, Geoffrey (pf)
- London OS-26053; 33s; rel 1968; del 1971

Poet's Song (1927)
[2107] Beardslee, Bethany (sop); Helps, Robert (pf)
- New World NW-243; 33s; rel 1977

[2108] Dickinson, Meriel (m sop); Dickinson, Peter (pf)
Rec 3/28/77
- Unicorn RHS-353; 33s; rel 1978
- Unicorn UNI-72017; 33s; rel 1978
- Unicorn RHS-253; 33s; rel 1978*

Preamble for a Solemn Occasion (1949)
[2109] London Symphony Orchestra; Copland, Aaron (cond)
Rec 6/14/64
- Columbia M-31714; 33s; rel 1973; cip
- Columbia (English) 73116; 33

Quartet, Piano and Strings (1950)
[2110] Cardiff Festival Ensemble
- Argo ZRG-794; 33s; rel 1975

[2111] Chodack, Walter (pf); Trio a Cordes de Paris
- Ades (French) 14.002; 33s; rel 1976

[2112] Copland, Aaron (pf); Juilliard String Quartet (members of)
Rec 10/28/66
- CBS 32-11-0041/32-11-0042; 33m/s; rel 1967; del 1970
- Columbia M-30376; 33s; rel 1970; cip

Quartet, Piano and Strings (1950)
(cont'd)
[2113] New York Piano Quartet
Rec 10/50
- Columbia ML-4421; 33m; rel
1951; del 1965

Quiet City (1939)
[2114] Academy of St. Martin-in-the-Fields;
Marriner, Neville (cond)
- Argo ZRG-845; 33s; rel 1976;
cip
- Time-Life STL-570; 33s; rel
1979

[2115] Buffalo Philharmonic Orchestra;
Foss, Lukas (cond)
- Turnabout TVS-34398; 33s; rel
1971; cip
- Turnabout (English) TVS-34398;
33s

[2116] Chamber Orchestra of
Copenhagen; Moriarty, John
(cond)
- Cambridge CRS-2823; 33s; rel
1970; cip

[2117] Concert Arts Orchestra;
Golschmann, Vladimir (cond)
- Capitol P-8245; 33m; rel 1954;
del 1969
- Capitol CTL-7056; 33m; rel
pre-1956

[2118] Eastman-Rochester Symphony
Orchestra; Hanson, Howard
(cond)
- Mercury MG-40003; 33m; rel
1953; del 1957
- Mercury MG-50076; 33m; rel
1957; del 1963
- Mercury MG-50421/SR-90421;
33m/s; rel 1965; del 1971
- Eastman-Rochester Archives
ERA-1001; 33s; rel 1974; cip

[2119] Hamburg Philharmonia; Korn,
Richard (cond)
- Allegro ALG-3149; 33m; rel
1954?

[2120] Janssen Symphony Orchestra of
Los Angeles; Janssen, Werner
(cond)
- Artist 1401-04 (in set JS-13);
78; 4 discs; rel 1949
- Artist 100; 33m; rel pre-1949;
del 1952
- Everest LPBR-6118/SDBR-3118;
33m/s; rel 1965; del 1975

[2121] London Symphony Orchestra;
Copland, Aaron (cond)
Rec 11/6/65
- Columbia MS-7375; 33s; rel
1970; cip
- Columbia (English) 72809; 33s

[2122] Utah Symphony Orchestra;
Abravanel, Maurice (cond)
- Vanguard VRS-1088/VSD-2115;
33m/s; rel 1963; cip
- Vanguard SRV-348-SD; 33s; rel
1976; cip

Red Pony, The (Suite) (1948)
[2123] Little Orchestra Society; Scherman,
Thomas (cond)
- Decca DL-9616; 33m; rel 1952;
del 1971
- Brunswick AXTL-1022; 33m; rel
pre-1956
- Decca DCM-3207; 33m; rel
1962; del 1970

[2124] New Philharmonia Orchestra;
Copland, Aaron (cond)
- Columbia M-33586; 33s; rel
1975; cip

[2125] St. Louis Symphony Orchestra;
Previn, Andre (cond)
- Columbia ML-5983/MS-6583;
33m/s; rel 1964; del 1970
- Odyssey Y-31016; 33s; rel
1972; cip

Rodeo (Four Dance Episodes) (1942)
[2126] Ballet Theatre Orchestra; Levine,
Joseph (cond)
- Capitol L-8198; 33m; 10"; rel
1953; del 1957
- Capitol P-8196; 33m; rel 1953;
del 1963
- Capitol CCL-7516; 33m; rel
pre-1956
- Capitol SAL-9020; 33m; rel
pre-1956 (excerpts)
- Capitol HDR-21004; 33m; 4
discs; rel 1966; del 1970

[2127] Concert Arts Orchestra; Irving,
Robert (cond)
- Capitol SP-8702; 33s; rel 1969;
del 1970
- EMI/Studio Two TWO-302; 33s;
rel 1969
- Seraphim S-60198; 33s; rel
1972; cip
- Angel S-36084; 33s; rel 1975;
del 1978

[2128] Dallas Symphony Orchestra; Dorati,
Antal (cond)
- Victor 12-0267-69 (in set
DM-1214); 78; 3 discs; rel 1948
- Victor 12-0270-72 (in set
M-1214); 78; 3 discs; rel 1948
- Victor WDM-1214; 45; 3-7"; rel
1950
- RCA LM-32; 33m; 10"; rel
1950; del 1956

[2129] Dallas Symphony Orchestra;
Johanos, Donald (cond)
- Turnabout TVS-34169; 33s; rel
1967; cip

[2130] Dallas Symphony Orchestra; Mata,
Eduardo (cond)
- RCA ARL-1-2862; 33s; rel 1978;
cip
- RCA CRL-3-3270; 33s; 3 discs;
rel 1979; cip (excerpts)
- Time-Life STL-570; 33s; rel
1979

Rodeo (Four Dance Episodes) (1942) *(cont'd)*
[2131] London Symphony Orchestra;
Copland, Aaron (cond)
Rec 10/29/68
- Columbia MS-7521; 33s; rel
1970; cip
- Columbia M-30114; 33s; rel
1970; cip
- Columbia D3M-33720; 33s; 3
discs; rel 1975; cip
- Columbia (English) 72888; 33

[2132] Minneapolis Symphony Orchestra;
Dorati, Antal (cond)
Rec 12/21/57
- Mercury MG-50172/SR-90172;
33m/s; rel 1958/1959; del
1971

[2133] Morton Gould and his Orchestra;
Gould, Morton (cond)
- RCA LM-2195/LSC-2195;
33m/s; rel 1958; del 1976
- RCA AGL-1-1335; 33s; rel 1976;
cip

[2134] New York Philharmonic; Bernstein,
Leonard (cond)
- Columbia ML-5575/MS-6175;
33m/s; rel 1960; del 1979
- Columbia MG-30071; 33s; 2
discs; rel 1970; cip
- Columbia M-31823; 33s; rel
1973; cip
- Columbia (English) 72411; 33

[2135] Utah Symphony Orchestra;
Abravanel, Maurice (cond)
- Westminster
XWN-18840/WST-14058;
33m/s; rel 1959; del 1967
- Music Guild MS-164; 33s; rel
1970; del 1971
- Westminster WGS-8170; 33s; rel
1972; cip

Rodeo (Four Dance Episodes): Excerpts
[2136] Boston Pops Orchestra; Fiedler,
Arthur (cond)
- RCA LM-1726; 33m; rel 1953;
del 1961 (Excerpts: Saturday
Night Waltz and Hoedown)
- Victor 49-4003-06 (in set
WDM-1726); 45; 4-7"; rel
1953? (Excerpts: Saturday Night
Waltz and Hoedown)
- RCA LM-2294/LSC-2294;
33m/s; rel 1959; del 1964
(Excerpt: Hoedown)
- RCA LM-2744/LSC-2744;
33m/s; rel 1964; del 1975
(Excerpt: Hoedown)
- RCA LSC-3277; 33s; rel 1972;
cip (Excerpt: Hoedown)
- RCA ARL-1-0109; 33s; rel 1973;
cip (Excerpt: Hoedown)

[2137] Capitol Symphony Orchestra;
Dragon, Carmen (cond)
- Capitol P-8523/SP-8523;
33m/s; rel 1960; del 1970
(Excerpt: Hoedown)

**Rodeo (Four Dance Episodes):
Excerpts** *(cont'd)*
[2138] Cleveland Pops Orchestra; Lane,
Louis (cond)
Rec 8/58
- Epic LC-3539/BC-1013; 33m/s;
rel 1959; del 1968 (Excerpts:
Buckaroo Holiday, Saturday Night
Waltz, and Hoedown)

[2139] National Symphony Orchestra;
Mitchell, Howard (cond)
- RCA LM-2704/LSC-2704;
33m/s; rel 1964; del 1968
(Excerpt: Hoedown)

[2140] New York Philharmonic; Bernstein,
Leonard (cond)
- Columbia ML-6271/MS-6871;
33m/s; rel 1966; del 1976
(Excerpt: Hoedown)
- Columbia MS-7213-14 (in set
M2X-795); 33s; 2 discs; rel
1969; cip (Excerpt: Hoedown)
- Columbia M3X-31068; 33s; 3
discs; rel 1972; cip (Excerpt:
Hoedown)
- Columbia MG-35186; 33s; 2
discs; rel 1978 (Excerpts:
Saturday Night Waltz and
Hoedown)

[2141] Philadelphia Orchestra; Ormandy,
Eugene (cond)
- Columbia MS-7289; 33s; rel
1969; cip (Excerpt: Hoedown)

[2142] orchestra
- RCA LSC-3300; 33s; rel 1972
(Excerpt: Hoedown)

**Rodeo: Hoedown (string-orchestra
version) (1945)**
[2143] New Concert String Ensemble;
Wilber, Jay (cond)
- Boosey & Hawkes S-2095; 78;
10''; rel 1949

**Rodeo: Hoedown (arr for 4 pfs by
Marga Richter)**
[2144] Manhattan Piano Quartet
- MGM E-3224; 33m; rel 1956;
del 1959

**Rodeo: Hoedown (arr for vln and
orch by Arthur Harris)**
[2145] Stern, Isaac (vln); Columbia
Symphony Orchestra; Katims,
Milton (cond)
- Columbia ML-5896/MS-6496;
33m/s; rel 1963; del 1966
- Columbia ML-6225/MS-6825;
33m/s; rel 1966; cip

**Rodeo: Hoedown (arr for vln and
pf)**
[2146] Haendel, Ida (vln); Moore, Gerald
(pf)
- Gramophone B-9994; 78; 10'';
rel pre-1952

[2147] Kaufman, Louis (vln); Kaufman,
Annette (pf)
- Vox 627; 78; 3 discs; rel 1948

**Rodeo: Hoedown (arr for vln and
pf)** *(cont'd)*
- Concert Hall CHC-58; 33m; rel
1950; del 1957
- Concert Hall CHS-1140; 33m; rel
1952; del 1957
- Concert Hall H-1640; 33m; rel
1957; del 1959

Salon Mexico, El (1933-36)
[2148] Berlin Symphony Orchestra; Balzer,
Joseph (cond)
- Allegro-Royale 1517; 33m; rel
1954

[2149] Boston Pops Orchestra; Fiedler,
Arthur (cond)
- RCA LM-1928; 33m; rel 1955;
del 1968
- RCA LM-6129; 33m; 3 discs; rel
1956; del 1958
- RCA LM-2294/LSC-2294;
33m/s; rel 1959; del 1964
- RCA LSC-3303; 33s; rel 1972;
cip
- RCA ARL-1-0109; 33s; rel 1973;
cip

[2150] Boston Symphony Orchestra;
Koussevitzky, Serge (cond)
- Victor 15363-64 (in set M-546);
78; 2 discs; rel 1939
- Victor 18448-49A (in set
DM-546); 78; 2 discs; rel 1939
- Gramophone DB-3812-13; 78; 2
discs; rel 1939
- RCA LCT-1134; 33m; rel 1954;
del 1960
- Gramophone 7ERL-1040; 45; 7'';
rel pre-1956
- RCA AVM-1-1739; 33m; rel
1976; del 1980

[2151] Dallas Symphony Orchestra; Mata,
Eduardo (cond)
- Silver Burdett 76289; 33; rel
1969
- RCA ARL-1-2862; 33s; rel 1978;
cip
- Time-Life STL-570; 33s; rel
1979

[2152] London Philharmonic Orchestra;
Pritchard, John (cond)
- EMI CFP-40240; 33s; rel 1976

[2153] Minneapolis Symphony Orchestra;
Dorati, Antal (cond)
Rec 12/21/57
- Mercury MG-50172/SR-90172;
33m/s; rel 1958/1959; del
1971

[2154] National Symphony Orchestra;
Mitchell, Howard (cond)
- Westminster WL-5286; 33m; rel
1954; del 1956
- Nixa WLP-5286; 33m; rel
pre-1956
- Westminster XWN-18284; 33m;
rel 1956; del 1968
- Westminster WST-14284; 33s;
rel 1968; del 1970
- Westminster W-9727; 33m; rel
1970; del 1971

Salon Mexico, El (1933-36) *(cont'd)*
[2155] New Philharmonia Orchestra;
Copland, Aaron (cond)
- Columbia M-33269; 33s; rel
1975; cip
- Columbia D3M-33720; 33s; 3
discs; rel 1975; cip

[2156] New York Philharmonic; Bernstein,
Leonard (cond)
Rec 5/20/61
- Columbia ML-5755/MS-6355;
33m/s; rel 1962; cip
- Columbia ML-5841/MS-6441;
33m/s; rel 1963; del 1979
- Columbia MGP-13; 33s; 2 discs;
rel 1969; del 1976
- Columbia MG-30071; 33s; 2
discs; rel 1970; cip
- Columbia MS-7521; 33s; rel
1970; cip
- Columbia (English) 72074; 33

[2157] Utah Symphony Orchestra;
Abravanel, Maurice (cond)
- Westminster
XWN-18840/WST-14063;
33m/s; rel 1959; del 1967
- Music Guild MS-167; 33s; rel
1970; del 1971
- Angel S-37314; 33s; rel 1978;
cip

[2158] Vienna State Opera Orchestra;
Litschauer, Franz (cond)
- Vanguard VRS-439; 33m; rel
1953; del 1965

**Salon Mexico, El (arr by Johnny
Green as Fantasia Mexicana for
the film Fiesta)**
[2159] Al Goodman Orchestra; Goodman,
Al (cond)
- Victor 28-0419; 78; rel 1947
- Victor 52-0065; 45; 7''; rel
1950?

[2160] Columbia Symphony Orchestra;
Bernstein, Leonard (cond)
- Columbia ML-2203; 33m; 10'';
rel 1952; del 1956
- Philips N-02600R; 33m; 10''; rel
pre-1956
- Philips (English) NBR-6019;
33m; 10''; rel pre-1956
- Columbia CL-920; 33m; rel
1956; del 1965

[2161] MGM Orchestra; Marrow, Macklin
(cond)
- MGM 30016; 78; 10''; rel
1947?

[2162] orchestra; Morales, Novo (cond)
- RCA; 33m; rel 1953

**Salon Mexico, El (arr for pf by
Leonard Bernstein)**
[2163] Rivers, James (pf)
- Educo 3069; 33

Salon Mexico, El (arr for pf and orch by Johnny Green)

[2164] Hambro, Leonid (pf); MGM Orchestra; Marrow, Macklin (cond)
- MGM E-539; 33m; rel pre-1953
- MGM 9144 (in set E-3136); 33m; rel 1954; del 1958
- MGM (Italian) ESPQ-502; 45; 7"; rel pre-1956

[2165] Semprini, A. (pf?); orchestra
- Fonit LP-110; 33m; rel pre-1956

Scherzo humoristique (Le chat et la souris) (1920)

[2166] Nishry, Varda (pf)
- Ace of Diamonds (Decca); 33; rel 1970

[2167] Sanroma, Jesus Maria (pf)
- Victor 15861 (in set M-646); 78; rel 1940

[2168] Silverman, Robert (pf)
- Orion ORS-7280; 33s; rel 1972; cip

[2169] Singer, Joan (pf)
- Golden Age GAR-1008-09; 33s; 2 discs; rel 1977?

[2170] Smit, Leo (pf)
Rec 1/78
- Columbia M2-35901; 33s; 2 discs; rel 1979; cip

Scherzo humoristique (arr for orch)

[2171] Decca Symphony Orchestra
- Decca 23106 (in set A-85); 78; 10"; rel pre-1952

Second Hurricane, The (1936)

[2172] High School of Music and Art (New York) Soloists and Chorus; narrator; New York Philharmonic; Bernstein, Leonard (cond)
Rec 4/30/60
- Columbia ML-5581/MS-6181; 33m/s; rel 1960; del 1971
- New World NW-241; 33s; rel 1978 (Excerpts: Jeff's Song, Queenie's Song, Sextet, and Two Willow Hill)

Sentimental Melody (1926)

[2173] Singer, Joan (pf)
- Golden Age GAR-1008-09; 33s; 2 discs; rel 1977?

[2174] Smit, Leo (pf)
- Concert Hall CHC-51; 33m; 10"; rel 1950; del 1953

Sextet, Clarinet, Piano, and String Quartet (1937)

[2175] Oppenheim, David (cl); Hambro, Leonid (pf); Juilliard String Quartet
- Columbia ML-4492; 33m; rel 1952; del 1958

Sextet, Clarinet, Piano, and String Quartet (1937) (cont'd)

[2176] Wright, Harold (cl); Copland, Aaron (pf); Juilliard String Quartet
Rec 10/27/66
- CBS 32-11-0041/32-11-0042; 33m/s; rel 1967; del 1970
- Columbia M-30376; 33s; rel 1970; cip

Short Symphony (Symphony No 2) (1932-33)

[2177] London Symphony Orchestra; Copland, Aaron (cond)
Rec 11/5/65
- Columbia MS-7223; 33s; rel 1969; cip

Sonata, Piano (1939-41)

[2178] Aitken, Webster (pf)
- Walden W-101; 33m; rel 1953; del 1961
- Lyrichord LL-104; 33m; rel 1962; cip

[2179] Bernstein, Leonard (pf)
- Camden CAL-214; 33m; rel 1955; del 1958

[2180] Fleisher, Leon (pf)
- Epic LC-3862/BC-1262; 33m/s; rel 1963; del 1966

[2181] Foldes, Andor (pf)
- Deutsche Grammophon; 33m; rel 1956

[2182] Knardahl, Eva (pf)
Rec 4/3-4/76
- BIS LP-52; 33s; rel 1977

[2183] Lee, Noel (pf)
- Valois (French) MB-430; 33m; rel 1962

[2184] Silverman, Robert (pf)
- Orion ORS-7280; 33s; rel 1972; cip

[2185] Singer, Joan (pf)
- Golden Age GAR-1008-09; 33s; 2 discs; rel 1977?

[2186] Smit, Leo (pf)
- Concert Hall A-2; 78; 4 discs; rel 1946

[2187] Smit, Leo (pf)
Rec 1/78
- Columbia M2-35901; 33s; 2 discs; rel 1979; cip

[2188] Somer, Hilde (pf)
- CRI-171; 33m/s; rel 1963/1974; cip

Sonata, Violin and Piano (1942-43)

[2189] Fuchs, Joseph (vln); Smit, Leo (pf)
- Decca DL-8503; 33m; rel 1950; del 1970
- Decca AXT-233048; 33m; rel pre-1953
- Brunswick AXTL-1047; 33m; rel pre-1956

[2190] Glenn, Carroll (vln); Somer, Hilde (pf)
- CRI-171; 33m/s; rel 1963/1974; cip

Sonata, Violin and Piano (1942-43) (cont'd)

[2191] Kaufman, Louis (vln); Copland, Aaron (pf)
Rec ca 1948
- Concert Hall 1356-60 (in set C-10); 78; 3 discs; rel pre-1950

[2192] Lack, Fredell (vln); Hambro, Leonid (pf)
- Allegro AL-33; 33m; rel 1950; del 1959
- Allegro-Elite LEG-9001; 33m; rel 1964; del 1970

[2193] Laredo, Jaime (vln); Schein, Ann (pf)
- Desto DC-6439; 33s; rel 1975; cip

[2194] Menuhin, Yehudi (vln); Gazelle, Marcel (pf)
- RCA LM-6092; 33m; 2 discs; rel 1960; cip
- London HLP-27

[2195] Sandler, Myron (vln); Maury, Lowndes (pf)
- Crystal S-631; 33s; rel 1970; cip

[2196] Stern, Isaac (vln); Copland, Aaron (pf)
Rec 1/16-17/68
- Columbia M-32737; 33s; rel 1974; cip

Statements (1932-35)

[2197] London Symphony Orchestra; Copland, Aaron (cond)
Rec ca 1958
- Everest LPBR-6015/SDBR-3015; 33m/s; rel 1959; cip

[2198] London Symphony Orchestra; Copland, Aaron (cond)
Rec 11/5/65
- CBS 32-11-0001/32-11-0002; 33m/s; rel 1966; del 1970
- Columbia M-30374; 33s; rel 1970; cip
- Columbia (English) 72466; 33

Statements: (No 5) Jingo

[2199] Victor Symphony Orchestra; Bernstein, Leonard (cond)
- Victor 12-1032 (in set DM-1333); 78; rel pre-1950
- Victor M-1333; 78; rel pre-1952
- Victor 49-0680-82 (in set WDM-1333); 45; 3-7"; rel 1950

Symphonic Ode (1927-29, rev 1955)

[2200] London Symphony Orchestra; Copland, Aaron (cond)
Rec 10/2-3/67
- Columbia M-31714; 33s; rel 1973; cip
- Columbia (English) 73116; 33

Symphony No 3 (1944-46)

[2201] Berlin Symphony Orchestra; Rubahn, Gerd (cond)
- Allegro-Royale 1513; 33m; rel 1954

Symphony No 3 (1944-46) (cont'd)

[2202] London Symphony Orchestra;
Copland, Aaron (cond)
Rec ca 1958
- Everest LPBR-6018/SDBR-3018;
33m/s; rel 1959; cip
- Time-Life STL-570; 33s; rel
1979

[2203] Minneapolis Symphony Orchestra;
Dorati, Antal (cond)
- Mercury MG-50018; 33m; rel
1953; del 1965
- Mercury MG-50421/SR-90421;
33m/s; rel 1965; del 1971

[2204] New York Philharmonic; Bernstein,
Leonard (cond)
- Columbia ML-6354/MS-6954;
33m/s; rel 1967; cip
- Columbia (English) 72559; 33

[2205] Philharmonia Orchestra; Copland,
Aaron (cond)
- Columbia M-35113; 33s; rel
1979; cip

Symphony, Organ and Orchestra (1924)

[2206] Biggs, E. Power (org); New York
Philharmonic; Bernstein, Leonard
(cond)
Rec 1/3/67
- Columbia ML-6458/MS-7058;
33m/s; rel 1968; cip
- Columbia (English) 72643; 33

Tender Land, The (1952-54, rev 1955)

[2207] Clements, Joy (sop); Turner,
Claramae (m sop); Cassilly,
Richard (ten); Fredericks, Richard
(bar); Treigle, Norman (b bar);
Choral Art Society; New York
Philharmonic; Copland, Aaron
(cond)
Rec 7/31/65
- Columbia ML-6214/MS-6814;
33m/s; rel 1966; del 1970
- Columbia (English) 72433; 33
- New World NW-241; 33s; rel
1978 (Excerpts: It Promises to
be a Fine Night and The Promise
of Living)

Tender Land, The (Orchestral Suite) (1956)

[2208] Boston Symphony Orchestra;
Copland, Aaron (cond)
Rec 11/13/59
- RCA LM-2401/LSC-2401;
33m/s; rel 1960; cip
- RCA-Victrola (English)
VICS-1488; 33s; rel 1970*
- Time-Life STL-570; 33s; rel
1979

Variations, Orchestra (1957)

[2209] Hartford Symphony Orchestra;
Mahler, Fritz (cond)
- Vanguard VRS-1067/VSD-2085;
33m/s; rel 1961; del 1969

Variations, Orchestra (1957) (cont'd)

[2210] London Symphony Orchestra;
Copland, Aaron (cond)
Rec 10/26/68
- Columbia M-31714; 33s; rel
1973; cip
- Columbia (English) 73116; 33

[2211] Louisville Orchestra; Whitney,
Robert (cond)
Rec 1957?
- LOU-59-1; 33m (Louisville
Orchestra First Edition Records
1959 No 1); rel 1959; del 1980

Variations, Piano (1930)

[2212] Aitken, Webster (pf)
- Walden W-101; 33m; rel 1953;
del 1961
- Lyrichord LL-104; 33m; rel
1962; cip

[2213] Copland, Aaron (pf)
Rec 4/2/35 and 4/5/35
- Columbia 68320-21D (in set
X-48); 78; 2 discs; rel 1935
- Columbia M-220; 78; 2 discs; rel
1935
- New World NW-277; 33m; rel
1976

[2214] Fierro, Charles (pf)
- Delos DEL-25436; 33s; rel
1979; cip

[2215] Glazer, Frank (pf)
- Concert-Disc M-1217/CS-217;
33m/s; rel 1960; del 1977
- Everest (English) SDBR-4217;
33s

[2216] Johannesen, Grant (pf)
- Golden Crest CRS-4111; 33q; rel
1972; cip
- Golden Crest CRSD-1, CRSTT-1;
33s; 2 discs; rel 1977; cip

[2217] Lee, Noel (pf)
- Valois (French) MB-775; 33; rel
1966

[2218] McCabe, John (pf)
- Pye (English) GSGC-1416; 33

[2219] Masselos, William (pf)
- Columbia ML-5568/MS-6168;
33m/s; rel 1960; del 1965
- Odyssey
32-16-0039/32-16-0040;
33m/s; rel 1967; cip

[2220] Shields, Roger (pf)
- Vox SVBX-5303; 33s; 3 discs; rel
1977; cip
- Time-Life STL-570; 33s; rel
1979

[2221] Singer, Joan (pf)
- Golden Age GAR-1008-09; 33s;
2 discs; rel 1977?

[2222] Smit, Leo (pf)
Rec 1/78
- Columbia M2-35901; 33s; 2
discs; rel 1979; cip

Variations, Piano (1930) (cont'd)

[2223] Webster, Beveridge (pf)
- Dover HCR-5265/HCRST-7265;
33m/s; rel 1966/1967; del
1975
- Dover HCRST-7014; 33s; rel
1966; del 1967

Variations on a Shaker Song (1967)

[2224] Cornell University Wind Ensemble;
Stith, Marice (cond)
- Cornell CUWE-6; 33s; rel 1971;
cip

Vitebsk (Study on a Jewish Theme) (1928)

[2225] Carlyss, Earl (vln); Adam, Claus
(vcl); Copland, Aaron (pf)
Rec 10/26/66
- CBS 32-11-0041/32-11-0042;
33m/s; rel 1967; del 1970
- Columbia M-30376; 33s; rel
1970; cip

[2226] Gerle, Robert (vln); University of
Oklahoma Trio
- University of Oklahoma 1; 33m;
rel 1957; del 1978

[2227] Glenn, Carroll (vln); McCracken,
Charles (vcl); Somer, Hilde (pf)
- CRI-171; 33m/s; rel
1963/1974; cip

[2228] Karman, Ivor (vln); Freed, David
(vcl); Copland, Aaron (pf)
Rec 4/22/35
- Columbia 68741-42D (in set
X-68); 78; 2 discs; rel 1937

[2229] Pintavalle, John (vln); Joachim,
Heinrich (vcl); Mocsany, Edith (pf)
- Decca DL-10126/DL-710126;
33m/s; rel 1966; del 1973

[2230] Silverstein, Joseph (vln); Eskin,
Jules (vcl); Frank, Claude (pf)
- RCA LM-6167/LSC-6167;
33m/s; 3 discs; rel 1966; del
1976
- Time-Life STL-570; 33s; rel
1979

[2231] Western Arts Trio
- Laurel LR-109; 33s; rel 1980;
cip

Vocalise (1928)

[2232] Luening, Ethel (sop); Copland,
Aaron (pf)
Rec ca 10/35
- New Music Quarterly Recordings
1211 (2-1); 78; rel 1936

Vocalise (flute and piano version) (1972)

[2233] Padorr, Laila (fl); Swearingen, Anita
(pf)
- Laurel-Protone LP-14; 33s; rel
1977; cip

CORDLE, Andrew E.*

Interlude for Flute and Bassoon
[2234] Schrock, Sheryl (fl); Cordle, Andrew
E. (bsn)
- Orion ORS-77269; 33s; rel
1977; cip

CORIGLIANO, John (1938-)

**Concerto, Oboe and Orchestra
(1975)**
[2235] Lucarelli, Bert (ob); American
Symphony Orchestra; Akiyama,
Kazuyoshi (cond)
- RCA ARL-1-2534; 33s; rel 1978;
cip

**Concerto, Piano and Orchestra
(1968)**
[2236] Somer, Hilde (pf); San Antonio
Symphony; Alessandro, Victor
(cond)
- Mercury SR-90517; 33s; rel
1969; del 1974
- Mercury SRI-75118; 33s; rel
1979; cip

Naked Carmen, The
[2237] Hess, David; Moore, Melba; Walker,
William; Detroit Symphony
Orchestra; Corigliano, John (cond)
- Mercury SRM-1-604; 33s; rel
1970; del 1972

Poem in October (1969)
[2238] White, Robert (ten); Nyfenger,
Thomas (fl); Lucarelli, Bert (ob);
Rabbai, Joseph (cl); American
String Quartet; Peress, Maurice
(hpschd) (cond)
- RCA ARL-1-2534; 33s; rel 1978;
cip

Psalm 8
[2239] San Antonio Symphony
Mastersingers; Melone, Roger
(cond)
- Telarc 5026; 33s; rel 1978; cip

Sonata, Violin and Piano (1963)
[2240] Corigliano, John, Sr. (vln); Votapek,
Ralph (pf)
- CRI-215; 33m/s; rel 1968; cip

CORNER, Philip (1933-)

Gamelan II
[2241] Gamelan Son of Lion
- Folkways FTS-31313; 33s; rel
1980; cip

CORTES, Ramiro (1933-)

**Chamber Concerto, Violoncello and
Twelve Wind Instruments (1958)**
[2242] McCracken, Charles (vcl);
Contemporary Chamber
Ensemble; Weisberg, Arthur
(cond)
- CRI-181; 33m/s; rel 1964/?; cip

Duo, Flute and Oboe (1967)
[2243] Westwood Wind Quintet (members
of)
- Crystal S-812; 33s; rel 1973; cip

Meditation (1963)
[2244] United States International
Orchestra; Lambro, Phillip (cond)
- Crystal S-861; 33s; rel 1973; cip

(Three) Movements for Five Winds
[2245] Westwood Wind Quintet
- Crystal S-812; 33s; rel 1973; cip

Sonata, Violin and Piano
[2246] Goldman (vln); Brown (pf)
- Orion ORS-76212; 33s; rel
1977; cip

**Sonata, Violoncello and Piano, E
Minor**
[2247] Members of the Angelus Trio
- Orion ORS-77279; 33s; rel
1978; cip

**Trio, Piano and Strings (1959, rev
1965)**
[2248] Angelus Trio
- Orion ORS-77279; 33s; rel
1978; cip

CORY, George (1920-)

Most Men
[2249] Reardon, John (bar); Hebert, Bliss
(pf)
- Serenus SRE-1019/SRS-12019;
33m/s; rel 1967; cip

(Two) Songs for Children
[2250] Tozzi, Giorgio (b); Walmer, Max
(pf)
- Serenus SRS-12030; 33s; rel
1971; cip

(Four) Songs of Night
[2251] Tozzi, Giorgio (b); Walmer, Max
(pf)
- Serenus SRS-12030; 33s; rel
1971; cip

COTEL, Morris Moshe (1943-)

**August 12, 1952 (The Night of the
Murdered Poets) (1978)**
[2252] Wallach, Eli (nar); Hein, Richard
(hn); Masuzzo, Dennis (cb);
McCauley, John (pf); Gibbs,
Ronald (vib) (xyl); Goldstein,
Mark (perc); Cotel, Morris Moshe
(cond)
- Grenadilla GS-1051; 33s; rel
1979

Sonata, Piano (1976)
[2253] Cotel, Morris Moshe (pf)
- Grenadilla GS-1051; 33s; rel
1979

COUSINS, M. Thomas (1914-72)

Glorious Everlasting (1950)
[2254] Mormon Tabernacle Choir;
Schreiner, Alexander (org); Asper,
Frank (org); Cornwall, J. Spencer
(cond)
- Columbia ML-5203; 33m; rel
1957; del 1962

COWELL, Henry (1897-1965)

Advertisement (1914)
[2255] Cowell, Henry (pf)
- Concert Hall B-9; 78; 4 discs; rel
pre-1948
- Circle L-51-101; 33m; rel 1952;
del 1955
- CRI-109; 33m/s; rel 1957/?; cip
- Folkways FM-3349; 33m; rel
1963; cip

[2256] Hays, Doris (pf)
- Finnadar SR-9016; 33s; rel
1977; cip

[2257] Shields, Roger (pf)
- Vox SVBX-5303; 33s; 3 discs; rel
1977; cip

Aeolian Harp (1923)
[2258] Cowell, Henry (pf)
- Concert Hall B-9; 78; 4 discs; rel
pre-1948
- Circle L-51-101; 33m; rel 1952;
del 1955
- CRI-109; 33m/s; rel 1957/?; cip
- Folkways FX-6160; 33m; rel
1958; cip
- Folkways FM-3349; 33m; rel
1963; cip

[2259] Hays, Doris (pf)
- Finnadar SR-9016; 33s; rel
1977; cip

[2260] Miller, Robert (pf)
- New World NW-203; 33s; rel
1977

[2261] Shields, Roger (pf)
- Vox SVBX-5303; 33s; 3 discs; rel
1977; cip

**Air and Scherzo, Alto Saxophone
and Piano (1961)**
[2262] Black, Robert (al sax); Black,
Patricia (pf)
- Brewster; 33; rel 197?

Amiable Conversation (1917)
[2263] Cowell, Henry (pf)
- Circle L-51-101; 33m; rel 1952;
del 1955
- Folkways FM-3349; 33m; rel
1963; cip

[2264] Hays, Doris (pf)
- Finnadar SR-9016; 33s; rel
1977; cip

Ancient Desert Drone (1939-40)
[2265] Janssen Symphony Orchestra of
Los Angeles; Janssen, Werner
(cond)
- Artist 1401-04 (in set JS-13);
78; 4 discs; rel 1949
- Artist 100; 33m; rel pre-1949;
del 1952
- Everest LPBR-6118/SDBR-3118;
33m/s; rel 1965; del 1975

Anger Dance (1914)
[2266] Cowell, Henry (pf)
- Circle L-51-101; 33m; rel 1952;
del 1955
- Folkways FM-3349; 33m; rel
1963; cip

[2267] Hays, Doris (pf)
- Finnadar SR-9016; 33s; rel
1977; cip

Antinomy (1914)
[2268] Cowell, Henry (pf)
- Circle L-51-101; 33m; rel 1952;
del 1955
- Folkways FM-3349; 33m; rel
1963; cip

[2269] Hays, Doris (pf)
- Finnadar SR-9016; 33s; rel
1977; cip

Ballad, String Orchestra (1954)
[2270] Louisville Orchestra; Mester, Jorge
(cond)
- LOU-68-2/LS-68-2; 33m/s
(Louisville Orchestra First Edition
Records 1968 No 2); rel 1968;
cip

[2271] Vienna Orchestral Society; Adler, F.
Charles (cond)
- Unicorn UNLP-1011; 33m; rel
1955; del 1957
- Unicorn UNLP-1045; 33m; rel
1957; del 1959

Ballad, Woodwind Quintet (1956)
[2272] Lawrence, Eleanor (fl); Arrowsmith,
William (ob); Neidich, Irving (cl);
Vrotney, Richard (bsn); Tillotson,
Brooks (hn)
- Musical Heritage Society
MHS-3578; 33s; rel 1977

Ballad and Dance
[2273] Eastman-Rochester Symphony
Orchestra; Hanson, Howard
(cond)
- Mercury EP-1-5063; 45; 7''; rel
pre-1956

Banshee, The (1925)
[2274] Cowell, Henry (pf)
- Circle L-51-101; 33m; rel 1952;
del 1955
- CRI-109; 33m/s; rel 1957/?; cip
- Folkways FX-6160; 33m; rel
1958; cip
- Folkways FM-3349; 33m; rel
1963; cip

Banshee, The (1925) *(cont'd)*
[2275] Hays, Doris (pf)
- Finnadar SR-9016; 33s; rel
1977; cip

[2276] Miller, Robert (pf)
- New World NW-203; 33s; rel
1977

(Six) Casual Developments (1933)
[2277] Russo, John (cl); Ignacio, Lydia
Walton (pf)
- Capra 1204; 33s; rel 1976; cip

Celestial Violin (1944)
[2278] Szigeti, Joseph (vln); Cowell, Henry
(pf)
- Columbia MM-920; 78; rel 1948

**(Four) Declamations with Return
(1949)**
[2279] Barab, Seymour (vcl); Masselos,
William (pf)
- Paradox X-102; 78; 3-10''
- Paradox PL-10001; 33m; 10'';
rel 1950; del 1957

[2280] King, Terry (vcl); Jensen, John (pf)
- CRI-386; 33s; rel 1978; cip

Donkey, The (1946)
[2281] McCollum, John (ten); Biltcliffe,
Edwin (pf)
- St/And SPL-411-12; 33m; 2
discs; rel 1963; del 1964
- Desto D-411-12/DST-6411-12;
33m/s; 2 discs; rel 1964; cip

Dynamic Motion (1914)
[2282] Cowell, Henry (pf)
- Circle L-51-101; 33m; rel 1952;
del 1955
- Folkways FM-3349; 33m; rel
1963; cip

[2283] Hays, Doris (pf)
- Finnadar SR-9016; 33s; rel
1977; cip

Episode (1916)
[2284] Rogers, Herbert (pf)
- CRI-281; 33s; rel 1972; cip

Exultation (1919)
[2285] Cowell, Henry (pf)
- Circle L-51-101; 33m; rel 1952;
del 1955
- Folkways FM-3349; 33m; rel
1963; cip

[2286] Gowen, Bradford (pf)
- New World NW-304; 33s; rel
1979

[2287] Shields, Roger (pf)
- Vox SVBX-5303; 33s; 3 discs; rel
1977; cip

Fabric (1917?)
[2288] Cowell, Henry (pf)
- Circle L-51-101; 33m; rel 1952;
del 1955

Fabric (1917?) *(cont'd)*
- Folkways FM-3349; 33m; rel
1963; cip

[2289] Hays, Doris (pf)
- Finnadar SR-9016; 33s; rel
1977; cip

Fairy Answer (1929)
[2290] Cowell, Henry (pf)
- Circle L-51-101; 33m; rel 1952;
del 1955
- Folkways FM-3349; 33m; rel
1963; cip

Fiddler's Jig (1952)
[2291] Vienna Orchestral Society; Adler, F.
Charles (cond)
- Unicorn UNLP-1008; 33m; rel
1955; del 1957
- Unicorn UNLP-1045; 33m; rel
1957; del 1959

Gravely and Vigorously (1963)
[2292] King, Terry (vcl)
- CRI-386; 33s; rel 1978; cip

Harp of Life, The (1924)
[2293] Cowell, Henry (pf)
- Circle L-51-101; 33m; rel 1952;
del 1955
- Folkways FM-3349; 33m; rel
1963; cip

[2294] Hays, Doris (pf)
- Finnadar SR-9016; 33s; rel
1977; cip

Harper Minstrel Sings, The (1934)
[2295] Martin, Charlotte (pf)
- Educo 3021; 33m; rel 1968; del
1972

Hero Sun, The (1922)
[2296] Hays, Doris (pf)
- Finnadar SR-9016; 33s; rel
1977; cip

Homage to Iran (1957)
[2297] Avakian, Leopold (vln); Andrews,
Mitchell (pf); Bahar, Basil (Persian
dr)
- CRI-173; 33m/s; rel 1963/?; cip

**Hymn and Fuguing Tune No 1
(1943)**
[2298] Leeds Concert Band; Todd, Peter
(cond)
- Columbia ML-4254; 33m; rel
1950; del 1956

**Hymn and Fuguing Tune No 2
(1944)**
[2299] Boston Symphony Orchestra;
Koussevitzky, Serge (cond)
- CRI-248(78); 33s; rel 1979; cip

Hymn and Fuguing Tune No 2 (1944) (cont'd)

[2300] Louisville Orchestra; Mester, Jorge (cond)
- LOU-68-2/LS-68-2; 33m/s (Louisville Orchestra First Edition Records 1968 No 2); rel 1968; cip

[2301] Vienna Orchestral Society; Adler, F. Charles (cond)
- Unicorn UNLP-1011; 33m; rel 1955; del 1957
- Unicorn UNLP-1045; 33m; rel 1957; del 1959

Hymn and Fuguing Tune No 3 (1944)

[2302] Louisville Orchestra; Mester, Jorge (cond)
- LOU-68-2/LS-68-2; 33m/s (Louisville Orchestra First Edition Records 1968 No 2); rel 1968; cip

Hymn and Fuguing Tune No 5 (1945)

[2303] Randolph Singers; Randolph, David (cond)
- Concert Hall CHC-52; 33m; rel 1950; del 1957

[2304] Vienna Orchestral Society; Adler, F. Charles (cond)
- Unicorn UNLP-1011; 33m; rel 1955; del 1957
- Unicorn UNLP-1045; 33m; rel 1957; del 1959

Hymn and Fuguing Tune No 9 (1950)

[2305] King, Terry (vcl); Jensen, John (pf)
- CRI-386; 33s; rel 1978; cip

Hymn and Fuguing Tune No 10 (1955)

[2306] Academy of St. Martin-in-the-Fields; Marriner, Neville (cond)
- Argo ZRG-845; 33s; rel 1976; cip

. . . if He Please (1955)

[2307] Norwegian Choir of Solo Singers; Oslo Philharmonic Orchestra; Strickland, William (cond)
- CRI-165; 33m; rel 1963; cip
- CRI-217; 33m/s; rel 1968; cip

(Six) Ings (1916)

[2308] Hays, Doris (pf)
- Finnadar SR-9016; 33s; rel 1977; cip

(Six) Ings Plus One (1916)

[2309] Rogers, Herbert (pf)
- CRI-281; 33s; rel 1972; cip

Irishman Dances, The (1934)

[2310] Martin, Charlotte (pf)
- Educo 3021; 33m; rel 1968; del 1972

Irishman Dances, The (1934) (cont'd)

[2311] Richter, Marga (pf)
- MGM E-3147; 33m; rel 1955; del 1959

Jig (1925)

[2312] Cowell, Henry (pf)
- Concert Hall B-9; 78; 4 discs; rel pre-1948
- Circle L-51-101; 33m; rel 1952; del 1955
- Folkways FM-3349; 33m; rel 1963; cip

Lilt of the Reel (1925)

[2313] Cowell, Henry (pf)
- Circle L-51-101; 33m; rel 1952; del 1955
- CRI-109; 33m/s; rel 1957/?; cip
- Folkways FM-3349; 33m; rel 1963; cip

[2314] Hays, Doris (pf)
- Finnadar SR-9016; 33s; rel 1977; cip

Luther's Carol for his Son (1947)

[2315] Columbia University Men's Glee Club; Smith, Gregg (cond) Rec 1976
- Vox SVBX-5353; 33s; 3 discs; rel 1979; cip

Maestoso (1929)

[2316] Hays, Doris (pf)
- Finnadar SR-9016; 33s; rel 1977; cip

Ongaku (1957)

[2317] Japan Philharmonic Symphony Orchestra; Watanabe, Akeo (cond)
- CRI-132; 33m/s; rel 1960/?; cip

[2318] Louisville Orchestra; Whitney, Robert (cond)
- LOU-59-5; 33m (Louisville Orchestra First Edition Records 1959 No 5); rel 1960; del 1975

(Three) Ostinati with Chorales (1937): Two Chorales and Ostinato

[2319] Marx, Josef (ob); Fine, Vivian (pf)
- New Music Quarterly Recordings 1413 (18-19); 78; rel 1938

(Three) Ostinati with Chorales: No 2

[2320] McBride, Robert (ob); Nowak, Lionel (pf)
- Yaddo II-4; 78; 10''; rel 1940

Ostinato pianissimo (1934)

[2321] Manhattan Percussion Ensemble; Cage, John (cond); Price, Paul (cond)
- Time 58000/S-8000; 33m/s; rel 1961; del 1970

Ostinato pianissimo (1934) (cont'd)

- Mainstream MS-5011; 33s; rel 1970; del 1979

[2322] New Jersey Percussion Ensemble; DesRoches, Raymond (cond)
- Nonesuch H-71291/HQ-1291; 33s/q; rel 1974/1976; cip

[2323] Percussions-Ensemble?; Fink, Siegfried (cond)
- Thorofon MTH-149; 33s; rel 197?

Persian Set (1956-57)

[2324] Leopold Stokowski and his Orchestra; Stokowski, Leopold (cond)
- CRI-114; 33m/s; rel 1957/?; cip

Piece pour piano avec cordes (1924)

[2325] Hays, Doris (pf)
- Finnadar SR-2-720; 33s; 2 discs; rel 1980; cip

[2326] Miller, Robert (pf)
- New World NW-203; 33s; rel 1977

Processional (1944)

[2327] Ellsasser, Richard (org)
- MGM E-3064; 33m; rel 1953; del 1959

Quartet, Strings, No 2 (Movement for String Quartet) (1934)

[2328] Beaux-Arts String Quartet
- CRI-173; 33m/s; rel 1963/?; cip

[2329] Dorian String Quartet
- Columbia 69747D (in set M-388); 78; rel pre-1942

Quartet, Strings, No 3 (Mosaic Quartet) (1935)

[2330] Beaux-Arts String Quartet
- CRI-173; 33m/s; rel 1963/?; cip

Quartet, Strings, No 4 (United Quartet) (1936)

[2331] Beaux-Arts String Quartet
- CRI-173; 33m/s; rel 1963/?; cip

Quartet, Strings, No 5 (1955-56)

[2332] Beaux-Arts String Quartet
- Columbia ML-5788/MS-6388; 33m/s; rel 1962; del 1966

Quartet Euphometric (1916-19)

[2333] Composers Quartet
- Golden Crest NEC-115; 33s/q; rel 1977; cip

[2334] Emerson String Quartet
- New World NW-218; 33s; rel 1978

Quartet Romantic (1915-17)
[2335] Dunkel, Paul (fl); Palma, Susan (fl); Schulte, Rolf (vln); Graham, John (vla)
- New World NW-285; 33s; rel 1978

Saturday Night at the Firehouse (1948)
[2336] Vienna Philharmonic Orchestra; Adler, F. Charles (cond)
- SPA-47; 33m; rel 1953; del 1970

Set of Five (1952)
[2337] Ajemian, Anahid (vln); Ajemian, Maro (pf); Bailey, Elden (perc)
- MGM E-3454; 33m; rel 1957; del 1959

Set of Two: Prelude (1955)
[2338] Brink, Robert (vln); Pinkham, Daniel (pf)
- CRI-109; 33m/s; rel 1957/?; cip

Sinfonietta (1928)
[2339] Louisville Orchestra; Mester, Jorge (cond)
- LOU-68-1/LS-68-1; 33m/s (Louisville Orchestra First Edition Records 1968 No 1); rel 1968; cip

Sinister Resonance (1930?)
[2340] Cowell, Henry (pf)
- Circle L-51-101; 33m; rel 1952; del 1955
- CRI-109; 33m/s; rel 1957/?; cip
- Folkways FM-3349; 33m; rel 1963; cip

[2341] Hays, Doris (pf)
- Finnadar SR-9016; 33s; rel 1977; cip

Snows of Fujiyama, The (1922)
[2342] Cowell, Henry (pf)
- Circle L-51-101; 33m; rel 1952; del 1955
- Folkways FM-3349; 33m; rel 1963; cip

Sonata, Violin and Piano, No 1 (1945)
[2343] Szigeti, Joseph (vln); Bussotti, Carlo (pf)
- Columbia ML-4841; 33m; rel 1954; del 1968
- Columbia CML-4841; 33m; rel 1968; del 1974
- Columbia AML-4841; 33m; rel 1974; del 1979

Suite, Wind Quintet (1931)
[2344] Barrere Woodwind Ensemble
- New Music Quarterly Recordings 1111 (11-1); 78; rel 1935

[2345] New Art Wind Quintet
- Classic Editions CE-2003; 33m; 2 discs; rel 1953; del 1961

Symphony No 4 (Short Symphony) (1946)
[2346] Eastman-Rochester Symphony Orchestra; Hanson, Howard (cond)
- Mercury MG-40005; 33m; rel 1953; del 1957
- Mercury MG-50078; 33m; rel 1957; del 1963
- Mercury SRI-75111; 33s; rel 1978; cip

Symphony No 5 (1948)
[2347] Vienna Symphony Orchestra; Dixon, Dean (cond)
- American Recording Society ARS-2; 33m; 10"; rel 1952*
- American Recording Society ARS-112; 33m; rel pre-1956
- Desto D-406/DST-6406; 33m/s; rel 1964; cip

Symphony No 7 (1952)
[2348] Vienna Symphony Orchestra; Strickland, William (cond)
- MGM E-3084; 33m; rel 1956; del 1959
- CRI-142; 33m/s; rel 1961/?; cip

Symphony No 8 (Choral) (1952)
[2349] Ohio High School Folk Chorus and Orchestra; Johnson, Thor (cond) Rec 3/1/53
- Wilmington College 1; 33m; 10"

Symphony No 10 (1952-53)
[2350] Vienna Orchestral Society; Adler, F. Charles (cond)
- Unicorn UNLP-1008; 33m; rel 1955; del 1957
- Unicorn UNLP-1045; 33m; rel 1957; del 1959

Symphony No 11 (Seven Rituals of Music) (1953-54)
[2351] Louisville Orchestra; Whitney, Robert (cond)
- Columbia ML-5039; 33m; rel 1955; del 1965
- LOU-545-2; 33m (Louisville Orchestra First Edition Records 1955 No 2); rel 1959; del 1972

Symphony No 15 (Thesis) (1960)
[2352] Louisville Orchestra; Whitney, Robert (cond)
- LOU-62-2; 33m (Louisville Orchestra First Edition Records 1962 No 2); rel 1962; del 1978

Symphony No 16 (Icelandic) (1962)
[2353] Iceland Symphony Orchestra; Strickland, William (cond)
- CRI-179; 33m/s; rel 1964/?; cip

Synchrony (1929-30)
[2354] Polish National Radio Orchestra; Strickland, William (cond)
- CRI-217; 33m/s; rel 1968; cip

Tales of Our Countryside (1941)
[2355] Cowell, Henry (pf); All-American Orchestra; Stokowski, Leopold (cond)
- Columbia 11964-65D (in set X-235); 78; 2 discs; rel pre-1943
- Columbia 11966-67D; 78; 2 discs; rel pre-1943

Tides of Manaunan (1912?)
[2356] Cowell, Henry (pf)
- Circle L-51-101; 33m; rel 1952; del 1955
- CRI-109; 33m/s; rel 1957/?; cip
- Folkways FM-3349; 33m; rel 1963; cip

[2357] Hays, Doris (pf)
- Finnadar SR-9016; 33s; rel 1977; cip

Tiger (1928?)
[2358] Cowell, Henry (pf)
- Circle L-51-101; 33m; rel 1952; del 1955
- Folkways FM-3349; 33m; rel 1963; cip

[2359] Hays, Doris (pf)
- Finnadar SR-9016; 33s; rel 1977; cip

Toccanta (1938)
[2360] Boatwright, Helen (sop); Smith, Carleton Sprague (fl); Parisot, Aldo (vcl); Kirkpatrick, John (pf)
- Columbia ML-4986; 33m; rel 1955; del 1968
- Columbia CML-4986; 33m; rel 1968; del 1974
- Columbia AML-4986; 33m; rel 1974; cip

Trio, Violin, Violoncello, and Piano (1964-65)
[2361] Philharmonia Trio
- CRI-211; 33m/s; rel 1966/?; cip

Triple Rondo (1961)
[2362] Polin, Claire (fl); Schlomovitz, Phyllis (hp)
- Ars Nova/Ars Antiqua AN-1004; 33m; rel 1971; del 1973
- Educo 4031; 33s; rel 1974*

Trumpet of Angus Og (1924)
[2363] Cowell, Henry (pf)
- Consolidated 7338; 78; 10"
- Circle L-51-101; 33m; rel 1952; del 1955
- Folkways FM-3349; 33m; rel 1963; cip

[2364] Hays, Doris (pf)
- Finnadar SR-9016; 33s; rel 1977; cip

Twilight in Texas (1966)
[2365] Andre Kostelanetz and his
Orchestra; Kostelanetz, Andre
(cond)
- Columbia MG-33728; 33s; 2
discs; rel 1976; del 1979

**Two-Part Invention in Three Parts
(1950)**
[2366] Rogers, Herbert (pf)
- CRI-281; 33s; rel 1972; cip

[2367] Shields, Roger (pf)
- Vox SVBX-5303; 33s; 3 discs; rel
1977; cip

Variations, Orchestra (1956)
[2368] Polish National Radio Orchestra;
Strickland, William (cond)
- CRI-217; 33m/s; rel 1968; cip

Vocalise (1937)
[2369] Luening, Ethel (sop); Luening, Otto
(fl); Johansen, Gunnar (pf)
- Yaddo M-1; 78; 10"; rel 1938

Voice of Lir (1919)
[2370] Cowell, Henry (pf)
- Circle L-51-101; 33m; rel 1952;
del 1955
- Folkways FM-3349; 33m; rel
1963; cip

[2371] Hays, Doris (pf)
- Finnadar SR-9016; 33s; rel
1977; cip

What's This? (1914)
[2372] Cowell, Henry (pf)
- Circle L-51-101; 33m; rel 1952;
del 1955
- Folkways FM-3349; 33m; rel
1963; cip

[2373] Hays, Doris (pf)
- Finnadar SR-9016; 33s; rel
1977; cip

COWLES, Eugene (1860-1948)
Crossing the Bar
[2374] Stanley, Frank C. (b)
- Victor 4556; 78; 10"; rel
pre-1925?

Forgotten
[2375] House, Judson (ten)
- Columbia A-2011; 78

[2376] Williams, Evan (ten); orchestra
- Victor 6309; 78; rel 1907-10
- Victor 74160; 78; rel 1907-10

CRANDELL, Robert E. (1910-)
Carnival Suite
[2377] Baker, Robert (org)
Rec 7/28/57
- Mirrosonic DRE-1004; 33m; 2
discs; rel 1958; del 1965

[2378] Mason, Marilyn (org)
- Aeolian-Skinner AS-7; 33m; rel
1956; del 1958

Carnival Suite *(cont'd)*
- Washington WAS-7; 33m; rel
1958; del 1962

CRAWFORD SEEGER, Ruth (1901-53)
Chant (1930)
[2379] Magdamo, Priscilla (al); Gregg
Smith Singers; Smith, Gregg
(cond)
Rec 1976
- Vox SVBX-5353; 33s; 3 discs; rel
1979; cip

Diaphonic Suite No 1 (1930)
[2380] Ostryniec, James (ob)
- CRI-423; 33s; rel 1980; cip

Etude in Mixed Accents (1930)
[2381] Bloch, Joseph (pf)
- CRI-247; 33s; rel 1969; cip

**(Two) Movements for Chamber
Orchestra**
[2382] Boston Musica Viva; Pittman,
Richard (cond)
- Delos DEL-25405; 33s; rel
1975; cip

(Nine) Preludes, Piano (1924-28)
[2383] Bloch, Joseph (pf)
- CRI-247; 33s; rel 1969; cip

(Nine) Preludes, Piano: Nos 6-9
[2384] Mandel, Alan (pf)
- Desto DC-6445-47; 33s; 3 discs;
rel 1975; cip

Quartet, Strings (1931)
[2385] Amati String Quartet
- Columbia ML-5477/MS-6142;
33m/s; rel 1960; del 1968
- Columbia CML-5477/CMS-6142;
33m/s; rel 1968; del 1974
- Columbia AMS-6142; 33s; rel
1974; del 1976

[2386] Composers Quartet
- Nonesuch H-71280; 33s; rel
1973; cip

Quartet, Strings: Andante
[2387] New World String Quartet
- New Music Quarterly Recordings
1011 (1-1); 78; rel 1934

(Three) Songs (1930-32)
[2388] Morgan, Beverly (m sop);
Speculum Musicae (members of);
Dunkel, Paul (cond)
- New World NW-285; 33s; rel
1978

Suite, Wind Quintet (1952)
[2389] Lark Quintet
- CRI-249; 33s; rel 1970; cip

CRESHEVSKY, Noah (1945-)
Broadcast (1973)
[2390] Electronic music
- Opus One 47; 33s; rel 1980; cip

Chaconne (1974)
[2391] Violette, Andrew (pf)
- Opus One 50; 33s; rel 1979; cip

Circuit (1971)
[2392] Rosett, Marianna (hpschd)
- Opus One 45; 33s; rel 1978; cip

Great Performances (1977)
[2393] Sheldon, Paul (cl); Hindell, Leonard
(cbsn); electronic music
- Opus One 47; 33s; rel 1980; cip

Highway (1978)
[2394] Electronic music
- Opus One 50; 33s; rel 1979; cip

**In Other Words (Portrait of John
Cage) (1976)**
[2395] Cage, John (speaker); electronic
music
- Opus One 45; 33s; rel 1978; cip

Portrait of Rudy Perez (1978)
[2396] Electronic music
- Opus One 50; 33s; rel 1979; cip

CRESTON, Paul (1906-)
Bird of the Wilderness (1937)
[2397] Luening, Ethel (sop)
- Yaddo 26A; 78; 10"; rel 1937

**Celebration Overture (Op 61)
(1954)**
[2398] North Texas State University
Concert Band; McAdow, Maurice
(cond)
- Austin 6104; 33m; rel 1961; del
1971

[2399] Ohio State University Concert
Band; McGinnis, Donald E. (cond)
- Coronet S-1501; 33s; rel 1969;
del 1978

[2400] Texas Tech Concert Band; Killion,
Dean (cond)
- Austin 6388; 33m; rel 1964; del
1971

[2401] Yale University Band; Wilson, Keith
(cond)
- Carillon 109; 33m; rel 1960; del
1971

**(Three) Chorales (Op 11) (1936):
Here is thy Footstool**
[2402] De Paur Infantry Chorus; De Paur,
Leonard (cond)
- Columbia 72349D (in set
M-709); 78; rel pre-1948
- Columbia MM-709; 78; 3 discs;
rel pre-1948
- Columbia ML-4144; 33m; rel
pre-1949; del 1958

(Three) Chorales (Op 11) (1936): Here is thy Footstool *(cont'd)*

[2403] Notre Dame Glee Club; Pedtke, Daniel H. (cond)
- MGM E-3212; 33m; rel 1956; del 1959

(Two) Choric Dances (Op 17) (1938)

[2404] Arizona Chamber Orchestra; Hull, Robert (cond)
Rec 9/17/78
- Laurel LR-110; 33s; rel 1979; cip

[2405] Concert Arts Orchestra; Golschmann, Vladimir (cond)
- Capitol P-8245; 33m; rel 1954; del 1969
- Capitol CTL-7056; 33m; rel pre-1956

[2406] Yaddo Orchestra; Shepherd, Arthur (cond)
- Yaddo M-2-3; 78; 2-10"; rel 1938

Concertino, Marimba and Orchestra (Op 21) (1940)

[2407] Owen, Charles (mrmb); Philadelphia Orchestra; Ormandy, Eugene (cond)
- Columbia ML-6377/MS-6977; 33m/s; rel 1967; cip

[2408] Stuber, Ruth (mrmb); Yaddo Chamber Orchestra
- Yaddo II-7; 78; 2 discs; rel 1940

Concerto, Alto Saxophone and Band (Op 26) (1941)

[2409] Underwood, Dale (al sax); Metropolitan Wind Ensemble; Mugol, Rodrigo C. (cond)
- Golden Crest CRS-4136; 33s/q; rel 1975; cip

Corinthians XIII (Op 82) (1963)

[2410] Louisville Orchestra; Whitney, Robert (cond)
- LOU-65-5/LS-65-5; 33m/s (Louisville Orchestra First Edition Records 1965 No 5); rel 1965; cip

Dance Overture (Op 62) (1954)

[2411] Oslo Philharmonic Orchestra; Antonini, Alfredo (cond)
- CRI-111; 33m/s; rel 1957/?; cip

(Five) Dances (Op 1) (1932): Toy Dance, Pastoral Dance, and Festive Dance

[2412] Bennett, Bob L. (pf)
- Educo 3110; 33

Dedication

[2413] Pfeiffer College Concert Choir; Brewer, Richard (cond)
- Pfeiffer 1; 33m; rel 1966; del 1968

Invocation and Dance (Op 58) (1953)

[2414] Louisville Orchestra; Whitney, Robert (cond)
- Columbia ML-5039; 33m; rel 1955; del 1965
- LOU-545-1; 33m (Louisville Orchestra First Edition Records 1955 No 1); rel 1959; del 1975

Legend (Op 31) (1942)

[2415] Leeds Concert Band; Todd, Peter (cond)
- Columbia ML-4254; 33m; rel 1950; del 1956

Lydian Ode (Op 67) (1956)

[2416] Academy Symphony Orchestra of Rome; Rescigno, Nicola (cond)
- RCA LM-2426; 33m; rel 1960; del 1962

Metamorphoses (Op 84) (1964)

[2417] Labrecque, Candida (pf)
- Rhythmicon R-101; 33; rel 1974

Midnight-Mexico

[2418] Andre Kostelanetz and his Orchestra; Kostelanetz, Andre (cond)
- Columbia MG-33728; 33s; 2 discs; rel 1976; del 1979

Partita, Flute, Violin, and Strings (Op 12) (1937)

[2419] Silberberg, Robert (fl); Porter, Lois (vln); Yaddo Orchestra; Creston, Paul (cond)
- Yaddo 103-04; 78; 2-10"; rel 1937 (1st, 2nd, 3rd, and 4th movements)
- Yaddo 7A-B; 78; 10"; rel 1937 (1st and 2nd movements)
- Yaddo 120A; 78; 10"; rel 1937 (1st movement)
- Yaddo 105A; 78; 10"; rel 1937 (5th movement)

[2420] Vienna Symphony Orchestra; Hendl, Walter (cond)
- American Recording Society ARS-23; 33m; 10"; rel 1953
- Desto D-424/DST-6424; 33m/s; rel 1967; cip

Prelude and Dance (Op 76) (1959)

[2421] Cornell University Symphonic Band; Stith, Marice (cond)
- Cornell CUWE-10; 33s; rel 1973; cip

[2422] North Texas State University Concert Band; McAdow, Maurice (cond)
- Austin 6226; 33m; rel 1963; del 1971

Quartet, Strings (Op 8) (1936)

[2423] Hollywood String Quartet
- Capitol P-8260; 33m; rel 1954; del 1958

Quartet, Strings (Op 8) (1936) *(cont'd)*

- Capitol CTL-7063; 33m; rel pre-1956

Rhythmicon, Book 5: Nos 78 and 81-89

[2424] Labrecque, Candida (pf)
- Rhythmicon R-101; 33; rel 1974

Rumor, A (1941)

[2425] Academy of St. Martin-in-the-Fields; Marriner, Neville (cond)
- Argo ZRG-845; 33s; rel 1976; cip

[2426] Hamburg Philharmonia; Korn, Richard (cond)
- Allegro ALG-3148; 33m; rel 1955?

Sonata, Saxophone and Piano (Op 19) (1939)

[2427] Abato, Vincent J. (sax); Creston, Paul (pf)
- Columbia ML-4989; 33m; rel 1955; del 1968
- Columbia CML-4989; 33m; rel 1968; del 1974
- Columbia AML-4989; 33m; rel 1974; del 1976

[2428] Brodie, Paul (sax); Shechter, Myriam (pf)
- Golden Crest RE-7037; 33s; rel 1970; cip

[2429] Londeix, Jean Marie (sax); Pontier, Pierre (pf)
- EMI/His Master's Voice (French) 2C-065-12.805; 33s; rel 1974

[2430] Mule, Marcel (sax); Robin, Solange (pf)
- London LLP-1479; 33m; rel 1957; del 1958

[2431] Pittel, Harvey (sax); Rothfuss, Levering (pf)
- Crystal S-157; 33s; rel 1979; cip

[2432] Rascher, Sigurd (sax); piano
- Award 33-708; 33m; rel 1958; del 1970

[2433] Sinta, Donald (sax); True, Nelita (pf)
- Mark MRS-22868; 33m; rel 1968; cip

Suite, Organ (Op 70)

[2434] Mason, Marilyn (org)
- Mirrosonic CM-7001; 33m; rel 1959

Suite, Organ: Toccata

[2435] Thalben-Ball, George (org)
- Vista VPS-1046; 33s; rel 1977

**Suite, Saxophone and Piano (Op 6)
(1935)**
[2436] Leeson, Cecil (sax); Creston, Paul
(pf)
- New Music Quarterly Recordings
1313 (5-6); 78; rel 1937

**Suite, Saxophone and Piano:
Pastorale and Scherzoso**
[2437] McBride, Robert (sax); Creston,
Paul (pf)
- Yaddo 24A; 78; rel 1937
- Yaddo 34A; 78; rel 1937
- Yaddo 43A; 78; rel 1937
- Yaddo 150B; 78; 10''; rel 1937
(Excerpt: Pastorale)

**Suite, Violin and Piano (Op 18)
(1939)**
[2438] Steiner, Diana (vln); Berfield, David
(pf)
- Orion ORS-74160; 33s; rel
1975; cip

**Symphony No 1 (Op 20) (1940):
Scherzo**
[2439] All-American Orchestra; Stokowski,
Leopold (cond)
- Columbia 11713D; 78; rel
pre-1942

Symphony No 2 (Op 35) (1944)
[2440] National Symphony Orchestra;
Mitchell, Howard (cond)
- Westminster WL-5272; 33m; rel
1954; del 1956
- Nixa WLP-5272; 33m; rel
pre-1956
- Westminster XWN-18456; 33m;
rel 1957; del 1961
- Westminster W-9708; 33m; rel
1964; del 1971

Symphony No 3 (Op 48) (1950)
[2441] National Symphony Orchestra;
Mitchell, Howard (cond)
- Westminster WL-5272; 33m; rel
1954; del 1956
- Nixa WLP-5272; 33m; rel
pre-1956
- Westminster XWN-18456; 33m;
rel 1957; del 1961
- Westminster W-9708; 33m; rel
1964; del 1971

Walt Whitman (Op 53) (1952)
[2442] Academy Symphony Orchestra of
Rome; Rescigno, Nicola (cond)
- RCA LM-2426; 33m; rel 1960;
del 1962

CRIST, Bainbridge (1883-1969)
C'est mon ami
[2443] Muzio, Claudia (sop); orchestra;
Molajoli, Lorenzo (cond)
- Columbia 9114M (in set 289);
78; rel 1937
- Columbia 9171M (in set M-289);
78; rel pre-1948
- Columbia BQX-2523; 78; rel
pre-1948

C'est mon ami *(cont'd)*
- Columbia LCX-30; 78; rel
pre-1948
- Columbia BQX-2509; 78; rel
pre-1948
- Columbia ML-4634; 33m; rel
1953; del 1957

CROSS, Lowell M. (1938-)
(Three) Etudes, Tape (1965)
[2444] Electronic music
- CRI-342; 33s; rel 1975; cip

CRUMB, George (1929-)
Ancient Voices of Children (1970)
[2445] DeGaetani, Jan (m sop); Dash,
Michael (boy sop); Contemporary
Chamber Ensemble; Weisberg,
Arthur (cond)
- Nonesuch H-71255; 33s; rel
1971; cip

Black Angels (Images I) (1970)
[2446] Concord String Quartet
- Vox SVBX-5306; 33s; 3 discs; rel
1973; cip
- Turnabout TVS-34610; 33s; rel
1976; cip

[2447] Gaudeamus String Quartet
- Philips 6500.881; 33s; rel
1975; cip

[2448] New York String Quartet
- CRI-283; 33s; rel 1972; cip

**Dream Sequence (Images II)
(1976)**
[2449] Aeolian Chamber Players; Kaplan,
Lewis (cond)
- Odyssey Y-35201; 33s; rel
1978; cip

**(Eleven) Echoes of Autumn (Echoes
I) (1966)**
[2450] Aeolian Chamber Players
- CRI-233; 33s; rel 1969; cip

**Echoes of Time and the River
(Echoes II) (1967)**
[2451] Louisville Orchestra; Mester, Jorge
(cond)
- LS-71-1; 33s (Louisville
Orchestra First Edition Records
1971 No 1); rel 1971; cip

Lux aeterna (1971)
[2452] DeGaetani, Jan (sop); Penn
Contemporary Players; Wernick,
Richard (cond)
- Odyssey Y-35201; 33s; rel
1978; cip

**Madrigals, Books I, II, III, and IV
(1965-69)**
[2453] DeGaetani, Jan (m sop); University
of Pennsylvania Chamber Players;
Wernick, Richard (cond)
- Acoustic Research AR-0654.085;
33s; rel 1971

**Madrigals, Books I, II, III, and IV
(1965-69)** *(cont'd)*
[2454] Suderburg, Elizabeth (sop);
Skowronek, Felix (fl); Vokolek,
Pamela (hp); Warner, W. Ring
(cb); Shrader, David (perc)
- Turnabout TVS-34523; 33s; rel
1975; cip

Makrokosmos I (1972)
[2455] Burge, David (pf)
- Nonesuch H-71293/HQ-1293;
33s/q; rel 1974/1976; cip

Makrokosmos II (1973)
[2456] Miller, Robert (pf)
- Odyssey Y-34135; 33s; rel
1976; cip

**Music for a Summer Evening
(Makrokosmos III) (1974)**
[2457] Kalish, Gilbert (pf); Freeman,
James (pf); DesRoches, Raymond
(perc); Fitz, Richard (perc)
Rec 1/6-8/75
- Nonesuch H-71311; 33s; rel
1975; cip

Night Music I (1963)
[2458] DeGaetani, Jan (m sop); Orchestra
of Our Time; Thome, Joel (cond)
- Candide CE-31113; 33s; rel
1979; cip

[2459] Toth, Louise (sop); Parmelee, Paul
(pf) (cel); Burge, David (perc);
MacClusky, Thomas (perc);
Crumb, George (cond)
- CRI-218; 33s; rel 1968; cip

Night of the Four Moons (1969)
[2460] DeGaetani, Jan (m sop);
DesRoches, Raymond (perc);
Aeolian Chamber Players; Crumb,
George (cond)
- Columbia M-32739/MQ-32739;
33s/q; rel 1974; cip

**(Four) Nocturnes (Night Music II)
(1964)**
[2461] Rosenblith, Eric (vln); Hagen, David
(pf)
- Odyssey Y-35201; 33s; rel
1978; cip

[2462] Zukofsky, Paul (vln); Kalish, Gilbert
(pf)
- Mainstream MS-5016; 33s; rel
1974*
- Desto DC-6435-37; 33s; 3 discs;
rel 1975; cip

(Five) Pieces, Piano (1962)
[2463] Burge, David (pf)
- Advance FGR-3; 33m; rel 1967;
cip

Sonata, Violoncello (1955)
[2464] Christensen, Roy (vcl)
- Gasparo GS-101; 33s; rel 1975

Sonata, Violoncello (1955) *(cont'd)*
[2465] Helmerson, Frans (vcl)
Rec 1977
- BIS LP-65; 33s; rel 1977

[2466] Sylvester, Robert (vcl)
- Desto DC-7169; 33s; rel 1974; cip

Songs, Drones, and Refrains of Death (1968)
[2467] Weller, Lawrence (bar); Philadelphia Composers' Forum; Thome, Joel (cond)
- Desto DC-7155; 33s; rel 1973; cip

Vox balaenae (Voice of the Whale) (1971)
[2468] Aeolian Chamber Players; Crumb, George (cond)
- Columbia M-32739/MQ-32739; 33s/q; rel 1974; cip

CUMMING, Richard (1928-)
Go, Lovely Rose! (1956)
[2469] Hanks, John Kennedy (ten); Friedberg, Ruth (pf)
- Duke University Press DWR-7306; 33s; rel 1974

Knight's Page
[2470] Livesey (voice?); Cumming, Richard (pf)
- Music Library MLR-7027; 33m; rel 1953; del 1974

Little Black Boy, The (1966)
[2471] Hanks, John Kennedy (ten); Friedberg, Ruth (pf)
- Duke University Press DWR-7306; 33s; rel 1974

Loveliest of Trees
[2472] Gramm, Donald (b); Cumming, Richard (pf)
- Music Library MLR-7033; 33m; rel 1954; del 1974

Memory, Hither Come (1966)
[2473] Hanks, John Kennedy (ten); Friedberg, Ruth (pf)
- Duke University Press DWR-7306; 33s; rel 1974

(Twenty-Four) Preludes, Piano (1966-68)
[2474] Browning, John (pf)
- Desto DC-7120; 33s; rel 1971; cip

(Twenty-Four) Preludes, Piano: F-sharp Major
[2475] Waldoff, Stanley (pf)
- Musical Heritage Society MHS-3808; 33s; rel 1978

Sonata, Piano (1951)
[2476] Cumming, Richard (pf)
- Music Library MLR-7027; 33m; rel 1953; del 1974

CUNDICK, Robert (1926-)
Sonatina, Organ
[2477] Munns, Robert (org)
- Pye TPLS-13022; 33s; rel 1970; del 1971

West Wind, The
[2478] Mormon Tabernacle Choir; Cundick, Robert (pf); Ottley, Jerold D. (cond)
- Columbia M-34134; 33s; rel 1976; cip

CUNNINGHAM, Arthur (1928-)
Engrams (1970)
[2479] Hinderas, Natalie (pf)
- Desto DC-7102-03; 33s; 2 discs; rel 1970; cip

Lullabye for a Jazz Baby (1970)
[2480] Bedford, Cynthia (m sop); Oakland Youth Orchestra; Hughes, Robert (cond)
- Desto DC-7107; 33s; rel 1970; cip

Thisby (1968)
[2481] Trio Pro Viva
- Eastern ERS-513; 33s; 2 discs; rel 1973*

CURRAN, Alvin (1938-)
Fiori chiari, fiori oscuri
[2482] tape and instruments
- Ananda No 4; 33; rel 197?

Songs and Views from the Magnetic Garden
[2483] tape and instruments
- Ananda No 1; 33; rel 197?

CURRAN, Pearl Gildersleeve (1875-1941)
Life
[2484] Gigli, Beniamino (ten); Fedri, Dino (pf)
Rec 4/55
- RCA LM-1972; 33m; rel 1956; del 1958

Nocturne
[2485] Wilson, Robert (ten); orchestra; Geehl, Henry (cond)
- Gramophone BD-1098; 78; 10''

CURTIS-SMITH, Curtis O. B. (1941-)
Masquerades (1978)
[2486] Albright, William (org)
- CRI-409; 33s; rel 1979; cip

Music for Handbells (1976-77)
[2487] Handbell Choir; Curtis-Smith, Curtis (cond)
Rec 1978
- CRI-388; 33s; rel 1978; cip

Rhapsodies
[2488] Burge, David (pf)
Rec 10/16-17/75
- CRI-345; 33s; rel 1976; cip

(Five) Sonorous Inventions (1973)
[2489] Fischbach, Gerald (vln); Curtis-Smith, Curtis (pf)
- CRI-346; 33s; rel 1976; cip

Unisonics (1976)
[2490] Kynaston, Trent (al sax); Curtis-Smith, Curtis (pf)
Rec 1978
- CRI-388; 33s; rel 1978; cip

CUSHING, Charles (1905-)
Cereus (1960)
[2491] San Francisco Symphony Orchestra; Jorda, Enrique (cond)
- CRI-152; 33m; rel 1962; cip

Hommage a A. Roussel (1954)
[2492] Deffayet, Daniel (sax); Gobet, F. (pf)
- Pathe G-1052; 45; 7''; rel pre-1956

Sonata, Clarinet and Piano (1957)
[2493] Rosen, Jerome (cl); Schwartz, Nathan (pf)
- Fantasy 5008; 33m; rel 1960; del 1970

CUSTER, Arthur R. (1923-)
Comments on This World
[2494] Forrester, Maureen (al); Phoenix String Quartet
- Serenus SRS-12031; 33s; rel 1973; cip

Concerto, Brass Quintet (1968)
[2495] New York Brass Quintet
- Serenus SRS-12031; 33s; rel 1973; cip

Cycle for Nine Instruments (1964)
[2496] Francis Chagrin Ensemble; Farberman, Harold (cond)
- Serenus SRS-12024; 33s; rel 1969; cip

Found Objects No 3 (1971)
[2497] Turetzky, Bertram (cb); tape
- Serenus SRS-12045; 33s; rel 1976; cip

Found Objects No 5
[2498] Perkins, Barbara (vln); McClintock, Philip (cl); Pellegrino, John (tpt); Pezzullo, Louis (tbn); Preston, Victor (cb); Custer, Arthur (pf)
- Serenus SRS-12045; 33s; rel 1976; cip

Found Objects No 6 (1973)
[2499] Shansky, Marjorie (fl); tape
- Serenus SRS-12045; 33s; rel 1976; cip

Found Objects No 7 (1974)
[2500] Peltzer, Dwight (pf); tape
- Serenus SRS-12071; 33s; rel 1978; cip

I Used to Play by Ear (1971)
[2501] Peltzer, Dwight (pf)
- Serenus SRS-12031; 33s; rel 1973; cip

(Four) Ideas (1965)
[2502] Peltzer, Dwight (pf)
- Serenus SRS-12024; 33s; rel 1969; cip

(Two) Movements, Woodwind Quintet (1964)
[2503] Interlochen Arts Quintet
- CRI-253; 33s; rel 1970; cip

Parabolas (1969)
[2504] Sackson, David (vla); Peltzer, Dwight (pf)
- Serenus SRS-12031; 33s; rel 1973; cip

Permutations (1967)
[2505] Douglas, Bonnie (vln); Gray, Gary (cl); Davis, Douglas (vcl)
- CRI-253; 33s; rel 1970; cip

(Three) Pieces for Six Brass (1959)
[2506] American Brass Quintet (augmented)
- Serenus SRS-12024; 33s; rel 1969; cip

Rhapsodality Brown! (1969)
[2507] Peltzer, Dwight (pf)
- Serenus SRS-12024; 33s; rel 1969; cip

Rhapsody and Allegro (1957)
[2508] Bialkin, Maurice (vcl); Peltzer, Dwight (pf)
- Serenus SRS-12031; 33s; rel 1973; cip

Quartet, Strings, No 2 (1964)
[2509] St. Louis Quartet
- Serenus SRS-12024; 33s; rel 1969; cip

Sextet, Piano and Winds (1959)
[2510] Moore (pf); Interlochen Arts Quintet
- Serenus SRS-12028; 33s; rel 1972; cip

CYR, Gordon (1925-)
Peter Quince at the Clavier (1954)
[2511] Jones, Edgar (bar); Cyr, Helen (pf)
- Fantasy 5008; 33m; rel 1960; del 1970

CZAJKOWSKI, Michael (1939-)
People the Sky
[2512] Electronic music
- Vanguard Cardinal VCS-10069; 33s; rel 1970; del 1975

DA COSTA, Noel (1930-)
(Three) Short Pieces for Alto Flute Alone (1968)
[2513] Handy, D. Antoinette (fl)
- Eastern ERS-513; 33s; 2 discs; rel 1973*

Silver-Blue (1965)
[2514] Handy, D. Antoinette (fl); Lipscomb, Ronald (vcl)
- Eastern ERS-513; 33s; 2 discs; rel 1973*

DAHL, Ingolf (1912-70)
Allegro and Arioso (1942)
[2515] New Art Wind Quintet
- Classic Editions CE-2003; 33m; 2 discs; rel 1953; del 1961

[2516] New York Woodwind Quintet
- Concert-Disc M-1216/CS-216; 33m/s; rel 1960; cip

Concerto, Alto Saxophone and Winds (1949, rev 1953)
[2517] Sinta, Donald (al sax); University of Michigan Wind Ensemble; Reynolds, H. Robert (cond)
- University of Michigan SM-0009; 33s; rel 1979; cip

[2518] Timmons, Tim (al sax); Ithaca College Band; Gobrecht, Edward (cond)
- Golden Crest CRS-4124; 33q; rel 1979; cip

Concerto, Alto Saxophone and Winds (arr for al sax and pf)
[2519] Hemke, Frederick (al sax); Granger, Milton (pf)
- Brewster BR-1203; 33s; rel 1972; del 1978

Concerto a tre (1946)
[2520] Lurie, Mitchell (cl); Shapiro, Eudice (vln); Gottlieb, Victor (vcl)
- Columbia ML-4493; 33m; rel 1952; del 1958
- New World NW-281; 33m; rel 1976

Divertimento (1948)
[2521] Thomas, Milton (vla); Akst, Georgia (pf)
- Protone 145-LP2S; 33s; rel 1972; cip

Duettino concertante (1966)
[2522] Boston Symphony Chamber Players
- RCA LSC-6189; 33s; 3 discs; rel 1969; del 1976

[2523] Di Tullio, Louise (fl); Ervin, Karen (perc)
- Crystal S-641; 33s; rel 1973; cip

[2524] Stackhouse, Holly (fl); Frazeur, Theodore (perc)
- Grenadilla GS-1042; 33s; rel 1979; cip

Fanfares (1958)
[2525] Helps, Robert (pf)
- RCA LM-7042/LSC-7042; 33m/s; 2 discs; rel 1966; del 1971
- CRI-288; 33s; 2 discs; rel 1972; cip

Hymn and Toccata (1947): Hymn
[2526] Fierro, Charles (pf)
- Orion ORS-76209; 33s; rel 1976; cip

Music for Brass Instruments (1944)
[2527] American Brass Quintet
- Desto DC-6474-77; 33s; 4 discs; rel 1969; cip
- BASF KMB-20812; 33s; rel 1975; del 1976

[2528] Annapolis Brass Quintet
- Crystal S-202; 33s; rel 1975; cip

[2529] Canadian Brass
- Vanguard VSD-71253; 33s; rel 1979; cip

[2530] brass ensemble; Voisin, Roger (cond)
- Unicorn UNLP-1031; 33m; rel 1956; del 1959
- Kapp KCL-9020; 33m; rel 1959; del 1963
- Kapp KL-1391; 33m; rel 1965; del 1971

Sinfonietta (1961)
[2531] Eastman Symphonic Wind Ensemble; Hunsberger, Donald (cond)
- Decca DL-710163; 33s; rel 1969; del 1973

Sonata da camera (1970)
[2532] Long Island Chamber Ensemble of New York
- Grenadilla GS-1025; 33s; rel 1980; cip

Sonata pastorale (1959)
[2533] Fierro, Charles (pf)
- Orion ORS-76209; 33s; rel 1976; cip

Sonata seria (1953)
[2534] Fierro, Charles (pf)
- Orion ORS-76209; 33s; rel 1976; cip

Tower of Saint Barbara, The (1954)
[2535] Louisville Orchestra; Whitney, Robert (cond)
- LOU-56-2; 33m (Louisville Orchestra First Edition Records 1956 No 2); rel 1959; del 1978

Variations on a Swedish Folk Tune (1945)
[2536] Dwyer, Doriot (fl)
- Claremont 1205; 33m; rel 1953; del 1965

DAMROSCH, Walter (1862-1950)

Danny Deever (Op 2, No 7)
[2537] Bispham, David (bar)
Rec ca 1906
- Columbia A-5021; 78; rel 1906-10
- Columbia A-5778; 78; rel 1911-15
- Columbia 5010M; 78; rel 1911-15
- New World NW-247; 33m; rel 1976

[2538] Bonelli, Richard (bar)
- Brunswick 5166; 78; 10''; rel pre-1927

[2539] Brownlee, John (voice)
- Gramophone E-553; 78; 10''; rel pre-1936

[2540] Cordon, Norman (b); Black, Frank (pf)
- Victor 10-1182 (in set M-1030); 78; 10''; rel pre-1948
- Camden CAL-269; 33m; rel 1955; del 1957

[2541] Graveure, Louis (bar)
- Columbia 5038M; 78; rel pre-1927

[2542] Kisselburgh, Alexander (bar)
- Columbia 5101M; 78; rel pre-1936

[2543] McEachern, M.; chorus
- Columbia DX-701; 78; rel pre-1936

[2544] Warren, Leonard (bar); Victor Orchestra; Black, Frank (cond)
- RCA LM-147; 33m; 10''; rel 1952; del 1956
- Victor WDM-1630; 45; 7''

[2545] Werrenrath, Reinald (bar)
- Victor 74827; 78; rel 1919-25
- Victor 6638; 78; rel ca 1925-27
- Victor 35476; 78

DANIELS, Mabel Wheeler (1878-1971)

Deep Forest (1931)
[2546] Imperial Philharmonic Orchestra of Tokyo; Strickland, William (cond)
- CRI-145; 33m/s; rel 1961/?; cip

(Three) Observations (1943)
[2547] Roseman, Ronald (ob); Rabbai, Joseph (cl); McCord, Donald (bsn)
- Desto DC-7117; 33s; rel 1971; cip

DARTER, Thomas (1949-)

Sonatina, Trumpet (1970)
[2548] Stith, Marice (tpt)
- Golden Crest RE-7068; 33s; rel 1977; cip

DAVIDOVSKY, Mario (1934-)

Chacona (1973)
[2549] Benjamin, Jeanne (vln); Krosnick, Joel (vcl); Miller, Robert (pf)
- CRI-305; 33s; rel 1974; cip

Inflexions (1965)
[2550] instrumental ensemble; Gilbert, David (cond)
- CRI-305; 33s; rel 1974; cip

Junctures (1966)
[2551] Sollberger, Harvey (fl); Blustine, Allen (cl); Benjamin, Jeanne (vln)
- Nonesuch HB-73028; 33s; 2 discs; rel 1975; cip

Pennplay
[2552] Parnassus; Korf, Anthony (cond)
- New World NW-306; 33s; rel 1980

Study No 1 (1961)
[2553] Electronic music
- Columbia ML-5966/MS-6566; 33m/s; rel 1964; del 1979

Study No 2 (1962)
[2554] Electronic music
- Son-Nova 3/S-3; 33m/s; rel 1963; del 1970
- Orpheum SN-3; 33s; rel 1968; del 1970
- CRI-356; 33s; rel 1977; cip

Study No 3 (1965)
[2555] Electronic music
- Turnabout TVS-34487; 33s; rel 1972; del 1978
- Finnadar CD-4; 33q; rel 1976
- Finnadar QD-9010; 33q; rel 1976; cip

Synchronism No 1 (1962)
[2556] Baron, Samuel (fl); tape
- Nonesuch H-71289; 33s; rel 1974; cip

[2557] Sollberger, Harvey (fl); tape
- CRI-204; 33m/s; rel 1966; cip

Synchronism No 2 (1964)
[2558] Sollberger, Sophie (fl); Drucker, Stanley (cl); Zukofsky, Paul (vln); Martin, Robert L. (vcl); tape; Guigi, Efrain (cond)
- CRI-204; 33m/s; rel 1966; cip

Synchronism No 3 (1964)
[2559] Humeston, Jay (vcl); tape
- Delos DEL-25406; 33s; rel 1975; cip

[2560] Martin, Robert L. (vcl); tape
- CRI-204; 33m/s; rel 1966; cip

[2561] Moore, David (vcl); tape
- Opus One 6; 33s; rel 1970; cip

Synchronism No 5 (1969)
[2562] Group for Contemporary Music at Columbia University; tape; Sollberger, Harvey (cond)
- Turnabout TVS-34487; 33s; rel 1972; del 1978

[2563] Percussion Ensemble; tape; Sollberger, Harvey (cond)
- CRI-268; 33s; 2 discs; rel 1972; cip

Synchronism No 6 (1970)
[2564] Miller, Robert (pf); tape
- Turnabout TVS-34487; 33s; rel 1972; del 1978

Synchronism No 8 (1974)
[2565] Dorian Woodwind Quintet; tape
- Vox SVBX-5307; 33s; 3 discs; rel 1977; cip

DAVIDSON, Charles S. (1929-)

I Never Saw Another Butterfly (1973)
[2566] Columbus Boychoir; Hanson, Donald (cond)
- CBP-DB-6174; 33s; rel 1975

DAVIS, Katherine K. (1892-1980)

Carol of the Drum
[2567] Augustana Choir; Veld, Henry (cond)
- RCA LBC-1075; 33m; rel 1955; del 1957

Raising of Lazarus, The
[2568] Jagel, Frederick (ten); Phelps, Ruth Barrett (org)
- Washington WAS-13; 33m; rel 1959; del 1962
- Aeolian-Skinner AS-313; 33s; rel 1963; del 1966

DAVIS, Sharon (1937-)

(Three) Poems of William Blake
[2569] Stevenson, Delcina (sop); Spear, Julian (cl)
- WIM Records WIMR-10; 33s; rel 1978; cip

Though Men Call Us Free
[2570] Stevenson, Delcina (sop); Atkins, David (cl); Davis, Sharon (pf)
- WIM Records WIMR-13; 33s; rel 1977; cip

DAVISON, John H. (1930-)
Introduction and Dance
[2571] Ignacio, Lydia Walton (pf)
- Orion ORS-77275; 33s; rel 1978; cip

Sonata, Trombone and Piano (1958)
[2572] Smith, Henry Charles (tbn); Kuehefuhs, Gertrude C. (pf)
- Coronet S-1410; 33s; rel 1969; cip

DAWES, Charles Gates (1865-1951)
Melody, A Major (1912)
[2573] Kreisler, Fritz (vln); Lamson, Carl (pf)
- Victor 64961; 78
- Victor 725; 78; 10''; rel 1917-25

Melody
[2574] Dorsey, Tommy (tbn); Tommy Dorsey Orchestra
- Victor 10-1045; 78; 10''

DAWSON, William Levi (1898-)
Negro Folk Symphony (1934)
[2575] American Symphony Orchestra; Stokowski, Leopold (cond)
- Decca DL-10077/DL-710077; 33m/s; rel 1964; del 1975
- Varese Sarabande VC-81056; 33s; rel 1979; cip

Out in the Fields
[2576] Bedford, Cynthia (m sop); Oakland Youth Orchestra; Hughes, Robert (cond)
- Desto DC-7107; 33s; rel 1970; cip

DEDRICK, Christopher (1947-)
Sensitivity
[2577] New York Saxophone Quartet
- Mark MES-32322; 33s; rel 1969; cip

DEDRICK, Lyle (Rusty) (1918-)
Modern Art Suite
[2578] New York Saxophone Quartet
- Mark MES-32322; 33s; rel 1969; cip

DE KOVEN, Reginald (1859-1920)
Marching Song
[2579] Howard, Ann (sop); piano
- Victor 36032; 78; rel pre-1936

Owl and the Pussycat, The
[2580] Hayden Quartet
- Victor 16105; 78; 10''

Recessional
[2581] Warren, Leonard (bar); Victor Orchestra; Black, Frank (cond)
- RCA LM-147; 33m; 10''; rel 1952; del 1956

Robin Hood (1890): Excerpts
[2582] Victor Light Opera Company
- Victor 35784; 78

Robin Hood: Oh Promise Me
[2583] Baker, Elsie (al); orchestra
- Victor 16196A; 78; 10''

[2584] Claire, Marian (sop); WGN Concert Orchestra; Weber, Henry (cond)
- Victor 4566; 78; 10''

[2585] Homer, Louise (al); orchestra
- Victor 680; 78; 10''; rel 1912-18
- Victor 87255; 78; 10''; rel 1912-18
- Victor 1295; 78; 10''

[2586] MacDonough, Harry (ten); piano
- Monarch 724; 78; 10''; rel pre-1910

[2587] Peerce, Jan (ten); orchestra; chorus; Bass, Warner (cond)
- Victor 12-0795; 78; rel 1949

[2588] Robeson, Paul (b); orchestra
- Gramophone B-9059; 78; 10''; rel pre-1952
- Gramophone EA-2839; 78; rel pre-1952

[2589] Stevens, Rise (m sop); orchestra; King, Dudley (cond)
- Columbia 4515M; 78; 10''

[2590] Swarthout, Gladys (m sop); Victor Orchestra; Katims, Milton (cond)
- RCA LM-116; 33m; 10''; rel 1951; del 1953

DEL BORGO, Anthony (1938-)
Canto
[2591] Stolti, James (al sax)
- Coronet LPS-3036; 33s; rel 1978; cip

DELLO JOIO, Justin (1954-)
Quartet, Strings (Op 1) (1974)
[2592] Primavera String Quartet
- Grenadilla GS-1023; 33s; rel 1979; cip

DELLO JOIO, Norman (1913-)
Air Power (Suite) (1957)
[2593] Philadelphia Orchestra; Ormandy, Eugene (cond)
- Columbia ML-5214/MS-6029; 33m/s; rel 1957/1959; del 1965

Assassination, The
[2594] Druary, John (ten); Rogell, Peter (pf)
- Concert Hall CHD-6; 33m; rel 1950*

Colonial Ballads for Band
[2595] West Texas State University Symphonic Band; Garner, Gary (cond)
- Golden Crest ATH-5054; 33s; rel 1978; cip

Come to Me, My Love (1973)
[2596] Boston University Concert Choir and Chorus; Priest, Glen (pf); Dello Joio, Norman (cond)
- Golden Crest ATH-5059; 33s; rel 1979; cip

Concertante (1973)
[2597] West Texas State University Symphonic Band; Garner, Gary (cond)
- Golden Crest ATH-5054; 33s; rel 1978; cip

Concertante, Clarinet and Orchestra (1952) (arr for cl and pf)
[2598] Russo, John (cl); Ignacio, Lydia Walton (pf)
- Orion ORS-79330; 33s; rel 1980; cip

Concerto, Harp and Orchestra (1945)
[2599] Vito, Edward (hp); Little Orchestra Society; Scherman, Thomas (cond)
- Columbia 73014D-15D (in set MX-339); 78; 2 discs; rel 1948
- Columbia ML-4303; 33m; rel 1950; del 1956

Developing Flutist, The (Suite) (1972)
[2600] Padorr, Laila (fl); Swearingen, Anita (pf)
- Laurel-Protone LP-14; 33s; rel 1977; cip

Duo Concertato, Violoncello and Piano (1945)
[2601] Solow, Jeffrey (vcl); Dominguez, Albert (pf)
- Pelican LP-2010; 33s; rel 1980; cip

Epigraph (1951)
[2602] Vienna Symphony Orchestra; Swarowsky, Hans (cond)
- American Recording Society ARS-31; 33m; rel 1953
- Desto D-416/DST-6416; 33m/s; rel 1965; cip

Eyebright
[2603] Hanks, John Kennedy (ten);
Friedberg, Ruth (pf)
- Duke University Press
DWR-6417-18; 33m; 2 discs; rel
1966; del 1975

Fantasy and Variations, Piano and Orchestra (1961)
[2604] Hollander, Lorin (pf); Boston
Symphony Orchestra; Leinsdorf,
Erich (cond)
- RCA LM-2667/LSC-2667;
33m/s; rel 1963; del 1975

Fantasies on a Theme by Haydn (1968)
[2605] West Texas State University
Symphonic Band; Garner, Gary
(cond)
- Golden Crest ATH-5054; 33s; rel
1978; cip

From Every Horizon
[2606] West Texas State University
Symphonic Band; Garner, Gary
(cond)
- Golden Crest ATH-5054; 33s; rel
1978; cip

Homage to Haydn (1968)
[2607] Louisville Orchestra; Slatkin,
Leonard (cond)
Rec 5/14/74
- LS-74-2; 33s (Louisville
Orchestra First Edition Records
1974 No 2); rel 1975; cip

Jubilant Song, A (1946)
[2608] Ottley, Jo Ann (sop); Mormon
Tabernacle Choir; Cundick, Robert
(pf); Ottley, Jerold D. (cond)
- Columbia M-34134; 33s; rel
1976; cip

Lament
[2609] Druary, John (ten); Rogell, Peter
(pf)
- Concert Hall CHD-6; 33m; rel
1950*

Listeners, The
[2610] Parker, William (bar); Baldwin,
Dalton (pf)
- New World NW-300; 33s; rel
1978

Mass in Honor of the Eucharist
[2611] Boston University Concert Choir
and Chorus; Miller, Max (org);
Dello Joio, Norman (cond)
Rec 10/26/78
- Golden Crest ATH-5059; 33s; rel
1979; cip

Meditations on Ecclesiastes (1956)
[2612] Boston University Symphony
Orchestra; Silverstein, Joseph
(cond)
- Boston University BU-101; 33s;
2 discs; rel 1976

[2613] Oslo Philharmonic Orchestra;
Antonini, Alfredo (cond)
- CRI-110; 33m/s; rel 1957/?; cip

[2614] Princeton Chamber Orchestra;
Harsanyi, Nicholas (cond)
- Decca DL-10138/DL-710138;
33m/s; rel 1967; del 1973

Meeting at Night
[2615] Hanks, John Kennedy (ten);
Friedberg, Ruth (pf)
- Duke University Press
DWR-6417-18; 33m; 2 discs; rel
1966; del 1975

New York Profiles (1949)
[2616] La Jolla Musical Arts Festival
Orchestra; Sokoloff, Nicolai (cond)
- Alco ALP-1001; 33m; 10"; rel
1950; del 1955

[2617] Oslo Philharmonic Orchestra;
Lipkin, Arthur Bennett (cond)
- CRI-209; 33m/s; rel 1966; cip

Nocturne, E Major (1949)
[2618] Johannesen, Grant (pf)
- Golden Crest CRS-4111; 33q; rel
1972; cip

Nocturne, F-sharp (1949)
[2619] Johannesen, Grant (pf)
- Golden Crest CRS-4111; 33q; rel
1972; cip

Notes from Tom Paine (1975)
[2620] De Paur Chorus; Wingreen, Harriet
(pf); De Paur, Leonard (cond)
- Columbia M-33838; 33s; rel
1975; cip

Of Crows and Cluster
[2621] Boston University Concert Choir
and Chorus; Priest, Glen (pf);
Dello Joio, Norman (cond)
Rec 10/26/78
- Golden Crest ATH-5059; 33s: rel
1979; cip

Poet's Song, The
[2622] Boston University Concert Choir
and Chorus; Priest, Glen (pf);
Dello Joio, Norman (cond)
Rec 10/26/78
- Golden Crest ATH-5059; 33s; rel
1979; cip

(Two) Preludes, Piano (To a Young Musician and To a Young Dancer) (1945-46)
[2623] Dello Joio, Norman (pf)
- Concert Hall B-9; 78; 4 discs; rel
pre-1948

Psalm of David, A (1950)
[2624] Crane Chorus (State University of
New York at Potsdam); State
University of New York at
Potsdam Orchestra; Hosmer,
Helen M. (cond)
- Concert Hall CHS-1118; 33m;
10"; rel 1952; del 1957

Ricercari, Piano and Orchestra (1946)
[2625] Smadja, Germaine (pf); Concert
Hall Symphony Orchestra;
Swoboda, Henry (cond)
- Concert Hall D-6; 78; 3 discs; rel
pre-1950
- Concert Hall CHD-6; 33m; rel
1950*

Satiric Dances (1975)
[2626] Concord Band; Toland, William M.
(cond)
Rec 10/20/75
- Vogt Quality Recordings
CSRV-2503; 33s; rel 1975

[2627] West Texas State University
Symphonic Band; Garner, Gary
(cond)
- Golden Crest ATH-5054; 33s; rel
1978; cip

Serenade (1947-48)
[2628] Vienna Symphony Orchestra;
Swarowsky, Hans (cond)
- American Recording Society
ARS-36; 33m; rel 1953
- Desto D-413-14/DST-6413-14;
33m/s; 2 discs; rel 1965; cip

Sonata, Piano, No 2 (1944): Adagio
[2629] True, Nelita (pf)
- Educo 3068; 33
- Educo 3115; 33

Sonata, Piano, No 3 (1948)
[2630] Glazer, Frank (pf)
- Concert-Disc M-1217/CS-217;
33m/s; rel 1960; del 1977

[2631] Purves, Del (pf)
- Music Library MLR-7021; 33m;
rel 1953; del 1974

Song of the Open Road (1952)
[2632] Boston University Concert Choir
and Chorus; Priest, Glen (pf);
Morrison, John (tpt); Dello Joio,
Norman (cond)
Rec 10/26/78
- Golden Crest ATH-5059; 33s; rel
1979; cip

Songs of Abelard (1969)
[2633] Oderkirk (m sop); University of
South Florida Chamber Winds;
Croft, James (cond)
- Golden Crest CRS-4186; 33s; rel
1980; cip

Suite, Piano (1940)
[2634] Towlen, Gary (pf)
- Wardle TW-63; 33m; rel 1964;
del 1968

Suite for the Young: Invention No 2
[2635] Fuszek, Rita (pf)
- Educo 3108; 33

There is a Lady Sweet and Kind
[2636] Druary, John (ten); Rogell, Peter
(pf)
- Concert Hall CHD-6; 33m; rel
1950*

[2637] Valletti, Cesare (ten); Taubman,
Leo (pf)
Rec 10/28/60
- RCA LM-2540/LSC-2540;
33m/s; rel 1962; del 1963

To Saint Cecilia (1958)
[2638] Springer, Barbara (sop); Mallon,
Catherine (al); Bullard, Gene
(ten); Doe, Edward (b); Columbia
University Chapel Choir; brass
and percussion ensemble; Wright,
Serle (cond)
- Kapp KL-9057/KC-S-9057;
33m/s; rel 1961; del 1964

**Trio, Flute, Violoncello, and Piano
(1944)**
[2639] Baker, Julius (fl); Saidenberg,
Daniel (vcl); Hambro, Leonid (pf)
Concert Hall 1203-06 (in set
B-13); 78; 2 discs; rel pre-1948

**Triumph of Saint Joan Symphony,
The (1951)**
[2640] Louisville Orchestra; Whitney,
Robert (cond)
- Columbia ML-4615; 33m; rel
1952; del 1968
- Columbia CML-4615; 33m; rel
1968; del 1974
- Columbia AML-4615; 33m; rel
1974; cip

**Variants on a Medieval Tune
(1963)**
[2641] Yale University Band; Wilson, Keith
(cond)
- Carillon 128; 33m; rel 1965

Variations and Capriccio (1948)
[2642] Travers, Patricia (vln); Dello Joio,
Norman (pf)
- Columbia ML-4845; 33m; rel
1954; del 1968
- Columbia CML-4845; 33m; rel
1968; del 1974
- Columbia AML-4845; 33m; rel
1974; del 1976

**Variations, Chaconne, and Finale
(Three Symphonic Dances)
(1947)**
[2643] Philadelphia Orchestra; Ormandy,
Eugene (cond)
- Columbia ML-5263; 33m; rel
1958; del 1965

DELMAR, Dezso (1891-)
Hungarian Sketches (1947)
[2644] Frankenland Symphony Orchestra;
Kloss, Erich (cond)
- Lyrichord LL-29; 33m; rel 1952;
del 1957

Sonata, Violin and Piano
[2645] Fostofsky, Stuart (vln); piano
- Dorian 1022; 33m; rel 1968; del
1974

DEL MONACO, Alfredo (1938-)
Electronic Study No 2 (1970)
[2646] Electronic music
- CRI-328; 33s; rel 1975; cip

Metagrama
[2647] Sanoja, Sonia (voice); tape
- CRI-328; 33s; rel 1975; cip

DEL TREDICI, David (1937-)
Fantasy Pieces (1962)
[2648] Bennette, George (pf)
- Desto DC-7110; 33s; rel 1971;
cip

I Hear an Army (1964)
[2649] Bryn-Julson, Phyllis (sop);
Composers Quartet
- CRI-294; 33s; rel 1973; cip

Night Conjure-Verse (1965)
[2650] Valente, Benita (sop); Burgess,
Mary (m sop); Marlboro Festival
(players from); Del Tredici, David
(cond)
- CRI-243; 33s; rel 1970; cip

Scherzo (1960)
[2651] Helps, Robert (pf); Del Tredici,
David (pf)
- CRI-294; 33s; rel 1973; cip

Syzygy (1966)
[2652] Bryn-Julson, Phyllis (sop); Festival
Chamber Ensemble; Dufallo,
Richard (cond)
- Columbia MS-7281; 33s; rel
1969; del 1973

DE MARINIS, Paul (1948-)
Great Masters of Melody
[2653] multiple keyboards
Rec 8-9/78
- Vital VR-1062; 33s; rel 1979

DEMPSTER, Stuart (1936-)
Didjeridervish (1976)
[2654] Dempster, Stuart (tbn)
- 1750 Arch S-1775; 33s; rel
1979; cip

Standing Waves (1976)
[2655] Dempster, Stuart (tbn)
- 1750 Arch S-1775; 33s; rel
1979; cip

DENNI, Lucien (1886-1947)
My Skylark Love (Barcarolle)
[2656] Romaine, Margaret (sop)
- Victor 60135; 78; rel pre-1925

DENNIS, Robert (1933-)
**Improvisation and Variations,
Violoncello and Piano (1962-65)**
[2657] Moore, David (vcl); Thomas,
Andrew (pf)
- Opus One 6; 33s; rel 1970; cip

**(Three) Views from the Open
Window: (No 2) Pennsylvania
Station**
[2658] Louisville Orchestra; Mester, Jorge
(cond)
- LS-69-1; 33s (Louisville
Orchestra First Edition Records
1969 No 1); rel 1969; cip

DENNY, William D. (1910-80)
Overture for Strings (1945)
[2659] Janssen Symphony Orchestra of
Los Angeles; Janssen, Werner
(cond)
- Artist JS-15; 78; 3 discs; rel
1949

Partita, Organ
[2660] Moe, Lawrence (org)
- Fantasy 5010; 33m; rel 1960;
del 1970

Quartet, Strings, No 2
[2661] Juilliard String Quartet
- Epic LC-3325; 33m; rel 1957;
del 1961

DETT, Robert Nathaniel
(1882-1943)
Adagio cantabile
[2662] Behrend, Jeanne (pf)
- Victor 17912 (in set M-764);
78; rel 1941

Follow Me
[2663] Werrenrath, Reinald (bar)
- Victor 6472; 78; rel 1919-20

In the Bottoms (1913)
[2664] Hinderas, Natalie (pf)
- Desto DC-7102-03; 33s; 2 discs;
rel 1970; cip

In the Bottoms (1913) *(cont'd)*
[2665] Lythgoe, Clive (pf)
- Philips 9500.096; 33s; rel 1976; cip

In the Bottoms: Prelude (Night) and Juba Dance
[2666] Grainger, Percy (pf)
- Columbia A-6145; 78; rel 1919-25 (Excerpt: Prelude)
- Decca A-586; 78; rel pre-1948

In the Bottoms: Juba Dance
[2667] Dubal, David (pf)
- Musical Heritage Society MHS-3808; 33s; rel 1978

[2668] Steinhardt, Victor (pf)
- University of Washington Press OLY-104; 33q; 2 discs; rel 1976; cip

In the Bottoms: Juba Dance (arr for orch)
[2669] Hamburg Philharmonia; Walther, Hans-Jurgen (cond)
- Music Sound Books 78024; 78; rel pre-1956
- MGM E-3195; 33m; rel 1955; del 1959

[2670] Victor Symphony Orchestra; Bourdon, Rosario (cond)
- Victor 21750; 78; 10"; rel pre-1948
- Victor E-76; 78; 10"; rel pre-1948

Listen to the Lambs
[2671] De Paur Infantry Chorus; De Paur, Leonard (cond)
- Columbia ML-2119; 33m; 10"; rel 1950; del 1956

[2672] Mormon Tabernacle Choir; Philadelphia Orchestra; Condie, Richard P. (cond)
- Columbia ML-5048; 33m; rel 1955; del 1967
- Philips (English) NBL-5012; 33m; 10"; rel pre-1956
- Philips N-02125L; 33m; rel pre-1956
- Columbia ML-6235/MS-6835; 33m/s; rel 1966; cip

DIAMOND, Arline (1928-)
Composition for Clarinet
[2673] Rehfeldt, Phillip (cl)
- Advance FGR-5; 33m; rel 1964

DIAMOND, David (1915-)
Brigid's Song (1946)
[2674] Miller, Mildred (m sop); Biltcliffe, Edwin (pf)
- St/And SPL-411-12; 33m; 2 discs; rel 1963; del 1964
- Desto D-411-12/DST-6411-12; 33m/s; 2 discs; rel 1964; cip

Concerto, Chamber Orchestra (1940)
[2675] Yaddo Orchestra
- Yaddo II-6; 78; 2-10"; rel 1940

David Weeps for Absalom (1946)
[2676] Gramm, Donald (b); Cumming, Richard (pf)
- Music Library MLR-7033; 33m; rel 1954; del 1974

[2677] Miller, Mildred (m sop); Biltcliffe, Edwin (pf)
- St/And SPL-411-12; 33m; 2 discs; rel 1963; del 1964
- Desto D-411-12/DST-6411-12; 33m/s; 2 discs; rel 1964; cip

Elegy in Memory of Maurice Ravel (1938-39)
[2678] Rome Chamber Orchestra; Flagello, Nicolas (cond)
- Peters Internationale PLE-059; 33s; rel 1978; cip

Mad Maid's Song, The (1937)
[2679] Luening, Ethel (sop); Luening, Otto (fl); Tucker, Gregory (pf)
- Yaddo 117B; 78; 10"; rel 1937

Night Music (1961)
[2680] Davine, Robert (acc); Lamont String Quartet
- Crystal S-106; 33s; rel 1979; cip

Nonet (1961-62)
[2681] string ensemble; Wuorinen, Charles (cond)
- CRI-294; 33s; rel 1973; cip

(Eight) Piano Pieces for Children (1935)
[2682] Richter, Marga (pf)
- MGM E-3147; 33m; rel 1955; del 1959

(Eight) Piano Pieces for Children: Pease-Porridge Hot
[2683] Fuszek, Rita (pf)
- Educo 3108; 33

Preludes and Fugues (1939): Prelude and Fugue No 3
[2684] Bernstein, Leonard (pf)
- New Music Quarterly Recordings 1611; 78; rel 1941

Quartet, Strings, No 3 (1946)
[2685] Guilet String Quartet
- Concert Hall CHE-8; 33m; rel 1953*

Quartet, Strings, No 4 (1951)
[2686] Beaux-Arts String Quartet
- Epic LC-3907/BC-1307; 33m/s; rel 1965; del 1968

Quartet, Strings, No 9 (1966-68)
[2687] Composers Quartet
- CRI-294; 33s; rel 1973; cip

Quintet, Clarinet, Two Violas, and Two Violoncellos (1950)
[2688] Long Island Chamber Ensemble of New York
- Grenadilla GS-1007; 33s; rel 1977; cip

Quintet, Flute, String Trio, and Piano (1937)
[2689] Gilbert, David (fl); Kooper, Kees (vln); Doktor, Paul (vla); Sherry, Fred (vcl); Boehm-Kooper, Mary Louise (pf)
- Turnabout TVS-34508; 33s; rel 1973; del 1978

Romeo and Juliet (1947)
[2690] Little Orchestra Society; Scherman, Thomas (cond)
- Columbia M-751; 78; 3 discs; rel 1948
- Columbia ML-4303; 33m; rel 1950; del 1956

[2691] Polish National Radio Orchestra; Krenz, Jan (cond)
- CRI-216; 33m/s; rel 1968; cip

Rounds (1944)
[2692] Concert Arts Orchestra; Golschmann, Vladimir (cond)
- Capitol P-8245; 33m; rel 1954; del 1969
- Capitol CTL-7056; 33m; rel pre-1956

[2693] MGM String Orchestra; Solomon, Izler (cond)
- MGM E-3117; 33m; rel 1954; del 1959

[2694] Vienna Symphony Orchestra; Hendl, Walter (cond)
- American Recording Society ARS-7; 33m; 10"; rel 1953
- American Recording Society ARS-116; 33m; rel 1953

Sonata, Violoncello and Piano (1936-38)
[2695] Clark, Harry (vcl); Schuldmann, Sanda (pf)
- Musical Heritage Society MHS-3378; 33s; rel 1976

Sonatina, Violin and Piano
[2696] Donaldson, Hildegarde (vln); Johansen, Gunnar (pf)
- Yaddo D-10; 78; rel 1938

Symphony No 4 (1945)
[2697] New York Philharmonic; Bernstein, Leonard (cond)
Rec 1/13/58
- Columbia ML-5412/MS-6089; 33m/s; rel 1960; del 1968
- Columbia CML-5412/CMS-6089; 33m/s; rel 1968; del 1973

Symphony No 4 (1945) (cont'd)
- New World NW-258; 33s; rel 1976

Then and Now (1962): Three Camels and Three Kings
[2698] Fuszek, Rita (pf)
- Educo 3107; 33

Tempest, The (1944): Overture
[2699] Little Orchestra Society; Scherman, Thomas (cond)
- Columbia M-751; 78; 3 discs; rel 1948

Timon of Athens (1949)
[2700] Louisville Orchestra; Whitney, Robert (cond)
- LOU-60-5; 33m (Louisville Orchestra First Edition Records 1960 No 5); rel 1961; del 1978

Vocalises (1935)
[2701] Long Island Chamber Ensemble of New York
- Grenadilla GS-1025; 33s; rel 1980; cip

World of Paul Klee, The (1957)
[2702] Portland Junior Symphony; Avshalomov, Jacob (cond)
- CRI-140; 33m/s; rel 1961/?; cip

DIAMOND, Stuart S. (1950-)
Fragments from a Lost Adventure
[2703] Bolotowsky, Andrew (fl); Karpienia, Joseph (gtr)
- Orion ORS-78304; 33s; rel 1979; cip

DICK, Marcel (1898-)
Suite, Piano (1959)
[2704] Loesser, Arthur (pf)
- CRI-183; 33m/s; rel 1964/?; cip

Symphony for Strings (1964)
[2705] London Sinfonietta; Atherton, David (cond)
- CRI-274; 33s; rel 1972; cip

DICK, Robert (1950-)
Afterlight (1973)
[2706] Dick, Robert (fl)
- CRI-400; 33s; rel 1979; cip

DICKINSON, Clarence (1873-1969)
Berceuse
[2707] Courboin, Charles (org)
- Victor 14578; 78; rel 1937

[2708] Dickinson, Clarence (org) Rec 4/64
- RR4M-4497-98 (matrix no); 33m; rel 1964?

Joy of the Redeemed, The
[2709] Barnes, William H. (org)
- Replica FB-512-13; 33m; rel 1957?

[2710] Dickinson, Clarence (org) Rec 4/64
- RR4M-4497-98 (matrix no); 33m; rel 1964?

Storm King Symphony (1921): Allegro and Intermezzo
[2711] Dickinson, Clarence (org) Rec 4/64
- RR4M-4497-98 (matrix no); 33m; rel 1964?

DI DOMENICA, Robert (1927-)
Concerto, Violin and Chamber Orchestra (1962)
[2712] Rosenblith, Eric (vln); New England Conservatory Contemporary Ensemble; Schuller, Gunther (cond)
- Golden Crest NEC-119; 33s; rel 1979; cip

DIEMENTE, Edward (1923-)
Diary Part II
[2713] Kynaston, Trent (ten sax); Fisch, David (al sax)
- Coronet LPS-3035; 33s; rel 1978; cip

Quartet, Flute, Clarinet, Vibraphone, and Contrabass (1966)
[2714] Turetzky, Nancy (fl); Larsen, Henry (cl); Lesbines, Tele (vib); Turetzky, Bertram (cb)
- Ars Nova/Ars Antiqua AN-1001; 33s; rel 1969; del 1973

DIEMER, Emma Lou (1927-)
Fragments from the Mass
[2715] West Texas State University Chorale; Sanders, Hugh (cond)
- Golden Crest ATH-5063; 33s; rel 1980; cip

Hast Thou Not Known?
[2716] West Texas State University Chorale; Sanders, Hugh (cond)
- Golden Crest ATH-5063; 33s; rel 1980; cip

Laughing Song
[2717] West Texas State University Chorale; Sanders, Hugh (cond)
- Golden Crest ATH-5063; 33s; rel 1980; cip

Madrigals
[2718] West Texas State University Chorale; Sanders, Hugh (cond)
- Golden Crest ATH-5063; 33s; rel 1980; cip

O Come, Let Us Sing unto the Lord
[2719] West Texas State University Chorale; Sanders, Hugh (cond)
- Golden Crest ATH-5063; 33s; rel 1980; cip

(Three) Poems by Alice Meynell
[2720] West Texas State University Chorale; Sanders, Hugh (cond)
- Golden Crest ATH-5063; 33s; rel 1980; cip

Psalm 134
[2721] West Texas State University Chorale; Sanders, Hugh (cond)
- Golden Crest ATH-5063; 33s; rel 1980; cip

Sound Pictures: Infinity
[2722] Fuszek, Rita (pf)
- Educo 3107; 33

Toccata for Flute Chorus
[2723] Armstrong Flute Ensemble
- Golden Crest CRS-4088; 33s; rel 1970; cip

Wild Nights! Wild Nights!
[2724] West Texas State University Chorale; Sanders, Hugh (cond)
- Golden Crest ATH-5063; 33s; rel 1980; cip

DILLON, Fannie Charles (1881-1947)
Birds at Dawn
[2725] Hofmann, Josef (pf)
- Columbia A-6125; 78; rel 1912-22

From the Chinese (Op 93)
[2726] Andrews, Mitchell (pf)
- Dorian 1014; 33m; rel 1968; del 1974

Woodland Flute Call (arr for org by Alexander Schreiner)
[2727] Schreiner, Alexander (org)
- Columbia ML-5425/MS-6101; 33m/s; rel 1960; cip

DILLON, Robert M. (1922-)
Quartz Mountain
[2728] Ohio State University Concert Band; McGinnis, Donald E. (cond)
- Coronet S-1502; 33s; rel 1969; del 1978

DI PASQUALE, James (1941-)
Sonata, Tenor Saxophone and Piano
[2729] Hemke, Frederick (sax); Granger, Milton (pf)
- Brewster BR-1204; 33s; rel 1972; del 1978

DIRKSEN, Richard Wayne (1921-)
Child My Choice, A
[2730] Cathedral Choral Society;
　　　Washington Cathedral Choir of
　　　Men and Boys; various
　　　instruments; Callaway, Paul
　　　(cond)
　　　Rec 12/76
　　　- Washington Cathedral Archives
　　　CAR-006; 33s; rel 1977?

Christ is Made the Sure Foundation
[2731] Washington Cathedral Choir;
　　　Dirksen, Richard W. (org) (cond)
　　　- Washington Cathedral Archives
　　　CAR-009; 33s; rel 1979?

Jonah
[2732] Stillwell, Richard (bar); Knapp,
　　　Wallace (b); Bell, Cornelia (nar);
　　　All Saints' Episcopal Church
　　　(Chevy Chase, MD) Senior Girls
　　　Choir; All Saints' Episcopal
　　　Church Men and Boys Choir;
　　　chamber orchestra; Roeckelein,
　　　Richard (cond)
　　　Rec 4/31/68 and 5/1/68
　　　- CSM-349; 33s; rel 1968

Welcome!
[2733] Cathedral Choral Society;
　　　Washington Cathedral Choir of
　　　Men and Boys; various
　　　instruments; Callaway, Paul
　　　(cond)
　　　Rec 12/76
　　　- Washington Cathedral Archives
　　　CAR-006; 33s; rel 1977?

DISSEVELT, Tom* and BALTAN, Kid
Song of the Second Moon
[2734] Electronic music
　　　- Philips
　　　PHM-200047/PHS-600047;
　　　33m/s; rel 1968*
　　　- Limelight LS-86050; 33s

DLUGOSZEWSKI, Lucia (1931-)
Angels of the Inmost Heaven (1972)
[2735] Gould, Mark (tpt); Ranger, Louis
　　　(tpt); Brevig, Per (tbn); Taylor,
　　　David (tbn); Smith, Martin (hn);
　　　Schwarz, Gerard (cond)
　　　- Folkways FTS-33902; 33s; rel
　　　1976; cip

Fire Fragile Flight (1973)
[2736] Orchestra of Our Time; Thome,
　　　Joel (cond)
　　　- Candide CE-31113; 33s; rel
　　　1979; cip

Space is a Diamond (1970)
[2737] Schwarz, Gerard (tpt); Oppens,
　　　Ursula (pf)
　　　- Nonesuch H-71275; 33s; rel
　　　1973; cip

Tender Theatre Flight Nageire (1971)
[2738] Schwarz, Gerard (tpt); Carroll,
　　　Edward (tpt); Smith, Norman
　　　(tpt); Rouch, Robert (hn);
　　　Langlitz, David (ten tbn); Taylor,
　　　David (b tbn); Dlugoszewski,
　　　Lucia (perc); Schwarz, Gerard
　　　(cond)
　　　Rec 5/78
　　　- CRI-388; 33s; rel 1978; cip

DOCKSTADER, Tod (1932-)
Apocalypse (1961)
[2739] Electronic music
　　　- Owl ORLP-6; 33s; rel 1966; del
　　　1976

Drone (1962)
[2740] Electronic music
　　　- Owl ORLP-7; 33s; rel 1966; del
　　　1976

(Eight) Electronic Pieces (1960)
[2741] Electronic music
　　　Rec 1960
　　　- Folkways FM-3434; 33m; rel
　　　1962; del 1971

(Two) Fragments from Apocalypse (1961)
[2742] Electronic music
　　　- Owl ORLP-7; 33s; rel 1966; del
　　　1976

Luna Park (1961)
[2743] Electronic music
　　　- Owl ORLP-6; 33s; rel 1966; del
　　　1976

Quatermass (1964)
[2744] Electronic music
　　　- Owl ORLP-8; 33s; rel 1966; del
　　　1976

Traveling Music (1960)
[2745] Electronic music
　　　- Owl ORLP-6; 33s; rel 1966; del
　　　1976

Water Music (1963)
[2746] Electronic music
　　　- Owl ORLP-7; 33s; rel 1966; del
　　　1976

DOCKSTADER, Tod and REICHERT, James
Omniphony I
[2747] Electronic music
　　　- Owl ORLP-11; 33s; rel 1969; del
　　　1976

DODGE, Charles (1942-)
Changes (1969-70)
[2748] Electronic music
　　　- Nonesuch H-71245; 33s; rel
　　　1970; cip

Earth's Magnetic Field (1970)
[2749] Electronic music
　　　- Nonesuch H-71250; 33s; rel
　　　1970; cip

Extensions (1973)
[2750] Anderson, Ronald (tpt); tape
　　　- CRI-300; 33s; rel 1974; cip

[2751] Stevens, Thomas (tpt); tape
　　　Rec 10/78
　　　- Crystal S-366; 33s; rel 1979; cip

Folia (1965)
[2752] instrumental ensemble; Monod,
　　　Jacques (cond)
　　　- CRI-300; 33s; rel 1974; cip

In Celebration (1975)
[2753] Electronic music
　　　- CRI-348; 33s; rel 1976; cip

Story of Our Lives, The (1974)
[2754] Electronic music
　　　- CRI-348; 33s; rel 1976; cip

Speech Songs (1973)
[2755] Electronic music
　　　- CRI-348; 33s; rel 1976; cip

Speech Songs: When I Am with You and He Destroyed Her Image
[2756] Electronic music
　　　- 1750 Arch S-1752; 33s; rel
　　　1975*

DOLAN, Robert E. (1906-)
Message for Liza, A
[2757] Hollywood Bowl Symphony
　　　Orchestra; Stokowski, Leopold
　　　(cond)
　　　- Victor 10-1302A; 78; 10"

DONOVAN, Richard Frank (1891-1970)
Allegro-Fugato
[2758] Mariotti, Arno (ob); Yaddo
　　　Orchestra
　　　- Yaddo M-4; 78; rel 1938

Antiphon and Chorale (1955)
[2759] Krigbaum, Charles (org)
　　　- CRI-262; 33s; rel 1970; cip

(Five) Elizabethan Lyrics (1932-57)
[2760] Addison, Adele (sop); Galimir
　　　String Quartet
　　　- Columbia ML-6359/MS-6959;
　　　33m/s; rel 1967; del 1970
　　　- CRI-290; 33s; rel 1972; cip

Epos (1963)
[2761] Polish National Radio Orchestra;
　　　Krenz, Jan (cond)
　　　- CRI-203; 33m/s; rel 1966; cip

**Fantasy on American Folk Ballads
(1940)**
[2762] Columbia University Glee Club
- Carillon 117; 33m; rel 1961; del
1970

Farr a Diddle Dino
[2763] Donovan, Grace (sop); string
quartet
- New Music Quarterly Recordings
1114 (4-1); 78; rel 1935

Magnificat
[2764] Battell Chapel Choir (men's
voices); Krigbaum, Charles (org)
(cond)
- CRI-262; 33s; rel 1970; cip

Mass (1955)
[2765] Battell Chapel Choir (men's
voices); Krigbaum, Charles (org)
(cond)
- CRI-262; 33s; rel 1970; cip

Music for Six (1961)
[2766] Columbia Chamber Ensemble;
Schuller, Gunther (cond)
- Columbia ML-6359/MS-6959;
33m/s; rel 1967; del 1970
- CRI-290; 33s; rel 1972; cip

New England Chronicle (1947)
[2767] Eastman-Rochester Symphony
Orchestra; Hanson, Howard
(cond)
- Mercury MG-40013; 33m; rel
1955; del 1957
- Mercury MG-50086; 33m; rel
1957; del 1963

On Her Dancing
[2768] Donovan, Grace (sop); string
quartet
- New Music Quarterly Recordings
1114 (4-1); 78; rel 1935

**Passacaglia on Vermont Folk
Themes (1948)**
[2769] Polish National Radio Orchestra;
Krenz, Jan (cond)
- CRI-203; 33m/s; rel 1966; cip

Quartet, Woodwinds (1953)
[2770] Yale Woodwind Quartet
- Contemporary AP-121; 33m; rel
1953; del 1958

Serenade (1939)
[2771] Wann, Lois (ob); Tinterow, Bernard
(vln); Porter, Quincy (vla);
Bodenhorn, Aaron (vcl)
- New Music Quarterly Recordings
1514; 78; rel 1939
- Yaddo I-5; 78; rel 1940
- CRI-390; 33s; rel 1978; cip

Soundings (1953)
[2772] MGM Chamber Orchestra;
Surinach, Carlos (cond)
- MGM E-3371; 33m; rel 1956;
del 1959

Suite, Piano
[2773] Gerschefski, Edwin (pf)
- New Music Quarterly Recordings
1114 (4-2); 78; rel 1935

**Suite, Oboe and String Orchestra
(1944-45)**
[2774] Genovese, Alfred (ob); Baltimore
Little Symphony; Stewart,
Reginald (cond)
- Vanguard VRS-468; 33m; rel
1955; del 1965

**Symphony, Chamber Orchestra
(1937)**
[2775] Yaddo Orchestra; Donovan, Richard
(cond)
- Yaddo 35A-B; 78; rel 1937

**Symphony, Chamber Orchestra:
Adagio**
[2776] Yaddo Orchestra; Donovan, Richard
(cond)
- Yaddo 5A; 78; rel 1937
- Yaddo 38B; 78; rel 1937
- Yaddo 41A; 78; rel 1937

Trio, Violin, Viola, and Piano (1937)
[2777] no performers given
- Yaddo 11B; 78; rel 1937

DORAN, Matt (1921-)
Andante, Flute and Guitar
[2778] Stancliff, Floyd (fl); Macaluso,
Vincenzo (gtr)
- Klavier KS-537; 33s; rel 1975;
cip

Sonata, Clarinet and Piano (1963)
[2779] Atkins, David (cl); Davis, Sharon
(pf)
- WIM Records WIMR-1; 33s; rel
1971; cip

Sonatina, Flute and Violoncello
[2780] Andrus, Gretel Shanley (fl); Davis,
Douglas (vcl)
- WIM Records WIMR-2; 33s; rel
1971; cip

Suite, Flute and Guitar: Finale
[2781] Stancliff, Floyd (fl); Macaluso,
Vincenzo (gtr)
- Klavier KS-537; 33s; rel 1975;
cip

DORATI, Antal (1906-)
**Concerto, Piano and Orchestra
(1974)**
[2782] Alpenheim, Ilse von (pf); National
Symphony Orchestra; Dorati,
Antal (cond)
Rec 4/3/76
- Turnabout TVS-34669; 33s; rel
1977; cip

**Concerto, Violoncello and Orchestra
(1946)**
[2783] Starker, Janos (vcl); Louisville
Orchestra; Mester, Jorge (cond)
- LS-75-9; 33s (Louisville
Orchestra First Edition Records
1975 No 9); rel 1977; cip

Nocturne and Capriccio (1920)
[2784] Lord, Roger (ob); Allegri String
Quartet
- Mercury MG-50248/SR-90248;
33m/s; rel 1963; del 1965
- Mercury SR-90499; 33s; rel
1968; del 1972

Symphony (1957)
[2785] Minneapolis Symphony Orchestra;
Dorati, Antal (cond)
- Mercury MG-50248/SR-90248;
33m/s; rel 1963; del 1965
- Mercury SR-90499; 33s; rel
1968; del 1972

Variations on a Theme by Bartok
[2786] Alpenheim, Ilse von (pt)
Rec 6/76
- Turnabout TVS-34669; 33s; rel
1977; cip

DOROUGH, Robert
Eons Ago Blue
[2787] College Consort; Buckton, Roger
(cond)
- Kiwi SLD-38; 33s; rel 1975

[2788] Krainis Recorder Consort; Krainis,
Bernard (rec)
- Columbia ML-5875/MS-6475;
33m/s; rel 1963; del 1968
- Odyssey
32-16-0143/32-16-0144;
33m/s; rel 1967; cip

DOUGHERTY, Celius (1902-)
K'e, The
[2789] Williams, Camilla (sop); Bazala,
Borislav (pf)
- MGM E-140; 33m; 10''; rel
1952; del 1957

Minor Bird, A
[2790] Gorin, Igor (bar); Straight, Willard
(pf)
- Golden Crest CRS-4135; 33s; rel
1976; cip

Serenader
[2791] Hanks, John Kennedy (ten);
Friedberg, Ruth (pf)
- Duke University Press
DWR-6417-18; 33m; 2 discs; rel
1966; del 1975

Uncle Joe's Reel
[2792] Lear, Evelyn (sop); Stewart,
Thomas (bar); Katz, Martin (pf)
Rec 1/17/78
- Pelican LP-2012; 33s; rel 1979;
cip

DOUGLAS, Bill (1944-)
Improvisations III (1969)
[2793] Stoltzman, Richard (cl); Douglas,
Bill (pf)
- Orion ORS-73125; 33s; rel
1973; cip

Vajra (1969)
[2794] Stoltzman, Richard (cl); Douglas,
Bill (pf)
- Orion ORS-73125; 33s; rel
1973; cip

DOWNEY, John W. (1927-)
Adagio lyrico (1953)
[2795] Paratore, Anthony (pf); Paratore,
Joseph (pf)
- Orion ORS-77267; 33s; rel
1977; cip

Agort (1972)
[2796] Woodwind Arts Quintet
- Orion ORS-73123; 33s; rel
1973; cip

Dolphin, A (1974)
[2797] Nelson, Daniel (ten); instrumental
ensemble; Downey, John (pf)
(cond)
- Orion ORS-77267; 33s; rel
1977; cip

Octet, Winds (1954, rev 1976)
[2798] wind octet; De Rusha, Stanley
(cond)
- Orion ORS-77267; 33s; rel
1977; cip

Quartet, Strings, No 2 (1975)
[2799] Fine Arts Quartet
- Gasparo GS-205; 33s; rel 1980

**Sonata, Violoncello and Piano
(1966)**
[2800] Sopkin, George (vcl); Basile,
Armand (pf)
- CRI-234; 33s; rel 1969; cip

What If? (1973)
[2801] University of Wisconsin-Milwaukee
Concert Choir; brass ensemble;
percussion; Balko, Eldon (cond)
- Orion ORS-77267; 33s; rel
1977; cip

DOWNS, Hugh
Elegiac Prelude, An
[2802] National High School Orchestra;
Maddy, Joseph (cond)
Rec 1960
- Interlochen National Music Camp
NMC-6161; 33m; rel 1961

DREWS, Steve (1945-)
Ceres Motion
[2803] Drews, Steve (syn); Fisher, Linda
(syn); Borden, David (syn) (elec
pf)
- Earthquack EQ-0001; 33s; rel
1974*

Train
[2804] Drews, Steve (syn); Fisher, Linda
(syn); Borden, David (syn) (elec
pf)
- Earthquack EQ-0001; 33s; rel
1974*

DROSSIN, Julius (1918-)
**Quartet, Strings, No 6 (Op 33)
(1963)**
[2805] Severance String Quartet
- Advent USR-5004; 33s; rel
1973; cip

DRUCKMAN, Jacob (1928-)
Animus I (1966)
[2806] Smith, Andre (tbn); tape
- Turnabout TVS-34177; 33s; rel
1967; del 1975

Animus II (1968)
[2807] DeGaetani, Jan (m sop); Fitz,
Richard (perc); Gottlieb, Gordon
(perc); tape
- CRI-255; 33s; rel 1971; cip

Animus III (1969)
[2808] Bloom, Arthur (cl); tape
- Nonesuch H-71253; 33s; rel
1971; cip

Antiphonies (1963)
[2809] Tanglewood Festival Chorus; Oliver,
John (cond)
- Deutsche Grammophon
2530.912; 33s; rel 1979; cip

Dark upon the Harp (1962)
[2810] DeGaetani, Jan (m sop); New York
Brass Quintet; Carlyss, Gerald
(perc); Ayers, Robert (perc)
- CRI-167; 33m/s; rel 1963/?; cip

**Delizie contente che l'alme beate
(1973)**
[2811] Dorian Woodwind Quintet; tape
- Vox SVBX-5307; 33s; 3 discs; rel
1977; cip

Incenters (1968)
[2812] Contemporary Chamber Ensemble;
Weisberg, Arthur (cond)
- Nonesuch H-71221; 33s; rel
1969; cip

Lamia (1974)
[2813] DeGaetani, Jan (m sop); Louisville
Orchestra; Mester, Jorge (cond);
Spurlock, Daniel (cond)
- LS-76-4; 33s (Louisville
Orchestra First Edition Records
1976 No 4); rel 1979; cip

(Four) Madrigals (1959)
[2814] Rees, Rosalind (sop); Gregg Smith
Singers; Smith, Gregg (cond)
Rec 4/76
- Vox SVBX-5354; 33s; 3 discs; rel
1979

Quartet, Strings, No 2 (1966)
[2815] Concord String Quartet
- Vox SVBX-5306; 33s; 3 discs; rel
1973; cip

Synapse (1971)
[2816] Electronic music
- Nonesuch H-71253; 33s; rel
1971; cip

Valentine (1969)
[2817] Brehm, Alvin (cb)
- Nonesuch H-71253; 33s; rel
1971; cip

DRUMWRIGHT, George
Dance
[2818] Skipworth, George (pf)
- Educo 3096; 33; rel 1963

Song for a Bird
[2819] Skipworth, George (pf)
- Educo 3096; 33; rel 1963

DUBENSKY, Arcady (1890-1966)
Fugue for Eighteen Violins (1932)
[2820] Indianapolis Symphony Orchestra;
Sevitzky, Fabien (cond)
- Victor 11-8366 (in set M-912);
78; rel 1942
- Victor 11-8229 (in set DM-912);
78; rel 1942

Gossips (1928)
[2821] Hamburg Chamber Orchestra;
Walther, Hans-Jurgen (cond)
- Music Sound Books 78024; 78;
rel pre-1956

[2822] Philadelphia String Sinfonietta;
Sevitzky, Fabien (cond)
- Victor 4186; 78; 10''; rel 1930

**Gossips (arr for 2 pfs by Arthur
Whittemore and Jack Lowe)**
[2823] Whittemore, Arthur (pf); Lowe,
Jack (pf)
- Victor 10-1041; 78; 10''; rel
pre-1948

Raven, The
[2824] De Loache, Benjamin (speaker);
Philadelphia Orchestra;
Stokowski, Leopold (cond)
- Victor 2000-01; 78; 2-10''; rel
pre-1936

**Stephen Foster: Theme, Variations,
and Finale (1941)**
[2825] Indianapolis Symphony Orchestra;
Sevitzky, Fabien (cond)
- Victor 11-8365-66 (in set
M-912); 78; 2 discs; rel 1942
- Victor 11-8228-29 (in set
DM-912); 78; 2 discs; rel 1942

DUBLE, Charles Edward
(1884-1960)

Bravura
[2826] Eastman Symphonic Wind
Ensemble; Fennell, Frederick
(cond)
- Mercury MG-50314/SR-90314;
33m/s; rel 1963; del 1976
- Mercury SRI-75087; 33s; rel
1977; cip

DUCKWORTH, William E. (1943-)

**Ballad in Time and Space, A
(1968)**
[2827] Hemke, Frederick (sax); Granger,
Milton (pf)
- Brewster BR-1204; 33s; rel
1972; del 1978

Gambit (1967)
[2828] Electronic music
- Capra 1201; 33s; rel 1969; cip

Pitt County Excursions
[2829] Houlik, James (ten sax); Tardif,
Paul (pf)
- Golden Crest RE-7060; 33s; rel
1977; cip

Reel Music (1970)
[2830] Chicago Saxophone Quartet
- Brewster BR-184; 33s; rel 1972;
del 1978

DUGGER, Edwin (1940-)

Abwesenheiten und Wiedersehen
[2831] Berkeley Contemporary Chamber
Players; Khuner, Jonathan (cond)
Rec 11/77
- CRI-378; 33s; rel 1978; cip

Intermezzi (1969)
[2832] San Francisco Contemporary Music
Players; Le Roux, Jean-Louis
(cond)
Rec 11/77
- CRI-378; 33s; rel 1978; cip

**Music for Synthesizer and Six
Instruments**
[2833] instrumental ensemble; Epstein,
David (cond)
- Acoustic Research AR-0654.084;
33s; rel 1971

DUKE, John Woods (1899-)

Bird, The
[2834] Sayao, Bidu (sop); Charnley, Milne
(pf)
- Columbia ML-4154; 33m; rel
pre-1949; del 1956

(Four) Chinese Love Lyrics
[2835] Bogard, Carole (sop); Duke, John
Woods (pf)
- Cambridge CRS-2776; 33s; rel
1980; cip

I Carry Your Heart (1962)
[2836] Hanks, John Kennedy (ten);
Friedberg, Ruth (pf)
- Duke University Press
DWR-7306; 33s; rel 1974

In Just Spring (1954)
[2837] Hanks, John Kennedy (ten);
Friedberg, Ruth (pf)
- Duke University Press
DWR-7306; 33s; rel 1974

Loveliest of Trees
[2838] De Loache, Benjamin (bar); Duke,
John Woods (pf)
- Yaddo 102A; 78; 10''; rel 1937

[2839] Hanks, John Kennedy (ten);
Friedberg, Ruth (pf)
- Duke University Press
DWR-6417-18; 33m; 2 discs; rel
1966; del 1975
- Duke University Press
DWR-7306; 33s; rel 1974

Luke Havergal
[2840] Gramm, Donald (bar); Hassard,
Donald (pf)
- New World NW-243; 33s; rel
1977

[2841] Moore, Dale (bar); Tomfohrde,
Betty Ruth (pf)
- Cambridge CRS-2715; 33s; rel
1973; cip

Miniver Cheevy
[2842] Gramm, Donald (bar); Hassard,
Donald (pf)
- New World NW-243; 33s; rel
1977

**Mountains Are Dancing, The
(1956)**
[2843] Hanks, John Kennedy (ten);
Friedberg, Ruth (pf)
- Duke University Press
DWR-7306; 33s; rel 1974

(Four) Poems by e. e. cummings
[2844] Bogard, Carole (sop); Duke, John
Woods (pf)
- Cambridge CRS-2776; 33s; rel
1980; cip

(Four) Poems by Emily Dickinson
[2845] Bogard, Carole (sop); Duke, John
Woods (pf)
- Cambridge CRS-2776; 33s; rel
1980; cip

(Six) Poems by Emily Dickinson
[2846] Bogard, Carole (sop); Duke, John
Woods (pf)
- Cambridge CRS-2776; 33s; rel
1980; cip

Richard Cory
[2847] Gramm, Donald (bar); Hassard,
Donald (pf)
- New World NW-243; 33s; rel
1977

(Five) Songs
[2848] Bogard, Carole (sop); Duke, John
Woods (pf)
- Cambridge CRS-2776; 33s; rel
1980; cip

(Seventeen) Songs
[2849] Boothman, Donald (bar); Duke,
John Woods (pf)
- Golden Age GAR-1004; 33s; rel
1976?

**Stopping by Woods on a Snowy
Evening**
[2850] Bogard, Carole (sop); Duke, John
Woods (pf)
- Cambridge CRS-2776; 33s; rel
1980; cip

Suite, Viola (1933)
[2851] Rood, Louise (vla)
- Yaddo II-1; 78; rel 1940

Suite, Violoncello (1934): Aria
[2852] De Ronde, Marion (vcl)
- Yaddo 102B; 78; 10''; rel 1937

There Will Be Stars
[2853] Hanks, John Kennedy (ten);
Friedberg, Ruth (pf)
- Duke University Press
DWR-6417-18; 33m; 2 discs; rel
1966; del 1975
- Duke University Press
DWR-7306; 33s; rel 1974

Trio, Strings (1937)
[2854] Porter, Lois (vln); Rood, Louise
(vla); De Ronde, Marion (vcl)
- Yaddo 2A-B; 78; 1-10'' and
1-12''; rel 1937 (1st and 3rd
movements)
- Yaddo 57A; 78; rel 1937 (2nd
movement)

Viennese Waltz
[2855] Hanks, John Kennedy (ten);
Friedberg, Ruth (pf)
- Duke University Press
DWR-6417-18; 33m; 2 discs; rel
1966; del 1975
- Duke University Press
DWR-7306; 33s; rel 1974

White in the Moon
[2856] Hanks, John Kennedy (ten);
Friedberg, Ruth (pf)
- Duke University Press
DWR-6417-18; 33m; 2 discs; rel
1966; del 1975
- Duke University Press
DWR-7306; 33s; rel 1974

Yellow Hair
[2857] Hanks, John Kennedy (ten);
Friedberg, Ruth (pf)
- Duke University Press
DWR-6417-18; 33m; 2 discs; rel
1966; del 1975
- Duke University Press
DWR-7306; 33s; rel 1974

DUKE, Lewis Byron (1924-)
Sonata, Violin and Piano (Op 21)
[2858] Plummer, Stanley (vln);
Vallecillo-Gray, Irma (pf)
- Byron 5; 33s; rel 1971; del
1975

DUKE, Vernon (1903-69)
(Three) Caprices, Piano (1944)
[2859] Duke, Vernon (pf)
- Contemporary C-6004; 33m; rel
1959; del 1969
- Stereo S-7024; 33s; rel 1959;
del 1966
- Contemporary S-7024; 33s; rel
1966; del 1978

Etude (1939)
[2860] Baker, Israel (vln); Christlieb, Don
(bsn)
- Contemporary M-6007/S-8007;
33m/s; rel 1961; cip

Parisian Suite (1955)
[2861] Ryshna, Natalie (pf)
- Contemporary M-6007/S-8007;
33m/s; rel 1961; cip

Quartet, Strings, C Major (ca 1956)
[2862] Roth Quartet
- Contemporary C-6004; 33m; rel
1959; del 1969
- Stereo S-7024; 33s; rel 1959;
del 1966
- Contemporary S-7024; 33s; rel
1966; del 1978

**Sonata, Violin and Piano, D Major
(1948)**
[2863] Baker, Israel (vln); Duke, Vernon
(pf)
- Contemporary M-6007/S-8007;
33m/s; rel 1961; cip

**Souvenir de Monte Carlo
(1949-56)**
[2864] MGM Chamber Orchestra;
Surinach, Carlos (cond)
- MGM E-3497; 33m; rel 1957;
del 1959

Souvenir de Venise (1955)
[2865] Ryshna, Natalie (pf)
- Contemporary M-6007/S-8007;
33m/s; rel 1961; cip

Surrealist Suite (1940)
[2866] Duke, Vernon (pf)
- Contemporary C-6004; 33m; rel
1959; del 1969
- Stereo S-7024; 33s; rel 1959;
del 1966
- Contemporary S-7024; 33s; rel
1966; del 1978

**Variations on Old Russian Chant
(1958)**
[2867] Gassman, Bert (ob); Roth Chamber
Players
- Contemporary C-6004; 33m; rel
1959; del 1969
- Stereo S-7024; 33s; rel 1959;
del 1966
- Contemporary S-7024; 33s; rel
1966; del 1978

DUNCAN, John (1913-)
Black Bards
[2868] flute; violoncello; piano
- Eastern ERS-513; 33s; 2 discs;
rel 1973*

DUNLAP, William Paul (1919-)
Tequila
[2869] Columbus Philharmonic Orchestra;
Solomon, Izler (cond)
- Discovery DL-4004; 33m; rel
1950; del 1956

DUNN, James Philip
(1884-1936)
Bitterness of Love, The
[2870] McCormack, John (ten); Schneider,
Edwin (pf)
Rec 12/30
- Gramophone AGSA-21; 78
- Victor 1568; 78; 10"
- Gramophone DA-1175; 78
- New World NW-247; 33m; rel
1976

DUTTON, Frederic (1928-)
Fanfares 1969 *see* REYNOLDS,
Jeffrey, et al

DVORKIN, Judith (1930-)
Maurice (1955)
[2872] Randolph Singers; Randolph, David
(cond)
- CRI-102; 33m/s; rel 1956/?; cip

DYER, Susan H. (?-1923)
**Outlandish Suite, An: Florida Night
Song (Chuck Will's Widow)**
[2873] Heifetz, Jascha (vln); Bay, Emanuel
(pf)
- Decca DA-23659 (in set
DA-454); 78; 10"; rel pre-1948
- Decca DL-9760; 33m; rel 1955;
del 1971

EAKIN, Charles (1927-)
Frames (1977)
[2874] Burge, David (pf)
- CRI-407; 33s; rel 1979; cip

EARLS, Paul (1934-)
And on the Seventh Day (1959)
[2875] Eastman-Rochester Symphony
Orchestra; Hanson, Howard
(cond)
Rec 1958
- Mercury MG-50053/SR-90053;
33m/s; rel 1959; del 1964
- Eastman-Rochester Archives
ERA-1003; 33s; rel 1974; cip

Arise, My Love (1967)
[2876] Hanks, John Kennedy (ten);
Friedberg, Ruth (pf)
- Duke University Press
DWR-7306; 33s; rel 1974

**Entreat Me Not To Leave You
(1967)**
[2877] Hanks, John Kennedy (ten);
Friedberg, Ruth (pf)
- Duke University Press
DWR-7306; 33s; rel 1974

EASTHAM, Clark
Andante, Strings
[2878] Yaddo Orchestra; Holmes, M.
(cond)
- Yaddo IV-7; 78; 10"; rel 1940

EATON, John (1935-)
Blind Man's Cry (1969)
[2879] Hirayama, Michiko (sop); ensemble
of synthesizers
- CRI-296; 33s; rel 1973; cip

**Concert Music for Solo Clarinet
(1961)**
[2880] Smith, William O. (cl)
- CRI-296; 33s; rel 1973; cip

**Concert Piece for Solo Syn-Ket
(1966)**
[2881] Eaton, John (syn-ket)
- Decca DL-10154/DL-710154;
33m/s; rel 1968; del 1972

**Concert Piece for Syn-Ket and
Symphony Orchestra (1966)**
[2882] Dallas Symphony Orchestra;
Johanos, Donald (cond)
- Turnabout TVS-34428; 33s; rel
1971; del 1977

Danton and Robespierre (1978)
[2883] Indiana University Opera Theater;
Baldner, Thomas (cond)
Rec 1978
- CRI-421; 33s; 3 discs; rel 1980;
cip

Duet (1968)
[2884] Eaton, John (syn-ket) (syn)
- Decca DL-710165; 33s; rel
1969; del 1975

Mass (1970)
[2885] Hirayama, Michiko (sop); Smith,
William O. (cl); ensemble of
synthesizers; tape; White, John
Reeves (cond)
- CRI-296; 33s; rel 1973; cip

Microtonal Fantasy (1965)
[2886] Eaton, John (pf)
- Decca DL-10154/DL-710154;
33m/s; rel 1968; del 1972

Myshkin (1970): Prelude
[2887] Eaton, John (syn-ket)
- Decca DL-10154/DL-710154;
33m/s; rel 1968; del 1972

Soliloquy (1967)
[2888] Eaton, John (syn-ket)
- Decca DL-710165; 33s; rel
1969; del 1975

Songs for R. P. B. (1965)
[2889] Hirayama, Michiko (sop); Eaton,
John (syn-ket)
- Decca DL-10154/DL-710154;
33m/s; rel 1968; del 1972

Thoughts on Rilke (1967)
[2890] Hirayama, Michiko (sop); Eaton,
John (syn-ket) (syn-mil); Smith,
Jane (syn-ket); Ketoff, Paolo
(vibrator) (reverberation plate)
- Decca DL-710165; 33s; rel
1969; del 1975

Vibrations (1966)
[2891] University of Washington
Contemporary Group; Smith,
William O. (cond)
- Decca DL-710165; 33s; rel
1969; del 1975

EDMUNDS, John (1913-)
Adam's Lament
[2892] Renzi, Dorothy (sop) or Crader,
Jeannine (sop) or Langstaff, John
(bar); Crowder, Charles (pf) or
Garvey, David (pf)
- Desto D-430/DST-6430; 33m/s;
rel 1968; cip

As Dew in Aprille
[2893] Renzi, Dorothy (sop) or Crader,
Jeannine (sop) or Langstaff, John
(bar); Crowder, Charles (pf) or
Garvey, David (pf)
- Desto D-430/DST-6430; 33m/s;
rel 1968; cip

Drummer, The (1952)
[2894] Gramm, Donald (bar); Cumming,
Richard (pf)
- St/And SPL-411-12; 33m; 2
discs; rel 1963; del 1964
- Desto D-411-12/DST-6411-12;
33m/s; 2 discs; rel 1964; cip

Everlasting Voices, The
[2895] Renzi, Dorothy (sop) or Crader,
Jeannine (sop) or Langstaff, John
(bar); Crowder, Charles (pf) or
Garvey, David (pf)
- Desto D-430/DST-6430; 33m/s;
rel 1968; cip

Faucon, The (1939-44)
[2896] Gramm, Donald (bar); Cumming,
Richard (pf)
- St/And SPL-411-12; 33m; 2
discs; rel 1963; del 1964
- Desto D-411-12/DST-6411-12;
33m/s; 2 discs; rel 1964; cip

Fish, The
[2897] Renzi, Dorothy (sop) or Crader,
Jeannine (sop) or Langstaff, John
(bar); Crowder, Charles (pf) or
Garvey, David (pf)
- Desto D-430/DST-6430; 33m/s;
rel 1968; cip

Gay Hornpipe (1950)
[2898] Willett, William C. (cl); Staples,
James (pf)
- Mark MRS-32638; 33s; rel
1970; del 1975

Isle of Portland, The
[2899] Renzi, Dorothy (sop) or Crader,
Jeannine (sop) or Langstaff, John
(bar); Crowder, Charles (pf) or
Garvey, David (pf)
- Desto D-430/DST-6430; 33m/s;
rel 1968; cip

Magi, The
[2900] Renzi, Dorothy (sop) or Crader,
Jeannine (sop) or Langstaff, John
(bar); Crowder, Charles (pf) or
Garvey, David (pf)
- Desto D-430/DST-6430; 33m/s;
rel 1968; cip

Milk Maids
[2901] Renzi, Dorothy (sop) or Crader,
Jeannine (sop) or Langstaff, John
(bar); Crowder, Charles (pf) or
Garvey, David (pf)
- Desto D-430/DST-6430; 33m/s;
rel 1968; cip

Molly Samways
[2902] Renzi, Dorothy (sop) or Crader,
Jeannine (sop) or Langstaff, John
(bar); Crowder, Charles (pf) or
Garvey, David (pf)
- Desto D-430/DST-6430; 33m/s;
rel 1968; cip

O Death, Rock Me Asleep
[2903] Renzi, Dorothy (sop) or Crader,
Jeannine (sop) or Langstaff, John
(bar); Crowder, Charles (pf) or
Garvey, David (pf)
- Desto D-430/DST-6430; 33m/s;
rel 1968; cip

On the Nature of Truth
[2904] Renzi, Dorothy (sop) or Crader,
Jeannine (sop) or Langstaff, John
(bar); Crowder, Charles (pf) or
Garvey, David (pf)
- Desto D-430/DST-6430; 33m/s;
rel 1968; cip

Why Canst Thou Not?
[2905] Renzi, Dorothy (sop) or Crader,
Jeannine (sop) or Langstaff, John
(bar); Crowder, Charles (pf) or
Garvey, David (pf)
- Desto D-430/DST-6430; 33m/s;
rel 1968; cip

EDMUNDSON, Garth (1900-)
Apostolic Symphony
[2906] Sunderland, Raymond (org)
Rec 10/2/72
- Vista VPS-1006; 33s; rel 1973

**Christus advenit (Christmas Suite
No 2): Von Himmel hoch**
[2907] Friedell, Harold (org)
- Grayco LPM-101; 33m; 10"; rel
1954

[2908] Rawsthorne, Noel (org)
- EMI/Studio Two TWO-338; 33s;
rel 1971

[2909] Spedding, Alan (org)
- RCA-Victrola VICS-1738; 33s; rel
1973

**(Seven) Classic Preludes on Old
Chorales: Fairest Lord Jesus**
[2910] Becker, C. Warren (org)
- Chapel LP-5-134/ST-134;
33m/s; rel 1968

[2911] Swann, Frederick (org)
Rec 8/63
- Sheldon Recording Studios
S-3165-66 (matrix no); 33m; rel
1963

**(Seven) Contrapuntal Preludes: Now
Woods and Fields Are Sleeping**
[2912] Springer, J. Herbert (org)
- Helffrich Recording Labs
HRL-1556; 33m; rel 1959

Impressions gothiques: Gargoyles
[2913] Crozier, Catharine (org)
- Kendall KRC-LP-2555; 33m; rel 1953; del 1958

EDWARDS, Clara (1887-1974)
By the Bend of the River
[2914] White, Robert (ten); Sanders, Samuel (pf)
- RCA ARL-1-1698; 33s; rel 1976; cip

Into the Night
[2915] Pinza, Ezio (b); King, Gibner (pf) or orchestra; Cleva, Fausto (cond) or Pelletier, Wilfred (cond)
- Columbia ML-2142; 33m; 10"; rel 1950; del 1956

EDWARDS, George (1943-)
Exchange-misere (1974)
[2916] Persichilli, Angelo (fl) (al fl) (pic); Incenzo, Michele (cl) (b cl); Coen, Massimo (vln) (vla); Uitti, Frances (vcl); Saperstein, David (pf)
- CRI-336; 33s; rel 1977; cip

Kreuz und Quer (1971)
[2917] Boston Musica Viva; Pittman, Richard (cond)
Rec 11/24/74
- CRI-323; 33s; rel 1975; cip

Quartet, Strings (1967)
[2918] Composers Quartet
- CRI-265; 33s; rel 1971; cip

EFFINGER, Cecil (1914-)
Invisible Fire, The (1957)
[2919] National Methodist Student Movement Chorus; soloists; Kansas City Philharmonic; Johnson, Thor (cond)
- Methodist Student Movement; 33m; rel 1958*

Little Symphony No 1 (1945)
[2920] Columbia Symphony Orchestra of Vienna; Rozsnyai, Zoltan (cond)
- Columbia ML-5997/MS-6597; 33m/s; rel 1964; del 1968
- Columbia CML-5997/CMS-6597; 33m/s; rel 1968; del 1974
- Columbia AMS-6597; 33s; rel 1974; del 1979

Nocturne
[2921] Davine, Robert (acc)
- Crystal S-106; 33s; rel 1979; cip

Paul of Tarsus (1968)
[2922] Lawrence, Douglas (bar); William Hall Chorale and String Orchestra; Ladd, Thomas (org)
- Owl ORLP-25; 33s; rel 197?

Quartet, Strings, No 5 (1963)
[2923] Hungarian Quartet
- Owl ORLP-10; 33s; rel 1967; del 1977

EHRHARDT, C. Michael (1914-)
Balletti (Suite for Piano) (1954)
[2924] Ehrhardt, C. Michael (pf)
- Educo EP-1001; 33m; 10"; rel 1954; del 1971

Trio, Violin, Violoncello, and Piano, D Minor (Op 17)
[2925] Compinsky Trio
- Alco ALP-1025; 33m; rel 1950; del 1955

EHRLICH, Jesse (1920-)
(Six) Short Pieces for Three Violoncellos
[2926] Cellisti, I; Kessler, Jerome (cond)
- Orion ORS-7037; 33s; rel 1971; cip

EICHHEIM, Henry (1870-1942)
Bali (Symphonic Variations) (1933)
[2927] Philadelphia Orchestra; Stokowski, Leopold (cond)
- Victor 14141-42; 78; 2 discs; rel pre-1942

Japanese Nocturne (orchestral version) (1922)
[2928] Philadelphia Orchestra; Stokowski, Leopold (cond)
- Victor 7260; 78; rel pre-1936

EL-DABH, Halim (1921-)
Leiyla and the Poet (1959-61)
[2929] Electronic music
- Columbia ML-5966/MS-6566; 33m/s; rel 1964; del 1979

Symphonies in Sonic Vibration: Spectrum No 1
[2930] Electronic music
- Folkways FX-6160; 33m; rel 1958; cip

ELKUS, Jonathan (1931-)
After their Kind
[2931] Jones, Edgar (bar); Schwartz, Nathan (pf)
- Fantasy 5008; 33m; rel 1960; del 1969

Dorados (1961)
[2932] Lehigh University Glee Club; Cutler (cond)
- Lehigh 1660; 33m; rel 1968; del 1969

ELLIS, Merrill (1916-81)
Kaleidoscope
[2933] Wall, Joan (m sop); Louisville Orchestra; synthesizer; Mester, Jorge (cond)
- LS-71-1; 33s (Louisville Orchestra First Edition Records 1971 No 1); rel 1971; cip

ELLSASSER, Richard (1926-72)
Chorale Prelude on an English Lullabye (1950)
[2934] Ellsasser, Richard (org)
- MGM E-3031; 33m; rel 1953; del 1959

Concert Study on a Theme of Pietro Yon (1942)
[2935] Ellsasser, Richard (org)
- MGM E-3031; 33m; rel 1953; del 1959
- Conciertos Mexicanos 4; 33m; rel pre-1956
- Elite LPE-116; 33m; rel pre-1956

Erin, O Erin (A Thomas Moore Suite)
[2936] Ellsasser, Richard (org)
- MGM E-3205; 33m; rel 1955; del 1959
- MGM X-314; 45; 7"; rel pre-1956 (excerpts)

Icarus (A Tone Poem) (1945)
[2937] Ellsasser, Richard (org)
- MGM E-3066; 33m; rel 1954; del 1965

Improvisation on a Theme of M. B. Jimenez
[2938] Ellsasser, Richard (org)
- Conciertos Mexicanos 4; 33m; rel pre-1956
- Elite LPE-116; 33m; rel pre-1956

Marche fantastique (1948)
[2939] Ellsasser, Richard (org)
- MGM E-3005; 33m; rel 1953; del 1959

Recreation on Turkey in the Straw
[2940] Ellsasser, Richard (org)
- MGM E-3031; 33m; rel 1953; del 1959

Toward Evening
[2941] Ellsasser, Richard (org)
- MGM E-3127; 33m; rel 1955; del 1959

Variations on a Theme by Chopin
[2942] Ellsasser, Richard (org)
- MGM E-3417; 33m; rel 1957; del 1959

Variations on a Theme by Paganini
[2943] Ellsasser, Richard (org)
- MGM E-3417; 33m; rel 1957;
del 1959

ELLSTEIN, Abraham (1907-63)
Negev Concerto
[2944] Original Piano Quartet
- Decca DL-10047/DL-710047;
33m/s; rel 1962; del 1971

V'liyerusholayim ircho
[2945] Cantica Hebraica; Michno, Dennis
(cond)
- JML-3812; 33s; rel 1977?

ELMAN, Mischa (1891-1967)
In a Gondola
[2946] Elman, Mischa (vln)
- Victor 64530; 78; 10''; rel
1914-19
- Victor 603; 78; 10''; rel
1914-19

Tango (1930)
[2947] Elman, Mischa (vln); Seiger, Joseph
(pf)
- London LLP-1629; 33m; rel
1957; del 1959

ELMORE, Robert Hall (1913-)
**Chorale Prelude on
Seelenbraeutigam**
[2948] Jones, Joyce (org)
- Word WST-8611; 33s; rel 1973

Donkey Dance
[2949] Prince-Joseph, Bruce (org)
- Hi-Fi R-709/S-709; 33m/s; rel
1957/1960; del 1965
- Everest LPBR-6158/SDBR-3158;
33m/s; rel 1967; cip

Fantasy on Nursery Themes
[2950] Elmore, Robert (org)
Rec 11/24/56
- Mercury MG-50109/SR-90109;
33m/s; rel 1957/1959; del
1963

(Three) Miniatures
[2951] Elmore, Robert (org)
- Word W-4026/WST-9026;
33m/s; rel 1965; del 1976

Rhumba
[2952] Linzel, Edward (org)
- Discuriosities BCL-7201; 33m;
rel 1955

Rhythmic Suite
[2953] Elmore, Robert (org)
- Canterbury MMR-270; 33m; rel
pre-1956
- Allen Organ Co AO-3600; 33m;
rel 197? (Excerpt: Pavane)

Rhythmic Suite *(cont'd)*
[2954] Linzel, Edward (org)
- Discuriosities BCL-7201; 33m;
rel 1955

Rhythmic Suite: Pavane
[2955] Purvis, Richard (org)
- Hi-Fi R-703/S-703; 33m/s; rel
1956/1960; del 1970

[2956] White, Ernest (org)
- Moeller Organ Co E4QP-3442-43
(matrix no); 33m; rel 1954

ELSTON, Arnold (1907-71)
Quartet, Strings (1961)
[2957] Pro Arte Quartet
- CRI-289; 33s; rel 1972; cip

ELWELL, Herbert (1898-1974)
Blue Symphony (1944)
[2958] Vanni, Helen (m sop); Cerone,
David (vln); Sharon, Linda (vln);
Skernick, Abraham (vla); Geber,
Stephen (vcl)
- Golden Crest GCCL-201; 33s; rel
1976*

Bus Ride
[2959] Martin, Charlotte (pf)
- Educo 3021; 33m; rel 1968; del
1972

Child's Grace, A
[2960] Makas, Maxine (sop); Makas,
Anthony (pf)
- CRI-270; 33s; rel 1971; cip

Concert Suite (1957)
[2961] Harth, Sidney (vln); Louisville
Orchestra; Whitney, Robert (cond)
- LOU-59-3; 33m (Louisville
Orchestra First Edition Records
1959 No 3); rel 1960; cip

**Happy Hypocrite, The (Suite)
(1927)**
[2962] Vienna Symphony Orchestra;
Hendl, Walter (cond)
- American Recording Society
ARS-37; 33m; rel 1953*

[2963] Cleveland Pops Orchestra; Lane,
Louis (cond)
- Epic LC-3819/BC-1154; 33m/s;
rel 1962; del 1965

I Look Back
[2964] Makas, Maxine (sop); Makas,
Anthony (pf)
- CRI-270; 33s; rel 1971; cip

Ousel-Cock, The
[2965] Luening, Ethel (sop); Nowak, Lionel
(pf)
- Yaddo IV-2; 78; 10''; rel 1940

[2966] Makas, Maxine (sop); Makas,
Anthony (pf)
- CRI-270; 33s; rel 1971; cip

Pastorale (1948)
[2967] Marshall, Lois (sop); Toronto
Symphony Orchestra; MacMillan,
Ernest C. (cond)
- Hallmark CS-1; 33m; rel 1954*

Service of All the Dead
[2968] Makas, Maxine (sop); Makas,
Anthony (pf)
- CRI-270; 33s; rel 1971; cip

Tarantella
[2969] Martin, Charlotte (pf)
- Educo 3021; 33m; rel 1968; del
1972

This Glittering Grief (1969)
[2970] Makas, Maxine (sop); Makas,
Anthony (pf)
- CRI-270; 33s; rel 1971; cip

Wistful
[2971] Makas, Maxine (sop); Makas,
Anthony (pf)
- CRI-270; 33s; rel 1971; cip

ENGEL, Carl (1883-1944)
**Sea Shell (arr for vln and pf by
Efrem Zimbalist)**
[2972] Rabin, Michael (vln); Balsam, Artur
(pf)
- Columbia AAL-30; 33m; 10''; rel
1953; del 1957

[2973] Rabin, Michael (vln); Pommers,
Leon (pf)
- Capitol P-8506/SP-8506;
33m/s; rel 1959; del 1961

[2974] Steiner, Diana (vln); Berfield, David
(pf)
- Orion ORS-74160; 33s; rel
1975; cip

Triptych
[2975] Kroll, William (vln); Sheridan, Frank
(pf)
- Schirmer 15; 78; 3 discs; rel
pre-1942

ENGELMAN, John*
Fanfare
[2976] Ithaca Percussion Ensemble;
Benson, Warren (cond)
- Golden Crest
CR-4016/CRS-4016; 33m/s; rel
1960/1961; cip

EPHROS, Gershon (1890-78)
Aeolian Quartet (1961)
[2977] Silvermine String Quartet
- Tikva T-87; 33m; rel 1965; del
1974

Cantorial Anthology: Uvashofor godol, Ovos, Ashre, Kiddush, and Lo amus
[2978] Segal, Robert H. (voice); Wolfson, Arthur (voice); Meisels, Saul (voice); Ganchoff, Moshe (voice); Temple Bnai Jeshurun (New York) Chorus; Temple on the Heights (Cleveland) Choir
- Tikva T-70; 33m; rel 1961; del 1974

Children's Suite (1936)
[2979] Brall, Ruth (al); Eisner, Bruno (pf)
- Tikva T-87; 33m; rel 1965; del 1974

Halleluyah (1960)
[2980] Marcus, Jacob (ten); Kosakoff, Reuven (pf)
- Tikva T-87; 33m; rel 1965; del 1974

Introduction, Andante, and Fugue (1957)
[2981] Kohon Quartet
- Tikva T-70; 33m; rel 1961; del 1974

Suite, Piano (1951)
[2982] Brown, Lucy (pf)
- Tikva T-70; 33m; rel 1961; del 1974

Variations, Piano (1932)
[2983] Brown, Lucy (pf)
- Tikva T-70; 33m; rel 1961; del 1974

Vocalise (1962)
[2984] Lavanne, Antonia (sop); Kosakoff, Reuven (pf)
- Tikva T-87; 33m; rel 1965; del 1974

EPSTEIN, Alvin (1926-)
Dialogue (1965)
[2985] Turetzky, Bertram (cb); Lesbines, Tele (perc)
- Medea MCLP-1001; 33m/s; rel 1966; del 1971

EPSTEIN, David (1930-)
Night Voices (1974)
[2986] Bookspan, Janet (nar); Boston Archdiocesan Boys Choir; MIT Symphony Orchestra; Epstein, David (cond)
- Candide CE-31116; 33s; rel 1980; cip

Quartet, Strings (1971)
[2987] Philadelphia String Quartet
- Desto DC-7148; 33s; rel 1974; cip

Seasons, The (1956)
[2988] DeGaetani, Jan (m sop); Freeman, Robert (pf)
- Desto DC-7148; 33s; rel 1974; cip

Trio, Strings (1964)
[2989] Pacific String Trio
- Desto DC-7148; 33s; rel 1974; cip

Vent-ures
[2990] Eastman Symphonic Wind Ensemble; Hunsberger, Donald (cond)
- Desto DC-7148; 33s; rel 1974; cip

ERB, Donald (1927-)
Basspiece (1969)
[2991] Turetzky, Bertram (cb); tape
- Desto DC-7128; 33s; rel 1972; cip

Concerto, Percussion and Orchestra (1966)
[2992] Dahlgren, David (perc); Dallas Symphony Orchestra; Johanos, Donald (cond)
- Turnabout TVS-34433; 33s; rel 1971; cip

Diversion for Two (Other Than Sex) (1966)
[2993] Murtha, Roger (tpt); Lesbines, Tele (perc)
- Opus One 1/S-1; 33m/s; rel 1966; cip

Harold's Trip to the Sky (1972)
[2994] Ferritto, Marcia (vla); Benedict, Allyn (pf); Williams, Kent (perc)
- Crystal S-531; 33s; rel 1977; cip

In No Strange Land (1968)
[2995] Dempster, Stuart (tbn); Turetzky, Bertram (cb); tape
- Nonesuch H-71223; 33s; rel 1969; cip

Kyrie (1965)
[2996] University Circle Singers; Weiner, Richard (perc); tape; Appling, William (cond)
- Ars Nova/Ars Antiqua AN-1008; 33s; rel 1971; del 1973

Phantasma (1965)
[2997] Turetzky, Nancy (fl) (al fl) (pic); Korman, Fred (ob) (E hn); Turetzky, Bertram (cb); White, John Reeves (hpschd)
- Opus One 1/S-1; 33m/s; rel 1966; cip

(Three) Pieces, Piano and Brass Quintet (1968)
[2998] Smolko, James (pf); New York Brass Quintet; Bamert, Matthias (cond)
- CRI-323; 33s; rel 1975; cip

Reconnaissance (1967)
[2999] instrumental ensemble (including electronic instruments); Erb, Donald (cond)
- Nonesuch H-71223; 33s; rel 1969; cip

VII Miscellaneous (1964)
[3000] Turetzky, Nancy (fl); Turetzky, Bertram (cb)
- Medea MCLP-1001; 33m/s; rel 1966; del 1971

Seventh Trumpet, The (1969)
[3001] Dallas Symphony Orchestra; Johanos, Donald (cond)
- Turnabout TVS-34433; 33s; rel 1971; cip

Sonata, Harpsichord and String Quartet (1963)
[3002] White, John Reeves (hpschd); Koch String Quartet
- CRI-183; 33m/s; rel 1964/?; cip

Sonneries (1961)
[3003] Cleveland Orchestra (brass section); Bamert, Matthias (cond)
- Crystal S-531; 33s; rel 1977; cip

Stargazing (1966)
[3004] Cornell University Symphonic Band; tape; Stith, Marice (cond)
- Cornell CUWE-3; 33s; rel 1975; cip

Summer Music (1966)
[3005] Priest, Maxine (pf)
- Golden Crest GCCL-202; 33s; rel 1978; cip

[3006] Smolko, James (pf)
- Ars Nova/Ars Antiqua AN-1008; 33s; rel 1971; del 1973

Symphony of Overtures (1964)
[3007] Dallas Symphony Orchestra; Johanos, Donald (cond)
- Turnabout TVS-34433; 33s; rel 1971; cip

Trio, Strings (1966)
[3008] Pollikoff, Max (vln); Tekula, Joseph (vla); Hall, James (elec gtr)
- Opus One 1/S-1; 33m/s; rel 1966; cip

Trio for Two (1968)
[3009] Turetzky, Nancy (fl) (timp); Turetzky, Bertram (cb)
- Ars Nova/Ars Antiqua AN-1008; 33s; rel 1971; del 1973

Trio for Two (1968) (cont'd)
- Finnadar SR-9015; 33s; rel 1977; cip

ERICKSON, Frank (1923-)

Air for Band
[3010] Tennessee Tech Symphonic Wind Ensemble; McGuffey, Patrick (cond)
- Tennessee Tech 2638-39/S-2638-39; 33m/s; rel 1967; del 1975

Balladair
[3011] Tennessee Tech Symphonic Wind Ensemble; McGuffey, Patrick (cond)
- Tennessee Tech 2638-39/S-2638-39; 33m/s; rel 1967; del 1975

Chanson and Bourree
[3012] Ohio State University Concert Band; McGinnis, Donald E. (cond)
- Coronet S-1258; 33s; rel 1969; del 1978

Chroma
[3013] Cornell University Wind Ensemble; Stith, Marice (cond)
- Cornell CUWE-6; 33s; rel 1971; cip

Earth-Song
[3014] Cornell University Wind Ensemble; Stith, Marice (cond)
- Cornell CUWE-6; 33s; rel 1971; cip

Golden Gate
[3015] Tennessee Tech Symphonic Wind Ensemble; McGuffey, Patrick (cond)
- Tennessee Tech 2638-39/S-2638-39; 33m/s; rel 1967; del 1975

Mexican Folk Fantasy
[3016] Cornell University Wind Ensemble; Stith, Marice (cond)
- Cornell CUWE-6; 33s; rel 1971; cip

Presidio
[3017] Tennessee Tech Symphonic Wind Ensemble; McGuffey, Patrick (cond)
- Tennessee Tech 2638-39/S-2638-39; 33m/s; rel 1967; del 1975

Rondo giocoso
[3018] Tennessee Tech Symphonic Wind Ensemble; McGuffey, Patrick (cond)
- Tennessee Tech 2638-39/S-2638-39; 33m/s; rel 1967; del 1975

Symphony, Band, No 2: Finale
[3019] Tennessee Tech Symphonic Wind Ensemble; McGuffey, Patrick (cond)
- Tennessee Tech 2638-39/S-2638-39; 33m/s; rel 1967; del 1975

Thunderbird
[3020] Tennessee Tech Symphonic Wind Ensemble; McGuffey, Patrick (cond)
- Tennessee Tech 2638-39/S-2638-39; 33m/s; rel 1967; del 1975

Toccata, Band
[3021] Tennessee Tech Symphonic Wind Ensemble; McGuffey, Patrick (cond)
- Tennessee Tech 2638-39/S-2638-39; 33m/s; rel 1967; del 1975

ERICKSON, Robert (1917-)

Chamber Concerto (1960)
[3022] Hartt Chamber Players; Shapey, Ralph (cond)
- CRI-218; 33s; rel 1968; cip

End of the Mime
[3023] New Music Choral Ensemble I; Gaburo, Kenneth (cond)
- CRI-325; 33s; rel 1974; cip

General Speech (1969)
[3024] Dempster, Stuart (tbn) (speaker)
- New World NW-254; 33s; rel 1978

Oceans
[3025] Logan, Jack (tpt)
- Orion ORS-7294; 33s; rel 1972; cip

Ricercar a 3 (1967)
[3026] Turetzky, Bertram (cb)
- Ars Nova/Ars Antiqua AN-1001; 33s; rel 1969; del 1973

Ricercar a 5 (1966)
[3027] Dempster, Stuart (tbn); instrumental ensemble
- Acoustic Research AR-0654.084; 33s; rel 1971

ERNST, David (1945-)

Exit
[3028] Logan, Jack (tpt)
- Orion ORS-7294; 33s; rel 1972; cip

ETLER, Alvin (1913-73)

Concerto, Brass Quintet, Strings, and Percussion (1967)
[3029] American Brass Quintet; National Orchestral Association Alumni; Barnett, John (cond)
- CRI-229; 33s; rel 1968; cip

Concerto, Clarinet and Chamber Ensemble (1962)
[3030] Shifrin, David A. (cl); University of Michigan Wind Ensemble; Reynolds, H. Robert (cond)
- University of Michigan SM-0009; 33s; rel 1979; cip

Concerto, Wind Quintet and Orchestra (1960)
[3031] Louisville Orchestra; Whitney, Robert (cond)
- LOU-65-1; 33m (Louisville Orchestra First Edition Records 1965 No 1); rel 1965; cip

Five Speeds Forward
[3032] Van Vactor, David (fl); Etler, Alvin (ob); Rood, Louise (vla); Reines, Joseph (bsn)
- Yaddo III-2; 78; rel 1940

Music for Chamber Orchestra
[3033] Yaddo Orchestra; Shepherd, Arthur (cond)
- Yaddo M-5-6; 78; 2-10"; rel 1938

Quintet, Brass (1963)
[3034] New York Brass Quintet
- CRI-205; 33m/s; rel 1966; cip

Quintet, Winds (1955)
[3035] New York Woodwind Quintet
- Concert-Disc M-1216/CS-216; 33m/s; rel 1960; cip

Six from Ohio
[3036] Etler, Alvin (ob); Walden String Quartet
- Yaddo 109-11; 78; 3-10"; rel 1937

Sonata, Bassoon and Piano (1951)
[3037] Schoenbach, Sol (bsn); Levine, Joseph (pf)
- Columbia ML-5821/MS-6421; 33m/s; rel 1963; del 1968
- Columbia CML-5821/CMS-6421; 33m/s; rel 1968; del 1974
- Columbia AMS-6421; 33s; rel 1974; cip

[3038] Sharrow, Leonard (bsn); Robert, Walter (pf)
- Coronet M-1294; 33m; rel 1969; cip

Sonata, Clarinet and Piano (1952)
[3039] Pino, David (cl); Webb, Frances Mitchum (pf)
- Orion ORS-76256; 33s; rel 1977; cip

Sonic Sequence (1967)
[3040] American Brass Quintet; National Orchestral Association Alumni; Barnett, John (cond)
- CRI-229; 33s; rel 1968; cip

Triptych (1961)
[3041] Louisville Orchestra; Whitney,
Robert (cond)
- LOU-67-4/LS-67-4; 33m/s
(Louisville Orchestra First Edition
Records 1967 No 4); rel 1967;
cip

EVANS, Merle (1893-)
Symphonia
[3042] Incredible Columbia All-Star Band;
Schuller, Gunther (cond)
- Columbia M-33513/MQ-33513;
33s/q; rel 1975; cip

EVETT, Robert (1922-75)
Anniversary Concerto–Seventy-Five
[3043] National Symphony Orchestra;
Mitchell, Howard (cond)
- Basic-Witz BW-1889; 33m; rel
1964

Billy in the Darbies
[3044] Parker, William (bar); Blackwell,
Virgil (cl); Huckaby, William (pf);
Columbia String Quartet
- New World NW-305; 33s; rel
1980

Chaconne
[3045] Gowen, Bradford (pf)
- New World NW-304; 33s; rel
1979

Quintet, Piano and Strings
[3046] Parris, Robert (pf); University of
Maryland String Quartet
- Turnabout TVS-34568; 33s; rel
1975; del 1978

Sonata, Harpsichord (1961)
[3047] Parris, Robert (hpschd)
- CRI-237; 33s; rel 1969; cip

FAIRCHILD, Blair (1877-1933)
**Moustiques (arr for vln and pf by
Dushkin)**
[3048] Candela, Miguel (vln); Benvenuti,
Joseph (pf)
- Columbia LF-138; 78; 10''; rel
pre-1936

FARBERMAN, Harold (1929-)
Alea
[3049] Pugwash Percussion Ensemble;
Farberman, Harold (cond)
- Serenus SRS-12064; 33s; rel
1976; cip

August 30, 1964 (1964)
[3050] Curry, Corrine (sop); Miller, Robert
(pf); Farberman, Harold (perc)
- Serenus SRE-1011/SRS-12011;
33m/s; rel 1965; cip

**Concerto, Alto Saxophone and
String Orchestra (1966)**
[3051] Estrin, Harvey (al sax); Stuttgart
Philharmonia (strings);
Farberman, Harold (cond)
- Serenus SRE-1016/SRS-12016;
33m/s; rel 1967; cip

Elegy, Fanfare, and March (1965)
[3052] Stuttgart Philharmonia; Farberman,
Harold (cond)
- Serenus SRE-1016/SRS-12016;
33m/s; rel 1967; cip

Evolution (1954)
[3053] Baldyga, Dolores (sop); Stagliano,
James (hn); Boston Percussion
Group
- Boston B-207; 33m; rel 1954;
del 1968

[3054] Curry, Corrine (sop); Boston
Percussion Ensemble; Farberman,
Harold (cond)
- Mercury
MGW-36144/SRW-80015;
33m/s; rel 1961; del 1964

[3055] Curtin, Phyllis (sop); Pottle, Ralph
(hn); Boston Chamber Ensemble;
Farberman, Harold (cond)
- Cambridge CRM-805/CRS-1805;
33m/s; rel 1965; del 1975

Evolution: Section 1
[3056] Leopold Stokowski and his
Orchestra; Stokowski, Leopold
(cond)
- Capitol SAL-8385/SSAL-8385;
33m/s; rel 1957/1959; del
1961
- Capitol PAR-8385/SPAR-8385;
33m/s; rel 1961; del 1964

Greek Scene (1957)
[3057] Curry, Corrine (sop); Miller, Robert
(pf); Farberman, Harold (perc)
- Serenus SRE-1011/SRS-12011;
33m/s; rel 1965; cip

Images for Brass (1964)
[3058] New York Brass Quintet
- Serenus SRE-1011/SRS-12011;
33m/s; rel 1965; cip

Impressions (1959)
[3059] Gomberg, Ralph (ob); Boston
Chamber Ensemble; Farberman,
Harold (cond)
- Cambridge CRM-805/CRS-1805;
33m/s; rel 1965; del 1975

Music Inn Suite
[3060] Boston Percussion Ensemble;
Farberman, Harold (cond)
- Mercury
MGW-36144/SRW-80015;
33m/s; rel 1961; del 1964

Progressions (1960)
[3061] Perras, John (fl); Boston Chamber
Ensemble; Farberman, Harold
(cond)
- Cambridge CRM-805/CRS-1805;
33m/s; rel 1965; del 1975

Quintessence (1962)
[3062] Dorian Woodwind Quintet
- Serenus SRE-1011/SRS-12011;
33m/s; rel 1965; cip

Theme and Variations (1959)
[3063] Goodman, Saul (perc)
- Columbia CL-1533/CS-8333;
33m/s; rel 1961; del 1962

. . . Then Silence (1964)
[3064] instrumental ensemble; Farberman,
Harold (cond); Schuller, Gunther
(cond)
- Cambridge CRM-820/CRS-1820;
33m/s; rel 1967; del 1971

3 + 2
[3065] Blades, James (perc); assisting
instrumentalists
Rec 1972
- Discourses ABK-13; 33s; rel
1973

Three States of Mind
[3066] New York Studio Sextet
- Serenus SRE-1016/SRS-12016;
33m/s; rel 1967; cip

**Trio, Violin, Piano, and Percussion
(1963)**
[3067] New York Studio Trio
- Serenus SRE-1016/SRS-12016;
33m/s; rel 1967; cip

Variations on a Familiar Theme
[3068] Boston Percussion Ensemble;
Farberman, Harold (cond)
- Mercury
MGW-36144/SRW-80015;
33m/s; rel 1961; del 1964

FARLEY, Roland (1892-1932)
Night Wind, The
[3069] Ponselle, Rosa (sop); Chicagov,
Igor (pf)
Rec 10/54
- RCA LM-1889; 33m; rel 1955;
del 1957

**FARNAM, Lynnwood
(1885-1930)**
Toccata on O filii et filiae
[3070] Farnam, Lynnwood (org) (from
Welte player rolls made in 1925)
- Ultra Fidelity UF-1; 33m; rel
1959

[3071] Hamme, A. (org)
- Sound Recordings Specialists H-1;
33m; rel pre-1956

A Discography

Toccata on O filii et filiae (cont'd)
[3072] Harmon, Thomas (org)
- Orion ORS-76255; 33s; rel 1977; cip

FARRAND, Noel (1928-)
Allegro assai
[3073] Earle, B. (vln) or Loft, A. (vla); piano
- New Editions 4; 33m; rel pre-1953

Sonata, Piano (Op 40)
[3074] Berg, Christopher (pf)
- Opus One 49; 33s; rel 1979; cip

FARRAR, O. R.
Bombasto (1895)
[3075] Eastman Symphonic Wind Ensemble; Fennell, Frederick (cond)
- Mercury MG-50314/SR-90314; 33m/s; rel 1963; del 1976
- Mercury SRI-75087; 33s; rel 1977; cip

[3076] University of Michigan Winds and Percussion; Lillya, Clifford P. (cond)
Rec 2/18-19/75
- University of Michigan SM-0002; 33s; rel 1978; cip

FARWELL, Arthur (1877-1952)
Alabaster Chambers
[3077] Luening, Ethel (sop); Nowak, Lionel (pf)
- Yaddo IV-2; 78; 10''; rel 1940

Americana (Op 78) (1927): (No 3) Sourwood Mountain
[3078] Behrend, Jeanne (pf)
- Victor 17913 (in set M-764); 78; rel 1941

(Two) Blake Songs (Op 88) (1930): A Cradle Song
[3079] Luening, Ethel (sop); Nowak, Lionel (pf)
- Yaddo IV-2; 78; 10''; rel 1940

From Mesa and Plain (Op 20) (1905): Navajo War Dance and Pawnee Horses
[3080] Basquin, Peter (pf)
- New World NW-213; 33s; rel 1977

From Mesa and Plain: Navajo War Dance
[3081] Behrend, Jeanne (pf)
- Victor 17913 (in set M-764); 78; rel 1941

[3082] Johannesen, Grant (pf)
- Golden Crest CR-4065/CRS-4065; 33m/s; rel 1963/1966; cip

(Three) Indian Songs (Op 32) (1908)
[3083] Parker, William (bar); Huckaby, William (pf)
- New World NW-213; 33s; rel 1977

(Four) Indian Songs (Op 102) (1937): Navajo War Dance and The Old Man's Love Song
[3084] New World Singers; Miner, John (cond)
- New World NW-213; 33s; rel 1977

Quintet, Piano and Strings (Op 103) (1937)
[3085] James, Aileen (pf); Erickson, Ronald (vln); Rosenberger, Celia (vln); Kissling, Elizabeth (vla); Warkentin, Wanda (vcl)
- Musical Heritage Society MHS-3827; 33s; rel 1978

FAWICK, Thomas L.
Musical Impressions
[3086] Kerekjarto, Duci de (vln); Freeman, Charles Kennedy (pf)
- Omega OMLX-4; 33; rel 1959

Musicale 1967
[3087] Harth, Sidney (vln); Harth, Teresa (vln); U.S. Marine Band; Harpham, Capt. Dale (cond)
- Pride RKL-140848 (matrix no); 33m; rel 1967

Musicale 1969
[3088] Harth, Sidney (vln); Harth, Teresa (vln)
- Pride 143583 (matrix no); 33s; rel 1969

Romance in Music
[3089] Kerekjarto, Duci de (vln); accordion; piano
- M-5; 33; rel 1961

Violin Musicale
[3090] Kerekjarto, Duci de (vln); accordion; piano
- CN-104/CMS-105; 33m/s; rel 1960

FAX, Mark (1911-74)
Prelude, Piano (1968)
[3091] Norman, Ruth (pf)
- Opus One 35; 33s; rel 1978; cip

Whatsoever a Man Soweth
[3092] Virginia Union University Choir; Hobbs, Odell (cond)
- Gerald Lewis Recording MC-8806; 33

FAXON, Nancy Plummer (1914-)
Adagio espressivo
[3093] Phelps, Ruth Barrett (org)
- Washington WAS-13; 33m; rel 1959; del 1962
- Aeolian-Skinner AS-313; 33s; rel 1963; del 1966

FEARIS, John S. (1867-1932)
Beautiful Isle of Somewhere
[3094] Jarvis, Harold (voice); orchestra
- Victor 16008; 78; 10''

[3095] McCormack, John (ten)
- Victor 64428; 78; 10''; rel 1913-15
- Victor 744; 78; 10''; rel 1913-15

[3096] Miller, William (ten); Hymns of all Churches Choir; Jacky, Frederick J. (cond)
- Victor P-162; 78; 10''

[3097] Robyn, William (ten); orchestra
- Cameo S-412; 78; 10''

[3098] Steber, Eleanor (sop); Harshaw, Margaret (al)
- Victor 10-1449A; 78; 10''

[3099] Williams, Evan (ten); orchestra
- Victor 64411; 78; 10''; rel 1911-18
- Victor 865; 78; 10''; rel 1911-18

FELCIANO, Richard (1930-)
And from the Abyss (1976)
[3100] Cooley, Floyd (tu); tape
- Opus One 29; 33s; rel 1976; cip

Chod (1975)
[3101] Philadelphia Composers' Forum; Thome, Joel (cond)
- CRI-349; 33s; rel 1976; cip

Crasis
[3102] Subke, David (fl); O'Brien, Donald (cl); Bloch, Robert (vln); Hampton, Bonnie (vcl); Bellows, Beverly (hp); Sparrow, Naomi (pf); Blackshere, Lawrence (perc); Felciano, Richard (cond)
- CRI-349; 33s; rel 1976; cip

Glossolalia (1967)
[3103] Klebe, Marvin (bar); Maund, Peter (perc); Moe, Lawrence (org); tape
- Cambridge CRS-2560; 33s; rel 1978; cip

God of the Expanding Universe
[3104] Davis, Merrill N., III (org); tape
Rec 5/20/72
- Aeolian-Skinner AS-330; 33s; rel 1975

[3105] Pizarro, David (org); tape
- Grosvenor GRS-1017; 33s; rel 1973

Gravities
[3106] Salkind, Milton (pf); Salkind, Peggy
(pf)
- CRI-349; 33s; rel 1976; cip

In Celebration of Golden Rain
[3107] Moe, Lawrence (org); Scripps
Gamelan of the University of
California; Felciano, Richard
(cond)
- Cambridge CRS-2560; 33s; rel
1978; cip

Spectra (1966)
[3108] Turetzky, Nancy (fl); Turetzky,
Bertram (cb)
- Ars Nova/Ars Antiqua AN-1001;
33s; rel 1969; del 1973
- CRI-349; 33s; rel 1976; cip

FELDMAN, Morton (1926-)
Chorus and Instruments II (1967)
[3109] Brandeis University Chamber
Chorus; Lucier, Alvin (cond)
- Odyssey
32-16-0155/32-16-0156;
33m/s; rel 1967; cip

**Christian Wolff in Cambridge
(1963)**
[3110] Brandeis University Chamber
Chorus; Lucier, Alvin (cond)
- Odyssey
32-16-0155/32-16-0156;
33m/s; rel 1967; cip

Durations I-IV (1960-62)
[3111] Hammond, Don (al fl); Butterfield,
Don (tu); Kraus, Philip (vib);
Raimondi, Matthew (vln); Soyer,
David (vcl); Tudor, David (pf)
- Time 58007/S-8007; 33m/s; rel
1963; del 1970
- Mainstream MS-5007; 33s; rel
1970; del 1979

Extensions I (1951)
[3112] Raimondi, Matthew (vln); Tudor,
David (pf)
- Columbia ML-5403/MS-6090;
33m/s; rel 1960; del 1963
- Odyssey 32-16-0302; 33s; rel
1969; del 1971

Extensions IV (1960)
[3113] Hymovitz, Edwin (pf); Sherman,
Russell (pf); Tudor, David (pf)
- Columbia ML-5403/MS-6090;
33m/s; rel 1960; del 1963
- Odyssey 32-16-0302; 33s; rel
1969; del 1971

**False Relationships and the
Extended Ending (1968)**
[3114] Raimondi, Matthew (vln); Barab,
Seymour (vcl); Jacobs, Paul (pf);
Takahashi, Yuji (pf); Tudor, David
(pf); Fromme, Arnold (tbn); Fitz,
Richard (perc)
- CRI-276; 33s; rel 1971; cip

For Frank O'Hara (1973)
[3115] Buffalo Center of the Creative and
Performing Arts (members of);
Williams, Jan (cond)
- Odyssey Y-34138; 33s; rel
1976; cip

Four Instruments (1965)
[3116] Cantilena Chamber Players
- Grenadilla GS-1029-30; 33s; 2
discs

Intersection III (1953)
[3117] Tudor, David (pf)
- Columbia ML-5403/MS-6090;
33m/s; rel 1960; del 1963
- Odyssey 32-16-0302; 33s; rel
1969; del 1971

[3118] Zacher, Gerd (org)
- Deutsche Grammophon
SLPM-139442; 33s; rel 1970;
del 1975

King of Denmark, The (1964)
[3119] Amemiya (perc)
- RCA (Japanese) RVC-2154; 33s;
rel 1979; cip

[3120] Neuhaus, Max (perc)
- Columbia MS-7139; 33s; rel
1968; cip

Out of Last Pieces (1958)
[3121] New York Philharmonic; Bernstein,
Leonard (cond)
- Columbia ML-6133/MS-6733;
33m/s; rel 1965; del 1975

**Piano Piece (To Philip Guston)
(1963)**
[3122] Hays, Doris (pf)
- Finnadar SR-2-720; 33s; 2 discs;
rel 1980; cip

Piece, Four Pianos (1957)
[3123] Hymovitz, Edwin (pf); Sherman,
Russell (pf); Tudor, David (pf);
Feldman, Morton (pf)
- Columbia ML-5403/MS-6090;
33m/s; rel 1960; del 1963
- Odyssey 32-16-0302; 33s; rel
1969; del 1971

(Two) Pieces, Two Pianos (1954)
[3124] Sherman, Russell (pf); Tudor, David
(pf)
- Columbia ML-5403/MS-6090;
33m/s; rel 1960; del 1963
- Odyssey 32-16-0302; 33s; rel
1969; del 1971

**(Three) Pieces, String Quartet
(1956)**
[3125] Raimondi, Matthew (vln); Rabushka
(vln); Trampler, Walter (vla);
Barab, Seymour (vcl)
- Columbia ML-5403/MS-6090;
33m/s; rel 1960; del 1963
- Odyssey 32-16-0302; 33s; rel
1969; del 1971

Projection IV (1951)
[3126] Raimondi, Matthew (vln); Tudor,
David (pf)
- Columbia ML-5403/MS-6090;
33m/s; rel 1960; del 1963
- Odyssey 32-16-0302; 33s; rel
1969; del 1971

Rothko Chapel, The (1971-72)
[3127] Phillips, Karen (vla); Holland,
James (perc); Gregg Smith
Singers; Smith, Gregg (cond)
- Odyssey Y-34138; 33s; rel
1976; cip

Structures (1951)
[3128] Concord String Quartet
- Vox SVBX-5306; 33s; 3 discs; rel
1973; cip

[3129] Raimondi, Matthew (vln); Rabushka
(vln); Trampler, Walter (vla);
Barab, Seymour (vcl)
- Columbia ML-5403/MS-6090;
33m/s; rel 1960; del 1963
- Odyssey 32-16-0302; 33s; rel
1969; del 1971

Vertical Thoughts II (1963)
[3130] Zukofsky, Paul (vln); Kalish, Gilbert
(pf)
- Desto DC-6435-37; 33s; 3 discs;
rel 1975; cip

Vertical Thoughts IV (1963)
[3131] Hays, Doris (pf)
- Finnadar SR-2-720; 33s; 2 discs;
rel 1980; cip

Viola in My Life I-III, The (1970)
[3132] Phillips, Karen (vla); Ajemian,
Anahid (vln); Barab, Seymour
(vcl); Robison, Paula (fl); Bloom,
Arthur (cl); Tudor, David (pf);
DesRoches, Raymond (perc)
- CRI-276; 33s; rel 1971; cip

FELDSTEIN, Saul (1940-)
Insight (1967)
[3133] instrumental ensemble; Feldstein,
Saul (cond)
- Golden Crest
CR-1005/CRS-1005; 33m/s; rel
1967/1979; cip

**Variations on a Four-Note Theme
(1963)**
[3134] instrumental ensemble; Feldstein,
Saul (cond)
- Golden Crest
CR-1005/CRS-1005; 33m/s; rel
1967/1979; cip

FENNELLY, Brian (1937-)
Empirical Rag
[3135] Tidewater Brass Quintet
- Golden Crest CRSQ-4179; 33q

Evanescences (1969)
[3136] Da Capo Chamber Players
(members of); tape; Murray,
Edward (cond)
- CRI-322; 33s; rel 1974; cip

Prelude and Elegy (1973)
[3137] Empire Brass Quintet
- Advance FGR-19S; 33s; rel
1976; cip

Quintet, Winds (1967)
[3138] Dorian Woodwind Quintet
- CRI-318; 33s; rel 1974; cip

Scintilla Prisca (1979)
[3139] Moore, David (vcl); Fennelly, Brian
(pf)
- Orion ORS-80368; 33s; rel
1980; cip

FENNIMORE, Joseph (1940-)
Concerto piccolo
[3140] Fennimore, Joseph (pf); Royal
Philharmonic Orchestra; Freeman,
Paul (cond)
- Spectrum SR-119; 33s; rel 1980

Quartet (After Vinteuil)
[3141] Guy, Larry (cl); Gallagher, Maureen
(vla); Hoyle, Ted (vcl); Helmrich,
Dennis (pf)
- Spectrum SR-119; 33s; rel 1980

FERRITTO, John (1937-)
Oggi (Op 9) (1969)
[3142] Pilgrim, Neva (m sop); Blustine,
Allen (cl); Oppens, Ursula (pf)
- CRI-325; 33s; rel 1974; cip

FETLER, Paul (1920-)
April
[3143] Hamline Singers; Holliday, Robert
(cond)
- SPAMH MIA-116; 33s; rel 1961

Contrasts (1958)
[3144] Minneapolis Symphony Orchestra;
Dorati, Antal (cond)
- Mercury MG-50282/SR-90282;
33m/s; rel 1961; del 1965

Make a Joyful Noise
[3145] Capital University Chapel Choir;
Snyder, Ellis Emanuel (cond)
- Coronet S-1504; 33s; rel 1969;
cip

Nothing but Nature (1961)
[3146] Jaeger, John (bar); Hamline
Chorus; St. Paul Chamber
Orchestra; Sipe, Leopold (cond)
- St. Paul 96585-86/S-96583-84;
33m/s; rel 1964; del 1970

Pastoral Suite
[3147] Macalester Trio
- Golden Crest CRS-4153; 33s; rel
1977; cip

You Did Not Miss Jerusalem
[3148] Capital University Chapel Choir;
Snyder, Ellis Emanuel (cond)
- Westminster
XWN-19024/WST-17024;
33m/s; rel 1963; del 1967

FICKENSCHER, Arthur (1871-1954)
From the Seventh Realm (1920-29)
[3149] Fickenscher, Arthur (pf); string
quartet
- Music Library MLR-5004; 33m;
10"; rel 1952; del 1974

Willow Wood
[3150] Porter, Caryl (m sop); viola;
bassoon; piano
- Music Library MLR-7020; 33m;
rel 1952; del 1974

FILLMORE, Henry (1881-1956)
Americans We
[3151] Eastman Symphonic Wind
Ensemble; Fennell, Frederick
(cond)
Rec 10/19/57
- Mercury MG-50170/SR-90170;
33m/s; rel 1958/1959; del
1965

[3152] U.S. Army Band; Laboda, Samuel R.
(cond)
- Department of Defense
Bicentennial Edition 50-1776;
33s; 2 discs; rel 1976*

[3153] University of Michigan Winds and
Percussion; Lillya, Clifford P.
(cond)
Rec 2/18-19/75
- University of Michigan SM-0002;
33s; rel 1978; cip

Bones Trombone (1922)
[3154] Eastman Symphonic Wind
Ensemble; Fennell, Frederick
(cond)
- Mercury MG-50314/SR-90314;
33m/s; rel 1963; del 1976
- Mercury SRI-75087; 33s; rel
1977; cip

Circus Bee, The (1908)
[3155] Eastman Symphonic Wind
Ensemble; Fennell, Frederick
(cond)
- Mercury MG-50314/SR-90314;
33m/s; rel 1963; del 1976
- Mercury SR-2-9131; 33s; 2
discs; rel 1968; del 1971
- Mercury SRI-75087; 33s; rel
1977; cip

Footlifter, The
[3156] Incredible Columbia All-Star Band;
Schuller, Gunther (cond)
- Columbia M-33513/MQ-33513;
33s/q; rel 1975; cip

His Excellency
[3157] Goldman Band; Goldman, Richard
Franko (cond)
- New World NW-266; 33s; rel
1977

His Honor
[3158] Eastman Symphonic Wind
Ensemble; Fennell, Frederick
(cond)
- Mercury MG-50113; 33m; rel
1956; del 1969

**Lassus Trombone - De Cullud Valet
to Teddy Trombone (ca 1918)**
[3159] Barron, Ronald (tbn); Cooper,
Kenneth (pf)
- Nonesuch H-71341; 33s; rel
1977

Men of Ohio
[3160] University of Miami Symphonic
Band
- King 682; 33m/s; rel 1960; del
1965

Miss Trombone
[3161] Dempster, Stuart (tbn); Steinhardt,
Victor (pf)
- University of Washington Press
OLY-104; 33q; 2 discs; rel 1976;
cip

Rolling Thunder (1916)
[3162] Eastman Symphonic Wind
Ensemble; Fennell, Frederick
(cond)
- Mercury MG-50314/SR-90314;
33m/s; rel 1963; del 1976
- Mercury SRI-75087; 33s; rel
1977; cip

**Shoutin' Liza Trombone - One-Step
(Mose Trombone's Ah-Finity)**
[3163] Barron, Ronald (tbn); Cooper,
Kenneth (pf)
Rec 12/76
- Nonesuch H-71341; 33s; rel
1977
- Nonesuch H-7-14; 33s; 2 discs;
rel 1978; cip

**Teddy Trombone - A Brother to
Miss Trombone (ca 1918)**
[3164] Barron, Ronald (tbn); Cooper,
Kenneth (pf)
- Nonesuch H-71341; 33s; rel
1977

FINE, Irving (1914-62)
**Childhood Fables for Grownups
(1954-55): Two Worms, The Duck
and the Yak, Lenny the Leopard,
and Tigeroo**
[3165] Parker, William (bar); Baldwin,
Dalton (pf)
- New World NW-300; 33s; rel
1978

Choral New Yorker, The (1944)
[3166] Price, Patricia (sop); Eckard, Linda (al); Magdamo, Priscilla (al); Muenz, Richard (bar); Gregg Smith Singers; Cybriwsky, Oresta (pf); Smith, Gregg (cond)
Rec 1976
- Vox SVBX-5353; 33s; 3 discs; rel 1979; cip

(Three) Choruses from Alice in Wonderland (1942)
[3167] Gregg Smith Singers; Beegle, Raymond (pf); Smith, Gregg (cond)
- Odyssey 32-16-0272; 33s; rel 1968; del 1971
- CRI-376; 33s; rel 1978; cip

(Three) Choruses from Alice in Wonderland, Second Series (1953)
[3168] Gregg Smith Singers; Beegle, Raymond (pf); Smith, Gregg (cond)
- Odyssey 32-16-0272; 33s; rel 1968; del 1971
- CRI-376; 33s; rel 1978; cip

Diversions (1959-60)
[3169] Louisville Orchestra; Whitney, Robert (cond)
- LOU-64-3; 33m (Louisville Orchestra First Edition Records 1964 No 3); rel 1964; del 1975

Fantasia, String Trio (1956)
[3170] Boston Symphony Chamber Players
- RCA LM-6167/LSC-6167; 33m/s; 3 discs; rel 1966; del 1976

[3171] Schmitt, Homer (vln); Garvey, John (vla); Swenson, Robert (vcl)
- University of Illinois CRS-5; 33m; rel 1958*

Frog and the Snake, The (1954)
[3172] Miller, Mildred (m sop); Biltcliffe, Edwin (pf)
- St/And SPL-411-12; 33m; 2 discs; rel 1963; del 1964
- Desto D-411-12/DST-6411-12; 33m/s; 2 discs; rel 1964; cip

Hour Glass, The (1949)
[3173] Gregg Smith Singers; Beegle, Raymond (pf); Smith, Gregg (cond)
- Odyssey 32-16-0272; 33s; rel 1968; del 1971
- CRI-376; 33s; rel 1978; cip

[3174] New England Conservatory Chorus; De Varon, Lorna Cooke (cond)
- Golden Crest NEC-117; 33s; rel 1979; cip

Lullaby for a Baby Panda
[3175] Bennett, Bob L. (pf)
- Educo 3109; 33

McCord's Menagerie (1957)
[3176] Gregg Smith Singers; Beegle, Raymond (pf); Smith, Gregg (cond)
- Odyssey 32-16-0272; 33s; rel 1968; del 1971
- CRI-376; 33s; rel 1978; cip

Music for Piano (1947): Variations and Waltz-Gavotte
[3177] Fine, Irving (pf)
- CRI-106; 33m/s; rel 1957/?; cip

Mutability (1952)
[3178] Alberts, Eunice (al); Fine, Irving (pf)
- CRI-106; 33m/s; rel 1957/?; cip

Partita, Wind Quintet (1949)
[3179] Dorian Woodwind Quintet
- Vox SVBX-5307; 33s; 3 discs; rel 1977; cip

[3180] Interlochen Arts Quintet
- Mark 28486; 33s; rel 1968; del 1976

[3181] New Art Wind Quintet
- Classic Editions CE-1003; 33m; rel 1951; del 1959

[3182] New York Woodwind Quintet
- Concert-Disc M-1229/CS-229; 33m/s; rel 1963; del 1973

Polaroli (1954)
[3183] Miller, Mildred (m sop); Biltcliffe, Edwin (pf)
- St/And SPL-411-12; 33m; 2 discs; rel 1963; del 1964
- Desto D-411-12/DST-6411-12; 33m/s; 2 discs; rel 1964; cip

Quartet, Strings (1952)
[3184] Juilliard String Quartet
- Columbia ML-4843; 33m; rel 1954; del 1968
- Columbia CML-4843; 33m; rel 1968; del 1974
- Columbia AML-4843; 33m; rel 1974; del 1976
- CRI-395; 33s; rel 1979; cip

Romanza (1958)
[3185] Musical Arts Quintet
- Now 9632; 33s; rel 1966; del 1976

Serious Song (1955)
[3186] Boston Symphony Orchestra; Leinsdorf, Erich (cond)
- RCA LM-2829/LSC-2829; 33m/s; rel 1966; del 1970
- Desto DC-7167; 33s; rel 1973; cip

[3187] Louisville Orchestra; Whitney, Robert (cond)
- LOU-57-6; 33m (Louisville Orchestra First Edition Records 1957 No 6); rel 1959; del 1972

Symphony (1962)
[3188] Boston Symphony Orchestra; Fine, Irving (cond)
Rec 8/12/62
- RCA LM-2829/LSC-2829; 33m/s; rel 1966; del 1970
- Desto DC-7167; 33s; rel 1973; cip

Toccata concertante (1947)
[3189] Boston Symphony Orchestra; Leinsdorf, Erich (cond)s
- RCA LM-2829/LSC-2829; 33m/s; rel 1966; del 1970
- Desto DC-7167; 33s; rel 1973; cip

FINE, Vivian (1913-)
Alcestis (1960)
[3190] Imperial Philharmonic Orchestra of Tokyo; Strickland, William (cond)
- CRI-145; 33m/s; rel 1961/?; cip

Concertante, Piano and Orchestra (1944)
[3191] Honsho, Reiko (pf); Japan Philharmonic Symphony Orchestra; Watanabe, Akeo (cond)
- CRI-135; 33m/s; rel 1960/1973; cip

Paean (1969)
[3192] Baker, Frank S. (ten) (speaker); Bennington Choral Ensemble; Eastman Brass Ensemble; Fine, Vivian (cond)
- CRI-260; 33s; rel 1971; cip

Sinfonia and Fugato (1963)
[3193] Helps, Robert (pf)
- RCA LM-7042/LSC-7042; 33m/s; 2 discs; rel 1966; del 1971
- CRI-288; 33s; 2 discs; rel 1972; cip

Spring's Welcome
[3194] Luening, Ethel (sop); Johansen, Gunnar (pf)
- Yaddo M-1; 78; 10"; rel 1938

FINLAYSON, W.
Thunder Song March
[3195] Royal Artillery Band; Geary, Col. Owen W. (cond)
- Boosey & Hawkes BH-MTLP-2030; 33m; rel 1954

FINNEY, Charles H.
Improvisations
[3196] Finney, Charles H. (org)
- Advent 5015-SQ; 33s/q; rel 1975

FINNEY, Ross Lee (1906-)

Bleheris (ca 1935)
[3197] Finney, Ross Lee (ten); Yaddo
Chamber Orchestra
- Yaddo I-6; 78; 2 discs; rel 1940

Chromatic Fantasy, Violoncello
[3198] Jelinek, Jerome (vcl)
- CRI-311; 33s; rel 1974; cip

**Concerto, Alto Saxophone, Winds,
and Percussion (1974)**
[3199] Hemke, Frederick (al sax);
Northwestern University
Symphonic Wind Ensemble;
Paynter, John P. (cond)
Rec 11/76
- New World NW-211; 33s; rel
1977

Drinking Song
[3200] Hanks, John Kennedy (ten);
Friedberg, Ruth (pf)
- Duke University Press
DWR-6417-18; 33m; 2 discs; rel
1966; del 1975

**(Twenty-Four) Inventions, Piano
(1970): Holiday**
[3201] Fuszek, Rita (pf)
- Educo 3107; 33

Quartet, Strings, No 2 (1937)
[3202] Yaddo String Quartet
- Yaddo 47A-B; 78; rel 1937 (1st
and 2nd movements)
- Yaddo 5B; 10"; rel 1937 (2nd
movement)
- Yaddo 52A; 78; rel 1937 (3rd
movement)

Quartet, Strings, No 6 (1950)
[3203] Stanley Quartet of the University of
Michigan
- CRI-116; 33m/s; rel 1957/?; cip

Quintet, Piano and Strings
[3204] Webster, Beveridge (pf); Stanley
Quartet of the University of
Michigan
- Columbia ML-5477/MS-6142;
33m/s; rel 1960; del 1968
- Columbia CML-5477/CMS-6142;
33m/s; rel 1968; del 1974
- Columbia AMS-6142; 33s; rel
1974; del 1976

**So Long as the Mind Keeps Silent
(1967)**
[3205] Noehren, Robert (org)
- Lyrichord LL-191/LLST-7191;
33m/s; rel 1968; cip

**Sonata, Viola and Piano, No 1
(1937)**
[3206] Rood, Louise (vla); Johansen,
Gunnar (pf)
- Yaddo D-11-12; 78; 2 discs; rel
1938

**Sonata, Violoncello and Piano, No 2
(1950)**
[3207] Jelinek, Jerome (vcl); Gurt, Joseph
(pf)
- CRI-311; 33s; rel 1974; cip

**Symphony No 1 (Communique)
(1943)**
[3208] Louisville Orchestra; Whitney,
Robert (cond)
- LOU-65-2; 33m (Louisville
Orchestra First Edition Records
1965 No 2); rel 1965; cip

Symphony No 2 (1960)
[3209] Louisville Orchestra; Whitney,
Robert (cond)
- LOU-62-5; 33m (Louisville
Orchestra First Edition Records
1962 No 5); rel 1962; cip

Symphony No 3 (1964)
[3210] Louisville Orchestra; Whitney,
Robert (cond)
- LOU-67-2/LS-67-2; 33m/s
(Louisville Orchestra First Edition
Records 1967 No 2); rel 1967;
cip

Wedlock
[3211] Hanks, John Kennedy (ten);
Friedberg, Ruth (pf)
- Duke University Press
DWR-6417-18; 33m; 2 discs; rel
1966; del 1975

FIORILLO, Dante (1905-)

Concerto, Harpsichord and Strings
[3212] Kirkpatrick, Ralph (hpschd); Yaddo
Orchestra; Donovan, Richard
(cond)
- Yaddo D-9 (23); 78; rel 1938

FIRESTONE, Idabelle
(1874-1954)

Bluebirds
[3213] Stevens, Rise (m sop); orchestra;
Barlow, Howard (cond)
- Victor ERA-149; 45; 7"; rel
1953?

If I Could Tell You
[3214] Stevens, Rise (m sop); orchestra;
Barlow, Howard (cond)
- Victor ERA-149; 45; 7"; rel
1953?

In My Garden
[3215] Stevens, Rise (m sop); orchestra;
Barlow, Howard (cond)
- Victor ERA-149; 45; 7"; rel
1953?

You Are the Song in My Heart
[3216] Stevens, Rise (m sop); orchestra;
Barlow, Howard (cond)
- Victor ERA-149; 45; 7"; rel
1953?

FISCHER, Adolphe*

By the Brook (Op 6)
[3217] Mukle, May (vcl); Falkenstein,
George (pf)
- Victor 17844; 78; rel pre-1925

FISCHER, Carl (1912-)

**Reflections of an Indian Boy (Suite)
(arr by Young)**
[3218] Paul Weston and his Orchestra;
Weston, Paul (cond)
- Columbia CL-788; 33m; rel
1956; del 1965

FISCHER, Irwin (1903-)

**Hungarian Set (The Pearly Bouquet)
(1938)**
[3219] Peninsula Festival Orchestra;
Johnson, Thor (cond)
- CRI-122; 33m; rel 1958; cip

**Overture on an Exuberant Tone Row
(1964)**
[3220] Louisville Orchestra; Whitney,
Robert (cond)
- LOU-67-6/LS-67-6; 33m/s
(Louisville Orchestra First Edition
Records 1967 No 6); rel 1968;
cip

FISCHER, William (1935-)

Quiet Movement, A (1966)
[3221] Oakland Youth Orchestra; Hughes,
Robert (cond)
- Desto DC-7107; 33s; rel 1970;
cip

FISHER, Truman (1927-)

Lincoln, Man of the People
[3222] Pasadena City Symphony
Orchestra and College Concert
Choir
- Capra 1202; 33s; rel 1971; del
1973

FISSINGER, Alfred (1925-)

Suite, Marimba (1953)
[3223] Chenoweth, Vida (mrmb)
- Epic LC-3818/BC-1153; 33m/s;
rel 1962; del 1965

FLAGELLO, Nicolas (1928-)

As I Walked Forth
[3224] Reardon, John (bar); Hebert, Bliss
(pf)
- Serenus SRE-1019/SRS-12019;
33m/s; rel 1967; cip

Burlesca (Op 34) (1961)
[3225] Ketchum, Janet (fl); Segal, Peter
(gtr)
- Orion ORS-78324; 33s; rel
1979; cip

[3226] Sigurdson, Gary (fl); Rome
Symphony Orchestra; Flagello,
Nicolas (cond)
- Serenus SRE-1004/SRS-12004;
33m/s; rel 1965; cip

Capriccio, Violoncello and Orchestra (Op 32) (1962)
[3227] Koutzen, George (vcl); Rome Symphony Orchestra; Flagello, Nicolas (cond)
- Serenus SRE-1003/SRS-12003; 33m/s; rel 1965; cip

Chorale and Episode (1948)
[3228] Rome Symphony Orchestra; Flagello, Nicolas (cond)
- Serenus SRE-1003/SRS-12003; 33m/s; rel 1965; cip

Concertino, Piano, Brass, and Tympani (Op 40) (1963)
[3229] Marshall, Elizabeth (pf); Rome Symphony Orchestra; Flagello, Nicolas (cond)
- Serenus SRE-1003/SRS-12003; 33m/s; rel 1965; cip

Concerto, Flute and Orchestra (Op 12) (1953)
[3230] Sigurdson, Gary (fl); Rome Symphony Orchestra; Flagello, Nicolas (cond)
- Serenus SRE-1004/SRS-12004; 33m/s; rel 1965; cip

Concerto, Strings (Op 27) (1959)
[3231] Rome Symphony Orchestra; Flagello, Nicolas (cond)
- Serenus SRE-1002/SRS-12002; 33m/s; rel 1965; cip

Contemplations (Op 42) (1964)
[3232] Rome Symphony Orchestra; Flagello, Nicolas (cond)
- Serenus SRE-1005/SRS-12005; 33m/s; rel 1965; cip

(Three) Dances, Piano (1945)
[3233] Marshall, Elizabeth (pf)
- Serenus SRE-1003/SRS-12003; 33m/s; rel 1965; cip

(Three) Episodes, Piano (1957)
[3234] Marshall, Elizabeth (pf)
- Serenus SRE-1003/SRS-12003; 33m/s; rel 1965; cip

Good English Hospitality
[3235] Reardon, John (bar); Hebert, Bliss (pf)
- Serenus SRE-1019/SRS-12019; 33m/s; rel 1967; cip

L'Infinito (1956)
[3236] Flagello, Ezio (b bar); orchestra; Flagello, Nicolas (cond)
- Internos INT-0002; 33m/s; rel 1963; del 1971

Island in the Moon, An (Op 43) (1964)
[3237] Tatum, Nancy (sop); Rome Symphony Orchestra; Flagello, Nicolas (cond)
- Serenus SRE-1005/SRS-12005; 33m/s; rel 1965; cip

Judgment of St. Francis, The (Op 28) (1959): Adoration
[3238] Rome Chamber Orchestra; Flagello, Nicolas (cond)
- Peters Internationale PLE-071; 33s; rel 1978; cip

Land, The (Op 16) (1954)
[3239] Flagello, Ezio (b bar); I Musici di Firenze; Flagello, Nicolas (cond)
- Internos INT-0002; 33m/s; rel 1963; del 1971
- Musical Heritage Society MHS-1559; 33s; rel 1973

Lautrec (Op 47) (1965)
[3240] Rome Symphony Orchestra; Flagello, Nicolas (cond)
- Serenus SRE-1014/SRS-12014; 33m/s; rel 1966; cip

Leave O Leave Me to My Sorrow
[3241] Reardon, John (bar); Hebert, Bliss (pf)
- Serenus SRE-1019/SRS-12019; 33m/s; rel 1967; cip

Lyra (1945)
[3242] Rome Symphony Orchestra; Flagello, Nicolas (cond)
- Serenus SRE-1008/SRS-12008; 33m/s; rel 1965; cip

Philos
[3243] American Brass Quintet
- Serenus SRS-12041; 33s; rel 1972

Prelude, Ostinato, and Fugue (Op 30) (1960)
[3244] Marshall, Elizabeth (pf)
- Serenus SRE-1004/SRS-12004; 33m/s; rel 1965; cip

Prisma II
[3245] New York Harp Ensemble; Wurtzler, Aristid von (cond)
- Musical Heritage Society MHS-3307; 33s; rel 1975

Sonata, Piano (Op 38) (1962)
[3246] Marshall, Elizabeth (pf)
- Serenus SRE-1002/SRS-12002; 33m/s; rel 1965; cip

Symphony No 2 (Op 63) (1970)
[3247] Cornell University Wind Ensemble; Stith, Marice (cond)
- Cornell CUWE-23; 33s; rel 197?

FLANAGAN, William (1923-69)

Another August (1966)
[3248] Barton, June (sop); Lee, Noel (pf); Royal Philharmonic Orchestra; Jenkins, Newell (cond)
- CRI-250; 33s; rel 1970; cip

Chaconne (1948)
[3249] Earle, B. (vln); piano
- New Editions 4; 33m; rel pre-1953

Chapters from Ecclesiastes (1962)
[3250] King's Chapel Choir, Boston; Cambridge Festival Strings; Pinkham, Daniel (cond) Rec 1963
- Cambridge CRM-416/CRS-1416; 33m/s; rel 1964; del 1971

Concert Ode, A (1951)
[3251] Imperial Philharmonic Orchestra of Tokyo; Strickland, William (cond)
- CRI-143; 33m/s; rel 1961/?; cip

Dugout, The
[3252] Carter, Sara (sop); Weiser, Bernhard (pf)
- New Editions 2; 33m; rel 1953; del 1959

Go, and Catch a Falling Star (1949)
[3253] Carter, Sara (sop); Weiser, Bernhard (pf)
- New Editions 2; 33m; rel 1953; del 1959

Goodbye, My Fancy (1959)
[3254] Bogard, Carole (sop); Del Tredici, David (pf)
- Desto DC-6468; 33s; rel 1968; cip

Heaven Haven (1948)
[3255] Carter, Sara (sop); Weiser, Bernhard (pf)
- New Editions 2; 33m; rel 1953; del 1959

Horror Movie
[3256] Bogard, Carole (sop); Del Tredici, David (pf)
- Desto DC-6468; 33s; rel 1968; cip

If You Can
[3257] Bogard, Carole (sop); Del Tredici, David (pf)
- Desto DC-6468; 33s; rel 1968; cip

Lady of Tearful Regret, The (1959)
[3258] Larson, Eva Toerklep (sop); Krogh, Yngvar (bar); Oslo Philharmonic Orchestra (members of); Strickland, William (cond)
- CRI-163; 33m/s; rel 1963/?; cip

Plants Cannot Travel
[3259] Bogard, Carole (sop); Del Tredici,
         David (pf)
         - Desto DC-6468; 33s; rel 1968;
         cip

See How They Love Me
[3260] Bogard, Carole (sop); Del Tredici,
         David (pf)
         - Desto DC-6468; 33s; rel 1968;
         cip

**Send Home My Long Strayed Eyes
(1949)**
[3261] Carter, Sara (sop); Weiser,
         Bernhard (pf)
         - New Editions 2; 33m; rel 1953;
         del 1959

[3262] Miller, Mildred (m sop); Biltcliffe,
         Edwin (pf)
         - St/And SPL-411-12; 33m; 2
         discs; rel 1963; del 1964
         - Desto D-411-12/DST-6411-12;
         33m/s; 2 discs; rel 1964; cip

Sonata, Piano (1950)
[3263] Weiser, Bernhard (pf)
         - New Editions 1; 33m; rel 1952;
         del 1959

Times Long Ago (1951)
[3264] Bogard, Carole (sop); Del Tredici,
         David (pf)
         - Desto DC-6468; 33s; rel 1968;
         cip

Upside-Down Man, The
[3265] Bogard, Carole (sop); Del Tredici,
         David (pf)
         - Desto DC-6468; 33s; rel 1968;
         cip

**Valentine to Sherwood Anderson, A
(1949)**
[3266] Carter, Sara (sop); Weiser,
         Bernhard (pf)
         - New Editions 2; 33m; rel 1953;
         del 1959

[3267] Miller, Mildred (m sop); Biltcliffe,
         Edwin (pf)
         - St/And SPL-411-12; 33m; 2
         discs; rel 1963; del 1964
         - Desto D-411-12/DST-6411-12;
         33m/s; 2 discs; rel 1964; cip

Weeping Pleiades, The (1953)
[3268] Beattie, Herbert (b bar);
         instrumental ensemble
         - Desto DC-6468; 33s; rel 1968;
         cip

FLETCHER, Grant (1913-)
Habanera
[3269] Bennett, Bob L. (pf)
         - Educo 3109; 33

**Marching Music for Johnny
Appleseed**
[3270] Bennett, Bob L. (pf)
         - Educo 3109; 33

Son (1972)
[3271] Epperson, Gordon (vcl); Burnett,
         Frances (pf)
         - Orion ORS-78314; 33s; rel
         1978; cip

FLICK-FLOOD, Dora
Huajilla
[3272] Flick-Flood, Dora (pf)
         - Standard 406; 33m; rel 1960;
         del 1964

Theme and Variations
[3273] Flick-Flood, Dora (pf)
         - Standard 406; 33m; rel 1960;
         del 1964

Waterfall
[3274] Flick-Flood, Dora (pf)
         - Standard 406; 33m; rel 1960;
         del 1964

FLOYD, Carlisle (1926-)
Episodes, Volume One
[3275] Grove, Roger (pf)
         - Educo 3112; 33

In Celebration (1971)
[3276] Louisville Orchestra; Mester, Jorge
         (cond)
         - LS-71-6; 33s (Louisville
         Orchestra First Edition Records
         1971 No 6); rel 1972; cip

Mystery, The (1960)
[3277] Curtin, Phyllis (sop); Louisville
         Orchestra; Whitney, Robert (cond)
         - LOU-63-5; 33m (Louisville
         Orchestra First Edition Records
         1963 No 5); rel 1963; del 1978

**Pilgrimage (1956): Man That Is
Born of a Woman, O Lord Thou
Hast Searched, and For I Am
Persuaded**
[3278] Treigle, Norman (b bar); New
         Orleans Philharmonic-Symphony
         Orchestra; Torkanowsky, Werner
         (cond)
         - Orion ORS-7268; 33s; rel 1972;
         cip

FLYNN, George (1937-)
Wound (1968)
[3279] Flynn, George (pf)
         - Finnadar QD-9006; 33q; rel
         1975; cip

**FOERSTER, Adolph M.
(1854-1927)**
On the Sea
[3280] Frager, Malcolm (pf)
         - New World NW-206; 33s; rel
         1978

FOLEY, David (1945-)
**(Four) Pieces for Saturday
Afternoon**
[3281] Composers Festival Orchestra;
         Brehm, Alvin (cond)
         - Trilogy CTS-1002; 33s; rel
         1973; del 1975

FOOTE, Arthur (1853-1937)
Arabesque (Op 42, No 2)
[3282] Dayton, Norma (pf)
         - SPAMH MIA-123; 33s; rel 1965

Aubade (Op 77) (1912)
[3283] Moore, Douglas (vcl); Dwyer, Paula
         Ennis (pf)
         - Musical Heritage Society
         MHS-4018; 33s; rel 1979

Caprice (Op 27, No 9)
[3284] Bennette, George (pf)
         - Grenadilla GS-1026; 33s; rel
         1978; cip

**(Four) Character Pieces after the
Rubaiyat of Omar Khayyam (Op
48) (1900)**
[3285] Royal Philharmonic Orchestra;
         Krueger, Karl (cond)
         - SPAMH MIA-127; 33s; rel 1965

**(Three) Characteristic Pieces, Piano
Duo (Op 21)**
[3286] Hersh, Paul (pf); Montgomery,
         David (pf)
         - Orion ORS-76247; 33s; rel
         1977; cip

Compositions (Op 71): Cantilena
[3287] Smith, Rollin (org)
         Rec 8/73
         - Repertoire Recording Society
         RRS-12; 33s; rel 1974

Compositions: Canzonetta
[3288] Beck, Janice (org)
         - Musical Heritage Society
         OR-A-263; 33s; rel 1972

Compositions: Toccata
[3289] Gay, Harry W. (org)
         - Cleveland Sound and Recording
         Co CRC-2051; 33m; rel 1966

Gavotte (Op 8, No 1)
[3290] Dayton, Norma (pf)
         - SPAMH MIA-123; 33s; rel 1965

Irish Folk Song, An (1891)
[3291] Gadski, Johanna (sop)
         - Victor 88117; 78; rel 1908

Irish Folk Song, An (1891) *(cont'd)*
[3292] White, Robert (ten); Sanders, Samuel (pf)
- RCA ARL-1-1698; 33s; rel 1976; cip

May Song, A (When Spring Comes Laughing) (Op 60, No 2)
[3293] Dayton, Norma (pf)
- SPAMH MIA-123; 33s; rel 1965

(Trois) Morceaux (Op 3) (1877-80): Impromptu, G Minor
[3294] Dayton, Norma (pf)
- SPAMH MIA-123; 33s; rel 1965

Night Piece, A (1922)
[3295] Baker, Julius (fl); Schulman Quartet; Saidenberg, Daniel (cond)
- Decca DL-4013; 33m; 10"; rel 1952; del 1957
- Brunswick AXL-2015; 33m; 10"; rel pre-1956

[3296] Gold, Diane (fl); Alard Quartet
- Leonarda LPI-105; 33s; rel 1980

[3297] Sharp, Maurice (fl); Cleveland Sinfonietta; Lane, Louis (cond)
- Epic LC-3754/BC-1116; 33m/s; rel 1961; del 1970
- Columbia (English) 33SX-1682/SCX-3539; 33m/s; rel 1964*

[3298] Wummer, John (fl); Dorian String Quartet
- Columbia 70339D; 78; rel ca 1940

(Three) Pieces, Oboe and Piano (Op 31): Pastorale
[3299] Mariotti, Arno (ob); La Gore, Lawrence (pf)
- Golden Crest RE-7027; 33m/s; rel 1968/1979; cip

(Five) Pieces, Piano (Op 6) (1883): Sarabande
[3300] Dayton, Norma (pf)
- SPAMH MIA-123; 33s; rel 1965

(Three) Pieces, Violoncello and Piano (Op 1) (1881)
[3301] Moore, Douglas (vcl); Dwyer, Paula Ennis (pf)
- Musical Heritage Society MHS-4018; 33s; rel 1979

(Five) Poems after Omar Khayyam (Op 41)
[3302] Bennette, George (pf)
- Grenadilla GS-1026; 33s; rel 1978; cip

Quartet, Strings (Op 70) (1907-10)
[3303] Kohon Quartet
- Vox SVBX-5301; 33s; 3 discs; rel 1971; cip

Quintet, Piano and Strings (Op 38) (1897)
[3304] Boehm-Kooper, Mary Louise (pf); Kooper Quartet
- Turnabout TVS-34556; 33s; rel 1974; cip

Romance and Scherzo (Op 22) (1887-90): Scherzo
[3305] Moore, Douglas (vcl); Dwyer, Paula Ennis (pf)
- Musical Heritage Society MHS-4018; 33s; rel 1979

Romanza (Op 33)
[3306] Moore, Douglas (vcl); Dwyer, Paula Ennis (pf)
- Musical Heritage Society MHS-4018; 33s; rel 1979

Sonata, Violin and Piano (Op 20) (1889)
[3307] Gratovich, Eugene (vln); Benoit, Regis (pf)
- Orion ORS-76243; 33s; rel 1977; cip

[3308] Silverstein, Joseph (vln); Kalish, Gilbert (pf)
- New World NW-268; 33s; rel 1977

Sonata, Violoncello and Piano (Op 78) (ca 1913)
[3309] Moore, Douglas (vcl); Dwyer, Paula Ennis (pf)
- Musical Heritage Society MHS-4018; 33s; rel 1979

(Five) Songs (Op 13): I'm Wearin' Awa'
[3310] Traubel, Helen (sop); orchestra; Armbruster, Robert (cond)
- Victor 49-4046-48 (in set WDM-4013); 45; 3-7"; rel 1953
- RCA LM-7013; 33m; 10"; rel 1953; del 1956

Suite, Orchestra, D Minor (Op 36) (1895)
[3311] Royal Philharmonic Orchestra; Krueger, Karl (cond)
- SPAMH MIA-122; 33s; rel 1963

Suite, Orchestra, E Major (Op 63) (1907-08)
[3312] Boston Symphony Orchestra; Koussevitzky, Serge (cond)
Rec 1944
- Victor 11-8571-72 (in set M-962); 78; 2 discs; rel 1944
- Victor 11-8573-74B (in set DM-962); 78; 2 discs; rel 1944
- RCA LM-2900; 33m; rel 1966; del 1970
- RCA VCM-6174; 33m; 3 discs; rel 1966; del 1972

Suite, Orchestra, E Major (Op 63) (1907-08) *(cont'd)*
[3313] Eastman-Rochester Symphony Orchestra; Hanson, Howard (cond)
- Mercury MG-40001; 33m; rel 1953; del 1957
- Mercury MG-50074; 33m; rel 1957; del 1963

[3314] Vienna Symphony Orchestra; Hendl, Walter (cond)
- American Recording Society ARS-22; 33m; 10"; rel 1952

Suite, Organ, D Major (Op 54) (1904)
[3315] Osborne, William (org)
- Orion ORS-78309; 33s; rel 1978; cip

Suite, Piano, D Minor (Op 15) (1886)
[3316] Dayton, Norma (pf)
- SPAMH MIA-123; 33s; rel 1965

Symphonic Prologue (Francesca da Rimini) (Op 24) (1890)
[3317] Louisville Orchestra; Mester, Jorge (cond)
Rec 10/29/75
- LS-75-4; 33s (Louisville Orchestra First Edition Records 1975 No 4); rel 1976; cip

[3318] Royal Philharmonic Orchestra; Krueger, Karl (cond)
- SPAMH MIA-127; 33s; rel 1965

Trio, Violin, Violoncello, and Piano (Op 5) (1882)
[3319] Macalester Trio
- Golden Crest CRS-4153; 33s; rel 1977; cip

FORMAN, Joanne (1934-)
Arbole, Arbole
[3320] Bissell, Sally (sop); McFarland, Glenn (gtr)
- Opus One 44; 33s; rel 1980; cip

Es verdad
[3321] Bissell, Sally (sop); McFarland, Glenn (gtr)
- Opus One 44; 33s; rel 1980; cip

I Thank You God for Most This Amazing
[3322] Woolf, Kristen (sop); Scaletti, Carla (hp); Butcher, Geoffrey (org)
- Opus One 34; 33s; rel 1978; cip

In Time of Daffodils/Who Know
[3323] Woolf, Kristen (sop); Scaletti, Carla (hp); Butcher, Geoffrey (org)
- Opus One 34; 33s; rel 1978; cip

Luna asoma, La
[3324] Bissell, Sally (sop); McFarland,
      Glenn (gtr)
      - Opus One 44; 33s; rel 1980; cip

Maggie and Milly and Molly and May
[3325] Woolf, Kristen (sop); Scaletti, Carla
      (hp); Butcher, Geoffrey (org)
      - Opus One 34; 33s; rel 1978; cip

Noche
[3326] Woolf, Kristen (sop); Scaletti, Carla
      (hp)
      - Opus One 34; 33s; rel 1978; cip

FORSLAND, Rolf Bruce*
Concert Portrayal, A
[3327] Forsland, Rolf Bruce (pf)
      - RF-83076; 33s; rel 1976

Portrait of a Composer
[3328] Forsland, Rolf Bruce (pf)
      - RBF-11377; 33s; rel 1977

FORST, Rudolf (1900-73)
Divertimento, Chamber Orchestra (1938)
[3329] Yaddo Orchestra; Donovan, Richard
      (cond)
      - Yaddo D-13-14; 78; rel 1938

FORSTER, Glad
Each Shining Hour
[3330] De Gogorza, Emilio (bar); orchestra
      - Victor 64888; 78; 10''; rel
      1916-20
      - Victor 577; 78; 10''; rel
      1916-20

FOSS, Lukas (1922-)
Baroque Variations (1967)
[3331] Buffalo Philharmonic Orchestra;
      Foss, Lukas (cond)
      Rec 3/68
      - Nonesuch H-71202; 33s; rel
      1968; cip

Behold I Build an House (1950)
[3332] Peabody Conservatory Concert
      Singers; Landen, Michael (org);
      Smith, Gregg (cond)
      Rec 1976
      - Vox SVBX-5353; 33s; 3 discs; rel
      1979; cip

[3333] Roger Wagner Chorale; MacInnes,
      James (pf); Foss, Lukas (pf);
      Wagner, Roger (cond)
      - CRI-123; 33m/s; rel
      1958/1959; cip

Capriccio (1946)
[3334] Kates, Stephen (vcl); Sanders,
      Samuel (pf)
      - RCA LM-2940/LSC-2940;
      33m/s; rel 1967; del 1975

Capriccio (1946) *(cont'd)*
[3335] Piatigorsky, Gregor (vcl); Foss,
      Lukas (pf)
      - RCA LM-2293/LSC-2293;
      33m/s; rel 1960; del 1963
      - New World NW-281; 33s; rel
      1976

Cave of the Winds, The (1972)
[3336] Dorian Woodwind Quintet
      - Vox SVBX-5307; 33s; 3 discs; rel
      1977; cip

Concerto, Oboe and Orchestra (1950)
[3337] Gassman, Bert (ob); Crystal
      Chamber Orchestra; Endo, Akira
      (cond)
      - Crystal S-851; 33s; rel 1971; cip

Concerto, Piano and Orchestra, No 2 (1951)
[3338] Foss, Lukas (pf); Los Angeles
      Festival Orchestra; Waxman,
      Franz (cond)
      - Decca DL-9889; 33m; rel 1957;
      del 1960
      - Varese Sarabande VC-81052;
      33m; rel 1978; cip

Curriculum vitae
[3339] Klucevsek, Guy (acc)
      - CRI-413; 33s; rel 1980; cip

Echoi (1961-63)
[3340] Group for Contemporary Music at
      Columbia University
      - Epic LC-3886/BC-1286; 33m/s;
      rel 1964; del 1970

Echoi: Movements 1-4
[3341] Yadzinsky, Edward (cl); Davis,
      Douglas (vcl); Foss, Lukas (pf);
      Williams, Jan (perc)
      Rec 5/68
      - Wergo WER-60-040; 33s; rel
      196?
      - Heliodor 2549.001; 33s; rel
      1970; del 1973

Elytres (1964)
[3342] New York Philomusica Chamber
      Ensemble; Foss, Lukas (cond)
      - Turnabout TVS-34514; 33s; rel
      1973; cip

Encore 1 (Bagatelle)
[3343] Improvisation Chamber Ensemble;
      Foss, Lukas (pf)
      - RCA LM-2558/LSC-2558;
      33m/s; rel 1961; del 1965

Encore 2 (Air Antique)
[3344] Calf, Howard (vcl); Foss, Lukas (pf)
      - RCA LM-2558/LSC-2558;
      33m/s; rel 1961; del 1965

Encore 3 (Circus Pieces)
[3345] Improvisation Chamber Ensemble;
      Foss, Lukas (pf)
      - RCA LM-2558/LSC-2558;
      33m/s; rel 1961; del 1965

Fantasy and Fugue
[3346] Improvisation Chamber Ensemble;
      Foss, Lukas (pf)
      - RCA LM-2558/LSC-2558;
      33m/s; rel 1961; del 1965

Fantasy Rondo (1946)
[3347] Foss, Lukas (pf)
      - Concert Hall B-9; 78; 4 discs; rel
      pre-1948

Fragments of Archilochos (1965)
[3348] Abramowitsch, Miriam (speaker);
      Strauss, Melvin (speaker); Betts,
      Robert (ct); Crane Collegiate
      Singers (State University of New
      York at Potsdam); Rantucci,
      Oswald (mand); Marcus, Jonathan
      (gtr); Williams, Jan (perc);
      Burnham, Edward (perc); Harbold,
      Lynn (perc); McElheran, Brock
      (cond)
      Rec 5/68
      - Wergo WER-60-040; 33s; rel
      196?
      - Heliodor 2549.001; 33s; rel
      1970; del 1973

Fugue
[3349] Improvisation Chamber Ensemble
      - RCA LM-2558/LSC-2558;
      33m/s; rel 1961; del 1965

Geod (1969)
[3350] Buffalo Philharmonic Orchestra;
      Foss, Lukas (cond)
      - Candide CE-31042; 33s; rel
      1970; del 1977

Jumping Frog of Calaveras County, The (1950)
[3351] After Dinner Opera Company;
      Kurzwell, Frederic (pf); Flusser,
      Richard (cond)
      - Lyrichord LL-11/LLST-711;
      33m/s; rel 1951/1980; cip

Moirai (The Fates)
[3352] Improvisation Chamber Ensemble;
      Foss, Lukas (pf)
      - RCA LM-2558/LSC-2558;
      33m/s; rel 1961; del 1965

Music for Clarinet, Percussion, and Piano
[3353] Improvisation Chamber Ensemble;
      Foss, Lukas (pf)
      - RCA LM-2558/LSC-2558;
      33m/s; rel 1961; del 1965

Music for Six (1977)
[3354] University of Buffalo Percussion
      Ensemble
      - CRI-413; 33s; rel 1980; cip

Ni bruit ni vitesse (1972)
[3355] Foss, Lukas (pf); Williams, Jan
(perc)
- Turnabout TVS-34514; 33s; rel
1973; cip

Non-Improvisation
[3356] Yadzinsky, Edward (cl); Davis,
Douglas (vcl); Foss, Lukas (pf);
Williams, Jan (perc)
Rec 5/68
- Wergo WER-60-040; 33s; rel
196?
- Heliodor 2549.001; 33s; rel
1970; del 1973

Parable of Death, A (1952)
[3357] Hayes, Marvin (nar); Robinson,
Richard (ten); Pomona College
Glee Clubs; Steiner, Armin (vln);
Sandler, Myron (vln); Ailman,
Carroll (vla); Koff, Howard (vcl);
Ailman, Suzanne (cb); Priest,
Anita (org); Limonick, Natalie
(pf); Lommell, Thomas (perc);
Foss, Lukas (cond)
Rec 3/6/54
- Educo ECM-4002; 33m; rel
1954; del 1964

[3358] Zorina, Vera (nar); Stevens, Farrold
(ten); Southern Baptist
Theological Seminary Choir;
Louisville Orchestra; Whitney,
Robert (cond)
- Columbia ML-4859; 33m; rel
1954; del 1968
- Columbia CML-4859; 33m; rel
1968; del 1974
- Columbia AML-4859; 33m; rel
1974; del 1976

Paradigm (1968)
[3359] Buffalo Center of the Creative and
Performing Arts
- Deutsche Grammophon
2543.005; 33s; rel 1971; del
1975

[3360] New York Philomusica Chamber
Ensemble
- Turnabout TVS-34514; 33s; rel
1973; cip

**Phorion (Baroque Variations III)
(1967)**
[3361] New York Philharmonic; Bernstein,
Leonard (cond)
- Columbia ML-6452/MS-7052;
33m/s; rel 1967; del 1973

**(Three) Pieces, Violin and Piano
(1944): Dedication**
[3362] Ortenberg, Edgar (vln); Foss, Lukas
(pf)
- Hargail MW-300; 78; 2 discs; rel
pre-1948

Prairie, The (1944)
[3363] Gregg Smith Singers; Long Island
Symphonic Choral Association;
soloists; Foss, Lukas (cond)
- Turnabout TVS-34649; 33s; rel
1977; cip

Psalms (1955-56)
[3364] Roger Wagner Chorale; MacInnes,
James (pf); Foss, Lukas (pf);
Wagner, Roger (cond)
- CRI-123; 33m/s; rel
1958/1959; cip

Quartet, Strings, No 1 (1947)
[3365] American Art Quartet
- Columbia ML-5476; 33m; rel
1960; del 1968
- Columbia CML-5476; 33m; rel
1968; del 1974
- Columbia AML-5476; 33m; rel
1974; del 1976

Quartet, Strings, No 3
[3366] Columbia String Quartet
- CRI-413; 33s; rel 1980; cip

Song of Songs (1947)
[3367] Tourel, Jennie (m sop); New York
Philharmonic; Bernstein, Leonard
(cond)
- Columbia ML-5451/MS-6123;
33m/s; rel 1962; del 1966
- CRI-284; 33s; rel 1972; cip

Time Cycle (1959-60)
[3368] Addison, Adele (sop); Improvisation
Chamber Ensemble; Columbia
Symphony Orchestra; Bernstein,
Leonard (cond)
- Columbia ML-5680/MS-6280;
33m/s; rel 1962; del 1971
- Columbia CMS-6280; 33s; rel
1971; del 1974
- Columbia AMS-6280; 33s; rel
1974; cip

**Time Cycle (chamber version)
(1960)**
[3369] Martin, Grace Lynne (sop);
Improvisation Chamber Ensemble;
Foss, Lukas (pf)
- Epic LC-3886/BC-1286; 33m/s;
rel 1964; del 1970

Variations on a Theme in Unison
[3370] Improvisation Chamber Ensemble;
Foss, Lukas (pf)
- RCA LM-2558/LSC-2558;
33m/s; rel 1961; del 1965

FOSTER, Dudley (1935-)
Piece in Free Form, A (1961)
[3371] Foster, Dudley (org)
- Contemporary Composers Guild
1; 33m; rel 1962; del 1975

FOSTER, Fay (1886-1960)
Americans Come, The
[3372] Crooks, Richard (ten); Victor
Orchestra; Pilzer, Maximilian
(cond)
- Victor 10-1150; 78; 10"

[3373] Graveure, Louis (bar); orchestra
- Columbia A-2709; 78; rel
pre-1925

[3374] Werrenrath, Reinald (bar);
orchestra
- Victor 45157; 78; rel pre-1925

FOX, Jim (1913-)
Nine-Fifty
[3375] no performers given
- Zanja ZR-2; 33; rel 197?

FRABIZIO, William (1929-)
Quartet, Strings (Op 23)
[3376] Amado String Quartet
- Apex S-1243; 33s; rel 1972*

FRACKENPOHL, Arthur (1924-)
Cantilena
[3377] University of Maryland Concert
Band; Ostling, Acton, Jr. (cond)
- Coronet 955; 33m; rel 1969; del
1978

Prelude and Allegro
[3378] Capital University Clarinet Choir;
Hite, David (cond)
- Coronet S-1509; 33s; rel 1969;
del 1978

Quintet, Brass (1966)
[3379] Ithaca Brass Quintet
- Mark MES-32558; 33s; rel
1969; del 1976

FRANCHETTI, Arnold (1906-)
Chamber Concerto (1965)
[3380] Kobialka, Daniel (vln); Hartt
Chamber Players; Larsen, Henry
(cond)
- Ars Nova/Ars Antiqua AN-1002;
33s; rel 1969; del 1973

(Three) Italian Masques (1953)
[3381] Hanson, Raymond (pf); New York
Brass Quintet; New York
Percussion Ensemble; Baron,
Samuel (cond)
- CRI-125; 33m; rel 1960; cip

FRANCO, Johan (1908-)
As the Prophets Foretold (1955)
[3382] Meyer, Shirley (sop); McDonald,
William (ten); Graham, William
Harvey (b); Chapman, Charles T.
(car); New York Avenue
Presbyterian Church (Washington,
DC) Choir; brass ensemble;
Prussing, Stephen H. (cond)
- CRI-222; 33s; rel 1968; cip

Cranbrook Nocturne
[3383] Barnes, Ronald (car) or Strauss,
Richard (car)
- Washington Cathedral Archives
CAR-0002; 33s; rel 1975

Fantasy, Violoncello and Orchestra
[3384] Brill, Samuel (vcl); Rotterdam
Philharmonic Orchestra; Flipse,
Eduard (cond)
- CRI-124; 33m; rel 1959; cip

Symphony No 5 (Cosmos) (1958)
[3385] North Holland Philharmonic
Orchestra; Arends, Henri (cond)
- CRI-135; 33m/s; rel
1960/1973; cip

**Virgin Queen's Dream Monologue,
The (1947; 1952)**
[3386] Lenchner, Paula (sop); Rotterdam
Philharmonic Orchestra; Flipse,
Eduard (cond)
- CRI-124; 33m; rel 1959; cip

FRANK, Andrew (1946-)
Arcadia (1977)
[3387] Miller, Robert (pf)
- CRI-419; 33s; rel 1980; cip

Orpheum (Night Music I) (1970)
[3388] Burge, Lois Svard (pf)
Rec 10/16-17/75
- CRI-345; 33s; rel 1976; cip

Sonata da camera (1978)
[3389] Quan, Linda (vln); Dunkel, Paul (fl);
Miller, Robert (pf)
- CRI-419; 33s; rel 1980; cip

FRAZEUR, Theodore (1929-)
Frieze
[3390] Joseph, Charles (vln); Frazeur,
Theodore (perc)
- Grenadilla GS-1042; 33s; rel
1979; cip

(Four) Sea Fragments
[3391] East, James (cl); Frazeur, Theodore
(perc)
- Grenadilla GS-1042; 33s; rel
1979; cip

FREDRICKSON, Thomas (1928-)
Sinfonia concertante
[3392] University of Illinois Symphony
Orchestra; Goodman, Bernard
(cond)
- Illini Union Bookstore CRS-7;
33m; rel 1960?

Triptych
[3393] University of Illinois Contemporary
Chamber Players; London, Edwin
(cond)
- CRI-405; 33s; rel 1979; cip

FREED, Arnold (1926-)
Angels We Have Heard on High
[3394] Whikehart Chorale; Whikehart,
Lewis E. (cond)
- Lyrichord LL-151/LLST-7151;
33m/s; rel 1965; cip

FREED, Isadore (1900-60)
Around the Maypole
[3395] Martin, Charlotte (pf)
- Educo 3021; 33m; rel 1968; del
1972

Jolie comme un coeur
[3396] Jeunnesse, L. (bar)
- Festival RA-16; 78; rel pre-1952

(Five) Pieces, Piano: March
[3397] Behrend, Jeanne (pf)
- Victor 17912 (in set M-764);
78; rel 1941

Rebel
[3398] Luening, Ethel (sop); Duke, John
Woods (pf)
- Yaddo 117A; 78; 10''; rel 1937
- Yaddo 27A; 78; 10''; rel 1937

Waltz on White Keys
[3399] Bennett, Bob L. (pf)
- Educo 3109; 33

FREEDMAN, Robert M. (1934-)
Journeys of Odysseys, The
[3400] Currier, Terry (nar); chamber
orchestra; Freedman, Robert M.
(cond)
- Cobblestone CST-9009; 33s; rel
1972

FREEMAN, John (1928-)
Quartet, Strings (1950)
[3401] Koeckert Quartet
- Varese Sarabande VC-81046;
33m; rel 1979; cip

FRIEDELL, Harold W. (1905-58)
King of Glory
[3402] St. Bartholomew's Episcopal
Church (New York) Choir; Friedell,
Harold (org) (cond)
- Grayco LPM-101; 33m; 10''; rel
1954

**FRIEDMAN, Stanleigh P.
(1884-1960)**
Down the Field March
[3403] Arthur Pryor's Band; Pryor, Arthur
(cond)
Rec 9/13/12
- Victor 17289; 78
- New World NW-282; 33m; rel
1976

FRIESE, Alfred
Timpani Studies
[3404] Friese, Alfred (timp); McArthur,
Edwin (pf); James, Philip (nar)
- Benjamin Sachs-Artist Recordings
AF-101-06; 78; 3 discs; rel
1950

**FRITSCHELL, James Erwin
(1929-)**
Be Still (1971)
[3405] Wartburg College Choir; Fritschell,
James (cond)
- Musical Heritage Society
MHS-3167; 33s; rel 1975

FROHNE, Vincent
Study, Clarinet (Op 17)
[3406] Ludewig-Verdehr, Elsa (cl)
- Grenadilla GS-1018; 33s; rel
1979; cip

FROMM, Herbert (1905-)
**Atonement Music: V'al kulom and
Psach lonu**
[3407] Boothman, Donald (bar); Berlinski,
Herman (org)
- Musical Heritage Society
MHS-1775; 33s; rel 1972

Crimson Sap (1954)
[3408] Blum, Margot (m sop)
- Music Library MLR-7112; 33m;
rel 1965; del 1974

Fantasy, Piano
[3409] List, Eugene (pf)
- Lyrichord LLST-7241; 33s; rel
1973; cip

**Let All Mortal Flesh Keep Silent
(1940)**
[3410] Noehren, Robert (org)
- Lyrichord LL-191/LLST-7191;
33m/s; rel 1968; cip

Quartet, Strings
[3411] Pro Arte Quartet
- Lyrichord LL-203/LLST-7203;
33m/s; rel 1968; cip

(Six) Shakespeare Songs
[3412] North Texas State University
Chorus; McKinley, Frank A. (cond)
- Lyrichord LLST-7241; 33s; rel
1973; cip

Transience
[3413] Williams, Grant (ten); North Texas
State University Chorus;
McKinley, Frank A. (cond)
- Lyrichord LLST-7241; 33s; rel
1973; cip

FRYXELL, Regina (1899-)

Christmas Wish (1957)
[3414] Augustana Choir; Veld, Henry
(cond)
- Word 4012; 33m; rel 1957; del
1969

FUERSTNER, Carl (1912-)

Nocturne and Dance (Op 36)
[3415] Pellerite, James (fl); Webb, Charles
(pf)
- Coronet S-1713; 33s; rel 1972;
cip

FULEIHAN, Anis (1901-70)

**For Talented Young Bipeds: Casual
Walk**
[3416] Fuszek, Rita (pf)
- Educo 3107; 33

From the Aegean (1946)
[3417] Rigai, Amiram (pf)
- Vox PL-12570/STPL-512570;
33m/s; rel 1963; del 1970

FULKERSON, James (1945-)

Antiphonies and Streams
[3418] Fulkerson, James (tbn)
- Irida 0017; 33; rel 197?

Coordinative Systems No 10
[3419] Fulkerson, James (tbn)
- Irida 0017; 33; rel 197?

Music for Brass II
[3420] Fulkerson, James (tbn)
- Irida 0017; 33; rel 197?

Patterns VII
[3421] Hellermann, William (gtr)
- Folkways FTS-33902; 33s; rel
1976; cip

Suite, Violoncello
[3422] no performer given
- Irida 0017; 33; rel 197?

FUSSELL, Charles (1938-)

(Three) Processionals (1972-73)
[3423] Springfield Symphony Orchestra;
Gutter, Robert (cond)
- Opus One 21; 33s; rel 1975; cip

GABER, Harley (1943-)

Kata (1969)
[3424] Cummiskey, Linda (vln)
- CRI-299; 33s; rel 1973; cip

Ludus primus (1966)
[3425] Gilbert, David (fl); Kraber, Karl (fl);
DesRoches, Raymond (vib)
- CRI-299; 33s; rel 1973; cip

**Winds Rise in the North, The
(revised version)**
[3426] Cummiskey, Linda (vln); Goldstein,
Malcolm (vln); Seplow, Kathy
(vln); Reynolds, Stephen (vla);
Gibson, David (vcl)
Rec 6/21-27/76
- Titanic Ti-16-17; 33s; 2 discs; rel
1977; cip

GABRILOWITSCH, Ossip
(1878-1936)

Caprice burlesque (Op 3, No 1)
[3427] Gabrilowitsch, Ossip (pf)
(transferred from the Welte
reproducing piano)
- RCA LM-2824; 33m; rel 1965;
del 1966
- Recorded Treasures
GCP-771B-15; 33m; rel 1972?

Good-Bye (Op 11, No 1)
[3428] Crooks, Richard (ten); orchestra;
Pelletier, Wilfred (cond)
- Victor 1912; 78; 10"; rel 1939

GABURO, Kenneth (1926-)

**Antiphony III (Pearl-White
Moments) (1962)**
[3429] New Music Choral Ensemble;
electronic music; Gaburo,
Kenneth (cond)
- Nonesuch H-71199; 33s; rel
1968; cip

Antiphony IV (Poised) (1966)
[3430] University of Illinois Contemporary
Chamber Players; tape; Gaburo,
Kenneth (cond)
- Nonesuch H-71199; 33s; rel
1968; cip

**(Three) Dedications to Lorca
(1953)**
[3431] Hamline A Cappella Choir; Holliday,
Robert (cond)
- SPAMH MIA-116; 33s; rel 1961

Fat Millie's Lament (1964)
[3432] Electronic music
- Nonesuch H-71199; 33s; rel
1968; cip

For Harry (1965)
[3433] Electronic music
- Heliodor H-25047/HS-25047;
33m/s; rel 1967; del 1970
- CRI-356; 33s; rel 1977; cip

Lemon Drops (1965)
[3434] Electronic music
- Heliodor H-25047/HS-25047;
33m/s; rel 1967; del 1970
- CRI-356; 33s; rel 1977; cip

Line Studies (1957)
[3435] Baker, Julius (fl); Glazer, David (cl);
Trampler, Walter (vla); Price,
Erwin L. (tbn)
- Columbia ML-5821/MS-6421;
33m/s; rel 1963; del 1968
- Columbia CML-5821/CMS-6421;
33m/s; rel 1968; del 1974
- Columbia AMS-6421; 33s; rel
1974; cip

Lingua II (Maledetto) (1967-68)
[3436] New Music Choral Ensemble III;
Gaburo, Kenneth (cond)
- CRI-316; 33s; rel 1974; cip

Mouthpiece (1970)
[3437] Logan, Jack (tpt)
- Orion ORS-7294; 33s; rel 1972;
cip

Two (1962)
[3438] Sudock, Shirley (sop); Purswell,
Patrick (fl) or Turetzky, Nancy
(fl); Turetzky, Bertram (cb);
Meier, Gustav (cond)
- Advance FGR-1; 33m; rel 1966;
del 1972

Wasting of Lucrecetzia, The (1964)
[3439] Electronic music
- Nonesuch H-71199; 33s; rel
1968; cip

GANZ, Rudolph (1877-1972)

Peasant Dance (Op 24, No 3)
[3440] Ganz, Rudolph (pf) (transferred
from the Welte reproducing
piano)
- Recorded Treasures
GCP-771B-15; 33m; rel 1972?

GARCIA, Russell (1916-)

Adventure in Emotion
[3441] Los Angeles Neophonic Orchestra;
Kenton, Stan (cond)
- Capitol MAS-2424/SMAS-2424;
33m/s; rel 1965; del 1970

Variations on a Five-Note Theme
[3442] Horn Club of Los Angeles
- Capitol P-8525/SP-8525;
33m/s; rel 1960; del 1963
- Seraphim S-60095; 33s; rel
1969; del 1973

GARDNER, Samuel (1891-)

From the Canebrake (Op 5, No 1)
[3443] Heifetz, Jascha (vln); Kaye, Milton
(pf)
- Decca 23386 (in set A-385); 78;
10"; rel pre-1948
- Decca DL-5214; 33m; 10"; rel
1950; del 1957

From the Canebrake (arr for orch)
[3444] Victor Orchestra; Bourdon, Rosario
(cond)
- Victor 21750; 78; 10"; rel
pre-1948
- Victor E-76; 78; 10"; rel
pre-1948

GARLAND, Peter (1952-)
Apple Blossom (1972)
[3445] Blackearth Percussion Group
Rec 5/27-28/74
- Opus One 22; 33s; rel 1975; cip

GASSMANN, Remi (1908-)
Music to the Ballet (1961)
[3446] Electronic music
- Westminster
XWN-18962/WST-14143;
33m/s; rel 1961; del 1977
- Westminster WGS-8110; 33s; rel
1971; del 1977

GATES, Crawford M. (1921-)
Oh, My Love's Like a Red, Red Rose
[3447] Mormon Tabernacle Choir; Ottley,
Jerold D. (cond)
- Columbia M-34134; 33s; rel
1976; cip

GATES, Everett
Declamation and Dance (1961)
[3448] Rascher Saxophone Quartet
- Coronet LPS-3021; 33s; rel
1975; cip

Incantation and Ritual
[3449] Stolti, James (sax)
- Coronet LPS-3036; 33s; rel
1978; cip

GAUDLIN, Robert (1931-)
Pavane
[3450] Eastman-Rochester Symphony
Orchestra; Hanson, Howard
(cond)
Rec 1958
- Mercury MG-50053/SR-90053;
33m/s; rel 1959; del 1964
- Eastman-Rochester Archives
ERA-1003; 33s; rel 1974; cip

GAY, Harry W.
Carol Paraphrase on Silent Night
[3451] Gay, Harry W. (org)
- Cleveland Sound and Recording
Co XCTV-82411-12 (matrix no);
33m; rel 1963

Prelude on an Old Carol
[3452] Gay, Harry W. (org)
- Cleveland Sound and Recording
Co CRC-2051; 33m; rel 1966

GEISSLER, Frederick (1946-)
**Variations on a Modern American
Trumpet Tune**
[3453] Stith, Marice (tpt); Cornell
University Wind Ensemble;
Geissler, Frederick (cond)
Rec 3/24/74
- Cornell CUWE-14; 33s; rel 1975;
cip

GEORGE, Earl (1924-)
Declamations
[3454] Cornell University Wind Ensemble;
Stith, Marice (cond)
- Cornell CUWE-11; 33s; rel 1973;
cip

Tuckets and Sennets (1973)
[3455] Stith, Marice (tpt); Raleigh, Stuart
W. (pf)
- Redwood RRES-5; 33s; rel 1977;
cip

GERSCHEFSKI, Edwin (1909-)
**Alexander Suite, The (Op 66)
(1971)**
[3456] Andrie, Karen (vcl); Gerschefski,
Martha (vcl)
Rec 5/21/72
- Mark MC-6804; 33s; rel 1972

**American Tarantella (Op 11, No
2b)**
[3457] Yerlow, Stanley (pf)
Rec 5/21/72
- Mark MC-6804; 33s; rel 1972

**And Thou Shalt Love the Lord (Op
57)**
[3458] Georgia Singers
Rec 5/21/72
- Mark MC-6804; 33s; rel 1972

Border Raid (Op 57, No 1) (1965)
[3459] University of Georgia Vocalists
- Rite 32329 (matrix no); 33s; rel
1973?

Celebration (Op 51) (1964)
[3460] violin; orchestra
Rec 1962-69
- Rite 34103-06 (matrix no); 33s;
rel 1974

Classic Overture
[3461] Yaddo Orchestra
- Yaddo 21B; 78; 10"; rel 1937

Crossing the Bar (Op 3, No 2)
[3462] University of Georgia Vocalists and
Instrumentalists
- Rite 32329 (matrix no); 33s; rel
1973?

Dedication (Op 36, No 3a)
[3463] University of Georgia Vocalists and
Instrumentalists
Rec 1/31/71
- Mark MC-6705; 33s; rel 1971

Fanfare, Fugato, and Finale (1937)
[3464] Polish National Radio Orchestra;
Krenz, Jan (cond)
- CRI-228; 33s; rel 1968; cip

Guadalcanal Fantasy (Op 6, No 6c)
[3465] band
Rec 1962-69
- Rite 34103-06 (matrix no); 33s;
rel 1974

**Half Moon Mountain (Op 33)
(1947-48)**
[3466] University of Georgia Vocalists and
Instrumentalists
Rec 5/29/69
- Project 70 Custom Records
PS-4038; 33s; rel 1969

Lai (Op 20, No 1a)
[3467] De Loache, Benjamin (bar)
- Yaddo 8B; 78; 10"; rel 1937

[3468] University of Georgia Vocalists and
Instrumentalists
Rec 1/31/71
- Mark MC-6705; 33s; rel 1971

**Lord's Controversy with His People,
The (Op 34, No 1) (1947-49)**
[3469] University of Georgia Vocalists and
Instrumentalists
Rec 1/31/71
- Mark MC-6705; 33s; rel 1971

Lord's Prayer, The (Op 36, No 2)
[3470] chorus
Rec 1962-69
- Rite 34103-06 (matrix no); 33s;
rel 1974

Man on the Cross, A (Op 34, No 2)
[3471] University of Georgia Vocalists and
Instrumentalists
Rec 1/31/71
- Mark MC-6705; 33s; rel 1971

Manhattan Flats
[3472] no performers given
- Yaddo 17A; 78; 10"; rel 1937

**Moderato, Violoncello and Piano
(Op 63, No 1)**
[3473] University of Georgia
Instrumentalists
Rec 5/29/69
- Project 70 Custom Records
PS-4038; 33s; rel 1969

Mountain, The (Op 50)
[3474] Eicher, Eugene (vcl); Karlas, Despy
(pf)
Rec 2/12/70
- Mark UMC-2254; 33s; rel 1970

Music for a Stately Occasion (Op 29, No 2b) (1968)
[3475] band
Rec 1962-69
- Rite 34103-06 (matrix no); 33s; rel 1974

New Music for Piano
[3476] Gerschefski, Edwin (pf)
- New Music Quarterly Recordings 1312; 78; rel 1937

Nocturne (Op 42, No 2b)
[3477] violoncello; cordovox
Rec 1962-69
- Rite 34103-06 (matrix no); 33s; rel 1974

On his Blindness (Op 31, No 1)
[3478] University of Georgia Vocalist and Instrumentalist
Rec 5/29/69
- Project 70 Custom Records PS-4038; 33s; rel 1969
- Rite 34103-06 (matrix no); 33s; rel 1974

Piece, Saxophone and Piano
[3479] McBride, Robert (sax); Gerschefski, Edwin (pf)
- Yaddo 121B; 78; 10''; rel 1937

(Three) Pieces, Piano
[3480] Gerschefski, Edwin (pf)
- Yaddo 121A; 78; 10''; rel 1937

Preludes, Piano (Op 6) (1931)
[3481] Yerlow, Stanley (pf)
Rec 5/21/72
- Mark MC-6804; 33s; rel 1972

Psalm 100 (Op 53) (1965)
[3482] University of Georgia Vocalists and Instrumentalists
Rec 1/31/71
- Mark MC-6705; 33s; rel 1971

Quintet, Piano and Strings (Op 16)
[3483] Karlas, Despy (pf); University of Georgia String Quartet
Rec 2/12/70
- Mark UMC-2254; 33s; rel 1970

Saugatuck Suite (1938)
[3484] Vienna Orchestra; Adler, F. Charles (cond)
- CRI-115; 33m/s; rel 1957/?; cip

Septet, Brass (Op 26) (1938)
[3485] no performers given
Rec 1962-69
- Rite 34103-06 (matrix no); 33s; rel 1974

Sonata, Piano, No 1 (Op 22) (1936): Menuetto-Trio
[3486] no performer given
Rec 1962-69
- Rite 34103-06 (matrix no); 33s; rel 1974

(Six) Songs (Op 39a)
[3487] Georgia Singers
Rec 5/21/72
- Mark MC-6804; 33s; rel 1972

[3488] University of Georgia Vocalists and Instrumentalists
Rec 5/29/69
- Project 70 Custom Records PS-4038; 33s; rel 1969

Streamline (Op 17) (1935)
[3489] University of Georgia Instrumentalists
- Rite 32329 (matrix no); 33s; rel 1973?

(Twelve) Studies, Piano (Op 58): Allegro giocoso, Andante con moto, and Allegro ma non troppo
[3490] no performer given
Rec 1962-69
- Rite 34103-06 (matrix no); 33s; rel 1974

To Belshazzar (Op 32, No 4)
[3491] University of Georgia Vocalists and Instrumentalists
- Rite 32329 (matrix no); 33s; rel 1973?

Toccata and Fugue (After Bach) (Op 40a)
[3492] University of Georgia Instrumentalists
- Rite 32329 (matrix no); 33s; rel 1973?

Trio, Violin, Violoncello, and Piano (Op 43)
[3493] University of Georgia Instrumentalists
Rec 5/29/69
- Project 70 Custom Records PS-4038; 33s; rel 1969
- Rite 32329 (matrix no); 33s; rel 1973?

Variations, String Quartet (Op 25) (1937)
[3494] University of Georgia String Quartet
Rec 2/12/70
- Mark UMC-2254; 33s; rel 1970

Wanting Is – What? (Op 8, No 1)
[3495] Luening, Ethel (sop); Gerschefski, Edwin (pf)
- Yaddo 106A; 78; 10''; rel 1937
- Yaddo 127A; 78; 10''; rel 1937

Wanting Is – What? (Op 8, No 1) *(cont'd)*
[3496] tenor; piano
Rec 1962-69
- Rite 34103-06 (matrix no); 33s; rel 1974

GERSHWIN, George (1898-1937)
American in Paris, An (1928)
[3497] American Radio Symphony Orchestra; Brown, M. (cond)
- Vox STPL-513030; 33s; rel 1968; cip

[3498] Andre Kostelanetz and his Orchestra; Kostelanetz, Andre (cond)
- Columbia 7713-14M (in set MM-1020); 78; 2 discs; rel 1951
- Columbia ML-4455; 33m; rel 1952; del 1955
- Columbia A-1020; 45; 7''; rel pre-1953
- Columbia CL-795; 33m; rel 1955; del 1962

[3499] Berlin Concert Orchestra; Kevehazy, Lajos (cond)
- Rondo-lette 47; 33s; rel 1959; del 1963

[3500] Berlin Symphony Orchestra; Buschkoetter (cond)
- EMI/Odeon O-3691-92; 78; 2 discs; rel pre-1952

[3501] Big Symphonic Band; Beeler, Walter (cond)
- Golden Crest CR-4022/CRS-4022; 33m/s; rel 1960; cip

[3502] Boston Pops Orchestra; Fiedler, Arthur (cond)
- RCA LM-2367/LSC-2367; 33m/s; rel 1960; cip
- RCA LM-2702/LSC-2702; 33m/s; rel 1964; del 1966
- RCA-Victrola VICS-1423; 33s; rel 1969; cip
- RCA LSC-5001; 33s; rel 1971; cip
- RCA LSC-3319; 33s; rel 1972; cip
- RCA VCS-7097; 33s; 2 discs; rel 1972; cip

[3503] Cleveland Orchestra; Maazel, Lorin (cond)
- London CS-6946; 33s; rel 1975; cip

[3504] Elite Concert Orchestra; Marschner, Max (cond)
- Allegro ALG-3063; 33m; rel 1953; del 1959
- Pacific (French) LDAA-71; 33m; rel pre-1956

[3505] Elliot Everett Orchestra; Everett, Elliot (cond)
- Rondo 538; 33s; rel 1959; del 1963

American in Paris, An (1928)
(cont'd)

[3506] Grand Symphony; Legrand, Michel (cond)
- Mercury SRW-18089; 33s; rel 1968; del 1970

[3507] Hamburg International Philharmonic Orchestra; Von Luden, Wilhelm (cond)
- Milton Cross 5001/6001; 33m/s; rel 1961; del 1964

[3508] Hamburg Philharmonia; Walther, Hans-Jurgen (cond)
Rec 1955
- MGM E-3253; 33m; rel 1956; del 1959
- MGM 3E-1; 33m; 3 discs; rel 1957; del 1959

[3509] Hollywood Bowl Symphony Orchestra; Newman, Alfred (cond)
- Mercury MG-20037; 33m; rel 1951; del 1968
- Mercury (French) MLP-7068; 33m; rel pre-1956

[3510] Hollywood Bowl Symphony Orchestra; Slatkin, Felix (cond)
- Capitol P-8343/SP-8343; 33m/s; rel 1956/1959; del 1970
- Time-Life TL-146/STL-146; 33m/s; rel 1967
- Seraphim S-60174; 33s; rel 1971; cip

[3511] International Philharmonic Orchestra
- Tops 1544; 33m; rel 1958; del 1961

[3512] Kingsway Symphony Orchestra; Camarata, Salvador (cond)
- Decca DL-8519; 33m; rel 1951; del 1970
- Brunswick LAT-8014; 33m; rel pre-1953
- Decca UMT-263036; 33m; rel pre-1956
- Decca ED-3538; 45; 7"; rel pre-1956
- Decca DCM-3206; 33m; rel 1962; del 1970

[3513] London Festival Orchestra; Black, Stanley (cond)
- London SPC-21009; 33s; rel 1967; cip

[3514] London Symphony Orchestra; Previn, Andre (cond)
- Angel S-36810; 33s; rel 1971; cip

[3515] Los Angeles Philharmonic Orchestra; Mehta, Zubin (cond)
- London CSA-2246; 33s; 2 discs; rel 1976; del 1980
- London CS-7031; 33s; rel 1977; cip

[3516] MGM Orchestra; Green, Johnny (cond)
- MGM 425-26; 78; 2 discs; rel pre-1953
- MGM 5080-81; 78; 2 discs; rel pre-1953

American in Paris, An (1928)
(cont'd)

- MGM 9030-31; 78; 2 discs; rel pre-1953
- MGM E-93; 33m; rel pre-1953
- MGM K-93; 45; 7"; rel pre-1953

[3517] Minneapolis Symphony Orchestra; Dorati, Antal (cond)
- Mercury MG-50071; 33m; rel 1958; del 1963
- Mercury MG-50290/SR-90290; 33m/s; rel 1962; del 1967
- Mercury MG-50431/SR-90431; 33m/s; rel 1965; del 1969

[3518] Morton Gould and his Orchestra; Gould, Morton (cond)
- RCA LM-6033; 33m; 2 discs; rel 1955; del 1961
- RCA LM-2002; 33m; rel 1956; del 1961

[3519] NBC Symphony Orchestra; Toscanini, Arturo (cond)
Rec 1945
- Victor WDM-1657; 45; 7"; rel 1952*
- RCA LM-9020; 33m; rel 1952; del 1970
- Gramophone ALP-1107; 33m; rel pre-1956
- RCA (Italian) A12R-0101; 33m; rel pre-1956
- RCA AVM-1-1737; 33m; rel 1976; cip

[3520] New Symphony Society Orchestra; Walther, Hans-Jurgen (cond)
- Concert Hall RG-123; 33m; rel 1957; del 1959

[3521] New York Philharmonic; Bernstein, Leonard (cond)
- Columbia ML-5413/MS-6091; 33m/s; rel 1960; cip
- Columbia MG-31155; 33s; 2 discs; rel 1972; cip
- Columbia M-31804; 33s; rel 1973; cip

[3522] New York Philharmonic; Thomas, Michael Tilson (cond)
- Columbia M-34205/QBL-34205; 33s/q; rel 1976; cip

[3523] Paris Conservatory Orchestra; Cluytens, Andre (cond)
- Columbia (French) GFX-132-33; 78; 2 discs; rel pre-1950

[3524] Paul Whiteman Orchestra; Whiteman, Paul (cond)
- Decca 29054-55 (in set 31); 78; 2 discs; rel pre-1942
- Decca 29088-91 (in set DA-31); 78; 4 discs; rel pre-1948
- Brunswick 0143-44; 78; 2 discs; rel pre-1952
- Decca DL-8024; 33m; rel 1950; del 1970
- Capitol H-301; 33m; 10"; rel 1952; del 1957
- Capitol P-303; 33m; rel 1952; del 1956
- Capitol (French) LDC-04; 33m; rel pre-1953

American in Paris, An (1928)
(cont'd)

- Capitol EBF-301; 45; 7"; rel pre-1953
- Telefunken LCA-303; 33m; rel pre-1953
- Capitol LC-6550; 33m; 10"; rel pre-1956
- Decca UMT-263072; 33m; rel pre-1956
- Decca ED-2196; 45; 7"; rel pre-1956
- Decca EUM-10551; 45; 7"; rel pre-1956
- Capitol T-303; 33m; rel 1956; del 1962
- Capitol T-1678/DT-1678; 33m/s; rel 1962; del 1970
- Pickwick 3399; 33m; rel 1976; del 1979

[3525] Philadelphia Orchestra; Ormandy, Eugene (cond)
- Columbia MS-7258; 33s; rel 1969; cip
- Columbia MS-7518; 33s; rel 1970; cip
- Columbia MG-30073; 33s; 2 discs; rel 1970; cip

[3526] Philharmonic Symphony Orchestra of New York; Rodzinski, Artur (cond)
- Columbia 12106-07 (in set X-246); 78; 2 discs; rel pre-1948
- Columbia 12108-09D; 78; 2 discs; rel pre-1948
- Columbia (English) GQX-11161-62; 78; 2 discs; rel pre-1952
- Columbia ML-4026; 33m; rel pre-1949; del 1954
- Columbia ML-4879; 33m; rel 1954; del 1955
- Columbia CL-700/CS-8641; 33m/s; rel 1955/1962; cip
- Columbia (English) S-1003; 33m; rel pre-1956
- Columbia (English) VS-801; 33m; rel pre-1956
- Columbia (English) FA-1001; 33m; rel pre-1956
- Columbia (English) QS-6002; 33m; rel pre-1956

[3527] Pittsburgh Symphony Orchestra; Steinberg, William (cond)
- Everest LPBR-6067/SDBR-3067; 33m/s; rel 1960; cip
- Command CC33-11037/CC-SD-11037; 33m/s; rel 1967; del 1973
- Westminster WGS-8243; 33s

[3528] Pro Musica Orchestra of Hamburg; Byrd, George (cond)
- Forum F-70008/SF-70008; 33m/s; rel 1959; del 1962

[3529] Royal Danish Symphony Orchestra; Kreutzer, Joseph (cond)
- Summit SUM-3011; 33s; rel 1978

American in Paris, An (1928)
(cont'd)

[3530] Royal Farnsworth Symphony
Orchestra; D'Artega, Alfonso
(cond)
- Design DLP-44/DCF-33; 33m/s;
rel 1959; del 1961

[3531] St. Louis Symphony Orchestra;
Slatkin, Leonard (cond)
Rec 1974
- Vox QSVBX-5132; 33q; 3 discs;
rel 1975; cip
- Turnabout QTVS-34594; 33q; rel
1979; cip

[3532] San Francisco Symphony
Orchestra; Ozawa, Seiji (cond)
- Deutsche Grammophon
2530.788; 33s; rel 1977; cip

[3533] Slovak Philharmonic Orchestra;
Burkh, Dennis (cond)
- Musical Heritage Society
MHS-4158; 33s

[3534] Utah Symphony Orchesra;
Abravanel, Maurice (cond)
- Westminster XWN-18686; 33m;
rel 1958; del 1961
- Westminster
XWN-18687/WST-14002;
33m/s; rel 1958; del 1967
- Vanguard Cardinal VCS-10017;
33s; rel 1968; cip
- Music Guild MS-151; 33s; rel
1970; del 1971
- Westminster WGS-8122; 33s; rel
1971; cip

[3535] Victor Symphony Orchestra;
Bernstein, Leonard (cond)
- Victor 12-0369-70 (in set
M-1237); 78; 2 discs; rel 1948*
- Victor 12-0371-72 (in set
DM-1237); 78; 2 discs; rel
1948*
- Gramophone C-3881-82; 78; 2
discs; rel pre-1952
- Gramophone FKX-220-21; 78; 2
discs; rel pre-1952
- Victor WDM-1237; 45; 2-7"; rel
pre-1950
- RCA LM-1031; 33m; rel 1950;
del 1958
- Camden CAL-439; 33m; rel
1958; del 1961
- RCA-Victrola VICS-1669(e); 33s;
rel 1972; del 1976

[3536] Victor Symphony Orchestra;
Shilkret, Nathaniel (cond)
Rec 2/4/29
- Victor 35963-64; 78; 2 discs; rel
1929
- Gramophone C-1698-99; 78; 2
discs; rel pre-1952
- RCA LPT-29; 33m; 10"; rel
1951; del 1957
- Victor WPT-38; 45; 7"; rel
pre-1953
- RCA AVM-1-1740; 33m; rel
1976; cip

American in Paris, An (1928)
(cont'd)

[3537] Vienna Symphony Orchestra;
Dixon, Dean (cond)
- Vox VLP-3130; 33m; 10"; rel
1952; del 1954
- Pathe-Vox VPO-3000; 33m; rel
pre-1953
- Olympic OL-8121; 33s; rel 1974

[3538] Warner Brothers Orchestra;
Heindorf, Ray (cond)
- Warner Bros B-1243/BS-1243;
33m/s; rel 1959; del 1970

[3539] orchestra; Shankson, Louis (cond)
- Allegro-Royale 1609; 33m; rel
pre-1956
- Allegro-Royale 1806; 33m; rel
pre-1956
- Plymouth 12-140; 33m; rel
pre-1956

[3540] orchestra
- Fonit LP-109; 33m; rel pre-1956
- Fonit LP-110; 33m; rel pre-1956

American in Paris, An (Abridged)
[3541] Symphony of the Air Pops
Orchestra; D'Artega, Alfonso
(cond)
- Epic LN-3621-22 (in set
SN-6034)/BSN-549-50 (in set
BSN-104); 33m/s; 2 discs; rel
1959; del 1965
- Epic LN-3652/BN-553; 33m/s;
rel 1960; del 1963

American in Paris, An (arr by Frank Campbell-Watson)
[3542] National Opera Orchestra of Monte
Carlo; Waart, Edo de (cond)
- Philips 6500.290; 33s; rel
1972; del 1977

American in Paris, An (arr for harmonica)
[3543] Sebastian, John (harmonica)
- Decca DL-10025/DL-710025;
33m/s; rel 1960; del 1975

American in Paris, An (arr for 2 pfs by Livingston Gearhart)
[3544] Morley, Virginia (pf); Gearhart,
Livingston (pf)
- Columbia ML-2197; 33m; 10";
rel 1951; del 1955

American in Paris, An (arr for 2 pfs by Gregory Stone)
[3545] Grierson, Ralph (pf); Kane, Artie
(pf)
- Angel S-36083; 33s; rel 1975;
cip

American in Paris, An (arr for 4 pfs)
[3546] First Piano Quartet
- RCA LM-125; 33m; 10"; rel
1951; del 1956
- Victor WDM-1574; 45; 7"; rel
1951*

American in Paris, An (arr for 4 pfs) *(cont'd)*
- Victor WEPR-8; 45; 7"; rel
pre-1953
- Gramophone 7EP-7005; 45; 7";
rel pre-1956
- Camden CAL-654; 33m; rel
1961; del 1963

Blue Monday (1922)
[3547] Andrews, Joyce (sop); Bogdan,
Thomas (ten); Meyer, Jeffrey
(ten); Mason, Patrick (bar);
Richardson, Walter (b); orchestra;
Gregg Smith Singers; Smith,
Gregg (cond)
- Turnabout TVS-34638; 33s; rel
1977; cip

Catfish Row (Suite from Porgy and Bess) (1936)
[3548] Andre Kostelanetz and his
Orchestra; Kostelanetz, Andre
(cond)
- Columbia CL-2133/CS-8933;
33m/s; rel 1964; del 1967

[3549] St. Louis Symphony Orchestra;
Slatkin, Leonard (cond)
Rec 1974
- Vox QSVBX-5132; 33q; 3 discs;
rel 1975; cip
- Turnabout QTVS-34594; 33q; rel
1979; cip

[3550] Utah Symphony Orchestra;
Abravanel, Maurice (cond)
- Westminster
XWN-18850/WST-14063;
33m/s; rel 1959; del 1967
- Music Guild MS-167; 33s; rel
1970; del 1971

Concerto in F, Piano and Orchestra (1925)
[3551] Bargy, Roy (pf); Paul Whiteman
Orchestra; Whiteman, Paul (cond)
- Columbia 50139-41D (in set
M-3); 78; 3 discs; rel pre-1936
- Columbia 9665-67; 78; 3 discs;
rel pre-1936
- Columbia 7315-17M (in set
M-280); 78; 3 discs; rel
pre-1942

[3552] Bianca, Sondra (pf); Hamburg
Philharmonia; Walther,
Hans-Jurgen (cond)
- MGM E-3237; 33m; rel 1955;
del 1959
- Parlophone PMC-1026; 33m; rel
pre-1956
- MGM 3E-1; 33m; 3 discs; rel
1957; del 1959

[3553] Bianca, Sondra (pf); New
Symphony Society Orchestra;
Goehr, Walter (cond)
- Concert Hall RG-123; 33m; rel
1957; del 1959

Concerto in F, Piano and Orchestra (1925) *(cont'd)*

[3554] Davis, Ivan (pf); Andre Kostelanetz and his Orchestra; Kostelanetz, Andre (cond)
- Columbia ML-6226/MS-6826; 33m/s; rel 1966; cip

[3555] Entremont, Philippe (pf); Philadelphia Orchestra; Ormandy, Eugene (cond)
- Columbia ML-6413/MS-7013; 33m/s; rel 1967; cip
- Columbia MG-30073; 33s; 2 discs; rel 1970; cip

[3556] Gould, Morton (pf); Morton Gould and his Orchestra; Gould, Morton (cond)
- Victor DC-31; 78
- RCA LM-6033; 33m; 2 discs; rel 1955; del 1961
- RCA LM-2017; 33m; rel 1956; del 1961

[3557] Haas, Werner (pf); National Opera Orchestra of Monte Carlo; Waart, Edo de (cond)
- Philips 6500.118; 33s; rel 1971; cip

[3558] Katchen, Julius (pf); Mantovani and his Orchestra; Mantovani, Annunzio Paolo (cond)
- London LLP-1262; 33m; rel 1955; del 1969
- Decca LXT-5069; 33m; rel pre-1956
- Decca LK-40108; 33m; rel pre-1956

[3559] Knor, Stanislav (pf); Prague Symphony Orchestra; Neumann, Vaclav (cond)
- Everest SDBR-3405; 33s; rel 1977; cip

[3560] Levant, Oscar (pf); Philharmonic Symphony Orchestra of New York; Kostelanetz, Andre (cond)
- Columbia 11818-21D (in set M-512); 78; 4 discs; rel pre-1943
- Columbia ML-4025; 33m; rel pre-1949; del 1954
- Columbia LOX-575-58; 78; 4 discs; rel pre-1952
- Columbia FCX-118; 33m; rel pre-1953
- Columbia ML-4879; 33m; rel 1954; del 1955
- Columbia CL-700/CS-8641; 33m/s; rel 1955/1962; cip
- Columbia A-1047; 45; 7"; rel pre-1956

[3561] List, Eugene (pf); Berlin Symphony Orchestra; Adler, Samuel (cond)
- Turnabout TVS-34457; 33s; rel 1971; cip

Concerto in F, Piano and Orchestra (1925) *(cont'd)*

[3562] List, Eugene (pf); Eastman-Rochester Symphony Orchestra; Hanson, Howard (cond) Rec 5/4/57
- Mercury MG-50138/SR-90002; 33m/s; rel 1957/1958; del 1972

[3563] Lowenthal, Jerome (pf); Utah Symphony Orchestra; Abravanel, Maurice (cond)
- Vanguard Cardinal VCS-10017; 33s; rel 1968; cip

[3564] Nero, Peter (pf); Boston Pops Orchestra; Fiedler, Arthur (cond)
- RCA LSC-3025; 33s; rel 1968; del 1974
- RCA LSC-3319; 33s; rel 1972; cip

[3565] Nibley, Reid (pf); Utah Symphony Orchestra; Abravanel, Maurice (cond)
- Westminster XWN-18684/WST-14038; 33m/s; rel 1958; del 1967
- Westminster XWN-18685; 33m; rel 1958; del 1967
- Westminster XWN-18686; 33m; rel 1958; del 1961

[3566] Pechersky, Piotr (pf); Moscow Philharmonic; Kondrashin, Kiril (cond)
- Westminster WGS-8355; 33s; rel 1979; cip

[3567] Pennario, Leonard (pf); Pittsburgh Symphony Orchestra; Steinberg, William (cond)
- Capitol P-8219; 33m; rel 1953; del 1960
- Capitol CTL-7046; 33m; rel pre-1956
- Capitol (Australian) CLCX-036; 33m; rel pre-1956
- Telefunken LCE-8219; 33m; rel pre-1956
- Everest SDBR-3288; 33s; rel 1971; del 1977

[3568] Previn, Andre (pf); Andre Kostelanetz and his Orchestra; Kostelanetz, Andre (cond)
- Columbia CL-1495/CS-8286; 33m/s; rel 1960; cip
- Columbia MS-7518; 33s; rel 1970; cip (Excerpt: 3rd Movement)
- Columbia MG-33728; 33s; 2 discs; rel 1976; del 1979

[3569] Previn, Andre (pf); London Symphony Orchestra; Previn, Andre (cond)
- Angel S-36810; 33s; rel 1971; cip

[3570] Reims, H. (pf); Philharmonic Symphony
- Allegro ALG-3096; 33m; rel 1954; del 1959

Concerto in F, Piano and Orchestra (1925) *(cont'd)*

[3571] Sanroma, Jesus Maria (pf); Boston Pops Orchestra; Fiedler, Arthur (cond)
- Victor 17208-11S (in set M-690); 78; 4 discs; rel 1940*
- Victor 17216-19; 78; 4 discs; rel 1940*
- Camden CAL-304; 33m; rel 1956; del 1961

[3572] Siegel, Jeffrey (pf); St. Louis Symphony Orchestra; Slatkin, Leonard (cond)
- Vox QSVBX-5132; 33q; 3 discs; rel 1975; cip
- Turnabout QTVS-34703; 33q; rel 1978; cip

[3573] Silver, Eric (pf) (cond); orchestra
- Rondo-lette 110; 33s; rel 1959; del 1963

[3574] Sosina, F. (pf); USSR Radio Symphony Orchestra; Yansons, Alexander (cond)
- Matrix No 5674(a)-5675(a); 33m; rel 196?

[3575] Szidon, Robert (pf); London Philharmonic Orchestra; Downes, Edward (cond)
- Deutsche Grammophon 2530.055; 33s; rel 1970; cip

[3576] Templeton, Alec (pf); Cincinnati Symphony Orchestra; Johnson, Thor (cond)
- Remington 199-184; 33m; rel 1955; del 1956

[3577] Wild, Earl (pf); Boston Pops Orchestra; Fiedler, Arthur (cond)
- RCA LM-2586/LSC-2586; 33m/s; rel 1962; del 1980
- RCA VCS-7097; 33s; 2 discs; rel 1972; cip

[3578] piano; Sauter-Finegan Orchestra
- RCA LPM-1051; 33m; rel 1955; del 1959
- Victor EPC-1051; 45; 7"; rel pre-1956
- Gramophone 7EG-8152; 45; 7"; rel pre-1956

[3579] piano; orchestra
- Silver Burdett 76289; 33; rel 1969 (Excerpt: 3rd Movement)

Concerto in F (Abridged)

[3580] Bargy, Roy (pf); Paul Whiteman Orchestra; Whiteman, Paul (cond)
- Decca 57; 78; 2 discs; rel pre-1942
- Decca A-57; 78; 2 discs; rel pre-1948
- Brunswick 0145-46; 78; 2 discs; rel pre-1952

[3581] Scime, Roger (pf); Symphony of the Air Pops Orchestra; D'Artega, Alfonso (cond)
- Epic LN-3621-22 (in set SN-6034)/BSN-549-50 (in set BSN-104); 33m/s; 2 discs; rel 1959; del 1965

Concerto in F (Abridged) *(cont'd)*
- Epic LN-3652/BN-553; 33m/s; rel 1960; del 1963

Concerto in F: Excerpt (arr for pf)
[3582] Schuyler, D. (pf)
- EMI/Odeon (Argentinian) 66070; 78; rel pre-1956

Cuban Overture, A (Rumba) (1932)
[3583] Andre Kostelanetz and his Orchestra; Kostelanetz, Andre (cond)
- Columbia ML-4481; 33m; rel 1952; del 1955
- Columbia CL-783; 33m; rel 1955; del 1959

[3584] Boston Pops Orchestra; Fiedler, Arthur (cond)
- RCA LM-2586/LSC-2586; 33m/s; rel 1962; del 1980

[3585] Cleveland Orchestra; Maazel, Lorin (cond)
- London CS-6946; 33s; rel 1975; cip

[3586] Cleveland Pops Orchestra; Lane, Louis (cond)
- Epic LC-3626/BC-1047; 33m/s; rel 1959; del 1970

[3587] Eastman-Rochester Symphony Orchestra; Hanson, Howard (cond)
- Mercury MG-50166; 33m; rel 1958; del 1963
- Mercury MG-50290/SR-90290; 33m/s; rel 1962; del 1967

[3588] National Opera Orchestra of Monte Carlo; Waart, Edo de (cond)
- Philips 6500.290; 33s; rel 1972; del 1977

[3589] Prague Symphony Orchestra; Neumann, Vaclav (cond)
- Supraphon SUAST-50479; 33s; rel 1963
- Everest SDBR-3405; 33s; rel 1977; cip

[3590] Pro Musica Orchestra of Hamburg; Walther, Hans-Jurgen (cond)
- MGM E-3307; 33m; rel 1956; del 1959
- MGM 3E-1; 33m; 3 discs; rel 1957; del 1959

[3591] St. Louis Symphony Orchestra; Slatkin, Leonard (cond)
- Vox QSVBX-5132; 33q; 3 discs; rel 1975; cip

Cuban Overture, A (two-piano version)
[3592] Veri, Frances (pf); Jamanis, Michael (pf)
- Connoisseur Society CSQ-2067-SQ; 33q; rel 1975; del 1979

Cuban Overture, A (arr for pf and orch by Rosa Linda)
[3593] Linda, Rosa (pf); Paul Whiteman Orchestra; Whiteman, Paul (cond)
- Decca 29053-54 (in set 31); 78; 2 discs; rel pre-1942
- Decca 29088-91 (in set DA-31); 78; 4 discs; rel pre-1948
- Brunswick 0141-42; 78; 2 discs; rel pre-1952
- Decca DL-8024; 33m; rel 1950; del 1970
- Decca UMT-263072; 33m; rel pre-1956
- Coral 57021; 33m; rel pre-1956

Cuban Overture, A (arr for pf and orch by Greig McRitchie)
[3594] Pennario, Leonard (pf); Hollywood Bowl Symphony Orchestra; Newman, Alfred (cond)
- Capitol P-8581/SP-8581; 33m/s; rel 1962; del 1970
- Angel S-36070; 33s; rel 1974; cip

Dawn of a New Day (1938)
[3595] Horace Heidt and his Musical Knights
- Brunswick 8313; 78; 10"; rel pre-1942

I Got Rhythm Variations (1934)
[3596] Bianca, Sondra (pf); Pro Musica Orchestra of Hamburg; Walther, Hans-Jurgen (cond)
- MGM E-3307; 33m; rel 1956; del 1959
- MGM 3E-1; 33m; 3 discs; rel 1957; del 1959

[3597] Levant, Oscar (pf); Morton Gould and his Orchestra; Gould, Morton (cond)
- Columbia 72873-74D (in set MM-867); 78; 2 discs; rel 1949
- Columbia M-10037; 78; rel pre-1953
- Columbia GFX-184; 78; rel pre-1953
- Columbia ML-2073; 33m; 10"; rel pre-1949; del 1956

[3598] Moussov, Teodor (pf); TVR Symphony Orchestra; Vladigerov, Alexander (cond)
- Monitor MCS-2153; 33s; rel 1977; cip

[3599] Parkhouse, David (pf); London Festival Recording Ensemble; Herrmann, Bernard (cond)
- London SPC-21077/4-SPC-21077; 33s/q; rel 1973; del 1979

[3600] Pennario, Leonard (pf); Hollywood Bowl Symphony Orchestra; Newman, Alfred (cond)
- Capitol P-8581/SP-8581; 33m/s; rel 1962; del 1970
- Time-Life LT-156/SLT-156; 33m/s; rel 1968
- Angel S-36070; 33s; rel 1974; cip

I Got Rhythm Variations (1934) *(cont'd)*
- Angel S-36062; 33s; rel 1977; cip

[3601] Siegel, Jeffrey (pf); St. Louis Symphony Orchestra; Slatkin, Leonard (cond)
- Vox QSVBX-5132; 33q; 3 discs; rel 1975; cip
- Turnabout QTVS-34703; 33q; rel 1978; cip

[3602] Wild, Earl (pf); Boston Pops Orchestra; Fiedler, Arthur (cond)
- RCA LM-2586/LSC-2586; 33m/s; rel 1962; del 1980
- RCA VCS-7097; 33s; 2 discs; rel 1972; cip

[3603] Wild, Earl (pf); Paul Whiteman Orchestra; Whiteman, Paul (cond)
- Coral 57021; 33m; rel pre-1956

I Got Rhythm Variations (arr for 2 pfs by George Gershwin)
[3604] Veri, Frances (pf); Jamanis, Michael (pf)
- Connoisseur Society CSQ-2067-SQ; 33q; rel 1975; del 1979

I Got Rhythm Variations (arr by William C. Shoenfeld)
[3605] Haas, Werner (pf); National Opera Orchestra of Monte Carlo; Waart, Edo de (cond)
- Philips 6500.118; 33s; rel 1971; cip

In the Mandarin's Orchid Garden (1929)
[3606] Rees, Rosalind (sop); Cybriwsky, Oresta (pf)
- Turnabout TVS-34638; 33s; rel 1977; cip

Lullaby (1919)
[3607] Juilliard String Quartet
- Columbia M-32596; 33s; rel 1974; cip

[3608] Kohon Quartet
- Vox SVBX-5305; 33s; 3 discs; rel 1974; cip

Lullaby (arr for orch)
[3609] St. Louis Symphony Orchestra; Slatkin, Leonard (cond)
- Vox QSVBX-5132; 33q; 3 discs; rel 1975; cip

Lullaby (arr for harmonica and orch by Morton Gould)
[3610] Adler, Larry (harmonica); Morton Gould and his Orchestra; Gould, Morton (cond)
- RCA LM-2986/LSC-2986; 33m/s; rel 1968; del 1973

Porgy and Bess (1935)

[3611] Albert, Donnie Ray (bar); Dale, Clamma (sop); Shakesnider, Wilma (sop); Lane, Betty (sop); Brice, Carol (al); Marshall, Larry (ten); Smith, Andrew (bar); Smalls, Alexander B. (bar); chorus; Houston Grand Opera Orchestra; De Main, John (cond)
- RCA ARL-3-2109; 33s; 3 discs; rel 1977; cip

[3612] Duncan, Todd (b); Brown, Anne Wiggins (sop); other members of original cast; orchestra
- Design DCF-53; 33s; rel 1959; del 1961
- Design DLP-110; 33m; rel 1960; del 1962
- Design DLP-1002/DCF-1002; 33m/s; rel 1960; del 1963

[3613] McFerrin, Robert; Addison, Adele; Bailey, Pearl; Matthews, Inez; Thigpen, Helen; Price, Loulie Jean Norman; Calloway, Cab; Scott, Leslie; Smith, Merritt; chorus; orchestra; Previn, Andre (cond)
- Columbia OL-5410/OS-2016; 33m/s; rel 1959/1960; cip

[3614] White, Willard (b); Mitchell, Leona (sop); Boatwright, McHenry (b bar); Clemmons, Francois (ten); other soloists; Cleveland Orchestra Chorus; Cleveland Orchestra; Maazel, Lorin (cond)
- London OS-26461-63 (in set OSA-13116); 33s; 3 discs; rel 1976; cip

[3615] Winters, Lawrence (bar); Williams, Camilla (sop); Matthews, Inez (sop); Long, Avon (ten); other soloists; J. Rosamond Johnson Chorus and Orchestra; Engel, Lehman (cond)
- Columbia OL-4427-29 (in set OSL-162); 33m; 3 discs; rel 1951; del 1968
- Columbia AAL-31; 33m; 10"; rel 1953; del 1957 (excerpts)
- Columbia ML-4766; 33m; rel 1954; del 1956 (excerpts)
- Philips A-01115-17L; 33m; 3 discs; rel pre-1956
- Philips S-06600R; 33m; rel pre-1956 (excerpts)
- Philips (English) NBL-5016-18; 33m; 3-10"; rel pre-1956
- Columbia A-1045; 45; 7"; rel pre-1956 (excerpts)
- Columbia CL-922; 33m; rel 1956; del 1961
- Columbia OL-4766; 33m; rel 1956; del 1957 (excerpts)
- Odyssey 32-16-0242-44 (in set 32-36-0018); 33s; 3 discs; rel 1968; cip

Porgy and Bess (Abridged)

[3616] Trendler, Robert (cond)
- Pilotone 103; 78; 4 discs; rel pre-1952
- Grand Award 33-304; 33m; rel 1955; del 1962

Porgy and Bess (arr by Russell Garcia)

[3617] Torme, Mel; Faye, Frances; Roche, Betty; Blair, Sallie; Price, Loulie Jean Norman; Kirby, George; Hartman, Johnny; Rosolino, Frank; Derise, Joe; Dorough, Bob; Collins, Al; Bethlehem Orchestra; Garcia, Russell (cond)
- Bethlehem EXLP-1; 33m; 3 discs; rel 1956; del 1965
- Bethlehem 6040; 33m; rel 1960; del 1963 (excerpts)
- Bethlehem 3BP-1; 33m; 3 discs; rel 1976; cip

Porgy and Bess: Selections

[3618] Belafonte, Harry; Horne, Lena
- RCA LOP-1507/LSO-1507; 33m/s; rel 1959; del 1972

[3619] Booth, Webster (ten); Zeigler, A. (sop); Savoy Hotel Orpheans; Gibbons, Carroll (cond)
- Columbia 69194D; 78; rel pre-1952
- Columbia (English) DX-824; 78; rel pre-1952

[3620] Calloway, Cab; Thigpen, Helen; Scott, Leslie; orchestra; Blackton, Jay (cond)
- RCA LPM-3156; 33m; 10"; rel 1953; del 1956
- Victor EPA-3156; 45; 7"; rel pre-1956

[3621] Charles, Ray (voice) (pf); Laine, Cleo; Reverend James Cleveland Singers; orchestra; De Vol, Frank (cond)
Rec 4/20-23/76 and 7/13/76
- RCA CPL-2-1831; 33s; 2 discs; rel 1976

[3622] Davis, Sammy, Jr.; McRae, Carmen; chorus; orchestra; Evans, Gil (cond)
- Decca DL-8854/DL-78854; 33m/s; rel 1959

[3623] Douglas Singers; orchestra
- World Wide 20010; 33s; rel 1959; del 1976

[3624] Duncan, Todd (b); Brown, Anne Wiggins (sop); other members of original cast; Eva Jessye Choir; Decca Symphony Orchestra; Smallens, Alexander (cond)
- Decca 29067-70 (in set A-145); Vol I (of 2); 78; 4 discs; rel 1940*
- Decca 23250-52 (in set A-283); Vol II (of 2); 78; 3-10"; rel pre-1948
- Decca 40128-31 (in set DU-739); Vol I (of 2); 78; 4-10"; rel 1949
- Brunswick 05045-46; 78; 2 discs; rel pre-1956
- Decca DL-7006; 33m; 10"; rel 1951; del 1957
- Decca DL-8042; 33m; rel 1952; del 1956
- Brunswick LAT-8021; 33m; rel pre-1953

Porgy and Bess: Selections *(cont'd)*

- Decca DL-9024/DL-79024; 33m/s; rel 1955/1959; del 1974
- Decca UM-233028; 33m; 10"; rel pre-1956
- Decca ED-808; 45; 7"; rel pre-1956
- MCA 2035; 33s; rel 1974; cip

[3625] Duncan, Todd (b); Brown, Anne Wiggins (sop); Mitchell, Abbie; Matthews, Edward; Elzy, Ruby; Gershwin, George (pf)
Rec 7/19/35 (Recording of rehearsal)
- Mark 56 Records 667; 33m; rel 1977; cip

[3626] Hayes, Richard; Stewart, Paula; Roberts, Lynn; chorus; orchestra; Bassman, George (cond)
- Decca DL-8910-12 (in set DXZ-160)/DL-78910-12 (in set DXSZ-7160); 33m/s; rel 1959

[3627] Long, Avon (b); Dowdy, Helen (sop); Leo Reisman Orchestra; Reisman, Leo (cond)
- Decca A-351; 78; 3-10"; rel pre-1948 (issued as Vol III of Decca set with Todd Duncan and Anne Brown)

[3628] Merrill, Robert (bar); Stevens, Rise (m sop); Robert Shaw Chorale; Victor Orchestra; Bennett, Robert Russell (cond)
- Victor DM-1496; 78; rel pre-1952
- RCA LM-1124; 33m; rel 1951; del 1961

[3629] Peters, Brock (bar); Tynes, Margaret (sop); Burton, Miriam (sop); Merritte, Theresa (sop); Crawford, Joseph (ten); Dillard, William (bar); Colman, Charles (bar); Opera Society Chorus and Orchestra; Belanger, Paul (cond)
- Musical Masterpiece Society MMS-2035; 33m; rel pre-1956
- Concert Hall CHS-1247; 33m; rel 1956; del 1957
- Concert Hall H-1647; 33m; rel 1957; del 1959

[3630] Royale Operetta Singers and Orchestra
- Royale 1242; 33m; rel 1952; del 1957
- Royale 6095; 33m; 10"; rel 1952; del 1957
- Royale 14588; 45; 3-7"; rel pre-1953

[3631] Schuyler, Sonny; Froman, Jane (sop); Knight, Felix; Victor Orchestra; Shilkret, Nathaniel (cond)
- Victor 12334 (in set C-29); 78; rel 1939
- RCA LPT-3055; 33
- Victor EPBT-3055; 45; 7"

Porgy and Bess: Selections *(cont'd)*
[3632] Soennerstedt, Bernhardt (bar);
Quensel, I. (bar); Tibell, E. (al)
- Symfoni & Artist (Swedish)
RT-1006-07; 78; 2 discs; rel
pre-1956

[3633] Stewart-Williams Company
- Warner Bros W-1260/WS-1260;
33m/s; rel 1959; del 1962

[3634] Tibbett, Lawrence (bar); Jepson,
Helen (sop); chorus; orchestra;
Smallens, Alexander (cond)
Rec 1935
- Victor 11878-81 (in set C-25);
78; 4 discs; rel 1935
- Victor 11-8860 (in set M-1015);
78; rel pre-1948 (side 6 of
4-disc set)
- Gramophone DB-2735-38; 78; 4
discs; rel pre-1952
- Gramophone DB-3395; 78; rel
pre-1952 (sides 1 and 6 of the
complete 4-disc set)
- Gramophone DB-3396; 78; rel
pre-1952 (sides 3 and 8 of
4-disc set)
- Victor ERAT-23; 45; 7"; rel
pre-1956 (excerpts)
- Camden CAL-500; 33m; rel
1959; del 1961

[3635] Tibbett, Lawrence (bar); Steber,
Eleanor (sop); Jepson, Helen
(sop); Merrill, Robert (bar);
Calloway, Cab; Stevens, Rise (m
sop); Robert Shaw Chorale;
various orchestras; various
conductors
Rec 1935-53
- RCA AVM-1-1742; 33m; rel
1976; cip

[3636] Warfield, William (bar); Price,
Leontyne (sop); Bubbles, John W.
(ten); Boatwright, McHenry (bar);
other soloists; Victor Orchestra;
Victor Chorus; De Paur, Leonard
(choral cond); Henderson, Skitch
(cond)
- RCA LM-2679/LSC-2679;
33m/s; rel 1963; cip
- RCA LSC-5001; 33s; rel 1971;
cip

[3637] Williams; Hollywood Grand Studio
Orchestra
- Tops 1641; 33m; rel 1958; del
1963
- Mayfair 9641; 33s; rel 1958;
del 1963

[3638] Winters, Lawrence; Lucas, Isabelle;
Elsy, Barbara; Stevens, Pauline;
Ellington, Ray; chorus; orchestra;
Alwyn, Kenneth (cond)
- Heliodor H-25052/HS-25052;
33m/s; rel 1967; del 1970

**Porgy and Bess: Selections (arr for
vocals and tpt by Russell Garcia)**
[3639] Fitzgerald, Ella; Armstrong, Louis
(tpt); orchestra; Garcia, Russell
(cond)
Rec 9/57
- Verve
MGV-4011-12/VS-64011-12;
33m/s; 2 discs; rel 1959; del
1968
- Verve MGV-4068/VS-64068;
33m/s; rel 1965; del 1968
- Verve VE-2-2507; 33s; 2 discs;
rel 1976; cip

**Porgy and Bess: Bess, You Is My
Woman Now**
[3640] Lawrence, N.; Thomson, M.
- Durium (Italian) Al-10239; 78;
rel pre-1956

[3641] Seattle Chamber Singers;
Shangrow, George (cond)
Rec 8/1-8/76
- Voyager VRLP-701S; 33s; rel
1976

[3642] Stevens, Rise (m sop); Merrill,
Robert (bar); chorus
- Victor WEPR-34; 45; 7"; rel
pre-1953
- Gramophone 7EB-6015; 45; 7";
rel pre-1956

Porgy and Bess: Duet
[3643] Norby, Einar (bar); Brems, Elsa
(sop)
- Sonora (Swedish) K-9524; 78;
rel pre-1952
- Tono (Danish) X-25028; 78; rel
pre-1952

**Porgy and Bess: I Got Plenty o'
Nuttin'**
[3644] Bennett, R. (b)
- RCA LM-9002; 33m; rel
pre-1956
- Victor WDM-1341; 45; 7"; rel
pre-1956

[3645] Dawson, P. (bar)
- Gramophone B-8715; 78; 10";
rel pre-1952

[3646] Duncan, Todd (b); Allen, W. (pf)
- Parlophone R-3055 (in set 82);
78; rel pre-1952

[3647] Lawrence, N. (b)
- Durium (Italian) Al-10239; 78;
rel pre-1956

[3648] Matthews, Edward (bar); Leo
Reisman Orchestra; Reisman, Leo
(cond)
- Brunswick 7562; 78; 10"; rel
pre-1936

[3649] Merrill, Robert (bar); chorus
- Victor WEPR-34; 45; 7"; rel
pre-1953
- Gramophone 7EB-6015; 45; 7";
rel pre-1956

**Porgy and Bess: I Got Plenty o'
Nuttin'** *(cont'd)*
[3650] Norby, Einar (bar)
- Sonora (Swedish) K-9524; 78;
rel pre-1952
- Tono (Danish) X-25028; 78; rel
pre-1952

[3651] Spencer, Kenneth
- Columbia DW-5240; 33m; rel
pre-1956
- Columbia SCMW-506; 45; 7"; rel
pre-1956

[3652] Tibbett, Lawrence (bar)
- Allegro-Royale 1627; 33m; rel
pre-1956
- Allegro-Royale EP-388; 45; 7";
rel pre-1956

**Porgy and Bess: It Ain't Necessarily
So**
[3653] Matthews, Edward (bar); Leo
Reisman Orchestra; Reisman, Leo
(cond)
- Brunswick 7562; 78; 10"; rel
pre-1936

[3654] Merrill, Robert (bar)
- Victor WEPR-34; 45; 7"; rel
pre-1953
- Gramophone 7EB-6015; 45; 7";
rel pre-1956

[3655] Robeson, Paul (b bar); Columbia
Concert Orchestra; Balaban,
Emanuel (cond)
- Columbia 17517D (in set
MM-732); 78; rel 1948*
- Columbia ML-4105; 33m; rel
1952; del 1971

[3656] Robeson, Paul (b); orchestra
- Victor 26358A; 78; 10"; rel
pre-1943
- Gramophone B-8711; 78; 10";
rel pre-1948

[3657] Tibbett, Lawrence (bar)
- Allegro-Royale 1627; 33m; rel
pre-1956
- Allegro-Royale EP-388; 45; 7";
rel pre-1956

**Porgy and Bess: It Takes a Long
Pull to Get There**
[3658] Robeson, Paul (b); orchestra
- Victor 26359A; 78; 10"; rel
pre-1943

Porgy and Bess: Jazzbo Brown
[3659] Bolcom, William (pf)
Rec 3/73
- Nonesuch H-71284/HQ-1284;
33s/q; rel 1973; cip
- Nonesuch H-7-14; 33s; 2 discs;
rel 1978; cip

[3660] Gould, Morton (pf)
- RCA LM-6033; 33m; 2 discs; rel
1955; del 1961

Porgy and Bess: My Man's Gone Now

[3661] Brown, Anne Wiggins (sop);
Copenhagen Royal Orchestra;
Hye-Knudsen, Johan (cond)
- Mercury (French) M-4123; 78;
rel pre-1956
- Tono (Danish) X-25112; 78; rel
pre-1956

[3662] Eamon, Deltra (sop); Almeida,
Laurindo (gtr)
- Orion ORS-7260; 33s; rel 1972;
cip

[3663] Kirsten, Dorothy (sop)
- Pelican LP-2005; 33m; rel 1976

Porgy and Bess: Summertime

[3664] Berberian, Cathy (m sop); Canino,
Bruno (pf)
Rec 1970
- Wergo WER-60-054; 33s; rel
1977*

[3665] Brown, Anne Wiggins (sop);
Copenhagen Royal Orchestra;
Hye-Knudsen, Johan (cond)
- Mercury (French) M-4123; 78;
rel pre-1956
- Tono (Danish) X-25112; 78; rel
pre-1956

[3666] Farrell, Eileen (sop); Trovillo,
George (pf)
- Angel 35608; 33m; rel 1959;
del 1966

[3667] Pons, Lily (sop)
- Columbia 71491D; 78; rel
pre-1948

[3668] Ray, E.
- Vega (French) P-1506; 45; 7";
rel pre-1956

[3669] Robeson, Paul (b); orchestra
- Victor 26359A; 78; 10"; rel
pre-1943

[3670] Rowe, Genevieve (sop); Columbia
Symphony Orchestra; Rodzinski,
Artur (cond)
- Columbia ML-4337; 33m; rel
1950*
- Columbia A-1003; 45; 7"; rel
pre-1953

[3671] Seattle Chamber Singers;
Shangrow, George (cond)
Rec 8/1-8/76
- Voyager VRLP-701S; 33s; rel
1976

[3672] Steber, Eleanor (sop)
- Victor 11-9186; 78; rel
pre-1948
- RCA LCT-6701; 33m; rel
pre-1956

[3673] Stevens, Rise (m sop)
- Victor 12-3160 (in set
DM-1496); 78; rel pre-1953
- Victor WEPR-34; 45; 7"; rel
pre-1953
- Gramophone 7EB-6015; 45; 7";
rel pre-1956

Porgy and Bess: Summertime
(cont'd)

[3674] Williams, Camilla (sop)
- Victor 46-0004; 78; rel
pre-1948

Porgy and Bess: Summertime (arr by Oswald Cheesman)

[3675] Te Kanawa, Kiri (sop); orchestra;
Cheesman, Oswald (cond)
- Musical Heritage Society
MHS-3631; 33s; rel 1977

Porgy and Bess: Where's My Bess

[3676] Bennett, R. (bar)
- RCA LM-9002; 33m; rel
pre-1956
- Victor WDM-1341; 45; 7"; rel
pre-1956

[3677] Duncan, Todd (b); Allen, W. (pf)
- Parlophone R-3055 (in set 82);
78; rel pre-1952

[3678] Melton, James (ten); two pianos
- Victor 11-9224; 78; rel
pre-1948

[3679] Merrill, Robert (bar)
- Victor 12-3160 (in set
DM-1496); 78; rel pre-1953

Porgy and Bess: A Woman is a Sometime Thing

[3680] Robeson, Paul (b); orchestra
- Victor 26358A; 78; 10"; rel
pre-1943
- Gramophone B-8711; 78; 10";
rel pre-1948

Porgy and Bess (arr for orch by Robert Russell Bennett, A Symphonic Picture of Porgy and Bess)

[3681] Big Symphonic Band; Beeler,
Walter (cond)
- Golden Crest
CR-4022/CRS-4022; 33m/s; rel
1960; cip

[3682] Boston Pops Orchestra; Fiedler,
Arthur (cond)
- RCA LSC-3130; 33s; rel 1970;
del 1975
- RCA VCS-7097; 33s; 2 discs; rel
1972; cip

[3683] Hamburg Philharmonic Orchestra;
Walther, Hans-Jurgen (cond)
Rec 1955
- Music Sound Books 78163-64;
78; 2 discs; rel pre-1956
- MGM E-3253; 33m; rel 1956;
del 1959
- MGM 3E-1; 33m; 3 discs; rel
1957; del 1959

[3684] Hollywood Bowl Pops Concert
Orchestra; Green, Johnny (cond)
- Decca DL-4051; 33m; 10"; rel
1953; del 1957
- Brunswick LA-8690; 33m; rel
pre-1956

Porgy and Bess (arr for orch by Robert Russell Bennett, A Symphonic Picture of Porgy and Bess) *(cont'd)*

[3685] Hollywood Bowl Symphony
Orchestra; Slatkin, Felix (cond)
- Capitol P-8474/SP-8474;
33m/s; rel 1959; del 1963
- Pickwick 4044; 33s; rel 1968;
del 1972

[3686] Indianapolis Symphony Orchestra;
Sevitzky, Fabien (cond)
- Victor 11-8789-91 (in set
M-999); 78; 3 discs; rel
pre-1948
- RCA LBC-1059; 33m; rel 1953;
del 1956
- Victor WBC-1059; 45; 7"; rel
pre-1956

[3687] Ira Wright Orchestra; Wright, Ira
(cond)
- Rondo-lette 76; 33s; rel 1959;
del 1963

[3688] Los Angeles Philharmonic
Orchestra; Wallenstein, Alfred
(cond)
- Decca 29176-77 (in set
DA-397); 78; 2 discs; rel
pre-1948
- Decca DL-7002; 33m; 10"; rel
pre-1956

[3689] MGM Orchestra; Ashley, Robert
(cond)
- MGM E-3131; 33m; rel 1954;
del 1959

[3690] Minneapolis Symphony Orchestra;
Dorati, Antal (cond)
- Mercury MG-50016; 33m; rel
1953; del 1963
- Mercury (English) MG-50016;
33m; rel pre-1956
- Mercury (French) MLP-7508;
33m; rel pre-1956
- Mercury EP-2-501; 45; 7"; rel
pre-1956
- Mercury (French)
MEP-14534-35; 45; 2-7"; rel
pre-1956
- Mercury MG-50071; 33m; rel
1958; del 1963
- Mercury MG-50394/SR-90394;
33m/s; rel 1964; del 1969

[3691] National Opera Orchestra of Monte
Carlo; Waart, Edo de (cond)
- Philips 6500.290; 33s; rel
1972; del 1977

[3692] Philadelphia Orchestra; Ormandy,
Eugene (cond)
- Columbia MS-7258; 33s; rel
1969; cip
- Columbia MS-7518; 33s; rel
1970; cip
- Columbia MG-30073; 33s; 2
discs; rel 1970; cip

[3693] Philharmonic Symphony Orchestra
of New York; Kostelanetz, Andre
(cond)
- Columbia ML-4904; 33m; rel
1954; del 1955

Porgy and Bess (arr for orch by Robert Russell Bennett, A Symphonic Picture of Porgy and Bess) *(cont'd)*
- Columbia CL-721; 33m; rel 1955; del 1959
- Columbia A-1102; 45; 7"; rel pre-1956
- Columbia A-1921; 45; 7"; rel pre-1956
- Philips (English) NBL-5020; 33m; 10"; rel pre-1956

[3694] Pittsburgh Symphony Orchestra; Reiner, Fritz (cond)
- Columbia 12118-20D (in set M-572); 78; 3 discs; rel 1945
- Columbia 12121-23D (in set MM-572); 78; 3 discs; rel 1945*
- Columbia ML-2019; 33m; 10"; rel pre-1949; del 1956

[3695] Pittsburgh Symphony Orchestra; Steinberg, William (cond)
- Command CC33-11037/CC-SD-11037; 33m/s; rel 1967; del 1973
- Westminster WGS-8243; 33s

[3696] Royal Farnsworth Symphony Orchestra; D'Artega, Alfonso (cond)
- Design DLP-44/DCF-33; 33m/s; rel 1959; del 1961

[3697] Symphony of the Air Pops Orchestra; D'Artega, Alfonso (cond)
- Epic LN-3621-22 (in set SN-6034)/BSN-549-50 (in set BSN-104); 33m/s; 2 discs; rel 1959; del 1965
- Epic LN-3651/BN-552; 33m/s; rel 1960; del 1963

[3698] Utah Symphony Orchestra; Abravanel, Maurice (cond)
- Vanguard Cardinal VCS-10023; 33s; rel 1968; del 1977
- Vanguard SRV-345-SD; 33s; rel 1976; cip

[3699] Victor Symphony Orchestra; Bennett, Robert Russell (cond)
- RCA LM-2340/LSC-2340; 33m/s; rel 1959; del 1963
- RCA-Victrola VICS-1491; 33s; rel 1970; del 1975
- RCA-Victrola VICS-1669(e); 33s; rel 1972; del 1976

Porgy and Bess (arr for orch by Robert Farnon)
[3700] London Festival Orchestra; Farnon, Robert (cond)
- London SPC-21013; 33s; rel 1966; del 1979

Porgy and Bess (arr for orch by Morton Gould)
[3701] Morton Gould and his Orchestra; Gould, Morton (cond)
- RCA LM-6033; 33m; 2 discs; rel 1955; del 1961
- RCA LM-2002; 33m; rel 1956; del 1961

Porgy and Bess (arr for orch)
[3702] Andre Kostelanetz and his Orchestra; Kostelanetz, Andre (cond)
- Columbia 7326M; 78; rel pre-1952
- Columbia (English) CQX-16637; 78; rel pre-1952
- Columbia DX-1176; 78; rel pre-1952
- Columbia ML-4481; 33m; rel 1952; del 1955
- Columbia CL-783; 33m; rel 1955; del 1959
- Columbia KG-32825; 33s; rel 1974

[3703] Boston Pops Orchestra; Fiedler, Arthur (cond)
- Victor 10-4215; 78; 10"; rel pre-1956 (excerpts)
- RCA LM-1879; 33m; rel 1955; del 1972
- Victor ERA-179; 45; 7"; rel pre-1956
- Victor (Italian) A72R-0020; 45; 7"; rel pre-1956
- Victor (French) A-95201; 45; 7"; rel pre-1956
- Victor 49-4215; 45; 7"; rel pre-1956 (excerpts)
- RCA LM-2071; 33m; rel 1956

[3704] Bravo Pops Symphony Orchestra; Senati, John (cond)
- Bravo K-119; 33m; rel pre-1977

[3705] C. Spivak Orchestra
- Victor 20-1650-51 (in set SP-6); 78; 2-10"; rel pre-1952

[3706] G. Melachrino Orchestra
- Gramophone C-4211; 78; rel pre-1956
- Gramophone EH-1439; 78; rel pre-1956
- Gramophone 7GF-170; 45; 7"; rel pre-1956
- Gramophone 7PQ-2015; 45; 7"; rel pre-1956

[3707] Monty Kelly and his Orchestra; Kelly, Monty (cond)
- Carlton STLP-12-111; 33s; rel 1958

[3708] Percy Faith and his Orchestra; Faith, Percy (cond)
- Columbia CL-1298/CS-8105; 33m/s; rel 1959; del 1962

[3709] orchestra; Gibbons (cond)
- Columbia AAL-39; 33m; 10"; rel 1954; del 1957

Porgy and Bess (arr for pf and orch by Greig McRitchie)
[3710] Pennario, Leonard (pf); Hollywood Bowl Symphony Orchestra; Newman, Alfred (cond)
- Capitol P-8581/SP-8581; 33m/s; rel 1962; del 1970
- Capitol SP-8689; 33s; rel 1968; del 1970
- Angel S-36070; 33s; rel 1974; cip

Porgy and Bess: Bess, You Is My Woman Now (arr for orch)
[3711] Percy Faith and his Orchestra; Faith, Percy (cond)
- Columbia C2L-1; 33m; 2 discs; rel 1957; del 1966

[3712] Philadelphia Orchestra; Ormandy, Eugene (cond)
- Columbia MS-7289; 33s; rel 1969; cip

Porgy and Bess: I Got Plenty o' Nuttin' (arr for orch)
[3713] Guy Lombardo Orchestra
- Victor 25204; 78; 10"; rel pre-1936

[3714] orchestra; Shankson, Louis (cond)
- Allegro-Royale 1609; 33m; rel pre-1956

Porgy and Bess: It Ain't Necessarily So (arr for orch)
[3715] Billie Butterfield and his Orchestra; Butterfield, Billie (cond)
- Capitol BD-10; 78; 10"; rel pre-1948

[3716] Guy Lombardo Orchestra
- Victor 25204; 78; 10"; rel pre-1936

Porgy and Bess: Summertime (arr for orch by Hill Bowen)
[3717] Living Voices with Living Strings; Bowen, Hill (cond)
- Camden CAS-675; 33s
- RCA Camden ACL-1-0423; 33s; rel 1974

Porgy and Bess: Summertime (arr for orch by Richard Jones)
[3718] Pittsburgh Symphony Orchestra (members of); Jones, Richard (cond)
- Capitol L-419; 33m; 10"; rel 1953*

Porgy and Bess: Summertime (arr for orch)
[3719] Percy Faith and his Orchestra; Faith, Percy (cond)
- Columbia C2L-1; 33m; 2 discs; rel 1957; del 1966

Porgy and Bess: Where's My Bess (arr for orch)
[3720] Andre Kostelanetz and his Orchestra; Kostelanetz, Andre (cond)
- Columbia ML-4819; 33m; rel 1954; del 1955
- Columbia KG-32825; 33s; rel 1974

Porgy and Bess (Various Instrumental Arrangements)
[3721] Arr for Clavichord and Guitar
Peterson, Oscar (clav); Pass, Joe (gtr)
Rec 1/26/76
- Pablo 2310-779; 33s; rel 1976

Porgy and Bess (Various Instrumental Arrangements)
(cont'd)

[3722] Arr for 2 Harps
Vito, Edward (hp); Vito, J. (hp)
- Cook 1031; 33m; rel pre-1956
- Cook 10301; 33m; rel pre-1956

[3723] Arr for Jazz Orchestra and Piano by Ralph Burns
jazz orchestra; Burns, Ralph (pf)
- Decca DL-9215; 33m; rel 1958

[3724] Arr for Piano by Earl Wild
Wild, Earl (pf)
Rec 10/18-20/76
- Quintessence PMC-7060; 33s; rel 1978; cip

[3725] Arr for Piano
Abadi, Marden (pf)
- Orion ORS-77265; 33s; rel 1977; cip
- Sine Qua Non Superba SAS-2022; 33s; rel 1978

[3726] recorded from player-piano rolls (no pianist given)
- Biograph BLP-1022Q; 33; rel 1977

[3727] Arr for 4 Pianos
First Piano Quartet
- RCA LM-125; 33m; 10"; rel 1951; del 1956
- Victor WDM-1574; 45; 7"; rel 1951*

[3728] Arr for Synthesizer
Kingsley, Gershon (syn)
- Avco 33021; 33s; rel 1971; del 1974

[3729] Arr for Violin and Piano by Jascha Heifetz
Heifetz, Jascha (vln); Bay, Emanuel (pf)
- Decca 29195, 23521-22 (in set A-435); 78; 1-10" and 2-12"; rel pre-1948
- Decca UAT-273572; 33m; rel pre-1956
- Decca DL-7003; 33m; 10"; rel pre-1949; del 1957
- Decca DL-9760; 33m; rel 1955; del 1971
- Brunswick LAT-8066; 33m; rel pre-1956
- Decca UM-233070; 33m; 10"; rel pre-1956
- RCA LM-2856/LSC-2856; 33m/s; rel 1965; cip
- RCA LSC-3256; 33s; rel 1973; del 1977

Porgy and Bess: Bess, You Is My Woman Now (Various Instrumental Arrangements)

[3730] Arr for Harmonica
Adler, Larry (harmonica)
- Angel 70025; 45; 7"; rel pre-1956

Porgy and Bess: Bess, You Is My Woman Now (Various Instrumental Arrangements) *(cont'd)*

[3731] Arr for Violin and Orchestra by Arthur Harris
Stern, Isaac (vln); Columbia Symphony Orchestra; Katims, Milton (cond)
- Columbia ML-5896/MS-6496; 33m/s; rel 1963; del 1966
- Columbia ML-6225/MS-6825; 33m/s; rel 1966; cip

[3732] Arr for Violin and Piano by Jascha Heifetz
Ferraresi, A. (vln); Galdieri, E. (pf)
- Gramophone HN-3537; 78; rel pre-1956

[3733] Suk, Josef (vln); Holecek, Alfred (pf)
- Epic LC-3967/BC-1367; 33m/s; rel 1967
- Supraphon SUAST-50882; 33s; rel 1967

Porgy and Bess: It Ain't Necessarily So (Various Instrumental Arrangements)

[3734] Arr for Harmonica
Adler, Larry (harmonica)
- Angel 70025; 45; 7"; rel pre-1956

[3735] Arr for Violin and Piano by Jascha Heifetz
Heifetz, Jascha (vln); Smith, Brooks (pf)
- RCA LSC-3205; 33s; rel 1971; cip

Porgy and Bess: Summertime (arr for qnt)

[3736] Sidney Bechet Quintet
- Blue Note 6; 78; rel pre-1943

(Three) Preludes, Piano (1926)

[3737] Behrend, Jeanne (pf)
- Victor 17910 (in set M-764); 78; rel 1941

[3738] Bianca, Sondra (pf)
- MGM E-3307; 33m; rel 1956; del 1959
- MGM 3E-1; 33m; 3 discs; rel 1957; del 1959

[3739] Bolcom, William (pf)
- Nonesuch H-71284/HQ-1284; 33s/q; rel 1973; cip

[3740] Chodack, Walter (pf)
- Ades (French) 14.002; 33s; rel 1976

[3741] Gershwin, George (pf)
- Columbia C-50107D; 78; rel pre-1936
- Columbia 7192M; 78; rel pre-1936

[3742] Gershwin, George (pf)
Rec 1926 or 1928
- RCA AVM-1-1740; 33m; rel 1976; cip

[3743] Glazer, Frank (pf)
- Concert-Disc M-1217/CS-217; 33m/s; rel 1960; del 1977

(Three) Preludes, Piano (1926)
(cont'd)

[3744] Gould, Morton (pf)
- RCA LM-6033; 33m; 2 discs; rel 1955; del 1961 (Excerpts: Nos 2 and 3)
- RCA LM-2017; 33m; rel 1956; del 1961

[3745] Jamanis, Michael (pf)
- Connoisseur Society CSQ-2067-SQ; 33q; rel 1975; del 1979

[3746] Johannesen, Grant (pf)
- Golden Crest CR-4065/CRS-4065; 33m/s; rel 1963/1966; cip

[3747] Leichner, Emil (pf)
Rec 6/72-3/73
- Supraphon 111.1721-22; 33s; 2 discs; rel 1975

[3748] Levant, Oscar (pf)
- Columbia 12125D (in set X-251); 78; rel pre-1948 (Excerpt: No 2)
- Columbia MX-251; 78; rel pre-1948 (Excerpt: No 2)
- Columbia 17333D; 78; 10"; rel pre-1948
- Columbia 17452D (in set M-508); 78; 10"; rel pre-1948
- Columbia GFX-129; 78; rel pre-1952 (Excerpt: No 2)
- Columbia LOX-598; 78; rel pre-1952 (Excerpt: No 2)
- Columbia (English) DX-1213; 78; rel pre-1952 (Excerpt: No 2)
- Columbia 72639D; 78 (Excerpts: Nos 2 and 3)
- Columbia ML-2073; 33m; 10"; rel pre-1949; del 1956
- Columbia A-1047; 45; 7"; rel pre-1956
- Columbia MS-7518; 33s; rel 1970; cip

[3749] List, Eugene (pf)
- Turnabout TVS-34457; 33s; rel 1971; cip

[3750] Mayorga, Lincoln (pf)
- Sheffield M-4; 33m; rel 1965; del 1979
- Town Hall M-4; 33m; rel 1979; cip

[3751] O'Neil, Perry (pf)
- Kapp KCL-9029/KC-S-9029; 33m/s; rel 1959; del 1962

[3752] Pennario, Leonard (pf)
- Capitol FAP-8206; 45; 7"; rel pre-1956
- Capitol P-8391; 33m; rel 1962; del 1970
- RCA LM-2731/LSC-2731; 33m/s; rel 1964; del 1975
- RCA LSC-5001; 33s; rel 1971; cip
- RCA-Victrola VICS-1669(e); 33s; rel 1972; del 1976 (Excerpt: No 2)

(Three) Preludes, Piano (1926)
(cont'd)

[3753] Ribbing, Stig (pf)
- Telefunken A-8855; 78; 10"; rel pre-1952

[3754] Shields, Roger (pf)
- Vox SVBX-5303; 33s; 3 discs; rel 1977; cip

[3755] Smit, Leo (pf)
- Dot DLP-3111; 33m; rel 1958; del 1966

[3756] Stepan, Russell (pf)
- Sonic LS-10; 33s; rel 1979; cip

[3757] Towlen, Gary (pf)
- Wardle TW-63; 33m; rel 1964; del 1968

[3758] Watts, Andre (pf)
- Columbia M-34221; 33s; rel 1976; cip

[3759] Werner, Ken (pf)
- Finnadar SR-9019; 33s; rel 1978; cip

(Three) Preludes: No 1
[3760] Foldes, Andor (pf)
- Continental 5033 (in set 22); 78; rel pre-1948
- Remington 149-4; 33m; 10"; rel 1950; del 1956

(Three) Preludes: No 2
[3761] Entremont, Philippe (pf)
- Columbia ML-6286/MS-6886; 33m/s; rel 1966; cip

[3762] Gershwin, George (pf)
Rec 11/10/32
- Mark 56 Records 667; 33m; rel 1977; cip

[3763] Goldsand, Robert (pf)
- Desto DM-200/DS-6200; 33m/s; 2 discs; rel 1964*

[3764] Rubinstein, Artur (pf)
- Victor 11-9420; 78; rel pre-1948

[3765] Schuyler, D. (pf)
- EMI/Odeon (Argentinian) 66070; 78; rel pre-1956

[3766] Waldoff, Stanley (pf)
- Musical Heritage Society MHS-3808; 33s; rel 1978

(Three) Preludes (arr for 2 pfs by Gregory Stone)
[3767] Grierson, Ralph (pf); Kane, Artie (pf)
- Angel S-36083; 33s; rel 1975; cip

(Three) Preludes (arr for orch)
[3768] Boston Pops Orchestra; Fiedler, Arthur (cond)
- London SPC-21185; 33s; rel 1979; cip

(Three) Preludes: Nos 2 and 3 (arr for orch)
[3769] Percy Faith and his Orchestra; Faith, Percy (cond)
- Columbia C2L-1; 33m; 2 discs; rel 1957; del 1966

(Three) Preludes (arr for vln and pf by Jascha Heifetz)
[3770] Besrodni, Igor (vln); Makarov, Abram (pf)
- Monitor MC-2028; 33m; rel 1959; del 1978

[3771] Heifetz, Jascha (vln); Bay, Emanuel (pf)
- Decca 23522-23 (in set A-435); 78; 2 discs; rel 1946*
- Decca DL-7003; 33m; 10"; rel pre-1949; del 1957
- Decca DL-9760; 33m; rel 1955; del 1971
- Decca UM-233070; 33m; 10"; rel pre-1956
- Decca UAT-273572; 33m; rel pre-1956
- Brunswick LAT-8066; 33m; rel pre-1956

[3772] Heifetz, Jascha (vln); Smith, Brooks (pf)
- RCA LM-2856/LSC-2856; 33m/s; rel 1965; cip
- RCA ARL-2-1421; 33s; 2 discs; rel 1976; del 1979

(Three) Preludes: No 2 (Various Instrumental Arrangements)
[3773] Arr for Harmonica
Adler, Larry (harmonica)
- Angel 64014; 33m; rel pre-1956
- Angel 70025; 45; 7"; rel pre-1956

[3774] Arr for Harp Ensemble
New York Harp Ensemble; Wurtzler, Aristid von (cond)
- Musical Heritage Society MHS-3890; 33s

[3775] Arr for Horn and Orchestra by S. Hunkins
Eger, Joseph (hn); Victor Orchestra; Rosenstock, Joseph (cond)
- RCA LM-2146; 33m; rel 1957; del 1960

[3776] Arr for Orchestra by Stone
Hamburg Philharmonia; Korn, Richard (cond)
- Allegro ALG-3149; 33m; rel 1954?

[3777] Arr for Orchestra
Hollywood Bowl Symphony Orchestra; Newman, Alfred (cond)
- Mercury MG-20036; 33m; rel pre-1958

[3778] orchestra; Camarata, Salvador (cond)
- London 40368; 78

(Three) Preludes: No 2 (Various Instrumental Arrangements)
(cont'd)

[3779] orchestra; Shankson, Louis (cond)
- Allegro-Royale 1609; 33m; rel pre-1956

[3780] Arr for Saxophone and Piano by Sigurd Rascher
Rascher, Sigurd (sax); Tudor, David (pf)
- Concert Hall CHS-1156; 33m; rel 1952; del 1957

[3781] Arr for Saxophone and Piano
Brodie, Paul (sax); Kubalek, Antonin (pf)
- Golden Crest RE-7056; 33s; rel 1979; cip

[3782] Arr for Violin and Piano
Szeryng, Henryk (vln); Berthelier, M. (pf)
- Pacific (French) LDPC-50; 33m; rel pre-1956

[3783] Arr for Violoncello and Piano
Fournier, Pierre (vcl); Lush, Ernest (pf)
- London LLP-700; 33m; rel 1953; del 1957
- Decca LXT-2766; 33m; rel pre-1956

Rhapsody in Blue (1924)
[3784] Atwell (pf); orchestra; Heath, Ted (cond)
- London LLP-1749; 33m; rel 1958; del 1959
- Richmond 20037; 33m; rel 1959; del 1975

[3785] Bargy, Roy (pf); Paul Whiteman Orchestra; Whiteman, Paul (cond)
- Decca 29051 (in set 31); 78; rel pre-1942
- Decca A-31; 78; rel pre-1948
- Decca 29088-91 (in set DA-31); 78; 4 discs; rel pre-1948
- Brunswick 0140; 78; rel pre-1948
- Decca DL-8024; 33m; rel 1950; del 1970
- Decca UMT-263072; 33m; rel pre-1956
- Decca ED-2195; 45; 7"; rel pre-1956
- Pickwick 3399; 33m; rel 1976; del 1979

[3786] Barnes, B. (pf); Ambrose Orchestra
- Decca F-5454; 78; rel pre-1936

[3787] Bernstein, Leonard (pf); New York Philharmonic; Bernstein, Leonard (cond)
- Columbia ML-5413/MS-6091; 33m/s; rel 1960; cip
- Columbia MS-7518; 33s; rel 1970; cip
- Columbia M-31804; 33s; rel 1973; cip

Rhapsody in Blue (1924) *(cont'd)*

[3788] Bianca, Sondra (pf); Hamburg Philharmonic Orchestra; Walther, Hans-Jurgen (cond)
- MGM E-3237; 33m; rel 1955; del 1959
- Parlophone PMC-1026; 33m; rel pre-1956
- MGM 3E-1; 33m; 3 discs; rel 1957; del 1959

[3789] Binz, G. (pf); orchestra; Thomassen, T. (cond)
- Telefunken E-1808; 78; rel pre-1936
- Ultraphon G-18128; 78; rel pre-1948

[3790] Black, Stanley (pf); London Festival Orchestra; Black, Stanley (cond)
- London SPC-21009; 33s; rel 1967; cip

[3791] Davis, Ivan (pf); Cleveland Orchestra; Maazel, Lorin (cond)
- London CS-6946; 33s; rel 1975; cip

[3792] Entremont, Philippe (pf); New Symphony Society Orchestra; Goehr, Walter (cond)
- Concert Hall RG-123; 33m; rel 1957; del 1959

[3793] Entremont, Philippe (pf); Philadelphia Orchestra; Ormandy, Eugene (cond)
- Columbia ML-6413/MS-7013; 33m/s; rel 1967; cip
- Columbia MS-7197; 33s; rel 1969; del 1979
- Columbia MG-30073; 33s; 2 discs; rel 1970; cip

[3794] Evarts, Donald (pf); National High School Orchestra; Wilson, George C. (cond)
- Interlochen National Music Camp NMC-1957-19; 33m; rel 1957

[3795] Fox, William (pf); International Philharmonic Orchestra; Stein, Gustave (cond)
- Tops 1536; 33m; rel 1957; del 1961

[3796] Gershwin, George (pf) (1925 piano roll); Columbia Jazz Band; Thomas, Michael Tilson (cond)
- Columbia M-34205/QBL-34205; 33s/q; rel 1976; cip

[3797] Gershwin, George (pf); Paul Whiteman Orchestra; Whiteman, Paul (cond) Rec 6/10/24
- Victor 55225; 78; rel pre-1927
- RCA AVM-1-1740; 33m; rel 1976; cip

[3798] Gershwin, George (pf); Paul Whiteman Orchestra; Whiteman, Paul (cond) Rec 4/21/27
- Victor 35822; 78; rel 1927
- Gramophone C-1395; 78; rel pre-1936
- Victor 87-5009; 78; rel pre-1942
- Gramophone S-10037; 78; rel pre-1948

Rhapsody in Blue (1924) *(cont'd)*

- Gramophone L-634; 78; rel pre-1948
- RCA LPT-29; 33m; 10"; rel 1951; del 1957
- Victor WPT-39; 45; 7"; rel pre-1953
- RCA LPV-555; 33m; rel 1969; del 1971

[3799] Gershwin, George (pf); Winter Garden Theatre Orchestra; Ansell, John (cond)
- World SH-214; 33m; rel 197? (Excerpt: Andante)

[3800] Gould, Morton (pf); Morton Gould and his Orchestra; Gould, Morton (cond)
- RCA LM-6033; 33m; 2 discs; rel 1955; del 1961
- RCA LM-2017; 33s; rel 1956; del 1961
- RCA-Victrola VICS-1669(e); 33s; rel 1972; del 1976

[3801] Graffman, Gary (pf); New York Philharmonic; Mehta, Zubin (cond)
- Columbia JS-36020; 33s; rel 1979

[3802] Haas, Werner (pf); National Opera Orchestra of Monte Carlo; Waart, Edo de (cond)
- Philips 6500.118; 33s; rel 1971; cip

[3803] Haines, David (pf); Hamburg Philharmonia
- Somerset 1800; 33m; rel 1957; del 1969
- Stereo-Fidelity 1800; 33s; rel 1959; del 1971

[3804] Hala, Josef (pf); Slovak Philharmonic Orchestra; Burkh, Dennis (cond)
- Musical Heritage Society MHS-4158; 33s

[3805] Hatto, Joyce (pf); Pro Musica Orchestra of Hamburg; Byrd, George (cond)
- Forum F-70008/SF-70008; 33m/s; rel 1959; del 1962

[3806] Heinemann, H. (pf); N. W. German Philharmonic Orchestra; Schuechter, Wilhelm (cond)
- Imperial ILP-116; 33m; rel pre-1956
- Gramophone FFLP-1059; 33m; rel pre-1956

[3807] Janis, Byron (pf); Hugo Winterhalter Orchestra; Winterhalter, Hugo (cond)
- RCA LBC-1045; 33m; rel 1953; del 1957
- Victor (French) A-530201; 33m; rel pre-1956
- Victor WBC-1045; 45; 7"; rel pre-1956
- Victor EPA-565; 45; 7"; rel pre-1956
- Victor (Italian) A72R-0001; 45; 7"; rel pre-1956
- RCA LPM-1429; 33s; rel 1957; del 1960

Rhapsody in Blue (1924) *(cont'd)*

[3808] Katchen, Julius (pf); London Symphony Orchestra; Kertesz, Istvan (cond)
- London CS-6633; 33s; rel 1970; del 1978

[3809] Katchen, Julius (pf); Mantovani and his Orchestra; Mantovani, Annunzio Paolo (cond)
- London LLP-1262; 33m; rel 1955; del 1969
- Decca LK-40108; 33m; rel pre-1956
- Decca LF-1226; 33m; rel pre-1956
- London BEP-6289; 45; 7"; rel pre-1956

[3810] Kiessling, H. (pf); orchestra; Edelhagen (cond)
- Philips P-44104G; 78; rel pre-1953
- Epic EG-7067; 45; 7"; rel pre-1953

[3811] Legrand, Michel (pf); Grand Symphony; Legrand, Michel (cond)
- Mercury SRW-18089; 33s; rel 1968; del 1970

[3812] Levant, Oscar (pf); F. Black Orchestra
- Brunswick 20058; 78; rel pre-1936

[3813] Levant, Oscar (pf); Philadelphia Orchestra; Ormandy, Eugene (cond)
- Columbia 12124-25D (in set X-251); 78; 2 discs; rel pre-1948
- Columbia 12126-27D; 78; 2 discs; rel pre-1948
- Columbia (English) DX-1212-13; 78; 2 discs; rel pre-1952
- Columbia (English) GFX-128-29; 78; 2 discs; rel pre-1952
- Columbia ML-4026; 33m; rel pre-1949; del 1954
- Columbia ML-4879; 33m; rel 1954; del 1955
- Columbia CL-700/CS-8641; 33m/s; rel 1955/1962; cip
- Columbia S-1003; 33m; rel pre-1956
- Columbia VS-801; 33m; rel pre-1956
- Columbia FA-1001; 33m; rel pre-1956
- Columbia QS-6002; 33m; rel pre-1956
- Columbia A-1643; 45; 7"; rel pre-1956

[3814] List, Eugene (pf); Berlin Symphony Orchestra; Adler, Samuel (cond)
- Turnabout TVS-34457; 33s; rel 1971; cip

[3815] List, Eugene (pf); Eastman-Rochester Symphony Orchestra; Hanson, Howard (cond)
- Mercury MG-50138/SR-90002; 33m/s; rel 1957/1958; del 1972

Rhapsody in Blue (1924) *(cont'd)*

- Mercury MG-50290/SR-90290; 33m/s; rel 1962; del 1967

[3816] Liter, M. (pf); G. Melachrino Orchestra
- Gramophone C-3929; 78; rel pre-1952

[3817] Lowenthal, Jerome (pf); Utah Symphony Orchestra; Abravanel, Maurice (cond)
- Vanguard Cardinal VCS-10017; 33s; rel 1968; cip

[3818] Moussov, Teodor (pf); TVR Symphony Orchestra; Vladigerov, Alexander (cond)
- Monitor MCS-2153; 33s; rel 1977; cip

[3819] Nero, Peter (pf); Boston Pops Orchestra; Fiedler, Arthur (cond)
- RCA LM-2821/LSC-2821; 33m/s; rel 1965; del 1975
- RCA LSC-5001; 33s; rel 1971; cip
- RCA LSC-3319; 33s; rel 1972; cip
- RCA ANL-1-1970; 33s; rel 1978; cip

[3820] Nibley, Reid (pf); Utah Symphony Orchestra; Abravanel, Maurice (cond)
- Westminster XWN-18685; 33m; rel 1958; del 1967
- Westminster XWN-18687/WST-14002; 33m/s; rel 1958; del 1967
- Music Guild MS-151; 33s; rel 1970; del 1971
- Westminster WGS-8122; 33s; rel 1971; cip

[3821] Panenka, Jan (pf); Prague Film and Concert Orchestra; Smetacek, Vaclav (cond)
- Ultraphon/Supraphon H-24436-37; 78; 2 discs; rel pre-1956

[3822] Pennario, Leonard (pf); Hollywood Bowl Symphony Orchestra; Slatkin, Felix (cond)
- Capitol P-8343/SP-8343; 33m/s; rel 1956/1959; del 1970
- Capitol SP-8675; 33s; rel 1968; del 1970
- Seraphim S-60174; 33s; rel 1971; cip
- Angel S-36084; 33s; rel 1975; del 1978

[3823] Pennario, Leonard (pf); Paul Whiteman Orchestra; Whiteman, Paul (cond)
- Capitol H-302; 33m; 10''; rel 1952; del 1957
- Capitol P-303; 33m; rel 1952; del 1956
- Capitol (French) LDC-04; 33m; rel pre-1953
- Telefunken LCA-303; 33m; rel pre-1953
- Capitol EBF-302; 45; 7''; rel pre-1953

Rhapsody in Blue (1924) *(cont'd)*

- Capitol LC-6551; 33m; 10''; rel pre-1956
- Capitol T-303; 33m; rel 1956; del 1962
- Capitol T-1678/DT-1678; 33m/s; rel 1962; del 1970

[3824] Perkins, K. (pf); American Radio Symphony Orchestra; Brown, M. (cond)
- Vox STPL-513030; 33s; rel 1968; cip

[3825] Previn, Andre (pf); Andre Kostelanetz and his Orchestra; Kostelanetz, Andre (cond)
- Columbia CL-1495/CS-8286; 33m/s; rel 1960; cip
- Columbia MG-31415; 33s; 2 discs; rel 1972; cip
- Columbia KG-32825; 33s; rel 1974

[3826] Previn, Andre (pf); London Symphony Orchestra; De Peyer, Gervaise (cl); Previn, Andre (cond)
- Angel S-36810; 33s; rel 1971; cip
- Angel SS-45001; 33s; rel 1979; cip

[3827] Rivkin, Vivian (pf); Vienna Symphony Orchestra; Dixon, Dean (cond)
- Vox VLP-3130; 33m; 10''; rel 1952; del 1954
- Pathe-Vox VPO-3000; 33m; rel pre-1953
- Vox VIP-30200; 45; 7''; rel pre-1956
- Olympic OL-8121; 33s; rel 1974

[3828] Rothmueller, H. (pf); Berlin Radio Orchestra; Kudritzi (cond)
- Polydor 57387; 78; rel pre-1953

[3829] Roy, H. (pf); orchestra
- Parlophone E-11320; 78; rel pre-1952
- EMI/Odeon O-7732; 78; rel pre-1952

[3830] Sandford, Arthur (pf); Kingsway Symphony Orchestra; Camarata, Salvador (cond)
- Decca AK-24082-83; 78; 2 discs; rel pre-1953
- Decca DL-8519; 33m; rel 1951; del 1970
- Brunswick LAT-8014; 33m; rel pre-1953
- Decca ED-3539; 45; 7''; rel pre-1953
- Decca UMT-263036; 33m; rel pre-1956
- Decca DCM-3206; 33m; rel 1962; del 1970

[3831] Sanroma, Jesus Maria (pf); Boston Pops Orchestra; Fiedler, Arthur (cond)
- Gramophone C-2806-07; 78; 2 discs; rel pre-1936
- Victor 11822-23 (in set M-358); 78; 2 discs; rel pre-1936

Rhapsody in Blue (1924) *(cont'd)*

- Victor 13834-35 (in set DM-358); 78; 2 discs; rel 1937
- Gramophone EH-953-54; 78; 2 discs; rel pre-1948
- Gramophone FKX-46-47; 78; 2 discs; rel pre-1948
- Victor 11-8749-50 (in set SP-3); 78; 2 discs; rel pre-1952
- Victor DM-1408; 78; rel pre-1952 (excerpt)
- Victor WDM-1408; 45; 7''; rel 1950* (excerpt)
- RCA LM-1105; 33m; rel 1950; del 1959 (excerpt)
- Camden CAL-113; 33m; rel pre-1956 (excerpt)
- Camden CAL-304; 33m; rel 1956; del 1961

[3832] Sanroma, Jesus Maria (pf); Pittsburgh Symphony Orchestra; Steinberg, William (cond)
- Everest LPBR-6067/SDBR-3067; 33m/s; rel 1960; cip

[3833] Schioler, Victor (pf); Concert Orchestra; Tuxen, Erik (cond)
- Polydor Z-60105; 78; rel pre-1952

[3834] Seguirini, N. (pf); Rome Radio Orchestra; Nicelli, Ernesto (cond)
- Parlophone AB-30008-09; 78; 2 discs; rel pre-1952
- Cetra (Italian) LPC-55004; 33m; rel pre-1956

[3835] Semprini, A. (pf); orchestra
- Fonit LP-109; 33m; rel pre-1956

[3836] Shefter, Bert (pf); Warner Brothers Orchestra; Heindorf, Ray (cond)
- Warner Bros B-1243/BS-1243; 33m/s; rel 1959; del 1970

[3837] Siegel, Jeffrey (pf); St. Louis Symphony Orchestra; Slatkin, Leonard (cond)
- Vox QSVBX-5132; 33q; 3 discs; rel 1975; cip
- Turnabout QTVS-34703; 33q; rel 1978; cip

[3838] Silver, Eric (pf); orchestra; Schmidt, Otto (cond)
- Rondo-lette 101; 33s; rel 1959; del 1963

[3839] Sokoloff, Vladimir (pf); Al Goodman Orchestra
- Victor 46-0004; 78; rel pre-1948
- Victor 52-0014; 45; 7''; rel pre-1952

[3840] Spoliansky, M. (pf); J. Fuhs Orchestra
- Parlophone E-10645; 78; rel pre-1936
- Decca 25062; 78; rel pre-1942

[3841] Stein, Gerhard (pf); Elite Concert Orchestra; Marschner, Max (cond)
- Allegro ALG-3063; 33m; rel 1953; del 1959
- Pacific (French) LDAA-71; 33m; rel pre-1956

Rhapsody in Blue (1924) *(cont'd)*

[3842] Templeton, Alec (pf); Andre
Kostelanetz and his Orchestra;
Kostelanetz, Andre (cond)
- Columbia 7376-77M (in set
MX-196); 78; 2 discs; rel
pre-1942
- Columbia MM-1020; 78; 2 discs;
rel pre-1942
- Columbia (English) DX-1045-46;
78; 2 discs; rel pre-1948
- Columbia ML-4455; 33m; rel
1952; del 1955
- Columbia A-1020; 45; 7"; rel
pre-1953
- Columbia CL-795; 33m; rel
1955; del 1962

[3843] Von Kurtz, Johann (pf); Hamburg
International Philharmonic
Orchestra; Von Luden, Wilhelm
(cond)
- Milton Cross 5001/6001;
33m/s; rel 1961; del 1964

[3844] Wild, Earl (pf); Boston Pops
Orchestra; Fiedler, Arthur (cond)
- RCA LM-2367/LSC-2367;
33m/s; rel 1960; cip
- RCA LM-2746/LSC-2746;
33m/s; rel 1964; del 1975
- RCA VCS-7097; 33s; 2 discs; rel
1972; cip

[3845] Williams, R. (pf); Symphony of the
Air; Page, Willis (cond)
- Kapp 1088; 33m/s; rel 1958;
del 1971

[3846] Zwassman, Alexander (pf); USSR
State Symphony Orchestra;
Rozhdestvensky, Gennady (cond)
- Westminster WGS-8355; 33s; rel
1979; cip

[3847] piano; Berlin Symphony Orchestra
- Royale 1421; 33m; rel 1956; del
1958

[3848] piano; Bravo Pops Symphony
Orchestra; Senati, John (cond)
- Bravo K-119; 33m; rel pre-1977

[3849] piano; Hylton Orchestra
- Decca F-3763; 78; rel pre-1936

[3850] piano; Jazz Orchestra
- Pathe X-97304; 78; rel
pre-1936

[3851] piano; P. Green Orchestra
- Decca F-8586; 78; rel pre-1952

[3852] piano; Royale Concert Orchestra;
Everett (cond)
- Allegro-Royale 1421; 33m; rel
1954; del 1956
- Varsity 69139; 33m; rel
pre-1956

[3853] piano; Royal Danish Symphony
Orchestra; Kreutzer, Joseph
(cond)
- Summit SUM-3011; 33s; rel
1978

[3854] piano; Schubert's Concert
Orchestra
- Banner 2153; 78; rel pre-1927

Rhapsody in Blue (Abridged)

[3855] Scime, Roger (pf); Symphony of
the Air Pops Orchestra; D'Artega,
Alfonso (cond)
- Epic LN-3621-22 (in set
SN-6034)/BSN-549-50 (in set
BSN-104); 33m/s; 2 discs; rel
1959; del 1965
- Epic LN-3652/BN-553; 33m/s;
rel 1960; del 1963

Rhapsody in Blue (arr for pf)

[3856] Abadi, Marden (pf)
- Orion ORS-77265; 33s; rel
1977; cip
- Sine Qua Non Superba
SAS-2022; 33s; rel 1978

[3857] Gershwin, George (pf)
- Twentieth Century-Fox
FX-3013/SFX-3013; 33m/s; rel
1959; del 1965
- RCA LPM-2058/LSP-2058;
33m/s; rel 1959; del 1966
- Distinguished DR-107; 33m; rel
1962; del 1966
- Everest X-914; 33s; rel 1968;
cip
- Klavier KS-124; 33s; rel 1975;
cip
- Everest SDBR-3371; 33s

[3858] Pennario, Leonard (pf)
- Capitol FAP-8206; 45; 7"; rel
pre-1956

[3859] Suchman, Harry (pf)
- Artist 3001; 78

[3860] Watts, Andre (pf)
- Columbia M-34221; 33s; rel
1976; cip

Rhapsody in Blue: Andante (arr for pf)

[3861] Gershwin, George (pf)
- Columbia 50107D; 78; rel
pre-1936
- Columbia 7192M; 78; rel
pre-1936
- Klavier KS-133; 33

Rhapsody in Blue (arr for 2 pfs by Jose Iturbi)

[3862] Iturbi, Jose (pf); Iturbi, Amparo (pf)
- Victor 15215-16 (in set M-517);
78; 2 discs; rel pre-1942
- Victor 18446-47 (in set
DM-517); 78; 2 discs; rel
pre-1942
- Gramophone DB-6220-21; 78; 2
discs; rel pre-1952
- Victor DM-1366; 78; 2 discs; rel
pre-1952
- RCA LM-23; 33m; 10"; rel
1950; del 1956
- RCA LM-9018; 33m; rel 1953;
del 1960
- Victor ERA-145; 45; 7"; rel
pre-1956

Rhapsody in Blue (arr for 2 pfs)

[3863] Ferrante, Arthur (pf); Teicher, Louis
(pf)
- Urania UR-8011; 33m; rel 1958;
del 1969
- Urania USD-1009; 33s; rel
1958; del 1960
- Urania US-58011; 33s; rel
1961; del 1972

[3864] Herzer, Clifford (pf); Zayde, Jascha
(pf)
- Royale 1861-62; 78; 2-10"; rel
pre-1952

[3865] Rawicz, M. (pf); Landauer, W. (pf)
- Columbia DB-2104; 78; 10"; rel
pre-1948
- Philips
PHM-200005/PHS-600005;
33m/s; rel 1962; del 1968

[3866] Stech, Willi (pf); Rokovic, Borislav
(pf)
- MGM E-4230/SE-4230; 33m/s;
rel 1964; del 1966

[3867] Veri, Frances (pf); Jamanis,
Michael (pf)
- Connoisseur Society
CSQ-2054-SQ; 33q; rel 1975;
del 1979

Rhapsody in Blue (arr for 4 pfs)

[3868] First Piano Quartet
- Gramophone EP-7005; 78; rel
pre-1956
- RCA LM-125; 33m; 10"; rel
1951; del 1956
- Victor WDM-1574; 45; 7"; rel
1951*
- Victor WEPR-8; 45; 7"; rel
pre-1953

Rhapsody in Blue (arr for 8 pfs)

[3869] no performers given
- Victor 36123; 78; rel pre-1936
- Gramophone C-2616; 78; rel
pre-1936
- Decca F-5097; 78; rel pre-1936

Rhapsody in Blue (arr for pf orch)

[3870] Philadelphia Piano Orchestra;
Knisley (cond)
- Epic LN-3435; 33m; rel 1958;
del 1961
- Perfect 12012/14012; 33m/s;
rel 1960; del 1963

Rhapsody in Blue (Various Instrumental Arrangements)

[3871] Arr for Banjo
Peabody, E. (banjo)
- Columbia B-812; 78; rel
pre-1936

[3872] Arr for Harmonica and Orchestra
Adler, Larry (harmonica); orchestra
- Columbia DB-1560; 78; rel
pre-1936
- Columbia 35513 (in set 18); 78;
rel pre-1948
- Hamilton 149/12149; 33m/s;
rel 1965; del 1967

Rhapsody in Blue (Various Instrumental Arrangements)
(cont'd)

[3873] Arr for Harmonica Orchestra
Minnevitch Harmonica Orchestra
- Brunswick 6705; 78; 10"; rel
pre-1936

[3874] Arr for 2 Harps
Vito, Edward (hp); Vito, J. (hp)
- Cook 1031; 33m; rel pre-1956
- Cook 10301; 33m; rel pre-1956

[3875] Arr for Organ
Crawford, J. (org)
- Victor 22343; 78; 10"; rel
pre-1936
- Gramophone B-3435; 78; 10";
rel pre-1936

[3876] Arr for Piano and Organ
Maclean, Q. (pf); organ
- Columbia 6329M; 78; rel
pre-1936
- Columbia DX-116; 78; rel
pre-1936

[3877] Rossborough, R. (pf); Ramsay, H.
(org)
- Parlophone R-1895; 78; rel
pre-1936
- EMI/Odeon 25226; 78; rel
pre-1936

[3878] Arr for Piano and Synthesizer
Hambro, Leonid (pf); Kingsley,
Gershon (syn)
- Avco 33021; 33s; rel 1971; del
1974

[3879] Arr for Piano, Orchestra, and
Chorus
Wild, Earl (pf); Paul Whiteman
Orchestra; chorus
- Signature GP1; 78; 2 discs; rel
pre-1948
- Coral 56053; 33m; 10"; rel
1952; del 1957
- Coral 58063; 33m; rel pre-1953
- Coral 57021; 33m; rel pre-1956
- Coral EC-8111; 45; 7"; rel
pre-1956
- Signal 10; 33m; rel pre-1956

Rhapsody in Blue: Andante (arr for chorus)

[3880] Schuyler, Sonny; Knight, Felix;
Victor Orchestra; Shilkret,
Nathaniel (cond)
- Victor 12333 (in set C-29); 78;
rel 1939

Second Rhapsody (1931)

[3881] Bargy, Roy (pf); Paul Whiteman
Orchestra; Whiteman, Paul (cond)
- Decca 29052 (in set 31); 78; rel
pre-1942
- Decca 29088-91 (in set DA-31);
78; 4 discs; rel pre-1948
- Brunswick 0144; 78; rel
pre-1952
- Decca DL-8024; 33m; rel 1950;
del 1970
- Decca UMT-263072; 33m; rel
pre-1956

Second Rhapsody (1931) *(cont'd)*

[3882] Bianca, Sondra (pf); Pro Musica
Orchestra of Hamburg; Walther,
Hans-Jurgen (cond)
- MGM E-3307; 33s; rel 1956; del
1959
- MGM 3E-1; 33m; 3 discs; rel
1957; del 1959

[3883] Levant, Oscar (pf); Morton Gould
and his Orchestra; Gould, Morton
(cond)
- Columbia 72874-75D (in set
MM-867); 78; 2 discs; rel 1949
- Columbia ML-2073; 33m; 10";
rel pre-1949; del 1956

[3884] Moussov, Teodor (pf); TVR
Symphony Orchestra; Vladigerov,
Alexander (cond)
- Monitor MCS-2153; 33s; rel
1977; cip

[3885] Pennario, Leonard (pf); Hollywood
Bowl Symphony Orchestra;
Newman, Alfred (cond)
- Capitol P-8581/SP-8581;
33m/s; rel 1962; del 1970
- Angel S-36070; 33s; rel 1974;
cip

[3886] Reims, H. (pf); Berlin Symphony
Orchestra; Rubahn, Gerd (cond)
- Allegro-Royale 1512; 33m; rel
pre-1956

[3887] Siegel, Jeffrey (pf); St. Louis
Symphony Orchestra; Slatkin,
Leonard (cond)
- Vox QSVBX-5132; 33q; 3 discs;
rel 1975; cip

[3888] Votapek, Ralph (pf); Boston Pops
Orchestra; Fiedler, Arthur (cond)
- London SPC-21185; 33s; rel
1979; cip

Second Rhapsody (two-piano version)

[3889] Veri, Frances (pf); Jamanis,
Michael (pf)
- Connoisseur Society
CSQ-2067-SQ; 33q; rel 1975;
del 1979

Short Story (1925)

[3890] Dushkin, Samuel (vln); piano
- Gramophone P-794; 78; rel
pre-1936
- Gramophone ER-261; 78; rel
pre-1936

[3891] Gautier, J. (vln); Todd, J. D. (pf)
- Columbia DO-2362; 78; rel
pre-1952

GERSTER, Robert (1945-)

Bird in the Spirit (1972)

[3892] Skowronek, Felix (fl); Grossman,
Arthur (bsn)
- Crystal S-351; 33s; rel 1975; cip

GESENSWAY, Louis (1906-76)

Four Squares of Philadelphia (1951)

[3893] Treadwell, Oscar (nar); Philadelphia
Orchestra; Ormandy, Eugene
(cond)
- Columbia ML-5108; 33m; rel
1956; del 1965

GHENT, Emmanuel (1925-)

Helices (1969)

[3894] Golub, Elliot (vln); Cobb, John (pf);
tape
- Desto DC-7124; 33s; rel 1971;
cip

GHEZZO, Dinu (1940-)

Aphorisms

[3895] Kreiselman, Jack (cl); Boardman,
Roger (pf)
- Orion ORS-80368; 33s; rel
1980; cip

Kanones (1972)

[3896] Andrus, Gretel Shanley (fl);
Hurford, Selene (vcl); Shapiro,
Susanne (hpschd)
- Orion ORS-75172; 33s; rel
1975; cip

Music for Flutes and Tapes (1971)

[3897] Andrus, Gretel Shanley (fl); tape
- Orion ORS-75172; 33s; rel
1975; cip

Ritualen (1969)

[3898] Tipei, Sever (pf)
- Orion ORS-75172; 33s; rel
1975; cip

Thalla (1974)

[3899] Tipei, Sever (pf); Contemporary
Directions Ensemble; Mayer, Uri
(cond)
- Orion ORS-75172; 33s; rel
1975; cip

GIANNINI, Vittorio (1903-66)

Dedication Overture

[3900] Ohio State University Concert
Band; McGinnis, Donald E. (cond)
- Coronet M-1157; 33m; rel
1969; del 1978

Divertimento No 2 (1961)

[3901] Louisville Orchestra; Whitney,
Robert (cond)
- LOU-64-2; 33m (Louisville
Orchestra First Edition Records
1964 No 2); rel 1964; cip

Fantasia

[3902] University of Maryland Concert
Band; Ostling, Acton, Jr. (cond)
- Coronet 955; 33m; rel 1969; del
1978

Symphony No 2 (1956)
[3903] National High School Orchestra;
Wilson, George C. (cond)
 - Interlochen National Music Camp
NMC-1957-20; 33m; rel 1957

Symphony No 3 (1959)
[3904] Eastman Symphonic Wind
Ensemble; Roller, A. Clyde (cond)
 - Mercury MG-50366/SR-90366;
33m/s; rel 1964; del 1973
 - Mercury SRI-75010; 33s; rel
1973; cip

Taming of the Shrew, The (1953)
[3905] Jennings, Mary (sop); Christensen,
Catherine (m sop); Harris, Lowell
(ten); McGowen, Adair (bar);
Davis, J. B. (b bar); Kansas City
Lyric Theatre Chorus and
Orchestra; Patterson, Russell
(cond)
 - CRI-272; 33s; 2 discs; rel 1971;
cip

[3906] Rome Symphony Orchestra;
Savino, Domenico (cond)
 - Kapp KCL-9026/KC-S-9026;
33m/s; rel 1959; del 1962

Tell Me, O Blue, Blue Sky
[3907] Sektberg, Willard (pf)
Rec 5/58
 - RCA LM-2266; 33m; rel 1958;
del 1961

GIANNINI, Walter (1917-)
Modal Variations
[3908] Burton, Catherine (pf)
 - American Recording Edition
ARE-1001; 33m; rel pre-1956

GIBSON, Archer (1875-1952)
Fantasy and Fugue
[3909] Smith, Rollin (org)
Rec 8/73
 - Repertoire Recording Society
RRS-12; 33s; rel 1974

GIBSON, Jon (1940-)
Visitations (1968)
[3910] Gibson, Jon; Peck, Richard;
Munkasci, Kurt; Fullerman, John;
Girouard, Tina (playing various
instruments)
 - Chatham Square LP-12; 33s; rel
1973*

GIDEON, Miriam (1906-)
Adorable Mouse, The (1960)
[3911] Reardon, John (bar); Ariel Quintet;
harpsichord; percussion; Heller,
Marsha (cond)
 - Serenus SRS-12050; 33s; rel
1974; cip

**Condemned Playground, The
(1963)**
[3912] Bryn-Julson, Phyllis (sop);
Cassolas, Constantine (ten);
Galimir, Felix (vln); Shapiro, Jack
(vln); Tolomeo, Michael (vla);
Arico, Fortunato (vcl); Dunkel,
Paul (fl); Heller, Alexander (bsn);
Jahoda, Fritz (cond)
Rec 3/26/75
 - CRI-343; 33s; rel 1976; cip

**Fantasy on a Javanese Motive
(1948)**
[3913] Barab, Seymour (vcl); Masselos,
William (pf)
 - Paradox X-102; 78; 3-10"
 - Paradox PL-10001; 33m; 10";
rel 1950; del 1957

Hound of Heaven, The (1945)
[3914] Metcalf, William (bar); Roseman,
Ronald (ob); Cohen, Isidore (vln);
Phillips, Karen, (vla); Sherry, Fred
(vcl); Jahoda, Fritz (cond)
 - CRI-286; 33s; rel 1972; cip

How Goodly Are Thy Tents (1947)
[3915] Chizuk Amuno Congregation
(Baltimore) Choral Society;
Weisgall, Hugo (cond)
 - Westminster W-9634; 33m; rel
1970; del 1971

Lyric Piece (1941)
[3916] Imperial Philharmonic Orchestra of
Tokyo; Strickland, William (cond)
 - CRI-170; 33m; rel 1963; cip

Nocturnes (1976)
[3917] Raskin, Judith (sop); Roseman,
Ronald (ob); Gottlieb, Gordon
(vib); Da Capo Chamber Players;
De Main, John (cond)
 - CRI-401; 33s; rel 1979; cip

Questions on Nature (1965)
[3918] DeGaetani, Jan (m sop); West,
Philip (ob); Lipman, Samuel (pf);
Jekofsky, Barry (perc)
Rec 9/27/74
 - CRI-343; 33s; rel 1976; cip

Rhymes from the Hill (1968)
[3919] DeGaetani, Jan (m sop); Bloom,
Arthur (cl); DesRoches, Raymond
(mrmb); Sherry, Fred (vcl);
Gilbert, David (cond)
 - CRI-286; 33s; rel 1972; cip

Seasons of Time, The (1969)
[3920] Mandac, Evelyn (sop); Kraber, Karl
(fl); Arico, Fortunato (vcl);
Jahoda, Fritz (pf)
 - Desto DC-7117; 33s; rel 1971;
cip

[3921] Sperry, Paul (ten); flute;
violoncello; piano
 - Serenus SRS-12078; 33s; rel
1980; cip

Slow, Slow, Fresh Fount (1941)
[3922] Bushnell Choir; Dashnaw,
Alexander (cond)
Rec 8/22/76
 - Golden Crest CRS-4172; 33s; rel
1979; cip

**Songs of Youth and Madness
(1977)**
[3923] Raskin, Judith (sop); American
Composers Orchestra; Dixon,
James (cond)
 - CRI-401; 33s; rel 1979; cip

Suite, Piano, No 3 (ca 1963)
[3924] Helps, Robert (pf)
 - RCA LM-7042/LSC-7042;
33m/s; 2 discs; rel 1966; del
1971
 - CRI-288; 33s; 2 discs; rel 1972;
cip

Symphonia brevis (1953)
[3925] Zurich Radio Orchestra; Monod,
Jacques (cond)
 - CRI-128; 33m; rel 1960; cip

GILBERT, David (1936-)
Centering I (1969)
[3926] Kaplan, Lewis (vln); Abramowitz,
Jonathan (vcl); Greenberg, Lloyd
(cl); Gilbert, David (fl)
 - Opus One 8; 33s; rel 1972; cip

Centering II (1970)
[3927] Ellert, Michael (bsn); List, Garrett
(tbn); Greenberg, Lloyd (cl);
Deak, Jon (cb); Heldrich, Claire
(perc); Kaplan, Lewis (vln);
Romm, Ronald (tpt); Gilbert,
David (cond)
 - Opus One 8; 33s; rel 1972; cip

Poem VI (1966)
[3928] Gilbert, David (al fl)
 - Opus One 13; 33s; rel 1976; cip

Poem VII (1970)
[3929] Lucarelli, Bert (ob)
 - Opus One 13; 33s; rel 1976; cip

**(Two) Unaccompanied Songs
(1965)**
[3930] Regni, Charlotte (sop)
 - Opus One 8; 33s; rel 1972; cip

GILBERT, Henry F. (1868-1928)
**Americanesque (Op 5) (ca
1902-08)**
[3931] Royal Philharmonic Orchestra;
Krueger, Karl (cond)
 - SPAMH MIA-128; 33s; rel 1965

GILBERT, Henry F.

Dance in Place Congo, The (Op 15) (ca 1908, rev 1916)

[3932] Janssen Symphony Orchestra of Los Angeles; Janssen, Werner (cond)
- Artist 1404 (in set JS-13); 78; rel 1949
- Artist 100; 33m; rel pre-1949; del 1952
- Everest LPBR-6118/SDBR-3118; 33m/s; rel 1965; del 1975

[3933] Los Angeles Philharmonic Orchestra; Simmons, Calvin (cond)
Rec 8/77
- New World NW-228; 33s; rel 1978

Mazurka (1902)

[3934] Frager, Malcolm (pf)
- New World NW-206; 33s; rel 1978

Nocturne (1925-26)

[3935] Royal Philharmonic Orchestra; Krueger, Karl (cond)
- SPAMH MIA-141; 33s; rel 1968

Pirate Song, The (1902)

[3936] Bispham, David (bar)
- Columbia A-5019; 78; rel 1900-15
- Columbia A-5778; 78; rel 1911-15

[3937] Werrenrath, Reinald (bar)
- Victor 1104; 78; 10"; rel pre-1927

[3938] Witherspoon, Herbert (b)
- Victor 64472; 78; 10"; rel 1912-18

GILBERT, John

Suonare

[3939] Kreiselman, Jack (cl); tape
- Orion ORS-80368; 33s; rel 1980; cip

GILLIS, Don (1912-78)

Alamo, The (1947)

[3940] National High School Orchestra; Gillis, Don (cond)
Rec 1960
- Interlochen National Music Camp NMC-6161; 33m; rel 1961

[3941] New Symphony Orchestra; Gillis, Don (cond)
- London LPS-177; 33m; 10"; rel 1950; del 1957

Dance Symphony, A

[3942] Rexford Symphony; Gillis, Don (cond)
- Rexford 2; 33m; rel 1951; del 1957

Man Who Invented Music, The (1950)

[3943] New Symphony Orchestra; Gillis, Don (cond)
- London LLP-176; 33m; rel 1950; del 1957
- London 5008; 33m; rel 1957; del 1962

Portrait of a Frontier Town (1940)

[3944] New Symphony Orchestra; Gillis, Don (cond)
- London LLP-176; 33m; rel 1950; del 1957
- London 5008; 33m; rel 1957; del 1962

[3945] no performers given
- Boosey & Hawkes O-2128; 78; 10"

Short Overture (To an Unwritten Opera)

[3946] New Concert Orchestra
- Boosey & Hawkes OT-2092; 78

(Three) Sketches

[3947] no performers given
- Boosey & Hawkes S-2097; 78

Symphony No 5 1/2 (A Symphony for Fun) (1948)

[3948] New Symphony Orchestra; Gillis, Don (cond)
- London LPS-177; 33m; 10"; rel 1950; del 1957

Symphony No 7 (Saga of a Prairie School)

[3949] New Symphony Orchestra; Gillis, Don (cond)
- London LPS-175; 33m; 10"; rel 1950; del 1957

This Is Our America

[3950] Middleton, Ray (nar); Rhys Morgan Singers; Gillis, Don (cond)
- Rexford 2; 33m; rel 1951; del 1957

Tulsa (A Symphonic Portrait in Oil) (1957)

[3951] North Texas State University Concert Band; McAdow, Maurice (cond)
- Austin 6328; 33m/s; rel 1964; del 1975

[3952] Viennese Symphonic Society Symphony Orchestra; Brown, H. Arthur (cond)
- Remington 149-13; 33m; 10"; rel 1951; del 1956
- Varese Sarabande VC-81046; 33m; rel 1979; cip

GIORNI, Aurelio (1895-1938)

Minuet, G Major (1935)

[3953] Hunkins, Sterling (vcl); Lief, Arthur (pf)
- Musicraft 1115 (in set 33); 78; rel pre-1942

Trio, Violin, Violoncello, and Piano, C Major (1934)

[3954] Hollaender, Max (vln); Hunkins, Sterling (vcl); Kusmiak, Eugene (pf)
- Musicraft 33; 78; 4 discs; rel pre-1942

GIOVANNINI, Caesar (1925-)

Overture in B-flat

[3955] Ohio State University Concert Band; McGinnis, Donald E. (cond)
- Coronet S-1258; 33s; rel 1969; del 1978

GLANVILLE-HICKS, Peggy (1912-)

Choral Suite (1937)

[3956] chorus; orchestra
- L'Oiseau-lyre 100; 78; 10"; rel pre-1948

Concertino da camera (1945)

[3957] Bussotti, Carlo (pf); New York Wind Ensemble
- Columbia ML-4990; 33m; rel 1955; del 1965

Concerto romantico (1957)

[3958] Trampler, Walter (vla); MGM Chamber Orchestra; Surinach, Carlos (cond)
- MGM E-3559; 33m; rel 1957; del 1959

Etruscan Concerto (1956)

[3959] Bussotti, Carlo (pf); MGM Chamber Orchestra; Surinach, Carlos (cond)
- MGM E-3357; 33m; rel 1956; del 1959

(Trois) Gymnopedies (1934)

[3960] Berlin Radio Orchestra; Perlea, Jonel (cond)
- Remington 199-188; 33m; rel 1956; del 1959
- Varese Sarabande VC-81046; 33m; rel 1979; cip

[3961] MGM Chamber Orchestra; Surinach, Carlos (cond)
- MGM E-3336; 33m; rel 1956; del 1959

Letters from Morocco (1952)

[3962] Driscoll, Loren (ten); MGM Chamber Orchestra; Surinach, Carlos (cond)
- MGM E-3549; 33m; rel 1958; del 1960

Nausicaa (1960): Excerpts
[3963] Stratas, Teresa (sop); Modenos,
John (bar); chorus; Athens
Symphony Orchestra; Surinach,
Carlos (cond)
Rec 1961
- CRI-175; 33m/s; rel 1963/?; cip

Prelude for a Pensive Pupil (1963)
[3964] Helps, Robert (pf)
- RCA LM-7042/LSC-7042;
33m/s; 2 discs; rel 1966; del
1971
- CRI-288; 33s; 2 discs; rel 1972;
cip

Sinfonia da pacifica (1953)
[3965] MGM Chamber Orchestra;
Surinach, Carlos (cond)
- MGM E-3336; 33m; rel 1956;
del 1959

Sonata, Harp (1951)
[3966] Zabaleta, Nicanor (hp)
Rec 12/53
- Esoteric ES-523; 33m; rel 1954;
del 1964
- Counterpoint/Esoteric
CPT-523/CPST-5523; 33m/s;
rel 1964/1966; del 1972

Sonata, Piano and Percussion (1952)
[3967] Bussotti, Carlo (pf); New York
Percussion Group; Surinach,
Carlos (cond)
- Columbia ML-4990; 33m; rel
1955; del 1965

Transposed Heads, The (1953)
[3968] Harlan, Monas (ten); Pickett,
William (bar); Nossaman, Audrey
(sop); Anderson, Dwight (nar);
Sutton, Robert (nar); Kentucky
Opera Association (members of);
Louisville Orchestra; Bomhard,
Moritz (cond)
- LOU-545-6; 33m; 2 discs
(Louisville Orchestra First Edition
Records 1955 No 6); rel 1959;
del 1975

GLASOW, Glen (1924-)

Rakka
[3969] Kobialka, Daniel (vln); Marconi,
Don (perc); Neff, Jerome (perc)
- Desto DC-7144; 33s; rel 1973;
cip

Two Egrets
[3970] Hamline Singers; Holliday, Robert
(cond)
- SPAMH MIA-116; 33s; rel 1961

GLASS, Philip (1937-)

Einstein on the Beach (1975)
[3971] Philip Glass Ensemble
- Tomato TOM-101; 33s; rel
1979; cip

Music in Fifths (1969)
[3972] Philip Glass Ensemble
- Chatham Square LP-1003; 33s;
rel 1973*

Music in Similar Motion (1969)
[3973] Philip Glass Ensemble
- Chatham Square LP-1003; 33s;
rel 1973*

Music with Changing Parts (1970)
[3974] Philip Glass Ensemble
- Chatham Square LP-1001-02;
33s; 2 discs; rel 1973*

North Star (1975)
[3975] Philip Glass Ensemble
- Virgin PZ-34669; 33s; rel 1977;
del 1979

Strung Out
[3976] Zukofsky, Paul (amplified vln)
Rec 6/29/76
- CP2 6; 33s; rel 1976

Two Pages (1969)
[3977] Philip Glass Ensemble
- Folkways FTS-33902; 33s; rel
1976; cip

GLUSHANOK, Peter

In Memoriam for my Friend Henry Saia
[3978] Electronic music
- Turnabout TVS-34427; 33s; rel
1972; del 1975

GNAZZO, Anthony (1936-)

Population Explosion, The (1969)
[3979] Electronic music
- 1750 Arch S-1752; 33s; rel
1975*

GODFREY, Daniel (1949-)

Celebration, A (1977)
[3980] Avery, James (pf)
- Orion ORS-79340; 33s; rel
1979; cip

(Five) Character Pieces (1976)
[3981] Preucil, William (vla); Avery, James
(pf)
- Orion ORS-79340; 33s; rel
1979; cip

Progression
[3982] Electronic music
- Orion ORS-77262; 33s; rel
1977; cip

Quartet, Strings (1974)
[3983] Rowe String Quartet
- Orion ORS-77262; 33s; rel
1977; cip

Trio, Viola, Clarinet, and Horn (1976)
[3984] Preucil, William (vla); Ross, David
(cl); Hundemer, Thomas (hn)
- Orion ORS-79340; 33s; rel
1979; cip

GODOWSKY, Leopold (1870-1938)

Java Suite (1925): Gamelan and Chattering Monkeys at the Sacred Lake of Wendit
[3985] Pines, Doris (pf)
- Genesis GS-1000; 33s; rel
1970; cip

Java Suite: Gardens of Buitenzorg
[3986] Godowsky, Leopold (pf)
- Veritas VM-103; 33m; rel 1968;
del 1974

Java Suite: Wayang Purwa
[3987] Kann, Hans (pf)
- Musical Heritage Society
MHS-3501; 33s; rel 1976

Miniatures (1918): Seven Dances
[3988] Kann, Hans (pf); Wuensch, Gerhard
(pf)
- Musical Heritage Society
MHS-3501; 33s; rel 1976

Miniatures: Humoresque
[3989] Pines, Doris (pf); Friedman, Linda
(pf)
- Genesis GS-1000; 33s; rel
1970; cip

Passacaglia (1928)
[3990] Glover, Stephen (pf)
- International Piano
Library/International Piano
Archives IPL-1001; 33m; rel
1970

Sonata, Piano, E Minor (1911): Excerpts
[3991] Kann, Hans (pf)
- Musical Heritage Society
MHS-3501; 33s; rel 1976

[3992] Pines, Doris (pf)
- Genesis GS-1000; 33s; rel
1970; cip

Triakontameron (1920): (1) Nocturnal Tangier, (2) Sylvan Tyrol, (3) Paradoxical Moods, (8) A Watteau paysage, (11) Alt Wien, (12) Ethiopian Serenade, (13) Terpsichorean Vindobona, (25) Memories, and (28) Lament
[3993] Kann, Hans (pf)
- Musical Heritage Society
MHS-3501; 33s; rel 1976

Triakontameron: (11) Alt Wien
[3994] Tillius, Carl (pf)
- Gramophone X-7326; 78; 10";
rel pre-1948

[3995] Waldoff, Stanley (pf)
- Musical Heritage Society
MHS-3681; 33s; rel 1977?

Triakontameron: (11) Alt Wien (arr for 2 pfs)
[3996] Appleton, Vera (pf); Field, Michael
(pf)
- Vox VX-540; 33m; rel pre-1956

[3997] Madeleine, J. (pf); Therese, F. (pf)
- Conlin (Convent) SF-1; 33m; rel
pre-1953

Triakontameron: (11) Alt Wien (arr for vln and pf by Jascha Heifetz)
[3998] Heifetz, Jascha (vln); Bay, Emanuel
(pf)
- Victor 10-1345; 78; 10"; rel
pre-1948
- Gramophone DA-2037; 78; 10";
rel pre-1956
- Gramophone EC-208; 78; 10";
rel pre-1956
- Gramophone FALP-248; 33m; rel
pre-1956
- Victor ERA-57; 45; 7"; rel
pre-1956
- RCA LSC-3233(e); 33s; rel
1971; cip
- RCA ARM-4-0943; 33m; 4 discs;
rel 1975; cip

[3999] Heifetz, Jascha (vln); Kaye, Milton
(pf)
- Decca 23385 (in set A-385); 78;
10"; rel pre-1948
- Decca DL-5214; 33m; 10"; rel
1950; del 1957
- Brunswick AXL-2017; 33m; rel
pre-1956
- Decca UA-243086; 33m; 10";
rel pre-1956
- Decca DL-9780; 33m; rel 1958;
del 1971

[4000] Heifetz, Jascha (vln); Sandor,
Arpad (pf)
- Victor 1645; 78; 10"; rel
pre-1936

Triakontameron: (11) Alt Wien (arr for orch)
[4001] H. Horlick Orchestra
- Decca 1995; 78; rel pre-1952
- Decca (English) F-6944; 78;
10"; rel pre-1952

[4002] MGM Orchestra; Marrow, Macklin
(cond)
- MGM E-3138; 33m; rel 1955;
del 1960

Walzermasken (1912): (12) Legende, (15) Elegie, (18) Schuhplattler, and (21) Orientale
[4003] Kann, Hans (pf)
- Musical Heritage Society
MHS-3501; 33s; rel 1976

Walzermasken: (22) Wienerisch
[4004] Pines, Doris (pf)
- Genesis GS-1000; 33s; rel
1970; cip

Walzermasken: (22) Wienerisch (arr for vln and pf by Jascha Heifetz)
[4005] Heifetz, Jascha (vln); Kaye, Milton
(pf)
- Decca DL-5214; 33m; 10"; rel
1950; del 1957

Walzermasken: Valse in D (arr for vln and pf by Jascha Heifetz)
[4006] Heifetz, Jascha (vln); Bay, Emanuel
(pf)
- RCA ARM-4-0942; 33m; 4 discs;
rel 1975; cip

GODWIN, Joscelyn (1945-)

Epistle to Harmodius (1966)
[4007] Philharmonic Chorale; Koch,
Frederick (pf)
- Advent USR-5005; 33s; rel
1973; cip

GOEB, Roger (1914-)

(Three) American Dances (1952)
[4008] MGM String Orchestra; Solomon,
Izler (cond)
- MGM E-3117; 33m; rel 1954;
del 1959

Concertino, Orchestra, No 2 (1956)
[4009] Louisville Orchestra; Whitney,
Robert (cond)
- LOU-58-5; 33m (Louisville
Orchestra First Edition Records
1958 No 5); rel 1959; cip

Concertino, Trombone and Strings (1949)
[4010] Shuman, Davis (tbn); WQXR
Strings
- Golden Crest RE-7011; 33m/s;
rel 1962/1979; cip

Prairie Songs (1947)
[4011] Five-Wind Ensemble
- American Recording Society
ARS-10; 33m; rel 1953
- Desto D-422/DST-6422; 33m/s;
rel 1967; cip

Quintet, Trombone and Strings (1950)
[4012] Shuman, Davis (tbn); Radio Artists
String Quartet
- Circle L-51-102; 33m; rel
pre-1953

Quintet, Winds, No 1 (1948)
[4013] New Art Wind Quintet
- Classic Editions CE-2003; 33m;
2 discs; rel 1953; del 1961
- CRI-158; 33m/s; rel 1962/?; cip

Symphony No 3 (1950)
[4014] Leopold Stokowski and his
Orchestra; Stokowski, Leopold
(cond)
- Victor 49-3984-87 (in set
WDM-1727); 45; 2-7"; rel
1953?
- RCA LM-1727; 33m; rel 1953;
del 1957
- CRI-120; 33m; rel 1957; cip

Symphony No 4 (1954)
[4015] Japan Philharmonic Symphony
Orchestra; Watanabe, Akeo
(cond)
- CRI-167; 33m/s; rel 1963/?; cip

GOLD, Ernest (1921-)

Boston Pops March
[4016] Boston Pops Orchestra; Fiedler,
Arthur (cond)
- RCA LSC-3130; 33s; rel 1970;
del 1975

Songs of Love and Parting: Excerpts
[4017] Tatum, Nancy (sop); Parsons,
William (pf)
- London OS-26053; 33s; rel
1968; del 1971

Songs of Love and Parting (orchestral version)
[4018] Nixon, Marni (sop); Vienna
Volksoper Orchestra; Gold, Ernest
(cond)
Rec 9/28-29/74
- Crystal S-501; 33s; rel 1975; cip

Symphony for Five Instruments (1952)
[4019] Rudnytsky, Roman (pf); Israel
Baker Ensemble
- Crystal S-862; 33s; rel 1973; cip

GOLDMAN, Edwin Franko (1878-1956)

Boy Scouts of America
[4020] Eastman Symphonic Wind
Ensemble; Fennell, Frederick
(cond)
Rec 10/19/57
- Mercury MG-50170/SR-90170;
33m/s; rel 1958/1959; del
1965

Bugles and Drums
[4021] Eastman Symphonic Wind
Ensemble; Fennell, Frederick
(cond)
Rec 10/19/57
- Mercury MG-50170/SR-90170;
33m/s; rel 1958/1959; del
1965

Children's March
[4022] Eastman Symphonic Wind
Ensemble; Fennell, Frederick
(cond)
Rec 10/19/57
- Mercury MG-50170/SR-90170;
33m/s; rel 1958/1959; del
1965

Chimes of Liberty, The
[4023] Goldman Band; Goldman, Richard
Franko (cond)
- New World NW-266; 33s; rel
1977

[4024] Morton Gould and his Symphonic
Band; Gould, Morton (cond)
- RCA LM-2080/LSC-2080;
33m/s; rel 1957/1959; del
1963

[4025] U.S. Marine Band; Schoepper, Lt.
Col. Albert F. (cond)
- RCA LPM-2687/LSP-2687;
33m/s; rel 1963; del 1975

Happy Go Lucky
[4026] Morton Gould and his Symphonic
Band; Gould, Morton (cond)
- RCA LM-2080/LSC-2080;
33m/s; rel 1957/1959; del
1963

Illinois March
[4027] Eastman Symphonic Wind
Ensemble; Fennell, Frederick
(cond)
Rec 10/19/57
- Mercury MG-50170/SR-90170;
33m/s; rel 1958/1959; del
1965

[4028] Royal Artillery Band; Geary, Col.
Owen W. (cond)
- Boosey & Hawkes
BH-MTLP-2030; 33m; rel 1954

Interlochen Bowl, The
[4029] Eastman Symphonic Wind
Ensemble; Fennell, Frederick
(cond)
Rec 10/19/57
- Mercury MG-50170/SR-90170;
33m/s; rel 1958/1959; del
1965

Jubilee
[4030] Morton Gould and his Symphonic
Band; Gould, Morton (cond)
- RCA LM-2080/LSC-2080;
33m/s; rel 1957/1959; del
1963

On Guard
[4031] Leeds Concert Band; Todd, Peter
(cond)
- Columbia ML-4254; 33m; rel
1950; del 1956

On the Mall (1924)
[4032] Eastman Symphonic Wind
Ensemble; Fennell, Frederick
(cond)
- Mercury MG-50113; 33m; rel
1956; del 1969
- Mercury MG-50337/SR-90337;
33m/s; rel 1963; del 1967
- Mercury SR-2-9131; 33s; 2
discs; rel 1968; del 1971
- Mercury SRI-75004; 33s; rel
1974; cip

[4033] Morton Gould and his Symphonic
Band; Gould, Morton (cond)
- RCA LM-2080/LSC-2080;
33m/s; rel 1957/1959; del
1963

Onward-Upward
[4034] Eastman Symphonic Wind
Ensemble; Fennell, Frederick
(cond)
Rec 10/19/57
- Mercury MG-50170/SR-90170;
33m/s; rel 1958/1959; del
1965

Pride of America, The
[4035] Goldman Band; Goldman, Richard
Franko (cond)
- New World NW-266; 33s; rel
1977

GOLDMAN, Richard Franko (1910-80)
Introduction and Tarantella
[4036] Benedetti, Donald (tpt); Sanders,
Samuel (pf)
- Golden Crest RE-7029; 33s; rel
1968; cip

Sonata, Violin and Piano (1952)
[4037] Senofsky, Berl (vln); Mack, Ellen
(pf)
Rec 10/9/75
- CRI-353; 33s; rel 1976; cip

Sonatina, Two Clarinets (1945)
[4038] Falcone, Thomas (cl); Cole,
Theodore (cl)
Rec 1/30/76
- CRI-353; 33s; rel 1976; cip

GOMEZ, Vincente (1911-)
Calypso Fantasy
[4039] Gomez, Vincente (gtr); McManus,
Dorothy (pf)
- Decca DL-4088/DL-74088;
33m/s; rel 1961*

Concierto flamenco
[4040] Gomez, Vincente (gtr); McManus,
Dorothy (pf)
- Decca DL-4088/DL-74088;
33m/s; rel 1961*

GOODE, Daniel (1936-)
Circular Thoughts (1973)
[4041] Gamelan Son of Lion
- Folkways FTS-31313; 33s; rel
1980; cip

GOODENOUGH, Forrest (1918-)
Elegy (1960)
[4042] Oslo Philharmonic Orchestra;
Fjeldstad, Oivin (cond)
- CRI-159; 33m; rel 1962; cip

GOODMAN, Joseph (1918-)
Jadis III
[4043] Skowronek, Felix (fl); Grossman,
Arthur (bsn)
- Crystal S-351; 33s; rel 1975; cip

Quintet, Winds (1954)
[4044] Soni Ventorum Wind Quintet
- Lyrichord LL-158/LLST-7158;
33m/s; rel 1966; cip

GOOSSEN, Frederic (1927-)
Clausulae for Violin and Piano
[4045] Steinerius Duo
Rec 1/77
- CRI-371; 33s; rel 1977; cip

Fantasy, Aria, and Fugue (1973)
[4046] Gowen, Bradford (pf)
- New World NW-304; 33s; rel
1979

Temple Music for Violin and Piano
[4047] Steinerius Duo
Rec 1/77
- CRI-371; 33s; rel 1977; cip

GORDON, Philip (1894-)
Colonial Diary
[4048] University of Maryland Concert
Band; Ostling, Acton, Jr. (cond)
- Coronet 955; 33m; rel 1969; del
1978

GOSLEE, George*
(Three) Sketches
[4049] Luening, Otto (fl); Etler, Alvin (ob);
Korn, Richard (cl); Goslee, George
(bsn)
- Yaddo D-15; 78; 10"; rel 1938

GOTTSCHALK, Arthur (1952-)
Substructures for Ten Tubas
[4050] University of Michigan Tuba
Ensemble; Mayer, Uri (cond)
- Golden Crest CRSQ-4145; 33q;
rel 1977; cip

GOULD, Morton (1913-)
American Caprice
[4051] Gould, Morton (pf)
- Decca DL-5067; 33m; 10"; rel
1950; del 1957

American Salute (Fantasy on When Johnny Comes Marching Home) (1947)

[4052] Boston Pops Orchestra; Fiedler, Arthur (cond)
- Victor 11-8762 (in set M-554); 78; rel 1945
- RCA LM-2229/LSC-2229; 33m/s; rel 1958; del 1975
- RCA VCS-7068; 33s; 2 discs; rel 1971; cip
- RCA LSC-3200; 33s; rel 1971; cip

[4053] Cleveland Pops Orchestra; Lane, Louis (cond)
Rec 8/58
- Epic LC-3539/BC-1013; 33m/s; rel 1959; del 1968

[4054] Cornell University Wind Ensemble; Stith, Marice (cond)
- Cornell CUWE-18; 33s; rel 1977; cip

[4055] Philadelphia Orchestra; Ormandy, Eugene (cond)
- Columbia ML-5874/MS-6474; 33m/s; rel 1963; cip
- Columbia ML-6121/MS-6721; 33m/s; rel 1965
- Columbia MS-7289; 33s; rel 1969; cip
- Columbia MG-32314; 33s; 2 discs; rel 1973; cip

[4056] Robin Hood Dell Orchestra (of Philadelphia); Gould, Morton (cond)
- Columbia M-668; 78; 4 discs; rel pre-1948
- Columbia ML-4218; 33m; rel 1948; del 1958

[4057] University of Miami Symphonic Band
- King 682; 33m/s; rel 1960; del 1965

[4058] U.S. Air Force Band; Howard, Col. George S. (cond)
- RCA LPM-2686/LSP-2686; 33m/s; rel 1963; del 1975

[4059] Utah Symphony Orchestra; Abravanel, Maurice (cond)
- Turnabout TVS-34459; 33s; rel 1972; cip

American Symphonette No 2 (1935)

[4060] Louisville Orchestra; Mester, Jorge (cond)
Rec 5/15/75
- LS-75-1; 33s (Louisville Orchestra First Edition Records 1975 No 1); rel 1976; cip

American Symphonette No 2: Pavane

[4061] Boston Pops Orchestra; Fiedler, Arthur (cond)
- Victor 4456 (in set M-554); 78; 10"; rel 1940

American Symphonette No 2: Pavane (cont'd)

[4062] Capitol Symphony Orchestra; Dragon, Carmen (cond)
- Capitol P-8523/SP-8523; 33m/s; rel 1960; del 1970

[4063] Morton Gould and his Orchestra; Gould, Morton (cond)
- Columbia 55030 (in set C-96); 78; rel pre-1948
- Columbia ML-2190; 33m; 10"; rel 1951; del 1956

American Symphonette No 2: Pavane (Various Arrangements)

[4064] Arr for Harpsichord
Crossan, Jack (hpschd)
- Westminster WGS-8255; 33s; rel 1973

[4065] Arr for Piano
Gould, Morton (pf)
- Decca DL-5067; 33m; 10"; rel 1950; del 1957

[4066] Litwin, Leo (pf)
- Boston B-500; 33m; 10"; rel 1958; del 1960

[4067] Arr for Trumpet and Orchestra
Hirt, Al (tpt); Boston Pops Orchestra; Fiedler, Arthur (cond)
- RCA LM-2729/LSC-2729; 33m/s; rel 1964; del 1975

[4068] Arr for Wind Quintet
Chicago Symphony Woodwind Quintet
- Audiophile AP-17; 33m; rel pre-1955

American Youth March

[4069] Morton Gould and his Orchestra; Gould, Morton (cond)
- RCA LM-2080/LSC-2080; 33m/s; rel 1957/1959; del 1963

Ballad for Band (1946)

[4070] Eastman Symphonic Wind Ensemble; Fennell, Frederick (cond)
- Mercury MG-40006; 33m; rel 1953; del 1957
- Mercury MG-50079; 33m; rel 1957; del 1969
- Mercury SRI-75086; 33s; rel 1977

Ballerina, The

[4071] Gould, Morton (pf)
- Decca DL-5067; 33m; 10"; rel 1950; del 1957

Big City Blues

[4072] Morton Gould and his Orchestra; Gould, Morton (cond)
- Columbia ML-2144; 33m; 10"; rel 1950; del 1956

Boogie-Woogie Etude

[4073] Iturbi, Jose (pf)
- Victor 10-1127; 78; 10"; rel pre-1948
- Gramophone B-9466; 78; 10"; rel pre-1948

Buckaroo Blues

[4074] Morton Gould and his Orchestra; Gould, Morton (cond)
- Columbia ML-4858; 33m; rel 1954; del 1963

Calypso Souvenir

[4075] Morton Gould and his Orchestra; Gould, Morton (cond)
- RCA LM-2768/LSC-2768; 33m/s; rel 1964; del 1974

Child Prodigy, The

[4076] Gould, Morton (pf)
- Decca DL-5067; 33m; 10"; rel 1950; del 1957

[4077] Litwin, Leo (pf)
- Boston B-500; 33m; 10"; rel 1958; del 1960

Columbia (Broadsides for Orchestra) (1967)

[4078] Louisville Orchestra; Gould, Morton (cond)
- LS-71-6; 33s (Louisville Orchestra First Edition Records 1971 No 6); rel 1972; cip

Concertette

[4079] Vardi, Emanuel (vla); MGM Band; Winograd, Arthur (cond)
- MGM E-3714; 33m; rel 1959; del 1959

Cowboy Rhapsody (1942)

[4080] Robin Hood Dell Orchestra (of Philadelphia); Gould, Morton (cond)
- Columbia M-668; 78; 4 discs; rel pre-1948
- Columbia ML-4218; 33m; rel 1948; del 1958

Crinoline and Old Lace

[4081] Litwin, Leo (pf)
- Boston B-500; 33m; 10"; rel 1958; del 1960

Dance Variations (1953)

[4082] Whittemore, Arthur (pf); Lowe, Jack (pf); San Francisco Symphony Orchestra; Stokowski, Leopold (cond)
- RCA LM-1858; 33m; rel 1955; del 1959

Declaration (Suite) (1957)

[4083] National Symphony Orchestra; Mitchell, Howard (cond)
- RCA LM-2264; 33m; rel 1959; del 1961

Derivations (1956)

[4084] Goodman, Benny (cl); Columbia
Symphony Orchestra Jazz
Ensemble; Gould, Morton (cond)
- Columbia ML-6205/MS-6805;
33m/s; rel 1966; cip

Deserted Ballroom

[4085] Gould, Morton (pf)
- Decca DL-5067; 33m; 10"; rel
1950; del 1957

Fall River Legend (Suite) (1948)

[4086] Ballet Theatre Orchestra; Levine,
Joseph (cond)
- Capitol P-8320; 33m; rel 1956;
del 1960
- Capitol HDR-21004; 33m; 4
discs; rel 1966; del 1970

[4087] Eastman-Rochester Symphony
Orchestra; Hanson, Howard
(cond)
- Mercury MG-50263/SR-90263;
33m/s; rel 1960; del 1964
- Mercury MG-50326/SR-90326;
33m/s; rel 1963; del 1966
(excerpts)
- Mercury SR-2-9127; 33s; 2
discs; rel 1968; del 1971

[4088] Morton Gould and his Orchestra;
Gould, Morton (cond)
- RCA LM-2532/LSC-2532;
33m/s; rel 1961; del 1976
- RCA CRL-3-3270; 33s; 3 discs;
rel 1979; cip

[4089] New York Philharmonic;
Mitropoulos, Dimitri (cond)
Rec 3/31/52
- Columbia ML-4616; 33m; rel
1953; del 1965
- New World NW-253; 33m; rel
1978

Fall River Legend: Cotillion

[4090] London Symphony Orchestra;
Gould, Morton (cond)
- Varese Sarabande
VCDM-1000.10; digital; rel
1980; cip

Family Album

[4091] Rochester Pops Orchestra; Gould,
Morton (cond)
Rec 1/19/53
- Columbia ML-2215; 33m; 10";
rel 1953; del 1956

Fanfare

[4092] London Symphony Orchestra;
Gould, Morton (cond)
- Chalfont/Varese Sarabande
CVS-55001; digital

Festive Music (1965)

[4093] London Symphony Orchestra;
Gould, Morton (cond)
- Varese Sarabande
VCDM-1000.10; digital; rel
1980; cip

Formations (1964)

[4094] Knightsbridge Symphonic Band;
Gould, Morton (cond)
- Gallery GS-6202; 33s; rel 1968*
- Everest SDBR-3253; 33s; rel
1969; cip

Fourth of July

[4095] Morton Gould and his Symphonic
Band; Gould, Morton (cond)
- Columbia 4516M (in set M-743);
78; 10"; rel 1948*
- Columbia ML-2029; 33m; 10";
rel pre-1949; del 1956
- RCA LM-2080/LSC-2080;
33m/s; rel 1957/1959; del
1963

Gavotte

[4096] Gould, Morton (pf)
- Decca DL-5067; 33m; 10"; rel
1950; del 1957

Interplay (American Concertette) (1943)

[4097] Gould, Morton (pf); Morton Gould
and his Orchestra; Gould, Morton
(cond)
- RCA CRL-3-3270; 33s; 3 discs;
rel 1979; cip

[4098] Gould, Morton (pf); Robin Hood
Dell Orchestra (of Philadelphia);
Gould, Morton (cond)
- Columbia X-289; 78; 2 discs; rel
pre-1948
- Columbia ML-4218; 33m; rel
1948; del 1958
- RCA LM-2532/LSC-2532;
33m/s; rel 1961; del 1976

[4099] Groot, Cor de (pf); Hague
Philharmonic Orchestra; Otterloo,
Willem van (cond)
- Epic LC-3021; 33m; rel 1954;
del 1961

Interplay (American Concertette): Gavotte and Blues

[4100] Boston Pops Orchestra; Fiedler,
Arthur (cond)
- Victor 49-4003-06 (in set
WDM-1726); 45; 4-7"; rel
1953?
- RCA LM-1726; 33m; rel 1953;
del 1961
- RCA LM-2744/LSC-2744;
33m/s; rel 1964; del 1975

Interplay (American Concertette): Blues (arr for pf)

[4101] Iturbi, Jose (pf)
- Victor 10-1127; 78; 10"; rel
pre-1948
- Gramophone B-9466; 78; 10";
rel pre-1948

Jekyll and Hyde Variations (1957)

[4102] National Symphony Orchestra;
Mitchell, Howard (cond)
- RCA LM-2264; 33m; rel 1959;
del 1961

Jericho

[4103] Morton Gould and his Orchestra;
Gould, Morton (cond)
- RCA LM-2308/LSC-2308;
33m/s; rel 1959; del 1962

[4104] North Texas State University
Concert Band; McAdow, Maurice
(cond)
- Austin 6016; 33m; rel 1960; del
1971

Latin-American Symphonette (1941)

[4105] Boston Pops Orchestra; Fiedler,
Arthur (cond)
- RCA LM-2988/LSC-2988;
33m/s; rel 1968; del 1976

[4106] Eastman-Rochester Symphony
Orchestra; Hanson, Howard
(cond)
- Mercury MG-40002; 33m; rel
1953; del 1957
- Mercury MG-50075; 33m; rel
1957; del 1963
- Mercury MG-50166; 33m; rel
1958; del 1963
- Mercury MG-50394/SR-90394;
33m/s; rel 1964; del 1969

[4107] Hollywood Bowl Symphony
Orchestra; Slatkin, Felix (cond)
- Capitol P-8474/SP-8474;
33m/s; rel 1959; del 1963
- Pickwick 4044; 33s; rel 1968;
del 1972

[4108] London Symphony Orchestra;
Gould, Morton (cond)
- Varese Sarabande
VCDM-1000.10; digital; rel
1980; cip
- Chalfont/Varese Sarabande
CVS-55001; digital (Excerpt:
Conga)

[4109] Rochester Philharmonic Orchestra;
Iturbi, Jose (cond)
- Victor M-964; 78; 3 discs; rel
pre-1948

[4110] Utah Symphony Orchestra;
Abravanel, Maurice (cond)
- Vanguard VRS-1103/VSD-2141;
33m/s; rel 1963; del 1970
- Vanguard SRV-275-SD; 33s; rel
1968; cip

Latin-American Symphonette: Tango and Guaracha

[4111] Morton Gould and his Orchestra;
Gould, Morton (cond)
- RCA LM-2532/LSC-2532;
33m/s; rel 1961; del 1976

Latin-American Symphonette: Guaracha

[4112] All-American Orchestra; Stokowski,
Leopold (cond)
- Columbia 11713D; 78; rel
pre-1942

Latin-American Symphonette: Guaracha *(cont'd)*

[4113] Cleveland Pops Orchestra; Lane, Louis (cond)
- Epic LC-3626/BC-1047; 33m/s; rel 1959; del 1970

Latin-American Symphonette (arr for 2 pfs)

[4114] Whittemore, Arthur (pf); Lowe, Jack (pf)
- Victor 11-9759; 78; rel pre-1948
- RCA LM-1926; 33m; rel 1956; del 1958 (Excerpt: Guaracha)

Legend

[4115] Rochester Pops Orchestra; Gould, Morton (cond)
- Columbia AAL-36; 33m; 10"; rel 1953; del 1956

Manhattan Polka

[4116] Litwin, Leo (pf)
- Boston B-500; 33m; 10"; rel 1958; del 1960

Mediterranean Concerto

[4117] Rochester Pops Orchestra; Gould, Morton (cond)
- Columbia AAL-36; 33m; 10"; rel 1953; del 1956

Minstrel Show (1946)

[4118] Minneapolis Symphony Orchestra; Mitropoulos, Dimitri (cond)
- Victor 11-9654; 78; rel pre-1948

New China March

[4119] Robin Hood Dell Orchestra (of Philadelphia); Gould, Morton (cond)
- Columbia M-668; 78; 4 discs; rel pre-1948
- Columbia ML-4218; 33m; rel 1948; del 1958

Nightwalk

[4120] Adler, Larry (harmonica); Morton Gould and his Orchestra; Gould, Morton (cond)
- RCA LM-2986/LSC-2986; 33m/s; rel 1968; del 1973

Night Watch

[4121] Morton Gould and his Orchestra; Gould, Morton (cond)
- RCA LM-2542/LSC-2542; 33m/s; rel 1961; del 1975

Parade

[4122] Morton Gould and his Symphonic Band; Gould, Morton (cond)
- RCA LM-2080/LSC-2080; 33m/s; rel 1957/1959; del 1963

Philharmonic Waltzes (1948)

[4123] London Symphony Orchestra; Gould, Morton (cond)
- Varese Sarabande VCDM-1000.10; digital; rel 1980; cip
- Chalfont/Varese Sarabande CVS-55001; digital (excerpt)

[4124] New York Philharmonic; Mitropoulos, Dimitri (cond)
- Columbia ML-2167; 33m; 10"; rel 1951; del 1956

Prima Donna, The

[4125] Gould, Morton (pf)
- Decca DL-5067; 33m; 10"; rel 1950; del 1957

Rag-Blues-Rag (ca 1963)

[4126] Helps, Robert (pf)
- RCA LM-7042/LSC-7042; 33m/s; 2 discs; rel 1966; del 1971
- CRI-288; 33s; 2 discs; rel 1972; cip

Red Cavalry March

[4127] Robin Hood Dell Orchestra (of Philadelphia); Gould, Morton (cond)
- Columbia M-668; 78; 4 discs; rel pre-1948
- Columbia ML-4218; 33m; rel 1948; del 1958

Rhapsodies, Piano and Orchestra

[4128] Gould, Morton (pf); Morton Gould and his Orchestra; Gould, Morton (cond)
- Columbia ML-4657; 33m; rel 1953; del 1957

St. Lawrence Suite (1958)

[4129] Morton Gould and his Orchestra; Gould, Morton (cond)
- RCA LM-2308/LSC-2308; 33m/s; rel 1959; del 1962

[4130] North Texas State University Concert Band; McAdow, Maurice (cond)
- Austin 6016; 33m; rel 1960; del 1971

Santa Fe Saga (1956)

[4131] Knightsbridge Symphonic Band; Gould, Morton (cond)
- Gallery GS-6202; 33s; rel 1968*
- Everest SDBR-3253; 33s; rel 1969; cip

Sonatina, Piano (1939): Spiritual

[4132] Waldoff, Stanley (pf)
- Musical Heritage Society MHS-3808; 33s; rel 1978

Soundings (1969)

[4133] Louisville Orchestra; Gould, Morton (cond)
- LS-71-6; 33s (Louisville Orchestra First Edition Records 1971 No 6); rel 1972; cip

Spirituals (1941)

[4134] Chicago Symphony Orchestra; Gould, Morton (cond)
- RCA LM-2850/LSC-2850; 33m/s; rel 1965; del 1970
- RCA AGL-1-1965; 33s; rel 1976; del 1979

[4135] Eastman-Rochester Symphony Orchestra; Hanson, Howard (cond)
- Mercury MG-50263/SR-90263; 33m/s; rel 1960; del 1964

[4136] Hague Philharmonic Orchestra; Otterloo, Willem van (cond)
- Epic LC-3021; 33m; rel 1954; del 1961

[4137] London Philharmonic Orchestra; Gould, Morton (cond)
Rec 10/24/78 and 10/29/78
- Crystal Clear CCS-7005; 33s; rel 1979; cip

[4138] London Symphony Orchestra; Susskind, Walter (cond)
- Everest LPBR-6002/SDBR-3002; 33m/s; rel 1958; cip

[4139] Minneapolis Symphony Orchestra; Dorati, Antal (cond)
- Mercury MG-50016; 33m; rel 1953; del 1963
- Mercury MGW-14034/SRW-18034; 33m/s; rel 1963; del 1968

[4140] Morton Gould and his Orchestra; Gould, Morton (cond)
- RCA LM-2686/LSC-2686; 33m/s; rel 1963; del 1967

[4141] New York Philharmonic; Rodzinski, Artur (cond)
- Columbia M-832; 78; 3 discs; rel pre-1950
- Columbia ML-2042; 33m; 10"; rel pre-1949; del 1956

Spring Morning

[4142] Litwin, Leo (pf)
- Boston B-500; 33m; 10"; rel 1958; del 1960

Suite, Tuba and Three Horns (1971)

[4143] Phillips, Harvey (tu); New York Horn Trio
- Golden Crest CRS-4122; 33s/q; rel 1974; cip

Symphony No 2 (Symphony on Marching Tunes) (1944): Quickstep

[4144] London Symphony Orchestra; Gould, Morton (cond)
 - Varese Sarabande VCDM-1000.10; digital; rel 1980; cip

[4145] New York Philharmonic; Gould, Morton (cond)
 - Columbia M-832; 78; 3 discs; rel pre-1950

[4146] New York Philharmonic; Mitropoulos, Dimitri (cond)
 - Columbia ML-2167; 33m; 10''; rel 1951; del 1956

Symphony for Band (West Point) (1952)

[4147] Eastman Symphonic Wind Ensemble; Fennell, Frederick (cond)
 - Mercury MG-50220/SR-90220; 33m/s; rel 1960; del 1972
 - Mercury SRI-75094; 33s; rel 1978; cip

[4148] Ithaca College Band; Beeler, Walter (cond)
 - Mark MCBS-21360; 33s; rel 1968; del 1976

Tap Dance Concerto (1952)

[4149] Daniels, Danny (tap dancer); Rochester Pops Orchestra; Gould, Morton (cond) Rec 1/19/53
 - Columbia ML-2215; 33m; 10''; rel 1953; del 1956

Theme

[4150] Rochester Pops Orchestra; Gould, Morton (cond)
 - Columbia AAL-36; 33m; 10''; rel 1953; del 1956

Tropical

[4151] Gould, Morton (pf)
 - Decca DL-5067; 33m; 10''; rel 1950; del 1957

[4152] Litwin, Leo (pf)
 - Boston B-500; 33m; 10''; rel 1958; del 1960

[4153] Morton Gould and his Orchestra; Gould, Morton (cond)
 - Columbia ML-2015; 33m; 10''; rel pre-1949; del 1956

Venice (1967)

[4154] Seattle Symphony Orchestra; Katims, Milton (cond)
 - RCA LSC-3079; 33s; rel 1969; del 1975

GOUPIL, Auguste

Jungle Drums

[4155] Knudson, Thurston (perc); Goupil, Auguste (perc); Jungle Rhythmists
 - Decca DL-8216; 33m; rel 1956?

GOWER, Albert E., Jr. (1935-)

(Three) Short Pieces, Baritone Horn and Piano

[4156] Young, Raymond G. (bar hn); Fraschillo, Tom (pf)
 - Golden Crest RE-7025; 33m/s; rel 1968/1979; cip

GRAHAM, Robert (1912-)

Golgotha

[4157] Broadman Chorale; narrator; organ; Green, Paul (cond)
 - Broadman 452-041; 33m; rel 1962

Sower and the Seed, The

[4158] First Baptist Church (Tulsa, OK) Chapel Choir; organ; Woodward, James D. (cond)
 - Broadman 452-045; 33m; rel 1963

GRAINGER, Percy (1882-1961)

Arrival Platform Humlet (1908-12)

[4159] Forbes, Watson (vla)
 - Decca M-540; 78; 10''; rel pre-1948

Children's March (Over the Hills and Far Away) (two-piano version) (1916-18)

[4160] Howard, Leslie (pf); Stanhope, David (pf) Rec 1976
 - EMI/His Master's Voice HQS-1402; 33s; rel 1978

Children's March (Over the Hills and Far Away) (piano version) (1918)

[4161] Adni, Daniel (pf)
 - EMI/Odeon HQS-1363; 33q; rel 1976
 - Seraphim S-60295; 33q; rel 1979; cip

[4162] List, Eugene (pf)
 - Vanguard VRS-1072; 33m; rel 1961; del 1965

Children's March (Over the Hills and Far Away) (band and piano version) (1916-19)

[4163] University of Illinois Symphonic Band; Begian, Harry (cond)
 - University of Illinois Bands 24089-90; 33s; 2 discs; rel 1975?

Children's March (Over the Hills and Far Away) (orchestral version)

[4164] Eastman-Rochester Pops Orchestra; Fennell, Frederick (cond)
 - Mercury MG-50219/SR-90219; 33m/s; rel 1959; del 1965
 - Mercury MG-50325/SR-90325; 33m/s; rel 1963; del 1967
 - Mercury MGW-14060/SRW-18060; 33m/s; rel 1966; del 1970
 - Mercury SRI-75102; 33s; rel 1977; cip

[4165] Goldman Band
 - Decca DL-8663/DL-78633; 33m/s; rel 1958; del 1973

[4166] Rochester Pops Orchestra; Gould, Morton (cond)
 - Columbia AAL-49; 33m; 10''; rel 1954; del 1957
 - Columbia A-1912; 45; 7''; rel pre-1956

[4167] Victor Symphony Orchestra
 - Victor 36035; 78; rel pre-1936

Colonial Song (version for soprano, tenor, harp, and orchestra) (1905-12, rev 1914)

[4168] Atwater, A. (sop); Sanchez, L. O. (ten); orchestra; Grainger, Percy (cond)
 - Columbia 2066M; 78; rel pre-1936

[4169] Dargavel, Joan (sop); Stirling, Lance (ten); Melbourne Symphony Orchestra; Hopkins, John (cond)
 - Australian Broadcasting Commission RRCS-131; 33s; rel 197?

Colonial Song (orchestral version) (1905-12, rev ca 1928)

[4170] Eastman-Rochester Pops Orchestra; Fennell, Frederick (cond)
 - Mercury MG-50219/SR-90219; 33m/s; rel 1959; del 1965
 - Mercury MG-50325/SR-90325; 33m/s; rel 1963; del 1967
 - Mercury MGW-14060/SRW-18060; 33m/s; rel 1966; del 1970
 - Mercury SRI-75102; 33s; rel 1977; cip

[4171] Victor Symphony Orchestra
 - Victor 36035; 78; rel pre-1936

Colonial Song (piano version) (1914)

[4172] Grainger, Percy (pf)
 - Everest X-913; 33s; rel 1967; cip

Colonial Song (band version) (1918)

[4173] University of Illinois Symphonic Band; Begian, Harry (cond)
- University of Illinois Bands 24089-90; 33s; 2 discs; rel 1975?

Eastern Intermezzo (1922)

[4174] Adni, Daniel (pf)
- EMI/Odeon HQS-1363; 33q; rel 1976
- Seraphim S-60295; 33q; rel 1979; cip

English Waltz (1947)

[4175] Howard, Leslie (pf); Stanhope, David (pf)
Rec 1976
- EMI/His Master's Voice HQS-1402; 33s; rel 1978

Fantasy on Gershwin's Porgy and Bess

[4176] Phillips, Robert (pf); Renzulli, Franco (pf)
- Crystal Clear CCS-6002; 33s; rel 1979; cip

Handel in the Strand (piano version) (1930)

[4177] Adni, Daniel (pf)
- EMI/Odeon HQS-1363; 33q; rel 1976
- Seraphim S-60295; 33q; rel 1979; cip

[4178] Howard, Leslie (pf)
Rec 1976
- EMI/His Master's Voice HQS-1402; 33s; rel 1978

[4179] List, Eugene (pf)
- Vanguard VRS-1072; 33m; rel 1961; del 1965

Handel in the Strand (string-orchestra version) (1932)

[4180] Boyd Neel String Orchestra; Neel, Boyd (cond)
- Decca K-1216; 78; rel pre-1948
- London T-5229; 78; rel pre-1952
- London 12017; 78; rel pre-1953
- London 40357; 45; 7"; rel pre-1953

[4181] Eastman-Rochester Pops Orchestra; Fennell, Frederick (cond)
- Mercury MG-50219/SR-90219; 33m/s; rel 1959; del 1965
- Mercury MG-50325/SR-90325; 33m/s; rel 1963; del 1967
- Mercury MGW-14060/SRW-18060; 33m/s; rel 1966; del 1970
- Mercury SRI-75102; 33s; rel 1977; cip

[4182] New Light Symphony Orchestra; Sargent, Malcolm (cond)
- Gramophone C-2002; 78; rel pre-1936

Handel in the Strand (string-orchestra version) (1932) *(cont'd)*

[4183] New Queen's Hall Orchestra; Wood, Sir Henry (cond)
- Decca 25609; 78; rel pre-1936
- Decca (English) K-767; 78; rel pre-1936

[4184] Philharmonia Orchestra; Braithwaite, Warwick (cond)
- Columbia (English) DX-1660; 78; rel pre-1952
- Columbia RL-3042; 33m; rel 1952*

Handel in the Strand (piano and orchestra version)

[4185] Grainger, Percy (pf); Leopold Stokowski and his Orchestra; Stokowski, Leopold (cond)
Rec 5/31/50 and 11/8/50
- RCA LM-1238; 33m; rel 1952; del 1956
- Victor WDM-1663; 45; 7"; rel pre-1953
- Victor ERA-124; 45; 2-7"; rel 1953
- Gramophone 7E-5046; 45; 7"; rel pre-1956
- RCA ARL-1-3059; 33m; rel 1979; cip

Handel in the Strand (arr for band)

[4186] University of Illinois Symphonic Band; Begian, Harry (cond)
- University of Illinois Bands 24089-90; 33s; 2 discs; rel 1975?

Handel in the Strand (arr for sextet)

[4187] V. Olof Sextet
- Parlophone R-429; 78; rel pre-1936

Harvest Hymn (piano version) (1936)

[4188] Howard, Leslie (pf)
Rec 1976
- EMI/His Master's Voice HQS-1402; 33s; rel 1978

Hill Song No 2 (band version) (1907, rev 1911, 1940-46)

[4189] Eastman Symphonic Wind Ensemble; Fennell, Frederick (cond)
- Mercury MG-50221/SR-90221; 33m/s; rel 1960; del 1964
- Mercury MG-50388/SR-90388; 33m/s; rel 1964; del 1974
- Mercury SRI-75011; 33s; rel 1973; cip

[4190] University of Illinois Symphonic Band; Begian, Harry (cond)
- University of Illinois Bands 24089-90; 33s; 2 discs; rel 1975?

Hill Song No 2 (arr for orch)

[4191] Melbourne Symphony Orchestra; Hopkins, John (cond)
- Australian Broadcasting Commission RRCS-131; 33s; rel 197?

Immovable Do, The (orchestral version) (ca 1939)

[4192] Eastman-Rochester Pops Orchestra; Fennell, Frederick (cond)
- Mercury MG-50219/SR-90219; 33m/s; rel 1959; del 1965
- Mercury MG-50325/SR-90325; 33m/s; rel 1963; del 1967
- Mercury MGW-14060/SRW-18060; 33m/s; rel 1966; del 1970
- Mercury SRI-75102; 33s; rel 1977; cip

[4193] English Sinfonia; Dilkes, Neville (cond)
- EMI/His Master's Voice ASD-3651; 33s; rel 1979

Immovable Do, The (band version) (1939)

[4194] University of Illinois Symphonic Band; Begian, Harry (cond)
- University of Illinois Bands 24089-90; 33s; 2 discs; rel 1975?

Lads of Wamphray March, The (1906-07, rev 1937-38)

[4195] Cornell University Symphonic Band; Stith, Marice (cond)
- Cornell CUWE-10; 33s; rel 1973; cip

[4196] Goldman Band
- Decca DL-8931/DL-78931; 33m/s; rel 1960; del 1971

[4197] University of Illinois Symphonic Band; Begian, Harry (cond)
- University of Illinois Bands 24089-90; 33s; 2 discs; rel 1975?

Lullaby from Tribute to Foster (1915)

[4198] Adni, Daniel (pf)
- EMI/Odeon HQS-1363; 33q; rel 1976
- Seraphim S-60295; 33q; rel 1979; cip

Mock Morris (piano version) (1910)

[4199] Grainger, Percy (pf)
Rec 1914-22
- Pearl GEM-143; 33m; rel 1978

[4200] List, Eugene (pf)
- Vanguard VRS-1072; 33m; rel 1961; del 1965

Mock Morris (string-orchestra version) (1910)

[4201] Boyd Neel String Orchestra; Neel, Boyd (cond)
- Decca K-1215; 78; rel pre-1948

[4202] Sydney Civic Symphony Strings; Beck (cond)
- Diaphon DPM-1; 33m; rel pre-1953

Mock Morris (orchestral version) (1914)

[4203] Eastman-Rochester Pops Orchestra; Fennell, Frederick (cond)
- Mercury MG-50219/SR-90219; 33m/s; rel 1959; del 1965
- Mercury MG-50325/SR-90325; 33m/s; rel 1963; del 1967
- Mercury MGW-14060/SRW-18060; 33m/s; rel 1966; del 1970
- Mercury SRI-75102; 33s; rel 1977; cip

[4204] New Light Symphony Orchestra; Sargent, Malcolm (cond)
- Gramophone C-2002; 78; rel pre-1936

[4205] New Queen's Hall Orchestra; Wood, Sir Henry (cond)
- Decca 25609; 78; rel pre-1936
- Decca (English) K-767; 78; rel pre-1936
- Columbia 7338M; 78; rel pre-1936
- Columbia (English) LX-200; 78; rel pre-1936

[4206] Philharmonia Orchestra; Braithwaite, Warwick (cond)
- Columbia DB-2572; 78; rel pre-1952
- Columbia RL-3042; 33m; rel 1952*

[4207] Rochester Pops Orchestra; Gould, Morton (cond)
- Columbia AAL-49; 33m; 10"; rel 1954; del 1957
- Columbia A-1912; 45; 7"; rel pre-1956

Mock Morris (piano and orchestra version)

[4208] Grainger, Percy (pf); Leopold Stokowski and his Orchestra; Stokowski, Leopold (cond)
Rec 5/31/50 and 11/8/50
- RCA LM-1238; 33m; rel 1952; del 1956
- Victor WDM-1663; 45; 7"; rel pre-1953
- Victor ERA-124; 45; 2-7"; rel 1953
- Gramophone 7E-5046; 45; 7"; rel pre-1956
- RCA ARL-1-3059; 33m; rel 1979; cip

Power of Rome and the Christian Heart, The (band version) (1948)

[4209] University of Illinois Symphonic Band; Begian, Harry (cond)
- University of Illinois Bands 24089-90; 33s; 2 discs; rel 1975?

Sailor's Song

[4210] Adni, Daniel (pf)
- EMI/Odeon HQS-1363; 33q; rel 1976
- Seraphim S-60295; 33q; rel 1979; cip

Suite (In a Nutshell) (orchestral version) (1905-16)

[4211] English Sinfonia; Dilkes, Neville (cond)
- EMI/His Master's Voice ASD-3651; 33s; rel 1979

Suite (In a Nutshell) (piano version) (1916): The Gum-Suckers March

[4212] Grainger, Percy (pf)
Rec 1914-22
- Columbia A-3381; 78; rel 1919-25
- Columbia 2002M; 78; rel 1919-25
- Columbia 7147M; 78; rel pre-1936
- Pearl GEM-143; 33m; rel 1978

To a Nordic Princess (piano version) (1927-28)

[4213] Adni, Daniel (pf)
- EMI/Odeon HQS-1363; 33q; rel 1976
- Seraphim S-60295; 33q; rel 1979; cip

Walking Tune (wind-quintet version) (1900-05)

[4214] Philadelphia Woodwind Quintet
- Columbia ML-5984/MS-6584; 33m/s; rel 1964; del 1968

Walking Tune (piano version) (ca 1905)

[4215] Adni, Daniel (pf)
- EMI/Odeon HQS-1363; 33q; rel 1976
- Seraphim S-60295; 33q; rel 1979; cip

Warriors, The (1912-16)

[4216] Melbourne Symphony Orchestra; Hopkins, John (cond)
- Australian Broadcasting Commission RRCS-131; 33s; rel 197?

Youthful Rapture (1901, 1929)

[4217] Harrison, B. (vcl); orchestra
- Gramophone C-1929; 78; rel pre-1936

GRANDJANY, Marcel (1891-1975)

Aria in Classic Style (arr for hp and strings)

[4218] Kling, Taka (hp); Louisville Orchestra; Mester, Jorge (cond)
- LS-70-1; 33s (Louisville Orchestra First Edition Records 1970 No 1); rel 1970; cip

(Deux) Chansons populaires francaises

[4219] Grandjany, Marcel (hp)
- Capitol P-8401; 33m; rel 1957; del 1962

(Deux) Chansons populaires francaises: Le Bon petit roi d'Yvetot

[4220] Robles, Marisa (hp)
- Argo RG-458/ZRG-5458; 33m/s; rel 1967; del 1980

Children's Hour, The (Op 25) (1950)

[4221] Grandjany, Marcel (hp)
- Capitol P-8492/SP-8492; 33m/s; rel 1959; del 1963
- Paperback Classics SL-9217; 33s; rel 1963
- Seraphim S-60142; 33s; rel 1970; cip

Dans la foret du charme et de l'enchantement (1922)

[4222] Grandjany, Marcel (hp)
- Capitol PAO-8420; 33m; rel 1958; del 1961

Divertissement

[4223] Grandjany, Marcel (hp)
- Capitol PAO-8420; 33m; rel 1958; del 1961

Fantasie on a Theme by Haydn (Homage to Xavier Desargus)

[4224] Grandjany, Marcel (hp)
- Capitol PAO-8420; 33m; rel 1958; del 1961

[4225] Spitzerova, Magdalena (hp)
Rec 1973
- Panton 11-0380; 33s; rel 1973

On an Old Christmas Song

[4226] Remsen, Dorothy (hp)
- Avant AV-1000; 33s; rel 1967; cip

Rhapsodie pour la harpe (1922)

[4227] Grandjany, Marcel (hp)
- Camden CAL-338; 33m; rel 1957; del 1958
- Paperback Classics SL-9217; 33s; rel 1963
- Seraphim S-60142; 33s; rel 1970; cip

Rhapsodie pour la harpe (1922)
(cont'd)
[4228] Vito, Edward (hp)
- Period SPL-721; 33m; rel 1955;
del 1968
- Orion ORS-7039; 33s; rel 1971;
cip

GRANT, William Parks (1910-)
Brevities Suite No 3 (Op 44)
[4229] Love, Randolph (tpt); Walford,
David (tpt); Wagnitz, Ralph (hn);
Keller, Jeffrey (tbn)
- Coronet S-2738; 33s; rel 1973;
cip

Essay (Op 25)
[4230] Held, Wilbur (org); Jones, James
(hn)
Rec 10/9/70
- Coronet S-2738; 33s; rel 1973;
cip

Excursions (1951)
[4231] Schwarz, Gerard (tpt); Eckert, John
W. (tpt); Birdwell, Edward (hn);
Fromme, Arnold (tbn)
- CRI-222; 33s; rel 1968; cip

Laconic Suite (Op 31)
[4232] Love, Randolph (tpt); Wolford,
David (tpt); Wagnitz, Ralph (hn);
Keller, Jeffrey (tbn)
- Coronet S-2738; 33s; rel 1973;
cip

Prelude and Canonic Piece (Op 51)
[4233] Owen, Beth Russell (fl); Hite, David
(cl)
- Coronet S-2738; 33s; rel 1973;
cip

GRANTHAM, Donald (1947-)
(Cuatro) Caprichos de Francisco Goya
[4234] Clapp, Stephen (vln)
- Orion ORS-77279; 33s; rel
1978; cip

Trio, Violin, Violoncello, and Piano (1972)
[4235] Angelus Trio
- Orion ORS-77279; 33s; rel
1978; cip

GRASSE, Edwin (1884-1954)
Wellenspiel
[4236] Heifetz, Jascha (vln); Bay, Emanuel
(pf)
- Decca DL-8521; 33m; rel 1951;
del 1970

GRAUER, Victor (1937-)
Inferno
[4237] Electronic music
- Folkways FM-3436/FMS-33436;
33m/s; rel 1967; cip

GRAYSON, Richard (1941-)
Homage to J. S. Bach
[4238] Grayson, Richard (syn)
- Orion ORS-74142; 33s; rel
1974; cip

Improvisation after Satie
[4239] Grayson, Richard (pf); tape
- Orion ORS-74142; 33s; rel
1974; cip

Meadow Music
[4240] Grayson, Richard (pf); tape
- Orion ORS-74142; 33s; rel
1974; cip

Ostinato
[4241] Grayson, Richard (syn)
- Orion ORS-74142; 33s; rel
1974; cip

Promenade
[4242] Nightingale, James (acc); tape
- Orion ORS-77263; 33s; rel
1977; cip

Rain
[4243] Grayson, Richard (syn)
- Orion ORS-74142; 33s; rel
1974; cip

GREEN, Bernard (1908-75)
Symphony
[4244] Westphalian Symphony Orchestra;
Green, Bernard (cond)
- Vox PL-14080; 33m; rel 1964?

Waltz Etudes
[4245] Westphalian Symphony Orchestra;
Green, Bernard (cond)
- Vox PL-14080; 33m; rel 1964?

GREEN, George (1930-)
Perihelion (1973)
[4246] Cornell University Wind Ensemble;
Stith, Marice (cond)
Rec 3/24/74
- Cornell CUWE-15; 33s; rel 1975;
cip

Triptych
[4247] Stith, Marice (tpt)
- Golden Crest RE-7042; 33s; rel
1972; cip

GREEN, Ray (1909-)
Festival Fugues (An American Toccata)
[4248] Green, Ray (pf)
- American Recording Edition
ARE-1002; 33m; rel pre-1956

Holiday for Four
[4249] Weiss, Abraham (vla); Peterson,
Alfred (cl); Weiss, Adolph (bsn);
Furman, Maxine (pf)
- American Recording Edition
ARE-1002; 33m; rel pre-1956

Holiday for Four *(cont'd)*
[4250] no performers given
- Alco AR-102; 78; rel pre-1956

Hymn Tunes for Strings
[4251] Rome Chamber Orchestra; Flagello,
Nicolas (cond)
- Peters Internationale PLE-059;
33s; rel 1978; cip

(Twelve) Inventions, Piano
[4252] Green, Ray (pf)
- American Recording Edition
ARE-1002; 33m; rel pre-1956

Pieces for Children . . . and for Grownups to Make a Note Of
[4253] Green, Ray (pf)
- American Recording Edition
ARE-1002; 33m; rel pre-1956

Sea Calm
[4254] Greek Byzantine Chorus; Vriondes,
Christos (cond)
- New Music Quarterly Recordings
1014 (1-8); 78; rel 1934

Short Sonata in F
[4255] Burton, Catherine (pf)
- American Recording Edition
ARE-1001; 33m; rel pre-1956

Sunday-Sing Symphony (1946)
[4256] Hessian Radio Symphony
Orchestra; Van Vactor, David
(cond)
- CRI-169; 33m/s; rel 1963/?; cip

[4257] Vienna Symphony Orchestra;
Schoenherr, Max (cond)
- American Recording Society
ARS-31; 33m; rel 1953
- Desto D-420/DST-6420; 33m/s;
rel 1966; cip

GRELL, G.*
Larghetto
[4258] Arizona Cello Society Orchestra;
Varga, Laszlo (cond)
Rec 4/14/71
- Arizona Cello Society ARA-171;
33; rel 1971?

GRESSEL, Joel (1943-)
Crossings (1976)
[4259] Electronic music
- CRI-393; 33s; rel 1979; cip

Points in Time (1974)
[4260] Electronic music
- Odyssey Y-34139; 33s; rel
1976; cip

P-Vibes (Three Canons) (1971-72)
[4261] Electronic music
- CRI-393; 33s; rel 1979; cip

GRIFFES, Charles T. (1884-1920)

Am Kreuzweg wird begraben (1906?)
[4262] Milnes, Sherrill (bar); Spong, Jon (pf)
- New World NW-273; 33s; rel 1977

An den Wind (1906?)
[4263] Milnes, Sherrill (bar); Spong, Jon (pf)
- New World NW-273; 33s; rel 1977

Auf geheimem Waldespfade (1906?)
[4264] Darwin, Glenn (b); Fiedler, Elsa (pf)
- Victor 36224; 78; rel 1939

[4265] Hanks, John Kennedy (ten); Friedberg, Ruth (pf)
- Duke University Press DWR-6417-18; 33m; 2 discs; rel 1966; del 1975

[4266] Kisselburgh, Alexander (bar); piano
- Columbia C-2041D; 78; 10"; rel pre-1936
- Columbia C-189M; 78; 10"; rel pre-1936

[4267] Milnes, Sherrill (bar); Spong, Jon (pf)
- New World NW-273; 33s; rel 1977

[4268] Myrvik, Norman (ten); Levenson, Emanuel (pf)
- EMS Recordings EMS-501; 33m; rel 1962; del 1970

[4269] Rethberg, Elisabeth (sop); Persson, Fred (pf)
- Brunswick AMB-15146; 78; 10"; rel pre-1936
- Brunswick A-62651; 78; 10"; rel pre-1936

[4270] Steber, Eleanor (sop); Quillian, James (pf)
Rec 3/31/41 and 4/14/41
- Victor 10-1071A; 78; 10"; rel pre-1948
- New World NW-247; 33m; rel 1976

Bacchanale (1919?)
[4271] Eastman-Rochester Symphony Orchestra; Hanson, Howard (cond)
Rec 10/28/54
- Mercury MG-40012; 33m; rel 1955; del 1957
- Mercury MG-50085; 33m; rel 1957; del 1969
- Mercury (English) MRL-2544; 33m; rel 1957*
- Mercury MG-50422/SR-90422; 33m/s; rel 1965; del 1974
- Mercury SRI-75090; 33s; rel 1976*

Clouds (orchestral version) (1919?)
[4272] Eastman-Rochester Symphony Orchestra; Hanson, Howard (cond)
Rec 10/28/54
- Mercury MG-40012; 33m; rel 1955; del 1957
- Mercury MG-50085; 33m; rel 1957; del 1969
- Mercury (English) MRL-2544; 33m; rel 1957*
- Mercury SRI-75090; 33s; rel 1976*

Das ist ein Brausen und Heulen (1906?)
[4273] Parker, William (bar); Huckaby, William (pf)
- New World NW-305; 33s; rel 1980

Elfe (1906?)
[4274] Myrvik, Norman (ten); Levenson, Emanuel (pf)
- EMS Recordings EMS-501; 33s; rel 1962; del 1970

Evening Song (pre-1912)
[4275] Hunt, Alexandra (sop); Benoit, Regis (pf)
- Orion ORS-77272; 33s; rel 1978; cip

[4276] Myrvik, Norman (ten); Levenson, Emanuel (pf)
- EMS Recordings EMS-501; 33m; rel 1962; del 1970

Fantasy Pieces (Op 6) (1912-15)
[4277] Engdahl, Leonore (pf)
- MGM E-3225; 33m; rel 1955; del 1959

[4278] Mancinelli, Aldo (pf)
- Musical Heritage Society MHS-3695; 33s; rel 1978?

[4279] Ranck, John (pf)
- Zodiac Z-1002; 33m; rel 1955; del 1960

First Snowfall, The (pre-1912)
[4280] Parker, William (bar); Huckaby, William (pf)
- New World NW-305; 33s; rel 1980

(Four) Impressions (1912-16)
[4281] Stapp, Olivia (m sop); Richardson, Diane (pf)
- New World NW-273; 33s; rel 1977

(Four) Impressions: Impressions du matin
[4282] Suderburg, Elizabeth (sop); Suderburg, Robert (pf)
- University of Washington Press OLY-104; 33q; 2 discs; rel 1976; cip

(Zwei) Koenige sassen auf Orkadahl (1906?)
[4283] Parker, William (bar); Huckaby, William (pf)
- New World NW-305; 33s; rel 1980

Meeres Stille (1906?)
[4284] Milnes, Sherrill (bar); Spong, Jon (pf)
- New World NW-273; 33s; rel 1977

Mueden Abendlied, Des (1906?)
[4285] Parker, William (bar); Huckaby, William (pf)
- New World NW-305; 33s; rel 1980

Nocturne (1919)
[4286] American Arts Orchestra; Krueger, Karl (cond)
- SPAMH MIA-104; 33s; rel 1959

Notturno (1918?)
[4287] American Arts Orchestra; Krueger, Karl (cond)
- SPAMH MIA-104; 33s; rel 1959

Pleasure-Dome of Kubla Khan, The (orchestral version) (Op 8) (1917)
[4288] Andre Kostelanetz and his Orchestra; Kostelanetz, Andre (cond)
- Columbia MG-33728; 33s; 2 discs; rel 1976; del 1979

[4289] Boston Symphony Orchestra; Ozawa, Seiji (cond)
- New World NW-273; 33s; rel 1977

[4290] Eastman-Rochester Symphony Orchestra; Hanson, Howard (cond)
Rec 10/28/54
- Mercury MG-40012; 33m; rel 1955; del 1957
- Mercury MG-50085; 33m; rel 1957; del 1969
- Mercury (English) MRL-2544; 33m; rel 1957*
- Mercury MG-50422/SR-90422; 33m/s; rel 1965; del 1974
- Mercury SRI-75090; 33s; rel 1976*

[4291] Minneapolis Symphony Orchestra; Ormandy, Eugene (cond)
- Victor 7957; 78; rel pre-1936

Poem (1918)
[4292] Baker, Julius (fl); Saidenberg Chamber Orchestra; Saidenberg, Daniel (cond)
- Decca DL-4013; 33m; 10"; rel 1952; del 1957
- Brunswick AXL-2015; 33m; rel 1954*

Poem (1918) *(cont'd)*

[4293] Kincaid, William (fl); Philadelphia
Orchestra; Ormandy, Eugene
(cond)
- Columbia ML-4629; 33m; rel
1953; del 1970

[4294] Mariano, Joseph (fl);
Eastman-Rochester Symphony
Orchestra; Hanson, Howard
(cond)
- Victor 11-8349; 78; rel 1943*
- Mercury MG-50379/SR-90379;
33m/s; rel 1964; del 1973
- Mercury MG-50422/SR-90422;
33m/s; rel 1965; del 1974
- Mercury SRI-75020; 33s; rel
1974; cip

[4295] Sharp, Maurice (fl); Cleveland
Sinfonietta; Lane, Louis (cond)
- Epic LC-3754/BC-1116; 33m/s;
rel 1961; del 1970
- Columbia (English)
33SX-1682/SCX-3539; 33m/s;
rel 1964*

[4296] Wanausek, Camille (fl); Vienna
Symphony Orchestra; Hendl,
Walter (cond)
- American Recording Society
ARS-22; 33m; 10"; rel 1952
- Desto D-424/DST-6424; 33m/s;
rel 1967; cip

**(Two) Poems by John Masefield: An
Old Song Re-Sung (1918)**

[4297] Hanks, John Kennedy (ten);
Friedberg, Ruth (pf)
- Duke University Press
DWR-6417-18; 33m; 2 discs; rel
1966; del 1975

[4298] Myrvik, Norman (ten); Levenson,
Emanuel (pf)
- EMS Recordings EMS-501; 33m;
rel 1962; del 1970

[4299] Parker, William (bar); Huckaby,
William (pf)
- New World NW-305; 33s; rel
1980

[4300] Stenberg, Donald (bar); Crossman,
Joann (pf)
- Educo 4006; 33

[4301] Warren, Leonard (bar); Sektberg,
Willard (pf)
- RCA LM-2266; 33m; rel 1958;
del 1961

**(Three) Poems (Op 9) (1916): In a
Myrtle Shade and Waikiki**

[4302] Hunt, Alexandra (sop); Benoit,
Regis (pf)
- Orion ORS-77272; 33s; rel
1978; cip

(Three) Poems (Op 9): Waikiki

[4303] Steber, Eleanor (sop); Biltcliffe,
Edwin (pf)
- St/And SPL-411-12; 33m; 2
discs; rel 1963; del 1964
- Desto D-411-12/DST-6411-12;
33m/s; 2 discs; rel 1964; cip

**(Three) Poems of Fiona MacLeod
(Op 11) (1918)**

[4304] Myrvik, Norman (ten); Levenson,
Emanuel (pf)
- EMS Recordings EMS-501; 33m;
rel 1962; del 1970

**(Three) Poems of Fiona MacLeod:
The Lament of Ian the Proud**

[4305] Hain, William (ten); Bohm, Jerome
(pf)
- Friends of Recorded Music FRM-5;
78; rel pre-1942

[4306] Hanks, John Kennedy (ten);
Friedberg, Ruth (pf)
- Duke University Press
DWR-6417-18; 33m; 2 discs; rel
1966; del 1975

[4307] Moore, Dale (bar); Tomfohrde,
Betty Ruth (pf)
- Cambridge CRS-2715; 33s; rel
1973; cip

[4308] Suderburg, Elizabeth (sop);
Suderburg, Robert (pf)
- University of Washington Press
OLY-104; 33q; 2 discs; rel 1976;
cip

**(Three) Poems of Fiona MacLeod:
Thy Dark Eyes to Mine**

[4309] Hunt, Alexandra (sop); Benoit,
Regis (pf)
- Orion ORS-77272; 33s; rel
1978; cip

**(Three) Poems of Fiona MacLeod
(orchestral version) (1918)**

[4310] Bryn-Julson, Phyllis (sop); Boston
Symphony Orchestra; Ozawa, Seiji
(cond)
- New World NW-273; 33s; rel
1977

(Three) Preludes, Piano (1919)

[4311] Jochum, Veronica (pf)
- Golden Crest CRS-4168; 33s; rel
1978; cip

[4312] Mandel, Alan (pf)
- Desto DC-6445-47; 33s; 3 discs;
rel 1975; cip

[4313] Ranck, John (pf)
- Zodiac Z-1002; 33m; rel 1955;
del 1960
- International Piano
Library/International Piano
Archives IPA-2002; 33m; rel
1977

Roman Sketches (Op 7) (1915-16)

[4314] Engdahl, Leonore (pf)
- MGM E-3225; 33m; rel 1955;
del 1959

[4315] Hambro, Leonid (pf)
- Walden W-100; 33m; rel 1952;
del 1961
- Lyrichord LL-105/LLST-7105;
33m/s; rel 1962/1976; cip

Roman Sketches (Op 7) (1915-16)
(cont'd)

[4316] Jochum, Veronica (pf)
- Golden Crest CRS-4168; 33s; rel
1978; cip

[4317] Mancinelli, Aldo (pf)
- Musical Heritage Society
MHS-3695; 33s; rel 1978?

[4318] Stearns, Duncan (pf)
- Orion ORS-79352; 33s; rel
1980; cip

**Roman Sketches: The White
Peacock and The Fountain of the
Acqua Paola**

[4319] Shields, Roger (pf)
- Vox SVBX-5303; 33s; 3 discs; rel
1977; cip

**Roman Sketches: The White
Peacock**

[4320] Dubal, David (pf)
- Musical Heritage Society
MHS-3808; 33s; rel 1978

[4321] Hess, Myra (pf)
- Columbia 50149D; 78; 10"; rel
pre-1936
- Columbia 9072M; 78; 10"; rel
pre-1936

[4322] Iturbi, Amparo (pf)
- Victor 12-3273; 78; rel
pre-1952

[4323] Pressler, Menahem (pf)
- MGM E-3129; 33m; rel 1954;
del 1959

[4324] Samaroff, Olga (pf)
- Victor 7384; 78; rel pre-1936

[4325] Snyder, Barry (pf)
- Golden Crest RE-7063; 33q; rel
1976

[4326] Wells, Howard (pf)
- Educo 3012; 33m; rel 1958; del
1972

**Roman Sketches: The Fountain of
the Acqua Paola**

[4327] Gruen, Rudolph (pf)
- Roycroft 171; 78; 10"; rel
pre-1936

**Roman Sketches: The White
Peacock (orchestral version)
(1919?)**

[4328] Andre Kostelanetz and his
Orchestra; Kostelanetz, Andre
(cond)
- Columbia MG-33728; 33s; 2
discs; rel 1976; del 1979

[4329] CBS Symphony Orchestra; Barlow,
Howard (cond)
- Columbia 17140D; 78; 10"; rel
pre-1940

Roman Sketches: The White Peacock (orchestral version) (1919?) *(cont'd)*

[4330] Eastman-Rochester Symphony Orchestra; Hanson, Howard (cond)
- Victor 15659 (in set M-608); 78; rel 1939
- Victor 12-0155-58 (in set DM-608); 78; 4 discs; rel pre-1942

[4331] Eastman-Rochester Symphony Orchestra; Hanson, Howard (cond) Rec 10/28/54
- Mercury MG-40012; 33m; rel 1955; del 1957
- Mercury MG-50085; 33m; rel 1957; del 1969
- Mercury (English) MRL-2544; 33m; rel 1957*
- Mercury MG-50422/SR-90422; 33m/s; rel 1965; del 1974
- Mercury SRI-75090; 33s; rel 1976*

[4332] National Symphony Orchestra; Mitchell, Howard (cond)
- RCA LE-1009/LES-1009; 33m/s

[4333] New York Philharmonic; Stokowski, Leopold (cond)
- Columbia 19012D; 78; 10"; rel 1948*
- Columbia LP3-117; 78; 7"; rel 1949*
- Columbia ML-2167; 33m; 10"; rel 1951; del 1956
- Columbia A-1516; 45; 7"; rel pre-1953

[4334] Royal Philharmonic Orchestra; Krueger, Karl (cond)
- SPAMH MIA-129; 33s; rel 1966

[4335] orchestra; Piastro, Mishel (cond)
- Decca DL-8573; 33m; rel 1957; del 1962

Roman Sketches: The White Peacock (arr for 2 pfs by Arthur Whittemore and Jack Lowe)

[4336] Whittemore, Arthur (pf); Lowe, Jack (pf)
- Capitol P-8550/SP-8550; 33m/s; rel 1961; del 1967

(Two) Sketches Based on Indian Themes (1918-19?)

[4337] Coolidge String Quartet
- Victor 15416-17 (in set M-558); 78; 2 discs; rel pre-1942
- Victor (Japanese) SD-3067 (in set JAS-236); 78; rel pre-1953 (Excerpt: No 2)

[4338] Delme String Quartet
- SPAMH MIA-117; 33s; rel 1965

[4339] Kohon Quartet
- Vox SVBX-5301; 33s; 3 discs; rel 1971; cip

(Two) Sketches Based on Indian Themes: (No 1) Lento e mesto

[4340] Kreiner String Quartet
- Friends of Recorded Music FRM-5; 78; rel pre-1942

Sonata, Piano (1917-18)

[4341] Behrend, Jeanne (pf)
- Allegro ALG-3024; 33m; rel 1951; del 1952
- Concord 3017; 33m; rel 1957; del 1959

[4342] Hambro, Leonid (pf)
- Walden W-100; 33m; rel 1952; del 1961
- Lyrichord LL-105/LLST-7105; 33m/s; rel 1962/1976; cip

[4343] Lythgoe, Clive (pf)
- Philips 9500.096; 33s; rel 1976; cip

[4344] Mancinelli, Aldo (pf)
- Musical Heritage Society MHS-3695; 33s; rel 1978?

[4345] Masselos, William (pf)
- MGM E-3556; 33m; rel 1958; del 1960

[4346] Potter, Harrison (pf)
- Friends of Recorded Music FRM-10-11; 78; 2 discs; rel pre-1940

[4347] Purves, Del (pf)
- Music Library MLR-7021; 33m; rel 1953; del 1974

[4348] Starr, Susan (pf)
- Orion ORS-77270; 33s; rel 1977; cip

Song of the Dagger (1916)

[4349] Milnes, Sherrill (bar); Spong, Jon (pf)
- New World NW-273; 33s; rel 1977

Symphonische Phantasie (1907)

[4350] Royal Philharmonic Orchestra; Krueger, Karl (cond)
- SPAMH MIA-129; 33s; rel 1966

Tone-Images (Op 3): Symphony in Yellow (1912?)

[4351] Hanks, John Kennedy (ten); Friedberg, Ruth (pf)
- Duke University Press DWR-6417-18; 33m; 2 discs; rel 1966; del 1975

[4352] Myrvik, Norman (ten); Levenson, Emanuel (pf)
- EMS Recordings EMS-501; 33m; rel 1962; del 1970

(Three) Tone-Pictures (Op 5) (1911-12?)

[4353] Engdahl, Leonore (pf)
- MGM E-3225; 33m; rel 1955; del 1959

[4354] Jochum, Veronica (pf)
- Golden Crest CRS-4168; 33s; rel 1978; cip

[4355] Mancinelli, Aldo (pf)
- Musical Heritage Society MHS-3695; 33s; rel 1978?

(Three) Tone-Pictures (Op 5) (1911-12?) *(cont'd)*

[4356] Starr, Susan (pf)
- Orion ORS-77270; 33s; rel 1977; cip

(Three) Tone-Pictures: The Night Winds

[4357] Wells, Howard (pf)
- Educo 3012; 33m; rel 1958; del 1972

(Three) Tone-Pictures (version for piano and double quintet) (1919?)

[4358] American Arts Orchestra; Krueger, Karl (cond)
- SPAMH MIA-104; 33s; rel 1959

[4359] New World Chamber Ensemble
- New World NW-273; 33s; rel 1977

(Three) Tone-Pictures: The Vale of Dreams (arr for orch)

[4360] Hamburg Philharmonic Orchestra; Korn, Richard (cond)
- Allegro ALG-3150; 33m; rel 1955*
- Concord 3007; 33m; rel 1957; del 1959

Wo ich bin, mich rings umdunkelt (1906?)

[4361] Parker, William (bar); Huckaby, William (pf)
- New World NW-305; 33s; rel 1980

Wohl lag ich einst in Gram und Schmerz (1906?)

[4362] Tatum, Nancy (sop); Parsons, Geoffrey (pf)
- London OS-26053; 33s; rel 1968; del 1971
- Decca (English) LXT-6336/SXL-6336; 33m/s; rel 1968*

GRIFFIS, Elliot (1893-1967)

Aztec Flute, The (1942)

[4363] Lewis, Harold (fl)
- Music Library MLR-7076; 33m; rel 1959; del 1974

Frustration

[4364] Griffis, Elliot (pf)
- Salem SR-100; 33m; rel 1959; del 1961

Letters from a Maine Farm

[4365] Carpenter, Richard (pf)
- Educo 3102; 33

[4366] Griffis, Elliot (pf)
- Music Library MLR-7076; 33m; rel 1959; del 1974

Nocturne
[4367] Griffis, Elliot (pf)
- Salem SR-100; 33m; rel 1959; del 1961

Nostalgia
[4368] Griffis, Elliot (pf)
- Salem SR-100; 33m; rel 1959; del 1961

Piece, Piano
[4369] Griffis, Elliot (pf)
- Salem SR-100; 33m; rel 1959; del 1961

Playa Laguna–Arabesque
[4370] Griffis, Elliot (pf)
- Salem SR-100; 33m; rel 1959; del 1961
- Music Library MLR-7076; 33m; rel 1959; del 1974

Set of Eight, A (Poems and Studies) (1921-30)
[4371] Martin, Charlotte (pf)
- Educo ECM-4008; 33m; rel 1961; del 1964

Sonata, Violin and Piano (1931)
[4372] Chassman, Joachim (vln); Griffis, Elliot (pf)
- Educo ECM-4008; 33m; rel 1961; del 1964

Suite, Piano Trio (1941)
[4373] Schoenfeld Trio
- Music Library MLR-7076; 33m; rel 1959; del 1974

Tapestry
[4374] Griffis, Elliot (pf)
- Salem SR-100; 33m; rel 1959; del 1961

Transmutations
[4375] Griffis, Elliot (pf)
- Salem SR-100; 33m; rel 1959; del 1961

Yellow Rose
[4376] Griffis, Elliot (pf)
- Salem SR-100; 33m; rel 1959; del 1961

GRIFFITH, Peter (1943-)
One String Quartet (ca 1970)
[4377] Composers Quartet
- CRI-265; 33s; rel 1971; cip

GRIFFITH, Robert B. (1914-)
Courier Journal March
[4378] Eastern Brass Quintet
- Klavier KS-539; 33s; rel 1975; cip

GRILLER, Arnold (1937-)
Symphony, Eight Celli and Piano
[4379] San Francisco Chamber Ensemble; Griller, Arnold (cond)
- Music Library MLR-7070; 33m; rel 1961; del 1974

GRISELLE, Thomas (1891-1955)
(Two) American Sketches (1928)
[4380] Victor Orchestra; Shilkret, Nathaniel (cond)
- Victor Special (Autographed); 78
- Victor 36000; 78

(Two) American Sketches: Nocturne
[4381] Morton Gould and his Orchestra; Gould, Morton (cond)
- Columbia ML-2144; 33m; 10"; rel 1950; del 1956

GROFE, Ferde (1892-1972)
Atlantic Crossing
[4382] Dolin, Anton (nar); Le Vane, Ethel (nar); George Mitchell Chorus; New Symphony Orchestra; Grofe, Ferde (cond)
- London LLP-277; 33m; rel 1951; del 1957
- Decca LK-4037; 33m; rel pre-1952
- Everest LPBR-6139/SDBR-3139; 33m/s; rel 1966; del 1979

Aviation Suite
[4383] Hollywood Studio Orchestra; Grofe, Ferde (cond)
- Remington 3; 33m; 10"; rel 1950; del 1951

Concerto, Piano and Orchestra
[4384] Sanroma, Jesus Maria (pf); Rochester Philharmonic Orchestra; Grofe, Ferde (cond)
- Everest LPBR-6044/SDBR-3044; 33m/s; rel 1960; cip

Death Valley Suite
[4385] Capitol Symphony Orchestra; Grofe, Ferde (cond)
- Capitol H-271; 33m; 10"; rel 1951; del 1955
- Capitol P-272; 33m; rel 1951; del 1956
- Capitol EBF-271; 45; 7"; rel pre-1953
- Capitol L-271; 33m; 10"; rel 1955; del 1957
- Capitol T-272/DT-272; 33m/s; rel 1956/1966; del 1970
- Angel S-36089; 33s; rel 1975; cip

Grand Canyon Suite (1931)
[4386] Andre Kostelanetz and his Orchestra; Kostelanetz, Andre (cond)
- Columbia 7381-84M (in set M-463); 78; 4 discs; rel pre-1942

Grand Canyon Suite (1931) *(cont'd)*
- Columbia (English) DOX-707-10; 78; 4 discs; rel pre-1942
- Columbia 7390M; 78; rel pre-1942 (Excerpt: On the Trail)
- Columbia DX-1878; 78; rel pre-1956 (Excerpt: On the Trail)
- Columbia CQX-16669; 78; rel pre-1956 (Excerpt: On the Trail)
- Columbia ML-4059; 33m; rel pre-1949; del 1955
- Columbia CL-716; 33m; rel 1955; del 1965
- Columbia A-1088; 45; 7"; rel pre-1956
- Columbia CL-1622/CS-8422; 33m/s; rel 1961; del 1968
- Harmony HL-7395/HS-11195; 33m/s; rel 1966; del 1975
- Columbia MS-7425; 33s; rel 1970; del 1973

[4387] Boston Pops Orchestra; Fiedler, Arthur (cond)
- RCA LM-1928; 33m; rel 1955; del 1968
- Victor ERB-66; 45; 7"; rel pre-1956
- RCA LM-2789/LSC-2789; 33m/s; rel 1965; cip
- RCA-Victrola VICS-1423; 33s; rel 1969; cip
- RCA LSC-3303; 33s; rel 1972; cip

[4388] Capitol Symphony Orchestra; Grofe, Ferde (cond)
- Capitol P-272; 33m; rel 1951; del 1956
- Capitol L-270; 33m; 10"; rel 1951; del 1956
- Capitol LC-6536; 33m; 10"; rel pre-1953
- Capitol ECF-270; 45; 7"; rel pre-1953
- Capitol (Australian) CLP-002; 33m; rel pre-1956
- Capitol FAP-8207; 45; 7"; rel pre-1956 (excerpts)
- Capitol H-270; 33m; 10"; rel 1956; del 1957
- Capitol T-272/DT-272; 33m/s; rel 1956/1966; del 1970
- Capitol P-8523/SP-8523; 33m/s; rel 1960; del 1970 (Excerpt: On the Trail)
- Angel S-36089; 33s; rel 1975; cip

[4389] Eastman-Rochester Symphony Orchestra; Hanson, Howard (cond)
Rec 5/5/58
- Mercury MG-50049/SR-90049; 33m/s; rel 1959; del 1971

[4390] Graunke Symphony Orchestra; Stark, Frederick (cond)
- Disneyland 4019; 33m/s; rel 1959; cip

[4391] Hamburg Philharmonic Orchestra; Walther, Hans-Jurgen (cond)
- Design DCF-61; 33s; rel 1960; del 1961
- Design DLP-123; 33m; rel 1960; del 1962

Grand Canyon Suite (1931) (cont'd)
- Design DLP-1005/DCF-1005; 33m/s; rel 1960; del 1963
- Summit SUM-1062; 33s; rel 1977

[4392] Hollywood Bowl Symphony Orchestra; Slatkin, Felix (cond)
- Capitol P-8347/SP-8347; 33m/s; rel 1956/1958; del 1970
- Capitol P-8591/SP-8591; 33m/s; rel 1963 (Excerpt: On the Trail)
- Angel S-36084; 33s; rel 1975; del 1978

[4393] Ira Wright Orchestra; Wright, Ira (cond)
- Rondo-lette 91; 33s; rel 1959; del 1963

[4394] London Festival Orchestra; Black, Stanley (cond)
- London SPC-21002; 33s; rel 1964; cip

[4395] Morton Gould and his Orchestra; Gould, Morton (cond)
- RCA LM-2433/LSC-2433; 33m/s; rel 1960; del 1975
- Quintessence PMC-7043; 33s; rel 1978; cip

[4396] NBC Symphony Orchestra; Toscanini, Arturo (cond)
- Victor 11-9074-77 (in set M-1038); 78; 4 discs; rel pre-1948
- Gramophone DB-6327-30; 78; 4 discs; rel pre-1948
- Victor WDM-1038; 45; 4-7"; rel pre-1948
- RCA LM-1004; 33m; rel 1950; del 1970
- Victor ERC-3; 45; 4-7"; rel pre-1953
- Victor WEPR-15; 45; 7"; rel pre-1953 (Excerpt: On the Trail)
- Gramophone ALP-1232; 33m; rel pre-1956
- RCA (Italian) A12R-0075; 33m; rel pre-1956
- RCA (Dutch) L-16466; 33m; rel pre-1956
- Gramophone 7ER-5012; 45; 7"; rel pre-1956 (Excerpt: On the Trail)
- Victor (Italian) A72R-0041; 45; 7"; rel pre-1956 (Excerpt: On the Trail)
- RCA AVM-1-1737; 33m; rel 1976; cip

[4397] New York Philharmonic; Bernstein, Leonard (cond)
- Columbia ML-6018/MS-6618; 33m/s; rel 1964; cip
- Columbia ML-6388/MS-6988; 33m/s; rel 1967; cip (Excerpt: On the Trail)
- Columbia MG-31155; 33s; 2 discs; rel 1972 (Excerpt: On the Trail)
- Columbia M3X-31068; 33s; 3 discs; rel 1972; cip (Excerpt: On the Trail)

Grand Canyon Suite (1931) (cont'd)
- Columbia M-31824; 33s; rel 1973; cip

[4398] Oslo Philharmonic Orchestra; Fjeldstad, Oivin (cond)
- Camden CAL-468/CAS-468; 33m/s; rel 1959; del 1970

[4399] Paul Whiteman Orchestra; Whiteman, Paul (cond)
- Victor 36052-55 (in set C-18); 78; 4 discs; rel pre-1936
- Gramophone C-2473-76 (in set 165); 78; 4 discs; rel pre-1936
- Victor 36095; 78; rel pre-1936 (Excerpt: On the Trail)

[4400] Philadelphia Orchestra; Ormandy, Eugene (cond)
- Columbia ML-5286/MS-6003; 33m/s; rel 1958; cip
- Columbia MS-7289; 33s; rel 1969; cip (Excerpt: On the Trail)
- Columbia M-30446; 33s; rel 1971; cip

[4401] Rochester Philharmonic Orchestra; Grofe, Ferde (cond)
- Everest LPBR-6044/SDBR-3044; 33m/s; rel 1960; cip

[4402] Utah Symphony Orchestra; Abravanel, Maurice (cond)
- Westminster XWN-18850/WST-14065; 33m/s; rel 1959; del 1967
- Music Guild MS-169; 33s; rel 1970; del 1971
- Westminster WGS-8186; 33s; rel 1973; cip
- Angel S-37314; 33s; rel 1978; cip
- Angel SS-45028; 33s; rel 1979; cip

Grand Canyon Suite: Painted Desert, On the Trail, and Cloudburst
[4403] Hugo Winterhalter Orchestra
- RCA LBC-1045; 33m; rel 1953; del 1957
- RCA (French) A-530201; 33m; rel pre-1956
- RCA LPM-1020; 33m; rel pre-1956 (Excerpt: On the Trail)
- Victor WBC-1045; 45; 7"; rel pre-1956

Grand Canyon Suite: On the Trail
[4404] New York Philharmonic; Kostelanetz, Andre (cond)
- Columbia ML-5463/MS-6133; 33m/s; rel 1960; del 1965

[4405] orchestra; Shankson, Louis (cond)
- Allegro-Royale 1609; 33m; rel pre-1956
- Allegro-Royale EP-357; 45; 7"; rel pre-1956

Grand Canyon Suite: On the Trail (arr for voice and orch)
[4406] Jones, Allan (ten); Armbruster, Robert (cond)
- RCA LM-95; 33m; rel 1951*

Hudson River Suite (1955)
[4407] New York Philharmonic; Kostelanetz, Andre (cond)
- Columbia CL-763; 33m; rel 1955; del 1959

March for Americans
[4408] Meredith Willson Orchestra; Willson, Meredith (cond)
- Decca 29104 (in set A-219); 78; rel pre-1952
- Decca DL-8025; 33m; rel 1950; del 1961

Metropolis (A Blue Fantasia)
[4409] Paul Whiteman Orchestra
- Victor 35933-34; 78; 2 discs; rel pre-1936

Mississippi Suite
[4410] Andre Kostelanetz and his Orchestra; Kostelanetz, Andre (cond)
- Columbia 7569-70M (in set X-284); 78; 2 discs; rel pre-1948
- Columbia MX-284; 78; rel pre-1952
- Columbia ML-2046; 33m; 10"; rel pre-1949; del 1956
- Columbia ML-4059; 33m; rel pre-1949; del 1955
- Columbia ML-4625; 33m; rel 1953; del 1956
- Columbia CL-864; 33m; rel 1957; del 1962

[4411] Eastman-Rochester Symphony Orchestra; Hanson, Howard (cond)
Rec 5/5/58
- Mercury MG-50049/SR-90049; 33m/s; rel 1959; del 1971

[4412] Hollywood Bowl Symphony Orchestra; Slatkin, Felix (cond)
- Capitol P-8347/SP-8347; 33m/s; rel 1956/1958; del 1970

[4413] New York Philharmonic; Kostelanetz, Andre (cond)
- Columbia ML-5463/MS-6133; 33m/s; rel 1960; del 1965

[4414] Paul Whiteman Orchestra; Whiteman, Paul (cond)
- Victor 35859; 78; rel pre-1936

Mississippi Suite: Huckleberry Finn and Mardi Gras
[4415] orchestra; Shankson, Louis (cond)
- Allegro-Royale 1609; 33m; rel pre-1956
- Allegro-Royale EP-357; 45; 7"; rel pre-1956 (Excerpt: Mardi Gras)

Mississippi Suite: Huckleberry Finn

[4416] Hamburg Philharmonia; Korn, Richard (cond)
- Allegro ALG-3149; 33m; rel 1954?

Mississippi Suite: Mardi Gras

[4417] New Century Orchestra; Torch, Sydney (cond)
- FDH 001; 78; rel pre-1956

[4418] Pro Arte Orchestra; Vinter, Gilbert (cond)
- Capitol P-8642/SP-8642; 33m/s; rel 1966; del 1969

(Three) Shades of Blue (Suite)

[4419] Paul Whiteman Orchestra; Whiteman, Paul (cond)
- Victor 35952; 78; rel pre-1936
- Gramophone C-4874; 78; rel pre-1952

Trick or Treat

[4420] Andre Kostelanetz and his Orchestra; Kostelanetz, Andre (cond)
- Columbia MG-33728; 33s; 2 discs; rel 1976; del 1979

World's Fair Suite (1964) (arr for orch by Glasser)

[4421] World's Fair Symphony Orchestra; Lavalle, Paul (cond)
- RCA LM-2764/LSC-2764; 33m/s; rel 1964; del 1966

GROSS, Robert (1914-)

Chacounne, a Song, Ooh

[4422] Gross, Robert (vln); Bush, Norelee (sop)
- Orion ORS-76239; 33s; rel 1977; cip

Epode (1955)

[4423] Rejto, Gabor (vcl)
- CRI-208; 33m/s; rel 1966/?; cip

Passacaglia

[4424] Gross, Robert (vln); Grayson, Richard (org)
- Orion ORS-76239; 33s; rel 1977; cip

3-4-2

[4425] Gross, Robert (vln); Solow, Jeffrey (vcl)
- Orion ORS-76239; 33s; rel 1977; cip

GRUEN, John (1927-)

Birds, The

[4426] Concert Chorus
- Contemporary AP-122; 33m; rel pre-1956

Chansons de geishas

[4427] Bannister, Georgiana (sop); Gruen, John (pf)
- Elektra EKL-1; 33m; rel 1952; del 1957

Haelfte des Lebens

[4428] Bannister, Georgiana (sop); Gruen, John (pf)
- Elektra EKL-1; 33m; rel 1952; del 1957

(Three) Poems by e. e. cummings

[4429] McCollum, John (ten); Biltcliffe, Edwin (pf)
- St/And SPL-411-12; 33m; 2 discs; rel 1963; del 1964
- Desto D-411-12/DST-6411-12; 33m/s; 2 discs; rel 1964; cip

(Seven) Poems Penyeach

[4430] Neway, Patricia (sop); Gruen, John (pf)
- Contemporary AP-121; 33m; rel 1953; del 1958

(Seven) Poems Penyeach: Alone, Bahnhofstrasse, and Watching the Needleboats at San Sabba

[4431] Neway, Patricia (sop); Colston, Robert (pf)
- Lyrichord LL-83; 33m; rel 1959; del 1978

Sirenen, Die

[4432] Bannister, Georgiana (sop); Gruen, John (pf)
- Elektra EKL-1; 33m; rel 1952; del 1957

(Four) Songs

[4433] Bannister, Georgiana (sop); Gruen, John (pf)
- Elektra EKL-1; 33m; rel 1952; del 1957

(Four) Stundenbuch-Lieder

[4434] Bannister, Georgiana (sop); Gruen, John (pf)
- Elektra EKL-1; 33m; rel 1952; del 1957

Sweet Was the Song

[4435] Concert Chorus
- Contemporary AP-122; 33m; rel pre-1956

Thirteen Ways of Looking at a Blackbird

[4436] Neway, Patricia (sop); Gruen, John (pf)
- Contemporary AP-121; 33m; rel 1953; del 1958

GRUENBERG, Louis (1884-1964)

Concerto, Violin and Orchestra (Op 47) (1944)

[4437] Heifetz, Jascha (vln); San Francisco Symphony Orchestra; Monteux, Pierre (cond)
Rec 12/45
- Victor 11-9376-79 (in set M-1079); 78; 4 discs; rel pre-1948
- RCA LCT-1160; 33m; rel 1955; del 1956
- RCA (French) A-630291; 33m; rel pre-1956
- RCA LVT-1017; 33m; rel 1956; cip

Daniel Jazz, The (Op 21) (1924)

[4438] Lewis, William (ten); Kohon Ensemble
- Amrex LTG-0100-101; 33s; rel 1974

Emperor Jones, The (Op 36) (1931): Scenes

[4439] Tibbett, Lawrence (bar)
- Rococo 5324; 33m; rel 1970; del 1975

Emperor Jones, The: Standin' in the Need of Prayer

[4440] London, George (bar); Columbia Symphony Orchestra; Morel, Jean (cond)
- Columbia ML-4999; 33m; rel 1955; del 1958
- Odyssey Y-32669; 33m; rel 1974; cip

[4441] Tibbett, Lawrence (bar); Metropolitan Opera Orchestra; Pelletier, Wilfred (cond)
Rec 1/19/34
- Victor 7959; 78; rel pre-1936
- New World NW-241; 33m; rel 1978

Polychromatics (Op 16) (1924)

[4442] Shaulis, Zola (pf)
- CRI-295; 33s; rel 1973; cip

(Five) Variations on a Popular Theme (1942)

[4443] Kohon Quartet
- Amrex LTG-0100-101; 33s; rel 1974

GRUNDMAN, Clare Ewing (1913-)

American Civil War Suite (The Blue and the Gray)

[4444] H. M. Royal Marines Band; Neville, Paul (cond)
- Arabesque 8006; 33s; rel 1980; cip

Blue-Tail Fly, The
[4445] Royal Artillery Band; Geary, Col.
Owen W. (cond)
- Boosey & Hawkes
BH-MTLP-2030; 33m; rel 1954

Fantasy on American Sailing Songs
[4446] Royal Artillery Band; Geary, Col.
Owen W. (cond)
- Boosey & Hawkes
BH-MTLP-2030; 33m; rel 1954

Spirit of '76, The
[4447] Concord Band; Toland, William M.
(cond)
Rec 10/20/75
- Vogt Quality Recordings
CSRV-2503; 33s; rel 1975

Westchester Overture, A (1952)
[4448] Royal Artillery Band; Geary, Col.
Owen W. (cond)
- Boosey & Hawkes
BH-MTLP-2030; 33m; rel 1954

GUINALDO, Norberto (1937-)

Chorale Prelude on Come Thou Almighty King
[4449] Guinaldo, Norberto (org)
- Advent USR-5002; 33s; rel 1972

Chorale Prelude on How Great the Wisdom
[4450] Guinaldo, Norberto (org)
- Advent USR-5002; 33s; rel 1972

Chorale Prelude on How Long, O Lord
[4451] Guinaldo, Norberto (org)
- Advent USR-5002; 33s; rel 1972

Chorale Prelude on Oh, How Lovely
[4452] Guinaldo, Norberto (org)
- Advent USR-5002; 33s; rel 1972

Chorale Prelude on Praise to the Man
[4453] Guinaldo, Norberto (org)
- Advent USR-5002; 33s; rel 1972

Chorale Prelude on Prayer is the Soul's Sincere Desire
[4454] Guinaldo, Norberto (org)
- Advent USR-5002; 33s; rel 1972

Chorale Prelude on While of These Emblems
[4455] Guinaldo, Norberto (org)
- Advent USR-5002; 33s; rel 1972

Fantasia on Come, Come Ye Saints
[4456] Guinaldo, Norberto (org)
- Advent USR-5002; 33s; rel 1972

Prelude for the Passion of Our Lord
[4457] Guinaldo, Norberto (org)
- Advent USR-5002; 33s; rel 1972

GUION, David W. (1892-1981)

All Day Long on the Prairie
[4458] Melton, James (ten)
- Victor 10-1237 (in set M-1060);
78; 10''; rel pre-1948

Country Jig
[4459] Behrend, Jeanne (pf)
- Victor 17911 (in set M-764);
78; rel 1941

Mary Alone
[4460] Tatum, Nancy (sop); Parsons,
Geoffrey (pf)
- London OS-26053; 33s; rel
1968; del 1971

Mother Goose Suite: Hickory Dickory Dock and The North Wind Doth Blow
[4461] Bianca, Sondra (pf)
- Music Sound Books 21; 78; rel
pre-1956
- Music Sound Books 60041;
33m; rel pre-1956

(Three) Scenes from the South: The Harmonica Player
[4462] Janis, Byron (pf)
- Mercury MG-50305/SR-90305;
33m/s; rel 1962; del 1967

(Three) Scenes from the South: The Harmonica Player (arr for harmonica)
[4463] Sebastian, John (harmonica)
- Victor P-166; 78; 10''; rel
pre-1952

(Three) Scenes from the South: The Harmonica Player (arr for hn and orch by Eger-Rosenthal)
[4464] Eger, Joseph (hn); Victor
Orchestra; Rosenstock, Joseph
(cond)
- RCA LM-2146; 33m; rel 1957;
del 1960

Sheep and Goat Walkin' to Pasture
[4465] Eaver, Myrtle (pf)
- Victor 24532; 78; 10''; rel
pre-1936

[4466] Grainger, Percy (pf)
- Columbia 7134M; 78; rel
pre-1936

Sheep and Goat Walkin' to Pasture (arr for orch)
[4467] Boston Pops Orchestra; Fiedler,
Arthur (cond)
- Victor 10-1092 (in set M-968);
78; 10''; rel 1944

Texas (Suite)
[4468] Houston Summer Symphony
Orchestra; Rachlin, Ezra (cond)
- Carsan LP-1002; 33m; rel 1966

GUTCHE, Gene (1907-)

Bongo Divertimento (Op 35) (1962)
[4469] Dahlgren, Marvin (perc); St. Paul
Chamber Orchestra; Sipe, Leopold
(cond)
- St. Paul 96585-86/S-96583-84;
33m/s; rel 1964; del 1970

Genghis Khan (Op 37)
[4470] Louisville Orchestra; Mester, Jorge
(cond)
- LS-72-2; 33s (Louisville
Orchestra First Edition Records
1972 No 2); rel 1973; cip

Icarus (Op 48)
[4471] Rochester Philharmonic Orchestra;
Zinman, David (cond)
Rec 4/4/77
- Turnabout TVS-34705; 33s; rel
1978; cip

Symphony No 5 (Op 34) (1962)
[4472] Cincinnati Symphony Orchestra;
Rudolf, Max (cond)
- CRI-189; 33s; rel 1965; cip

GYRING, Elizabeth (1886-1970)

Sonata, Piano, No 2 (1957)
[4473] Andrews, Mitchell (pf)
- CRI-252; 33s; rel 1970; cip

HA, Jae Eun (1937-)

(Three) Pieces, Tuba
[4474] Cummings, Barton (tu)
- Crystal S-391; 33s; rel 1978; cip

HABER, Louis (1915-)

(Six) Miniatures, Flute and Violin
[4475] Musical Arts Trio
- Serenus SRE-1018/SRS-12018;
33m/s; rel 1967; cip

Trio, Flute, Violin, and Piano
[4476] Musical Arts Trio
- Serenus SRE-1018/SRS-12018;
33m/s; rel 1967; cip

HACKBARTH, Glenn (1949-)

Double Concerto, Trumpet, Tuba, and Chamber Orchestra
[4477] Hickman, David (tpt); Perantoni,
Daniel (tu); Illinois Contemporary
Chamber Players; Zonn, Paul
(cond)
- Crystal S-394; 33s; rel 1978

HADDAD, Don (1935-)

Blues au vent
[4478] American Woodwind Quintet
- Golden Crest
CR-4075/CRS-4075; 33m/s; rel
1966/1967; cip

Suite, Tuba
[4479] Conner, Rex (tu)
- Coronet M-1259; 33m; rel 1969; cip

HADLEY, Henry (1871-1937)

Concertino, Piano and Orchestra (Op 131) (1937)
[4480] Howard, Eunice (pf); Victor Symphony Orchestra; James, Philip (cond)
- Victor 12599-600 (in set M-634); 78; 2 discs; rel pre-1942

Culprit Fay, The (1909)
[4481] National High School Orchestra; Maddy, Joseph (cond)
- Interlochen National Music Camp NMC-1957-19; 33m; rel 1957

Elegie (arr for org by Charles Courboin)
[4482] Courboin, Charles (org)
- Victor 18085; 78; rel pre-1942
- Gramophone ED-331; 78; rel pre-1952

Evening Song (Op 53, No 3)
[4483] McCormack, John (ten)
- Victor 64496; 78; 10"; rel 1913-15
- Victor 760; 78; 10"; rel 1913-15

I Sing of a Maiden That Is Makeless
[4484] St. Luke's Chapel Choir of Men and Boys; Clark (cond)
- Lyrichord LLST-7249; 33s; rel 1973*

Marguerites
[4485] orchestra
- Ginn Educational Series G-12A; 78; rel pre-1927

October Twilight (Op 95, No 2)
[4486] Victor Symphony Orchestra; James, Philip (cond)
- Victor 12600 (in set M-634); 78; rel pre-1942

Quintet, Piano and Strings (Op 50) (1920)
[4487] Byman, Isabelle (pf); Kohon Quartet
- Vox SVBX-5301; 33s; 3 discs; rel 1971; cip

Salome (1905)
[4488] Royal Philharmonic Orchestra; Krueger, Karl (cond)
- SPAMH MIA-138; 33s; rel 1968*

Scherzo diabolique (1934)
[4489] Hamburg Philharmonia; Korn, Richard (cond)
- Allegro ALG-3150; 33m; rel 1955*

Scherzo diabolique (1934) (cont'd)
- Concord 3007; 33m; rel 1957; del 1959

Symphony No 2 (The Four Seasons) (Op 30) (1901)
[4490] Royal Philharmonic Orchestra; Krueger, Karl (cond)
- SPAMH MIA-145; 33s; rel 1969

HAGEMAN, Richard (1882-1966)

At the Well
[4491] Cotlow, Marilyn (sop); Stafford, Claire (pf)
- Victor 10-1467A; 78; 10"; rel 1949
- Victor 49-0679; 45; 7"; rel pre-1952

Caponsacchi (1931): This Very Vivid Morn and Lullaby
[4492] Jepson, Helen (sop); orchestra; Smallens, Alexander (cond)
- Victor 14183; 78; rel pre-1942

Christ Went Up into the Hills
[4493] McCormack, John (ten); orchestra
- Victor 6708; 78; rel pre-1942
- Camden CAL-635; 33m; rel 1960; del 1972

Do Not Go, My Love (1917)
[4494] Bampton, Rose (al); Pelletier, Wilfred (pf)
Rec 9/22/32
- Victor 10-1118 (in set 1607); 78; 10"; rel pre-1948
- Gramophone DA-1855; 78; 10"; rel pre-1952
- New World NW-247; 33m; rel 1976

[4495] D'Alvarez, Marguerite (al); piano
- Victor 1116; 78; 10"; rel 1925

[4496] Evans, Nancy (al); Moore, Gerald (pf)
- Decca K-866; 78; rel pre-1948
- Decca Z-775; 78; rel pre-1952

[4497] Hanks, John Kennedy (ten); Friedberg, Ruth (pf)
- Duke University Press DWR-6417-18; 33m; 2 discs; rel 1966; del 1975

[4498] MacDonald, Jeanette (sop); Bamboschek, Giuseppe (pf)
- Victor 2047 (in set M-642); 78; 10"; rel pre-1942

[4499] Milanov, Zinka (sop); Kunc, Bozidar (pf)
- RCA LM-1915; 33m; rel 1955; del 1958

[4500] Moore, Dale (bar); Tomfohrde, Betty Ruth (pf)
- Cambridge CRS-2715; 33s; rel 1973; cip

[4501] Warenskjold, Dorothy (sop); Crossan, Jack (pf)
- Capitol P-8333; 33m; rel 1956; del 1961

Donkey, The
[4502] Hammond, Joan (sop); Moore, Gerald (pf)
- Gramophone B-9503; 78; 10"; rel pre-1948

Miranda
[4503] Melton, James (ten); Hill, Robert (pf)
- Victor 10-1051 (in set M-947); 78; 10"; rel pre-1948

Music I Heard with You
[4504] Amara, Lucine (sop); Benedict, David (pf)
- Cambridge CRM-704/CRS-1704; 33m/s; rel 1963; del 1975

HAGEN, Earle H.

Claudia's Letter
[4505] Lord, Marjorie (nar); chorus; orchestra; Hagen, Earle H. (cond)
Rec 3/62
- Fan Record FAN-ST-1002; 33; rel 1962

HAGER, Fred W.

Assembly March, The
[4506] Prince's Band
- Columbia S-3042; 78; 10"

HAIEFF, Alexei (1914-)

(Three) Bagatelles, Harpsichord (1955)
[4507] Marlowe, Sylvia (hpschd)
- Decca DL-10001/DL-710001; 33m/s; rel 1959; del 1972

Bagatelles, Oboe and Bassoon (1940-55)
[4508] Boston Symphony Chamber Players
- RCA LM-6184/LSC-6184; 33m/s; 3 discs; rel 1968; del 1976

Ballet in E (1955)
[4509] Louisville Orchestra; Whitney, Robert (cond)
- LOU-58-1; 33m (Louisville Orchestra First Edition Records 1958 No 1); rel 1959; del 1975

Concerto, Piano and Orchestra (1951)
[4510] Bianca, Sondra (pf); Hamburg Philharmonia; Walther, Hans-Jurgen (cond)
- MGM E-3243; 33m; rel 1955; del 1959

[4511] Smit, Leo (pf); Vienna Symphony Orchestra; Hendl, Walter (cond)
- American Recording Society ARS-9; 33m; rel 1952*
- Desto D-420/DST-6420; 33m/s; rel 1966; cip
- Serenus SRS-12086; 33s; rel 1979; cip

Divertimento, Small Orchestra (1944)
[4512] Louisville Orchestra; Whitney, Robert (cond)
- LOU-61-1; 33m (Louisville Orchestra First Edition Records 1961 No 1); rel 1961; del 1975

(Four) Juke Box Pieces
[4513] Smit, Leo (pf)
- MGM E-3243; 33m; rel 1955; del 1959

(Five) Pieces, Piano
[4514] Smit, Leo (pf)
- MGM E-3243; 33m; rel 1955; del 1959

Quartet, Strings, No 1 (1951)
[4515] Juilliard String Quartet
- Columbia ML-4988; 33m; rel 1955; del 1968
- Columbia CML-4988; 33m; rel 1968; del 1976

Sonata, Two Pianos (1945)
[4516] Gold, Arthur (pf); Fizdale, Robert (pf)
Rec 9/10/52
- Columbia ML-4853-55 (in set SL-198); 33m; 3 discs; rel 1954; del 1958

Symphony No 2 (1958)
[4517] Boston Symphony Orchestra; Munch, Charles (cond)
- RCA LM-2352/LSC-2352; 33m/s; rel 1960; del 1963
- Serenus SRS-12086; 33s; rel 1979; cip

HAILSTORK, Adolphus C. (1941-)

Celebration!
[4518] Detroit Symphony Orchestra; Freeman, Paul (cond)
- Columbia M-34556; 33s; rel 1978; del 1979

HAINES, Edmund (1914-74)

Concertino, Seven Solo Instruments and Orchestra (1959)
[4519] Oklahoma City Symphony Orchestra; Harrison, Guy Fraser (cond)
- CRI-153; 33m/s; rel 1962/?; cip

Promenade, Air, and Toccata
[4520] Crozier, Catharine (org)
- Kendall KRC-LP-2555; 33m; rel 1953; del 1958

Quartet, Strings, No 4 (1957)
[4521] Oxford String Quartet
- CRI-188; 33m; rel 1965; cip

Sonata, Harp
[4522] Chertok, Pearl (hp)
- Orion ORS-75207; 33s; rel 1976; cip

Toccata, Brass
[4523] Ars Nova Brass Quintet
- Musical Heritage Society MHS-1446; 33s; rel 1972
[4524] Chicago Symphony Brass Ensemble
- Audiophile AP-21; 33m; rel pre-1956
[4525] Dallas Brass Quintet
- Crystal S-203; 33s; rel 1979; cip
[4526] New York Brass Quintet
- Golden Crest CR-4023/CRS-4023; 33m/s; rel 1960; cip

HAKIM, Talib Rasul (1940-)

Placements (1970)
[4527] Chambers, Joe (perc); Clay, Omar (perc); Smith, Warren (perc); Burton, Barbara (perc); Moorman, Wilson (perc); Cowell, Stanley (pf); Hakim, Talib Rasul (cond)
- Folkways FTS-33903; 33s; rel 1976; cip

Shapes (1965)
[4528] Oakland Youth Orchestra; Hughes, Robert (cond)
- Desto DC-7107; 33s; rel 1970; cip

Sound-Gone (1967)
[4529] Hinderas, Natalie (pf)
- Desto DC-7102-03; 33s; 2 discs; rel 1970; cip

Visions of Ishwara (1970)
[4530] Baltimore Symphony Orchestra; Freeman, Paul (cond)
- Columbia M-33434; 33s; rel 1975; del 1979

HALL, James (1930-)

Piece, Guitar and Strings
[4531] Hall, James (gtr); Contemporary String Quartet
- Atlantic 1365/SD-1365; 33m/s; rel 1961; del 1968

HALL, John T.

Wedding of the Winds
[4532] Deiro, Pietro (acc)
- Victor 17865; 78

HALLEY, Glenn

March of the Legionnaires
[4533] American Legion Band; Colling, Joe (cond)
- Decca 25426-29 (in set A-713); 78; 4-10"; rel 1949

HAMILTON, Thomas (1946-)

Pieces for Kohn
[4534] Electronic music
- Somnath KH-120; 33s; rel 1978; cip

HAMM, Charles (1925-)

Canto (1963)
[4535] Electronic music
- Heliodor H-25047/HS-25047; 33m/s; rel 1967; del 1970

Something Else for Ellsworth Snyder
[4536] Snyder, Ellsworth (pf)
- Advance FGR-21S; 33s; rel 197?

HAMMOND, Don (1917-)

Quintet, Brass
[4537] New York Brass Quintet
- Golden Crest CR-4017/CRS-4017; 33m/s; rel 1960/1961; cip

HAMPTON, Calvin (1938-)

Catch-Up (1967)
[4538] Pappastavrou, George C. (pf); Lanning, Stuart Warren (pf); tape
- Odyssey 32-16-0161/32-16-0162; 33m/s; rel 1967; cip

Triple Play (1967)
[4539] Pappastavrou, George C. (pf); Lanning, Stuart Warren (pf); McGill, Helen (ondes martenot); Macero, Teo (cond)
- Odyssey 32-16-0161/32-16-0162; 33m/s; rel 1967; cip

HANCOCK, Gerre (1934-)

Air
[4540] Swann, Frederick (org)
- Saville Organ Corp 853S-2000; 33s; rel 1968

Improvisations
[4541] Hancock, Gerre (org)
Rec 7/26-27/71
- Audiocraft; 33s; rel 1972

HANNA, Stephen (1950-)

Sonic Sauce (1976)
[4542] Sonic Boom Percussion Ensemble
- Crystal S-140; 33s; rel 1977; cip

HANSON, Howard (1896-1981)

Bell, The
[4543] Martin, Charlotte (pf)
- Educo 3021; 33m; rel 1968; del 1972

Centennial Ode (1950)
[4544] Treash, Leonard (speaker); Myers, D. (bar); Eastman School of Music Chorus; Eastman-Rochester Symphony Orchestra; Hanson, Howard (cond)
- Eastman LP-1; 33m; rel 1951; del 1959

Cherubic Hymn, The (Op 37) (1949)
[4545] Bach Chorus; Carnegie Institute of Technology Chorus and Orchestra; Hanson, Howard (cond)
- ASCAP CB-162; 33m (Pittsburgh International Contemporary Music Festival); rel 1954

[4546] Eastman School of Music Chorus; Eastman-Rochester Symphony Orchestra; Hanson, Howard (cond)
Rec 1954
- Mercury MG-40014; 33m; rel 1956; del 1957
- Mercury MG-50087; 33m; rel 1957; del 1964
- Eastman-Rochester Archives ERA-1014; 33s; rel 1978; cip

Chorale and Alleluia (1953)
[4547] Eastman Symphonic Wind Ensemble; Fennell, Frederick (cond)
Rec Spring 1954
- Mercury MG-40011; 33m; rel 1954; del 1957
- Mercury MG-50084; 33m; rel 1957; del 1969

[4548] Royal Canadian Air Force Concert Band; Hunt, Clifford (cond)
- CBC Transcription Programme 256; 33s; rel 196?

Clap Your Hands
[4549] Cantica Hebraica; Michno, Dennis (cond)
- JML-3812; 33s; rel 1977?

Concerto, Organ, Harp, and Strings (1921)
[4550] Ellsasser, Richard (org); Hamburg Philharmonia; Winograd, Arthur (cond)
- MGM E-3361; 33m; rel 1956; del 1959

Concerto, Piano and Orchestra (Op 36) (1948)
[4551] Firkusny, Rudolf (pf); Eastman-Rochester Symphony Orchestra; Hanson, Howard (cond)
- Columbia ML-4403; 33m; rel 1951; del 1956

Concerto, Piano and Orchestra (Op 36) (1948) *(cont'd)*
[4552] Mouledous, Alfred (pf); Eastman-Rochester Symphony Orchestra; Hanson, Howard (cond)
- Mercury MG-50430/SR-90430; 33m/s; rel 1965; del 1969
- Eastman-Rochester Archives ERA-1006; 33s; rel 1976; cip

Dance of the Warriors
[4553] Martin, Charlotte (pf)
- Educo 3021; 33m; rel 1968; del 1972

Elegy (Op 44) (1956)
[4554] Eastman-Rochester Symphony Orchestra; Hanson, Howard (cond)
- Mercury MG-50150/SR-90150; 33m/s; rel 1957/1960; del 1964
- Eastman-Rochester Archives ERA-1010; 33s; rel 1976; cip

Enchantment
[4555] Martin, Charlotte (pf)
- Educo 3021; 33m; rel 1968; del 1972

Fantasy-Variations on a Theme of Youth (Op 40) (1951)
[4556] Burge, David (pf); Eastman-Rochester Symphony Orchestra; Hanson, Howard (cond)
Rec Spring 1956
- Mercury MG-50114; 33m; rel 1957; del 1963
- Mercury MG-50165/SR-90165; 33m/s; rel 1961; del 1965
- Eastman-Rochester Archives ERA-1002; 33s; rel 1974; cip

For the First Time (1963)
[4557] Eastman Philharmonia; Hanson, Howard (cond)
- Mercury MG-50357/SR-90357; 33m/s; rel 1963; del 1967
- Eastman-Rochester Archives ERA-1015; 33s; rel 1978; cip

How Excellent Thy Name (Op 41) (1952)
[4558] Augustana Choir; Veld, Henry (cond)
- Word 4012; 33m; rel 1957; del 1969

[4559] Mormon Tabernacle Choir; Schreiner, Alexander (org); Asper, Frank (org); Condie, Richard P. (cond)
- Columbia ML-6019/MS-6619; 33m/s; rel 1964; del 1966

Lament for Beowulf, The (Op 25) (1925)
[4560] Eastman School of Music Chorus; Eastman-Rochester Symphony Orchestra; Hanson, Howard (cond)
- Victor 11-8114-16 (in set M-889); 78; 3 discs; rel pre-1942
- Mercury MG-50192/SR-90192; 33m/s; rel 1959; del 1973
- Mercury SRI-75007; 33s; rel 1973; cip

Merry Mount (Op 31) (1933): Excerpts
[4561] soloists; Eastman School of Music Chorus; Eastman-Rochester Symphony Orchestra; Hanson, Howard (cond)
- Mercury SR-90524; 33s; rel 1970; del 1974
- Eastman-Rochester Archives ERA-1013; 33s; rel 1978*

Merry Mount: 'Tis an Earth Defiled
[4562] Tibbett, Lawrence (bar); orchestra; Pelletier, Wilfred (cond)
Rec 1/19/34
- Victor 7959; 78; rel pre-1936
- Victor 11-8932 (in set M-1015); 78; rel pre-1948
- Gramophone ED-24; 78; rel pre-1952
- Camden CAL-171; 33m; rel 1955; del 1958
- New World NW-241; 33m; rel 1978

Merry Mount (Suite) (1938)
[4563] Eastman-Rochester Symphony Orchestra; Hanson, Howard (cond)
- Victor 17995-96 (in set M-781); 78; 2 discs; rel pre-1942

[4564] Eastman-Rochester Symphony Orchestra; Hanson, Howard (cond)
Rec 10/20/57
- Mercury MG-50175/SR-90175; 33m/s; rel 1958/1959; del 1965
- Mercury MG-50423/SR-90423; 33m/s; rel 1965; del 1972
- Eastman-Rochester Archives ERA-1005; 33s; rel 1974; cip

Mosaics (1958)
[4565] Eastman-Rochester Symphony Orchestra; Hanson, Howard (cond)
- Mercury MG-50267/SR-90267; 33m/s; rel 1961; del 1964
- Mercury MG-50430/SR-90430; 33m/s; rel 1965; del 1969
- Eastman-Rochester Archives ERA-1006; 33s; rel 1976; cip

Pastorale, Oboe, Harp, and Strings (Op 38) (1949)
[4566] Sprenkle, Robert (ob); Malone, Eileen (hp); Eastman-Rochester Symphony Orchestra; Hanson, Howard (cond)
- Mercury MG-40003; 33m; rel 1953; del 1957

Pastorale, Oboe, Harp, and Strings (Op 38) (1949) *(cont'd)*
- Mercury EP-1-5064; 45; 7"; rel pre-1956
- Mercury MG-50076; 33m; rel 1957; del 1963
- Eastman-Rochester Archives ERA-1001; 33s; rel 1974; cip

Psalm 150 (1965)
[4567] Capital University Chapel Choir; Snyder, Ellis Emanuel (cond)
- Coronet S-1504; 33s; rel 1969; cip

[4568] Mormon Tabernacle Choir; Schreiner, Alexander (org); Ottley, Jerold D. (cond)
- Columbia M-34134; 33s; rel 1976; cip

(Four) Psalms (1964)
[4569] Boucher, Gene (bar); Eastman-Rochester Symphony Orchestra; Hanson, Howard (cond)
- Mercury MG-50429/SR-90429; 33m/s; rel 1965; del 1971
- Mercury SRI-75063; 33s; rel 1976; cip

Quartet, Strings (Op 23) (1923)
[4570] Kohon Quartet
- Vox SVBX-5305; 33s; 3 discs; rel 1974; cip

Serenade, Flute, Harp, and Strings (Op 35) (1945)
[4571] Kincaid, William (fl); Philadelphia Orchestra; Ormandy, Eugene (cond)
- Columbia 12983D (in set M-841); 78; rel pre-1950

[4572] Laurent, Georges (fl); Zighera, Bernard (hp); Boston Symphony Orchestra; Koussevitzky, Serge (cond)
Rec 1938-47
- RCA LM-2900; 33m; rel 1966; del 1970
- RCA VCM-6174; 33m; 3 discs; rel 1966; del 1972

[4573] Mariano, Joseph (fl); Malone, Eileen (hp); Eastman-Rochester Symphony Orchestra; Hanson, Howard (cond)
- Mercury MG-40003; 33m; rel 1953; del 1957
- Mercury EP-1-5065; 45; 7"; rel pre-1956
- Mercury MG-50076; 33m; rel 1957; del 1963
- Eastman-Rochester Archives ERA-1001; 33s; rel 1974; cip

[4574] Sharp, Maurice (fl); Chalifoux, Alice (hp); Cleveland Sinfonietta; Lane, Louis (cond)
- Epic LC-3754/BC-1116; 33m/s; rel 1961; del 1970

Serenade, Flute and Wind Ensemble
[4575] Pellerite, James (fl); Indiana University Wind Ensemble; Ebbs, Frederick (cond)
- Coronet S-1724; 33s; rel 1971; cip

Song of Democracy (1957)
[4576] Eastman School of Music Chorus; Eastman-Rochester Symphony Orchestra; Hanson, Howard (cond)
- Mercury MG-50150/SR-90150; 33m/s; rel 1957/1960; del 1964
- Mercury SRW-18113; 33s; rel 1969; del 1970
- Eastman-Rochester Archives ERA-1010; 33s; rel 1976; cip

Songs from Drum Taps (Op 32) (1935)
[4577] Eastman School of Music Chorus; Eastman-Rochester Symphony Orchestra; Hanson, Howard (cond)
- Mercury MG-40000; 33m; rel 1952; del 1957
- Mercury MG-50073; 33m; rel 1957; del 1969
- Eastman-Rochester Archives ERA-1007; 33m; rel 1976; cip

Symphony No 1 (Nordic) (Op 21) (1922)
[4578] Eastman-Rochester Symphony Orchestra; Hanson, Howard (cond)
- Victor 11-8623-25 (in set M-973); 78; 3 discs; rel pre-1948
- Mercury MG-50165/SR-90165; 33m/s; rel 1961; del 1965
- Mercury SRI-75112; 33s; rel 1978; cip

[4579] Hamburg Philharmonia; Walther, Hans-Jurgen (cond)
- Music Sound Books 78160-62; 78; 3 discs; rel pre-1956
- MGM E-3141; 33m; rel 1955; del 1959

Symphony No 1 (arr for band): 2nd Movement
[4580] Fredonia Concert Band; Harp, Herbert Winters (cond)
- Fredonia State Teachers College XTV-21899; 33m; rel 1954

Symphony No 2 (Romantic) (Op 30) (1930)
[4581] Eastman-Rochester Symphony Orchestra; Hanson, Howard (cond)
- Victor 15865-68 (in set M-648); 78; 4 discs; rel pre-1942
- Victor (Japanese) SD-3018-21; 78; 4 discs; rel pre-1942
- Columbia ML-4638; 33m; rel 1953; del 1965

Symphony No 2 (Romantic) (Op 30) (1930) *(cont'd)*
- Mercury MG-50192/SR-90192; 33m/s; rel 1959; del 1973
- Mercury SRI-75007; 33s; rel 1973; cip

[4582] National High School Orchestra; Maddy, Joseph (cond)
- Interlochen National Music Camp NMC-1957-20; 33m; rel 1957

[4583] National Philharmonic Orchestra; Gerhardt, Charles (cond)
Rec 12/18/67
- Quintessence PMC-7062; 33s; rel 1978; cip

Symphony No 3 (Op 33) (1937-38)
[4584] Boston Symphony Orchestra; Koussevitzky, Serge (cond)
Rec 3/20/40
- Victor 11-9875-79 (in set M-1170); 78; 5 discs; rel pre-1948
- RCA LCT-1153; 33m; rel 1954; del 1956
- RCA LVT-1016; 33m; rel 1956; del 1960

[4585] Eastman-Rochester Symphony Orchestra; Hanson, Howard (cond)
- Mercury MG-50449/SR-90449; 33m/s; rel 1966; del 1971
- Mercury SRI-75112; 33s; rel 1978; cip

Symphony No 4 (The Requiem) (Op 34) (1943)
[4586] Eastman-Rochester Symphony Orchestra; Hanson, Howard (cond)
- Mercury MG-40004; 33m; rel 1953; del 1957
- Mercury MG-50077; 33m; rel 1957; del 1968
- Mercury SRI-75107; 33s; rel 1978; cip

[4587] Vienna Symphony Orchestra; Dixon, Dean (cond)
- American Recording Society ARS-6; 33m; 10"; rel 1953?
- American Recording Society ARS-114; 33m; rel pre-1956

Symphony No 5 (Sinfonia sacra) (Op 43) (1954)
[4588] Eastman-Rochester Symphony Orchestra; Hanson, Howard (cond)
Rec 1954
- Mercury MG-40014; 33m; rel 1956; del 1957
- Mercury MG-50087; 33m; rel 1957; del 1964
- Eastman-Rochester Archives ERA-1014; 33s; rel 1978; cip

Symphony No 6 (1968)
[4589] Westchester Symphony Orchestra;
Landau, Siegfried (cond)
- Turnabout TVS-34534; 33s; rel
1973; cip

**Young Person's Guide to the
Six-Tone Scale (1972)**
[4590] Eastman Symphonic Wind
Ensemble; Hunsberger, Donald
(cond)
Rec 11/6-7/78
- Mercury SRI-75132; 33s; rel
1980; cip

**(Two) Yuletide Pieces (Op 19)
(1920): (No 2) March Carillon
(arr for band)**
[4591] Cornell University Symphonic Band;
Stith, Marice (cond)
- Cornell CUWE-10; 33s; rel 1973;
cip

[4592] Eastman Symphonic Wind
Ensemble; Fennell, Frederick
(cond)
- Mercury MG-40007; 33m; rel
1954; del 1957

HARBISON, John (1938-)
Bermuda Triangle (1970)
[4593] Regni, Albert (ten sax); Harbison,
Helen (vcl); Levin, Robert (elec
org)
- CRI-313; 33s; rel 1974; cip

Confinement (1965)
[4594] Contemporary Chamber Ensemble;
Weisberg, Arthur (cond)
- Nonesuch H-71221; 33s; rel
1969; cip

Flower-Fed Buffaloes, The
[4595] Evitts, David (bar); Emmanuel
Choir of Boston; Speculum
Musicae; Harbison, John (cond)
- Nonesuch H-71366; 33s; rel
1979; cip

Parody-Fantasia (1968)
[4596] Miller, Robert (pf)
- CRI-293; 33s; rel 1973; cip

Quintet, Winds
[4597] Aulos Wind Quintet
- CRI-436; 33s; rel 1980; cip

(Five) Songs of Experience (1973)
[4598] Cantata Singers and Ensemble;
Harbison, John (cond)
- CRI-313; 33s; rel 1974; cip

**Trio, Violin, Violoncello, and Piano
(1969)**
[4599] Wheaton Trio
- CRI-313; 33s; rel 1974; cip

HARKNESS, Rebekah (1915-)
Barcelona Suite (1958)
[4600] orchestra; Levin, Sylvan (cond)
- Vanguard VRS-1058/VSD-2071;
33m/s; rel 1960; del 1964

Gift of the Magi (1959)
[4601] orchestra; Levin, Sylvan (cond)
- Vanguard VRS-1058/VSD-2071;
33m/s; rel 1960; del 1964

Journey to Love (1958)
[4602] Symphony of the Air; D'Artega,
Alfonso (cond)
- Westminster XWN-18745; 33m;
rel 1958; del 1960

**HARLING, W. Franke
(1887-1958)**
Corps, The
[4603] U.S. Military Academy Glee Club;
Gaillard, Cadet Frank (cond)
- Columbia CL-6118; 33m; rel
1950; del 1956

HARMAN, Carter (1918-)
Hymn to the Virgin (1952)
[4604] Randolph Singers; Randolph, David
(cond)
- CRI-102; 33m/s; rel 1956/?; cip

**HARMONIC, Phil (pseud for
Kenneth Werner) (1949-)**
Timing
[4605] multiple keyboards
Rec 8-9/78
- Vital VR-1062; 33s; rel 1979

HARRIS, Albert (1916-)
Sonatina, Guitar
[4606] Almeida, Laurindo (gtr)
- Capitol P-8392; 33m; rel 1957;
del 1962
- Everest SDBR-3287; 33s; rel
1971; del 1972

Suite, Guitar
[4607] Kneubuhl, John (gtr)
- Orion ORS-78323; 33s; rel
1979; cip

**Variations and Fugue on a Theme of
Handel**
[4608] Segovia, Andres (gtr)
- Decca DL-710167; 33s; rel
1969; del 1974
- MCA 2501; 33s; rel 1974; cip

HARRIS, Arthur (1927-)
Jazz Suite
[4609] Harris-Lee Chamber Group
- Epic LN-3200; 33m; rel 1956;
del 1958

March of the Mandarins
[4610] Philadelphia Orchestra; Ormandy,
Eugene (cond)
- Columbia ML-6157/MS-6757;
33m/s; rel 1965; del 1970

(Four) Moods and Finale
[4611] Metropolitan Brass Quintet
- Crystal S-208; 33s; rel 1978; cip

[4612] New York Brass Quintet
- Golden Crest
CR-4023/CRS-4023; 33m/s; rel
1960; cip

Strict Forms
[4613] Harris-Lee Chamber Group
- Epic LN-3200; 33m; rel 1956;
del 1958

HARRIS, Donald (1931-)
Fantasy, Violin and Piano (1957)
[4614] Zukofsky, Paul (vln); Kalish, Gilbert
(pf)
- CRI-307; 33s; rel 1973; cip

Ludus (1966)
[4615] St. Paul Chamber Orchestra;
Hodkinson, Sydney (cond)
- CRI-274; 33s; rel 1972; cip

Ludus II (1973)
[4616] Boston Musica Viva; Pittman,
Richard (cond)
- Delos DEL-25406; 33s; rel
1975; cip

Quartet, Strings (1965)
[4617] Composers Quartet
- CRI-274; 33s; rel 1972; cip

Sonata, Piano (1956)
[4618] Von Moltke, Veronica Jochum (pf)
- Golden Crest NEC-107; 33s; rel
1974; cip

HARRIS, Roger (1940-)
Kroma II
[4619] Bigler (tpt); Bowers (perc); Yaw
(perc); Bothwell (perc); Rhodes
(perc); Harris, Roger (cond)
- Capra 1202; 33s; rel 1971; del
1973

HARRIS, Roy (1898-1979)
**Abraham Lincoln Walks at Midnight
(1953)**
[4620] Tangeman, Nell (m sop); Thaviu,
Samuel (vln); Salzman, Theo
(vcl); Harris, Johana (pf)
- MGM E-3210; 33m; rel 1955;
del 1959

**(Ten) American Ballads (1946):
Nos 1-5**
[4621] Johannesen, Grant (pf)
- Golden Crest CRS-4111; 33q; rel
1972; cip

(Ten) American Ballads: Nos 1 and 3
[4622] Foldes, Andor (pf)
- Vox 16069 (in set 174); 78; 10"; rel 1947

Chorale, Organ and Brass (1944)
[4623] Harmon, Thomas (org); UCLA Brass Ensemble; Westbrook, James (cond)
Rec 11/78
- Varese Sarabande VC-81085; 33s; rel 1979; cip

Chorale, Strings (Op 3) (1932)
[4624] Kreiner Sextette
Rec 8/14/37
- Victor 12537; 78; rel 1939

Cimarron (1941)
[4625] UCLA Wind Ensemble; Westbrook, James (cond)
Rec 1/79
- Varese Sarabande VC-81100; 33s; rel 1980

Concerto, Amplified Piano, Brass, Contrabasses, and Percussion (1968)
[4626] Harris, Johana (pf); U.S. Air Force Academy Band (members of); Harris, Roy (cond)
Rec 1971
- Varese Sarabande VC-81085; 33s; rel 1979; cip

Concerto, Piano, Clarinet, and String Quartet (Op 2) (1927)
[4627] Basquin, Peter (pf); Sobol, Lawrence (cl); Long Island Chamber Ensemble of New York
Rec ca 2/76
- Grenadilla GS-1007; 33s; rel 1977; cip

[4628] Cumpson, Harry (pf); Gorodner, Aaron (cl); Aeolian Quartet
Rec 7/17/33 and 7/25/33
- Columbia 68138-40D (in set M-281); 78; 3 discs; rel pre-1936
- Columbia M-6; 78; rel pre-1936

Concerto, Piano and String Orchestra (195?)
[4629] Harris, Johana (pf); International String Congress Orchestra; Harris, Roy (cond)
Rec 1960
- Varese Sarabande VC-81100; 33s; rel 1980

Elegy and Dance (1958)
[4630] Portland Junior Symphony; Avshalomov, Jacob (cond)
- CRI-140; 33m/s; rel 1961/?; cip

Epilogue to Profiles in Courage (J.F.K.) (1964)
[4631] Louisville Orchestra; Whitney, Robert (cond)
- LOU-66-6/LS-66-6; 33m/s (Louisville Orchestra First Edition Records 1966 No 6); rel 1967; cip

Fantasy, Organ, Brass, and Timpani (1964)
[4632] Harmon, Thomas (org); UCLA Brass Ensemble; Westbrook, James (cond)
Rec 11/78
- Varese Sarabande VC-81085; 33s; rel 1979; cip

Fantasy, Piano and Orchestra (1954)
[4633] Harris, Johana (pf); MGM Orchestra; Solomon, Izler (cond)
- MGM E-3210; 33m; rel 1955; del 1959

Fog (1946)
[4634] Hanks, John Kennedy (ten); Friedberg, Ruth (pf)
- Duke University Press DWR-6417-18; 33m; 2 discs; rel 1966; del 1975

Four Minutes Twenty Seconds (1942)
[4635] Laurent, Georges (fl); Burgin Quartet
- Columbia 68186D (in set M-191); 78; rel pre-1936

Kentucky Spring (1949)
[4636] Louisville Orchestra; Whitney, Robert (cond)
- LOU-60-2; 33m (Louisville Orchestra First Edition Records 1960 No 2); rel 1960; del 1978

Little Suite, Piano (1938)
[4637] Harris, Johana (pf)
Rec 1/24/39
- Victor 12446B (in set M-568); 78; rel 1939
- Victor 17753B (in set M-752); 78; rel 1941
- Victor 17754 (in set AM-752); 78; rel 1941
- Victor 17758B (in set DM-752); 78; rel 1941

Poem, Violin and Piano (1935)
[4638] Spalding, Albert (vln); Benoist, Andre (pf)
Rec 1/28/36
- Victor 8997; 78; rel 1936

Quartet, Strings, No 2 (Three Variations on a Theme) (1933)
[4639] Emerson String Quartet
5/17-20/77
- New World NW-218; 33s; rel 1978

Quartet, Strings, No 2 (Three Variations on a Theme) (1933)
(cont'd)
[4640] Roth Quartet
Rec 5/14,16,18/34
- Victor 8502-04 (in set M-244); 78; 3 discs; rel 1934
- Victor 8505-07 (in set AM-244); 78; 3 discs; rel 1934

Quartet, Strings, No 3 (1937)
[4641] Blair String Quartet
- Varese Sarabande VC-81123; 33s

[4642] Roth Quartet
Rec 6/6/40 and 6/13/40
- Columbia 71050-53D (in set M-450); 78; 4 discs; rel pre-1942

Quintet, Piano and Strings (1936)
[4643] Harris, Johana (pf); Blair String Quartet
- Varese Sarabande VC-81123; 33s

[4644] Harris, Johana (pf); Coolidge String Quartet
Rec 1/24/39
- Victor 17750-53S (in set M-752); 78; 4 discs; rel 1941
- Victor 17754-57S (in set AM-752); 78; 4 discs; rel 1941
- Victor 17758-61 (in set DM-752); 78; 4 discs; rel 1941

[4645] Harris, Johana (pf); Shapiro, Eudice (vln); Ross, Nathan (vln); Schonbach, Sanford (vla); Lustgarten, Edgar (vcl)
Rec 1963
- Contemporary M-6012/S-8012; 33m/s; rel 1964; del 1978

Soliloquy and Dance, Viola and Piano (1938)
[4646] Primrose, William (vla); Harris, Johana (pf)
Rec 1/12/42
- Victor 11-9212-13 (in set M-1061); 78; 2 discs; rel 1946
- Victor 11-9214-17B (in set DM-1061); 78; 4 discs; rel 1946

Sonata, Piano (1928)
[4647] Harris, Johana (pf)
Rec 12/15/37
- Victor 12445-46 (in set M-568); 78; 2 discs; rel 1939

[4648] Shields, Roger (pf)
- Vox SVBX-5303; 33s; 3 discs; rel 1977; cip

Sonata, Violin and Piano (1941)
[4649] Gingold, Josef (vln); Harris, Johana (pf)
Rec 9/14/50
- Columbia ML-4842; 33m; rel 1954; del 1968
- Columbia CML-4842; 33m; rel 1968; del 1974

Sonata, Violin and Piano (1941)
(cont'd)
- Columbia AML-4842; 33m; rel
  1974; del 1976

[4650] Shapiro, Eudice (vln); Harris,
Johana (pf)
Rec 1963
- Contemporary M-6012/S-8012;
  33m/s; rel 1964; del 1978

Song for Occupations, A (1934)
[4651] Westminster Choir; Williamson,
John Finley (cond)
Rec 6/4/35
- Columbia 68349-56D (in set
  M-227); 78; 8 discs; rel
  pre-1936
- Columbia 68347-48D (in set
  MM-227); 78; 2 discs; rel
  pre-1936

Symphony No 1 (1933)
[4652] Boston Symphony Orchestra;
Koussevitzky, Serge (cond)
Rec 2/2/34
- Columbia 68183-86D (in set
  M-191); 78; 4 discs; rel
  pre-1936
- Columbia ML-5095; 33m; rel
  1956; del 1965
- Columbia CML-5095; 33m; rel
  1968; del 1974
- Columbia AML-5095; 33m; rel
  1974; cip

Symphony No 3 (1937)
[4653] Boston Symphony Orchestra;
Koussevitzky, Serge (cond)
Rec 11/8/39
- Victor 15885-86 (in set M-651);
  78; 2 discs; rel pre-1942
- Victor 18454-55 (in set
  DM-651); 78; 2 discs; rel
  pre-1942
- Gramophone DB-6137-38; 78; 2
  discs; rel 1942*
- Gramophone (Australian)
  DB-5775-76; 78; 2 discs; rel
  pre-1952
- RCA LCT-1153; 33m; rel 1954;
  del 1956
- RCA LVT-1016; 33m; rel 1956;
  del 1960
- RCA-Victrola VIC-1047; 33m; rel
  1969*

[4654] Eastman-Rochester Symphony
Orchestra; Hanson, Howard
(cond)
- Mercury MG-40004; 33m; rel
  1953; del 1957
- Mercury (English) MG-40004;
  33m; rel 1954*
- Mercury MG-50077; 33m; rel
  1957; del 1968
- Mercury (German) MG-50077;
  33m
- Pye-Mercury (English) MRL-2520;
  33m; rel 1957*
- Mercury (English) MMA-11097;
  33m; rel 1960*
- Mercury MG-50421/SR-90421;
  33m/s; rel 1965; del 1971

Symphony No 3 (1937) *(cont'd)*
[4655] New York Philharmonic; Bernstein,
Leonard (cond)
Rec 9/28/60
- Columbia ML-5703/MS-6303;
  33m/s; rel 1962; cip
- Columbia (French)
  ML-5703/MS-6303; 33m/s; rel
  1962
- Columbia (English)
  BRG-72399/SBRG-72399;
  33m/s; rel 1966*
- Columbia (English and German)
  61681; 33s; rel 1976*

[4656] Philadelphia Orchestra; Ormandy,
Eugene (cond)
Rec 3/20/74
- RCA ARL-1-1682; 33s; rel 1976;
  cip

[4657] Vienna Symphony Orchestra;
Hendl, Walter (cond)
- American Recording Society
  ARS-28; 33m; 10"; rel 1952
- American Recording Society
  ARS-115; 33m; rel 1953
- Desto D-404/DST-6404; 33m/s;
  rel 1964; cip

**Symphony No 4 (Folksong
Symphony) (1940)**
[4658] American Festival Chorus and
Orchestra; Golschmann, Vladimir
(cond)
- Vanguard VRS-1064/VSD-2082;
  33m/s; rel 1960; del 1968
- Vanguard SRV-347-SD; 33s; rel
  1976; cip

[4659] Utah Chorale; Utah Symphony
Orchestra; Abravanel, Maurice
(cond)
Rec 5/6/75
- Angel S-36091; 33q; rel 1975;
  cip

Symphony No 4: Interlude No 1
[4660] Hamburg Philharmonia; Korn,
Richard (cond)
- Allegro ALG-3149; 33m; rel
  1954?

Symphony No 5 (1942)
[4661] Louisville Orchestra; Whitney,
Robert (cond)
- LOU-65-5/LS-65-5; 33m/s
  (Louisville Orchestra First Edition
  Records 1965 No 5); rel 1965;
  cip
- RCA (English) GL-25058; 33s;
  rel 1977*

[4662] Pittsburgh Symphony Orchestra;
Steinberg, William (cond)
Rec 1952
- ASCAP CB-165; 33m (Pittsburgh
  International Contemporary Music
  Festival); rel 1954

Symphony No 7 (1952)
[4663] Philadelphia Orchestra; Ormandy,
Eugene (cond)
Rec 10/22/55
- Columbia ML-5095; 33m; rel
  1956; del 1965
- Columbia CML-5095; 33m; rel
  1968; del 1974
- Columbia AML-5095; 33m; rel
  1974; cip

Symphony for Voices (1935)
[4664] Westminster Choir; Williamson,
John Finley (cond)
Rec 5/20/37
- Victor 4803-04 (in set M-427);
  78; 2 discs; rel 1938

Toccata, Organ and Brass (1944)
[4665] Harmon, Thomas (org); UCLA
Brass Ensemble; Westbrook,
James (cond)
- Varese Sarabande VC-81085;
  33s; rel 1979; cip

Toccata, Violin and Piano
[4666] Carabo-Cone, Madeleine (vln);
Lumsden, Ronald (pf)
Rec 6/1/70
- Executive Recording, Ltd
  CHC-002; 33s; rel 1970

**Trio, Violin, Violoncello, and Piano
(1934)**
[4667] Italian Trio
Rec 10/13/34 and 10/16/34
- Columbia 62247-49D (in set
  M-7); 78; 3 discs; rel pre-1936
- Columbia 68247-49D (in set
  M-282); 78; 3 discs; rel
  pre-1952

[4668] New England Trio
- HNH Records HNH-4070; 33s;
  rel 1979

[4669] University of Oklahoma Trio
- University of Oklahoma 1; 33m;
  rel 1957; del 1978

West Point Symphony (1952)
[4670] UCLA Wind Ensemble; Westbrook,
James (cond)
Rec 1/79
- Varese Sarabande VC-81100;
  33s; rel 1980

[4671] U.S. Military Academy Band; Harris,
Roy (cond)
Rec 1952
- ASCAP CB-175; 33m (Pittsburgh
  International Contemporary Music
  Festival); rel 1954

**When Johnny Comes Marching
Home (orchestral version) (1935)**
[4672] Louisville Orchestra; Mester, Jorge
(cond)
Rec 1/78
- LS-76-6; 33s (Louisville
  Orchestra First Edition Records
  1976 No 6); rel 1979; cip

When Johnny Comes Marching Home (orchestral version) (1935)
(cont'd)
[4673] Minneapolis Symphony Orchestra; Ormandy, Eugene (cond)
Rec 1/12/35
- Victor 8629; 78; rel 1935

When Johnny Comes Marching Home (choral version) (1935)
[4674] Westminster Choir; Williamson, John Finley (cond)
Rec 12/15/37
- Victor 1883; 78; 10"; rel 1938

HARRIS, Russell (1914-)
It Was Beginning Winter (1961)
[4675] Hamline A Cappella Choir; Holliday, Robert (cond)
- SPAMH MIA-116; 33s; rel 1961

Moon Is Hiding, The (1961)
[4676] Hamline A Cappella Choir; Holliday, Robert (cond)
- SPAMH MIA-116; 33s; rel 1961

Tarye No Lenger
[4677] Hamline A Cappella Choir; Holliday, Robert (cond)
- New NRLP-306; 33m; 10"; rel 1957; del 1963

HARRIS, Sydney
Cavalier March, The
[4678] Arthur Pryor's Band
- Victor 5757; 78; 10"

HARRISON, Lou (1917-)
Canticle No 1 (1940)
[4679] Manhattan Percussion Ensemble; Cage, John (cond); Price, Paul (cond)
- Time 58000/S-8000; 33m/s; rel 1961; del 1970
- Mainstream MS-5011; 33s; rel 1970; del 1979

Canticle No 3 (1941)
[4680] American Percussion Society; Price, Paul (cond)
- Urania UX-106; 33m; rel 1957; del 1969
- Urania USD-1007; 33s; rel 1958; del 1960
- Urania US-5106; 33s; rel 1961; del 1970

[4681] Illinois University Ensemble; Price, Paul (cond)
- Illini Union Bookstore CRS-3; 33m; rel 1955*

Concerto, Organ and Percussion Orchestra
[4682] Craighead, David (org); Los Angeles Percussion Ensemble; Kraft, William (cond)
- Crystal S-858; 33s; rel 1977; cip

Concerto in slendro (1961)
[4683] Kobialka, Daniel (vln); Barbagallo, James (tack pf); Kobialka, Machiko (tack pf)
- Desto DC-7144; 33s; rel 1973; cip

Elegiac Symphony (1975)
[4684] Oakland Youth Orchestra; De Coteau, Denis M. (cond)
- 1750 Arch S-1772; 33s; rel 1978; cip

Fugue, Percussion (1941)
[4685] Blackearth Percussion Group
Rec 5/27-28/74
- Opus One 22; 33s; rel 1975; cip

Gending pak chokro (Music for kyai hudan mas) (1976)
[4686] Berkeley Gamelan
- Cambridge CRS-2560; 33s; rel 1978; cip

Koncherto por la violino kun perkuta orkestro (1959)
[4687] Glenn, Carroll (vln); Eastman School of Music Percussion Ensemble (members of); Beck, John (cond)
Rec 4/72
- Turnabout QTVS-34653; 33q; rel 1977; cip

[4688] Shapiro, Eudice (vln); Los Angeles Percussion Ensemble; Kraft, William (cond)
- Crystal S-853; 33s; rel 1972; cip

Mass (1939-54)
[4689] Gregg Smith Singers; Kittelson, Fay (al); Magdamo, Priscilla (al); Lieberson, Harold (tpt); Allen, Nancy (hp); Orpheus Ensemble; Smith, Gregg (cond)
Rec 4/76
- Vox SVBX-5354; 33s; 3 discs; rel 1979

[4690] New York Concert Choir and Orchestra; Kutik, Ronald (tpt); Hillis, Margaret (cond)
- Epic LC-3307; 33m; rel 1957; del 1961

Only Jealousy of Emer, The (1949)
[4691] Reed College (Oregon) Summer Workshop in Dance and Drama; Harrison, Lou (cond)
Rec 2/51
- Esoteric ES-506; 33m; rel 1951-53

Pacifika rondo (1963)
[4692] Oakland Youth Orchestra; Hughes, Robert (cond)
- Desto DC-6478; 33s; rel 1969; cip

(Four) Pieces, Harp (1968)
[4693] Bellows, Beverly (hp)
- Desto DC-6478; 33s; rel 1969; cip

(Two) Pieces, Psaltery (1961-69)
[4694] Bellows, Beverly (hp)
- Desto DC-6478; 33s; rel 1969; cip

Serenade (1952)
[4695] Starobin, David (gtr)
Rec 1976
- Turnabout TVS-34727; 33s; rel 1978

Song of Quetzalcoatl (1940)
[4696] Percussion Ensemble; Price, Paul (cond)
- Period SPL-743/SPLS-743; 33m/s; rel 1958; del 1968
- Orion ORS-7276; 33s; rel 1972; cip

(Four) Strict Songs (1955)
[4697] Bingham, David (soloist); Southern Baptist Theological Seminary Choir; Louisville Orchestra; Whitney, Robert (cond)
- LOU-58-2; 33m (Louisville Orchestra First Edition Records 1958 No 2); rel 1959; del 1978

Suite, Percussion (1940)
[4698] Manhattan Percussion Ensemble; Price, Paul (cond)
- CRI-252; 33s; rel 1970; cip

Suite, String Quartet, No 2 (1949-50)
[4699] New Music String Quartet
- Columbia ML-4491; 33m; rel 1952; del 1958

Suite, Symphonic Strings (1936-60)
[4700] Louisville Orchestra; Whitney, Robert (cond)
- LOU-62-1; 33m (Louisville Orchestra First Edition Records 1962 No 1); rel 1962; del 1978

Suite, Violin, Piano, and Small Orchestra (1951)
[4701] Ajemian, Anahid (vln); Ajemian, Maro (pf); Leopold Stokowski and his Orchestra; Stokowski, Leopold (cond)
- RCA LM-1785; 33m; rel 1954; del 1956
- CRI-114; 33m/s; rel 1957/?; cip

Suite, Violoncello and Harp (1949)
[4702] Barab, Seymour (vcl); Lawrence, Lucille (hp)
Rec 1951
- Columbia ML-4491; 33m; rel 1952; del 1958
- New World NW-281; 33m; rel 1976

Symphony on G (1948-61)
[4703] Royal Philharmonic Orchestra;
　　　Samuel, Gerhard (cond)
　　　- CRI-236; 33s; rel 1969; cip

HARRISON, Lou and CAGE, John
see CAGE, John and HARRISON, Lou

HARTLEY, Gerald (1921-)
Divertissement, Wind Quintet
[4704] Chicago Symphony Wind Ensemble
　　　- Audiophile AP-16; 33m; rel 1958; del 1970

[4705] Ohio State University Faculty
　　　Woodwind Quintet
　　　- Coronet 543; 33m; rel 1969; cip

HARTLEY, Walter Sinclair (1927-)
Canzona for Eight Trombones (1969)
[4706] Eastman Trombone Choir
　　　- Mark 50500; 33s; rel 1972; del 1975

Caprice (1967)
[4707] Levy, Robert (tpt); Levy, Amy Lou (pf)
　　　- Golden Crest RE-7045; 33q; rel 1972; cip

Concerto, Alto Saxophone and Band (1966)
[4708] Sinta, Donald (al sax); Ithaca
　　　College Band; Beeler, Walter (cond)
　　　- Golden Crest
　　　CR-4077/CRS-4077; 33m/s; rel 1967; cip

Concerto, Twenty-Three Winds (1957)
[4709] Eastman Symphonic Wind
　　　Ensemble; Fennell, Frederick (cond)
　　　- Mercury MG-50221/SR-90221; 33m/s; rel 1960; del 1964

Divertissement, Brass (1965)
[4710] Ithaca Brass Quintet
　　　- Mark MES-32558; 33s; rel 1969; del 1976

Double Concerto, Alto Saxophone, Tuba, and Wind Octet (1969)
[4711] Underwood, Dale (al sax); Erickson,
　　　Martin D. (tu); Metropolitan Wind
　　　Ensemble; Mugol, Rodrigo C. (cond)
　　　- Golden Crest CRS-4136; 33s/q; rel 1975; cip

Duo, Saxophone and Piano (1964)
[4712] Sinta, Donald (sax); True, Nelita (pf)
　　　- Mark MRS-22868; 33m; rel 1968; cip

Duo, Saxophone and Piano (1964)
(cont'd)
[4713] Underwood, Dale (sax); Lee,
　　　Marjorie (pf)
　　　Rec 8/15/76
　　　- Golden Crest RE-7067; 33s; rel 1978; cip

Miniatures, Four Valve Instruments
[4714] Atlantic Tuba Quartet
　　　- Golden Crest CRSQ-4173; 33q; rel 1979; cip

Octet, Saxophones (1975)
[4715] Rascher Saxophone Ensemble
　　　- Coronet LPS-3031; 33s; rel 1977; cip

Orpheus (1960)
[4716] Annapolis Brass Quintet
　　　- Crystal S-206; 33s; rel 1977; cip

(Two) Pieces, Wind Quintet
[4717] Interlochen Arts Quintet
　　　- Mark 28486; 33s; rel 1968; del 1976

Poem, Tenor Saxophone and Piano
[4718] Hemke, Frederick (ten sax);
　　　Granger, Milton (pf)
　　　- Brewster BR-1204; 33s; rel 1972; del 1978

[4719] Houlik, James (ten sax); Tardif,
　　　Paul (pf)
　　　- Golden Crest RE-7060; 33s; rel 1977; cip

Sinfonia No 4 (1965)
[4720] Eastman Symphonic Wind
　　　Ensemble; Hunsberger, Donald (cond)
　　　- Decca DL-710163; 33s; rel 1969; del 1973

Sonata, Tenor Saxophone and Piano
[4721] Houlik, James (ten sax); Tardif,
　　　Paul (pf)
　　　- Golden Crest RE-7060; 33s; rel 1977; cip

Sonata, Tuba and Piano
[4722] Le Blanc, Robert (tu); Baker, Myra (pf)
　　　- Coronet S-1721; 33s; rel 1973; cip

Sonata breve, Bass Trombone
[4723] Reynolds, Jeffrey (b tbn)
　　　- Crystal S-383; 33s; rel 1979; cip

Sonata concertante, Trombone and Piano (1958)
[4724] Cramer, William F. (tbn);
　　　Glotzbach, Robert (pf)
　　　- Coronet S-1506; 33s; rel 1969; cip

Sonata concertante, Trombone and Piano (1958) *(cont'd)*
[4725] Smith, Henry Charles (tbn);
　　　Kuehefuhs, Gertrude C. (pf)
　　　- Coronet S-1711; 33s; rel 1973; cip

Sonatina, Tuba and Piano
[4726] Popiel, Peter J. (tu); Fuchs, Henry (pf)
　　　- Mark MRS-28437; 33s; rel 1968; cip

Sonorities II
[4727] Smith, Calvin (hn); Dressler, John (pf)
　　　- Crystal S-371; 33s; rel 1976; cip

Suite, Flute and Tuba
[4728] Lolya, Andrew J. (fl); Phillips,
　　　Harvey (tu)
　　　- Golden Crest RE-7054; 33s; rel 1973*

Suite, Saxophone Quartet (1970)
[4729] Rascher Saxophone Quartet
　　　- Coronet LPS-3021; 33s; rel 1975; cip

Suite, Tuba
[4730] Conner, Rex (tu)
　　　- Coronet M-1259; 33m; rel 1969; cip

[4731] Popiel, Peter J. (tu)
　　　- Mark MRS-28437; 33s; rel 1968; cip

HARTWAY, James (1944-)
Three Ways of Looking at a Blackbird
[4732] Grimes, Carolyn (sop); Gregory, Liz
　　　(fl); Ball, Gerrie (pf); Wencel, Mike
　　　(perc); Claeys, Keith (perc);
　　　Hartway, James (cond)
　　　- Advance FGR-24S; 33s; rel 1978

HASKINS, Robert (1937-)
Sonata, Brass Quartet: 1st Movement
[4733] Georgia State College Brass
　　　Ensemble; Hill, William H. (cond)
　　　- Golden Crest CRS-4084; 33s; rel 1969; cip

HAUBIEL, Charles (1892-78)
1865 A.D. (1941)
[4734] Roberts, Carol (pf)
　　　- Orion ORS-74158; 33s; rel 1975; cip

Elves Spinning
[4735] Kramer, Selma (pf)
　　　- Orion ORS-7261; 33s; rel 1972; cip

Gothic Variations (1943) (arr for vln and orch)

[4736] Granat, Endre (vln); Westphalian Symphony Orchestra; Freeman, Paul (cond)
- Orion ORS-74158; 33s; rel 1975; cip

In the French Manner (1942)

[4737] Marsius Trio
- Dorian 1007; 33m; rel 1962; del 1974

[4738] no performers given
- Orion ORS-74165; 33s; rel 1974; cip

Karma (1928)

[4739] orchestra; Haubiel, Charles (cond)
- Columbia 9065-67M (in set M-1); 78; 3 discs; rel pre-1936
- Columbia M-278; 78

Masks

[4740] Kaplan, Melvin (ob); Tarack, Gerald (vln); Kougell, Alexander (vcl); Wingreen, Harriet (pf)
- Orion ORS-74165; 33s; rel 1974; cip

Metamorphoses (1948)

[4741] Dowis, Jeaneane (pf)
- Orion ORS-75188; 33s; rel 1975; cip

Miniatures (1938) (arr for string orch)

[4742] Graunke Symphony Orchestra; Swift, James (cond)
- Orion ORS-75197; 33s; rel 1975; cip

Noche en Espana

[4743] Kramer, Selma (pf)
- Orion ORS-7261; 33s; rel 1972; cip

Nuances (1941)

[4744] Granat, Endre (vln); Westphalian Symphony Orchestra; Freeman, Paul (cond)
- Orion ORS-74158; 33s; rel 1975; cip

Pioneers (1946, rev 1956)

[4745] Hamburg Philharmonia; Walther, Hans-Jurgen (cond)
- Dorian 1008; 33m; rel 1962; del 1974
- Orion ORS-75197; 33s; rel 1975; cip

Portraits (piano version)

[4746] Rogers, Herbert (pf)
- Dorian 1006; 33m; rel 1962; del 1970

Portraits (orchestral version) (1935)

[4747] Hamburg Philharmonia; Walther, Hans-Jurgen (cond)
- Dorian 1008; 33m; rel 1962; del 1974
- Orion ORS-74143; 33s; rel 1974; cip

Shadows

[4748] Roberts, Carol (pf)
- Orion ORS-74158; 33s; rel 1975; cip

Solari (piano version) (1932-34)

[4749] Andrews, Mitchell (pf)
- Dorian 1014; 33m; rel 1968; del 1974

Solari (orchestral version) (1938)

[4750] Hamburg Philharmonia; Walther, Hans-Jurgen (cond)
- Orion ORS-74143; 33s; rel 1974; cip

Sonata, Violin and Piano, D Minor (1948)

[4751] Granat, Endre (vln); Roberts, Carol (pf)
- Orion ORS-74158; 33s; rel 1975; cip

Sonata, Violoncello and Piano, C Minor (1944)

[4752] Manucci, Livio (vcl); Haubiel, Charles (pf)
- Dorian 1009; 33m; rel 1962; del 1974
- Orion ORS-74165; 33s; rel 1974; cip

Suite passecaille (1935): Minuet

[4753] Graunke Symphony Orchestra; Swift, James (cond)
- Orion ORS-75197; 33s; rel 1975; cip

HAUFRECHT, Herbert (1909-)

Square Set (1941)

[4754] Accademia Nazionale di Santa Cecilia Orchestra, Roma; Antonini, Alfredo (cond)
- CRI-111; 33m/s; rel 1957/?; cip

Strange Lullaby

[4755] Randolph Singers; Randolph, David (cond)
- Concert Hall CHC-52; 33m; rel 1950; del 1957

Symphony, Brass and Timpani (1956)

[4756] Brass Ensemble Society of New York; Karasick, Simon (cond)
- CRI-192/CRI-192(78); 33m/s; rel 1965/1979; cip

Walkin' the Road (1944)

[4757] Leeds Concert Band; Todd, Peter (cond)
- Columbia ML-4254; 33m; rel 1950; del 1956

HAYS, Doris (1941-)

Sunday Nights (1977)

[4758] Hays, Doris (pf)
- Finnadar SR-2-720; 33s; 2 discs; rel 1980; cip

HEIDEN, Bernhard (1910-)

(Five) Canons, Horns (1971): Nos 2 and 5

[4759] Smith, Calvin (hn); Zsembery, William (hn)
- Crystal S-371; 33s; rel 1976; cip

Intrada (1970)

[4760] Pittel, Harvey (sax); Westwood Wind Quintet
- Crystal S-353; 33s; rel 1979; cip

Quintet, Horn and String Quartet (1952)

[4761] Leuba, Christopher (hn); Philadelphia String Quartet
- Olympic OLY-102; 33s; rel 1973; cip

Quintet, Winds (1965)

[4762] Clarion Wind Quintet
- Golden Crest CRS-4125; 33s; rel 1974; cip

(Five) Short Pieces, Flute and Piano (1933)

[4763] Pellerite, James (fl); Webb, Charles (pf)
- Golden Crest RE-7023; 33m/s; rel 1968/1979; cip

Sinfonia, Wind Quintet (1949)

[4764] Musical Arts Quintet
- Now 9632; 33s; rel 1966; del 1976

Sonata, Alto Saxophone and Piano (1937)

[4765] Kynaston, Trent (al sax); Turner-Jones, Terry (pf)
- Coronet LPS-3044; 33s; rel 1978; cip

[4766] Rascher, Sigurd (al sax)
- Award 33-708; 33m; rel 1958; del 1970

[4767] Sinta, Donald (al sax); True, Nelita (pf)
- Mark MRS-22868; 33m; rel 1968; cip

[4768] Underwood, Dale (al sax); Lee, Marjorie (pf)
Rec 8/15/76
- Golden Crest RE-7067; 33s; rel 1978; cip

Sonata, Horn and Piano (1939)
[4769] Chambers, James (hn)
  - Award 33-704; 33m; rel 1958; del 1970

[4770] Kavalovski, Charles (hn); Wolff, Andrew (pf)
  - Musical Heritage Society MHS-3547; 33s; rel 1977

Variations, Tuba and Nine Horns (1974)
[4771] Phillips, Harvey (tu); Valhalla Horn Choir; Heiden, Bernhard (cond)
  - Golden Crest CRSQ-4147; 33q; rel 1979; cip

HEIFETZ, Robin Julian (1951-)
Flykt (1979)
[4772] Heifetz, Robin Julian (pf); tape
  - Orion ORS-80366; 33s; rel 1980; cip

For Anders Lundberg: Mardrom 29 30 10 (1978)
[4773] Electronic music
  - Orion ORS-80366; 33s; rel 1980; cip

Susurrus (1978)
[4774] Heifetz, Robin Julian (pf); tape
  - Orion ORS-80366; 33s; rel 1980; cip

Wasteland (1979)
[4775] Electronic music
  - Orion ORS-80366; 33s; rel 1980; cip

HEILNER, Irwin (1908-)
(Four) Chinese Songs (1947)
[4776] Maki, Mitsuko (sop); Imperial Philharmonic Orchestra of Tokyo; Strickland, William (cond)
  - CRI-143; 33m/s; rel 1961/?; cip

HEINTZ, James R.*
Fanfare and Raga
[4777] Heintz, James R. (bsn); tape
  - Music Guild MS-877; 33s; rel 1970; del 1971
  - Westminster WGS-8129; 33s; rel 1971; del 1977

HEISINGER, Brent
Essay
[4778] Ohio State University Concert Band; McGinnis, Donald E. (cond)
  - Coronet S-1403; 33s; rel 1969; cip

HEISS, John (1938-)
Inventions, Contours, and Colors (1973)
[4779] Speculum Musicae; Fitz, Richard (cond)
  Rec 5/3/76
  - CRI-363; 33s; rel 1977; cip

(Four) Movements, Three Flutes (1966-69)
[4780] Heiss, John (fl); Dunkel, Paul (fl); Kout, Trix (fl)
  - CRI-321; 33s; rel 1974; cip

Quartet, Flute, Clarinet, Violoncello, and Piano (1971)
[4781] Boston Musica Viva; Pittman, Richard (cond)
  - CRI-321; 33s; rel 1974; cip

Songs of Nature (1974)
[4782] Fortunato, D'Anna (m sop); Boston Musica Viva; Pittman, Richard (cond)
  Rec 1/78
  - Nonesuch H-71351; 33s; rel 1978; cip

HELD, Wilbur (1914-)
Nativity Suite
[4783] Wichmann, Russell G. (org)
  - True Image LP-125; 33m; rel 1966

HELF, Fred
New Tipperary March
[4784] Arthur Pryor's Band
  - Victor 16024; 78; 10"

HELLER, Kenneth (1949-)
Labyrinth (1969)
[4785] Ischar, Douglas (vcl); tape
  - Orion ORS-7021; 33s; rel 1970; cip

HELLERMANN, William (1939-)
Ariel (1967)
[4786] Electronic music
  - Turnabout TVS-34301; 33s; rel 1969; del 1975

Ek-stasis II (1970)
[4787] Corner, Philip (pf); Levenson, Michael (perc); tape
  - CRI-299; 33s; rel 1973; cip

On the Edge of a Node (1974)
[4788] Street, Tison (vln); Uitti, Frances (vcl); Hellermann, William (gtr)
  - CRI-336; 33s; rel 1977; cip

Passages 13 - The Fire (1970-71)
[4789] Schwarz, Gerard (tpt); tape
  - Nonesuch H-71275; 33s; rel 1973; cip

HELM, Everett (1913-)
Comment on Two Spirtuals
[4790] Kaufman, Louis (vln); Kaufman, Annette (pf)
  - Vox 627; 78; 3 discs; rel 1948
  - Concert Hall CHC-58; 33m; rel 1950; del 1957

Concerto, Piano and Orchestra, No 2 (1956)
[4791] Owen, Benjamin (pf); Louisville Orchestra; Whitney, Robert (cond)
  - LOU-58-3; 33m (Louisville Orchestra First Edition Records 1958 No 3); rel 1959; cip

Trio, Flute and Strings
[4792] Luening, Otto (fl); Levine, Morris (vln); Finney, Ross Lee (vcl)
  - Yaddo I-4; 78; 10"; rel 1940

HELPS, Robert (1928-)
(Three) Etudes, Piano (1956)
[4793] Del Tredici, David (pf)
  - Desto DC-7122; 33s; rel 1972; cip

Gossamer Noons (1974)
[4794] Beardslee, Bethany (sop); American Composers Orchestra; Schuller, Gunther (cond)
  Rec 5/24/78
  - CRI-384; 33s; rel 1979; cip

Image (1958)
[4795] Helps, Robert (pf)
  - RCA LM-7042/LSC-7042; 33m/s; 2 discs; rel 1966; del 1971
  - CRI-288; 33s; 2 discs; rel 1972; cip

Portrait (1960)
[4796] Bennette, George (pf)
  - Desto DC-7110; 33s; rel 1971; cip

Quartet, Piano Solo (1970)
[4797] Helps, Robert (pf)
  - Desto DC-7122; 33s; rel 1972; cip

Recollections (1959)
[4798] Masselos, William (pf)
  - Desto DC-7122; 33s; rel 1972; cip

Running Sun, The (1972)
[4799] Beardslee, Bethany (sop); Helps, Robert (pf)
  - New World NW-243; 33s; rel 1977

Saccade (1967)
[4800] Chinn, Genevieve (pf); Brings, Allen (pf)
  Rec 10/77
  - CRI-383; 33s; rel 1978; cip

Symphony No 1 (1955)
[4801] Columbia Symphony Orchestra; Rozsnyai, Zoltan (cond)
  - Columbia ML-6201/MS-6801; 33m/s; rel 1966; del 1971
  - CRI-411; 33s; rel 1980; cip

HEMMER, Eugene (1929-77)

Divertimento, Harp, Marimba, Celesta, and Piano
[4802] Otis, Cynthia (hp); Traber, William (mrmb); Green, Ray (cel); Hemmer, Eugene (pf)
- American Recording Edition ARE-1001; 33m; rel pre-1956

Remembrance of Things Present
[4803] Hemmer, Eugene (pf); Kaplan, Leigh (pf)
- Charade CH-1012; 33s; rel 1975

Suggestion and Fugue
[4804] Hemmer, Eugene (pf); Kaplan, Leigh (pf)
- Charade CH-1012; 33s; rel 1975

HENDERSON, Robert

Fanfare (1964)
[4805] Los Angeles Philharmonic Brass Ensemble; Henderson, Robert (cond)
- Avant AV-1005; 33s; rel 1976; cip

Variation Movements
[4806] Stevens, Thomas (tpt); Grierson, Ralph (pf); Peters, Mitchell (perc)
- Avant AV-1003; 33s; rel 1972; cip

HENDL, Walter (1917-)

Dark of the Moon: Prelude
[4807] Hendl, Walter (pf)
- Hargail 1100-01; 78; rel 1948

In the Passing of a Sigh
[4808] Hess, William (ten); Fizdale, Robert (pf)
- Hargail HN-707 (in set 0090); 78; 10"; rel 1946

Short Story No 2
[4809] Hendl, Walter (pf)
- Hargail 1100-01; 78; rel 1948

HENNAGIN, Michael (1936-)

Crossing the Han River
[4810] King Chorale; King, Gordon (cond)
- Orion ORS-75205; 33s; rel 1978; cip

House on the Hill, The (1969)
[4811] Mason, Patrick (bar); Gregg Smith Singers; Smith, Gregg (cond) Rec 1975
- Vox SVBX-5354; 33s; 3 discs; rel 1979

Walking on the Green Grass
[4812] King Chorale; King, Gordon (cond)
- Orion ORS-75205; 33s; rel 1978; cip

HENNINGS, Nancy and WOLFF, Henry

see WOLFF, Henry and HENNINGS, Nancy

HERBERT, Victor (1859-1924)

Air de Ballet (publ 1912) (arr by Nathaniel Shilkret)
[4813] Victor Orchestra; Shilkret, Nathaniel (cond)
- Victor 9147 (in set M-C1); 78; rel pre-1936
- Victor 12591 (in set M-C33); 78; rel pre-1942

Al fresco (publ 1904)
[4814] Columbia Symphony Orchestra; Bowers, R. H. (cond)
- Columbia 1297D; 78; 10"; rel pre-1936

[4815] Rochester Pops Orchestra; Gould, Morton (cond)
- Columbia AAL-50; 33m; 10"; rel 1954; del 1957

Al fresco (arr by Nathaniel Shilkret)
[4816] Victor Orchestra; Shilkret, Nathaniel (cond)
- Victor 9147 (in set M-C1); 78; rel pre-1936
- Victor 12591 (in set M-C33); 78; rel pre-1942

American Fantasia (publ 1898)
[4817] Detroit Symphony Orchestra; Kolar, Victor (cond)
- Decca 29071; 78; rel pre-1942

[4818] Philadelphia Pops Orchestra; Ormandy, Eugene (cond)
- Columbia AAL-21; 33m; 10"; rel 1952; del 1957
- Columbia A-1030; 45; 7"; rel 1953*
- Columbia ML-5376; 33m; rel 1959; del 1966

[4819] Victor Herbert's Orchestra; Herbert, Victor (cond)
- Victor 55093; 78; rel pre-1927

[4820] Victor Symphony Orchestra; O'Connell, Charles (cond)
- Victor 36409; 78

American Fantasia (arr for band)
[4821] Columbia Band
- Columbia 50043D; 78; rel 1927

Badinage (publ 1895)
[4822] Capitol Grand Orchestra
- Brunswick 2656; 78; 10"; rel pre-1927

[4823] Columbia Symphony Orchestra; Bowers, R. H. (cond)
- Columbia 1297D; 78; 10"; rel pre-1936

[4824] Rochester Pops Orchestra; Gould, Morton (cond)
- Columbia AAL-50; 33m; 10"; rel 1954; del 1957

Badinage (publ 1895) *(cont'd)*
- Columbia CL-560; 33m; rel 1954

[4825] Victor Herbert's Orchestra; Herbert, Victor (cond)
- Victor 55104; 78; rel pre-1927

Badinage (arr by Nathaniel Shilkret)
[4826] Victor Orchestra; Shilkret, Nathaniel (cond)
- Victor 9147 (in set M-C1); 78; rel pre-1936
- Victor 12591 (in set M-C33); 78; rel pre-1942

Badinage (arr for sop and orch)
[4827] MacDonald, Jeanette (sop); orchestra; Pilzer, Maximilian (cond)
- Victor 10-1134; 78; 10"; rel pre-1948

Concerto, Violoncello and Orchestra, No 2 (Op 30) (publ 1898)
[4828] Greenhouse, Bernard (vcl); Vienna Symphony Orchestra; Schoenherr, Max (cond)
- American Recording Society ARS-24; 33m; rel 1953
- American Recording Society ARS-110; 33m; rel pre-1956
- American Recording Society ARS-111; 33m; rel pre-1956
- Desto D-417/DST-6417; 33m/s; rel 1965; cip

[4829] Miquelle, Georges (vcl); Eastman-Rochester Symphony Orchestra; Hanson, Howard (cond)
- Mercury MG-50163/SR-90163; 33m/s; rel 1958/1959; del 1963
- Mercury MG-50286/SR-90286; 33m/s; rel 1962; del 1964
- Eastman-Rochester Archives ERA-1014; 33s; rel 1978; cip

Czardas
[4830] Andre Kostelanetz and his Orchestra; Kostelanetz, Andre (cond)
- Columbia 7367M (in set M-415); 78; rel pre-1942
- Columbia MM-1012; 78; rel pre-1952
- Columbia ML-4430; 33m; rel 1951; del 1955
- Columbia CL-765; 33m; rel 1955; del 1965
- Columbia (English) SX-1036; 33m; rel pre-1956
- Columbia A-1012; 45; 7"; rel pre-1956

L'Encore
[4831] Decca Symphony Orchestra
- Decca 23123; 78; 10"

Fleurette (Valse lente) (publ 1903) (arr for orch)

[4832] Paul Lavalle Orchestra
- Musicraft 81; 78; 10"; rel pre-1948

[4833] Rochester Pops Orchestra; Gould, Morton (cond)
- Columbia AAL-50; 33m; 10"; rel 1954; del 1957

[4834] Victor Orchestra; Shilkret, Nathaniel (cond)
- Victor 9906 (in set M-C11); 78; rel pre-1936

Foreign Children

[4835] Howard, Ann (sop) (pf)
- Victor 36032; 78; rel pre-1936

Heart O' Mine (publ 1924)

[4836] Werrenrath, Reinald (bar)
- Victor 1055; 78; 10"; rel 1919-25

Hero and Leander (Op 33) (1901)

[4837] Royal Philharmonic Orchestra; Krueger, Karl (cond)
- SPAMH MIA-121; 33s; rel 1965

Indian Summer (An American Idyll) (publ 1919) (arr for orch)

[4838] Andre Kostelanetz and his Orchestra; Kostelanetz, Andre (cond)
- Columbia 7365M (in set M-415); 78; rel pre-1942
- Columbia MM-1012; 78; rel pre-1952
- Columbia ML-4430; 33m; rel 1951; del 1955
- Columbia CL-765; 33m; rel 1955; del 1965
- Columbia (English) SX-1036; 33m; rel pre-1956
- Columbia A-1012; 45; 7"; rel pre-1956

[4839] Percy Faith and his Orchestra; Faith, Percy (cond)
- Columbia CL-1196-97 (in set C2L-10); 33m; 2 discs; rel 1958

[4840] Victor Herbert's Orchestra; Herbert, Victor (cond)
- Victor 55200; 78; rel pre-1925
- Victor 55220; 78; rel pre-1927

[4841] Victor Young and his Orchestra; Young, Victor (cond)
- Decca 2319 (in set 38); 78; 10"; rel pre-1942

Indian Summer (An American Idyll) (arr for vocalists and orch)

[4842] Kirsten, Dorothy (sop); Russ Case and his Orchestra and Chorus; Case, Russ (cond)
- Victor 1069; 78; 10"; rel pre-1948

Irish Rhapsody (1892)

[4843] Cleveland Pops Orchestra; Lane, Louis (cond)
- Epic LC-3879/BC-1279; 33m/s; rel 1964; del 1967

[4844] Philadelphia Orchestra; Ormandy, Eugene (cond)
- Columbia AAL-21; 33m; 10"; rel 1952; del 1957
- Columbia A-1030; 45; 7"; rel 1953*
- Columbia ML-5376; 33m; rel 1959; del 1966

[4845] Victor Symphony Orchestra; Shilkret, Nathaniel (cond)
- Gramophone C-1889; 78; rel pre-1936
- Victor 35997; 78; rel pre-1936

Madeleine (1913-14): A Perfect Day

[4846] Alda, Frances (sop)
- Victor 74385; 78; rel 1914-16
- Victor 6370; 78; rel 1914-16

Molly (publ 1919)

[4847] Werrenrath, Reinald (bar)
- Victor 64830; 78; 10"; rel 1919-25

Natoma (1911): Habanera, Vaquero's Song, Natoma Theme, Dagger Dance, and Finale

[4848] Victor Orchestra; Shilkret, Nathaniel (cond)
- Victor 9907 (in set M-C11); 78; rel pre-1936

Natoma: Dagger Dance and Habanera

[4849] Percy Faith and his Orchestra; Faith, Percy (cond)
- Columbia CL-1196-97 (in set C2L-10); 33m; 2 discs; rel 1958

Natoma: Habanera and Sunset

[4850] Andre Kostelanetz and his Orchestra; Kostelanetz, Andre (cond)
- Columbia 7366M (in set M-415); 78; rel pre-1942
- Columbia MM-1012; 78; rel pre-1952
- Columbia ML-4430; 33m; rel 1951; del 1955
- Columbia CL-765; 33m; rel 1955; del 1965
- Columbia (English) SX-1036; 33m; rel pre-1956
- Columbia A-1012; 45; 7"; rel pre-1956

Natoma: Dagger Dance

[4851] Aeolian Orchestra
- Vocalion 14227; 78; 10"; rel pre-1927

[4852] Boston Pops Orchestra; Fiedler, Arthur (cond)
- Victor 11932 (in set M-554); 78; rel pre-1942

Natoma: Dagger Dance *(cont'd)*
- Gramophone EB-100; 78; rel pre-1952
- RCA LM-1790; 33m; rel 1954
- Victor (Danish) 16062; 45; 7"; rel pre-1956
- Victor 49-1438; 45; 7"; rel pre-1956

[4853] Carnegie Pops Orchestra; O'Connell, Charles (cond)
- Columbia ML-2176; 33m; 10"; rel 1951; del 1956

[4854] Frederick Fennell and his Orchestra; Fennell, Frederick (cond)
- Mercury PP-2007/PPS-6007; 33m/s; rel 1961
- Mercury SR-60954; 33s; rel 1964

[4855] Victor Herbert's Orchestra; Herbert, Victor (cond)
- Victor 55220; 78; rel pre-1927

Natoma: I List the Trill of Golden Throat

[4856] Gluck, Alma (sop); orchestra; Herbert, Victor (cond) Rec 6/10/12
- Victor 74274; 78; rel 1912-15
- Cantilena CF-6215; 33m; rel 1969; del 1975
- Belcantodisc BC-247; 33m; rel 197?
- New World NW-241; 33m; rel 1978

Natoma: No Country Can My Own Outvie

[4857] McCormack, John (ten); orchestra; Herbert, Victor (cond) Rec 4/3/12
- Victor 74295; 78; rel 1912
- Gramophone AGSB-3; 78; rel pre-1925
- New World NW-241; 33m; rel 1978
- RCA-Victrola VIC-1472; 33m; rel 1979; cip

Natoma: Spring Song

[4858] Gluck, Alma (sop)
- Victor 74274; 78; rel 1912-15
- Victor 6147; 78; rel 1912-15

Natoma: Vaquero's Song

[4859] Cartwright, Earl (bar)
- Victor 5871; 78; 10"; rel 1911-13

[4860] Fanning, Cecil (bar)
- Columbia A-1070; 78; rel pre-1925
- Columbia 19376; 78; rel pre-1925

Pan-Americana (Morceau characteristique) (publ 1901)

[4861] Capitol Grand Orchestra
- Brunswick 2656; 78; 10"; rel pre-1927

Pan-Americana (Morceau characteristique) (publ 1901)
(cont'd)
[4862] Columbia Symphony Orchestra;
       Bowers, R. H. (cond)
       - Columbia 50060D; 78; rel
         pre-1936

[4863] Philadelphia Orchestra; Ormandy,
       Eugene (cond)
       - Columbia AAL-21; 33m; 10"; rel
         1952; del 1957
       - Columbia A-1030; 45; 7"; rel
         1953*
       - Columbia ML-5376; 33m; rel
         1959; del 1966

[4864] Victor Orchestra; Shilkret,
       Nathaniel (cond)
       - Victor 9903 (in set M-C11); 78;
         rel pre-1936

Pan-Americana (Morceau characteristique) (arr for band)
[4865] Decca Band
       - Decca 18494; 78

Pensee amoureuse (publ 1906)
[4866] Herbert, Victor (vcl)
       - Victor 74286; 78; rel 1912

Petite valse (publ 1906)
[4867] Herbert, Victor (vcl)
       - Victor 64297; 78; 10"; rel 1912
       - Victor 677; 78; 10"; rel 1912

[4868] Powell, Maud (vln)
       - Victor 64617; 78; 10"; rel
         1913-17

(Two) Pieces, Violin: A la valse (publ 1915)
[4869] Elman, Mischa (vln)
       - Victor 1079; 78; 10"; rel
         1920-25

[4870] Heifetz, Jascha (vln); Kaye, Milton
       (pf)
       - Decca DL-9760; 33m; rel 1955;
         del 1971

President's March, The (publ 1898)
[4871] Goldman Band; Goldman, Richard
       Franko (cond)
       - New World NW-266; 33s; rel
         1977

Punchinello (publ 1900) (arr by Nathaniel Shilkret)
[4872] Victor Orchestra; Shilkret,
       Nathaniel (cond)
       - Victor 9904 (in set M-C11); 78;
         rel pre-1936

Slumber Song
[4873] Wilson, M.; Rodgers, R.
       - Victor 24542; 78; 10"; rel
         pre-1936

Suite, Violoncello (Op 3) (1894): 4th Movement (Serenade)
[4874] Victor Orchestra; Shilkret,
       Nathaniel (cond)
       - Victor 9907 (in set M-C11); 78;
         rel pre-1936

Suite, Violoncello: 4th Movement (arr for string quartet)
[4875] Musical Arts Quartet
       - Columbia 190M; 78; 10"; rel
         pre-1936

Suite of Serenades (publ 1924)
[4876] Life Guards Band
       - Vocalion (English) K-05293; 78;
         rel pre-1927

[4877] Paul Whiteman Orchestra;
       Whiteman, Paul (cond)
       - Victor 55226; 78; rel pre-1927
       - Victor 35926; 78; rel pre-1936

[4878] Rochester Pops Orchestra; Gould,
       Morton (cond)
       - Columbia AAL-50; 33m; 10"; rel
         1954; del 1957
       - Columbia CL-560; 33m; rel
         1954

Suite of Serenades: Spanish Serenade and Cuban Serenade
[4879] Percy Faith and his Orchestra;
       Faith, Percy (cond)
       - Columbia CL-1196-97 (in set
         C2L-10); 33m; 2 discs; rel 1958

Suite of Serenades: Spanish Serenade
[4880] Allegro Concert Orchestra; Bath,
       John (cond)
       - Allegro-Elite 4013; 33m; 10"; rel
         1954; del 1957

Sunset (publ 1912)
[4881] string orchestra; Kostelanetz,
       Andre (cond)
       - Columbia M-30075; 33s; rel
         1970

Under the Elms (Souvenir de Saratoga) (publ 1903) (arr by Nathaniel Shilkret)
[4882] Victor Orchestra; Shilkret,
       Nathaniel (cond)
       - Victor 9906 (in set M-C11); 78;
         rel pre-1936

When You're Away
[4883] Andre Kostelanetz and his
       Orchestra; Kostelanetz, Andre
       (cond)
       - Columbia 7365M (in set M-415);
         78; rel pre-1942
       - Columbia MM-1012; 78; rel
         pre-1952
       - Columbia ML-4430; 33m; rel
         1951; del 1955
       - Columbia CL-765; 33m; rel
         1955; del 1965
       - Columbia (English) SX-1036;
         33m; rel pre-1956

When You're Away *(cont'd)*
       - Columbia A-1012; 45; 7"; rel
         pre-1956

Willow Plate, The (publ 1924)
[4884] Allegro Concert Orchestra; Bath,
       John (cond)
       - Allegro-Elite 4013; 33m; 10"; rel
         1954; del 1957
       - Festival (Australian) CFR-10-578;
         33m; rel pre-1956

Yesterthoughts (publ 1900)
[4885] Percy Faith and his Orchestra;
       Faith, Percy (cond)
       - Columbia CL-1196-97 (in set
         C2L-10); 33m; 2 discs; rel 1958

[4886] Rochester Pops Orchestra; Gould,
       Morton (cond)
       - Columbia AAL-50; 33m; 10"; rel
         1954; del 1957
       - Columbia CL-560; 33m; rel
         1954

[4887] Victor Orchestra; Shilkret,
       Nathaniel (cond)
       - Victor 9906 (in set M-C11); 78;
         rel pre-1936

[4888] Victor Young and his Orchestra;
       Young, Victor (cond)
       - Decca 2319 (in set 38); 78;
         10"; rel pre-1942

HERDER, Ronald (1930-)
Movements (1963)
[4889] Louisville Orchestra; Whitney,
       Robert (cond)
       - LOU-66-5/LS-66-5; 33m/s
         (Louisville Orchestra First Edition
         Records 1966 No 5); rel 1967;
         cip

HERRMANN, Bernard (1911-75)
Echoes (1965)
[4890] Amici Quartet
       - Pye GSGC-14101; 33s; rel 1967
       - Unicorn RHS-332; 33s; rel
         1976*

Fantasticks, The (1944)
[4891] Humphreys, Gillian (sop);
       Dickinson, Meriel (al); Amis, John
       (ten); Rippon, Michael (b);
       Thames Chamber Choir; National
       Philharmonic Orchestra;
       Herrmann, Bernard (cond)
       Rec 6/26/75
       - Unicorn RHS-340; 33s; rel 1976

For the Fallen (1943)
[4892] National Philharmonic Orchestra;
       Herrmann, Bernard (cond)
       Rec 6/26/75
       - Unicorn RHS-340; 33s; rel 1976

Moby Dick (1936-38)
[4893] Amis, John (ten); Bowman, Robert
(ten); Kelly, David (b); Rippon,
Michael (b); Aeolian Singers;
London Philharmonic Orchestra;
Herrmann, Bernard (cond)
- Pye TPLS-13006; 33s; rel 1970
- Unicorn UNI-72015; 33s; rel
1979

Souvenirs de voyage (1967)
[4894] Hill, Robert (cl); Ariel Quartet
- Unicorn RHS-332; 33s; rel
1976*

Symphony (1940)
[4895] National Philharmonic Orchestra;
Herrmann, Bernard (cond)
Rec 1/10/74
- Unicorn RHS-331; 33s; rel 1975
- Unicorn UNI-75003; 33s; rel
1978; del 1980

Wuthering Heights (1940-52)
[4896] Beaton; Bowen; Bainbridge; Bell;
Kitchiner; Ward; Rippon, Michael;
Kelly, David; Elizabethan Singers;
Pro Arte Orchestra; Herrmann,
Bernard (cond)
- Pye CSCL-301731-34; 33s; 4
discs; rel 1970

HERSTEIN, Peter
Wall Fantasy
[4897] Cornell University Wind Ensemble;
Stith, Marice (cond)
- Cornell CUWE-8; 33s; rel 1971;
cip

HERVIG, Richard (1917-)
**Chamber Music for Six Players
(1976)**
[4898] Mather, Betty Bang (fl); Ayres,
Thomas (cl); Simms, John (pf);
Davis, Thomas L. (perc); La
Fosse, Leopold (vln); Obrecht,
Eldon (cb); Hibbard, William
(cond)
Rec 1/77
- CRI-380; 33s; rel 1978; cip

Quartet, Strings (1955)
[4899] Stradivari Quartet
- Orion ORS-79340; 33s; rel
1979; cip

**Sonata, Clarinet and Piano, No 1
(1953)**
[4900] Ayres, Thomas (cl); Avery, James
(pf)
- Orion ORS-79340; 33s; rel
1979; cip

HEUSSENSTAM, George (1926-)
(Seven) Etudes, Woodwind Trio
[4901] Westwood Wind Quintet
- Crystal S-811; 33s; rel 1971; cip

Set for Double-Reeds (Op 39)
[4902] Los Angeles Philharmonic
Orchestra (members of); Endo,
Akira (cond)
- Crystal S-871; 33s; rel 1972; cip

Tetralogue
[4903] Los Angeles Clarinet Society; Ervin,
Karen (perc)
- WIM Records WIMR-7; 33s; rel
1973; cip

Tubafour (Op 30) (1969)
[4904] New York Tuba Quartet
- Crystal S-221; 33s; rel 1977; cip

HIBBARD, William (1939-)
Quartet, Strings (1971)
[4905] Stradivari Quartet
- CRI-322; 33s; rel 1974; cip

**Trio, Bass Clarinet, Bass Trombone,
and Harp (1973)**
[4906] University of Iowa Center for New
Music Ensemble (members of);
Hibbard, William (cond)
- CRI-324; 33s; rel 1975; cip

**HILL, Edward Burlingame
(1872-1960)**
Jazz Study, A (1922-24)
[4907] Maier, Guy (pf); Pattison, Lee (pf)
- Victor 45346; 78; rel pre-1927

Prelude (1952-53)
[4908] Columbia Symphony Orchestra;
Bernstein, Leonard (cond)
- Columbia ML-4996; 33m; rel
1955; del 1966

**Sextet, Piano and Winds (Op 39)
(1934)**
[4909] Kalir, Lilian (pf); New York
Woodwind Quintet
- Columbia ML-4846; 33m; rel
1954; del 1968
- Columbia CML-4846; 33m; rel
1968; del 1974
- Columbia AML-4846; 33m; rel
1974; del 1976

**Stevensoniana Suite No 1 (Op 24)
(1916-17)**
[4910] Royal Philharmonic Orchestra;
Krueger, Karl (cond)
- SPAMH MIA-142; 33s; rel 1969

HILL, William H. (1925-)
Concerto, Euphonium and Band
[4911] Royall, Dennis (euph); California
State University (Los Angeles)
Wind Ensemble; Hill, William H.
(cond)
- Golden Crest ATH-5053; 33s; rel
1978; cip

Dances Sacred and Profane
[4912] California State University (Los
Angeles) Wind Ensemble; Hill,
William H. (cond)
- Golden Crest ATH-5053; 33s; rel
1978; cip

Sioux Variants
[4913] California State University (Los
Angeles) Wind Ensemble; Hill,
William H. (cond)
- Golden Crest ATH-5053; 33s; rel
1978; cip

Sonitus revelationis
[4914] California State University (Los
Angeles) Wind Ensemble; Hill,
William H. (cond)
- Golden Crest ATH-5053; 33s; rel
1978; cip

HILLER, Lejaren (1924-)
**Algorithms I (1968): Versions I and
IV**
[4915] Buffalo Center of the Creative and
Performing Arts (members of)
- Deutsche Grammophon
2543.005; 33s; rel 1971; del
1975

(Five) Appalachian Ballads (1958)
[4916] Simpson, Winifred (sop); Sussman,
David (gtr)
- Orion ORS-78287; 33s; rel
1978; cip

Avalanche, An (1968)
[4917] MacDonald, Royal (nar); Marder,
Norma (sop); Rosen (perc); player
piano; tape
- Heliodor 2549.006; 33s; rel
1970; del 1973
- Capra 1206; 33s; rel 1979; cip

**Computer Music (After Computer
Cantata) (1963)**
[4918] percussion; tape
- Heliodor 2549.006; 33s; rel
1970; del 1973

Jesse James (1950)
[4919] Bane, Jane (sop); Rosenberg,
Marjorie (al); Daniel, Keith (ten);
Schultze, Andrew (b); Cary, Jane
(pf)
- Orion ORS-78287; 33s; rel
1978; cip

Machine Music (1964)
[4920] Rappeport, Phyllis (pf); Siwe,
Thomas (perc); tape
- Heliodor H-25047/HS-25047;
33m/s; rel 1967; del 1970

[4921] Shields, Roger (pf); Kowalsky,
Jeffrey (perc); tape
- Turnabout TVS-34536; 33s; rel
1973; del 1978

Malta (1975)
[4922] Cummings, Barton (tu); tape
- Capra 1206; 33s; rel 1979; cip

Quartet, Strings, No 5 (1962)
[4923] Concord String Quartet
- Vox SVBX-5306; 33s; 3 discs; rel 1973; cip

Quartet, Strings, No 6 (1972)
[4924] Concord String Quartet
- CRI-332; 33s; rel 1975; cip

Sonata, Piano, No 4 (1950)
[4925] Boldt, Frina Arschanska (pf)
- Orion ORS-75176; 33s; rel 1975; cip

Sonata, Piano, No 5 (1961)
[4926] Boldt, Kenwyn (pf)
- Orion ORS-75176; 33s; rel 1975; cip

Sonata, Violin and Piano, No 3 (1970)
[4927] Sokol, Mark (vln); Shields, Roger (pf)
- Turnabout TVS-34536; 33s; rel 1973; del 1978

Suite, Two Pianos and Tape (After A Triptych for Hieronymus) (1966)
[4928] Shields, Roger (pf); Bruce, Neely (pf)
- Heliodor 2549.006; 33s; rel 1970; del 1973
- Capra 1206; 33s; rel 1979; cip

Time of the Heathen (1961): Nightmare Music
[4929] Electronic music
- Heliodor 2549.006; 33s; rel 1970; del 1973

Twelve-Tone Variations (1954)
[4930] Shields, Roger (pf)
- Turnabout TVS-34536; 33s; rel 1973; del 1978

HILLER, Lejaren and BAKER, Robert
Computer Cantata (1963)
[4931] Hamm, Helen (sop); University of Illinois Contemporary Chamber Players; University of Illinois Composition String Quartet; McKenzie, Jack (cond)
- Heliodor H-25053/HS-25053; 33m/s; rel 1967; del 1970
- CRI-310; 33s; rel 1973; cip

HILLER, Lejaren and CAGE, John
see CAGE, John and HILLER, Lejaren

HILLER, Lejaren and ISAACSON, Leonard M.
Illiac Suite (String Quartet No 4) (1957)
[4932] University of Illinois Composition String Quartet
- Heliodor H-25053/HS-25053; 33m/s; rel 1967; del 1970

HIVELY, Wells (1902-69)
(Tres) Himnos (1946-47)
[4933] Eastman-Rochester Symphony Orchestra; Hanson, Howard (cond)
- Mercury MG-40013; 33m; rel 1955; del 1957
- Mercury MG-50086; 33m; rel 1957; del 1963
- Eastman-Rochester Archives ERA-1015; 33s; rel 1978; cip

Icarus (1961)
[4934] Polish National Radio Orchestra; Wodiczko, Bodhan (cond)
- CRI-254; 33s; rel 1970; cip

Summer Holiday (Rive gauche) (1944)
[4935] Accademia Nazionale di Santa Cecilia Orchestra, Roma; Antonini, Alfredo (cond)
- CRI-111; 33m/s; rel 1957/?; cip

HOBBS, Christopher (1950-)
(Six) Preludes and Five Chorales
[4936] no performers given
- Zanja ZR-2; 33; rel 197?

HOBBS, Odell*
Halls of Ivy
[4937] Virginia Union University Choir; Hobbs, Odell (cond)
- Richmond Sound Stages RSSWO-626; 33

HODKINSON, Sydney (1934-)
Dance Variations (On a Chopin Fragment) (1977)
[4938] Snyder, Barry (pf); Zeitlin, Zvi (vln); Sylvester, Robert (vcl)
- CRI-432; 33s; rel 1980; cip

Dissolution of the Serial, The (1967)
[4939] Errante, F. Gerard (cl) (b cl) (sax); Albright, William (pf)
- CRI-292; 33s; rel 1973; cip

Edge of the Olde One, The (1977)
[4940] Stacy, Thomas (E hn); Eastman Musica Nova; Phillips, Paul (cond)
- Grenadilla GS-1048; 33s; rel 1979

Megalith Trilogy (1973)
[4941] Albright, William (org)
Rec 3/15/76
- CRI-363; 33s; rel 1977; cip

(Two) Structures (1958)
[4942] University of Illinois Percussion Ensemble; McKenzie, Jack (cond)
- Illini Union Bookstore CRS-6; 33m; rel 1960*

Valence (1970)
[4943] St. Paul Chamber Orchestra; Hodkinson, Sydney (cond)
- CRI-292; 33s; rel 1973; cip

HOFFMANN, Richard (1925-)
In memoriam patris (1976)
[4944] Electronic music
- CRI-393; 33s; rel 1979; cip

Orchestra Piece (1961)
[4945] Oberlin Orchestra; Baustian, Robert (cond)
- Acoustic Research AR-0654.084; 33s; rel 1971

Trio, Strings (1961-63)
[4946] Zukofsky, Paul (vln); Dupouy, Jean (vla); Sylvester, Robert (vcl)
- CRI-240; 33s; rel 1969; cip

HOIBY, Lee (1926-)
After Eden (Op 25) (1966)
[4947] London Symphony Orchestra; Foster, Lawrence (cond)
- Desto DC-6434; 33s; rel 1970; cip

At the Round Earth's Imagined Corners
[4948] Washington Cathedral Choir; Dirksen, Richard W. (org) (cond)
- Washington Cathedral Archives CAR-009; 33s; rel 1979?

Beatrice (1959)
[4949] Kentucky Opera Association (members of); Louisville Orchestra (members of); Bomhard, Moritz (cond)
- LOU-60-3; 33m; 2 discs (Louisville Orchestra First Edition Records 1960 No 3); rel 1960; del 1972

Concerto, Piano and Orchestra (Op 17) (1957)
[4950] Atkins, John (pf); Polish National Radio Orchestra; Krenz, Jan (cond)
- CRI-214; 33m/s; rel 1968; cip

Summer and Smoke (Op 27) (1971): Anatomy Lesson and Scene
[4951] Parker, William (bar); Huckaby, William (pf)
- New World NW-305; 33s; rel 1980

HOLDRIDGE, Lee (1944-)

Andante
[4952] London Symphony Orchestra;
Holdridge, Lee (cond)
- Varese Sarabande VC-81081;
33s; rel 1979; cip
- Varese Sarabande DBX-81081;
33s; rel 1980; cip

Concerto, Violin and Orchestra, No 2
[4953] Dicterow, Glenn (vln); London
Symphony Orchestra; Holdridge,
Lee (cond)
- Varese Sarabande Digital
VCDM-1000.40; 33 and 45
digital

Grand Waltz
[4954] London Symphony Orchestra;
Holdridge, Lee (cond)
- Varese Sarabande VC-81081;
33s; rel 1979; cip
- Varese Sarabande DBX-81081;
33s; rel 1980; cip

**Lazarus and his Beloved
(Symphonic Suite)**
[4955] London Symphony Orchestra;
Holdridge, Lee (cond)
- Varese Sarabande Digital
VCDM-1000.40; 33 and 45
digital

Scenes of Summer (1973)
[4956] London Symphony Orchestra;
Holdridge, Lee (cond)
- Varese Sarabande VC-81081;
33s; rel 1979; cip
- Varese Sarabande DBX-81081;
33s; rel 1980; cip

HOLLANDER, Lorin (1944-)

Up against the Wall
[4957] Hollander, Lorin (pf)
- Angel S-36025; 33s; rel 1969;
del 1974

HOLLINGSWORTH, Stanley (1924-)

Stabat mater (1957)
[4958] Syracuse Music Festival Chorus;
Brown, Elaine (cond)
- Desto 102; 33m/s; rel 1964; del
1969

HOLMES, Paul (1923-)

Lento, Tuba and Piano
[4959] Conner, Rex (tu)
- Coronet M-1259; 33m; rel
1969; cip

[4960] Le Blanc, Robert (tu); Baker, Myra
(pf)
- Coronet S-1721; 33s; rel 1973;
cip

HOLMES, Robert L.

Citizens' Threshold
[4961] Fisk Jubilee Singers; Holmes,
Robert (cond)
- NR-2597; 33s; rel 1972

Eye of the Storm
[4962] Fisk Jubilee Singers; Jones, Quincy
(cond)
- NR-2597; 33s; rel 1972

Yesterday's Mansions
[4963] Trio Pro Viva
- Eastern ERS-513; 33s; 2 discs;
rel 1973*

HOLZMAN, Abe (1874-1939)

Alagazam March
[4964] Arthur Pryor's Band; Pryor, Arthur
(cond)
Rec 12/11/03
- Victor 2645; 78; 10"
- New World NW-282; 33m; rel
1976

HOMER, Sidney (1864-1953)

Banjo Song, A
[4965] Bispham, David (bar)
- Columbia 30767; 78; rel
1911-15
- Columbia A-5320; 78; rel
1911-15

[4966] Homer, Louise (al)
- Victor 87074; 78; 10"; rel
1906-11
- Victor 680; 78; 10"; rel
1906-11
- Victor 87572; 78; 10"; rel
1919-25
- Victor 3016; 78; 10"; rel
1919-25

Boats Sail
[4967] Homer, Louise (al)
- Victor 87205; 78; 10"; rel
1912-18

Dearest
[4968] Homer, Louise (al)
- Victor 88407; 78; rel 1912-18

[4969] Witherspoon, Herbert (b)
- Victor 64185; 78; 10"; rel
1907-11

Mother Goose Songs
[4970] Homer, Louise (al)
- Victor 88640; 78; rel 1919-25

Pauper's Drive, The
[4971] Bispham, David (bar)
- Columbia 30333; 78; rel
1906-10
- Columbia A-5166; 78; rel
1906-10

Requiem
[4972] De Gogorza, Emilio (bar); orchestra
- Victor 992; 78; 10"; rel
1921-25
- Victor 66228; 78; 10"; rel
1921-25

[4973] Homer, Louise (al)
- Victor 88407; 78; rel 1912-18

[4974] Witherspoon, Herbert (b)
- Victor 64185; 78; 10"; rel
1907-11

Sheep and Lambs
[4975] Homer, Louise (al)
- Victor 87376; 78; 10"; rel
1919-25
- Victor 979; 78; 10"; rel
1919-25

Sick Rose, The
[4976] Moore, Dale (bar); Tomfohrde,
Betty Ruth (pf)
- Cambridge CRS-2715; 33s; rel
1973; cip

Sing Me a Song
[4977] Homer, Louise (al)
- Victor 64026; 78; 10"; rel
1903-05
- Victor 81036; 78; 10"; rel
1903-05

Sing to Me, Sing
[4978] Farrell, Eileen (sop); Trovillo,
George (pf)
- Angel 35608; 33m; rel 1959;
del 1966

Uncle Rome
[4979] Thomas, John Charles (bar)
- Vocalion (English) B-60055; 78;
rel pre-1925

[4980] Whitehill, Clarence (bar)
- Victor 64388; 78; 10"; rel
pre-1925

HOOD, Boyde W. (1939-)

Pange lingua (1968)
[4981] Ball State University Choir and
Instrumental Ensemble; Corwin,
George (cond)
- Golden Crest CRS-4087; 33s; rel
1970; cip

Puer nobis nascitur (1967)
[4982] Ball State University Choir and
Instrumental Ensemble; Corwin,
George (cond)
- Golden Crest CRS-4087; 33s; rel
1970; cip

HOOVER, Katherine (1937-)

Divertimento, Flute and String Trio
[4983] Gold, Diane (fl); Alard Quartet
(members of)
- Leonarda LPI-105; 33s; rel 1980

**On the Betrothal of Princess
Isabelle of France, Aged Six**
[4984] Eskin, Virginia (pf)
- Leonarda LPI-104; 33s; rel 1980

Sinfonia
[4985] New York Bassoon Quartet
- Leonarda LPI-102; 33s; rel 1980

Trio (1978)
[4986] Rogeri Trio
Rec 3/23/79
- Leonarda LPI-103; 33s; rel 1980

HOPKINS, James (1939-)

Diferencias (1973)
[4987] Western Arts Trio
- Laurel LR-104; 33s; rel 1976;
cip

HORN, Paul (1930-)

Haida
[4988] Electronic music
- Epic KE-31600; 33s; rel 1972

Mahabhutas, The (Elements)
[4989] Electronic music
- Epic KE-31600; 33s; rel 1972

HOROWITZ, Vladimir (1904-)

Danse excentrique
[4990] Horowitz, Vladimir (pf)
Rec 1928-47
- RCA LM-2993; 33m; rel 1968;
cip

[4991] MacKenzie, Arthur (pf)
- Westminster WGS-8261; 33s; rel
1975; del 1977

HORVIT, Michael (1932-)

Antiphon II
[4992] Rehfeldt, Phillip (cl); tape
- Grenadilla GS-1017; 33s; rel
1980; cip

HORWOOD, Michael (1947-)

**Overture for Piano Player and Two
Assistants (1972)**
[4993] Kubera, Joseph (pf); Horwood,
Michael (assistant)
- Opus One 36; 33s; rel 1978; cip

HOSKINS, William Barnes (1917-)

Eastern Reflections
[4994] Electronic music
- Spectrum SR-106; 33s; rel 1979

Galactic Fantasy
[4995] Electronic music
- Spectrum SR-106; 33s; rel 1979

HOSMER, Lucius (1870-1935)

Romanza
[4996] McGinnis, Robert (cl); Baker, Myra
(pf)
- Coronet S-1705; 33s; rel 1970*

HOVEY, Serge (1920-)

**Tevya and his Daughters (Incidental
Music) (1957)**
[4997] no performers given
- Columbia OL-5225; 33m; rel
1957

HOVHANESS, Alan (1911-)

Achtamar (Op 64, No 1) (1948)
[4998] Ajemian, Maro (pf)
- Dial 6; 33m; rel 1950; del 1956
- Metronome CLP-505; 33m; rel
pre-1953

[4999] Masselos, William (pf)
- MGM E-3160; 33m; rel 1955;
del 1959

**Allegro on a Pakistan Lute Tune
(Op 104, No 6) (1951)**
[5000] Helps, Robert (pf)
- RCA LM-7042/LSC-7042;
33m/s; 2 discs; rel 1966; del
1971
- CRI-288; 33s; 2 discs; rel 1972;
cip

**Alleluia and Fugue (Op 40b)
(1941)**
[5001] MGM Orchestra; Surinach, Carlos
(cond)
- MGM E-3504; 33m; rel 1957;
del 1959

Anahid (Op 57) (1945)
[5002] MGM Orchestra; Surinach, Carlos
(cond)
- MGM E-3504; 33m; rel 1957;
del 1959

**And God Created Great Whales (Op
229) (1970)**
[5003] Andre Kostelanetz and his
Orchestra; taped whale sounds;
Kostelanetz, Andre (cond)
- Columbia M-30390; 33s; rel
1971; cip
- Columbia M-34537; 33s; rel
1977; cip

**(Twelve) Armenian Folk Songs (Op
43) (1943): Nos 3, 7, 10, 11, and
12**
[5004] Bennett, Bob L. (pf)
- Educo 3110; 33

**Armenian Rhapsody No 1 (Op 45)
(1944)**
[5005] Crystal Chamber Orchestra
(strings); Gold, Ernest (cond)
- Crystal S-800; 33s; rel 1976; cip

**Armenian Rhapsody No 2 (Op 51)
(1944)**
[5006] MGM String Orchestra; Surinach,
Carlos (cond)
- MGM E-3517; 33m; rel 1958;
del 1959

**Armenian Rhapsody No 3 (Op 189)
(1944)**
[5007] Royal Philharmonic Orchestra;
Hovhaness, Alan (cond)
- Poseidon 1004; 33s; rel 1971;
cip

**As on the Night (Christmas Ode)
(Op 100, No 1b) (1952)**
[5008] Valente, Benita (sop); Bayerischer
Rundfunk Singers; Bamberg
Symphony (members of);
Antonini, Alfredo (cond)
- CRI-221; 33s; rel 1968; cip

**Avak the Healer (Op 64) (1945,
rev 1946)**
[5009] Farris, Mary Lee (m sop); Rapier,
Leon (tpt); Louisville Orchestra;
Mester, Jorge (cond)
- LS-73-5; 33s (Louisville
Orchestra First Edition Records
1973 No 5); rel 1974; cip

[5010] Nixon, Marni (sop); Stevens,
Thomas (tpt); Crystal Chamber
Orchestra (strings); Gold, Ernest
(cond)
- Crystal S-800; 33s; rel 1976; cip

Ave Maria (Op 100, No 1a) (1952)
[5011] Valente, Benita (sop); Bayerischer
Rundfunk Singers; Bamberg
Symphony (members of);
Antonini, Alfredo (cond)
- CRI-221; 33s; rel 1968; cip

Bacchanale (1968)
[5012] Gardiner; Tristan Fry Percussion
Ensemble; Eliot, John (cond)
- Gale 004; 33s; rel 1979; cip

**Black Pool of Cat (Op 84, No 1)
(1949)**
[5013] Berberian, Ara (b); Hovhaness,
Alan (pf)
- Poseidon 1005; 33s; rel 1971;
cip

**Celestial Fantasy (Op 44) (1935,
orchd 1944)**
[5014] MGM String Orchestra; Surinach,
Carlos (cond)
- MGM E-3517; 33m; rel 1958;
del 1959

**Concerto No 1, Orchestra
(Arevakal) (Op 88) (1951)**
[5015] Eastman-Rochester Symphony
Orchestra; Hanson, Howard
(cond)
- Mercury MG-40005; 33m; rel
1953; del 1957

Concerto No 1, Orchestra (Arevakal) (Op 88) (1951) *(cont'd)*
- Mercury MG-50078; 33m; rel 1957; del 1963

Concerto No 2, Violin and Orchestra (Op 89a) (1951)
[5016] Ajemian, Anahid (vln); MGM String Orchestra; Surinach, Carlos (cond)
- MGM E-3674; 33m; rel 1958; del 1959
- Heliodor H-25040/HS-25040; 33m/s; rel 1966; del 1970

Concerto No 7, Orchestra (Op 116) (1953)
[5017] Louisville Orchestra; Whitney, Robert (cond)
- LOU-545-4; 33m (Louisville Orchestra First Edition Records 1955 No 4); rel 1959; del 1978

Concerto, Harp and Strings (Op 267) (1973)
[5018] Wurtzler, Aristid von (hp); Festival Orchestra; Valante, Harrison R. (cond)
- Musical Heritage Society MHS-3370; 33s; rel 1976

(Six) Dances (Op 79) (1967)
[5019] Dallas Brass Quintet
- Crystal S-203; 33s; rel 1979; cip

Dawn at Laona (Op 153) (1957)
[5020] Berberian, Ara (b); Hovhaness, Alan (pf)
- Poseidon 1005; 33s; rel 1971; cip

Distant Lake of Sighs
[5021] Berberian, Ara (b); Hovhaness, Alan (pf)
- Poseidon 1009; 33s; rel 1972; cip

Duet, Violin and Harpsichord (Op 122) (1954)
[5022] Brink, Robert (vln); Pinkham, Daniel (hpschd)
- CRI-109; 33m/s; rel 1957/?; cip

Easter Cantata (Op 100, No 3) (1953)
[5023] Valente, Benita (sop); Bayerischer Rundfunk Singers; Bamberg Symphony (members of); Antonini, Alfredo (cond)
- CRI-221; 33s; rel 1968; cip

Fantasy, Piano (To Tumburu) (Op 16) (1953)
[5024] Hovhaness, Alan (pf)
- Poseidon 2; 33m; rel 1970; del 1978
- Poseidon 1007; 33m; rel 1978; cip

Fantasy on an Ossetin Tune (Op 85) (1951)
[5025] Masselos, William (pf)
- MGM E-3160; 33m; rel 1955; del 1959

Fantasy on Japanese Woodprints (Op 211) (1965)
[5026] Hiraoka, Yoichi (xyl); Andre Kostelanetz and his Orchestra; Kostelanetz, Andre (cond)
- Columbia CL-2581/CS-9381; 33m/s; rel 1967; del 1974
- Columbia M-34537; 33s; rel 1977; cip

Firdausi (Op 252, No 2) (1972)
[5027] Long Island Chamber Ensemble of New York
- Grenadilla GS-1008; 33s; rel 1977; cip

Floating World (Ukiyo) (Op 209) (1964)
[5028] Andre Kostelanetz and his Orchestra; Kostelanetz, Andre (cond)
- Columbia MS-7162; 33s; rel 1968; del 1971
- Columbia M-34537; 33s; rel 1977; cip

Flowering Peach, The (Op 125) (1954)
[5029] chamber ensemble; Hovhaness, Alan (cond)
- MGM E-3164; 33m; rel 1955; del 1959

Flute Player of the Armenian Mountains, The (Op 239) (1946, rev 1971)
[5030] Berberian, Ara (b); Hovhaness, Alan (pf)
- Poseidon 1008; 33s; rel 1972; cip

Fra Angelico (Op 220) (1967)
[5031] New Orleans Philharmonic-Symphony Orchestra; Torkanowsky, Werner (cond)
- Orion ORS-7268; 33s; rel 1972; cip

[5032] Royal Philharmonic Orchestra; Hovhaness, Alan (cond)
- Poseidon 1002; 33s; rel 1970; cip

From High Armenia Mountain
[5033] Berberian, Ara (b); Hovhaness, Alan (pf)
- Poseidon 1009; 33s; rel 1972; cip

(Six) Greek Folk Dances (Op 150) (1956)
[5034] Sebastian, John (harmonica); Josi, Renato (pf)
- Deutsche Grammophon DGM-12015/DGS-712015; 33m/s; rel 1959; del 1961

Hercules (Op 56, No 4)
[5035] Malfitano, Catherine (sop); Malfitano, Joseph (vln)
- Musical Heritage Society MHS-1976; 33s; rel 1974

Holy City, The (Op 218) (1965)
[5036] Royal Philharmonic Orchestra; Lipkin, Arthur Bennett (cond)
- CRI-259; 33s; rel 1970; cip

How I Adore Thee (Op 7) (1936)
[5037] Berberian, Ara (b); Hovhaness, Alan (pf)
- Poseidon 1005; 33s; rel 1971; cip

Hymn to a Celestial Musician (Op 111, No 2) (1952)
[5038] Masselos, William (pf)
- MGM E-3160; 33m; rel 1955; del 1959

Hymn to Yerevan (Op 83) (1969)
[5039] North Jersey Wind Symphony; Brion, Keith (cond)
- Mace MXX-9099; 33s; rel 1971; del 1975

In Early Dawn Time
[5040] Berberian, Ara (b); Hovhaness, Alan (pf)
- Poseidon 1009; 33s; rel 1972; cip

In the Beginning Was the Word (Op 206) (1963)
[5041] Harsanyi, Janice (sop); Berberian, Ara (b); National Methodist Student Movement Chorus; Lincoln Symphony Orchestra (members of); Johnson, Thor (cond)
- Methodist Student Movement 100-01; 33m; 2 discs; rel 1965; del 1970

Invocations to Vahaken (Op 54) (1945): Nos 4 and 5
[5042] Ajemian, Maro (pf); Hovhaness, Alan (perc)
- Disc 3058 (in set 675); 78; rel pre-1948

Is There Survival? (King Vahaken) (Op 59) (1949)
[5043] chamber ensemble; Hovhaness, Alan (cond)
- MGM E-3164; 33m; rel 1955; del 1959

Island of Mysterious Bells (Op 244) (1971)
[5044] New York Harp Ensemble; Wurtzler, Aristid von (cond)
- Musical Heritage Society MHS-1844; 33s; rel 1974

Island Sunrise (Op 107) (1965)
[5045] Andre Kostelanetz and his Orchestra; Kostelanetz, Andre (cond)
- Columbia M-34537; 33s; rel 1977; cip

Jhala (Op 103) (1952)
[5046] Masselos, William (pf)
- MGM E-3160; 33m; rel 1955; del 1959

Khaldis (Op 91) (1951) (revised version)
[5047] Berkofsky, Martin (pf); Rohdin, Willia (tpt); Cahn, Dan (tpt); Bonny, Francis (tpt); Dougherty, Patrick (tpt); Boyar, Neal (perc); Sobol, Lawrence (cond)
- Poseidon 1011; 33s; rel 1973; cip

[5048] Masselos, William (pf); chamber ensemble; Solomon, Izler (cond)
- MGM E-3160; 33m; rel 1955; del 1959
- Heliodor H-25027/HS-25027; 33m/s; rel 1966; del 1970

Khirgiz Suite (Op 73) (1951)
[5049] Ajemian, Anahid (vln); Ajemian, Maro (pf)
- MGM E-3454; 33m; rel 1957; del 1959
- MGM E-3517; 33m; rel 1958; del 1959

Koke no niwa (Moss Garden) (Op 181) (1954, rev 1960)
[5050] Kaplan, Melvin (E hn); Rosenberger, Walter (perc); Bailey, Elden (perc); Negri, Ruth (hp)
- CRI-186; 33m/s; rel 1964/1971; cip

Lady of Light (Op 227)
[5051] Clark, Patricia (sop); Fyson, Leslie (bar); Ambrosian Singers; Royal Philharmonic Orchestra; Hovhaness, Alan (cond)
- Poseidon 1006; 33s; rel 1971; cip

Lament (Op 20b) (1937)
[5052] Ignacio, Lydia Walton (pf)
- Capra 1205; 33s; rel 1979; cip

Live in the Sun (Op 169) (1954, rev 1960)
[5053] Berberian, Ara (b); Hovhaness, Alan (pf)
- Poseidon 1009; 33s; rel 1972; cip

Lousadzak (Op 48) (1944)
[5054] Ajemian, Maro (pf); MGM String Orchestra; Surinach, Carlos (cond)
- MGM E-3674; 33m; rel 1958; del 1959
- Heliodor H-25040/HS-25040; 33m/s; rel 1966; del 1970

[5055] Ajemian, Maro (pf); orchestra; Hovhaness, Alan (cond)
- Disc 876; 78; 3 discs; rel pre-1948
- Dial 6; 33m; rel 1950; del 1956
- Metronome CLP-505; 33m; rel pre-1953
- Folkways FM-3369; 33m; rel 1967; cip

(Seven) Love Songs of Hafiz (Op 33, Version 1) (1935)
[5056] Berberian, Ara (b); Hovhaness, Alan (pf)
- Poseidon 1005; 33s; rel 1971; cip

Lullaby (Op 52, No 7) (1951)
[5057] Richter, Marga (pf)
- MGM E-3147; 33m; rel 1955; del 1959

Lullaby of the Lake (Op 74, No 4) (1948)
[5058] Berberian, Ara (b); Hovhaness, Alan (pf)
- Poseidon 1005; 33s; rel 1971; cip

Macedonian Mountain Dance (Op 144, No 2)
[5059] Carpenter, Richard (pf)
- Educo 3104; 33

[5060] Manhattan Piano Quartet
- MGM E-3224; 33m; rel 1956; del 1959
- MGM E-3517; 33m; rel 1958; del 1959

Magnificat (Op 157) (1958)
[5061] Nossaman, Audrey (sop); Johnson, Elizabeth (al); East, Thomas (ten); Dales, Richard (bar); University of Louisville Choir; Louisville Orchestra; Whitney, Robert (cond)
- LOU-61-4; 33m (Louisville Orchestra First Edition Records 1961 No 4); rel 1961; del 1975
- Poseidon 1018; 33s; rel 1976; cip

Meditation on Orpheus (Op 155) (1957)
[5062] Andre Kostelanetz and his Orchestra; Kostelanetz, Andre (cond)
- Columbia MG-33728; 33s; 2 discs; rel 1976; del 1979
- Columbia M-34537; 33s; rel 1977; cip

Meditation on Orpheus (Op 155) (1957) *(cont'd)*
[5063] Japan Philharmonic Symphony Orchestra; Strickland, William (cond)
- CRI-134; 33m/s; rel 1960/?; cip

Mihr (Op 60, No 1) (1945)
[5064] Ajemian, Maro (pf); Hovhaness, Alan (pf)
- Disc 3057 (in set 675); 78; rel pre-1948

Mountain Idylls (Op 52, Nos 4-6) (1932-53)
[5065] Richter, Marga (pf)
- MGM E-3181; 33m; rel 1955; del 1959
- MGM E-3517; 33m; rel 1958; del 1959

Mountains and Rivers without End (Op 225) (1968)
[5066] Royal Philharmonic Orchestra; Hovhaness, Alan (cond)
- Poseidon 1004; 33s; rel 1971; cip

Nocturne (Op 20) (1938)
[5067] McDonald, Susann (hp)
- Klavier KS-507; 33s; rel 1972; cip

October Mountain (Op 135) (1942)
[5068] Manhattan Percussion Ensemble; Price, Paul (cond)
- Urania UX-134; 33m; rel 1959; del 1969
- Urania USD-1034; 33s; rel 1959; del 1960
- Urania US-5134; 33s; rel 1961; del 1972

[5069] Tristan Fry Percussion Ensemble; Eliot, John (cond)
- Gale 004; 33s; rel 1979; cip

(Three) Odes of Solomon (Op 30) (1935, rev 1937)
[5070] Berberian, Ara (b); Hovhaness, Alan (pf)
- Poseidon 1005; 33s; rel 1971; cip

Orbit No 1 (Op 90, No 2) (1952)
[5071] chamber ensemble; Hovhaness, Alan (cond)
- MGM E-3164; 33m; rel 1955; del 1959

Orbit No 2 (Op 102) (1952)
[5072] Masselos, William (pf)
- MGM E-3160; 33m; rel 1955; del 1959

Out of the Depths (Op 142, No 3) (1938, rev 1958)

[5073] Berberian, Ara (b); Hovhaness, Alan (pf)
- Poseidon 1005; 33s; rel 1971; cip

Pagan Saint (Op 74, No 1) (1948)

[5074] Berberian, Ara (b); Hovhaness, Alan (pf)
- Poseidon 1009; 33s; rel 1972; cip

Pastoral No 1 (Op 111, No 1) (1952)

[5075] Masselos, William (pf)
- MGM E-3160; 33m; rel 1955; del 1959

Prayer of Saint Gregory (Op 62b) (1946)

[5076] Chestnut, Walter (tpt); May, Ernest (org)
- Afka SK-4634; 33s; rel 1980; cip

[5077] Nashville Symphony Orchestra (members of); Peninsula Festival Orchestra (members of)
- Nashville Symphony Orchestra 5525; 33s; rel 1975

[5078] Plog, Anthony (tpt); Swearingen, Madolyn (org)
- Avant AV-1014; 33s; rel 1978; cip

[5079] Polyphonia Orchestra; Hovhaness, Alan (cond)
- Poseidon 1017; 33s; rel 1975; cip

[5080] Stevens, Thomas (tpt); Crystal Chamber Orchestra (strings); Gold, Ernest (cond)
- Crystal S-800; 33s; rel 1976; cip

Prelude and Fugue (Op 13) (1935, rev 1937)

[5081] Etler, Alvin (ob); Reines, Joseph (bsn)
- Yaddo IV-4; 78; rel 1940

Prelude and Quadruple Fugue (Op 128) (1936, orchd 1954)

[5082] Eastman-Rochester Symphony Orchestra; Hanson, Howard (cond)
- Mercury MG-50106; 33m; rel 1956; del 1964
- Mercury MG-50423/SR-90423; 33m/s; rel 1965; del 1972

Quartet, Flute, Oboe, Violoncello, and Harpsichord, No 1 or 2 (Op 97 or 112) (1952)

[5083] Bennett, Harold (fl); Schulman, Harry (ob); Greenhouse, Bernard (vcl); Marlowe, Sylvia (hpschd)
- New Editions 3; 33m; rel 1953; del 1959

Quartet, Flute, Oboe, Violoncello, and Harpsichord, No 2 (Op 112) (1952)

[5084] MGM Chamber Ensemble
- MGM E-3517; 33m; rel 1958; del 1959

Requiem and Resurrection (Op 224) (1968)

[5085] North Jersey Wind Symphony; Hovhaness, Alan (cond)
- Poseidon 1002; 33s; rel 1970; cip

Return and Rebuild the Desolate Places (Op 213) (1944, rev 1965)

[5086] Schwarz, Gerard (tpt); North Jersey Wind Symphony; Brion, Keith (cond)
- Mace MXX-9099; 33s; rel 1971; del 1975

Rubayiyat of Omar Khayyam, The

[5087] Fairbanks, Douglas, Jr. (nar); Carrozza, Carmen (acc); Andre Kostelanetz and his Orchestra; Kostelanetz, Andre (cond)
- Columbia M-34537; 33s; rel 1977; cip

Saturn (Op 243) (1971)

[5088] Hurney, Kate (sop); Long Island Chamber Ensemble of New York; Berkofsky, Martin (cond)
- Poseidon 1010; 33s; rel 1972; cip

(Two) Shakespeare Sonnets (Op 31) (1942)

[5089] Berberian, Ara (b); Hovhaness, Alan (pf)
- Poseidon 1009; 33s; rel 1972; cip

Sharagan and Fugue (Op 58) (1949)

[5090] MGM Brass Ensemble; Surinach, Carlos (cond)
- MGM E-3517; 33m; rel 1958; del 1959

[5091] New York Brass Quintet
- Desto D-401/DST-6401; 33m/s; rel 1964; cip

Shatakh (Op 63) (1948)

[5092] Ajemian, Anahid (vln); Ajemian, Maro (pf)
- Dial 6; 33m; rel 1950; del 1956
- Metronome CLP-505; 33m; rel pre-1953

Siris Dance (Op 52, No 3) (1943)

[5093] Richter, Marga (pf)
- MGM E-3147; 33m; rel 1955; del 1959
- MGM E-3517; 33m; rel 1958; del 1959

Slumber Song (Op 52, No 2) (1938)

[5094] Richter, Marga (pf)
- MGM E-3147; 33m; rel 1955; del 1959
- MGM E-3517; 33m; rel 1958; del 1959

Sonata, Flute (Op 118) (1964)

[5095] Baron, Samuel (fl)
- CRI-212; 33m/s; rel 1966/?; cip

Sonata, Harp (Op 127) (1954)

[5096] McDonald, Susann (hp)
- Klavier KS-507; 33s; rel 1972; cip

Sonata, Trumpet and Organ (Op 200) (1962)

[5097] Stith, Marice (tpt); Paterson, Donald (org)
Rec 4/18/67
- Redwood RRES-2; 33s; rel 1969; cip

Sonata, Trumpet and Organ: 1st Movement

[5098] Plog, Anthony (tpt); Thomas, Ladd (org)
- Crystal S-362; 33s; rel 1977; cip

(Four) Songs (Op 35) (1938)

[5099] Berberian, Ara (b); Hovhaness, Alan (pf)
- Poseidon 1008; 33s; rel 1972; cip

Spirit of Ink, The (Op 230)

[5100] Baron, Samuel (fl)
- Poseidon 1011; 33s; rel 1973; cip

Suite, Violin, Piano, and Percussion (Op 99) (1952)

[5101] Ajemian, Anahid (vln); Ajemian, Maro (pf); Bailey, Elden (perc)
- Columbia ML-5179; 33m; rel 1957; del 1968
- Columbia CML-5179; 33m; rel 1968; del 1974
- Columbia AML-5179; 33m; rel 1974; del 1976

Symphony No 2 (Mysterious Mountain) (Op 132) (1955)

[5102] Chicago Symphony Orchestra; Reiner, Fritz (cond)
- RCA LM-2251/LSC-2251; 33m/s; rel 1958/1959; cip

[5103] World Youth Symphony Orchestra; Roller, A. Clyde (cond)
- Golden Crest GCIN-402; 33s; rel 1975; cip

Symphony No 4 (Op 165) (1958)

[5104] Cornell University Wind Ensemble; Stith, Marice (cond)
- Cornell CUWE-2; 33s; rel 1971; cip

Symphony No 4 (Op 165) (1958)
(cont'd)

[5105] Eastman Symphonic Wind
Ensemble; Roller, A. Clyde (cond)
- Mercury MG-50366/SR-90366;
33m/s; rel 1964; del 1973
- Mercury SRI-75010; 33s; rel
1973; cip

**Symphony No 6 (Celestial Gate)
(Op 173) (1959, rev 1960)**

[5106] Polyphonia Orchestra; Hovhaness,
Alan (cond)
- Poseidon 1017; 33s; rel 1975;
cip

**Symphony No 7 (Nanga Parvat) (Op
175) (1959)**

[5107] North Jersey Wind Symphony;
Brion, Keith (cond)
- Mace MXX-9099; 33s; rel 1971;
del 1975

**Symphony No 9 (St. Vartan) (Op
180) (1950)**

[5108] MGM Chamber Orchestra;
Surinach, Carlos (cond)
- MGM E-3453; 33m; rel 1957;
del 1959

[5109] National Philharmonic Orchestra of
London; Wilbraham, John (tpt);
Hovhaness, Alan (pf) (cond)
- Poseidon 1013; 33s; rel 1973;
cip

**Symphony No 11 (All Men Are
Brothers) (Op 186) (1960, rev
1969)**

[5110] Royal Philharmonic Orchestra;
Hovhaness, Alan (cond)
- Poseidon 1001; 33s; rel 1970;
cip

**Symphony No 14 (Ararat) (Op 194)
(1961)**

[5111] North Jersey Wind Symphony;
Brion, Keith (cond)
- Mace MXX-9099; 33s; rel 1971;
del 1975

**Symphony No 15 (Silver
Pilgrimage) (Op 199) (1962)**

[5112] Louisville Orchestra; Whitney,
Robert (cond)
- LOU-66-2/LS-66-2; 33m/s
(Louisville Orchestra First Edition
Records 1966 No 2); rel 1966;
cip

**Symphony No 17 (Symphony for
Metal Orchestra) (Op 203)
(1963)**

[5113] Ithaca High School Concert Band;
Socciarelli, Ronald P. (cond)
- Mark MM-1112; 33s; rel 1970;
del 1976

**Symphony No 19 (Vishnu) (Op
217) (1966)**

[5114] Sevan Philharmonic; Hovhaness,
Alan (cond)
- Poseidon 1012; 33s; rel 1973;
cip

**Symphony No 20 (Three Journeys
to a Holy Mountain) (Op 223)
(1968)**

[5115] Ithaca High School Concert Band;
Socciarelli, Ronald P. (cond)
- Mark MM-1112; 33s; rel 1970;
del 1976

**Symphony No 21 (Etchmiadzin) (Op
234) (1970)**

[5116] Royal Philharmonic Orchestra;
Hovhaness, Alan (cond)
- Poseidon 1004; 33s; rel 1971;
cip

**Symphony No 23 (Ani) (Op 249)
(1972)**

[5117] Highland and Shoreline College
Bands; Hovhaness, Alan (cond)
- Poseidon 1015; 33s; rel 1974;
cip

**Symphony No 24 (Majnun) (Op
273) (1973)**

[5118] Hill, Martyn (ten); Wilbraham, John
(tpt); Sax, Sidney (vln); John
Alldis Choir; National
Philharmonic Orchestra of
London; Hovhaness, Alan (cond)
- Poseidon 1016; 33s; rel 1975;
cip

**Symphony No 25 (Odysseus) (Op
275) (1973)**

[5119] Polyphonia Orchestra; Hovhaness,
Alan (cond)
- Poseidon 1014; 33s; rel 1974;
cip

Symphony No 39 (Op 314) (1978)

[5120] Northwest Chamber Orchestra;
Hovhaness, Alan (cond)
- Pandora 3001; 33s; rel 1979;
cip

Talin (Op 93) (1952)

[5121] Vardi, Emanuel (vla); MGM String
Orchestra; Solomon, Izler (cond)
- MGM E-3432; 33m; rel 1957;
del 1959

**Talin (clarinet and string orchestra
version) (1971)**

[5122] Sobol, Lawrence (cl); Rome
Chamber Orchestra; Flagello,
Nicolas (cond)
- Peters Internationale PLE-071;
33s; rel 1978; cip

**To the God Who is in the Fire (Op
146) (1956)**

[5123] Miller, William (ten); Varsity Men's
Glee Club and Percussion
Ensemble; Shaw, Robert (cond)
- Illini Union Bookstore CRS-5;
33m; rel 1958*

Tower Music (Op 129) (1954)

[5124] MGM Orchestra; Surinach, Carlos
(cond)
- MGM E-3504; 33m; rel 1957;
del 1959

Tumburu (Op 264, No 1) (1973)

[5125] Macalester Trio
- CRI-326; 33s; rel 1974; cip

Tzaikerk (Op 53) (1945)

[5126] Andrus, Gretel Shanley (fl);
Shapiro, Eudice (vln); Peters,
Mitchell (timp); Crystal Chamber
Orchestra (strings); Gold, Ernest
(cond)
- Crystal S-800; 33s; rel 1976; cip

[5127] Kaplan, Phillip (fl); Ajemian, Anahid
(vln); Goodman, Saul (timp);
orchestra; Hovhaness, Alan
(cond)
- Disc 876; 78; 3 discs; rel
pre-1948
- Dial 6; 33m; rel 1950; del 1956
- Metronome CLP-505; 33m; rel
pre-1953

Under a Byzantine Dome

[5128] Berberian, Ara (b); Hovhaness,
Alan (pf)
- Poseidon 1009; 33s; rel 1972;
cip

**Upon Enchanted Ground (Op 90,
No 1) (1951)**

[5129] Baron, Samuel (fl); Adam, Claus
(vcl); Lawrence, Lucille (hp);
Bailey, Elden (tamtam)
- Columbia ML-5179; 33m; rel
1957; del 1968
- Columbia CML-5179; 33m; rel
1968; del 1974
- Columbia AML-5179; 33m; rel
1974; del 1976

Varuna (Op 264, No 2) (1973)

[5130] Macalester Trio
- CRI-326; 33s; rel 1974; cip

HOWE, Hubert S., Jr. (1942-)
Canons Four (1974)

[5131] Electronic music
- Opus One 47; 33s; rel 1980; cip

**Improvisation on the Overtone
Series (1977)**

[5132] Electronic music
- Opus One 53; 33s; rel 1980; cip

(Three) Studies in Timbre (1970-73): No 3
[5133] Electronic music
- Opus One 47; 33s; rel 1980; cip

HOWE, Mary (1882-1964)
Castellana (1935)
[5134] Dougherty, Celius (pf); Ruzicka, Vincenz (pf); Vienna Orchestra; Strickland, William (cond)
- CRI-124; 33m; rel 1959; cip

Cavaliers
[5135] Howard University Choir; Lawson, Warner (cond)
- WCFM-13; 33m; rel 1952; del 1955

Chain Gang Song (1925)
[5136] Howard University Choir; Lawson, Warner (cond)
- WCFM-13; 33m; rel 1952; del 1955

Fragment
[5137] Hansel, Katherine (sop); Schaefer, Theodore (pf)
- WCFM-13; 33m; rel 1952; del 1955

Horseman, The
[5138] Howard University Choir; Lawson, Warner (cond)
- WCFM-13; 33m; rel 1952; del 1955

Innisfree
[5139] Ronk, Harold (ten); Schaefer, Theodore (pf)
- WCFM-13; 33m; rel 1952; del 1955

Interlude Between Two Pieces
[5140] Catholic University of America Chamber Arts Society; Meyers, Emerson (cond)
Rec 7/21-22/51
- WCFM-9; 33m; rel 1951; del 1955

Lullaby for a Forester's Child
[5141] Ronk, Harold (ten); Schaefer, Theodore (pf)
- WCFM-13; 33m; rel 1952; del 1955

Ma douleur
[5142] Hansel, Katherine (sop); Schaefer, Theodore (pf)
- WCFM-13; 33m; rel 1952; del 1955

Mein Herz
[5143] Hansel, Katherine (sop); Schaefer, Theodore (pf)
- WCFM-13; 33m; rel 1952; del 1955

Movement for Quartet
[5144] Galimir String Quartet
- Yaddo IV-1; 78; rel 1940

Music When Soft Voices Die
[5145] Howard University Choir; Lawson, Warner (cond)
- WCFM-13; 33m; rel 1952; del 1955

O Proserpina
[5146] Hansel, Katherine (sop); Schaefer, Theodore (pf)
- WCFM-13; 33m; rel 1952; del 1955

(Three) Pieces after Emily Dickinson
[5147] Catholic University of America Chamber Arts Society; Meyers, Emerson (cond)
Rec 7/21-22/51
- WCFM-9; 33m; rel 1951; del 1955

Quartet, Strings: 2nd Movement (Allegro inevitable)
[5148] Coolidge String Quartet
- Victor 11-8126 (in set M-891); 78; rel pre-1942

Rag Picker, The
[5149] Ronk, Harold (ten); Schaefer, Theodore (pf)
- WCFM-13; 33m; rel 1952; del 1955

Sand (1938)
[5150] Vienna Orchestra; Strickland, William (cond)
- CRI-103; 33m/s; rel 1956/?; cip
- CRI-124; 33m; rel 1959; cip

Song of Ruth
[5151] Howard University Choir; Lawson, Warner (cond)
- WCFM-13; 33m; rel 1952; del 1955

Spring Pastoral (1936)
[5152] Imperial Philharmonic Orchestra of Tokyo; Strickland, William (cond)
- CRI-145; 33m/s; rel 1961/?; cip

Stars (1937)
[5153] Maganini Chamber Symphony; Maganini, Quinto (cond)
- New Music Quarterly Recordings 1514; 78; rel 1939

[5154] National Symphony Orchestra; Kindler, Hans (cond)
- Victor 11-8608; 78; rel pre-1948

[5155] Vienna Orchestra; Strickland, William (cond)
- CRI-103; 33m/s; rel 1956/?; cip
- CRI-124; 33m; rel 1959; cip

Suite, Piano and String Quartet (1923)
[5156] Catholic University of America Chamber Arts Society; Meyers, Emerson (cond)
Rec 7/21-22/51
- WCFM-9; 33m; rel 1951; del 1955

To the Unknown Soldier
[5157] Ronk, Harold (ten); Schaefer, Theodore (pf)
- WCFM-13; 33m; rel 1952; del 1955

When I Died in Berners Street
[5158] Hansel, Katherine (sop); Schaefer, Theodore (pf)
- WCFM-13; 33m; rel 1952; del 1955

Williamsburg Sunday
[5159] Howard University Choir; Lawson, Warner (cond)
- WCFM-13; 33m; rel 1952; del 1955

HOY, Bonnee (1936-)
De Mazia Quintet, The
[5160] Hoy, Bonnee (pf); Amado String Quartet
- Encore EN-3003; 33s; rel 1975*

Freeman Celebration, The (1971)
[5161] Bouleyn, Kathryn (sop); Barg, David (fl); Wiley, Peter (vcl); Hoy, Bonnee
- Encore EN-2002; 33s; rel 1975*

Lament
[5162] Stein, Carol (vln)
- Encore EN-3003; 33s; rel 1975*

(Eight) Preludes, Piano (1969)
[5163] Hoy, Bonnee (pf)
- Encore EN-1001; 33s; rel 1973*

Sonata, Piano, No 2 (1971)
[5164] Hoy, Bonnee (pf)
- Encore EN-1001; 33s; rel 1973*

Verlaine Songs, The
[5165] Webb, Bailus (bar); Hoy, Bonnee (pf)
- Encore EN-2002; 33s; rel 1975*

Winter Cycle, The
[5166] Bouleyn, Kathryn (sop); Hoy, Bonnee (pf)
- Encore EN-2002; 33s; rel 1975*

HOYSTRADT, John
Night Life in New York
[5167] Hoystradt, John (pf)
- Musicraft N-1; 78; rel pre-1943

HUDSON, Joseph A. (1952-)
Fantasy/Refrain
[5168] Quan, Linda (vln); Graham, John
(vla); Emelianoff, Andre (vcl)
- CRI-414; 33s; rel 1980; cip

Reflexives
[5169] Burge, David (pf); tape
Rec 10/16-17/75
- CRI-345; 33s; rel 1976; cip

Sonare (1977)
[5170] Schulte, Rolf (vln); Dunkel, Paul
(fl); Flax, Laura (cl); Oppens,
Ursula (pf); Passaro, Joseph
(perc); tape; Shulman, Daniel
(cond)
Rec 6/77
- CRI-382; 33s; rel 1978; cip

HUFF, Will
Squealer, The (1912)
[5171] Eastman Symphonic Wind
Ensemble; Fennell, Frederick
(cond)
- Mercury MG-50314/SR-90314;
33m/s; rel 1963; del 1976
- Mercury SRI-75087; 33s; rel
1977; cip

HUFFER, F. K.
Black Jack
[5172] University of Michigan Winds and
Percussion; Lillya, Clifford P.
(cond)
Rec 2/18-19/75
- University of Michigan SM-0002;
33s; rel 1978; cip

HUFFINE, G. H.
Them Basses (1924)
[5173] Eastman Symphonic Wind
Ensemble; Fennell, Frederick
(cond)
- Mercury MG-50314/SR-90314;
33m/s; rel 1963; del 1976
- Mercury SRI-75087; 33s; rel
1977; cip

[5174] Incredible Columbia All-Star Band;
Schuller, Gunther (cond)
- Columbia M-33513/MQ-33513;
33s/q; rel 1975; cip

HUGGLER, John (1928-)
Celebration (Op 68) (1966)
[5175] Ithaca High School Band; Battisti,
Frank (cond)
- Golden Crest 6001; 33m/s; rel
1967; cip

Quintet, Brass, No 1 (1955)
[5176] Cambridge Brass Quintet
- Crystal S-204; 33s; rel 1977; cip

Quintet, Brass, No 2 (Op 58)
[5177] Iowa Brass Quintet
- Trilogy CTS-1001; 33s; rel
1973; del 1976

Quintet, Brass, No 2 (Op 58)
(cont'd)
[5178] Tidewater Brass Quintet
- Golden Crest CRSQ-4179; 33q

HUGHES, Mark (1934-)
**Divertimento, Trumpet, Horn, and
Trombone**
[5179] Florida State University Brass Trio
- Golden Crest CRS-4081; 33s; rel
1969; cip

HUGHES, Robert
Cadences
[5180] Oakland Youth Orchestra; tape;
Hughes, Robert (cond)
- 1750 Arch S-1772; 33s; rel
1978; cip

Sonitudes (1970)
[5181] Millard, Janet (fl); Brown (vcl)
- 1750 Arch S-1760; 33s; rel
1979; cip

HUHN, Bruno (1871-1950)
Invictus (1910)
[5182] De Gogorza, Emilio (bar); orchestra
- Victor 992; 78; 10"; rel
1921-25

[5183] Merrill, Robert (bar); Edwards, Leila
(pf)
- Victor 10-1462; 78; 10"

HULICK, Terry*
Rondino, Percussion Quartet
[5184] Ithaca Percussion Ensemble;
Benson, Warren (cond)
- Golden Crest
CR-4016/CRS-4016; 33m/s; rel
1960/1961; cip

**HUMBERT, Jacqueline and
ROSENBOOM, David**
see ROSENBOOM, David and
HUMBERT, Jacqueline

HUMEL, Gerald (1931-)
Preludium und Scherzo (1960)
[5185] Baron, Samuel (fl)
- CRI-237; 33s; rel 1969; cip

**Sonata, Violin and Piano (Journey
to Praha) (1961)**
[5186] Gross, Robert (vln); Hewitt, Peter
(pf)
- CRI-237; 33s; rel 1969; cip

HUNDLEY, Richard (1931-)
Ballad on Queen Anne's Death
[5187] Sperry, Paul (ten)
- Seraphim SRS-12078; 33s; rel
1980; cip

For Your Delight (1965)
[5188] Reardon, John (bar); Hebert, Bliss
(pf)
- Serenus SRE-1019/SRS-12019;
33m/s; rel 1967; cip

Postcard from Spain (1965)
[5189] Reardon, John (bar); Hebert, Bliss
(pf)
- Serenus SRE-1019/SRS-12019;
33m/s; rel 1967; cip

Some Sheep Are Loving
[5190] Sperry, Paul (ten)
- Seraphim SRS-12078; 33s; rel
1980; cip

Spring
[5191] Sperry, Paul (ten)
- Seraphim SRS-12078; 33s; rel
1980; cip

Wild Plum
[5192] Sperry, Paul (ten)
- Seraphim SRS-12078; 33s; rel
1980; cip

HUNT, Jerry (1943-)
Lattice (1979)
[5193] Hunt, Jerry (pf)
- Irida 0026; 33s

HURD* and PRITCHARD, Robert
see PRITCHARD, Robert and HURD

HUSA, Karel (1921-)
Apotheosis of this Earth (1970)
[5194] University of Michigan Symphony
Band; Husa, Karel (cond)
- Golden Crest CRS-4134; 33s; rel
1975; cip

Chanson melancolique overture
[5195] Rascher Saxophone Ensemble
- Coronet LPS-3022; 33s; rel
1975; cip

**Concerto, Alto Saxophone and Band
(1967)**
[5196] Timmons, Tim (al sax); Ithaca
College Concert Band; Gobrecht,
Edward (cond)
- Golden Crest CRS-4124; 33q; rel
1979; cip

**Concerto, Alto Saxophone and Band
(arr for sax and pf)**
[5197] Black, Robert (sax); Black, Patricia
(pf)
- Brewster; 33; rel 197?

[5198] Hemke, Frederick (sax); Granger,
Milton (pf)
- Brewster BR-1203; 33s; rel
1972; del 1978

Divertimento, Brass Quintet (1968)
[5199] Iowa Brass Quintet
- University of Iowa Press 29001; 33s; rel 1977; cip

[5200] Ithaca Brass Quintet
- Golden Crest CRS-4114; 33q; rel 1979; cip

Elegie (1957)
[5201] Covert, Mary Ann (pf)
- Golden Crest CRS-4175; 33s; rel 1978

Evocations of Slovakia (1951)
[5202] Long Island Chamber Ensemble of New York
- Grenadilla GS-1008; 33s; rel 1977; cip

Fantasies (1956)
[5203] Orchestre des Solistes de Paris; Husa, Karel (cond)
- Cornell N80P-5536-37 (matrix no); 33m; rel 1962; del 1976
- CRI-261; 33s; rel 1971; cip (Excerpt: Nocturne)

Landscapes (1977)
[5204] Western Brass Quintet
- CRI-192(78); 33s; rel 1979; cip

(Four) Little Pieces, Strings (1955)
[5205] Chamber Orchestra of Albuquerque; Oberg, David (cond)
- Opus One 51; 33s; rel 197?

Mosaiques (1961)
[5206] Stockholm Radio Symphony Orchestra; Husa, Karel (cond)
- CRI-221; 33s; rel 1968; cip

Music for Prague (band version) (1968)
[5207] University of Michigan Symphony Band; Husa, Karel (cond)
- Golden Crest CRS-4134; 33s; rel 1975; cip

Music for Prague (orchestral version) (1968)
[5208] Louisville Orchestra; Mester, Jorge (cond)
- LS-72-2; 33s (Louisville Orchestra First Edition Records 1972 No 2); rel 1973; cip

(Two) Preludes, Flute, Clarinet, and Bassoon (1966)
[5209] Dorian Woodwind Quintet
- Vox SVBX-5307; 33s; 3 discs; rel 1977; cip

Quartet, Strings, No 2 (1953)
[5210] Fine Arts Quartet
- Everest SDBR-3290; 33s; rel 1971; cip

Quartet, Strings, No 3 (1968)
[5211] Fine Arts Quartet
- Everest SDBR-3290; 33s; rel 1971; cip

Serenade, Wind Quintet and String Orchestra (1963)
[5212] Foerster Woodwind Quintet; Prague Symphony Orchestra; Husa, Karel (cond)
- CRI-261; 33s; rel 1971; cip

Sonata, Piano, No 1 (Op 11) (1949)
[5213] Covert, Mary Ann (pf)
- Golden Crest CRS-4175; 33s; rel 1978

Sonata, Piano, No 2 (1975)
[5214] Basquin, Peter (pf)
- Grenadilla GS-1025; 33s; rel 1980; cip

[5215] Covert, Mary Ann (pf)
- Golden Crest CRS-4175; 33s; rel 1978

Sonata, Violin and Piano (1972-73)
[5216] Oliveira, Elmar (vln); Oei, David (pf)
- Grenadilla GS-1032; 33s; rel 1978; cip

Sonatina, Piano (Op 1) (1943)
[5217] Covert, Mary Ann (pf)
- Golden Crest CRS-4175; 33s; rel 1978

(Two) Sonnets from Michelangelo (1971)
[5218] Louisville Orchestra; Mester, Jorge (cond)
Rec 11/7/72
- LS-72-5; 33s (Louisville Orchestra First Edition Records 1972 No 5); rel 1973; cip

Symphony No 1 (1953)
[5219] Prague Symphony Orchestra; Husa, Karel (cond)
- CRI-261; 33s; rel 1971; cip

HUSS, Henry Holden (1862-1953)

Crossing the Bar (arr by Richard P. Condie)
[5220] Mormon Tabernacle Choir; Schreiner, Alexander (org); Asper, Frank (org); Condie, Richard P. (cond)
- Columbia ML-6019/MS-6619; 33m/s; rel 1964; del 1966

Prelude, Piano, No 2 (Op 17, No 2)
[5221] Frager, Malcolm (pf)
- New World NW-206; 33s; rel 1978

HUSTON, Scott (1916-)

For Our Times (1974)
[5222] Indianapolis Brass Ensemble
- Serenus SRS-12066; 33s; rel 1976; cip

Game of Circles, A (1971)
[5223] Williams, Floyd (cl); Loewy, Donna Hallen (pf) (cel)
- Music Now CFS-3037; 33s; rel 1974*

Idioms (1968)
[5224] Dominitz, Benzion (vln); Lavoie, Jean (cl); Little, Myra Beth (hn)
- Music Now CFS-3037; 33s; rel 1974*

Life-Styles I-IV (1972)
[5225] Plasko, George M. F. (cl); Miller, Ken (vcl); Loewy, Donna Hallen (pf)
- Serenus SRS-12064; 33s; rel 1976; cip

Penta-Tholoi (1966)
[5226] Leland, William (pf)
- Opus One 4; 33s; rel 1970; cip

Phenomena (1967)
[5227] Heritage Chamber Quartet
- Opus One 4; 33s; rel 1970; cip

Sounds at Night (1971)
[5228] Indianapolis Brass Ensemble
- Serenus SRS-12066; 33s; rel 1976; cip

HUTCHESON, Jere T. (1938-)

Fantaisie-Impromptu (1974)
[5229] Burge, Lois Svard (pf)
Rec 10/78
- CRI-407; 33s; rel 1979; cip

HUTCHINS, Guy Starr (1905-)

Spirit of Transylvania, The (1954)
[5230] Cornell University Wind Ensemble; Stith, Marice (cond)
- Cornell CUWE-8; 33s; rel 1971; cip

HUTCHINSON, Terry*

Tuba Juba Duba
[5231] Tennessee Tech Tuba Ensemble; Morris, R. Winston (cond)
- Golden Crest CRSQ-4139; 33q; rel 1977; cip

HUTCHISON, Warner (1930-)

Sonatina, Baritone Horn and Piano
[5232] Young, Raymond G. (bar hn); Fraschillo, Tom (pf)
- Golden Crest RE-7025; 33m/s; rel 1968/1979; cip

HYDE, George

Color Contrasts

[5233] Horn Club of Los Angeles
- Seraphim S-60095; 33s; rel 1969; del 1973

IANNACCONE, Anthony (1943-)

Bicinia, Flute and Alto Saxophone

[5234] Hill, Rodney (fl); Plank, Max (al sax)
- Coronet LPS-3038; 33s; rel 1976; cip

Hades

[5235] University of Michigan Tuba Ensemble; Mayer, Uri (cond)
- Golden Crest CRSQ-4145; 33q; rel 1977; cip

(Three) Mythical Sketches

[5236] University of Michigan Tuba Ensemble; Mayer, Uri (cond)
- Golden Crest CRSQ-4145; 33q; rel 1977; cip

Parodies (1975)

[5237] Clarion Wind Quintet
- Golden Crest CRS-4191; 33s; rel 1980; cip

Partita, Piano

[5238] Gurt, Joseph (pf)
- Coronet LPS-3038; 33s; rel 1976; cip

Rituals

[5239] Pignotti, Alfio (vln); Mehta, Dady (pf)
- Coronet LPS-3038; 33s; rel 1976; cip

Sonatine, Trumpet and Tuba

[5240] Eggers, Carter (tpt); Smith, J. R. (tu)
- Coronet LPS-3038; 33s; rel 1976; cip

IMBRIE, Andrew (1921-)

Concerto, Violin and Orchestra (1954)

[5241] Glenn, Carroll (vln); Columbia Symphony Orchestra; Rozsnyai, Zoltan (cond)
- Columbia ML-5997/MS-6597; 33m/s; rel 1964; del 1968
- Columbia CML-5997/CMS-6597; 33m/s; rel 1968; del 1974
- Columbia AMS-6597; 33s; rel 1974; del 1979

Dandelion Wine (1967)

[5242] Lucarelli, Bert (ob); Bloom, Arthur (cl); Kooper, Kees (vln); Rogers, Alvin (vln); Maximoff, Richard (vla); Sherry, Fred (vcl); Boehm-Kooper, Mary Louise (pf)
- Turnabout TVS-34520; 33s; rel 1974; del 1978

Impromptu, Violin and Piano (1960)

[5243] Gross, Robert (vln); Grayson, Richard (pf)
- Orion ORS-73107; 33s; rel 1973; cip

Legend (1959)

[5244] San Francisco Symphony Orchestra; Jorda, Enrique (cond)
- CRI-152; 33m; rel 1962; cip

On the Beach at Night (1948)

[5245] Gregg Smith Singers; Orpheus Ensemble; Smith, Gregg (cond) Rec 4/76
- Vox SVBX-5354; 33s; 3 discs; rel 1979

Quartet, Strings, No 1 (1942)

[5246] Juilliard String Quartet
- Columbia ML-4844; 33m; rel 1954; del 1968
- Columbia CML-4844; 33m; rel 1968; del 1974
- Columbia AML-4844; 33m; rel 1974; del 1976

Quartet, Strings, No 2 (1953)

[5247] California String Quartet
- Contemporary C-6003/S-7022; 33m/s; rel 1959/1961; cip
- Stereo S-7022; 33s; rel 1959; del 1961

Quartet, Strings, No 3 (1957)

[5248] Walden String Quartet
- Contemporary C-6003/S-7002; 33m/s; rel 1959/1961; cip
- Stereo S-7022; 33s; rel 1959; del 1961

Quartet, Strings, No 4 (1969)

[5249] Emerson String Quartet
- New World NW-212; 33s; rel 1978

Serenade, Flute, Viola, and Piano (1952)

[5250] Di Tullio, Louise (fl); Trampler, Walter (vla); Brandwynne, Lois (pf)
- Desto DC-7150; 33s; rel 1973; cip

(Three) Sketches (1967)

[5251] Dempster, Stuart (tbn); Aanerud, Kevin (pf)
- New World NW-254; 33s; rel 1978

Sonata, Piano (1947)

[5252] Imbrie, Andrew (pf)
- Fantasy 5009; 33m; rel 1960; del 1970

Sonata, Violoncello and Piano (1967)

[5253] Sayre, Robert (vcl); Bogas, Roy (pf)
- Desto DC-7150; 33s; rel 1973; cip

Symphony No 3 (1970)

[5254] London Symphony Orchestra; Farberman, Harold (cond)
- CRI-308; 33s; rel 1973; cip

Tell Me Where Is Fancy Bred (1964)

[5255] Rees, Rosalind (sop); Wagner, Richard (cl); Starobin, David (gtr) Rec 1976
- Turnabout TVS-34727; 33s; rel 1978

ISAACSON, Leonard M. and HILLER, Lejaren

see HILLER, Lejaren and ISAACSON, Leonard M.

ISRAEL, Brian (1951-)

Dance Variations (1973)

[5256] Stith, Marice (tpt); tape
- Golden Crest RE-7068; 33s; rel 1977; cip

Symphony No 1 (1974)

[5257] Cornell University Wind Ensemble; Stith, Marice (cond) Rec 3/24/74
- Cornell CUWE-14; 33s; rel 1975; cip

ITURBI, Jose (1895-1980)

Cancion de cuna

[5258] Iturbi, Jose (pf)
- RCA LRM-7057; 33m; 10"; rel 1954; del 1956

Seguidillas

[5259] Andre Kostelanetz and his Orchestra; Kostelanetz, Andre (cond)
- Columbia CL-943; 33m; rel 1958; del 1959

[5260] Valencia Symphony Orchestra; Iturbi, Jose (cond)
- RCA LM-1138; 33m; rel 1951; del 1956
- RCA LM-1937; 33m; rel 1955; del 1958

IVES, Charles (1874-1954)

Abide with Me (1890?)

[5261] Fischer-Dieskau, Dietrich (bar); Ponti, Michael (pf)
- Deutsche Grammophon 2530.696; 33s; rel 1976; cip

Adeste fidelis (1897)

[5262] Baker, George C. (org)
- Delos DEL-FY-025; 33s; rel 1977; cip

Adeste fidelis (1897) *(cont'd)*
[5263] Beck, Janice (org)
Rec 7/9-10/71
- Musical Heritage Society
OR-A-264; 33s; rel 1972

[5264] Hillsman, Walter (org)
Rec 5/10-11/76
- Vista VPS-1038; 33s; rel 1976

[5265] Smith, Rollin (org)
Rec 8/73
- Repertoire Recording Society
RRS-12; 33s; rel 1974

Ann Street (1921)
[5266] Bauman, Mordecai (bar); Hirsh,
Albert (pf)
Rec 1938
- CRI-390; 33s; rel 1978; cip

[5267] DeGaetani, Jan (m sop); Kalish,
Gilbert (pf)
- Nonesuch H-71325; 33s; rel
1976; cip

[5268] Fischer-Dieskau, Dietrich (bar);
Ponti, Michael (pf)
- Deutsche Grammophon
2530.696; 33s; rel 1976; cip

**Ann Street (arr for instrumental
ensemble by Gunther Schuller)**
[5269] New England Conservatory
Ragtime Ensemble; Schuller,
Gunther (cond)
Rec 10/74-3/75
- Golden Crest CRS-31042; 33q; 2
discs; rel 1976; cip

At the River (1916?)
[5270] DeGaetani, Jan (m sop); Kalish,
Gilbert (pf)
- Nonesuch H-71325; 33s; rel
1976; cip

[5271] Eberley, Helen Kay (sop); Isaak,
Donald (pf)
- Eb-Sko Productions 1001; 33s;
rel 1976; cip

[5272] Fischer-Dieskau, Dietrich (bar);
Ponti, Michael (pf)
- Deutsche Grammophon
2530.696; 33s; rel 1976; cip

[5273] Laine, Cleo (sop); Hymas, Anthony
(pf)
- RCA LRL-1-5058; 33s; rel 1975;
del 1979

[5274] Parker, William (bar); Baldwin,
Dalton (pf)
- New World NW-300; 33s; rel
1978

August (1920)
[5275] Grande, Peter del (bar); Pleshakov,
Vladimir (pf)
- CST-106; 33s; rel 1971

Autumn (1907)
[5276] Fischer-Dieskau, Dietrich (bar);
Ponti, Michael (pf)
- Deutsche Grammophon
2530.696; 33s; rel 1976; cip

**Bells of Yale, The (or Chapel
Chimes) (1897-98?) (arr for piano
by Nina Deutsch)**
[5277] Deutsch, Nina (pf)
Rec 6/76
- Vox SVBX-5482; 33s; 3 discs; rel
1977; cip

Cage, The (1906)
[5278] DeGaetani, Jan (m sop); Kalish,
Gilbert (pf)
- Nonesuch H-71325; 33s; rel
1976; cip

[5279] Eberley, Helen Kay (sop); Isaak,
Donald (pf)
- Eb-Sko Productions 1001; 33s;
rel 1976; cip

Camp Meeting, The (1912)
[5280] Grande, Peter del (bar); Pleshakov,
Vladimir (pf)
- CST-106; 33s; rel 1971

[5281] Parker, William (bar); Baldwin,
Dalton (pf)
- New World NW-300; 33s; rel
1978

**Canon (Not Only in My Lady's Eyes)
(1893)**
[5282] Boatwright, Helen (sop);
Kirkpatrick, John (pf)
Rec 11/69
- Columbia M4-32504; 33s; 4
discs; rel 1974; cip

**Canon (Oh the Days Are Gone)
(1894?)**
[5283] Gregg Smith Singers; New York
Vocal Arts Ensemble; Smith,
Gregg (cond)
- Vox SVBX-5304; 33s; 3 discs; rel
1974; cip

Celestial Country, The (1898-99)
[5284] Holt, Hazel (sop); Hodgson, Alfreda
(al); Elwes, John (ten); Noble,
John (bar); Schuetz Choir of
London; London Symphony
Orchestra; Farberman, Harold
(cond)
- CRI-314; 33s; rel 1974; cip

[5285] Rees, Rosalind (sop); Eckard, Linda
(m sop); Bogdan, Thomas (ten);
Fifer, Bruce (bar); De Ruiter,
Albert (cb); Gregg Smith Singers;
Columbia Chamber Orchestra;
Smith, Gregg (cond)
- Columbia M4-32504; 33s; 4
discs; rel 1974; cip

Central Park in the Dark (1906)
[5286] Boston Symphony Orchestra;
Ozawa, Seiji (cond)
- Deutsche Grammophon
2530.787; 33s; rel 1977; cip

Chanson de Florian (1898?)
[5287] Parker, William (bar); Baldwin,
Dalton (pf)
- New World NW-300; 33s; rel
1978

Charlie Rutlage (1920-21)
[5288] Bauman, Mordecai (bar); Hirsh,
Albert (pf)
Rec 1938
- CRI-390; 33s; rel 1978; cip

**Charlie Rutlage (theater-orchestra
version by Kenneth Singleton)**
[5289] Yale Theater Orchestra; Sinclair,
James (cond)
- Columbia M-32969/MQ-32969;
33s/q; rel 1974; cip

Children's Hour, The (1901)
[5290] Fischer-Dieskau, Dietrich (bar);
Ponti, Michael (pf)
- Deutsche Grammophon
2530.696; 33s; rel 1976; cip

Christmas Carol, A (1894)
[5291] DeGaetani, Jan (m sop); Kalish,
Gilbert (pf)
- Nonesuch H-71325; 33s; rel
1976; cip

[5292] Fischer-Dieskau, Dietrich (bar);
Ponti, Michael (pf)
- Deutsche Grammophon
2530.696; 33s; rel 1976; cip

**Christmas Carol, A (arr for chorus
by Paul Echols)**
[5293] Western Wind
- Musical Heritage Society
MHS-4077; 33s

Chromatimelodtune (1919?)
[5294] Yale Theater Orchestra; Sinclair,
James (cond)
- Columbia M-32969/MQ-32969;
33s/q; rel 1974; cip

Circus Band, The (1894?)
[5295] DeGaetani, Jan (m sop); Kalish,
Gilbert (pf)
Rec 10/75
- Nonesuch H-71325; 33s; rel
1976; cip
- Nonesuch H-7-14; 33s; 2 discs;
rel 1978; cip

[5296] Laine, Cleo (sop); Hymas, Anthony
(pf)
- RCA LRL-1-5058; 33s; rel 1975;
del 1979

[5297] Lear, Evelyn (sop) or Stewart,
Thomas (bar); Katz, Martin (pf)
Rec 1/17/78
- Pelican LP-2012; 33s; rel 1979;
cip

[5298] Saeden, Erik (bar); Envik, Sten (pf)
Rec 9/12/66
- EMI/His Master's Voice
4E-053-35162; 33m; rel 1976

Circus Band, The (arr for chorus)
[5299] C. W. Post College Chorus and Chamber Singers; Klauss, Walter (org); Dashnaw, Alexander (cond)
- Golden Crest CCS-8050; 33s; rel 1978; cip

[5300] Cornell Sage Chapel Choir; Cornell University Wind Ensemble; Stith, Marice (cond)
Rec 3/24/74
- Cornell CUWE-14; 33s; rel 1975; cip

[5301] Drake, Archie (b); Gregg Smith Singers; Columbia Chamber Orchestra; Smith, Gregg (cond)
Rec 7/7/65
- Columbia M4-32504; 33s; 4 discs; rel 1974; cip

[5302] Gregg Smith Singers; New York Vocal Arts Ensemble; Smith, Gregg (cond)
- Vox SVBX-5304; 33s; 3 discs; rel 1974; cip

Country Band March (1903)
[5303] Cornell University Wind Ensemble; Cornell University Symphonic Band; Stith, Marice (cond)
- Cornell CUWE-17; 33s; rel 1975; cip

[5304] Yale Theater Orchestra; Sinclair, James (cond)
- Columbia M-32969/MQ-32969; 33s/q; rel 1974; cip

Cradle Song (1919)
[5305] Grande, Peter del (bar); Pleshakov, Vladimir (pf)
- CST-106; 33s; rel 1971

December (1913?)
[5306] Grande, Peter del (bar); Pleshakov, Vladimir (pf)
- CST-106; 33s; rel 1971

Disclosure (1921)
[5307] Fischer-Dieskau, Dietrich (bar); Ponti, Michael (pf)
- Deutsche Grammophon 2530.696; 33s; rel 1976; cip

Down East (1919)
[5308] Boatwright, Helen (sop); Kirkpatrick, John (pf)
Rec 11/69
- Columbia M4-32504; 33s; 4 discs; rel 1974; cip

[5309] Grande, Peter del (bar); Pleshakov, Vladimir (pf)
- CST-106; 33s; rel 1971

Down East (arr for chorus by Gregg Smith)
[5310] Gregg Smith Singers; New York Vocal Arts Ensemble; Smith, Gregg (cond)
- Vox SVBX-5304; 33s; 3 discs; rel 1974; cip

Dreams (1897)
[5311] New York Vocal Arts Ensemble
- Turnabout TVS-34630; 33s; rel 1976; cip

Election, An (1920)
[5312] Saeden, Erik (bar); Envik, Sten (pf)
Rec 9/12/66
- EMI/His Master's Voice 4E-053-35162; 33m; rel 1976

Election, An (choral version)
[5313] Gregg Smith Singers; Ithaca College Concert Choir; American Symphony Orchestra; Stokowski, Leopold (cond)
Rec 10/18/67
- Columbia M4-32504; 33s; 4 discs; rel 1974; cip

Elegie (1901)
[5314] Fischer-Dieskau, Dietrich (bar); Ponti, Michael (pf)
- Deutsche Grammophon 2530.696; 33s; rel 1976; cip

[5315] Parker, William (bar); Baldwin, Dalton (pf)
- New World NW-300; 33s; rel 1978

Evening (1921)
[5316] Bauman, Mordecai (bar); Hirsh, Albert (pf)
Rec 1938
- CRI-390; 33s; rel 1978; cip

Evening (theater-orchestra version by Kenneth Singleton)
[5317] Yale Theater Orchestra; Sinclair, James (cond)
- Columbia M-32969/MQ-32969; 33s/q; rel 1974; cip

Farewell to Land, A (1909)
[5318] DeGaetani, Jan (m sop); Kalish, Gilbert (pf)
- Nonesuch H-71325; 33s; rel 1976; cip

[5319] Fischer-Dieskau, Dietrich (bar); Ponti, Michael (pf)
- Deutsche Grammophon 2530.696; 33s; rel 1976; cip

Feldeinsamkeit (1897)
[5320] Boatwright, Helen (sop); Kirkpatrick, John (pf)
Rec 11/69
- Columbia M4-32504; 33s; 4 discs; rel 1974; cip

[5321] Fischer-Dieskau, Dietrich (bar); Ponti, Michael (pf)
- Deutsche Grammophon 2530.696; 33s; rel 1976; cip

Fugue in Four Keys, on The Shining Shore (1897)
[5322] Yale Theater Orchestra; Sinclair, James (cond)
- Columbia M-32969/MQ-32969; 33s/q; rel 1974; cip

General William Booth Enters into Heaven (solo version) (1914)
[5323] Pazmor, Radiana (sop); Pitot, Genevieve (pf)
Rec 1934
- New World NW-247; 33m; rel 1976
- CRI-390; 33s; rel 1978; cip

General William Booth Enters into Heaven (choral version) (1914)
[5324] Bushnell Choir; Pappastavrou, George C. (pf); Dashnaw, Alexander (cond)
Rec 8/22/76
- Golden Crest CRS-4172; 33s; rel 1979; cip

[5325] Drake, Archie (b); Gregg Smith Singers; Columbia Chamber Orchestra; Smith, Gregg (cond)
Rec 5/4/66
- Columbia M4-32504; 33s; 4 discs; rel 1974; cip

Gong on the Hook and Ladder, The (Firemen's Parade on Main Street) (1911?)
[5326] New York Philharmonic; Bernstein, Leonard (cond)
Rec 1/31/67
- Columbia M3X-31068; 33s; 3 discs; rel 1972; cip

Greatest Man, The (1921)
[5327] Bauman, Mordecai (bar); Hirsh, Albert (pf)
Rec 1938
- CRI-390; 33s; rel 1978; cip

[5328] Laine, Cleo (sop); Hymas, Anthony (pf)
- RCA LRL-1-5058; 33s; rel 1975; del 1979

[5329] Saeden, Erik (bar); Envik, Sten (pf)
Rec 9/12/66
- EMI/His Master's Voice 4E-053-35162; 33m; rel 1976

Halloween (1906)
[5330] Taylor, Millard (vln); Celentano, John (vln); Tursi, Francis (vla); Harris, Alan (vcl); Glazer, Frank (pf)
Rec 1974
- Vox SVBX-564; 33s; 3 discs; rel 1976; cip

His Exaltation (1913)
[5331] Grande, Peter del (bar); Pleshakov, Vladimir (pf)
- CST-106; 33s; rel 1971

His Exaltation (1913) (cont'd)
[5332] Parker, William (bar); Baldwin,
Dalton (pf)
- New World NW-300; 33s; rel
1978

Holiday Quickstep (1887)
[5333] Yale Theater Orchestra; Sinclair,
James (cond)
- Columbia M-32969/MQ-32969;
33s/q; rel 1974; cip

Holidays Symphony (New England Holidays) (1904-13)
[5334] Philadelphia Orchestra; Ormandy,
Eugene (cond)
- RCA ARL-1-1249/ARD-1-1249;
33s/q; rel 1975; cip

Holidays Symphony: Washington's Birthday and The Fourth of July
[5335] New York Philharmonic; Bernstein,
Leonard (cond)
Rec 11/23/64
- Columbia MG-31155; 33s; 2
discs; rel 1972; cip
- Columbia M4-32504; 33s; 4
discs; rel 1974; cip (Excerpt: The
Fourth of July)

Holidays Symphony: Decoration Day
[5336] Los Angeles Philharmonic
Orchestra; Mehta, Zubin (cond)
- London CS-6982 (in set
CSA-2246); 33s; rel 1976; del
1980

[5337] no performers given
- Opus Musicum OM-104-06; 33s;
3 discs; rel 1973

Housatonic at Stockbridge, The (1921)
[5338] DeGaetani, Jan (m sop); Kalish,
Gilbert (pf)
- Nonesuch H-71325; 33s; rel
1976; cip

[5339] Grande, Peter del (bar); Pleshakov,
Vladimir (pf)
- CST-106; 33s; rel 1971

Hymn (1921)
[5340] Grande, Peter del (bar); Pleshakov,
Vladimir (pf)
- CST-106; 33s; rel 1971

Ich grolle nicht (1898)
[5341] Fischer-Dieskau, Dietrich (bar);
Ponti, Michael (pf)
- Deutsche Grammophon
2530.696; 33s; rel 1976; cip

Immortality (1921)
[5342] Saeden, Erik (bar); Envik, Sten (pf)
Rec 9/12/66
- EMI/His Master's Voice
4E-053-35162; 33m; rel 1976

Improvisations X, Y, Z
[5343] Ives, Charles (pf)
Rec 5/11/38
- Columbia M4-32504; 33s; 4
discs; rel 1974; cip

In Flanders Fields (1917)
[5344] Fischer-Dieskau, Dietrich (bar);
Ponti, Michael (pf)
- Deutsche Grammophon
2530.696; 33s; rel 1976; cip

[5345] Stewart, Thomas (bar); Mandel,
Alan (pf)
- Columbia M4-32504; 33s; 4
discs; rel 1974; cip

In re con moto et al (1913)
[5346] Taylor, Millard (vln); Celentano,
John (vln); Tursi, Francis (vla);
Harris, Alan (vcl); Glazer, Frank
(pf)
Rec 1974
- Vox SVBX-564; 33s; 3 discs; rel
1976; cip

In the Alley (1896)
[5347] Gregg Smith Singers; New York
Vocal Arts Ensemble; Smith,
Gregg (cond)
- Vox SVBX-5304; 33s; 3 discs; rel
1974; cip

In the Mornin' (1929)
[5348] DeGaetani, Jan (m sop); Kalish,
Gilbert (pf)
Rec 10/75
- Nonesuch H-71325; 33s; rel
1976; cip
- Nonesuch H-7-14; 33s; 2 discs;
rel 1978; cip

Incantation (1921)
[5349] Boatwright, Helen (sop);
Kirkpatrick, John (pf)
Rec 11/69
- Columbia M4-32504; 33s; 4
discs; rel 1974; cip

Indians, The (1921)
[5350] DeGaetani, Jan (m sop); Kalish,
Gilbert (pf)
- Nonesuch H-71325; 33s; rel
1976; cip

Innate, The (1916)
[5351] DeGaetani, Jan (m sop); Kalish,
Gilbert (pf)
- Nonesuch H-71325; 33s; rel
1976; cip

[5352] Grande, Peter del (bar); Pleshakov,
Vladimir (pf)
- CST-106; 33s; rel 1971

Kaeren (or Little Kaeren) (1895?)
[5353] Gregg Smith Singers; New York
Vocal Arts Ensemble; Smith,
Gregg (cond)
- Vox SVBX-5304; 33s; 3 discs; rel
1974; cip

Largo, Clarinet, Violin, and Piano (1902?)
[5354] Boston Musica Viva; Pittman,
Richard (cond)
- Delos DEL-25406; 33s; rel
1975; cip

[5355] Compinsky Ensemble
- Town Hall S-3; 33s; 2 discs; rel
1978; cip

[5356] D'Antonio, Roy (cl); Sandler, Myron
(vln); Stevens, Delores (pf)
- Laurel LR-103; 33s; rel 1975;
cip

[5357] Hasty, Stanley (cl); Taylor, Millard
(vln); Glazer, Frank (pf)
Rec 1974
- Vox SVBX-564; 33s; 3 discs; rel
1976; cip

Largo Risoluto No 1 (As to the Law of Diminishing Returns) (1906)
[5358] Taylor, Millard (vln); Celentano,
John (vln); Tursi, Francis (vla);
Harris, Alan (vcl); Glazer, Frank
(pf)
Rec 1974
- Vox SVBX-564; 33s; 3 discs; rel
1976; cip

Largo Risoluto No 3 (A Shadow Made–a Silhouette) (1906)
(= Largo Risoluto No 2)
[5359] Taylor, Millard (vln); Celentano,
John (vln); Tursi, Francis (vla);
Harris, Alan (vcl); Glazer, Frank
(pf)
Rec 1974
- Vox SVBX-564; 33s; 3 discs; rel
1976; cip

Last Reader, The (1921)
[5360] Grande, Peter del (bar); Pleshakov,
Vladimir (pf)
- CST-106; 33s; rel 1971

Light That Is Felt, The (1903)
[5361] Grande, Peter del (bar); Pleshakov,
Vladimir (pf)
- CST-106; 33s; rel 1971

Like a Sick Eagle (1913?)
[5362] DeGaetani, Jan (m sop); Kalish,
Gilbert (pf)
- Nonesuch H-71325; 33s; rel
1976; cip

[5363] Saeden, Erik (bar); Envik, Sten (pf)
Rec 9/12/66
- EMI/His Master's Voice
4E-053-35162; 33m; rel 1976

Lincoln, the Great Commoner (1912)
[5364] Gregg Smith Singers; Ithaca
College Concert Choir; American
Symphony Orchestra; Stokowski,
Leopold (cond)
Rec 10/18/67
- Columbia M4-32504; 33s; 4
discs; rel 1974; cip

Luck and Work (1913?)

[5365] Boatwright, Helen (sop); Kirkpatrick, John (pf)
Rec 11/69
- Columbia M4-32504; 33s; 4 discs; rel 1974; cip

Majority (The Masses) (1914-15)

[5366] Gregg Smith Singers; Ithaca College Concert Choir; American Symphony Orchestra; Stokowski, Leopold (cond)
Rec 10/18/67
- Columbia M4-32504; 33s; 4 discs; rel 1974; cip

Majority (1921)

[5367] DeGaetani, Jan (m sop); Kalish, Gilbert (pf)
- Nonesuch H-71325; 33s; rel 1976; cip

March No 2 (With: A Son of a Gambolier) (1892)

[5368] New England Conservatory Wind Ensemble
- Golden Crest NEC-111; 33s; rel 1975; cip

[5369] Yale Theater Orchestra; Sinclair, James (cond)
- Columbia M-32969/MQ-32969; 33s/q; rel 1974; cip

March No 3 (With: My Old Kentucky Home) (1892)

[5370] Yale Theater Orchestra; Sinclair, James (cond)
- Columbia M-32969/MQ-32969; 33s/q; rel 1974; cip

March No 5 or March Intercollegiate (With: Annie Lisle) (1892)

[5371] Incredible Columbia All-Star Band; Schuller, Gunther (cond)
- Columbia M-33513/MQ-33513; 33s/q; rel 1975; cip

[5372] New England Conservatory Wind Ensemble
- Golden Crest NEC-111; 33s; rel 1975; cip

March No 6 (With: Here's to Good Old Yale) (1892-97?)

[5373] Deutsch, Nina (pf)
Rec 6/76
- Vox SVBX-5482; 33s; 3 discs; rel 1977; cip

[5374] Ives, Charles (pf)
Rec 4/24/43
- Columbia M4-32504; 33s; 4 discs; rel 1974; cip

March: The Circus Band (1894?)

[5375] New York Philharmonic; Bernstein, Leonard (cond)
Rec 1/31/67
- Columbia M3X-31068; 33s; 3 discs; rel 1972; cip

March, F and C (With: Omega Lambda Chi) (1896)

[5376] Cornell University Wind Ensemble; Cornell University Symphonic Band; Stith, Marice (cond)
- Cornell CUWE-17; 33s; rel 1975; cip

[5377] Incredible Columbia All-Star Band; Schuller, Gunther (cond)
- Columbia M-33513/MQ-33513; 33s/q; rel 1975; cip

Marie (1896)

[5378] Gregg Smith Singers; New York Vocal Arts Ensemble; Smith, Gregg (cond)
- Vox SVBX-5304; 33s; 3 discs; rel 1974; cip

Memories (A, Very Pleasant; B, Rather Sad) (1897)

[5379] DeGaetani, Jan (m sop); Kalish, Gilbert (pf)
- Nonesuch H-71325; 33s; rel 1976; cip

[5380] Gregg Smith Singers; New York Vocal Arts Ensemble; Smith, Gregg (cond)
- Vox SVBX-5304; 33s; 3 discs; rel 1974; cip

Mists (1910)

[5381] Boatwright, Helen (sop); Kirkpatrick, John (pf)
Rec 11/69
- Columbia M4-32504; 33s; 4 discs; rel 1974; cip

Mists (theater-orchestra version by Kenneth Singleton)

[5382] Yale Theater Orchestra; Sinclair, James (cond)
- Columbia M-32969/MQ-32969; 33s/q; rel 1974; cip

New River, The (1913)

[5383] Boatwright, Helen (sop); Kirkpatrick, John (pf)
Rec 11/69
- Columbia M4-32504; 33s; 4 discs; rel 1974; cip

[5384] Grande, Peter del (bar); Pleshakov, Vladimir (pf)
- CST-106; 33s; rel 1971

Night Song (1895)

[5385] Gregg Smith Singers; New York Vocal Arts Ensemble; Smith, Gregg (cond)
- Vox SVBX-5304; 33s; 3 discs; rel 1974; cip

No More (1897)

[5386] Boatwright, Helen (sop); Kirkpatrick, John (pf)
Rec 11/69
- Columbia M4-32504; 33s; 4 discs; rel 1974; cip

Old Flame, An (or A Retrospect) (1896)

[5387] Gregg Smith Singers; New York Vocal Arts Ensemble; Smith, Gregg (cond)
- Vox SVBX-5304; 33s; 3 discs; rel 1974; cip

Old Home Day (1913?)

[5388] Boatwright, Helen (sop); Kirkpatrick, John (pf)
Rec 11/69
- Columbia M4-32504; 33s; 4 discs; rel 1974; cip

[5389] Grande, Peter del (bar); Davies, Nan (fl); Pleshakov, Vladimir (pf)
- CST-106; 33s; rel 1971

[5390] Gregg Smith Singers; New York Vocal Arts Ensemble; Smith, Gregg (cond)
- Vox SVBX-5304; 33s; 3 discs; rel 1974; cip

Old Song Deranged, An (1903?)

[5391] Yale Theater Orchestra; Sinclair, James (cond)
- Columbia M-32969/MQ-32969; 33s/q; rel 1974; cip

On Judges' Walk (1893-98?)

[5392] Boatwright, Helen (sop); Kirkpatrick, John (pf)
Rec 11/69
- Columbia M4-32504; 33s; 4 discs; rel 1974; cip

On the Counter (1920) (arr for brass quintet by Kenneth Singleton)

[5393] Eastern Brass Quintet
- Klavier KS-539; 33s; rel 1975; cip

One Way, The (1923)

[5394] Boatwright, Helen (sop); Kirkpatrick, John (pf)
Rec 11/69
- Columbia M4-32504; 33s; 4 discs; rel 1974; cip

Orchestral Set No 1 (A New England Symphony: Three Places in New England) (1908-14)

[5395] Eastman-Rochester Symphony Orchestra; Hanson, Howard (cond)
- Mercury SRI-75035; 33s; rel 1974; cip

[5396] Philadelphia Orchestra; Ormandy, Eugene (cond)
- RCA ARL-1-1682; 33s; rel 1976; cip

[5397] St. Paul Chamber Orchestra; Davies, Dennis Russell (cond)
- Sound 80 DLR-101; 33 digital; rel 1979; cip

Orchestral Set No 2 (1909-15)
[5398] London Symphony Orchestra and
Chorus; Stokowski, Leopold
(cond)
- London SPC-21060; 33s; rel
1972; del 1979

Overture and March 1776 (1903)
[5399] Cornell University Wind Ensemble;
Cornell University Symphonic
Band; Stith, Marice (cond)
- Cornell CUWE-17; 33s; rel 1975;
cip

[5400] Yale Theater Orchestra; Sinclair,
James (cond)
- Columbia M-32969/MQ-32969;
33s/q; rel 1974; cip

Paracelsus (1921)
[5401] DeGaetani, Jan (m sop); Kalish,
Gilbert (pf)
- Nonesuch H-71325; 33s; rel
1976; cip

Peaks (1923)
[5402] Boatwright, Helen (sop);
Kirkpatrick, John (pf)
Rec 11/69
- Columbia M4-32504; 33s; 4
discs; rel 1974; cip

Pictures (1906)
[5403] Boatwright, Helen (sop);
Kirkpatrick, John (pf)
Rec 11/69
- Columbia M4-32504; 33s; 4
discs; rel 1974; cip

Pond, The (1906)
[5404] chamber orchestra; Schuller,
Gunther (cond)
- Columbia M4-32504; 33s; 4
discs; rel 1974; cip

Premonitions (1921)
[5405] Grande, Peter del (bar); Pleshakov,
Vladimir (pf)
- CST-106; 33s; rel 1971

Psalm 24 (1894?)
[5406] Tanglewood Festival Chorus; Oliver,
John (cond)
- Deutsche Grammophon
2530.912; 33s; rel 1979; cip

Psalm 67 (1894?)
[5407] New England Conservatory Chorus;
De Varon, Lorna Cooke (cond)
- Golden Crest NEC-104; 33s; rel
1974; cip

[5408] Tanglewood Festival Chorus; Oliver,
John (cond)
- Deutsche Grammophon
2530.912; 33s; rel 1979; cip

Psalm 90 (1894-1924)
[5409] C. W. Post College Chorus and
Chamber Singers; Klauss, Walter
(org); Dashnaw, Alexander (cond)
- Golden Crest CCS-8050; 33s; rel
1978; cip

[5410] Tanglewood Festival Chorus; Oliver,
John (cond)
- Deutsche Grammophon
2530.912; 33s; rel 1979; cip

(Three) Quarter-Tone Pieces, Two Pianos (1923-24)
[5411] Glazer, Frank (pf); Balsam, Artur
(pf)
Rec 1974
- Vox SVBX-564; 33s; 3 discs; rel
1976; cip

(Three) Quarter-Tone Pieces, Two Pianos: Chorale
[5412] Bunger, Richard (pf); Bunger, L.
(pf)
- Avant AV-1008; 33s; rel 1973;
del 1979

Quartet, Strings, No 1 (From the Salvation Army) (1896)
[5413] Concord String Quartet
- Nonesuch H-71306; 33s; rel
1975; cip

Quartet, Strings, No 2 (1907-13)
[5414] Cleveland Quartet
- RCA ARL-1-1599; 33s; rel 1976;
cip

[5415] Concord String Quartet
- Nonesuch H-71306; 33s; rel
1975; cip

Qu'il m'irait bien (1897?)
[5416] Grande, Peter del (bar); Pleshakov,
Vladimir (pf)
- CST-106; 33s; rel 1971

[5417] Parker, William (bar); Baldwin,
Dalton (pf)
- New World NW-300; 33s; rel
1978

Remembrance (1921) (theater-orchestra version by Kenneth Singleton)
[5418] Yale Theater Orchestra; Sinclair,
James (cond)
- Columbia M-32969/MQ-32969;
33s/q; rel 1974; cip

Requiem (1911)
[5419] Boatwright, Helen (sop);
Kirkpatrick, John (pf)
Rec 11/69
- Columbia M4-32504; 33s; 4
discs; rel 1974; cip

[5420] Saeden, Erik (bar); Envik, Sten (pf)
Rec 9/12/66
- EMI/His Master's Voice
4E-053-35162; 33m; rel 1976

Resolution (1921)
[5421] Bauman, Mordecai (bar); Hirsh,
Albert (pf)
Rec 1938
- CRI-390; 33s; rel 1978; cip

[5422] Boatwright, Helen (sop);
Kirkpatrick, John (pf)
Rec 11/69
- Columbia M4-32504; 33s; 4
discs; rel 1974; cip

Romanzo di Central Park (1900)
[5423] Gregg Smith Singers; New York
Vocal Arts Ensemble; Smith,
Gregg (cond)
- Vox SVBX-5304; 33s; 3 discs; rel
1974; cip

Rosamunde (1898)
[5424] Grande, Peter del (bar); Pleshakov,
Vladimir (pf)
- CST-106; 33s; rel 1971

[5425] Parker, William (bar); Baldwin,
Dalton (pf)
- New World NW-300; 33s; rel
1978

Rough Wind (1902)
[5426] Grande, Peter del (bar); Pleshakov,
Vladimir (pf)
- CST-106; 33s; rel 1971

Sea Dirge, A (1925)
[5427] Boatwright, Helen (sop);
Kirkpatrick, John (pf)
Rec 11/69
- Columbia M4-32504; 33s; 4
discs; rel 1974; cip

Sea of Sleep, The (1903)
[5428] Boatwright, Helen (sop);
Kirkpatrick, John (pf)
Rec 11/69
- Columbia M4-32504; 33s; 4
discs; rel 1974; cip

See'r, The (1913?) (arr for instrumental ensemble by Gunther Schuller)
[5429] New England Conservatory
Ragtime Ensemble; Schuller,
Gunther (cond)
Rec 10/74-3/75
- Golden Crest CRS-31042; 33q; 2
discs; rel 1976; cip

September (1920)
[5430] Boatwright, Helen (sop);
Kirkpatrick, John (pf)
Rec 11/69
- Columbia M4-32504; 33s; 4
discs; rel 1974; cip

Serenity (1919)
[5431] DeGaetani, Jan (m sop); Kalish,
Gilbert (pf)
- Nonesuch H-71325; 33s; rel
1976; cip

Serenity (1919) *(cont'd)*
[5432] Lear, Evelyn (sop) or Stewart,
Thomas (bar); Katz, Martin (pf)
Rec 1/17/78
- Pelican LP-2012; 33s; rel 1979;
cip

[5433] New England Conservatory
Chamber Singers; De Varon,
Lorna Cooke (cond)
- Golden Crest NEC-111; 33s; rel
1975; cip

[5434] New Music Choral Ensemble;
Gaburo, Kenneth (cond)
- Ars Nova/Ars Antiqua AN-1005;
33s; rel 1971; del 1973

**Set No 2: Gyp the Blood or Hearst!?
Which is Worst?! (1912?)**
[5435] Yale Theater Orchestra; Sinclair,
James (cond)
- Columbia M-32969/MQ-32969;
33s/q; rel 1974; cip

**Set of Three Short Pieces, A: (No
1) Largo cantabile (Hymn) (1904)**
[5436] New York String Quartet; Brehm,
Alvin (cb)
- Columbia M4-32504; 33s; 4
discs; rel 1974; cip

**Set of Three Short Pieces, A: (No
2) Scherzo (Holding Your Own)
(1903-14)**
[5437] Cleveland Quartet
- RCA ARL-1-1599; 33s; rel 1976;
cip

[5438] Kohon Quartet
- Vox SVBX-5305; 33s; 3 discs; rel
1974; cip

**Set of Three Short Pieces, A: (No
3) Adagio cantabile (The Innate)
(1908)**
[5439] Taylor, Millard (vln); Celentano,
John (vln); Tursi, Francis (vla);
Harris, Alan (vcl); Glazer, Frank
(pf)
Rec 1974
- Vox SVBX-564; 33s; 3 discs; rel
1976; cip

Side-Show, The (1921)
[5440] Boatwright, Helen (sop);
Kirkpatrick, John (pf)
Rec 11/69
- Columbia M4-32504; 33s; 4
discs; rel 1974; cip

[5441] Eberley, Helen Kay (sop); Isaak,
Donald (pf)
- Eb-Sko Productions 1001; 33s;
rel 1976; cip

[5442] Lear, Evelyn (sop) or Stewart,
Thomas (bar); Katz, Martin (pf)
Rec 1/17/78
- Pelican LP-2012; 33s; rel 1979;
cip

**Side-Show, The (arr for brass
quintet by Kenneth Singleton)**
[5443] Eastern Brass Quintet
- Klavier KS-539; 33s; rel 1975;
cip

Slow March (1887?)
[5444] Boatwright, Helen (sop);
Kirkpatrick, John (pf)
Rec 11/69
- Columbia M4-32504; 33s; 4
discs; rel 1974; cip

**Slow March (arr for brass quintet
by Kenneth Singleton)**
[5445] Eastern Brass Quintet
- Klavier KS-539; 33s; rel 1975;
cip

Son of a Gambolier, A (1895)
[5446] Gregg Smith Singers; New York
Vocal Arts Ensemble; Smith,
Gregg (cond)
- Vox SVBX-5304; 33s; 3 discs; rel
1974; cip

Sonata, Piano, No 1 (1901-09)
[5447] Deutsch, Nina (pf)
Rec 6/76
- Vox SVBX-5482; 33s; 3 discs; rel
1977; cip

**Sonata, Piano, No 2 (Concord,
Mass., 1840-60) (1910-15)**
[5448] Deutsch, Nina (pf)
Rec 6/76
- Vox SVBX-5482; 33s; 3 discs; rel
1977; cip

[5449] Kalish, Gilbert (pf); Baron, Samuel
(fl); Graham, John (vla)
- Nonesuch H-71337; 33s; rel
1977; cip

[5450] Kontarsky, Aloys (pf); Schwegler,
Willy (fl); Plumacher, Theo (vla)
Rec 11/61
- Mainstream MS-5013; 33s; rel
1970; del 1979

[5451] Sahr, Hadassah (pf); Adams, Carl
(fl)
- Critics Choice CC-1705; 33s; rel
1976*

[5452] Szidon, Robert (pf); Sonntag, Dieter
(fl); Stangl, Walter (vla)
- Deutsche Grammophon
2530.215; 33s; rel 1972; del
1978

Sonata, Piano, No 2: Excerpts
[5453] Ives, Charles (pf)
Rec 6/12/33?
- Columbia M4-32504; 33s; 4
discs; rel 1974; cip

Sonata, Piano, No 2: The Alcotts
[5454] Shields, Roger (pf)
- Vox SVBX-5303; 33s; 3 discs; rel
1977; cip

**Sonata, Violin and Piano, Pre-First:
Largo in G (1901)**
[5455] Taylor, Millard (vln); Glazer, Frank
(pf)
Rec 1974
- Vox SVBX-564; 33s; 3 discs; rel
1976; cip

[5456] Zukofsky, Paul (vln); Kalish, Gilbert
(pf)
- Nonesuch HB-73025; 33s; 2
discs; rel 1974; cip

**Sonata, Violin and Piano, No 1
(1902-08)**
[5457] Negyesy, Janos (vln); Cardew,
Cornelius (pf)
Rec 4/75
- Thorofon ATHK-136-37; 33s; 2
discs; rel 1975?

[5458] Taylor, Millard (vln); Glazer, Frank
(pf)
Rec 1974
- Vox SVBX-564; 33s; 3 discs; rel
1976; cip

[5459] Zukofsky, Paul (vln); Kalish, Gilbert
(pf)
- Nonesuch HB-73025; 33s; 2
discs; rel 1974; cip

**Sonata, Violin and Piano, No 2
(1907-10)**
[5460] Dubow, Marilyn (vln); Winokur,
Marsha Cheraskin (pf)
- Musical Heritage Society
MHS-3160; 33s; rel 1975

[5461] Negyesy, Janos (vln); Cardew,
Cornelius (pf)
Rec 4/75
- Thorofon ATHK-136-37; 33s; 2
discs; rel 1975?

[5462] Taylor, Millard (vln); Glazer, Frank
(pf)
Rec 1974
- Vox SVBX-564; 33s; 3 discs; rel
1976; cip

[5463] Zukofsky, Paul (vln); Kalish, Gilbert
(pf)
- Nonesuch HB-73025; 33s; 2
discs; rel 1974; cip

**Sonata, Violin and Piano, No 3
(1913-14?)**
[5464] Carabo-Cone, Madeleine (vln);
Lumsden, Ronald (pf)
- Executive Recording, Ltd
CHC-002; 33s; rel 1970

[5465] Dubow, Marilyn (vln); Winokur,
Marsha Cheraskin (pf)
- Musical Heritage Society
MHS-3160; 33s; rel 1975

[5466] Negyesy, Janos (vln); Cardew,
Cornelius (pf)
Rec 4/75
- Thorofon ATHK-136-37; 33s; 2
discs; rel 1975?

Sonata, Violin and Piano, No 3 (1913-14?) *(cont'd)*
[5467] Taylor, Millard (vln); Glazer, Frank (pf)
Rec 1974
- Vox SVBX-564; 33s; 3 discs; rel 1976; cip

[5468] Zukofsky, Paul (vln); Kalish, Gilbert (pf)
- Nonesuch HB-73025; 33s; 2 discs; rel 1974; cip

Sonata, Violin and Piano, No 4 (Children's Day at the Camp Meeting) (1906-16?)
[5469] Gross, Robert (vln); Grayson, Richard (pf)
- Orion ORS-76239; 33s; rel 1977; cip

[5470] Laredo, Jaime (vln); Schein, Ann (pf)
- Desto DC-6439; 33s; rel 1975; cip

[5471] Negyesy, Janos (vln); Cardew, Cornelius (pf)
Rec 4/75
- Thorofon ATHK-136-37; 33s; 2 discs; rel 1975?

[5472] Szigeti, Joseph (vln); Bogas, Roy (pf)
Rec 3/59
- Philips 13PC-95; 33s; rel 1979

[5473] Szigeti, Joseph (vln); Foldes, Andor (pf)
- CRI-390; 33s; rel 1978; cip

[5474] Taylor, Millard (vln); Glazer, Frank (pf)
Rec 1974
- Vox SVBX-564; 33s; 3 discs; rel 1976; cip

[5475] Zukofsky, Paul (vln); Kalish, Gilbert (pf)
- Nonesuch HB-73025; 33s; 2 discs; rel 1974; cip

Study No 9 (The Anti-Abolitionist Riots) (1908)
[5476] Ives, Charles (pf)
Rec 4/24/43
- Columbia M4-32504; 33s; 4 discs; rel 1974; cip

[5477] Shields, Roger (pf)
- Vox SVBX-5303; 33s; 3 discs; rel 1977; cip

Study No 11
[5478] Ives, Charles (pf)
- Columbia M4-32504; 33s; 4 discs; rel 1974; cip

Study No 20: Excerpts
[5479] Ives, Charles (pf)
- Columbia M4-32504; 33s; 4 discs; rel 1974; cip

Study No 21 (Some Southpaw Pitching) (1909?)
[5480] Shields, Roger (pf)
- Vox SVBX-5303; 33s; 3 discs; rel 1977; cip

Study No 23 (1909?): Excerpts
[5481] Ives, Charles (pf)
- Columbia M4-32504; 33s; 4 discs; rel 1974; cip

Sunrise (1926)
[5482] Parker, William (bar); Kavafian, Ani (vln); Baldwin, Dalton (pf)
- New World NW-300; 33s; rel 1978

Swimmers (1915, rev 1921)
[5483] Fischer-Dieskau, Dietrich (bar); Ponti, Michael (pf)
- Deutsche Grammophon 2530.696; 33s; rel 1976; cip

[5484] Saeden, Erik (bar); Envik, Sten (pf)
Rec 9/12/66
- EMI/His Master's Voice 4E-053-35162; 33m; rel 1976

Swimmers (theater-orchestra version by James Sinclair)
[5485] Yale Theater Orchestra; Sinclair, James (cond)
- Columbia M-32969/MQ-32969; 33s/q; rel 1974; cip

Symphony No 1 (1895-98)
[5486] Los Angeles Philharmonic Orchestra; Mehta, Zubin (cond)
- London CS-6816; 33s; rel 1973; cip

Symphony No 2 (1900-02)
[5487] London Symphony Orchestra; Herrmann, Bernard (cond)
Rec 5/9/56
- London SPC-21086; 33s; rel 1972; del 1979

[5488] Los Angeles Philharmonic Orchestra; Mehta, Zubin (cond)
- London CS-6982 (in set CSA-2246); 33s; rel 1976; del 1980

[5489] Philadelphia Orchestra; Ormandy, Eugene (cond)
- RCA ARL-1-0663/ARD-1-0663; 33s/q; rel 1974; del 1977

Symphony No 2 (Improvisations on Themes from the Symphony)
[5490] Ives, Charles (pf)
- Columbia M4-32504; 33s; 4 discs; rel 1974; cip

Symphony No 3 (The Camp Meeting) (1904)
[5491] Academy of St. Martin-in-the-Fields; Marriner, Neville (cond)
- Argo ZRG-845; 33s; rel 1976; cip

Symphony No 3 (The Camp Meeting) (1904) *(cont'd)*
[5492] Eastman-Rochester Symphony Orchestra; Hanson, Howard (cond)
- Mercury SRI-75035; 33s; rel 1974; cip

Symphony No 4 (1909-16)
[5493] John Alldis Choir; London Philharmonic Orchestra; Serebrier, Jose (cond)
- RCA ARL-1-0589/ARD-1-0589; 33s/q; rel 1974; del 1979

[5494] Tanglewood Festival Chorus; Boston Symphony Orchestra; Ozawa, Seiji (cond)
- Deutsche Grammophon 2530.787; 33s; rel 1977; cip

Take-Offs: The Seen and Unseen (1906)
[5495] Deutsch, Nina (pf)
Rec 6/76
- Vox SVBX-5482; 33s; 3 discs; rel 1977; cip

Tarrant Moss (1898?) (arr for brass quintet by Kenneth Singleton)
[5496] Eastern Brass Quintet
- Klavier KS-539; 33s; rel 1975; cip

There Is a Certain Garden (1893)
[5497] Boatwright, Helen (sop); Kirkpatrick, John (pf)
Rec 11/69
- Columbia M4-32504; 33s; 4 discs; rel 1974; cip

They Are There! (solo version) (1942)
[5498] Ives, Charles (voice) (pf)
- Columbia M4-32504; 33s; 4 discs; rel 1974; cip

They Are There! (choral version) (1942)
[5499] Bushnell Choir; Pappastavrou, George C. (pf); Dashnaw, Alexander (cond)
Rec 8/22/76
- Golden Crest CRS-4172; 33s; rel 1979; cip

[5500] Gregg Smith Singers; Ithaca College Concert Choir; American Symphony Orchestra; Stokowski, Leopold (cond)
Rec 10/18/67
- Columbia M4-32504; 33s; 4 discs; rel 1974; cip

[5501] Gregg Smith Singers; New York Vocal Arts Ensemble; Smith, Gregg (cond)
- Vox SVBX-5304; 33s; 3 discs; rel 1974; cip

They Are There! (choral version) (1942) (cont'd)

[5502] Seattle Chamber Singers; piano; Shangrow, George (cond)
Rec 8/1-8/76
- Voyager VRLP-701S; 33s; rel 1976

They Are There! (War Song March)

[5503] Cornell University Wind Ensemble; Cornell University Symphonic Band; Stith, Marice (cond)
- Cornell CUWE-17; 33s; rel 1975; cip

Things Our Fathers Loved, The (1917)

[5504] Boatwright, Helen (sop); Kirkpatrick, John (pf)
Rec 11/69
- Columbia M4-32504; 33s; 4 discs; rel 1974; cip

[5505] DeGaetani, Jan (m sop); Kalish, Gilbert (pf)
- Nonesuch H-71325; 33s; rel 1976; cip

Thoreau (1915)

[5506] DeGaetani, Jan (m sop); Kalish, Gilbert (pf)
- Nonesuch H-71325; 33s; rel 1976; cip

[5507] Grande, Peter del (bar); Pleshakov, Vladimir (pf)
- CST-106; 33s; rel 1971

Those Evening Bells (1907)

[5508] Grande, Peter del (bar); Pleshakov, Vladimir (pf)
- CST-106; 33s; rel 1971

Three-Page Sonata (1905)

[5509] Deutsch, Nina (pf)
Rec 6/76
- Vox SVBX-5482; 33s; 3 discs; rel 1977; cip

[5510] Lythgoe, Clive (pf)
- Philips 9500.096; 33s; rel 1976; cip

[5511] Szidon, Robert (pf); Metzler, Richard (asst pf)
- Deutsche Grammophon 2530.215; 33s; rel 1972; del 1978

Tom Sails Away (1917)

[5512] Fischer-Dieskau, Dietrich (bar); Ponti, Michael (pf)
- Deutsche Grammophon 2530.696; 33s; rel 1976; cip

[5513] Saeden, Erik (bar); Envik, Sten (pf)
Rec 9/12/66
- EMI/His Master's Voice 4E-053-35162; 33m; rel 1976

(Four) Transcriptions from Emerson (1917?, 1922?)

[5514] Deutsch, Nina (pf)
Rec 6/76
- Vox SVBX-5482; 33s; 3 discs; rel 1977; cip

Trio, Violin, Violoncello, and Piano (1904-05, rev 1911)

[5515] Beaux-Arts Trio
- Philips 6500.860; 33s; rel 1975; cip

[5516] New England Trio
- HNH Records HNH-4070; 33s; rel 1979

[5517] Pacific Art Trio
- Delos DEL-25402; 33s; rel 1975; cip

[5518] Taylor, Millard (vln); Harris, Alan (vcl); Glazer, Frank (pf)
Rec ca 1974
- Vox SVBX-564; 33s; 3 discs; rel 1976; cip

Two Little Flowers (1921)

[5519] Bauman, Mordecai (bar); Hirsh, Albert (pf)
Rec 1938
- CRI-390; 33s; rel 1978; cip

[5520] Fischer-Dieskau, Dietrich (bar); Ponti, Michael (pf)
- Deutsche Grammophon 2530.696; 33s; rel 1976; cip

Unanswered Question, The (1906)

[5521] Moscow Radio Chamber Ensemble; Rozhdestvensky Orchestra or Bolshoi Symphony Orchestra; Rozhdestvensky, Gennady (cond)
- Westminster WGS-8338; 33s; rel 1977; cip

[5522] New York Philharmonic; Bernstein, Leonard (cond)
- Columbia M3X-33028; 33s; 3 discs; rel 1972; cip
- Columbia M4-32504; 33s; 4 discs; rel 1974; cip

[5523] no performers given
- Opus Musicum OM-113-15; 33s; 3 discs; rel 1974

Variations on America (1891?)

[5524] Anderson, Robert (org)
Rec 1971
- Aeolian-Skinner AS-328; 33s; rel 1971

[5525] Baker, George C. (org)
- Delos DEL-FY-025; 33s; rel 1977; cip

[5526] Beck, Janice (org)
Rec 7/9-10/71
- Musical Heritage Society OR-A-264; 33s; rel 1971

[5527] Biggs, E. Power (org)
Rec 11/68
- Columbia M4-32504; 33s; 4 discs; rel 1974; cip

Variations on America (1891?) (cont'd)

[5528] Fox, Virgil (org)
Rec 5/11/74
- RCA ARL-1-0666; 33s; rel 1974; del 1979

[5529] Hillsman, Walter (org)
Rec 5/10-11/76
- Vista VPS-1038; 33s; rel 1976

[5530] Obetz, John (org)
- Celebre/Century 36707; 33s; rel 197?

[5531] Roubos, Robert (org)
Rec 5/12/73
- Wicks Organ Co TS-73-723-24; 33s; rel 1973

Variations on America (arr for pf by Nina Deutsch)

[5532] Deutsch, Nina (pf)
Rec 6/76
- Vox SVBX-5482; 33s; 3 discs; rel 1977; cip

Variations on America (arr for 4-hand pf)

[5533] Hersh, Paul (pf); Montgomery, David (pf)
- Orion ORS-76247; 33s; rel 1977; cip

Variations on America (arr for orch by William Schuman)

[5534] Andre Kostelanetz and his Orchestra; Kostelanetz, Andre (cond)
Rec 4/15/75
- Columbia MG-33728; 33s; 2 discs; rel 1976; del 1979

[5535] Boston Pops Orchestra; Fiedler, Arthur (cond)
- London SPC-21178; 33s; rel 1978; cip

[5536] Chicago Symphony Orchestra; Gould, Morton (cond)
- RCA LM-2893/LSC-2893; 33m/s; rel 1966; del 1979
- RCA (English) RB-6687/SB-6687; 33m/s; rel 1966*
- RCA CRL-3-3270; 33s; 3 discs; rel 1979; cip

[5537] Los Angeles Philharmonic Orchestra; Mehta, Zubin (cond)
Rec 5/75
- London CS-6982 (in set CSA-2246); 33s; rel 1976; del 1980
- Decca (English) SXL-6753; 33s; rel 1976*

[5538] Louisville Orchestra; Whitney, Robert (cond)
Rec 11/24/64
- LOU-65-1; 33m (Louisville Orchestra First Edition Records 1965 No 1); rel 1965; cip

Variations on America (arr for orch by William Schuman) (cont'd)
[5539] Philadelphia Orchestra; Ormandy, Eugene (cond)
Rec 5/8/68
- CBS (English) 72683; 33s; rel 1968*
- Columbia MS-7289; 33s; rel 1969; cip

Vote for Names (1912)
[5540] Gregg Smith Singers; Akos, Catherine (sop); Smith, Gregg (cond)
Rec 1976
- Vox SVBX-5353; 33s; 3 discs; rel 1979; cip

Waiting Soul, The (1908)
[5541] Grande, Peter del (bar); Pleshakov, Vladimir (pf)
- CST-106; 33s; rel 1971

Walt Whitman (1921)
[5542] Suderburg, Elizabeth (sop); Suderburg, Robert (pf)
- University of Washington Press OLY-104; 33q; 2 discs; rel 1976; cip

Waltz (1894?)
[5543] Gregg Smith Singers; New York Vocal Arts Ensemble; Smith, Gregg (cond)
- Vox SVBX-5304; 33s; 3 discs; rel 1974; cip

Waltz-Rondo (1911)
[5544] Deutsch, Nina (pf)
Rec 6/76
- Vox SVBX-5482; 33s; 3 discs; rel 1977; cip

Watchman (1913)
[5545] Grande, Peter del (bar); Pleshakov, Vladimir (pf)
- CST-106; 33s; rel 1971

[5546] Parker, William (bar); Baldwin, Dalton (pf)
- New World NW-300; 33s; rel 1978

Weil' auf mir (1901?)
[5547] Fischer-Dieskau, Dietrich (bar); Ponti, Michael (pf)
- Deutsche Grammophon 2530.696; 33s; rel 1976; cip

[5548] Grande, Peter del (bar); Pleshakov, Vladimir (pf)
- CST-106; 33s; rel 1971

West London (1921)
[5549] Boatwright, Helen (sop); Kirkpatrick, John (pf)
Rec 11/69
- Columbia M4-32504; 33s; 4 discs; rel 1974; cip

West London (1921) (cont'd)
[5550] Fischer-Dieskau, Dietrich (bar); Ponti, Michael (pf)
- Deutsche Grammophon 2530.696; 33s; rel 1976; cip

Where the Eagle (1906)
[5551] Fischer-Dieskau, Dietrich (bar); Ponti, Michael (pf)
- Deutsche Grammophon 2530.696; 33s; rel 1976; cip

White Gulls, The (1921)
[5552] Fischer-Dieskau, Dietrich (bar); Ponti, Michael (pf)
- Deutsche Grammophon 2530.696; 33s; rel 1976; cip

[5553] Suderburg, Elizabeth (sop); Suderburg, Robert (pf)
- University of Washington Press OLY-104; 33q; 2 discs; rel 1976; cip

Widmung (1897?)
[5554] Boatwright, Helen (sop); Kirkpatrick, John (pf)
Rec 11/69
- Columbia M4-32504; 33s; 4 discs; rel 1974; cip

William Will (1896)
[5555] Kittelson, Fay (al); Mason, Patrick (bar); Gregg Smith Singers; Smith, Gregg (cond)
Rec 1976
- Vox SVBX-5353; 33s; 3 discs; rel 1979; cip

Yellow Leaves (1923)
[5556] Boatwright, Helen (sop); Kirkpatrick, John (pf)
Rec 11/69
- Columbia M4-32504; 33s; 4 discs; rel 1974; cip

IVEY, Jean Eichelberger (1923-)
Aldebaran (1973)
[5557] Glick, Jacob (vla); tape
- Folkways FTS-33439; 33s; rel 1974; cip

Cortege for Charles Kent (1969)
[5558] Electronic music
- Folkways FTS-33439; 33s; rel 1974; cip

Hera, Hung from the Sky (Op 9) (1974)
[5559] Bonazzi, Elaine (m sop); Notes from Underground Group; instrumental ensemble; tape; Thomas, Andrew (cond)
- CRI-325; 33s; rel 1974; cip

Pinball (1965)
[5560] Electronic music
- Folkways FM-3436/FMS-33436; 33m/s; rel 1967; cip

(Three) Songs of Night (1971)
[5561] Rowe, Catherine (sop); Peabody Conservatory Contemporary Music Ensemble; tape; Pearlman, Leonard (cond)
- Folkways FTS-33439; 33s; rel 1974; cip

Terminus (1971)
[5562] Bonazzi, Elaine (m sop); tape
- Folkways FTS-33439; 33s; rel 1974; cip

JACOBI, Frederick (1891-1952)
Ballade, Violin and Piano (1942)
[5563] Lack, Fredell (vln); Jacobi, Irene (pf)
- CRI-146; 33m/s; rel 1961/1970; cip

Concertino, Piano and String Orchestra (1946)
[5564] Jacobi, Irene (pf); Belgian National Radio Orchestra; Andre, Franz (cond)
- SPA-7; 33m; rel 1952; del 1970

Concerto, Violin and Orchestra (1936-37)
[5565] Gertler, Andre (vln); Belgian National Radio Orchestra; Andre, Franz (cond)
- SPA-7; 33m; rel 1952; del 1970

Concerto, Violoncello and Orchestra (1932)
[5566] Vecchi, Guido (vcl); Oslo Philharmonic Orchestra; Strickland, William (cond)
- CRI-174; 33m; rel 1963; cip

Fantasy, Viola and Piano (1941)
[5567] Rood, Louise (vla); Jacobi, Irene (pf)
- CRI-146; 33m/s; rel 1961/1970; cip

Hagiographia (Three Biblical Narratives) (1938)
[5568] Jacobi, Irene (pf); Claremont String Quartet
- CRI-174; 33m; rel 1963; cip

[5569] Jacobi, Irene (pf); Coolidge String Quartet
- Victor 17999-18001S (in set M-782); 78; 3 discs; rel pre-1942

Music Hall (1948)
[5570] Vienna Philharmonic Orchestra; Adler, F. Charles (cond)
- SPA-47; 33m; rel 1953; del 1970

Nocturne in Nineveh and Dance
[5571] Stoefs, Francis (fl); Belgian National Radio Orchestra; Andre, Franz (cond)
- SPA-7; 33m; rel 1952; del 1970

Quartet, Strings, No 3 (1945)
[5572] Lyric Art Quartet
   - CRI-146; 33m/s; rel
   1961/1970; cip

Quintet, Winds (1936)
[5573] Yaddo Woodwind Quintet
   - Yaddo 13A; 78; 10''; rel 1937

Scherzo, Wind Quintet (1936)
[5574] Juilliard Wind Ensemble
   - New Music Quarterly Recordings
   1611; 78; rel 1941

JACOBS, Henry*

Chan (1956)
[5575] Electronic music
   - Folkways 6301; 33s; rel 1969;
   cip

Electronic Kabuki Mambo (1955)
[5576] Electronic music
   - Folkways 6301; 33s; rel 1969;
   cip

Logos (1956)
[5577] Electronic music
   - Folkways 6301; 33s; rel 1969;
   cip

Rhythm Study No 8 (1957)
[5578] Electronic music
   - Folkways 6301; 33s; rel 1969;
   cip

JAMES, Philip (1890-1975)

Meditation a Sainte Clothilde (1915)
[5579] Smith, Rollin (org)
   Rec 10/71
   - Repertoire Recording Society
   RRS-6; 33m; rel 1972

Pastorale (1949)
[5580] Baker, Robert (org)
   Rec 7/28/57
   - Mirrosonic DRE-1004; 33m; 2
   discs; rel 1958; del 1965

[5581] Smith, Rollin (org)
   Rec 10/71
   - Repertoire Recording Society
   RRS-6; 33m; rel 1972

Solemn Prelude (1948, rev 1951)
[5582] Smith, Rollin (org)
   Rec 10/71
   - Repertoire Recording Society
   RRS-6; 33m; rel 1972

Suite, Organ (Op 28) (1921): Fete, Ostinato, and Dithyramb
[5583] Smith, Rollin (org)
   Rec 10/71
   - Repertoire Recording Society
   RRS-6; 33m; rel 1972

Symphony No 1 (1943)
[5584] Vienna Philharmonic Orchestra;
   Adler, F. Charles (cond)
   - SPA-38; 33m; rel 1954; del
   1970

Variations on a Theme by Schubert (1969)
[5585] Smith, Rollin (org)
   Rec 10/71
   - Repertoire Recording Society
   RRS-6; 33m; rel 1972

JANSSEN, Werner (1899-)

New Year's Eve in New York (1928)
[5586] Victor Symphony Orchestra;
   Shilkret, Nathaniel (cond)
   - Victor 35986-87; 78; 2 discs; rel
   pre-1936

JENKINS, Joseph W. (1928-)

American Overture
[5587] Cornell University Wind Ensemble;
   Stith, Marice (cond)
   - Cornell CUWE-6; 33s; rel 1971;
   cip

[5588] Ithaca Symphonic Winds; Beeler,
   Walter (cond)
   - Golden Crest
   CR-4015/CRS-4015; 33m/s; rel
   1959/1961; cip

[5589] North Hills High School Symphonic
   Band; Mercer, Warren, Jr. (cond)
   Rec 5/30/79
   - Golden Crest ATH-5065; 33s; rel
   1980; cip

Arioso
[5590] North Hills High School Symphonic
   Band; Mercer, Warren, Jr. (cond)
   Rec 5/30/79
   - Golden Crest ATH-5065; 33s; rel
   1980; cip

Cuernavaca
[5591] North Hills High School Symphonic
   Band; Mercer, Warren, Jr. (cond)
   Rec 5/30/79
   - Golden Crest ATH-5065; 33s; rel
   1980; cip

In Traskwood County
[5592] North Hills High School Symphonic
   Band; Mercer, Warren, Jr. (cond)
   Rec 5/30/79
   - Golden Crest ATH-5065; 33s; rel
   1980; cip

Pieces of Eight
[5593] North Hills High School Symphonic
   Band; Mercer, Warren, Jr. (cond)
   Rec 5/30/79
   - Golden Crest ATH-5065; 33s; rel
   1980; cip

Tartan Suite
[5594] North Hills High School Symphonic
   Band; Mercer, Warren, Jr. (cond)
   Rec 5/30/79
   - Golden Crest ATH-5065; 33s; rel
   1980; cip

Toccata, Winds
[5595] North Hills High School Symphonic
   Band; Mercer, Warren, Jr. (cond)
   Rec 5/30/79
   - Golden Crest ATH-5065; 33s; rel
   1980; cip

JENNI, Donald (1937-)

Cucumber Music (1969)
[5596] University of Iowa Center for New
   Music Ensemble
   - CRI-324; 33s; rel 1975; cip

Musique printaniere
[5597] Mather, Betty Bang (fl); Simms,
   John (pf)
   - CRI-329; 33s; rel 1975; cip

JENNINGS, Arthur B.

Springs in the Desert
[5598] St. Bartholomew's Episcopal
   Church (New York) Choir; Friedell,
   Harold (org) (cond)
   - Grayco LPM-101; 33m; 10''; rel
   1954

JEPSON, Harry Benjamin (1870-1952)

Pantomime
[5599] Ragatz, Oswald (org)
   - Schantz Organ Co FR-1522;
   33m; rel 1964

JERGENSON, Dale

Requiem for a City
[5600] Gregg Smith Singers; Peabody
   Conservatory Choir; tape; Smith,
   Gregg (cond)
   - Grenadilla GS-1013; 33s; rel
   1978; cip

Tanka Pieces
[5601] Rees, Rosalind (sop); Hoover,
   Katherine (fl); Wagner, Richard
   (cl)
   - Grenadilla GS-1013; 33s; rel
   1978; cip

Vision, The
[5602] Gregg Smith Singers; Smith, Gregg
   (cond)
   - Grenadilla GS-1013; 33s; rel
   1978; cip

JEWELL, Fred (1876-1936)

Screamer, The (1921)
[5603] Eastman Symphonic Wind
   Ensemble; Fennell, Frederick
   (cond)
   - Mercury MG-50314/SR-90314;
   33m/s; rel 1963; del 1976

Screamer, The (1921) *(cont'd)*
- Mercury SR-2-9131; 33s; 2
  discs; rel 1968; del 1971
- Mercury SRI-75087; 33s; rel
  1977; cip

JOHANNESEN, Grant (1921-)
**Improvisations over a Mormon
Hymn**
[5604] Johannesen, Grant (pf)
- Golden Crest
  CR-4065/CRS-4065; 33m/s; rel
  1963/1966; cip
- Golden Crest CRS-40866; 33s; 2
  discs; rel 1969; cip

JOHANSEN, Gunnar (1906-)
Sonata, Piano
[5605] Johansen, Gunnar (pf)
- Artist Direct 108; 33m; rel
  1967; del 1970

Sonata, Piano, No 108
[5606] Johansen, Gunnar (pf)
- Artist Direct 25; 33m; rel 1969;
  cip

(Three) Studies, Piano
[5607] Johansen, Gunnar (pf)
- Artist Direct 108; 33m; rel
  1967; del 1970

JOHNS, Louis Edgar (1886-)
Medieval Suite
[5608] Philharmonia Orchestra; Walther,
  Hans-Jurgen (cond)
- Dorian 1008; 33m; rel 1962; del
  1974

JOHNSON, David N. (1922-)
Fairest Lord Jesus
[5609] Johnson, David N. (org)
  Rec 6/8/71
- Wicks Organ Co TS-74-943-44;
  33s; rel 1971

Lord, Keep Us Steadfast
[5610] Johnson, David N. (org)
  Rec 6/8/71
- Wicks Organ Co TS-74-943-44;
  33s; rel 1971

O Sons and Daughters
[5611] Johnson, David N. (org)
  Rec 6/8/71
- Wicks Organ Co TS-74-943-44;
  33s; rel 1971

**Prelude on Of the Father's Love
Begotten**
[5612] Obetz, John (org)
- Celebre 8006; 33s; rel 197?

Procession in E-flat Major
[5613] Johnson, David N. (org)
  Rec 6/8/71
- Wicks Organ Co TS-74-943-44;
  33s; rel 1971

Thee We Adore
[5614] Johnson, David N. (org)
  Rec 6/8/71
- Wicks Organ Co TS-74-943-44;
  33s; rel 1971

Trumpet Tune in C Major
[5615] Hindmarsh, Jack (org)
  Rec 1975
- Wealden WS-142; 33s; rel 1976

Unto the Hills I Lift Mine Eyes
[5616] Augustana Evangelical Lutheran
  Church Choir; Wagner, Albert
  (cond)
- Golden Age GAR-153102; 33s;
  rel 1977?

Voluntary in D-flat Major
[5617] Johnson, David N. (org)
  Rec 6/8/71
- Wicks Organ Co TS-74-943-44;
  33s; rel 1971

Wondrous Love
[5618] Johnson, David N. (org)
  Rec 6/8/71
- Wicks Organ Co TS-74-943-44;
  33s; rel 1971

JOHNSON, Hunter (1906-)
**Concerto, Piano and Chamber
Orchestra (1935-36)**
[5619] Kirkpatrick, John (pf); Rochester
  Chamber Orchestra; Hull, Robert
  (cond)
- Concert Hall CHS-1189; 33m; rel
  1954; del 1957

Letter to the World (Suite) (1952)
[5620] Concert Hall Chamber Orchestra;
  Hull, Robert (cond)
- Concert Hall CHS-1151; 33m; rel
  1952; del 1957
- Nixa CLP-1151; 33m; rel 1952*
- Concert Hall H-1651; 33m; rel
  1957; del 1959

Past the Evening Sun (1964)
[5621] Louisville Orchestra; Mester, Jorge
  (cond)
  Rec 5/10/77
- LS-76-3; 33s (Louisville
  Orchestra First Edition Records
  1976 No 3); rel 1978; cip

Trio, Flute, Oboe, and Piano (1954)
[5622] Baker, Julius (fl); Bloom, Robert
  (ob); Nordli, Douglas (pf)
- CRI-125; 33m; rel 1960; cip

**JOHNSON, J. Rosamond
(1873-1954)**
Lit'l Gal (1917)
[5623] Robeson, Paul (bar); Brown,
  Lawrence (pf)
  Rec 7/27/25 and 1/25/26
- Victor 19824B; 78

Lit'l Gal (1917) *(cont'd)*
- New World NW-247; 33m; rel
  1976

Since You Went Away
[5624] McCormack, John (ten); Kreisler,
  Fritz (vln)
- Victor 87573; 78; 10"; rel
  1920-25
- Victor 3022; 78; 10"; rel
  1920-25

JOHNSON, Roger (1941-)
Quintet, Winds
[5625] Dorian Woodwind Quintet
- CRI-293; 33s; rel 1973; cip

Suite, Six Horns (1959)
[5626] Horn Club of Los Angeles; Kraft,
  William (cond)
- Angel S-36036; 33s; rel 1970;
  cip

JOHNSON, Romilly (1883-1929)
Boat Song
[5627] Farrar, Geraldine (sop)
- Victor 87289; 78; 10"; rel
  1918-23
- Victor 909; 78; 10"; rel
  1918-23

JOHNSON, Roy Hamlin (1929-)
Summer Fanfares
[5628] Barnes, Ronald (car) or Strauss,
  Richard (car)
- Washington Cathedral Archives
  CAR-0002; 33s; rel 1975

Te Deum laudamus
[5629] Barnes, Ronald (car) or Strauss,
  Richard (car)
- Washington Cathedral Archives
  CAR-0002; 33s; rel 1975

JOHNSTON, Ben (1926-)
Carmilla (1970)
[5630] ETC Company of La Mama
- Vanguard
  VSD-79322/VSQ-40017; 33s/q;
  rel 1973; cip

Casta Bertram (1969)
[5631] Turetzky, Bertram (cb); tape
- Nonesuch H-71237; 33s; rel
  1970; cip

Ci-Git-Satie (1967)
[5632] New Music Choral Ensemble;
  Gaburo, Kenneth (cond)
- Ars Nova/Ars Antiqua AN-1005;
  33s; rel 1971; del 1973

Dirge (1952)
[5633] University of Illinois Percussion
  Ensemble; McKenzie, Jack (cond)
- Illini Union Bookstore CRS-6;
  33m; rel 1960*

Duo, Flute and Contrabass (1963)
[5634] Purswell, Patrick (fl); Turetzky,
Bertram (cb)
- Advance FGR-1; 33m; rel 1966;
del 1972

[5635] University of Illinois Contemporary
Chamber Players
- CRI-405; 33s; rel 1979; cip

Quartet, Strings, No 2 (1964)
[5636] Composers Quartet
- Nonesuch H-71224; 33s; rel
1969; cip

Sonata, Microtonal Piano (1965)
[5637] Miller, Robert (pf)
- New World NW-203; 33s; rel
1977

JOHNSTONE, Arthur Edward (1860-1944)
Salute to the Flag
[5638] Thibault, Conrad (bar); Eaver,
Myrtle (pf)
- Victor 11830; 78; rel 1935

JOLLES, Jerome
Wordsworth Songs
[5639] Jubal Trio
- Grenadilla GS-1015; 33s; rel
1978; cip

JONES, Charles (1910-)
On the Morning of Christ's Nativity (1953)
[5640] Concert Chorus
- Contemporary AP-122; 33m; rel
pre-1956

Quartet, Strings, No 6 (1970)
[5641] New York String Quartet
- CRI-283; 33s; rel 1972; cip

Shepherd's Carol, The
[5642] Concert Chorus
- Contemporary AP-122; 33m; rel
pre-1956

Sonatina, Violin and Piano (1942)
[5643] Zukofsky, Paul (vln); Kalish, Gilbert
(pf)
- CRI-283; 33s; rel 1972; cip

JONES, Charles (1931-)
Symphony No 6 (1969)
[5644] Budapest Philharmonic Orchestra;
Steinberg, Benjamin (cond)
- Silhouettes in Courage
SIL-K-5001-02 (matrix no); 33s;
rel 1970; del 1974

JONES, Collier (1928-)
(Four) Movements for Five Brass (1957)
[5645] New York Brass Choir
- Golden Crest CRS-4148; 33s; rel
1979; cip

(Four) Movements for Five Brass (1957) *(cont'd)*
[5646] New York Brass Quintet
- Desto D-401/DST-6401; 33m/s;
rel 1964; cip

JONES, J. Randolph (1910-)
Prelude to Night
[5647] Hamburg Philharmonic Orchestra;
Jones, J. Randolph (cond)
- Mansions 1300; 33m; rel 1959*

Symphony No 1 (Southern Scenes)
[5648] Hamburg Philharmonic Orchestra;
Jones, J. Randolph (cond)
- Mansions 1300; 33m; rel 1959*

JONES, Jeffrey (1944-)
Ambiance (Quatre poemes de Samuel Beckett) (1968-69)
[5649] Bryn-Julson, Phyllis (sop);
Contemporary Chamber
Ensemble; Weisberg, Arthur
(cond)
- Nonesuch H-71302; 33s; rel
1974; cip

Piece mouvante (1974)
[5650] Hiraga, Noriko (pf)
- CRI-336; 33s; rel 1977; cip

JONES, Samuel (1935-)
Elegy
[5651] Houston Symphony Orchestra;
Jones, Samuel (cond)
Rec 11/25/75
- CRI-347; 33s; rel 1976; cip

Let Us Now Praise Famous Men
[5652] Houston Symphony Orchestra;
Jones, Samuel (cond)
Rec 11/25/75
- CRI-347; 33s; rel 1976; cip

JOPLIN, Scott (1868-1917)
Treemonisha (1911, rev 1911-15)
[5653] Balthrop, Carmen (sop); Allen,
Betty (m sop); Rayam, Curtis
(ten); White, Willard (b); Houston
Grand Opera Chorus and
Orchestra; Schuller, Gunther
(cond)
- Deutsche Grammophon
2530.620-21 (in set 2707.083);
33s; 2 discs; rel 1976; cip

[5654] Christopher, Barbara (sop); Dale,
Clamma (m sop); Gordon,
Michael (bar); chorus; Moorman,
Dennis (pf); Motley, John (cond)
- New York Public Library; 33; rel
1972*

Treemonisha: Excerpts
[5655] Lewis, Carolyn (voice); Utah State
University Concert Chorale;
Puffer, Ted (pf) (cond)
- Portents 3; 33; rel 1965 or
1966

Treemonisha: Excerpts (arr for pf)
[5656] Zimmerman, Richard (pf)
- Murray Hill 931079; 33q; rel
1975*

Treemonisha: Marching Onward (A Real Slow Drag) (arr for org)
[5657] Biggs, E. Power (org)
- Columbia M-34129/MQ-34129;
33s/q; rel 1976; cip

JOSTEN, Werner (1885-1963)
Adoration
[5658] Hanks, John Kennedy (ten);
Friedberg, Ruth (pf)
- Duke University Press
DWR-6417-18; 33m; 2 discs; rel
1966; del 1975

Canzona seria (A Hamlet Monologue) (1957)
[5659] American Symphony Orchestra
(members of); Stokowski, Leopold
(cond)
- CRI-267; 33s; rel 1972; cip

Concerto sacro I-II (1925)
[5660] American Symphony Orchestra;
Stokowski, Leopold (cond)
- CRI-200; 33m/s; rel 1965; cip

Endymion (Suite) (1933)
[5661] Vienna Philharmonia Orchestra;
Haefner, Herbert (cond)
- SPA-16; 33m; rel 1952; del
1970

Fruehlingsnetz
[5662] Endich, Sara Mae (sop); Josten,
Werner (pf)
- SPA-34; 33m; rel 1953; del
1970

Gefunden
[5663] Endich, Sara Mae (sop) or
McGrath, William (ten); Josten,
Werner (pf)
- SPA-34; 33m; rel 1953; del
1970

Guarda che bianca luna
[5664] McGrath, William (ten); Josten,
Werner (pf)
- SPA-34; 33m; rel 1953; del
1970

Heiligen drei Koenige, Die
[5665] Endich, Sara Mae (sop); Josten,
Werner (pf)
- SPA-34; 33m; rel 1953; del
1970

Hingabe
[5666] Endich, Sara Mae (sop); Josten,
Werner (pf)
- SPA-34; 33m; rel 1953; del
1970

Im Herbst
[5667] Endich, Sara Mae (sop); Josten, Werner (pf)
- SPA-34; 33m; rel 1953; del 1970

Indian Serenade, The (1922)
[5668] McGrath, William (ten); Josten, Werner (pf)
- SPA-34; 33m; rel 1953; del 1970

Jungle (1928)
[5669] American Symphony Orchestra; Stokowski, Leopold (cond)
- CRI-267; 33s; rel 1972; cip

Lament of Ian the Proud, The
[5670] Hanks, John Kennedy (ten); Friedberg, Ruth (pf)
- Duke University Press DWR-6417-18; 33m; 2 discs; rel 1966; del 1975

Lied
[5671] McGrath, William (ten); Josten, Werner (pf)
- SPA-34; 33m; rel 1953; del 1970

Old Song Re-Sung, An
[5672] Hanks, John Kennedy (ten); Friedberg, Ruth (pf)
- Duke University Press DWR-6417-18; 33m; 2 discs; rel 1966; del 1975

Partenza delle rondinelle, La
[5673] McGrath, William (ten); Josten, Werner (pf)
- SPA-34; 33m; rel 1953; del 1970

Roundelay
[5674] McGrath, William (ten); Josten, Werner (pf)
- SPA-34; 33m; rel 1953; del 1970

Sonata, Piano (1937)
[5675] Wolfram, Victor (pf)
- Educo 3026; 33m; rel 1968; del 1972

Sonatina, Violin and Piano (1940)
[5676] Elman, Mischa (vln); Seiger, Joseph (pf)
- London LLP-1467; 33m; rel 1957; del 1959

Sumer is icumen in
[5677] McGrath, William (ten); Josten, Werner (pf)
- SPA-34; 33m; rel 1953; del 1970

Symphony in F (1936)
[5678] Polish National Radio Orchestra; Strickland, William (cond)
- CRI-225; 33s; rel 1969; cip

Symphony in Yellow
[5679] Hanks, John Kennedy (ten); Friedberg, Ruth (pf)
- Duke University Press DWR-6417-18; 33m; 2 discs; rel 1966; del 1975

Verschwiegende Nachtigall, Die
[5680] Endich, Sara Mae (sop); Josten, Werner (pf)
- SPA-34; 33m; rel 1953; del 1970

Waldeinsamkeit
[5681] Endich, Sara Mae (sop); McGrath, William (ten); Josten, Werner (pf)
- SPA-34; 33m; rel 1953; del 1970

Weihnachten
[5682] Endich, Sara Mae (sop); Josten, Werner (pf)
- SPA-34; 33m; rel 1953; del 1970

JULIAN, Joseph (1948-)
Akasha
[5683] Turetzky, Bertram (cb); tape
- Finnadar SR-9015; 33s; rel 1977; cip

Wave Canon (1977)
[5684] Ostryniec, James (ob); tape
- CRI-423; 33s; rel 1980; cip

KAHN, Erich Itor (1905-56)
Ciaccona dei tempi di guerra (Op 10) (1943)
[5685] Kahn, Erich Itor (pf)
Rec 1965
- CRI-188; 33m; rel 1965; cip

(Eight) Inventions (Op 7) (1937-38): Nos 1-3 and 5-6
[5686] Kahn, Erich Itor (pf)
Rec 1965
- CRI-188; 33m; rel 1965; cip

(Five) Short Piano Pieces (Op 12) (1955)
[5687] Kahn, Erich Itor (pf)
Rec 1965
- CRI-188; 33m; rel 1965; cip

KALAJIAN, Berge (1924-)
Suite, Piano
[5688] Chodack, Walter (pf)
- Ades (French) 14.002; 33s; rel 1976

KANITZ, Ernest (1894-1978)
Sinfonietta da camera (1972)
[5689] Pittel, Harvey (sax); instrumental ensemble; Popper, Jan (cond)
- Orion ORS-75190; 33s; rel 1975; cip

Sonata, Violin and Piano, No 2 (1965)
[5690] Baker, Israel (vln); Stevens, Delores (pf)
- Orion ORS-75190; 33s; rel 1975; cip

Visions at Twilight (1962)
[5691] Stevens, Delores (pf) (cel); unison women's chorus; instrumental ensemble; Popper, Jan (cond)
- Orion ORS-75190; 33s; rel 1975; cip

KANTOR, Joseph (1930-)
Playthings of the World
[5692] Los Angeles Orchestra Camerata and Chorus; Mitzelfelt, H. Vincent (cond)
- Crystal S-890; 33s; rel 1977; cip

KAPLAN, Nathan Ivan (1948-)
(Eighteen) Concert Etudes, Clarinet
[5693] Sobol, Lawrence (cl)
- Grenadilla GS-1001; 33s; rel 1975; cip

KAPLAN, Sol (1919-)
Piece in the Form of a Rhapsody
[5694] Slatkin, Felix (vln); Kaplan, Sol (pf)
- Co-Art 5024; 78; rel pre-1943

KARLINS, M. William (1932-)
Music for Tenor Saxophone and Piano
[5695] Hemke, Frederick (sax); Granger, Milton (pf)
- Brewster BR-1204; 33s; rel 1972; del 1978

Solo Piece with Passacaglia
[5696] Rehfeldt, Phillip (cl)
- Advance FGR-15S; 33s; rel 1973; cip

Variations on Obiter dictum (1956)
[5697] Krosnick, Joel (amplf vcl); Buccheri, Elizabeth (pf); Siwe, Thomas (perc)
- CRI-329; 33s; rel 1975; cip

KARPIENIA, Joseph
(Three) Pieces, Bass Flute and Guitar
[5698] Bolotowsky, Andrew (b fl); Karpienia, Joseph (gtr)
- Orion ORS-78304; 33s; rel 1979; cip

KATZ, Erich (1900-73)
Pastorale
[5699] Katz, Erich (rec); Wann, Lois (ob)
- Gallery 5001; 78; rel pre-1950

Quick Dance
[5700] Katz, Erich (rec); Wann, Lois (ob)
- Gallery 5001; 78; rel pre-1950

Sonatina, Recorder and Oboe
[5701] Katz, Erich (rec); Wann, Lois (ob)
- Gallery 5001; 78; rel pre-1950

KAUFMAN, Jeffrey (1947-)
In Time Past Time Remembered (1973)
[5702] Martin, Barbara (sop); Long Island Chamber Ensemble of New York
- Grenadilla GS-1022; 33s; rel 1978; cip

Pastorale, Strings (1977)
[5703] Rome Chamber Orchestra; Flagello, Nicolas (cond)
- Peters Internationale PLE-071; 33s; rel 1978; cip

Reflections
[5704] Sobol, Lawrence (cl); Basquin, Peter (pf)
- Grenadilla GS-1009; 33s; rel 1977; cip

KAY, Hershy (1919-81)
Western Symphony (Suite) (1954)
[5705] New York City Ballet Orchestra; Barzin, Leon (cond)
- Vox PLP-9050; 33m; rel 1955; del 1965

[5706] New York City Ballet Orchestra; Irving, Robert (cond)
- Kapp KCL-9036/KC-S-9036; 33m/s; rel 1959; del 1963

Western Symphony: Saturday Night
[5707] Andre Kostelanetz and his Orchestra; Kostelanetz, Andre (cond)
- Columbia CL-763; 33m; rel 1955; del 1959
- Columbia B-763; 45; 7''; rel pre-1956

KAY, Ulysses (1917-)
Choral Triptych (1962)
[5708] King's Chapel Choir, Boston; Cambridge Festival Strings; Pinkham, Daniel (cond)
Rec 1963
- Cambridge CRM-416/CRS-1416; 33m/s; rel 1964; del 1971

Concerto, Orchestra (1954)
[5709] Berlin Radio Orchestra; Perlea, Jonel (cond)
- Varese Sarabande VC-81047; 33m; rel 1979; cip

[5710] Teatro La Fenice Orchestra; Perlea, Jonel (cond)
- Remington 199-173; 33m; rel 1954; del 1956

(Six) Dances, String Orchestra (1954)
[5711] Westphalian Symphony Orchestra; Freeman, Paul (cond)
- Turnabout TVS-34546; 33s; rel 1974; cip

(Six) Dances, String Orchestra: (No 1) Round Dance and (No 2) Polka
[5712] New Symphony Chamber Orchestra; Camarata, Salvador (cond)
- London LLP-1213; 33m; rel 1955; del 1957
- CRI-119; 33m; rel 1957; cip

Fantasy Variations (1963)
[5713] Oslo Philharmonic Orchestra; Lipkin, Arthur Bennett (cond)
- CRI-209; 33m/s; rel 1966; cip

How Stands the Glass Around? (1954)
[5714] Randolph Singers; Randolph, David (cond)
- CRI-102; 33m/s; rel 1956/?; cip

(Four) Inventions (1964): No 3
[5715] Norman, Ruth (pf)
- Opus One 35; 33s; rel 1978; cip

Markings (1966)
[5716] London Symphony Orchestra; Freeman, Paul (cond)
- Columbia M-32783; 33s; rel 1974; cip

Prelude, Flute (1957)
[5717] Handy, D. Antoinette (fl)
- Eastern ERS-513; 33s; 2 discs; rel 1973*

Quartet, Brass (1950)
[5718] American Brass Quintet
- Folkways FM-3651; 33m; rel 1965; cip

Serenade (1954)
[5719] Louisville Orchestra; Whitney, Robert (cond)
- LOU-545-8; 33m (Louisville Orchestra First Edition Records 1955 No 8); rel 1959; del 1972

Short Overture, A (1947)
[5720] Oakland Youth Orchestra; Hughes, Robert (cond)
- Desto DC-7107; 33s; rel 1970; cip

Sinfonia in E (1951)
[5721] Oslo Philharmonic Orchestra; Barati, George (cond)
- CRI-139; 33m; rel 1961; cip

Suite, Organ, No 1 (1959)
[5722] Harmon, Thomas (org)
- Orion ORS-76255; 33s; rel 1977; cip

Umbrian Scene (1963)
[5723] Louisville Orchestra; Whitney, Robert (cond)
- LOU-65-1; 33m (Louisville Orchestra First Edition Records 1965 No 1); rel 1965; cip

What's in a Name? (1954)
[5724] Randolph Singers; Randolph, David (cond)
- CRI-102; 33m/s; rel 1956/?; cip

KEATS, Donald (1929-)
Quartet, Strings, No 2 (1965)
[5725] Beaux-Arts String Quartet
- CRI-256; 33s; rel 1970; cip

KEENEY, Wendell (1903-)
Sonatina, Piano
[5726] Gowen, Bradford (pf)
- New World NW-304; 33s; rel 1979

[5727] Harris, Johana (pf)
- Yaddo II-2; 78; rel 1940

KEEZER, Ronald (1940-)
For Four Percussionists
[5728] Sonic Boom Percussion Ensemble
- Crystal S-140; 33s; rel 1977; cip

KELLAWAY, Roger (1939-)
Esque (1971)
[5729] Anderson, Miles (tbn); Nadel, Mickey (cb)
- Avant AV-1006; 33s; rel 1978; cip

KELLER, Homer (1915-)
Interplay
[5730] University of Oregon Woodwind Quintet
- Advance FGR-11S; 33s; rel 1973; cip

Serenade, Clarinet and Strings
[5731] Arey, Rufus (cl); Eastman-Rochester Symphony Orchestra; Hanson, Howard (cond)
- Victor 18102 (in set M-802); 78; rel 1941

[5732] Osseck, William (cl); Eastman-Rochester Symphony Orchestra; Hanson, Howard (cond)
- Mercury MG-40003; 33m; rel 1953; del 1957
- Mercury MG-50076; 33m; rel 1957; del 1963
- Eastman-Rochester Archives ERA-1001; 33s; rel 1974; cip

Symphony No 3 (1956)
[5733] Japan Philharmonic Symphony Orchestra; Strickland, William (cond)
- CRI-134; 33m/s; rel 1960/?; cip

KELLY, Robert (1916-)
Patterns
[5734] Paul, Mary Jane (sop); Illinois University Symphony Orchestra; Ansermet, Ernest (cond)
- Illini Union Bookstore CRS-4; 33m; rel 1955*

KELLY, Robert (1916-)

Symphony No 2 (1958)
[5735] Japan Philharmonic Symphony
Orchestra; Watanabe, Akeo
(cond)
- CRI-132; 33m/s; rel 1960/?; cip

Toccata, Marimba and Percussion (1959)
[5736] University of Illinois Percussion
Ensemble; McKenzie, Jack (cond)
- Illini Union Bookstore CRS-6;
33m; rel 1960*

KENNAN, Kent Wheeler (1913-)

Campo dei fiori, II (1937)
[5737] Austin, James (tpt);
Eastman-Rochester Symphony
Orchestra; Hanson, Howard
(cond)
- Mercury MG-50147/SR-90147;
33m/s; rel 1957/1960; del
1963
- Eastman-Rochester Archives
ERA-1004; 33s; rel 1974; cip

Concertino, Piano and Wind Ensemble (1963)
[5738] Covert, Mary Ann (pf); Ithaca
College Concert Band; Beeler,
Walter (cond)
- Golden Crest 9003; 33s; rel
1973; cip

Night Soliloquy (1938)
[5739] Kincaid, William (fl); Philadelphia
Orchestra; Ormandy, Eugene
(cond)
- Columbia MM-940; 78; rel
pre-1952

[5740] Mariano, Joseph (fl);
Eastman-Rochester Symphony
Orchestra; Hanson, Howard
(cond)
- Victor 15659 (in set M-608);
78; rel 1939
- Victor 12-0155-58 (in set
DM-608); 78; 4 discs; rel
pre-1942
- Mercury MG-40003; 33m; rel
1953; del 1957
- Mercury MG-50076; 33m; rel
1957; del 1963
- Mercury MG-50299/SR-90299;
33m/s; rel 1962; del 1964
- Eastman-Rochester Archives
ERA-1001; 33s; rel 1974; cip

[5741] Pellerite, James (fl); Indiana
University Wind Ensemble; Ebbs,
Frederick (cond)
- Coronet S-1724; 33s; rel 1971;
cip

Night Soliloquy (arr for fl and pf)
[5742] Kincaid, William (fl); Sokoloff,
Vladimir (pf)
- Award 33-706; 33m; rel 1958;
del 1970

Nocturne (1937)
[5743] Tursi, Francis (vla);
Eastman-Rochester Symphony
Orchestra; Hanson, Howard
(cond)
- Mercury MG-50147/SR-90147;
33m/s; rel 1957/1960; del
1963
- Eastman-Rochester Archives
ERA-1004; 33s; rel 1974; cip

(Two) Preludes, Piano (1951)
[5744] Helps, Robert (pf)
- RCA LM-7042/LSC-7042;
33m/s; 2 discs; rel 1966; del
1971
- CRI-288; 33s; 2 discs; rel 1972;
cip

Promenade (1938)
[5745] Eastman-Rochester Symphony
Orchestra; Hanson, Howard
(cond)
- Mercury MG-50147/SR-90147;
33m/s; rel 1957/1960; del
1963
- Eastman-Rochester Archives
ERA-1004; 33s; rel 1974; cip

Sonata, Trumpet and Piano (1957)
[5746] Darling, James (tpt); Sidoti,
Genevieve (pf)
- Advent 5006; 33s; rel 1974; del
1976
- Telarc 5032; 33s; rel 1978; cip

[5747] Stith, Marice (tpt); Bilson, Malcolm
(pf)
- Golden Crest RE-7042; 33s; rel
1972; cip

KENNEDY, Joseph J.

Dialogue
[5748] Trio Pro Viva
- Eastern ERS-513; 33s; 2 discs;
rel 1973*

KERN, Jerome (1885-1945)

Mark Twain Suite (Portrait for Orchestra) (1942)
[5749] Andre Kostelanetz and his
Orchestra; Kostelanetz, Andre
(cond)
- Columbia X-227; 78; 2 discs; rel
pre-1943
- Columbia ML-2046; 33m; 10";
rel pre-1949; del 1956
- Columbia CL-864; 33m; rel
1957; del 1962

Show Boat (Scenario for Orchestra) (1941)
[5750] Cleveland Orchestra; Rodzinski,
Artur (cond)
- Columbia M-495; 78; 3 discs; rel
pre-1943

[5751] Janssen Symphony Orchestra of
Los Angeles; Janssen, Werner
(cond)
- Victor M-906; 78; 3 discs; rel
pre-1943

Show Boat (Scenario for Orchestra) (1941) *(cont'd)*
- Camden CAL-205; 33m; rel
1955; del 1957

[5752] Philadelphia Pops Orchestra;
Kostelanetz, Andre (cond)
- Columbia CL-806; 33m; rel
1955; del 1961

[5753] Utah Symphony Orchestra;
Abravanel, Maurice (cond)
- Vanguard Cardinal VCS-10023;
33s; rel 1968; del 1977
- Vanguard SRV-345-SD; 33s; rel
1976; cip

KERNOCHAN, Marshall (1880-1955)

Smuggler's Song
[5754] Warren, Leonard (b); Vienna
Orchestra; Black, Frank (cond)
- RCA LM-147; 33m; 10"; rel
1952; del 1956

KERR, Harrison (1897-1978)

Concerto, Violin and Orchestra (1950-51, rev 1956)
[5755] Stavenhagen, Wolfgang (vln);
Imperial Philharmonic Orchestra
of Tokyo; Strickland, William
(cond)
- CRI-142; 33m/s; rel 1961/?; cip

Etude, Violoncello (1937)
[5756] Aue, Margaret (vcl)
- New Music Quarterly Recordings
1314; 78; rel 1937

Overture, Arioso, and Finale (1944-51)
[5757] Fink, E. (vcl); Billing, C. (pf)
- Remington 199-211; 33m; rel
1956; del 1959

Sinfonietta (1967-68)
[5758] University of Oklahoma Chamber
Orchestra; Mills (cond)
- Century 31380; 33s; rel 1968;
del 1977

Sonata, Violin and Piano (1956)
[5759] Joseph, Charles (vln); Eschenbach,
Christoph (pf)
- Century 31380; 33s; rel 1968;
del 1977

Trio, Clarinet, Violoncello, and Piano (1936)
[5760] Gorodner, Aaron (cl); Aue,
Margaret (vcl); Wagner, Josef (pf)
- New Music Quarterly Recordings
1613A-B; 78; rel 1942?

Trio, Clarinet, Violoncello, and Piano: 2nd and 3rd Movements
[5761] Korn, Richard (cl); Bodenhorn,
Aaron (vcl); Johansen, Gunnar
(pf)
- Yaddo D-16; 78; rel 1938

**Trio, Violin, Violoncello, and Piano
(1938, rev 1949)**
[5762] University of Oklahoma Trio
- University of Oklahoma 1; 33m;
rel 1957; del 1978

KERR, Thomas H., Jr.
Easter Monday Swagger
[5763] Hinderas, Natalie (pf)
- Desto DC-7102-03; 33s; 2 discs;
rel 1970; cip

Scherzino
[5764] Hinderas, Natalie (pf)
- Desto DC-7102-03; 33s; 2 discs;
rel 1970; cip

KESSNER, Daniel (1946-)
Chamber Concerto (1972)
[5765] Cutler, Victoria-Diane (sop);
California State University
(Northridge) New Music
Ensemble; Kessner, Daniel (cond)
- Orion ORS-78302; 33s; rel
1978; cip

KEYES, Nelson (1928-)
Abysses, Bridges, Chasms
[5766] Philharmonic Bridge (members of);
Louisville Orchestra; Mester,
Jorge (cond)
- LS-71-2; 33s (Louisville
Orchestra First Edition Records
1971 No 2); rel 1971; del 1979

Music for Monday Evenings (1959)
[5767] Louisville Orchestra; Whitney,
Robert (cond)
- LOU-63-1; 33m (Louisville
Orchestra First Edition Records
1963 No 1); rel 1963; cip

KIM, Earl (1920-)
(Two) Bagatelles (1948-50)
[5768] Helps, Robert (pf)
- RCA LM-7042/LSC-7042;
33m/s; 2 discs; rel 1966; del
1971
- CRI-288; 33s; 2 discs; rel 1972;
cip

Earthlight (1973)
[5769] Sargon, Merja (sop); Potter,
Martha (vln); Kim, Earl (pf)
- New World NW-237; 33s; rel
1978

KINDER, Ralph (1876-1952)
In Springtime
[5770] Asper, Frank (org)
- Columbia ML-5615/MS-6215;
33m/s; rel 1961; cip

KING, Karl (1891-1971)
Barnum and Bailey's Favorite
[5771] Eastern Brass Quintet
- Klavier KS-539; 33s; rel 1975;
cip

Barnum and Bailey's Favorite
(cont'd)
[5772] Eastman Symphonic Wind
Ensemble; Fennell, Frederick
(cond)
- Mercury MG-50113; 33m; rel
1956; del 1969
- Mercury SRI-75004; 33s; rel
1974; cip

Big Cage, The (1934)
[5773] Eastman Symphonic Wind
Ensemble; Fennell, Frederick
(cond)
- Mercury MG-50314/SR-90314;
33m/s; rel 1963; del 1976
- Mercury SRI-75087; 33s; rel
1977; cip

Circus Days (1954)
[5774] Eastman Symphonic Wind
Ensemble; Fennell, Frederick
(cond)
- Mercury MG-50314/SR-90314;
33m/s; rel 1963; del 1976
- Mercury SRI-75087; 33s; rel
1977; cip

Hosts of Freedom
[5775] University of Michigan Winds and
Percussion; Lillya, Clifford P.
(cond)
Rec 2/18-19/75
- University of Michigan SM-0002;
33s; rel 1978; cip

Invictus (1921)
[5776] Eastman Symphonic Wind
Ensemble; Fennell, Frederick
(cond)
- Mercury MG-50314/SR-90314;
33m/s; rel 1963; del 1976
- Mercury SRI-75087; 33s; rel
1977; cip

Pride of the Illini
[5777] Eastman Symphonic Wind
Ensemble; Fennell, Frederick
(cond)
- Mercury MG-50113; 33m; rel
1956; del 1969

Robinson's Grand Entree (1911)
[5778] Eastman Symphonic Wind
Ensemble; Fennell, Frederick
(cond)
- Mercury MG-50314/SR-90314;
33m/s; rel 1963; del 1976
- Mercury SRI-75087; 33s; rel
1977; cip

KINGMAN, Daniel C. (1924-)
Quintet, Winds
[5779] Philharmonic Wind Quintet
- WIM Records WIMR-9; 33s; rel
1974; cip

KINGSLEY, Gershon (1925-)
God and Abraham
[5780] Cantica Hebraica; Michno, Dennis
(cond)
- BOU-1212; 33s; rel 1977?

KINSELLA, John
Quartet, Strings, No 2
[5781] RTE String Quartet
- NIRC NIR-002; 33; rel 1971?

KIRCHNER, Leon (1919-)
**Concerto, Piano and Orchestra, No
1 (1953)**
[5782] Kirchner, Leon (pf); New York
Philharmonic; Mitropoulos, Dimitri
(cond)
Rec 2/24/56
- Columbia ML-5185; 33m; rel
1957; del 1965
- Columbia CML-5185; 33m; rel
1970; del 1974
- New World NW-286; 33m; rel
1977

**Concerto, Violin, Violoncello, Ten
Winds, and Percussion (1960)**
[5783] Spivakovsky, Tossy (vln); Parisot,
Aldo (vcl); winds; percussion;
Kirchner, Leon (cond)
- Epic LC-3830/BC-1157; 33m/s;
rel 1962; del 1965

Duo, Violin and Piano (1947)
[5784] Kobialka, Daniel (vln); Press,
Myron (pf)
- Medea MCLP-1002; 33m/s; rel
1966; del 1971

Lily (1973)
[5785] Hoagland, Diana (sop); The
Ensemble; Kirchner, Leon (cond)
- Columbia M-32740/MQ-32740;
33s/q; rel 1974; del 1976

Quartet, Strings, No 1 (1949)
[5786] American Art Quartet
- Columbia ML-4843; 33m; rel
1954; del 1968
- Columbia CML-4843; 33m; rel
1968; del 1974
- Columbia AML-4843; 33m; rel
1974; del 1976
- CRI-395; 33s; rel 1979; cip

Quartet, Strings, No 2 (1958)
[5787] Lenox String Quartet
- Columbia M-32740/MQ-32740;
33s/q; rel 1974; del 1976

Quartet, Strings, No 3 (1966)
[5788] Beaux-Arts String Quartet; tape
- Columbia MS-7284; 33s; rel
1969; del 1973

[5789] Concord String Quartet; tape
- Vox SVBX-5306; 33s; 3 discs; rel
1973; cip

Sonata, Piano (1948)
[5790] Fleisher, Leon (pf)
- Epic LC-3862/BC-1262; 33m/s; rel 1963; del 1966

[5791] Race, William (pf)
- Educo 3081; 33m; rel 1971; del 1972

Sonata concertante, Violin and Piano (1952)
[5792] Laredo, Jaime (vln); Laredo, Ruth (pf)
- Desto DC-7151; 33s; rel 1973; cip

[5793] Shapiro, Eudice (vln); Kirchner, Leon (pf)
- Epic LC-3306; 33m; rel 1957; del 1961

Toccata, Strings, Winds, and Percussion (1955)
[5794] Louisville Orchestra; Mester, Jorge (cond)
- LOU-68-3/LS-68-3; 33m/s (Louisville Orchestra First Edition Records 1968 No 3); rel 1968; cip

Trio, Violin, Violoncello, and Piano (1954)
[5795] Rubin, Nathan (vln); Neikrug, George (vcl); Kirchner, Leon (pf)
- Epic LC-3306; 33m; rel 1957; del 1961

KIRK, Theron (1919-)
O Sing Praises
[5796] Capital University Chapel Choir; Snyder, Ellis Emanuel (cond)
- Coronet S-1504; 33s; rel 1969; cip

Unto Thee, O Lord
[5797] Capital University Chapel Choir; Snyder, Ellis Emanuel (cond)
- Coronet S-1405; 33s; rel 1969; cip

KLAUSMEYER, Peter (1942-)
Cambrian Sea
[5798] Electronic music
- Turnabout TVS-34427; 33s; rel 1972; del 1975

KLEIN, Lothar (1932-)
Erlkoenig, Der
[5799] Markus, Karl (ten); Hecker, Wilhelm (pf)
- Musical Heritage Society MHS-1962; 33s

(Six) Exchanges (1972)
[5800] Brodie, Paul (sax)
- Golden Crest RE-7056; 33s; rel 1979; cip

Musique a Go-Go
[5801] Louisville Orchestra; Whitney, Robert (cond)
- LOU-67-2/LS-67-2; 33m/s (Louisville Orchestra First Edition Records 1967 No 2); rel 1967; cip

KLEINSINGER, George (1914-)
Absalom, My Son
[5802] London, George (bar); Blatt, Josef (pf)
- Victor 12-0238; 78

I Hear America Singing
[5803] Thomas, John Charles (bar); ILGWU Radio Chorus; Victor Symphony Orchestra; Shilkret, Nathaniel (cond)
- Victor M-777; 78; 2 discs; rel pre-1942
- Camden CAL-367; 33m; rel 1957; del 1958

Pavane for Seskia
[5804] Chertok, Pearl (hp)
- Orion ORS-76231; 33s; rel 1976; cip

KLENZ, William (1915-)
Hush
[5805] Hanks, John Kennedy (ten); Friedberg, Ruth (pf)
- Duke University Press DWR-6417-18; 33m; 2 discs; rel 1966; del 1975

Walk the Silver Night
[5806] Hanks, John Kennedy (ten); Friedberg, Ruth (pf)
- Duke University Press DWR-6417-18; 33m; 2 discs; rel 1966; del 1975

KLOHR, John N. (1869-1956)
Billboard, The
[5807] Eastman Symphonic Wind Ensemble; Fennell, Frederick (cond)
- Mercury MG-50113; 33m; rel 1956; del 1969
- Mercury SR-2-9131; 33s; 2 discs; rel 1968; del 1971
- Mercury SRI-75004; 33s; rel 1974; cip

[5808] University of Michigan Winds and Percussion; Lillya, Clifford P. (cond)
Rec 2/18-19/75
- University of Michigan SM-0002; 33s; rel 1978; cip

KNEUBUHL, John (1943-)
Variations on A Pretty Bird
[5809] Kneubuhl, John (gtr)
- Orion ORS-78323; 33s; rel 1979; cip

KNIGHT, Jim
Music for an Unwritten Play
[5810] Los Angeles Neophonic Orchestra; Kenton, Stan (cond)
- Capitol MAS-2424/SMAS-2424; 33m/s; rel 1965; del 1970

KNIGHT, Morris (1933-)
After Guernica (1969)
[5811] Knight, Morris (speaker); Sweetkind, David (cl); tape
- Golden Crest CRS-4092; 33s; rel 1971; cip

Assortments No 1
[5812] Legbandt, Rolf (cl); Greenhoe, David (tpt); Silpigni, Constance (vln)
- Now 10; 33s; rel 1974; del 1976

Assortments No 2
[5813] Pence, Judith (ob); Pavolka, David (tbn); Silpigni, Constance (vla)
- Now 10; 33s; rel 1974; del 1976

Binaries
[5814] Pence, Judith (ob); Pence, Homer (bsn)
- Now 10; 33s; rel 1974; del 1976

Cassation, Trumpet, Horn, and Trombone
[5815] Florida State University Brass Trio
- Golden Crest CRS-4081; 33s; rel 1969; cip

Duo, Violin and Violoncello
[5816] Silpigni, Constance (vln); Silpigni, Salvatore (vcl)
- Now 10; 33s; rel 1974; del 1976

Instances (1965)
[5817] Musical Arts Quintet
- Now 9632; 33s; rel 1966; del 1976

Luminescences (1967)
[5818] Knight, Morris (speaker); Sweetkind, David (cl); tape
- Golden Crest CRS-4092; 33s; rel 1971; cip

Miracles (1968)
[5819] Ball State University Choir and Instrumental Ensemble; Corwin, George (cond)
- Golden Crest CRS-4087; 33s; rel 1970; cip

Origin of Prophecy, The (1964)
[5820] Knight, Morris (speaker); Sweetkind, David (cl); tape
- Golden Crest CRS-4092; 33s; rel 1971; cip

Quartet, Brass, No 4
[5821] Georgia State College Brass
Ensemble; Hill, William H. (cond)
- Golden Crest CRS-4084; 33s; rel
1969; cip

Quintet, Brass, No 1 (1972)
[5822] New York Brass Quintet
- Now 9; 33s; rel 1974; del 1976

Quintet, Brass, No 2 (1972)
[5823] New York Brass Quintet
- Now 9; 33s; rel 1974; del 1976

Quintet, Brass, No 3 (1972)
[5824] New York Brass Quintet
- Now 9; 33s; rel 1974; del 1976

**Refractions, Clarinet and Tape
(1962)**
[5825] Sweetkind, David (cl); tape
- Golden Crest CRS-4092; 33s; rel
1971; cip

**Sonata, Alto Saxophone and Piano
(1964)**
[5826] Leeson, Cecil (al sax); Kohler, Jean
(pf)
- Enchante ENS-2003; 33s; rel
1970; del 1978

Suite, Clarinet and Violoncello
[5827] Legbandt, Rolf (cl); Legbandt,
Phyllis (vcl)
- Now 10; 33s; rel 1974; del
1976

Toccata, Brass Quintet and Tape
[5828] New York Brass Quintet; tape
- Now 9; 33s; rel 1974; del 1976

Varieties
[5829] Boyer, Paul (fl); Silpigni, Constance
(vla); Silpigni, Salvatore (vcl)
- Now 10; 33s; rel 1974; del
1976

KNOX, Charles (1929-)
Solo for Trumpet with Brass Trio
[5830] Georgia State College Brass
Ensemble; Hill, William H. (cond)
- Golden Crest CRS-4084; 33s; rel
1969; cip

**Symphony, Brass and Percussion
(1965)**
[5831] Baldwin-Wallace Brass
- Mark 32565; 33s; rel 1969; del
1976

[5832] Georgia State College Brass
Ensemble; Hill, William H. (cond)
- Golden Crest CRS-4085; 33s; rel
1969; cip

KNUDSON, Thurston
Jungle Drums
[5833] Knudson, Thurston; Goupil,
Auguste; Jungle Rhythmists
- Decca DL-8216; 33m; rel 1956?

KOCH, Frederick (1923-)
Quartet, Strings, No 2 (1966)
[5834] McMurray, Peggy Anne (m sop);
Cleveland Orchestra String
Quartet
- Crystal S-531; 33s; rel 1977; cip

Sonics for Piano (1976)
[5835] Dahlman, Barbro (pf)
- Opus One 38; 33s

Trio of Praise (1966)
[5836] McMurray, Peggy Anne (m sop);
Beck, Thomas (vla); Koch,
Frederick (pf)
- Advent USR-5004; 33s; rel
1973; cip

KOCH, John (1928-)
Immorality, An
[5837] Reardon, John (bar); Hebert, Bliss
(pf)
- Serenus SRE-1019/SRS-12019;
33m/s; rel 1967; cip

Silver
[5838] Reardon, John (bar); Hebert, Bliss
(pf)
- Serenus SRE-1019/SRS-12019;
33m/s; rel 1967; cip

Tame Cat
[5839] Reardon, John (bar); Hebert, Bliss
(pf)
- Serenus SRE-1019/SRS-12019;
33m/s; rel 1967; cip

Tea Shop, The
[5840] Reardon, John (bar); Hebert, Bliss
(pf)
- Serenus SRE-1019/SRS-12019;
33m/s; rel 1967; cip

KOHN, Karl (1926-)
Little Suite, Wind Quintet (1963)
[5841] Los Angeles Wind Quintet
- Orion ORS-7263; 33s; rel 1972;
cip

Madrigal (1966)
[5842] Gregg Smith Singers; Fink, Myron
(pf); Smith, Gregg (cond)
- CRI-241; 33s; rel 1970; cip

KOHS, Ellis (1916-)
**Chamber Concerto, Viola and Nine
Strings (1949)**
[5843] Molnar, Ferenc (vla); San Francisco
Symphony Orchestra (members
of)
- Music Library MLR-17-21; 78; 2
discs; rel pre-1952

**Chamber Concerto, Viola and Nine
Strings (1949)** *(cont'd)*
- Music Library MLR-7004; 33m;
rel 1952; del 1974

[5844] Molnar, Ferenc (vla); string
ensemble
- Columbia ML-4492; 33m; rel
1952; del 1958

Psalm 23 (1957)
[5845] Mid-America Chorale; Dexter, John
(cond)
- CRI-191; 33m/s; rel 1964/?; cip

**Quartet, Strings, No 2 (A Short
Concert) (1948)**
[5846] Shapiro, Eudice (vln); Ross, Nathan
(vln); Schonbach, Sanford (vla);
Rejto, Gabor (vcl)
- CRI-176; 33m/s; rel
1964/1973; cip

Symphony No 1 (1950)
[5847] Vienna Orchestra; Adler, F. Charles
(cond)
- CRI-104; 33m/s; rel 1956/?; cip

KOLB, Barbara (1939-)
Chansons bas (1966)
[5848] Lamoree, Valarie (sop); chamber
group; Kolb, Barbara (cond)
- Desto DC-7143; 33s; rel 1973;
cip

Figments (1967)
[5849] Herlinger, Jan (fl); Seltzer, Cheryl
(pf)
- Desto DC-7143; 33s; rel 1973;
cip

Looking for Claudio (1975)
[5850] Ivanoff, Alexandria (sop); Mason,
Patrick (bar); Starobin, David
(gtr) (mand); Gottlieb, Gordon
(perc)
Rec 1975-76
- CRI-361; 33s; rel 1977; cip

Rebuttal (1964)
[5851] Hirner, George (cl); McGee, Gary
(cl)
- Opus One 14; 33s; rel 1976; cip

Sentences, The (1976)
[5852] Rees, Rosalind[2] (sop); Starobin,
David (gtr)
Rec 1976
- Turnabout TVS-34727; 33s; rel
1978

Solitaire (1971)
[5853] Seltzer, Cheryl (pf); Fitz, Richard
(vib); tape
- Turnabout TVS-34487; 33s; rel
1972; del 1978

Spring River Flowers Moon Night (1975-76)

[5854] Phillips, Robert (pf); Renzulli, Franco (pf); Brooklyn College Percussion Ensemble; Kolb, Barbara (cond)
Rec 1975-76
- CRI-361; 33s; rel 1977; cip

Three Place Settings (1968)

[5855] Eastman, Julius (nar); chamber soloists; Kolb, Barbara (cond)
- Desto DC-7143; 33s; rel 1973; cip

Trobar clus (1970)

[5856] University of Chicago Contemporary Chamber Players; Kolb, Barbara (cond)
- Turnabout TVS-34487; 33s; rel 1972; del 1978

KORN, Peter Jona (1922-)

Concertino, Horn and Strings (Op 15) (1952)

[5857] Eger, Joseph (hn); Vienna Radio Orchestra; Loibner, Wilhelm (cond)
- Westminster XWN-19131/WST-17131; 33m/s; rel 1968; del 1969
- Music Guild MS-858; 33s; rel 1969; del 1971

In medias res (Op 21) (1953)

[5858] Vienna Radio Orchestra; Eger, Joseph (cond)
- Westminster XWN-19131/WST-17131; 33m/s; rel 1968; del 1969
- Music Guild MS-858; 33s; rel 1969; del 1971

Variations on a Tune from The Beggar's Opera (Op 26) (1954)

[5859] Louisville Orchestra; Whitney, Robert (cond)
- LOU-58-2; 33m (Louisville Orchestra First Edition Records 1958 No 2); rel 1959; del 1978 (Variations III and IV omitted at the composer's consent)

KORTE, Karl (1928-)

Aspects of Love (1965): Four Songs

[5860] University of Texas Chamber Singers; Beachy, Morris (cond)
- Golden Crest CRS-4141; 33q; rel 1975; cip

Concerto, Piano and Winds

[5861] Perry, John (pf); University of Texas Wind Ensemble; Lee, Thomas (cond)
Rec 6/1/77
- Turnabout TVS-34704; 33s; rel 1978; cip

Gestures (1970)

[5862] Frock, George (perc); University of Texas Wind Ensemble; Lee, Thomas (cond)
- Golden Crest CRS-4141; 33q; rel 1975; cip

I Think You Would Have Understood (1971)

[5863] Winters, Mel (tpt); University of Texas Jazz Ensemble; tape; Daum, Glen (cond)
- Golden Crest CRS-4141; 33q; rel 1975; cip

Libera me (1974)

[5864] Seigl; University of Texas Symphony and Chorus; Korte, Karl (cond)
- Golden Crest CRS-4141; 33q; rel 1975; cip

Matrix (1968)

[5865] New York Woodwind Quintet; Korte, Elizabeth (pf); DesRoches, Raymond (perc)
- CRI-249; 33s; rel 1970; cip

Pale Is This Good Prince

[5866] Temple University Concert Choir; vocal soloists; instrumentalists; Page, Robert (cond)
- Golden Crest CRS-4120; 33s/q; rel 1974; cip

Remembrances (1971)

[5867] Baron, Samuel (fl); tape
- Nonesuch H-71289; 33s; rel 1974; cip

KOSINS, Martin Scot (1947-)

Love Letters

[5868] Shostac, David (fl); Swearingen, Anita (pf)
- Crystal S-314; 33s; rel 1979; cip

Shadows of the Heart

[5869] Gordon, Marjorie (sop); Detroit Symphony Orchestra (members of); Resnick, Felix (cond)
Rec 7/22/77
- Orion ORS-78287; 33s; rel 1978; cip

KOSTECK, Gregory (1937-)

Concert Music

[5870] Reynolds, Jeffrey (b tbn)
- Crystal S-383; 33s; rel 1979; cip

KOSTELANETZ, Andre (1901-80)

Lake Louise

[5871] Marson, John (hp)
Rec 9/5/72
- Discourses ABK-15; 33s; rel 1973

Roumanian Fantasy

[5872] Andre Kostelanetz and his Orchestra; Kostelanetz, Andre (cond)
- Columbia 7427M; 78; rel pre-1948
- Columbia AAL-4; 33m; 10"; rel 1951; del 1957

KOTIK, Petr (1942-)

There Is Singularly Nothing No 1 (1971)

[5873] Kotik, Petr (fl)
- Cramps 5206-114; 33s; rel 1977

There Is Singularly Nothing No 11

[5874] Kotik, Petr (fl)
- Cramps 5206-114; 33s; rel 1977

KOUNTZ, Richard (1896-1950)

Come to the Manger

[5875] Augustana Choir; Veld, Henry (cond)
- Word 4005; 33m; rel 1955; del 1968

KOUSSEVITZKY, Serge (1874-1951)

Chanson triste (Op 2)

[5876] Koussevitzky, Serge (cb); Luboschutz, Pierre (pf)
Rec 9/29
- Victor 7159; 78; rel pre-1956
- RCA LCT-1145; 33m; rel 1954; del 1956

[5877] Posta, Frantisek (cb); Panenka, Jan (pf)
Rec 8/25-29/75
- Supraphon 111.1949; 33s; rel 1976

[5878] Wolfe, Lawrence (cb); Feldman, Jonathan (pf)
- Titanic Ti-23; 33s; rel 1979; cip

Concerto, Contrabass and Orchestra (Op 3) (1902)

[5879] Karr, Gary (cb); Oslo Philharmonic Orchestra; Antonini, Alfredo (cond)
- CRI-248(78); 33s; rel 1970; cip

Concerto, Contrabass and Orchestra (arr for cb and pf)

[5880] Goliav, Yoan (cb); piano
- Summit SUM-5066; 33s; rel 1978

[5881] Koussevitzky, Serge (cb); Luboschutz, Pierre (pf)
Rec 9/29
- RCA LCT-1145; 33m; rel 1954; del 1956

Humoresque (Op 4)

[5882] Wolfe, Lawrence (cb); Feldman, Jonathan (pf)
- Titanic Ti-23; 33s; rel 1979; cip

Valse miniature (Op 1, No 2)

[5883] Goliav, Yoan (cb); piano
- Summit SUM-5066; 33s; rel 1978

[5884] Karr, Gary (cb); Siegel, Jeffrey (pf)
- Golden Crest RE-7012; 33m/s; rel 1962/1979; cip

[5885] Koussevitzky, Serge (cb); Luboschutz, Pierre (pf) Rec 9/29
- Victor 1476; 78; 10''; rel pre-1956
- RCA LCT-1145; 33m; rel 1954; del 1956

[5886] Wolfe, Lawrence (cb); Feldman, Jonathan (pf)
- Titanic Ti-23; 33s; rel 1979; cip

KOUTZEN, Boris (1901-66)

Concertino, Piano and Strings (1959)

[5887] Guralnik, Robert (pf); Lamoureux Concerts Orchestra; Barzin, Leon (cond)
- Serenus SRE-1010/SRS-12010; 33m/s; rel 1965; cip

Eidolons (1953)

[5888] Maxin, Jacob (pf)
- Serenus SRE-1010/SRS-12010; 33m/s; rel 1965; cip

Quartet, Strings, No 2 (1936)

[5889] Koutzen, Boris (vln); Robbins, Bernard (vln); Cooley, Carlton (vla); Shapiro, Harvey (vcl)
- Society for Publication of American Music R-1; 33m; rel 1953

Sonata, Violin

[5890] Rosand, Aaron (vln)
- Serenus SRE-1010/SRS-12010; 33m/s; rel 1965; cip

Sonatina, Piano (1931)

[5891] Guralnik, Robert (pf)
- Serenus SRE-1010/SRS-12010; 33m/s; rel 1965; cip

Sonatina, Two Pianos (1944)

[5892] Guralnik, Robert (pf); Maxin, Jacob (pf)
- Serenus SRE-1010/SRS-12010; 33m/s; rel 1965; cip

KRAEHENBUEHL, David (1932-)

Canzona (1953)

[5893] Yale Woodwind Quintet
- Contemporary AP-121; 33m; rel 1953; del 1958

Ideo gloria in excelsis deo

[5894] Abbey Singers
- Decca DL-10073/DL-710073; 33m/s; rel 1963; del 1973

Ideo gloria in excelsis deo (cont'd)

[5895] Concert Chorus
- Contemporary AP-122; 33m; rel pre-1956

Song against Bores, A

[5896] Concert Chorus
- Contemporary AP-122; 33m; rel pre-1956

Star Song, The

[5897] Concert Chorus
- Contemporary AP-122; 33m; rel pre-1956

There Is No Rose

[5898] Concert Chorus
- Contemporary AP-122; 33m; rel pre-1956

KRAFT, Leo (1922-)

Allegro giocoso (1957)

[5899] Helps, Robert (pf)
- RCA LM-7042/LSC-7042; 33m/s; 2 discs; rel 1966; del 1971
- CRI-288; 33s; 2 discs; rel 1972; cip

Concerto No 3, Violoncello, Wind Quintet, and Percussion (1969)

[5900] Kougell, Alexander (vcl); New Wind Quintet of New York; DesRoches, Raymond (perc)
- Serenus SRS-12037; 33s; rel 1974; cip

Dialogues (1968)

[5901] Levy, Gerardo (fl); tape
- CRI-292; 33s; rel 1973; cip

Fantasy, Flute and Piano (1963)

[5902] Baron, Samuel (fl); Baron, Carol (pf)
- Serenus SRS-12082; 33s; rel 1980; cip

Let Me Laugh (1954)

[5903] Pfeiffer College Concert Choir; Brewer, Richard (cond)
- Pfeiffer 3; 33s; rel 1970; cip

Line Drawings (1972)

[5904] Dunkel, Paul (fl); Fitz, Richard (perc)
- Opus One 14; 33s; rel 1976; cip

Partita No 3, Wind Quintet (1964)

[5905] New Wind Quintet of New York
- Serenus SRS-12037; 33s; rel 1974; cip

Sestina (1974)

[5906] Peltzer, Dwight (pf)
- Serenus SRS-12085; 33s; rel 1980; cip

Spring in the Harbor (1970)

[5907] Rowe, Catherine (sop); Levy, Gerardo (fl); Kougell, Alexander (vcl); Thomas, Andrew (pf)
- CRI-292; 33s; rel 1973; cip

Statements and Commentaries (1965)

[5908] Peltzer, Dwight (pf)
- Serenus SRS-12037; 33s; rel 1974; cip

Trios and Interludes (1965)

[5909] Baron, Samuel (fl); Sackson, David (vla); Peltzer, Dwight (pf)
- Serenus SRS-12037; 33s; rel 1974; cip

KRAFT, William (1923-)

Concerto, Four Percussion Soloists and Orchestra (1966)

[5910] Kraft, William (perc); other soloists; Los Angeles Philharmonic Orchestra; Mehta, Zubin (cond)
- London CS-6613; 33s; rel 1969; cip

Concerto grosso (1961)

[5911] Louisville Orchestra; Whitney, Robert (cond)
- LOU-65-3/LS-65-3; 33m/s (Louisville Orchestra First Edition Records 1965 No 3); rel 1965; cip

Contextures (Riots—Decade 60) (1968)

[5912] Los Angeles Philharmonic Orchestra; Mehta, Zubin (cond)
- London CS-6613; 33s; rel 1969; cip

Encounters II (1966)

[5913] Bobo, Roger (tu)
- Crystal S-125; 33s; rel 1969; cip
- Crystal S-392; 33s; rel 1978; cip

Encounters III (Duel for Trumpet and Percussion) (1972)

[5914] Stevens, Thomas (tpt); Peters, Mitchell (perc)
- Avant AV-1003; 33s; rel 1972; cip

Encounters IV (Duel for Trombone and Percussion) (1972)

[5915] Ervin, Thomas (tbn); Ervin, Karen (perc)
- Crystal S-641; 33s; rel 1973; cip

Fanfares 1969 see **REYNOLDS, Jeffrey, et al**

Games (Collage No 1) (1969)

[5916] Horn Club of Los Angeles; Kraft, William (cond)
- Angel S-36036; 33s; rel 1970; cip

Imagistes, Des (1974)
[5917] Geer, Ellen (nar); Kermoyan,
Michael (nar); Los Angeles
Percussion Ensemble; Kraft,
William (cond)
- Delos DEL-25432; 33q; rel
1977; cip

In memoriam Igor Stravinsky
[5918] Goldman (vln); Brown (pf)
- Orion ORS-76212; 33s; rel
1977; cip

Momentum (1966)
[5919] Pacific Percussion Ensemble; Kraft,
William (cond)
- Crystal S-104; 33s; rel 1970; cip

[5920] University of Michigan Percussion
Ensemble; Owen, Charles (cond)
- Golden Crest CRSQ-4145; 33q;
rel 1977; cip

Morris Dance (1963)
[5921] Ervin, Karen (perc)
- WIM Records WIMR-5; 33s; rel
1972; cip

**Nonet, Brass and Percussion
(1958)**
[5922] Los Angeles Brass Quintet; Los
Angeles Percussion Ensemble;
Kraft, William (cond)
- Crystal S-821; 33s; rel 1971; cip

**Requiescat (Let the Bells Mourn for
Us for We Are Remiss) (1974)**
[5923] Grierson, Ralph (elec pf)
Rec 5/31/78
- Town Hall S-24; 33s; rel 1979;
cip

Suite for Weatherkings (1958)
[5924] University of Illinois Percussion
Ensemble; McKenzie, Jack (cond)
- Illini Union Bookstore CRS-6;
33m; rel 1960*

Theme and Variations (1956)
[5925] Pacific Percussion Ensemble; Kraft,
William (cond)
- Crystal S-104; 33s; rel 1970; cip

Triangles (1969)
[5926] Silverman, Barry (perc); Los
Angeles Philharmonic Orchestra;
Kraft, William (cond)
- Crystal S-104; 33s; rel 1970; cip

KRAMER, A. Walter (1890-1969)
Chant negre (Op 32, No 1)
[5927] Zimbalist, Efrem (vln); Chotzinoff,
Samuel (pf)
- Victor 64736; 78; 10''; rel
1912-14
- Victor 884; 78; 10''; rel
1912-24

Eklog, C Major (Op 41, No 1)
[5928] Elmore, Robert (org)
- Mercury MG-50109/SR-90109;
33m/s; rel 1957/1959; del
1963

Entr'acte
[5929] Zimbalist, Efrem (vln)
- Victor 1054; 78; 10''; rel
1912-24

Last Hour, The
[5930] McCormack, John (ten); Kreisler,
Fritz (vln)
- Victor 87576; 78; 10''; rel
1920-25
- Victor 3023; 78; 10''; rel
1920-25

Now Like a Lantern (Op 44, No 5)
[5931] Flagstad, Kirsten (sop); McArthur,
Edwin (pf)
Rec 3/18/52 and 4/19/52
- RCA LM-2825; 33m; rel 1965;
del 1967

Swans (Op 44, No 4)
[5932] Bampton, Rose (al); Pelletier,
Wilfred (pf)
- Victor 1607; 78; 10''

[5933] McCormack, John (ten); Schneider,
Edwin (pf)
Rec 9/26/23
- Victor 1081; 78; 10''; rel
1923-25
- New World NW-247; 33m; rel
1976

KRAMER, Jonathan D. (1942-)
**Canons of Blackearth, The
(1972-73)**
[5934] Blackearth Percussion Group
- Opus One 31; 33s; rel 1978; cip

**Renascence for Clarinet, Tape
Delay System, and Prerecorded
Tape (1974)**
[5935] Rehfeldt, Phillip (cl); Kramer,
Jonathan (mixer); Kimball, Gene
(electronics)
- Grenadilla GS-1017; 33s; rel
1980; cip

KRAUS, Phil (1918-)
Kriss-Kraus
[5936] percussion ensemble; Kraus, Phil
(cond)
- Golden Crest
CR-4004/CRS-4004; 33m/s; rel
1957/1979; cip

KREIGER, Arthur (1945-)
Short Piece (1974)
[5937] Electronic music
- Odyssey Y-34139; 33s; rel
1976; cip

KREMER, Rudolf
(Three) Fantasias
[5938] Kremer, Rudolf (org)
Rec 8/64
- Schlicker Organ Co/Cook No
1118; 33m; rel 1964

KROLL, William (1901-80)
Banjo and Fiddle
[5939] D'Andurain, Pedro (vln); Oxley,
Carlos (pf)
- Capitol P-18010; 33m; rel
1956; del 1959

[5940] Gordon, Kenneth (vln); Greenslade,
Hubert (pf)
- Parlophone R-3308; 78; rel
pre-1952

[5941] Haendel, Ida (vln); Holecek, Alfred
(pf)
- Supraphon SUAST-50465; 33s;
rel 196?

[5942] Haendel, Ida (vln); Moore, Gerald
(pf)
- Gramophone C-4021; 78; rel
pre-1952
- RCA LBC-1013; 33m; rel 1952;
del 1956

[5943] Heifetz, Jascha (vln); Bay, Emanuel
(pf)
- Victor 12-0430; 78; rel
pre-1952
- Victor 18-1068; 78; rel
pre-1952
- Gramophone DB-6878; 78; rel
pre-1952
- Victor ERA-126; 45; 7''; rel
1953?
- RCA LSC-3233(e); 33s; rel
1971; cip

[5944] Heifetz, Jascha (vln); Smith, Brooks
(pf)
- RCA LM-2382; 33m; rel 1960;
cip

[5945] Rabin, Michael (vln); Balsam, Artur
(pf)
- Columbia AAL-30; 33m; 10''; rel
1953; del 1957

[5946] Ricci, Ruggiero (vln); Lush, Ernest
(pf)
- London CS-6039; 33s; rel 1958;
del 1962
- London STS-15049; 33s

[5947] Staples, Gordon (vln); Silfies,
George (pf)
- McIntosh Music MM-101; 33m;
rel 1955; del 1958

**(Four) Characteristic Pieces, String
Quartet (1932): Little March**
[5948] Gordon String Quartet
- Schirmer 2524 (in set 6); 78; rel
pre-1942

KRUEGER, Karl (1894-1979)
Suite, Flute and Piano
[5949] Hoberman, Arthur (fl); Stannard,
       Neil (pf)
       - Orion ORS-76257; 33s; rel
       1978; cip

KRUMM, Phillip*
Sound Machine (1966)
[5950] Electronic music
       - Irida 0026; 33s; rel 197?

KUBIK, Gail (1914-)
Celebrations and Epilogue
(1938-50)
[5951] Maxin, Jacob (pf)
       Rec 1/28-30/59
       - Contemporary M-6006/S-8006;
       33m/s; rel 1960; del 1978

Divertimento No 1 (1959)
[5952] Kubik Chamber Ensemble; Kubik,
       Gail (cond)
       - Contemporary M-6013/S-8013;
       33m/s; rel 1964; cip

Divertimento No 2 (1959)
[5953] Kubik Chamber Ensemble; Kubik,
       Gail (cond)
       - Contemporary M-6013/S-8013;
       33m/s; rel 1964; cip

Fanfare for the Century
[5954] Malmo Brass Ensemble
       Rec 6/74
       - BIS LP-59; 33s; rel 1976

Scholastica (1972)
[5955] Claremont, Harvey Mudd, Pitzer,
       and Scripps Colleges' Concert
       Choir; Lilley, John (cond) Choir
       - Desto DC-7172; 33s; rel 1974;
       cip

Sonata, Piano (1947)
[5956] Maxin, Jacob (pf)
       Rec 1/28-30/59
       - Contemporary M-6006/S-8006;
       33m/s; rel 1960; del 1978

Sonatina, Clarinet and Piano
(1959)
[5957] Smith, William O. (cl); Dahl, Ingolf
       (pf)
       - Contemporary M-6013/S-8013;
       33m/s; rel 1964; cip

Sonatina, Piano (1941)
[5958] Dahl, Ingolf (pf)
       - Contemporary M-6013/S-8013;
       33m/s; rel 1964; cip

Symphony No 2 (1955)
[5959] Louisville Orchestra; Whitney,
       Robert (cond)
       - LOU-58-5; 33m (Louisville
       Orchestra First Edition Records
       1958 No 5); rel 1959; cip

Symphony concertante (1952, rev
1953)
[5960] Orchestre de la Radiodiffusion
       Francaise; Kubik, Gail (cond)
       - RCA LM-2426; 33m; rel 1960;
       del 1962
       - CRI-267; 33s; rel 1972; cip

(Five) Theatrical Sketches (1971)
[5961] Pacific Art Trio
       - Desto DC-7172; 33s; rel 1974;
       cip

Trivialities (1934)
[5962] Van Vactor, David (fl); Dunlap,
       Ralph (hn); Holmes, Malcolm
       (vln); Rossi, Urico (vln); Rood,
       Louise (vla); Bodenhorn, Aaron
       (vcl)
       - Yaddo III-5; 78; rel 1940

KUPFERMAN, Meyer (1926-)
Abracadabra (1976)
[5963] Cantilena Chamber Players
       - Grenadilla GS-1029-30; 33s; 2
       discs

Chamber Concerto (1955)
[5964] Baron, Samuel (fl); Kalish, Gilbert
       (pf); string quartet
       - Serenus SRS-12034; 33s; rel
       1974; cip

Chamber Symphony (1950)
[5965] Prisma Chamber Players of
       Copenhagen; Farberman, Harold
       (cond)
       - Serenus SRE-1017/SRS-12017;
       33m/s; rel 1966; cip

Concerto, Violoncello and Jazz
Band
[5966] Wells, David (vcl); Hartt Jazz
       Ensemble; Mattran, David (cond)
       - Serenus SRS-12025; 33s; rel
       1971; cip

Concerto, Violoncello, Tape, and
Orchestra (1974)
[5967] Varga, Laszlo (vcl); Westchester
       Symphony Orchestra; tape;
       Landau, Siegfried (cond)
       Rec 12/15/75
       - Turnabout QTVS-34653; 33q; rel
       1977; cip

Curtain Raiser (1960)
[5968] Conjunto Cameristico de Barcelona
       - Serenus SRS-12034; 33s; rel
       1974; cip

Divertimento, Orchestra (1948)
[5969] Stuttgart Philharmonia; Farberman,
       Harold (cond)
       - Serenus SRE-1017/SRS-12017;
       33m/s; rel 1966; cip

Evocation (1951)
[5970] Moore, David (vcl); Thomas,
       Andrew (pf)
       - Opus One 6; 33s; rel 1970; cip

Fantasy Concerto
[5971] Varga, Laszlo (vcl); Hersh, Paul
       (pf); tape
       - Serenus SRS-12059; 33s; rel
       1977; cip

Fantasy Sonata (1970)
[5972] Mann, Robert (vln); Masselos,
       William (pf)
       - Desto DC-7142; 33s; rel 1973;
       cip

Grand Guignols of Love, The
[5973] Carshon, Charles (voice);
       Kupferman, Meyer (cl)
       - Serenus SRS-12082; 33s; rel
       1980; cip

(Three) Ideas (1967)
[5974] Levy, Robert (tpt); Levy, Amy Lou
       (pf)
       - Golden Crest RE-7045; 33q; rel
       1972; cip

[5975] Stevens, Thomas (tpt);
       Swiatkowski, Chet (pf)
       Rec 10/78
       - Crystal S-366; 33s; rel 1979; cip

Infinities 1 (1961): Line Fantasy
[5976] Baron, Samuel (fl)
       - CRI-212; 33m/s; rel 1966/?; cip

Infinities 15 (1965)
[5977] Wentworth, Jean (pf); Wentworth,
       Kenneth (pf)
       Rec 3/24/78
       - Grenadilla GS-1050; 33s; rel
       1979

Infinities 22 (1967)
[5978] Nagel, Robert (tpt); Kalish, Gilbert
       (pf)
       - Serenus SRS-12044; 33s; rel
       1973; cip

Libretto (1951)
[5979] New Philharmonia Orchestra
       (members of); Farberman, Harold
       (cond)
       - Serenus SRS-12025; 33s; rel
       1971; cip

Little Sonata (1948)
[5980] Estrin, Morton (pf)
       - Serenus SRE-1001/SRS-12001;
       33m/s; rel 1965; cip

Little Symphony (1952)
[5981] Vienna State Opera Orchestra;
       Litschauer, Franz (cond)
       - Vanguard VRS-434; 33m; rel
       1953; del 1960

Lyric Symphony (1956)
[5982] Japan Philharmonic Symphony
Orchestra; Watanabe, Akeo
(cond)
- Serenus SRE-1000/SRS-12000;
33m/s; rel 1965; cip

Madrigal (1974)
[5983] Indianapolis Brass Ensemble
- Serenus SRS-12066; 33s; rel
1976; cip

Mask of Electra
[5984] DeGaetani, Jan (m sop); Roseman,
Ronald (ob); Spiegelman, Joel
(elec hpschd)
- Serenus SRS-12034; 33s; rel
1974; cip

Ostinato burlesco
[5985] Japan Philharmonic Symphony
Orchestra; Watanabe, Akeo
(cond)
- Serenus SRE-1000/SRS-12000;
33m/s; rel 1965; cip

Quartet, Strings, No 4 (1958)
[5986] Ravina String Quartet
- Serenus SRE-1001/SRS-12001;
33m/s; rel 1965; cip

Quiet Piece
[5987] Baron, Samuel (fl); Sanders,
Samuel (pf)
- Serenus SRS-12082; 33s; rel
1980; cip

Second Thoughts
[5988] Hayami, Kazuko (pf)
- Serenus SRS-12085; 33s; rel
1980; cip

Short Suite, Piano (1968)
[5989] Hayami, Kazuko (pf)
- Serenus SRS-12085; 33s; rel
1980; cip

Quintet, Brass
[5990] American Brass Quintet
- Serenus SRS-12041; 33s; rel
1972

Quintet, Winds, No 1 (1958)
[5991] Ariel Quintet
- Serenus SRS-12044; 33s; rel
1973; cip

Sonata, Two Pianos (1958)
[5992] Wentworth, Jean (pf); Wentworth,
Kenneth (pf)
- Serenus SRS-12044; 33s; rel
1973; cip

Sonata on Jazz Elements (1958)
[5993] Estrin, Morton (pf)
- Serenus SRE-1001/SRS-12001;
33m/s; rel 1965; cip

Superflute
[5994] Baron, Samuel (fl); tape
- Nonesuch H-71289; 33s; rel
1974; cip

Symphony No 4 (1955)
[5995] Louisville Orchestra; Whitney,
Robert (cond)
- LOU-58-4; 33m (Louisville
Orchestra First Edition Records
1958 No 4); rel 1959; del 1975

Variations, Orchestra (1959)
[5996] Japan Philharmonic Symphony
Orchestra; Watanabe, Akeo
(cond)
- Serenus SRE-1000/SRS-12000;
33m/s; rel 1965; cip

Variations, Piano (1948)
[5997] Estrin, Morton (pf)
- Serenus SRE-1017/SRS-12017;
33m/s; rel 1966; cip

KURKA, Robert (1921-57)
Good Soldier Schweik, The (Suite)
[5998] Louisville Orchestra; Whitney,
Robert (cond)
- LOU-65-6/LS-65-6; 33m/s
(Louisville Orchestra First Edition
Records 1965 No 6); rel 1965;
cip

[5999] Westchester Symphony Orchestra;
Landau, Siegfried (cond)
- Candide CE-31089; 33s; rel
1975; cip

**Serenade, Small Orchestra (Op 25)
(1954)**
[6000] Louisville Orchestra; Whitney,
Robert (cond)
- LOU-63-2; 33m (Louisville
Orchestra First Edition Records
1963 No 2); rel 1963; cip

Symphony No 2 (Op 24) (1958)
[6001] Louisville Orchestra; Whitney,
Robert (cond)
- LOU-61-6; 33m (Louisville
Orchestra First Edition Records
1961 No 6); rel 1962; cip

KYNASTON, Trent (1946-)
Dawn and Jubilation (1973)
[6002] Kynaston, Trent (sax)
- Coronet LPS-3035; 33s; rel
1978; cip

**Sonata, Alto Saxophone and Piano
(1977)**
[6003] Kynaston, Trent (al sax); Ricci,
Robert (pf)
- Coronet LPS-3044; 33s; rel
1978; cip

LA BARBARA, Joan (1947-)
Cathing (1977)
[6004] La Barbara, Joan (voice); tape
- Chiaroscuro CR-196; 33s; rel
1978; cip

Circular Song (1975)
[6005] La Barbara, Joan (voice)
Rec 2/26/76
- Wizard RVW-2266; 33s; rel
1976

Thunder (1976)
[6006] La Barbara, Joan (voice); tape
- Chiaroscuro CR-196; 33s; rel
1978; cip

Vocal Extensions
[6007] La Barbara, Joan (voice); electronic
music
Rec 2/26/76
- Wizard RVW-2266; 33s; rel
1976

**Voice Piece (One-Note Internal
Resonance Investigation)**
[6008] La Barbara, Joan (voice)
Rec 2/26/76
- Wizard RVW-2266; 33s; rel
1976

LABUNSKI, Felix (1892-1979)
Canto di aspirazione (1963)
[6009] Louisville Orchestra; Mester, Jorge
(cond)
- LS-72-1; 33s (Louisville
Orchestra First Edition Records
1972 No 1); rel 1973; cip

LACY, Steve (1934-)
Straws
[6010] Lacy, Steve (sax); instrumental
ensemble; tape
- Cramps 6206; 33s; rel 1977

LADERMAN, Ezra (1924-)
**Duo, Violin and Piano (Les Adieux
1970)**
[6011] Laredo, Jaime (vln); Laredo, Ruth
(pf)
- Desto DC-7125; 33s; rel 1971;
cip

From the Psalms (1970)
[6012] Raskin, Judith (sop); Edwards,
Ryan (pf)
- Desto DC-7105; 33s; rel 1970;
cip

Magic Prison (1966-67)
[6013] O'Brien, Adale (speaker); Jory, Jon
(speaker); Louisville Orchestra;
Mester, Jorge (cond)
- LS-71-2; 33s (Louisville
Orchestra First Edition Records
1971 No 2); rel 1971; del 1979

Quartet, Strings, No 1 (1958-59)
[6014] Beaux-Arts String Quartet
- CRI-126; 33m/s; rel 1960/?; cip

Quartet, Strings, No 2 (1964-65)
[6015] Cohen, Isidore (vln); Yajima, Hiroko
(vln); Rhodes, Samuel (vla);
Sylvester, Robert (vcl)
- CRI-244; 33s; rel 1969; cip

**Satire (Concerto for Orchestra)
(1968)**
[6016] Baltimore Symphony Orchestra;
Comissiona, Sergiu (cond)
- Desto DC-7168; 33s; rel 1973;
cip

Sonata, Flute and Piano (1955)
[6017] Baron, Samuel (fl); Baron, Carol
(pf) or Sanders, Samuel (pf)
- Desto DC-7104; 33s; rel 1970;
cip

Songs for Eve (1962-63)
[6018] Raskin, Judith (sop); Edwards,
Ryan (pf)
- Desto DC-7105; 33s; rel 1970;
cip

Stanzas (1960)
[6019] chamber orchestra; Mester, Jorge
(cond)
- Desto DC-7129; 33s; rel 1972;
cip

**Theme, Variations, and Finale
(1954)**
[6020] New York Woodwind Quintet;
Saidenberg Chamber Players;
Baron, Samuel (cond)
- CRI-130; 33m/s; rel 1960/?; cip

LA FORGE, Frank (1879-1953)
Before the Crucifix
[6021] Powers, Marie (al); La Forge, Frank
(pf)
- Atlantic 1207; 33m; rel 1952;
del 1959

[6022] Schumann-Heink, Ernestine (al)
- Victor 88548; 78; rel 1912-16
- Victor 6275; 78; rel 1912-16

Bird Song
[6023] Pons, Lily (sop); Andre Kostelanetz
and his Orchestra; Kostelanetz,
Andre (cond)
- Columbia ML-2138; 33m; 10";
rel 1950; del 1956

Come Unto These Yellow Sands
[6024] Houston, Marie (sop); Gelfius,
Julius (fl); La Forge, Frank
(hpschd)
- Victor 26711 (in set P-39); 78;
10"; rel pre-1943

Gavotte
[6025] La Forge, Frank (pf)
- Victor 64083; 78; 10"; rel 1908

How Much I Love You
[6026] Gadski, Johanna (sop); piano
- Victor 87026; 78; 10"; rel
1907-10

**I Came with a Song (orchd by
Douglas Gamley)**
[6027] Sutherland, Joan (sop); New
Philharmonia Orchestra; Bonynge,
Richard (cond)
- London OS-26367; 33s; rel
1974; cip

Into the Light
[6028] Melchior, Lauritz (ten); Strasvogel,
Ignace (pf)
- RCA CRM-3-0308; 33m; 3 discs;
rel 1974; del 1979

Take, O Take Those Lips Away
[6029] Houston, Marie (sop); Gelfius,
Julius (fl); La Forge, Frank
(hpschd) (pf)
- Victor 26711 (in set P-39); 78;
10"; rel pre-1943

LAIDLAW, Robert
Trio, Strings
[6030] Galimir String Quartet (members
of)
- Yaddo II-3; 78; 2 discs; rel 1940

**LAKE, Mayhew Lester
(1879-1955)**
Roosters Lay Eggs in Kansas, The
[6031] Perez, Antonio (bar); University of
Kansas Symphonic Band; Foster,
Robert E. (cond)
- Golden Crest CRS-4187; 33s; rel
1979

LAMB, John David (1935-)
Madrigal for Three Saxophones
[6032] Rascher Saxophone Quartet
- Coronet LPS-3030; 33s; rel
1978; cip

LAMBRO, Phillip (1935-)
**Music for Winds, Brass, and
Percussion**
[6033] United States International
Orchestra; Lambro, Phillip (cond)
- Crystal S-861; 33s; rel 1973; cip

Structures
[6034] United States International
Orchestra; Lambro, Phillip (cond)
- Crystal S-861; 33s; rel 1973; cip

Trumpet Voluntary
[6035] Plog, Anthony (tpt)
- Crystal S-364; 33s; rel 1980; cip

LA MONTAINE, John (1920-)
Birds' Courting Song
[6036] Anders, Lynne (sop)
- Golden Age GAR-1002; 33s; rel
1976

Birds of Paradise (Op 34) (1964)
[6037] La Montaine, John (pf);
Eastman-Rochester Symphony
Orchestra; Hanson, Howard
(cond)
- Mercury MG-50430/SR-90430;
33m/s; rel 1965; del 1969
- Eastman-Rochester Archives
ERA-1006; 33s; rel 1976; cip

Child's Picture Book, A
[6038] La Montaine, John (pf)
- Dorian DR-332; 33m; rel 1951;
del 1958

**Concerto, Piano and Orchestra (Op
9) (1958-59)**
[6039] Keys, Karen (pf); Oklahoma City
Symphony Orchestra; Harrison,
Guy Fraser (cond)
- CRI-166; 33m; rel 1963; cip
- CRI-189; 33s; rel 1965; cip

Conversations for Viola and Piano
[6040] Tatton (vla); La Montaine, John
(pf)
- Fredonia FD-8; 33s; rel 1979; cip

Conversations for Violin and Piano
[6041] Brostoff, Arnold (vln); Shkolnik,
Sheldon (pf)
- Fredonia FD-5; 33s; rel 1977; cip

**Copycats (Op 26): Sing No More
and It's Time to Dance**
[6042] Fuszek, Rita (pf)
- Educo 3108; 33

Even Song
[6043] Hebblethwaite, John E. (org)
- United Sound USR-4289; 33s; rel
1972?

[6044] Swann, Frederick (org)
- Mirrosonic CS-7230; 33s; rel
1972

[6045] Teague, William (org)
Rec 2/20/67
- Wicks Organ Co 832W-9785;
33s; rel 1967
- Wicks Organ Co S-V1S4; 33s; rel
1968; del 1974

Fuguing Set (Op 14)
[6046] La Montaine, John (pf)
- Fredonia FD-5; 33s; rel 1977; cip

Incantation (Op 39) (1971)
[6047] Eastman Jazz Ensemble; Wright,
Rayburn (cond)
- Fredonia FD-3; 33s; rel 1977; cip

**(Nine) Lessons of Christmas (Op
44)**
[6048] Baker, Polly Jo (sop); Griffith,
David (ten); Fredonia Singers; La
Montaine, John (cond)
- Fredonia FD-6; 33s; rel 1977; cip

Music for the Dance
[6049] La Montaine, John (pf)
- Fredonia FD-3; 33s; rel 1977; cip

(Twelve) Relationships (Op 10)
[6050] La Montaine, John (pf)
- Fredonia FD-5; 33s; rel 1977; cip

Sonata, Piano
[6051] La Montaine, John (pf)
- Dorian DR-332; 33m; rel 1951; del 1958

Songs of the Rose of Sharon (Op 29) (1957)
[6052] Steber, Eleanor (sop); Greater Trenton Symphony Orchestra; Harsanyi, Nicholas (cond)
Rec 1/13/62
- St/And SPL-420/SLS-7420; 33m/s; rel 1962; del 1964

(Six) Sonnets of Shakespeare (Op 12)
[6053] Baker, Polly Jo (sop); La Montaine, John (pf)
- Fredonia FD-8; 33s; rel 1979; cip

Stopping by Woods on a Snowy Evening
[6054] Steber, Eleanor (sop); Biltcliffe, Edwin (pf)
- St/And SPL-411-12; 33m; 2 discs; rel 1963; del 1964
- Desto D-411-12/DST-6411-12; 33m/s; 2 discs; rel 1964; cip

Teaching Pieces for Budding Pianists
[6055] La Montaine, John (pf)
- Fredonia FD-4; 33s; rel 1977; cip

Toccata, Piano
[6056] La Montaine, John (pf)
- Dorian DR-332; 33m; rel 1951; del 1958

LANDRY, Richard (1938-)
Alto Flute Quad Delay
[6057] Landry, Richard (al fl)
- Northern Light FSA-87003; 33s; rel 1977

Fifteen Saxophones
[6058] Landry, Richard (sax)
- Northern Light FSA-87003; 33s; rel 1977

Kitchen Solos
[6059] Landry, Richard
- Northern Light FSA-87003; 33s; rel 1977

Solos
[6060] Landry, Richard (sax); Peck, Richard; Prado, Robert; Gilder, Rusty; Lee, David; Smith, Jon; Brafman, Allan
- Chatham Square LP-17; 33s; 2 discs; rel 1973*

LANE, Richard B. (1933-)
(Four) Songs (1955-56)
[6061] Berlin, Patricia (m sop); Eastman-Rochester Symphony Orchestra; Hanson, Howard (cond)
- Mercury MG-50150/SR-90150; 33m/s; rel 1957/1960; del 1964
- Eastman-Rochester Archives ERA-1010; 33s; rel 1976; cip

Suite, Saxophone and Piano
[6062] Underwood, Dale (sax); Lee, Màrjorie (pf)
Rec 8/15/76
- Golden Crest RE-7067; 33s; rel 1978; cip

LANG, Craig Sellar
Fanfare (Op 85)
[6063] Farrell, Timothy (org)
- Vista VPS-1002; 33s; rel 1973

Tuba Tune (Op 15)
[6064] Bielby, Jonathan (org)
Rec 11/74
- Vista VPS-1034; 33s; rel 1976

LANG, Margaret Ruthven (1867-1972)
Irish Love Song (Op 22)
[6065] Beddoe, Dan (ten)
- Victor 64195; 78; 10"; rel 1911-14
- Victor 64391; 78; 10"; rel 1911-14

[6066] Gluck, Alma (sop); Zimbalist, Efrem (pf)
- Victor 64346; 78; 10"; rel 191?

[6067] Schumann-Heink, Ernestine (al)
- Pelican LP-2008; 33m; rel 1978; cip

[6068] Van Gordon, Cyrena (al)
- Columbia 79M; 78; rel pre-1927

Sie liebt mich
[6069] Bramson, Bernice (sop) or Johns, Mertine (m sop); May, Michael (pf) or Rundle, Roger (pf); Vieuxtemps String Quartet
- Gemini Hall RAP-1010; 33s; 2 discs; rel 1976*

LANG, P. F.
Trumpet and Drum
[6070] H. M. Royal Marines Band; Neville, Paul (cond)
- Arabesque 8006; 33s; rel 1980; cip

LANSKY, Paul (1944-)
Crossworks (1974-75)
[6071] Boston Musica Viva; Pittman, Richard (cond)
Rec 1/78
- Nonesuch H-71351; 33s; rel 1978; cip

Mild und leise (1973-74)
[6072] Electronic music
- Odyssey Y-34139; 33s; rel 1976; cip

Modal Fantasy (1970)
[6073] Miller, Robert (pf)
Rec 1/29/75
- CRI-342; 33s; rel 1975; cip

Quartet, Strings (1971, rev 1977)
[6074] Pro Arte Quartet
Rec 11/78
- CRI-402; 33s; rel 1979; cip

LAPHAM, Claude (1890-1957)
Japanese Concerto (Op 35)
[6075] Lapham, Claude (pf); orchestra
- Victor 4306-08 (in set 302); 78; 3-10"; rel pre-1936
- Victor JK-12-14; 78; 3-10"; rel pre-1936

Mihara yama (Op 34)
[6076] orchestra; Lapham, Claude (cond)
- Victor 11895; 78; rel pre-1936

LATEEF, Yusef (1921-)
Trio, Flute, Violin, and Piano, No 1
[6077] Handy, D. Antoinette (fl); Kennedy, Joseph (vln); Terry, William (pf)
- Eastern ERS-513; 33s; 2 discs; rel 1973*

LATHAM, William Peters (1917-)
(Three) Chorale Preludes, Band
[6078] Chicago Symphonic Band
- Summy 2; 33m/s; rel 1958; del 1966

[6079] North Texas State University Concert Band; McAdow, Maurice (cond)
- Austin 6104; 33m; rel 1961; del 1971

Court Festival (1957)
[6080] North Texas State University Concert Band; McAdow, Maurice (cond)
- Austin 6164; 33m; rel 1963; del 1971

Proud Heritage (1955)
[6081] University of Miami Symphonic Band
- King 682; 33m/s; rel 1960; del 1965

Sisyphus (1971)
[6082] Francois, Daneels (sax); Capelle, Claudine (pf)
- Buffet Crampon BCB-105; 33s; rel 1973?

LAVALLE, Paul (1908-)
Ballyhoo March, The
[6083] Cities Service Band of America; Lavalle, Paul (cond)
- Victor 547-0264-65 (in set EPB-3120); 45; 2-7"; rel 1953?

United Press March
[6084] Cities Service Band of America; Lavalle, Paul (cond)
- Victor 547-0264-65 (in set EPB-3120); 45; 2-7"; rel 1953?

LA VIOLETTE, Wesley (1894-1978)
Music from the High Sierras
[6085] Frankenland Symphony Orchestra; Kloss, Erich (cond)
- Lyrichord LL-29; 33m; rel 1952; del 1957

LAWRENCE, Harold (1906-)
Butterfly
[6086] Richter, Marga (pf)
- MGM E-3147; 33m; rel 1955; del 1959

March
[6087] Richter, Marga (pf)
- MGM E-3147; 33m; rel 1955; del 1959

Seagull
[6088] Richter, Marga (pf)
- MGM E-3147; 33m; rel 1955; del 1959

LAYMAN, Pamela
Gravitation I (1974)
[6089] Oliveira, Elmar (vln)
- Grenadilla GS-1032; 33s; rel 1978; cip

LAYTON, Billy Jim (1924-)
Quartet, Strings (Op 4) (1956)
[6090] Claremont String Quartet
- CRI-136; 33m; rel 1960; cip

(Three) Studies, Piano (Op 5) (1957)
[6091] Wyner, Yehudi (pf)
- CRI-257; 33s; rel 1970; cip

(Five) Studies, Violin and Piano (Op 1) (1952)
[6092] Raimondi, Matthew (vln); Wyner, Yehudi (pf)
- CRI-257; 33s; rel 1970; cip

LAZAROF, Henri (1932-)
Adieu (1974)
[6093] Gray, Gary (cl); Vallecillo-Gray, Irma (pf)
- Avant AV-1019; 33s; rel 1977; cip

Cadence II, Viola and Tape (1969)
[6094] Thomas, Milton (vla); tape
- Desto DC-7109; 33s; rel 1970; cip

Cadence III, Violin and Two Percussion Players (1970)
[6095] Plummer, Stanley (vln); Watson, Kenneth (perc); Bunker, Larry (perc)
- Candide CE-31072; 33s; rel 1973; del 1977

Cadence IV, Piano and Tape (1970)
[6096] Bunger, Richard (pf); tape
- Avant AV-1008; 33s; rel 1973; del 1979

Cadence V, Flute and Tape (1972)
[6097] Galway, James (fl); tape
Rec 1973
- CRI-381; 33s; rel 1978; cip

Cadence VI, Tuba and Tape
[6098] Bobo, Roger (tu); tape
- Avant AV-1019; 33s; rel 1977; cip
- Crystal S-392; 33s; rel 1978; cip

Chamber Concerto No 3 (1974)
[6099] chamber ensemble; Lazarof, Henri (cond)
- Avant AV-1019; 33s; rel 1977; cip

Concertazioni (1973)
[6100] Giles, Ann Diener (fl) (al fl); Buxbaum, Merritt (cl) (b cl); Stevens, Thomas (tpt) (flhn); Pyle, Ralph (hn); Rothmuller, Daniel (vcl); Remsen, Dorothy (hp); tape; Lazarof, Henri (cond)
- Avant AV-1009; 33s; rel 1977; cip
- Crystal S-366; 33s; rel 1979; cip

Concerto, Flute and Orchestra
[6101] Galway, James (fl); New Philharmonia Orchestra; Lazarof, Henri (cond)
- CRI-373; 33s; rel 1977; cip

Concerto, Violoncello and Orchestra (1968)
[6102] Lesser, Laurence (vcl); Oakland Symphony Orchestra; Samuel, Gerhard (cond)
- Desto DC-7109; 33s; rel 1970; cip

Continuum (1970)
[6103] Plummer, Stanley (vln); Thomas, Milton (vla); Lesser, Laurence (vcl)
- Desto DC-7109; 33s; rel 1970; cip

Duo 1973
[6104] Rejto, Gabor (vcl); Rejto, Alice (pf)
- Avant AV-1019; 33s; rel 1977; cip

Espaces (1967)
[6105] Los Angeles Chamber Ensemble; Lazarof, Henri (cond)
- CRI-263; 33s; rel 1971; cip

Inventions, Viola and Piano (1962)
[6106] Thomas, Milton (vla); Akst, Georgia (pf)
- Counterpoint/Esoteric CPT-605/CPTS-5605; 33m/s; rel 1964; del 1975
- Everest LPBR-6160/SDBR-3160; 33m/s; rel 1967; del 1975

Octet (1967)
[6107] UCLA Wind Ensemble; Lazarof, Henri (cond)
- CRI-263; 33s; rel 1971; cip

Partita, Brass Quintet and Tape (1971)
[6108] Los Angeles Brass Quintet; tape
- Candide CE-31072; 33s; rel 1973; del 1977

Rhapsody, Violin and Piano (1966)
[6109] Plummer, Stanley (vln); Steinhardt, Victor (pf)
- Everest LPBR-6160/SDBR-3160; 33m/s; rel 1967; del 1975

Spectrum (1972)
[6110] Stevens, Thomas (tpt); Utah Symphony Orchestra; tape; Lazarof, Henri (cond)
- CRI-373; 33s; rel 1977; cip

Structures sonores (1966)
[6111] Utah Symphony Orchestra; Abravanel, Maurice (cond)
- Vanguard Cardinal VCS-10047; 33s; rel 1969; cip

Tempi concertati (1964)
[6112] Plummer, Stanley (vln); Johnson, Maxine (vla); instrumental ensemble; Lazarof, Henri (cond)
- Everest LPBR-6160/SDBR-3160; 33m/s; rel 1967; del 1975

Textures (1970)
[6113] Ogdon, John (pf); Utah Symphony Orchestra; Lazarof, Henri (cond)
- Candide CE-31072; 33s; rel 1973; del 1977

LEACH, Rowland (1885-)

(Seven) Casual Brevities: Nos 2-5
[6114] Richardson, Harriette S. (org)
- Century Recording Service 20738/20739; 33m/s; rel 1965

(Seven) Casual Brevities: (No 2) Chollas Dance for You
[6115] Ellsasser, Richard (org)
- MGM E-3005; 33m; rel 1953; del 1959

LEAF, Robert

Let the Whole Creation Cry (1971)
[6116] Mormon Tabernacle Choir; Schreiner, Alexander (org); Ottley, Jerold D. (cond)
- Columbia M-34134; 33s; rel 1976; cip

LEBOW, Leonard (1929-)

Suite, Brass (1956)
[6117] Pacific Brass Quintet
- Avant AV-1004; 33s; rel 1972*

LEE, Dai-keong (1915-)

Polynesian Suite (1959)
[6118] Nuremberg Symphony Orchestra; Barati, George (cond)
- CRI-195; 33m/s; rel 1964/1970; cip

Prelude and Hula
[6119] National Symphony Orchestra; Kindler, Hans (cond)
- Victor 11-8452; 78; rel pre-1948

Symphony No 1 (1942)
[6120] Nuremberg Symphony Orchestra; Barati, George (cond)
- CRI-195; 33m/s; rel 1964/1970; cip

LEE, Eugene (1942-)

Composition for Flute Solo
[6121] Spencer, Patricia (fl)
Rec 1/78
- CRI-400; 33s; rel 1979; cip

LEE, Noel (1924-)

Caprices on the Name Schoenberg
[6122] Lee, Noel (pf); Nouvel Orchestre Philharmonique; Marty, Jean Pierre (cond)
Rec 11/23/76
- CRI-408; 33s; rel 1979; cip

Convergences
[6123] Adorjan, Andras (fl); Lee, Noel (hpschd)
- CRI-408; 33s; rel 1979; cip

Dialogues (1958)
[6124] Boehn, Ole (vln); Lee, Noel (pf)
- CRI-408; 33s; rel 1979; cip

Errances
[6125] Cornell University Wind Ensemble; Stith, Marice (cond)
- Cornell CUWE-13; 33s; rel 1973; cip

(Five) Songs from Lorca (1955)
[6126] Addison, Adele (sop); Baron, Samuel (fl); Torre, Rey de la (gtr)
- CRI-147; 33m; rel 1962; cip

LEE, Norman (1895-)

Fantasia
[6127] Cope, M. J.
- Capra 1202; 33s; rel 1971; del 1973

Temple Song
[6128] Gozesky, Betty (pf)
- Capra 1203; 33s; rel 1975; cip

LEEDY, Douglas (1938-)

Entropical Paradise (Six Sonic Environments) (1970)
[6129] Electronic music
- Seraphim SIC-6060; 33s; 3 discs; rel 1971; del 1976

LEES, Benjamin (1924-)

Concerto, Orchestra (1959)
[6130] Louisville Orchestra; Whitney, Robert (cond)
- LOU-66-5/LS-66-5; 33m/s (Louisville Orchestra First Edition Records 1966 No 5); rel 1967; cip

Concerto, String Quartet and Orchestra (1964)
[6131] Ronayne, John (vln); Grey, Geoffrey (vln); Riddle, Frederick (vla); Jones, Norman (vcl); Royal Philharmonic Orchestra; Buketoff, Igor (cond)
- RCA LSC-3095; 33s; rel 1969; del 1974

Concerto, Violin and Orchestra (1958)
[6132] Ricci, Ruggiero (vln); American Symphony Orchestra; Akiyama, Kazuyoshi (cond)
- Turnabout TVS-34692; 33s; rel 1977; cip

Odyssey (1970)
[6133] Mandel, Alan (pf)
- Desto DC-6445-47; 33s; 3 discs; rel 1975; cip

Prologue, Capriccio, and Epilogue (1959)
[6134] Portland Junior Symphony; Avshalomov, Jacob (cond)
- CRI-140; 33m/s; rel 1961/?; cip

Quartet, Strings, No 1 (1952)
[6135] Juilliard String Quartet
- Epic LC-3325; 33m; rel 1957; del 1961

Quartet, Strings, No 2 (1955)
[6136] Paganini Quartet
- Liberty 15004; 33m; rel 1957; del 1959

Sonata, Piano, No 3 (Sonata breve) (1956)
[6137] Mandel, Alan (pf)
- Desto DC-6445-47; 33s; 3 discs; rel 1975; cip

Sonata, Piano, No 4 (1963)
[6138] Graffman, Gary (pf)
- Odyssey Y-35203; 33s; rel 1978; cip

Sonata, Violin and Piano, No 2 (1972)
[6139] Druian, Rafael (vln); Alpenheim, Ilse von (pf)
- Desto DC-7174; 33s; rel 1974; cip

Symphony No 2 (1958)
[6140] Louisville Orchestra; Whitney, Robert (cond)
- LOU-59-5; 33s (Louisville Orchestra First Edition Records 1959 No 5); rel 1960; del 1975

Symphony No 3 (1968)
[6141] Louisville Orchestra; Mester, Jorge (cond)
Rec 5/15/75
- LS-75-2; 33s (Louisville Orchestra First Edition Records 1975 No 2); rel 1976; cip

LEGINSKA, Ethel (1886-1970)

(Three) Victorian Portraits (1959)
[6142] Dowis, Jeaneane (pf)
- Orion ORS-75188; 33s; rel 1975; cip

LEICH, Roland (1911-)

Elusive Sleep
[6143] Luening, Ethel (sop); Nowak, Lionel (pf)
- Yaddo I-2; 78; 10''; rel 1940

LEICHTLING, Alan (1947-)

(Eleven) Songs from A Shropshire Lad (Op 50) (1969)
[6144] Hyer, John (ten); Juilliard Orchestra; Leichtling, Alan (cond)
- Turnabout TVS-34420; 33s; rel 1971; del 1975

LEIDZEN, Erik (1894-1962)

Doxology
[6145] Leeds Concert Band; Todd, Peter
(cond)
- Columbia ML-4254; 33m; rel
1950; del 1956

LEIGH, Mitch (1928-)

Dream of America, The (arr by Lew Anderson)
[6146] De Paur Chorus; Wingreen, Harriet
(pf); De Paur, Leonard (cond)
- Columbia M-33838; 33s; rel
1975; cip

LEMARE, Edwin Henry (1865-1934)

Andantino in D-flat
[6147] Lemare, Edwin (org)
Rec 6/4/27
- Victor 35843; 78; rel 1927

[6148] Meale, Arthur (org)
- Gramophone B-2353; 78; 10";
rel 1927?

[6149] Pattman, G. T. (org)
- Columbia 9135; 78; rel 1927

Andantino in D-flat (arr for vln and pf by Saenger)
[6150] Kreisler, Fritz (vln); Lamson, Carl
(pf)
- Victor 1165; 78; 10"; rel
pre-1948

Chant de bonheur
[6151] Lemare, Edwin (org)
Rec 8/12/27
- Victor 21121; 78; 10"; rel
1927?

Gavotte moderne
[6152] Cunningham, G. D. (org)
- Gramophone B-2522; 78; 10";
rel 1927

Madrigal
[6153] Mason, Berkeley (org)
- Gramophone B-8022; 78; 10";
rel 1934

Marche moderne
[6154] Herrick, Christopher (org)
- Musical Heritage Society
MHS-3855; 33s; rel 1978

Pastorale in F
[6155] Meale, Arthur (org)
- Gramophone B-2399; 78; 10";
rel 1927

Reverie
[6156] Alcock, Sir W. G. (org)
- Gramophone C-1376; 78; rel
1927

Summer Sketches: Dawn, The Bee, The Cuckoo, and Evening
[6157] Curtis, Stanley (org)
- Apollo Sound AS-1004; 33s; rel
1968

LENGSFELDER, Hans (1903-79)

Musical Notes from a Tourist's Sketch
[6158] World Symphony Orchestra
- Request 10027; 33m; rel 1954*

LENTZ, Daniel (1942-)

Song of the Sirens (1975)
[6159] Montagnana Trio
Rec 6/75
- ABC Command COMS-9005;
33q; rel 1975; del 1977
- ABC 67013; 33q; rel 1977; del
1979
- MCA 67013; 33s; rel 1979; cip

LEONARD, Clair (1901-)

Recitativo and Abracadabra
[6160] Rascher, Sigurd (sax); Tudor, David
(pf)
- Concert Hall CHS-1156; 33m; rel
1952; del 1957

LERDAHL, Fred (1943-)

Eros (1975)
[6161] Morgan, Beverly (m sop); Collage;
Lerdahl, Fred (cond)
Rec 4/78
- CRI-378; 33s; rel 1978; cip

Fantasy, Piano (1964)
[6162] Miller, Robert (pf)
- CRI-319; 33s; rel 1974; cip

Trio, Strings (1965-66)
[6163] Raimondi, Matthew (vln); Dupouy,
Jean (vla); Rudiakov, Michael (vcl)
- CRI-319; 33s; rel 1974; cip

Wake
[6164] Beardslee, Bethany (sop); Boston
Symphony Chamber Players;
Epstein, David (cond)
- Acoustic Research AR-0654.083;
33s; rel 1971

LESEMANN, Frederick (1936-)

Nataraja (1975)
[6165] Grierson, Ralph (pf)
Rec 6/2/78
- Town Hall S-24; 33s; rel 1979;
cip

Sonata, Clarinet and Percussion (1972)
[6166] Lurie, Mitchell (cl); Ervin, Karen
(perc)
- Crystal S-641; 33s; rel 1973; cip

LESSARD, John (1920-)

Concerto, Woodwind Trio and Strings (1952)
[6167] Peninsula Festival Orchestra;
Johnson, Thor (cond)
- CRI-122; 33m; rel 1958; cip

Fragments from the Cantos of Ezra Pound (1969)
[6168] Murray, Matthew (bar);
Philharmonia Virtuosi of New
York; Kapp, Richard (cond)
- Serenus SRS-12026; 33s; rel
1971; cip

Octet, Winds (1952)
[6169] Rome Symphony Orchestra;
Flagello, Nicolas (cond)
- Serenus SRE-1008/SRS-12008;
33m/s; rel 1965; cip

Partita, Wind Quintet
[6170] Rome Symphony Orchestra
(members of); Flagello, Nicolas
(cond)
- Serenus SRE-1008/SRS-12008;
33m/s; rel 1965; cip

Prelude, Piano, III
[6171] Fuszek, Rita (pf)
- Educo 3108; 33

Quintet, Brass
[6172] American Brass Quintet
- Serenus SRS-12041; 33s; rel
1972

Quintet, Winds, II
[6173] New York Woodwind Quintet
- Serenus SRS-12032; 33s; rel
1973; cip

Quodlibets, Two Trumpets and Trombone (1967)
[6174] American Brass Quintet
- Serenus SRS-12026; 33s; rel
1971; cip

Sinfonietta concertante (1961)
[6175] New Philharmonia Orchestra
(members of); Farberman, Harold
(cond)
- Serenus SRS-12026; 33s; rel
1971; cip

Sonata, Violoncello and Piano (1954)
[6176] Greenhouse, Bernard (vcl);
Pressler, Menahem (pf)
- CRI-208; 33m/s; rel 1966/?; cip

Toccata, Harpsichord (1951)
[6177] Marlowe, Sylvia (hpschd)
- New Editions 3; 33m; rel 1953;
del 1959
- Decca DL-10021/DL-710021;
33m/s; rel 1961; del 1971

Toccata, Harpsichord (1951)
(cont'd)
[6178] Spiegelman, Joel (hpschd)
- Serenus SRS-12032; 33s; rel 1973; cip

Trio in sei parti (1966)
[6179] Zukofsky, Paul (vln); Eddy, Timothy (vcl); Kalish, Gilbert (pf)
- Serenus SRS-12032; 33s; rel 1973; cip

LEVANT, Oscar (1906-72)
Sonatina, Piano: 1st Movement
[6180] Levant, Oscar (pf)
- Columbia 17336D (in set M-508); 78; 10"; rel pre-1943

LEVITCH, Leon (1927-)
Fantasy, Oboe and Strings (Op 12)
[6181] Muggeridge, Donald (ob); Valley String Quartet
- Orion ORS-6914; 33s; rel 1969; cip

Little Suite, Piano (Op 1/2) (1948-50)
[6182] Guzelimian, Armen (pf)
- Orion ORS-74150; 33s; rel 1974; cip

Quartet, Flute, Viola, Violoncello, and Piano (Op 3) (1953)
[6183] Stokes, Sheridan (fl); Reher, Sven (vla); Solow, Jeffrey (vcl); Vallecillo-Gray, Irma (pf)
- Orion ORS-7288; 33s; rel 1972; cip

Quartet, Strings, No 1 (Op 13)
[6184] Valley String Quartet
- Orion ORS-6914; 33s; rel 1969; cip

Quintet, Flute and Strings (Op 5) (1954)
[6185] Stokes, Sheridan (fl); Lenski, Kathleen (vln); Watanabe, Miwako (vln); Polivnick, Paul (vla); Solow, Jeffrey (vcl)
- Orion ORS-74150; 33s; rel 1974; cip

Sonata, Flute and Piano, No 1
[6186] Stokes, Sheridan (fl); Pleshakov, Vladimir (pf)
- Orion ORS-6914; 33s; rel 1969; cip

Sonata, Piano, No 1 (Op 4) (1953)
[6187] Guzelimian, Armen (pf)
- Orion ORS-74150; 33s; rel 1974; cip

Sonata, Viola and Piano (Op 11) (1957)
[6188] Reher, Sven (vla); Levitch, Leon (pf)
- Orion ORS-7031; 33s; rel 1970; cip

Sonata, Violin and Piano (Op 6) (1955)
[6189] Plummer, Stanley (vln); Levitch, Leon (pf)
- Orion ORS-7031; 33s; rel 1970; cip

Trio, Flute, Clarinet, and Piano (Op 2) (1952)
[6190] Stokes, Sheridan (fl); Gray, Gary (cl); Vallecillo-Gray, Irma (pf)
- Orion ORS-7288; 33s; rel 1972; cip

LEVITZKI, Mischa (1898-1941)
Arabesque valsante (Op 6)
[6191] Levitzki, Mischa (pf)
- RCA LM-2585; 33m; rel 1962; del 1968

Do You Remember?
[6192] Pinza, Ezio (b); King, Gibner (pf)
- Columbia ML-2142; 33m; 10"; rel 1950; del 1956

Gypsy Dance
[6193] Luboschutz, Pierre (pf); Nemenoff, Genia (pf)
- Victor 2096; 78; 10"; rel pre-1952

Valse de concert
[6194] Levitzki, Mischa (pf)
- Columbia 65024D; 78; rel 1923-25
- Columbia 7009M; 78; rel 1923-25

Valse tzigane
[6195] Luboschutz, Pierre (pf); Nemenoff, Genia (pf)
- Camden CAL-198; 33m; rel 1955; del 1958

Waltz in A
[6196] Levitzki, Mischa (pf)
- Columbia 65024D; 78; rel 1923-25
- Columbia 7009M; 78; rel 1923-25

LEVY, Burt (1936-)
(Six) Moments
[6197] Snyder, Ellsworth (pf)
- Advance FGR-21S; 33s; rel 197?

Orbs with Flute
[6198] Sollberger, Harvey (fl)
- Nonesuch HB-73028; 33s; 2 discs; rel 1975; cip

LEVY, Frank (1930-)
Adagio and Rondo, Two Clarinets and Bass Clarinet
[6199] Weiss, Mitchell (cl) (b cl)
- Sound Master SMP-1003; 33s; rel 1973*

Duo, Violins (1967)
[6200] Vamos, Almita (vln); Vamos, Roland (vln)
- Coronet S-2750; 33s; rel 1978; cip

Quintet, Brass
[6201] Brass Arts Quintet
- Grenadilla GS-1027; 33s; rel 1979; cip

Sonata, Clarinet and Piano (1967)
[6202] Weiss, Mitchell (cl); Carno, Zita (pf)
- Sound Master SMP-1003; 33s; rel 1973*

Suite, Horn and Piano (1960)
[6203] Smith, Calvin (hn); Dressler, John (pf)
- Crystal S-371; 33s; rel 1976; cip

LEVY, Marvin David (1932-)
Mourning Becomes Electra (1967): Too Weak to Kill the Man I Hate
[6204] Milnes, Sherrill (bar); New Philharmonia Orchestra; Guadagno, Anton (cond)
- RCA LSC-3076; 33s; rel 1969; del 1979

LEWIN, David (1933-)
Study No 1
[6205] Electronic music
- Decca DL-9103/DL-79103; 33m/s; rel 1962

Study No 2
[6206] Electronic music
- Decca DL-9103/DL-79103; 33m/s; rel 1962

LEWIN, Frank (1925-)
Dramatic Suite for New Violins
[6207] new family of violins designed and constructed by Carleen M. Hutchins; Glickman, Loren (cond)
- Musical Heritage Society MHS-4102; 33s; rel 1979

Innocence and Experience (1961)
[6208] Wyner, Susan Davenny (sop); instrumental ensemble; Wyner, Yehudi (cond)
- Musical Heritage Society MHS-4102; 33s; rel 1979

Introduction on a Psalm Tune
[6209] new family of violins designed and constructed by Carleen M. Hutchins; Glickman, Loren (cond)
- Musical Heritage Society MHS-4102; 33s; rel 1979

Mass for the Dead (1969)
[6210] Princeton High School Choir; Parrella, Nancianne (org); Trego, William R. (cond)
- Demeter Music 102; 33s; rel 1970; del 1977

LEWIN-RICHTER, Andres*
Study No 1 (1963)
[6211] Electronic music
- Turnabout TV-4004/TVS-34004; 33m/s; rel 1965; del 1975

LEWIS, Malcolm (1925-)
Movement, Brass Quintet and Piano (1966)
[6212] Ithaca Brass Quintet; Covert, Mary Ann (pf)
- Mark MES-32558; 33s; rel 1969; del 1976

LEWIS, Merrills (1908-)
(Two) Preludes on Southern Hymn Tunes
[6213] Yaddo Orchestra
- Yaddo D-17; 78; rel 1938
- Yaddo M-4; 78; rel 1938

LEWIS, Peter Tod (1932-)
Gestes (1973)
[6214] Electronic music
- CRI-324; 33s; rel 1975; cip

Quartet, Strings, No 2 (Signs and Circuits) (1969)
[6215] Columbia String Quartet; tape
Rec 1978
- CRI-392; 33s; rel 1979; cip

LEWIS, Robert Hall (1926-)
Combinazioni I, Clarinet, Violin, Violoncello, and Piano (1973)
[6216] Penn Contemporary Players
Rec 5/11/78
- Orion ORS-79363; 33s; rel 1980; cip

Combinazioni II, Percussion Ensemble and Piano
[6217] Eastman School of Music Percussion Ensemble
Rec 5/19/75
- Orion ORS-79363; 33s; rel 1980; cip

Combinazioni IV, Violoncello and Piano
[6218] Kates, Stephen (vcl); Senofsky, Ellen Mack (pf)
Rec 10/26/78
- Orion ORS-79363; 33s; rel 1980; cip

Divertimento, Six Instruments (1969)
[6219] Aeolian Chamber Players
- CRI-263; 33s; rel 1971; cip

Inflections I (1969)
[6220] Turetzky, Bertram (cb)
- New World NW-254; 33s; rel 1978

Monophony VII
[6221] Stevens, Thomas (tpt)
- Crystal S-361; 33s; rel 1976; cip

Nuances II (1975)
[6222] Royal Philharmonic Orchestra; Lewis, Robert Hall (cond)
Rec 6/28/77
- CRI-389; 33s; rel 1978; cip

Sonata, Violin (1968)
[6223] Banat, Gabriel (vln)
- Turnabout TVS-34429; 33s; rel 1971; del 1974

Symphony No 2 (1971)
[6224] London Symphony Orchestra; Lewis, Robert Hall (cond)
Rec 7/3/74
- CRI-331; 33s; rel 1975; cip

Toccata, Violin and Percussion
[6225] Banat, Gabriel (vln); Goodman, Saul (perc); Rosenberger, Walter (perc)
- CRI-263; 33s; rel 1971; cip

LIEBERSON, Goddard (1911-77)
Quartet, Strings (1938)
[6226] Galimir String Quartet
- Columbia ML-5821/MS-6421; 33m/s; rel 1963; del 1968
- Columbia CMS-6421; 33s; rel 1968; del 1974
- Columbia AMS-6421; 33s; rel 1974; cip

(Five) Songs without Mendelssohn
[6227] Previn, Andre (pf)
- Columbia ML-5986/MS-6586; 33m/s; rel 1964; del 1968
- Columbia CMS-6586; 33s; rel 1968; del 1974
- Columbia AMS-6586; 33s; rel 1974; del 1976

(Eight) Studies in Musicology (Which Will Teach You a Good Deal)
[6228] Previn, Andre (pf)
- Columbia ML-5986/MS-6586; 33m/s; rel 1964; del 1968
- Columbia CMS-6586; 33s; rel 1968; del 1974
- Columbia AMS-6586; 33s; rel 1974; del 1976

(Six) Technical Studies (Which Will Teach You Nothing)
[6229] Previn, Andre (pf)
- Columbia ML-5986/MS-6586; 33m/s; rel 1964; del 1968
- Columbia CMS-6586; 33s; rel 1968; del 1974
- Columbia AMS-6586; 33s; rel 1974; del 1976

LIEBERSON, Peter (1946-)
Concerto for Four Groups of Instruments (1973)
[6230] Speculum Musicae; Lieberson, Peter (cond)
Rec 6/5/75 and 11/11/75
- CRI-350; 33s; rel 1976; cip

Fantasy, Piano
[6231] Oppens, Ursula (pf)
Rec 6/5/75 and 11/11/75
- CRI-350; 33s; rel 1976; cip

LIEURANCE, Thurlow (1878-1963)
A-oo-ah
[6232] Watawaso, Princess (sop); Small, Hubert (fl); Lieurance, Thurlow (pf)
- Victor 18418; 78; 10"; rel pre-1927
- Victor 22316; 78; 10"; rel pre-1936

By the Waters of the Minnetonka
[6233] Alda, Frances (sop); male quartet; orchestra
- Victor 64908; 78; 10"; rel 1917-20
- Victor 527; 78; 10"; rel 1917-20
- Victor 1268; 78; 10"; rel pre-1936

[6234] Bennett, Mavis (sop)
- Gramophone B-2453; 78; 10"; rel pre-1936

[6235] Culp, Julia (al)
- Victor 64721; 78; 10"; rel 1914-18
- Victor 564; 78; 10"; rel 1914-18

[6236] Eddy, Nelson (b); Paxson, Theodore (pf)
- Victor 4366 (in set M-C27); 78; 10"; rel pre-1948
- Gramophone DA-1579; 78; 10"; rel pre-1948

By the Waters of the Minnetonka
(cont'd)
[6237] Lennox, Elizabeth (al)
- Brunswick 2575; 78; 10"; rel
pre-1927

[6238] Nielsen, Alice (sop)
- Columbia 39874; 78; rel
1911-15
- Columbia A-1732; 78; rel
1911-15

[6239] Os-ke-non-ton (voice)
- Columbia A-3173; 78; rel
pre-1927

[6240] Rider-Kelsey, Corinne (sop)
- Columbia 121M; 78; rel
pre-1936

[6241] Schumann-Heink, Ernestine (al)
- Victor 1198; 78; 10"; rel
pre-1936
- Pelican LP-2008; 33m; rel
1978; cip

[6242] Watawaso, Princess (sop)
- Victor 18431; 78; rel pre-1927

By the Waters of the Minnetonka
(Various Arrangements)
[6243] Arr for Chorus and Organ
Mormon Tabernacle Choir; organ
- Victor 19829; 78; 10"; rel
pre-1936

[6244] Arr for 2 Flutes
Lieurance, Thurlow (Indian fl);
Barone, Clement (fl)
- Victor 21972; 78; 10"; rel
pre-1936

[6245] Arr for Orchestra
Andre Kostelanetz and his
Orchestra; Kostelanetz, Andre
(cond)
- Columbia 7569-70M (in set
X-284); 78; 2 discs; rel
pre-1948
- Columbia MX-284; 78; rel
pre-1952

[6246] Arr for Organ
Velasco, E. (org)
- Columbia 1627D; 78; rel
pre-1936

[6247] Arr for Organ and Piano
Harding Sisters (org) (pf)
- Victor 22949; 78; 10"; rel
pre-1936
- Gramophone B-4228; 78; 10";
rel pre-1936

[6248] Arr for Piano Duet
Fairchild, Edgar (pf); Lindblom,
Robert (pf)
- Gramophone B-3279; 78; 10";
rel pre-1936

[6249] Arr for Trio
Cherniavsky Trio
- Columbia 3368; 78; rel
pre-1936

[6250] Arr for Violin
Chemet, Renee (vln)
- Victor 66259; 78; 10"; rel
1922-25

By the Waters of the Minnetonka
(Various Arrangements) *(cont'd)*
- Victor 1015; 78; 10"; rel
1922-25
- Victor 1228; 78; 10"; rel
pre-1936

By the Weeping Waters
[6251] Os-ke-non-ton (voice)
- Columbia A-3173; 78; rel
pre-1927

[6252] Watawaso, Princess (sop); Small,
Hubert (fl); Lieurance, Thurlow
(pf)
- Victor 18418; 78; 10"; rel
pre-1927
- Victor 22316; 78; 10"; rel
pre-1936

Her Blanket
[6253] Watawaso, Princess (sop); Small,
Hubert (fl); Lieurance, Thurlow
(pf)
- Victor 18418; 78; 10"; rel
pre-1927
- Victor 22316; 78; 10"; rel
pre-1936

Love with Tears
[6254] Lieurance, Thurlow (Indian fl);
Barone, Clement (fl); piano
- Victor 21972; 78; 10"; rel
pre-1936
- Victor E-89; 78; rel pre-1948

Lullaby
[6255] Culp, Julia (al)
- Victor 64491; 78; 10"; rel
1914-18
- Victor 564; 78; 10"; rel
1914-18

Omaha Ceremonial
[6256] Lieurance, Thurlow (Indian fl);
Barone, Clement (fl); piano
- Victor 21972; 78; 10"; rel
pre-1936
- Victor E-89; 78; rel pre-1948

Pueblo Lullaby
[6257] Lieurance, Thurlow (Indian fl);
Barone, Clement (fl); piano
- Victor 21972; 78; 10"; rel
pre-1936
- Victor E-89; 78; rel pre-1948

Sioux Serenade
[6258] Watawaso, Princess (sop)
- Victor 18431; 78; rel pre-1927

Winnebago Love Song
[6259] Lieurance, Thurlow (Indian fl);
Barone, Clement (fl); piano
- Victor 21972; 78; 10"; rel
pre-1936
- Victor E-89; 78; rel pre-1948

LINDENFELD, Harris (1945-)
Combinations I (The Last Gold of
Perished Stars)
[6260] Stith, Marice (tpt); Lindenfeld,
Harris (perc); Rouse, Christopher
(perc)
- Golden Crest RE-7068; 33s; rel
1977; cip

Directions (1973)
[6261] Cornell University Wind Ensemble;
Stith, Marice (cond)
Rec 3/24/74
- Cornell CUWE-15; 33s; rel 1975;
cip

Symphonia (1971)
[6262] Cornell University Symphonic Band;
Stith, Marice (cond)
- Cornell CUWE-3; 33s; rel 1975;
cip

LINN, Robert (1925-)
Concertino, Violin and Wind Octet
(1965)
[6263] Shapiro, Eudice (vln); Crystal
Chamber Orchestra; Kraft,
William (cond)
- Crystal S-853; 33s; rel 1972; cip

Dithyramb (1965)
[6264] Cellisti, I; Kessler, Jerome (cond)
- Orion ORS-7037; 33s; rel 1971;
cip

Quintet, Winds (1963)
[6265] Westwood Wind Quintet
- Crystal S-811; 33s; rel 1971; cip

Saxifrage Blue
[6266] Watters, Mark (bar sax); piano
- Crystal S-152; 33s; rel 1979

Vino (1975)
[6267] Goldman (vln); Brown (pf)
- Orion ORS-76212; 33s; rel
1977; cip

LIST, Garrett
Your Own Self (1973)
[6268] La Barbara, Joan (voice); Clayton,
Jay (voice); Kaplan, Jerry (voice);
ensemble
- Opus One 15; 33s; rel 1974; cip

LIST, Kurt (1913-70)
Remember (1956)
[6269] Randolph Singers; Randolph, David
(cond)
- CRI-102; 33m/s; rel 1956/?; cip

LOCKWOOD, Larry (1943-)
Suite, Band (1973)
[6270] Cornell University Wind Ensemble;
Cornell University Symphonic
Band; Stith, Marice (cond)
- Cornell CUWE-17; 33s; rel 1975;
cip

LOCKWOOD, Normand (1906-)

Concerto, Organ and Brass (1950)
[6271] Mason, Marilyn (org); Ware, John
(tpt); Prager, Nathan (tpt); Pulis,
Gordon (tbn); Haney, Lewis (tbn)
- Remington 199-173; 33m; rel
1954; del 1956
- Varese Sarabande VC-81047;
33m; rel 1979; cip

Hosanna
[6272] Concordia Choir; Christiansen, Paul
J. (cond)
- Concordia CDLP-3; 33m; 10''; rel
1953; del 1971

Inscriptions from the Catacombs (1935)
[6273] Concordia Choir; Christiansen, Paul
J. (cond)
- Concordia CDLP-8; 33m; rel
1964; del 1974
- Concordia S-2; 33s; rel 1964;
del 1976

Lullaby for Christmas
[6274] Whikehart Chorale; Whikehart,
Lewis E. (cond)
- Lyrichord LL-151/LLST-7151;
33m/s; rel 1965; cip

Praise to the Lord
[6275] Mormon Tabernacle Choir;
Schreiner, Alexander (org); Asper,
Frank (org); Condie, Richard P.
(cond)
- Columbia ML-6019/MS-6619;
33m/s; rel 1964; del 1966

Quartet, Strings
[6276] Walden String Quartet
- Yaddo D-18-20; 78; 3 discs; rel
1940
- Yaddo II-5; 78; 3 discs; rel 1940

Quiet Design
[6277] Mason, Marilyn (org)
- Remington 199-173; 33m; rel
1954; del 1956

Sing unto the Lord a New Song (1952)
[6278] Mid-America Chorale; Dexter, John
(cond)
- CRI-191; 33m/s; rel 1964/?; cip

Sonata-Fantasia
[6279] Davine, Robert (acc)
- Crystal S-106; 33s; rel 1979; cip

LOEB, David J. (1939-)

Quartet, Strings, No 4 (1972)
[6280] Primavera String Quartet
- Grenadilla GS-1023; 33s; rel
1979; cip

Quartet, Strings, No 8 (1974)
[6281] Primavera String Quartet
- Grenadilla GS-1023; 33s; rel
1979; cip

LOEFFLER, Charles Martin (1861-1935)

Adieu pour jamais (Op 10, No 2) (arr for vln and pf by Jacques Gordon)
[6282] Gordon, Jacques (vln); Deis, Carl
(pf)
- Schirmer 2533 (in set 10); 78;
rel pre-1942

Dream within a Dream, A
[6283] Hanks, John Kennedy (ten);
Friedberg, Ruth (pf)
- Duke University Press
DWR-6417-18; 33m; 2 discs; rel
1966; del 1975

(Five) Irish Fantasies (1935)
[6284] Farrell, Eileen (sop); CBS
Symphony Orchestra; Herrmann,
Bernard (cond)
Rec 11/28/45
- Rockhill; 78; 4 discs

Memories of My Childhood (1925)
[6285] Eastman-Rochester Symphony
Orchestra; Hanson, Howard
(cond)
Rec 10/28/54
- Mercury MG-40012; 33m; rel
1955; del 1957
- Mercury MG-50085; 33m; rel
1957; del 1969
- Mercury SRI-75090; 33s; rel
1976*

Music for Four Stringed Instruments (1917)
[6286] Coolidge String Quartet
- Victor 15349-51 (in set M-543);
78; 3 discs; rel pre-1942

[6287] Kohon Quartet
- Vox SVBX-5301; 33s; 3 discs; rel
1971; cip

Pagan Poem, A (Op 14) (1906)
[6288] Gedney, Irene (pf); Swingley,
Richard (E hn);
Eastman-Rochester Symphony
Orchestra; Hanson, Howard
(cond)
- Victor 18479-81 (in set M-876);
78; 3 discs; rel pre-1942

[6289] Hunter, Robert (pf); Kosinski,
William (E hn); Leopold Stokowski
and his Orchestra; Stokowski,
Leopold (cond)
- Capitol PAO-8433; 33m; rel
1958; del 1959
- Capitol P-8433/SP-8433;
33m/s; rel 1960; del 1963
- Seraphim S-60080; 33s; rel
1968; cip

Pagan Poem, A (Op 14) (1906)
(cont'd)
[6290] piano; English horn; Paris
Philharmonic Orchestra;
Rosenthal, Manuel (cond)
- Capitol P-8188; 33m; rel 1953;
del 1959
- Capitol CTL-7033; 33m; rel
pre-1956

Partita, Violin and Piano (1930)
[6291] Gordon, Jacques (vln); Pattison,
Lee (pf)
- Columbia 68820-23D (in set
M-275); 78; 4 discs; rel
pre-1948

Peacocks (Op 10, No 4) (arr for vln and pf by Jacques Gordon)
[6292] Gordon, Jacques (vln); Pattison,
Lee (pf)
- Columbia 68820-23D (in set
M-275); 78; 4 discs; rel
pre-1948

Poem (1901, rev 1918)
[6293] Eastman-Rochester Symphony
Orchestra; Hanson, Howard
(cond)
Rec 10/28/54
- Mercury MG-40012; 33m; rel
1955; del 1957
- Mercury MG-50085; 33m; rel
1957; del 1969
- Mercury SRI-75090; 33s; rel
1976*

Quintet, Strings (1894)
[6294] Gordon String Quartet; Rickert, Kay
(vln)
- Schirmer 2534-35 (in set 13);
78; 2 discs; rel pre-1942

(Two) Rhapsodies (1905)
[6295] Gomberg, Harold (ob); Katims,
Milton (vla); Mitropoulos, Dimitri
(pf)
- Columbia ML-5603; 33m; rel
1961; del 1965

[6296] La Bate, Bruno (ob); Gordon,
Jacques (vla); Boynet, Emma (pf)
- Schirmer 2531-33 (in set 10);
78; 3 discs; rel pre-1942

[6297] Mack, John (ob); Skernick,
Abraham (vla); Podis, Eunice (pf)
- Advent S-5017; 33s; rel 1976;
cip

[6298] Sprenkle, Robert (ob); Tursi,
Francis (vla); Basile, Armand (pf)
Rec 5/58
- Mercury MG-50277/SR-90277;
33m/s; rel 1961; del 1964
- Eastman-Rochester Archives
ERA-1011; 33s; rel 1978; cip

songs
[6299] Mock, Alice (sop); Boyes, Shibley
(pf)
- Claremont 1206; 33m; rel
1952; del 1965

LOGAN, Wendell (1940-)
Duo Exchanges (1978)
[6300] McDonald, Lawrence (cl); Rosen,
Michael (perc)
Rec 5/6/79
- Orion ORS-80373; 33s; rel
1980; cip

(Five) Pieces, Piano (1977)
[6301] Walker, Frances (pf)
Rec 3/23/79
- Orion ORS-80373; 33s; rel
1980; cip

**(Three) Pieces, Violin and Electric
Piano (1977)**
[6302] Young, Richard (vln); Margolis,
Sanford (elec pf)
- Orion ORS-80373; 33s; rel
1980; cip

**Proportions for Nine Players
(1968)**
[6303] Willoughby, Robert (fl); McDonald,
Lawrence (cl); Young, Gene (tpt);
Roosa, James (tbn); Cooper,
Dianne (vln); Henderson, Aaron
(vcl); Price, Wilbur (pf); Rosen,
Michael (perc); Whatley, Andre
(perc); Moore, Kenneth (cond)
Rec 1/30/79
- Orion ORS-80373; 33s; rel
1980; cip

Songs of our Time
[6304] Ball State University Choir and
Instrumental Ensemble; Corwin,
George (cond)
- Golden Crest CRS-4087; 33s; rel
1970; cip

LOMBARDO, Robert (1932-)
Largo, String Quartet (1969)
[6305] American Chamber Virtuosi
- Crystal S-861; 33s; rel 1973; cip

Nocturne (1966)
[6306] Turetzky, Bertram (cb)
- Ars Nova/Ars Antiqua AN-1001;
33s; rel 1969; del 1973

LONDON, Edwin (1929-)
Better Is (1974)
[6307] Smith College Chamber Singers;
Hiatt, Iva Dee (cond)
- Ubres CS-302; 33s; rel 1979;
cip

Day of Desolation (1970)
[6308] University of Connecticut Concert
Choir; Poellein, John (cond)
- Ubres CS-302; 33s; rel 1979;
cip

Dream Thing on Biblical Episodes
[6309] Smith College Chamber Singers;
London, Edwin (cond)
- Ubres CS-302; 33s; rel 1979;
cip

Portraits of Three American Ladies
[6310] Coles, Marilyn (sop); MacDonald,
Royal (nar); University of Illinois
Contemporary Chamber
Ensemble; London, Edwin (cond)
- Acoustic Research AR-0654.085;
33s; rel 1971

Psalm of These Days III
[6311] University of Illinois Contemporary
Chamber Players; London, Edwin
(cond)
- CRI-405; 33s; rel 1979; cip

Sacred Hair (1973)
[6312] University of Illinois Concert Choir;
Decker, Harold (cond)
- Ubres CS-302; 33s; rel 1979;
cip

Sonatina, Viola and Piano
[6313] Wallfisch, Ernst (vla); Wallfisch,
Lory (pf)
- Advance FGR-7; 33m; rel 1969;
cip

**Trio, Flute, Clarinet, and Piano
(With ad lib Improvisation by
Other Instruments) (1956)**
[6314] Zonn, Paul (cl); Zonn, Wilma (ob);
University of Illinois
Contemporary Chamber Players
(members of)
- Ubres CS-301; 33s; rel 1976;
cip

LOPATNIKOFF, Nikolai (1903-76)
**Concertino, Orchestra (Op 30)
(1944)**
[6315] Columbia Symphony Orchestra;
Bernstein, Leonard (cond)
- Columbia ML-4996; 33m; rel
1955; del 1966

**Divertimento, Orchestra (Op 34)
(1951)**
[6316] La Jolla Musical Arts Festival
Orchestra; Sokoloff, Nikolai
(cond)
- Concert Hall CHG-4; 33m; rel
1953*

**Music for Orchestra (Op 39)
(1958)**
[6317] Louisville Orchestra; Whitney,
Robert (cond)
- LOU-59-6; 33m (Louisville
Orchestra First Edition Records
1959 No 6); rel 1960; del 1978

**Sonata, Violin and Piano, No 2 (Op
32) (1948)**
[6318] Fuchs, Joseph (vln); Balsam, Artur
(pf)
- Decca DL-9541; 33m; rel 1951;
del 1960

**Variations and Epilogue (Op 31)
(1946)**
[6319] Graudan, Nikolai (vcl); Graudan,
Joanna (pf)
- Columbia ML-4990; 33m; rel
1955; del 1965
- Orion ORS-73120; 33s; rel
1973; cip

**Variazioni concertanti (Op 38)
(1958)**
[6320] Louisville Orchestra; Whitney,
Robert (cond)
- LOU-65-4/LS-65-4; 33m/s
(Louisville Orchestra First Edition
Records 1965 No 4); rel 1965;
cip

Vocalise in modo russo (1952)
[6321] South Hills High School Chorus;
Crawford (cond)
- ASCAP CB-161; 33m (Pittsburgh
International Contemporary Music
Festival); rel pre-1956

LO PRESTI, Ronald (1933-)
Masks, The (1955)
[6322] Eastman-Rochester Symphony
Orchestra; Hanson, Howard
(cond)
- Mercury MG-50106; 33m; rel
1956; del 1964

Sketch (1956)
[6323] Manhattan Percussion Ensemble;
Price, Paul (cond)
- Urania UX-134; 33m; rel 1959;
del 1969
- Urania USD-1034; 33s; rel
1959; del 1960
- Urania US-5134; 33s; rel 1961;
del 1972

Suite, Eight Horns (1952)
[6324] Horn Club of Los Angeles
- Capitol P-8525/SP-8525;
33m/s; rel 1960; del 1963
- Seraphim S-60095; 33s; rel
1969; del 1973

LORA, Antonio John
(1899-1965)
**Concerto, Piano and Orchestra
(1948)**
[6325] Wollmann, Eva (pf); Vienna
Orchestra; Adler, F. Charles
(cond)
- CRI-113; 33m; rel 1957; cip

LOUGHBOROUGH, William
For the Big Horn (1957)
[6326] Electronic music
- Folkways 6301; 33s; rel 1969;
cip

LUCIER, Alvin (1931-)

North American Time Capsule 1967

[6327] Brandeis University Chamber Chorus; electronic music; Lucier, Alvin (cond)
- Odyssey 32-16-0155/32-16-0156; 33m/s; rel 1967; cip

Vespers (1967)

[6328] Electronic music
- Mainstream MS-5010; 33s; rel 1972; del 1979

LUENING, Otto (1900-)

Divine Image, The (1949)

[6329] Miller, Mildred (m sop); Biltcliffe, Edwin (pf)
- St/And SPL-411-12; 33m; 2 discs; rel 1963; del 1964
- Desto D-411-12/DST-6411-12; 33m/s; 2 discs; rel 1964; cip

Fantasia, Organ (1929)

[6330] Kneeream, Ralph (org)
- CRI-219; 33s; rel 1968; cip

Fantasy in Space (1952)

[6331] Electronic music
- Innovations GB-1; 33m; 10''; rel 1955*
- Folkways FX-6160; 33m; rel 1958; cip
- Desto DC-6466; 33s; rel 1968; cip

Fugue and Chorale Fantasy (1971)

[6332] Wyton, Alec (org); tape
Rec 11/4/74
- CRI-334; 33s; rel 1975; cip

Gargoyles (1960)

[6333] Pollikoff, Max (vln); tape
- Columbia ML-5966/MS-6566; 33m/s; rel 1964; del 1979

Impersonations (1937): Chinese Opera and Visit from S. K. (Serge Koussevitzky)

[6334] Luening, Otto
- Yaddo 115A-B; 78; 10''; rel 1937

Invention in Twelve Notes (1952)

[6335] Electronic music
- Innovations GB-1; 33m; 10''; rel 1955*
- Desto DC-6466; 33s; rel 1968; cip

(Three) Inventions, Piano (1938)

[6336] Nowak, Lionel (pf)
- Yaddo III-4; 78; 10''; rel 1940

Kentucky Rondo (1951)

[6337] Vienna Orchestra; Adler, F. Charles (cond)
- CRI-103; 33m/s; rel 1956/?; cip

Legend (1952)

[6338] Larsen, Erik (ob); Oslo Philharmonic Orchestra; Serebrier, Jose (cond)
- Desto DC-6466; 33s; rel 1968; cip

Love's Secret (1949)

[6339] Miller, Mildred (m sop); Biltcliffe, Edwin (pf)
- St/And SPL-411-12; 33m; 2 discs; rel 1963; del 1964
- Desto D-411-12/DST-6411-12; 33m/s; 2 discs; rel 1964; cip

Low Speed (1952)

[6340] Electronic music
- Innovations GB-1; 33m; 10''; rel 1955*
- Desto DC-6466; 33s; rel 1968; cip

Lyric Scene (1958)

[6341] Oien, Per (fl); Oslo Philharmonic Orchestra; Serebrier, Jose (cond)
- Desto DC-6466; 33s; rel 1968; cip

Monologue (1947)

[6342] LeRoy, Rene (fl)
- New Music Quarterly Recordings 1000C-D; 78; rel 1949

Moonflight (1969)

[6343] Luening, Otto (fl); tape
- Desto DC-6466; 33s; rel 1968; cip

Prelude and Fugue (1974)

[6344] Bennington Woodwind Trio
- Golden Crest CRS-4140; 33q; rel 1976; cip

Prelude to a Hymn Tune (1937)

[6345] Vienna Symphony Orchestra; Dixon, Dean (cond)
- American Recording Society ARS-8; 33m; rel 1953
- Desto D-429/DST-6429; 33m/s; rel 1967; cip

[6346] no performers given
- Yaddo 9B; 78; rel 1937

Preludes, Piano: Nos 2-8 (1936)

[6347] Gerschefski, Edwin (pf)
- Yaddo 26B; 78; 10''; rel 1937
- Yaddo 123A-B; 78; 10''; rel 1937

Quartet, Strings, No 2 (1923)

[6348] Sinnhoffer Quartet
- CRI-303; 33s; rel 1973; cip

Quartet, Strings, No 3 (1928)

[6349] Sinnhoffer Quartet
- CRI-303; 33s; rel 1973; cip

[6350] no performers given
- Yaddo 12A-B; 78; rel 1937

Short Sonata, Flute and Harpsichord, No 1 (1937)

[6351] Luening, Otto (fl); Kirkpatrick, Ralph (hpschd)
- Yaddo M-8; 78; 2-10''; rel 1938

Short Suite, Woodwind Trio (1974)

[6352] Bennington Woodwind Trio
- Golden Crest CRS-4140; 33q; rel 1976; cip

Sonata, Piano (In memoriam: Ferruccio Busoni) (1943)

[6353] Oppens, Ursula (pf)
Rec 11/5/72
- CRI-334; 33s; rel 1975; cip

Sonata, Violin, No 3 (1970)

[6354] Pollikoff, Max (vln)
- CRI-303; 33s; rel 1973; cip

Sonata, Violin and Piano, No 3 (1943): Andante and Variations

[6355] Gawriloff, Saschko (vln); Pietsch, K. P. (pf)
- Remington 199-211; 33m; rel 1956; del 1959

(Four) Songs (1929, 1936)

[6356] Luening, Ethel (sop); Luening, Otto (fl) (pf)
- New Music Quarterly Recordings 1211 (111-2); 78; rel 1936

Suite, Flute, No 3

[6357] Sollberger, Harvey (fl)
- CRI-400; 33s; rel 1979; cip

Suite, Flute, No 4

[6358] Sollberger, Harvey (fl)
- CRI-400; 33s; rel 1979; cip

Suite, Flute, No 5

[6359] Sollberger, Harvey (fl)
- CRI-400; 33s; rel 1979; cip

Suite, Soprano and Flute (1936-37)

[6360] Luening, Ethel (sop); Luening, Otto (fl)
- New Music Quarterly Recordings 1513; 78; rel 1939

Symphonic Fantasia I (1924)

[6361] Vienna Orchestra; Adler, F. Charles (cond)
- CRI-103; 33m/s; rel 1956/?; cip

(Two) Symphonic Interludes (1935)

[6362] Vienna Symphony Orchestra; Dixon, Dean (cond)
- American Recording Society ARS-8; 33m; rel 1953
- Desto D-429/DST-6429; 33m/s; rel 1967; cip

Synthesis (1962)
[6363] Hessian Radio Symphony
Orchestra; tape; Van Vactor,
David (cond)
- CRI-219; 33s; rel 1968; cip

**Theater Piece No 2 (1956): In the
Beginning**
[6364] Electronic music
- CRI-268; 33s; 2 discs; rel 1972;
cip

**Trio, Flute, Violoncello, and Piano
(1962)**
[6365] Sollberger, Harvey (fl); Sherry, Fred
(vcl); Wuorinen, Charles (pf)
- CRI-303; 33s; rel 1973; cip

**LUENING, Otto and
USSACHEVSKY, Vladimir
(1911-)**
**Concerted Piece for Tape and
Orchestra (1960)**
[6366] Oslo Philharmonic Orchestra; tape;
Serebrier, Jose (cond)
- CRI-227; 33s; rel 1968; cip

Incantation (1953)
[6367] Electronic music
- Innovations GB-1; 33m; 10''; rel
1955*
- Desto DC-6466; 33s; rel 1968;
cip

**King Lear (Incidental Music) (Suite)
(1956)**
[6368] Electronic music
- CRI-112; 33m/s; rel 1957/?; cip

Poem in Cycles and Bells, A (1954)
[6369] Royal Danish Radio Orchestra;
tape; Luening, Otto (cond)
- CRI-112; 33m/s; rel 1957/?; cip

Rhapsodic Variations (1953-54)
[6370] Louisville Orchestra; tape; Whitney,
Robert (cond)
- LOU-545-5; 33m (Louisville
Orchestra First Edition Records
1955 No 5); rel 1959; del 1978

LUKE, Ray (1928-)
**Concerto, Bassoon and Orchestra
(1965)**
[6371] Sharrow, Leonard (bsn); Crystal
Chamber Orchestra; Gold, Ernest
(cond)
Rec 9/13-15/76
- Crystal S-852; 33s; rel 1977; cip

Symphony No 2
[6372] Louisville Orchestra; Whitney,
Robert (cond)
- LOU-63-4/LS-63-4; 33m/s
(Louisville Orchestra First Edition
Records 1963 No 4); rel
1963/1965; cip

LUNDBORG, Charles Erik (1948-)
**Music Forever No 2 (1972):
Excerpts**
[6373] Light Fantastic Players; Shulman,
Daniel (cond)
Rec 6/7/73
- CRI-350; 33s; rel 1976; cip

Passacaglia (1974)
[6374] Light Fantastic Players; Shulman,
Daniel (cond)
Rec 9/24/75
- CRI-350; 33s; rel 1976; cip

Soundsoup
[6375] Parnassus; Korf, Anthony (cond)
- New World NW-306; 33s; rel
1980

LUNDE, Lawson (1935-)
Sonata, Alto Saxophone and Piano
[6376] Jackson, Reginald (sax); Mainous,
Jean Harris (pf)
- Musical Heritage Society
MHS-3623; 33s; rel 1977

[6377] Leeson, Cecil (al sax); Kohler, Jean
(pf)
- Enchante ENS-2003; 33s; rel
1970; del 1978

LYBBERT, Donald (1923-81)
Lines for the Fallen (1967)
[6378] Bryn-Julson, Phyllis (sop);
Pappastavrou, George C. (pf);
Lanning, Stuart Warren (pf)
- Odyssey
32-16-0161/32-16-0162;
33m/s; rel 1967; cip

Sonata brevis (1962)
[6379] Rogers, Herbert (pf)
- CRI-281; 33s; rel 1972; cip

LYON, M.
Suite, Low Brass
[6380] Atlantic Tuba Quartet
- Golden Crest CRSQ-4173; 33q;
rel 1979; cip

McAFEE, Donald (1935-)
Prayer of St. Francis, A
[6381] Singing City Choir of Philadelphia;
Brown, Elaine (cond)
- Fellowship FM-1/FS-1; 33m/s; rel
1961

McAMIS, Hugh (1899-1942)
Dreams
[6382] Barnes, William H. (org)
- H08P-0144-45 (matrix no);
33m; rel 196?

[6383] Fox, Virgil (org)
- Columbia AAL-18; 33m; 10''; rel
1952; del 1957
- Capitol P-8557/SP-8557;
33m/s; rel 1961; del 1970

McARTHUR, Edwin (1907-)
Night
[6384] Flagstad, Kirsten (sop); McArthur,
Edwin (pf)
- RCA LM-1870; 33m; rel 1955;
del 1960

We Have Turned Again Home
[6385] Flagstad, Kirsten (sop); McArthur,
Edwin (pf)
- Victor 49-4082-85 (in set
WDM-1738); 45; 4-7''; rel 1953
- RCA LM-1738; 33m; rel 1953;
del 1957

McBETH, W. Francis (1933-)
Chant and Jubilo (1962)
[6386] Ohio State University Concert
Band; McGinnis, Donald E. (cond)
- Coronet S-1502; 33s; rel 1969;
del 1978

**(Four) Frescoes for Five Brass
(1969)**
[6387] Annapolis Brass Quintet
- Crystal S-206; 33s; rel 1977; cip

Suite, Band, No 2
[6388] University of Maryland Symphony
Band; Ostling, Acton, Jr. (cond)
- Coronet S-1411; 33s; rel 1969;
del 1978

McBRIDE, Robert (1911-)
Aria and Toccata in Swing
[6389] Kaufman, Louis (vln); Kaufman,
Annette (pf)
- Vox 627; 78; 3 discs; rel 1948
- Concert Hall CHC-58; 33m; rel
1950; del 1957
- Concert Hall CHS-1140; 33m; rel
1952; del 1957
- Concert Hall H-1640; 33m; rel
1957; del 1959

**Concerto, Violin and Orchestra
(1954)**
[6390] Wilk, Maurice (vln); Vienna
Symphony Orchestra; Hendl,
Walter (cond)
- American Recording Society
ARS-27; 33m; 10''; rel 1953
- American Recording Society
ARS-116; 33m; rel 1953
- Desto D-417/DST-6417; 33m/s;
rel 1965; cip

Farm Stories
[6391] no performers given
- Yaddo 122B; 78; 10''; rel 1937

**Fugato on a Well Known Theme
(1935)**
[6392] Boston Pops Orchestra; Fiedler,
Arthur (cond)
- Victor 4378; 78; 10''; rel
pre-1942

Jingle-Jangle
[6393] White, Lawrence (vib); Boston Pops
Orchestra; Fiedler, Arthur (cond)
- Victor 12597; 78; rel pre-1942

Let Down
[6394] McBride, Robert (E hn); Creston,
Paul (pf)
- New Music Quarterly Recordings
1314; 78; rel 1937

[6395] McBride, Robert (E hn); Tucker,
Gregory (pf)
- Yaddo 42B; 78; 10"; rel 1937

Lonely Landscape
[6396] Leeds Concert Band; Todd, Peter
(cond)
- Columbia ML-4254; 33m; rel
1950; del 1956

March of the Be-Bops (1948)
[6397] Polish National Radio Orchestra;
Szostak, Zdzislav (cond)
- CRI-228; 33s; rel 1968; cip

Mexican Rhapsody (1935)
[6398] Boston Pops Orchestra; Fiedler,
Arthur (cond)
- Victor 13825 (in set M-554);
78; rel pre-1942
- Gramophone EB-196; 78; rel
1942

[6399] Eastman-Rochester Symphony
Orchestra; Hanson, Howard
(cond)
Rec 10/28/56
- Mercury MG-50134/SR-90134;
33m/s; rel 1957/1959; del
1963
- Mercury MG-50166; 33m; rel
1958; del 1963
- Eastman-Rochester Archives
ERA-1012; 33s; rel 197?

Panorama of Mexico (1960)
[6400] Polish National Radio Orchestra;
Szostak, Zdzislav (cond)
- CRI-228; 33s; rel 1968; cip

**Pumpkin Eaters Little Fugue
(1952)**
[6401] New Symphony Orchestra;
Camarata, Salvador (cond)
- London LLP-1213; 33m; rel
1955; del 1957
- CRI-119; 33m; rel 1957; cip

**Punch and the Judy (1941):
Excerpts**
[6402] Vienna Orchestra; Adler, F. Charles
(cond)
- CRI-107; 33m/s; rel 1957/?; cip

Quintet, Oboe and Strings (1937)
[6403] McBride, Robert (ob); Coolidge
String Quartet
- Victor 2159; 78; 10"; rel
pre-1942

Quintet, Oboe and Strings (1937)
(cont'd)
[6404] McBride, Robert (ob); Yaddo String
Quartet
- Yaddo 23B; 78; rel 1937
- Yaddo 38A; 78; rel 1937

[6405] Schuster, Earl (ob); Classic Quartet
- Classic Editions CE-1030; 33m;
rel 1957; del 1959

Swing Stuff
[6406] McBride, Robert (cl); Boston Pops
Orchestra; Fiedler, Arthur (cond)
- Victor 12597; 78; rel pre-1942

**Swing Stuff (clarinet and piano
version)**
[6407] clarinet; piano
- Yaddo 42A; 78; rel 1937

Warm-Up
[6408] McBride, Robert (E hn)
- New Music Quarterly Recordings
1314; 78; rel 1937

Way Out, But Not Too Far (1970)
[6409] Droste, Paul (euph); Droste, A. (pf)
- Coronet LPS-3026; 33s; rel
1977; cip

Wise-Apple Five
[6410] McBride, Robert (cl); Porter, Lois
(vln); Harper, Claire (vln); Porter,
Quincy (vla); Bodenhorn, Aaron
(vcl)
- Yaddo IV-6; 78; rel 1940

**Workout (chamber-orchestra
version) (1936)**
[6411] New Symphony Chamber
Orchestra; Camarata, Salvador
(cond)
- London LLP-1213; 33m; rel
1955; del 1957
- CRI-119; 33m; rel 1957; cip

[6412] Yaddo Orchestra
- Yaddo 31; 78; rel 1937 (1st and
3rd movements)
- Yaddo 15B; 78; 10"; rel 1937
(2nd movement)

McCARTY, Patrick (1928-)
Sonata, Bass Trombone and Piano
[6413] Reynolds, Jeffrey (b tbn); Carno,
Zita (pf)
- Crystal S-383; 33s; rel 1979; cip

McCLELLAN, Randall (1938-)
Distant Voices (1971)
[6414] Electronic music
- Opus One 17; 33s; rel 1975; cip

Genesis (1974)
[6415] Electronic music
- Opus One 24; 33s; rel 1975; cip

Interruptions (1971)
[6416] Electronic music
- Opus One 24; 33s; rel 1975; cip

**Tortoise Journies: Music of the
Spheres and Processional**
[6417] Electronic music
- CRI-382; 33s; rel 1978; cip

McDONALD, Harl (1899-1955)
**Builders of America (Washington
and Lincoln)**
[6418] Rains, Claude (nar); Columbia
Chamber Orchestra and Chorus;
McDonald, Harl (cond)
- Columbia ML-2220; 33m; 10";
rel 1954; del 1956

**Children's Symphony on Familiar
Themes (1948)**
[6419] Philadelphia Orchestra; McDonald,
Harl (cond)
- Columbia MX-348; 78; rel
pre-1952
- Columbia ML-2141; 33m; 10";
rel 1950; del 1956
- Columbia ML-2220; 33m; 10";
rel 1954; del 1956

**Concerto, Two Pianos and
Orchestra (1936)**
[6420] Behrend, Jeanne (pf); Kelberine,
Alexander (pf); Philadelphia
Orchestra; Stokowski, Leopold
(cond)
- Victor 15410-12 (in set M-557);
78; 3 discs; rel pre-1942
- Gramophone ED-84-86; 78; 3
discs; rel pre-1952

**Festival of the Workers (1932):
Dance of the Workers**
[6421] Philadelphia Orchestra; Stokowski,
Leopold (cond)
- Victor 8919; 78; rel pre-1936
- Gramophone DB-2913; 78; rel
pre-1952

From Childhood (1940)
[6422] Phillips, Edna (hp); Philadelphia
Orchestra; McDonald, Harl (cond)
- Victor 18256-58 (in set M-839);
78; 3 discs; rel pre-1942
- Gramophone ED-313-15; 78; 3
discs; rel pre-1952

[6423] Stockton, Ann Mason (hp); Concert
Arts Orchestra; Slatkin, Felix
(cond)
- Capitol P-8255; 33m; rel 1954;
del 1959
- Capitol CTL-7057; 33m; rel
pre-1956
- Avant AV-1017; 33s; rel 1977;
cip

**Legend of the Arkansas Traveler,
The (1939)**
[6424] Philadelphia Orchestra; Ormandy,
Eugene (cond)
- Victor 18069; 78; rel pre-1942

Legend of the Arkansas Traveler, The (1939) *(cont'd)*
- Victor 18395 (in set M-867);
  78; rel 1946
- Gramophone ED-130; 78; rel
  pre-1952
- Camden CAL-238; 33m; rel
  1956; del 1957

My Country at War (1943)
[6425] Philadelphia Orchestra; Ormandy,
  Eugene (cond)
- Columbia 12241-43 (in set
  M-592); 78; 3 discs; rel
  pre-1948

(Two) Nocturnes (San Juan Capistrano) (1938)
[6426] Boston Symphony Orchestra;
  Koussevitzky, Serge (cond)
- Victor 17229; 78; rel pre-1942

(Three) Poems on Aramaic Themes (1935): Two Poems
[6427] Philadelphia Orchestra; Ormandy,
  Eugene (cond)
- Victor 14903; 78; rel pre-1942

Songs of Conquest (1938)
[6428] University of Pennsylvania Choral
  Society; McDonald, Harl (cond)
- Victor 18164-65 (in set M-823);
  78; 2 discs; rel pre-1942

Symphony No 1 (The Santa Fe Trail) (1932)
[6429] Philadelphia Orchestra; Ormandy,
  Eugene (cond)
- Victor 17765-67 (in set M-754);
  78; 3 discs; rel pre-1942

Symphony No 2 (The Rhumba) (1934): Rhumba
[6430] Philadelphia Orchestra; Stokowski,
  Leopold (cond)
- Victor 8919; 78; rel pre-1936
- Gramophone DB-2913; 78; rel
  pre-1952
- Camden CAL-238; 33m; rel
  1956; del 1957

Symphony No 4 (1937): Cakewalk
[6431] Philadelphia Orchestra; Ormandy,
  Eugene (cond)
- Victor 15377; 78; rel 1939*
- Gramophone DB-5777; 78; rel
  pre-1948
- Camden CAL-238; 33m; rel
  1956; del 1957

MacDOUGALL, Robert (1941-)
Anacoluthon (A Confluence) (1972)
[6432] Contemporary Music Ensemble;
  Weisberg, Arthur (cond)
  Rec 1/15/75
- CRI-323; 33s; rel 1975; cip

McGILL, Josephine (1877-1919)
Duna
[6433] Werrenrath, Reinald (bar);
  orchestra
- Victor 64863; 78; 10"; rel
  1923?
- Victor 844; 78; 10"; rel 1923?

MacGIMSEY, Robert (1898-1979)
Shadrack
[6434] Eddy, Nelson (bar); orchestra;
  Armbruster, Robert (cond)
- Columbia 4584-87M (in set
  MM-873); 78; 4-10"; rel 1950
- Columbia ML-2091; 33m; 10";
  rel 1950; del 1956

Sweet Little Jesus Boy
[6435] De Paur Infantry Chorus; De Paur,
  Leonard (cond)
- Columbia ML-2119; 33m; 10";
  rel 1950; del 1956

Thunderin' Wonderin'
[6436] Pinza, Ezio (b); King, Gibner (pf)
- Columbia 17383; 78; 10"

[6437] Symonette, Randolph (b bar);
  Harnley, Lesley (pf)
- Colosseum CLPS-1008; 33m; rel
  1951; del 1958

Tower of Babel
[6438] Eddy, Nelson (bar); orchestra;
  Armbruster, Robert (cond)
- Columbia 4584-87M (in set
  MM-873); 78; 4-10"; rel 1950
- Columbia ML-2091; 33m; 10";
  rel 1950; del 1956

McGRATH, Joseph J. (1889-1968)
Adoration
[6439] Courboin, Charles (org)
- Victor 11-9402-04 (in set
  M-1091); 78; 3 discs; rel 1947

(Six) Brevities (Op 81)
[6440] New York Brass Quintet
- Desto D-401/DST-6401; 33m/s;
  rel 1964; cip

MacINNIS, Donald (1923-)
Collide-a-Scope (1971)
[6441] Georgia State College Brass
  Ensemble; tape; Hill, William H.
  (cond)
- Golden Crest CRS-4085; 33s; rel
  1969; cip

Variations, Brass and Percussion
[6442] Georgia State College Brass
  Ensemble; Hill, William H. (cond)
- Golden Crest CRS-4084; 33s; rel
  1969; cip

MacKAY, Eugene
Ballads, Piano
[6443] Gerschefski, Edwin (pf)
- Yaddo 112A-B; 78; 10"; rel
  1937

McKAY, George F. (1899-1970)
Dance Pastorale
[6444] Bennett, Bob L. (pf)
- Educo 3109; 33

McKAY, Neil (1924-)
Larghetto
[6445] Eastman-Rochester Symphony
  Orchestra; Hanson, Howard
  (cond)
  Rec 1958
- Mercury MG-50053/SR-90053;
  33m/s; rel 1959; del 1964
- Eastman-Rochester Archives
  ERA-1003; 33s; rel 1974; cip

McKENZIE, Jack H. (1930-)
(Three) Dances
[6446] Percussion Ensemble; Kraus, Paul
  (cond)
- Golden Crest
  CR-4004/CRS-4004; 33m/s; rel
  1957/1979; cip

Introduction and Allegro (1951)
[6447] American Percussion Society; Price,
  Paul (cond)
- Urania UX-106; 33m; rel 1957;
  del 1969
- Urania USD-1007; 33s; rel
  1958; del 1960
- Urania US-5106; 33s; rel 1961;
  del 1970

[6448] University of Illinois Percussion
  Ensemble; Price, Paul (cond)
- Illini Union Bookstore CRS-3;
  33m; rel 1955*

Nonet
[6449] Percussion Ensemble; Kraus, Paul
  (cond)
- Golden Crest
  CR-4004/CRS-4004; 33m/s; rel
  1957/1979; cip

Rites (1957)
[6450] University of Illinois Percussion
  Ensemble; McKenzie, Jack (cond)
- Illini Union Bookstore CRS-6;
  33m; rel 1960*

McKINLEY, Carl (1895-1966)
(Ten) Hymn Tune Fantasies: The King of Love My Shepherd Is
[6451] Titus, Parvin (org)
- Chime 1003; 33m; rel 1958; del
  1962

McKINLEY, William T. (1939-)

Paintings No 2 (1975)
[6452] New England Conservatory
Contemporary Ensemble;
Schuller, Gunther (cond)
- Golden Crest NEC-119; 33s; rel
1979; cip

McKUEN, Rod (1933-)

City, The (Op 42)
[6453] Seibel, Paula (sop); McKuen, Rod
(nar); Louisville Orchestra;
Mester, Jorge (cond)
- LS-73-2; 33s (Louisville
Orchestra First Edition Records
1973 No 2); rel 1974; cip
- Stanyan SR-9021; 33s; rel 1976
(Excerpt: Night)

Concerto, Balloon and Orchestra
[6454] Hymas, Tony (syn); National
Philharmonic Orchestra;
Greenslade, Arthur (cond)
- Stanyan SR-9023; 33s; rel 1977

Concerto, Guitar and Orchestra, No 2
[6455] Marias, Juan (gtr); Symphonie de
Madrid; Greenslade, Arthur (cond)
- Stanyan SR-9006; 33s; rel
1971; cip

Concerto, Four Harpsichords and Orchestra, No 1
[6456] London Arts Orchestra; Greenslade,
Arthur (cond)
- Stanyan 10009; 33s; rel 1971;
del 1976
- Stanyan SR-9001; 33s; rel
1972; del 1976
- Stanyan SR-9007; 33s; rel
1977; cip

Concerto, Piano and Orchestra, No 3
[6457] Pearson, Leslie (pf); Westminster
Philharmonic Orchestra;
Greenslade, Arthur (cond)
- Stanyan SR-9012; 33s; rel
1973; cip

Concerto, Violoncello and Orchestra
[6458] Harvey, Keith (vcl); National
Philharmonic Orchestra;
Standford, Patric (cond)
Rec 1973-76
- Stanyan SR-9021; 33s; rel 1976

Flower Suite, The: Fiore Serenade
[6459] Stanyan Strings; Byers, Billy (cond)
Rec 1973-76
- Stanyan SR-9021; 33s; rel 1976

I Hear America Singing (Op 43)
[6460] Seibel, Paula (sop); McKuen, Rod
(nar); Louisville Orchestra;
Mester, Jorge (cond)
- LS-73-2; 33s (Louisville
Orchestra First Edition Records
1973 No 2); rel 1974; cip

(Five) Pieces, Orchestra
[6461] London Arts Orchestra; Greenslade,
Arthur (cond)
- Stanyan SR-9006; 33s; rel
1971; cip

Plains of My Country, The (arr by Dick Walter)
[6462] Westminster Symphony Orchestra;
Greenslade, Arthur (cond)
- Stanyan SR-9015; 33s; rel
1975; cip

Rigadoon and Serenade
[6463] Westminster Symphony Orchestra
(strings); Greenslade, Arthur
(cond)
Rec 1973-76
- Stanyan SR-9021; 33s; rel 1976

Seascapes (arr by Reg Guest)
[6464] Redwine, Skip (pf); Hollywood Wind
Ensemble
- Stanyan SR-9015; 33s; rel
1975; cip

(Four) Statements from Three Books
[6465] London Arts Orchestra; Greenslade,
Arthur (cond)
- Stanyan 10009; 33s; rel 1971;
del 1976

Symphony No 1 (All Men Love Something)
[6466] Westminster Symphony Orchestra;
Greenslade, Arthur (cond)
- Stanyan SR-9005; 33s; rel
1971; cip

McLEAN, Barton (1938-)

Dimensions I
[6467] Clapp, Stephen (vln); tape
- Advance FGR-25S; 33s; rel
1979; cip

Dimensions II (1974)
[6468] Burge, David (pf); tape
- CRI-407; 33s; rel 1979; cip

[6469] Hamilton, Robert (pf); tape
- Orion ORS-75192; 33s; rel
1975; cip

Genesis
[6470] McLean, Barton (syn)
- Orion ORS-75192; 33s; rel
1975; cip

Song of the Nahuatl
[6471] Electronic music
- Folkways FTS-33450; 33s; rel
1979; cip

Sorcerer Revisited, The
[6472] McLean, Barton (syn)
- Orion ORS-75192; 33s; rel
1975; cip

Spirals (1973)
[6473] Electronic music
- CRI-335; 33s; rel 1975; cip

McLEAN, Priscilla (1942-)

Dance of Dawn (1974)
[6474] Electronic music
- CRI-335; 33s; rel 1975; cip

Interplanes (1970)
[6475] Hamilton, Robert (pf); Douberteen,
Christine (pf)
- Advance FGR-19S; 33s; rel
1976; cip

Invisible Chariots
[6476] Electronic music
- Folkways FTS-33450; 33s; rel
1979; cip

Variations and Mozaics on a Theme of Stravinsky (1975)
[6477] Louisville Orchestra; Mester, Jorge
(cond)
Rec 3/24/77
- LS-76-2; 33s (Louisville
Orchestra First Edition Records
1976 No 2); rel 1979; cip

McLIN, Lena Johnson

Glory, Glory, Hallelujah
[6478] Virginia Union University Choir;
Hobbs, Odell (cond)
- Richmond Sound Stages
RSSWO-626; 33

Sanctus
[6479] Virginia Union University Choir;
Hobbs, Odell (cond)
- Gerald Lewis Recording
MC-8806; 33

McMILLAN, Ann (1923-)

Amber '75
[6480] Electronic music
- Folkways FTS-33451; 33s; rel
1980; cip

Carrefours (1971)
[6481] Electronic music
- Folkways FTS-33904; 33s; rel
1976; cip

Episode
[6482] Electronic music
- Folkways FTS-33451; 33s; rel
1980; cip

Gateway Summer Sound
[6483] Electronic music
- Folkways FTS-33451; 33s; rel
1980; cip

Gong Song (1969)
[6484] Electronic music
- Folkways FTS-33451; 33s; rel
1980; cip

Syrinx
[6485] Electronic music
- Folkways FTS-33451; 33s; rel 1980; cip

Whale I
[6486] Electronic music
- Folkways FTS-33904; 33s; rel 1976; cip

McPHEE, Colin (1900-64)
Balinese Transcriptions: Pemungkah, Rebong, Gambangan, Lagu delem, Tabu teloe, Lagu arja, Kambing slem
[6487] McPhee, Colin (pf); Britten, Benjamin (pf); Barrere, Georges (fl)
- Schirmer 17; 78; rel 1941

Balinese Transcriptions: Lagu delem
[6488] Marlowe, Sylvia (hpschd)
- Decca DL-10001/DL-710001; 33m/s; rel 1959; del 1972

Concerto, Piano and Wind Octet (1928)
[6489] Johannesen, Grant (pf); wind octet; Surinach, Carlos (cond)
- Columbia ML-5105; 33m; rel 1956; del 1970
- CRI-315; 33s; rel 1974; cip

Nocturne (1958)
[6490] Hessian Radio Symphony Orchestra; Van Vactor, David (cond)
- CRI-219; 33s; rel 1968; cip

Symphony No 2 (Pastoral) (1958)
[6491] Louisville Orchestra; Whitney, Robert (cond)
- LOU-59-2; 33m (Louisville Orchestra First Edition Records 1959 No 2); rel 1960; cip

Tabuh-Tabuhan (1936)
[6492] Eastman-Rochester Symphony Orchestra; Hanson, Howard (cond)
Rec 1/22/56
- Mercury MG-50103/SR-90103; 33m/s; rel 1956/1959; del 1964
- Mercury SRI-75116; 33s; rel 1980; cip

MADDEN, Edward (1877-1952)
Symphonic Variations on a Theme by Purcell
[6493] Cornell University Wind Ensemble; Stith, Marice (cond)
- Cornell CUWE-7; 33s; rel 1971; cip

MADER, Clarence (1904-71)
Prelude, Tune, and a Masquerade
[6494] Calligaris, Sergio (pf)
- Orion ORS-7142; 33s; rel 1971; cip

MADISON, Carolyn
(Two) Pieces (1966)
[6495] Gregg Smith Singers; Smith, Gregg (cond)
- Vox SVBX-5354; 33s; 3 discs; rel 1979

MAILMAN, Martin (1932-)
Autumn Landscape (1954)
[6496] Eastman-Rochester Symphony Orchestra; Hanson, Howard (cond)
Rec 1958
- Mercury MG-50053/SR-90053; 33m/s; rel 1959; del 1964
- Mercury MG-50337/SR-90337; 33m/s; rel 1963; del 1967
- Eastman-Rochester Archives ERA-1003; 33s; rel 1974; cip

Decorations (Music for a Celebration) (Op 54)
[6497] Capital University Symphonic Wind Ensemble; Suddendorf, Richard J. (cond)
- Golden Crest ATH-5056; 33s; rel 1979; cip

Geometrics No 1 (1961)
[6498] Capital University Symphonic Wind Ensemble; Suddendorf, Richard J. (cond)
- Golden Crest ATH-5056; 33s; rel 1979; cip

Geometrics No 2 (1962)
[6499] University of Kentucky Symphonic Band; Miller, Phillip (cond)
- Coronet M-1260; 33m; rel 1969; del 1978

Geometrics No 4 (1968)
[6500] Capital University Symphonic Wind Ensemble; Suddendorf, Richard J. (cond)
- Golden Crest ATH-5056; 33s; rel 1979; cip

Liturgical Music (1964)
[6501] Ohio State University Concert Band; Suddendorf, Richard J. (cond)
- Coronet S-1403; 33s; rel 1969; del 1978

Petite Partita (1961)
[6502] Carpenter, Richard (pf)
- Educo 3103; 33

Shouts, Hymns, and Praises (1972)
[6503] Capital University Symphonic Wind Ensemble; Suddendorf, Richard J. (cond)
- Golden Crest ATH-5056; 33s; rel 1979; cip

MAIS, Chester L. (1936-)
Fantasy on Jewish Tunes
[6504] Cornell University Wind Ensemble; Stith, Marice (cond)
- Cornell CUWE-23; 33s; rel 197?

MALOTTE, Albert Hay (1895-1964)
Among the Living
[6505] Gorin, Igor (b); piano
- Victor 4554; 78; 10"; rel pre-1942

Blow Me Eyes
[6506] Lynch, Christopher (ten); Bossart, Eugene (pf)
- Columbia 7637M; 78; rel pre-1952
- Columbia 3-247; 33m; rel pre-1952

Little Song of Life, A
[6507] Thomas, John Charles (bar); Hollister, Carroll (pf)
- Victor 2054; 78; 10"; rel pre-1952

Lord's Prayer, The
[6508] Bailey, Norman (b bar); Parsons, Geoffrey (pf)
- L'Oiseau-lyre DSLO-20; 33s; rel 1977

[6509] Booth, Webster (ten); organ; piano
- Gramophone B-9201; 78; 10"; rel pre-1942

[6510] Canterbury Choir; White, Ernest (org); Marrow, Macklin (cond)
- MGM E-102; 33m; 10"; rel 1952*

[6511] Creegan, George (ten); Prosser, Carol (org)
- Crest CR-1000; 33; rel 1970

[6512] Eddy, Nelson (b)
- Columbia 70369D; 78; rel pre-1948

[6513] Fields, Gracie
- Decca F-8763; 78; rel pre-1948

[6514] Gorin, Igor (bar); orchestra; Voorhees, Donald (cond)
- Allied 2000; 33m; 10"; rel 1953; del 1957
- Allied EP-2000; 45; 7"

[6515] Lanza, Mario (ten); orchestra; Callinicos, Constantine (cond)
- RCA LM-7015; 33m; rel 1952; del 1957
- Victor ERA-51; 45; 7"

Lord's Prayer, The (cont'd)

[6516] Lawrence, Marjorie (sop); male
       quartet
       - Columbia 72090D (in set
       M-579); 78; rel pre-1948

[6517] Melton, James (ten); Victor
       Orchestra; Black, Frank (cond)
       - RCA LM-82; 33m; 10''; rel
       1951; del 1956

[6518] Milnes, Sherrill (bar); Spong, Jon
       (org)
       - RCA ARL-1-0562; 33s; rel 1975;
       del 1979

[6519] Mormon Tabernacle Choir;
       Philadelphia Orchestra; Ormandy,
       Eugene (cond)
       - Columbia ML-6235/MS-6835;
       33m/s; rel 1966; cip
       - Columbia ML-6351/MS-6951;
       33m/s; rel 1967; cip

[6520] Robert Shaw Chorale; Victor
       Orchestra; Weinrich, Carl (org);
       Shaw, Robert (cond)
       - Victor ERA-56; 45; 7''; rel 1953?

[6521] Robinson, Forbes (b); Davies,
       William (pf) or (org)
       - Musical Heritage Society
       MHS-2343; 33s; rel 1975

[6522] Shilling, Arthur; Columbus
       Boychoir; men's choir; string
       quintet; organ; Huffman, Herbert
       (cond)
       - Decca DL-8106; 33m; rel 1955;
       del 1969

[6523] Swarthout, Gladys (m sop);
       Hodges, Lester (pf)
       - Victor 16781 (in set M-679);
       78; rel pre-1942

[6524] Thibault, Conrad
       - Decca 24189; 78; 10''; rel
       pre-1948

[6525] Thomas, John Charles (b);
       Hollister, Carroll (pf)
       - Victor 1736; 78; 10''; rel
       pre-1942

[6526] Traubel, Helen (sop); Victor
       Orchestra; Black, Frank (cond)
       - Victor DM-1453; 78
       - Victor WDM-1453; 45; 7''
       - RCA LM-118; 33m; 10''; rel
       1951; del 1953
       - Camden CAL-469/CAS-469;
       33m/s; rel 1959*

[6527] U.S. Military Academy Glee Club;
       Gaillard, Cadet Frank (cond)
       - Columbia CL-6118; 33m; rel
       1950; del 1956

[6528] Victor Chorale and Orchestra;
       Shaw, Robert (cond)
       - Victor 11-9155; 78; rel
       pre-1948

[6529] Voices of Walter Schumann;
       Schumann, Walter (cond)
       - Capitol L-382; 33m; 10''; rel
       1953; del 1957

Lord's Prayer, The (cont'd)

[6530] Warenskjold, Dorothy (sop);
       Crossan, Jack (pf)
       - Capitol P-8333; 33m; rel 1956;
       del 1961

**Lord's Prayer, The (arr by Leonard
De Paur)**

[6531] De Paur Infantry Chorus; De Paur,
       Leonard (cond)
       - Columbia M-709; 78; 3 discs; rel
       pre-1948
       - Columbia 72349-51D (in set
       MM-709); 78; 3 discs; rel
       pre-1948
       - Columbia ML-4144; 33m; rel
       pre-1949; del 1958
       - Columbia CL-725; 33m; rel
       1955; del 1960

**Lord's Prayer, The (arr for chorus
and hp by K. Darby)**

[6532] Hollywood Presbyterian Church
       Choir; harp; Hirt, Charles C.
       (cond)
       - RCA LPM-1258; 33m; rel 1956;
       del 1958

Lord's Prayer, The (arr for org)

[6533] Crawford, Jesse (org)
       - Decca 24191; 78; 10''; rel
       pre-1948

My Friend

[6534] Gorin, Igor (b); piano
       - Victor 4554; 78; 10''; rel
       pre-1942

Sing a Song of Sixpence

[6535] Lynch, Christopher (ten); Bossart,
       Eugene (pf)
       - Columbia RL-3016; 33m; rel
       1952; del 1957

[6536] Thomas, John Charles (bar);
       Hollister, Carroll (pf)
       - Victor 2054; 78; 10''; rel
       pre-1952

Song of the Open Road

[6537] Gorin, Igor (b)
       - Victor 10-1179 (in set M-1125);
       78; 10''; rel pre-1948

[6538] Gorin, Igor (b); orchestra;
       Voorhees, Donald (cond)
       - Allied 2000; 33m; 10''; rel
       1953; del 1957
       - Allied EP-2000; 45; 7''

MAMLOK, Ursula (1928-)
Haiku Settings

[6539] Jubal Trio
       - Grenadilla GS-1015; 33s; rel
       1978; cip

Stray Birds (1963)

[6540] Bryn-Julson, Phyllis (sop);
       Sollberger, Harvey (fl); Sherry,
       Fred (vcl)
       - CRI-301; 33s; rel 1973; cip

Variations, Flute (1961)

[6541] Baron, Samuel (fl)
       - CRI-212; 33m/s; rel 1966/?; cip

MANN, Robert (1920-)
Tales

[6542] Lyric Trio
       - Bartok BRS-928; 33m; rel 1962;
       cip

**MANNING, Kathleen L.
(1890-1951)**
Shoes

[6543] Tatum, Nancy (sop); Parsons,
       Geoffrey (pf)
       - London OS-26053; 33s; rel
       1968; del 1971

MANZ, Paul (1919-)
Chorale Improvisations

[6544] Manz, Paul (org)
       - Concordia 79-9885-88; 33s; 4
       discs; rel 1973-74

E'en So, Lord Jesus, Quickly Come

[6545] Augustana Evangelical Lutheran
       Church Choir; Wagner, Albert
       (cond)
       - Golden Age GAR-153102; 33s;
       rel 1977?

MARDIROSIAN, Haig
Fantasia, Organ and Tape

[6546] Mardirosian, Haig (org); tape
       - Music Guild MS-877; 33s; rel
       1970; del 1971
       - Westminster WGS-8129; 33s; rel
       1971; del 1977

MAREN, Roger*
Natural Pipes

[6547] Electronic music
       - Folkways FX-6160; 33m; rel
       1958; cip

MARKAITIS, Bruno (1922-)
Community Mass (1967)

[6548] no performers given
       - Avant Garde
       AVM-102-04/AVS-102-04;
       33m/s; 3 discs; rel 1967

MARKOV, Albert
**Rhapsody No 2 (On Themes by
Gershwin)**

[6549] Markov, Albert (vln); Kaye, Milton
       (pf)
       - Musical Heritage Society
       MHS-4023; 33s; rel 1979

MARSHALL, Frank* (1883-)
Mazurka

[6550] Marshall, Frank (pf)
       - Recorded Treasures
       GCP-771B-15; 33m; rel 1972?

Suite Catalonia: Foc follets

[6551] De Larrocha, Alicia (pf)
- International Piano
Library/International Piano
Archives IPL-5005-06; 33s; 2
discs; rel 1974*

MARTIN, David L. (1926-)

Suite, Euphonium and Small Orchestra (1961) (arr for euph and pf)

[6552] Young, Raymond G. (bar hn);
Fraschillo, Tom (pf)
- Golden Crest RE-7025; 33m/s;
rel 1968/1979; cip

MARTIN, E.*

Evensong

[6553] New Symphony Orchestra; Goehr,
Walter (org) (cond)
- Victor 36338; 78; rel pre-1952
- Gramophone C-2897; 78; rel
pre-1952

MARTINO, Donald (1931-)

B,a,b,b,i,t,t (1966)

[6554] Rehfeldt, Phillip (cl)
- Advance FGR-17S; 33s; rel
1976; cip

Concerto, Wind Quintet (1964)

[6555] Contemporary Chamber Ensemble;
Weisberg, Arthur (cond)
- CRI-230; 33m/s; rel 1968; cip

Fantasy-Variations (1962)

[6556] Kobialka, Daniel (vln)
- Advance FGR-6S; 33s; rel 1970;
cip

[6557] Zukofsky, Paul (vln)
- CRI-240; 33s; rel 1969; cip

(Cinque) Frammenti (1962)

[6558] Marx, Josef (ob); Turetzky,
Bertram (cb)
- Advance FGR-1; 33m; rel 1966;
del 1972

Notturno (1973)

[6559] Speculum Musicae; Shulman,
Daniel (cond)
Rec 1974
- Nonesuch H-71300; 33s; rel
1974; cip

Paradiso Choruses (1974)

[6560] New England Conservatory Chorus;
New England Conservatory Opera
Department; children's choir;
orchestra; tape; De Varon, Lorna
Cooke (cond)
Rec 5/7/75
- Golden Crest NEC-114; 33s/q;
rel 1976; cip

(Seven) Pious Pieces (1971)

[6561] John Oliver Chorale; Oliver, John
(cond)
- New World NW-210; 33s; rel
1978

Quodlibets (1954)

[6562] Baron, Samuel (fl)
- CRI-212; 33m/s; rel 1966/?; cip

Set, A (1954)

[6563] Rehfeldt, Phillip (cl)
- Advance FGR-4; 33m; rel 1966;
cip
- Advance FGR-15S; 33s; rel
1973; cip

[6564] Webster, Michael (cl)
Rec 1974
- CRI-374; 33s; rel 1977; cip

Trio, Clarinet, Violin, and Piano (1959)

[6565] Bloom, Arthur (cl); Zukofsky, Paul
(vln); Kalish, Gilbert (pf)
- CRI-240; 33s; rel 1969; cip

Triple Concerto, Three Clarinets and Chamber Orchestra (1977)

[6566] Devendra, Anand (cl); Smylie (b cl);
Thimmig (cb cl); Group for
Contemporary Music at Columbia
University; Sollberger, Harvey
(cond)
- Nonesuch H-71372; 33s; rel
1980; cip₇

MARTIRANO, Salvatore (1927-)

Ballad (1966)

[6567] Smith, Donald (voice); chamber
ensemble; Martirano, Salvatore
(cond)
- Polydor 24.5001; 33s; rel 1970;
del 1976

Chansons innocentes (1957)

[6568] Nightbay, Candace (sop);
Marchand, Andreas (pf)
- CRI-324; 33s; rel 1975; cip

Cocktail Music (1962)

[6569] Burge, David (pf)
- Advance FGR-3; 33m; rel 1967;
cip

L's GA for Gas-Masked Politico, Helium Bomb, and Two-Channel Tape (1967-68)

[6570] Holloway, Michael (actor); Smith,
Donald (voice); chamber
ensemble; tape; Martirano,
Salvatore (cond)
- Polydor 24.5001; 33s; rel 1970;
del 1976

Mass (1952-55)

[6571] Ineluctable Modality; London, Edwin
(cond)
- New World NW-210; 33s; rel
1978

O, O, O, O, That Shakespeherian Rag (1958)

[6572] Princeton Chamber Singers;
instrumental ensemble; Hilbish,
Thomas (cond)
- CRI-164; 33m/s; rel
1963/1976; cip

Octet (1963)

[6573] chamber ensemble; Martirano,
Salvatore (cond)
- Polydor 24.5001; 33s; rel 1970;
del 1976

Underworld (1959)

[6574] actors; tenor saxophone;
contrabass; percussion; tape
- Heliodor H-25047/HS-25047;
33m/s; rel 1967; del 1970

MARVEL, Robert (1918-)

Suite, Wind Quintet and Piano: Arietta

[6575] Marvel, Robert (pf); Fredonia
Faculty Woodwind Quintet
- Fredonia State Teachers College
XTV-21902; 33m; rel 1954

MASON, Daniel Gregory (1873-1953)

Chanticleer (Op 27) (1926)

[6576] Vienna Symphony Orchestra;
Dixon, Dean (cond)
- American Recording Society
ARS-20; 33m; 10"; rel 1953
- American Recording Society
ARS-113; 33m; rel pre-1956
- Desto D-409/DST-6409; 33m/s;
rel 1965; cip

Country Pictures (Op 9)

[6577] Bennette, George (pf)
- Grenadilla GS-1026; 33s; rel
1978; cip

Country Pictures: (No 4) The Whippoorwill

[6578] Behrend, Jeanne (pf)
- Victor 17911 (in set M-764);
78; rel 1941

Pastorale (Op 8) (1909-12)

[6579] Reynolds, Richard James (cl);
Wehlan, John (vln); Gilbert, Joan
(pf)
- Musical Heritage Society
MHS-3143; 33s; rel 1975?

(Three) Pieces, Flute, Harp, and String Quartet (Op 13) (1911-12)

[6580] Wummer, John (fl); Vito, Edward
(hp); Eddy Brown Ensemble
- Royale 1867-68; 78; 2-10"; rel
pre-1943

Prelude and Fugue, Piano and Orchestra (Op 20) (1921)
[6581] Boehm-Kooper, Mary Louise (pf); Westphalian Symphony Orchestra; Landau, Siegfried (cond) Rec 5/76
- Turnabout QTVS-34665; 33q; rel 1977; cip

Quartet on Negro Themes (Op 19) (1918-19)
[6582] Coolidge String Quartet
- Victor 11-8124-26 (in set M-891); 78; 3 discs; rel pre-1942

[6583] Kohon Quartet
- Turnabout TVS-34398; 33s; rel 1971; cip
- Vox SVBX-5301; 33s; 3 discs; rel 1971; cip

Say a Little Prayer
[6584] McCormack, John (ten); Moore, Gerald (pf)
- Gramophone DA-1820; 78; 10"; rel pre-1948

Sonata, Clarinet and Piano (Op 14) (1912-15)
[6585] Reynolds, Richard James (cl); Gilbert, Joan (pf)
- Musical Heritage Society MHS-3143; 33s; rel 1975?

Whippoorwill, The (Op 9a)
[6586] Reynolds, Richard James (cl); Gilbert, Joan (pf)
- Musical Heritage Society MHS-3143; 33s; rel 1975?

MATHEWS, Max V. (1926-)
Masquerades (1963)
[6587] Electronic music
- Decca DL-710180; 33s; rel 1971; del 1973

May Carol
[6588] Electronic music
- Decca DL-9103/DL-79103; 33m/s; rel 1962

Numerology
[6589] Electronic music
- Decca DL-9103/DL-79103; 33m/s; rel 1962

Second Law, The
[6590] Electronic music
- Decca DL-9103/DL-79103; 33m/s; rel 1962

Slider (1965)
[6591] Electronic music
- Decca DL-710180; 33s; rel 1971; del 1973

Swansong (1966)
[6592] Electronic music
- Decca DL-710180; 33s; rel 1971; del 1973

MATTHEWS, Thomas (1915-)
Improvisations
[6593] Matthews, Thomas (org)
- XCTV-97395-96 (matrix no); 33m; rel 1963

Lord Is My Shepherd, The (1956)
[6594] Mormon Tabernacle Choir; Schreiner, Alexander (org); Asper, Frank (org); Condie, Richard P. (cond)
- Columbia ML-5302/MS-6019; 33m/s; rel 1958; cip

MATTHEWS, William (1950-)
Field Guide
[6595] Electronic music
- CRI-375; 33s; rel 1978; cip

Letters from Home (1973)
[6596] University of Iowa Center for New Music Ensemble; Dixon, James (cond) Rec 4/77
- CRI-375; 33s; rel 1978; cip

Sumer is icumen in - lhude sing
[6597] Polisi, Joseph (bsn)
- Crystal S-341; 33s; rel 1979; cip

MAULDIN, Michael (1947-)
Glyph
[6598] Williams, Floyd (cl); Mauldin, Michael (pf); Schulkoski, Robyn (vib)
- Opus One 52; 33s; rel 1979; cip

(Three) New Mexico Landscapes (1975)
[6599] Mauldin, Bonnie (cl); Mauldin, Michael (pf)
- Opus One 42; 33s; rel 1978; cip

Petroglyph (1978)
[6600] Chamber Orchestra of Albuquerque; Oberg, David (cond)
- Opus One 51; 33s; rel 1980

MAURY, Lowndes (1911-75)
Sonata in Memory of the Korean War Dead (1952)
[6601] Sandler, Myron (vln); Maury, Lowndes (pf)
- Crystal S-631; 33s; rel 1970; cip

MAXFIELD, Richard (1927-69)
Amazing Grace (1960)
[6602] Electronic music
- Advance FGR-8S; 33s; rel 1970; cip

Bacchanale (1963)
[6603] Electronic music
- Advance FGR-8S; 33s; rel 1970; cip

Night Music (1961-62)
[6604] Electronic music
- Odyssey 32-16-0160; 33s; rel 1967; cip

Pastoral Symphony (1959)
[6605] Electronic music
- Advance FGR-8S; 33s; rel 1970; cip

Piano Concert for David Tudor (1961)
[6606] Electronic music
- Advance FGR-8S; 33s; rel 1970; cip

MAYER, William R. (1925-)
Always, Always
[6607] Renzi, Dorothy (sop) or Crader, Jeannine (sop) or Langstaff, John (bar); Crowder, Charles (pf) or Garvey, David (pf)
- Desto D-430/DST-6430; 33m/s; rel 1968; cip

Andante, Strings (1956)
[6608] Minnesota Orchestra; Skrowaczewski, Stanislaw (cond)
- Desto DC-7126; 33s; rel 1971; cip

Appalachian Echoes
[6609] Chertok, Pearl (hp)
- Orion ORS-75207; 33s; rel 1976; cip

Barbara
[6610] Renzi, Dorothy (sop) or Crader, Jeannine (sop) or Langstaff, John (bar); Crowder, Charles (pf) or Garvey, David (pf)
- Desto D-430/DST-6430; 33m/s; rel 1968; cip

Brief Candle (1964)
[6611] soloists; chorus; Princeton Chamber Orchestra; Harsanyi, Nicholas (cond)
- Desto D-430/DST-6430; 33m/s; rel 1968; cip

Concert Piece, Trumpet (1957)
[6612] Levy, Robert (tpt); Levy, Amy Lou (pf)
- Golden Crest RE-7045; 33s; rel 1972; cip

Country Fair (1957)
[6613] Robert Nagel Brass Trio
- CRI-185; 33m/s; rel 1964/1971; cip

Dream's End
[6614] Teco, Romuald (vln); Howard, Peter
(vcl); Killmer, Richard E. (ob);
Paradise, Timothy J. (cl); Rybka,
Priscilla (hn); James, Layton (pf);
McGlaughlin, William (cond)
- CRI-415; 33s; rel 1980; cip

Essay for Brass and Winds (1954)
[6615] New York Brass and Woodwind
Ensemble; Balaban, Emanuel
(cond)
- CRI-185; 33m/s; rel
1964/1971; cip

**Eve of St. Agnes, The (A
Remembrance) (1969)**
[6616] Peabody Conservatory Chorus and
Orchestra; De Ruiter, Albert (nar)
(bar); Price, Patricia (sop); Rees,
Rosalind (sop); Hudson, David
(ten); Smith, Gregg (cond)
- Vox SVBX-5354; 33s; 3 discs; rel
1979

For a Young Man
[6617] Renzi, Dorothy (sop) or Crader,
Jeannine (sop) or Langstaff, John
(bar); Crowder, Charles (pf) or
Garvey, David (pf)
- Desto D-430/DST-6430; 33m/s;
rel 1968; cip

**Greatest Sound Around, The
(1954)**
[6618] Langstaff, John (bar); Roosevelt, E.
(voice); Little Orchestra Society;
Scherman, Thomas (cond)
- RCA LM-2332/LSC-2332;
33m/s; rel 1959; del 1962

Hello, World! (1956)
[6619] Langstaff, John (bar); Roosevelt, E.
(voice); Little Orchestra Society;
Scherman, Thomas (cond)
- RCA LM-2332/LSC-2332;
33m/s; rel 1959; del 1962

Khartoum (1968)
[6620] Renzi, Dorothy (sop) or Crader,
Jeannine (sop) or Langstaff, John
(bar); Crowder, Charles (pf) or
Garvey, David (pf)
- Desto D-430/DST-6430; 33m/s;
rel 1968; cip

[6621] Rowe, Catherine (sop);
instrumental ensemble; Weisberg,
Arthur (cond)
- CRI-291; 33s; rel 1973; cip

(Five) Miniatures (1968)
[6622] Renzi, Dorothy (sop) or Crader,
Jeannine (sop) or Langstaff, John
(bar); Crowder, Charles (pf) or
Garvey, David (pf)
- Desto D-430/DST-6430; 33m/s;
rel 1968; cip

(Six) Miniatures (1968)
[6623] Rowe, Catherine (sop);
instrumental ensemble; Weisberg,
Arthur (cond)
- CRI-291; 33s; rel 1973; cip

(Two) News Items (1972)
[6624] Rowe, Catherine (sop);
instrumental ensemble; Weisberg,
Arthur (cond)
- CRI-291; 33s; rel 1973; cip

Octagon (1971)
[6625] Masselos, William (pf); Milwaukee
Symphony Orchestra;
Schermerhorn, Kenneth (cond)
- Turnabout QTVS-34564; 33q; rel
1974; del 1978

Overture for an American (1958)
[6626] London Philharmonic Orchestra;
Stanger, Russell (cond)
- CRI-185; 33m/s; rel
1964/1971; cip

Paradox
[6627] Renzi, Dorothy (sop) or Crader,
Jeannine (sop) or Langstaff, John
(bar); Crowder, Charles (pf) or
Garvey, David (pf)
- Desto D-430/DST-6430; 33m/s;
rel 1968; cip

(Two) Pastels (1961)
[6628] Minnesota Orchestra;
Skrowaczewski, Stanislaw (cond)
- Desto DC-7126; 33s; rel 1971;
cip

Quintet, Brass (1964)
[6629] Iowa Brass Quintet
- CRI-291; 33s; rel 1973; cip

Sonata, Piano (1959)
[6630] Masselos, William (pf)
- CRI-198; 33m/s; rel
1965/1972; cip

That Purple Bird
[6631] Renzi, Dorothy (sop) or Crader,
Jeannine (sop) or Langstaff, John
(bar); Crowder, Charles (pf) or
Garvey, David (pf)
- Desto D-430/DST-6430; 33m/s;
rel 1968; cip

MAYS, Walter (1941-)
**Concerto, Alto Saxophone and
Chamber Ensemble (1974)**
[6632] Sampen, John (sax); Wichita State
University Faculty Chamber
Ensemble; Mays, Walter (cond)
Rec 5/76
- CRI-361; 33s; rel 1977; cip

**(Six) Invocations to the Svara
Mandala (1973)**
[6633] Wichita State University Percussion
Orchestra; Combs, J. C. (cond)
Rec 11/23/75
- CRI-344; 33s; rel 1976; cip

MECHEM, Kirke L. (1925-)
**Make a Joyful Noise unto the Lord
(Psalm 100)**
[6634] Mormon Tabernacle Choir; Ottley,
Jerold D. (cond)
- Columbia M-34134; 33s; rel
1976; cip

MEKEEL, Joyce (1931-)
Corridors of Dream (1972)
[6635] Curtis, Jan (m sop); Boston Musica
Viva; Pittman, Richard (cond)
- Delos DEL-25405; 33s; rel
1975; cip

Planh (1975)
[6636] Cirillo, Nancy (vln)
- Delos DEL-25405; 33s; rel
1975; cip

MELBY, John (1941-)
91 Plus 5 (1971)
[6637] Contemporary Brass Quintet; tape;
Pawlowski, Roman (cond)
- CRI-310; 33s; rel 1973; cip

(Two) Stevens Songs (1975)
[6638] Bryn-Julson, Phyllis (sop); tape
- CRI-364; 33s; rel 1977; cip

**MENASCE, Jacques de
(1905-60)**
**Concerto, Piano and Orchestra, No
2 (1939)**
[6639] Menasce, Jacques de (pf); Vienna
State Opera Orchestra; Appia,
Edmund (cond)
- Vanguard VRS-442; 33m; rel
1953; del 1960

**Divertimento on a Children's Song
(1940)**
[6640] Vienna State Opera Orchestra;
Appia, Edmund (cond)
- Vanguard VRS-442; 33m; rel
1953; del 1960

**Instantanes (Six Children's Pieces
for Piano) (1956-59)**
[6641] Bloch, Joseph (pf)
- CRI-154; 33m/s; rel 1962/?; cip

(Deux) Lettres d'enfants
[6642] Cuenod, Hugues (ten); Parsons,
Geoffrey (pf)
- Nimbus 2112; 33q; rel 1977

Petite Suite, Piano
[6643] Menasce, Jacques de (pf)
- Vanguard VRS-442; 33m; rel
1953; del 1960

Sonata, Viola and Piano (1955)
[6644] Fuchs, Lillian (vla); Balsam, Artur
(pf)
- CRI-154; 33m/s; rel 1962/?; cip

**Sonata, Violin and Piano, No 1
(1940)**
[6645] Fuchs, Joseph (vln); Balsam, Artur
(pf)
- CRI-154; 33m/s; rel 1962/?; cip

Sonatina, Piano, No 2 (1942)
[6646] Bloch, Joseph (pf)
- CRI-154; 33m/s; rel 1962/?; cip

MENNIN, Peter (1923-)

Canto (1963)
[6647] Cincinnati Symphony Orchestra;
Rudolf, Max (cond)
- Decca DL-710168; 33s; rel
1970; del 1973

Canzona (1951)
[6648] Eastman Symphonic Wind
Ensemble; Fennell, Frederick
(cond)
Rec 1954
- Mercury MG-40011; 33m; rel
1954; del 1957
- Mercury MG-50084; 33m; rel
1957; del 1969

Concertato (Moby Dick) (1952)
[6649] Vienna Symphony Orchestra;
Swarowsky, Hans (cond)
- American Recording Society
ARS-31; 33m; rel 1953
- Desto D-416/DST-6416; 33m/s;
rel 1965; cip

**Concerto, Piano and Orchestra
(1958)**
[6650] Ogdon, John (pf); Royal
Philharmonic Orchestra; Buketoff,
Igor (cond)
- RCA LSC-3243; 33s; rel 1971;
del 1976
- CRI-399; 33s; rel 1980; cip

**Concerto, Violoncello and Orchestra
(1956)**
[6651] Starker, Janos (vcl); Louisville
Orchestra; Mester, Jorge (cond)
- LS-69-3; 33s (Louisville
Orchestra First Edition Records
1969 No 3); rel 1969; cip

**(Five) Pieces, Piano (1949): Canto
and Toccata**
[6652] Johannesen, Grant (pf)
- Golden Crest
CR-4065/CRS-4065; 33m/s; rel
1963/1966; cip

Quartet, Strings, No 2 (1951)
[6653] Juilliard String Quartet
- Columbia ML-4844; 33m; rel
1954; del 1968
- Columbia CML-4844; 33m; rel
1968; del 1974

Quartet, Strings, No 2 (1951)
(cont'd)
- Columbia AML-4844; 33m; rel
1974; del 1976

[6654] Kohon Quartet
- Vox SVBX-5305; 33s; 3 discs; rel
1974; cip

Sonata concertante (1959)
[6655] Zukofsky, Paul (vln); Kalish, Gilbert
(pf)
- Desto DC-6435-37; 33s; 3 discs;
rel 1975; cip

Symphony No 3 (1946)
[6656] New York Philharmonic;
Mitropoulos, Dimitri (cond)
- Columbia ML-4902; 33m; rel
1954; del 1965
- CRI-278; 33s; rel 1972; cip

**Symphony No 4 (The Cycle)
(1948)**
[6657] Camerata Singers and Symphony
Orchestra; Kaplan, Abraham
(cond)
- Desto DC-7149; 33s; rel 1974;
cip

Symphony No 5 (1950)
[6658] Eastman-Rochester Symphony
Orchestra; Hanson, Howard
(cond)
- Mercury MG-50379/SR-90379;
33m/s; rel 1964; del 1973
- Mercury SRI-75020; 33s; rel
1974; cip

[6659] Louisville Orchestra; Whitney,
Robert (cond)
- LOU-61-3; 33m (Louisville
Orchestra First Edition Records
1961 No 3); rel 1961; del 1978

Symphony No 6 (1958)
[6660] Louisville Orchestra; Whitney,
Robert (cond)
- LOU-545-3; 33m (Louisville
Orchestra First Edition Records
1955 No 3); rel 1959; del 1978

**Symphony No 7
(Variation-Symphony) (1963)**
[6661] Chicago Symphony Orchestra;
Martinon, Jean (cond)
Rec 11/29/67
- RCA LSC-3043; 33s; rel 1968;
del 1971
- New World NW-258; 33s; rel
1976
- CRI-399; 33s; rel 1980; cip

MENNINI, Louis (1920-)
Arioso for String Orchestra (1948)
[6662] Eastman-Rochester Symphony
Orchestra; Hanson, Howard
(cond)
- Mercury MG-40001; 33m; rel
1953; del 1957
- Mercury MG-50074; 33m; rel
1957; del 1963

MENOTTI, Gian Carlo (1911-)
**Amahl and the Night Visitors
(1951)**
[6663] Yaghjian, Kurt (sop); King, Martha
(sop); McCollum, John (ten);
Patrick, Julian (bar); Cross,
Richard (b); Patterson, Willis (b);
NBC Opera Company Chorus and
Orchestra; Grossman, Herbert
(cond)
Rec 12/63
- RCA LM-2762/LSC-2762;
33m/s; rel 1964; cip

[6664] vocalists; orchestra; Peretti (cond)
- Mercury CM-41; 33m; rel
pre-1958

**Amahl and the Night Visitors
(Abridged)**
[6665] Allen, Chet (sop); Kuhlmann,
Rosemary (m sop); Aiken, David
(bar); Lishner, Leon (b); McKinley,
Andrew (ten); NBC Telecast
Chorus and Orchestra; Schippers,
Thomas (cond)
Rec 12/51
- RCA LM-1701; 33m; rel 1952;
del 1964
- Victor ERA-120; 45; 7"; rel
1952? (excerpts)
- Victor WDM-1701; 45; 7"; rel
pre-1953
- Gramophone ALP-1196; 33m; rel
pre-1956
- RCA-Victrola VIC-1512; 33m; rel
1970; cip

**Amahl and the Night Visitors:
Introduction, March, and
Shepherd's Dance**
[6666] Atlanta Symphony Orchestra and
Chorus; Shaw, Robert (cond)
- Turnabout QTVS-34647-48; 33q;
2 discs; rel 1977

**Amahl and the Night Visitors
(Suite)**
[6667] Cleveland Pops Orchestra; Lane,
Louis (cond)
- Epic LC-3819/BC-1154; 33m/s;
rel 1962; del 1965

Amelia al ballo (1936)
[6668] Carosio, Margherita (sop); Zanolli,
Silvana (m sop); Mazzoni, Elena
(m sop); Amadini, Maria (al);
Prandelli, Giacinto (ten); Panerai,
Rolando (bar); Campi, Enrico (b);
La Scala Orchestra and Chorus;
Sanzogno, Nino (cond)
- Angel 35140; 33m; rel 1954;
del 1959
- Columbia CX-1166; 33m; rel
pre-1956
- Columbia QCX-10070; 33m; rel
pre-1956
- Columbia FCX-335; 33m; rel
pre-1956

Amelia al ballo: Overture
[6669] Columbia Symphony Orchestra; Schippers, Thomas (cond)
- Columbia ML-5638/MS-6238; 33m/s; rel 1961; del 1966

[6670] Philadelphia Orchestra; Ormandy, Eugene (cond)
- Victor 15377; 78; rel 1939*
- Gramophone DB-5777; 78; rel pre-1948
- Camden CAL-238; 33m; rel 1956; del 1957

Amelia al ballo: Amelia cara
[6671] Malaspina, G. (bar)
- Parlophone AT-0275; 78; rel pre-1953

Concerto, Piano and Orchestra (1945)
[6672] Boukoff, Yury (pf); Paris Conservatory Orchestra; Cluytens, Andre (cond)
- Gramophone FALP-176; 33m; rel pre-1953
- Gramophone QALP-176; 33m; rel pre-1956

[6673] Wild, Earl (pf); Symphony of the Air; Mester, Jorge (cond)
- Vanguard VRS-1070/VSD-2094; 33m/s; rel 1961; cip

Concerto, Violin and Orchestra (1952)
[6674] Spivakovsky, Tossy (vln); Boston Symphony Orchestra; Munch, Charles (cond)
- RCA LM-1868; 33m; rel 1955; del 1960
- RCA (French) A-630275; 33m; rel pre-1956
- RCA (Italian) A12R-0115; 33m; rel pre-1956

Consul, The (1949)
[6675] Powers, Marie; Neway, Patricia; Lane, Gloria; McKinley, Andrew; Lishner, Leon; Jongeyans, George; MacNeil, Cornell; soloists and orchestra of the original NY production; Engel, Lehman (cond) Rec 4/11/50
- Decca DAU-769; 78; 8 discs; rel 1950
- Decca DL-9500-01 (in set DXA-101); 33m; 2 discs; rel 1950; del 1975
- Brunswick LAT-8012-13; 33m; 2 discs; rel pre-1952
- New World NW-241; 33s; rel 1978 (Excerpt: To This We've Come)

Consul, The: Frustration Theme and Lullaby (Act II)
[6676] Neway, Patricia (sop); Powers, Marie (al)
- Brunswick 0815; 78; rel pre-1952

Consul, The: To This We've Come
[6677] Borkh, Inge; trio
- Gramophone DB-11537; 78; rel pre-1953
- Gramophone 7RW-518; 45; 7"; rel pre-1956

[6678] Farrell, Eileen (sop); Philharmonia Orchestra; Schippers, Thomas (cond)
- Angel 35589; 33m; rel 1959; del 1969

Death of the Bishop of Brindisi, The (1963)
[6679] Chookasian, Lili (m sop); London, George (b); New England Conservatory Chorus; Catholic Memorial High School Glee Club (members of); St. Joseph's High School Glee Club (members of); Boston Symphony Orchestra; Leinsdorf, Erich (cond)
- RCA LM-2785/LSC-2785; 33m/s; rel 1965; del 1967

Maria Golovin (1958)
[6680] Duval, Franca (sop); Cross, Richard (b bar); Muti, Lorenzo (sop); Las, Genia (m sop); Neway, Patricia (al); Handt, Herbert (ten); Chapman, William (bar); chorus; orchestra; Adler, Peter Hermann (cond)
- RCA LM-6142; 33m; 3 discs; rel 1959; del 1960

Medium, The (1945)
[6681] Alberghetti, Anna Maria (sop); Dame, Beverly (sop); Kibler, Belva (sop); Powers, Marie (al); Morgan, Mac (bar); Rome Radio Orchestra; Schippers, Thomas (cond)
- Mercury MGL-7; 33m; 2 discs; rel 1951; del 1956
- Classic (French) CL-6278-79; 33m; 2 discs; rel pre-1956
- Mercury EP-1-5054; 45; 7"; rel pre-1956 (excerpts)
- Mercury (French) MEP-14532; 45; 7"; rel pre-1956 (excerpts)

[6682] Keller, Evelyn (sop); Powers, Marie (al); Dame, Beverly (sop); Mastice, Catherine; Rogier, Frank (bar); orchestra; Balaban, Emanuel (cond)
- Columbia 72475-81 (in set M-726); 78; 7 discs; rel pre-1948
- Columbia OL-4174-75 (in set OSL-154); 33m; 2 discs; rel 1949; del 1978
- Odyssey Y2-35239; 33m; 2 discs; rel 1979; cip

Medium, The (1945) (cont'd)
[6683] Resnik, Regina (sop); Blegen, Judith (sop); Derr, Emily (sop); Carlson, Claudine (m sop); Patrick, Julian (bar); Opera Society of Washington; Mester, Jorge (cond)
- Columbia MS-7387; 33s; rel 1970; cip

Old Maid and the Thief, The (1939)
[6684] Baker, Margaret (sop); Blegen, Judith (sop); Reynolds, Anna (al); Reardon, John (bar); Teatro Verdi di Trieste Orchestra; Mester, Jorge (cond)
- Mercury SR-90521; 33s; rel 1971; del 1973
- Turnabout TVS-34745; 33s; rel 1979; cip

Old Maid and the Thief, The: Overture
[6685] Turin Radio Orchestra; Simonetti, Alfredo (cond)
- Parlophone CB-20502; 78; rel pre-1952

Ricercare and Toccata on a Theme from The Old Maid and the Thief (1953)
[6686] Dorfmann, Ania (pf)
- Victor 49-4118-21 (in set WDM-1758); 45; 4-7"; rel 1953*
- RCA LM-1758; 33m; rel 1953; del 1956

[6687] Lewenthal, Raymond (pf)
- Westminster XWN-18362; 33m; rel 1957; del 1960

Saint of Bleecker Street, The (1954)
[6688] Ruggiero, Gabrielle (sop); Di Gerlando, Maria (sop); Marlo, Maria (sop); Becque, Lucy (sop); Carron, Elizabeth (sop); Lane, Gloria (m sop); Akos, Catherine (m sop); Poleri, David (ten); Gonzales, Ernesto (ten); Kaldenberg, Keith (ten); Cassilly, Richard (ten); Aiken, David (bar); Goodwin, Russell (bar); Reardon, John (bar); Lishner, Leon (b); orchestra; chorus; Schippers, Thomas (cond)
- RCA LM-6032; 33m; 2 discs; rel 1955; del 1960
- RCA CBM-2-2714; 33m; 2 discs; rel 1978; cip

Sebastian (Suite) (1944)
[6689] London Symphony Orchestra; Serebrier, Jose (cond)
- Desto DC-6432; 33s; rel 1969; cip

[6690] NBC Symphony Orchestra; Stokowski, Leopold (cond)
- RCA LM-1858; 33m; rel 1955; del 1959

Sebastian (Suite) (1944) *(cont'd)*
- RCA ARL-1-2715; 33s; rel 1978; cip

[6691] Robin Hood Dell Orchestra (of Philadelphia); Mitropoulos, Dimitri (cond)
- Columbia 12571-72D (in set X-278); 78; 2 discs; rel 1947*
- Columbia ML-2053; 33m; 10''; rel pre-1949; del 1956

Sebastian (Suite): Barcarolle
[6692] Boston Pops Orchestra; Fiedler, Arthur (cond)
- RCA LM-1726; 33m; rel 1953; del 1961
- Victor WDM-1726; 45; 4-7''; rel 1953?

[6693] Philadelphia Orchestra; Ormandy, Eugene (cond)
- Columbia M-31633; 33s; rel 1973; cip

Telephone, The (1946)
[6694] Cotlow, Marilyn (sop); Rogier, Frank (bar); orchestra; Balaban, Emanuel (cond)
- Columbia 72482-84D (in set M-726); 78; 3 discs; rel pre-1948
- Columbia OL-4174 (in set OSL-154); 33m; rel 1949; del 1978
- Odyssey Y2-35239; 33m; 2 discs; rel 1979; cip

[6695] Seibel, Paula (sop); Orth, Robert (bar); Louisville Orchestra; Mester, Jorge (cond)
- LS-76-7; 33s (Louisville Orchestra First Edition Records 1976 No 7); rel 1979; cip

Unicorn, the Gorgon, and the Manticore, The (or The Three Sundays of a Poet) (1956)
[6696] Hodges, Betty (sop); Nowland, Hallie (sop); Hensley, Mary (al); Karian, Frank (ten); Baker, Julius (fl); Shulman, Harry (ob); Lewis, Walter (cl); Glickman, Loren (bsn); Weis, Theodore (tpt); McCracken, Charles (vcl); Sankey, Stuart (cb); Koor (perc); Agostini, Gloria (hp); Schippers, Thomas (cond)
- Angel 35437; 33m; rel 1957; del 1974

[6697] Paul Hill Chorale and Orchestra; Hill, Paul (cond)
- Golden Crest CRS-4180; 33s; rel 1978

MEYERS, Emerson (1910-)
Marches militaires metaphoriquement (1977)
[6698] Gifford, Al (fl) (pic); Merz, Albert (perc); Marcellus, John (b tbn)
- Opus One 40; 33s

Rhapsodie fantastique (1974)
[6699] Dahlman, Barbro (pf)
- Opus One 33; 33s; rel 1979; cip

MICHALSKY, Donal (1928-)
Divertimento, Three Clarinets (1952)
[6700] Los Angeles Clarinet Society
- WIM Records WIMR-7; 33s; rel 1973; cip

Fantasia a due, Horn and Bass Trombone (1968)
[6701] Henderson, Robert (hn); Reynolds, Jeffrey (b tbn)
- Crystal S-383; 33s; rel 1979; cip

Partita piccola (1964)
[6702] Andrus, Gretel Shanley (fl); Davis, Sharon (pf)
- WIM Records WIMR-2; 33s; rel 1971; cip

MICHELET, Michel L. (1894-)
Chinoiserie
[6703] Adcock, Lynne Cole (sop); Pelta, Henriette (pf)
- Orion ORS-73135; 33s; rel 1974; cip

Elegy
[6704] Lawrence, Douglas (b bar); Lawrence, Darlene (pf)
- Orion ORS-73135; 33s; rel 1974; cip

Hannele (1972): Gottwald's Aria, Hannele's Aria, and Stranger's Aria
[6705] Lawrence, Douglas (b bar); Lawrence, Darlene (pf)
- Orion ORS-73135; 33s; rel 1974; cip

Headsman's Song, The
[6706] Lawrence, Douglas (b bar); Lawrence, Darlene (pf)
- Orion ORS-73135; 33s; rel 1974; cip

Lotus
[6707] Adcock, Lynne Cole (sop); Pelta, Henriette (pf)
- Orion ORS-73135; 33s; rel 1974; cip

Newspaper Clippings
[6708] Adcock, Lynne Cole (sop); Pelta, Henriette (pf)
- Orion ORS-73135; 33s; rel 1974; cip

MILBURN, Ellsworth (1938-)
Soli III, Clarinet, Violoncello, and Piano (1971)
[6709] Montagnana Trio
- Grenadilla GS-1021; 33s; rel 1979; cip

Quartet, Strings (1974)
[6710] Concord String Quartet
Rec 3/14/77
- CRI-369; 33s; rel 1978; cip

Quintet, Strings (1969)
[6711] Findlay, Mary (vln); Dominitz, Benzion (vln); Sepsenwol, Noah (vla); Mulliken, David (vcl); Green, Barry (cb)
- Music Now CFS-3037; 33s; rel 1974*

MILLER, Charles (1899-)
Cubanaise (1951)
[6712] Elman, Mischa (vln); Seiger, Joseph (pf)
- London LLP-1629; 33m; rel 1957; del 1959

MILLER, Edward Jay (1930-)
Folly Stone, The (1966)
[6713] New York Brass Quintet
- CRI-302; 33s; rel 1973; cip

Piece, Clarinet and Tape
[6714] Rehfeldt, Phillip (cl); tape
- Advance FGR-17S; 33s; rel 1976; cip

Quartet-Variations (1972)
[6715] Blackearth Percussion Group
Rec 5/27-28/74
- Opus One 22; 33s; rel 1975; cip

Song (1960)
[6716] Krainis, Bernard (rec)
- Columbia ML-5875/MS-6475; 33m/s; rel 1963; del 1968
- Odyssey 32-16-0143/32-16-0144; 33m/s; rel 1967; cip

Trio, Recorders, No 1 (1958)
[6717] Krainis Recorder Consort
- Kapp KC-9049/KC-S-9049; 33m/s; rel 1960; del 1963

MILLER, Jacques (1900-)
Badinage staccato
[6718] Rigai, Amiram (pf)
- Musical Heritage Society MHS-3749; 33s; rel 1978

Fantasie
[6719] Rigai, Amiram (pf)
- Musical Heritage Society MHS-3749; 33s; rel 1978

Impromptu, E-flat Minor
[6720] Rigai, Amiram (pf)
- Musical Heritage Society MHS-3749; 33s; rel 1978

Poeme romantique
[6721] Rigai, Amiram (pf)
- Musical Heritage Society MHS-3749; 33s; rel 1978

Profile, A
[6722] Rigai, Amiram (pf)
- Musical Heritage Society MHS-3749; 33s; rel 1978

Rhapsody, Piano and Orchestra (arr for 2 pfs)
[6723] Rigai, Amiram (pf); Kepalaite, Aldona (pf)
- Musical Heritage Society MHS-3749; 33s; rel 1978

Scherzo pittoresque
[6724] Rigai, Amiram (pf)
- Musical Heritage Society MHS-3749; 33s; rel 1978

MILLER, Malloy (1918-)
Prelude, Percussion (1956)
[6725] Percussion Ensemble; Price, Paul (cond)
- Period SPL-743/SPLS-743; 33m/s; rel 1958; del 1968
- Orion ORS-7276; 33s; rel 1972; cip

MILLS, Charles (1914-)
Prologue and Dithyramb (1954)
[6726] Zurich Radio Orchestra; Monod, Jacques (cond)
- CRI-128; 33m; rel 1960; cip

Sonata, Violin and Piano, No 1 (ca 1940)
[6727] Porter, Lois (vln); Nowak, Lionel (pf)
- Yaddo (169-171); 78; rel 1940

True Beauty, The (1950)
[6728] Randolph Singers; Randolph, David (cond)
- CRI-102; 33m/s; rel 1956/?; cip

MIMAROGLU, Ilhan (1926-)
Bowery Bum (1964)
[6729] voice; tape
- Turnabout TV-4004/TVS-34004; 33m/s; rel 1965; del 1975

Bowery Bum (revised version) (1976)
[6730] voice; tape
- Finnadar SR-9012; 33s; rel 1977; cip

Coucou Bazar (1973)
[6731] Electronic music
- Finnadar SR-9003; 33s; rel 1973; cip

Hyperboles (1972)
[6732] Electronic music
- Finnadar SR-9001; 33s; rel 1973; cip

Intermezzo (1964)
[6733] Electronic music
- Turnabout TV-4004/TVS-34004; 33m/s; rel 1965; del 1975

Intermezzo (revised version) (1976)
[6734] Electronic music
- Finnadar SR-9012; 33s; rel 1977; cip

Music Plus One (1970)
[6735] Banat, Gabriel (vln); tape
- Turnabout TVS-34429; 33s; rel 1971; del 1974

Piano Music for Performer and Composer (1967)
[6736] Flynn, George (pf); tape
- Turnabout TVS-34177; 33s; rel 1967; del 1975

Pieces sentimentales (1957)
[6737] Rigai, Amiram (pf)
- Vox PL-12570/STPL-512570; 33m/s; rel 1963; del 1970
- Folkways 3360; 33s; rel 1979; cip

Prelude, Tape
[6738] Electronic music
- Finnadar SR-9001; 33s; rel 1973; cip

Preludes, Tape (1966-67): Nos 1, 2, 6, 9, 11, and 12
[6739] Bozkurt, Guengoer (voice); tape
- Turnabout TVS-34177; 33s; rel 1967; del 1975

Preludes, Tape (revised version) (1976): Nos 1, 2, 6, 9, 11, 12, 14, and 16
[6740] Bozkurt, Guengoer (voice); Siegel, J. (voice); tape
- Finnadar SR-9012; 33s; rel 1977; cip

Provocations (1971)
[6741] Electronic music
- Finnadar SR-9001; 33s; rel 1973; cip

Rosa (1978)
[6742] Hays, Doris (pf)
- Finnadar SR-2-720; 33s; 2 discs; rel 1980; cip

Ruche, La
[6743] Wiederkehr, Jacques (vcl); Merlet, Michel (hpschd); Joste, Martine (pf); tape
- Folkways FTQ-33951; 33q; rel 1977; cip

Session
[6744] Biret, Idil (pf)
- Finnadar SR-9021; 33s; rel 1979; cip

Sing Me a Song of Songmy (1971)
[6745] Hoxworth, Mary Ann (speaker); Nha-Khe (speaker); Gran, Charles (speaker); Bozkurt, Guengoer (speaker); Hubbard, Freddie (speaker); organ; string orchestra; tape; Orloff, Gene (cond); Clarke, Selwart (cond); Mardin, Arif (cond); Freddie Hubbard and his Quintet; Barnard-Columbia Chorus; Paget, Daniel (cond)
- Atlantic SD-1576; 33s; rel 1971; del 1977

[6746] no performers given; tape
- Finnadar SR-9001; 33s; rel 1973; cip

To Kill a Sunrise (1974)
[6747] Hoxworth, Mary Ann (voice); Washington, Chris (speaker); Gursoy, Geoffrey (speaker); speaking choir; tape
- Folkways FTQ-33951; 33q; rel 1977; cip

Tombeau d'Edgar Poe, Le (1964)
[6748] Buri, Erdem (speaker); tape
- Turnabout TV-4004/TVS-34004; 33m/s; rel 1965; del 1975

Tombeau d'Edgar Poe, Le (revised version) (1976)
[6749] Buri, Erdem (speaker); tape
- Finnadar SR-9012; 33s; rel 1977; cip

Tract (1972-74)
[6750] Sand, Tuly (speaker-singer); Mimaroglu, Ilhan (speaker); Buri, Erdem (speaker); Topsy Turvy Moon; tape
- Folkways FTS-33441; 33s; rel 1975; cip

Visual Studies (1964-66): (No 4) Agony
[6751] Electronic music
- Turnabout TV-4046/TVS-34046; 33m/s; rel 1966; del 1975

Visual Studies: (No 4) Agony (revised version) (1976)
[6752] Electronic music
- Finnadar SR-9012; 33s; rel 1977; cip

White Cockatoo (1966)
[6753] Electronic music
- Finnadar SR-9001; 33s; rel 1973; cip

Wings of the Delirious Demon (1969)
[6754] Electronic music
- Finnadar SR-9001; 33s; rel 1973; cip

MITCHELL, Ian Douglas (1926-)

American Folk Song Mass, The

[6755] Northwestern University
Canterbury Choir; Mitchell, Ian
Douglas (gtr)
- North-American
CM-6806/CS-6806; 33m/s; rel
196?

MITCHELL, Lyndol C. (1923-64)

Kentucky Mountain Portraits

[6756] Eastman-Rochester Symphony
Orchestra; Hanson, Howard
(cond)
Rec 10/28/56
- Mercury MG-50134/SR-90134;
33m/s; rel 1957/1959; del
1963
- Eastman-Rochester Archives
ERA-1012; 33s; rel 197?

MOEVS, Robert (1920-)

Brief Mass, A (1968)

[6757] Kirkpatrick Chapel Choir (Rutgers);
vibraphone; guitar; contrabass;
organ; Drinkwater, David (cond)
- CRI-262; 33s; rel 1970; cip

**Collana musicale, Una (1977): Nos
2, 5, 6, 10, 11, and 12**

[6758] Maximilien, Wanda (pf)
Rec 11/78 and 2/79
- CRI-404; 33s; rel 1979; cip

Fantasia sopra uno motivo (1951)

[6759] Maximilien, Wanda (pf)
Rec 11/78 and 2/79
- CRI-404; 33s; rel 1979; cip

Musica da camera (1965)

[6760] Contemporary Chamber Ensemble;
Weisberg, Arthur (cond)
- CRI-223; 33s; rel 1968; cip

Phoenix (1971)

[6761] Maximilien, Wanda (pf)
Rec 11/78 and 2/79
- CRI-404; 33s; rel 1979; cip

Sonata, Piano (1950)

[6762] Bloch, Joseph (pf)
- CRI-136; 33m; rel 1960; cip

**Variazioni sopra una melodia
(1961)**

[6763] Glick, Jacob (vla); Sylvester, Robert
(vcl)
- CRI-223; 33s; rel 1968; cip

MOHAUPT, Richard (1904-57)

Double Trouble (1954)

[6764] Pulliam, Margaret (sop); Beierfield,
Abby (al); Riesley, Charme; Dales,
Richard (ten); Elliott, W. D.;
Pickett, William (bar); Harlan,
Monas; Kentucky Opera
Association (members of);
Louisville Orchestra; Bomhard,
Moritz (cond)
- LOU-545-12; 33m (Louisville
Orchestra First Edition Records
1955 No 12); rel 1955; del
1978

**Stadtpfeifermusik (1939, rev
1953)**

[6765] Louisville Orchestra; Whitney,
Robert (cond)
- LOU-64-5/LS-64-5; 33m/s
(Louisville Orchestra First Edition
Records 1964 No 5); rel 1964;
cip

MOLARSKY, Delmar*

Quintet, Voice and String Quartet

[6766] Molarsky, Delmar (b); Cambourakis
String Quartet
- Technichord T-1105; 78; 2 discs;
rel pre-1948

MOLINEUX, Allen (1950-)

Encounter (1972)

[6767] Annapolis Brass Quintet
- Crystal S-207; 33s; rel 1979; cip

MONDELLO, Nuncio (1929-)

Siciliana

[6768] Chertok, Pearl (hp)
- Orion ORS-75207; 33s; rel
1976; cip

MONK, Meredith (1944-)

Our Lady of Late

[6769] Monk, Meredith (voice); Walcott,
Collin (glass harmonica)
Rec 4/1/72
- Minona MN-1001; 33s; rel 1973

MONOD, Jacques L. (1927-)

Cantus contra cantum I (1972)

[6770] Sargon, Merja (sop); chamber
orchestra; Monod, Jacques (cond)
Rec 9/22-24/75
- CRI-358; 33s; rel 1976; cip

MONROE, Ervin

Sketches

[6771] Monroe, Ervin (fl)
- Golden Crest RE-7064; 33s; rel
1979; cip

MOODY, James (1925-)

Little Suite

[6772] Reilly, Tommy (harmonica);
Academy of St.
Martin-in-the-Fields; Marriner,
Neville (cond)
Rec 6/1-2/76
- Argo ZRG-856; 33s; rel 1977;
cip

**Quintet, Harmonica and String
Quartet**

[6773] Reilly, Tommy (harmonica); Hindar
Quartet
- Argo ZDA-206; 33s; rel 1976;
del 1980

MOORE, Carman (1936-)

**(Four) Movements for a
Fashionable Five-Toed Dragon**

[6774] Rivers, Sam (fl) (sax); Randal,
Elliott (elec gtr) (pi'pa); Bichel,
Kenneth (kbds); Davis, Richard
(cb); Smith, Warren (perc);
American Symphony Orchestra;
Jackson, Isaiah (cond)
- Hong Kong Trade Development
Council HKTDC-A1; 33s; rel
1976

Youth in a Merciful House

[6775] Baron, Samuel (fl); MacCourt,
Donald (bsn); Scribner, William
(bsn); Fitz, Richard (perc) (vib);
Friedman, David (perc) (vib);
Thompson, Marcus (vla); Gilbert,
David (cond)
- Folkways FTS-33902; 33s; rel
1976; cip

MOORE, Douglas S. (1893-1969)

Ballad of Baby Doe, The (1956)

[6776] Sills, Beverly (sop); Bible, Frances
(m sop); Cassel, Walter (bar);
Hecht, Joshua (b); New York City
Opera Chorus and Orchestra;
Buckley, Emerson (cond)
- MGM 3GC-1/S3GC-1; 33m/s; 3
discs; rel 1959; del 1966
- Heliodor
H-25035-3/HS-25035-3;
33m/s; 3 discs; rel 1966; del
1970
- Deutsche Grammophon
2584.009-11 (in set 2709.061);
33s; 3 discs; rel 1976; cip

Ballads

[6777] Moore, Douglas (pf?)
- Yaddo 126A-b; 78; rel 1937

Carrie Nation (1966)

[6778] Faull, Ellen (sop); Wolff, Beverly (m
sop); Patrick, Julian (bar);
Voketaitis, Arnold (b bar); other
soloists; New York City Opera
Chorus and Orchestra;
Krachmalnick, Samuel (cond)
- Desto DC-6463-65; 33s; 3 discs;
rel 1968; cip

Come Away, Death (1925)
[6779] Gramm, Donald (bar); Cumming, Richard (pf)
- St/And SPL-411-12; 33m; 2 discs; rel 1963; del 1964
- Desto D-411-12/DST-6411-12; 33m/s; 2 discs; rel 1964; cip

Cotillion (1952)
[6780] Oslo Philharmonic Orchestra; Antonini, Alfredo (cond)
- CRI-107; 33m/s; rel 1957/?; cip

Decoration Day
[6781] Bennett, Bob L. (pf)
- Educo 3109; 33

Devil and Daniel Webster, The (1938)
[6782] Young, Doris (sop); Weidner, Frederick (ten); Winters, Lawrence (bar); Blankenship, Joe (b); De Groat, James; Festival Choir and Orchestra; Aliberti, Armando (cond)
- Westminster OPW-11032/WST-14050; 33m/s; rel 1958/1959; del 1961
- Desto D-450/DST-6450; 33m/s; rel 1965; cip

Farm Journal (1947)
[6783] Oslo Philharmonic Orchestra; Antonini, Alfredo (cond)
- CRI-101; 33m/s; rel 1956/?; cip

Fiddlin' Joe
[6784] Martin, Charlotte (pf)
- Educo 3021; 33m; rel 1968; del 1972

Grievin' Annie
[6785] Martin, Charlotte (pf)
- Educo 3021; 33m; rel 1968; del 1972

In memoriam (1943)
[6786] Japan Philharmonic Symphony Orchestra; Strickland, William (cond)
- CRI-127; 33m/s; rel 1960/?; cip

Mississippi
[6787] Bennett, Bob L. (pf)
- Educo 3109; 33

Pageant of P. T. Barnum, The (1924)
[6788] Eastman-Rochester Symphony Orchestra; Hanson, Howard (cond)
- Mercury MG-50206/SR-90206; 33m/s; rel 1959; del 1965
- Mercury SRI-75095; 33s; rel 1977; cip

People's Choice, The
[6789] Goldman Band
- Decca DL-8931/DL-78931; 33m/s; rel 1960; del 1971

Quartet, Strings (1933)
[6790] Walden String Quartet
- Yaddo 124A-B; 78; 10"; rel 1937

Quintet, Clarinet and Strings (1946)
[6791] Oppenheim, David (cl); New Music String Quartet
- Columbia ML-4494; 33m; rel 1952; del 1958
- Desto D-425/DST-6425; 33m/s; rel 1966; del 1977

(Three) Sonnets of John Donne (1942): Death Be Not Proud
[6792] Steber, Eleanor (sop); Biltcliffe, Edwin (pf)
- St/And SPL-411-12; 33m; 2 discs; rel 1963; del 1964
- Desto D-411-12/DST-6411-12; 33m/s; 2 discs; rel 1964; cip

Suite, Piano: Prelude, Dancing School, and Air
[6793] Carpenter, Richard (pf)
- Educo 3102; 33

Symphony in A (1945)
[6794] Californian Symphony; Jomelli (cond)
- Music Library MLR-7037; 33m; rel pre-1956

[6795] Japan Philharmonic Symphony Orchestra; Strickland, William (cond)
- CRI-133; 33m/s; rel 1960/1973; cip

[6796] Vienna Symphony Orchestra; Dixon, Dean (cond)
- American Recording Society ARS-5; 33m; 10"; rel pre-1952
- American Recording Society ARS-45; 33m; rel 1951

MOORE, Glen (1941-)
Flageolet
[6797] Seifert, Zbigniew (vln)
- Vanguard VSD-79397; 33s; rel 1978

MOORE, Thomas (1933-)
Metamorphosis over the Symphony of Webern
[6798] Chinn, Genevieve (pf); Brings, Allen (pf)
Rec 1974
- CRI-383; 33s; rel 1978; cip

MOORE, Undine Smith (1904-)
Afro-American Suite
[6799] Trio Pro Viva
- Eastern ERS-513; 33s; 2 discs; rel 1973*

MORAN, Robert (1937-)
L'Apres-midi du Dracoula (1966)
[6800] San Francisco Conservatory New Music Ensemble; Moran, Robert (cond)
Rec 12/70
- Wergo WER-60-057; 33s; rel 1971?

MORGAN, Robert P. (1934-)
Trio, Flute, Violoncello, and Harpsichord (1974)
[6801] Morgan, Carole (fl); Haffner, Barbara (vcl); Orkis, Lambert (hpschd)
- CRI-414; 33s; rel 1980; cip

MORGENSTERN, Sam
Toccata Guatemala
[6802] Melnick, Bertha (pf)
- Vanguard 2A; 78; 10"

[6803] Philharmonic Piano Quartet
- Columbia ML-2071; 33m; 10"; rel pre-1949; del 1956

MOROSS, Jerome (1913-)
Concerto, Flute and String Quartet (1978)
[6804] Zlotkin, Frances (fl); Sortomme, Richard (vln); Hudson, Benjamin (vln); Appel, Toby (vla); Zlotkin, Frederick (vcl)
- Varese Sarabande VC-81101; 33s; rel 1979; cip

Frankie and Johnny (1937-38)
[6805] Vienna Symphony Orchestra; Hendl, Walter (cond)
- American Recording Society ARS-12; 33m; rel 1952
- Desto D-408/DST-6408; 33m/s; rel 1965; del 1972

Sonata, Piano Duet and String Quartet (1975)
[6806] Arzruni, Sahan (pf); Gianattosio (pf); Sortomme, Richard (vln); Hudson, Benjamin (vln); Appel, Toby (vla); Zlotkin, Frederick (vcl)
- Varese Sarabande VC-81101; 33s; rel 1979; cip

Sonatina for Divers Instruments No 1, Clarinet Choir (1966)
[6807] Capital University Clarinet Choir; Hite, David (cond)
- Coronet S-1509; 33s; rel 1969; del 1978

[6808] London Pro Musica
- Desto DC-6469; 33s; rel 1973; cip

A Discography

Sonatina for Divers Instruments No 2, Contrabass and Piano (1966)
[6809] London Pro Musica
- Desto DC-6469; 33s; rel 1973; cip

Sonatina for Divers Instruments No 3, Wind Quintet (1970)
[6810] London Pro Musica
- Desto DC-6469; 33s; rel 1973; cip

Sonatina for Divers Instruments No 4, Brass Quintet (1969)
[6811] London Pro Musica
- Desto DC-6469; 33s; rel 1973; cip

MORRILL, Dexter (1938-)
Divertimento, Band (1964)
[6812] Cornell University Wind Ensemble; Stith, Marice (cond)
- Cornell CUWE-11; 33s; rel 1973; cip

(Three) Lyric Pieces, Violin and Piano (1969)
[6813] Berg, Bruce (vln); Slater, Vivien (pf)
- Musical Heritage Society MHS-3804; 33s; rel 1978

Quartet, Strings, No 1
[6814] Madison String Quartet
- Musical Heritage Society MHS-3804; 33s; rel 1978

Studies, Trumpet and Computer (1974-75)
[6815] Stith, Marice (tpt); tape
- Golden Crest RE-7068; 33s; rel 1977; cip

MORRIS, Franklin E. (1920-)
(Five) Esoteric Pieces, Wind Quintet (1941, 1955)
[6816] Soni Ventorum Wind Quintet
- Desto D-401/DST-6401; 33m/s; rel 1964; cip

MORRIS, Harold (1890-1964)
Passacaglia, Adagio, and Finale (1955)
[6817] Riesley, Charme (sop); Louisville Orchestra; Whitney, Robert (cond)
- LOU-57-6; 33m (Louisville Orchestra First Edition Records 1957 No 6); rel 1959; del 1972

Quartet, Strings, No 2 (1937)
[6818] Walden String Quartet
- Yaddo D-21-22; 78; 2 discs; rel 1938

Sonata, Piano, No 4 (1939)
[6819] Ranck, John (pf)
- Dorian 1006; 33m; rel 1962; del 1970

MORRIS, Robert (1943-)
Motet on Doo-Dah (1973)
[6820] Sollberger, Harvey (fl); Palma, Donald (cb); Shulman, Daniel (pf)
- New World NW-254; 33s; rel 1978

Phases (1970)
[6821] Albright, William (pf); Morris, Robert (pf)
- CRI-346; 33s; rel 1976; cip

MORRISON, C. S.
Meditation
[6822] Seidel, Toscha (vln)
- Columbia 49685; 78; rel 1918-25
- Columbia 68075D; 78; rel 1918-25

MORRISSEY, John J. (1906-)
Medieval Fresco
[6823] Ohio State University Concert Band; McGinnis, Donald E. (cond)
- Coronet S-1501; 33s; rel 1969; del 1978

Soliloquy
[6824] Stith, Marice (tpt); Paterson, Donald (pf)
- Redwood RRES-1; 33s; rel 1969; cip

MORSE, Robert G. (1931-)
Up the Street
[6825] Boston Pops Orchestra; Fiedler, Arthur (cond)
- RCA LM-2229/LSC-2229; 33m/s; rel 1958; del 1975
- RCA VCS-7068; 33s; 2 discs; rel 1971; cip

MORTON, Lawrence (1942-)
Psalm 150
[6826] Voices of Walter Schumann
- Capitol L-382; 33m; 10"; rel 1953; del 1957

MORYL, Richard (1929-)
Choralis
[6827] West Connecticut State College Chorus
- Desto DC-7121; 33s; rel 1971; cip

Chroma (1972)
[6828] New England Conservatory Contemporary Ensemble; Moryl, Richard (cond)
- Desto DC-7143; 33s; rel 1973; cip

Contacts
[6829] Moryl, Joanne (pf); DesRoches, Raymond (perc)
- Desto DC-7121; 33s; rel 1971; cip

Fluorescences
[6830] West Connecticut State College Chorus
- Desto DC-7121; 33s; rel 1971; cip

Illuminations
[6831] Stellato, Jeannette (sop); New England Conservatory Contemporary Ensemble; Moryl, Richard (cond)
- Desto DC-7143; 33s; rel 1973; cip

Lied, Das (1976)
[6832] DeGaetani, Jan (m sop); New England Conservatory Contemporary Ensemble; Schwarz, Gerard (cond)
Rec 5/78
- CRI-397; 33s; rel 1979; cip

Modules (1969)
[6833] Turetzky, Nancy (pic); Williams (tbn); Turetzky, Bertram (cb); Lesbines, Tele (perc)
- Serenus SRS-12028; 33s; rel 1972; cip

Multiples
[6834] Contemporary Chamber Ensemble; Weisberg, Arthur (cond)
- Desto DC-7121; 33s; rel 1971; cip

Salvos (1969)
[6835] Schwarz, Gerard (tpt)
- Desto DC-7133; 33s; rel 1973; cip

MOSS, Lawrence (1927-)
Auditions (1971)
[6836] Dorian Woodwind Quintet; tape
- CRI-318; 33s; rel 1974; cip

Elegy (1969)
[6837] Zukofsky, Paul (vln); Teco, Romuald (vln); Dupouy, Jean (vla)
- CRI-307; 33s; rel 1973; cip

Evocation and Song (1972)
[6838] Etheridge, George (sax); tape
- Opus One 16; 33s; rel 1974; cip

Fantasy, Piano (1973)
[6839] Welgert, Dionne Laufman (pf)
- Opus One 34; 33s; rel 1978; cip

Omaggio
[6840] Wentworth, Jean (pf); Wentworth, Kenneth (pf)
- Desto DC-7131; 33s; rel 1973; cip

(Four) Scenes (1961)
[6841] Fink, Seymour (pf)
- CRI-186; 33m/s; rel 1964/1971; cip

Sonata, Violin and Piano (1959)
[6842] Raimondi, Matthew (vln); Wyner, Yehudi (pf)
- CRI-186; 33m/s; rel 1964/1971; cip

Symphonies for Brass Quintet and Chamber Orchestra (1977)
[6843] Annapolis Brass Quintet; American Camerata for New Music; Stephens, John (cond)
- Orion ORS-79362; 33s; rel 1980; cip

Timepiece (1970)
[6844] Zukofsky, Paul (vln); Kalish, Gilbert (pf); DesRoches, Raymond (perc)
- CRI-307; 33s; rel 1973; cip

Toot Sweet (1976)
[6845] Ostryniec, James (ob); Bick, Donald (perc); Merz, Albert (perc)
- Opus One 31; 33s; rel 1978; cip

Unseen Leaves (1975)
[6846] Ostryniec, James (ob); Drucker, Ruth (sop); tape
Rec 12/21/76
- Orion ORS-78288; 33s; rel 1978; cip

MOTT, David (1945-)
Night Flowers (1973)
[6847] Shansky, Marjorie (al fl); Macchia, Salvatore (cb)
- Opus One 45; 33s; rel 1978; cip

(Five) Pieces, Violin, Clarinet, and Piano (1971)
[6848] Braunlich, Helmut (vln); Bates, Stephen (cl); Dahlman, Barbro (pf)
- Opus One 40; 33s

MOURANT, Walter (1910-)
Air and Scherzo (1955)
[6849] New Symphony Orchestra; Camarata, Salvador (cond)
- London LLP-1213; 33m; rel 1955; del 1957
- CRI-157; 33m/s; rel 1962/?; cip

Blue Haze
[6850] Kell, Reginald (cl); Camarata and his Orchestra; Camarata, Salvador (cond)
- Decca DL-7550; 33m; 10"; rel 1954*

Ecstasy
[6851] Kell, Reginald (cl); Camarata and his Orchestra; Camarata, Salvador (cond)
- Decca 16048; 78
- Decca DL-7550; 33m; 10"; rel 1954*

Elegy
[6852] Jones, Harold (fl); Chertok, Pearl (hp)
- Orion ORS-76227; 33s; rel 1976; cip

Harper's Ferry, W. Va. (Aria for Orchestra) (1960)
[6853] Hamburg Symphony Orchestra; Balazs, Frederic (cond)
- CRI-192/CRI-192(78); 33m/s; rel 1965/1979; cip

In the Valley of the Moon (1955)
[6854] New Symphony Orchestra; Camarata, Salvador (cond)
- London LLP-1213; 33m; rel 1955; del 1957
- CRI-157; 33m/s; rel 1962/?; cip

Pied Piper, The
[6855] Kell, Reginald (cl); Camarata and his Orchestra; Camarata, Salvador (cond)
- Decca DL-7550; 33m; 10"; rel 1954*

Sleepy Hollow (1955)
[6856] New Symphony Orchestra; Camarata, Salvador (cond)
- London LLP-1213; 33m; rel 1955; del 1957
- CRI-157; 33m/s; rel 1962/?; cip

MUCZYNSKI, Robert (1929-)
American Songs
[6857] Atwood, Harry (pf); Muczynski, Robert (pf)
- Music Library MLR-7104; 33m; rel 1963; del 1974

Concerto, Piano and Orchestra, No 1 (1955)
[6858] Muczynski, Robert (pf); Louisville Orchestra; Whitney, Robert (cond)
- LOU-56-5; 33m (Louisville Orchestra First Edition Records 1956 No 5); rel 1959; cip

Dance Movements (Op 17) (1963)
[6859] Arizona Chamber Orchestra; Hull, Robert (cond)
Rec 9/17/78
- Laurel LR-110; 33s; rel 1979; cip

Fables (Op 21): Nos 1-5 and 9
[6860] Grove, Roger (pf)
- Educo 3113; 33

Fantasy Trio (Op 26) (1959)
[6861] Fain, Samuel (cl); Epperson, Gordon (vcl); Muczynski, Robert (pf)
- Coronet LPS-3004; 33s; rel 1974; del 1980

Fuzzette, the Tarantula
[6862] Baksa; Eaton; Coffee, Curtis Webb (fl); Muczynski, Robert (pf)
- Music Library MLR-7104; 33m; rel 1963; del 1974

Great Unfenced
[6863] University of Arizona Symphony; Johnson, Henry (cond)
- Music Library MLR-7110; 33m; rel 1964; del 1974

(Three) Preludes, Flute (Op 18) (1962)
[6864] Padorr, Laila (fl)
- Laurel-Protone LP-14; 33s; rel 1977; cip

(Six) Preludes, Piano (Op 6) (1954)
[6865] Muczynski, Robert (pf)
- Music Library MLR-6998; 33m; rel 1962; del 1974

Serenade for Summer, A (Op 38) (1976)
[6866] Arizona Chamber Orchestra; Hull, Robert (cond)
Rec 9/17/78
- Laurel LR-110; 33s; rel 1979; cip

Sonata, Alto Saxophone and Piano (Op 29)
[6867] Kynaston, Trent (al sax); Muczynski, Robert (pf)
- Coronet LPS-3004; 33s; rel 1974; del 1980

Sonata, Flute and Piano (Op 14) (1961)
[6868] Coffee, Curtis Webb (fl); Muczynski, Robert (pf)
- Music Library MLR-6998; 33m; rel 1962; del 1974

[6869] Swanson, Philip (fl); Muczynski, Robert (pf)
- Coronet LPS-3004; 33s; rel 1974; del 1980

Sonata, Piano, No 1 (Op 9) (1957)
[6870] Muczynski, Robert (pf)
- Music Library MLR-6998; 33m; rel 1962; del 1974

Sonata, Piano, No 2 (Op 22)
[6871] Muczynski, Robert (pf)
- Coronet LPS-3004; 33s; rel 1974; del 1980

Sonata, Violoncello and Piano (Op 25)
[6872] Epperson, Gordon (vcl); Muczynski, Robert (pf)
- Coronet LPS-3000; 33s; rel 1973; cip

Suite, Piano (Op 13) (1960)
[6873] Drake, Paulina (pf)
- Orion ORS-75168; 33s; rel 1975; cip

[6874] Muczynski, Robert (pf)
- Music Library MLR-6998; 33m; rel 1962; del 1974

Toccata, Piano (Op 15) (1961)
[6875] Muczynski, Robert (pf)
- Music Library MLR-6998; 33m; rel 1962; del 1974

Trio, Piano and Strings, No 2 (Op 26) (1975)
[6876] Western Arts Trio
- Laurel LR-106; 33s; rel 1978; cip

Yankee Painter
[6877] Wyszynski; Cine Quartet
- Music Library MLR-7110; 33m; rel 1964; del 1974

MUELLER, Frederick A. (1921-)
Concert Music
[6878] Conner, Rex (tu)
- Coronet M-1259; 33m; rel 1969; cip

MUMMA, Gordon (1935-)
Cybersonic Cantilevers (1973)
[6879] Electronic music
- Folkways FTS-33904; 33s; rel 1976; cip

Hornpipe (1967)
[6880] Electronic music
- Mainstream MS-5010; 33s; rel 1972; del 1979

Mesa (1966)
[6881] Tudor, David (bandoneon); Mumma, Gordon (cybersonic console)
- Odyssey 32-16-0157/32-16-0158; 33m/s; rel 1967; del 1978

Music for the Venezia Space Theater (1964)
[6882] Electronic music
- Advance FGR-5; 33m; rel 1966; cip

MURRAY, A.
I'll Walk Beside You
[6883] Bailey, Norman (b bar); Parsons, Geoffrey (pf)
- L'Oiseau-lyre DSLO-20; 33s; rel 1977

MURRAY, Bain (1926-)
Fence, A
[6884] McCoy, Seth (ten); Shirey, Richard (pf)
- Crystal S-532; 33s; rel 1978; cip

He Wishes for the Cloths of Heaven
[6885] McCoy, Seth (ten); Shirey, Richard (pf)
- Crystal S-532; 33s; rel 1978; cip

Now Close the Windows
[6886] McCoy, Seth (ten); Shirey, Richard (pf)
- Crystal S-532; 33s; rel 1978; cip

On the Divide (1970)
[6887] Philharmonic Chorale and Chamber Ensemble
- Advent USR-5005; 33s; rel 1973; cip

Safe in their Alabaster Chambers (1962)
[6888] Kulas Choir; McGuire, Harvey (E hn); Downs, Warren (vcl); Shaw, Robert (cond)
- CRI-182; 33m/s; rel 1964; cip

MUSSER, Clair
Etudes, Marimba (Op 6): Nos 2, 9, and 10
[6889] Chenoweth, Vida (mrmb)
- Epic LC-3818/BC-1153; 33m/s; rel 1962; del 1965

Preludes, Marimba (Op 11): No 3
[6890] Chenoweth, Vida (mrmb)
- Epic LC-3818/BC-1153; 33m/s; rel 1962; del 1965

MYERS, Robert (1941-)
Percussion Piece
[6891] University of Michigan Percussion Ensemble; Owen, Charles (cond)
- Golden Crest CRSQ-4145; 33q; rel 1977; cip

MYERS, Theldon (1927-)
Andante and Allegro
[6892] Day, Timothy (fl); Palanker, Edward (cl); Minger, Frederick (pf)
- Golden Crest RE-7086; 33s; rel 1980; cip

Cadenza and Lament
[6893] Palanker, Edward (cl); Minger, Frederick (pf)
- Golden Crest RE-7086; 33s; rel 1980; cip

Efflorescence
[6894] Day, Timothy (fl)
- Golden Crest RE-7086; 33s; rel 1980; cip

Night Song
[6895] Palanker, Edward (cl); Minger, Frederick (pf)
- Golden Crest RE-7086; 33s; rel 1980; cip

Sonata, Clarinet and Piano
[6896] Palanker, Edward (cl); Minger, Frederick (pf)
- Golden Crest RE-7086; 33s; rel 1980; cip

Sonatine, Alto Saxophone and Piano
[6897] Briscuso, Joseph (al sax); Minger, Frederick (pf)
- Golden Crest RE-7086; 33s; rel 1980; cip

Valse
[6898] Palanker, Edward (cl); Minger, Frederick (pf)
- Golden Crest RE-7086; 33s; rel 1980; cip

MYGRANT, W. S.
My Maryland
[6899] Goldman Band; Cox, Ainslee (cond)
- New World NW-266; 33s; rel 1977

MYHRE, Milford
Aupres de ma blonde
[6900] Barnes, Ronald (car) or Strauss, Richard (car)
- Washington Cathedral Archives CAR-0002; 33s; rel 1975

Leoni (arr for car)
[6901] Barnes, Ronald (car) or Strauss, Richard (car)
- Washington Cathedral Archives CAR-0002; 33s; rel 1975

MYROW, Frederic (1939-)
Songs from the Japanese (1965)
[6902] Bryn-Julson, Phyllis (sop); Contemporary Chamber Ensemble; Weisberg, Arthur (cond)
- Nonesuch H-71219; 33s; rel 1969; cip

NABOKOV, Nicolas (1903-78)
Holy Devil, The (1958)
[6903] Kentucky Opera Association; Louisville Orchestra; Bomhard, Moritz (cond)
- LOU-59-4; 33m (Louisville Orchestra First Edition Records 1959 No 4); rel 1960; del 1972

Symboli christiani (1956)
[6904] Pickett, William (bar); Louisville Orchestra; Whitney, Robert (cond)
- LOU-58-1; 33m (Louisville Orchestra First Edition Records 1958 No 1); rel 1959; del 1975

NAGEL, Robert (1924-)
Concerto, Trumpet and Strings (Op 8) (1951)
[6905] Blee, Eugene (tpt); Peninsula Festival Orchestra; Johnson, Thor (cond)
- CRI-122; 33m; rel 1958; cip

March
[6906] Swallow, John (tbn); Wingreen,
　　　　Harriet (pf)
　　　　- Golden Crest RE-7015; 33m/s;
　　　　　rel 1965/1979; cip

NAGINSKI, Charles (1909-40)
Nonsense Alphabet Suite
[6907] Martin, Betty (sop); Kagen, Sergius
　　　　(pf)
　　　　- Columbia J-12; 78; 2-10''; rel
　　　　　pre-1942

Pasture, The
[6908] Farrell, Eileen (sop); Trovillo,
　　　　George (pf)
　　　　- Angel 35608; 33m; rel 1959;
　　　　　del 1966

[6909] Frijsh, Povla (sop); Dougherty,
　　　　Celius (pf)
　　　　- Victor 2157 (in set M-789); 78;
　　　　　10''; rel 1941
　　　　- Victor MO-789; 78; 10''; rel
　　　　　1941

[6910] Yeend, Frances (sop); Benner,
　　　　James (pf)
　　　　- Da Vinci DRC-203; 33m; rel
　　　　　1962; del 1964

Sinfonietta (1937)
[6911] Yaddo Chamber Orchestra
　　　　- Yaddo I-7; 78; 2 discs; rel 1940
　　　　- Yaddo IV-8; 78; 2 discs; rel
　　　　　1940

NAJERA, Edmund (1936-)
In dulci jubilo (1959)
[6912] Gregg Smith Singers; Smith, Gregg
　　　　(cond)
　　　　Rec 1975
　　　　- Vox SVBX-5354; 33s; 3 discs; rel
　　　　　1979

Secundum lucam (1970)
[6913] Gregg Smith Singers; Peabody
　　　　Conservatory Choir and Chamber
　　　　Orchestra; Smith, Gregg (cond)
　　　　- Grenadilla GS-1012; 33s; rel
　　　　　1978; cip

NANCARROW, Conlon (1912-)
Studies for Player Piano: Nos 2, 7, 8, 10, 12, 15, 19, 21, 23-25 and 33
[6914] player piano
　　　　- Columbia MS-7222; 33s; rel
　　　　　1969; del 1973

Studies for Player Piano: Nos 4-6, 14, 22, 26, 31, 32, 35, 37, 40a-b
[6915] player piano
　　　　- 1750 Arch S-1777; 33s; rel
　　　　　1980*

Studies for Player Piano: Nos 3a-3e, 20, and 41a-41c
[6916] player piano
　　　　- 1750 Arch S-1768; 33s; rel
　　　　　1978; cip

Studies for Player Piano: Nos 1, 27, and 36
[6917] player piano
　　　　- New World NW-203; 33s; rel
　　　　　1977

NAUMANN, Joel
Miniatures, Violin and Piano (1974)
[6918] Braunlich, Helmut (vln); Dahlman,
　　　　Barbro (pf)
　　　　- Opus One 40; 33s

Variations, Piano (1973)
[6919] Dahlman, Barbro (pf)
　　　　- Opus One 38; 33s

NEAR, Gerald
Passacaglia
[6920] Noehren, Robert (org)
　　　　- Lyrichord LL-191/LLST-7191;
　　　　　33m/s; rel 1968; cip

Suite, Organ: Sarabande and Final
[6921] Roubos, Robert (org)
　　　　Rec 5/12/73
　　　　- Wicks Organ Co TS-73-723-24;
　　　　　33s; rel 1973

NEIKRUG, Marc (1946-)
Quartet, Strings (1972)
[6922] Madison String Quartet
　　　　- Musical Heritage Society
　　　　　MHS-3084; 33s; rel 1978

NELHYBEL, Vaclav (1919-)
Adagio and Allegro
[6923] University of Maryland Symphony
　　　　Band; Ostling, Acton, Jr. (cond)
　　　　- Coronet S-1411; 33s; rel 1969;
　　　　　del 1978

Arco and Pizzicato
[6924] Phoenix String Trio
　　　　- Serenus SRS-12062; 33s; rel
　　　　　1976; cip

Auriel
[6925] Western Illinois University
　　　　Symphonic Wind Ensemble; Izzo,
　　　　Christopher (cond)
　　　　Rec 4/4/79
　　　　- Golden Crest ATH-5060; 33s; rel
　　　　　1980; cip

Brass Piano Quartet
[6926] Rome Symphony Orchestra
　　　　(members of); Flagello, Nicolas
　　　　(cond)
　　　　- Serenus SRE-1006/SRS-12006;
　　　　　33m/s; rel 1965; cip

Caroli antiqui varii
[6927] John Alldis Choir
　　　　- Serenus SRE-1015/SRS-12015;
　　　　　33m/s; rel 1971; cip

Chorale, Brass and Percussion
[6928] Rome Symphony Orchestra
　　　　(members of); Flagello, Nicolas
　　　　(cond)
　　　　- Serenus SRE-1008/SRS-12008;
　　　　　33m/s; rel 1965; cip

[6929] University of Kentucky Symphonic
　　　　Band; Miller, Phillip (cond)
　　　　- Coronet M-1260; 33m; rel
　　　　　1969; del 1978

Concert Etudes, Four Bassoons
[6930] New York Bassoon Quartet
　　　　- Leonarda LPI-102; 33s; rel 1980

Concertino, Piano and Chamber Orchestra (1949)
[6931] Rome Symphony Orchestra
　　　　(members of); Flagello, Nicolas
　　　　(cond)
　　　　- Serenus SRE-1007/SRS-12007;
　　　　　33m/s; rel 1965; cip

Concertino da camera (1971)
[6932] Cooke, Antony (vcl); University of
　　　　South Florida Chamber Winds;
　　　　Croft, James (cond)
　　　　Rec 5/26/79
　　　　- Golden Crest CRS-4189; 33s; rel
　　　　　1980; cip

Concerto spirituoso No 1 (1974)
[6933] Western Illinois University
　　　　Symphonic Wind Ensemble; Izzo,
　　　　Christopher (cond)
　　　　Rec 4/4/79
　　　　- Golden Crest ATH-5060; 33s; rel
　　　　　1980; cip

Concerto spirituoso No 3 (1975)
[6934] Western Illinois University
　　　　Symphonic Wind Ensemble; Izzo,
　　　　Christopher (cond)
　　　　Rec 4/4/79
　　　　- Golden Crest ATH-5060; 33s; rel
　　　　　1980; cip

Counterpoint No 5
[6935] Western Illinois University
　　　　Symphonic Wind Ensemble; Izzo,
　　　　Christopher (cond)
　　　　Rec 4/4/79
　　　　- Golden Crest ATH-5060; 33s; rel
　　　　　1980; cip

Etude symphonique (1949)
[6936] Utah Symphony Orchestra;
　　　　Abravanel, Maurice (cond)
　　　　- Turnabout TVS-34459; 33s; rel
　　　　　1972; cip

Festivo
[6937] Ohio State University Concert
Band; McGinnis, Donald E. (cond)
- Coronet S-1501; 33s; rel 1969;
del 1978

Gran Intrada and Tower Music
[6938] Western Illinois University
Symphonic Wind Ensemble; Izzo,
Christopher (cond)
Rec 4/4/79
- Golden Crest ATH-5060; 33s; rel
1980; cip

House that Jack Built, The
[6939] Reardon, John (bar); Ariel Quintet;
harpsichord; percussion; Heller,
Marsha (cond)
- Serenus SRS-12050; 33s; rel
1974; cip

Impromptus, Six Woodwinds (1963)
[6940] Rome Symphony Orchestra
(members of); Flagello, Nicolas
(cond)
- Serenus SRE-1006/SRS-12006;
33m/s; rel 1965; cip

(Three) Intradas
[6941] Rome Symphony Orchestra
(members of); Flagello, Nicolas
(cond)
- Serenus SRE-1006/SRS-12006;
33m/s; rel 1965; cip

**Kaleidoscope for Young Pianists,
Vol I: Nos 41 and 42**
[6942] Fuszek, Rita (pf)
- Educo 3108; 33

**(Three) Miniatures for Three
Strings**
[6943] Phoenix String Trio
- Serenus SRS-12062; 33s; rel
1976; cip

**(Three) Modes for Orchestra
(1952)**
[6944] Stuttgart Philharmonia; Farberman,
Harold (cond)
- Serenus SRE-1015/SRS-12015;
33m/s; rel 1971; cip

**(Two) Movements, Chamber
Orchestra**
[6945] Rome Symphony Orchestra
(members of); Flagello, Nicolas
(cond)
- Serenus SRE-1007/SRS-12007;
33m/s; rel 1965; cip

(Three) Movements, Strings
[6946] Rome Symphony Orchestra
(members of); Flagello, Nicolas
(cond)
- Serenus SRE-1007/SRS-12007;
33m/s; rel 1965; cip

Numismata (1961)
[6947] Rome Symphony Orchestra
(members of); Flagello, Nicolas
(cond)
- Serenus SRE-1008/SRS-12008;
33m/s; rel 1965; cip

Outer Space
[6948] Electronic music
- Folkways FTS-33440; 33s; rel
1975; cip

Prelude and Fugue
[6949] University of Maryland Symphony
Band; Ostling, Acton, Jr. (cond)
- Coronet S-1411; 33s; rel 1969;
del 1978

Quartet, Horns (1957)
[6950] Rome Symphony Orchestra
(members of); Flagello, Nicolas
(cond)
- Serenus SRE-1007/SRS-12007;
33m/s; rel 1965; cip

Quintetto concertante (1965)
[6951] Cinque Solisti di Roma
- Serenus SRE-1015/SRS-12015;
33m/s; rel 1971; cip

**(Four) Readings from Marlowe's Dr.
Faustus**
[6952] D'Armand, John (ten); Tanner,
Peter (pf)
- Serenus SRS-12049; 33s; rel
1973; cip

Scherzo concertante (1963)
[6953] Kavalovski, Charles (hn); Wolff,
Andrew (pf)
- Musical Heritage Society
MHS-3547; 33s; rel 1977

[6954] Smith, Calvin (hn); Dressler, John
(pf)
- Crystal S-371; 33s; rel 1976; cip

Slavic March
[6955] Rome Symphony Orchestra
(members of); Flagello, Nicolas
(cond)
- Serenus SRE-1006/SRS-12006;
33m/s; rel 1965; cip

Study in Blues
[6956] Goebels, Franzpeter (hpschd)
- Folkways FM-3327; 33m; rel
1964*

**Suite, Trombone and Piano (arr for
tbn and band)**
[6957] McDunn, Mark (tbn); Coe College
Concert Band; Slattery, Thomas
C. (cond)
- Golden Crest CRS-4091; 33s; rel
1970; cip

Trio, Brass (1961)
[6958] Rome Symphony Orchestra
(members of); Flagello, Nicolas
(cond)
- Serenus SRE-1006/SRS-12006;
33m/s; rel 1965; cip

Trittico
[6959] University of Kentucky Symphonic
Band; Miller, Phillip (cond)
- Coronet M-1260; 33m; rel
1969; del 1978

Valse sentimentale
[6960] Rath, Richard (ob); Edwards, Karin
(pf)
- Golden Crest RE-7073; 33s; rel
1978; cip

NELSON, Leon

Improvisations
[6961] Nelson, Leon (org)
- Recorded Publications
Z-80481-82 (matrix no); 33s; rel
1974

NELSON, Oliver E. (1932-)

Black Suite, A
[6962] Stokes, Carl (nar); string quartet;
jazz orchestra; Nelson, Oliver
(cond)
- Flying Dutchman FDS-130; 33s;
rel 1971

NELSON, Ron (1929-)

Christmas Story, The (1959)
[6963] Brown-Pembroke Choir; brass
ensemble; Kunzel, Erich (cond)
- Carillon 123; 33m; rel 1962; del
1966

Rocky Point Holiday (1969)
[6964] Cornell University Wind Ensemble;
Stith, Marice (cond)
- Cornell CUWE-18; 33s; rel 1977;
cip

[6965] University of Minnesota Concert
Band; Bencriscutto, Frank A.
(cond)
- Mark 40400; 33s; 2 discs; rel
1970; del 1976

Sarabande (For Katharine in April)
[6966] Eastman-Rochester Symphony
Orchestra; Hanson, Howard
(cond)
Rec 1958
- Mercury MG-50053/SR-90053;
33m/s; rel 1959; del 1964
- Mercury MG-50337/SR-90337;
33m/s; rel 1963; del 1969
- Eastman-Rochester Archives
ERA-1003; 33s; rel 1974; cip

Savannah River Holiday (1957)
[6967] Eastman-Rochester Symphony
Orchestra; Hanson, Howard
(cond)
Rec 10/28/56
- Mercury MG-50134/SR-90134;
33m/s; rel 1957/1959; del
1963
- Mercury MG-50361/SR-90361;
33m/s; rel 1964; del 1966
- Mercury SRI-75095; 33s; rel
1977; cip
- Eastman-Rochester Archives
ERA-1012; 33s; rel 197?

NERO, Peter (1934-)
Fantasy and Improvisations (Blue Fantasy)
[6968] Nero, Peter (pf); Cherico, Gene
(cb); Cusatis, Joe (perc); Boston
Pops Orchestra; Fiedler, Arthur
(cond)
- RCA LSC-3025; 33s; rel 1968;
del 1974

NESTICO, Samuel (1924-)
Study in Contrasts
[6969] New York Saxophone Quartet
- Mark MES-32322; 33s; rel
1969; cip

NEUMANN, Richard (1914-)
Noches, noches
[6970] Cantica Hebraica; Michno, Dennis
(cond)
- JML-3812; 33s; rel 1977?

NEVIN, Gordon Balch (1892-1943)
Will-o'-the-Wisp
[6971] Ellsasser, Richard (org)
- MGM E-3031; 33m; rel 1953;
del 1959

[6972] Prince-Joseph, Bruce (org)
- Hi-Fi R-720/S-720; 33m/s; rel
1959; del 1967
- Everest LPBR-6156/SDBR-3156;
33m/s; rel 1967; cip

NEWBURY, Kent A. (1925-)
Psalm 150
[6973] Capital University Chapel Choir;
Snyder, Ellis Emanuel (cond)
- Westminster
XWN-19024/WST-17024;
33m/s; rel 1963; del 1967

NEWELL, Robert (1940-)
Spirals
[6974] no performers given
- Advance FGR-25S; 33s; rel
1979; cip

NEWLIN, Dika (1923-)
Machine Shop
[6975] Gamelan Son of Lion
- Folkways FTS-31313; 33s; rel
1980; cip

Trio, Piano and Strings (Op 2) (1948)
[6976] London Czech Trio
- CRI-170; 33m; rel 1963; cip

NEWMAN, Anthony (1941-)
Barricades
[6977] Pryor, Cecelia (voice); Newman,
Anthony (kbds); Mann, Bob (gtr);
Austria, Jaime (cb); Cox, Dave
(perc)
- Columbia M-32439/MQ-32439;
33s/q; rel 1973; del 1976

Bhajebochstiannanas
[6978] Newman, Anthony (org); Akright,
Mr. and Mrs. James (bells)
- Columbia M-32439/MQ-32439;
33s/q; rel 1973; del 1976

Chimaeras I and II
[6979] Newman, Anthony (hpschd)
- Columbia M-30062; 33s; rel
1970; del 1976

Habitat
[6980] Newman, Anthony (pf) (perc);
Austria, Jaime (cb); Corigliano,
John (perc)
- Columbia M-32439/MQ-32439;
33s/q; rel 1973; del 1976

Piano Cycle No 1
[6981] Newman, Anthony (pf)
- Cambridge CRS-B-2833; 33s; rel
1979; cip

Sonata, Violin and Piano
[6982] Berg, Bruce (vln); Newman,
Anthony (pf)
- Cambridge CRS-B-2833; 33s; rel
1979; cip

Sonata, Violoncello and Piano
[6983] Zlotkin, Frederick (vcl); Newman,
Anthony (pf)
- Cambridge CRS-B-2833; 33s; rel
1979; cip

Variations and Grand Contrapunctus
[6984] Verdery, Benjamin (gtr)
- Cambridge CRS-B-2833; 33s; rel
1979; cip

NEWSOM, Hugh Raymond (1891-1978)
Concertante in Three Movements, Harp and Piano
[6985] Newsom, Marjorie Brunton (hp);
Newsom, Hugh Raymond (pf)
- Performance 4032-3; 33s; rel
1973

Divine Tragedy, The
[6986] Grether, Olga (al); Smith-Spencer,
Harvey (ten); Chalmers, William
(bar); Gange, Fraser (b); Thomas,
Matt (b); Grosheff, Anatol (b);
chorus; orchestra; Newsom, Hugh
Raymond (cond)
- Performance 5052; 33s; rel
1972

(Ten) Nocturnes, Piano
[6987] Newsom, Hugh Raymond (pf)
- Performance 4101N34; 33s; rel
1974

(Fifteen) Preludes, Piano
[6988] Newsom, Hugh Raymond (pf)
- Performance 6103N7; 33s; rel
1976

NICHOL, J.
Summer of Timothy Once, The
[6989] no performers given
- Minnesota Public Radio 29203;
33s; rel 1976

NIGHTINGALE, James (1948-)
Entente
[6990] Nightingale, James (acc); harp
- Orion ORS-77263; 33s; rel
1977; cip

NIKOLAIS, Alwin (1912-)
Choreosonic Music of the New Dance
[6991] Henry Street Playhouse Theatre
Dance Company (members of);
Nikolais, Alwin (cond)
- Hanover 5005; 33m; rel 1960;
del 1961

NILES, John Jacob (1892-1980)
Evening
[6992] Parker, William (bar); Huckaby,
William (pf)
- New World NW-305; 33s; rel
1980

For My Brother (Reported Missing in Action, 1943)
[6993] Parker, William (bar); Huckaby,
William (pf)
- New World NW-305; 33s; rel
1980

Go 'Way from My Window
[6994] Souez, Ina (sop); Simpson, Loyd
(pf)
- New Sound 5001; 33m; rel
1956; del 1958

Love Winter When the Plant Says Nothing
[6995] Parker, William (bar); Huckaby,
William (pf)
- New World NW-305; 33s; rel
1980

NIN-CULMELL, Joaquin Maria (1908-)

Diferencias (1962)
[6996] Louisville Orchestra; Mester, Jorge (cond)
Rec 1/21/76
- LS-76-1; 33s (Louisville Orchestra First Edition Records 1976 No 1); rel 1978; cip

Tonadas (1956-61): (Vol II) Nos 14, 15, 19, 21, 22, and 24
[6997] De Larrocha, Alicia (pf)
- London CS-6677; 33s; rel 1971; cip

Variations on a Theme by Milan
[6998] Brouwer, Leo (gtr)
- Musical Heritage Society MHS-3839; 33s; rel 1978

[6999] Torre, Rey de la (gtr)
- Philharmonia 106; 33m; rel 1952; del 1958
- Epic LC-3815/BC-1151; 33m/s; rel 1962; del 1963
- Elektra EKL-244; 33m; rel 1964; del 1971
- Nonesuch H-71233; 33s; rel 1969; cip

NIXON, Roger (1921-)

Centennial Fanfare-March (1970)
[7000] Baylor University Wind Ensemble; Floyd, Richard (cond)
- Golden Crest ATH-5062; 33s; rel 1980; cip

Dances Sacred and Profane
[7001] Baylor University Wind Ensemble; Floyd, Richard (cond)
- Golden Crest ATH-5062; 33s; rel 1980; cip

Elegy and Fanfare-March (1967)
[7002] Ohio State University Concert Band; McGinnis, Donald E. (cond)
- Coronet S-1501; 33s; rel 1969; del 1978

Fiesta del Pacifico (1966)
[7003] Baylor University Wind Ensemble; Floyd, Richard (cond)
- Golden Crest ATH-5062; 33s; rel 1980; cip

[7004] Eastman Symphonic Wind Ensemble; Hunsberger, Donald (cond)
- Decca DL-710157; 33s; rel 1968; del 1973

(Six) Moods of Love (1950)
[7005] Blum, Margot (m sop)
- Music Library MLR-7112; 33m; rel 1965; del 1974

[7006] Renzi, Dorothy (sop); Pierce, Raylene (pf)
- Fantasy 5009; 33m; rel 1960; del 1970

Music for a Civic Celebration
[7007] Goldman Band; Cox, Ainslee (cond)
- Columbia M-33838; 33s; rel 1975; cip

Pacific Celebration Suite
[7008] Baylor University Wind Ensemble; Floyd, Richard (cond)
- Golden Crest ATH-5062; 33s; rel 1980; cip

Quartet, Strings, No 1 (1949)
[7009] California String Quartet
- Music Library MLR-3-7; 78; 3 discs; rel pre-1952
- Music Library MLR-7005; 33m; rel 1952; del 1974

Reflections (1962)
[7010] Baylor University Wind Ensemble; Floyd, Richard (cond)
- Golden Crest ATH-5062; 33s; rel 1980; cip

Solemn Processional, A (1971)
[7011] Baylor University Wind Ensemble; Floyd, Richard (cond)
- Golden Crest ATH-5062; 33s; rel 1980; cip

Wine of Astonishment, The (1960)
[7012] San Francisco State College A Cappella Choir; Tegnell, John Carl (cond)
- Music Library MLR-6997; 33m; rel 1963; del 1974

NOEHREN, Robert (1910-)

Fantasia, Organ (Homage to Hindemith)
[7013] Noehren, Robert (org)
- Lyrichord LL-191/LLST-7191; 33m/s; rel 1968; cip

Sonata, Organ
[7014] Craighead, David (org)
Rec 7/31/57
- Mirrosonic DRE-1012; 33m; 2 discs; rel 1958; del 1965

NOON, David (1946-)

Motets and Monodies (Op 31)
[7015] Roseman, Ronald (ob); Snow, John (E hn); Polisi, Joseph (bsn)
- Crystal S-341; 33s; rel 1979; cip

NORDENSTROM, Gladys (1924-)

Zeit XXIV (Renata Pandula) (1976)
[7016] Pilgrim, Neva (sop); Helmrich, Dennis (pf)
Rec 12/22/78
- Orion ORS-79348; 33s; rel 1979; cip

NORDOFF, Paul (1909-77)

There Shall Be More Joy
[7017] Farrell, Eileen (sop); Trovillo, George (pf)
- Angel 35608; 33m; rel 1959; del 1966

White Nocturne
[7018] Hanks, John Kennedy (ten); Friedberg, Ruth (pf)
- Duke University Press DWR-6417-18; 33m; 2 discs; rel 1966; del 1975

Winter Symphony (1954)
[7019] Louisville Orchestra; Whitney, Robert (cond)
- LOU-57-1; 33m (Louisville Orchestra First Edition Records 1957 No 1); rel 1957; del 1978

NORMAN, Ruth

Molto allegro (1970)
[7020] Norman, Ruth (pf)
- Opus One 35; 33s; rel 1978; cip

Prelude IV (1974)
[7021] Norman, Ruth (pf)
- Opus One 35; 33s; rel 1978; cip

NORMAN, Theodore (1912-)

(Two) Moods in Twelve-Tone
[7022] Kneubuhl, John (gtr)
- Orion ORS-78323; 33s; rel 1979; cip

Samba
[7023] Kneubuhl, John (gtr)
- Orion ORS-78323; 33s; rel 1979; cip

Toccata, Guitar
[7024] Kneubuhl, John (gtr)
- Orion ORS-78323; 33s; rel 1979; cip

NORTH, Alex (1910-)

Holiday Set (1948)
[7025] Vienna Philharmonic Orchestra; Adler, F. Charles (cond)
- SPA-47; 33m; rel 1953; del 1970

If You Are There
[7026] Booth, Webster (ten); piano
- Gramophone B-9777; 78; 10"; rel pre-1952

Symphony No 2 (1968)
[7027] orchestra; North, Alex (cond)
- MGM E-4462; 33m; rel 1967

NORTON, Spencer (1909-)

Dance Suite (1939): Prologue

[7028] Eastman-Rochester Symphony
Orchestra; Hanson, Howard
(cond)
- Victor 11-8116 (in set M-889);
78; rel pre-1942

Partita, Two Pianos and Orchestra (1959)

[7029] Zaremba, Sylvia (pf); Bell, Digby
(pf); Oklahoma City Symphony
Orchestra; Harrison, Guy Fraser
(cond)
- CRI-151; 33m/s; rel 1962/?; cip

NOWAK, Lionel (1911-)

Concert Piece for Kettledrums (1961)

[7030] Calabro, Louis (timp); Bennington
String Ensemble; Nowak, Lionel
(cond)
- CRI-260; 33s; rel 1971; cip

Soundscape

[7031] Bennington Woodwind Trio
- Golden Crest CRS-4140; 33q; rel
1976; cip

Suite, Flute and Piano

[7032] Luening, Otto (fl); Nowak, Lionel
(pf)
- Yaddo III-3; 78; 10''; rel 1940

NUNLIST, Juli (1916-)

(Two) Pieces, Piano (1961)

[7033] Loesser, Arthur (pf)
- CRI-183; 33m/s; rel 1964/?; cip

Spells (1963)

[7034] Philharmonic Chorale
- Advent USR-5005; 33s; rel
1973; cip

NUROCK, Kirk (1948-)

Scat Melisma

[7035] Natural Sound Workshop
- Minnesota Public Radio 29203;
33s; rel 1976

NYQUIST, Roger (1934-)

Adagio

[7036] Nyquist, Roger (org)
Rec 10/9/69
- Chapel S-5158; 33s; rel 1970

OAK, Kilsung (1942-)

Amorphosis (1973)

[7037] Moss, Danielle (sop); New Jersey
Percussion Ensemble; DesRoches,
Raymond (cond)
- Nonesuch H-71291/HQ-1291;
33s/q; rel 1974/1976; cip

O'BRIEN, Eugene (1945-)

Ambages (1972)

[7038] Priest, Maxine (pf); Abbott, Michael
(pf)
- Golden Crest GCCL-202; 33s; rel
1978; cip

Lingual (1971)

[7039] Nuove Forme Sonore
- Crystal S-532; 33s; rel 1978; cip

OGDON, Wilbur (1921-)

By the Isar

[7040] Turetzky, Bertram (cb); soprano;
alto flute
- Desto DC-7128; 33s; rel 1972;
cip

OLAN, David (1948-)

Composition for Clarinet and Tape (1975-76)

[7041] Flax, Laura (cl); tape
- CRI-419; 33s; rel 1980; cip

Octet

[7042] Parnassus; Korf, Anthony (cond)
- New World NW-306; 33s; rel
1980

Sonata, Violin and Piano (1974)

[7043] Schulte, Rolf (vln); Miller, Robert
(pf)
- CRI-419; 33s; rel 1980; cip

OLIVEROS, Pauline (1932-)

Bye Bye Butterfly (1965)

[7044] Electronic music
- 1750 Arch S-1765; 33s; rel
1978; cip

I of IV (1967)

[7045] Electronic music
- Odyssey 32-16-0160; 33s; rel
1967; cip

Outline (1963)

[7046] Turetzky, Nancy (fl); Turetzky,
Bertram (cb); George, Ronald
(perc)
- Nonesuch H-71237; 33s; rel
1970; cip

Sound Patterns (1961)

[7047] Brandeis University Chamber
Chorus; Lucier, Alvin (cond)
- Odyssey
32-16-0155/32-16-0156;
33m/s; rel 1967; cip

[7048] New Music Choral Ensemble;
Gaburo, Kenneth (cond)
- Ars Nova/Ars Antiqua AN-1005;
33s; rel 1971; del 1973

Trio, Flute, Piano, and Page Turner (1961)

[7049] no performers given
- Advance FGR-9S; 33s; rel 197?

OREM, Preston Ware (1865-1938)

American Indian Rhapsody (publ 1918)

[7050] Basquin, Peter (pf)
- New World NW-213; 33s; rel
1977

ORNSTEIN, Leo (1892-)

A la chinoise (Op 39) (ca 1918)

[7051] Sellers, Michael (pf)
- Orion ORS-75194; 33s; rel
1976; cip

[7052] Verbit, Martha Anne (pf)
- Genesis GS-1066; 33s; rel
1977; cip

Arabesques (Op 42)

[7053] Verbit, Martha Anne (pf)
- Genesis GS-1066; 33s; rel
1977; cip

Biography in Sonata Form (1974)

[7054] Sellers, Michael (pf)
- Orion ORS-78285; 33s; rel
1979; cip

Chant of the Hindu Priests

[7055] Sellers, Michael (pf)
- Orion ORS-75194; 33s; rel
1976; cip

Impressions de Notre Dame (Op 16, Nos 1-2) (1914)

[7056] Hays, Doris (pf)
- Finnadar SR-2-720; 33s; 2 discs;
rel 1980; cip

Melancholy Landscape

[7057] Sellers, Michael (pf)
- Orion ORS-75194; 33s; rel
1976; cip

(Three) Moods (1914)

[7058] Sellers, Michael (pf)
- Orion ORS-75194; 33s; rel
1976; cip

[7059] Westney, William (pf)
Rec 6/18/75
- CRI-339; 33s; rel 1976; cip

Morning in the Woods, A (1971)

[7060] Verbit, Martha Anne (pf)
- Genesis GS-1066; 33s; rel
1977; cip

Nocturne and Dance of the Fates (ca 1937)

[7061] Louisville Orchestra; Mester, Jorge
(cond)
Rec 1/20/76
- LS-75-4; 33s (Louisville
Orchestra First Edition Records
1975 No 4); rel 1976; cip

Poems of 1917 (Op 41) (1917)
[7062] Sellers, Michael (pf)
- Orion ORS-75194; 33s; rel 1976; cip

(Six) Preludes, Violoncello and Piano (1931): Three Preludes
[7063] Hampton, Bonnie (vcl); Schwartz, Nathan (pf)
- Orion ORS-76211; 33s; rel 1976; cip

Quintet, Piano and Strings (Op 92) (1927)
[7064] Westney, William (pf); Stepner, Daniel (vln); Strauss, Michael (vln); Sacco, Peter John (vla); Mansbacher, Thomas (vcl)
Rec 6/10-12/75
- CRI-339; 33s; rel 1976; cip

Sonata, Piano, No 4 (ca 1924)
[7065] Verbit, Martha Anne (pf)
- Genesis GS-1066; 33s; rel 1977; cip

Sonata, Violoncello and Piano (Op 52) (ca 1918)
[7066] Hampton, Bonnie (vcl); Schwartz, Nathan (pf)
- Orion ORS-76211; 33s; rel 1976; cip

Wild Men's Dance (Danse sauvage) (Op 13, No 2) (ca 1915)
[7067] Sellers, Michael (pf)
- Orion ORS-75194; 33s; rel 1976; cip

OSBORNE, Willson (1906-)
Rhapsody, Bassoon
[7068] Grossman, Arthur (bsn)
- Ravenna RAVE-761; 33s; rel 1977; cip

[7069] Sharrow, Leonard (bsn)
- Coronet M-1294; 33m; rel 1969; cip

OSTERLING, Eric (1926-)
Bandology
[7070] H. M. Royal Marines Band; Neville, Paul (cond)
- Arabesque 8006; 33s; rel 1980; cip

OVERTON, Hall (1920-72)
Polarities No 1 (1959)
[7071] Helps, Robert (pf)
- RCA LM-7042/LSC-7042; 33m/s; 2 discs; rel 1966; del 1971
- CRI-288; 33s; 2 discs; rel 1972; cip

Pulsations (1972)
[7072] Ensemble, The; Davies, Dennis Russell (cond)
- CRI-298; 33s; rel 1973; cip

Quartet, Strings, No 2 (1954)
[7073] Beaux-Arts String Quartet
- CRI-126; 33m/s; rel 1960/?; cip

Sonata, Viola and Piano (1960)
[7074] Trampler, Walter (vla); Greene, Lucy (pf)
- EMS Recordings EMS-403/EMS-S-403; 33m/s; rel 1962; del 1968

Sonata, Violoncello and Piano (1960)
[7075] McCracken, Charles (vcl); Greene, Lucy (pf)
- EMS Recordings EMS-403/EMS-S-403; 33m/s; rel 1962; del 1968

Sonorities (1964)
[7076] Orchestra USA; Farberman, Harold (cond)
- Columbia CL-2395/CS-9195; 33m/s; rel 1965; del 1967

Symphony No 2 (1962)
[7077] Louisville Orchestra; Whitney, Robert (cond)
- LOU-63-3/LS-63-3; 33m/s (Louisville Orchestra First Edition Records 1963 No 3); rel 1963/1965; del 1975

OWEN, Blythe (1898-)
Festal Prelude
[7078] Becker, C. Warren (org)
Rec 3/66
- STCP-662; 33m; rel 1966

OWEN, Harold (1931-)
Chamber Music, Four Clarinets
[7079] Los Angeles Clarinet Society
- WIM Records WIMR-7; 33s; rel 1973; cip

OWEN, Richard (1922-)
Fisherman Called Peter, A
[7080] Owen, L.; orchestra; chorus; Egermann (cond)
- Serenus SRS-12027; 33s; rel 1971; cip

I Saw a Man Pursuing the Horizon
[7081] Reardon, John (bar); Hebert, Bliss (pf)
- Serenus SRE-1019/SRS-12019; 33m/s; rel 1967; cip

There Were Many Who Went in Huddled Procession
[7082] Reardon, John (bar); Hebert, Bliss (pf)
- Serenus SRE-1019/SRS-12019; 33m/s; rel 1967; cip

PALMER, Courtlandt (1872-)
Chorale with Interludes
[7083] Barnes, William H. (org)
- Replica FB-512-13; 33m; rel 1957?

PALMER, Robert (1915-)
Chamber Concerto, Violin, Oboe, and Chamber Orchestra (1949)
[7084] Taylor, Millard (vln); Sprenkle, Robert (ob); Rochester Chamber Orchestra; Hull, Robert (cond)
- Concert Hall CHS-1190; 33m; rel 1954; del 1957
- Concert Hall H-1690; 33m; rel 1957; del 1959

Choric Song and Toccata (1968)
[7085] Cornell University Wind Ensemble; Stith, Marice (cond)
- Cornell CUWE-2; 33s; rel 1971; cip

Memorial Music (1960)
[7086] Orchestre des Solistes de Paris; Husa, Karel (cond)
- Cornell N80P-5536-37 (matrix no); 33m; rel 1962; del 1976

Nabuchodonosor (1964)
[7087] Rochester Symphonic Brass Ensemble; Cornell University Glee Club; Sokol, Thomas A. (cond)
- Fleetwood 6001; 33m; rel 1967; del 1971

(Three) Preludes, Piano (1941)
[7088] Behrend, Jeanne (pf)
- Allegro ALG-3024; 33m; rel 1951; del 1952
- Concord 3017; 33m; rel 1957; del 1959

Quartet, Piano and Strings, No 1 (1947)
[7089] Walden String Quartet
- Columbia ML-4842; 33m; rel 1954; del 1968
- Columbia CML-4842; 33m; rel 1968; del 1974
- Columbia AML-4842; 33m; rel 1974; del 1976

Quintet, Clarinet, String Trio, and Piano (1952)
[7090] Bloom, Arthur (cl); Kooper, Kees (vln); Doktor, Paul (vla); Lash, Warren (vcl); Boehm-Kooper, Mary Louise (pf)
- Turnabout TVS-34508; 33s; rel 1973; del 1978

Slow, Slow, Fresh Fount (1953)
[7091] Cornell A Cappella Choir; Hull, Robert (cond)
- Concert Hall CHS-1190; 33m; rel 1954; del 1957
- Concert Hall H-1690; 33m; rel 1957; del 1959

Sonata, Piano, No 1 (1938)
[7092] Kirkpatrick, John (pf)
- Yaddo III-6; 78; 2-10''; rel 1940

Sonata, Trumpet and Piano (1972)
[7093] Stith, Marice (tpt); Palmer, Robert (pf)
- Redwood RRES-4; 33s; rel 1977; cip

Toccata ostinato (1945)
[7094] Mandel, Alan (pf)
- Desto DC-6445-47; 33s; 3 discs; rel 1975; cip

PALMER, Rudolph (1952-)
Contrasts
[7095] New York Bassoon Quartet
- Leonarda LPI-102; 33s; rel 1980

PALOMBO, Paul M. (1937-)
Metathesis (1970)
[7096] Heritage Chamber Quartet
- Piper 3081; 33s; rel 1973; del 1978

Morphosis (1970)
[7097] Electronic music
- Music Now CFS-3037; 33s; rel 1974*

PANELLA, Frank A. (1878-1953)
My Maryland Fantasia
[7098] Arthur Pryor's Band
- Victor 35028; 78

On the Square
[7099] University of Michigan Winds and Percussion; Lillya, Clifford P. (cond)
Rec 2/18-19/75
- University of Michigan SM-0002; 33s; rel 1978; cip

PARKER, Horatio W. (1863-1919)
(Four) Compositions, Organ (Op 28) (1891): (No 3) Pastorale
[7100] Smith, Rollin (org)
Rec 8/73
- Repertoire Recording Society RRS-12; 33s; rel 1974

(Four) Compositions, Organ (Op 36) (1893): (No 3) Fugue in C Minor
[7101] Beck, Janice (org)
- Musical Heritage Society OR-A-263; 33s; rel 1972

[7102] Harmon, Thomas (org)
- Orion ORS-76255; 33s; rel 1977; cip

[7103] Morris, Richard (org)
- New World NW-280; 33s; rel 1978

Hora novissima (Op 30) (1893)
[7104] Hopf, Gertrude (sop); Wien, Erika (al); Kent, Edward (ten); Berry, Walter (b); Vienna Symphony Orchestra; Strickland, William (cond)
- American Recording Society ARS-335; 33m; 2 discs; rel 1953
- Desto D-413-14/DST-6413-14; 33m/s; 2 discs; rel 1965; cip

Hora novissima: Urbs syon and Pars mea
[7105] no performers given
- Washington Cathedral Archives CAR-004-05; 33s; 2 discs; rel 1976

Legend of St. Christopher, The (Op 43) (1897): Jam sol recedit igneus
[7106] Washington Cathedral Choir of Men and Boys; Callaway, Paul (cond)
- Vanguard VRS-1036/VSD-2021; 33m/s; rel 1959; del 1968

Mona (Op 71) (1910): Prelude
[7107] Eastman-Rochester Symphony Orchestra; Hanson, Howard (cond)
- Mercury SR-90524; 33s; rel 1970; del 1974

Mona: Interlude
[7108] Hamburg Philharmonia; Korn, Richard (cond)
- Allegro ALG-3150; 33m; rel 1955*
- Concord 3007; 33m; rel 1957; del 1959

(Trois) Morceaux caracteristiques (Op 49) (1899): (No 3) Valse gracile
[7109] Frager, Malcolm (pf)
- New World NW-206; 33s; rel 1978

[7110] Hofmann, Josef (pf)
- Columbia A-6125; 78; rel 1912-22

Northern Ballad, A (Op 46) (1899)
[7111] Royal Philharmonic Orchestra; Krueger, Karl (cond)
- SPAMH MIA-132; 33s; rel 1966

(Six) Old English Songs (Op 47) (1897-99): (No 6) The Lark
[7112] Casey, Ethel (sop); Siddell, Bill (pf)
- Carolina 712C-1713; 33m; rel 1965

[7113] De Gogorza, Emilio (bar)
Rec 5/18/08
- Victor 74118; 78; rel 1908-09
- Victor 6072; 78; rel 1908-09
- New World NW-247; 33m; rel 1976

(Three) Part Songs (Op 48) (1901): (No 2) The Lamp in the West
[7114] Syracuse University Glee Club
- Brunswick 3165; 78; 10''; rel pre-1927

[7115] University of Kansas Glee Club
- Columbia 691D; 78; rel pre-1927

(Five) Short Pieces, Organ (Op 68) (1908): (No 2) Slumber Song and (No 4) Arietta
[7116] Beck, Janice (org)
- Musical Heritage Society OR-A-263; 33s; rel 1972

Sonata, Organ, E-flat (Op 65) (1908)
[7117] Osborne, William (org)
- Orion ORS-78309; 33s; rel 1978; cip

Sonata, Organ, E-flat: 1st Movement
[7118] Gay, Harry W. (org)
- Erico BPC-101; 33s; rel 1974

Sonata, Organ, E-flat: 3rd Movement
[7119] Beck, Janice (org)
- Musical Heritage Society OR-A-263; 33s; rel 1972

[7120] Miller, Max (org)
- Organ Historical Society/Redwood OHS-ST-1; 33s; rel 1976

(Four) Songs (Op 51) (1901): (No 4) Love in May
[7121] Eames, Emma (sop)
Rec 5/18/08
- Victor 88131; 78
- New World NW-247; 33m; rel 1976

Vathek (Op 56) (1903)
[7122] Royal Philharmonic Orchestra; Krueger, Karl (cond)
- SPAMH MIA-138; 33s; rel 1968*

PARKER, Muriel (1908-)
Toccata, Interlude, and Fugue
[7123] Parker, Muriel (pf)
- Yaddo 40A-B; 78; rel 1937

PARKS, James A. (ca 1863-1945)
King of Glory, The (Psalm 24)
[7124] Smith, Jessie Evans (voice); Mormon Tabernacle Choir; Philadelphia Orchestra; Condie, Richard P. (cond)
- Columbia ML-6235/MS-6835; 33m/s; rel 1966; cip

PARRIS, Robert (1924-)

Book of Imaginary Beings, The (1972)

[7125] Skidmore, Dorothy (fl); Barnett, Ronald (perc); Jones, Thomas (perc); University of Maryland Trio
- Turnabout TVS-34568; 33s; rel 1975; del 1978
- Orion ORS-78301; 33s; rel 1978; cip

Concerto, Percussion, Violin, and Violoncello

[7126] Barnett, Ronald (perc); University of Maryland Trio
- Orion ORS-78301; 33s; rel 1978; cip

Concerto, Trombone and Chamber Orchestra (1964)

[7127] Siwek, Roman (tbn); Polish National Radio Orchestra; Szostak, Zdzislav (cond)
- CRI-231; 33s; rel 1968; cip

Fantasy and Fugue

[7128] Christensen, Roy (vcl)
- Gasparo GS-104; 33s; rel 1977

PARRY, Roland

All Faces West: Excerpts

[7129] Gorin, Igor (bar); Larsen, Jack (ten); Devereux, Wayne (org); Thuesen, Dean (nar); Weber College Singers; Utah Symphony Orchestra (string ensemble); Parry, Roland (cond)
- Par-Go; 33m; rel 1952*

PARTCH, Harry (1901-76)

And on the Seventh Day Petals Fell in Petaluma (1964)

[7130] Gate 5 Ensemble; Partch, Harry (cond)
- CRI-213; 33m/s; rel 1968; cip

Barstow (Eight Hitchhiker Inscriptions from a Highway Railing at Barstow, California) (1941)

[7131] ensemble of instruments developed by the composer: McAllister, John; Ranta, Michael; Schell, Linda; Partch, Harry (nar); Stannard, John (nar); Mitchell, Danlee (cond)
- Columbia MS-7207; 33s; rel 1969; cip
- Columbia MQ-31227; 33q; rel 1972; del 1976

Bewitched, The (1955)

[7132] Schell, Freda Pierce (sop); Gate 5 Ensemble; Garvey, John (cond)
Rec 1957
- Gate 5 Issue 3; 33m; rel 1957
- Gate 5 Issue E; 33; rel 1962 (excerpts)

Bewitched, The (1955) *(cont'd)*
- CRI-193; 33m/s; rel 1964/?; cip (Excerpts: Scene 10 and Epilogue)
- CRI-304; 33s; 2 discs; rel 1974; cip

Bless This House (1961)

[7133] Gate 5 Ensemble
- Gate 5 Issue A; 33; rel 1962

By the Rivers of Babylon (Psalm 137) (1931)

[7134] Gate 5 Ensemble
- Gate 5 Issue A; 33; rel 1962

Cloud-Chamber Music (1950)

[7135] Johnston, Ben; Johnston, Betty; Pippin, Donald; Partch, Harry
Rec 1950
- CRI-193; 33m/s; rel 1964/?; cip

Delusion of the Fury (1969)

[7136] ensemble of instruments developed by the composer; Mitchell, Danlee (cond)
- Columbia M2-30576; 33s; 2 discs; rel 1971; cip

Dreamer That Remains, The (1972)

[7137] Partch, Harry (intoning voice) (nar); Hoffman, Mark (voice); Mitchell, Danlee (voice) (new kithara I); Szanto, Jon (voice) (ektara and boo II); Bjornson, Katherine (voice); Glattly, Alexis (voice); Crosier, Michael (voice); Caruso, Ron (gourd tree); Dunn, David (adapted vla); Dunn, Dennis (new harmonic canon I); Francois, Jean-Charles (quadrangularis reversum); Glasier, Jonathan (new harmonic canon I); Hoffman, Randy (eucal blossom) (mbira bass dyad); Richards, Emil (cloud-chamber bowls); Thomas, Duane (harmonic canon II); Thumm, Francis (chromelodeon); Logan, Jack (cond)
Rec 1973
- New World NW-214; 33s; rel 1978

(Fourteen) Intrusions (1950): The Rose, The Street, The Waterfall, and The Wind

[7138] Partch, Harry (intoning voice) (adapted gtr II) (harmonic canon II) (harmonic canon I); Johnston, Ben (diamond mrmb) (b mrmb)
- Gate 5 Issue A; 33; rel 1962
- New World NW-214; 33s; rel 1978

Letter, The (1943)

[7139] Partch, Harry (nar); Gate 5 Ensemble; McKenzie, Jack (cond)
Rec 1950
- Gate 5 Issue B; 33; rel 196?
- CRI-193; 33m/s; rel 1964/?; cip

(Seventeen) Lyrics by Li Po (1931): Six Lyrics

[7140] Partch, Harry (intoning voice) (adapted vla); Wendlandt, William (ten); Johnston, Ben; Johnston, Betty; Pippin, Donald; Garvey, John (cond)
- Gate 5 Issue A; 33; rel 1962

(Seventeen) Lyrics by Li Po: The Intruder, I Am a Peach Tree, A Midnight Farewell, and Before the Cask of Wine

[7141] Wendlandt, William (intoning voice); Partch, Harry (intoning voice) (adapted vla)
Rec 1947
- New World NW-214; 33s; rel 1978

Oedipus (1951)

[7142] Louw, Allan (voice); Stark, Sue Bell (voice); Gate 5 Ensemble; Hohensee, Jack (cond)
- Gate 5 Issue 2; 33m; rel 1954
- Partch LP-2-3; 33m; 2 discs; rel pre-1956
- Gate 5 Issue D; 33; rel 1962 (excerpts)

Plectra and Percussion Dances (1952): Castor and Pollux

[7143] ensemble of instruments developed by the composer; Coleman, Gary; Drummond, Dean; McAllister, John; Richards, Emil; Ranta, Michael; Schell, Linda; Mitchell, Danlee (cond)
- Columbia MS-7207; 33s; rel 1969; cip
- Columbia MQ-31227; 33q; rel 1972; del 1976

[7144] Ludlow, L (nar); Ludlow, A. (nar); Gate 5 Ensemble; Schwartz, Horace (cond)
Rec 1953
- Gate 5 Issue 1; 33m; rel 1953*
- Partch LP-9; 33m; rel pre-1956
- Gate 5 Issue 4; 33m; rel 1957
- Gate 5 Issue C; 33; rel 1962
- CRI-193; 33m/s; rel 1964/?; cip

Revelation in the Courthouse Square (1962)

[7145] Schell, Freda Pierce (sop); Foote, Jeffrey (b bar); University of Illinois Ensemble; Garvey, John (cond)
- Gate 5 Issue F; 33; rel 1962

Rotate the Body in All Its Planes (1963): Excerpts

[7146] University of Illinois Ensemble; Garvey, John (cond)
- Gate 5 Issue G; 33; rel 196?

Ulysses at the Edge of the World (1955)
[7147] Gate 5 Ensemble; McKenzie, Jack (cond)
Rec 1958
- Gate 5 Issue B; 33; rel 196?

[7148] Logan, Jack (tpt); other instrumentalists
- Orion ORS-7294; 33s; rel 1972; cip

US Highball (1943)
[7149] Coleman, Thomas (ten); Gate 5 Ensemble; McKenzie, Jack (cond)
Rec 1958
- Gate 5 Issue 6; 33m; rel 1956
- Gate 5 Issue B; 33; rel 196?

[7150] Hoiby, Lee (kithara); Wendlandt, William (voice); Charnstrom, Christine (chromelodeon); Gieschen, Hulda (harmonic canon); Partch, Harry (intoning voice) (adapted gtr)
- Gilsonophone GME-2-130-35; 78; 3 discs

Water! Water! (1961): Excerpts
[7151] University of Illinois Ensemble; Garvey, John (cond)
- Gate 5 Issue G; 33; rel 196?

Windsong (Daphne of the Dunes) (1958)
[7152] ensemble of instruments developed by the composer: Partch, Harry; Berberich, Frank; Coleman, Gary; Drummond, Dean; Lapore, Richard; McAllister, John; McCormick, Robert; Miller, Todd; Richards, Emil; Ranta, Michael; Schell, Linda; Mitchell, Danlee (cond)
- Columbia MS-7207; 33s; rel 1969; cip
- Columbia MQ-31227; 33q; rel 1972; del 1976

Windsong (Daphne of the Dunes): Excerpts
[7153] Partch, Harry (instruments)
Rec 1958
- Gate 5 Issue A; 33; rel 1962
- CRI-193; 33m/s; rel 1964/?; cip

PECK, Russell (1945-)
Automobile (1965)
[7154] Ragains, Diane (sop); Middleton, Peter (fl); Johnson, David (perc); Calvetti, Aventino (cb)
Rec 6/76
- CRI-367; 33s; rel 1977; cip

Quotations from the Electronic Chairman
[7155] no performers given
- Advance FGR-19S; 33s; rel 1976; cip

Suspended Sentence (1973)
[7156] Hays, Doris (pf)
- Finnadar SR-2-720; 33s; 2 discs; rel 1980; cip

PEEK, Richard M. (1927-)
Prelude and Fugue on St. Thomas
[7157] Peek, Richard M. (org)
- Century; 33m; rel 1966

PELUSI, Mario (1951-)
Concert Piece, Baritone Saxophone, Brass Quartet, and Percussion
[7158] Watters, Mark (bar sax)
- Crystal S-152; 33s; rel 1979

PENN, William (1943-)
Chamber Music II (1972)
[7159] violoncello; piano
- Advance FGR-19S; 33s; rel 1976; cip

Crystal Rainbows
[7160] no performers given
- Sounds Reasonable Associates SR-7801; 33s; rel 1978

Fantasy, Harpsichord
[7161] Louwenaar, Karyl (hpschd)
- CRI-367; 33s; rel 1977; cip

(Four) Preludes, Marimba
[7162] Stevens, Leigh Howard (mrmb)
- CRI-367; 33s; rel 1977; cip

Ultra mensuram (1971)
[7163] Western Michigan University Wind Ensemble; Bjerregaard, Carol (cond)
- CRI-340; 33s; rel 1975; cip

PENNARIO, Leonard (1924-)
Keyboard Fantasies
[7164] Pennario, Leonard (pf)
- Capitol P-8391; 33m; rel 1957; del 1969

PEPE, Carmine
Rue de la Tombe Issoire (1959)
[7165] Violette, Andrew (pf)
- Opus One 32; 33s; rel 1978; cip

Sonata, Violin and Piano (1965)
[7166] Quan, Linda (vln); Carno, Zita (pf)
- Opus One 18; 33s; rel 1974; cip

PERERA, Ronald (1941-)
Alternate Routes (1971)
[7167] Electronic music
- CRI-364; 33s; rel 1977; cip

Apollo Circling (1971-72)
[7168] D'Armand, Gretchen (sop); La Salle, Constance (pf)
- Opus One 27; 33s; rel 1976; cip

(Three) Poems of Guenter Grass (1974)
[7169] Charlston, Elsa (sop); Boston Musica Viva; tape; Pittman, Richard (cond)
- CRI-420; 33s; rel 1980; cip

Reflex (1973)
[7170] Wallfisch, Ernst (vla); tape
- Opus One 14; 33s; rel 1976; cip

PERKINS, Bill (1941-)
Textures (1970)
[7171] Turner, Jim (musical saw); Electric Percussion Ensemble
- Owl QS-22; 33q; rel 1972; del 1978

PERKINS, Frank (1908-)
Dusty Road
[7172] Warfield, William (bar); Columbia Symphony Orchestra; Engel, Lehman (cond)
- Columbia AAL-32; 33m; 10"; rel 1953; del 1957

Fandango
[7173] Original Piano Quartet
- Decca DL-10055/DL-710055; 33m/s; rel 1962; del 1971

PERKINS, John M. (1935-)
Caprice (1963)
[7174] Blackwood, Easley (pf)
- CRI-232; 33s; rel 1969; cip

Divertimento (1958)
[7175] Cole, Matilda; Papas, Arthur; O'Brien, Nicholas; Rinzler, Alan; Ticknor, Malcolm; orchestra
Rec 4/17-20/58
- Audience R-58001; 33; rel 1959?

Music for Thirteen Players (1964)
[7176] University of Chicago Contemporary Chamber Players; Shapey, Ralph (cond)
- CRI-232; 33s; rel 1969; cip

PERLE, George (1915-)
(Thirteen) Dickinson Songs (1977-78)
[7177] Beardslee, Bethany (sop); Ritt, Morey (pf)
Rec 12/78 and 1/79
- CRI-403; 33s; rel 1979; cip

(Six) Etudes, Piano (1976)
[7178] Gowen, Bradford (pf)
- New World NW-304; 33s; rel 1979

(Three) Inventions, Bassoon (1962)
[7179] Cordle, Andrew E. (bsn)
- Orion ORS-77269; 33s; rel 1977; cip

**(Three) Inventions, Bassoon
(1962)** *(cont'd)*
[7180] Grossman, Arthur (bsn)
  - Coronet S-2741; 33s; rel 1973;
    cip

Lyric Piece (1946)
[7181] Barab, Seymour (vcl); Masselos,
    William (pf)
  - Paradox X-102; 78; 3-10"
  - Paradox PL-10001; 33m; 10";
    rel 1950; del 1957

Monody I (1960)
[7182] Baron, Samuel (fl)
  - CRI-212; 33m/s; rel 1966/?; cip

Monody II (1962)
[7183] Turetzky, Bertram (cb)
  - Advance FGR-1; 33m; rel 1966;
    del 1972

**(Three) Movements for Orchestra
(1960)**
[7184] Royal Philharmonic Orchestra;
    Epstein, David (cond)
    Rec 12/20/74
  - CRI-331; 33s; rel 1975; cip

**(Six) Preludes, Piano (Op 20b)
(1946)**
[7185] Helps, Robert (pf)
  - RCA LM-7042/LSC-7042;
    33m/s; 2 discs; rel 1966; del
    1971
  - CRI-288; 33s; 2 discs; rel 1972;
    cip

**Quartet, Strings, No 5 (1960, rev
1967)**
[7186] Composers Quartet
  - Nonesuch H-71280; 33s; rel
    1973; cip

Quartet, Strings, No 7 (1973)
[7187] New York String Quartet
    Rec 4-5/77
  - CRI-387; 33s; rel 1978; cip

Quintet, Strings (Op 35) (1958)
[7188] Beaux-Arts String Quartet;
    Trampler, Walter (vla)
  - CRI-148; 33m/s; rel 1962/?; cip

Quintet, Winds, No 3 (1967)
[7189] Clarion Wind Quintet
  - Golden Crest CRS-4191; 33s; rel
    1980; cip

Rhapsody (1953)
[7190] Louisville Orchestra; Whitney,
    Robert (cond)
  - LOU-545-9; 33m (Louisville
    Orchestra First Edition Records
    1955 No 9); rel 1959; del 1980

(Two) Rilke Songs (1941)
[7191] Beardslee, Bethany (sop); Perle,
    George (pf)
    Rec 12/78 and 1/79
  - CRI-403; 33s; rel 1979; cip

Toccata (1969)
[7192] Miller, Robert (pf)
  - CRI-306; 33s; rel 1974; cip

PERLMAN, George
Dance of the Rebitzen
[7193] Elman, Mischa (vln); Seiger, Joseph
    (pf)
  - Vanguard VRS-1099/VSD-2137;
    33m/s; rel 1963; del 1965

PERRY, Julia (1924-79)
Homunculus C. F. (1969)
[7194] Manhattan Percussion Ensemble;
    Price, Paul (cond)
  - CRI-252; 33s; rel 1970; cip

Short Piece, A (1952)
[7195] Imperial Philharmonic Orchestra of
    Tokyo; Strickland, William (cond)
  - CRI-145; 33m/s; rel 1961/?; cip

Stabat mater (1951)
[7196] Asakura, Makiko (m sop); Japan
    Philharmonic Symphony
    Orchestra; Strickland, William
    (cond)
  - CRI-133; 33m/s; rel
    1960/1973; cip

PERSICHETTI, Vincent (1915-)
Bagatelles (Op 87) (1961)
[7197] Ohio State University Concert
    Band; Persichetti, Vincent (cond)
  - Coronet M-1247/S-1247;
    33m/s; rel 1969; cip

[7198] University of Kansas Symphonic
    Band; Foster, Robert E. (cond)
  - Golden Crest ATH-5055; 33s; rel
    1979; cip

**Chorale Prelude (So Pure the Star)
(Op 91) (1962)**
[7199] Ohio State University Concert
    Band; Persichetti, Vincent (cond)
  - Coronet M-1247/S-1247;
    33m/s; rel 1969; cip

[7200] University of Kansas Symphonic
    Band; Foster, Robert E. (cond)
  - Golden Crest ATH-5055; 33s; rel
    1979; cip

**Chorale Prelude (Turn Not Thy
Face) (Op 105) (1966)**
[7201] University of Kansas Symphonic
    Band; Foster, Robert E. (cond)
  - Golden Crest ATH-5055; 33s; rel
    1979; cip

**Concerto, English Horn and String
Orchestra (1977)**
[7202] Stacy, Thomas (E hn); String
    Orchestra of New York;
    Persichetti, Vincent (cond)
  - Grenadilla GS-1048; 33s; rel
    1979

**Concerto, Piano, Four Hands (Op
56) (1952)**
[7203] Persichetti, Dorothea (pf);
    Persichetti, Vincent (pf)
  - ASCAP CB-184; 33m (Pittsburgh
    International Contemporary Music
    Festival); rel 1954
  - Columbia ML-4989; 33m; rel
    1955; del 1968
  - Columbia CML-4989; 33m; rel
    1968; del 1974
  - Columbia AML-4989; 33m; rel
    1974; del 1976

[7204] Wentworth, Jean (pf); Wentworth,
    Kenneth (pf)
  - Grenadilla GS-1050; 33s; rel
    1979

(Four) cummings Choruses (1964)
[7205] no performers given
  - USC Sound Enterprises
    KM-1558; 33

Divertimento, Band (1950)
[7206] Eastman Symphonic Wind
    Ensemble; Fennell, Frederick
    (cond)
  - Mercury MG-40006; 33m; rel
    1953; del 1957
  - Mercury MG-50079; 33m; rel
    1957; del 1969
  - Mercury SRI-75086; 33s; rel
    1977

Divertimento, Band: March
[7207] Leopold Stokowski and his
    Orchestra; Stokowski, Leopold
    (cond)
  - Capitol SAL-8385/SSAL-8385;
    33m/s; rel 1957/1959; del
    1961
  - Capitol PAR-8385/SPAR-8385;
    33m/s; rel 1961; del 1964

Drop, Drop, Slow Tears (Op 104)
[7208] Baker, George C. (org)
  - Delos DEL-FY-025; 33s; rel
    1977; cip

Grass, The (1958)
[7209] Hanks, John Kennedy (ten);
    Friedberg, Ruth (pf)
  - Duke University Press
    DWR-7306; 33s; rel 1974

Harmonium (Op 50): The Death of a Soldier (1957), Of the Surface of Things (1957), and The Snow Man (1957)
[7210] Hanks, John Kennedy (ten); Friedberg, Ruth (pf)
- Duke University Press DWR-7306; 33s; rel 1974

Harmonium: Sonatina to Hans Christian (1951)
[7211] Miller, Mildred (m sop); Biltcliffe, Edwin (pf)
- St/And SPL-411-12; 33m; 2 discs; rel 1963; del 1964
- Desto D-411-12/DST-6411-12; 33m/s; 2 discs; rel 1964; cip

Hollow Men, The (Op 25) (1944)
[7212] Baker, S. (tpt); MGM String Orchestra; Solomon, Izler (cond)
- MGM E-3117; 33m; rel 1954; del 1959

[7213] Parker, R. Ted (tpt); Philharmonia Virtuosi of New York; Karrenin, Robert (cond)
Rec 5/22/76
- Turnabout TVS-34705; 33s; rel 1978; cip

Hollow Men, The (arr for tpt and org)
[7214] Plog, Anthony (tpt); Swearingen, Madolyn (org)
- Avant AV-1014; 33s; rel 1978; cip

[7215] Stith, Marice (tpt); Paterson, Donald (org)
Rec 4/18/67
- Redwood RRES-2; 33s; rel 1969; cip

Hollow Men, The (arr for tpt and pf)
[7216] Levy, Robert (tpt); Levy, Amy Lou (pf)
- Golden Crest RE-7045; 33q; rel 1972; cip

Little Piano Book (Op 60) (1953)
[7217] Richter, Marga (pf)
- MGM E-3147; 33m; rel 1955; del 1959

Little Piano Book: Fanfare
[7218] Fuszek, Rita (pf)
- Educo 3108; 33

Masquerade (Op 102) (1965)
[7219] Eastman Symphonic Wind Ensemble; Hunsberger, Donald (cond)
- Decca DL-710163; 33s; rel 1969; del 1973

[7220] Ohio State University Concert Band; Persichetti, Vincent (cond)
- Coronet M-1247/S-1247; 33m/s; rel 1969; cip

O Cool is the Valley (Op 118) (1971)
[7221] University of Kansas Symphonic Band; Foster, Robert E. (cond)
- Golden Crest ATH-5055; 33s; rel 1979; cip

Pageant (1953)
[7222] North Texas State University Symphonic Band; McAdow, Maurice (cond)
- Austin 6008; 33m; rel 1960; del 1969

[7223] Northwestern University Symphonic Wind Ensemble; Paynter, John P. (cond)
Rec 11/76
- New World NW-211; 33s; rel 1977

Parable for Alto Saxophone (Op 123)
[7224] Stolti, James (sax)
- Coronet LPS-3036; 33s; rel 1978; cip

Parable for Band (Op 121) (1972)
[7225] University of Kansas Symphonic Band; Foster, Robert E. (cond)
- Golden Crest ATH-5055; 33s; rel 1979; cip

Parable for Bassoon (Op 110) (1969)
[7226] Grossman, Arthur (bsn)
- Coronet S-2741; 33s; rel 1973; cip

[7227] Weisberg, Arthur (bsn)
Rec 1/24/72
- CRI-353; 33s; rel 1976; cip

Parable for Brass Quintet (1968)
[7228] Dallas Brass Quintet
- Crystal S-203; 33s; rel 1979; cip

[7229] New York Brass Quintet
- Crystal S-210; 33s; rel 1980; cip

Parable for Oboe (1968)
[7230] Christ, Peter (ob)
- Crystal S-321; 33s; rel 1979; cip

Parable IX (1972)
[7231] no performers given
- USC Sound Enterprises KM-1558; 33

Pastoral (Op 21) (1943)
[7232] Fredonia Faculty Woodwind Quintet
- Fredonia State Teachers College XTV-21902; 33m; rel 1954

[7233] New Art Wind Quintet
- Classic Editions CE-2003; 33m; 2 discs; rel 1953; del 1961

[7234] Philadelphia Woodwind Quintet
- Columbia ML-5984/MS-6584; 33m/s; rel 1964; del 1968

Psalm (Op 53) (1952)
[7235] Eastman Symphonic Wind Ensemble; Fennell, Frederick (cond)
Rec 1954
- Mercury MG-40011; 33m; rel 1954; del 1957
- Mercury MG-50084; 33m; rel 1957; del 1969

[7236] Ohio State University Concert Band; Persichetti, Vincent (cond)
- Coronet M-1247/S-1247; 33m/s; rel 1969; cip

Quartet, Strings, No 1 (1939)
[7237] New Art String Quartet
- Arizona State University, Tempe, College of Fine Arts, Dept of Music ASU-1976-ARA; 33s; rel 1976

Quartet, Strings, No 2 (1944)
[7238] New Art String Quartet
- Arizona State University, Tempe, College of Fine Arts, Dept of Music ASU-1976-ARA; 33s; rel 1976

Quartet, Strings, No 3 (1959)
[7239] New Art String Quartet
- Arizona State University, Tempe, College of Fine Arts, Dept of Music ASU-1976-ARA; 33s; rel 1976

Quartet, Strings, No 4 (1973)
[7240] New Art String Quartet
- Arizona State University, Tempe, College of Fine Arts, Dept of Music ASU-1976-ARA; 33s; rel 1976

Sam Was a Man
[7241] Seattle Chamber Singers; Shangrow, George (cond)
Rec 8/1-8/76
- Voyager VRLP-701S; 33s; rel 1976

Serenade No 1 (1929)
[7242] University of Kansas Symphonic Band; Foster, Robert E. (cond)
- Golden Crest ATH-5055; 33s; rel 1979; cip

Serenade No 3 (Op 17) (1941)
[7243] Temple University Trio
- Golden Crest CRS-4117; 33s/q; rel 1974; cip

Serenade No 5 (1950)
[7244] Louisville Orchestra; Whitney, Robert (cond)
- LOU-60-6; 33m (Louisville Orchestra First Edition Records 1960 No 6); rel 1961; del 1980

Serenade No 6 (Op 44) (1950)
[7245] Sauer, Ralph (tbn); De Veritch,
        Alan (vla); Leonard, Ronald (vcl)
        - Crystal S-381; 33s; rel 1977; cip

Serenade No 10 (Op 79) (1957)
[7246] Baron, Samuel (fl); Maoyani, Ruth
        (hp)
        - Desto DC-7134; 33s; rel 1973;
        cip

[7247] Di Tullio, Louise (fl); McDonald,
        Susann (hp)
        - Klavier KS-560; 33s; rel 1978;
        cip

Serenade No 11 (Op 85) (1960)
[7248] Ithaca High School Concert Band;
        Battisti, Frank (cond)
        - Golden Crest 6001; 33m/s; rel
        1967; cip

[7249] Ohio State University Concert
        Band; Persichetti, Vincent (cond)
        - Coronet M-1247/S-1247;
        33m/s; rel 1969; cip

Serenade No 12 (Op 88) (1960)
[7250] Phillips, Harvey (tu)
        - Golden Crest RE-7018; 33m/s;
        rel 1965/1979; cip

Shimah B'koli (Psalm 130) (Op 89)
[7251] Anderson, Robert (org)
        - Aeolian-Skinner AS-327; 33s; rel
        1971

[7252] Rimmer, Frederick (org)
        - RCA-Victrola VICS-1663; 33s; rel
        1972

**Sonata, Two Pianos (Op 13)
(1940)**
[7253] Yarbrough, Joan (pf); Cowan,
        Robert (pf)
        - CRI-279; 33s; rel 1974; cip

Sonata, Violoncello (Op 54) (1952)
[7254] Moore, David (vcl)
        - Opus One 6; 33s; rel 1970; cip

Song of Peace (Op 82) (1959)
[7255] Hamilton College Men's Choir;
        Baldwin, John L. (cond) or Bonta,
        Stephen (cond)
        - Connoisseur Society CS-2056;
        33s; rel 1975; del 1979

Symphony No 4 (Op 51) (1954)
[7256] Philadelphia Orchestra; Ormandy,
        Eugene (cond)
        - Columbia ML-5108; 33m; rel
        1956; del 1965

Symphony No 5 (Op 61) (1954)
[7257] Louisville Orchestra; Whitney,
        Robert (cond)
        - LOU-545-7; 33m (Louisville
        Orchestra First Edition Records
        1955 No 7); rel 1959; del 1972

Symphony No 6 (Op 69) (1956)
[7258] Cornell University Wind Ensemble;
        Stith, Marice (cond)
        - Cornell CUWE-18; 33s; rel 1977;
        cip

[7259] Eastman Symphonic Wind
        Ensemble; Fennell, Frederick
        (cond)
        - Mercury MG-50221/SR-90221;
        33m/s; rel 1960; del 1964
        - Mercury SRI-75094; 33s; rel
        1978; cip

[7260] Harvard Concert Band; Walker
        (cond)
        - INC 7; 33s; rel 1972; del 1978

[7261] New England Conservatory Wind
        Ensemble; Battisti, Frank (cond)
        - Golden Crest NEC-103; 33s; rel
        1974; cip

[7262] Ohio State University Concert
        Band; Persichetti, Vincent (cond)
        - Coronet M-1247/S-1247;
        33m/s; rel 1969; cip

[7263] University of Minnesota Band;
        Bencriscutto, Frank A. (cond)
        - Mark 40400; 33s; 2 discs; rel
        1970; del 1976

Symphony No 6: Excerpts
[7264] no performers given
        - USC Sound Enterprises
        KM-1558; 33

Symphony No 8 (Op 107) (1970)
[7265] Louisville Orchestra; Mester, Jorge
        (cond)
        - LS-70-6; 33s (Louisville
        Orchestra First Edition Records
        1970 No 6); rel 1971; cip

**Symphony No 9 (Sinfonia:
Janiculum) (Op 113) (1971)**
[7266] Philadelphia Orchestra; Ormandy,
        Eugene (cond)
        - RCA LSC-3212; 33s; rel 1971;
        del 1977

Te Deum (1963)
[7267] no performers given
        - USC Sound Enterprises
        KM-1558; 33

Thou Child So Wise
[7268] Hanks, John Kennedy (ten);
        Friedberg, Ruth (pf)
        - Duke University Press
        DWR-7306; 33s; rel 1974

PETERSON, Theodore*
Psalm 150
[7269] Fredonia Choir; Gunn, George
        (cond)
        - Fredonia State Teachers College
        XTV-21900; 33m; rel 1954

PETERSON, Wayne (1927-)
Capriccio, Flute and Piano (1972)
[7270] Millard, Janet (fl); Peterson, Wayne
        (pf)
        Rec 1978
        - 1750 Arch S-1760; 33s; rel
        1979; cip

Free Variations
[7271] Minneapolis Symphony Orchestra;
        Dorati, Antal (cond)
        - Mercury MG-50288/SR-90288;
        33m/s; rel 1962; del 1965

Phantasmagoria
[7272] Baron, Samuel (fl); Bloom, Arthur
        (cl); Brehm, Alvin (cb)
        - Desto DC-7134; 33s; rel 1973;
        cip

PFEIFFER, John (1920-)
Electronomusic - 9 Images (1965)
[7273] Electronic music
        - RCA-Victrola VICS-1371; 33s; rel
        1969; del 1976

PHILLIPS, Barre (1934-)
Journal Violine (1968)
[7274] Phillips, Barre (cb)
        - Opus One 2; 33s; rel 1969; del
        1976

PHILLIPS, Burrill (1907-)
American Dance (1940)
[7275] Eastman-Rochester Symphony
        Orchestra; Hanson, Howard
        (cond)
        - Victor 18102 (in set M-802);
        78; rel 1941

Bucket of Water, A
[7276] South Hills High School Chorus;
        Crawford (cond)
        - ASCAP CB-161; 33m (Pittsburgh
        International Contemporary Music
        Festival); rel pre-1956

Canzona III (1964)
[7277] Basescu, Elinor (reader); Juilliard
        Ensemble; Davies, Dennis Russell
        (cond)
        - CRI-286; 33s; rel 1972; cip

**Concert Piece, Bassoon and String
Orchestra (1942)**
[7278] Schoenbach, Sol (bsn); Philadelphia
        Orchestra; Ormandy, Eugene
        (cond)
        - Columbia ML-4629; 33m; rel
        1953; del 1970

**Concert Piece, Piano and Chamber
Orchestra**
[7279] Pierlot, P. (pf); Paris Chamber
        Orchestra; Duvauchelle (cond)
        - Lumen (French) 2.08.015-16;
        78; 2 discs; rel pre-1952

Concerto, Piano and Orchestra (1942)
[7280] Richards, Claire (pf); Illinois University Symphony Orchestra; Ansermet, Ernest (cond)
- Illini Union Bookstore CRS-4; 33m; rel 1955*

Return of Odysseus, The (1956)
[7281] Foote, Bruce (bar); Tuttle, Preston (nar); University of Illinois Symphony Orchestra and University Choir; Shaw, Robert (cond)
- Illini Union Bookstore CRS-5; 33m; rel 1958*

Selections from McGuffey's Reader (1933)
[7282] Eastman-Rochester Symphony Orchestra; Hanson, Howard (cond)
Rec 10/28/56
- Mercury MG-50136/SR-90136; 33s/s; rel 1957/1959; del 1964
- Eastman-Rochester Archives ERA-1009; 33s; rel 1976; cip

[7283] Vienna Symphony Orchestra; Schoenherr, Max (cond)
- American Recording Society ARS-38; 33m; rel 1953*
- Desto D-423/DST-6423; 33m/s; rel 1966; cip

Sonata, Piano, No 1 (1942)
[7284] Sanders, Dean (pf)
- Trilogy CTS-1003; 33s; rel 1973; del 1975

Sonata, Piano, No 2 (1949)
[7285] Sanders, Dean (pf)
- Trilogy CTS-1003; 33s; rel 1973; del 1975

Sonata, Violin and Harpsichord (1965)
[7286] Van Bronkhorst, Warren (vln); Morgan, Wesley K. (hpschd)
- Pleiades P-101; 33s; rel 1969; cip

Sonata, Violoncello and Piano (1948)
[7287] Stern, Carl (vcl); Phillips, Burrill (pf)
- SPA-54; 33m; rel 1953; del 1970

Sonata da camera
[7288] Morgan, Wesley K. (org)
- Pleiades P-101; 33s; rel 1969; cip

Tunes
[7289] Vienna Symphony Orchestra; Schoenherr, Max (cond)
- Desto D-423/DST-6423; 33m/s; rel 1966; cip

PHILLIPS, Peter (1930-)
Music for Brass Quintet (1966)
[7290] American Brass Quintet
- Nonesuch H-71222; 33s; rel 1969; cip

Sonata, Contrabass (1964)
[7291] Turetzky, Bertram (cb)
- Medea MCLP-1001; 33m/s; rel 1966; del 1971

PICK, Richard (1915-)
Autumn Day Suite
[7292] Pick, Richard (gtr)
- Music Library MLR-7066; 33m; rel 1956; del 1971

Baca and Fiesta Day
[7293] Pick, Richard (gtr)
- Music Library MLR-7066; 33m; rel 1956; del 1971

PICKER, Tobias (1954-)
Rhapsody (1978)
[7294] Hudson, Benjamin (vln); Picker, Tobias (pf)
- CRI-427; 33s; rel 1980; cip

Romance (1978)
[7295] Quan, Linda (vln); Karis, Aleck (pf)
- CRI-427; 33s; rel 1980; cip

Sextet No 3 (1976)
[7296] Speculum Musicae
- CRI-427; 33s; rel 1980; cip

When Soft Voices Die (1977)
[7297] Oppens, Ursula (pf)
- CRI-427; 33s; rel 1980; cip

PIERCE, Alexandra (1934-)
Job 22:28
[7298] clarinet duo
- Zanja ZR-2; 33; rel 197?

PIERCE, J. R.*
Beat Canon
[7299] Electronic music
- Decca DL-9103/DL-79103; 33m/s; rel 1962

Eight-Tone Canon
[7300] Electronic music
- Decca DL-9103/DL-79103; 33m/s; rel 1962
- Decca DL-710180; 33s; rel 1971; del 1973

Five against Seven (Random Canon)
[7301] Electronic music
- Decca DL-9103/DL-79103; 33m/s; rel 1962

Melodie
[7302] Electronic music
- Decca DL-9103/DL-79103; 33m/s; rel 1962

Molto amoroso
[7303] Electronic music
- Decca DL-9103/DL-79103; 33m/s; rel 1962

Stochatta
[7304] Electronic music
- Decca DL-9103/DL-79103; 33m/s; rel 1962

Variations in Timbres and Attack
[7305] Electronic music
- Decca DL-9103/DL-79103; 33m/s; rel 1962

PIKET, Frederick (1903-74)
Twinkle, Twinkle, Little Star Variations
[7306] Ithaca Symphonic Winds; Beeler, Walter (cond)
- Golden Crest CR-4015/CRS-4015; 33m/s; rel 1959/1961; cip

PILLIN, Boris (1940-)
Duo, Percussion and Piano (1971)
[7307] Ervin, Karen (perc); Davis, Sharon (pf)
- WIM Records WIMR-5; 33s; rel 1972; cip

(Three) Pieces, Double-Reed Septet (1972)
[7308] Los Angeles Philharmonic (members of); Endo, Akira (cond)
- Crystal S-871; 33s; rel 1972; cip

Scherzo, Wind Quartet (1968)
[7309] Westwood Wind Quintet
- Crystal S-811; 33s; rel 1971; cip

Scherzo barbaro
[7310] Spear, Julian (b cl); Davis, Sharon (pf)
- WIM Records WIMR-10; 33s; rel 1978; cip

Serenade, Piano and Wind Quintet
[7311] Davis, Sharon (pf); Westwood Wind Quintet
- WIM Records WIMR-11; 33s; rel 1976; cip

Sonata, Clarinet and Piano (1965)
[7312] Atkins, David (cl); Davis, Sharon (pf)
- WIM Records WIMR-1; 33s; rel 1971; cip

Sonata, Violoncello and Piano (1973)
[7313] Davis, Douglas (vcl); Davis, Sharon (pf)
- WIM Records WIMR-11; 33s; rel 1976; cip

Tune, C Minor (1975)
[7314] Davis, Sharon (pf); Silverman,
       Barry (perc)
       - WIM Records WIMR-11; 33s; rel
       1976; cip

PIMSLEUR, Solomon (1900-62)

I Never See the Red Rose
[7315] Gregg Smith Singers; Smith, Gregg
       (cond)
       - CRI-241; 33s; rel 1970; cip

There Are Two Forces of Life
[7316] Gregg Smith Singers; Smith, Gregg
       (cond)
       - CRI-241; 33s; rel 1970; cip

PINKHAM, Daniel (1923-)

Agnus Dei
[7317] King Chorale; King, Gordon (cond)
       - Orion ORS-75205; 33s; rel
       1978; cip

Cantilena and Capriccio (1956)
[7318] Brink, Robert (vln); Pinkham,
       Daniel (hpschd)
       - CRI-109; 33m/s; rel 1957/?; cip

Christmas Cantata (1958)
[7319] Roger Wagner Chorale; Wagner,
       Roger (cond)
       - Angel 36016/S-36016; 33m/s;
       rel 1967; del 1978

Concertante No 1 (1954)
[7320] Brink, Robert (vln); Chiasson,
       Claude Jean (hpschd); Low,
       Edward (cel); MGM String
       Ensemble; Solomon, Izler (cond)
       - MGM E-3245; 33m; rel 1956;
       del 1959
       - CRI-143; 33m/s; rel 1961/?; cip

**Concerto, Celeste and Harpsichord
Soli (1955)**
[7321] Low, Edward (cel); Pinkham, Daniel
       (hpschd)
       - CRI-109; 33m/s; rel 1957/?; cip

Folk Song (Elegy) (1947)
[7322] Randolph Singers; Randolph, David
       (cond)
       - CRI-102; 33m/s; rel 1956/?; cip

For Evening Draws On (1973)
[7323] Roth, Kenneth (E hn); Phillips,
       Larry (org); tape
       - Golden Crest NEC-114; 33s/q;
       rel 1976; cip

**Glory Be to God (Motet for
Christmas Day) (1955)**
[7324] Mid-America Chorale; Dexter, John
       (cond)
       - CRI-191; 33m/s; rel 1964/?; cip

Henry Was a Worthy King
[7325] King Chorale; King, Gordon (cond)
       - Orion ORS-75205; 33s; rel
       1978; cip

In dulci jubilo
[7326] Biggs, E. Power (org); Columbia
       Chamber Orchestra; Rozsnyai,
       Zoltan (cond)
       - Columbia ML-5911/MS-6511;
       33m/s; rel 1963

Leaf, The
[7327] King Chorale; King, Gordon (cond)
       - Orion ORS-75205; 33s; rel
       1978; cip

Liturgies (1974)
[7328] Phillips, Larry (org); Grimes, John
       (timp); tape
       - Golden Crest NEC-114; 33s/q;
       rel 1976; cip

Madrigal (1955)
[7329] Randolph Singers; Randolph, David
       (cond)
       - CRI-102; 33m/s; rel 1956/?; cip

Partita, Harpsichord
[7330] Pinkham, Daniel (hpschd)
       Rec 1958
       - Cambridge CRM-412; 33m; rel
       1962; del 1970

Pastorale on Morning Star
[7331] Pinkham, Daniel (org)
       Rec 7/9/62
       - R-A Recording Co 1023; 33m; rel
       1962

Piping Anne and Husky Paul
[7332] King Chorale; King, Gordon (cond)
       - Orion ORS-75205; 33s; rel
       1978; cip

Revelations: Litany and Toccata
[7333] Hindmarsh, Jack (org)
       Rec 1975
       - Wealden WS-142; 33s; rel 1976

Signs of the Zodiac (1964)
[7334] Louisville Orchestra; Whitney,
       Robert (cond)
       - LOU-67-3/LS-67-3; 33m/s
       (Louisville Orchestra First Edition
       Records 1967 No 3); rel 1967;
       cip

Slow, Slow, Fresh Fount (1949)
[7335] McCollum, John (ten); Biltcliffe,
       Edwin (pf)
       - St/And SPL-411-12; 33m; 2
       discs; rel 1963; del 1964
       - Desto D-411-12/DST-6411-12;
       33m/s; 2 discs; rel 1964; cip

Symphony No 2 (1963)
[7336] Louisville Orchestra; Whitney,
       Robert (cond)
       - LOU-65-2; 33m (Louisville
       Orchestra First Edition Records
       1965 No 2); rel 1965; cip

**Toccatas for the Vault of Heaven
(1972)**
[7337] Phillips, Larry (org); tape
       - Golden Crest NEC-114; 33s/q;
       rel 1976; cip

**(Five) Voluntaries, Organ: Quick and
Cheerful, Wistful, and Nimble**
[7338] Thompson, Robert (org)
       Rec 8/73
       - Ethos ES-1002; 33s; rel 1973

PISK, Paul A. (1893-)

**(Three) Ceremonial Rites (Op 90)
(1958)**
[7339] Polish National Radio Orchestra;
       Ormicki, Wlodzimiertz (cond)
       - CRI-228; 33s; rel 1968; cip

From Old Mexicale
[7340] Martin, Charlotte (pf)
       - Educo 3021; 33m; rel 1968; del
       1972

From the Ozarks
[7341] Martin, Charlotte (pf)
       - Educo 3021; 33m; rel 1968; del
       1972

Nocturnal Interlude (1957)
[7342] Helps, Robert (pf)
       - RCA LM-7042/LSC-7042;
       33m/s; 2 discs; rel 1966; del
       1971
       - CRI-288; 33s; 2 discs; rel 1972;
       cip

**Passacaglia, Orchestra (Op 50)
(1944)**
[7343] Zurich Radio Orchestra; Monod,
       Jacques (cond)
       - CRI-128; 33m; rel 1960; cip

**(Two) Shakespeare Sonnets (Op
103) (1964)**
[7344] Chabay, Leslie (ten); Washington
       University Madrigal Singers;
       Johnson, Orland (cond)
       - Washington University 000; 33m;
       rel 1966; del 1976

**Sonata, Clarinet and Piano (Op 59)
(1947)**
[7345] Scott, Leslie (cl); Mitchell, Evelyn
       (pf)
       - Washington University 000; 33m;
       rel 1966; del 1976

Sonata, Flute and Piano (Op 82) (1954)
[7346] Scott, Janet (fl); Mitchell, Evelyn (pf)
- Washington University 000; 33m; rel 1966; del 1976

Songs from Chamber Music (Op 101)
[7347] Chabay, Leslie (ten)
- Washington University 000; 33m; rel 1966; del 1976

PISTON, Walter (1894-1976)
Carnival Song (1938)
[7348] Cornell University Glee Club; Rochester Symphonic Brass Ensemble; Sokol, Thomas A. (cond)
- Fleetwood 6001; 33m; rel 1967; del 1971

[7349] Harvard Glee Club; Boston Symphony Brass Ensemble; Woodworth, G. Wallace (cond)
- Victor 18013; 78; rel pre-1942

Ceremonial Fanfare (1969)
[7350] brass and percussion ensemble; Prausnitz, Frederik (cond)
Rec 1970
- Metropolitan Museum of Art AKS-10001; 33; rel 1970

Chromatic Study on the Name of Bach (1940)
[7351] Andrews, Mildred (org)
- University of Oklahoma 2; 33m; rel 1957; del 1978

[7352] Noehren, Robert (org)
- Lyrichord LL-191/LLST-7191; 33m/s; rel 1968; cip

Concertino, Piano and Chamber Orchestra (1937)
[7353] Jenner, Alexander (pf); Vienna State Academy Orchestra; Strickland, William (cond)
- Vox PLP-7750; 33m; rel 1952; del 1956

[7354] Mitchell, Marjorie (pf); Goteborg Symphony Orchestra; Strickland, William (cond)
- CRI-180; 33m/s; rel 1964/1973; cip

Concerto, Orchestra (1933)
[7355] Polish National Radio Orchestra; Strickland, William (cond)
- CRI-254; 33s; rel 1970; cip

Concerto, String Quartet, Winds, and Percussion (1976)
[7356] Emerson String Quartet; Juilliard Orchestra; Ehrling, Sixten (cond)
- CRI-248(78); 33s; rel 1979; cip

Concerto, Viola and Orchestra (1957)
[7357] Doktor, Paul (vla); Louisville Orchestra; Whitney, Robert (cond)
- LOU-63-3/LS-63-3; 33m/s (Louisville Orchestra First Edition Records 1963 No 3); rel 1963/1965; del 1975

Concerto, Violin and Orchestra, No 1 (1939)
[7358] Kolberg, Hugo (vln); Berlin Symphony Orchestra; Matzerath, Otto (cond)
- EMI/Odeon O-80610; 33m
- Mace MXX-9089; 33s; rel 1970; del 1975

Divertimento, Nine Instruments (1946)
[7359] Boston Symphony Chamber Players
- RCA LM-6167/LSC-6167; 33m/s; 3 discs; rel 1966; del 1976

Duo, Viola and Violoncello (1949)
[7360] Ilmer, Irving (vla); Teraspulsky, Leopold (vcl)
- Coronet S-1715; 33s; rel 1973; cip

Improvisation (1945)
[7361] Foldes, Andor (pf)
- Vox 16070 (in set 174); 78; 10''; rel 1947

Incredible Flutist, The (1938)
[7362] Louisville Orchestra; Mester, Jorge (cond)
- LS-75-5; 33s (Louisville Orchestra First Edition Records 1975 No 5); rel 1977; cip

Incredible Flutist, The (Suite) (1938)
[7363] Berlin Radio Orchestra; Rother, Arthur (cond)
- Urania URLP-7092; 33m; rel 1953; del 1960

[7364] Boston Pops Orchestra; Fiedler, Arthur (cond)
- Victor 12595-96 (in set M-621); 78; 2 discs; rel 1939*
- Gramophone EB-142-43; 78; 2 discs; rel pre-1942
- Camden CAL-145; 33m; rel 1955; del 1957

[7365] Boston Pops Orchestra; Pappoutsakis, James (fl); Fiedler, Arthur (cond)
- RCA LM-6113; 33m; 3 discs; rel 1954; del 1960
- RCA (French) A-630217; 33m; rel pre-1956
- RCA LM-2084/LSC-2084; 33m/s; rel 1957/1959; del 1961

Incredible Flutist, The (Suite) (1938) (cont'd)
[7366] Cleveland Pops Orchestra; Lane, Louis (cond)
- Epic LC-3539/BC-1013; 33m/s; rel 1959; del 1968

[7367] Eastman-Rochester Symphony Orchestra; Hanson, Howard (cond)
- Mercury MG-50206/SR-90206; 33m/s; rel 1959; del 1965
- Mercury MG-50423/SR-90423; 33m/s; rel 1965; del 1972
- Mercury SRI-75050; 33s; rel 1975; cip

[7368] MIT Symphony Orchestra; Epstein, David (cond)
- Turnabout QTVS-34670; 33q; rel 1977; cip

[7369] New York Philharmonic; Bernstein, Leonard (cond)
- Columbia ML-6343/MS-6943; 33m/s; rel 1967; cip
- Columbia MG-31155; 33s; 2 discs; rel 1972; cip

Partita, Violin, Viola, and Organ (1944)
[7370] Thaviu, Samuel (vln); Malno, Kras (vla); Fillinger, Valentina Woshner (org)
Rec 11/29/52
- ASCAP CB-190; 33m (Pittsburgh International Contemporary Music Festival); rel 1954

Passacaglia, Piano (1943)
[7371] Shields, Roger (pf)
- Vox SVBX-5303; 33s; 3 discs; rel 1977; cip

(Three) Pieces, Flute, Clarinet, and Bassoon (1926)
[7372] Barrere Woodwind Ensemble
- New Music Quarterly Recordings 1113 (11-5-6); 78; rel 1935

[7373] Bennington Woodwind Trio
- Golden Crest CRS-4140; 33q; rel 1976; cip

[7374] Berkshire Woodwind Ensemble (members of)
- Unicorn UNLP-1029; 33m; rel 1956; del 1959

[7375] New Art Wind Quintet (members of)
- Classic Editions CE-2003; 33m; 2 discs; rel 1953; del 1961

[7376] Soni Ventorum Wind Quintet (members of)
- Lyrichord LL-158/LLST-7158; 33m/s; rel 1966; cip

Prelude and Allegro, Organ and Strings (1943)
[7377] Biggs, E. Power (org); Boston Symphony Orchestra; Koussevitzky, Serge (cond)
Rec 4/24/45
- Victor 11-9262; 78; rel 1947

Psalm and Prayer of David (1958)
[7378] Peabody Conservatory Concert Singers; instrumental ensemble; Smith, Gregg (cond)
Rec 1976
- Vox SVBX-5353; 33s; 3 discs; rel 1979; cip

Quartet, Strings, No 1 (1933)
[7379] Dorian String Quartet
- Columbia 69745-47D (in set M-388); 78; 3 discs; rel pre-1942

[7380] Juilliard String Quartet
Rec 1952
- ASCAP CB-157; 33m (Pittsburgh International Contemporary Music Festival); rel 1954

Quartet, Strings, No 2 (1935)
[7381] Budapest String Quartet
Rec 10/18/45
- New World NW-302; 33m; rel 1979

Quartet, Strings, No 5 (1962)
[7382] Kohon Quartet
- Vox SVBX-5305; 33s; 3 discs; rel 1974; cip

Quintet, Piano and Strings (1949)
[7383] Harris, Johana (pf); New Music String Quartet
Rec 1952
- ASCAP CB-159; 33m (Pittsburgh International Contemporary Music Festival); rel 1954

[7384] Wild, Earl (pf); Walden String Quartet
- WCFM-14; 33m; rel 1953; del 1955
- McIntosh Music MM-109; 33m; rel 1956; del 1958
- Heliodor H-25027/HS-25027; 33m/s; rel 1966; del 1970

Quintet, Winds (1956)
[7385] Boehm Quintet
- Orion ORS-75206; 33s; rel 1976; cip

[7386] Boston Woodwind Quintet
- Boston B-407/BST-1005; 33m/s; rel 1958; del 1967

Serenata (1956)
[7387] Louisville Orchestra; Whitney, Robert (cond)
- LOU-58-6; 33m (Louisville Orchestra First Edition Records 1958 No 6); rel 1959; del 1978

Sonata, Flute and Piano (1930)
[7388] Baker, Julius (fl); Makas, Anthony (pf)
- Westminster XWN-19121/WST-17121; 33m/s; rel 1967; del 1971

[7389] Bryan, Keith (fl); Keys, Karen (pf)
- Orion ORS-76242; 33s; rel 1976; cip

[7390] Dingfelder, Ingrid (fl); Gordon, Anita (pf)
Rec 8/76
- CRI-394; 33s; rel 1978; cip

[7391] Dwyer, Doriot (fl); Korn, Barbara (pf)
- Claremont 1205; 33m; rel 1953; del 1965

[7392] Padorr, Laila (fl); Swearingen, Anita (pf)
- Laurel-Protone LP-14; 33s; rel 1977; cip

Sonata, Flute and Piano: 1st Movement (Allegro moderato e grazioso)
[7393] Fouse, Sarah Baird (fl); Ewing, Cecilia (pf)
- Coronet M-1245; 33m; rel 1969; del 1971

Sonata, Violin and Piano (1939)
[7394] Fuchs, Joseph (vln); Balsam, Artur (pf)
- Decca DL-9541; 33m; rel 1951; del 1960

[7395] Krasner, Louis (vln); Piston, Walter (pf)
- Columbia 71121-22D (in set X-199); 78; 2 discs; rel pre-1942

Sonatina, Violin and Harpsichord (1945)
[7396] Schneider, Alexander (vln); Kirkpatrick, Ralph (hpschd)
- Columbia ML-4495; 33m; rel 1952; del 1958

[7397] Zukofsky, Paul (vln); Kalish, Gilbert (pf)
- Desto DC-6435-37; 33s; 3 discs; rel 1975; cip

Suite, Oboe and Piano (1931)
[7398] Rapier, Wayne (ob); Perry, John (pf)
- Coronet S-1409; 33s; rel 1970; cip

[7399] Speyer, Louis (ob); Piston, Walter (pf)
- Technichord T-1561; 78; rel pre-1942

Symphony No 1 (1937)
[7400] Louisville Orchestra; Mester, Jorge (cond)
- LS-76-6; 33s (Louisville Orchestra First Edition Records 1976 No 6); rel 1979; cip

Symphony No 2 (1943)
[7401] Boston Symphony Orchestra; Thomas, Michael Tilson (cond)
- Deutsche Grammophon 2530.103; 33s; rel 1971; del 1979

[7402] Vienna Symphony Orchestra; Dixon, Dean (cond)
- American Recording Society ARS-1; 33m; 10"; rel 1951*
- American Recording Society ARS-112; 33m; rel pre-1956
- Desto D-410/DST-6410; 33m/s; rel 1965; cip

Symphony No 3 (1947)
[7403] Eastman-Rochester Symphony Orchestra; Hanson, Howard (cond)
Rec 5/54
- Mercury MG-40010; 33m; rel 1954; del 1957
- Mercury MG-50083; 33m; rel 1957; del 1963
- Mercury SRI-75107; 33s; rel 1978; cip

Symphony No 4 (1950)
[7404] Philadelphia Orchestra; Ormandy, Eugene (cond)
- Columbia ML-4992; 33m; rel 1955; del 1968
- Columbia CML-4992; 33m; rel 1968; del 1974
- Columbia AML-4992; 33m; rel 1974; cip

Symphony No 5 (1954)
[7405] Louisville Orchestra; Whitney, Robert (cond)
- LOU-65-3/LS-65-3; 33m/s (Louisville Orchestra First Edition Records 1965 No 3); rel 1965; cip

Symphony No 6 (1955)
[7406] Boston Symphony Orchestra; Mayes, Samuel (vcl); Munch, Charles (cond)
Rec 3/12/56
- RCA LM-2083; 33m; rel 1957; del 1961
- New World NW-286; 33m; rel 1977

Symphony No 7 (1960)
[7407] Louisville Orchestra; Mester, Jorge (cond)
- LS-74-6; 33s (Louisville Orchestra First Edition Records 1974 No 6); rel 1975; cip

Symphony No 8 (1965)
[7408] Louisville Orchestra; Mester, Jorge (cond)
- LS-74-6; 33s (Louisville Orchestra First Edition Records 1974 No 6); rel 1975; cip

Trio, Violin, Violoncello, and Piano (1935)
[7409] New York Trio
- Perspective PR-2004; 33m; rel 1954; del 1958

[7410] Temple University Trio
- Golden Crest CRS-4117; 33s/q; rel 1974; cip

[7411] Western Arts Trio
- Laurel LR-104; 33s; rel 1976; cip

Tunbridge Fair (Intermezzo for Band) (1950)
[7412] Eastman Symphonic Wind Ensemble; Fennell, Frederick (cond)
- Mercury MG-40006; 33m; rel 1953; del 1957
- Mercury EP-1-5062; 45; 7"; rel pre-1956
- Mercury MG-50079; 33m; rel 1957; del 1969
- Mercury SRI-75086; 33s; rel 1977

PITTAWAY, Rudolph
Sonata, Clarinet and Piano
[7413] McBride, Robert (cl); Pittaway, Rudolph (pf)
- Yaddo 101B; 78; 10"; rel 1937 (1st movement)
- Yaddo 128A; 78; rel 1937 (1st movement)
- Yaddo 21A; 78; rel 1937 (2nd and 3rd movements)

PLAIN, Gerald (1940-)
Showers of Blessings
[7414] Rehfeldt, Phillip (cl); tape
- Advance FGR-17S; 33s; rel 1976; cip

PLESKOW, Raoul (1931-)
Bagatelle, Violin, No 3 (1968)
[7415] Kaplan, Lewis (vln)
- CRI-293; 33s; rel 1973; cip

(Three) Bagatelles with Contrabass (1966)
[7416] Turetzky, Nancy (fl) (al fl) (pic); Larsen, Henry (cl) (b cl); Turetzky, Bertram (cb); Lesbines, Tele (perc)
- Ars Nova/Ars Antiqua AN-1001; 33s; rel 1969; del 1973

Cantata
[7417] C. W. Post College Chorus and Chamber Singers; Klauss, Walter (org); Dashnaw, Alexander (cond)
- Golden Crest CCS-8050; 33s; rel 1978; cip

Motet and Madrigal
[7418] Allen, Judith (sop); Sperry, Paul (ten); Spencer, Patricia (fl); Blustine, Allen (cl); Quan, Linda (vln); Sherry, Fred (vcl); Oppens, Ursula (pf); Wuorinen, Charles (cond)
Rec 11/18/74
- CRI-342; 33s; rel 1975; cip

Movement, Nine Players (1967)
[7419] Contemporary Chamber Ensemble; Weisberg, Arthur (cond)
- CRI-293; 33s; rel 1973; cip

Movement, Oboe, Violin, and Piano (1966)
[7420] Marx, Josef (ob); Moore, Thomas (vln); Rovics, Howard (pf)
- CRI-253; 33s; rel 1970; cip

(Three) Movements, Quintet (1971)
[7421] Sollberger, Sophie (fl); Blustine, Allen (cl); Schulte, Rolf (vln); Sherry, Fred (vcl); Miller, Robert (pf); Wuorinen, Charles (cond)
- CRI-302; 33s; rel 1973; cip

Pentimento (1974)
[7422] Peltzer, Dwight (pf)
- Serenus SRS-12069; 33s; rel 1978; cip

Per vege viene (1973)
[7423] Kaplan, Lewis (vln); Ponce, Walter (pf)
- CRI-293; 33s; rel 1973; cip

Piece, Piano (1966)
[7424] Chamberlain, Anne (pf)
- Ars Nova/Ars Antiqua AN-1007; 33s; rel 1971; del 1974

(Three) Pieces, Piano, Four Hands (1968)
[7425] Chinn, Genevieve (pf); Brings, Allen (pf)
Rec 1974
- CRI-383; 33s; rel 1978; cip

PLOG, Anthony
Animal Ditties
[7426] Smith, Hal (nar); Plog, Anthony (tpt); Davis, Sharon (pf)
- Crystal S-364; 33s; rel 1980; cip

Fanfare
[7427] Plog, Anthony (tpt); Kid, Russell (tpt)
- Crystal S-362; 33s; rel 1977; cip

Mini-Suite
[7428] Fine Arts Brass Quintet
- WIM Records WIMR-4; 33s; rel 1975; cip

(Two) Scenes
[7429] Bing, Barbara (sop); Plog, Anthony (tpt); Swearingen, Madolyn (org)
- Avant AV-1014; 33s; rel 1978; cip

POISTER, Arthur W. (1898-)
Christmas Cradle Song
[7430] Wichmann, Russell G. (org)
- True Image LP-125; 33m; rel 1966

POLIN, Claire C. (1926-)
Margo'a
[7431] Lind, Loren N. (fl)
- Orion ORS-79330; 33s; rel 1980; cip

Summer Settings (1966)
[7432] Polin, Claire (fl); Schlomovitz, Phyllis (hp)
- Ars Nova/Ars Antiqua AN-1004; 33m; rel 1971; del 1973
- Educo 4031; 33s; rel 1974*

Synaulia II
[7433] Russo, John (cl) (b cl); Lind, Loren N. (fl) (al fl); Ignacio, Lydia Walton (pf)
- Orion ORS-79330; 33s; rel 1980; cip

POLLOCK, Robert E. (1946-)
Bridgeforms (1972)
[7434] Pollock, Robert (pf)
- CRI-333; 33s; rel 1976; cip

Movement and Variations (1967)
[7435] Composers Quartet
- CRI-265; 33s; rel 1971; cip

PORTER, Quincy (1897-1966)
Anthony and Cleopatra (Incidental Music) (1934)
[7436] Yaddo Orchestra; Porter, Quincy (cond)
- Yaddo M-9-10; 78; 2-10"; rel 1938

Concerto, Harpsichord and Orchestra (1959)
[7437] Pleasants, Virginia (hpschd); Polish National Radio Orchestra; Krenz, Jan (cond)
- CRI-226; 33s; rel 1968; cip

Concerto, Viola and Orchestra (1948)
[7438] Angerer, Paul (vla); Vienna Symphony Orchestra; Schoenherr, Max (cond)
- American Recording Society ARS-36; 33m; rel 1953
- Desto D-410/DST-6410; 33m/s; rel 1965; cip

Concerto concertante (1953)
[7439] Terrasse, Andre (pf); Cohen, Jean
       Leon (pf); Orchestre des Concerts
       Colonne; Porter, Quincy (cond)
       Rec 6/55
       - Overtone LP-10; 33m; rel 1956;
       del 1974

Dance (arr for band by Keith Wilson)
[7440] Yale University Band; Wilson, Keith
       (cond)
       - Carillon 109; 33m; rel 1960; del
       1971

Dance in Three-Time (1937)
[7441] Orchestre des Concerts Colonne;
       Porter, Quincy (cond)
       Rec 6/55
       - Overtone LP-10; 33m; rel 1956;
       del 1974

[7442] no performers given
       - Yaddo 7B; 78; rel 1937

Lonesome (1940)
[7443] Martin, Charlotte (pf)
       - Educo 3021; 33m; rel 1968; del
       1972

Music for Strings (1941)
[7444] MGM String Orchestra; Solomon,
       Izler (cond)
       - MGM E-3117; 33m; rel 1954;
       del 1959

New England Episodes (1958)
[7445] Polish National Radio Orchestra;
       Wodiczko, Bodhan (cond)
       - Desto DC-7123; 33s; rel 1972;
       cip

Poem and Dance (1932)
[7446] Eastman-Rochester Symphony
       Orchestra; Hanson, Howard
       (cond)
       - Mercury MG-40013; 33m; rel
       1955; del 1957
       - Mercury MG-50086; 33m; rel
       1957; del 1963

Quartet, Strings, No 3 (1930)
[7447] Gordon String Quartet
       - Columbia 68395-96D (in set
       M-242); 78; 2 discs; rel
       pre-1936

[7448] Kohon Quartet
       - CRI-235; 33s; rel 1970; cip

Quartet, Strings, No 6 (1937)
[7449] Quatuor Pascal de la Radiodiffusion
       Francaise
       - Angel 35105; 33m; rel 1954;
       del 1961
       - Columbia FCX-220; 33m; rel
       pre-1956

[7450] Walden String Quartet
       - Yaddo 13B; 78; rel 1937 (1st
       movement)

Quartet, Strings, No 6 (1937)
(cont'd)
       - Yaddo 14A; 78; rel 1937 (2nd
       movement)
       - Yaddo 29A; 78; rel 1937 (3rd
       movement)

Quartet, Strings, No 7 (1943)
[7451] Hungarian Quartet
       - Owl ORLP-10; 33s; rel 1967; del
       1977

Quartet, Strings, No 8 (1950)
[7452] Stanley Quartet of the University of
       Michigan
       - CRI-118; 33m/s; rel 1957/?; cip

Quintet, Oboe and Strings (Elegiac) (1966)
[7453] Bloom, Robert (ob); Yale Quartet
       - CRI-235; 33s; rel 1970; cip

[7454] Boston Symphony Chamber
       Players (members of)
       - Deutsche Grammophon
       2530.104; 33s; rel 1971; del
       1976

Quintet in One Movement on a Childhood Theme (1937, rev 1940)
[7455] Van Vactor, David (fl); Yaddo
       String Quartet
       - Yaddo I-3; 78; rel 1940

Sonata, Piano (1930)
[7456] Von Moltke, Veronica Jochum (pf)
       - Golden Crest NEC-107; 33s; rel
       1974; cip

Sonata, Violin and Piano, No 2 (1929)
[7457] Druian, Rafael (vln); Simms, John
       (pf)
       - Mercury MG-50096; 33m; rel
       1956; del 1963

[7458] Flissler, Joyce (vln); Wingreen,
       Harriet (pf)
       - Artia/MK 1571; 33m; rel 1962;
       del 1971

[7459] Kaufman, Louis (vln); Balsam,
       Artur (pf)
       - Concert Hall D-16; 78; 2 discs;
       rel pre-1950
       - Concert Hall CHD-16; 33m; rel
       pre-1950
       - Orion ORS-79359; 33s; rel
       1980; cip

Suite, Viola (1930)
[7460] Porter, Quincy (vla)
       - New Music Quarterly Recordings
       1512; 78; rel 1939
       - CRI-390; 33s; rel 1978; cip

Symphony No 1 (1934)
[7461] Orchestre des Concerts Colonne;
       Porter, Quincy (cond)
       Rec 6/55
       - Overtone LP-10; 33m; rel 1956;
       del 1974

Symphony No 2 (1962)
[7462] Louisville Orchestra; Whitney,
       Robert (cond)
       - LOU-64-2; 33m (Louisville
       Orchestra First Edition Records
       1964 No 2); rel 1964; cip

Toccata, Andante, and Finale (1930): Andante
[7463] Smith, Melville (org)
       Rec 2/10/59
       - Organ Historical Society F-MS-I-II;
       33m; rel 1965

PORTNOFF, Mischa (1901-)

Perpetual Motion (On a Theme of Brahms)
[7464] Luboschutz, Pierre (pf); Nemenoff,
       Genia (pf)
       - Remington 199-143; 33m; rel
       1953; del 1959

POUND, Ezra (1885-1972)

Testament of Francois Villon, The (1923)
[7465] Western Opera Theater (soloists
       of); University of California
       Chamber Singers Associated
       Students; Hughes, Robert (cond)
       - Fantasy 12001; 33s; rel 1973;
       cip

POWELL, John (1882-1963)

At the Fair (1907): Banjo-Picker and Merry-Go-Round
[7466] Cook, Jean Carrington (pf)
       - Golden Age GAR-1003; 33s; rel
       1976
       - USR-8335; 33s; rel 1976?

In Old Virginia (Op 28) (1921)
[7467] Hamburg Philharmonia; Walther,
       Hans-Jurgen (cond)
       - Music Sound Books 78158-59;
       78; 2 discs; rel pre-1956

Rhapsodie negre (1918)
[7468] Carno, Zita (pf); Los Angeles
       Philharmonic Orchestra;
       Simmons, Calvin (cond)
       Rec 8/77
       - New World NW-228; 33s; rel
       1978

[7469] Powell, John (pf); Vienna
       Symphony Orchestra; Dixon, Dean
       (cond)
       - American Recording Society
       ARS-20; 33m; 10"; rel 1953
       - American Recording Society
       ARS-113; 33m; rel pre-1956
       - Desto D-409/DST-6409; 33m/s;
       rel 1965; cip

Sonata teutonica (Op 24) (1913)
[7470] Johnson, Roy Hamlin (pf)
Rec 1/77
- CRI-368; 33s; rel 1977; cip

Sonata virginianesque (Op 7) (1906?)
[7471] Brown, Eddy (vln); Powell, John (pf)
- Royale 29; 78; rel pre-1943

Sonate noble (Op 21) (1907)
[7472] Cook, Jean Carrington (pf)
- Golden Age GAR-1003; 33s; rel 1976
- USR-8335; 33s; rel 1976?

(Five) Traditional Children's Songs
[7473] Langstaff, John (bar); Powell, John (pf)
- John Powell Foundation P.S.-109; 33m; rel 196?

(Five) Virginian Folk Songs (With a Dedication to L.B.P.) (Op 34) (1938)
[7474] Langstaff, John (bar); Powell, John (pf)
- John Powell Foundation P.S.-109; 33m; rel 196?

POWELL, Mel (1923-)

Divertimento, Violin and Harp (1955)
[7475] Sorkin, Herbert (vln); Ross, Margaret (hp)
- CRI-121; 33m/s; rel 1957/?; cip

Divertimento, Wind Quintet (1957)
[7476] Fairfield Wind Ensemble; Karpilovsky, Murray (cl)
- CRI-121; 33m/s; rel 1957/?; cip

Electronic Setting (1961)
[7477] Electronic music
- Son-Nova 1/S-1; 33m/s; rel 1962; del 1967

Etude, Piano (1957)
[7478] Helps, Robert (pf)
- RCA LM-7042/LSC-7042; 33m/s; 2 discs; rel 1966; del 1971
- CRI-288; 33s; 2 discs; rel 1972; cip

Events (1963)
[7479] Electronic music
- CRI-227; 33s; rel 1968; cip

Filigree Setting (1958)
[7480] Claremont String Quartet
- Son-Nova 1/S-1; 33m/s; rel 1962; del 1967

Haiku Settings (1960)
[7481] Beardslee, Bethany (sop); Helps, Robert (pf)
- Son-Nova 1/S-1; 33m/s; rel 1962; del 1967

Improvisation (1962)
[7482] Wilson, Keith (cl); Schwartz, David (vla); Davenny, Ward (pf); tape
- CRI-227; 33s; rel 1968; cip

(Two) Prayer Settings (1962)
[7483] Bressler, Charles (ten); Kaplan, Melvin (ob); Tarack, Gerald (vln); Lynch, Ynez (vla); Kougell, Alexander (vcl); tape
- CRI-227; 33s; rel 1968; cip

Second Electronic Setting (1962)
[7484] Electronic music
- CRI-227; 33s; rel 1968; cip

Trio (1956)
[7485] Helura Trio
- CRI-121; 33m/s; rel 1957/?; cip

POWELL, Morgan (1938-)

Darkness II
[7486] University of Illinois Faculty Brass Quintet
- Ubres SN-203; 33s; rel 1976; cip

Inacabado
[7487] no performers given
- Ubres SN-203; 33s; rel 1976; cip

Loneliness
[7488] no performers given
- Ubres SN-203; 33s; rel 1976; cip

Midnight Realities
[7489] Persantoni, Daniel (tu)
- Ubres SN-203; 33s; rel 1976; cip
- Crystal S-394; 33s; rel 1978

Music for Brass and Percussion
[7490] no performers given
- Ubres SN-203; 33s; rel 1976; cip

Nocturnes
[7491] Persantoni, Daniel (tu); Illinois Contemporary Chamber Players; London, Edwin (cond)
- Crystal S-394; 33s; rel 1978

Old Man
[7492] no performers given
- Ubres SN-203; 33s; rel 1976; cip

Transitions
[7493] Illinois Contemporary Chamber Players; London, Edwin (cond)
- Crystal S-394; 33s; rel 1978

Zelanski Medley
[7494] Ineluctable Modality; London, Edwin (cond)
- Advance FGR-18S; 33s; rel 197?

POWELL, Roger

Cosmic Furnace
[7495] Powell, Roger (syn) (pf)
- Atlantic SD-7251; 33s; rel 1973

POZDRO, John (1923-)

Symphony No 3 (1959)
[7496] Oklahoma City Symphony Orchestra; Harrison, Guy Fraser (cond)
- CRI-151; 33m/s; rel 1962/?; cip

PRESS, Jacques (1903-)

Prelude and Fugue in Jazz
[7497] Boston Pops Orchestra; Fiedler, Arthur (cond)
- RCA LM-2789/LSC-2789; 33m/s; rel 1965; cip

PRESSER, William (1916-)

Prelude, Fugue, and Postlude
[7498] Florida State University Brass Trio
- Golden Crest CRS-4081; 33s; rel 1969; cip

Serenade: 3rd Movement (Allegro)
[7499] University of Michigan Tuba Ensemble; Mayer, Uri (cond)
- Golden Crest CRSQ-4145; 33q; rel 1977; cip

Sonatina, Trombone
[7500] Cramer, William F. (tbn); Glotzbach, Robert (pf)
- Coronet S-1506; 33s; rel 1969; cip

Suite, Brass Quintet (1964)
[7501] Georgia State College Brass Ensemble; Hill, William H. (cond)
- Golden Crest CRS-4084; 33s; rel 1969; cip

Suite, Trumpet (1967)
[7502] Hickman, David (tpt)
- Crystal S-363; 33s; rel 1978; cip

PREVIN, Andre (1929-)

Concerto, Guitar and Orchestra (1971)
[7503] Williams, John (gtr); London Symphony Orchestra; Previn, Andre (cond)
- Columbia M-31963/MQ-31963; 33s/q; rel 1973; cip

(Four) Outings for Brass Quintet (1974)
[7504] Philip Jones Brass Ensemble
- Argo ZRG-851; 33s; rel 1978; cip

Overture to a Comedy (1960)
[7505] Leicestershire Schools Symphony
Orchestra; Previn, Andre (cond)
- Argo ZRG-685; 33s; rel 1972;
del 1978

PRINCE, Robert (1929-)
Events (1961)
[7506] orchestra; Prince, Robert (cond)
- RCA LPM-2435/LSP-2435;
33m/s; rel 1961; del 1963

**New York Export (Opus Jazz)
(1958)**
[7507] orchestra; Prince, Robert (cond)
- Warner Bros B-1240/BS-1240;
33m/s; rel 1959; del 1969
- RCA LPM-2435/LSP-2435;
33m/s; rel 1961; del 1963

PRINCE-JOSEPH, Bruce (1925-)
Toccata, Organ
[7508] Prince-Joseph, Bruce (org)
- Hi-Fi R-709/S-709; 33m/s; rel
1957/1960; del 1965
- Everest LPBR-6158/SDBR-3158;
33m/s; rel 1967; cip

PRITCHARD, Robert
**Ti Jacques (Suite sur melodie
folklorique d'Haiti)**
[7509] Pritchard, Robert (pf)
- Spoken Arts 202; 33m; rel
1962; del 1971

PRITCHARD, Robert and HURD
Passacaglia monroviana
[7510] Pritchard, Robert (pf)
- Spoken Arts 202; 33m; rel
1962; del 1971

PROCTER, Leland H. (1914-)
Symphony No 1 (1948)
[7511] Polish National Radio Orchestra;
Ormicki, Wlodzimiertz (cond)
- CRI-224; 33s; rel 1968; cip

PROSTAKOFF, Joseph (1911-)
(Two) Bagatelles (ca 1963)
[7512] Helps, Robert (pf)
- RCA LM-7042/LSC-7042;
33m/s; 2 discs; rel 1966; del
1971
- CRI-288; 33s; 2 discs; rel 1972;
cip

PROTO, Frank (1941-)
Duet, Violin and Contrabass (1967)
[7513] Howard, Larrie (vln); Proto, Frank
(cb)
- QCA 375; 33s; rel 1978; cip

Nebula (1975)
[7514] Green, Barry (cb); Cook, James
(pf); tape
- Liben LS-001; 33s; rel 1977
- QCA 370; 33s; rel 1978; cip

Quartet, Contrabasses (1964)
[7515] Proto, Frank (cb)
- QCA 375; 33s; rel 1978; cip

Sonata 1963
[7516] Proto, Frank (cb); piano
- QCA 375; 33s; rel 1978; cip

**Trio, Violin, Viola, and Contrabass
(1974)**
[7517] Howard, Larrie (vln); Olson, Mary
(vla); Proto, Frank (cb)
Rec 6/74
- Liben LS-001; 33s; rel 1977
- QCA 370; 33s; rel 1978; cip

PURSELL, William (1926-)
Christ Looking Over Jerusalem
[7518] Eastman-Rochester Symphony
Orchestra; Hanson, Howard
(cond)
Rec 1958
- Mercury MG-50053/SR-90053;
33m/s; rel 1959; del 1964
- Eastman-Rochester Archives
ERA-1003; 33s; rel 1974; cip

PURSWELL, Patrick (1939-)
It Grew and Grew (1964)
[7519] Purswell, Patrick (fl)
- CRI-324; 33s; rel 1975; cip

PURVIS, Richard (1915-)
**American Organ Mass, An: Introit
and Elevation**
[7520] Purvis, Richard (org)
- Aeolian-Skinner AS-5; 33m; rel
1956; del 1958

American Organ Mass, An: Offertory
[7521] Purvis, Richard (org)
- Hi-Fi R-705; 33m; rel 1956

**Capriccio on the Notes of the
Cuckoo (1953)**
[7522] Purvis, Richard (org)
- Hi-Fi R-703/S-703; 33m/s; rel
1956/1960; del 1970
- Aeolian-Skinner AS-5; 33m; rel
1956; del 1958
- Word WST-9033; 33s; rel 1970

**(Four) Carol Preludes (1945):
Greensleeves**
[7523] Purvis, Richard (org)
- Key 13; 33m; rel 1951?
- Word 4004; 33m; rel 1955
- Hi-Fi R-703/S-703; 33m/s; rel
1956/1960; del 1970
- Word WST-9033; 33s; rel 1970

[7524] Wichmann, Russell G. (org)
- True Image LP-125; 33m; rel
1966

Carol Rhapsody (1939)
[7525] MacDonald, Robert (org)
- Mirrosonic CS-7232; 33s; rel
197?

Carol Rhapsody (1939) *(cont'd)*
[7526] Purvis, Richard (org)
- Hi-Fi R-705; 33m; rel 1956

**(Seven) Chorale Preludes (1945):
Contemplation (Tallis' Canon)**
[7527] Phelps, Ruth Barrett (org)
- Aeolian-Skinner AS-9; 33m; rel
1956; del 1958
- Washington WAS-9; 33m; rel
1958; del 1962

**(Seven) Chorale Preludes: Pastorale
(Forest Green)**
[7528] Purvis, Richard (org)
- Hi-Fi R-705; 33m; rel 1956
- Aeolian-Skinner AS-5; 33m; rel
1956; del 1958

[7529] Read, Robert (org)
- Jewel LPS-406; 33s; rel 1974

**(Seven) Chorale Preludes: Poeme
mystique (Manna)**
[7530] Barnes, William H. (org)
- Replica FB-512-13; 33m; rel
1957?

**(Seven) Chorale Preludes: Toccata
festiva (In Babilone)**
[7531] Purvis, Richard (org)
- Hi-Fi R-704/S-704; 33m/s; rel
1956/1960; del 1970

[7532] Snyder, Clarence (org)
- Key 15; 33m; rel 1951; del
1955
- Word 4003; 33m; rel 1955; del
1961

Dialogue monastique
[7533] Ness, Earl (org); Whitehead,
William (org)
Rec 3/7/65
- Rittenhouse RS-1003; 33s; rel
1966; del 1968
- Allen Organ Co AO-100; 33s; rel
1970

**(Four) Dubious Conceits (1953):
Les Petites cloches, Nocturne on
Night in Monterrey, and Marche
grotesque**
[7534] Purvis, Richard (org)
- Hi-Fi R-704/S-704; 33m/s; rel
1956/1960; del 1970
- Word WST-9033; 33s; rel 1970
(Excerpts: Les Petites cloches and
Nocturne on Night in Monterrey)

**(Four) Dubious Conceits: Les
Petites cloches**
[7535] Chapman, Keith (org)
- Stentorian SC-1685; 33s; rel
1973

[7536] Wichmann, Russell G. (org)
- True Image LP-125; 33m; rel
1966

Fanfare
[7537] Purvis, Richard (org)
- Word WST-9033; 33s; rel 1970

(Seven) Folktone Poems: Of Moor and Fen and Brigg Fayre
[7538] Purvis, Richard (org)
- Word WST-9033; 33s; rel 1970

Idyll
[7539] Rhoads, C. Thomas (org)
- Century V-12735; 33s; rel 1960

Partita on Christ ist erstanden (1953)
[7540] Purvis, Richard (org)
- Aeolian-Skinner AS-5; 33m; rel 1956; del 1958

[7541] Swann, Frederick (org)
Rec 12/66
- Westminster XWN-19125/WST-17125; 33m/s; rel 1967; del 1969

(Five) Pieces on Gregorian Themes (1940): Communion
[7542] Gay, Harry W. (org)
- B & C BC-12435; 33m; rel 1958

[7543] Purvis, Richard (org)
- Key 13; 33m; rel 1951?
- Word 4004; 33m; rel 1955

(Five) Pieces on Gregorian Themes: Divinum mysterium
[7544] Barnes, William H. (org)
- H08P-0144-45 (matrix no); 33m; 196?

[7545] Purvis, Richard (org)
- Key 13; 33m; rel 1951?
- Word 4004; 33m; rel 1955
- Aeolian-Skinner AS-5; 33m; rel 1956; del 1958

[7546] Swann, Frederick (org)
Rec 8/63
- Sheldon Recording Studios S-3167-68 (matrix no); 33m; rel 1963

(Four) Prayers in Tone (1952): Repentance, Supplication, and Thanksgiving
[7547] Purvis, Richard (org)
- Key 13; 33m; rel 1951?
- Word 4004; 33m; rel 1955
- Hi-Fi R-703/S-703; 33m/s; rel 1956/1960; del 1970 (Excerpt: Supplication)
- Word WST-9033; 33s; rel 1970 (Excerpts: Supplication and Thanksgiving)

(Four) Prayers in Tone: Adoration
[7548] Purvis, Richard (org)
- Aeolian-Skinner AS-5; 33m; rel 1956; del 1958

(Four) Prayers in Tone: Adoration
(cont'd)
[7549] Swann, Frederick (org)
Rec 8/63
- Sheldon Recording Studios S-3167-68 (matrix no); 33m; rel 1963

Romanza
[7550] Riley, Lowell (org)
- Mirrosonic CM-7002/CS-7002; 33m/s; rel 1960

Virgin's Slumber Song (1954)
[7551] Purvis, Richard (org)
- Hi-Fi R-705; 33m; rel 1956

PUTSCHE, Thomas (1929-)
Cat and the Moon, The (1957)
[7552] Charlston, Elsa (sop); MacBone, Thomas (ten); Mack, James (bar); University of Chicago Contemporary Chamber Players; Shapey, Ralph (cond)
- CRI-245; 33s; rel 1969; cip

RAFFMAN, Relly (1921-)
Triptych (1957)
[7553] Hamline A Cappella Choir; Holliday, Robert (cond)
- SPAMH MIA-116; 33s; rel 1961

RAKSIN, David (1912-)
Morning Revisited
[7554] Horn Club of Los Angeles
- Capitol P-8525/SP-8525; 33m/s; rel 1960; del 1963
- Seraphim S-60095; 33s; rel 1969; del 1973

Psalmist, The
[7555] Remsen, Dorothy (hp)
- Avant AV-1000; 33s; rel 1967; cip

RALEIGH, Stuart W. (1940-)
Maledictions (1970)
[7556] Cornell University Wind Ensemble; Stith, Marice (cond)
- Cornell CUWE-7; 33s; rel 1971; cip

Monoliths
[7557] Cornell University Wind Ensemble; Stith, Marice (cond)
Rec 3/24/74
- Cornell CUWE-15; 33s; rel 1975; cip

RAMEY, Phillip (1939-)
Fantasy, Piano (1972)
[7558] Atkins, John (pf)
- Opus One 37; 33s; rel 1978; cip

Leningrad Rag (1972)
[7559] Atkins, John (pf)
- Opus One 37; 33s; rel 1978; cip

Sonata, Piano, No 4 (1968)
[7560] Atkins, John (pf)
- Opus One 37; 33s; rel 1978; cip

RAMSEY, Gordon (1926-)
(Four) Descriptive Pieces, Violin and Viola
[7561] Wolf, Harold (vln); Rumpler, Harry (vla)
- Orion ORS-79354; 33s; rel 1980; cip

(Three) Movements, Flute and Piano
[7562] Hoberman, Arthur (fl); Gustetto, Martha (pf)
- Orion ORS-79353; 33s; rel 1979; cip

Petite collection, La
[7563] Gustetto, Martha (pf)
- Orion ORS-79353; 33s; rel 1979; cip

Quartet, Flute and Strings
[7564] Hoberman, Arthur (fl); Wolf, Harold (vln); Rumpler, Harry (vla); Assayas, Irit (vcl)
- Orion ORS-79354; 33s; rel 1980; cip

Quartet, Strings
[7565] Wolf, Harold (vln); Jones, Karon (vln); Rumpler, Harry (vla); Assayas, Irit (vcl)
- Orion ORS-79354; 33s; rel 1980; cip

Sonata, Violin and Piano (1964)
[7566] Wolf, Harold (vln); Gustetto, Martha (pf)
- Orion ORS-79353; 33s; rel 1979; cip

RAN, Shulamit (1949-)
Hatsvi Israel (1970)
[7567] Reid-Parsons, Susan (m sop); Dal Segno Ensemble; Hoffman, Stanley (cond)
- Critics Choice CC-1703; 33s; rel 1975*

O the Chimneys (1970)
[7568] Davy, Gloria (sop); New York Philomusica Chamber Ensemble; tape; Johnson, A. Robert (cond)
- Turnabout TVS-34492; 33s; rel 1973; del 1978

RANDALL, James K. (1929-)
Eakins (1972): Selections
[7569] Electronic music
- CRI-328; 33s; rel 1975; cip

Improvisation on a Poem by e. e. cummings (1960)
[7570] Beardslee, Bethany (sop); Blustine, Allen (cl); Regni, Albert (sax); Anderson, Ronald (tpt); Silverman, Stanley (gtr); James, Thomas (pf); Gilbert, David (cond)
- CRI-325; 33s; rel 1974; cip

Lyric Variations, Violin and Computer (1968)
[7571] Zukofsky, Paul (vln); tape
- Vanguard Cardinal VCS-10057; 33s; rel 1969; del 1977

Mudgett (Monologues by a Mass Murderer) (1965)
[7572] Electronic music
- Nonesuch H-71245; 33s; rel 1970; cip

Quartets in Pairs (1964)
[7573] Electronic music
- Nonesuch H-71245; 33s; rel 1970; cip

Quatersines (1969)
[7574] Electronic music
- Nonesuch H-71245; 33s; rel 1970; cip

RAPHLING, Sam (1910-)

American Album (1946): Three Pieces
[7575] Raphling, Sam (pf)
- Circle L-51-102; 33m; rel pre-1953

Concerto, Piano and Percussion
[7576] Montague, Gramiston (pf); London Percussion Ensemble
- Serenus SRS-12061; 33s; rel 1976; cip

(Twenty-Four) Etudes, Piano
[7577] Raphling, Sam (pf)
- Serenus SRE-1020; 33m; rel 1972; cip

(Four) Indiscretions
[7578] Raphling, Sam (pf)
- Serenus SRS-12061; 33s; rel 1976; cip

Movement, Piano and Brass Quintet
[7579] Raphling, Sam (pf); American Brass Quintet
- Serenus SRS-12061; 33s; rel 1976; cip

Remembered Scene for Piano and Small Dance Band (ca 1927)
[7580] Montague, Gramiston (pf); London Melody Group
- Serenus SRS-12061; 33s; rel 1976; cip

Sonatina, Piano
[7581] Raphling, Sam (pf)
- Serenus SRS-12061; 33s; rel 1976; cip

RARIG, John (1912-)
Introduction and March
[7582] Spear, Julian (b cl); Davis, Sharon (pf)
- WIM Records WIMR-10; 33s; rel 1978; cip

RASBACH, Oscar (1888-1975)
Trees
[7583] Bailey, Norman (b bar); Parsons, Geoffrey (pf)
- L'Oiseau-lyre DSLO-20; 33s; rel 1977

[7584] Eddy, Nelson (bar); Paxson, Theodore (pf) or Columbia Concert Orchestra; Arnaud, Leon (cond)
- Columbia ML-4343; 33m; rel 1950; del 1958
- Columbia CL-812; 33m; rel 1956; del 1958

[7585] Merrill, Robert (bar); Russ Case and his Orchestra
- Victor ERA-60; 45; 7"; rel 1947*
- RCA LM-92; 33m; 10"; rel 1951; del 1953

[7586] Robeson, Paul (b)
- Gramophone B-8830; 78; 10"; rel pre-1952

[7587] Schumann-Heink, Ernestine (al)
- Victor 1198; 78; 10"; rel pre-1936

[7588] Sievall, O. (bar)
- EMI/Odeon D-5386; 78; rel pre-1952

[7589] Stevens, Rise (m sop); orchestra; Shulman, Sylvan (cond)
- Columbia ML-4179; 33m; rel pre-1949; del 1956

[7590] Thebom, Blanche (m sop); London Symphony Orchestra; Braithwaite, Warwick (cond)
- RCA LM-58; 33m; 10"; rel 1951; del 1953
- RCA LM-104; 33m; 10"; rel 1951; del 1953
- RCA LBC-1054; 33m; rel 1953; del 1956
- Victor WBC-1054; 45; 7"

[7591] U.S. Military Academy Glee Club; Gaillard, Cadet Frank (cond)
- Columbia CL-6118; 33m; rel 1950; del 1956

RATHAUS, Karol (1895-1954)
Louisville Prelude (Op 71) (1953)
[7592] Louisville Orchestra; Whitney, Robert (cond)
- LOU-545-9; 33m (Louisville Orchestra First Edition Records 1955 No 9); rel 1959; del 1980

Tower Music
[7593] Berlin Brass Quintet
- Crystal S-201; 33s; rel 1975; cip

RATNER, Leonard (1916-)
Serenade, Oboe, Horn, and String Quartet
[7594] instrumental ensemble; Salgo, Sandor (cond)
- Music Library MLR-7023; 33m; rel 1952; del 1974

Sonata, Piano
[7595] Baller, Albert (pf)
- Music Library MLR-7023; 33m; rel 1952; del 1974

RAYMOND, Lewis (1908-56)
Short Suite, Brass Quartet
[7596] Fine Arts Brass Quintet
- WIM Records WIMR-4; 33s; rel 1975; cip

READ, Gardner (1913-)
Golden Harp, The (Op 93) (1952)
[7597] Peabody High School Chorus; Shute, Florence (cond)
- ASCAP CB-160; 33m (Pittsburgh International Contemporary Music Festival); rel pre-1956

Night Flight (Op 44) (1936-42)
[7598] Louisville Orchestra; Whitney, Robert (cond)
- LOU-63-2; 33m (Louisville Orchestra First Edition Records 1963 No 2); rel 1963; cip

(Eight) Preludes on Old Southern Hymns (Op 90) (1950): (No 1) My Soul Forsakes Her Vain Delight, (No 2) Thou Man of Grief, Remember Me, and (No 4) On Jordan's Stormy Banks I Stand
[7599] Craighead, David (org)
Rec 7/31/57
- Mirrosonic DRE-1012; 33m; 2 discs; rel 1958; del 1965

(Eight) Preludes on Old Southern Hymns: (No 1) My Soul Forsakes Her Vain Delight and (No 3) David, the King, Was Grieved and Moved
[7600] Swann, Frederick (org)
- Mirrosonic CS-7230; 33s; rel 1972

(Six) Preludes on Old Southern Hymns (Op 112): (No 2) How Happy Are the Souls Above
[7601] Swann, Frederick (org)
- Mirrosonic CS-7230; 33s; rel 1972

Suite, Organ (Op 81) (1949):
Toccata
[7602] Gehring, Philip (org)
- Valparaiso University
RR4M-6307-08 (matrix no);
33m; rel 1965

Toccata giocosa (Op 94) (1953)
[7603] Louisville Orchestra; Whitney,
Robert (cond)
- LOU-545-5; 33m (Louisville
Orchestra First Edition Records
1955 No 5); rel 1959; del 1978

RECK, David (1935-)
(Five) Studies, Tuba
[7604] Hanks, Toby (tu)
- Crystal S-395; 33s; rel 1980; cip

REED, Alfred (1921-)
Festival Prelude, A
[7605] Michigan State University
Symphonic Band; Reed, Alfred
(cond)
Rec 5/6/78
- Golden Crest ATH-5057; 33s; rel
1978; cip

Music Makers, The
[7606] Michigan State University
Symphonic Band; Hegerberg, A.
Thad (cond)
Rec 5/6/78
- Golden Crest ATH-5057; 33s; rel
1978; cip

Prelude and Capriccio (1977)
[7607] Michigan State University
Symphonic Band; Reed, Alfred
(cond)
Rec 5/6/78
- Golden Crest ATH-5057; 33s; rel
1978; cip

Punchinello (1973)
[7608] Michigan State University
Symphonic Band; Reed, Alfred
(cond)
Rec 5/6/78
- Golden Crest ATH-5057; 33s; rel
1978; cip

Seascape
[7609] Behrend, Roger (euph); Michigan
State University Symphonic Band;
Hegerberg, A. Thad (cond)
Rec 5/6/78
- Golden Crest ATH-5057; 33s; rel
1978; cip

Symphony No 2
[7610] Michigan State University
Symphonic Band; Bloomquist,
Kenneth Gene (cond)
Rec 5/6/78
- Golden Crest ATH-5057; 33s; rel
1978; cip

REED, Herbert Owen (1910-)
Concerto, Violoncello and Orchestra
(1949)
[7611] Potter, Louis J. (vcl); Michigan
State University Symphony
Orchestra; Reed, Herbert (cond)
- Dorian 1009; 33m; rel 1962; del
1974

Fiesta mexicana, La (1949)
[7612] Eastman Symphonic Wind
Ensemble; Fennell, Frederick
(cond)
Rec 1954
- Mercury MG-40011; 33m; rel
1954; del 1957
- Mercury MG-50084; 33m; rel
1957; del 1969

[7613] Eastman Symphonic Wind
Ensemble; Hunsberger, Donald
(cond)
- Decca DL-710157; 33s; rel
1968; del 1973

[7614] University of Minnesota Band;
Frank A. Bencriscutto (cond)
- Mark 40400; 33s; 2 discs; rel
1970; del 1976

REGNEY, Noel
Slovenly Peter and his Friends
[7615] Stuttgart Chamber Orchestra;
Reichert, Karl Paul (cond)
- Serenus SRS-12050; 33s; rel
1974; cip

REICH, Steve (1936-)
Come Out (1966)
[7616] Electronic music
- Odyssey 32-16-0160; 33s; rel
1967; cip

Drumming (1971)
[7617] Steve Reich and his Ensemble
- J Gibson & Multiples
46T2/14-16.2; T2-14 46-17.2
(matrix no); 33s; rel 1972
- Deutsche Grammophon
2563.301-03 (in set 2740.106);
33s; 3 discs; rel 1975; cip

Four Organs (1970)
[7618] Reich, Steve (elec org); Kellaway,
Roger (elec org); Thomas,
Michael Tilson (elec org);
Grierson, Ralph (elec org); Raney,
Tom (maracas)
- Angel S-36059; 33s; rel 1973;
cip

It's Gonna Rain (1965)
[7619] Electronic music
- Columbia MS-7265; 33s; rel
1969; del 1976

Music for Eighteen Musicians
(1975)
[7620] Steve Reich and his Ensemble
- ECM/Warner Bros 1129; 33s; rel
1978; cip

Music for Mallet Instruments,
Voices, and Organ (1973)
[7621] Steve Reich and his Ensemble
- Deutsche Grammophon
2563.301-03 (in set 2740.106);
33s; 3 discs; rel 1975; cip

Six Pianos (1973)
[7622] Steve Reich and his Ensemble
- Deutsche Grammophon
2563.301-03 (in set 2740.106);
33s; 3 discs; rel 1975; cip

Violin Phase (1967)
[7623] Zukofsky, Paul (vln); tape
- Columbia MS-7265; 33s; rel
1969; del 1976

REICHERT, James (1932-) and
DOCKSTADER, Tod
see DOCKSTADER, Tod and
REICHERT, James

REIF, Paul (1910-78)
And Be My Love
[7624] Tozzi, Giorgio (b); Walmer, Max
(pf)
- Serenus SRS-12030; 33s; rel
1971; cip

Banter (1966)
[7625] Baker, Julius (fl); Makas, Anthony
(pf)
- Westminster
XWN-19121/WST-17121;
33m/s; rel 1967; del 1971

Curse of Mauvais-Air, The (1974)
[7626] Gregg Smith Singers; Smith, Gregg
(cond)
- Grenadilla GS-1033; 33s; rel
1978; cip

(Five) Divertimenti, Four Strings
(1969)
[7627] Serenus Quartet
- Serenus SRS-12022; 33s; rel
1969; cip

Duo for Three (1974)
[7628] Long Island Chamber Ensemble of
New York (members of)
- Grenadilla GS-1009; 33s; rel
1977; cip

Figlia che piange, La
[7629] Tozzi, Giorgio (b); Walmer, Max
(pf)
- Serenus SRS-12030; 33s; rel
1971; cip

Five-Finger Exercises
[7630] Reardon, John (bar); Hebert, Bliss
(pf)
- Serenus SRE-1019/SRS-12019;
33m/s; rel 1967; cip

Monsieur le pelican (1960)
[7631] New York Wind Ensemble; Reif,
Paul (cond)
- Epic LC-3657/BC-1065; 33m/s;
rel 1960; del 1964
- Serenus SRS-12022; 33s; rel
1969; cip

Philidor's Defense (1965)
[7632] Rome Chamber Orchestra; Flagello,
Nicolas (cond)
- Serenus SRE-1018/SRS-12018;
33m/s; rel 1967; cip

Reverence for Life (1960)
[7633] Cassel, Walter (bar); Epic String
Quartet; Hambro, Leonid (pf);
Reif, Paul (cond)
- Epic LC-3657/BC-1065; 33m/s;
rel 1960; del 1964

**(Four) Songs on Words of Kenneth
Koch**
[7634] Reardon, John (bar); Hebert, Bliss
(pf)
- Serenus SRS-12022; 33s; rel
1969; cip

**(Eight) Vignettes for Four Singers
(1975)**
[7635] Gregg Smith Singers (soloists
from); Beegle, Raymond (pf);
Smith, Gregg (cond)
- Orion ORS-76228; 33s; rel
1977; cip

RENWICK, Wilke (1921-)
Dance (1973)
[7636] Annapolis Brass Quintet
- Crystal S-206; 33s; rel 1977; cip

REYNOLDS, Jeffrey (1943-)
**(in collaboration with Irving Bush,
Frank Campo, Frederic Dutton,
William Kraft, Leonard Rosenman,
and William Schmidt)**
Fanfares 1969
[7637] Los Angeles Brass Society;
Remsen, Lester (cond)
- Avant AV-1001; 33s; rel 1971;
cip

REYNOLDS, Roger (1934-)
Ambages (1965)
[7638] Sollberger, Harvey (fl)
- Nonesuch HB-73028; 33s; 2
discs; rel 1975; cip

Blind Men (1966)
[7639] Peabody Conservatory Concert
Singers and Chamber Ensemble;
Smith, Gregg (cond)
- CRI-241; 33s; rel 1970; cip

Fantasy for Pianist (1964)
[7640] Takahashi, Yuji (pf)
- Mainstream MS-5000; 33s; rel
1970; del 1979

From Behind the Unreasoning Mask
[7641] Anderson, Miles (tbn); Raney, Tom
(perc); Reynolds, Roger (perc);
tape
- New World NW-237; 33s; rel
1978

Ping (1969)
[7642] Reynolds, Karen (fl); Reynolds,
Roger (pf); Chihara, Paul (harm)
(perc); Johnson, Alan (electronics)
- CRI-285; 33s; rel 1972; cip

**Quick Are the Mouths of Earth
(1964-65)**
[7643] Contemporary Chamber Ensemble;
Weisberg, Arthur (cond)
- Nonesuch H-71219; 33s; rel
1969; cip

Traces (1969)
[7644] Reynolds, Karen (fl); Barron, Lin
(vcl); Takahashi, Yuji (pf);
Johnson, Alan (electronics)
- CRI-285; 33s; rel 1972; cip

REYNOLDS, Verne (1926-)
(Four) Caprices (1972)
[7645] Webster, Michael (cl); Webster,
Beveridge (pf)
Rec 1974
- CRI-374; 33s; rel 1977; cip

Music for Five Trumpets (1957)
[7646] Plog, Anthony (tpt); Los Angeles
Philharmonic Orchestra (trumpet
section); Henderson, Robert
(cond)
- Crystal S-362; 33s; rel 1977; cip

Signals
[7647] Stevens, Thomas (tpt); Bobo, Roger
(tu); brass ensemble; Henderson,
Robert (cond)
- Crystal S-392; 33s; rel 1978; cip

Suite, Brass (1963)
[7648] Iowa Brass Quintet
- Trilogy CTS-1001; 33s; rel
1973; del 1975

[7649] Ithaca Brass Quintet
- Golden Crest CRS-4114; 33q; rel
1979; cip

RHODES, Phillip (1940-)
Autumn Setting (1969)
[7650] Bryn-Julson, Phyllis (sop);
Speculum Musicae String Quartet
- CRI-301; 33s; rel 1973; cip

**Divertimento, Chamber Orchestra
(1971)**
[7651] St. Paul Chamber Orchestra;
Davies, Dennis Russell (cond)
Rec 10/75
- CRI-361; 33s; rel 1977; cip

Duo, Violin and Violoncello
[7652] Zukofsky, Paul (vln); Sylvester,
Robert (vcl)
- Acoustic Research AR-0654.087;
33s; rel 1971

From Paradise Lost
[7653] Speaight, Robert (nar); Bryn-Julson,
Phyllis (sop); McDonald, James
(ten); Horton, Gary (bar);
Chamber Singers of Louisville;
Louisville Orchestra; Mester,
Jorge (cond)
- LS-72-3-4; 33s; 2 discs
(Louisville Orchestra First Edition
Records 1972 Nos 3-4); rel
1973; cip

Lament of Michal, The
[7654] Bryn-Julson, Phyllis (sop); Louisville
Orchestra; Mester, Jorge (cond)
- LS-70-4; 33s (Louisville
Orchestra First Edition Records
1970 No 4); rel 1970; cip

Mountain Songs (1976)
[7655] Bryn-Julson, Phyllis (sop); Mayer,
Anne (pf)
Rec 10/31/76 and 11/1/76
- Orion ORS-77276; 33s; rel
1978; cip

Museum Pieces (1973)
[7656] Livingston, James (cl); Louisville
String Quartet
- LS-74-1; 33s (Louisville
Orchestra First Edition Records
1974 No 1); rel 1975; cip

**On the Morning of Christ's Nativity
(1976)**
[7657] McWilliams, Jane (sop); Rudzinsky,
John (ten); Sahlin, Kay (fl); Van
Tyn, Robert (ob); Bryce, Jackson
(bsn); Feiler, Wayne (tpt);
Ransom, Anne (hp); Carleton
Chamber Singers; Wells, William
(cond)
Rec 10/31/76 and 11/1/76
- Orion ORS-77276; 33s; rel
1978; cip

Visions of Remembrance
[7658] Wilson, Carol (sop); Manz, Lorraine
(m sop); Carleton Contemporary
Ensemble; Wells, William (cond)
- CRI-426; 33s; rel 1980; cip

RIBBLE, M. H.
Bennet's Triumphal (1925)
[7659] Eastman Symphonic Wind
Ensemble; Fennell, Frederick
(cond)
- Mercury MG-50314/SR-90314;
33m/s; rel 1963; del 1976
- Mercury SRI-75087; 33s; rel
1977; cip

RICH, Gladys (1892-)

American Lullaby
[7660] Forrester, Maureen (m sop);
Newmark, John (pf)
- Westminster WST-17137; 33s;
rel 1969; del 1971
- Westminster WGS-8124; 33s; rel
1971; del 1978

RICHARD, Edmund (1926-)

Hudson River Sketches
[7661] Richard, Edmund (pf)
- MGM E-3309; 33m; rel 1956;
del 1959

RICHARDS, Stephen (1935-)

Ballad of Ruth, The
[7662] Conner, Crail (voice); Richards,
Stephen, Jr. (cond)
- Tikva T-40; 33m; rel 1959

RICHARDSON, Harriette Slack

Rhapsody on a Chorale
[7663] Richardson, Harriette S. (org)
- Century Recording Service
20738/20739; 33m/s; rel
1965

RICHTER, Marga (1926-)

Aria and Toccata
[7664] Trampler, Walter (vla); MGM
Chamber Orchestra; Surinach,
Carlos (cond)
- MGM E-3559; 33m; rel 1957;
del 1959

**Concerto, Piano, Violas,
Violoncellos, and Contrabasses
(1955)**
[7665] Masselos, William (pf); MGM String
Orchestra; Surinach, Carlos
(cond)
Rec 1956
- MGM E-3547; 33m; rel 1957;
del 1959

Fishing Picture
[7666] Renzi, Dorothy (sop); Ajemian,
Maro (pf)
- MGM E-3546; 33m; rel 1958;
del 1959

Hermit, The
[7667] Renzi, Dorothy (sop); Ajemian,
Maro (pf)
- MGM E-3546; 33m; rel 1958;
del 1959

Lament (1956)
[7668] MGM String Orchestra; Solomon,
Izler (cond)
- MGM E-3422; 33m; rel 1956;
del 1959

**(Two) Short Studies for Young
Pianists**
[7669] Richter, Marga (pf)
- MGM E-3147; 33m; rel 1955;
del 1959

Sonata, Piano (1954)
[7670] Basquin, Peter (pf)
- Grenadilla GS-1010; 33s; rel
1978; cip

[7671] Pressler, Menahem (pf)
- MGM E-3244; 33m; rel 1956;
del 1959

Transmutation
[7672] Renzi, Dorothy (sop); Ajemian,
Maro (pf)
- MGM E-3546; 33m; rel 1958;
del 1959

RIEGGER, Wallingford (1885-1961)

Canon and Fugue (Op 33) (1941)
[7673] Oslo Philharmonic Orchestra
(members of); Strickland, William
(cond)
- CRI-177; 33m; rel 1964; cip

**Concerto, Piano and Wind Quintet
(Op 53) (1952)**
[7674] Glazer, Frank (pf); New York
Woodwind Quintet
- Concert-Disc M-1221/CS-221;
33m/s; rel 1961; del 1975
- Everest LPBR-6081/SDBR-3081;
33m/s; rel 1963; del 1977

[7675] Wingreen, Harriet (pf); New Art
Wind Quintet
- CRI-130; 33m/s; rel 1960/?; cip

**Cry, The (Op 22) (1935) (arr for 2
pfs)**
[7676] Schoettler, Frederic (pf); Dye,
Theresa (pf)
- Orion ORS-79337; 33s; rel
1980; cip

Dance Rhythms (Op 58) (1955)
[7677] Cleveland Pops Orchestra; Lane,
Louis (cond)
- Epic LC-3819/BC-1154; 33m/s;
rel 1962; del 1965

[7678] Oslo Philharmonic Orchestra;
Antonini, Alfredo (cond)
- CRI-117; 33m/s; rel 1957/?; cip

[7679] University of Kentucky Symphonic
Band; Miller, Phillip (cond)
- Coronet M-1260; 33m; rel
1969; del 1978

Dichotomy (Op 12) (1931-32)
[7680] London Sinfonietta; Prausnitz,
Frederik (cond)
- Argo ZRG-702; 33s; rel 1974;
cip

Dichotomy (Op 12) (1931-32)
(cont'd)
[7681] Louisville Chamber Orchestra;
Mester, Jorge (cond)
- LS-71-5; 33s (Louisville
Orchestra First Edition Records
1971 No 5); rel 1972; cip

**Divertissement, Flute, Harp, and
Violoncello (Op 15) (1933): Finale**
[7682] Barrere, Georges (fl); Salzedo,
Carlos (hp); Britt, Horace (vcl)
- New Music Quarterly Recordings
1012 (1-3); 78; rel 1934

Evocation (Op 17) (1933)
[7683] Gerschefski, Edwin (pf); Creston,
Paul (pf)
- New Music Quarterly Recordings
1214; 78; rel 1936

[7684] Schoettler, Frederic (pf); Dye,
Theresa (pf)
- Orion ORS-79337; 33s; rel
1980; cip

**Fantasy and Fugue, Orchestra and
Organ (Op 10) (1930-31)**
[7685] Polish National Radio Orchestra;
Krenz, Jan (cond)
- CRI-219; 33s; rel 1968; cip

**Introduction and Fugue, Violoncello
and Winds (Op 74) (1960)**
[7686] Cooke, Antony (vcl); University of
South Florida Chamber Winds;
Croft, James (cond)
Rec 5/26/79
- Golden Crest CRS-4189; 33s; rel
1980; cip

**Movement, Two Trumpets,
Trombone, and Piano (Op 66)
(1957)**
[7687] National Orchestral Association
Alumni; Barnett, John (cond)
- CRI-229; 33s; rel 1968; cip

**Music for Brass Choir (Op 45)
(1948-49)**
[7688] Lehigh University Instrumental
Ensemble; Elkus, Jonathan (cond)
Rec 5/19/58
- Lehigh RINC-1103; 33m; rel
1968; del 1976

[7689] National Orchestral Association
Alumni; Barnett, John (cond)
- CRI-229; 33s; rel 1968; cip

**Music for Orchestra (Op 50)
(1951)**
[7690] Accademia Nazionale di Santa
Cecilia Orchestra, Roma; Antonini,
Alfredo (cond)
- CRI-117; 33m/s; rel 1957/?; cip

New and Old (Op 38) (1944): Six Movements
[7691] Shields, Roger (pf)
- Vox SVBX-5303; 33s; 3 discs; rel 1977; cip

New Dance (two-piano version) (Op 18a) (1935)
[7692] Nemenoff, Genia (pf); Luboschutz, Pierre (pf)
- Victor 17993; 78; rel pre-1942

[7693] Schoettler, Frederic (pf); Dye, Theresa (pf)
- Orion ORS-79337; 33s; rel 1980; cip

New Dance (orchestral version) (Op 18b) (1935)
[7694] Eastman-Rochester Symphony Orchestra; Hanson, Howard (cond)
- Mercury MG-40005; 33m; rel 1953; del 1957
- Mercury EP-1-5063; 45; 7''; rel pre-1956
- Mercury MG-50078; 33m; rel 1957; del 1963
- Mercury SRI-75111; 33s; rel 1978; cip

[7695] Vienna Radio Orchestra; Eger, Joseph (cond)
Rec 6/67
- Westminster XWN-19131/WST-17131; 33m/s; rel 1968; del 1969
- Music Guild MS-858; 33s; rel 1969; del 1971

Nonet, Brass (Op 49) (1951)
[7696] National Orchestral Association Alumni; Barnett, John (cond)
- CRI-229; 33s; rel 1968; cip

Quartet, Strings, No 1 (Op 30) (1938-39)
[7697] Galimir String Quartet
- Yaddo IV-3; 78; 2 discs; rel 1940

Quartet, Strings, No 2 (Op 43) (1948)
[7698] Kroll Quartet
- Columbia ML-5589/MS-6189; 33m/s; rel 1961; del 1965

[7699] New Music String Quartet
- Columbia ML-4494; 33m; rel 1952; del 1958
- CRI-307; 33s; rel 1973; cip

Quintet, Winds (Op 51) (1952)
[7700] Dunkel, Paul (fl); Taylor, Stephen (ob); Blackwell, Virgil (cl); Morelli, Frank (bsn); Rose, Stewart (hn)
- New World NW-285; 33s; rel 1978

[7701] New Art Wind Quintet
- Classic Editions CE-2003; 33m; 2 discs; rel 1953; del 1961

Romanza (1953)
[7702] Accademia Nazionale di Santa Cecilia Orchestra, Roma; Antonini, Alfredo (cond)
- CRI-117; 33m/s; rel 1957/?; cip

Sonatina, Violin and Piano (Op 39) (1947)
[7703] Ajemian, Anahid (vln); Ajemian, Maro (pf)
- MGM E-3218; 33m; rel 1956; del 1959

[7704] Zukofsky, Paul (vln); Kalish, Gilbert (pf)
- Desto DC-6435-37; 33s; 3 discs; rel 1975; cip

Study in Sonority (Op 7) (1926-27)
[7705] Louisville Orchestra; Mester, Jorge (cond)
- LS-70-6; 33s (Louisville Orchestra First Edition Records 1970 No 6); rel 1971; cip

Suite, Flute (Op 8) (1929)
[7706] Baron, Samuel (fl)
- CRI-212; 33m/s; rel 1966/?; cip

Symphony No 3 (Op 42) (1946-47)
[7707] Eastman-Rochester Symphony Orchestra; Hanson, Howard (cond)
- Columbia ML-4902; 33m; rel 1954; del 1965
- CRI-284; 33s; rel 1972; cip

Symphony No 4 (Op 63) (1957)
[7708] Louisville Orchestra; Whitney, Robert (cond)
- LOU-64-6/LS-64-6; 33m/s (Louisville Orchestra First Edition Records 1964 No 6); rel 1964; cip

[7709] University of Illinois Symphony Orchestra; Goodman, Bernard (cond)
- Illini Union Bookstore CRS-5; 33m; rel 1958*

Trio, Violin, Violoncello, and Piano (Op 1) (1919-20)
[7710] Temple University Trio
- Golden Crest CRS-4117; 33s/q; rel 1974; cip

[7711] Kroll, William (vln); Kougell, Alexander (vcl); Covelli, John (pf)
- Columbia ML-5589/MS-6189; 33m/s; rel 1961; del 1965

Variations, Piano and Orchestra (Op 54) (1953)
[7712] Owen, Benjamin (pf); Louisville Orchestra; Whitney, Robert (cond)
- LOU-545-3; 33m (Louisville Orchestra First Edition Records 1955 No 3); rel 1959; del 1978

Variations, Two Pianos (Op 54a) (1952)
[7713] Yarbrough, Joan (pf); Cowan, Robert (pf)
- CRI-279; 33s; rel 1974; cip

Variations, Violin and Orchestra (Op 71) (1959)
[7714] Harth, Sidney (vln); Louisville Orchestra; Whitney, Robert (cond)
- LOU-60-1; 33m (Louisville Orchestra First Edition Records 1960 No 1); rel 1960; cip

Who Can Revoke (Op 44) (1951)
[7715] Gregg Smith Singers; Cybriwsky, Oresta (pf); Smith, Gregg (cond)
Rec 1976
- Vox SVBX-5353; 33s; 3 discs; rel 1979; cip

RIEPE, Russell (1945-)

(Three) Studies on Flight (1976)
[7716] Pino, David (cl)
- Orion ORS-76256; 33s; rel 1977; cip

RIETI, Vittorio (1898-)

Capers
[7717] London Philharmonic Orchestra; Mester, Jorge (cond)
- Desto DC-6434; 33s; rel 1970; cip

Capriccio, Violin and Piano (1941)
[7718] Ravina, Oscar (vln); Gzhashvili, Gleb (pf)
- Serenus SRS-12063; 33s; rel 1976; cip

Concertino, Flute, Viola, Violoncello, Harp, and Harpsichord (1963)
[7719] Chamber Players of Heilbronn; Flagello, Nicolas (cond)
- Serenus SRE-1013/SRS-12013; 33m/s; rel 1966; cip

Concerto, Harpsichord and Orchestra (1952-55)
[7720] Marlowe, Sylvia (hpschd); chamber orchestra; Baron, Samuel (cond)
- Decca DL-10135/DL-710135; 33m/s; rel 1967; del 1971
- CRI-312; 33s; rel 1974; cip

Concerto, Piano and Orchestra, No 3 (1955)
[7721] Santoliquido, Ornella Puliti (pf); Rome Symphony Orchestra; Flagello, Nicolas (cond)
- Serenus SRS-12033; 33s; rel 1972; cip

Concerto, Violoncello and Twelve Instruments, No 1 (1934)
[7722] Amfiteatrof, Massimo (vcl); Rome Symphony Orchestra; Flagello, Nicolas (cond)
- Serenus SRE-1013/SRS-12013; 33m/s; rel 1966; cip

Corale, variazioni e finale (1969)
[7723] Gold, Arthur (pf); Fizdale, Robert (pf)
- Serenus SRS-12033; 33s; rel 1972; cip

Conundrum (1961)
[7724] Harkness Ballet Orchestra; Mester, Jorge (cond)
- Serenus SRS-12073; 33s; rel 1977; cip

Dance Variations (1956)
[7725] MGM String Orchestra; Surinach, Carlos (cond)
- MGM E-3565; 33m; rel 1958; del 1959

L'Ecole des femmes (Incidental Music) (1936)
[7726] Louis Jouvet and his French Dramatic Company
Rec 3/16/51
- Harvard Vocarium RL-F-D1-6; 33m; 3 discs; rel pre-1956
- Pathe PCX-5003-05; 33m; 3 discs; rel pre-1956

Fontaine, La (1968)
[7727] Rome Symphony Orchestra; Flagello, Nicolas (cond)
- Serenus SRS-12023; 33s; rel 1969; cip

Incisioni (1967)
[7728] Cambridge Brass Quintet
- Crystal S-204; 33s; rel 1977; cip

[7729] no performers given
- Serenus SRS-12023; 33s; rel 1969; cip

Introduzione e gioco delle ore (1953)
[7730] Louisville Orchestra; Whitney, Robert (cond)
- LOU-545-11; 33m (Louisville Orchestra First Edition Records 1955 No 11); rel 1959; del 1978

(Quattro) Liriche italiane
[7731] Reardon, John (bar); Hebert, Bliss (pf)
- Serenus SRE-1019/SRS-12019; 33m/s; rel 1967; cip

(Sette) Liriche saffiche (1974)
[7732] Pecchioli, Benedetta (m sop); chamber orchestra; Rossi, Mario (cond)
- Serenus SRS-12063; 33s; rel 1976; cip

Madrigale (1927)
[7733] MGM Chamber Orchestra; Winograd, Arthur (cond)
- MGM E-3414; 33m; rel 1956; del 1959

Medieval Variations (1962)
[7734] Guralnik, Robert (pf)
- Serenus SRE-1013/SRS-12013; 33m/s; rel 1966; cip

Partita, Flute, Oboe, String Quartet, and Harpsichord (1945)
[7735] Baker, Julius (fl); Miller, Mitchell (ob); Kroll Quartet; Marlowe, Sylvia (hpschd)
- Mercury MG-10012; 33m; rel 1950; del 1956

[7736] Baron, Samuel (fl); Roseman, Ronald (ob); Libove, Charles (vln); Ajemian, Anahid (vln); Zaratzian, Harry (vla); McCracken, Charles (vcl); Marlowe, Sylvia (hpschd)
- Decca DL-10135/DL-710135; 33m/s; rel 1967; del 1971
- CRI-312; 33s; rel 1974; cip

[7737] Concert Arts Players; Marlowe, Sylvia (hpschd)
- Capitol P-8309; 33m; rel 1955; del 1960

Pastorale and Fughetta, Flute, Viola, and Piano (1966)
[7738] Trio della Casa Serena
- Serenus SRS-12063; 33s; rel 1976; cip

(Sei) Pezzi brevi (1932)
[7739] Guralnik, Robert (pf)
- Serenus SRE-1013/SRS-12013; 33m/s; rel 1966; cip

(Quatre) Poemes de Max Jacob
[7740] Sperry, Paul (ten)
- Serenus SRS-12078; 33s; rel 1980; cip

Quartet, Strings, F Major
[7741] Pro Arte Quartet
- Victor 1821-22; 78; 2-10"; rel pre-1943

Quartet, Strings, No 3 (1951)
[7742] Phoenix String Quartet
- Serenus SRS-12063; 33s; rel 1976; cip

Quartet, Strings, No 4 (1960)
[7743] St. Louis Quartet
- Serenus SRS-12023; 33s; rel 1969; cip

Second Avenue Waltzes (1942)
[7744] Baretta (pf); Madini-Moretti (pf)
- Serenus SRS-12073; 33s; rel 1977; cip

Second Avenue Waltzes (1942)
(cont'd)
[7745] Gold, Arthur (pf); Fizdale, Robert (pf)
- Columbia MM-956; 78; rel pre-1952
- Columbia ML-2147; 33m; 10"; rel 1952; del 1956
- Philips S-06614R; 33m; rel pre-1956

Sestetto pro Gemini (1975)
[7746] Gemini Ensemble
- Serenus SRS-12073; 33s; rel 1977; cip

Silografie (1967)
[7747] Ariel Wind Quintet
- Serenus SRS-12063; 33s; rel 1976; cip

Sonata, Flute, Oboe, Bassoon, and Piano (1924)
[7748] Berkshire Woodwind Ensemble
- Unicorn UNLP-1029; 33m; rel 1956; del 1959

Sonata, Piano, A-flat Major (1938)
[7749] Marshall, Elizabeth (pf)
- Serenus SRS-12043; 33s; rel 1975; cip

Sonata a cinque (1966)
[7750] Nyfenger, Thomas (fl); Roseman, Ronald (ob); Glazer, David (cl); Weisberg, Arthur (bsn); Kalish, Gilbert (pf)
- Serenus SRS-12043; 33s; rel 1975; cip

Sonata all'antica (1946)
[7751] Marlowe, Sylvia (hpschd)
- New Editions 3; 33m; rel 1953; del 1959
- Decca DL-10021/DL-710021; 33m/s; rel 1961; del 1971

Suite champetre (1948)
[7752] Gold, Arthur (pf); Fizdale, Robert (pf)
Rec 6/20/52
- Columbia ML-4853-55 (in set SL-198); 33m; 3 discs; rel 1954; del 1958

Symphony No 3 (Sinfonietta) (1932)
[7753] Prague Sinfonietta; Rohan, Jindrich (cond)
- Serenus SRS-12043; 33s; rel 1975; cip

Trio, Piano and Strings (1972)
[7754] Beaux-Arts Trio
- Serenus SRS-12043; 33s; rel 1975; cip

Valse fugitive (1970)
[7755] Gold, Arthur (pf); Fizdale, Robert (pf)
- Serenus SRS-12033; 33s; rel 1972; cip

(Three) Vaudeville Marches (1969)
[7756] Gold, Arthur (pf); Fizdale, Robert (pf)
- Serenus SRS-12033; 33s; rel 1972; cip

RILEY, Dennis (1943-)
Variations II, String Trio (1967)
[7757] University of Iowa Center for New Music Ensemble (members of)
- CRI-324; 33s; rel 1975; cip

RILEY, Terry (1935-)
In C (1964)
[7758] Buffalo Center of the Creative and Performing Arts; Riley, Terry (cond)
- Columbia MS-7178; 33s; rel 1968; cip

Persian Surgery Dervishes (1971)
[7759] Riley, Terry (elec org)
- Shandar 83-501-02; 33s; 2 discs; rel 1979*

Poppy Nogood's Phantom Band (1970)
[7760] Riley, Terry (elec instruments)
- Columbia MS-7315; 33s; rel 1969; cip

Rainbow in Curved Air, A (1970)
[7761] Riley, Terry (elec instruments)
- Columbia MS-7315; 33s; rel 1969; cip

Shri Camel
[7762] Riley, Terry (elec org)
- Columbia M-35164; 33s; rel 1980; cip

ROBB, John Donald (1892-)
Analogies
[7763] Electronic music
- Asch AHS-3438; 33s; rel 1971; del 1976

Better Banditree (ca 1953)
[7764] Ives, Eugene (bar); Robert, George (pf)
- Opus One 48; 33s; rel 1979; cip

Canon in Percussive Sound
[7765] Electronic music
- Asch AHS-3438; 33s; rel 1971; del 1976

Collage (1964)
[7766] Electronic music
- Folkways FM-3436/FMS-33436; 33m/s; rel 1967; cip

Collage No 2 (1965)
[7767] Electronic music
- Asch AHS-3438; 33s; rel 1971; del 1976

Concertino, Viola and Piano (1977)
[7768] Rosenberg, Joel (vla); Robert, George (pf)
- Opus One 44; 33s; rel 1980; cip

Dialogue for Guitar and Piano (1967)
[7769] Robb, John Donald (gtr) (pf)
- Opus One 13; 33s; rel 1976; cip

Drivers, The
[7770] Ives, Eugene (bar); Robert, George (pf)
- Opus One 48; 33s; rel 1979; cip

Elegy for String Orchestra with Violoncello Obbligato
[7771] Chamber Orchestra of Albuquerque; Oberg, David (cond)
- Opus One 51; 33s; rel 1980

Goodnight My Love
[7772] Ives, Eugene (bar); Robert, George (pf)
- Opus One 48; 33s; rel 1979; cip

Green Mansions (1968)
[7773] Electronic music
- Asch AHS-3438; 33s; rel 1971; del 1976

I Am Very Old Tonight (1968)
[7774] McRae, Donna (sop); Randall, Darrel (ob); Robert, George (pf)
- Opus One 48; 33s; rel 1979; cip

Ondes martenot, Les
[7775] Electronic music
- Asch AHS-3438; 33s; rel 1971; del 1976

Pleasant Obsession
[7776] Electronic music
- Asch AHS-3438; 33s; rel 1971; del 1976

Requiem
[7777] Ives, Eugene (bar); Robert, George (pf)
- Opus One 48; 33s; rel 1979; cip

Retrograde Sequence from a Tragedy
[7778] Electronic music
- Asch AHS-3438; 33s; rel 1971; del 1976

Rhythmania (1968)
[7779] Electronic music
- Folkways FMS-33435; 33s; rel 1976; cip

Richmond Hill
[7780] Ives, Eugene (bar); Robert, George (pf)
- Opus One 48; 33s; rel 1979; cip

Rondino
[7781] Electronic music
- Asch AHS-3438; 33s; rel 1971; del 1976

Shepherdess, The
[7782] Ives, Eugene (bar); Robert, George (pf)
- Opus One 48; 33s; rel 1979; cip

Snowy Mountain (ca 1963)
[7783] Ives, Eugene (bar); Robert, George (pf)
- Opus One 48; 33s; rel 1979; cip

Sonata, Violin and Piano, No 3 (1974)
[7784] Levinson, Herbert (vln); Robert, George (pf)
- Opus One 35; 33s; rel 1978; cip

Sonata, Violoncello and Piano (1975)
[7785] Kempter, Dorothy (vcl); Tung, Mimi (pf)
- Opus One 43; 33s; rel 1979; cip

Spatial Serenade (1965): Excerpt
[7786] Electronic music
- Asch AHS-3438; 33s; rel 1971; del 1976

Tarantella
[7787] Electronic music
- Asch AHS-3438; 33s; rel 1971; del 1976

Tears (1971)
[7788] McRae, Donna (sop); Randall, Darrel (ob); Robert, George (pf)
- Opus One 48; 33s; rel 1979; cip

Tecolote (1977)
[7789] McRae, Donna (sop); Randall, Darrel (ob); Robert, George (pf)
- Opus One 48; 33s; rel 1979; cip

To Elektra
[7790] Ives, Eugene (bar); Robert, George (pf)
- Opus One 48; 33s; rel 1979; cip

Toccata
[7791] Electronic music
- Opus One 42; 33s; rel 1978; cip

Tragedy
[7792] Ives, Eugene (bar); Robert, George (pf)
- Opus One 48; 33s; rel 1979; cip

Transmutations (1968): 2nd and 3rd Movements
[7793] Electronic music
- Asch AHS-3438; 33s; rel 1971; del 1976

Trio, Oboe, Violin, and Piano (1973)
[7794] Randall, Darrel (ob); Gref, Ann (vln); Morse, Dorenda (pf)
- Opus One 27; 33s; rel 1976; cip

What is this Glory
[7795] McRae, Donna (sop); Randall, Darrel (ob); Robert, George (pf)
- Opus One 48; 33s; rel 1979; cip

ROBERTS, Megan (1952-)
I Could Sit Here All Day (1976)
[7796] vocalists and instrumentalists; tape
- 1750 Arch S-1765; 33s; rel 1978; cip

ROBERTS, Myron J. (1912-)
Homage to Perotin
[7797] Munns, Robert (org)
- Pye TPLS-13022; 33s; rel 1970; del 1971

Improvisation on God Rest You Merry
[7798] Obetz, John (org)
- Celebre 8006; 33s; rel 197?

[7799] Wichmann, Russell G. (org)
- True Image LP-125; 33m; rel 1966

Litany
[7800] Copes, V. Earle (org)
- Graded Press SoN-33341-42, SoN-33351-52; 33m; 2 discs; rel 1959

Prelude and Trumpetings
[7801] Baker, George C. (org)
- Delos DEL-FY-025; 33s; rel 1977; cip

[7802] Russell, Albert (org)
- Aeolian-Skinner A-319/AS-319; 33m/s; rel 1964

ROBERTSON, Leroy (1896-1971)
American Serenade (1944)
[7803] Weicher Quartet
- SPAMH MIA-115; 33s; rel 1961

Book of Mormon (1953)
[7804] Mormon Tabernacle Choir; Utah Symphony Orchestra; Abravanel, Maurice (cond)
- Columbia M-35148; 33s; rel 1979; cip

Book of Mormon (1953) *(cont'd)*
[7805] Samuelsen, Roy (bar); Whitelock, Kenly (ten); Preston, Jean (m sop); Wood, Warren (b); University of Utah Chorus; South High Girls' Chorus; Utah Symphony Orchestra; Abravanel, Maurice (cond)
- Vanguard VRS-1077/VSD-2099; 33m/s; rel 1961; del 1964

Book of Mormon: Excerpts
[7806] University of Utah Chorus and Orchestra; Schreiner, Alexander (org); Shand, David A. (cond)
- SPAMH MIA-111; 33s; rel 1959

Concerto, Violin and Orchestra (1948)
[7807] Spivakovsky, Tossy (vln); Utah Symphony Orchestra; Abravanel, Maurice (cond)
- Vanguard VRS-1089/VSD-2116; 33m/s; rel 1962; del 1965

Punch and Judy (1945)
[7808] Utah Symphony Orchestra; Abravanel, Maurice (cond)
- Turnabout TVS-34459; 33s; rel 1972; cip

Quartet, Strings (1940)
[7809] Weicher Quartet
- SPAMH MIA-115; 33s; rel 1961

ROBINSON, Avery (1878-1965)
Water Boy
[7810] Robeson, Paul (b); Brown, Lawrence (pf)
- Victor 19824; 78

ROBINSON, Earl (1910-)
House I Live In, The
[7811] Melchior, Lauritz (ten); chorus; Blackton, Jay (cond)
- Victor 10-1227 (in set 1056); 78; 10"; rel pre-1948

[7812] Robinson, Earl (voice) (gtr)
- Keynote 538; 78; 10"; rel pre-1948

In the Folded and Quiet Yesterdays
[7813] Loring, Michael (bar); American People's Chorus; Grennell, Horace (cond)
- Keynote 1001; 78; rel pre-1943

Lonesome Train, The
[7814] Peters, Brock (nar); Odetta (voice); chorus; orchestra; De Paur, Leonard (cond)
- United Artists UA-LA-604G; 33s; rel 1976

Lonesome Train, The *(cont'd)*
[7815] Robinson, Earl (nar); Ives, Burl (voice); Johnson, Raymond Edward (voice); Huey, Richard (voice); Lyn Murray Chorus and Orchestra; Corwin, Norman (cond)
- Decca A-375; 78; 3 discs; rel pre-1948
- Decca DL-5054; 33m; 10"; rel 1950; del 1957

Man's a Man for a' That, A
[7816] Robinson, Earl (voice) (gtr)
- Keynote 538; 78; 10"; rel pre-1948

Sandhog
[7817] Salt, Waldo (nar); Robinson, Earl (voice) (pf)
- Vanguard VRS-9001; 33m; rel 1955; del 1962

ROBINSON, Edward (1905-79)
Chilmark Suite: Overture, Arietta, and Finale
[7818] Benton, Tom (harmonica); Benton, T. P. (fl); Robinson, Edward (hpschd)
- Decca 311; 78; 3-10"; rel 1942
- Decca 23247-49 (in set A-311); 78; 3-10"; rel 1942

Gay Head Dance
[7819] Benton, Tom (harmonica); Benton, T. P. (fl); Robinson, Edward (hpschd)
- Decca 311; 78; 3-10"; rel 1942
- Decca 23247-49 (in set A-311); 78; 3-10"; rel 1942

ROBINSON, Richard (1923-)
Ambience (1972)
[7820] Electronic music
- Turnabout TVS-34427; 33s; rel 1972; del 1975

ROCHBERG, George (1918-)
(Twelve) Bagatelles (1952)
[7821] Burge, David (pf)
- Advance FGR-3; 33m; rel 1967; cip

Black Sounds (1965)
[7822] Oberlin Wind Ensemble
- Grenadilla GS-1019; 33s; rel 1978; cip

Blake Songs (1961)
[7823] DeGaetani, Jan (m sop); Contemporary Chamber Ensemble; Weisberg, Arthur (cond)
- Nonesuch H-71302; 33s; rel 1974; cip

Bocca della verita, La (1958-59)
[7824] Ostryniec, James (ob); Wuorinen,
Charles (pf)
- CRI-423; 33s; rel 1980; cip

[7825] Roseman, Ronald (ob); Kalish,
Gilbert (pf)
- Ars Nova/Ars Antiqua AN-1008;
33s; rel 1971; del 1973

Caprice-Variations (1970)
[7826] Zeitlin, Zvi (vln)
- Musical Heritage Society
MHS-3719; 33s; rel 1978

Carnival Music (1971)
[7827] Mandel, Alan (pf)
- Grenadilla GS-1019; 33s; rel
1978; cip

**Chamber Symphony, Nine
Instruments (1953)**
[7828] Oberlin Chamber Orchestra
(members of); Moore, Kenneth
(cond)
- Desto DC-6444; 33s; rel 1975;
cip

**Concerto, Violin and Orchestra
(1975)**
[7829] Stern, Isaac (vln); Pittsburgh
Symphony Orchestra; Previn,
Andre (cond)
- Columbia M-35149; 33s; rel
1979; cip

Contra mortem et tempus (1965)
[7830] Aeolian Quartet of Sarah Lawrence
College
- CRI-231; 33s; rel 1968; cip

**Dialogues, Clarinet and Piano
(1957-58)**
[7831] Russo, John (cl); Ignacio, Lydia
Walton (pf)
- Capra 1204; 33s; rel 1976; cip

**Duo concertante, Violin and
Violoncello (1955)**
[7832] Kobialka, Daniel (vln); Kobialka,
Jan (vcl)
- Advance FGR-6S; 33s; rel 1970;
cip

[7833] Sokol, Mark (vln); Fischer, Norman
(vcl)
- CRI-337; 33s; rel 1975; cip

**Music for the Magic Theater
(1965)**
[7834] Owings, John (pf); Oberlin
Orchestra; Moore, Kenneth (cond)
- Desto DC-6444; 33s; rel 1975;
cip

Nach Bach (1966)
[7835] Kipnis, Igor (hpschd)
- Grenadilla GS-1019; 33s; rel
1978; cip

Night Music (1949)
[7836] Louisville Orchestra; Whitney,
Robert (cond)
- LOU-62-3; 33m (Louisville
Orchestra First Edition Records
1962 No 3); rel 1962; del 1978

Quartet, Strings, No 1 (1952)
[7837] Concord String Quartet
- CRI-337; 33s; rel 1975; cip

Quartet, Strings, No 2 (1959-61)
[7838] Bryn-Julson, Phyllis (sop); Concord
String Quartet
- Turnabout TVS-34524; 33s; rel
1974; del 1978

[7839] Harsanyi, Janice (sop); Philadelphia
String Quartet
- CRI-164; 33m/s; rel
1963/1976; cip

Quartet, Strings, No 3 (1972)
[7840] Concord String Quartet
- Nonesuch H-71283/HQ-1283;
33s/q; rel 1973; cip

Ricordanza soliloquy (1972)
[7841] Fischer, Norman (vcl); Rochberg,
George (pf)
- CRI-337; 33s; rel 1975; cip

Serenata d'estate (1955)
[7842] Contemporary Chamber Ensemble;
Weisberg, Arthur (cond)
- Nonesuch H-71220; 33s; rel
1969; cip

Slow Fires of Autumn (1978-79)
[7843] Wincenc, Carol (fl); Allen, Nancy
(hp)
- CRI-436; 33s; rel 1980; cip

Songs in Praise of Krishna (1970)
[7844] Pilgrim, Neva (sop); Rochberg,
George (pf)
Rec 6/9/72
- CRI-360; 33s; rel 1977; cip

Symphony No 1 (1949-57)
[7845] Louisville Orchestra; Whitney,
Robert (cond)
- LOU-63-4/LS-63-4; 33m/s
(Louisville Orchestra First Edition
Records 1963 No 4); rel
1963/1965; cip

Symphony No 2 (1955-56)
[7846] New York Philharmonic;
Torkanowsky, Werner (cond)
- Columbia ML-5779/MS-6379;
33m/s; rel 1962; del 1968
- Columbia CML-5779/CMS-6379;
33m/s; rel 1968; del 1974
- Columbia AMS-6379; 33s; rel
1974; del 1979

Tableaux (1968)
[7847] DeGaetani, Jan (sop); Penn
Contemporary Players; Wernick,
Richard (cond)
- Turnabout TVS-34492; 33s; rel
1973; del 1978

**Trio, Violin, Violoncello, and Piano
(1963)**
[7848] Kooper, Kees (vln); Sherry, Fred
(vcl); Boehm-Kooper, Mary Louise
(pf)
- Turnabout TVS-34520; 33s; rel
1974; del 1978

RODBY, John (1944-)

**Concerto, Saxophone and Orchestra
(1971)**
[7849] Pittel, Harvey (sax); London
Sinfonietta; Howarth, Elgar (cond)
- Crystal S-500; 33s; rel 1973; cip

Concerto for Twenty-Nine (1973)
[7850] London Sinfonietta; Howarth, Elgar
(cond)
- Crystal S-504; 33s; rel 1977; cip

Festivals (1970)
[7851] London Sinfonietta; Howarth, Elgar
(cond)
- Crystal S-500; 33s; rel 1973; cip

Variations, Orchestra (1969)
[7852] London Sinfonietta; Howarth, Elgar
(cond)
- Crystal S-500; 33s; rel 1973; cip

**RODRIGUEZ, Robert Xavier
(1946-)**

Canto (1973)
[7853] Harmon, Su (sop); Sells, Michael
(ten); Gruber, Emanuel (vcl);
Sanders, Michael (pf); Orion
Chamber Orchestra; Nord,
Edward (cond)
- Orion ORS-74138; 33s; rel
1974; cip

**Concerto III, Piano and Orchestra
(1974)**
[7854] Segall, Bernardo (pf); Orion
Chamber Orchestra; Nord,
Edward (cond)
- Orion ORS-74159; 33s; rel
1974; cip

Lyric Variations (1970)
[7855] Davis, Robert (ob); Orion Chamber
Orchestra; Nord, Edward (cond)
- Orion ORS-74138; 33s; rel
1974; cip

Sonata in One Movement (1973)
[7856] Pittel, Harvey (sop sax); Grierson,
Ralph (pf)
- Crystal S-105; 33s; rel 1975; cip

Variations, Violin and Piano
[7857] Goldman (vln); Brown (pf)
- Orion ORS-76212; 33s; rel 1977; cip

ROGERS, Bernard (1893-1968)

Apparitions (1967)
[7858] Royal Philharmonic Orchestra; Lipkin, Arthur Bennett (cond)
- CRI-259; 33s; rel 1970; cip

Dance Scenes (1953)
[7859] Louisville Orchestra; Whitney, Robert (cond)
- LOU-60-6; 33m (Louisville Orchestra First Edition Records 1960 No 6); rel 1961; del 1980

(Three) Japanese Dances (1933)
[7860] Eastman Symphonic Wind Ensemble; Fennell, Frederick (cond)
Rec 3/2/58
- Mercury MG-50173/SR-90173; 33m/s; rel 1958/1959; del 1974
- Mercury SRI-75093; 33s; rel 1977; cip

Leaves from the Tale of Pinocchio (1951)
[7861] MacKowan, Marjorie T. (nar); Eastman-Rochester Symphony Orchestra; Hanson, Howard (cond)
Rec 1956
- Mercury MG-50114; 33m; rel 1957; del 1963
- Eastman-Rochester Archives ERA-1002; 33s; rel 1974; cip

[7862] Vienna Symphony Orchestra; Schoenherr, Max (cond)
- American Recording Society ARS-30; 33m; 10"; rel 1953
- Desto D-424/DST-6424; 33m/s; rel 1967; cip

Light of Man, The (1964)
[7863] Harsanyi, Janice (sop); Berberian, Ara (b); National Methodist Student Movement Chorus; Lincoln Symphony Orchestra (members of); Johnson, Thor (cond)
- Methodist Student Movement 100-01; 33m; 2 discs; rel 1965; del 1967

Once upon a Time (1936)
[7864] Eastman-Rochester Symphony Orchestra; Hanson, Howard (cond)
- Mercury MG-50147/SR-90147; 33m/s; rel 1957/1960; del 1963
- Eastman-Rochester Archives ERA-1004; 33s; rel 1974; cip

Soliloquy No 1, Flute and Strings (1922)
[7865] Mariano, Joseph (fl); Eastman-Rochester Symphony Orchestra; Hanson, Howard (cond)
- Victor 18101 (in set M-802); 78; rel 1941
- Mercury MG-40003; 33m; rel 1953; del 1957
- Mercury EP-1-5065; 45; 7"; rel pre-1956
- Mercury MG-50076; 33m; rel 1957; del 1963
- Eastman-Rochester Archives ERA-1001; 33s; rel 1974; cip

Soliloquy No 1 (arr for fl and pf)
[7866] Pellerite, James (fl); Robert, Walter (pf)
- Coronet M-1291/S-1291; 33m/s; rel 1969/?; cip

Variations on a Song by Moussorgsky (1960)
[7867] Rochester Philharmonic Orchestra; Bloomfield, Theodore (cond)
- CRI-153; 33m/s; rel 1962/?; cip

ROGERS, Melville Reuben*

Prelude, Organ
[7868] Murray, Michael (org)
- Musical Heritage Society MHS-3344; 33s; rel 1976

ROGERS, Walter B.

War Songs March
[7869] Victor Drum, Fife, and Bugle Corps
- Victor 16154; 78; 10"

ROHE, Robert (1916-)

Mainescape (1966)
[7870] Louisville Orchestra; Whitney, Robert (cond)
- LOU-67-3/LS-67-3; 33m/s (Louisville Orchestra First Edition Records 1967 No 3); rel 1967; cip

ROLLIN, Robert (1947-)

Aquarelles
[7871] Cornell University Wind Ensemble; Stith, Marice (cond)
- Cornell CUWE-11; 33s; rel 1973; cip

Reflections on Ruin by the Sea
[7872] Stith, Marice (tpt); Raleigh, Stuart W. (pf)
- Redwood RRES-4; 33s; rel 1977; cip

RONSHEIN, John (1927-)

Bitter-Sweet (1969)
[7873] DeGaetani, Jan (m sop); DesRoches, Raymond (vib)
- CRI-301; 33s; rel 1973; cip

Easter-Wings (1964)
[7874] DeGaetani, Jan (m sop); DesRoches, Raymond (vib)
- CRI-301; 33s; rel 1973; cip

ROOSEVELT, Willard (1918-)

Suite, Piano (1963)
[7875] Violette, Andrew (pf)
- Opus One 44; 33s; rel 1980; cip

ROREM, Ned (1923-)

Alleluia (1946)
[7876] Steber, Eleanor (sop); Biltcliffe, Edwin (pf)
- St/And SPL-411-12; 33m; 2 discs; rel 1963; del 1964
- Desto D-411-12/DST-6411-12; 33m/s; 2 discs; rel 1964; cip

Ariel (1971)
[7877] Curtin, Phyllis (sop); Rabbai, Joseph (cl); Edwards, Ryan (pf)
- Desto DC-7147; 33s; rel 1973; cip

(Three) Barcarolles (1949)
[7878] Fleisher, Leon (pf)
- Epic LC-3862/BC-1262; 33m/s; rel 1963; del 1966

Blessed Art Thou
[7879] North Texas State University A Capella Choir; McKinley, Frank A. (cond)
- Boosey & Hawkes SNBH-5001; 33s; rel 1978

Book of Hours (1975)
[7880] Dingfelder, Ingrid (fl); Geliot, Martine (hp)
Rec 3/76
- CRI-362; 33s; rel 1977; cip

Call, The
[7881] Gramm, Donald (b bar); Rorem, Ned (pf)
- Columbia ML-5961/MS-6561; 33m/s; rel 1964; del 1966
- Odyssey 32-16-0274; 33s; rel 1968; del 1971

Canticle of the Lamb (1971)
[7882] North Texas State University A Capella Choir; McKinley, Frank A. (cond)
- Boosey & Hawkes SNBH-5001; 33s; rel 1978

Christmas Carol, A (1952)
[7883] Bressler, Charles (ten); Rorem, Ned (pf)
- Columbia ML-5961/MS-6561; 33m/s; rel 1964; del 1966
- Odyssey 32-16-0274; 33s; rel 1968; del 1971

[7884] Hanks, John Kennedy (ten); Friedberg, Ruth (pf)
- Duke University Press DWR-7306; 33s; rel 1974

Clouds (1953)
[7885] Hanks, John Kennedy (ten); Friedberg, Ruth (pf)
- Duke University Press DWR-7306; 33s; rel 1974

Concerto in Six Movements, Piano and Orchestra (1969)
[7886] Lowenthal, Jerome (pf); Louisville Orchestra; Mester, Jorge (cond)
Rec 4/9/73
- LS-73-3; 33s (Louisville Orchestra First Edition Records 1973 No 3); rel 1974; cip

Cycle of Holy Songs (1951): Psalms 134, 148, and 150
[7887] Curtin, Phyllis (sop); Rorem, Ned (pf)
- Columbia ML-5961/MS-6561; 33m/s; rel 1964; del 1966
- Odyssey 32-16-0274; 33s; rel 1968; del 1971

Day Music (1971)
[7888] Laredo, Jaime (vln); Laredo, Ruth (pf)
- Desto DC-7151; 33s; rel 1973; cip

Design for Orchestra (1953)
[7889] Louisville Orchestra; Whitney, Robert (cond)
- LOU-57-5; 33m (Louisville Orchestra First Edition Records 1957 No 5); rel 1959; del 1972

(Four) Dialogues, Two Voices and Two Pianos (1954)
[7890] Darian, Anita (sop); Stewart, John (ten); Rorem, Ned (pf); Cumming, Richard (pf)
- Desto DC-7101; 33s; rel 1970; cip

Early in the Morning (1955)
[7891] Gramm, Donald (b bar); Rorem, Ned (pf)
Rec 1962-63
- Columbia ML-5961/MS-6561; 33m/s; rel 1964; del 1966
- Odyssey 32-16-0274; 33s; rel 1968; del 1971
- New World NW-229; 33s; rel 1978

Echo's Song (1948)
[7892] Bressler, Charles (ten); Rorem, Ned (pf)
- Columbia ML-5961/MS-6561; 33m/s; rel 1964; del 1966
- Odyssey 32-16-0274; 33s; rel 1968; del 1971

Flight for Heaven (1950): Upon Julia's Clothes and To the Willow Tree
[7893] Gramm, Donald (b bar); Rorem, Ned (pf)
Rec 1962-63
- Columbia ML-5961/MS-6561; 33m/s; rel 1964; del 1966
- Odyssey 32-16-0274; 33s; rel 1968; del 1971
- New World NW-229; 33s; rel 1978

For Poulenc (1963)
[7894] Curtin, Phyllis (sop); Gramm, Donald (bar); Rorem, Ned (pf)
- CRI-238; 33s; rel 1969; cip

For Susan (1953)
[7895] Hanks, John Kennedy (ten); Friedberg, Ruth (pf)
- Duke University Press DWR-7306; 33s; rel 1974

From an Unknown Past (1951)
[7896] Modern Madrigal Quartet
- Desto DC-6480; 33s; rel 1969; cip

Gloria (1970)
[7897] Curtin, Phyllis (sop); Vanni, Helen (m sop); Rorem, Ned (pf)
- Desto DC-7147; 33s; rel 1973; cip

He Shall Rule from Sea to Sea (1967)
[7898] North Texas State University A Capella Choir; Harris, Charles (org); McKinley, Frank A. (cond)
- Boosey & Hawkes SNBH-5001; 33s; rel 1978

I Am Rose (1955)
[7899] Sarfaty, Regina (m sop); Rorem, Ned (pf)
Rec 1962-63
- Columbia ML-5961/MS-6561; 33m/s; rel 1964; del 1966
- Odyssey 32-16-0274; 33s; rel 1968; del 1971
- New World NW-229; 33s; rel 1978

Ideas for Easy Orchestra (1961): Four Ideas
[7900] Oakland Youth Orchestra; Hughes, Robert (cond)
- Desto DC-6462; 33s; rel 1968; cip

King Midas (1961)
[7901] Stewart, John (ten); Walker, Sandra (m sop); Schein, Ann (pf)
- Desto DC-6443; 33s; rel 1975; cip

Lift Up Your Heads (1963)
[7902] North Texas State University A Capella Choir; instrumental ensemble; McKinley, Frank A. (cond)
- Boosey & Hawkes SNBH-5001; 33s; rel 1978

Lions (1963)
[7903] New Orleans Philharmonic-Symphony Orchestra; Torkanowsky, Werner (cond)
- Orion ORS-7268; 33s; rel 1972; cip

Little Elegy (1949)
[7904] Curtin, Phyllis (sop); Gramm, Donald (bar); Rorem, Ned (pf)
- CRI-238; 33s; rel 1969; cip

Look Down, Fair Moon (1957)
[7905] Curtin, Phyllis (sop); Gramm, Donald (bar); Rorem, Ned (pf)
- CRI-238; 33s; rel 1969; cip

Lordly Hudson, The (1947)
[7906] Sarfaty, Regina (m sop); Rorem, Ned (pf)
- Columbia ML-5961/MS-6561; 33m/s; rel 1964; del 1966
- Odyssey 32-16-0274; 33s; rel 1968; del 1971

Love Divine, All Loves Excelling (1966)
[7907] North Texas State University A Capella Choir; McKinley, Frank A. (cond)
- Boosey & Hawkes SNBH-5001; 33s; rel 1978

Lovers (A Narrative in Ten Scenes) (1964): Six Scenes
[7908] Roseman, Ronald (ob); Kougell, Alexander (vcl); Marlowe, Sylvia (hpschd); Farberman, Harold (perc)
- Decca DL-10108/DL-710108; 33m/s; rel 1965; del 1973
- Serenus SRS-12056; 33s; rel 1975; cip

Lullaby of the Woman of the Mountain (1950)
[7909] Bressler, Charles (ten); Rorem, Ned (pf)
Rec 1962-63
- Columbia ML-5961/MS-6561; 33m/s; rel 1964; del 1966
- Odyssey 32-16-0274; 33s; rel 1968; del 1971
- New World NW-229; 33s; rel 1978

(Four) Madrigals (1947)
[7910] Modern Madrigal Quartet
- Desto DC-6480; 33s; rel 1969; cip

Missa brevis (1974)
[7911] Rees, Rosalind (sop); Magdamo, Priscilla (al); Bogdan, Thomas (ten); Garber, Lin (bar); Gregg Smith Singers; Smith, Gregg (cond)
Rec 1975
- Vox SVBX-5354; 33s; 3 discs; rel 1979

Mourning Scene from Samuel (1947)
[7912] Parker, William (bar); Huckaby, William (pf); Columbia String Quartet
- New World NW-305; 33s; rel 1980

My Papa's Waltz (1959)
[7913] Gramm, Donald (b bar); Rorem, Ned (pf)
Rec 1962-63
- Columbia ML-5961/MS-6561; 33m/s; rel 1964; del 1966
- Odyssey 32-16-0274; 33s; rel 1968; del 1971
- New World NW-229; 33s; rel 1978

Night Crow (1959)
[7914] Curtin, Phyllis (sop); Gramm, Donald (bar); Rorem, Ned (pf)
- CRI-238; 33s; rel 1969; cip

Night Music (1972)
[7915] Carlyss, Earl (vln); Schein, Ann (pf)
- Desto DC-7174; 33s; rel 1974; cip

Nightingale, The (1951)
[7916] Curtin, Phyllis (sop); Rorem, Ned (pf)
- Columbia ML-5961/MS-6561; 33m/s; rel 1964; del 1966
- Odyssey 32-16-0274; 33s; rel 1968; del 1971

O You Whom I Often and Silently Come (1957)
[7917] Sarfaty, Regina (m sop); Rorem, Ned (pf)
- Columbia ML-5961/MS-6561; 33m/s; rel 1964; del 1966
- Odyssey 32-16-0274; 33s; rel 1968; del 1971

Poems of Love and the Rain (1963)
[7918] Sarfaty, Regina (m sop); Rorem, Ned (pf)
- CRI-202; 33m/s; rel 1965/?; cip

[7919] Wolff, Beverly (m sop); Rorem, Ned (pf)
- Desto DC-6480; 33s; rel 1969; cip

(Two) Psalms and a Proverb (1963)
[7920] King's Chapel Choir, Boston; Cambridge Festival Strings; Pinkham, Daniel (cond)
Rec 1963
- Cambridge CRM-416/CRS-1416; 33m/s; rel 1964; del 1971

Quaker Reader, A (1976)
[7921] Raver, Leonard (org)
Rec 6/78
- CRI-396; 33s; rel 1979; cip

Quaker Reader, A: Six Selections
[7922] Crozier, Catharine (org)
- Gothic D-87904; 33 digital; 2 discs; rel 1980; cip

Rain in Spring (1949)
[7923] Sarfaty, Regina (m sop); Rorem, Ned (pf)
- Columbia ML-5961/MS-6561; 33m/s; rel 1964; del 1966
- Odyssey 32-16-0274; 33s; rel 1968; del 1971

Requiem (1948)
[7924] Bressler, Charles (ten); Rorem, Ned (pf)
- Columbia ML-5961/MS-6561; 33m/s; rel 1964; del 1966
- Odyssey 32-16-0274; 33s; rel 1968; del 1971

Romeo and Juliet (1977)
[7925] Dingfelder, Ingrid (fl); Levine, Herbert (gtr)
Rec 3/78
- CRI-394; 33s; rel 1978; cip

Root Cellar (1959)
[7926] Gramm, Donald (b bar); Rorem, Ned (pf)
Rec 1962-63
- Columbia ML-5961/MS-6561; 33m/s; rel 1964; del 1966
- Odyssey 32-16-0274; 33s; rel 1968; del 1971
- New World NW-229; 33s; rel 1978

Sally's Smile (1953)
[7927] Gramm, Donald (b bar); Rorem, Ned (pf)
- Columbia ML-5961/MS-6561; 33m/s; rel 1964; del 1966
- Odyssey 32-16-0274; 33s; rel 1968; del 1971

See How They Love Me (1956)
[7928] Bressler, Charles (ten); Rorem, Ned (pf)
- Columbia ML-5961/MS-6561; 33m/s; rel 1964; del 1966
- Odyssey 32-16-0274; 33s; rel 1968; del 1971

Serenade on Five English Poems (1976)
[7929] Bonazzi, Elaine (m sop); Cantilena Chamber Players; Glazer, Frank (pf)
Rec 12/21/77 and 3/6/78
- Grenadilla GS-1031; 33s; rel 1980; cip

Silver Swan, The (1949)
[7930] D'Angelo, Gianna (sop); Rorem, Ned (pf)
- Columbia ML-5961/MS-6561; 33m/s; rel 1964; del 1966
- Odyssey 32-16-0274; 33s; rel 1968; del 1971

Sing My Soul (1955)
[7931] King Chorale; King, Gordon (cond)
- Orion ORS-75205; 33s; rel 1978; cip

Snake (1959)
[7932] D'Angelo, Gianna (sop); Rorem, Ned (pf)
Rec 1962-63
- Columbia ML-5961/MS-6561; 33m/s; rel 1964; del 1966
- Odyssey 32-16-0274; 33s; rel 1968; del 1971
- New World NW-229; 33s; rel 1978

Some Trees (1968)
[7933] Curtin, Phyllis (sop); Wolff, Beverly (al); Gramm, Donald (bar); Rorem, Ned (pf)
- CRI-238; 33s; rel 1969; cip

Sonata, Piano, No 2 (1950)
[7934] Katchen, Julius (pf)
- London LLP-759; 33m; rel 1953; del 1957
- Decca LXT-2812; 33m; rel pre-1956
- CRI-202; 33m/s; rel 1965/?; cip

(Three) Songs by Demetrios Capetanakis (1954): Guilt
[7935] Hanks, John Kennedy (ten); Friedberg, Ruth (pf)
- Duke University Press DWR-7306; 33s; rel 1974

(Six) Songs for High Voice (1953): Pippa's Song, In a Gondola, and Song for a Girl
[7936] D'Angelo, Gianna (sop); Rorem, Ned (pf)
Rec 1962-63
- Columbia ML-5961/MS-6561; 33m/s; rel 1964; del 1966
- Odyssey 32-16-0274; 33s; rel 1968; del 1971
- New World NW-229; 33s; rel 1978 (Excerpt: Pippa's Song)

(Five) Songs to Poems of Walt Whitman (1954)
[7937] Gramm, Donald (b bar); Istomin, Eugene (pf)
- Desto DC-7101; 33s; rel 1970; cip

Spring (1947)
[7938] Curtin, Phyllis (sop); Rorem, Ned (pf)
Rec 1962-63
- Columbia ML-5961/MS-6561; 33m/s; rel 1964; del 1966
- Odyssey 32-16-0274; 33s; rel 1968; del 1971
- New World NW-229; 33s; rel 1978

Spring and Fall (1946)
[7939] Gramm, Donald (b bar); Rorem, Ned (pf)
Rec 1962-63
- Columbia ML-5961/MS-6561; 33m/s; rel 1964; del 1966
- Odyssey 32-16-0274; 33s; rel 1968; del 1971
- New World NW-229; 33s; rel 1978

(Eleven) Studies for Eleven Players (1960)
[7940] Louisville Orchestra (members of); Whitney, Robert (cond)
- LOU-64-4/LS-64-4; 33m/s (Louisville Orchestra First Edition Records 1964 No 4); rel 1964/1965; cip

Such Beauty as Hurts to Behold (1957)
[7941] Sarfaty, Regina (m sop); Rorem, Ned (pf)
- Columbia ML-5961/MS-6561; 33m/s; rel 1964; del 1966
- Odyssey 32-16-0274; 33s; rel 1968; del 1971

Symphony No 3 (1958)
[7942] Utah Symphony Orchestra; Abravanel, Maurice (cond)
- Turnabout TVS-34447; 33s; rel 1971; cip

To You (1957)
[7943] Gramm, Donald (b bar); Rorem, Ned (pf)
Rec 1962-63
- Columbia ML-5961/MS-6561; 33m/s; rel 1964; del 1966
- Odyssey 32-16-0274; 33s; rel 1968; del 1971
- New World NW-229; 33s; rel 1978

Trio, Flute, Violoncello, and Piano (1960)
[7944] New York Camarata
- Desto DC-6462; 33s; rel 1968; cip

Trio, Flute, Violoncello, and Piano (1960) (cont'd)
[7945] Tipton Trio
- Westminster WST-17147; 33s; rel 1968; del 1971

Tulip Tree, The (1953)
[7946] Curtin, Phyllis (sop); Gramm, Donald (bar); Rorem, Ned (pf)
- CRI-238; 33s; rel 1969; cip

Virelai (1961)
[7947] North Texas State University A Capella Choir; McKinley, Frank A. (cond)
- Boosey & Hawkes SNBH-5001; 33s; rel 1978

Visits to St. Elizabeth's (1957)
[7948] Miller, Mildred (m sop); Biltcliffe, Edwin (pf)
- St/And SPL-411-12; 33m; 2 discs; rel 1963; del 1964
- Desto D-411-12/DST-6411-12; 33m/s; 2 discs; rel 1964; cip

[7949] Sarfaty, Regina (m sop); Rorem, Ned (pf)
- Columbia ML-5961/MS-6561; 33m/s; rel 1964; del 1966
- Odyssey 32-16-0274; 33s; rel 1968; del 1971

War Scenes (1969)
[7950] Gramm, Donald (b bar); Istomin, Eugene (pf)
- Desto DC-7101; 33s; rel 1970; cip

Water Music (1966)
[7951] Oakland Youth Orchestra; Hughes, Robert (cond)
- Desto DC-6462; 33s; rel 1968; cip

What If Some Little Pain (1949)
[7952] Sarfaty, Regina (m sop); Rorem, Ned (pf)
- Columbia ML-5961/MS-6561; 33m/s; rel 1964; del 1966
- Odyssey 32-16-0274; 33s; rel 1968; del 1971

What Sparks and Wiry Cries (1956)
[7953] Curtin, Phyllis (sop); Gramm, Donald (bar); Rorem, Ned (pf)
- CRI-238; 33s; rel 1969; cip

[7954] Hanks, John Kennedy (ten); Friedberg, Ruth (pf)
- Duke University Press DWR-7306; 33s; rel 1974

Youth, Day, Old Age, and Night (1954)
[7955] Bressler, Charles (ten); Rorem, Ned (pf)
- Columbia ML-5961/MS-6561; 33m/s; rel 1964; del 1966
- Odyssey 32-16-0274; 33s; rel 1968; del 1971

ROSEN, Jerome (1921-)

(Five) Pieces, Violin and Piano (1970)
[7956] Gross, Robert (vln); Grayson, Richard (pf)
- Orion ORS-73110; 33s; rel 1973; cip

Quartet, Strings, No 1 (1955)
[7957] New Music String Quartet
- Epic LC-3333; 33m; rel 1957; del 1961

Sonata, Clarinet and Violoncello (ca 1954)
[7958] Rosen, Jerome (cl); Stross, Helen (vcl)
- Fantasy 5009; 33m; rel 1960; del 1970

ROSENBOOM, David (1947-)

And Out Come the Night Ears (1978)
[7959] Buchla, Donald (pf); tape
Rec 4/21/78
- 1750 Arch S-1774; 33s; rel 1979; cip

Etude, Piano, No 1 (1971)
[7960] no performer given
- ARC ST-1002; 33s; rel 1975

How Much Better if Plymouth Rock Had Landed on the Pilgrims (1969): Section V
[7961] Electronic music
Rec 4/21/78
- 1750 Arch S-1774; 33s; rel 1979; cip

Portable Gold and Philosophers' Stones
[7962] Electronic music
- ARC ST-1002; 33s; rel 1975

ROSENBOOM, David and HUMBERT, Jacqueline

Chilean Drought (1974)
[7963] no performers given
- ARC ST-1002; 33s; rel 1975

ROSENMAN, Leonard (1924-)

Chamber Music 2 (1968)
[7964] Harmon, Su (sop); New Muse; Rosenman, Leonard (cond)
- Delos DEL-25432; 33q; rel 1977; cip

Duo, Violin and Piano (1970)
[7965] Gross, Robert (vln); Grayson, Richard (pf)
- Orion ORS-73107; 33s; rel 1973; cip

Fanfares 1969 see REYNOLDS, Jeffrey, et al

ROSS, Richard (1914-54)

Invocation
[7966] Swann, Frederick (org)
- Mirrosonic CS-7015; 33s; rel 1963

ROSS, Walter (1936-)

Concerto, Trombone and Orchestra (1971)
[7967] Brevig, Per (tbn); Bergen Symphony Orchestra; Andersen, Karsten (cond)
Rec 9-10/72
- CRI-340; 33s; rel 1975; cip

Concerto, Tuba and Winds (1973)
[7968] Phillips, Harvey (tu); Cornell University Wind Ensemble; Cornell University Symphonic Band; Stith, Marice (cond)
- Cornell CUWE-17; 33s; rel 1975; cip

Concerto, Wind Quintet and Strings (1977)
[7969] Clarion Wind Quintet; Piedmont Chamber Orchestra; Harsanyi, Nicholas (cond)
- Golden Crest CRS-4188; 33s; rel 1979

Concerto basso (1974)
[7970] Tennessee Tech Tuba Ensemble; Morris, R. Winston (cond)
- Golden Crest CRSQ-4139; 33q; rel 1977; cip

Divertimento, Woodwind Quintet (1974)
[7971] Clarion Wind Quintet
- Golden Crest CRS-4191; 33s; rel 1980; cip

Fancy Dances (1972)
[7972] New York Tuba Quartet
- Crystal S-221; 33s; rel 1977; cip

Partita, Euphonium and Piano
[7973] Bowman, Brian (euph); Lee, Marjorie (pf)
- Crystal S-393; 33s; rel 1978; cip

Piltdown Fragments (1975)
[7974] Cummings, Barton (tu); tape
- Crystal S-391; 33s; rel 1978; cip

Prelude, Fugue, and Big Apple (1972)
[7975] Brevig, Per (tbn); tape
Rec 3/75
- CRI-340; 33s; rel 1975; cip

ROUSE, Christopher (1949-)

Subjectives VIII (1972-73)
[7976] Stith, Marice (tpt); Israel, Brian (perc); Lindenfeld, Harris (perc); Rouse, Christopher (perc); tape
- Golden Crest RE-7068; 33s; rel 1977; cip

Vulcan
[7977] Cornell University Wind Ensemble; Stith, Marice (cond)
- Cornell CUWE-16; 33s; rel 1975; cip

ROUSSAKIS, Nicolas (1934-)

Night Speech (1968)
[7978] Macalester Concert Choir; Warland, Dale (cond)
- CRI-255; 33s; rel 1971; cip

(Six) Short Pieces, Two Flutes (1969)
[7979] Sollberger, Harvey (fl); Sollberger, Sophie (fl)
- Nonesuch HB-73028; 33s; 2 discs; rel 1975; cip

Sonata, Harpsichord (1967)
[7980] Chaney, Harold (hpschd)
- CRI-255; 33s; rel 1971; cip

ROVICS, Howard (1936-)

Echo
[7981] Dougherty, Lee (sop); Alexander, Sylvia (fl); Chamberlain, Anne (pf)
- CRI-392; 33s; rel 1979; cip

Events (1971)
[7982] Chamberlain, Anne (pf)
- CRI-392; 33s; rel 1979; cip

Look, Friend, at Me (1973)
[7983] Dougherty, Lee (sop)
- CRI-392; 33s; rel 1979; cip

Piece, Violoncello, Piano, and Tape (1973)
[7984] Wells, David (vcl); Chamberlain, Anne (pf); tape
- CRI-392; 33s; rel 1979; cip

(Three) Studies, Piano (1966)
[7985] Chamberlain, Anne (pf)
- Ars Nova/Ars Antiqua AN-1007; 33s; rel 1971; del 1974

What Grandma Knew
[7986] Dougherty, Lee (sop)
- CRI-392; 33s; rel 1979; cip

ROXBURY, Ronald (1946-)

Leda and the Velvet Gentleman
[7987] Gregg Smith Singers; Smith, Gregg (cond)
- Grenadilla GS-1033; 33s; rel 1978; cip

(Four) Motets (1970)
[7988] Gregg Smith Singers; Smith, Gregg (cond)
Rec 4/76
- Vox SVBX-5354; 33s; 3 discs; rel 1979

ROY, Klaus George (1924-)

Canticle of the Sun (Op 17) (1950)
[7989] Kulas Choir; Skernick, Abraham (vla); Shaw, Robert (cond)
- CRI-182; 33m/s; rel 1964; cip

ROZSA, Miklos (1907-)

Background to Violence
[7990] Frankenland State Symphony Orchestra; Rozsa, Miklos (cond)
- Decca DL-10015/DL-710015; 33m/s; rel 1959; del 1973

Bagatellen, Piano (Op 12) (1932)
[7991] Dominguez, Albert (pf)
- Citadel CT-7004; 33s; rel 1979; cip

Capriccio pastorale e danza (1938)
[7992] RCA Italiana Orchestra; Rozsa, Miklos (cond)
- RCA LM-2802/LSC-2802; 33m/s; rel 1965; del 1967

Concerto, String Orchestra (Op 17) (1943)
[7993] London String Orchestra; Rozsa, Miklos (cond)
- Vox PLP-7690; 33m; rel 1952; del 1957

[7994] MGM String Orchestra; Surinach, Carlos (cond)
- MGM E-3565; 33m; rel 1958; del 1959

[7995] Vienna State Opera Orchestra; Rozsa, Miklos (cond)
- Westminster XWN-18805/WST-14035; 33m/s; rel 1959; del 1962
- Westminster WGS-8353; 33s; rel 1978; cip

Concerto, Violin and Orchestra, No 2 (Op 24) (1956)
[7996] Heifetz, Jascha (vln); Dallas Symphony Orchestra; Hendl, Walter (cond)
- RCA LM-2027; 33m; rel 1956; del 1969
- RCA LM-2767/LSC-2767; 33m/s; rel 1964; del 1977

Duo, Violin and Piano (Op 7) (1931)
[7997] Granat, Endre (vln); Pennario, Leonard (pf)
- Orion ORS-73127; 33s; rel 1973; cip

Duo, Violoncello and Piano (Op 8) (1931)
[7998] Compinsky, Alec (vcl); Compinsky, Sara (pf)
- Alco Y-1210; 33m; rel 1952; del 1955

[7999] Solow, Jeffrey (vcl); Dominguez, Albert (pf)
- Entr'acte ERS-6509; 33s; rel 1978; cip

Hungarian Serenade (Op 25) (1946)
[8000] Frankenland State Symphony Orchestra; Kloss, Erich (cond)
- MGM S-3645; 33s; rel 1960; del 1965

[8001] MGM Orchestra; Winograd, Arthur (cond)
- MGM E-3631; 33m; rel 1958; del 1960

[8002] Nuremberg Symphony Orchestra; Rozsa, Miklos (cond)
- Citadel CT-6001; 33s; rel 1976; cip

(Three) Hungarian Sketches (Op 14) (1938)
[8003] Frankenland State Symphony Orchestra; Rozsa, Miklos (cond)
- Decca DL-9966; 33m; rel 1958; del 1971
- Varese Sarabande VC-81058; 33s; rel 1979; cip

[8004] RCA Italiana Orchestra; Rozsa, Miklos (cond)
- RCA LM-2802/LSC-2802; 33m/s; rel 1965; del 1967

Jungle Book Suite (1942)
[8005] Genn, Leo (nar); Frankenland State Symphony Orchestra; Rozsa, Miklos (cond)
- RCA LM-2118; 33m; rel 1957; del 1959

[8006] Sabu (nar); Victor Symphony Orchestra; Rozsa, Miklos (cond)
- Entr'acte ERS-6002; 33s; rel 1979; cip

Kaleidoscope (Op 19) (ca 1948)
[8007] Dominguez, Albert (pf)
- Orion ORS-74137; 33s; rel 1974; cip

Kaleidoscope (Op 19a)
[8008] Vienna State Opera Orchestra; Rozsa, Miklos (cond)
- Westminster XWN-18805/WST-14035; 33m/s; rel 1959; del 1962
- Westminster WGS-8353; 33s; rel 1978; cip

North Hungarian Peasant Songs and Dances (Op 5) (1929) (violin and orchestra version)
[8009] Colbertson, Oliver (vln); Frankenland State Symphony Orchestra; Kloss, Erich (cond)
- MGM S-3645; 33s; rel 1960; del 1965

North Hungarian Peasant Songs and Dances (violin and piano version)
[8010] Granat, Endre (vln); Herbst, Erwin (pf)
- Orion ORS-73127; 33s; rel 1973; cip

Notturno ungherese (Op 28) (1964)
[8011] RCA Italiana Orchestra; Rozsa, Miklos (cond)
- RCA LM-2802/LSC-2802; 33m/s; rel 1965; del 1967

Overture to a Symphony Concert (Op 26) (1957)
[8012] Frankenland State Symphony Orchestra; Rozsa, Miklos (cond)
- Decca DL-9966; 33m; rel 1958; del 1971
- Varese Sarabande VC-81058; 33s; rel 1979; cip

[8013] RCA Italiana Orchestra; Rozsa, Miklos (cond)
- RCA LM-2802/LSC-2802; 33m/s; rel 1965; del 1967

Psalm 23 (Op 34) (1972)
[8014] Choir of the West; Skones (cond)
- Entr'acte ERS-6512; 33s; rel 1978; cip

Quartet, Strings (Op 22) (1950)
[8015] New World String Quartet
- Vox SVBX-5109; 33s; 3 discs; rel 1979; cip

Quintet, Piano and Strings (Op 2) (1928)
[8016] Pennario, Leonard (pf); Granat, Endre (vln); Sanov, Sheldon (vln); Thomas, Milton (vla); Rosen, Nathaniel (vcl)
- Orion ORS-75191; 33s; rel 1975; cip

Serenade for Small Orchestra (Op 10) (1932)
[8017] La Jolla Musical Arts Festival Orchestra; Sokoloff, Nikolai (cond)
- Concert Hall CHG-4; 33m; rel 1953*

Snow Is Falling
[8018] Budapest Children's Choir; Botka, Valeria (cond) or Czanyi, Laszlo (cond)
- RCA LM-2861/LSC-2861; 33m/s; rel 1966; del 1971

Sonata, Piano (Op 20) (ca 1949)
[8019] Dominguez, Albert (pf)
- Orion ORS-74137; 33s; rel 1974; cip

[8020] Parkin, Eric (pf)
- Unicorn UNI-72029; 33s; rel 1979; cip

[8021] Pennario, Leonard (pf)
- Capitol P-8376; 33m; rel 1957; del 1959

Sonata, Two Violins (Op 15) (1933, rev 1973)
[8022] Granat, Endre (vln); Sanov, Sheldon (vln)
- Entr'acte ERS-6509; 33s; rel 1978; cip

Sonata, Violoncello and Piano
[8023] Compinsky, Alec (vcl); Compinsky, Sara (pf)
- Alco AL-1210; 33m; rel pre-1956

Tema con variazioni (1962)
[8024] Heifetz, Jascha (vln); Piatigorsky, Gregor (vcl); orchestra
- RCA LM-2770/LSC-2770; 33m/s; rel 1964; cip

Theme, Variations, and Finale (Op 13) (1933, rev 1943)
[8025] Frankenland State Symphony Orchestra; Rozsa, Miklos (cond)
- Decca DL-9966; 33m; rel 1958; del 1971
- Varese Sarabande VC-81058; 33s; rel 1979; cip

[8026] RCA Italiana Orchestra; Rozsa, Miklos (cond)
- RCA LM-2802/LSC-2802; 33m/s; rel 1965; del 1967

[8027] Royal Philharmonic Orchestra; Rozsa, Miklos (cond)
- Vox PLP-7690; 33m; rel 1952; del 1957

To Everything There Is a Season (Op 21) (1945)
[8028] Choir of the West; Skones (cond)
- Entr'acte ERS-6512; 33s; rel 1978; cip

[8029] Columbia University Teachers College Concert Choir; Ohl, Dorothy (org); Wilson, Harry R. (cond)
Rec 3/55
- Music Library MLR-7071; 33m; rel 1956; del 1974

[8030] Hollywood First Methodist Church Choir; Wright, Norman Soereng (cond)
- Dot 3304/25304; 33m/s; rel 1960; del 1969

Toccata capricciosa (Op 36)
[8031] Solow, Jeffrey (vcl)
- Entr'acte ERS-6509; 33s; rel 1978; cip

Trio, Violin, Violoncello, and Piano (1927)
[8032] Granat, Endre (vln); Rosen, Nathaniel (vcl); Pennario, Leonard (pf)
- Orion ORS-75191; 33s; rel 1975; cip

Valse crepusculaire
[8033] Dominguez, Albert (pf)
- Citadel CT-7004; 33s; rel 1979;
cip

**Vanities of Life, The (Op 30)
(1967)**
[8034] Choir of the West; Skones (cond)
- Entr'acte ERS-6512; 33s; rel
1978; cip

Variations, Piano (Op 9) (1932)
[8035] Dominguez, Albert (pf)
- Citadel CT-7004; 33s; rel 1979;
cip

**Variations on a Hungarian Peasant
Song (Op 4) (1929) (violin and
orchestra version)**
[8036] Vienna State Opera Orchestra;
Rozsa, Miklos (cond)
- Westminster
XWN-18805/WST-14035;
33m/s; rel 1959; del 1962
- Westminster WGS-8353; 33s; rel
1978; cip

**Variations on a Hungarian Peasant
Song (violin and piano version)**
[8037] Granat, Endre (vln); Herbst, Erwin
(pf)
- Orion ORS-73127; 33s; rel
1973; cip

**Vintner's Daughter, The (Twelve
Variations on a French Folksong)
(Op 23) (1952)**
[8038] Frankenland State Symphony
Orchestra; Kloss, Erich (cond)
- MGM S-3645; 33s; rel 1960; del
1965

[8039] Nuremberg Symphony Orchestra;
Rozsa, Miklos (cond)
- Citadel CT-6001; 33s; rel 1976;
cip

RUBINSTEIN, Beryl (1898-1952)
Quartet, Strings (1924): Passepied
[8040] Kreiner String Quartet
- Victor 12131 (in set M-397);
78; rel pre-1942

Suite, Two Pianos (1939)
[8041] Rubinstein, Beryl (pf); Loesser,
Arthur (pf)
- Victor 18019-21 (in set M-784);
78; 3 discs; rel pre-1942

RUDHYAR, Dane (1895-)
Advent
[8042] Kronos String Quartet
Rec 7/2-3/79
- CRI-418; 33s; rel 1980; cip

Crisis and Overcoming
[8043] Kronos String Quartet
Rec 7/2-3/79
- CRI-418; 33s; rel 1980; cip

Granites (1929)
[8044] Masselos, William (pf)
- MGM E-3556; 33m; rel 1958;
del 1960
- CRI-247; 33s; rel 1969; cip

Paeans (1927)
[8045] Masselos, William (pf)
- CRI-247; 33s; rel 1969; cip

Pentagram No 3 (Release) (1926)
[8046] Sellers, Michael (pf)
- Orion ORS-7285; 33s; rel 1972;
cip

Sinfonietta (1928)
[8047] Berlin Radio Orchestra; Perlea,
Jonel (cond)
- Remington 199-188; 33m; rel
1956; del 1959
- Varese Sarabande VC-81046;
33m; rel 1979; cip

Stars (1925)
[8048] Masselos, William (pf)
- CRI-247; 33s; rel 1969; cip

Syntony (1929)
[8049] Sellers, Michael (pf)
- Orion ORS-7285; 33s; rel 1972;
cip

Tetragrams (Series 1)
[8050] Peltzer, Dwight (pf)
- Serenus SRS-12072; 33s; rel
1977; cip

**Tetragram No 4 (Adolescence)
(1925)**
[8051] Mikulak, Marcia (pf)
Rec 4/77
- CRI-372; 33s; rel 1977; cip

Tetragram No 5 (Solitude) (1927)
[8052] Mikulak, Marcia (pf)
Rec 4/77
- CRI-372; 33s; rel 1977; cip

Transmutation (1976)
[8053] Mikulak, Marcia (pf)
Rec 4/77
- CRI-372; 33s; rel 1977; cip

RUDIN, Andrew (1939-)
Tragoedia
[8054] Electronic music
- Nonesuch H-71198; 33s; rel
1968; cip

RUGER, Morris Hutchins (1902-)
Sonata, Piano
[8055] Rigai, Amiram (pf)
- Music Library MLR-7083; 33m;
rel 1956; del 1974

Suite, Piano, No 2
[8056] Rigai, Amiram (pf)
- Music Library MLR-7083; 33m;
rel 1956; del 1974

RUGGLES, Carl (1876-1971)
Angels (original version) (1920)
[8057] brass ensemble; Schwarz, Gerard
(leader); Thomas, Michael Tilson
(cond)
Rec 3/77
- Columbia M2-34591; 33s; 2
discs; rel 1980

Angels (revised version) (1938)
[8058] brass ensemble; Schwarz, Gerard
(leader); Thomas, Michael Tilson
(cond)
Rec 3/77
- Columbia M2-34591; 33s; 2
discs; rel 1980

[8059] Buffalo Philharmonic Orchestra;
Foss, Lukas (cond)
- Turnabout TVS-34398; 33s; rel
1971; cip

[8060] Lehigh University Instrumental
Ensemble; Elkus, Jonathan (cond)
Rec 4/30/60
- Lehigh RINC-1103; 33m; rel
1968; del 1976

**Evocations (piano version)
(1935-43, rev 1954)**
[8061] Kirpatrick, John (pf)
Rec 3/2/55
- Columbia ML-4986; 33m; rel
1955; del 1968
- Columbia CML-4986; 33m; rel
1968; del 1974
- Columbia AML-4986; 33m; rel
1974; cip

[8062] Kirkpatrick, John (pf)
Rec 10/77
- Columbia M2-34591; 33s; 2
discs; rel 1980

[8063] Mandel, Alan (pf)
- Desto DC-6445-47; 33s; 3 discs;
rel 1975; cip Shields, Roger (pf)
[8063a] Shields, Roger (pf)
- Vox SVBX-5303; 33s; 3 discs; rel
1977; cip

**Evocations (orchestral version)
(1942-45)**
[8064] Buffalo Philharmonic Orchestra;
Thomas, Michael Tilson (cond)
Rec 11/75
- Columbia M2-34591; 33s; 2
discs; rel 1980

Exaltation (1958)
[8065] Gregg Smith Singers; brass
ensemble; Schwarz, Gerard
(leader); Raver, Leonard (org);
Thomas, Michael Tilson (cond)
Rec 3/77
- Columbia M2-34591; 33s; 2
discs; rel 1980

Men and Angels (1920): Men

[8066] Buffalo Philharmonic Orchestra;
       Thomas, Michael Tilson (cond)
       Rec 5/76
       - Columbia M2-34591; 33s; 2
       discs; rel 1980

**Men and Mountains
(chamber-orchestra version)
(1924)**

[8067] New Hampshire Music Festival
       Orchestra; Nee, Thomas (cond)
       Rec 7/14/76
       - Hammar SD-150; 33s

**Men and Mountains (orchestral
version) (1936, rev 1941)**

[8068] Buffalo Philharmonic Orchestra;
       Foss, Lukas (cond)
       - Turnabout TVS-34398; 33s; rel
       1971; cip

[8069] Buffalo Philharmonic Orchestra;
       Thomas, Michael Tilson (cond)
       Rec 11/75
       - Columbia M2-34591; 33s; 2
       discs; rel 1980

[8070] Polish National Radio Orchestra;
       Strickland, William (cond)
       Rec 1968
       - CRI-254; 33s; rel 1970; cip

Men and Mountains: Lilacs

[8071] Juilliard String Orchestra;
       Prausnitz, Frederik (cond)
       - Columbia ML-4986; 33m; rel
       1955; del 1968
       - Columbia CML-4986; 33m; rel
       1968; del 1974
       - Columbia AML-4986; 33m; rel
       1974; cip

[8072] Pan American Chamber Orchestra;
       Lichter, Charles (cond)
       Rec 5/16/34
       - New Music Quarterly Recordings
       1013 (1-6); 78; rel 1934
       - Orion ORD-7150/ORS-7150;
       33m/s; rel 1971/?; cip

Organum (1944-47)

[8073] Buffalo Philharmonic Orchestra;
       Thomas, Michael Tilson (cond)
       Rec 5/76
       - Columbia M2-34591; 33s; 2
       discs; rel 1980

[8074] Japan Philharmonic Symphony
       Orchestra; Watanabe, Akeo
       (cond)
       - CRI-127; 33m/s; rel 1960/?; cip

**Portals (string-orchestra version)
(1929, rev 1941, rev 1952-53)**

[8075] Buffalo Philharmonic Orchestra;
       Thomas, Michael Tilson (cond)
       Rec 5/76
       - Columbia M2-34591; 33s; 2
       discs; rel 1980

**Portals (string-orchestra version)
(1929, rev 1941, rev 1952-53)**
   (cont'd)

[8076] Juilliard String Orchestra;
       Prausnitz, Frederik (cond)
       Rec 5/13/54
       - Columbia ML-4986; 33m; rel
       1955; del 1968
       - Columbia CML-4986; 33m; rel
       1968; del 1974
       - Columbia AML-4986; 33m; rel
       1974; cip

Sun-Treader (1926-31)

[8077] Boston Symphony Orchestra;
       Thomas, Michael Tilson (cond)
       Rec 3/24/70
       - Deutsche Grammophon
       2530.048; 33s; rel 1970; cip
       - Deutsche Grammophon
       2563.039 (in set 2721.020);
       33s

[8078] Buffalo Philharmonic Orchestra;
       Thomas, Michael Tilson (cond)
       Rec 11/75
       - Columbia M2-34591; 33s; 2
       discs; rel 1980

[8079] Columbia Symphony Orchestra;
       Rozsnyai, Zoltan (cond)
       Rec 3/8-9/65
       - Columbia ML-6201/MS-6801;
       33m/s; rel 1966; del 1971

Toys (1919)

[8080] Blegen, Judith (sop); Thomas,
       Michael Tilson (pf)
       Rec 5/78
       - Columbia M2-34591; 33s; 2
       discs; rel 1980

[8081] Litante, Judith (sop); Brant, Henry
       (pf)
       - New Music Quarterly Recordings
       1013 (1-6); 78; rel 1934

Vox clamans in deserto (1923)

[8082] Morgan, Beverly (voice); Speculum
       Musicae (members of); Thomas,
       Michael Tilson (cond)
       Rec 5/78
       - Columbia M2-34591; 33s; 2
       discs; rel 1980

RUSH, Loren (1935-)

Hexahedron (1964)

[8083] Peltzer, Dwight (pf)
       - Serenus SRS-12071; 33s; rel
       1978; cip

Little Traveling Music, A

[8084] Peltzer, Dwight (pf); tape
       - Serenus SRS-12070; 33s; rel
       1978; cip

Nexus 16 (1964)

[8085] San Francisco Conservatory New
       Music Ensemble; Hersh, Howard
       (cond)
       - Wergo WER-60-057; 33s; rel
       1971?

Oh, Susanna (1970)

[8086] Peltzer, Dwight (pf)
       - Serenus SRS-12070; 33s; rel
       1978; cip

Quartet, Strings (1961)

[8087] San Francisco Contemporary Music
       Players (members of); Le Roux,
       Jean-Louis (cond)
       Rec 10/76
       - CRI-381; 33s; rel 1978; cip

soft music, HARD MUSIC (1969)

[8088] Peltzer, Dwight (pf)
       - Serenus SRS-12070; 33s; rel
       1978; cip

RUSSELL, George (1923-)

All about Rosie

[8089] McKusik, Hal (sax); La Porta, John
       (sax); Mucci, Louis (tpt); Farmer,
       Art (tpt); Knepper, Jimmy (tbn);
       Di Domenico, Robert (fl); Zegler,
       Manuel (bsn); Evans, Bill (pf);
       Charles, Teddy (vib); Benjamin,
       Joe (cb); Ross, Margaret (hp);
       Buffington, James (hn); Galbraith,
       Barry (gtr); Sommer, Teddy
       (perc); Schuller, Gunther (cond)
       or Russell, George (cond)
       Rec 6/10/57
       - Columbia WL-127; 33m; rel
       1958*
       - Columbia CL-2109-10 (in set
       C2L-31)/CS-8909-10 (in set
       C2S-831); 33m/s; 2 discs; rel
       1963

**RUSSELL, George Alexander
(1880-1953)**

St. Lawrence Sketches (1916)

[8090] Ellsasser, Richard (org)
       - MGM E-3066; 33m; rel 1954;
       del 1965

**St. Lawrence Sketches: (No 2) The
Bells of Ste. Anne de Beaupre**

[8091] Cronham, Charles (org)
       Rec 1/31/27
       - Victor 35812; 78; rel 1927

**St. Lawrence Sketches: (No 3) Song
of the Basket Weaver**

[8092] Courboin, Charles (org)
       - Victor 14578; 78; rel 1937

RUSSELL, George H. (1919-)

Encounter Near Venus (1975)

[8093] Mayorga, Lincoln (pf); Feldman
       (perc); Mannes (perc); Bunker,
       Larry (perc); Balley (perc); Snow
       (perc); Russell, George (cond)
       - Sheffield S-17; 33s; 2 discs; rel
       1976; del 1978
       - Town Hall S-17; 33s; 2 discs; rel
       1978; cip

RUSSELL, William (1905-)

(Three) Cuban Pieces (1939)
[8094] Manhattan Percussion Ensemble;
Cage, John (cond); Price, Paul
(cond)
- Time 58000/S-8000; 33m/s; rel
1961; del 1970
- Mainstream MS-5011; 33s; rel
1970; del 1979

(Three) Dance Movements (1933)
[8095] Baetz, Jessie (perc); Cowell, Henry
(perc); Dresskell, Miles (perc);
Russell, William (perc)
- New Music Quarterly Recordings
1214; 78; rel 1936

[8096] Manhattan Percussion Ensemble;
Cage, John (cond); Price, Paul
(cond)
- Time 58000/S-8000; 33m/s; rel
1961; del 1970
- Mainstream MS-5011; 33s; rel
1970; del 1979

RUSSO, John (1943-)

Conversazione (1975)
[8097] Ignacio, Lydia Walton (pf)
- Capra 1204; 33s; rel 1976; cip

Elegy
[8098] Lancie, John de (ob)
- Orion ORS-78311; 33s; rel
1978; cip

(Three) Etudes, Clarinet and Piano
[8099] Russo, John (cl); Ignacio, Lydia
Walton (pf)
- Capra 1205; 33s; rel 1979; cip

Growing Up
[8100] Monasevitch (voice)
- Orion ORS-80367; 33s; rel
1980; cip

If You Never Talked with Fairies
[8101] Monasevitch (voice)
- Orion ORS-80367; 33s; rel
1980; cip

Larghetto (1964)
[8102] Russo, John (cl); Curtiss, Sidney
(vla); Ignacio, Lydia Walton (pf)
- Orion ORS-77275; 33s; rel
1978; cip

Little Elf, The
[8103] Monasevitch (voice)
- Orion ORS-80367; 33s; rel
1980; cip

(Four) Pieces, Clarinet
[8104] Russo, John (cl)
- Capra 1203; 33s; rel 1975; cip

(Three) Seasons
[8105] Schutt, Kenneth (fl); Russo, John
(cl); Ignacio, Lydia Walton (pf)
- Capra 1204; 33s; rel 1976; cip

Sonata, Clarinet and Piano, No 4 (1962-63)
[8106] Russo, John (cl); Ignacio, Lydia
Walton (pf)
- Orion ORS-77275; 33s; rel
1978; cip

Sonata, Clarinet, Piano, and Percussion, No 5 (1969)
[8107] Russo, John (cl); Ignacio, Lydia
Walton (pf); Ierardi, Florence
(perc); Power, Andrew J. (perc)
- Orion ORS-78294; 33s; rel
1978; cip

Sonata, Flute and Piano, No 1
[8108] Lind, Loren N. (fl); Ignacio, Lydia
Walton (pf)
- Capra 1205; 33s; rel 1979; cip

(Two) Studies, Clarinet and Piano
[8109] Russo, John (cl); Ignacio, Lydia
Walton (pf)
- Orion ORS-79330; 33s; rel
1980; cip

RUSSO, William (1928-)

(Three) Pieces, Blues Band and Symphony Orchestra (1967-68)
[8110] Siegel-Schwall Band; San Francisco
Symphony Orchestra; Ozawa, Seiji
(cond)
- Deutsche Grammophon
2530.309; 33s; rel 1973; cip

Street Music (Op 65) (1975)
[8111] Siegel, Corky (harmonica) (pf); San
Francisco Symphony Orchestra;
Ozawa, Seiji (cond)
- Deutsche Grammophon
2530.788; 33s; rel 1977; cip

RYAN, Thomas

Epitaph
[8112] Luening, Ethel (sop); Nowak, Lionel
(pf)
- Yaddo IV-2; 78; 10''; rel 1940

RYTERBAND, Roman (1914-)

(Trois) Ballades hebraiques
[8113] Glanz, Elemer (vln); Mersson, Boris
(pf)
- Orion ORS-74167; 33s; rel
1975; cip

Piece sans titre (1952)
[8114] Magnin, Alexandre (fl); Gueneux,
Georges (fl)
- Orion ORS-74167; 33s; rel
1975; cip

Sonata, Piano, No 1 (1951)
[8115] Pleshakov, Vladimir (pf)
- Orion ORS-76222; 33s; rel
1977; cip

Sonata breve, Violin and Harp (1961)
[8116] Glanz, Elemer (vln); Kauffungen,
Eva (hp)
- Orion ORS-74167; 33s; rel
1975; cip

(Two) Sonnets (1955)
[8117] Vernon, Lyn (m sop); Magnin,
Alexandre (fl); Kauffungen, Eva
(hp)
- Orion ORS-74167; 33s; rel
1975; cip

Suite polonaise
[8118] Pleshakov, Vladimir (pf)
- Orion ORS-76222; 33s; rel
1977; cip

Suite polonaise: Three Movements
[8119] Mersson, Boris (pf)
- Orion ORS-74167; 33s; rel
1975; cip

RZEWSKI, Frederic (1938-)

Apolitical Intellectuals
[8120] Holloway, David (bar); Rzewski,
Frederic (pf)
- Folkways FTS-33903; 33s; rel
1976; cip

Attica (1972)
[8121] Israel, Steve ben (speaker); Gibson,
Jon (al sax); List, Garrett (tbn);
Kalisch, Joan (vla); Youngstein,
Richard (cb); Curran, Alvin (syn)
(pic tpt); Rzewski, Frederic (pf);
Berger, Karl (vib)
- Opus One 20; 33s; rel 1974; cip

Coming Together (1972)
[8122] Israel, Steve ben (speaker); Gibson,
Jon (al sax); List, Garrett (tbn);
Kalisch, Joan (vla); Youngstein,
Richard (cb); Curran, Alvin (syn)
(pic tpt); Rzewski, Frederic (pf);
Berger, Karl (vib)
- Opus One 20; 33s; rel 1974; cip

Lullaby (God to a Hungry Child)
[8123] Holloway, David (bar); Braxton,
Anthony (cl); Berger, Karl (vib)
- Folkways FTS-33903; 33s; rel
1976; cip

Moutons de Panurge, Les (1969)
[8124] Blackearth Percussion Group
- Opus One 20; 33s; rel 1974; cip

People United Will Never Be Defeated, The (1975)
[8125] Oppens, Ursula (pf)
- Vanguard VSD-71248; 33s; rel
1979; cip

Song and Dance (1977)
[8126] Speculum Musicae
- Nonesuch H-71366; 33s; rel
1979; cip

Struggle: Struggle
[8127] Holloway, David (bar); Berger, Karl
(vib); Braxton, Anthony (cl);
Musician's Action Collective
(members of)
- Folkways FTS-33903; 33s; rel
1976; cip

**Variations on No Place to Go but
Around (1974)**
[8128] Rzewski, Frederic (pf)
- Finnadar SR-9011; 33s; rel
1976; cip

SACCO, John (1905-)
Maple Candy
[8129] Uppman, Theodor (bar); Rogers,
Allen (pf)
Rec 1/24/62, 2/2/62, and
2/7/62
- Internos INT-0001; 33m; rel
1962; del 1970

Rapunzel
[8130] Anders, Lynne (sop)
- Golden Age GAR-1002; 33s; rel
1976

SACCO, P. Peter (1928-)
Behold the Fowls of the Air
[8131] San Francisco State College A
Cappella Choir; Tegnell, John Carl
(cond)
- Music Library MLR-6997; 33m;
rel 1963; del 1974

(Three) Psalms
[8132] Sacco, P. Peter (ten); Los Angeles
Brass Society
- Avant AV-1005; 33s; rel 1976;
cip

SAHL, Michael (1934-)
Mitzvah for the Dead, A (1966-67)
[8133] Zukofsky, Paul (vln); tape
- Vanguard Cardinal VCS-10057;
33s; rel 1969; del 1977

Quartet, Strings
[8134] Zukofsky, Paul (vln); Teco,
Romuald (vln); Depony, Jean
(vla); Eddy, Timothy (vcl)
- Desto DC-6435-37; 33s; 3 discs;
rel 1975; cip

Tropes on the Salve regina
[8135] mixed media performers
- Lyrichord LLST-7210; 33s; rel
1969; cip

SALZEDO, Carlos (1885-1961)
Ballade
[8136] Salzedo, Carlos (hp)
- Mercury MG-80003; 33m; rel
1956; del 1957
- Mercury MG-50092; 33m; rel
1957; del 1963

Chanson dans la nuit
[8137] McDonald, Susann (hp)
- Klavier KS-525; 33s; rel 1973;
cip

[8138] Reardon, Casper (hp)
- Schirmer 5507; 78; rel
pre-1936

[8139] Robles, Marisa (hp)
- Argo RG-458/ZRG-5458; 33m/s;
rel 1967; del 1980

[8140] Salzedo, Carlos (hp)
- Columbia 68284D (in set M-8);
78; rel pre-1936

[8141] Zabaleta, Nicanor (hp)
- Decca DL-9929; 33m; rel 1959;
del 1963
- Deutsche Grammophon
SLPM-139419; 33s; rel 1969;
del 1975
- Deutsche Grammophon
2531.051; 33s; rel 1979; cip

**Concert Variations on O
Tannenbaum**
[8142] Remsen, Dorothy (hp)
- Avant AV-1000; 33s; rel 1967;
cip

**Concerto, Harp and Seven Winds,
No 1 (1925-26)**
[8143] Lawrence, Lucille (hp); Barrere
Woodwind Ensemble; Salzedo,
Carlos (cond)
- Columbia C-68282-84D (in set
M-8); 78; 3 discs; rel pre-1936

(Eight) Dances
[8144] Salzedo, Carlos (hp)
- Mercury MG-10144; 33m; rel
1954; del 1957
- Mercury MG-50093; 33m; rel
1957; del 1963

Jeu d'eau (1920)
[8145] Vito, Edward (hp)
- Period SPL-704; 33m; rel 1957;
del 1971

Petite valse (1943)
[8146] Salzedo, Carlos (hp)
- Mercury MG-80003; 33m; rel
1956; del 1957
- Mercury MG-50092; 33m; rel
1957; del 1963

Piece concertante (Op 27)
[8147] Anderson, Miles (tbn); Baley, Virko
(pf)
- Crystal S-385; 33s; rel 1980; cip

[8148] Barron, Ronald (tbn); Wanger,
Fredrik (pf)
- Boston Brass BB-1001; 33s; rel
1976; cip

**(Fifteen) Preludes for Beginners
(1927): La Desirade**
[8149] Salzedo, Carlos (hp)
- Mercury MG-80003; 33m; rel
1956; del 1957
- Mercury MG-50092; 33m; rel
1957; del 1963

Scintillation (1936)
[8150] Salzedo, Carlos (hp)
- Mercury MG-80003; 33m; rel
1956; del 1957
- Mercury MG-50092; 33m; rel
1957; del 1963

**Short Stories in Music for Young
Harpists**
[8151] Salzedo, Carlos (hp)
- Victor 14871; 78; rel pre-1936

Steel (two-harp version)
[8152] Salzedo, Carlos (hp); Lawrence,
Lucille (hp)
- Mercury MG-10144; 33m; rel
1954; del 1957
- Mercury MG-50093; 33m; rel
1957; del 1963

Traipsin' thru Arkansaw
[8153] Salzedo, Carlos (hp)
- Mercury MG-80003; 33m; rel
1956; del 1957
- Mercury MG-50092; 33m; rel
1957; del 1963

Transcriptions for Two Harps
[8154] Salzedo, Carlos (hp); Lawrence,
Lucille (hp)
- Mercury MG-10144; 33m; rel
1954; del 1957
- Mercury MG-50093; 33m; rel
1957; del 1963

Variations, Harp
[8155] Erdeli, Olga (hp)
- USSR/State Music Trust
17338-39; 78; rel pre-1953
- USSR/State Music Trust D-480;
78; rel pre-1956

**Variations on a Theme in Ancient
Style (Op 30)**
[8156] McDonald, Susann (hp)
- Klavier KS-525; 33s; rel 1973;
cip

Whirlwind
[8157] Goossens, Sidonie (hp)
- Columbia DB-565; 78; 10''; rel
pre-1936

SALZMAN, Eric (1933-)
Helix (1972)
[8158] Quog Music Theatre Ensemble
- Finnadar QD-9005; 33q; rel
1974; cip

Larynx Music (1966-67)
[8159] Ross, Elinor (sop); Silverman,
Stanley (gtr)
- Finnadar QD-9005; 33q; rel
1974; cip

Nude Paper Sermon, The (1969)
[8160] Keach, Stacy (nar); Nonesuch
Consort; New York Motet Singers;
Rifkin, Joshua (cond)
- Nonesuch H-71231; 33s; rel
1969; cip

Queens Collage (1966)
[8161] Electronic music
- Finnadar QD-9005; 33q; rel
1974; cip

Wiretap (1968)
[8162] Nagrin, Daniel (voice)
- Finnadar QD-9005; 33q; rel
1974; cip

SAMINSKY, Lazare (1882-1959)
By the Rivers of Babylon (1926)
[8163] Gravell, Hazel (sop); American Arts
Chorus; Saminsky, Lazare (cond)
- New NRLP-301; 33m; 10"; rel
1951; del 1956

Chassidic Suite (Op 24)
[8164] Waldman, Yuval (vln); Waldman,
Cathy (pf)
- Musique Internationale M-7502;
33s; rel 197?

SAMUEL, Gerhard (1924-)
Sun-Like (1975)
[8165] Phillips-Thornburgh (sop);
California Arts Faculty Ensemble;
Sequoia Quartet
- Orion ORS-78302; 33s; rel
1978; cip

What of my Music! (1979)
[8166] Lynn, Nelga (sop); Green, Barry
(cb); Ellison, Paul (cb);
International Society of Bassists
(36 cb from); Otte, Allen (perc);
Culley, James (perc); Hakes,
Michael (perc); Samuel, Gerhard
(cond)
- CRI-422; 33s; rel 1980; cip

SANDERS, Robert L. (1906-74)
Little Symphony No 1 (1936-37)
[8167] Louisville Orchestra; Whitney,
Robert (cond)
- LOU-63-5; 33m (Louisville
Orchestra First Edition Records
1963 No 5); rel 1963; del 1978

Little Symphony No 2 (1953)
[8168] Louisville Orchestra; Whitney,
Robert (cond)
- LOU-545-7; 33m (Louisville
Orchestra First Edition Records
1955 No 7); rel 1959; del 1972

Quintet, Brass (1942)
[8169] brass ensemble; Voisin, Roger
(cond)
- Unicorn UNLP-1031; 33m; rel
1956; del 1959
- Kapp KCL-9020; 33m; rel 1959;
del 1963
- Kapp KL-1391; 33m; rel 1965;
del 1971

Quintet, Brass: 3rd Movement
[8170] New York Philharmonic Brass
Ensemble
- Golden Crest
CR-4003/CRS-4003; 33m/s; rel
1957/1979; cip

Saturday Night (1933)
[8171] Vienna Symphony Orchestra;
Schoenherr, Max (cond)
- American Recording Society
ARS-30; 33m; 10"; rel 1953

Symphony in A (1954-55)
[8172] Knoxville Symphony Orchestra; Van
Vactor, David (cond)
- CRI-156; 33m; rel 1962; cip

SANDOVAL, Miguel (1903-53)
Cantiga
[8173] Ibarrondo, Lydia (m sop);
Sandoval, Miguel (pf)
- Columbia ML-2189; 33m; 10";
rel 1951*

Copla bailable
[8174] Ibarrondo, Lydia (m sop);
Sandoval, Miguel (pf)
- Columbia ML-2189; 33m; 10";
rel 1951*

Copla leonoesa
[8175] Ibarrondo, Lydia (m sop);
Sandoval, Miguel (pf)
- Columbia ML-2189; 33m; 10";
rel 1951*

Copla malaguena
[8176] Ibarrondo, Lydia (m sop);
Sandoval, Miguel (pf)
- Columbia ML-2189; 33m; 10";
rel 1951*

Danza del contrabandista
[8177] Orquesta Zarzuela de Madrid;
Machado, Roger (cond)
- Decca DL-9757; 33m; rel 1955;
del 1971

Mercado de los esclaves, El
[8178] Ibarrondo, Lydia (m sop);
Sandoval, Miguel (pf)
- Columbia ML-2189; 33m; 10";
rel 1951*

Solea
[8179] Ibarrondo, Lydia (m sop);
Sandoval, Miguel (pf)
- Columbia ML-2189; 33m; 10";
rel 1951*

Zamorana
[8180] Ibarrondo, Lydia (m sop);
Sandoval, Miguel (pf)
- Columbia ML-2189; 33m; 10";
rel 1951*

SANGSTER, John*
Lord of the Rings
[8181] ensemble; Sangster, John (cond)
- EMI EMC-2525-26; 33s; 2 discs;
rel 1975

SAPERSTEIN, David (1948-)
Antiphonies (1972)
[8182] New Jersey Percussion Ensemble;
DesRoches, Raymond (cond)
- Nonesuch H-71291/HQ-1291;
33s/q; rel 1974/1976; cip

SARGENT, Paul (1910-)
Hickory Hill
[8183] Farrell, Eileen (sop); Trovillo,
George (pf)
- Angel 35608; 33m; rel 1959;
del 1966

SATUREN, David (1939-)
Sonata, Clarinet and Piano
[8184] Russo, John (cl); Ignacio, Lydia
Walton (pf)
- Capra 1205; 33s; rel 1979; cip

**Trio, Clarinet, Piano, and Mallet
Percussion**
[8185] Russo, John (cl); Ignacio, Lydia
Walton (pf); Power, Andrew J.
(mrmb) (glock) (xyl)
- Orion ORS-78294; 33s; rel
1978; cip

SAUCEDO, Victor (1937-)
Ran I. X. (1976)
[8186] Rehfeldt, Phillip (cl); tape
- Grenadilla GS-1017; 33s; rel
1980; cip

SAUTER, Edward E. (1914-)
**Tanglewood Concerto, Saxophone
and Orchestra**
[8187] Getz, Stan (sax); Boston Pops
Orchestra; Fiedler, Arthur (cond)
- RCA LM-2925/LSC-2925;
33m/s; rel 1967; del 1971

SAYLOR, Bruce (1946-)
(Four) Psalms (1976-78)
[8188] Beavon, Constance (m sop);
Simonsen, Irene (fl)
- Orion ORS-80368; 33s; rel
1980; cip

SCALETTI, Carla
Motet (1977)
[8189] Ives-Clawson, Kathy (m sop);
Hoffman, Irwin (nar); Williams,
Floyd (b cl); Scaletti, Carla (hp)
- Opus One 42; 33s; rel 1978; cip

SCAVARDA, Donald (1928-)

Landscape Journey (1964)
[8190] Morgan, John (cl); Scavarda, Donald (pf)
- Advance FGR-5; 33m; rel 1966; cip

Matrix for Clarinetist (1962)
[8191] Rehfeldt, Phillip (cl)
- Advance FGR-4; 33m; rel 1966; cip

SCHELLING, Ernest (1876-1939)

Nocturne a Raguze
[8192] Paderewski, Ignace Jan (pf)
- Victor 6700; 78; rel pre-1936
- Gramophone DB-1029; 78; rel pre-1936

Victory Ball, A (1925)
[8193] New York Philharmonic; Mengelberg, Willem (cond)
- Victor 1127-28; 78; 2-10"; rel 1926

SCHICKELE, Peter (1935-)

Diversions (1963)
[8194] Clarion Wind Quintet
- Golden Crest CRS-4191; 33s; rel 1980; cip

Elegies (1974)
[8195] Stoltzman, Richard (cl); Schickele, Peter (pf)
- Vanguard VSD-71269; 33s; rel 1980; cip

Fantastic Garden, The
[8196] Open Window; Louisville Orchestra; Mester, Jorge (cond)
- LS-69-1; 33s (Louisville Orchestra First Edition Records 1969 No 1); rel 1969; cip

Lowest Trees Have Tops, The (1975)
[8197] Jubal Trio
- Grenadilla GS-1015; 33s; rel 1978; cip

Songs from The Knight of the Burning Pestle (1974)
[8198] Shelton, Lucy (sop); Rose; Hoffmeister; Kuehn; instrumental ensemble; Schickele, Peter (cond)
- Vanguard VSD-71269; 33s; rel 1980; cip

Summer Trio (1966)
[8199] Walden Trio
- Vanguard VSD-71269; 33s; rel 1980; cip

SCHIFRIN, Lalo (1932-)

Continuum
[8200] De Cray, Marcella (hp)
- Coronet S-2745; 33s; rel 1972*

Continuum (cont'd)
[8201] Stockton, Ann Mason (hp)
- Crystal S-107; 33s; rel 1973; cip

Dialogues, Jazz Quintet and Orchestra
[8202] Cannonball Adderley Quintet; orchestra; Schifrin, Lalo (cond)
- Capitol ST-484; 33s; rel 1970

Jazz Suite on Mass Texts (1965)
[8203] Horn, Paul (fl) (cl) (al sax); chorus; jazz ensemble; Schifrin, Lalo (cond)
- RCA LPM-3414/LSP-3414; 33m/s; rel 1965; del 1972

Rise and Fall of the Third Reich, The (1967)
[8204] Harvey, Laurence (nar); Chookasian, Lili (al); Cassilly, Richard (ten); Gregg Smith Singers; MGM Studio Symphony Orchestra; Foster, Lawrence (cond)
- MGM 1SE-12ST; 33s; rel 1968; del 1976

Rock Requiem (1971)
[8205] Mike Curb Congregation; orchestra; Schifrin, Lalo (cond)
- Verve V6-8801; 33s; rel 1972; del 1974

SCHINDLER, Allan (1944-)

Sextet, Strings
[8206] University of Chicago Contemporary Chamber Players
- Owl ORLP-20; 33s; rel 1972; del 1977

SCHMIDT, William J. (1926-)

Chamber Concerto, Organ and Brass: Spiritual Fantasy
[8207] Ladd, Thomas (org); Los Angeles Brass Society (members of); Remsen, Lester (cond)
- WIM Records WIMR-6; 33s; rel 1972; cip

Concertino, Piano and Brass Quintet
[8208] Davis, Sharon (pf); Los Angeles Brass Quintet
- Crystal S-821; 33s; rel 1971; cip

Fanfares 1969 see REYNOLDS, Jeffrey, et al

Ludus Americanus (1971)
[8209] Penney, Edmund (nar); Ervin, Karen (perc)
- WIM Records WIMR-5; 33s; rel 1972; cip

Music for Scrimshaw
[8210] Remsen, Dorothy (hp); Los Angeles Brass Society; Remsen, Lester (cond)
- WIM Records WIMR-6; 33s; rel 1972; cip

Rhapsody, Clarinet and Piano, No 1
[8211] Atkins, David (cl); Davis, Sharon (pf)
- WIM Records WIMR-1; 33s; rel 1971; cip

Septigrams (1956)
[8212] Andrus, Gretel Shanley (fl); Davis, Sharon (pf); Remsen, Eric (perc)
- WIM Records WIMR-2; 33s; rel 1971; cip

Sequential Fanfares
[8213] Los Angeles Philharmonic Brass Ensemble; Remsen, Lester (cond)
- Avant AV-1005; 33s; rel 1976; cip

Serenade, Tuba and Piano (1958)
[8214] Conner, Rex (tu)
- Coronet M-1259; 33m; rel 1969; cip
[8215] Johnson, Tommy (tu); Davis, Sharon (pf)
- WIM Records WIMR-14; 33s; rel 1979; cip

Short'nin' Bread Variations
[8216] Remsen, Dorothy (hp); Los Angeles Brass Society; percussion; Remsen, Lester (cond)
- WIM Records WIMR-6; 33s; rel 1972; cip

Sonata, Horn and Piano
[8217] Smith, Calvin (hn); Davis, Sharon (pf)
- WIM Records WIMR-14; 33s; rel 1979; cip

Sonatina, Contrabass Clarinet and Piano
[8218] Spear, Julian (cb cl); Davis, Sharon (pf)
- WIM Records WIMR-10; 33s; rel 1978; cip

Sonatina, Tenor Saxophone and Piano
[8219] Houlik, James (ten sax); Tardif, Paul (pf)
- Golden Crest RE-7060; 33s; rel 1977; cip

Sparrow and the Amazing Mr. Avaunt, The
[8220] Vlazinskaya, Valeria (nar); Christ, Peter (ob)
- Crystal S-321; 33s; rel 1979; cip

Suite, Brass, No 1
[8221] New York Brass Society
- WIM Records WIMR-3; 33s; rel 1972; cip

Suite, Brass, No 2 (Folksongs)
[8222] Los Angeles Brass Society; Remsen, Lester (cond)
- WIM Records WIMR-6; 33s; rel 1972; cip

(Seven) Variations on a Hexachord (1963)
[8223] Fine Arts Brass Quintet
- WIM Records WIMR-4; 33s; rel 1975; cip

Variations on a Negro Folk Song
[8224] Los Angeles Brass Quintet
- Crystal S-602; 33s; rel 1968; cip

Variations on St. Bone
[8225] Veeh, Alvin (tbn); Davis, Sharon (pf)
- WIM Records WIMR-14; 33s; rel 1979; cip

Vendor's Call (1968)
[8226] Davis, Sharon (pf); Los Angeles Clarinet Society
- WIM Records WIMR-13; 33s; rel 1977; cip

SCHOENFIELD, Paul (1947-)
Sonata, Piano, No 2
[8227] Schoenfield, Paul (pf)
- VLR 1520/S-1520; 33m/s; rel 1965/?; del 1976

SCHOOP, Paul (1909-76)
Fata Morgana
[8228] Frankenland Symphony Orchestra; Kloss, Erich (cond)
- Lyrichord LL-29; 33m; rel 1952; del 1957

March Ballet
[8229] Frankenland Symphony Orchestra; Kloss, Erich (cond)
- Lyrichord LL-29; 33m; rel 1952; del 1957

SCHRAMM, Harold (1935-)
Song of Tayumanavar
[8230] Addison, Adele (sop); Baron, Samuel (fl)
- Desto DC-7134; 33s; rel 1973; cip

SCHREINER, Alexander (1901-)
Lyric Interlude
[8231] Schreiner, Alexander (org)
- Columbia ML-5425/MS-6101; 33m/s; rel 1960; cip

[8232] Westfield, Donald L. (org)
- Allen Organ Co DLW-1014; 33s; rel 197?

SCHUBEL, Max (1932-)
Exotica (1967)
[8233] Wells, David (vcl); Thomas, Andrew (hpschd)
- Opus One 7; 33s; rel 1968; cip

F-Sharp (1968)
[8234] Electronic music
- Opus One 7; 33s; rel 1968; cip

Fracture (1969)
[8235] Springfield Symphony Orchestra; Gutter, Robert (cond)
- Opus One 21; 33s; rel 1975; cip

Guale (1976)
[8236] Bowen, Frank (fl) (pic); Randall, Darrel (E hn); Williams, Floyd (cl) (b cl); Gref, Warren (hn); Patrick, Susan (hpschd); Gref, Ann (pf) (voice); Scaletti, Carla (hp); Oberg, David (cb); Schulkoski, Robyn (perc); Wood, William (cond)
- Opus One 25; 33s; rel 1976; cip

Insected Surfaces (1965-66)
[8237] Goldstein, William (cl); Wells, David (vcl); Turetzky, Bertram (cb); White, John Reeves (hpschd); Gigliotti, Charles (pf); Larsen, Henry (cond)
- Opus One 1/S-1; 33m/s; rel 1966; cip

Joyeux Noel (1967)
[8238] Blustine, Allen (cl); Moore, David (vcl); tape
- Opus One 7; 33s; rel 1968; cip

Moonwave (1969)
[8239] Dunkel, Paul (fl)
- Opus One 14; 33s; rel 1976; cip

Omphaloskepsis (1964)
[8240] Moore, David (vcl)
- Opus One 6; 33s; rel 1970; cip

Paraplex (1977-78)
[8241] Pope, George (fl) (pic); Randall, Darrel (E hn); Wood, William (ten sax); Williams, Floyd (cl) (b cl); Piper, Jeffrey (tpt); Hinterbichler, Karl (tbn); Schulkoski, Robyn (perc); Forsman, Ron (perc); Brown, Robert (pf); Scaletti, Carla (hp); Patrick, Susan (hpschd); Gwin, Daniel (cb); Oberg, David (cond)
- Opus One 50; 33s; rel 1979; cip

Quartet, Strings, No 2 (High Ice) (1967)
[8242] Kohon Quartet
- Opus One 7; 33s; rel 1968; cip

Quashed Culch (1966)
[8243] Schecter, Peggy (fl); Phillips, Barre (cb)
- Opus One 7; 33s; rel 1968; cip

Ragwyrk (1977)
[8244] Scaletti, Carla (hp)
- Opus One 50; 33s; rel 1979; cip

Son of Quashed Culch (1966)
[8245] Williams, Averil (fl); Kok, Alexander (vcl); Phillips, Barre (cb)
- Opus One 3; 33s; rel 1969; cip

Zones (1972)
[8246] Dunkel, Paul (fl); Jekofsky, Barry (perc); Carno, Zita (pf); New York Brass Society; Thomas, Andrew (cond)
- Opus One 18; 33s; rel 1974; cip

SCHULE, Bernard (1909-)
Resonances (1962)
[8247] Modern Brass Ensemble
- Advance FGR-2; 33m; rel 1966; del 1978

SCHULLER, Gunther (1925-)
Abstraction (1959)
[8248] Dolphy, Eric (fl); Di Domenico, Robert (fl); Coleman, Ornette (sax); Brown, Alfred (vla); La Faro, Scott (cb); Brehm, Alvin (cb); Duvivier, George (cb); Contemporary String Quartet; Hall, James (gtr); Evans, Bill (pf); Costa, Eddie (vib); Evans, Sticks (perc)
- Atlantic 1365/SD-1365; 33m/s; rel 1961; del 1968

(Five) Bagatelles, Orchestra (1964)
[8249] Louisville Orchestra; Mester, Jorge (cond)
- LS-68-6; 33s (Louisville Orchestra First Edition Records 1968 No 6); rel 1969; cip

Concertino, Jazz Quartet and Orchestra (1959)
[8250] Modern Jazz Quartet; orchestra
- Atlantic 1359/SD-1359; 33m/s; rel 1961; del 1977

Contours (1958)
[8251] Contemporary Chamber Ensemble; Weisberg, Arthur (cond)
- Odyssey Y-34141; 33s; rel 1976; cip

Conversations (1959)
[8252] Modern Jazz Quartet; Beaux-Arts String Quartet
- Atlantic 1345/SD-1345; 33m/s; rel 1960; cip

Densities No 1 (1962)
[8253] instrumental ensemble; Farberman, Harold (cond) or Schuller, Gunther (cond)
- Cambridge CRM-820/CRS-1820; 33m/s; rel 1967; del 1971

Dramatic Overture (1951)
[8254] Louisville Orchestra; Whitney,
Robert (cond)
- LOU-66-6/LS-66-6; 33m/s
(Louisville Orchestra First Edition
Records 1966 No 6); rel 1967;
cip

**Duets, Unaccompanied Horns: Nos
1 and 3**
[8255] Smith, Calvin (hn); Zsembery,
William (hn)
- Crystal S-371; 33s; rel 1976; cip

**Fantasy, Violoncello (Op 19)
(1951)**
[8256] Christensen, Roy (vcl)
- Gasparo GS-101; 33s; rel 1975

Fantasy Quartet (1959)
[8257] Varga, Laszlo (vcl); Eskin, Jules
(vcl); Rudiakov, Michael (vcl);
Hunkins, Sterling (vcl)
- CRI-144; 33m/s; rel 1961/?; cip

(Tre) Invenzioni (1972)
[8258] instrumental ensemble; Schuller,
Gunther (cond)
- Odyssey Y-34141; 33s; rel
1976; cip

Journey into Jazz (1962)
[8259] Henderson, Skitch (nar); Hawkins,
Coleman (ten sax); Lewis, John
(pf); Orchestra USA; Schuller,
Gunther (cond) or Farberman,
Harold (cond)
- Columbia CL-2247/CS-9047;
33m/s; rel 1964; del 1966

Lines and Contrasts (1960)
[8260] Horn Club of Los Angeles; Schuller,
Gunther (cond)
- Angel S-36036; 33s; rel 1970;
cip

Meditation (1963)
[8261] Yale University Band; Wilson, Keith
(cond)
- Carillon 126; 33m; rel 1965

(Five) Moods (1972)
[8262] New York Tuba Quartet
- Crystal S-221; 33s; rel 1977; cip

Music for Brass Quintet (1961)
[8263] New York Brass Quintet
- CRI-144; 33m/s; rel 1961/?; cip

Night Music (1962)
[8264] instrumental ensemble; Farberman,
Harold (cond) or Schuller,
Gunther (cond)
- Cambridge CRM-820/CRS-1820;
33m/s; rel 1967; del 1971

Quartet, Contrabasses (1947)
[8265] Hollingsworth, Sam (cb); Spohr,
Clifford (cb); Carroll, James (cb);
Craver, Arnold (cb)
- Turnabout TVS-34412; 33s; rel
1971; del 1978

Quartet, Strings, No 1 (1957)
[8266] Composers Quartet
- Golden Crest NEC-115; 33s/q;
rel 1977; cip

[8267] Walden Quartet of the University of
Illinois
- Illini Union Bookstore CRS-5;
33m; rel 1958*

Quartet, Strings, No 2 (1966)
[8268] Emerson String Quartet
- New World NW-212; 33s; rel
1978

Quintet, Winds (1958)
[8269] Dorian Woodwind Quintet
- Vox SVBX-5307; 33s; 3 discs; rel
1977; cip

[8270] New York Woodwind Quintet
- Concert-Disc M-1229/CS-229;
33m/s; rel 1963; del 1973

Sonata, Oboe and Piano (1948-51)
[8271] Roseman, Ronald (ob); Kalish,
Gilbert (pf)
- Desto DC-7116; 33s; rel 1971;
cip

**(Seven) Studies on Themes of Paul
Klee (1959)**
[8272] Boston Symphony Orchestra;
Leinsdorf, Erich (cond)
- RCA LM-2879/LSC-2879;
33m/s; rel 1966; del 1975

[8273] Minneapolis Symphony Orchestra;
Dorati, Antal (cond)
- Mercury MG-50282/SR-90282;
33m/s; rel 1961; del 1965
- Mercury SRI-75116; 33s; rel
1980; cip

Suite, Wind Quintet (1958)
[8274] Pacific Art Woodwind Quintet
- Orion ORS-79345; 33s; rel
1980; cip

Symphony (1965)
[8275] Dallas Symphony Orchestra;
Johanos, Donald (cond)
- Turnabout TVS-34412; 33s; rel
1971; del 1978

**Symphony for Brass and Percussion
(Op 16) (1950)**
[8276] Jazz and Classical Music Society
Brass Ensemble; Mitropoulos,
Dimitri (cond) or Schuller,
Gunther (cond)
- Columbia CL-941; 33m; rel
1957; del 1959

**Symphony for Brass and Percussion
(Op 16) (1950)** *(cont'd)*
[8277] Philip Jones Brass Ensemble;
Howarth, Elgar (cond)
- Argo ZRG-731; 33s; rel 1973;
cip

Transformation (1957)
[8278] McKusik, Hal (sax); La Porta, John
(sax); Mucci, Louis (tpt); Farmer,
Art (tpt); Knepper, Jimmy (tbn);
Di Domenico, Robert (fl); Zegler,
Manuel (bsn); Evans, Bill (pf);
Charles, Teddy (vib); Benjamin,
Joe (cb); Ross, Margaret (hp);
Buffington, James (hn); Galbraith,
Barry (gtr); Sommer, Teddy
(perc); Schuller, Gunther (cond)
or Russell, George (cond)
Rec 6/20/57
- Columbia WL-127; 33m; rel
1958*
- Columbia CL-1209-10 (in set
C2L-31)/CS-8909-10 (in set
C2S-831); 33m/s; 2 discs; rel
1964; del 1969

Trio, Oboe, Horn, and Viola (1948)
[8279] Ostryniec, James (ob); Bakkegard,
David (hn); Chaves, Noah (vla)
- CRI-423; 33s; rel 1980; cip

Triplum (1967)
[8280] New York Philharmonic; Bernstein,
Leonard (cond)
- Columbia ML-6452/MS-7052;
33m/s; rel 1967; del 1973

**Variants on a Theme of John Lewis
(1960)**
[8281] Dolphy, Eric (fl); Di Domenico,
Robert (fl); Coleman, Ornette
(sax); Brown, Alfred (vla); La
Faro, Scott (cb); Brehm, Alvin
(cb); Duvivier, George (cb);
Contemporary String Quartet;
Hall, James (gtr); Evans, Bill (pf);
Costa, Eddie (vib); Evans, Sticks
(perc)
- Atlantic 1365/SD-1365; 33m/s;
rel 1961; del 1968

**Variants on a Theme of Thelonious
Monk (1960)**
[8282] Dolphy, Eric (fl); Di Domenico,
Robert (fl); Coleman, Ornette
(sax); Brown, Alfred (vla); La
Faro, Scott (cb); Brehm, Alvin
(cb); Duvivier, George (cb);
Contemporary String Quartet;
Hall, James (gtr); Evans, Bill (pf);
Costa, Eddie (vib); Evans, Sticks
(perc)
- Atlantic 1365/SD-1365; 33m/s;
rel 1961; del 1968

SCHUMAN, William (1910-)
American Festival Overture (1939)
[8283] National Symphony Orchestra;
Kindler, Hans (cond)
- Victor 18511; 78; rel pre-1942

American Festival Overture (1939)
(cont'd)
- Gramophone ED-350; 78; rel pre-1942
- Gramophone AF-562; 78; rel pre-1942

[8284] Vienna Symphony Orchestra; Hendl, Walter (cond)
- American Recording Society ARS-28; 33m; 10''; rel 1952
- American Recording Society ARS-115; 33m; rel 1953
- Desto D-404/DST-6404; 33m/s; rel 1964; cip

Anniversary Fanfare (1969)
[8285] brass and percussion ensemble; Prausnitz, Frederik (cond)
Rec 1970
- Metropolitan Museum of Art AKS-10001; 33; rel 1970

(Four) Canonic Choruses (Chorale Canons) (1932-33): Nos 1, 2, and 3
[8286] Concordia Choir; Christiansen, Paul J. (cond)
- Concordia S-1; 33s; rel 1961; del 1977

Carols of Death (1958)
[8287] Gregg Smith Singers; Smith, Gregg (cond)
- Everest LPBR-6129/SDBR-3129; 33m/s; rel 1965; cip
- Everest (English) LPBR-6129/SDBR-3129; 33m/s; rel 1972*

Casey at the Bat (1976) (Abridged)
[8288] Schuman, William (nar); soloists; Long Island Symphonic Choral Association and Orchestra; Cornell University Wind Ensemble; Smith, Gregg (cond); Stith, Marice (cond)
- EAV LE-77410; 33s; rel 1980

Choral Etude (1937)
[8289] Madrigal Singers; Engel, Lehman (cond)
Rec 3/22/39
- Columbia 17139D; 78; 10''; rel pre-1942

Concerto, Piano and Orchestra (1942)
[8290] Steigerwalt, Gary (pf); MIT Symphony Orchestra; Epstein, David (cond)
- Turnabout TVS-34733; 33s; rel 1979; cip

Concerto, Violin and Orchestra (1947, rev 1954 and 1958-59)
[8291] Zukofsky, Paul (vln); Boston Symphony Orchestra; Thomas, Michael Tilson (cond)
Rec 1970
- Deutsche Grammophon 2530.103; 33s; rel 1971; del 1979
- Deutsche Grammophon (English) 2530.103; 33s; rel 1971*
- Deutsche Grammophon (French) 2530.103; 33s

Concerto on Old English Rounds (1974)
[8292] McInnes, Donald (vla); Camerata Singers; New York Philharmonic; Bernstein, Leonard (cond)
Rec 4/17/76 and 4/22/76
- Columbia M-35101; 33s; rel 1978; cip

Credendum (Article of Faith) (1955)
[8293] Philadelphia Orchestra; Ormandy, Eugene (cond)
Rec 3/11/56
- Columbia ML-5185; 33m; rel 1957; del 1965
- Columbia CML-5185; 33m; rel 1970; del 1974
- CRI-308; 33s; rel 1973; cip

George Washington Bridge (1950)
[8294] Eastman Symphonic Wind Ensemble; Fennell, Frederick (cond)
- Mercury MG-40006; 33m; rel 1953; del 1957
- Mercury EP-1-5062; 45; 7''; rel pre-1956
- Mercury MG-50079; 33m; rel 1957; del 1969
- Mercury (English) MMA-11009; 33m; rel 1959
- Mercury SRI-75086; 33s; rel 1977

In Praise of Shahn (1969)
[8295] New York Philharmonic; Bernstein, Leonard (cond)
Rec 2/12/70
- Columbia M-30112; 33s; rel 1970; del 1979

Judith (1949)
[8296] Louisville Orchestra; Whitney, Robert (cond)
- Mercury MG-10088; 33m; rel 1952; del 1956
- LOU-60-4; 33m (Louisville Orchestra First Edition Records 1960 No 4); rel 1960; del 1974

Mail Order Madrigals (Sears, Roebuck 1897 Catalogue) (1971)
[8297] Gregg Smith Singers; Smith, Gregg (cond)
Rec 4/76
- Vox SVBX-5354; 33s; 3 discs; rel 1979

New England Triptych (1956)
[8298] Cincinnati Symphony Orchestra; Rudolf, Max (cond)
- Decca DL-710168; 33s; rel 1970; del 1973

[8299] Eastman-Rochester Symphony Orchestra; Hanson, Howard (cond)
- Mercury MG-50379/SR-90379; 33m/s; rel 1964; del 1973
- Mercury SRI-75020; 33s; rel 1974; cip

[8300] National Symphony Orchestra; Dorati, Antal (cond)
Rec 4/75
- London OS-26442; 33s; rel 1977; del 1979

[8301] New York Philharmonic; Kostelanetz, Andre (cond)
Rec 3/16/58
- Columbia ML-5347/MS-6040; 33m/s; rel 1959; del 1965
- Columbia 91-AO-2007; 33m; rel 1972; cip

[8302] Philadelphia Orchestra; Ormandy, Eugene (cond)
Rec 5/68
- RCA LSC-3060; 33s; rel 1969; del 1977
- RCA (English) SB-6798; 33s; rel 1969*
- RCA (French) 644529; 33s
- RCA (German) LSC-3060; 33s

New England Triptych: Be Glad, Then, America (band version)
[8303] Cornell University Wind Ensemble; Stith, Marice (cond)
Rec 3/20/76
- Cornell CUWE-19; 33s

New England Triptych: When Jesus Wept (band version) (1958)
[8304] Cornell University Wind Ensemble; Stith, Marice (cond)
- Cornell CUWE-9; 33s; rel 1971; cip

New England Triptych: Chester
[8305] Boston Pops Orchestra; Fiedler, Arthur (cond)
- RCA LM-2677/LSC-2677; 33m/s; rel 1963; del 1975
- RCA LSC-3277; 33s; rel 1972; cip

New England Triptych: Chester (band version)

[8306] Concord Band; Toland, William M. (cond)
Rec 10/20/75
- Vogt Quality Recordings CSRV-2503; 33s; rel 1975

[8307] Cornell University Symphonic Band; Stith, Marice (cond)
Rec 11/15/71
- Cornell CUWE-10; 33s; rel 1973; cip

[8308] Goldman Band; Goldman, Richard Franko (cond)
- Decca DL-8633/DL-78633; 33m/s; rel 1958; del 1973

[8309] University of Miami Symphonic Band
- King 682; 33m/s; rel 1960; del 1965

[8310] University of Michigan Band; Revelli, William (cond)
- Vanguard VRS-9114/VSD-2124; 33m/s; rel 1963; cip

Orpheus and his Lute (1944) (arr for voice and gtr)

[8311] Rees, Rosalind (sop); Starobin, David (gtr)
Rec 1976
- Turnabout TVS-34727; 33s; rel 1978

Prayer in Time of War (1943)

[8312] Louisville Orchestra; Mester, Jorge (cond)
Rec 3/16/72
- LS-72-1; 33s (Louisville Orchestra First Edition Records 1972 No 1); rel 1973; cip

Prelude (1939)

[8313] Concordia Choir; Christiansen, Paul J. (cond)
- Concordia CDLP-6; 33m; rel 1958; del 1974

[8314] Rees, Rosalind (sop); Gregg Smith Singers; Smith, Gregg (cond)
Rec 1976
- Vox SVBX-5353; 33s; 3 discs; rel 1979; cip

Quartet, Strings, No 3 (1939)

[8315] Gordon String Quartet
- Concert Hall AB; 78; 3 discs; rel 1946

[8316] Juilliard String Quartet
- RCA LM-2481/LSC-2481; 33m/s; rel 1961; del 1964

[8317] Kohon Quartet
- Vox SVBX-5305; 33s; 3 discs; rel 1974; cip

Quartet, Strings, No 4 (1950)

[8318] Juilliard String Quartet
- Columbia ML-4493; 33m; rel 1952; del 1958

Quartettino, Bassoons (1939)

[8319] Cohen, Sam (bsn); Knitzer, Jack (bsn); Kutzing, Erika (bsn); Sharrow, Leonard (bsn)
- New Music Quarterly Recordings 1415; 78; rel 1939

Song of Orpheus, A (1961)

[8320] Rose, Leonard (vcl); Cleveland Orchestra; Szell, George (cond)
Rec 1/11/64
- Columbia ML-6038/MS-6638; 33m/s; rel 1964; cip
- Columbia (English) CX-1937/SAX-2575; 33m/s; rel 1965*
- Epic (French) 82002/S-82002; 33m/s

Symphony No 3 (1941)

[8321] New York Philharmonic; Bernstein, Leonard (cond)
- Columbia ML-5645/MS-6245; 33m/s; rel 1961; del 1968
- Columbia CML-5645/CMS-6245; 33m/s; rel 1968; del 1973
- Columbia MS-7442; 33s; rel 1970; cip

[8322] Philadelphia Orchestra; Ormandy, Eugene (cond)
Rec 3/11/51
- Columbia ML-4413; 33m; rel 1951; del 1960

Symphony No 4 (1941)

[8323] Louisville Orchestra; Mester, Jorge (cond)
- LS-69-2; 33s (Louisville Orchestra First Edition Records 1969 No 2); rel 1969; cip

Symphony No 5 (Symphony for Strings) (1943)

[8324] Concert Hall Symphony Orchestra; Schenkman, Edgar (cond)
- Concert Hall A-11; 78; 2 discs; rel 1947
- Concert Hall CHS-1078; 33m; rel 1951; del 1957

[8325] New York Philharmonic; Bernstein, Leonard (cond)
Rec 10/20/66
- Columbia MS-7442; 33s; rel 1970; cip

[8326] Pittsburgh Symphony Orchestra String Sinfonia; Steinberg, William (cond)
Rec 11/52
- ASCAP CB-152; 33m (Pittsburgh International Contemporary Music Festival); rel 1952
- Capitol S-8212; 33m; rel 1953; del 1959
- Capitol CTL-7039; 33m; rel 1953*
- Telefunken LCE-8212; 33m; rel pre-1956

Symphony No 6 (1948)

[8327] Philadelphia Orchestra; Ormandy, Eugene (cond)
Rec 11/15/53
- Columbia ML-4992; 33m; rel 1955; del 1968
- Columbia CML-4992; 33m; rel 1968; del 1974
- Columbia AML-4992; 33m; rel 1974; cip

Symphony No 7 (1960)

[8328] Utah Symphony Orchestra; Abravanel, Maurice (cond)
- Turnabout TVS-34447; 33s; rel 1971; cip
- Turnabout (English) TVS-34447; 33s; rel 1973*
- Turnabout (German) TVS-34447; 33s

Symphony No 8 (1962)

[8329] New York Philharmonic; Bernstein, Leonard (cond)
Rec 10/14/62
- Columbia ML-5912/MS-6512; 33m/s; rel 1963; del 1970
- Columbia CMS-6512; 33s; rel 1970; del 1970
- Odyssey Y-34140; 33s; rel 1976; cip

Symphony No 9 (Le fosse ardeatine) (1968)

[8330] Philadelphia Orchestra; Ormandy, Eugene (cond)
- RCA LSC-3212; 33s; rel 1971; del 1977

Te Deum (1944)

[8331] Washington University Choir; Weiss, Don (cond)
- Aspen 1511; 33m; rel 1958; del 1960

Three-Score Set (1943)

[8332] Carpenter, Richard (pf)
- Educo 3105; 33

[8333] Foldes, Andor (pf)
- Vox 16070 (in set 174); 78; 10"; rel 1947

To Thee Old Cause (1968)

[8334] Gomberg, Harold (ob); New York Philharmonic; Bernstein, Leonard (cond)
Rec 10/22/68
- Columbia MS-7392; 33s; rel 1970; del 1973

Undertow (1945)

[8335] Ballet Theatre Orchestra; Levine, Joseph (cond)
Rec 4/21/53
- Capitol CTL-7040; 33m; rel 1953*
- Capitol P-8238; 33m; rel 1954; del 1960
- Capitol (Australian) CLCX-047; 33m; rel pre-1956

Undertow (1945) *(cont'd)*
- Capitol HDR-21004; 33m; 4 discs; rel 1966; del 1970
- New World NW-253; 33m; rel 1978

[8336] Louisville Orchestra; Schuman, William (cond)
- Mercury MG-10088; 33m; rel 1952; del 1956

Voyage (1953)
[8337] Webster, Beveridge (pf)
Rec 6/9/54 and 9/23/54
- Columbia ML-4987; 33m; rel 1955; del 1968
- Columbia CML-4987; 33m; rel 1968; del 1974
- Columbia AML-4987; 33m; rel 1974; cip

SCHUMANN, Walter (1913-58)

Apostle's Creed, The
[8338] Voices of Walter Schumann
- Capitol L-382; 33m; 10"; rel 1953; del 1957

SCHWANTER, Joseph (1943-)

. . . And the Mountains Rising Nowhere
[8339] Eastman Symphonic Wind Ensemble; Hunsberger, Donald (cond)
Rec 11/6-7/81
- Mercury SRI-75132; 33s; rel 1980; cip

Autumn Canticles (1974)
[8340] Western Arts Trio
- Laurel LR-104; 33s; rel 1976; cip

Consortium I (1968)
[8341] Boston Musica Viva; Pittman, Richard (cond)
- Delos DEL-25406; 33s; rel 1975; cip

Consortium III (Modus caelestis) (1972)
[8342] Shearer, Grieg (fl); New England Conservatory Repertory Orchestra; Pittman, Richard (cond)
Rec 5/73
- CRI-340; 33s; rel 1975; cip

Diaphonia intervallum (1965)
[8343] Morosco, Victor (sax); Contemporary Chamber Ensemble; Weisberg, Arthur (cond)
- Nonesuch H-71221; 33s; rel 1969; cip

In aeternam (1973)
[8344] Boston Musica Viva; Pittman, Richard (cond)
- Delos DEL-25406; 33s; rel 1975; cip

SCHWARTZ, Elliott (1936-)

Aria No 1, Clarinet and Piano
[8345] Blustine, Allen (cl); Schwartz, Elliott (pf)
- Advance FGR-7; 33m; rel 1969; cip

Aria No 2, Violin and Drums
[8346] Furney, Jo Anne (vln); Thrailkill, Gene (drs)
- Advance FGR-7; 33m; rel 1969; cip

Aria No 4, Bassoon
[8347] Pachman, Maurice (bsn)
- Advance FGR-7; 33m; rel 1969; cip

Concert Piece for Ten Players (1965)
[8348] New Cantata Orchestra of London; Dufallo, Richard (cond)
- Ars Nova/Ars Antiqua AN-1002; 33s; rel 1969; del 1973
- Opus One 23; 33s; rel 1975; cip

Essays (1966)
[8349] Patti, Douglas (tpt); Smith, Robert D. (tbn)
- Advance FGR-7; 33m; rel 1969; cip

Extended Oboe (1975)
[8350] Celli, Joseph (ob); tape
- Organic Oboe OO-1; 33s

Interruptions (1965)
[8351] University of Oregon Woodwind Quintet
- Advance FGR-11S; 33s; rel 1973; cip

Signals (1968)
[8352] Fulkerson, James (tbn); Molfese, Nicholas (cb)
- Deutsche Grammophon 2543.005; 33s; rel 1971; del 1975

(Four) Studies, Two Clarinets (1964)
[8353] Rehfeldt, Phillip (cl); Gates, John (cl)
- Advance FGR-15S; 33s; rel 1973; cip

Texture (1966)
[8354] New Cantata Orchestra of London; Dufallo, Richard (cond)
- Ars Nova/Ars Antiqua AN-1002; 33s; rel 1969; del 1973
- Opus One 23; 33s; rel 1975; cip

SCHWARTZ, Elliott and BROWN, Marion

see **BROWN, Marion and SCHWARTZ, Elliott**

SCHWARTZ, Paul (1907-)

Concertino, Chamber Orchestra (1937, rev 1947)
[8355] Zurich Radio Orchestra; Monod, Jacques (cond)
- CRI-128; 33m; rel 1960; cip

Vienna Baroque Suite
[8356] Capital University Clarinet Choir; Hite, David (cond)
- Coronet S-1509; 33s; rel 1969; del 1978

SCIANNI, Joseph (1928-)

Adagio cantabile
[8357] Eastman-Rochester Symphony Orchestra; Hanson, Howard (cond)
Rec 1958
- Mercury MG-50053/SR-90053; 33m/s; rel 1959; del 1964
- Eastman-Rochester Archives ERA-1003; 33s; rel 1974; cip

SCOTT, Raymond (1909-)

Soothing Sounds for Baby
[8358] Electronic music
- Epic LN-24083-85; 33m; 3 discs; rel 1964

Toy Trumpet, The
[8359] Boston Pops Orchestra; Fiedler, Arthur (cond)
- Victor 4456; 78; 10"; rel 1940
- Victor M-554; 78; 2-10" and 4-12"; rel 194?

SCOTT, Thomas Jefferson (1912-61)

Binorie Variations (1953)
[8360] Vienna Orchestra; Adler, F. Charles (cond)
- CRI-104; 33m/s; rel 1956/?; cip

Creation
[8361] Rhapsody in White and the Baylor Bards
- Austin 6241; 33m; rel 1963; del 1976

Go Down Death (1954)
[8362] Pfeiffer College Concert Choir; Brewer, Richard (cond)
- Pfeiffer 1; 33m; rel 1966; del 1968

Hornpipe and Chantey (1944)
[8363] Vienna Orchestra; Adler, F. Charles (cond)
- CRI-104; 33m/s; rel 1956/?; cip

Sea Shanties
[8364] Warren, Leonard (bar); chorus; orchestra; Levine, M. (cond)
- RCA LM-1168; 33m; rel 1951; del 1976

SCOVILLE, Margaret Lee (1944-)

Ostinato, Fantasy, and Fugue
[8365] Skipworth, George (pf)
- Educo 3097; 33

Pentacycle
[8366] Skipworth, George (pf)
- Educo 3097; 33

SEAVER, Blanche Ebert (1891-)

Calling Me Back To You
[8367] McCormack, John (ten); orchestra
- Victor 1197; 78; 10''; rel 1926

Just for Today
[8368] Gorin, Igor (bar); orchestra;
Voorhees, Donald (cond)
- Allied 2000; 33m; 10''; rel
1953; del 1957
- Allied EP-2000; 45; 7''

[8369] McCormack, John (ten); orchestra
- Camden CAL-635; 33m; rel
1960; del 1972

SEBASTIAN, John (1915-80)

Etude ala flamenca
[8370] Sebastian, John (harmonica); Josi,
Renato (hpschd) or (pf)
- Deutsche Grammophon
DGM-12015/DGS-712015;
33m/s; rel 1959; del 1961

Serenade
[8371] Sebastian, John (harmonica);
Clugston, Glen (pf)
- Decca DL-10025/DL-710025;
33m/s; rel 1960; del 1975

SECUNDA, Sholom (1894-1974)

Welcoming the Sabbath (Kabbalat shabbat)
[8372] Tucker, Richard (ten); choir;
Secunda, Sholom (cond)
- Columbia ML-5119; 33m; rel
1956; del 1971

SEEGER, Ruth Crawford
see CRAWFORD SEEGER, Ruth

SEITZ, Roland F. (1867-1946)

Grandioso
[8373] Eastman Symphonic Wind
Ensemble; Fennell, Frederick
(cond)
Rec 10/19/57
- Mercury MG-50170/SR-90170;
33m/s; rel 1958/1959; del
1965

[8374] Goldman Band; Cox, Ainslee (cond)
- New World NW-266; 33s; rel
1977

SELETSKY, Harold (1927-)

Christ in Concrete
[8375] Wallach, Eli (speaker); orchestra
- Da Vinci DRC-205; 33m; rel
1964

SELF, William (1906-)

Hymn of Praise
[8376] All Saints' Church Male Choir; Self,
William (cond)
- Classic Editions CE-1023; 33m;
rel 1953; del 1961

SELIG, Robert (1939-)

Mirage (1968)
[8377] Ghitalla, Armando (tpt); Chamber
Orchestra of Copenhagen;
Moriarty, John (cond)
- Cambridge CRS-2823; 33s; rel
1970; cip

SEMEGEN, Daria (1946-)

Arc (1977)
[8378] Electronic music
- Finnadar SR-9020; 33s; rel
1978; cip

**Electronic Composition No 1
(1971-72)**
[8379] Electronic music
- Odyssey Y-34139; 33s; rel
1976; cip$_s$

SEMMLER, Alexander (1900-77)

**Trio, Violin, Violoncello, and Piano
(Op 40) (1964)**
[8380] Philharmonia Trio
- CRI-211; 33m/s; rel 1966/?; cip

SEREBRIER, Jose (1938-)

Partita (1957-58)
[8381] Louisville Orchestra; Whitney,
Robert (cond)
- LOU-64-1; 33m (Louisville
Orchestra First Edition Records
1964 No 1); rel 1964; cip

Symphony for Percussion (1964)
[8382] Tristan Fry Percussion Ensemble;
Gardiner, John Eliot (cond)
- Gale 004; 33s; rel 1979; cip

SERLY, Tibor (1901-78)

American Elegy (1945)
[8383] New London Orchestra; Autori,
Franco (cond)
- Bartok BRS-304; 33m; rel 1952;
del 1953
- Musical Heritage Society
MHS-3590; 33m; rel 1977

**American Fantasy of Quodlibets
(1950)**
[8384] Vienna Volksoper Orchestra; Serly,
Tibor (cond)
- Musical Heritage Society
MHS-3590; 33s; rel 1977

Canonic Prelude (1967)
[8385] New York Harp Ensemble;
Wurtzler, Aristid von (cond)
- Musical Heritage Society
MHS-1844; 33s; rel 1974

Concertino 3 x 3 (1967)
[8386] Molin, Miriam (pf); Master Virtuosi
of London; Serly, Tibor (cond)
- Musical Heritage Society
MHS-3360; 33s; rel 1976

**Concerto, Two Pianos and
Orchestra (1943-58)**
[8387] Frid, Geza (pf); Ponse, Luctor (pf);
Vienna Volksoper Orchestra;
Serly, Tibor (cond)
- Keyboard K-102M/K-102S;
33m/s; rel 1968*
- Musical Heritage Society
MHS-3337; 33s; rel 1976

**Concerto, Trombone and Chamber
Orchestra (1953)**
[8388] Shuman, Davis (tbn); orchestra;
Serly, Tibor (cond)
- Audio Fidelity 1811; 33m; rel
1956; del 1962

**Concerto, Viola and Orchestra
(1929)**
[8389] Vardi, Emanuel (vla); Vienna
Symphony Orchestra; Serly, Tibor
(cond)
- Keyboard K-101M/K-101S;
33m/s; rel 1967
- Musical Heritage Society
MHS-3306; 33s; rel 1976

**Concerto, Violin and Winds
(1953-58)**
[8390] Vardi, Emanuel (vln); Vienna
Symphony Orchestra; Serly, Tibor
(cond)
- Musical Heritage Society
MHS-3306; 33s; rel 1976

David of the White Rock
[8391] Vardi, Emanuel (vla); Vardi, Pauline
(pf)
- Musical Heritage Society
MHS-3590; 33s; rel 1977

**Fantasy on a Double Quodlibet
(1973)**
[8392] New York Harp Ensemble;
Wurtzler, Aristid von (cond)
- Musical Heritage Society
MHS-3307; 33s; rel 1975

Forget-Me-Not
[8393] Stanford, Carolyn (m sop); Vienna
Volksoper Orchestra; Serly, Tibor
(cond)
- Musical Heritage Society
MHS-3447; 33s; rel 1976
- Musical Heritage Society
MHS-3590; 33s; rel 1977

Innovations (1933-34)
[8394] Wurtzler, Aristid von (hp);
Connecticut String Quartet
- Musical Heritage Society
MHS-3370; 33s; rel 1976

Lament (Homage to Bela Bartok) (1955)
[8395] Kunstmaand Chamber Orchestra of
Holland; Serly, Tibor (cond)
- Musical Heritage Society
MHS-3447; 33m; rel 1976

Miniature Suite, Twelve Wind Instruments (1947)
[8396] chamber orchestra; Serly, Tibor
(cond)
- Audio Fidelity 1811; 33m; rel
1956; del 1962

Rhapsody, Viola and Orchestra (1948) (arr for vla and pf)
[8397] Vardi, Emanuel (vla); Harrington,
Grace (pf)
- Musical Heritage Society
MHS-3590; 33s; rel 1977

Sonata, Violin (1947)
[8398] Magnes, Frances (vln)
- Bartok BRS-908; 33m; rel 1952;
cip

(Four) Songs from Chamber Music (1926)
[8399] Stanford, Carolyn (m sop); Vienna
Volksoper Orchestra; Serly, Tibor
(cond)
- Keyboard K-101M/K-101S;
33m/s; rel 1967
- Musical Heritage Society
MHS-3447; 33s; rel 1976

Strange Story (1927)
[8400] Stanford, Carolyn (m sop); Vienna
Volksoper Orchestra; Serly, Tibor
(cond)
- Keyboard K-101M/K-101S;
33m/s; rel 1967
- Musical Heritage Society
MHS-3447; 33s; rel 1976

Symphony No 2 (1932)
[8401] Vienna Symphony Orchestra; Serly,
Tibor (cond)
- Musical Heritage Society
MHS-3360; 33s; rel 1976

Symphony in Four Cycles (1960)
[8402] Kunstmaand Chamber Orchestra of
Holland; Serly, Tibor (cond)
- Musical Heritage Society
MHS-3447; 33m; rel 1976

SESSIONS, Roger (1896-)
Black Maskers, The (Suite) (1928)
[8403] Eastman-Rochester Symphony
Orchestra; Hanson, Howard
(cond)
- Mercury MG-50106; 33m; rel
1956; del 1964

Black Maskers, The (Suite) (1928)
(cont'd)
- Mercury SR-90103; 33s; rel
1959; del 1964
- Mercury MG-50423/SR-90423;
33m/s; rel 1965; del 1972
- Mercury SRI-75049; 33s; rel
1975; cip

[8404] Vienna Symphony Orchestra;
Hendl, Walter (cond)
- American Recording Society
ARS-11; 33m; 10"; rel 1953
- American Recording Society
ARS-115; 33m; rel 1953
- Desto D-404/DST-6404; 33m/s;
rel 1964; cip

Chorale No 1 (1926)
[8405] Andrews, Mildred (org)
- University of Oklahoma 2; 33m;
rel 1957; del 1978

[8406] Gay, Harry W. (org)
- B & C BC-12435; 33m; rel
1958

[8407] Hillsman, Walter (org)
Rec 5/10-11/76
- Vista VPS-1038; 33s; rel 1976

[8408] Mason, Marilyn (org)
Rec 12/53
- Esoteric ES-522; 33m; rel 1954;
del 1964
- Counterpoint/Esoteric
CPT-522/CPST-5522; 33m/s;
rel 1964/1966; del 1974

[8409] Smith, Melville (org)
Rec 2/10/59
- Organ Historical Society F-MS-I-II;
33m; rel 1965

(Three) Chorale Preludes (1926)
[8410] Fillinger, Valentina Woshner (org)
Rec 11/29/52
- ASCAP CB-189; 33m (Pittsburgh
International Contemporary Music
Festival); rel 1954

[8411] Mason, Marilyn (org)
Rec 12/53
- Esoteric ES-522; 33m; rel 1954;
del 1964
- Counterpoint/Esoteric
CPT-522/CPST-5522; 33m/s;
rel 1964/1966; del 1974

Concertino, Chamber Orchestra (1972)
[8412] University of Chicago
Contemporary Chamber Players;
Shapey, Ralph (cond)
- Desto DC-7155; 33s; rel 1973;
cip

Concerto, Violin and Orchestra (1935)
[8413] Zukofsky, Paul (vln); ORTF
Philharmonic Orchestra; Schuller,
Gunther (cond)
- CRI-220; 33s; rel 1968; cip

Duo, Violin and Piano (1942)
[8414] Travers, Patricia (vln); Herz, Otto
(pf)
- Columbia MM-987; 78; rel
pre-1952
- Columbia ML-2169; 33m; 10";
rel 1952; del 1956

[8415] Zukofsky, Paul (vln); Kalish, Gilbert
(pf)
- Desto DC-6435-37; 33s; 3 discs;
rel 1975; cip

From My Diary (1939-40)
[8416] Abramowitsch, Bernhard (pf)
- Music Library MLR-5000; 33m;
10"; rel 1952; del 1968
- Music Library MLR-7003; 33m;
rel 1952; del 1974

[8417] Ajemian, Maro (pf)
- MGM E-3218; 33m; rel 1956;
del 1959

[8418] Fleisher, Leon (pf)
- Epic LC-3862/BC-1262; 33m/s;
rel 1963; del 1966

[8419] Rogers, Herbert (pf)
- CRI-281; 33s; rel 1972; cip

[8420] Shields, Roger (pf)
- Vox SVBX-5303; 33s; 3 discs; rel
1977; cip

[8421] Weiser, Bernhard (pf)
- New Editions 1; 33m; rel 1952;
del 1959

From My Diary: No 1
[8422] Foldes, Andor (pf)
- Vox 16070 (in set 174); 78;
10"; rel 1947

Idyll of Theocritus (1954)
[8423] Nossaman, Audrey (sop); Louisville
Orchestra; Whitney, Robert (cond)
- LOU-57-4; 33m (Louisville
Orchestra First Edition Records
1957 No 4); rel 1959; del 1972

March
[8424] Martin, Charlotte (pf)
- Educo 3021; 33m; rel 1968; del
1972

On the Beach at Fontana (1929)
[8425] Beardslee, Bethany (sop); Helps,
Robert (pf)
- New World NW-243; 33s; rel
1977

(Six) Pieces, Violoncello (1966)
[8426] Christensen, Roy (vcl)
- Gasparo GS-102; 33s; rel 1976

Quartet, Strings, No 1 (1936)
[8427] Amado String Quartet
- Apex S-1243; 33s; rel 1972*

[8428] Galimir String Quartet
- Guild; 78; 4 discs; rel pre-1943

Quartet, Strings, No 1 (1936)
(cont'd)
[8429] Pro Arte Quartet
Rec 2/2/45
- New World NW-302; 33m; rel
1979

Quartet, Strings, No 2 (1951)
[8430] Kohon Quartet
- Vox SVBX-5305; 33s; 3 discs; rel
1974; cip

[8431] New Music String Quartet
- Columbia ML-5105; 33m; rel
1956; del 1970

Rhapsody, Orchestra (1970)
[8432] New Philharmonia Orchestra;
Prausnitz, Frederik (cond)
- Argo ZRG-702; 33s; rel 1974;
cip

Sonata, Piano, No 1 (1928-30)
[8433] Helps, Robert (pf)
- CRI-198; 33m/s; rel
1965/1972; cip

Sonata, Piano, No 2 (1946)
[8434] Abramowitsch, Bernhard (pf)
- Music Library MLR-49-50; 78; 2
discs; rel pre-1952
- Music Library MLR-5000; 33m;
10"; rel 1952; del 1968
- Music Library MLR-7003; 33m;
rel 1952; del 1974

[8435] Marks, Alan (pf)
Rec 1/77
- CRI-385; 33s; rel 1979; cip

[8436] Webster, Beveridge (pf)
- Dover HCR-5265/HCRST-7265;
33m/s; rel 1966/1967; del
1975
- Dover HCRST-7014; 33s; rel
1966; del 1967

Sonata, Piano, No 3 (1965)
[8437] Helps, Robert (pf)
- Acoustic Research AR-0654.086;
33s; rel 1971
- New World NW-307; 33s; rel
1980

Sonata, Violin (1953)
[8438] Bress, Hyman (vln)
- Folkways FM-3355; 33m; rel
1963; cip

[8439] Gross, Robert (vln)
- Orion ORS-73110; 33s; rel
1973; cip

[8440] Zukofsky, Paul (vln)
Rec 5/5/76
- CP2 1; 33s; rel 1976

Symphony No 1 (1927)
[8441] Japan Philharmonic Symphony
Orchestra; Watanabe, Akeo
(cond)
- CRI-131; 33m/s; rel
1960/1971; cip

Symphony No 2 (1946)
[8442] New York Philharmonic;
Mitropoulos, Dimitri (cond)
- Columbia MM-920; 78; rel 1948
- Columbia ML-2120; 33m; 10";
rel 1950; del 1954
- Columbia ML-4784; 33m; rel
1954; del 1961
- CRI-278; 33s; rel 1972; cip

Symphony No 3 (1957)
[8443] Royal Philharmonic Orchestra;
Buketoff, Igor (cond)
- RCA LSC-3095; 33s; rel 1969;
del 1974

Symphony No 8 (1968)
[8444] New Philharmonia Orchestra;
Prausnitz, Frederik (cond)
- Argo ZRG-702; 33s; rel 1974;
cip

Turn, O Libertad (1944)
[8445] Gregg Smith Singers; Cybriwsky,
Oresta (pf); Beegle, Raymond
(pf); Smith, Gregg (cond)
Rec 1976
- Vox SVBX-5353; 33s; 3 discs; rel
1979; cip

**When Lilacs Last in the Dooryard
Bloom'd (1970)**
[8446] Hinds, Esther (sop); Quivar,
Florence (m sop); Cossa, Dominic
(bar); Tanglewood Festival
Chorus; Boston Symphony
Orchestra; Ozawa, Seiji (cond)
- New World NW-296; 33s; rel
1978

SHACKELFORD, Rudy (1944-)
Tombeau de Stravinsky, Le (1971)
[8447] Palmer, Larry (hpschd)
- Musical Heritage Society
MHS-3222; 33s; rel 1975

SHADWELL, Nancy*
Theme and Variations
[8448] Endsley, Gerald (tpt)
- Clarino SLP-1006; 33s; rel
1974*

SHAFFER, Sherwood (1934-)
**Sonata, Contrabass and Piano
(1965)**
[8449] Peters, Lynn (cb); Barrow, Rebecca
(pf)
- Ubres SN-202; 33s; rel 1976;
cip

SHAHAN, Paul W. (1923-)
Leipzig Towers (1955)
[8450] Vienna State Opera Orchestra
Brass Ensemble; Stone, Sayard
(cond)
- Westminster
XWN-18931/WST-14113;
33m/s; rel 1960; del 1965

Leipzig Towers (1955) *(cont'd)*
- Westminster
WM-1008/WMS-1008; 33m/s; 3
discs; rel 1965; del 1971

SHALLENBERG, Robert (1930-)
Lilacs (1966)
[8451] New Music Choral Ensemble;
Gaburo, Kenneth (cond)
- Ars Nova/Ars Antiqua AN-1005;
33s; rel 1971; del 1973

SHAPERO, Harold (1920-)
Credo (1955)
[8452] Louisville Orchestra; Whitney,
Robert (cond)
- LOU-56-5; 33m (Louisville
Orchestra First Edition Records
1956 No 5); rel 1959; cip

**On Green Mountain (Chaconne after
Monteverdi) (1958)**
[8453] McKusik, Hal (sax); La Porta, John
(sax); Mucci, Louis (tpt); Farmer,
Art (tpt); Knepper, Jimmy (tbn);
Di Domenico, Robert (fl); Zegler,
Manuel (bsn); Evans, Bill (pf);
Charles, Teddy (vib); Benjamin,
Joe (cb); Ross, Margaret (hp);
Buffington, James (hn); Galbraith,
Barry (gtr); Sommer, Teddy (dr);
Schuller, Gunther (cond) or
Russell, George (cond)
Rec 6/20/57
- Columbia WL-127; 33m; rel
1958*
- Columbia CL-2109-10 (in set
C2L-31)/CS-8909-10 (in set
C2S-831); 33m/s; 2 discs; rel
1964; del 1969

**Partita, Piano and Chamber
Orchestra (1960)**
[8454] Owen, Benjamin (pf); Louisville
Orchestra; Whitney, Robert (cond)
- LOU-67-4/LS-67-4; 33m/s
(Louisville Orchestra First Edition
Records 1967 No 4); rel 1967;
cip

Quartet, Strings (1940)
[8455] Koff, Robert (vln); Bellam, Paul
(vln); Trampler, Walter (vla);
McCracken, Charles (vcl)
- Columbia ML-5576/MS-6176;
33m/s; rel 1960; del 1968
- Columbia CML-5576/CMS-6176;
33m/s; rel 1968; del 1974
- Columbia AMS-6176; 33s; rel
1974; cip

Serenade, Strings (1945)
[8456] Arthur Winograd String Orchestra;
Winograd, Arthur (cond)
- MGM E-3557; 33m; rel 1957;
del 1959

Sonata, Piano, No 1 (1942)
[8457] Glazer, Frank (pf)
- Concert-Disc M-1217/CS-217;
  33m/s; rel 1960; del 1977

[8458] Marlowe, Sylvia (hpschd)
- Decca DL-10021/DL-710021;
  33m/s; rel 1961; del 1971

[8459] Weiser, Bernhard (pf)
- New Editions 1; 33m; rel 1952;
  del 1959

Sonata, Piano, Four Hands (1941)
[8460] Shapero, Harold (pf); Smit, Leo (pf)
- Columbia ML-4841; 33m; rel
  1954; del 1968
- Columbia CML-4841; 33m; rel
  1968; del 1974
- Columbia AML-4841; 33m; rel
  1974; del 1979

Sonata, Trumpet and Piano (1939)
[8461] Stith, Marice (tpt); Raleigh, Stuart
  W. (pf)
- Redwood RRES-4; 33s; rel 1977;
  cip

Symphony, Classical Orchestra (1947)
[8462] Columbia Symphony Orchestra;
  Bernstein, Leonard (cond)
- Columbia ML-4889; 33m; rel
  1954; del 1966
- CRI-424; 33s; rel 1980; cip

SHAPEY, Ralph (1921-)
Configurations (1965)
[8463] Sollberger, Sophie (fl); Black,
  Robert (pf)
- New World NW-254; 33s; rel
  1978

Evocation (1959)
[8464] Raimondi, Matthew (vln); Wyner,
  Yehudi (pf); Price, Paul (perc)
- CRI-141; 33m; rel 1961; cip

[8465] Zukofsky, Paul (vln); Kalish, Gilbert
  (pf); DesRoches, Raymond (perc)
- Desto DC-6435-37; 33s; 3 discs;
  rel 1975; cip

Fromm Variations
[8466] Black, Robert (pf)
- CRI-428; 33s; rel 1980; cip

Incantations (1961)
[8467] Beardslee, Bethany (sop);
  University of Chicago
  Contemporary Chamber Players;
  Shapey, Ralph (cond)
- CRI-232; 33s; rel 1969; cip

Praise (1971)
[8468] Geiger, Paul (b bar); University of
  Chicago Contemporary Chamber
  Players; chorus; Shapey, Ralph
  (cond)
- CRI-355; 33s; rel 1976; cip

Quartet, Strings, No 6 (1963)
[8469] University of Chicago
  Contemporary Chamber Players
- CRI-275; 33s; rel 1972; cip

Quartet, Strings, No 7 (1972)
[8470] University of Chicago
  Contemporary Chamber Players
  Rec 4/77
- CRI-391; 33s; rel 1978; cip

Rhapsody, Oboe and Piano (1957)
[8471] Ostryniec, James (ob); Wuorinen,
  Charles (pf)
- CRI-423; 33s; rel 1980; cip

Rituals (1959)
[8472] London Sinfonietta; Shapey, Ralph
  (cond)
- CRI-275; 33s; rel 1972; cip

Seven (1963)
[8473] Salkind, Milton (pf); Salkind, Peggy
  (pf)
- Friends of Four-Hand Music
  SKD-1027; 33; rel 1965; del
  1974

Songs of Ecstasy (1967)
[8474] Pilgrim, Neva (sop); Cobb, John
  (pf); University of Chicago
  Contemporary Chamber Players;
  tape; Shapey, Ralph (cond)
- Desto DC-7124; 33s; rel 1971;
  cip

SHAPLEIGH, Bertram (1871-1940)
Andante
[8475] Majeske, Daniel (vln); Stein,
  Thelma (pf)
- Bertram Shapleigh Foundation
  B-13865-66 (matrix no); 33; rel
  196?

Arise, O Moon
[8476] Sehm, Isolde (sop); Stein, Thelma
  (pf)
- Bertram Shapleigh Foundation
  F8OP-8314-15 (matrix no);
  33m; rel 1963

Aubade
[8477] Majeske, Daniel (vln); Stein,
  Thelma (pf)
- Bertram Shapleigh Foundation
  B-13865-66 (matrix no); 33; rel
  196?

Ave Maria
[8478] Sehm, Isolde (sop); Olefsky, Paul
  (vcl); Stein, Thelma (pf)
- Bertram Shapleigh Foundation
  F8OP-8314-15 (matrix no);
  33m; rel 1963

Ebbrezze d'amore
[8479] Sehm, Isolde (sop); Orenstein,
  Martin (fl); Stein, Thelma (pf)
- Bertram Shapleigh Foundation
  F8OP-8314-15 (matrix no);
  33m; rel 1963

Fitnes Gesang: Fitnes sehnen
[8480] Sehm, Isolde (sop); Orenstein,
  Martin (fl); Stein, Thelma (pf)
- Bertram Shapleigh Foundation
  F8OP-8314-15 (matrix no);
  33m; rel 1963

Getaeuschtes Erwachen
[8481] Sehm, Isolde (sop); Stein, Thelma
  (pf)
- Bertram Shapleigh Foundation
  F8OP-8314-15 (matrix no);
  33m; rel 1963

Ha da venir
[8482] Sehm, Isolde (sop); Stein, Thelma
  (pf)
- Bertram Shapleigh Foundation
  F8OP-8314-15 (matrix no);
  33m; rel 1963

Intermezzo
[8483] Majeske, Daniel (vln); Stein,
  Thelma (pf)
- Bertram Shapleigh Foundation
  B-13865-66 (matrix no); 33; rel
  196?

Ishtar: Aria
[8484] Sehm, Isolde (sop); Stein, Thelma
  (pf)
- Bertram Shapleigh Foundation
  F8OP-8314-15 (matrix no);
  33m; rel 1963

Legende
[8485] Majeske, Daniel (vln); Stein,
  Thelma (pf)
- Bertram Shapleigh Foundation
  B-13865-66 (matrix no); 33; rel
  196?

Meditation
[8486] Majeske, Daniel (vln); Stein,
  Thelma (pf)
- Bertram Shapleigh Foundation
  B-13865-66 (matrix no); 33; rel
  196?

Minuet
[8487] Majeske, Daniel (vln); Stein,
  Thelma (pf)
- Bertram Shapleigh Foundation
  B-13865-66 (matrix no); 33; rel
  196?

Nachtigall und Rose
[8488] Sehm, Isolde (sop); Orenstein,
  Martin (fl); Stein, Thelma (pf)
- Bertram Shapleigh Foundation
  F8OP-8314-15 (matrix no);
  33m; rel 1963

Nachtlied
[8489] Sehm, Isolde (sop); Orenstein,
Martin (fl); Stein, Thelma (pf)
- Bertram Shapleigh Foundation
F8OP-8314-15 (matrix no);
33m; rel 1963

Nordic Cradle Song
[8490] Majeske, Daniel (vln); Stein,
Thelma (pf)
- Bertram Shapleigh Foundation
B-13865-66 (matrix no); 33; rel
196?

On the Terrace
[8491] Majeske, Daniel (vln); Stein,
Thelma (pf)
- Bertram Shapleigh Foundation
B-13865-66 (matrix no); 33; rel
196?

Pieces, Violoncello and Piano
[8492] Olefsky, Paul (vcl); Stein, Thelma
(pf)
- Bertram Shapleigh Foundation
F8OP-8999-9000 (matrix no);
33m; rel 1963

Quartet, Strings, G Major
[8493] Staples, Gordon (vln); Majeske,
Daniel (vln); Parnas, Richard
(vla); Olefsky, Paul (vcl)
- Bertram Shapleigh Foundation
F8OP-8299 (matrix no); 33m; rel
1963

Rapture
[8494] Sehm, Isolde (sop); Stein, Thelma
(pf)
- Bertram Shapleigh Foundation
F8OP-8314-15 (matrix no);
33m; rel 1963

Rest
[8495] Sehm, Isolde (sop); Stein, Thelma
(pf)
- Bertram Shapleigh Foundation
F8OP-8314-15 (matrix no);
33m; rel 1963

Romance
[8496] Majeske, Daniel (vln); Stein,
Thelma (pf)
- Bertram Shapleigh Foundation
B-13865-66 (matrix no); 33; rel
196?

Romanze
[8497] Majeske, Daniel (vln); Stein,
Thelma (pf)
- Bertram Shapleigh Foundation
B-13865-66 (matrix no); 33; rel
196?

Sleep
[8498] Sehm, Isolde (sop); Stein, Thelma
(pf)
- Bertram Shapleigh Foundation
F8OP-8314-15 (matrix no);
33m; rel 1963

**Sonata, Violoncello and Piano, E
Minor**
[8499] Olefsky, Paul (vcl); Stein, Thelma
(pf)
- Bertram Shapleigh Foundation
F8OP-8967 (matrix no); 33m; rel
1963

Twilight on the Marshes
[8500] Majeske, Daniel (vln); Stein,
Thelma (pf)
- Bertram Shapleigh Foundation
B-13865-66 (matrix no); 33; rel
196?

Wild Geese
[8501] Majeske, Daniel (vln); Stein,
Thelma (pf)
- Bertram Shapleigh Foundation
B-13865-66 (matrix no); 33; rel
196?

Willst du mit einem Male
[8502] Sehm, Isolde (sop); Stein, Thelma
(pf)
- Bertram Shapleigh Foundation
F8OP-8314-15 (matrix no);
33m; rel 1963

SHARLIN, William (1920-)
May the Time Not Be Distant
[8503] Cantica Hebraica; Michno, Dennis
(cond)
- JML-3812; 33s; rel 1977?

SHAUGHNESSY, Robert M.
(1925-)
Bacchae, The (Suite) (1970)
[8504] Kohon, Harold (vln); Shaughnessy,
Robert (gtr)
- Opus One 11; 33s; rel 1972; cip

SHAW, Clifford (1911-)
Lamb, The
[8505] Farrell, Eileen (sop); Trovillo,
George (pf)
- Angel 35608; 33m; rel 1959;
del 1966

**Third Street Rhumba (arr for 2 pfs
by Arthur Whittemore and Jack
Lowe)**
[8506] Whittemore, Arthur (pf); Lowe,
Jack (pf)
- RCA LM-1926; 33m; rel 1956;
del 1958

SHEINFELD, David (1910-)
Patterns for Harp
[8507] De Cray, Marcella (hp)
- Coronet S-2745; 33s; rel 1972*

SHELDON, Earl
Saraband
[8508] Chertok, Pearl (hp)
- Orion ORS-76231; 33s; rel
1976; cip

SHEPARD, R. N.*
Shepard's Tones
[8509] Electronic music
- Decca DL-710180; 33s; rel
1971; del 1973

SHEPHERD, Arthur (1880-1958)
April
[8510] Kraft, Marie Simmelink (m sop);
Mastics, Marianne Matousek (pf)
- Western Reserve University
JB-136-37 (matrix no); 33m; rel
1959?

Bacchus
[8511] Kraft, Marie Simmelink (m sop);
Mastics, Marianne Matousek (pf)
- Western Reserve University
JB-136-37 (matrix no); 33m; rel
1959?

Capriccio II (1941)
[8512] Slater, Vivien (pf)
- Western Reserve University
WRUD-M-1; 33m; rel 1967
- CRI-383; 33s; rel 1978; cip

Charm, The
[8513] Kraft, Marie Simmelink (m sop);
Mastics, Marianne Matousek (pf)
- Western Reserve University
JB-136-37 (matrix no); 33m; rel
1959?

Eclogue No 4 (1948)
[8514] Slater, Vivien (pf)
- Western Reserve University
WRUD-M-1; 33m; rel 1967
- CRI-383; 33s; rel 1978; cip

**(Three) Exotic Dances: Nos 1
(1928) and 3 (1941)**
[8515] Slater, Vivien (pf)
- Western Reserve University
WRUD-M-1; 33m; rel 1967
- CRI-383; 33s; rel 1978; cip

**Fantasia on The Garden Hymn
(1939)**
[8516] Smith, Melville (org); Chapin
Chapel Choir; Heywood,
Alexander (cond)
Rec 4/23/61
- Organ Historical Society F-MS-I-II;
33m; rel 1965

Fiddlers, The
[8517] Kraft, Marie Simmelink (m sop);
Mastics, Marianne Matousek (pf)
- Western Reserve University
JB-136-37 (matrix no); 33m; rel
1959?

Gentle Lady, The
[8518] Kraft, Marie Simmelink (m sop);
Mastics, Marianne Matousek (pf)
- Western Reserve University
JB-136-37 (matrix no); 33m; rel
1959?

Gigue fantasque (1931)
[8519] Slater, Vivien (pf)
- Western Reserve University
WRUD-M-1; 33m; rel 1967
- CRI-383; 33s; rel 1978; cip

Golden Stockings
[8520] Kraft, Marie Simmelink (m sop);
Mastics, Marianne Matousek (pf)
- Western Reserve University
JB-136-37 (matrix no); 33m; rel
1959?

He Came All So Still (1915)
[8521] Kraft, Marie Simmelink (m sop);
Mastics, Marianne Matousek (pf)
- Western Reserve University
JB-136-37 (matrix no); 33m; rel
1959?

**Horizons (Symphony No 1) (1927):
The Old Chisholm Trail**
[8522] Cleveland Pops Orchestra; Lane,
Louis (cond)
- Epic LC-3819/BC-1154; 33m/s;
rel 1962; del 1965

In modo ostinato (Rustic Ramble)
[8523] Johannesen, Grant (pf)
- Golden Crest
CR-4065/CRS-4065; 33m/s; rel
1963/1966; cip

[8524] Slater, Vivien (pf)
- Western Reserve University
WRUD-M-1; 33m; rel 1967
- CRI-383; 33s; rel 1978; cip

In the Scented Bud of Morning
[8525] Kraft, Marie Simmelink (m sop);
Mastics, Marianne Matousek (pf)
- Western Reserve University
JB-136-37 (matrix no); 33m; rel
1959?

Lento amabile (1938)
[8526] Slater, Vivien (pf)
- Western Reserve University
WRUD-M-1; 33m; rel 1967
- CRI-383; 33s; rel 1978; cip

Lost Child, The
[8527] Kraft, Marie Simmelink (m sop);
Mastics, Marianne Matousek (pf)
- Western Reserve University
JB-136-37 (matrix no); 33m; rel
1959?

Matin Song
[8528] Kraft, Marie Simmelink (m sop);
Mastics, Marianne Matousek (pf)
- Western Reserve University
JB-136-37 (matrix no); 33m; rel
1959?

Morning Glory
[8529] Kraft, Marie Simmelink (m sop);
Mastics, Marianne Matousek (pf)
- Western Reserve University
JB-136-37 (matrix no); 33m; rel
1959?

Reverie
[8530] Kraft, Marie Simmelink (m sop);
Mastics, Marianne Matousek (pf)
- Western Reserve University
JB-136-37 (matrix no); 33m; rel
1959?

Quartet, Strings, No 2 (1936)
[8531] Walden String Quartet
- Yaddo 6A-C; 78; rel 1937
- Yaddo 113A-B; 78; rel 1937
(1st and 2nd movements)
- Yaddo 114A-B; 78; rel 1937
(3rd and 4th movements)

Sonata, Piano, No 2 (1930)
[8532] Slater, Vivien (pf)
- Western Reserve University
WRUD-M-1; 33m; rel 1967

Sonata, Violin and Piano (ca 1918)
[8533] Cerone, David (vln); Johannesen,
Grant (pf)
- Golden Crest GCCL-201; 33s; rel
1976*

Starling Lake, The
[8534] Kraft, Marie Simmelink (m sop);
Mastics, Marianne Matousek (pf)
- Western Reserve University
JB-136-37 (matrix no); 33m; rel
1959?

Sunday up the River
[8535] Kraft, Marie Simmelink (m sop);
Mastics, Marianne Matousek (pf)
- Western Reserve University
JB-136-37 (matrix no); 33m; rel
1959?

To a Trout
[8536] Kraft, Marie Simmelink (m sop);
Mastics, Marianne Matousek (pf)
- Western Reserve University
JB-136-37 (matrix no); 33m; rel
1959?

Triptych (1925)
[8537] Kraft, Marie Simmelink (sop);
Walden String Quartet
- American Recording Society
ARS-18; 33m; rel 1953
- Society for Publication of
American Music R-1; 33m; rel
1953

[8538] Norden, Betsy (sop); Emerson
String Quartet
- New World NW-218; 33s; rel
1978

Where Loveliness Keeps House
[8539] Kraft, Marie Simmelink (m sop);
Mastics, Marianne Matousek (pf)
- Western Reserve University
JB-136-37 (matrix no); 33m; rel
1959?

SHERMAN, Robert W. (1921-)
Quintet, Winds (1963)
[8540] Musical Arts Quintet
- Now 9632; 33s; rel 1966; del
1976

SHIELDS, Alice (1943-)
Farewell to a Hill (1975)
[8541] Electronic music
- Finnadar CD-4; 33q; rel 1976
- Finnadar QD-9010; 33q; rel
1976; cip

Transformation of Ani, The (1970)
[8542] Electronic music
- CRI-268; 33s; 2 discs; rel 1972;
cip

Wildcat Songs (1966)
[8543] Turash, Stephanie (sop); Dunkel,
Paul (pic)
- Opus One 13; 33s; rel 1976; cip

SHIFRIN, Seymour (1926-79)
In eius memoriam (1967-68)
[8544] Boston Musica Viva; Pittman,
Richard (cond)
Rec 1/78
- Nonesuch H-71351; 33s; rel
1978; cip

Odes of Shang (1963)
[8545] University of Michigan Chamber
Choir; University of Michigan
Symphony Orchestra; Hilbish,
Thomas (cond)
- New World NW-219; 33s; rel
1978

(Three) Pieces, Orchestra (1958)
[8546] London Sinfonietta; Monod,
Jacques (cond)
- CRI-275; 33s; rel 1972; cip

Quartet, Strings, No 4 (1966-67)
[8547] Fine Arts Quartet
- CRI-358; 33s; rel 1976; cip

Satires of Circumstance (1964)
[8548] DeGaetani, Jan (m sop);
Contemporary Chamber
Ensemble; Weisberg, Arthur
(cond)
- Nonesuch H-71220; 33s; rel
1969; cip

Serenade, Five Instruments (1954)
[8549] Kaplan, Melvin (ob); Russo, Charles
(cl); Cecil, Robert (hn); Lynch,
Ynez (vla); Wingreen, Harriet (pf)
- CRI-123; 33m/s; rel
1958/1959; cip

SHILKRET, Nathaniel (1895-)
Lonesome Road, The
[8550] Traubel, Helen (sop); orchestra;
Armbruster, Robert (cond)
- Victor 49-4046-48 (in set
WDM-4013); 45; 3-7"; rel 1953

Lonesome Road, The *(cont'd)*
- RCA LM-7013; 33m; 10"; rel 1953; del 1956
- Camden CAL-485; 33m; rel 1959; del 1961

SHULMAN, Alan M. (1915-)

Cod Liver 'Ile
[8551] Heifetz, Jascha (vln); Smith, Brooks (pf)
- RCA LM-2382; 33m; rel 1960; cip

Mood in Question
[8552] Shaw, Artie (cl); New Music String Quartet
- Columbia ML-4260; 33m; rel 1950; del 1954

Nocturne for Strings, A
[8553] Stuyvesant Sinfonietta; Shulman, Sylvan (cond)
- Columbia ML-2121; 33m; 10"; rel 1950; del 1956

Rendezvous (1946)
[8554] Shaw, Artie (cl); New Music String Quartet
- Columbia ML-4260; 33m; rel 1950; del 1954

SHURE, Ralph Deane (1885-)

Galilean Easter Carol (1948)
[8555] Mormon Tabernacle Choir; Schreiner, Alexander (org); Asper, Frank (org); Condie, Richard P. (cond)
- Columbia ML-5302/MS-6019; 33m/s; rel 1958; cip

One of God's Best Mornings
[8556] Mormon Tabernacle Choir; Schreiner, Alexander (org); Asper, Frank (org); Condie, Richard P. (cond)
- Columbia ML-6019/MS-6619; 33m/s; rel 1964; del 1966

SIBBING, Robert (1929-)

Sonata, Tuba and Piano (1970)
[8557] Perantoni, Daniel (tu); Karp, Howard (pf)
- Ubres SN-101; 33s; rel 1976; cip

SIEGEL, Paul (1914-)

Concerto Between Two Worlds
[8558] Radluker, Guenther (pf); Vienna Symphony Orchestra; Moralt, Rudolf (cond)
- Abbey 3; 33m; rel 1952; del 1955

SIEGMEISTER, Elie (1909-)

American Harp (1966)
[8559] Chertok, Pearl (hp)
- Orion ORS-75207; 33s; rel 1976; cip

Concerto, Clarinet and Orchestra (1956)
[8560] Brymer, Jack (cl); London Symphony Orchestra; Siegmeister, Elie (cond)
Rec 12/16/73
- Turnabout TVS-34640; 33s; rel 1977; cip

Concerto, Flute and Orchestra (1960)
[8561] Lloyd, Peter (fl); London Symphony Orchestra; Siegmeister, Elie (cond)
Rec 12/16/73
- Turnabout TVS-34640; 33s; rel 1977; cip

(Five) cummings Songs (1970)
[8562] Kirkpatrick, Elizabeth (sop); Mandel, Alan (pf)
- Orion ORS-76220; 33s; rel 1977; cip

Elegies for Garcia Lorca (1938)
[8563] Beattie, Herbert (b); Mandel, Alan (pf)
- Orion ORS-76220; 33s; rel 1977; cip

Evil
[8564] Beattie, Herbert (b); Mandel, Alan (pf)
- Orion ORS-76220; 33s; rel 1977; cip

Face of War, The (1967-68)
[8565] Hinds, Esther (sop); Mandel, Alan (pf)
- CRI-416; 33s; rel 1980; cip

Fantasy and Soliloquy (1964)
[8566] Sylvester, Robert (vcl)
- Orion ORS-7284; 33s; rel 1972; cip

For My Daughters (1952)
[8567] Kirkpatrick, Elizabeth (sop); Mandel, Alan (pf)
- Orion ORS-76220; 33s; rel 1977; cip

John Reed
[8568] American Ballad Singers; Siegmeister, Elie (cond)
- Disc 725; 78; 3-10"; rel pre-1948

Johnny Appleseed (1940)
[8569] American Ballad Singers; Siegmeister, Elie (cond)
- Disc 725; 78; 3-10"; rel pre-1948
[8570] Beattie, Herbert (b); Mandel, Alan (pf)
- Orion ORS-76220; 33s; rel 1977; cip

Lazy Afternoon (1946)
[8571] American Ballad Singers; Siegmeister, Elie (cond)
- Disc 725; 78; 3-10"; rel pre-1948
[8572] Beattie, Herbert (b); Mandel, Alan (pf)
- Orion ORS-76220; 33s; rel 1977; cip

Lincoln Penny, The
[8573] American Ballad Singers; Siegmeister, Elie (cond)
- Disc 725; 78; 3-10"; rel pre-1948

Madam to You (1964)
[8574] Hinds, Esther (sop); Mandel, Alan (pf)
- CRI-416; 33s; rel 1980; cip

Nancy Hanks (1941)
[8575] American Ballad Singers; Siegmeister, Elie (cond)
- Disc 725; 78; 3-10"; rel pre-1948
[8576] Kirkpatrick, Elizabeth (sop); Mandel, Alan (pf)
- Orion ORS-76220; 33s; rel 1977; cip

On This Ground (1971)
[8577] Mandel, Alan (pf)
- Orion ORS-7284; 33s; rel 1972; cip

Ozark Set (1943)
[8578] Hamburg Philharmonia; Walther, Hans-Jurgen (cond)
- Music Sound Books 78129-30; 78; 2 discs; rel pre-1956
- MGM E-3141; 33m; rel 1955; del 1959
[8579] Minneapolis Symphony Orchestra; Mitropoulos, Dimitri (cond)
- Columbia CX-262; 78; 2 discs; rel pre-1948
- Columbia 12295-96D (in set X-262); 78; 2 discs; rel pre-1952
- Columbia ML-2123; 33m; 10"; rel 1950; del 1956
- Orion ORS-73116; 33s; rel 1973; cip

Paul Bunyan
[8580] American Ballad Singers; Siegmeister, Elie (cond)
- Disc 725; 78; 3-10"; rel pre-1948

Quartet, Strings, No 2 (1960)
[8581] Galimir String Quartet
- CRI-176; 33m/s; rel 1964/1973; cip

Quartet, Strings, No 3 (On Hebrew Themes) (1973)

[8582] Primavera String Quartet
- CRI-416; 33s; rel 1980; cip

Sextet, Brass and Percussion (1965)

[8583] American Brass Quintet; Gottlieb, Gordon (perc)
- Desto DC-6467; 33s; rel 1969; cip

Sonata, Piano (American) (1944)

[8584] Siegmeister, Elie (pf)
- Disc 4059-60 (in set 773); 78; 2 discs; rel pre-1948

Sonata, Piano, No 2 (1964)

[8585] Mandel, Alan (pf)
- Desto DC-6467; 33s; rel 1969; cip

Sonata, Violin and Piano, No 1 (1951)

[8586] Mandel, Nancy (vln); Mandel, Alan (pf)
- Grenadilla GS-1024; 33s; rel 1978; cip

Sonata, Violin and Piano, No 2 (1965)

[8587] Laredo, Jaime (vln); Laredo, Ruth (pf)
- Desto DC-7125; 33s; rel 1971; cip

Sonata, Violin and Piano, No 3 (1965)

[8588] Cohen, Isidore (vln); Mandel, Alan (pf)
- Desto DC-6467; 33s; rel 1969; cip

Sonata, Violin and Piano, No 4 (1971)

[8589] Mandel, Nancy (vln); Mandel, Alan (pf)
- Orion ORS-7284; 33s; rel 1972; cip

Sonata, Violin and Piano, No 5 (1972)

[8590] Mandel, Nancy (vln); Mandel, Alan (pf)
- Grenadilla GS-1024; 33s; rel 1978; cip

Song of the Dark Woods

[8591] Fuszek, Rita (pf)
- Educo 3108; 33

Songs of Experience (1966)

[8592] Cantilena Chamber Players
- Grenadilla GS-1029-30; 33s; 2 discs

(Two) Songs of the City

[8593] Kirkpatrick, Elizabeth (sop); Mandel, Alan (pf)
- Orion ORS-76220; 33s; rel 1977; cip

Strange Funeral in Braddock (1933)

[8594] Bauman, Mordecai (b); Siegmeister, Elie (pf)
- New Music Quarterly Recordings 1212; 78; rel 1936

[8595] Beattie, Herbert (b); Mandel, Alan (pf)
- Orion ORS-76220; 33s; rel 1977; cip

Street Games

[8596] Fuszek, Rita (pf)
- Educo 3108; 33

Sunday in Brooklyn (1946)

[8597] Vienna Philharmonic Orchestra; Adler, F. Charles (cond)
- SPA-47; 33m; rel 1953; del 1970
- Orion ORS-73116; 33s; rel 1973; cip

Symphony No 3 (1957)

[8598] Oslo Philharmonic Orchestra; Siegmeister, Elie (cond)
- CRI-185; 33m/s; rel 1964/1971; cip

Theme and Variations No 2 (1967)

[8599] Mandel, Alan (pf)
- Grenadilla GS-1020; 33s; rel 1978; cip

Western Suite (1945)

[8600] Utah Symphony Orchestra; Abravanel, Maurice (cond)
- Turnabout TVS-34459; 33s; rel 1972; cip

Wilderness Road (1944)

[8601] Leeds Concert Band; Todd, Peter (cond)
- Columbia ML-4254; 33m; rel 1950; del 1956

SIFLER, Paul J. (1911-)

Autumnal Song

[8602] Sifler, Paul J. (org)
- Fredonia FD-2; 33s; rel 1977; cip

Despair and Agony of Dachau, The

[8603] Sifler, Paul J. (org)
- Fredonia FD-2; 33s; rel 1977; cip

Fantasia

[8604] Sifler, Paul J. (org)
- Fredonia FD-2; 33s; rel 1977; cip

Gloria in excelsis deo

[8605] Sifler, Paul J. (org)
- Fredonia FD-2; 33s; rel 1977; cip

Joseph's Vigil

[8606] Sifler, Paul J. (org)
- Fredonia FD-2; 33s; rel 1977; cip

Last Supper, The

[8607] Sifler, Paul J. (org)
- Fredonia FD-2; 33s; rel 1977; cip

(Seven) Last Words of Christ (1976)

[8608] Sifler, Paul J. (org)
- Fredonia FD-7; 33s; rel 1979; cip

Prelude on God of Might

[8609] Sifler, Paul J. (org)
Fredonia FD-2; 33s; rel 1977; cip

Shepherd Pipers before the Manger

[8610] Sifler, Paul J. (org)
- Fredonia FD-2; 33s; rel 1977; cip

Suite, Marimba (1970)

[8611] Ervin, Karen (mrmb)
- WIM Records WIMR-5; 33s; rel 1972; cip

(Three) Tall Tales

[8612] Sifler, Paul J. (pf)
- Fredonia FD-4; 33s; rel 1977; cip

Toccata on Ein feste Burg

[8613] Sifler, Paul J. (org)
- Fredonia FD-2; 33s; rel 1977; cip

Young Pianist's Almanac, The

[8614] Sifler, Paul J. (pf)
- Fredonia FD-4; 33s; rel 1977; cip

SILVERMAN, Stanley (1938-)

Doctor Selavy's Magic Theatre, or Swinging at the Stock Exchange (1972)

[8615] Delapenha, Denise; Delson, Mary; Harper, Jessica; McGrath, George; Menken, Steve; Paris, Jackie; Primus, Barry; Schlee, Robert; Taubin, Amy; instrumental ensemble; Silverman, Stanley (cond)
- United Artists UA-LA-196G; 33s; rel 1974; del 1978

Elephant Steps (1968)

[8616] Belling, Susan; Altman, Karen; Sokol, Marilyn; Steele, Philip; Enstad, Luther; Marshall, Larry; Gagnon, Roland; Rix, Luther; chorus; instrumental ensemble; tape; Thomas, Michael Tilson (cond)
- Columbia M2X-33044; 33s; 2 discs; rel 1974; del 1978
- Columbia MG-33044; 33s; 2 discs; rel 1978; cip

Planh (Chamber Concerto for Guitar)
[8617] instrumental ensemble; Gagnon, Roland (cond)
- Folkways FTS-33902; 33s; rel 1976; cip

SIMON, Frank (1889-1967)
Willow Echoes (1918)
[8618] Schwarz, Gerard (cor); Bolcom, William (pf)
- Nonesuch H-71298/HQ-1298; 33s/q; rel 1974/1976; cip

SIMONDS, Bruce (1895-)
(Two) Preludes on Latin Hymns: Iam sol recedit igneus
[8619] Crozier, Catharine (org)
- Kendall KRC-LP-2555; 33m; rel 1953; del 1958

[8620] Perry, Roy (org)
- Aeolian-Skinner AS-10; 33m; rel 1956; del 1958

SIMONS, Gardell
Atlantic Zephyrs
[8621] Dempster, Stuart (tbn) or (euph); Steinhardt, Victor (pf)
- University of Washington Press OLY-104; 33q; 2 discs; rel 1976; cip

SIMONS, Netty (1913-)
Design Groups No 1, Percussion (1966)
[8622] percussion ensemble
- Desto DC-7128; 33s; rel 1972; cip

Design Groups No 2, Flute and Contrabass (1968)
[8623] Turetzky, Nancy (fl); Turetzky, Bertram (cb)
- Desto DC-7128; 33s; rel 1972; cip

Pied Piper of Hamelin, The (1955)
[8624] Gilbert, Lou (nar); Dunkel, Paul (fl); Simons, Netty (pf); string orchestra; Dufallo, Richard (cond)
- CRI-309; 33s; rel 1974*; cip

Puddintame (1972)
[8625] Britton, Barbara (speaker); Gilbert, Lou (speaker); Francois, Jean-Charles (perc); George, Ronald (perc)
- CRI-309; 33s; rel 1974*; cip

Set of Poems for Children (1949)
[8626] Britton, Barbara (nar); string and wind octet; London, Edwin (cond)
- CRI-309; 33s; rel 1974*; cip

Silver Thaw (1969)
[8627] Turetzky, Bertram (cb); tape
- Desto DC-7128; 33s; rel 1972; cip

SIMPSON, Dudley
Expose
[8628] Fry, Tristan (perc)
- Classics for Pleasure (English) CFP-40207; 33s; rel 1975

SIMS, Ezra (1928-)
Chamber Cantata on Chinese Poems (1954)
[8629] Conrad, Richard (ten); Preble, Elinor (fl); Viscuglia, Felix (cl); Hibbard, William (vla); Davidoff, Judith (vcl); Keany, Helen (hpschd); Pinkham, Daniel (cond)
- CRI-186; 33m/s; rel 1964/1971; cip

Elegie nach Rilke (1976)
[8630] Charlston, Elsa (sop); Boston Musica Viva; Pittman, Richard (cond)
- CRI-377; 33s; rel 1978; cip

Sonate concertante (1961-62): Quartet, Strings, No 2
[8631] Lenox String Quartet
- CRI-223; 33s; rel 1969; cip

"String Quartet No 2 (1962)" (1974)
[8632] Boston Musica Viva; Pittman, Richard (cond)
- CRI-377; 33s; rel 1978; cip

SINGER, Andre
(Nine) Parables to Franz Kafka's Amerika (1950)
[8633] Wentworth, Kenneth (nar); Wentworth, Jean (pf)
- Grenadilla GS-1011; 33s; rel 1978; cip

(Three) Serial Pieces, Piano (1963, 1967)
[8634] Wentworth, Jean (pf)
- Grenadilla GS-1011; 33s; rel 1978; cip

Sonata, Two Pianos (1949, rev 1952)
[8635] Wentworth, Jean (pf); Wentworth, Kenneth (pf)
- Grenadilla GS-1011; 33s; rel 1978; cip

SINGER, Lawrence
Work (1968)
[8636] Ostryniec, James (ob)
- CRI-423; 33s; rel 1980; cip

SKELLY, Alan
Buttinski March
[8637] Richter, Marga (pf)
- MGM E-3147; 33m; rel 1955; del 1959

Solemn Song
[8638] Richter, Marga (pf)
- MGM E-3147; 33m; rel 1955; del 1959

SKILTON, Charles S. (1868-1941)
Gambling Song
[8639] Victor Orchestra
- Victor 35749 or 19556; 78; rel pre-1927

Kickapoo Social Dance
[8640] Columbia Orchestra
- Columbia A-3106; 78; rel pre-1927
- Columbia A-6131; 78; rel pre-1927

Shawnee Indian Hunting Dance (1930)
[8641] Victor Orchestra; Bourdon, Rosario (cond)
- Victor 45-5075 (in set E-89); 78; rel pre-1948
- Victor 22144; 78; 10"; rel pre-1948
- Victor WE-89; 45; 7"; rel pre-1956

Sioux Flute Serenade (1920)
[8642] Columbia Orchestra
- Columbia A-3106; 78; rel pre-1927
- Columbia A-6131; 78; rel pre-1927

[8643] Victor Orchestra
- Victor 35749 or 19556; 78; rel pre-1927

Suite Primeval (1920): Deer Dance and War Dance
[8644] Columbia Orchestra
- Columbia A-3106; 78; rel pre-1927
- Columbia A-6131; 78; rel pre-1927

[8645] Hamburg Philharmonia; Walther, Hans-Jurgen (cond)
- Music Sound Books 78024; 78; rel pre-1956
- Music Sound Books 78202; 78; rel pre-1956
- MGM E-3141; 33m; rel 1955; del 1959

[8646] Victor Orchestra
- Victor 35749 or 19556; 78; rel pre-1927

[8647] Victor Orchestra; Bourdon, Rosario (cond)
- Victor 22174; 78; rel pre-1948 (Excerpt: Deer Dance)
- Victor 22144; 78; 10"; rel pre-1948 (Excerpt: War Dance)
- Victor 45-5075 (in set E-89); 78; rel pre-1948 (Excerpt: War Dance)
- Victor WE-89; 45; 7"; rel pre-1956 (Excerpt: War Dance)

Suite Primeval: War Dance and Sunrise Dance
[8648] Eastman-Rochester Symphony Orchestra; Hanson, Howard (cond)
- Victor 11-8302; 78; rel pre-1943

SKROWACZEWSKI, Stanislaw (1923-)

Concerto, English Horn and Orchestra (1969)
[8649] Stacy, Thomas (E hn); Minnesota Orchestra; Skrowaczewski, Stanislaw (cond)
- Desto DC-7126; 33s; rel 1971; cip

SLAWSON, Wayne (1932-)

Wishful Thinking about Winter
[8650] Electronic music
- Decca DL-710180; 33s; rel 1971; del 1973

SLONIMSKY, Nicolas (1894-)

(Five) Advertising Songs (1925)
[8651] Eamon, Deltra (sop); Slonimsky, Nicolas (pf)
- Orion ORS-72100; 33s; rel 1973; cip

Gravestones at Hancock, New Hampshire (1945)
[8652] Bramlage, Nancy (sop); Slonimsky, Nicolas (pf)
- Orion ORS-7145; 33s; rel 1971; cip

I Owe a Debt to a Monkey
[8653] Bramlage, Nancy (sop); Slonimsky, Nicolas (pf)
- Orion ORS-7145; 33s; rel 1971; cip

Impressions (1927): Silhouettes and The Flight of the Moon
[8654] Bramlage, Nancy (sop); Slonimsky, Nicolas (pf)
- Orion ORS-7145; 33s; rel 1971; cip

(Fifty) Minitudes (Thesaurus) (1971-77)
[8655] Slonimsky, Nicolas (pf)
- Orion ORS-72100; 33s; rel 1973; cip

Modinha russo-brasileira (1942) (arr for 2 gtrs by Laurindo Almeida)
[8656] Almeida, Laurindo (gtr)
- Orion ORS-72100; 33s; rel 1973; cip

My Little Pool
[8657] Bramlage, Nancy (sop); Slonimsky, Nicolas (pf)
- Orion ORS-7145; 33s; rel 1971; cip

Silhouettes iberiennes (1934) (arr for 2 gtrs by Laurindo Almeida)
[8658] Almeida, Laurindo (gtr)
- Orion ORS-72100; 33s; rel 1973; cip

Studies in Black and White (1928)
[8659] Slonimsky, Nicolas (pf)
- Orion ORS-7145; 33s; rel 1971; cip

Suite, Violoncello and Piano (1950)
[8660] Kessler, Jerome (vcl); Slonimsky, Nicolas (pf)
- Orion ORS-7145; 33s; rel 1971; cip

Variations on a Brazilian Tune (1942)
[8661] Slonimsky, Nicolas (pf)
- Orion ORS-7145; 33s; rel 1971; cip

Very Great Musician, A
[8662] Bramlage, Nancy (sop); Slonimsky, Nicolas (pf)
- Orion ORS-7145; 33s; rel 1971; cip

Vocalise
[8663] Bramlage, Nancy (sop); Slonimsky, Nicolas (pf)
- Orion ORS-7145; 33s; rel 1971; cip

SLY, Allan

Lyric Variations
[8664] viola; piano
- Yaddo 3A; 78; 10"; rel 1937

SMILEY, Pril (1943-)

Eclipse (1967)
[8665] Electronic music
- Turnabout TVS-34301; 33s; rel 1969; del 1974
- Finnadar CD-4; 33q; rel 1976
- Finnadar QD-9010; 33q; rel 1976; cip

Kolyosa (1970)
[8666] Electronic music
- CRI-268; 33s; 2 discs; rel 1972; cip

SMIT, Leo (1921-)

At the Corner of the Sky
[8667] Smit, Leo (speaker); Svitzer, Henrik (fl); Post, Nora (ob); St. Paul's Cathedral (Buffalo) Men and Boys Choir; Burgomaster, Frederick (cond)
- CRI-370; 33s; rel 1977; cip

Copernicus (1973)
[8668] Hoyle, Sir Fred (nar); Gregg Smith Singers and Orchestra; Smit, Leo (cond)
- Desto DC-7178; 33s; rel 1974; cip

In Woods (1978)
[8669] Post, Nora (ob); Falcao, Mario (hp); Williams, Jan (perc) Rec 8/19/78
- Orion ORS-79333; 33s; rel 1979; cip

Rondel (For a Young Girl)
[8670] Smit, Leo (pf)
- Concert Hall B-9; 78; 4 discs; rel pre-1948

Songs of Wonder (1976)
[8671] Hanneman, Martha (sop); Smit, Leo (pf)
- CRI-370; 33s; rel 1977; cip

Toccata Breakdown
[8672] Smit, Leo (pf)
- Concert Hall B-9; 78; 4 discs; rel pre-1948

SMITH, Claude T. (1932-)

Anthem for Winds and Percussion
[8673] Southwestern State University (Weatherford, OK) Wind Symphony; Jurrens, James W. (cond)
- Golden Crest ATH-5064; 33s; rel 1980; cip

Dance Prelude
[8674] Southwestern State University (Weatherford, OK) Wind Symphony; Jurrens, James W. (cond)
- Golden Crest ATH-5064; 33s; rel 1980; cip

Jubilant Prelude
[8675] Southwestern State University (Weatherford, OK) Wind Symphony; Jurrens, James W. (cond)
- Golden Crest ATH-5064; 33s; rel 1980; cip

March on an Irish Air (Minstrel Boy)
[8676] Southwestern State University (Weatherford, OK) Wind Symphony; Jurrens, James W. (cond)
- Golden Crest ATH-5064; 33s; rel 1980; cip

Overture on an Easy American Folk Hymn (My Shepherd Will Supply My Need)
[8677] Southwestern State University (Weatherford, OK) Wind Symphony; Jurrens, James W. (cond)
- Golden Crest ATH-5064; 33s; rel 1980; cip

Symphony, Band, No 1
[8678] Southwestern State University (Weatherford, OK) Wind Symphony; Jurrens, James W. (cond)
- Golden Crest ATH-5064; 33s; rel 1980; cip

SMITH, Gregg (1931-)
Beware of the Soldier (1969)
[8679] Rees, Rosalind (sop); Garretson, Chuck (sop); Perry, Douglas (ten); Greenwell, Charles (b); Texas Boys Choir; Columbia University Men's Glee Club; instrumental ensemble; Smith, Gregg (cond)
- CRI-341; 33s; rel 1975; cip

Bible Songs for Young Voices (1964)
[8680] Texas Boys Choir; Smith, Gregg (cond)
- Turnabout TVS-34544; 33s; rel 1975; cip

Legend (The Lion and the Unicorn)
[8681] Treadway, Kevin (sop); Texas Boys Choir; Buratto, Alan (pf); Smith, Gregg (cond)
- Vox SVBX-5354; 33s; 3 discs; rel 1979

Steps (1975)
[8682] Rees, Rosalind (sop); Starobin, David (gtr)
Rec 1976
- Turnabout TVS-34727; 33s; rel 1978

SMITH, Hale (1925-)
Brevities (1960)
[8683] Handy, D. Antoinette (fl)
- Eastern ERS-513; 33s; 2 discs; rel 1973*

Contours (1962)
[8684] Louisville Orchestra; Whitney, Robert (cond)
- LOU-63-2; 33m (Louisville Orchestra First Edition Records 1963 No 2); rel 1963; cip

Evocation (1970)
[8685] Hinderas, Natalie (pf)
- Desto DC-7102-03; 33s; 2 discs; rel 1970; cip

Expansions (1967)
[8686] Northwestern University Symphonic Wind Ensemble; Paynter, John P. (cond)
Rec 11/76
- New World NW-211; 33s; rel 1977

In memoriam–Beryl Rubenstein (1953)
[8687] Kulas Choir; chamber orchestra; Shaw, Robert (cond)
- CRI-182; 33m/s; rel 1964; cip

Ritual and Incantations (1974)
[8688] Detroit Symphony Orchestra; Freeman, Paul (cond)
- Columbia M-34556; 33s; rel 1978; del 1979

Somersault
[8689] Baldwin-Wallace Symphonic Band; Snap, Kenneth (cond)
- Educational Reference Record Library BP-102; 33m; rel 1969

Valley Wind, The (1955)
[8690] Harris, Hilda (sop); Carno, Zita (pf)
- CRI-301; 33s; rel 1973; cip

SMITH, Julia Frances (1911-)
Daisy (1973): Excerpts
[8691] Volkman, Elizabeth (sop); Smalley, Linda (m sop); Gerber, Larry (ten); Smith, David Rae (b bar); other soloists; Charlotte Opera Association Orchestra and Chorus; Rosekrans, Charles (cond)
- Orion ORS-76248; 33s; rel 1977; cip

Quartet, Strings (1964)
[8692] Kohon Quartet
- Desto DC-7117; 33s; rel 1971; cip

SMITH, Leland (1925-)
Trio, Strings (1953)
[8693] Rubin, Nathan (vln); James, Mary (vla); Hampton, Bonnie (vcl)
- Fantasy 5010; 33m; rel 1960; del 1970

SMITH, Richard Burney*
Versets on O filli et filiae
[8694] Smith, Richard B. (org)
- Vogt Quality Recordings; 33m; rel 1966

SMITH, Russell (1927-)
Concerto, Piano and Orchestra, No 2 (1956-57)
[8695] Stefanski, Andrzej (pf); Polish National Radio Orchestra; Krenz, Jan (cond)
- CRI-214; 33m/s; rel 1968; cip

Eclogue
[8696] Earle, B. (vln) or Loft, A. (vla); Weiser, Bernhard (pf)
- New Editions 4; 33m; rel pre-1953

(Six) Songs of Innocence (1950)
[8697] Carter, Sara (sop); Weiser, Bernhard (pf)
- New Editions 2; 33m; rel 1953; del 1959

Tetrameron (1957)
[8698] Japan Philharmonic Symphony Orchestra; Watanabe, Akeo (cond)
- CRI-131; 33m/s; rel 1960/1971; cip

SMITH, Stuart (1948-)
Faces (1975)
[8699] Zonn, Wilma (ob); Zonn, Paul (cl)
- Advance FGR-25S; 33s; rel 1979; cip

Gifts
[8700] Zonn, Wilma (ob); Zonn, Paul (cl); piano
- Ubres CS-301; 33s; rel 1976; cip

SMITH, William O. (1926-)
Capriccio, Violin and Piano (1952)
[8701] Rubin, Nathan (vln); Previn, Andre (pf)
Rec 6/12/57
- Contemporary C-6001; 33m; rel 1957; del 1969
- Stereo S-7015; 33s; rel 1959; del 1967
- Contemporary S-7015; 33s; rel 1967; del 1978

Concerto, Jazz Soloist and Orchestra (1962)
[8702] Smith, William O. (cl); Orchestra USA; Schuller, Gunther (cond)
- CRI-320; 33s; rel 1974; cip

Elegy for Eric (1964)
[8703] instrumental ensemble; Farberman, Harold (cond) or Schuller, Gunther (cond)
- Cambridge CRM-820/CRS-1820; 33m/s; rel 1967; del 1971

Fancies (1969)
[8704] Smith, William O. (cl)
- New World NW-209; 33s; rel 1977

Mosaic (1964)
[8705] Smith, William O. (cl); Suderburg, Robert (pf)
- CRI-320; 33s; rel 1974; cip

(Five) Pieces, Clarinet (1959)
[8706] Smith, William O. (cl)
- Contemporary M-6010/S-8010;
33m/s; rel 1963; del 1978

[8707] Warner, Melvin (cl)
- Crystal S-332; 33s; rel 1978; cip

(Four) Pieces, Clarinet, Violin, and Piano
[8708] Smith, William O. (cl); Shapiro,
Eudice (vln); Kaufman, Pearl (pf)
- Contemporary M-6010/S-8010;
33m/s; rel 1963; del 1978

Quartet, Clarinet, Violin, Violoncello, and Piano (1958)
[8709] Smith, William O. (cl); Shapiro,
Eudice (vln); Gottlieb, Victor (vcl);
Kaufman, Pearl (pf)
- Contemporary M-6010/S-8010;
33m/s; rel 1963; del 1978

Quartet, Strings (1952)
[8710] Amati String Quartet
Rec 3/13/57
- Contemporary C-6001; 33m; rel
1957; del 1969
- Stereo S-7015; 33s; rel 1959;
del 1967
- Contemporary S-7015; 33s; rel
1967; del 1978

(Five) Songs for Soprano and Violoncello (1959)
[8711] Nixon, Marni (sop); Gottlieb, Victor
(vcl)
- Contemporary M-6010/S-8010;
33m/s; rel 1963; del 1978

Straws
[8712] Skowronek, Felix (fl); Grossman,
Arthur (bsn)
- Crystal S-351; 33s; rel 1975; cip

Suite, Violin and Clarinet (1952)
[8713] Rubin, Nathan (vln); Smith, William
O. (cl)
Rec 6/7/57
- Contemporary C-6001; 33m; rel
1957; del 1969
- Stereo S-7015; 33s; rel 1959;
del 1967
- Contemporary S-7015; 33s; rel
1967; del 1978

Variants (1963)
[8714] Smith, William O. (cl)
- CRI-320; 33s; rel 1974; cip

SMOKER, Paul
Brass in Spirit
[8715] Iowa Brass Quintet
- University of Iowa Press 29001;
33s; rel 1977; cip

SNOW, David (1954-)
Passion and Transfiguration of a Post Apocalyptic Eunuch, The (1978-79)
[8716] Campellone, Mark (voice) (elec gtr)
(elec b gtr) (pf) (perc) (vln)
(ethnic appeal); Snow, David
(voice) (pf) (syn) (tpts) (perc)
(electronic effects) (pigs); Back,
Rachel (voice)
Rec 1-2/78
- Opus One 55; 33s; rel 1980

SOKOL, Thomas (1929-)
Sonatina, Trumpet and Piano
[8717] Stith, Marice (tpt); Israel, Brian (pf)
- Golden Crest RE-7068; 33s; rel
1977; cip

SOLLBERGER, Harvey (1939-)
Chamber Variations (1964)
[8718] Group for Contemporary Music at
Columbia University; Schuller,
Gunther (cond)
- CRI-204; 33m/s; rel 1966; cip

Divertimento, Flute, Violoncello, and Piano (1970)
[8719] Sollberger, Harvey (fl); Sherry, Fred
(vcl); Wuorinen, Charles (pf)
- CRI-319; 33s; rel 1974; cip

Grand Quartet for Flutes (1962)
[8720] Gilbert, David (fl); Nyfenger,
Thomas (fl); Sollberger, Harvey
(fl); Sollberger, Sophie (fl)
- Acoustic Research AR-0654.088;
33s; rel 1971

Impromptu (1968)
[8721] Wuorinen, Charles (pf)
- CRI-319; 33s; rel 1974; cip

Riding the Wind I (1974)
[8722] Spencer, Patricia (fl); Da Capo
Chamber Players; Sollberger,
Harvey (cond)
- CRI-352; 33s; rel 1976; cip

Solos for Violin and Five Instruments (1962)
[8723] Zukofsky, Paul (vln); Sollberger,
Sophie (fl); Blustine, Allen (cl);
Jolley, David (hn); Brehm, Alvin
(cb); Kalish, Gilbert (pf);
Sollberger, Harvey (cond)
- Desto DC-6435-37; 33s; 3 discs;
rel 1975; cip

Sunflowers (1976)
[8724] Sollberger, Harvey (fl); Heldrich,
Claire (vib)
- New World NW-254; 33s; rel
1978

SOUTHERS, Leroy W. (1941-)
Evolutions
[8725] Plog, Anthony (tpt); Swearingen,
Madolyn (org)
- Avant AV-1014; 33s; rel 1978;
cip

(Three) Spheres
[8726] Plog, Anthony (tpt); Wolfson, Ken
(bsn); Davis, Sharon (pf)
- Crystal S-362; 33s; rel 1977; cip

SOWERBY, Leo (1895-1968)
All on a Summer's Day (1954)
[8727] Louisville Orchestra; Whitney,
Robert (cond)
- LOU-56-6; 33m (Louisville
Orchestra First Edition Records
1956 No 6); rel 1959; del 1980

Arioso
[8728] Beck, Janice (org)
- Musical Heritage Society
OR-A-264; 33s; rel 1973

[8729] Whitley, Bob (org)
- Aeolian-Skinner AS-321; 33s; rel
1966

Ballade (1949)
[8730] Doktor, Paul (vla); Mason, Marilyn
(org)
- Mirrosonic RM-1013/RS-1013;
33m/s; rel 1961; del 1965

Canon, Chacony, and Fugue (1949)
[8731] Schaefer, Theodore (org)
- Den DR-3; 33m; rel pre-1956

Carillon (1917)
[8732] Bouchett, Richard (org)
- Mirrosonic CS-7232; 33s; rel
1971

[8733] Farnam, Lynnwood (org)
- Classic Editions CE-1040; 33m;
rel 1953; del 1961

[8734] Schaefer, Theodore (org)
- Den DR-3; 33m; rel pre-1956

[8735] Sowerby, Leo (org)
Rec 5/17/46
- Diapason 1; 78; 2 discs; rel
1946

[8736] no performer given
- Aeolian-Skinner AS-2; 33m; rel
1955; del 1958
- Washington WAS-2; 33m; rel
1958; del 1962

Classic Concerto, Organ and String Orchestra (1944)
[8737] Karlsen, Rolf (org); Oslo
Philharmonic Orchestra;
Strickland, William (cond)
- CRI-165; 33m; rel 1963; cip

Classic Concerto, Organ and String Orchestra (1944) *(cont'd)*
[8738] Mason, Marilyn (org); Harvey Phillips Orchestra; Sowerby, Leo (cond)
Rec 8/1/57
- Mirrosonic DRE-1001-03; 33m; 3 discs; rel 1958; del 1965

Comes Autumn Time (1917)
[8739] Noehren, Robert (org)
- Lyrichord LL-191/LLST-7191; 33m/s; rel 1968; cip

[8740] Smith, Rollin (org)
Rec 8/73
- Repertoire Recording Society RRS-12; 33s; rel 1974

Comes Autumn Time (orchestral version)
[8741] Eastman-Rochester Symphony Orchestra; Hanson, Howard (cond)
- Victor 2058; 78; 10"; rel pre-1942

Communion Service in C Major (1930): Sanctus
[8742] Washington Cathedral Choir of Men and Boys; Callaway, Paul (cond)
- Vanguard VRS-1036/VSD-2021; 33m/s; rel 1959; del 1968

From the Northland (1925)
[8743] Vienna Symphony Orchestra; Dixon, Dean (cond)
- American Recording Society ARS-14; 33m; rel 1953
- Desto D-429/DST-6429; 33m/s; rel 1967; cip

Lonely Fiddlemaker, The
[8744] Behrend, Jeanne (pf)
- Victor 17912 (in set M-764); 78; rel 1941

Pageant
[8745] Mason, Marilyn (org)
- Mirrosonic CM-7145/CS-7145; 33m/s; rel 1965

Pop Goes the Weasel (1927)
[8746] Westwood Wind Quintet
- Crystal 101/S-101; 33m/s; rel 1966; cip

[8747] Yaddo Woodwind Quartet
- Yaddo (168); 78; rel 1937

Prairie (1929)
[8748] Vienna Symphony Orchestra; Dixon, Dean (cond)
- American Recording Society ARS-14; 33m; rel 1953
- Desto D-421/DST-6421; 33m/s; rel 1965; cip

Prelude on Deus tuorum militum (1955)
[8749] Wyton, Alec (org)
- Aeolian-Skinner AS-6; 33m; rel 1956; del 1958
- Washington WAS-6; 33m; rel 1958; del 1962

Prelude on Psalm 46
[8750] Beck, Janice (org)
- Musical Heritage Society OR-A-264; 33s; rel 1973

Prelude on The King's Majesty (1944)
[8751] Harmon, Thomas (org)
- Orion ORS-76255; 33s; rel 1977; cip

[8752] Sowerby, Leo (org)
Rec 5/17/46
- Diapason 1; 78; 2 discs; rel 1946

Psalm 122
[8753] Washington Cathedral Choir; Dirksen, Richard W. (org) (cond)
- Washington Cathedral Archives CAR-009; 33s; rel 1979?

Requiescat in pace (1920)
[8754] Craighead, David (org)
Rec 7/31/57
- Mirrosonic DRE-1012; 33m; 2 discs; rel 1958; del 1965

[8755] Crozier, Catharine (org)
- Kendall KRC-LP-2555; 33m; rel 1953; del 1958

[8756] Friedell, Harold (org)
- Grayco LPM-101; 33m; 10"; rel 1954

[8757] Swann, Frederick (org)
- Mirrosonic CM-7058/CS-7058; 33m/s; rel 1964

Sonatina, Organ (1947)
[8758] Arnatt, Ronald (org)
- Aeolian-Skinner AS-323; 33s; rel 1969; del 1977

Suite, Organ (1937): Air with Variations
[8759] Beck, Janice (org)
- Musical Heritage Society OR-A-264; 33s; rel 1973

Suite, Organ: Fantasy for Flute Stops
[8760] Baker, George C. (org)
- Delos DEL-FY-025; 33s; rel 1977; cip

[8761] Crozier, Catharine (org)
- Kendall KRC-LP-2555; 33m; rel 1953; del 1958
- Washington WAS-16; 33m/s; rel 1961; del 1962
- Aeolian-Skinner AS-316; 33s; rel 1963; del 1970

Symphony, Organ, G Major (1930)
[8762] Biggs, E. Power (org)
- Victor 11-8142-45 (in set M-894); 78; 4 discs; rel 1942
- Victor 11-8146-49 (in set DM-894); 78; 4 discs; rel 1942

[8763] Crozier, Catharine (org)
Rec 12/53
- Kendall KRC-LP-2554; 33m; rel 1953; del 1955

[8764] Mulbury, David (org)
- Lyrichord LLST-7306; 33s; rel 1977; cip

[8765] Wilson, Gordon (org)
Rec 1/67
- Century-Advent GW-039-745; 33m; rel 1975

Symphony, Organ: Fast and Sinister
[8766] Beck, Janice (org)
- Musical Heritage Society OR-A-264; 33s; rel 1973

Symphony, Organ: Passacaglia
[8767] Huston, John (org)
Rec 7/30/57
- Mirrosonic DRE-1012; 33m; 2 discs; rel 1958; del 1965

[8768] Nyquist, Roger (org)
- Bridge S-2241; 33s; rel 1972

Toccata, Organ (1940)
[8769] Crozier, Catharine (org)
- Washington WAS-16; 33m/s; rel 1961; del 1962
- Aeolian-Skinner AS-316; 33s; rel 1963; del 1970

[8770] Jackson, Francis (org)
Rec 7/27/57
- Mirrosonic DRE-1008; 33m; 2 discs; rel 1958; del 1965

[8771] McVey, David (org)
- Orion ORS-74161; 33s; rel 1975; cip

SPALDING, Albert (1888-1953)
Alabama (Plantation Melody)
[8772] Zimbalist, Efrem (vln); Chotzinoff, Samuel (pf)
- Victor 74443; 78; rel 1912-24
- Discopaedia MB-1008; 33m; rel 197?

Dragon Fly (A Study in Arpeggios)
[8773] Spalding, Albert (vln)
- Victor 1914; 78; 10"; rel pre-1942

Etchings (Op 5)
[8774] Spalding, Albert (vln); Benoist, Andre (pf)
- Victor 1707-09 (in set 264); 78; 3-10"; rel pre-1936

Wind in the Pines (Prelude)
[8775] Spalding, Albert (vln); Benoist,
Andre (pf)
- Victor 1881; 78; 10"; rel
pre-1942

SPEETH, S. D.*
Theme and Variations
[8776] Electronic music
- Decca DL-9103/DL-79103;
33m/s; rel 1962

SPELMAN, Timothy (1891-1970)
Pervigilium veneris (1929)
[8777] Steingruber, Ilona (sop); Wiener,
Otto (bar); Vienna Academy
Chorus; Vienna State Opera
Orchestra; Fekete, Zoltan (cond)
- MGM E-3085; 33m; rel 1955;
del 1959

SPIEGEL, Laurie (1945-)
Appalachian Grove (1974)
[8778] Electronic music
- 1750 Arch S-1765; 33s; rel
1978; cip

SPIEGELMAN, Joel (1933-)
Kousochki (1966)
[8779] Wentworth, Jean (pf); Wentworth,
Kenneth (pf)
- Desto DC-7131; 33s; rel 1973;
cip

SPIES, Claudio (1925-)
Impromptu (1963)
[8780] Miller, Robert (pf)
- CRI-257; 33s; rel 1970; cip

Viopiacem (1965)
[8781] Rhodes, Samuel (vla); Miller,
Robert (pf) (hpschd)
- CRI-257; 33s; rel 1970; cip

SPILLMAN, Robert (1936-)
(Two) Songs
[8782] Bobo, Roger (tu); Grierson, Ralph
(pf)
- Crystal S-392; 33s; rel 1978; cip

SPRATLAN, Lewis (1940-)
(Two) Pieces, Orchestra (1970)
[8783] Springfield Symphony Orchestra;
Gutter, Robert (cond)
- Opus One 19; 33s; rel 1974; cip

**SPROSS, Charles G.
(1874-1961)**
Day Is Done
[8784] Nielsen, Alice (sop)
- Columbia A-5717; 78

Gunga Din
[8785] Cordon, Norman (b); Black, Frank
(pf)
- Victor 10-1182 (in set M-1030);
78; 10"; rel 1946

Gunga Din *(cont'd)*
- Camden CAL-269; 33m; rel
1955; del 1957

[8786] Warren, Leonard (bar); Victor
Orchestra; Black, Frank (cond)
- RCA LM-147; 33m; 10"; rel
1952; del 1956
- Victor WDM-1630; 45; 7"; rel
1952*

Will o' the Wisp
[8787] Anderson, Marian (al); Rupp, Franz
(pf)
- Victor 10-1123 (in set M-986);
78; 10"; rel pre-1952

[8788] Gluck, Alma (sop); Spross, Charles
(pf)
- Victor 64192; 78

STALVEY, Dorrance (1930-)
Points - Lines - Circles (1968)
[8789] instrumental ensemble; Stalvey,
Dorrance (cond)
- Ars Nova/Ars Antiqua AN-1008;
33s; rel 1971; del 1973

STARER, Robert (1924-)
Ariel (Visions of Isaiah) (1959)
[8790] Peters, Roberta (sop); Patrick,
Julian (bar); Camerata Singers
and Symphony Orchestra; Kaplan,
Abraham (cond)
- Desto DC-7135; 33s; rel 1973;
cip

**Concerto, Viola, Strings, and
Percussion (1958)**
[8791] Berger, Melvin (vla); English
Chamber Orchestra; Snashall,
John (cond)
- Pye GGC-4049/GSGC-14049;
33m/s; rel 1965/1969; del
1971
- Turnabout TVS-34692; 33s; rel
1977; cip

Concerto a tre (1954)
[8792] Rabbai, Joseph (cl); Schwarz,
Gerard (tpt); Brevig, Per (tbn);
Camerata Symphony Orchestra;
Kaplan, Abraham (cond)
- Desto DC-7135; 33s; rel 1973;
cip

Dialogues (1961)
[8793] Glazer, David (cl); Garvey, David
(pf)
- Desto DC-7106; 33s; rel 1970;
cip

Evanescents (1975)
[8794] Mandel, Alan (pf)
- Grenadilla GS-1020; 33s; rel
1978; cip

Fantasia concertante (1959)
[8795] Wentworth, Jean (pf); Wentworth,
Kenneth (pf)
Rec 3/24/78
- Grenadilla GS-1050; 33s; rel
1979

(Three) Israeli Sketches (1956)
[8796] Rigai, Amiram (pf)
- Musical Heritage Society
MHS-1653-54; 33s; 2 discs; rel
1973

Lullaby for Amittai (1952)
[8797] Pressler, Menahem (pf)
- MGM E-3010; 33m; rel 1953;
del 1959

(Five) Miniatures (1948)
[8798] American Brass Quintet
- Desto DC-6474-77; 33s; 4 discs;
rel 1969; del 1979

[8799] New York Philharmonic Brass
Ensemble
- Golden Crest
CR-4003/CRS-4003; 33m/s; rel
1957/1979; cip

[8800] Shuman Brass Choir; Starer,
Robert (cond)
- Circle L-51-102; 33m; rel
pre-1953

[8801] Symphony Artists Band; Serly,
Tibor (cond)
- Classic Editions CE-1041; 33m;
rel 1959; del 1963

Mutabili (1965)
[8802] Louisville Orchestra; Mester, Jorge
(cond)
- LOU-68-2/LS-68-2; 33m/s
(Louisville Orchestra First Edition
Records 1968 No 2); rel 1968;
cip

On the Nature of Things (1968)
[8803] Collegiate Chorale; Kaplan,
Abraham (cond)
- Desto DC-7106; 33s; rel 1970;
cip

(Five) Preludes, Piano (1952)
[8804] Mandel, Alan (pf)
- Desto DC-6445-47; 33s; 3 discs;
rel 1975; cip

Quartet, Piano and Strings (1977)
[8805] Glazer, Frank (pf); Cantilena
Chamber Players
Rec 3/28/78
- Grenadilla GS-1031; 33s; rel
1980; cip

Sonata, Piano, No 1 (1948)
[8806] Lewis, Dorothy (pf)
- VLR 1518/S-1518; 33m/s; rel
1966; del 1967

Sonata, Piano, No 2 (1965)
[8807] Schoenfield, Paul (pf)
- Desto DC-7106; 33s; rel 1970; cip

Variants (1963)
[8808] Buswell, James Oliver (vln); Garvey, David (pf)
- Desto DC-7106; 33s; rel 1970; cip

STARK, Richard* (1923-)
Psalm 8
[8809] Yale Divinity School Choir; Borden, James I. (cond)
Rec 5/52
- Overtone LP-2; 33m; rel 1954; del 1974

STEARNS, Peter P. (1931-)
Quintet, Winds (1966)
[8810] Dorian Woodwind Quintet
- CRI-318; 33s; rel 1974; cip

STEBBINS, George W. (1869-1930)
In Summer
[8811] Farnam, Lynnwood (org)
- Ultra Fidelity UF-1; 33m; rel 1959

[8812] Jerles, Ralph E. (org)
- Christian Science Publishing Society SH-123071; 33m; rel 1972

STEIN, Herman (1915-)
Mock March (1960)
[8813] Annapolis Brass Quintet
- Crystal S-207; 33s; rel 1979; cip

Sour Suite
[8814] Westwood Wind Quintet
- Crystal S-811; 33s; rel 1971; cip

STEIN, Leon (1910-)
(Three) Hassidic Dances (1940-41)
[8815] Cincinnati Symphony Orchestra; Johnson, Thor (cond)
- Remington 199-185; 33m; rel 1955; del 1957

Quartet, Strings, No 1 (1933)
[8816] Chicago Symphony String Quartet
- De Paul 23181-84 (in set 74S-100); 33s; 4 discs; rel 1974; del 1978

Quartet, Strings, No 2 (1962)
[8817] Chicago Symphony String Quartet
- De Paul 23181-84 (in set 74S-100); 33s; 4 discs; rel 1974; del 1978

[8818] Symphony String Quartet
- Music Library MLR-7118; 33m; rel 1969; del 1974

Quartet, Strings, No 3 (1964)
[8819] Chicago Symphony String Quartet
- De Paul 23181-84 (in set 74S-100); 33s; 4 discs; rel 1974; del 1978

Quartet, Strings, No 4 (1965)
[8820] Chicago Symphony String Quartet
- De Paul 23181-84 (in set 74S-100); 33s; 4 discs; rel 1974; del 1978

Quartet, Strings, No 5 (1967)
[8821] Perillo, Anne (sop); Chicago Symphony String Quartet
- De Paul 23181-84 (in set 74S-100); 33s; 4 discs; rel 1974; del 1978

Quintet, Saxophone and String Quartet (1957)
[8822] Leeson, Cecil (sax); Lyric Art Quartet
- Enchante EN-1001/ENS-2001; 33m/s; rel 1964; del 1978

Sonata, Violin (1960)
[8823] Moll, David (vln)
- Music Library MLR-7115; 33m; rel 1966; del 1974

Sonata, Violin and Piano
[8824] Moll, David (vln); Siegel, Clara (pf)
- Music Library MLR-7115; 33m; rel 1966; del 1974

Trio concertante (1961)
[8825] Minor, Brian (sax); Zlatoff-Mirsky, Everett (vln); Lunde, Lawson (pf)
- Music Library MLR-7118; 33m; rel 1969; del 1974

STERN, Robert (1934-)
Carom (1971)
[8826] Springfield Symphony Orchestra; tape; Gutter, Robert (cond)
- Opus One 19; 33s; rel 1974; cip

(Three) Chinese Poems (1970-71)
[8827] Indiana University Chorale (women); Knuth, Penelope (vla); Weeks, Douglas (pf) (cel); Vaughn, Ron (perc); Harler, Alan (cond)
- Advance FGR-24S; 33s; rel 1978

In memoriam Abraham (1956)
[8828] Eastman-Rochester Symphony Orchestra; Hanson, Howard (cond)
Rec 1958
- Mercury MG-50053/SR-90053; 33m/s; rel 1959; del 1964
- Eastman-Rochester Archives ERA-1003; 33s; rel 1974; cip

Terezin (1966)
[8829] Ornest, Dorothy (sop); Krosnick, Joel (vcl); Stern, Robert Lewis (pf)
- CRI-264; 33s; rel 1971; cip

STEVENS, Everett*
(Six) Modal Miniatures: An Ancient Roundelay, Highland Hornpipe, Forlana, and Country Fair
[8830] Bennett, Bob L. (pf)
- Educo 3109; 33

STEVENS, Halsey (1908-)
Concerto, Clarinet and Orchestra (1969)
[8831] Lurie, Mitchell (cl); Crystal Chamber Orchestra; Endo, Akira (cond)
- Crystal S-851; 33s; rel 1971; cip

Dittico (1972)
[8832] Pittel, Harvey (sax); Grierson, Ralph (pf)
- Crystal S-105; 33s; rel 1975; cip

Go, Lovely Rose (1942)
[8833] King Chorale; King, Gordon (cond)
- Orion ORS-75205; 33s; rel 1978; cip

Like as a Culver on the Bared Bough
[8834] King Chorale; King, Gordon (cond)
- Orion ORS-75205; 33s; rel 1978; cip

[8835] Randolph Singers; Randolph, David (cond)
- CRI-102; 33m/s; rel 1956/?; cip

Psalm 98 (O Sing unto the Lord a New Song) (1955)
[8836] Mid-America Chorale; Dexter, John (cond)
- CRI-191; 33m/s; rel 1964/?; cip

Sinfonia breve (1957)
[8837] Louisville Orchestra; Whitney, Robert (cond)
- LOU-59-3; 33m (Louisville Orchestra First Edition Records 1959 No 3); rel 1960; cip

Sonata, Horn and Piano (1953)
[8838] Decker, James (hn); Bricard, Nancy (pf)
- Entr'acte ERS-6505; 33s; rel 1978; cip

[8839] Leuba, Christopher (hn); Aanerud, Kevin (pf)
- Crystal S-372; 33s; rel 1977; cip

Sonata, Trombone and Piano (1965)
[8840] Brown, Keith (tbn); Fiorillo, Alexander (pf)
- Golden Crest RE-7043; 33s; rel 1972; cip

Sonata, Trumpet and Piano (1956)
[8841] Darling, James (tpt); Sidoti, Genevieve (pf)
- Advent 5006; 33s; rel 1974; del 1976

Sonata, Trumpet and Piano (1956)
(cont'd)
  - Telarc 5032; 33s; rel 1978; cip

[8842] Hickman, David (tpt); piano
  - Crystal S-363; 33s; rel 1978; cip

[8843] Stith, Marice (tpt); Bilson, Malcolm (pf)
  - Golden Crest RE-7042; 33s; rel 1972; cip

Sonata, Violoncello (1958)
[8844] Rejto, Gabor (vcl)
  - CRI-208; 33m/s; rel 1966/?; cip

Sonatina, Trombone and Piano
[8845] Knaub, Donald (b tbn); Snyder, Barry (pf)
  - Golden Crest RE-7040; 33s; rel 1971; cip

Sonatina, Tuba and Piano (1960)
[8846] Perantoni, Daniel (tu); Karp, Howard (pf)
  - Ubres SN-101; 33s; rel 1976; cip

Suite, Violin (1954)
[8847] Shapiro, Eudice (vln)
  - Entr'acte ERS-6505; 33s; rel 1978; cip

Symphonic Dances (1962)
[8848] London Philharmonic Orchestra; Barati, George (cond)
  - CRI-166; 33m; rel 1963; cip

Symphony No 1 (revised version) (1945)
[8849] Japan Philharmonic Symphony Orchestra; Watanabe, Akeo (cond)
  - CRI-129; 33m/s; rel 1960/1970; cip

Triskelion (1954)
[8850] Louisville Orchestra; Whitney, Robert (cond)
  - LOU-545-1; 33m (Louisville Orchestra First Edition Records 1955 No 1); rel 1959; del 1975

Weepe O Mine Eyes
[8851] King Chorale; King, Gordon (cond)
  - Orion ORS-75205; 33s; rel 1978; cip

STEVENS, John
Dances
[8852] Hanks, Toby (tu)
  - Crystal S-395; 33s; rel 1980; cip

Music Four Tubas
[8853] New York Tuba Quartet
  - Crystal S-221; 33s; rel 1977; cip

STEVENS, Noel*
Rhapsody, Violoncello and Winds
[8854] Cooke, Antony (vcl); University of South Florida Chamber Winds; Croft, James (cond)
Rec 5/26/79
  - Golden Crest CRS-4189; 33s; rel 1980; cip

STEVENS, Thomas (1938-)
Encore: Boz
[8855] Bobo, Roger (tu)
  - Crystal S-392; 33s; rel 1978; cip

STEWART, Robert (1918-)
Music for Brass No 4
[8856] Georgia State College Brass Ensemble; Hill, William H. (cond)
  - Golden Crest CRS-4085; 33s; rel 1969; cip

(Three) Pieces, Brass Quintet
[8857] Georgia State College Brass Ensemble; Hill, William H. (cond)
  - Golden Crest CRS-4084; 33s; rel 1969; cip

Quartet, Strings, No 3
[8858] Iowa Quartet
  - CRI-256; 33s; rel 1970; cip

Rondeau for Two Pianos (1968)
[8859] Ritacca, Jo Ann (pf); Jensen, John (pf)
  - Advance FGR-25S; 33s; rel 1979; cip

STILL, William Grant (1895-1978)
Carmela
[8860] Kaufman, Louis (vln); Kaufman, Annette (pf)
  - Orion ORS-7152; 33s; rel 1971; cip

Danzas de Panama (1948)
[8861] Kaufman, Louis (vln); Berres, George (vln); Neiman, Alexander (vla); King, Terry (vcl)
  - Orion ORS-7278; 33s; rel 1972; cip

Darker America (1924)
[8862] Westchester Symphony Orchestra; Landau, Siegfried (cond)
  - Turnabout TVS-34546; 33s; rel 1974; cip

Ennanga (1956)
[8863] Craft, Lois Adele (hp); Kaufman, Annette (pf); Berres, George (vln); Neiman, Alexander (vla); King, Terry (vcl); Kaufman, Louis (vln) (cond)
  - Orion ORS-7278; 33s; rel 1972; cip
  - Orion ORS-79359; 33s; rel 1980; cip

Festive Overture (1944)
[8864] Royal Philharmonic Orchestra; Lipkin, Arthur Bennett (cond)
  - CRI-259; 33s; rel 1970; cip

From the Black Belt (1926)
[8865] Westchester Symphony Orchestra; Landau, Siegfried (cond)
  - Turnabout TVS-34546; 33s; rel 1974; cip

From the Delta (1945): (No 1) Work Song
[8866] Morton Gould and his Symphonic Band; Gould, Morton (cond)
  - Columbia 4519M (in set MM-743); 78; rel 1948*
  - Columbia ML-2029; 33m; 10"; rel pre-1949; del 1956

Here's One (arr for vln and pf by Louis Kaufman)
[8867] Kaufman, Louis (vln); Kaufman, Annette (pf)
  - Vox 627; 78; 3 discs; rel 1948
  - Concert Hall CHC-58; 33m; rel 1950; del 1957
  - Concert Hall CHS-1140; 33m; rel 1952; del 1957
  - Concert Hall H-1640; 33m; rel 1957; del 1959
  - Orion ORS-7152; 33s; rel 1971; cip

Highway No 1, U.S.A. (1962): What Does He Know of Dreams and You're Wonderful, Mary
[8868] Brown, William (ten); London Symphony Orchestra; Freeman, Paul (cond)
  - Columbia M-32782; 33s; rel 1974; cip

Lenox Avenue (Suite) (1937): Blues (arr for pf)
[8869] Manley, Gordon (pf)
  - New NRLP-105; 33m; rel 1952; del 1962

Lenox Avenue (Suite): Blues (arr for vln and pf by Louis Kaufman)
[8870] Kaufman, Louis (vln); Kaufman, Annette (pf)
  - Vox 627; 78; 3 discs; rel 1948
  - Concert Hall CHC-58; 33m; rel 1950; del 1957
  - Concert Hall CHS-1140; 33m; rel 1952; del 1957
  - Concert Hall H-1640; 33m; rel 1957; del 1959
  - Orion ORS-7152; 33s; rel 1971; cip

Miniatures
[8871] Christ, Peter (ob); Andrus, Gretel Shanley (fl); Davis, Sharon (pf)
  - Crystal S-321; 33s; rel 1979; cip

Pastorela (1946)
[8872] Kaufman, Louis (vln); Kaufman,
Annette (pf)
- Orion ORS-7152; 33s; rel 1971;
cip

Sahdji (1930)
[8873] Eastman-Rochester Symphony
Orchestra; Eastman School of
Music Chorus; Hanson, Howard
(cond)
- Mercury MG-50257/SR-90257;
33m/s; rel 1960; del 1964

[8874] London Symphony Orchestra;
Morgan State College Choir;
Freeman, Paul (cond)
- Columbia M-33433; 33s; rel
1975; del 1979

Sahdji: Excerpt
[8875] Morgan State College Choir;
Houston, Annette (pf); Gray,
George (perc); Carter, Nathan
(cond)
- Audio House AHS-30F75; 33s;
rel 1975

Song for the Lonely, A
[8876] Carlson, Claudine (sop); Akst,
Georgia (pf)
- Orion ORS-7278; 33s; rel 1972;
cip

Songs of Separation (1949)
[8877] Bedford, Cynthia (m sop); Oakland
Youth Orchestra; Hughes, Robert
(cond)
- Desto DC-7107; 33s; rel 1970;
cip

[8878] Carlson, Claudine (sop); Akst,
Georgia (pf); Kaufman, Louis
(vln); Berres, George (vln);
Neiman, Alexander (vla); King,
Terry (vcl)
- Orion ORS-7278; 33s; rel 1972;
cip

Suite, Violin and Piano (1943)
[8879] Kaufman, Louis (vln); Kaufman,
Annette (pf)
- Orion ORS-7152; 33s; rel 1971;
cip

**Symphony No 1 (Afro-American
Symphony) (1930)**
[8880] London Symphony Orchestra;
Freeman, Paul (cond)
- Columbia M-32782; 33s; rel
1974; cip

[8881] Royal Philharmonic Orchestra;
Krueger, Karl (cond)
- SPAMH MIA-118; 33s; rel 1965

[8882] Vienna State Opera Orchestra;
Krueger, Karl (cond)
- New NRLP-105; 33m; rel 1952;
del 1962

**Symphony No 1 (Afro-American
Symphony): Scherzo**
[8883] All-American Orchestra; Stokowski,
Leopold (cond)
- Columbia 11992D; 78; rel
pre-1948

[8884] Eastman-Rochester Symphony
Orchestra; Hanson, Howard
(cond)
- Victor 2059; 78; 10"; rel
pre-1942

To You, America (1951)
[8885] U.S. Military Academy Band; Resta,
Francis E. (cond)
- ASCAP CB-177; 33m (Pittsburgh
International Contemporary Music
Festival); rel 1954

(Seven) Traceries (1939)
[8886] Walker, Frances (pf)
- Orion ORS-78306; 33s; rel
1979; cip

**(Seven) Traceries: (No 1) Cloud
Cradles, (No 2) Mystic Pool, (No
3) Muted Laughter, (No 4) Out of
the Silence, and (No 5) Woven
Silver**
[8887] Manley, Gordon (pf)
- New NRLP-105; 33m; rel 1952;
del 1962

**(Seven) Traceries: (No 1) Cloud
Cradles, (No 3) Muted Laughter,
(No 4) Out of the Silence, and (No
5) Woven Silver**
[8888] Arvey, Verna (pf)
- Co-Art 5037; 78; rel pre-1948

**(Seven) Traceries: (No 3) Muted
Laughter and (No 6) Wailing Dawn**
[8889] Norman, Ruth (pf)
- Opus One 39; 33s; rel 1979; cip

(Three) Visions (1936)
[8890] Hinderas, Natalie (pf)
- Desto DC-7102-03; 33s; 2 discs;
rel 1970; cip

[8891] Manley, Gordon (pf)
- New NRLP-105; 33m; rel 1952;
del 1962

**(Three) Visions: (No 2)
Summerland**
[8892] Norman, Ruth (pf)
- Opus One 39; 33s; rel 1979; cip

**(Three) Visions: (No 2)
Summerland (violin and piano
version)**
[8893] Kaufman, Louis (vln); Kaufman,
Annette (pf)
- Orion ORS-7152; 33s; rel 1971;
cip

We Sang Our Songs
[8894] Fisk Jubilee Singers; Kennedy,
Matthew (cond)
- NR-2597; 33s; rel 1972

STILLMAN, Mitya (1892-1936)
**(Four) Songs, Mezzo Soprano,
String Quartet, Flute, and Harp**
[8895] Reid-Parsons, Susan (m sop); Dal
Segno Ensemble; Hoffman,
Stanley (cond)
- Critics Choice CC-1703; 33s; rel
1975*

STOCK, David (1939-)
**Quintet, Clarinet and Strings
(1966)**
[8896] Blustine, Allen (cl); Contemporary
String Quartet
- CRI-329; 33s; rel 1975; cip

STOCK, Frederick (1872-1942)
Symphonic Waltz (Op 8)
[8897] Chicago Symphony Orchestra;
Stock, Frederick (cond)
- Victor 7387; 78; rel pre-1936
- Camden CAL-282; 33m; rel
1956*

STOESSEL, Albert (1894-1943)
Crinoline
[8898] Sinfonietta; Stoessel, Albert (cond)
- Royale 1856; 78; 10"

Suite antique (1922)
[8899] Brown, Eddy (vln); Stoessel, Albert
(vln); Sinfonietta; Schenkman,
Edgar (cond)
- Royale 1854-56; 78; 3-10"

**STOJOWSKI, Sigismund
(1870-1946)**
By the Brookside
[8900] Paderewski, Ignace Jan (pf)
Rec 1912-31
- Victor 1426; 78; 10"; rel 1931*
- Gramophone DA-869; 78; 10";
rel 1931*
- Camden CAL-310; 33m; rel
1956; del 1961

Chant d'amour
[8901] Paderewski, Ignace Jan (pf)
- Victor (Imported) 88436; 78; rel
1912-14
- Victor 6633; 78; rel pre-1936

Oriental (Op 10, No 2) (1894)
[8902] Hofmann, Josef (pf)
Rec 4/7/38
- Veritas VM-101; 33m; rel 1968;
del 1974
- International Piano
Library/International Piano
Archives IPA-5007-08; 33m; 2
discs; rel 1975*

STOKES, Eric (1930-)

Continental Harp and Band Report, The (An American Miscellany) (1975)
[8903] Louisville Orchestra (members of); Davies, Dennis Russell (cond) Rec 11/17/76
- LS-76-0; 33s (Louisville Orchestra First Edition Records); rel 1978; cip

Eldey Island (1971)
[8904] Stokes, Cynthia (fl) (pic); tape
- CRI-415; 33s; rel 1980; cip

On the Badlands - Parables (1972)
[8905] St. Paul Chamber Orchestra; Davies, Dennis Russell (cond)
- CRI-415; 33s; rel 1980; cip

STOUGHTON, Roy S. (1884-1953)

Within a Chinese Garden
[8906] Farnam, Lynnwood (org)
- Ultra Fidelity UF-1; 33m; rel 1959

STOUT, Alan (1932-)

Great Day of the Lord, The (Op 28a) (1956)
[8907] Mid-America Chorale; Dexter, John (cond)
- CRI-191; 33m/s; rel 1964/?; cip

Prologue (Op 75) (1963-64)
[8908] Harsanyi, Janice (sop); National Methodist Student Movement Chorus; Lincoln Symphony Orchestra (members of); Johnson, Thor (cond)
- Methodist Student Movement 100-01; 33m; 2 discs; rel 1966; del 1970

Sonata, Violoncello and Piano (1966)
[8909] Sopkin, George (vcl); Basile, Armand (pf)
- CRI-234; 33s; rel 1969; cip

STRAIGHT, Willard (1930-)

Development (1961)
[8910] London Philharmonic Orchestra; Stanger, Russell (cond)
- CRI-221; 33s; rel 1968; cip

STRANDBERG, Newton (1921-)

Ask (1972)
[8911] Mills, Linda (pic); Hall, Keith (b cl); Westbrook, Milton (tpt); Hale, Alana (tpt); Hardy, Gary (tpt); Marquart, Vincent (tpt); Haskell, Mike (tbn); Furr, Laney (tbn); Cantu, Glen (tbn); Zimmerman, Randy (tbn); Smith, Lovie (vib); Bachelder, Marlene (pf); Bachelder, Daniel (cond)
- Opus One 23; 33s; rel 1975; cip

Planh (1972)
[8912] Shugerman, Ruth (pf)
- Opus One 23; 33s; rel 1975; cip

Sea of Tranquility (1969)
[8913] Springfield Symphony Orchestra; Gutter, Robert (cond)
- Opus One 21; 33s; rel 1975; cip

Xerxes (1970)
[8914] Sam Houston State University Concert Band; Worthington, David (cond)
- Opus One 16; 33s; rel 1974; cip

STRANG, Gerald (1908-)

Concerto, Violoncello and Wind Quartet (1951)
[8915] Rejto, Gabor (vcl); Wade, Archie (fl); Benno, Norman (ob); Neufeld, John (cl); Christlieb, Don (bsn)
- CRI-215; 33m/s; rel 1968; cip

Percussion Music (1935)
[8916] The Percussion Ensemble; Price, Paul (cond)
- Period SPL-743/SPLS-743; 33m/s; rel 1958; del 1968
- Orion ORS-7276; 33s; rel 1972; cip

Sonatina, Clarinet (1932)
[8917] McBride, Robert (cl)
- New Music Quarterly Recordings 1312; 78; rel 1937
[8918] Rehfeldt, Phillip (cl)
- Advance FGR-17S; 33s; rel 1976; cip

STRANGE, Allen (1943-)

Two x Two
[8919] Electronic music
- Capra 1201; 33s; rel 1969; cip

STRAVINSKY, Soulima (1910-)

Piano Music for Children, Books 1 and 2: Tag (Book 1) and Pussy Cat, Pussy Cat (Book 2)
[8920] Fuszek, Rita (pf)
- Educo 3108; 33

Sonatina, Piano (arr for 2 gtrs)
[8921] Kneubuhl, John (gtr)
- Orion ORS-78323; 33s; rel 1979; cip

STREET, Tison (1943-)

Quartet, Strings (1972)
[8922] Concord String Quartet
- CRI-305; 33s; rel 1974; cip

Quintet, Strings (1974)
[8923] Concord String Quartet; Thompson, Marcus (vla) Rec 4/76
- CRI-381; 33s; rel 1978; cip

STRICKLAND, Lily Teresa (1887-1958)

Dreamin' Time
[8924] Galli-Curci, Amelita (sop); orchestra
- Victor 1144; 78; 10"; rel 1926
[8925] Mason, Edith (sop)
- Brunswick 10177; 78; 10"; rel 1924-25
[8926] Schumann-Heink, Ernestine (al)
- Victor 87374; 78; 10"; rel 1917-25
- Victor 969; 78; 10"; rel 1917-25

Mah Lindy Lou
[8927] Robeson, Paul (b bar); Columbia Concert Orchestra; Balaban, Emanuel (cond)
- Columbia ML-4105; 33m; rel 1952; del 1971
[8928] Warfield, William (bar); Columbia Symphony Orchestra; Engel, Lehman (cond)
- Columbia AAL-32; 33m; 10"; rel 1953; del 1957

STRICKLAND, William (1914-)

Electric Visit to the Zoo, An
[8929] Electronic music
- Spectrum SR-118; 33s; rel 1979

Sound Hypnosis
[8930] Electronic music
- Spectrum SR-118; 33s; rel 1979

STRILKO, Anthony (1931-)

Meditation of Hermes Trismegistis, The
[8931] Louisville Orchestra; Mester, Jorge (cond) Rec 5/19/76
- LS-75-8; 33s (Louisville Orchestra First Edition Records 1975 No 8); rel 1977; cip

STRINGFIELD, Lamar E. (1897-1959)

Chipmunks (1940)
[8932] Bennington Woodwind Trio
- Golden Crest CRS-4140; 33q; rel 1976; cip

From the Southern Mountains (Op 41) (1927): (No 4) Cripple Creek
[8933] Hamburg Philharmonia; Korn, Richard (cond)
- Allegro ALG-3150; 33m; rel 1955*
[8934] National High School Orchestra; Maddy, Joseph (cond)
- Victor 22095; 78; 10"; rel pre-1936

Moods of a Moonshiner (1933)
[8935] Stringfield, Lamar (fl); string
      quartet
      - Royale 35; 78; rel pre-1943

**STRONG, George Templeton
(1856-1948)**

**Chorale on a Theme by Leo Hassler
(1929)**
[8936] Eastman-Rochester Symphony
      Orchestra; Hanson, Howard
      (cond)
      - Mercury SR-90524; 33s; rel
      1970; del 1974

**Sintram (Symphony No 2) (Op 50)
(1887-88)**
[8937] Royal Philharmonic Orchestra;
      Krueger, Karl (cond)
      - SPAMH MIA-136; 33s; rel 1968

STROUD, Richard (1929-)

Treatments
[8938] Tennessee Tech Tuba Ensemble;
      Morris, R. Winston (cond)
      - Golden Crest
      CRS-4152/CRSQ-4152; 33s/q;
      rel 1977/1978; cip

SUBOTNICK, Morton (1933-)

(Four) Butterflies (1973)
[8939] Electronic music
      - Columbia M-32741/MQ-32741;
      33s/q; rel 1974; cip

Lamination I (1965)
[8940] Buffalo Philharmonic Orchestra;
      Foss, Lukas (cond)
      - Turnabout TVS-34428; 33s; rel
      1971; del 1977

Liquid Strata (1977)
[8941] Grierson, Ralph (pf); tape
      Rec 5/30/78
      - Town Hall S-24; 33s; rel 1979;
      cip

**Prelude, Piano and Tape, No 4
(1966)**
[8942] Bunger, Richard (pf); tape
      - Avant AV-1008; 33s; rel 1973;
      del 1979

Sidewinder (1970)
[8943] Electronic music
      - Columbia M-30683/MQ-30683;
      33s/q; rel 1971/1972; cip

Silver Apples of the Moon (1966)
[8944] Electronic music
      - Nonesuch H-1174/H-71174;
      33m/s; rel 1967; cip

Touch (1969)
[8945] Electronic music
      - Columbia MS-7316; 33s; rel
      1970; del 1977

Touch (1969) *(cont'd)*
      - Columbia MQ-31019; 33q; rel
      1972; del 1976

Until Spring (1974-75)
[8946] Electronic music
      - Odyssey Y-34158; 33s; rel
      1976; cip

Wild Bull, The (1967)
[8947] Electronic music
      - Nonesuch H-71208; 33s; rel
      1968; cip

SUDERBURG, Robert (1936-)

Chamber Music II (1967)
[8948] Philadelphia String Quartet
      - Turnabout TVS-34524; 33s; rel
      1974; del 1978

**Concerto, Piano and Orchestra
(Within the Mirror of Time)
(1974)**
[8949] Siki, Bela (pf); Seattle Symphony
      Orchestra; Katims, Milton (cond)
      - Odyssey Y-34140; 33s; rel
      1976; cip

SUESSE, Dana (1911-)

Young Man with a Harp
[8950] Suesse, Dana (pf); Reardon,
      Casper (hp); Morehouse (perc)
      - Schirmer 8; 78; rel pre-1943

SURINACH, Carlos (1915-)

(Tres) Cantos berberes (1952)
[8951] chamber ensemble; Surinach,
      Carlos (cond)
      - MGM E-3268; 33m; rel 1955;
      del 1959

**Concertino, Piano, Strings, and
Cymbals (1956)**
[8952] Masselos, William (pf); MGM String
      Orchestra; Surinach, Carlos
      (cond)
      - MGM E-3547; 33m; rel 1957;
      del 1959

Concerto, Orchestra (1959)
[8953] Orchestre de la Radiodiffusion
      Francaise; Surinach, Carlos (cond)
      - Montilla FM-163/FMS-2063;
      33m/s; rel 1960; del 1971

**Concerto, Piano and Orchestra
(1973)**
[8954] De Larrocha, Alicia (pf); Royal
      Philharmonic Orchestra; De
      Burgos, Fruehbeck (cond)
      - London CS-6990; 33s; rel 1977;
      cip

Danza andaluza (1946)
[8955] MGM Chamber Orchestra;
      Surinach, Carlos (cond)
      - MGM E-3419; 33m; rel 1956;
      del 1959

Doppio concertino (1954)
[8956] Ajemian, Anahid (vln); Ajemian,
      Maro (pf); MGM Chamber
      Orchestra; Surinach, Carlos
      (cond)
      - MGM E-3180; 33m; rel 1956;
      del 1959

Feria magica (1956)
[8957] Louisville Orchestra; Whitney,
      Robert (cond)
      - LOU-58-4; 33m (Louisville
      Orchestra First Edition Records
      1958 No 4); rel 1959; del 1975

[8958] Orchestre de la Radiodiffusion
      Francaise; Surinach, Carlos (cond)
      - Montilla FM-141/FMS-2041;
      33m/s; rel 1959; del 1971

Hollywood Carnival (1954)
[8959] MGM Chamber Orchestra;
      Surinach, Carlos (cond)
      - MGM E-3336; 33m; rel 1956;
      del 1959
      - MGM E-3419; 33m; rel 1956;
      del 1959

Madrid 1890 (1956)
[8960] MGM Chamber Orchestra;
      Surinach, Carlos (cond)
      - MGM E-3419; 33m; rel 1956;
      del 1959

Melorhythmic Dramas (1966)
[8961] Louisville Orchestra; Mester, Jorge
      (cond)
      - LOU-68-1/LS-68-1; 33m/s
      (Louisville Orchestra First Edition
      Records 1968 No 1); rel 1968;
      cip

**Paeans and Dances of Heathen
Iberia**
[8962] Eastman Symphonic Wind
      Ensemble; Hunsberger, Donald
      (cond)
      - Decca DL-710157; 33s; rel
      1968; del 1973

Quartet, Strings (1975)
[8963] New World String Quartet
      - Vox SVBX-5109; 33s; 3 discs; rel
      1979; cip

Ritmo jondo (Suite) (1952)
[8964] MGM Chamber Orchestra;
      Solomon, Izler (cond)
      - MGM E-3155; 33m; rel 1955;
      del 1965
      - MGM E-3419; 33m; rel 1956;
      del 1959

**Ritmo jondo (Suite) (revised
version) (1953)**
[8965] MGM Chamber Orchestra;
      Surinach, Carlos (cond)
      - MGM E-3268; 33m; rel 1955;
      del 1959

Romance, oracion y saeta (1958)
[8966] Mesler, Florence (sop)
- Mesler 155; 33s; 2 discs; rel 1973; del 1976

Sinfonietta flamenca (1953)
[8967] Hamburg Philharmonia; Winograd, Arthur (cond)
- MGM E-3435; 33m; rel 1956; del 1959

[8968] Louisville Orchestra; Whitney, Robert (cond)
- LOU-545-4; 33m (Louisville Orchestra First Edition Records 1955 No 4); rel 1959; del 1978

[8969] Orchestre de la Radiodiffusion Francaise; Surinach, Carlos (cond)
- Montilla FM-142/FMS-2042; 33m/s; rel 1959; del 1971

(Three) Spanish Songs and Dances (1950-51)
[8970] De Larrocha, Alicia (pf)
- London CS-6677; 33s; rel 1971; cip

[8971] Masselos, William (pf)
- MGM E-3165; 33m; rel 1955; del 1965
- MGM E-3419; 33m; rel 1956; del 1959

Spells and Rhymes for Dancers
[8972] Harkness Symphony Orchestra; Mester, Jorge (cond)
- Desto DC-6433; 33s; rel 1969; cip

Symphonic Variations (1962)
[8973] Louisville Orchestra; Whitney, Robert (cond)
- LOU-65-6/LS-65-6; 33m/s (Louisville Orchestra First Edition Records 1965 No 6); rel 1965; cip

Symphony No 2 (1950)
[8974] Hamburg Philharmonia; Winograd, Arthur (cond)
- MGM E-3510; 33m; rel 1957; del 1959

Tales from the Flamenco Kingdom (1954)
[8975] Richter, Marga (pf)
- MGM E-3181; 33m; rel 1955; del 1959
- MGM E-3419; 33m; rel 1956; del 1959

Tientos (1953)
[8976] Concert Arts Players
- Capitol P-8309; 33m; rel 1955; del 1960

[8977] chamber ensemble; Surinach, Carlos (cond)
- MGM E-3268; 33m; rel 1955; del 1959

SUTCLIFFE, James (1929-)
Gymnopedie
[8978] Eastman-Rochester Symphony Orchestra; Hanson, Howard (cond)
Rec 1958
- Mercury MG-50053/SR-90053; 33m/s; rel 1959; del 1964
- Eastman-Rochester Archives ERA-1003; 33s; rel 1974; cip

SWANSON, Howard (1907-78)
Concerto, Orchestra (1954)
[8979] Budapest Philharmonic Orchestra; Steinberg, Benjamin (cond)
- Silhouettes in Courage SIL-K-5001-02 (matrix no); 33s; rel 1970; del 1974

Ghosts in Love
[8980] Thigpen, Helen (sop); Allen, David (pf)
- American Recording Society ARS-10; 33m; rel 1953
- Desto D-422/DST-6422; 33m/s; rel 1967; cip

Joy
[8981] Thigpen, Helen (sop); Allen, David (pf)
- American Recording Society ARS-10; 33m; rel 1953
- Desto D-422/DST-6422; 33m/s; rel 1967; cip

Junk Man, The
[8982] Thigpen, Helen (sop); Allen, David (pf)
- American Recording Society ARS-10; 33m; rel 1953
- Desto D-422/DST-6422; 33m/s; rel 1967; cip

Negro Speaks of Rivers, The
[8983] Thigpen, Helen (sop); Allen, David (pf)
- American Recording Society ARS-10; 33m; rel 1953
- Desto D-422/DST-6422; 33m/s; rel 1967; cip

Night Music (1950)
[8984] New York Ensemble of the Philharmonic Scholarship Winners; Mitropoulos, Dimitri (cond)
- Decca DL-8511; 33m; rel 1954; del 1970
- Brunswick AXTL-1054; 33m; rel pre-1956
- Decca UAT-273045; 33m; rel pre-1956
- Decca DCM-3215; 33m; rel 1964; del 1970

Night Song
[8985] Thigpen, Helen (sop); Allen, David (pf)
- American Recording Society ARS-10; 33m; rel 1953

Night Song (cont'd)
- Desto D-422/DST-6422; 33m/s; rel 1967; cip

Short Symphony (Symphony No 2) (1948)
[8986] Vienna Symphony Orchestra; Dixon, Dean (cond)
- American Recording Society ARS-7; 33m; 10"; rel 1953
- American Recording Society ARS-116; 33m; rel 1953

[8987] Vienna State Opera Orchestra; Litschauer, Franz (cond)
- Vanguard VRS-434; 33m; rel 1953; del 1960
- CRI-254; 33s; rel 1970; cip

Still Life
[8988] Thigpen, Helen (sop); Allen, David (pf)
- American Recording Society ARS-10; 33m; rel 1953
- Desto D-422/DST-6422; 33m/s; rel 1967; cip

Suite, Violoncello and Piano (1948)
[8989] Stern, Carl (vcl); Bogin, Abba (pf) or O'Neil, Perry (pf)
- SPA-54; 33m; rel 1953; del 1970

Trio, Flute, Clarinet, and Piano
[8990] Rampal, Jean-Pierre (fl); clarinet; piano
- RCA CRL-3-1429; 33s; 3 discs; rel 1976; cip

Trio, Flute, Oboe, and Piano (1976)
[8991] Jones, Harold (fl); Smyles, Harry (ob); Booth, Alan (pf)
- Folkways FTS-33903; 33s; rel 1976; cip

Valley, The
[8992] Thigpen, Helen (sop); Allen, David (pf)
- American Recording Society ARS-10; 33m; rel 1953
- Desto D-422/DST-6422; 33m/s; rel 1967; cip

SWEELEY, Charles C. (pseud for Henry J. Linciln)
Repasz Band March
[8993] Arthur Pryor's Band; Pryor, Arthur (cond)
Rec 10/5/26
- Victor 20303; 78; 10"
- New World NW-282; 33m; rel 1976

SWICKARD, Ralph (1922-)
Hymn of Creation (1969)
[8994] Electronic music; Du Bay, William (nar)
- Orion ORS-7021; 33s; rel 1970; cip

Sermons of Saint Francis (1968)
[8995] Electronic music; Du Bay, William
(nar)
- Orion ORS-7021; 33s; rel 1970;
cip

SWIFT, Richard (1927-)
Great Praises (1977)
[8996] Dudley, Anna Carol (sop); Tartak,
Marvin (pf)
- CRI-412; 33s; rel 1980; cip

Quartet, Strings, No 4 (1973)
[8997] Composers Quartet
- Golden Crest NEC-115; 33s/q;
rel 1977; cip

Sonata, Violin (Op 15) (1957)
[8998] Gross, Robert (vln)
- Orion ORS-74147; 33s; rel
1974; cip

Summer Notes (1965)
[8999] Hersh, Paul (pf)
- CRI-412; 33s; rel 1980; cip

SWING, Raymond (1887-)
**Sonata, Violin and Piano, C Minor
(1928)**
[9000] Wigler, Jerome (vln); Reeves,
George (pf)
- Folkways FG-3506; 33m; rel
1962; del 1969

SYDEMAN, William (1928-)
**Concerto, Four-Hand Piano and
Orchestra (1967)**
[9001] Wentworth, Jean (pf); Wentworth,
Kenneth (pf); Contemporary
Music Ensemble; Weisberg, Arthur
(cond)
- Desto DC-7131; 33s; rel 1973;
cip

Concerto da camera (1959)
[9002] Pollikoff, Max (vln); CRI Chamber
Ensemble; Wolfe, Paul C. (cond)
- CRI-158; 33m/s; rel 1962/?; cip

Concerto da camera No 2 (1961)
[9003] Zukofsky, Paul (vln); Contemporary
Chamber Ensemble; Weisberg,
Arthur (cond)
- CRI-181; 33m/s; rel 1964/?; cip

Duo, Flute and Piano (1960)
[9004] Baron, Samuel (fl); Sanders,
Samuel (pf)
- Desto DC-7104; 33s; rel 1970;
cip

Duo, Violin and Piano (1963)
[9005] Banat, Gabriel (vln); Carno, Zita
(pf)
- Turnabout TVS-34429; 33s; rel
1971; del 1974

For Double Bass Alone (1957)
[9006] Turetzky, Bertram (cb)
- Advance FGR-1; 33m; rel 1966;
del 1972

**(Seven) Movements for Seven
Instruments (1958)**
[9007] CRI Chamber Ensemble; Wolfe,
Paul C. (cond)
- CRI-158; 33m/s; rel 1962/?; cip

**Music for Flute, Viola, Guitar, and
Percussion (1962)**
[9008] Contemporary Chamber Ensemble;
Weisberg, Arthur (cond)
- CRI-181; 33m/s; rel 1964/?; cip

Orchestral Abstractions (1958)
[9009] Louisville Orchestra; Whitney,
Robert (cond)
- LOU-64-4/LS-64-4; 33m/s
(Louisville Orchestra First Edition
Records 1964 No 4); rel
1964/1965; cip

Quartet, Oboe and Strings (1961)
[9010] Roseman, Ronald (ob); Lenox
String Quartet (members of)
- Desto DC-7116; 33s; rel 1971;
cip

Quintet, Brass
[9011] Brass Arts Quintet
- Grenadilla GS-1027; 33s; rel
1979; cip

Quintet, Winds, No 2 (1959-61)
[9012] University of Oregon Woodwind
Quintet
- Advance FGR-11S; 33s; rel
1973; cip

Sonata, Violoncello
[9013] Christensen, Roy (vcl)
- Gasparo GS-104; 33s; rel 1977

**Trio, Flute, Violin, and Contrabass
(1958)**
[9014] Turetzky, Nancy (fl); Kobialka,
Daniel (vln); Turetzky, Bertram
(cb)
- Medea MCLP-1001; 33m/s; rel
1966; del 1971

Trio Montagnana (1972)
[9015] Montagnana Trio
- Grenadilla GS-1021; 33s; rel
1979; cip

no title given
[9016] Rehfeldt, Phillip (cl)
- Advance FGR-17S; 33s; rel
1976; cip

TACKETT, Fred
Yellow Bird, The (1971-72)
[9017] Bobo, Roger (tu); Tackett, Fred
(gtr); Grierson, Ralph (pf);
Mosher, Skip (cb); Rich, Ray
(perc)
- Avant AV-1009; 33s; rel 1977;
cip

TALMA, Louise (1906-)
Alleluia in Form of Toccata (1944)
[9018] Fierro, Nancy (pf)
- Avant AV-1012; 33s; rel 1974*

Corona, La (1955)
[9019] Dorian Chorale; Aks, Harold (cond)
- CRI-187; 33m/s; rel 1964/?; cip

(Three) Duologues (1967)
[9020] Webster, Michael (cl); Webster,
Beveridge (pf)
Rec 1974
- CRI-374; 33s; rel 1977; cip

(Six) Etudes, Piano (1954)
[9021] Webster, Beveridge (pf)
- Desto DC-7117; 33s; rel 1971;
cip

Let's Touch the Sky (1952)
[9022] Gregg Smith Singers; Troxler,
Rebecka (fl); Reuter, Gerard (ob);
Simmons, Peter (bsn); Smith,
Gregg (cond)
Rec 1976
- Vox SVBX-5353; 33s; 3 discs; rel
1979; cip

Sonata, Piano, No 2 (1955)
[9023] Rogers, Herbert (pf)
- CRI-281; 33s; rel 1972; cip

Toccata, Orchestra (1944)
[9024] Imperial Philharmonic Orchestra of
Tokyo; Strickland, William (cond)
- CRI-145; 33m/s; rel 1961/?; cip

Toccata, Piano (1944)
[9025] Arzruni, Sahan (pf)
- Musical Heritage Society
MHS-1843; 33s; rel 1974?

TANG, Jordan Cho-tung (1948-)
Little Suite, A (1972)
[9026] Clarion Wind Quintet
- Golden Crest CRS-4191; 33s; rel
1980; cip

Piece, Violoncello and Harp (1972)
[9027] Kempter, Dorothy (vcl); Scaletti,
Carla (hp)
- Opus One 42; 33s; rel 1978; cip

TANENBAUM, Elias (1924-)
Blue Fantasy
[9028] Electronic music
- Desto DC-7130; 33s; rel 1972;
cip

Contrasts
[9029] Electronic music
- Desto DC-7130; 33s; rel 1972;
cip

Fantasy
[9030] New York Harp Ensemble; tape;
Wurtzler, Aristid von (cond)
- Musical Heritage Society
MHS-3307; 33s; rel 1975

For the Bird
[9031] Electronic music
- Desto DC-7130; 33s; rel 1972;
cip

Movements
[9032] Petitt, Marsha (sop); tape
- Desto DC-7130; 33s; rel 1972;
cip

Patterns and Improvisations
[9033] American Brass Quintet; tape
- Desto DC-6474-77; 33s; 4 discs;
rel 1969; cip

Rituals and Reactions (1975)
[9034] Reel, Elizabeth (sop); Manhattan
School of Music Chorus and
Instrumental Ensemble; Paget,
Daniel (cond)
Rec 4/76
- CRI-354; 33s; rel 1977; cip

Variations, Orchestra (1955)
[9035] Japan Philharmonic Symphony
Orchestra; Watanabe, Akeo
(cond)
- CRI-149; 33m/s; rel 1962/?; cip

TANNER, Peter H. (1936-)
Diversions
[9036] Stackhouse, Holly (fl); Frazeur,
Theodore (mrmb)
- Grenadilla GS-1042; 33s; rel
1979; cip

TAUB, Bruce (1948-)
Quintet I (1972)
[9037] Composers Ensemble
- Advance FGR-24S; 33s; rel 1978

TAYLOR, Dub
Lumiere
[9038] Electronic music
- Varese International VS-81001;
33s; rel 1973; cip

TAYLOR, Deems (1885-1966)
Ballet from Casanova (Op 22)
(1937)
[9039] Hamburg Philharmonia; Korn,
Richard (cond)
- Allegro ALG-3150; 33m; rel
1955*

Captain Stratton's Fancy
[9040] Eddy, Nelson (bar); orchestra;
Armbruster, Robert (cond)
- Columbia ML-2091; 33m; 10";
rel 1950; del 1956

[9041] Symonette, Randolph (b bar);
Harnley, Lesley (pf)
- Colosseum CLPS-1008; 33m; rel
1951; del 1958

[9042] Werrenrath, Reinald (bar)
- Victor 1104; 78; 10"; rel
pre-1927

King's Henchman, The (Op 19)
(1927): Oh! Caesar, Great Wert
Thou! (Act I) and Nay, Maccus,
Lay Him Down (Act III)
[9043] Tibbett, Lawrence (bar);
Metropolitan Opera Chorus and
Orchestra; Setti, Giulio (cond)
Rec 4/5/28
- Victor 8103; 78; rel pre-1936
- Victor 11-8932 (in set M-1015);
78; rel pre-1936 (Excerpt: Nay,
Maccus)
- Camden CAL-171; 33m; rel
1955; del 1958 (Excerpt: Nay,
Maccus)
- New World NW-241; 33m; rel
1978

Peter Ibbetson (Orchestral Suite)
(1931): Waltzes (Act I), Prelude
(Act II), Inn Music (Act II), and
Dream Music (Act III)
[9044] CBS Symphony Orchestra; Barlow,
Howard (cond)
- Columbia 71204-05D (in set
X-204); 78; 2 discs; rel
pre-1942

Portrait of a Lady (Op 14) (1918)
[9045] Vienna Symphony Orchestra;
Hendl, Walter (cond)
- American Recording Society
ARS-23; 33m; 10"; rel 1953
- Desto D-417/DST-6417; 33m/s;
rel 1965; cip

Smugglers, The
[9046] Martin, Charlotte (pf)
- Educo 3021; 33m; rel 1968; del
1972

Song for Lovers, A (Op 13, No 2)
[9047] Bampton, Rose (al); piano
- Victor 1648; 78; 10"; rel
pre-1936

[9048] Flagstad, Kirsten (sop); McArthur,
Edwin (pf)
- RCA LM-1870; 33m; rel 1955;
del 1960
- Gramophone ALP-1309; 33m; rel
pre-1956

Through the Looking Glass (Op 12)
(orchestral version) (1921-22)
[9049] CBS Symphony Orchestra; Barlow,
Howard (cond)
- Columbia 11127-30D (in set
M-350); 78; 4 discs; rel
pre-1942

[9050] Eastman-Rochester Symphony
Orchestra; Hanson, Howard
(cond)
Rec 11/21/53
- Mercury MG-40008; 33m; rel
1954; del 1957
- Mercury MG-50081; 33m; rel
1957; del 1963
- Eastman-Rochester Archives
ERA-1008; 33m; rel 1976; cip

[9051] National High School Orchestra;
Maddy, Joseph (cond)
- RCA LM-2807/LSC-2807;
33m/s; rel 1965; del 1967

Through the Looking Glass:
Dedication (arr for org)
[9052] Courboin, Charles (org)
- Victor 10-1007; 78; 10"; rel
pre-1948

TEMPLETON, Alec (1909-63)
Pocket Size Sonata
[9053] Kell, Reginald (cl); Smith, Brooks
(pf)
- Decca DL-9941; 33m; rel 1958;
del 1971

Quartet, Strings, No 1 (Quartet
Pastorale)
[9054] Phoenix String Quartet
- Esoteric ES-533; 33m; rel 1954;
del 1964
- Counterpoint/Esoteric
CPT-533/CPST-5533; 33m/s;
rel 1964/1966; cip

Roses in Wintertime
[9055] Steber, Eleanor (sop)
- Victor 49-0421; 45; 7"; rel
pre-1958

Scherzo
[9056] Goossens, Leon (ob); Moore,
Gerald (pf)
- Angel 35794/S-35794; 33m/s;
rel 1962; del 1966

Siciliana
[9057] Goossens, Leon (ob); Moore,
Gerald (pf)
- Angel 35794/S-35794; 33m/s;
rel 1962; del 1966

Trio, Flute, Oboe, and Piano
[9058] Baker, Julius (fl); Goltzer, Albert
(ob); Templeton, Alec (pf)
- Esoteric ES-533; 33m; rel 1954;
del 1964
- Counterpoint/Esoteric
CPT-533/CPST-5533; 33m/s;
rel 1964/1966; cip

Vienna in the Springtime
[9059] Steber, Eleanor (sop)
- Victor 49-0421; 45; 7"; rel
pre-1958

TENNEY, James (1934-)
Noise Study
[9060] Electronic music
- Decca DL-9103/DL-79103;
33m/s; rel 1962

Stochastic Quartet (1963)
[9061] Electronic music
- Decca DL-710180; 33s; rel
1971; del 1973

THAYER, William A. (1874-1933)
My Laddie
[9062] Easton, Florence (sop); Moore,
Gerald (pf)
- Victor 1705; 78; 10"; rel
1921-25
- Victor 10036; 78; rel 1921-25

[9063] Gluck, Alma (sop)
- Cantilena CF-6215; 33m; rel
1969; del 1975

THEMMEN, Ivana M.
Ode to Akhmatova (1977)
[9064] Kraft, Jean (m sop); Jones, Linda
(pf)
- Opus One 54; 33s

Shelter this Candle from the Wind
[9065] Seibel, Paula (sop); Louisville
Orchestra; Mester, Jorge (cond)
- LS-76-7; 33s (Louisville
Orchestra First Edition Records
1976 No 7); rel 1979; cip

THIMMIG, Leslie (1943-)
(Seven) Profiles
[9066] Composers Quartet
- CRI-265; 33s; rel 1971; cip

THOMAS, Andrew (1939-)
An Wasserfluessen Babylon (1973)
[9067] Thomas, Andrew (pf); Violette,
Andrew (pf)
- Opus One 34; 33s; rel 1978; cip

Death of Yukio Mishima, The
[9068] Notes from Underground Group;
Leonard, Peter (cond)
- Opus One 28; 33s; rel 1976; cip

Dirge in Woods (1973)
[9069] Notes from Underground Group;
Leonard, Peter (cond)
- Opus One 28; 33s; rel 1976; cip

Presido 27 (1970)
[9070] Rowe, Catherine (sop); New York
Brass Society
- Opus One 8; 33s; rel 1972; cip

Pricksong (1975)
[9071] Hess, Alyssa (hp)
- Opus One 30; 33s; rel 1977; cip

Roman de fauvel (1969)
[9072] Rowe, Catherine (sop); Heldrich,
Claire (perc); Thomas, Andrew
(pf)
- Opus One 8; 33s; rel 1972; cip

(Two) Studies for Woodwind Quintet (1969)
[9073] Gilbert, David (fl); Lucarelli, Bert
(ob); Greenberg, Lloyd (cl); Jolley,
David (hn); Ellert, Michael (bsn)
- Opus One 8; 33s; rel 1972; cip

THOMAS, Christopher J. (1894-)
Oh! Men from the Fields
[9074] Anderson, Marian (al); Rupp, Franz
(pf)
- Victor 10-1300; 78; 10"

THOMPSON, Leland*
(Two) Masques
[9075] Lang, Judith (pf); Lang, Doris (pf)
- Golden Crest
CR-4070/CRS-4070; 33m/s; rel
1963; cip

THOMPSON, Randall (1899-)
Agnus Dei
[9076] King Chorale; King, Gordon (cond)
- Orion ORS-75205; 33s; rel
1978; cip

Alleluia (1940)
[9077] Catawba College Choir; Weaver,
Robert (cond)
- Music Library MLR-7085; 33m;
rel 1957; del 1974

[9078] Fleet Street Choir; Lawrence, T. B.
(cond)
Rec 8/11/43
- Decca (English) M-541; 78; 10";
rel 1943

[9079] Gregg Smith Singers; Smith, Gregg
(cond)
Rec 1976
- Vox SVBX-5353; 33s; 3 discs; rel
1979; cip

[9080] Harvard Glee Club; Radcliffe Choral
Society; Thompson, Randall
(cond)
Rec 4/23/65
- Harvard Glee Club FH-RT; 33; rel
1965

[9081] Harvard Glee Club; Radcliffe Choral
Society; Woodworth, G. Wallace
(cond)
- Cambridge CRM-403; 33m; rel
1957; del 1980

[9082] Howard University Choir; Lawson,
Warner (cond)
- Key 12; 33m; rel 1951?
- Voice of America VOA-3030; 33

Alleluia (1940) (cont'd)
[9083] International University Choral
Festival Massed Choruses;
Woodworth, G. Wallace (cond)
Rec 9/26/65
- RCA LM-7043/LSC-7043;
33m/s; 2 discs; rel 1966; del
1976

[9084] Louisville Fourth Avenue Unitarian
Methodist Church Choir; St.
Mark's Episcopal Choir; Ruy
(cond)
- Educo 4504; 33; rel 197?

[9085] Peloquin Choir; Peloquin, C.
Alexander (cond)
- Gregorian Institute of America
EL-19 (in set EL-100); 33m; rel
1960; del 1978

[9086] San Antonio Symphony
Mastersingers; Melone, Roger
(cond)
Rec 5/77
- Telarc 5026; 33s; rel 1978; cip
- Mixtur (German) TA-5026; 33s;
rel 1978

[9087] Singing City Choir of Philadelphia;
Brown, Elaine (cond)
- Fellowship FM-1/FS-1; 33m/s; rel
1961

[9088] Stanford University Choir; Schmidt,
Harold C. (cond)
Rec 1962
- Music Library MLR-6995-96;
33m; 2 discs; rel 1967; del
1974

[9089] Vienna State Academy Chorus;
Grossman, Ferdinand (cond)
Rec 4/52
- Vox PLP-7750; 33m; rel 1952;
del 1956

[9090] Wellington Schola Cantorum;
Thompson, Randall (cond)
- Argo RG-115; 33m; rel 1956?

Americana (From The American Mercury) (1932)
[9091] University of Michigan Chamber
Choir; University of Michigan
Symphony Orchestra (members
of); Hilbish, Thomas (cond)
Rec 1977
- New World NW-219; 33s; rel
1978

Americana (From The American Mercury): (No 3) God's Bottles
[9092] Randolph Singers; Randolph, David
(cond)
- Concert Hall CHC-52; 33m; rel
1950; del 1957

Felices ter (Horace Ode for A. T. Davison) (1953)
[9093] King Chorale; King, Gordon (cond)
- Orion ORS-75205; 33s; rel
1978; cip

Felices ter (Horace Ode for A. T. Davison) (1953) *(cont'd)*
[9094] Stanford University Chorus; Schmidt, Harold C. (cond)
- Music Library MLR-7022; 33m; rel 1955; del 1974

Frostiana (1959)
[9095] Harvard Glee Club; Radcliffe Choral Society; Harvard-Radcliffe Orchestra; Thompson, Randall (cond)
Rec 4/23/65
- Harvard Glee Club FH-RT; 33; rel 1965

Glory to God in the Highest (1958)
[9096] Capital University Chapel Choir; Snyder, Ellis Emanuel (cond)
- Coronet S-1405; 33s; rel 1969; cip

[9097] Mormon Tabernacle Choir; Ottley, Jerold D. (cond)
Rec 1/27-31/76
- Columbia M-34134; 33s; rel 1976; cip

Last Words of David, The (1949)
[9098] Harvard Glee Club; Forbes, Elliot (cond)
Rec 1961
- Carillon 122; 33m; rel 1962; del 1970

[9099] Harvard Glee Club; Radcliffe Choral Society; Harvard-Radcliffe Orchestra; Thompson, Randall (cond)
Rec 4/23/65
- Harvard Glee Club FH-RT; 33; rel 1965

[9100] Mormon Tabernacle Choir; Schreiner, Alexander (org); Asper, Frank W. (org); Condie, Richard P. (cond)
- Columbia ML-5302/MS-6019; 33m/s; rel 1958; cip

[9101] Notre Dame Glee Club; Pedtke, Daniel H. (cond)
- MGM E-3212; 33m; rel 1956; del 1959

[9102] Pontarddulais Male Choir; Jones, D. Hugh (org); Davis, Noel G. (cond)
- Pye (English) GGL-0427; 33s; rel 1968

[9103] Rhapsody in White and the Baylor Bards; Barkema, Martha (cond)
- Austin 6241; 33m; rel 1963; del 1976

[9104] U.S. Military Academy Chapel Choir; Davis, John A. (cond)
- Vox VX-25590/STVX-425590; 33m/s; rel 1958; del 1962

[9105] Walter Ehret Chorale; Flath, Edwin (org); Ehret, Walter (cond)
- Golden Crest CR-4032/CRS-4032; 33m/s; rel 1962; del 1976

Little Prelude
[9106] Martin, Charlotte (pf)
- Educo 3021; 33m; rel 1968; del 1972

Mass of the Holy Spirit (1955-56)
[9107] Harvard Glee Club; Radcliffe Choral Society; Woodworth, G. Wallace (cond)
- Cambridge CRM-403; 33m; rel 1957; del 1980

Nativity According to Saint Luke, The (1961)
[9108] Covenant Methodist Church (Evanston, IL) Soloists, Chorus, and Chamber Orchestra; Thompson, Randall (cond)
Rec 12/9/62
- Festival Arts S-2693-95; 33s; 3 discs; rel 1963

(Five) Odes of Horace (1924): (No 2) Vitas hinnuleo me similis, Chloe, (No 4) O fons bandusiae, splendidior vitro, and (No 5) Montium custos memorumque
[9109] Harvard Glee Club; Radcliffe Choral Society; Thompson, Randall (cond)
Rec 4/23/65
- Harvard Glee Club FH-RT; 33; rel 1965

[9110] Vienna State Academy Chorus; Grossman, Ferdinand (cond)
Rec 4/52
- Vox PLP-7750; 33m; rel 1952; del 1956

(Five) Odes of Horace: (No 2) Vitas hinnuleo me similis, Chloe
[9111] Harvard Glee Club; Radcliffe Choral Society; Forbes, Elliot (cond)
Rec 9/25/65
- RCA LM-7043/LSC-7043; 33m/s; 2 discs; rel 1966; del 1976

Peaceable Kingdom, The (1936)
[9112] Harvard Glee Club; Radcliffe Choral Society; Thompson, Randall (cond)
Rec 4/23/65
- Harvard Glee Club FH-RT; 33; rel 1965

[9113] Macalester Radio Singers; Johnson, Hollis L. (cond)
- Schmitt Music Co MC-89546; 78; 10''; rel 1949

[9114] Pepperdine University A Cappella Choir; McCommas, Lawrence (cond)
Rec 5/76
- Orion ORS-76228; 33s; rel 1977; cip

[9115] San Jose State College A Cappella Choir; Erlendson, William (cond)
- Music Library MLR-7065; 33m; rel 1957; del 1974

Peaceable Kingdom, The (1936) *(cont'd)*
[9116] Singing City Choir of Philadelphia; Brown, Elaine (cond)
- Fellowship FM-1/FS-1; 33m/s; rel 1961

[9117] Whikehart Chorale; Whikehart, Lewis E. (cond)
Rec 1/64
- Lyrichord LL-124/LLST-7124; 33m/s; rel 1964; cip

Peaceable Kingdom, The: (No 7) Have Ye Not Known and (No 8) Ye Shall Have a Song
[9118] Capital University Chapel Choir; Whikehart, Lewis E. (cond)
Rec 1972
- Coronet LPS-3018; 33s; rel 1973

Peaceable Kingdom, The: (No 1) Say Ye to the Righteous
[9119] Wellington Schola Cantorum; Oliver (cond)
- Argo RG-115; 33m; rel 1956?

Peaceable Kingdom, The: (No 4) Howl Ye
[9120] Gregg Smith Singers; Smith, Gregg (cond)
- Verve MGV-2137/VS-6151; 33m/s; rel 1960; del 1965

Peaceable Kingdom, The: (No 5) The Paper Reeds by the Brook
[9121] Brown-Pembroke Choir; Fidlar (cond)
- Brown University 1000; 33s; rel 1971; del 1975

[9122] King Chorale; King, Gordon (cond)
- Orion ORS-75205; 33s; rel 1978; cip

[9123] Mormon Tabernacle Choir; Schreiner, Alexander (org); Asper, Frank (org); Condie, Richard P. (cond)
- Columbia ML-6019/MS-6619; 33m/s; rel 1964; del 1966

[9124] Washington University Choir; Weiss, Don (cond)
- Aspen 1511; 33m; rel 1958; del 1960

Pueri hebraeorum (1928)
[9125] Columbus Boychoir; Bryant, Donald (cond)
- Caedmon CBC-15; 33

[9126] University of North Carolina (Greensboro) Choir; Cox, Richard (cond)
Rec 3/65
- Copeland Sound Studios CSS-554; 33

A Discography

Quartet, Strings, No 1 (1941)
[9127] Guilet String Quartet
- Concert Hall C-3; 78; 3 discs; rel 1949
- Concert Hall CHS-1092; 33m; rel 1951; del 1956

Requiem (1957-58)
[9128] Harvard Glee Club; Radcliffe Choral Society; Forbes, Elliot (cond)
Rec 4/24/59
- Technichord TC-15-16; 33; rel 1959

Song after Sundown (1935)
[9129] Behrend, Jeanne (pf)
Rec 7/3/40
- Victor 17912 (in set M-764); 78; rel 1941

[9130] Martin, Charlotte (pf)
- Educo 3021; 33m; rel 1968; del 1972

Suite, Oboe, Clarinet, and Viola (1940)
[9131] Berkshire Woodwind Ensemble
- Unicorn UNLP-1029; 33m; rel 1956; del 1959
- Unicorn UNSR-2; 33m; rel 1956; del 1959

[9132] Christ, Peter (ob); Atkins, David (cl); De Veritch, Alan (vla)
Rec 11/78
- Crystal S-321; 33s; rel 1979; cip

Symphony No 1 (1929)
[9133] Utah Symphony Orchestra; Abravanel, Maurice (cond)
Rec 5/78
- Angel S-37315; 33s; rel 1978; cip

Symphony No 2 (1931)
[9134] New York Philharmonic; Bernstein, Leonard (cond)
Rec 10/22/68
- Columbia MS-7392; 33s; rel 1970; del 1973

[9135] Vienna Symphony Orchestra; Dixon, Dean (cond)
- American Recording Society ARS-4; 33m; 10''; rel 1951
- American Recording Society ARS-45; 33m; rel 1951
- Desto D-406/DST-6406; 33m/s; rel 1964; cip

Tarantella (1937)
[9136] Columbia University Glee Club; Harvey, J. Bailey (cond)
- Carillon 117; 33m; rel 1961; del 1970

Testament of Freedom, The (1943)
[9137] Eastman School of Music Male Chorus; Eastman-Rochester Symphony Orchestra; Hanson, Howard (cond)
- Mercury MG-40000; 33m; rel 1952; del 1957

Testament of Freedom, The (1943) (cont'd)
- Mercury MG-50073; 33m; rel 1957; del 1969
- Mercury SRW-18113; 33s; rel 1969; del 1970
- Eastman-Rochester Archives ERA-1007; 33s; rel 1976; cip

[9138] Harvard Glee Club; Boston Symphony Orchestra; Koussevitzky, Serge (cond)
Rec 4/24/45
- Victor 11-9176-78 (in set M-1054); 78; 3 discs; rel 1946
- Victor DM-1054; 78; 3 discs; rel 1946
- Victor VM-1054; 78; 3 discs; rel 1946

[9139] Pfeiffer College Concert Choir; Brewer, Richard (cond)
- Pfeiffer 8777; 33s; rel 1976; cip

[9140] University of Virginia Glee Club; Thompson, Randall (pf); Tuttle, Steven D. (cond)
Rec 4/13/43
- Columbia XP-3333-38; 78; rel 1943

[9141] Utah Chorale; Utah Symphony Orchestra; Abravanel, Maurice (cond)
Rec 5/78
- Angel S-37315; 33s; rel 1978; cip

Testament of Freedom, The: (No 2) We Have Counted the Cost and (No 3) We Fight Not for Glory
[9142] U.S. Military Academy Glee Club; Schempf, William (cond)
- Vox VX-26240/STVX-426240; 33m/s; rel 1960; del 1962

Testament of Freedom, The: (No 1) The God Who Gave Us Life
[9143] U.S. Military Academy Chapel Choir; Davis, John A. (cond)
- Vox VX-25980/STVX-425980; 33m/s; rel 1960; del 1962

Testament of Freedom, The: (No 3) We Fight Not for Glory
[9144] University of Pittsburgh Men's Glee Club; Weiss, David G. (cond)
Rec 11/52
- ASCAP CB-162; 33m (Pittsburgh International Contemporary Music Festival); rel 1954

Velvet Shoes (1927)
[9145] De Loache, Benjamin (bar)
- Yaddo 8A; 78; 10''; rel 1937

[9146] Frijsh, Povla (sop); Dougherty, Celius (pf)
Rec 4/12/40
- Victor 2157B (in set M-789); 78; 10''; rel 1941
- Victor MO-789; 78; 10''; rel 1941

Velvet Shoes (1927) (cont'd)
- RCA LCT-1158; 33m; rel 1955; del 1957
- Town Hall 002; 33m; rel 1961?
- New World NW-247; 33m; rel 1976

[9147] Lang, Edith (sop); Hempel, Gottfried (pf)
- Fan (German) 555112; 33; rel 196?

[9148] Tassie, Phalen (sop)
- Music Library MLR-7105; 33m; rel 1965; del 1974

THOMPSON, Van Denman (1890-1969)
Come Thou Almighty King
[9149] Hollywood Presbyterian Church Choir; Hirt, Charles C. (cond)
- RCA LPM-1258; 33m; rel 1956; del 1958

Hymn Meditations, Vol 1: I Am Coming to the Cross and More Love to Thee
[9150] Becker, C. Warren (org)
- Chapel LP-5-134/ST-134; 33m/s; rel 1968

THOMSON, Virgil (1896-)
Acadian Songs and Dances (from film score Louisiana Story) (1948)
[9151] Cleveland Pops Orchestra; Lane, Louis (cond)
- Epic LC-3809/BC-1147; 33m/s; rel 1961; del 1966

[9152] Little Orchestra Society; Scherman, Thomas (cond)
- Decca DL-9616; 33m; rel 1952; del 1971
- Brunswick AXTL-1022; 33m; rel pre-1956
- Decca DCM-3207; 33m; rel 1962; del 1970

(Three) Antiphonal Psalms (1922-24): (No 1) Psalm 123 and (No 3) Psalm 136
[9153] Yale Divinity School Choir; Borden, James I. (cond)
Rec 5/52
- Overtone LP-2; 33m; rel 1954; del 1974

At the Beach (1948)
[9154] Schwarz, Gerard (cor); Bolcom, William (pf)
- Nonesuch H-71298/HQ-1298; 33s/q; rel 1974/1976; cip

Autumn (1964)
[9155] Stockton, Ann Mason (hp); Los Angeles Chamber Orchestra; Marriner, Neville (cond)
- Angel SQ-37300; 33q; rel 1976; cip

Capital Capitals (1927)

[9156] Crawford, Joseph (ten); Turner, Clyde S. (ten); James, Joseph (bar); Smith, William C. (b); Thomson, Virgil (pf)
- Columbia ML-4491; 33m; rel 1952; del 1958

Concerto, Flute, Harp, Strings, and Percussion (1954)

[9157] Fuge, Francis (fl); Louisville Orchestra; Whitney, Robert (cond)
- LOU-66-3/LS-66-3; 33m/s (Louisville Orchestra First Edition Records 1966 No 3); rel 1966; cip

Concerto, Violoncello and Orchestra (1950)

[9158] Silva, Luigi (vcl); Janssen Symphony Orchestra of Los Angeles; Janssen, Werner (cond)
- Columbia ML-4468; 33m; rel 1952; del 1968
- Columbia CML-4468; 33m; rel 1968; del 1974
- Columbia AML-4468; 33m; rel 1974; del 1976

Eccentric Dance (1940)

[9159] Richter, Marga (pf)
- MGM E-3147; 33m; rel 1955; del 1959

(Nine) Etudes, Piano (1940, 1951)

[9160] Tollefson, Arthur (pf)
Rec 12/10-11/79
- Finnadar SR-9027; 33s; rel 1980

(Ten) Etudes, Piano (1943)

[9161] Schapiro, Maxim (pf)
- Decca DL-4083; 33m; 10"; rel 1954; del 1957
- Brunswick AXL-2009; 33m; rel pre-1956

[9162] Tollefson, Arthur (pf)
Rec 12/10-11/79
- Finnadar SR-9027; 33s; rel 1980

(Ten) Etudes, Piano: (No 7) Oscillating Arm (Spinning Song) and (No 10) Ragtime Bass

[9163] Foldes, Andor (pf)
- Vox 16068-71 (in set 174); 78; 4-10"; rel 1947
- Polydor/Deutsche Grammophon 46002; 78; rel pre-1953 (Excerpt: Ragtime Bass)
- Polydor/Deutsche Grammophon 36104; 78; rel pre-1956 (Excerpt: Ragtime Bass)

(Ten) Etudes, Piano: (No 9) Parallel Chords (Tango) and (No 10) Ragtime Bass

[9164] Johannesen, Grant (pf)
- Golden Crest CR-4065/CRS-4065; 33m/s; rel 1963/1966; cip (Excerpt: Ragtime Bass)
- Golden Crest CRS-4132; 33s; rel 1975; cip

[9165] Shields, Roger (pf)
- Vox SVBX-5303; 33s; 3 discs; rel 1977; cip

(Ten) Etudes, Piano: (No 6) For the Weaker Fingers (Music Box Lullaby)

[9166] Jonas, Maryla (pf)
- Columbia ML-4624; 33m; rel 1953; del 1956

(Ten) Etudes, Piano: (No 10) Ragtime Bass

[9167] Dubal, David (pf)
- Musical Heritage Society MHS-3808; 33s; rel 1978

(Ten) Etudes, Piano: (No 10) Ragtime Bass (arr for 4 pfs)

[9168] First Piano Quartet
- Victor 12-0588-90 (in set MO-1263); 78; 3 discs

Fanfare (1922)

[9169] Ellsasser, Richard (org)
- MGM E-3005; 33m; rel 1953; del 1959

[9170] Smith, Rollin (org)
Rec 8/73
- Repertoire Recording Society RRS-12; 33s; rel 1974

Feast of Love, The (1964)

[9171] Clatworthy, David (bar); Eastman-Rochester Symphony Orchestra; Hanson, Howard (cond)
- Mercury MG-50429/SR-90429; 33m/s; rel 1965; del 1971
- Mercury SRI-75063; 33s; rel 1976; cip

Filling Station (1937)

[9172] New York City Ballet Orchestra; Barzin, Leon (cond)
- Vox PLP-9050; 33m; rel 1955; del 1965

Four Saints in Three Acts (1927-28, orchd 1933) (Abridged)

[9173] Robinson-Wayne, Beatrice (sop); Matthews, Inez (sop); Hines, Altnoell (m sop); Greene, Ruby (al); Holland, Charles (ten); Bethea, David (ten); Matthews, Edward (bar); Robinson, Randolph (bar); Dorsey, Abner (b); double chorus; orchestra; Thomson, Virgil (cond)
Rec 6/47
- Victor 12-0451-55 (in set M-1244); 78; 5 discs; rel 1948*
- RCA LCT-1139; 33m; rel 1954; del 1955
- RCA LM-2756; 33m; rel 1964; del 1973

(Three) Hymns from the Old South (1949)

[9174] Peabody Conservatory Concert Singers; Smith, Gregg (cond)
Rec 1976
- Vox SVBX-5353; 33s; 3 discs; rel 1979; cip

(Three) Hymns from the Old South: (No 1) The Morning Star and (No 2) Death, 'Tis a Melancholy Day

[9175] Vienna Academy Chamber Chorus; Grossman, Ferdinand (cond)
- Vox PLP-7750; 33m; rel 1952; del 1956

Let's Take a Walk

[9176] Tatum, Nancy (sop); Parsons, Geoffrey (pf)
- London OS-26053; 33s; rel 1968; del 1971

Louisiana Story (Suite) (1948)

[9177] Philadelphia Orchestra; Ormandy, Eugene (cond)
- Columbia 13049-50D (in set MX-329); 78; 2 discs; rel pre-1952
- Columbia LX-8802-03; 78; 2 discs; rel pre-1952
- Columbia ML-2087; 33m; 10"; rel 1950; del 1956

[9178] Westphalian Symphony Orchestra; Landau, Siegfried (cond)
- Turnabout TVS-34534; 33s; rel 1973; cip

Metropolitan Museum Fanfare: Portrait of an American Artist (Portrait of Florine Stettheimer, Parades) (1941, orchd 1970)

[9179] brass and percussion ensemble; Prausnitz, Frederik (cond)
Rec 1970
- Metropolitan Museum of Art AKS-10001; 33; rel 1970

Missa brevis (1934)
[9180] King's Chapel Choir, Boston;
McCausland, Lloyd S. (perc);
Thomson, Virgil (cond)
- Cambridge CRM-412; 33m; rel
1962; del 1970

Mother of Us All, The (1947)
[9181] Santa Fe Opera; Leppard, Raymond
(cond)
- New World NW-288-89; 33s; 2
discs; rel 1977; cip

Mother of Us All, The (Suite) (1949)
[9182] Janssen Symphony Orchestra of
Los Angeles; Janssen, Werner
(cond)
- Columbia ML-4468; 33m; rel
1952; del 1968
- Columbia CML-4468; 33m; rel
1968; del 1974
- Columbia AML-4468; 33m; rel
1974; del 1976

My Shepherd Will Supply My Need (1937)
[9183] Heinz Chapel Choir; Finney,
Theodore (cond)
- ASCAP CB-162; 33m (Pittsburgh
International Contemporary Music
Festival); rel 1954

[9184] Peabody Conservatory Concert
Singers; Smith, Gregg (cond)
Rec 1976
- Vox SVBX-5353; 33s; 3 discs; rel
1979; cip

[9185] Stanford University Chorus;
Schmidt, Harold C. (cond)
- Music Library MLR-7022; 33m;
rel 1955; del 1974

Pastorale on a Christmas Plainsong (1922)
[9186] Ellsasser, Richard (org)
- MGM E-3064; 33m; rel 1953;
del 1959

Plow That Broke the Plains, The (Suite) (1936)
[9187] Hollywood Bowl Symphony
Orchestra; Stokowski, Leopold
(cond)
- Victor 11-9520-21 (in set
M-1116); 78; 2 discs; rel
pre-1948

[9188] Little Orchestra Society; Scherman,
Thomas (cond)
- Decca DL-7527; 33m; 10"; rel
1952; del 1957
- Brunswick AXL-2006; 33m; rel
pre-1956

[9189] Los Angeles Chamber Orchestra;
Marriner, Neville (cond)
- Angel SQ-37300; 33q; rel 1976;
cip

Plow That Broke the Plains, The (Suite) (1936) (cont'd)
[9190] Symphony of the Air; Stokowski,
Leopold (cond)
- Vanguard VRS-1071/VSD-2095;
33m/s; rel 1961; cip
- Vanguard VSD-707-08; 33s; 2
discs; rel 1971; cip

Portrait of F. B. (1929)
[9191] Dickinson, Meriel (m sop);
Dickinson, Peter (pf)
Rec 3/28/77
- Unicorn RHS-353; 33s; rel 1978
- Unicorn UNI-72017; 33s; rel
1978
- Unicorn RHS-253; 33s; rel
1978*

Portraits for Solo Keyboard
[9192] Alternations (Portrait of Maurice
Grosser), An Old Song (Portrait of
Carrie Stettheimer), Bugles and
Birds (Portrait of Pablo Picasso)
(1940), Cantabile (Portrait of
Nicolas de Chatelain) (1940),
Catalan Waltz (Portrait of Ramon
Senabre), and In a Bird Cage
(Portrait of Lise Deharme)
Tollefson, Arthur (pf)
Rec 12/10-11/79
- Finnadar SR-9027; 33s; rel
1980

[9193] Bugles and Birds (Portrait of Pablo
Picasso) (1940), Poltergeist
(Portrait of Hans Arp), and
Solitude (Portrait of Lou Harrison)
Mandel, Alan (pf)
- Desto DC-6445-47; 33s; 3 discs;
rel 1975

[9194] Cantabile (Portrait of Nicolas de
Chatelain) (1940)
Marlowe, Sylvia (hpschd)
- Decca DL-10021/DL-710021;
33m/s; rel 1961; del 1971

Portraits for Orchestra
[9195] Bugles and Birds (Portrait of Pablo
Picasso) (1940, orchd 1944),
Cantabile for Strings (Portrait of
Nicolas de Chatelain (1940,
orchd 1944), Fugue (Portrait of
Alexander Smallens) (1940,
orchd 1944), Percussion Piece
(Portrait of Jessie K. Lasell)
(1941, orchd 1944), and Tango
Lullaby (Portrait of Flavie Alvarez
de Toledo) (1940, orchd 1944)
Philadelphia Orchestra; Thomson,
Virgil (cond)
- Columbia 12154-55D (in set
255); 78; 2 discs; rel 1945*
- Columbia 12608D; 78 (Excerpts:
Bugles and Birds, and Cantabile
for Strings)
- Columbia ML-2087; 33m; 10"; rel
1950; del 1956
- CRI-398; 33s; rel 1979; cip
(Excerpts: Bugles and Birds,
Fugue, and Tango Lullaby)

Praises and Prayers (1963)
[9196] Allen, Betty (m sop); Thomson,
Virgil (pf)
- CRI-207; 33m/s; rel 1966/?; cip
- Hi-Fi/Stereo Review Editorial
Recording L-165; 33m; rel 1965

Praises and Prayers: Before Sleeping
[9197] Tatum, Nancy (sop); Parsons,
Geoffrey (pf)
- London OS-26053; 33s; rel
1968; del 1971

Quartet, Strings, No 1 (1931)
[9198] New Music String Quartet
- ASCAP CB-181; 33m (Pittsburgh
International Contemporary Music
Festival); rel 1952
- ASCAP CB-169; 33m (Pittsburgh
International Contemporary Music
Festival); rel 1954

Quartet, Strings, No 2 (1932)
[9199] Juilliard String Quartet
- Columbia ML-4987; 33m; rel
1955; del 1968
- Columbia CML-4987; 33m; rel
1968; del 1974
- Columbia AML-4987; 33m; rel
1974; cip

[9200] Kohon Quartet
- Vox SVBX-5305; 33s; 3 discs; rel
1974; cip

River, The (Suite) (1937)
[9201] Los Angeles Chamber Orchestra;
Marriner, Neville (cond)
- Angel SQ-37300; 33q; rel 1976;
cip

[9202] Symphony of the Air; Stokowski,
Leopold (cond)
- Vanguard VRS-1071/VSD-2095;
33m/s; rel 1961; cip

[9203] Vienna Symphony Orchestra;
Hendl, Walter (cond)
- American Recording Society
ARS-8; 33m; rel 1953
- Desto D-405/DST-6405; 33m/s;
rel 1964; cip

Scenes from the Holy Infancy According to St. Matthew (1937): Joseph and the Angels
[9204] Peloquin Choir; Peloquin, C.
Alexander (cond)
- Gregorian Institute of America
EL-19 (in set EL-100); 33m; rel
1960; del 1978

Sea Piece with Birds (1952)
[9205] Philadelphia Orchestra; Thomson,
Virgil (cond)
- Columbia ML-4919; 33m; rel
1954; del 1957
- CRI-398; 33s; rel 1979; cip

Seine at Night, The (1947)
[9206] Philadelphia Orchestra; Thomson, Virgil (cond)
- Columbia ML-4919; 33m; rel 1954; del 1957
- CRI-398; 33s; rel 1979; cip

Serenade, Flute and Violin (1931)
[9207] Gilbert, David (fl); Kooper, Kees (vln)
- Turnabout TVS-34508; 33s; rel 1973; del 1978

Solemn Music, A (1949, orchd 1962)
[9208] Eastman Symphonic Wind Ensemble; Fennell, Frederick (cond)
Rec 1954
- Mercury MG-40011; 33m; rel 1954; del 1957
- Mercury MG-50084; 33m; rel 1957; del 1969

Sonata, Flute (1943)
[9209] Moskovitz, Harvey (fl)
- Musical Heritage Society MHS-3578; 33s; rel 1977

Sonata, Piano, No 3 (1930)
[9210] Shields, Roger (pf)
- Vox SVBX-5303; 33s; 3 discs; rel 1977; cip

Sonata, Piano, No 4 (1940)
[9211] Marlowe, Sylvia (hpschd)
- New Editions 3; 33m; rel 1953; del 1959
- Decca DL-10021/DL-710021; 33m/s; rel 1961; del 1971

Sonata, Violin and Piano (1930)
[9212] Fuchs, Joseph (vln); Balsam, Artur (pf)
- CRI-207; 33m/s; rel 1966/?; cip
- Hi-Fi/Stereo Review Editorial Recording L-165; 33m; rel 1965

Sonata da chiesa (1926)
[9213] Fuchs, Lillian (vla); Simenauer, Peter (cl); Mills, Fred (tpt); Ingraham, Paul (hn); Erwin, Edward (tbn); Thomson, Virgil (cond)
- CRI-207; 33m/s; rel 1966/?; cip
- Hi-Fi/Stereo Review Editorial Recording L-165; 33m; rel 1965

(Five) Songs to Poems of William Blake (1951)
[9214] Harrell, Mack (bar); Philadelphia Orchestra; Ormandy, Eugene (cond)
- Columbia ML-4919; 33m; rel 1954; del 1957
- CRI-398; 33s; rel 1979; cip
(Excerpts: The Divine Image, Tiger! Tiger!, The Land of Dreams, and And Did Those Feet)

Stabat mater (1931)
[9215] Tourel, Jennie (m sop); New Music String Quartet
- Columbia ML-4491; 33m; rel 1952; del 1958

Symphony No 3 (1972)
[9216] New Hampshire Symphony Orchestra; Bolle, James (cond)
- CRI-411; 33s; rel 1980; cip

Symphony on a Hymn Tune (1928)
[9217] Eastman-Rochester Symphony Orchestra; Hanson, Howard (cond)
- Mercury MG-50429/SR-90429; 33m/s; rel 1965; del 1971
- Mercury SRI-75063; 33s; rel 1976; cip

Synthetic Waltzes (1925)
[9218] Gold, Arthur (pf); Fizdale, Robert (pf)
- Columbia MM-956; 78; rel pre-1952
- Columbia ML-2147; 33m; 10''; rel 1952; del 1956
- Philips S-06614R; 33m; rel pre-1956

Tiger, The (1926)
[9219] Steber, Eleanor (sop); Biltcliffe, Edwin (pf)
- St/And SPL-411-12; 33m; 2 discs; rel 1963; del 1964
- Desto D-411-12/DST-6411-12; 33m/s; 2 discs; rel 1964; cip

Two by Marianne Moore (1963)
[9220] Dickinson, Meriel (m sop); Dickinson, Peter (pf)
Rec 3/28/77
- Unicorn RHS-353; 33s; rel 1978
- Unicorn UNI-72017; 33s; rel 1978
- Unicorn RHS-253; 33s; rel 1978*

Variations and Fugues on Sunday School Tunes (1926)
[9221] Mason, Marilyn (org)
Rec 12/53
- Esoteric ES-522; 33m; rel 1954; del 1964
- Counterpoint/Esoteric CPT-522/CPST-5522; 33m/s; rel 1964/1966; del 1974

Wheat Field at Noon (1948)
[9222] Philadelphia Orchestra; Thomson, Virgil (cond)
- Columbia ML-4919; 33m; rel 1954; del 1957
- CRI-398; 33s; rel 1979; cip

THORNE, Francis (1922-)
Burlesque Overture (1963-64)
[9223] Polish National Radio Orchestra; Strickland, William (cond)
- CRI-216; 33m/s; rel 1968; cip

Concerto, Piano and Chamber Orchestra (1965-66)
[9224] Davies, Dennis Russell (pf); St. Paul Chamber Orchestra
- Serenus SRS-12058; 33s; rel 1976; cip

Elegy (1962-63)
[9225] Orquesta Sinfonica de la Escuela de Conjunto Orquestal de la Municipalidad de Avellaneda, Argentina; Faure, Jose Rodriguez (cond)
- Owl ORLP-2; 33s; rel 1965; del 1977

Fanfare, Fugue, and Funk (1972)
[9226] Springfield Symphony Orchestra; Gutter, Robert (cond)
- Opus One 19; 33s; rel 1974; cip

Fantasia, String Orchestra (1963)
[9227] Orquesta Sinfonica de la Escuela de Conjunto Orquestal de la Municipalidad de Avellaneda, Argentina; Faure, Jose Rodriguez (cond)
- Owl ORLP-2; 33s; rel 1965; del 1977

Liebesrock (1968-69)
[9228] Royal Philharmonic Orchestra; Dixon, James (cond)
- CRI-258; 33s; rel 1970; cip

Lyric Variations II (1971-72)
[9229] Boehm Quintet; Fitz, Richard (perc)
- Serenus SRS-12058; 33s; rel 1976; cip

Nocturnes
[9230] Rowe, Catherine (sop); Thorne, Francis (pf)
- Serenus SRS-12035; 33s; rel 1975; cip

Rhapsodic Variations (1964-65)
[9231] Thorne, Francis (pf); Polish National Radio Orchestra; Strickland, William (cond)
- CRI-216; 33m/s; rel 1968; cip

(Six) Set-Pieces (1967)
[9232] University of Chicago Contemporary Chamber Players; Shapey, Ralph (cond)
- Owl ORLP-20; 33s; rel 1968; del 1977
- CRI-397; 33s; rel 1979; cip

Simultaneities (1971)
[9233] American Brass Quintet
- Serenus SRS-12035; 33s; rel 1975; cip

Sonata, Piano (1972)
[9234] Peltzer, Dwight (pf)
- Serenus SRS-12071; 33s; rel 1978; cip

Sonatina, Flute
[9235] Sollberger, Harvey (fl)
- Serenus SRS-12058; 33s; rel
1976; cip

Songs and Dances (1969)
[9236] Rosenberger, Walter (perc); Moore,
David (vcl); Thomas, Andrew
(kbds); Gilbert, David (cond)
- Opus One 9; 33s; rel 1972; cip

Symphony No 3 (1969)
[9237] Prague Chamber Soloists; Rohan,
Jindrich (cond)
- Serenus SRS-12035; 33s; rel
1975; cip

**Symphony in One Movement
(1963)**
[9238] Orquesta Sinfonica de la Escuela
de Conjunto Orquestal de la
Municipalidad de Avellaneda,
Argentina; Faure, Jose Rodriguez
(cond)
- Owl ORLP-2; 33s; rel 1965; del
1977

TILLIS, Frederick C. (1930-)
**Music for Alto Flute, Violoncello,
and Piano (1966)**
[9239] Trio Pro Viva
- Eastern ERS-513; 33s; 2 discs;
rel 1973*

**Music for Violin, Violoncello, and
Piano**
[9240] Sackson, David (vln); Bialkin,
Maurice (vcl); Peltzer, Dwight (pf)
- Serenus SRS-12087; 33s; rel
1979; cip

Niger Symphony (1975)
[9241] Royal Philharmonic Orchestra;
Freeman, Paul (cond)
- Serenus SRS-12087; 33s; rel
1979; cip

Quintet, Brass (1962)
[9242] New York Brass Quintet
- Serenus SRS-12066; 33s; rel
1976; cip

TIMM, Kenneth N. (1934-)
**Joiner and the Die-Hard, The
(1972)**
[9243] percussion ensemble; Miller,
Donald D. (cond)
- Crystal S-531; 33s; rel 1977; cip

TITCOMB, Everett (1884-1968)
I Will Not Leave You Comfortless
[9244] All Saints' Church Male Choir; Self,
William (cond)
- Classic Editions CE-1023; 33m;
rel 1953; del 1961

**(Four) Improvisations on Gregorian
Themes: (No 4) Cibavit eos**
[9245] Jerles, Ralph E. (org)
- Christian Science Publishing
Society SH-123071; 33m; rel
1972

TOCH, Ernst (1887-1964)
Big Ben (Op 62) (1934)
[9246] RAI Orchestra; Kempe, Rudolf
(cond)
- Bruno Walter Society EMA-101;
33m; rel 1975*

Burlesken (Op 31) (1923)
[9247] Rehberg, Willy (pf)
- Polydor 62530; 78; rel
pre-1936

Burlesken: No 2
[9248] Spagnolo, Paolo (pf)
- Parlophone PE-158; 78; rel
pre-1953
- London LLP-1040; 33m; rel
1954; del 1957
- Decca LXT-2947; 33m; rel
pre-1956

Burkesken: No 3
[9249] Dymont, L. (pf)
- Polydor 23577; 78; rel
pre-1936

Capriccetti (Op 36) (1925)
[9250] Guzelimian, Armen (pf)
- Crystal S-502; 33s; rel 1976; cip

**Chinesische Floete, Die (Op 29)
(1921)**
[9251] Mock, Alice (sop); Pacific
Symphonietta; Compinsky,
Manuel (cond)
- Alco AC-203; 78; 3 discs; rel
1947*
- Alco ALP-1006; 33m; rel 1950;
del 1955

[9252] Renzi, Dorothy (sop); MGM
Chamber Orchestra; Surinach,
Carlos (cond)
- MGM E-3546; 33m; rel 1958;
del 1959

Circus Overture (1953)
[9253] New York Philharmonic;
Kostelanetz, Andre (cond)
- Columbia CL-758; 33m; rel
1955; del 1957
- Columbia A-2035; 45; 7"; rel
pre-1956

**Concerto, Piano and Orchestra (Op
38) (1926)**
[9254] Toch, Ernst (pf); Vienna Symphony
Orchestra; Haefner, Herbert
(cond)
- Contemporary M-6014/S-8014;
33m/s; rel 1968; del 1972

**Concerto, Violoncello and Chamber
Orchestra (Op 35) (1924)**
[9255] Mottier, Frederic (pf); Forum
Group, Zurich; Barth, Fred (cond)
- Contemporary M-6014/S-8014;
33m/s; rel 1968; del 1972

Covenant, The (1945)
[9256] Arnold, Edward (nar); Janssen
Symphony Orchestra of Los
Angeles; Janssen, Werner (cond)
- Artist JS-10; 78; 5 discs; rel
pre-1950
- Capitol P-8125; 33m; rel 1952;
del 1957

**(Two) Divertimentos (Op 37)
(1925): No 1 (arr for vln and vcl)**
[9257] Schoenfeld, Alice (vln); Schoenfeld,
Eleanore (vcl)
- Orion ORS-7267; 33s; rel 1972;
cip

**(Two) Divertimentos: No 2 (arr for
vln and vcl)**
[9258] Heifetz, Jascha (vln); Piatigorsky,
Gregor (vcl)
- RCA LM-3009/LSC-3009;
33m/s; rel 1968; cip

**Etudes, Piano (Op 56) (1931): (No
10) Etude Allegro (The Top)**
[9259] Gimpel, Jakob (pf)
- Vox 16021 (in set 164); 78;
10"; rel pre-1948

Etudes, Piano (Op 59) (1931)
[9260] Richter, Marga (pf)
- MGM E-3181; 33m; rel 1955;
del 1959

Fuge aus der Geographie (1930)
[9261] Abbey Singers
- Decca DL-10073/DL-710073;
33m/s; rel 1963; del 1973

[9262] Los Angeles Chorus Camerata;
Mitzelfelt, H. Vincent (cond)
- Crystal S-502; 33s; rel 1976; cip

**(Three) Impromptus (Op 90)
(1963): No 3 (arr for vcl and pf
by Jeffrey Solow)**
[9263] Solow, Jeffrey (vcl); Stevenson,
Doris (pf)
- Command COMS-9006; 33s; rel
1975; del 1977

**Jephta, Rhapsodic Poem (Symphony
No 5) (Op 89) (1963)**
[9264] Louisville Orchestra; Whitney,
Robert (cond)
- LOU-66-1/LS-66-1; 33m/s
(Louisville Orchestra First Edition
Records 1966 No 1); rel 1966;
cip

**(Three) Little Dances (Op 85)
(1961)**
[9265] Guzelimian, Armen (pf)
- Crystal S-502; 33s; rel 1976; cip

Miniature Overture (1932)
[9266] Louisville Orchestra; Mester, Jorge
(cond)
- LS-70-2; 33s (Louisville
Orchestra First Edition Records
1970 No 2); rel 1970; cip

Notturno (Op 77) (1953)
[9267] Louisville Orchestra; Whitney,
Robert (cond)
- LOU-545-3; 33m (Louisville
Orchestra First Edition Records
1955 No 3); rel 1959; del 1978

Peter Pan (Op 76) (1956)
[9268] Louisville Orchestra; Whitney,
Robert (cond)
- LOU-61-2; 33m (Louisville
Orchestra First Edition Records
1961 No 2); rel 1961; cip

**(Five) Pieces, Winds and
Percussion (Op 83) (1959)**
[9269] Philadelphia Woodwind Quintet;
Fearn, Ward O. (hn); Hinger, Fred
D. (perc); Owen, Charles (perc)
- Columbia ML-5788/MS-6388;
33m/s; rel 1962; del 1966

Pinocchio (1935)
[9270] Berlin Radio Orchestra; Romanski,
Ljubomir (cond)
- Bruno Walter Society EMA-101;
33m; rel 1975*

[9271] Chicago Symphony Orchestra;
Stock, Frederick (cond)
- Columbia 11665D; 78; rel
pre-1942
- Columbia (English) LOX-570; 78;
rel pre-1952

[9272] Hamburg Philharmonia; Walther,
Hans-Jurgen (cond)
- Music Sound Books 78045; 78;
rel pre-1956
- MGM E-3144; 33m; rel 1955;
del 1959

Poems to Martha (Op 66) (1942)
[9273] Tippey, James (bar); Compinsky
Ensemble (members of)
- Sheffield M-3/S-3; 33m/s; 2
discs; rel 1964; del 1978
- Town Hall S-3; 33s; 2 discs; rel
1978; cip

**Quartet, Strings, D-flat Major (Op
18) (1910)**
[9274] Westwood String Quartet
- Contemporary C-6002; 33m; rel
1958; del 1969
- Stereo S-7016; 33s; rel 1959;
del 1967
- Contemporary S-7016; 33s; rel
1967; del 1978

**Quartet, Strings, No 12 (Op 70)
(1946)**
[9275] London String Quartet
- Alco AC-203; 78; 3 discs; rel
1947*
- Alco A-5; 78; 3 discs; rel
pre-1952

[9276] Zurich String Quartet
Rec 5/11/58, 5/16/58, and
6/6/58
- Contemporary M-6005/S-8005;
33m/s; rel 1959; cip

**Quartet, Strings, No 13 (Op 74)
(1954)**
[9277] Roth Quartet
- Contemporary M-6008/S-8008;
33m/s; rel 1961; del 1978

**Quartet, Strings, on BASS (Op 23)
(1921)**
[9278] American Art Quartet
- Contemporary M-6008/S-8008;
33m/s; rel 1961; del 1978

**Quintet, Piano and Strings (Op 64)
(1938)**
[9279] Previn, Andre (pf); American Art
Quartet
- Contemporary M-6011/S-8011;
33m/s; rel 1963; del 1978

[9280] Toch, Ernst (pf); American Art
Quartet
- Alco 1212; 33m; rel 1951; del
1955

[9281] Toch, Ernst (pf); Kauffman Quartet
- Columbia 71149-52D (in set
M-460); 78; 4 discs; rel
pre-1942

**Serenade (Spitzweg Serenade) (Op
25) (1916)**
[9282] Kaufman, Louis (vln); Monasevitch,
Grischa (vln); Menhennick, Ray
(vla)
- Vox 16081-82 (in set 177); 78;
2-10"; rel pre-1948

[9283] Westwood String Trio
- Contemporary C-6002; 33m; rel
1958; del 1969
- Stereo S-7016; 33s; rel 1959;
del 1967
- Contemporary S-7016; 33s; rel
1967; del 1978

**Sonata, Violin and Piano, No 1 (Op
21) (1913)**
[9284] Shapiro, Eudice (vln); Berkowitz,
Ralph (pf)
- Crystal S-502; 33s; rel 1976; cip

**Sonatinetta, Flute, Clarinet, and
Bassoon (Op 84) (1959)**
[9285] Philadelphia Woodwind Quintet
- Columbia ML-5788/MS-6388;
33m/s; rel 1962; del 1966

Symphony No 1 (Op 72) (1950)
[9286] Vienna Symphony Orchestra;
Haefner, Herbert (cond)
- Bruno Walter Society EMA-101;
33m; rel 1975*

Symphony No 3 (Op 75) (1955)
[9287] Pittsburgh Symphony Orchestra;
Steinberg, William (cond)
- Capitol P-8364/SP-8364;
33m/s; rel 1957/1959; del
1961

**Tanz und Spielstuecke (Op 40)
(1926?): Sunbeam Play**
[9288] Bianca, Sondra (pf)
- Music Sound Books 23; 78; rel
pre-1956
- Music Sound Books 60041;
33m; rel pre-1956

Trio, Strings (Op 63) (1936)
[9289] Vienna String Trio
Rec 5/11/58, 5/16/58, and
6/6/58
- Contemporary M-6005/S-8005;
33m/s; rel 1959; cip

Valse (1961)
[9290] Los Angeles Chorus Camerata;
Mitzelfelt, H. Vincent (cond)
- Crystal S-502; 33s; rel 1976; cip

TOENSING, Richard (1940-)
Doxologies I (1965)
[9291] Cornell University Wind Ensemble;
Stith, Marice (cond)
- Cornell CUWE-9; 33s; rel 1971;
cip

TOURS, Frank E. (1877-1963)
Mother o' Mine
[9292] Warren, Leonard (bar); Victor
Orchestra; Black, Frank (cond)
- RCA LM-147; 33m; 10"; rel
1952; del 1956

[9293] White, Robert (ten); Sanders,
Samuel (pf)
- RCA ARL-1-1698; 33s; rel 1976;
cip

TOWER, Joan (1938-)
**Breakfast Rhythms I and II
(1974-75)**
[9294] Blustine, Allen (cl); Da Capo
Chamber Players; Shulman,
Daniel (cond)
Rec 10/76
- CRI-354; 33s; rel 1977; cip

Hexachords (1972)
[9295] Spencer, Patricia (fl)
Rec 10/76
- CRI-354; 33s; rel 1977; cip

Movements (1968)
[9296] Spencer, Patricia (fl); Tower, Joan
(pf)
- Advance FGR-24S; 33s; rel 1978

Prelude for Five Players (1971)
[9297] Da Capo Chamber Players
- CRI-302; 33s; rel 1973; cip

TOWNER, Ralph

Distant Hills
[9298] no performers given
- Vanguard
VSD-79341/VSQ-40031; 33s/q;
rel 1973

Friend of the Family
[9299] Seifert, Zbigniew (vln)
- Vanguard VSD-79397; 33s; rel
1978

Raven's Wood
[9300] Seifert, Zbigniew (vln)
- Vanguard VSD-79397; 33s; rel
1978

Serenade
[9301] Seifert, Zbigniew (vln)
- Vanguard VSD-79397; 33s; rel
1978

TRACK, Gerhard (1934-)

Festival Prelude and Fugue
[9302] Zamkochian, Berj (org)
- Gregorian Institute of America
M/S-119; 33s; rel 1970; del
1978

Festliches Spiel
[9303] piano; orchestra
- Gregorian Institute of America
M/S-119; 33s; rel 1970; del
1978

Hymn
[9304] no performers given
- Gregorian Institute of America
M/S-119; 33s; rel 1970; del
1978

**Mass in Honor of the Queen of
Peace (1966)**
[9305] St. John's Symphony; chorus;
Track, Gerhard (cond)
- Gregorian Institute of America
M/S-115; 33s; rel 1970; del
1978

Overture
[9306] no performers given
- Gregorian Institute of America
M/S-119; 33s; rel 1970; del
1978

Prelude
[9307] no performers given
- Gregorian Institute of America
M/S-119; 33s; rel 1970; del
1978

Seven Stars of the Assiniboine
[9308] St. John's Symphony; chorus;
Track, Gerhard (cond)
- Gregorian Institute of America
M/S-115; 33s; rel 1970; del
1978

Sonata, Violin and Piano, A Minor
[9309] no performers given
- Gregorian Institute of America
M/S-119; 33s; rel 1970; del
1978

There Is a God
[9310] St. John's Symphony; chorus;
Track, Gerhard (cond)
- Gregorian Institute of America
M/S-115; 33s; rel 1970; del
1978

TRAVIS, Roy (1922-)

African Sonata (1966)
[9311] Grayson, Richard (pf)
- Orion ORS-73121; 33s; rel
1974; cip

Collage
[9312] Royal Philharmonic Orchestra;
Lipkin, Arthur Bennett (cond)
- CRI-259; 33s; rel 1970; cip

**Concerto, Piano and Orchestra
(1970)**
[9313] Vallecillo-Gray, Irma (pf); Royal
Philharmonic Orchestra; Popper,
Jan (cond)
- Orion ORS-76219; 33s; rel
1976; cip

Duo concertante (1967)
[9314] Lateiner, Isidor (vln); Grosz, Edith
(pf)
- Orion ORS-73121; 33s; rel
1974; cip

(Five) Episodes (1961-62)
[9315] Masselos, William (pf)
- Desto DC-7132; 33s; rel 1972;
cip

**Passion of Oedipus, The (1965):
Flashback (The Murder of Laios)
and Denouement**
[9316] Lehane, Maureen (m sop); Du Pre,
William (ten); Mammen, Joy
(sop); Dunlap, John Robert (bar);
Lloyd, Robert (b); Hale, Richard
(speaker); Royal Philharmonic
Orchestra and Chorus; Popper,
Jan (cond)
- Orion ORS-73129; 33s; rel
1973; cip

Quartet, Strings, No 1 (1949)
[9317] New Forum Quartet
- Desto DC-7132; 33s; rel 1972;
cip

Songs and Epilogues
[9318] Enns, Harold (bar); Royal
Philharmonic Orchestra; Popper,
Jan (cond)
- Orion ORS-76219; 33s; rel
1976; cip

Switched-On Ashanti (1973)
[9319] Andrus, Gretel Shanley (fl); Travis,
Roy (syn); Badu, Kwasi (perc)
- Orion ORS-73121; 33s; rel
1974; cip

Symphonic Allegro
[9320] New York Philharmonic;
Mitropoulos, Dimitri (cond)
- Columbia AAL-16; 33m; 10"; rel
1952; del 1957

[9321] Royal Philharmonic Orchestra;
Popper, Jan (cond)
- Orion ORS-76219; 33s; rel
1976; cip

TREDINNICK, Noel*

Brief Encounters
[9322] Thalben-Ball, George (org)
- Vista VPS-1046; 33s; rel 1977

TREMBLAY, George (1911-)

Prelude and Dance (1935)
[9323] Crown, John (pf)
- Co-Art 5014; 78

Scherzo (1950)
[9324] Dufresme, Josephte (pf)
- CBC Transcription Programme
135; 33; rel 196?

**Symphony in One Movement
(1949)**
[9325] Hamburg Symphony Orchestra;
Balazs, Frederic (cond)
- CRI-224; 33s; rel 1968; cip

Vivace
[9326] Dufresme, Josephte (pf)
- CBC Transcription Programme
135; 33; rel 196?

TRIESTE, Robert

(Two) Pieces, Clarinet and Piano
[9327] McBride, Robert (cl); Tucker,
Gregory (pf)
- Yaddo 36A-B; 78; rel 1937
- Yaddo 37A; 78; rel 1937

TRIGGS, Harold (1900-)

Bright Land, The (1942)
[9328] Eastman-Rochester Symphony
Orchestra; Hanson, Howard
(cond)
Rec 1956
- Mercury MG-50114; 33m; rel
1957; del 1963
- Eastman-Rochester Archives
ERA-1002; 33s; rel 1974; cip

Danza braziliana (1947)
[9329] Besrodni, Igor (vln); Makarov,
Abram (pf)
- Monitor MC-2028; 33m; rel
1959; del 1978

[9330] Kaufman, Louis (vln); Kaufman,
Annette (pf)
- Vox 627; 78; 4 discs; rel 1948
- Concert Hall CHC-58; 33m; rel
1950; del 1957

TRIMBLE, Lester (1923-)
Closing Piece (1957)
[9331] Imperial Philharmonic Orchestra of
Tokyo; Strickland, William (cond)
- CRI-159; 33m; rel 1962; cip

(Five) Episodes (1962)
[9332] Japan Philharmonic Symphony
Orchestra; Watanabe, Akeo
(cond)
- CRI-187; 33m/s; rel 1964/?; cip

**(Four) Fragments from the
Canterbury Tales (1958)**
[9333] Addison, Adele (sop); Russo,
Charles (cl); Orenstein, Martin
(fl); Conant, Robert (hpschd)
- Columbia ML-5598/MS-6198;
33m/s; rel 1961; del 1968
- Columbia CML-5598/CMS-6198;
33m/s; rel 1968; del 1974
- Columbia AMS-6198; 33s; rel
1974; cip

**In Praise of Diplomacy and
Common Sense (1965)**
[9334] Frisch, Richard (bar); The
Ensemble; Davies, Dennis Russell
(cond)
- CRI-298; 33s; rel 1973; cip

Love Seeketh Not Itself to Please
[9335] Hanks, John Kennedy (ten);
Friedberg, Ruth (pf)
- Duke University Press
DWR-7306; 33s; rel 1974

Panels I (1969)
[9336] chamber ensemble; Trimble, Lester
(cond)
- Desto DC-7132; 33s; rel 1972;
cip

Quartet
[9337] New Forum Quartet
- Desto DC-7132; 33s; rel 1972;
cip

**Symphony in Two Movements
(1951)**
[9338] Japan Philharmonic Symphony
Orchestra; Watanabe, Akeo
(cond)
- CRI-187; 33m/s; rel 1964/?; cip

Tell Me Where Is Fancy Bred?
[9339] Hanks, John Kennedy (ten);
Friedberg, Ruth (pf)
- Duke University Press
DWR-7306; 33s; rel 1974

TROGAN, Roland (1933-)
(Five) Nocturnes (1969)
[9340] Woitach, Richard (pf)
- Opus One 11; 33s; rel 1972; cip

Seafarer, The (1965-66)
[9341] Wiederanders, William (b); Sullivan,
Jean (reader); Woitach, Richard
(pf)
- Opus One 5/S-5; 33m/s; rel
1968; cip

Sonata, Piano (1970)
[9342] Violette, Andrew (pf)
- Opus One 32; 33s; rel 1978; cip

Sonata, Violin (1959)
[9343] Kohon, Harold (vln)
- Opus One 11; 33s; rel 1972; cip

TROMBLY, Preston A. (1945-)
Kinetics III (1971)
[9344] Sollberger, Harvey (fl); tape
- Nonesuch HB-73028; 33s; 2
discs; rel 1975; cip

TROWBRIDGE, Luther (1892-)
Chromatico
[9345] Manucci, Livio (vcl); Haubiel,
Charles (pf)
- Dorian 1009; 33m; rel 1962; del
1974

TRYTHALL, Harry Gilbert (1930-)
Entropy
[9346] Georgia State College Brass
Ensemble; Hill, William H. (cond)
- Golden Crest CRS-4085; 33s; rel
1969; cip

Symphony No 1 (1958, rev 1961)
[9347] Knoxville Symphony Orchestra; Van
Vactor, David (cond)
- CRI-155; 33m; rel 1962; cip

TRYTHALL, Richard (1939-)
Coincidences (1969)
[9348] Trythall, Richard (pf)
- CRI-305; 33s; rel 1974; cip

Omaggio a Jerry Lee Lewis (1975)
[9349] Electronic music
Rec 6/77
- CRI-382; 33s; rel 1978; cip

**Variations on a Theme by Haydn
(1976)**
[9350] Dorian Woodwind Quintet; tape
Rec 6/77
- CRI-382; 33s; rel 1978; cip

TUCKER, Gregory (1908-71)
(Two) Pieces, Clarinet and Piano
[9351] McBride, Robert (cl); Tucker,
Gregory (pf)
- New Music Quarterly Recordings
1415; 78; rel 1939

(Three) Pieces, Clarinet and Piano
[9352] McBride, Robert (cl); Tucker,
Gregory (pf)
- Yaddo 24B; 78; rel 1937 (1st
movement)
- Yaddo 25A-B; 78; rel 1937 (2nd
and 3rd movements)
- Yaddo 39B; 78; rel 1937

TUDOR, David (1926-)
Microphone
[9353] Electronic music
- Cramps 5206; 33s; rel 1978

TUDOR, David and CAGE, John
see CAGE, John and TUDOR, David

TUFTS, Paul (1924-)
Sonata, Horn and Piano (1975)
[9354] Leuba, Christopher (hn); Aanerud,
Kevin (pf)
Rec 1977
- Crystal S-372; 33s; rel 1977; cip

Sonata, Viola and Piano (1967)
[9355] McInnes, Donald (vla); Siki, Bela
(pf)
- Laurel LR-107; 33s; rel 1978;
cip

Suite, Viola and Piano (1957)
[9356] McInnes, Donald (vla); Siki, Bela
(pf)
- Laurel LR-107; 33s; rel 1978;
cip

TULL, Fisher (1934-)
Capriccio, Chamber Orchestra
[9357] Tennessee Tech Chamber
Orchestra; Wattenberger, James
(cond)
- USC Sound Enterprises RPP-518;
33

Coup de Brass
[9358] Tidewater Brass Quintet
- Golden Crest CRSQ-4179; 33q

Credo
[9359] Sam Houston State University
Symphonic Band and Wind
Ensemble; Mills, Ralph L. (cond)
- Golden Crest ATH-5050; 33s; rel
1977; cip

Cryptic Essay
[9360] Tennessee Tech Symphonic Band;
Pegram, Wayne (cond) or Tull,
Fisher (cond)
- USC Sound Enterprises RPP-518;
33

Exhibition (1961)
[9361] Fine Arts Brass Quintet
- WIM Records WIMR-4; 33s; rel 1975; cip

Liturgical Symphony (1960)
[9362] Los Angeles Brass Society; Remsen, Lester (cond)
- Avant AV-1001; 33s; rel 1971; cip

March for Tripod
[9363] Sam Houston State University Symphonic Band and Wind Ensemble; Mills, Ralph L. (cond)
- Golden Crest ATH-5050; 33s; rel 1977; cip

Reflections on Paris
[9364] Sam Houston State University Symphonic Band and Wind Ensemble; Mills, Ralph L. (cond)
- Golden Crest ATH-5050; 33s; rel 1977; cip

[9365] Tennessee Tech Symphonic Band; Pegram, Wayne (cond) or Tull, Fisher (cond)
- USC Sound Enterprises RPP-518; 33

Sketches on a Tudor Psalm (1972)
[9366] Sam Houston State University Symphonic Band and Wind Ensemble; Mills, Ralph L. (cond)
- Golden Crest ATH-5050; 33s; rel 1977; cip

Terpsichore (1967)
[9367] Sam Houston State University Symphonic Band and Wind Ensemble; Mills, Ralph L. (cond)
- Golden Crest ATH-5050; 33s; rel 1977; cip

Toccata (1969)
[9368] Sam Houston State University Symphonic Band and Wind Ensemble; Mills, Ralph L. (cond)
- Golden Crest ATH-5050; 33s; rel 1977; cip

Variations on an Advent Hymn (1962)
[9369] Los Angeles Philharmonic Brass Ensemble; Remsen, Lester (cond)
- Avant AV-1005; 33s; rel 1976; cip

TURETZKY, Bertram (1933-)

Gamelan Music
[9370] Turetzky, Bertram (cb); Graves, Mel (cb)
- Finnadar SR-9015; 33s; rel 1977; cip

TURNER, Charles (1921-)

Serenade for Icarus (1960)
[9371] Kroll, William (vln); Johannesen, Grant (pf)
- Golden Crest CR-4072/CRS-4072; 33m/s; rel 1964; cip

TUROK, Paul (1929-)

Little Suite (Op 9)
[9372] Benoit, Regis (pf)
- Orion ORS-7274; 33s; rel 1972; cip

Lyric Variations (Op 32)
[9373] McAninch, Daniel (ob); Louisville Orchestra; Mester, Jorge (cond) Rec 5/4/73
- LS-73-3; 33s (Louisville Orchestra First Edition Records 1973 No 3); rel 1974; cip

Passacaglia (Op 10)
[9374] Benoit, Regis (pf)
- Orion ORS-7274; 33s; rel 1972; cip

(Three) Transcendental Etudes (Op 30)
[9375] Benoit, Regis (pf)
- Orion ORS-7274; 33s; rel 1972; cip

TUTHILL, Burnet (1888-)

Come Seven (1944)
[9376] Vienna Symphony Orchestra; Schoenherr, Max (cond)
- American Recording Society ARS-30; 33m; 10"; rel 1953

(Three) Moods
[9377] LeJeune, Claude (fl)
- SMP 209; 33s; rel 1971; del 1978

Sonata, Alto Saxophone and Piano (Op 20) (1939)
[9378] Leeson, Cecil (sax); Kohler, Jean (pf)
- Enchante ENS-2002; 33s; rel 1968; del 1977

TYSON, Mildred L. (1901-)

Sea Moods (arr for voice and pf)
[9379] Flagstad, Kirsten (sop); McArthur, Edwin (pf)
- RCA LM-1870; 33m; rel 1955; del 1960

ULEHLA, Ludmila (1923-)

Elegy for a Whale
[9380] Hoover, Katherine (fl); Brey, Carter (vcl); Weintraub, Barbara (pf); taped whale sounds
- Leonarda LPI-104; 33s; rel 1980

Gargoyles (1970)
[9381] Raskin, Judith (sop); Hindell, Leonard (bsn); Nygaard, Jens (pf)
- Mace MCS-9113; 33s; rel 1973

UNG, Chinary (1942-)

Mohori (1974)
[9382] Martin, Barbara (sop); Contemporary Chamber Ensemble; Weisberg, Arthur (cond)
- CRI-363; 33s; rel 1977; cip

USSACHEVSKY, Vladimir (1911-)

Conflict (1973-75)
[9383] Electronic music
- Folkways FTS-33904; 33s; rel 1976; cip

Creation Prologue (1960-61)
[9384] multiple choruses; tape
- Columbia ML-5966/MS-6566; 33m/s; rel 1964; del 1979

Improvisation 4711 (1958)
[9385] Electronic music
- Son-Nova 3/S-3; 33m/s; rel 1963; del 1970

Linear Contrasts (1958)
[9386] Electronic music
- Son-Nova 3/S-3; 33m/s; rel 1963; del 1970
- CRI-356; 33s; rel 1977; cip

Metamorphoses (1957)
[9387] Electronic music
- Son-Nova 3/S-3; 33m/s; rel 1963; del 1970
- CRI-356; 33s; rel 1977; cip

Missa brevis (1972)
[9388] Ottley, Jo Ann (sop); University of Utah Chorus; Utah Symphony Orchestra Brass Players; Wright, Newell (cond)
- CRI-297; 33s; rel 1974; cip

Of Wood and Brass (1964-65)
[9389] Electronic music
- CRI-227; 33s; rel 1968; cip

Piece for Computer (1968)
[9390] Electronic music
- CRI-268; 33s; 2 discs; rel 1972; cip

Piece for Tape Recorder (1956)
[9391] Electronic music
- CRI-112; 33m/s; rel 1957/?; cip
- Finnadar CD-4; 33q; rel 1976
- Finnadar QD-9010; 33q; rel 1976; cip

(Three) Scenes from the Creation: Prologue "Enuma Elish" (1960, rev 1973)
[9392] Macalester Chamber Chorus; Morton, Ian (cond)
- CRI-297; 33s; rel 1974; cip

(Three) Scenes from the Creation: Interlude (1960, rev 1973) and Epilogue "Spell of Creation" (1971)
[9393] University of Utah A Capella Chorus; Wright, Newell (cond)
- CRI-297; 33s; rel 1974; cip

(Two) Sketches for Computer Piece No 2 (1971)
[9394] Electronic music
- CRI-268; 33s; 2 discs; rel 1972; cip

Sonic Contours (1952)
[9395] Electronic music
- Innovations GB-1; 33m; 10"; rel 1955*
- Desto DC-6466; 33s; rel 1968; cip

Transposition, Reverberation, Experiment, Composition (1951-52)
[9396] Electronic music
- Folkways FX-6160; 33m; rel 1958; cip

Underwater Valse (1952)
[9397] Electronic music
- Folkways FX-6160; 33m; rel 1958; cip

Wireless Fantasy (De Forrest Murmurs) (1960)
[9398] Electronic music
- CRI-227; 33s; rel 1968; cip

USSACHEVSKY, Vladimir and LUENING, Otto

see LUENING, Otto and USSACHEVSKY, Vladimir

VAN APPLEDORN, Mary Jean (1927-)

Communique
[9399] Klinger, Judith (sop); Van Appledorn, Mary Jean (pf)
- Opus One 52; 33s; rel 1979; cip

Set of Five
[9400] Van Appledorn, Mary Jean (pf)
- Opus One 52; 33s; rel 1979; cip

Sonnet for Organ (1959)
[9401] Maynard, Judson (org)
- Opus One 43; 33s; rel 1979; cip

VAN HULSE, Camil (1897-)

Elegy
[9402] Clio Concert Trio
- Dorian 1007; 33m; rel 1962; del 1974

Festival Postlude on Veni, creator spiritus
[9403] Salvador, Mario (org)
- Technisonic Studios TMS-3-4; 33m; rel 1954

Saint Louis, roi de France: Marche
[9404] Salvador, Mario (org)
- Technisonic Studios TMS-1-2; 33m; rel 1954

Variations, Piano
[9405] Rogers, Herbert (pf)
- Dorian 1006; 33m; rel 1962; del 1970

VAN VACTOR, David (1906-)

(Five) Bagatelles, Strings (1938): Nos 3-5
[9406] Hessian Symphony Orchestra; Van Vactor, David (cond)
- Everest SDBR-3236; 33s; rel 1969; cip

Chorale and Allegro
[9407] Hessian Symphony Orchestra; Van Vactor, David (cond)
- Orion ORS-7029; 33s; rel 1970; cip

Concerto, Viola and Orchestra (1940)
[9408] Eurich, Hans (vla); Hessian Radio Symphony Orchestra; Van Vactor, David (cond)
- Orion ORS-7024; 33s; rel 1970; cip

Concerto grosso, Three Flutes, Harp, and Orchestra (1935)
[9409] Schmidt, Willy (fl); Peschke, Werner (fl); Seyfried, Karl-Hermann (fl); Cassedanne-Hasse, Charlotte (hp); Hessian Radio Symphony Orchestra; Van Vactor, David (cond)
- Orion ORS-7024; 33s; rel 1970; cip

Divertimento (1939)
[9410] Yaddo Chamber Orchestra; Van Vactor, David (cond)
- Yaddo III-8; 78; 1-10" and 1-12"; rel 1940

Economy Band (1968)
[9411] Georgia State College Brass Ensemble; Hill, William H. (cond)
- Golden Crest CRS-4085; 33s; rel 1969; cip

(Four) Etudes, Winds and Percussion (1963)
[9412] Hessian Symphony Orchestra; Van Vactor, David (cond)
- Orion ORS-7029; 33s; rel 1970; cip

Fantasia, Chaconne, and Allegro (1957)
[9413] Louisville Orchestra; Whitney, Robert (cond)
- LOU-58-6; 33m (Louisville Orchestra First Edition Records 1958 No 6); rel 1959; del 1978

Introduction and Presto
[9414] Hessian Symphony Orchestra; Van Vactor, David (cond)
- Orion ORS-6910; 33s; rel 1969; cip

Music for the Marines (1943): Ode
[9415] Hessian Symphony Orchestra; Van Vactor, David (cond)
- Orion ORS-7029; 33s; rel 1970; cip

Octet, Brass (1963)
[9416] Hessian Symphony Orchestra; Van Vactor, David (cond)
- Everest SDBR-3236; 33s; rel 1969; cip

Overture to a Comedy No 2 (1941)
[9417] Hessian Symphony Orchestra; Van Vactor, David (cond)
- Everest SDBR-3236; 33s; rel 1969; cip

Passacaglia, Chorale, and Allegro (1964)
[9418] Hessian Symphony Orchestra; Van Vactor, David (cond)
- Orion ORS-7029; 33s; rel 1970; cip

Pastoral and Dance (1947)
[9419] Hessian Symphony Orchestra; Van Vactor, David (fl) (cond)
- Orion ORS-6910; 33s; rel 1969; cip

Prelude and March (1950)
[9420] Hessian Symphony Orchestra; Van Vactor, David (cond)
- Orion ORS-7029; 33s; rel 1970; cip

Quintet, Flute and Strings (1932)
[9421] Hessian Symphony Orchestra; Van Vactor, David (cond)
- Everest SDBR-3236; 33s; rel 1969; cip

Recitativo and Saltarello (1947)
[9422] Hessian Symphony Orchestra; Van Vactor, David (cond)
- Orion ORS-6910; 33s; rel 1969; cip

Sarabande and Variations (1972)
[9423] Hessian Symphony Orchestra; Van
Vactor, David (cond)
- Orion ORS-7029; 33s; rel 1970;
cip

Scherzo
[9424] New York Woodwind Quintet
- Everest LPBR-6092/SDBR-3092;
33m/s; rel 1963; del 1978

Sinfonia breve (1964)
[9425] Hessian Symphony Orchestra; Van
Vactor, David (cond)
- Orion ORS-6910; 33s; rel 1969;
cip

Sonata, Flute and Piano (1945)
[9426] Bryan, Keith (fl); Keys, Karen (pf)
- Orion ORS-76242; 33s; rel
1976; cip

**Suite on Chilean Folk Themes
(1963)**
[9427] Hessian Symphony Orchestra; Van
Vactor, David (cond)
- Orion ORS-6910; 33s; rel 1969;
cip

Symphony No 1 (1937)
[9428] Frankfurt Radio Symphony
Orchestra; Van Vactor, David
(cond)
- CRI-225; 33s; rel 1969; cip

Symphony No 2 (1958)
[9429] Hessian Radio Symphony
Orchestra; Van Vactor, David
(cond)
- CRI-169; 33m/s; rel 1963/?; cip

Variazioni solenne (1941)
[9430] Hessian Symphony Orchestra; Van
Vactor, David (cond)
- Everest SDBR-3236; 33s; rel
1969; cip

VAN VEELEN, Paul (1939-)
Fantaisie, Organ
[9431] Van Veelen, Paul (org)
- Aeolian-Skinner AS-324; 33s; rel
1970

VANDERSLOOT, Carl D.
General Pershing March (1918)
[9432] American Legion Band; Colling, Joe
(cond)
- Decca 25426-29 (in set A-713);
78; 4-10"; rel 1949
[9433] Arthur Pryor's Band; Pryor, Arthur
(cond)
Rec 10/5/26
- Victor 20303; 78; 10"
- New World NW-282; 33m; rel
1976

VARDELL, Charles (1893-1962)
Joe Clark Steps Out (1933)
[9434] Eastman-Rochester Symphony
Orchestra; Hanson, Howard
(cond)
- Victor 2059; 78; 10"; rel
pre-1942
[9435] Eastman-Rochester Symphony
Orchestra; Hanson, Howard (cond)
Rec 10/28/56
- Mercury MG-50134/SR-90134;
33m/s; rel 1957/1959; del
1963
- Mercury MG-50326/SR-90326;
33m/s; rel 1963; del 1966
- Eastman-Rochester Archives
ERA-1012; 33s; rel 197?

VARDI, Emanuel (1917-)
**Americana: On the Banks of the Old
Pee Dee and The Unconstant
Lover**
[9436] Kapp Sinfonietta; Vardi, Emanuel
(cond)
- Kapp KCL-9059/KC-S-9059;
33m/s; rel 1961; del 1963

Prelude, Violoncello
[9437] Silberstein, Jascha (vcl) or
Cassado, Gaspar (vcl) or
Feuermann, Emanuel (vcl)
- Musical Heritage Society
MHS-3272; 33s

VARESE, Edgard (1883-1965)
Ameriques (1918?-21, rev 1927)
[9438] New York Philharmonic; Boulez,
Pierre (cond)
Rec 12/1/75
- Columbia M-34552; 33q; rel
1977; cip
- CBS (English, French, and
German) 76520; 33q
[9439] ORTF Philharmonic Orchestra;
Constant, Marius (cond)
- Erato (French) STU-70726; 33s;
rel 1973*
- Musical Heritage Society
MHS-3726; 33s; rel 1978
[9440] Utah Symphony Orchestra;
Abravanel, Maurice (cond)
- Vanguard
VRS-1156/VSD-71156; 33m/s;
rel 1966; del 1968
- Vanguard SRV-274-SD; 33s; rel
1968; cip
- Philips Vanguard (English)
VSL-11048; 33s; rel 1968*
- Vanguard SRV-308-SD; 33s; rel
1974; cip
- Barclay Vanguard (French)
VSD-71156; 33s
- Barclay Classic (French)
991-065; 33s

Arcana (1925-27, rev 1960)
[9441] Chicago Symphony Orchestra;
Martinon, Jean (cond)
Rec ca 3/66
- RCA LM-2914/LSC-2914;
33m/s; rel 1966; del 1974
- RCA (French) 645-064; 33s; rel
1966*

Arcana (1925-27, rev 1960)
(cont'd)
- RCA (English)
RB-6710/SB-6710; 33m/s; rel
1967*
- RCA (German)
LM-2914/LSC-2914; 33m/s
[9442] Columbia Symphony Orchestra;
Craft, Robert (cond)
Rec 6/28/61
- Columbia ML-5762/MS-6362;
33m/s; rel 1962; del 1977
- CBS (English and German)
BRG-72106/SBRG-72106;
33m/s; rel 1962*
- Columbia MG-31078; 33s; 2
discs; rel 1972; cip
- CBS (French) 72106; 33s
- CBS (French) 75106; 33s
- CBS (French and Italian) 77241;
33s
[9443] Los Angeles Philharmonic
Orchestra; Mehta, Zubin (cond)
- Decca (English and German)
SXL-6550; 33s; rel 1972*
- London CS-6752; 33s; rel 1973;
cip
- Orphic Egg OES-6913; 33s; rel
1974; del 1975
- JBL CSL-1010; 33s; rel 1977
(excerpt)
- Decca (French) 7146; 33s
[9444] New York Philharmonic; Boulez,
Pierre (cond)
Rec 2/12/77
- Columbia M-34552; 33q; rel
1977; cip
- CBS (English, French, and
German) 76520; 33q
[9445] ORTF Philharmonic Orchestra;
Constant, Marius (cond)
- Erato (French) STU-70726; 33s;
rel 1973*
- Musical Heritage Society
MHS-3726; 33s; rel 1978

Density 21.5 (1936)
[9446] Andersen, Alf (fl)
- Philips (Norwegian) 631-053NL;
33
[9447] Bourdin, Roger (fl)
- Arion (French) 30-A-071; 33s;
rel 1969*
- Arion 30-A-071; 33s; rel 1973
- Musical Heritage Society
MHS-3072; 33s; rel 1975
[9448] Castagner, Jacques (fl)
- Ades (French) 16.005; 33s; rel
1972*
[9449] Debost, Michel (fl)
- EMI/His Master's Voice (French)
C-061-10875; 33s; rel 1970*
- Angel S-36786; 33s; rel 1971;
cip
- Pathe C-061-10875; 33s; rel
1971
- Electrola (German)
C-063-10875; 33s

Density 21.5 (1936) *(cont'd)*

[9450] Gazzelloni, Severino (fl)
- Vega (French) C-37-S-173; 33;
7"; rel 1958*

[9451] Gazzelloni, Severino (fl)
Rec 5/67
- Wergo (French and German)
WER-60-029; 33s; rel 1968?
- Heliodor Wergo (English)
2549.002; 33s; rel 1969*
- Heliodor Wergo 2549.002; 33s;
rel 1970; del 1970

[9452] Gleghorn, Arthur (fl)
Rec 2/26-27/59
- Columbia ML-5478/MS-6146;
33m/s; rel 1960; cip
- Philips (English) ABL-3392; 33s;
rel 1961*
- Columbia MG-31078; 33s; 2
discs; rel 1972; cip
- Philips (French and German)
A-01494L; 33s
- CBS (French) 75695; 33s
- CBS (French and Italian) 77241;
33s

[9453] Graf, Peter-Lukas (fl)
- Claves (German) 0235/30235;
33m/s; rel 1972

[9454] LeRoy, Rene (fl)
- New Music Quarterly Recordings
1000A-B; 78; rel 1949

[9455] LeRoy, Rene (fl)
Rec 5/11/50
- EMS Recordings EMS-401; 33m;
rel 1950; del 1970
- Finnadar SR-9018; 33m; rel
1978; cip
- Boite a musique (French)
LD-024; 33m

[9456] Pellerite, James (fl)
- Coronet M-1291/S-1291;
33m/s; rel 1969/?; cip

[9457] Reissberger, Helmut (fl)
- Candide CE-31028; 33s; rel
1970; cip
- Vox (English) STGBY-643; 33s;
rel 1971*
- Candide (French and German)
CE-31028; 33s
- Vox (French) 36029; 33s

[9458] Sollberger, Harvey (fl)
- Nonesuch HB-73028; 33s; 2
discs; rel 1975; cip

[9459] Willoughby, Robert (fl)
- Coronet LPS-3006; 33s; rel
1977; cip

[9460] Zoeller, Karlheinz (fl)
- Electrola (German)
C-063-28950; 33s; rel 1972
- EMI/Odeon C-063-28950; 33s;
rel 1973
- EMI/His Master's Voice (French)
C-061-28950; 33s

[9461] no performer given
- Opus Musicum OM-113-15; 33s;
3 discs; rel 1974

Deserts (1950?-54, tape rev 1960, 1961)

[9462] Columbia Symphony Orchestra;
tape; Craft, Robert (cond)
Rec 3/21/61
- Columbia ML-5762/MS-6362;
33m/s; rel 1962; del 1977
- CBS (English and German)
BRG-72106/SBRG-72106;
33m/s; rel 1962*
- Columbia MG-31078; 33s; 2
discs; rel 1972; cip
- CBS (French) 72106; 33s
- CBS (French) 75106; 33s
- CBS (French and Italian) 77241;
33s

[9463] Group for Contemporary Music at
Columbia University; tape;
Wuorinen, Charles (cond)
- CRI-268; 33s; rel 1972; cip

[9464] Paris Instrumental Ensemble for
Contemporary Music; tape;
Simonovitch, Konstantin (cond)
- EMI/His Master's Voice (French)
C-061-10875; 33s; rel 1970*
- Angel S-36786; 33s; rel 1971;
cip
- Pathe C-061-10875; 33s; rel
1971
- Electrola (German)
C-063-10875; 33s

Deserts: Interpolations

[9465] Electronic music
- Finnadar SR-9018; 33s; rel
1978; cip

Ecuatorial (1932-34)

[9466] Paul, Thomas (b); Contemporary
Chamber Ensemble; Weisberg,
Arthur (cond)
- Nonesuch H-71269/HQ-1269;
33s/q; rel 1972/1973; cip

[9467] University-Civic Chorale (bass
ensemble); Utah Symphony
Orchestra; Abravanel, Maurice
(cond)
- Vanguard Cardinal VCS-10047;
33s; rel 1969; cip
- Philips Vanguard (English)
VSL-11073; 33s; rel 1969*
- Vanguard SRV-308-SD; 33s; rel
1974; cip

Hyperprism (1922-23)

[9468] Columbia Symphony Orchestra;
Craft, Robert (cond)
Rec 2/26-27/59
- Columbia ML-5478/MS-6146;
33m/s; rel 1960; cip
- Philips (English) ABL-3392; 33s;
rel 1961*
- Columbia MG-31078; 33s; 2
discs; rel 1972; cip
- Columbia AS-19; 33s; 7"
- Philips (English and German)
A-01494L; 33s
- CBS (French) 75695; 33s
- CBS (French and Italian) 77241;
33s

Hyperprism (1922-23) *(cont'd)*

[9469] Domaine Musicale Ensemble;
Boulez, Pierre (cond)
- Vega (French, German, and
Italian) C-30-A-271; 33; rel
1960*
- Wergo (German) WER-60-005;
33 (excerpt)

[9470] Ensemble Die Reihe; Cerha,
Friedrich (cond)
- Candide CE-31028; 33s; rel
1970; cip
- Vox (English) STGBY-643; 33s;
rel 1971*
- Candide (French and German)
CE-31028; 33s
- Vox (French) 36029; 33s

[9471] Paris Instrumental Ensemble for
Contemporary Music;
Simonovitch, Konstantin (cond)
- EMI/His Master's Voice (French)
C-061-10875; 33s; rel 1970*
- Angel S-36786; 33s; rel 1971;
cip
- Pathe C-061-10875; 33s; rel
1971
- Electrola (German)
C-063-10875; 33s

Integrales (1924-25)

[9472] Columbia Symphony Orchestra;
Craft, Robert (cond)
Rec 2/26-27/59
- Columbia ML-5478/MS-6146;
33m/s; rel 1960; cip
- Philips (English) ABL-3392; 33s;
rel 1961*
- Columbia MG-31078; 33s; 2
discs; rel 1972; cip
- Philips (English and German)
A-01494L; 33s
- CBS (French) 75695; 33s
- CBS (French and Italian) 77241;
33s

[9473] Contemporary Chamber Ensemble;
Weisberg, Arthur (cond)
- Nonesuch H-71269/HQ-1269;
33s/q; rel 1972/1973; cip
- Nonesuch (English)
H-71269/HQ-1269; 33s/q; rel
1973*

[9474] Domaine Musicale Ensemble;
Boulez, Pierre (cond)
- Vega (French, German, and
Italian) C-30-A-271; 33; rel
1960*

[9475] Ensemble Die Reihe; Cerha,
Friedrich (cond)
- Candide CE-31028; 33s; rel
1970; cip
- Vox (English) STGBY-643; 33s;
rel 1971*
- Candide (French and German)
CE-31028; 33s
- Vox (French) 36029; 33s

[9476] Los Angeles Philharmonic
Orchestra; Mehta, Zubin (cond)
Rec 4/20-21/71
- Decca (English and German)
SXL-6550; 33s; rel 1972*

Integrales (1924-25) *(cont'd)*
- London CS-6752; 33s; rel 1973; cip
- Orphic Egg OES-6913; 33s; rel 1974; del 1975
- Decca (French) 7146; 33s

[9477] New York Wind Ensemble; Juilliard Percussion Orchestra; Waldman, Frederic (cond)
Rec 6/21/50
- EMS Recordings EMS-401; 33m; rel 1950; del 1970
- Finnadar SR-9018; 33m; rel 1978; cip
- Boite a musique (French) LD-024; 33m

[9478] Paris Instrumental Ensemble for Contemporary Music; Simonovitch, Konstantin (cond)
- EMI/His Master's Voice (French) C-061-10875; 33s; rel 1970*
- Angel S-36786; 33s; rel 1971; cip
- Pathe C-061-10875; 33s; rel 1971
- Electrola (German) C-063-10875; 33s

Ionisation (1929-31)
[9479] Aarhus Conservatory Percussion Ensemble; Lylloff, Bent (cond)
Rec 4/4/71
- Cambridge CC-2824; 33s; rel 1972; cip

[9480] American Percussion Society; Price, Paul (cond)
- Urania UX-106; 33m; rel 1957; del 1969
- Urania USD-1007; 33s; rel 1958; del 1960
- Urania US-5106; 33s; rel 1961; del 1970

[9481] Ensemble Die Reihe; Cerha, Friedrich (cond)
- Candide CE-31028; 33s; rel 1970; cip
- Vox (English) STGBY-643; 33s; rel 1971*
- Candide (French and German) CE-31028; 33s
- Vox (French) 36029; 33s

[9482] Juilliard Percussion Orchestra; Waldman, Frederic (cond)
Rec 5/21/50
- EMS Recordings EMS-401; 33m; rel 1950; del 1970
- Folkways FX-6160; 33m; rel 1958; cip (excerpt)
- Finnadar SR-9018; 33m; rel 1978; cip
- Boite a musique (French) LD-024; 33m

[9483] Los Angeles Percussion Ensemble; Mehta, Zubin (cond)
Rec 4/20-21/71
- Decca (English and German) SXL-6550; 33s; rel 1972*
- London CS-6752; 33s; rel 1973; cip
- Orphic Egg OES-6913; 33s; rel 1974; del 1975

Ionisation (1929-31) *(cont'd)*
- Decca (French) 7146; 33s

[9484] New Jersey Percussion Ensemble; DesRoches, Raymond (cond)
- Nonesuch H-71291/HQ-1291; 33s/q; rel 1974/1976; cip

[9485] New York Philharmonic; Boulez, Pierre (cond)
Rec 2/12/77
- Columbia M-34552; 33q; rel 1977; cip
- CBS (English, French, and German) 76520; 33q

[9486] Percussions de Strasbourg
- Philips (English) 6526-017; 33s; rel 1971*

[9487] University of Illinois Percussion Ensemble; Price, Paul (cond)
- Illini Union Bookstore CRS-3; 33m; rel 1955*

[9488] percussion ensemble; Craft, Robert (cond)
Rec 2/26-27/59
- Columbia ML-5478/MS-6146; 33m/s; rel 1960; cip
- Philips (English) ABL-3392; 33s; rel 1961*
- Columbia MG-31078; 33s; 2 discs; rel 1972; cip
- Columbia AS-19; 33s; 7"
- Columbia P2-11687; 33s
- Philips (English and German) A-01494L; 33s
- CBS (French) 75695; 33s
- CBS (French and Italian) 77241; 33s

[9489] percussion ensemble; Slonimsky, Nicolas (cond)
Rec 6/1/34
- Columbia 4095M; 78; 10"; rel pre-1936
- Orion ORD-7150/ORS-7150; 33m/s; rel 1971/?; cip

Nocturnal (1961) (completed by Chou Wen-chung in 1973)
[9490] Bybee, Ariel (sop); University-Civic Chorale (bass ensemble); Utah Symphony Orchestra; Abravanel, Maurice (cond)
- Vanguard Cardinal VCS-10047; 33s; rel 1969; cip
- Philips Vanguard (English) VSL-11073; 33s; rel 1969*
- Vanguard SRV-308-SD; 33s; rel 1974; cip

Octandre (1923)
[9491] Contemporary Chamber Ensemble; Weisberg, Arthur (cond)
- Nonesuch H-71269/HQ-1269; 33s/q; rel 1972/1973; cip
- Nonesuch (English) H-71269/HQ-1269; 33s/q; rel 1973*

[9492] Domaine Musicale Ensemble; Boulez, Pierre (cond)
- Vega (French, German, and Italian) C-30-A-271; 33; rel 1960*

Octandre (1923) *(cont'd)*
[9493] Ensemble Die Reihe; Cerha, Friedrich (cond)
- Candide CE-31028; 33s; rel 1970; cip
- Vox (English) STGBY-643; 33s; rel 1971*
- Candide (French and German) CE-31028; 33s
- Vox (French) 36029; 33s

[9494] Musica Nova Stockholm; Naumann, Siegfried (cond)
Rec 5/5/66, 5/15/66, and 6/3/66
- Expo Norr Riks (Swedish) LP-4; 33
- Caprice (Swedish) CAP-1034; 33

[9495] New York Wind Ensemble; Waldman, Frederic (cond)
Rec 6/21/50
- EMS Recordings EMS-401; 33m; rel 1950; del 1970
- Finnadar SR-9018; 33m; rel 1978; cip
- Boite a musique (French) LD-024; 33m

[9496] wind ensemble; Craft, Robert (cond)
Rec 2/26-27/59
- Columbia ML-5478/MS-6146; 33m/s; rel 1960; cip
- Philips (English) ABL-3392; 33s; rel 1961*
- Columbia MG-31078; 33s; 2 discs; rel 1972; cip
- Philips (French and German) A-01494L; 33s
- CBS (French) 75695; 33s
- CBS (French and Italian) 77241; 33s

[9497] wind ensemble; Goehr, Walter (cond)
Rec ca 1938
- Columbia DB-1307 (in set M-361); 78; 10"; rel pre-1942 (Excerpt: 3rd Movement)
- Columbia (English) DB-1791 (in set CHM-5); 78; 10"; rel pre-1942 (Excerpt: 3rd Movement)

[9498] wind ensemble; Slonimsky, Nicolas (cond)
Rec ca 1936
- New Music Quarterly Recordings 1411; 78; rel 1938

Offrandes (1921)
[9499] DeGaetani, Jan (m sop); Contemporary Chamber Ensemble; Weisberg, Arthur (cond)
- Nonesuch H-71269/HQ-1269; 33s/q; rel 1972/1973; cip
- Nonesuch (English) H-71269/HQ-1269; 33s/q; rel 1973*

[9500] Eda-Pierre, Christiane (sop); Domaine Musicale Ensemble; Amy, Gilbert (cond)
- Ades (French) 12.001; 33s; rel 1969*

Offrandes (1921) (cont'd)
- Ades (French) 16.012; 33s
- Ades (French) 17.011; 33s; 7"

[9501] Escribano, Marie Therese (sop);
Ensemble Die Reihe; Cerha,
Friedrich (cond)
- Candide CE-31028; 33s; rel
1970; cip
- Vox (English) STGBY-643; 33s;
rel 1971*
- Candide (French and German)
CE-31028; 33s
- Vox (French) 36029; 33s

[9502] Precht, Donna (sop); Columbia
Symphony Orchestra; Craft,
Robert (cond)
Rec 1/26/62
- Columbia ML-5762/MS-6362;
33m/s; rel 1962; del 1977
- CBS (English and German)
BRG-72106/SBRG-72106;
33m/s; rel 1962*
- Columbia MG-31078; 33s; 2
discs; rel 1972; cip
- Columbia AS-19; 33s; 7"
(Excerpt: 1st Movement)
- CBS (French) 72106; 33s
- CBS (French) 75106; 33s
- CBS (French and Italian) 77241;
33s

Poeme electronique (1957-58)
[9503] Electronic music
- Columbia ML-5478/MS-6146;
33m/s; rel 1960; cip
- Philips (English) ABL-3392; 33s;
rel 1961*
- J & W Chester Ltd JWC-1001;
33; rel ca 1968 (excerpt)
- Columbia MG-31078; 33s; 2
discs; rel 1972; cip
- Carlton
LP-12-112/STLP-12-112;
33m/s (excerpt)
- Philips (English and German)
A-01494L; 33s
- CBS (French) 75695; 33s
- CBS (French and Italian) 77241;
33s

VAUGHAN, Clifford (1893-)
Oriental Translations
[9504] ensemble; Vaughan, Clifford (cond)
- Co-Art 5011-13; 78; 10"

Revery
[9505] Remsen, Dorothy (hp)
- Avant AV-1000; 33s; rel 1967;
cip

VAUGHAN, Rodger (1932-)
Concert Piece No 1
[9506] Conner, Rex (tu)
- Coronet M-1259; 33m; rel
1969; cip

VAZZANA, Anthony E. (1922-)
Incontri (1972)
[9507] Goldman (vln); Brown (pf)
- Orion ORS-76212; 33s; rel
1977; cip

VERCOE, Barry (1937-)
Synapse
[9508] Thompson, Marcus (vla); tape
- CRI-393; 33s; rel 1979; cip

Synthesism (1970)
[9509] Electronic music
- Nonesuch H-71245; 33s; rel
1970; cip

VERRALL, John (1908-)
Prelude and Allegro (1948)
[9510] MGM Chamber Orchestra;
Surinach, Carlos (cond)
Rec 1956
- MGM E-3371; 33m; rel 1956;
del 1959

Quartet, Strings, No 4 (1949)
[9511] Washington University String
Quartet
- Music Library MLR-7028; 33m;
rel 1953; del 1974

Quartet, Strings, No 7 (ca 1960)
[9512] Berkshire Quartet
- CRI-270; 33s; rel 1971; cip

Quintet, Piano and Strings (1953)
[9513] Balogh, S. (pf); Seattle Quartet
- North-West Recording Society 1;
33m; rel pre-1956

Sonata, Horn and Piano (1942)
[9514] Leuba, Christopher (hn); Aanerud,
Kevin (pf)
- Crystal S-372; 33s; rel 1977; cip

VINCENT, John (1902-77)
Consort for Piano and Strings (1960)
[9515] Foss, Lukas (pf); American Art
Quartet
Rec 4/10-11/61
- Contemporary M-6009/S-8009;
33m/s; rel 1961/?; del 1978

Quartet, Strings, No 1 (1936)
[9516] American Art Quartet
Rec 8/24/50
- Contemporary CE-2002; 33m;
10"; rel 1953; del 1959
- Contemporary M-6009/S-8009;
33m/s; rel 1961/?; del 1978

Symphonic Poem after Descartes (1958)
[9517] Philadelphia Orchestra; Ormandy,
Eugene (cond)
- Columbia ML-5579/MS-6179;
33m/s; rel 1960; del 1965

Symphony in D (1954)
[9518] Louisville Orchestra; Whitney,
Robert (cond)
- LOU-57-2; 33m (Louisville
Orchestra First Edition Records
1957 No 2); rel 1959; cip

[9519] Philadelphia Orchestra; Ormandy,
Eugene (cond)
- Columbia ML-5263; 33m; rel
1958; del 1965
- Columbia ML-5579/MS-6179;
33m/s; rel 1960; del 1965

VIOLETTE, Andrew
Amor dammi quel fazzolettino
[9520] Thomas, Andrew (pf); Violette,
Andrew (pf)
- Opus One 52; 33s; rel 1979; cip

Black Tea (1976)
[9521] Bettina, Judith (sop); Hess, Alyssa
(hp); Tamosaitis, Joseph (cb);
Violette, Andrew (perc)
- Opus One 53; 33s; rel 1980; cip

Piano Piece Two (1974)
[9522] Violette, Andrew (pf)
- Opus One 53; 33s; rel 1980; cip

Sonata, Two Pianos
[9523] Thomas, Andrew (pf); Violette,
Andrew (pf)
- Opus One 36; 33s; rel 1978; cip

VITO, Edward
Etude, Harp, in C
[9524] Vito, Edward (hp)
- Cook 1030; 33m; 10"; rel
1953; del 1955

Gigue in Olden Style
[9525] Vito, Edward (hp)
- Cook 1030; 33m; 10"; rel
1953; del 1955

VOEGELI, Don
Oscillations (Synthesized Themes and Bridges)
[9526] Electronic music
- National Center for Audio
Experimentation; 33s; rel 1972

VOIGHT, John
Bingo
[9527] Voight, John (cb); women's chorus
- Baller St Studios BSS-101; 33s;
rel 1978

Slum Settings
[9528] Voight, John (cb); narrator
- Baller St Studios BSS-101; 33s;
rel 1978

VOLLINGER, William

More Than Conquerors

[9529] Fifer, Bruce (bar); Sobol, Lawrence (cl); Basquin, Peter (pf)
- Grenadilla GS-1009; 33s; rel 1977; cip

VOLLRATH, Carl (1931-)

Concert Piece, Trombone and Piano

[9530] Cramer, William F. (tbn); Glotzbach, Robert (pf)
- Coronet LPS-3034; 33s; rel 1977; cip

Jaunts

[9531] Cramer, William F. (tbn); Glotzbach, Robert (pf)
- Coronet LPS-3034; 33s; rel 1977; cip

Jazz Mimics

[9532] Cramer, William F. (tbn); Glotzbach, Robert (pf)
- Coronet LPS-3034; 33s; rel 1977; cip

Sonata, Baritone Horn and Piano (1969)

[9533] Cramer, William F. (tbn); Glotzbach, Robert (pf)
- Coronet LPS-3034; 33s; rel 1977; cip

WADE, James

Martyred, The

[9534] Kim Cha Kyung Opera Company; National Symphony Orchestra of Korea; Yonsei University Chorus; Handbook Ilbo Children's Chorus; Shapiro, David (cond)
- Crane Koreana; 33m; 2 discs; rel 1972*

WAGENAAR, Bernard (1894-1971)

Concert Overture (1952)

[9535] Louisville Orchestra; Whitney, Robert (cond)
- LOU-545-2; 33m (Louisville Orchestra First Edition Records 1955 No 2); rel 1959; del 1972

Sonatina, Violoncello and Piano (1934)

[9536] Benditzky, Naoum (vcl); Wagenaar, Bernard (pf)
- Columbia 68331-32D (in set 223); 78; 2 discs; rel pre-1936
- Columbia X-49; 78; rel pre-1953

Symphony No 4 (1946)

[9537] Vienna Symphony Orchestra; Haefner, Herbert (cond)
- American Recording Society ARS-21; 33m; 10"; rel pre-1953
- American Recording Society ARS-114; 33m; rel pre-1956
- Desto D-415/DST-6415; 33m/s; rel 1965; cip

Tale, A

[9538] Wagenaar, Bernard (pf)
- Columbia 68332D (in set 223); 78; rel pre-1936
- Columbia X-49; 78; rel pre-1953

WAGNER, Joseph F. (1900-74)

Ballad of Brotherhood (1947)

[9539] Mormon Tabernacle Choir; Schreiner, Alexander (org); Asper, Frank (org); Condie, Richard P. (cond)
- Columbia ML-5302/MS-6019; 33m/s; rel 1958
- Harmony HS-11273; 33s; rel 1968; del 1974

Concert Piece, Violin and Violoncello (1966)

[9540] Schoenfeld, Alice (vln); Schoenfeld, Eleanore (vcl)
- Orion ORS-7036; 33s; rel 1971; cip

Concerto grosso (1949)

[9541] Kiltie Symphony Band (Carnegie-Mellon University); Strange, Richard E. (cond)
- Orion ORS-73118; 33s; rel 1973; cip

Festive Fanfare, A (1968)

[9542] University of Miami Symphonic Wind Ensemble; Fennell, Frederick (cond)
- Orion ORS-73118; 33s; rel 1973; cip

Liturgy for Organ

[9543] MacGowan, William (org)
- Dorian 1023; 33m; rel 1964; del 1974

Merlin and Sir Boss (1968)

[9544] University of Wisconsin Concert Band; Dvorak, Raymond (cond)
- Orion ORS-73118; 33s; rel 1973; cip

Missa sacra (1952)

[9545] Catholic University of America Modern Choir; Muller, Gerald (org); Cordovana, Michael (cond)
- Dorian 1023; 33m; rel 1964; del 1974

Preludes and Toccata, Harp, Violin, and Violoncello (1964)

[9546] McDonald, Susann (hp); Schoenfeld, Alice (vln); Schoenfeld, Eleanore (vcl)
- Orion ORS-7036; 33s; rel 1971; cip

Serenade, Oboe, Violin, and Violoncello: Pastoral and Burlesque

[9547] Etler, Alvin (ob); Holmes, Malcolm (vln); Bodenhorn, Aaron (vcl)
- Yaddo IV-5; 78; 10"; rel 1940

Sonata of Sonnets (1961)

[9548] Babikian, Virginia (sop); Limonick, Natalie (pf)
- Orion ORS-7036; 33s; rel 1971; cip

Symphonic Translations (1958)

[9549] California State University (Chico) Symphonic Band; Hiestand, Daniel (cond)
- Orion ORS-73118; 33s; rel 1973; cip

WALDEN, Stanley (1932-)

(Three) Views from the Open Window: (No 3) Circus

[9550] Louisville Orchestra; Mester, Jorge (cond)
- LS-69-1; 33s (Louisville Orchestra First Edition Records 1969 No 1); rel 1969; cip

WALKER, George (1922-)

Antifonys (1968)

[9551] Royal Philharmonic Orchestra; Freeman, Paul (cond)
- Serenus SRS-12081; 33s; rel 1979; cip

Concerto, Piano and Orchestra (1975)

[9552] Hinderas, Natalie (pf); Detroit Symphony Orchestra; Freeman, Paul (cond)
- Columbia M-34556; 33s; rel 1978; del 1979

Concerto, Trombone and Orchestra (1957)

[9553] Wick, Denis (tbn); London Symphony Orchestra; Freeman, Paul (cond)
- Columbia M-32783; 33s; rel 1974; cip

Lyric for Strings (1941)

[9554] London Symphony Orchestra; Freeman, Paul (cond)
- Columbia M-33433; 33s; rel 1975; del 1979

Music for Brass (Sacred and Profane) (1975)

[9555] American Brass Quintet
- Serenus SRS-12077; 33s; rel 1978; cip

Passacaglia

[9556] Oakland Youth Orchestra; Hughes, Robert (cond)
- Desto DC-7107; 33s; rel 1970; cip

Perimeters (1966)

[9557] Kupferman, Meyer (cl); Hayami, Kazuko (pf)
- Serenus SRS-12077; 33s; rel 1978; cip

Sonata, Piano, No 1 (1953)
[9558] Hinderas, Natalie (pf)
- Desto DC-7102-03; 33s; 2 discs;
rel 1970; cip

[9559] Walker, George (pf)
- Serenus SRS-12077; 33s; rel
1978; cip

Sonata, Piano, No 2 (1957)
[9560] Walker, George (pf)
- CRI-270; 33s; rel 1971; cip

Sonata, Piano, No 3 (1975)
[9561] Bates, Leon (pf)
- Orion ORS-76237; 33s; rel
1977; cip

**Sonata, Violoncello and Piano
(1957)**
[9562] Babini (vcl); Walker, George (pf)
- Serenus SRS-12081; 33s; rel
1979; cip

Spatials (1961)
[9563] Walker, George (pf)
- CRI-270; 33s; rel 1971; cip

Spektra (1971)
[9564] Walker, George (pf)
- CRI-270; 33s; rel 1971; cip

Variations, Orchestra (1971)
[9565] New Philharmonia Orchestra;
Freeman, Paul (cond)
- Serenus SRS-12077; 33s; rel
1978; cip

WALKER, Richard (1912-)
Danish Overture
[9566] Ohio State University Concert
Band; McGinnis, Donald E. (cond)
- Coronet S-1503; 33s; rel 1969;
del 1978

Scythian Overture
[9567] Marlborough Concert Band;
Cacavas, John (cond)
- Kapp KL-1455/KL-S-3455;
33m/s; rel 1966; del 1971

[9568] Ohio State University Concert
Band; McGinnis, Donald E. (cond)
- Coronet S-1258; 33s; rel 1969;
del 1978

WALLOWITCH, John (1930-)
(Four) Snappy Pieces
[9569] Wallowitch, John
- Serenus SRS-12085; 33s; rel
1980; cip

WALTERS, Harold L. (1918-)
Instant Concert
[9570] National Band of New Zealand;
Waters, Mervyn (cond)
- Five Star FSRS-1295; 33s; rel
1975

Trumpets Wild
[9571] National Band of New Zealand;
Waters, Mervyn (cond)
- Five Star FSRS-1295; 33s; rel
1975

WALTON, Kenneth (1904-)
If I But Had a Little Coat
[9572] Anders, Lynne (sop)
- Golden Age GAR-1002; 33s; rel
1976

WARD, Robert (1917-)
Adagio and Allegro (1943)
[9573] Vienna Symphony Orchestra;
Strickland, William (cond)
- MGM E-3084; 33m; rel 1956;
del 1959

Arioso and Tarantella (1954)
[9574] Ward, Mark (vcl); Garrett, Margo
(pf)
- Musical Heritage Society
MHS-4138; 33s; rel 1979

Clarinet Escapade
[9575] H. M. Royal Marines Band; Neville,
Paul (cond)
- Arabesque 8006; 33s; rel 1980;
cip

**Concerto, Piano and Orchestra
(1968)**
[9576] Mitchell, Marjorie (pf); Stuttgart
Radio Orchestra; Strickland,
William (cond)
- Desto DC-7123; 33s; rel 1972;
cip

Crucible, The (1961)
[9577] Brooks, Patricia (sop); Bible,
Frances (m sop); Ludgin, Chester
(bar); Alberts, Eunice; Wynder,
Gloria; Foster, Nancy; Kelly,
Norman; Macurdy, John; De Lon,
Jack; Krause, Richard; New York
City Opera Chorus and Orchestra;
Buckley, Emerson (cond)
- CRI-168; 33s; 2 discs; rel 1963;
cip

Divertimento (1960)
[9578] Portland Junior Symphony;
Avshalomov, Jacob (cond)
- CRI-194; 33m/s; rel 1964/?; cip

Euphony (1954)
[9579] Louisville Orchestra; Whitney,
Robert (cond)
- LOU-545-10; 33m (Louisville
Orchestra First Edition Records
1955 No 10); rel 1959; del
1975

Fantasia (1953)
[9580] Polish National Radio Orchestra;
Szostak, Zdzislav (cond)
- Musical Heritage Society
MHS-1600; 33s; rel 1973

Festive Ode (1966)
[9581] Polish National Radio Orchestra;
Szostak, Zdzislav (cond)
- Musical Heritage Society
MHS-1600; 33s; rel 1973

**He Who Gets Slapped (Pantaloon)
(1956): Ballad**
[9582] Parker, William (bar); Baldwin,
Dalton (pf)
- New World NW-300; 33s; rel
1978

**Hush'd Be the Camps Today
(1941)**
[9583] Norwegian Choir of Solo Singers;
Oslo Philharmonic Orchestra
(members of); Strickland, William
(cond)
- CRI-165; 33m; rel 1963; cip

Invocation and Toccata
[9584] Polish National Radio Orchestra;
Wodiczko, Bodhan (cond)
- Musical Heritage Society
MHS-1600; 33s; rel 1973

Jubilation (1946)
[9585] Vienna Symphony Orchestra;
Strickland, William (cond)
- MGM E-3084; 33m; rel 1956;
del 1959
- CRI-159; 33m; rel 1962; cip

Prairie Overture
[9586] Polish National Radio Orchestra;
Wodiczko, Bodhan (cond)
- Musical Heritage Society
MHS-1600; 33s; rel 1973

Quartet, Strings, No 1 (1966)
[9587] Razoumovsky Quartet
- Musical Heritage Society
MHS-4138; 33s; rel 1979

**Sacred Songs for Pantheists
(1951)**
[9588] Stahlman, Sylvia (sop); Polish
National Radio Orchestra;
Strickland, William (cond)
- CRI-206; 33m/s; rel 1966/?; cip

**Sonata, Violin and Piano, No 1
(1950)**
[9589] Manoogian, Vartan (vln); Epperson,
Anne (pf)
- Musical Heritage Society
MHS-4138; 33s; rel 1979

Sorrow of Mydath (1938)
[9590] McCollum, John (ten); Biltcliffe,
Edwin (pf)
- St/And SPL-411-12; 33m; 2
discs; rel 1963; del 1964
- Desto D-411-12/DST-6411-12;
33m/s; 2 discs; rel 1964; cip

Symphony No 1 (1941)

[9591] Vienna Symphony Orchestra;
Dixon, Dean (cond)
- American Recording Society
ARS-9; 33m; rel 1952*
- Desto D-405/DST-6405; 33m/s;
rel 1964; cip

Symphony No 2 (1947)

[9592] Japan Philharmonic Symphony
Orchestra; Strickland, William
(cond)
- CRI-127; 33m/s; rel 1960/?; cip

Symphony No 3 (1950)

[9593] Cincinnati Symphony Orchestra;
Johnson, Thor (cond)
- Remington 199-185; 33m; rel
1955; del 1957

[9594] Iceland Symphony Orchestra;
Buketoff, Igor (cond)
- CRI-206; 33m/s; rel 1966/?; cip

WARD, William R. (1918-)

Listen, Lord

[9595] San Francisco State College A
Cappella Choir; Tegnell, John Carl
(cond)
- Music Library MLR-6997; 33m;
rel 1963; del 1974

WARD-STEINMAN, David (1936-)

Child's Play

[9596] bassoon; piano
- Advance FGR-9S; 33s; rel 197?

**Duo, Violoncello and Piano
(1964-65)**

[9597] Lustgarten, Edgar (vcl); Williams,
John (pf)
- Orion ORS-74141; 33s; rel
1974; cip

Fragments from Sappho (1965)

[9598] Curtin, Phyllis (sop); Baron, Samuel
(fl); Glazer, David (cl);
Ward-Steinman, David (pf)
- CRI-238; 33s; rel 1969; cip

**Sonata, Clarinet and Piano
(1956-57)**

[9599] Robinette, Richard (cl);
Ward-Steinman, David (pf)
- Contemporary Composers Guild
1; 33m; rel 1962; del 1975

**(Three) Songs, Clarinet and Piano
(1957)**

[9600] Robinette, Richard (cl);
Ward-Steinman, David (pf)
- Contemporary Composers Guild
1; 33m; rel 1962; del 1975

WARE, Harriet (1877-1962)

Boat Song

[9601] Bispham, David (bar)
- Columbia A-5166; 78; rel
1906-10

WARFIELD, Gerald (1940-)

**Variations and Metamorphoses
(1973)**

[9602] Hoyle, Ted (vcl); Lensky, Larry
(vcl); Warfield, Gerald (pf)
- Advance FGR-19S; 33s; rel
1976; cip

WARNER, Richard L. (1908-)

**Prelude on Let All Mortal Flesh
Keep Silence**

[9603] Titus, Parvin (org)
- Chime 1003; 33m; rel 1958; del
1962

WARREN, Elinor Remick (1906-)

Abram in Egypt (1961)

[9604] Lewis, Ronald (bar); Roger Wagner
Chorale; London Philharmonic
Orchestra; Wagner, Roger (cond)
- CRI-172; 33m; rel 1963; cip

Suite, Orchestra (1954)

[9605] Oslo Philharmonic Orchestra;
Strickland, William (cond)
- CRI-172; 33m; rel 1963; cip

WASHBURN, Robert (1928-)

Ceremonial Music

[9606] Crane School of Music Wind
Ensemble; Maiello, Anthony
(cond)
- Golden Crest ATH-5052; 33s; rel
1978; cip

Chorale, Band

[9607] Crane School of Music Wind
Ensemble; Maiello, Anthony
(cond)
- Golden Crest ATH-5052; 33s; rel
1978; cip

Epigon IV

[9608] Crane School of Music Wind
Ensemble; Maiello, Anthony
(cond)
- Golden Crest ATH-5052; 33s; rel
1978; cip

March (Opus '76)

[9609] Crane School of Music Wind
Ensemble; Maiello, Anthony
(cond)
- Golden Crest ATH-5052; 33s; rel
1978; cip

Partita, Band

[9610] University of Maryland Concert
Band; Ostling, Acton, Jr. (cond)
- Coronet 955; 33m; rel 1969; del
1978

Saturn V

[9611] Crane School of Music Wind
Ensemble; Maiello, Anthony
(cond)
- Golden Crest ATH-5052; 33s; rel
1978; cip

Symphony, Band

[9612] Crane School of Music Wind
Ensemble; Maiello, Anthony
(cond)
- Golden Crest ATH-5052; 33s; rel
1978; cip

Trigon

[9613] Crane School of Music Wind
Ensemble; Maiello, Anthony
(cond)
- Golden Crest ATH-5052; 33s; rel
1978; cip

WATERS, James (1930-)

Dirge (1972)

[9614] Philharmonic Chorale and Chamber
Ensemble
- Advent USR-5005; 33s; rel
1973; cip

WATKINS, David*

Fire Dance

[9615] McDonald, Susann (hp)
- Klavier KS-507; 33s; rel 1972;
cip

Petite Suite

[9616] Watkins, David (hp)
Rec 1973
- RCA ARL-1-5087; 33s; rel 1975

WATSON, Walter R. (1933-)

**(Five) Japanese Love Poems
(1969)**

[9617] Kent State University Women's
Glee Club; Krehbiel, Clayton
(cond)
- Advent USR-5005; 33s; rel
1973; cip

Recital Suite

[9618] Watson, Kenneth (mrmb);
Swiatkowski, Chet (pf)
- Crystal S-532; 33s; rel 1978; cip

WATTERS, Clarence

Veni, creator spiritus

[9619] Watters, Clarence (org)
Rec 1/21/72
- Austin Organs/S & M Master
Recordings SM-225; 33s; rel
1973

WATTS, John (1930-)

**Elegy to Chimney (In memoriam)
(1972)**

[9620] trumpet; tape; synthesizer
- Serenus SRS-12080; 33s; rel
1979; cip

Mots d'heures: Gousses, Rames
[9621] voices; tape
- Serenus SRS-12080; 33s; rel 1979; cip

Piano for Te
[9622] piano; thirteen players; tape
- Serenus SRS-12080; 33s; rel 1979; cip

Signals
[9623] Rowe, Catherine (sop); Composers Festival Orchestra; Brehm, Alvin (cond)
- Trilogy CTS-1002; 33s; rel 1973; del 1975

Sonata, Piano
[9624] Peltzer, Dwight (pf)
- Serenus SRS-12069; 33s; rel 1978; cip

[9625] Sanders, Dean (pf)
- Trilogy CTS-1003; 33s; rel 1973; del 1975

WAXMAN, Donald (1925-)
First Piano Pageant: Peter's Song
[9626] Fuszek, Rita (pf)
- Educo 3108; 33

Second Year Piano Pageant: The Little Witch, The Mill Wheel, Kim's Lullaby, Kim Awake, and Finale
[9627] Bennett, Bob L. (pf)
- Educo 3110; 33

Thomas Hardy Songs
[9628] Genton, Samantha (sop); Edmonds, Kathie (al); Rohrer, Eugene (ten); Richardson, Walter (b); Gregg Smith Singers; Smith, Gregg (cond)
Rec 4/76
- Vox SVBX-5354; 33s; 3 discs; rel 1979

Trio, Oboe, Clarinet, and Bassoon (1960)
[9629] Lucarelli, Bert (ob); Bloom, Arthur (cl); MacCourt, Donald (bsn)
- Turnabout TVS-34520; 33s; rel 1974; del 1978

WAXMAN, Ernest (1918-)
Capriccio
[9630] Modern Brass Ensemble
- Advance FGR-2; 33m; rel 1966; del 1978

WAXMAN, Franz (1906-67)
Sinfonietta, Strings and Timpani

[9631] Los Angeles Festival Orchestra; Waxman, Franz (cond)
- Decca DL-9889; 33m; rel 1957; del 1960
- Varese Sarabande VC-81052; 33m; rel 1978; cip

(Three) Sketches (1955)
[9632] Los Angeles Festival Orchestra; Waxman, Franz (cond)
- Entr'acte ERS-6001; 33s; rel 1978; cip

Theme, Variations, and Fugato (1956)
[9633] Los Angeles Festival Orchestra; Waxman, Franz (cond)
- Entr'acte ERS-6001; 33m; rel 1978; cip

WAYDITCH, Gabriel von (1888-1969)
Caliph's Magician, The (1917)
[9634] Budapest National Opera; Korody, Andras (cond)
- Musical Heritage Society MHS-3565-66; 33s; 2 discs

Jesus Before Herod
[9635] San Diego Symphony Orchestra; San Diego Music Chorale; Eros, Peter (cond); Ketcham, Charles (cond)
- Musical Heritage Society MHS-4167; 33s

WEAVER, John (1889-)
Toccata, Organ
[9636] Weaver, John (org)
Rec 5/3/65
- Wicks Organ Co 832W-4267; 33s; rel 1967

WEAVER, Powell (1890-1951)
Squirrel, The
[9637] Elmore, Robert (org)
Rec 11/24/56
- Mercury MG-50109/SR-90109; 33m/s; rel 1957/1959; del 1963

[9638] Prince-Joseph, Bruce (org)
- Hi-Fi R-709/S-709; 33m/s; rel 1957/1960; del 1965
- Everest LPBR-6158/SDBR-3158; 33m/s; rel 1967; cip

[9639] Richardson, Harriette S. (org)
- Century Recording Service 20738/20739; 33m/s; rel 1965

WEBER, Ben (1916-79)
(Five) Bagatelles
[9640] Bennette, George (pf)
- Desto DC-7136; 33s; rel 1973; cip

Concert Aria after Solomon (Op 29) (1949)
[9641] Beardslee, Bethany (sop); instrumental ensemble; Brieff, Frank (cond)
- American Recording Society ARS-10; 33m; rel 1953
- Desto D-422/DST-6422; 33m/s; rel 1967; cip

Concertino, Flute, Oboe, Clarinet, and String Quartet (Op 45) (1956)
[9642] Baker, Julius (fl); Shulman, Harry (ob); Williams, Alexander (cl); Galimir String Quartet
- Epic LC-3567/BC-1022; 33m/s; rel 1959; del 1964

Concerto, Piano and Orchestra (Op 52) (1961)
[9643] Masselos, William (pf); Royal Philharmonic Orchestra; Samuel, Gerhard (cond)
- CRI-239; 33s; rel 1969; cip

Consort of Winds (Op 66) (1974)
[9644] Boehm Quintet
- Orion ORS-75206; 33s; rel 1976; cip

Dolmen (An Elegy) (Op 58) (1964)
[9645] Louisville Orchestra; Whitney, Robert (cond)
- LOU-67-6/LS-67-6; 33m/s (Louisville Orchestra First Edition Records 1967 No 6); rel 1968; cip

Episodes (Op 26a)
[9646] Masselos, William (pf)
- MGM E-3556; 33m; rel 1958; del 1960

Fantasia (Variations) (Op 25) (1945)
[9647] Bennette, George (pf)
- Desto DC-7136; 33s; rel 1973; cip

[9648] Masselos, William (pf)
- Epic LC-3567/BC-1022; 33m/s; rel 1959; del 1964

Humoreske (Op 49) (ca 1963)
[9649] Helps, Robert (pf)
- RCA LM-7042/LSC-7042; 33m/s; 2 discs; rel 1966; del 1971
- CRI-288; 33s; 2 discs; rel 1972; cip

Mourn! Mourn! (Op 53) (ca 1962)
[9650] McCollum, John (ten); Biltcliffe, Edwin (pf)
- St/And SPL-411-12; 33m; 2 discs; rel 1963; del 1964
- Desto D-411-12/DST-6411-12; 33m/s; 2 discs; rel 1964; cip

(Three) Pieces, Piano (Op 23)
[9651] Bennette, George (pf)
- Desto DC-7136; 33s; rel 1973; cip

(Five) Pieces, Violoncello and Piano (Op 12) (1940-41): Nos 3 and 5
[9652] Barab, Seymour (vcl); Masselos, William (pf)
- Paradox X-102; 78; 3-10"

(Five) Pieces, Violoncello and Piano (Op 12) (1940-41): Nos 3 and 5
(cont'd)
- Paradox PL-10001; 33m; 10"; rel 1950; del 1957

Prelude and Passacaglia (Op 42) (1954)
[9653] Louisville Orchestra; Whitney, Robert (cond)
- LOU-56-6; 33m (Louisville Orchestra First Edition Records 1956 No 6); rel 1959; del 1980

Quartet, Strings, No 2 (Op 35) (1951)
[9654] New Music String Quartet
Rec 3/5/61
- CRI-358; 33s; rel 1976; cip

Rapsodie concertante (Op 47) (1957)
[9655] Trampler, Walter (vla); MGM Chamber Orchestra; Winograd, Arthur (cond)
- MGM E-3559; 33m; rel 1957; del 1959

Serenade, Flute, Oboe, Violoncello, and Harpsichord (Op 39) (1953)
[9656] Monteux, Claude (fl); Shulman, Harry (ob); Greenhouse, Bernard (vcl); Marlowe, Sylvia (hpschd)
- Decca DL-10021/DL-710021; 33m/s; rel 1961; del 1971

Serenade, Strings (Op 46) (1956)
[9657] Galimir String Quartet; Walter, David (cb)
- Epic LC-3567/BC-1022; 33m/s; rel 1959; del 1964

Sonata da camera (Op 30)
[9658] Schneider, Alexander (vln); Horszowski, Mieczyslaw (pf)
Rec 1954
- New World NW-281; 33m; rel 1976

Symphony on Poems of William Blake (Op 33) (1950)
[9659] Galjour, Warren (bar); orchestra; Stokowski, Leopold (cond)
- RCA LM-1785; 33m; rel 1954; del 1956
- CRI-120; 33m; rel 1957; cip

WEBSTER, Michael (1944-)
(Five) Pieces, Clarinet
[9660] Webster, Michael (cl)
Rec 1974
- CRI-374; 33s; rel 1977; cip

WEIDENAAR, Reynold (1945-)
Tinsel Chicken Coop, The
[9661] Electronic music
- Crystal S-532; 33s; rel 1978; cip

WEIGEL, Eugene J. (1910-)
Prairie Symphony (1953)
[9662] University of Illinois Symphony Orchestra; Goodman, Bernard (cond)
- Illini Union Bookstore CRS-2; 33m; rel 1953*

WEINBERG, Henry (1931-)
Cantus commemorabilis I (1966)
[9663] University of Chicago Contemporary Chamber Players; Shapey, Ralph (cond)
- CRI-245; 33s; rel 1969; cip

Quartet, Strings, No 2 (1960-64)
[9664] Composers Quartet
- Columbia MS-7284; 33s; rel 1969; del 1973

Vox in Rama (Jeremiah XXXI) (1956)
[9665] Ineluctable Modality; London, Edwin (cond)
- Advance FGR-18S; 33s; rel 197?

WEINER, Lazar (1897-1982)
Amos
[9666] Kwartin, Paul (voice); Cantica Hebraica; Michno, Dennis (cond)
- BOU-1212; 33s; rel 1977?

Ashrei hoish
[9667] Bloch, Robert (voice); Cantica Hebraica; Michno, Dennis (cond)
- BOU-1212; 33s; rel 1977?

Etschayim
[9668] Boothman, Donald (bar); Berlinski, Herman (org)
- Musical Heritage Society MHS-1775; 33s; rel 1972

Ya'aleh
[9669] Dubrow, Samuel (voice); Cantica Hebraica; Michno, Dennis (cond)
- BOU-1212; 33s; rel 1977?

WEINER, Stanley (1925-)
Latin American Suite: Basso ostinato
[9670] Weiner, Stanley (vln); Demoulin, Giselle (pf)
- Musical Heritage Society MHS-3294; 33s

WEISGALL, Hugo (1912-)
End of Summer (1973-74)
[9671] Bressler, Charles (ten); New York Chamber Soloists
Rec 5/22-23/75
- CRI-343; 33s; rel 1976; cip

Fancies and Inventions (1970)
[9672] Patrick, Julian (bar); Aeolian Chamber Players; Weisgall, Hugo (cond)
- CRI-273; 33s; rel 1972; cip

Golden Peacock, The (1960, 1976)
[9673] Raskin, Judith (sop); Ritt, Morey (pf)
Rec 11/78
- CRI-417; 33s; rel 1980; cip

Overture in F (1942-43)
[9674] Czech Radio Orchestra; Weisgall, Hugo (cond)
- Supraphon H-18131; 78; rel ca 1946

Stronger, The (1952)
[9675] Bishop, Adelaide (sop); Columbia Chamber Orchestra; Antonini, Alfredo (cond)
- Columbia ML-5106; 33m; rel 1956; del 1967

[9676] Meier, Johanna (sop); Aeolian Chamber Players; Weisgall, Hugo (cond)
- CRI-273; 33s; rel 1972; cip

Tenor, The (1948-50)
[9677] Cassilly, Richard (ten); Cross, Richard (b bar); Coulter, Dorothy (sop); Young, Doris (sop); Ludgin, Chester (bar); Kuhn, John (ten); Vienna State Opera Orchestra; Grossman, Herbert (cond)
- Westminster OPW-1206/WST-208; 33m/s; 2 discs; rel 1959; del 1961
- CRI-197; 33m/s; 2 discs; rel 1965; cip

Translations (1971-72)
[9678] Raskin, Judith (sop); Ritt, Morey (pf)
Rec 6/79
- CRI-417; 33s; rel 1980; cip

WEISGARBER, Elliot (1919-)
Epigrams (1973)
[9679] Weisgarber, Karen (fl); Hoy, Vance (pf)
- Opus One 46; 33s; rel 1979; cip

WEISS, Adolph (1891-1971)
American Life (Scherzoso jazzoso) (1928)
[9680] Los Angeles Philharmonic Orchestra; Simmons, Calvin (cond)
Rec 8/77
- New World NW-228; 33s; rel 1978

(Seven) Songs (1928): Cemetery, The Railway Train, and Mysteries
[9681] Bell, Mary (sop); New World String Quartet
- New Music Quarterly Recordings 1011 (1-2); 78; rel 1934

(Seven) Songs: Elysium and I Taste a Liquor
[9682] Luening, Ethel (sop); Yaddo String
        Quartet
        - Yaddo 101A; 78; 10''; rel 1937

Theme and Variations (1933)
[9683] Vienna Orchestra; Adler, F. Charles
        (cond)
        - CRI-113; 33m; rel 1957; cip

Trio, Clarinet, Viola, and Violoncello (1948)
[9684] Bloch, Kalman (cl); Weiss,
        Abraham (vla); Reher, Kurt (vcl)
        - CRI-116; 33m/s; rel 1957/?; cip

WEISS, Helen L. (1920-48)
I Am the People
[9685] Singing City Choir of Philadelphia;
        Brown, Elaine (cond)
        - Fellowship FM-1/FS-1; 33m/s; rel
        1961

WELCHER, Dan (1948-)
Concerto, Flute and Orchestra (1973)
[9686] Fuge, Francis (fl); Louisville
        Orchestra; Mester, Jorge (cond)
        Rec 5/14/74
        - LS-74-2; 33s (Louisville
        Orchestra First Edition Records
        1974 No 2); rel 1975; cip

Concerto da camera (1975)
[9687] Sharrow, Leonard (bsn); Crystal
        Chamber Orchestra; Gold, Ernest
        (cond)
        Rec 9/13-15/76
        - Crystal S-852; 33s; rel 1977; cip

Dervishes (1976)
[9688] Louisville Orchestra; Mester, Jorge
        (cond)
        Rec 5/10/77
        - LS-76-3; 33s (Louisville
        Orchestra First Edition Records
        1976 No 3); rel 1978; cip

WELDON, Alfred F.
Gate City
[9689] Goldman Band; Cox, Ainslee (cond)
        - New World NW-266; 33s; rel
        1977

[9690] University of Michigan Winds and
        Percussion; Lillya, Clifford P.
        (cond)
        Rec 2/18-19/75
        - University of Michigan SM-0002;
        33s; rel 1978; cip

WELSH, Wilmer H. (1932-)
Passion Music
[9691] Welsh, Wilmer H. (org)
        - Wicks Organ Co 832W-2426;
        33s; rel 1972

Sonata, Organ, No 2 (Isaiah the Prophet)
[9692] Welsh, Wilmer H. (org)
        - Wicks Organ Co 832W-2426;
        33s; rel 1972

WERLE, Floyd E. (1929-)
Divertimento, Eight Soloists
[9693] Kent State University Wind
        Ensemble; Boyd, John (cond)
        Rec 5/26/78
        - Golden Crest ATH-5058; 33s; rel
        1978; cip

Glider Pilot's Reunion
[9694] Kent State University Wind
        Ensemble; Boyd, John (cond)
        Rec 5/26/78
        - Golden Crest ATH-5058; 33s; rel
        1978; cip

Symphony No 2
[9695] Kent State University Wind
        Ensemble; Boyd, John (cond)
        Rec 5/26/78
        - Golden Crest ATH-5058; 33s; rel
        1978; cip

WERLE, Frederick (1914-)
Sonata brevis No 2
[9696] Ranck, John (pf)
        - Zodiac Z-1002; 33m; rel 1955;
        del 1960
        - International Piano
        Library/International Piano
        Archives IPA-2002; 33m; rel
        1977

WERNER, Kenneth
see HARMONIC, Phil (pseud)

WERNICK, Richard F. (1934-)
Haiku of Basho (1967)
[9697] Pilgrim, Neva (sop); University of
        Chicago Contemporary Chamber
        Players; Wernick, Richard (cond)
        Rec 5/23/77
        - CRI-379; 33s; rel 1978; cip

Kaddish-Requiem (A Secular Service for the Victims of Indochina) (1969)
[9698] DeGaetani, Jan (m sop); Gilbert,
        Ramon (cantor); Contemporary
        Chamber Ensemble; Weisberg,
        Arthur (cond)
        - Nonesuch H-71303; 33s; rel
        1974; cip

Moonsongs from the Japanese (1969)
[9699] Pilgrim, Neva (sop); tape
        Rec 1/78
        - CRI-379; 33s; rel 1978; cip

Prayer for Jerusalem, A (1970-71)
[9700] DeGaetani, Jan (sop); Steele, Glenn
        (perc)
        Rec 12/17/75
        - CRI-344; 33s; rel 1976; cip

Songs of Remembrance (1974)
[9701] DeGaetani, Jan (m sop); West,
        Philip (shawm) (E hn) (ob)
        - Nonesuch H-71342; 33s; rel
        1977; cip

WESTERGAARD, Peter (1931-)
Divertimento on Discobbolos Fragments (1967)
[9702] Sollberger, Harvey (fl); Wuorinen,
        Charles (pf)
        - Nonesuch HB-73028; 33s; 2
        discs; rel 1975; cip

Mr. and Mrs. Discobbolos (1966)
[9703] Lamoree, Valarie (sop); Litten, Jack
        (ten); Group for Contemporary
        Music at Columbia University
        (members of); Sollberger, Harvey
        (cond)
        - CRI-271; 33s; rel 1971; cip

Variations for Six Players (1963)
[9704] Group for Contemporary Music at
        Columbia University; Sollberger,
        Harvey (cond)
        - Acoustic Research AR-0654.088;
        33s; rel 1971

WHEAR, Paul W. (1925-)
Bellerophon
[9705] Ohio State University Concert
        Band; McGinnis, Donald E. (cond)
        - Coronet S-1502; 33s; rel 1969;
        del 1978

Catharsis Suite (1967)
[9706] London Concert Orchestra; Whear,
        Paul W. (cond)
        - Advent USR-5001; 33s; rel
        1973; cip

Czech Suite: 1st and 3rd Movements
[9707] Ohio State University Concert
        Band; McGinnis, Donald E. (cond)
        - Coronet M-1411; 33m; rel
        1969; del 1978

Decade Overture
[9708] London Concert Orchestra; Whear,
        Paul W. (cond)
        - Advent USR-5001; 33s; rel
        1973; cip

Joyful-Jubilate (1969)
[9709] London Concert Orchestra and
        Chorus; Whear, Paul W. (cond)
        - Advent USR-5001; 33s; rel
        1973; cip

Psalms of Celebration (1965)
[9710] London Concert Orchestra and
Chorus; Whear, Paul W. (cond)
- Advent USR-5001; 33s; rel
1973; cip

WHITE, Clarence Cameron (1880-1960)

Concerto, Violin and Orchestra, G Minor (Op 63) (arr for vln and pf)
[9711] Zimmer, Robert (vln); Atkinson,
Carl (pf)
- Stark Fort Wayne SW-101-06;
78; 4-10"

WHITE, Donald H. (1921-)

Dichotomy (1964)
[9712] Ohio State University Concert
Band; McGinnis, Donald E. (cond)
- Coronet S-1258; 33s; rel 1969;
cip

Miniature Set (1957)
[9713] Ohio State University Concert
Band; McGinnis, Donald E. (cond)
- Coronet M-1157; 33m; rel
1969; del 1978

Three for Five (1958)
[9714] American Woodwind Quintet
- Golden Crest
CR-4075/CRS-4075; 33m/s; rel
1966/1967; cip

WHITE, John D. (1931-)

Variations, Clarinet and Piano (1971)
[9715] Cohen, Frederick (cl); Cohen, Enid
(pf)
- Advent USR-5004; 33s; rel
1973; cip

WHITE, Michael (1931-)

Songs and Dances of the Middle Ages
[9716] Ketchum, Janet (fl); Segal, Peter
(gtr)
- Orion ORS-78324; 33s; rel
1979; cip

WHITE, Paul (1895-1973)

Bella cubana
[9717] Columbia Symphony Orchestra;
Kurtz, Efrem (cond)
- Columbia CL-773; 33m; rel
1956; del 1958

Levee Dance
[9718] Heifetz, Jascha (vln); Kaye, Milton
(pf)
- Decca 23387 (in set 385); 78
- Decca DL-9780; 33m; rel 1958;
del 1971

(Five) Miniatures (arr for orch)
[9719] Boston Pops Orchestra; Fiedler,
Arthur (cond)
- Victor 4429 (in set M-554); 78;
10"; rel pre-1943
- Victor 4319; 78; 10"; rel
pre-1948 (Excerpt: Mosquito
Dance)
- Gramophone B-8488; 78; 10";
rel pre-1952 (Excerpt: Mosquito
Dance)
- RCA LM-1790; 33m; rel 1954;
del 1960 (Excerpt: Mosquito
Dance)
- RCA LM-2677/LSC-2677;
33m/s; rel 1963; del 1975
(Excerpt: Mosquito Dance)

(Five) Miniatures (arr for orch): Mosquito Dance
[9720] Andre Kostelanetz and his
Orchestra; Kostelanetz, Andre
(cond)
- Columbia CL-763; 33m; rel
1955; del 1959

Sea Chanty (1942)
[9721] Phillips, Edna (hp); Hilsberg,
Alexander (vln); Ruden, S. (vln);
Roens, S. (vla); Mayes, Samuel
(vcl); Torello, Anton (cb);
Ormandy, Eugene (cond)
- Columbia X-259; 78; 2 discs; rel
pre-1948

WHITE, Ruth S. (1925-)

Flowers of Evil (1969)
[9722] Electronic music
- Limelight LS-86066; 33s; rel
1969; del 1977

Motifs for Dance Composition
[9723] no performers given
- Rhythms Productions CC-611;
33m; rel 1965

Motivations for Modern Dance
[9724] no performers given
- Rhythms Productions CC-610;
33m; rel 1962

Music for Contemporary Dance
[9725] no performers given
- Rhythms Productions CC-612-13;
33m; 2 discs; rel 1966-67

Pinions (A Choreography about Symbolic Flight) (1968)
[9726] no performers given
- Limelight LS-86058; 33s; rel
1969; del 1972

Short Circuits (1970)
[9727] Electronic music
- Angel S-36042; 33s; rel 1970;
del 1979

(Seven) Trumps from the Tarot Cards (1968)
[9728] Electronic music
- Limelight LS-86058; 33s; rel
1969; del 1972

Variations on Couperin's Rondeau
[9729] Electronic music
- Angel S-36042; 33s; rel 1970;
del 1979

WHITFORD, Homer P. (1892-)

(Five) Chorale Paraphrases, Set 1: A Mighty Fortress and Now Thank We All Our God
[9730] Becker, C. Warren (org)
- Pioneer Memorial Church
STCP-662; 33m; rel 1966
(Excerpt: A Mighty Fortress)
- Chapel LP-5-134/ST-134;
33m/s; rel 1968

WHITHORNE, Emerson (1884-1958)

Drowsy Shepherdess
[9731] Martin, Charlotte (pf)
- Educo 3021; 33m; rel 1968; del
1972

New York Days and Nights (1923): Pell Street
[9732] Borodkin, Samuel (perc); Decca
Symphony Orchestra; Mendoza,
David (cond)
- Decca 93; 78

WHITNEY, Robert (1904-)

Concertino (1961)
[9733] Louisville Orchestra; Whitney,
Robert (cond)
- LOU-61-6; 33m (Louisville
Orchestra First Edition Records
1961 No 6); rel 1962; cip

WHITTAKER, Howard (1922-)

Behold, He Cometh with Clouds (1953)
[9734] McCoy, Seth (ten); Dietz, John
(bar); Kulas Male Choir; Hawk,
Marcellene (pf); Shelhorn, Donald
(pf); Shaw, Robert (cond)
- CRI-182; 33m/s; rel 1964; cip

WHITTENBERG, Charles (1927-)

Electronic Study II (1962)
[9735] Turetzky, Bertram (cb); tape
- Advance FGR-1; 33m; rel 1966;
del 1972

Games of Five (Op 44) (1968)
[9736] University of Oregon Woodwind
Quintet
- Advance FGR-11S; 33s; rel
1973; cip

[9737] no performers given
- Serenus SRS-12028; 33s; rel
1972; cip

(Three) Pieces, Clarinet (1963)
[9738] Rehfeldt, Phillip (cl)
- Advance FGR-4; 33m; rel 1966; cip

Polyphony (1965)
[9739] Schwarz, Gerard (tpt)
- Desto DC-7133; 33s; rel 1973; cip

Quartet, Strings, in One Movement (1965)
[9740] Composers Quartet
- CRI-257; 33s; rel 1970; cip

Set for Two
[9741] Sackson, David (vla); Peltzer, Dwight (pf)
- Serenus SRS-12064; 33s; rel 1976; cip

Triptych (1962)
[9742] American Brass Quintet
- Folkways FM-3651; 33m; rel 1965; cip
- Desto DC-6474-77; 33s; 4 discs; rel 1969; cip

Variations for Nine Players (1964, rev 1970)
[9743] Contemporary Chamber Ensemble; Weisberg, Arthur (cond)
- Acoustic Research AR-0654.087; 33s; rel 1971

WIDDOES, Lawrence (1932-)
From a Time of Snow (1971-72)
[9744] Notes from Underground Group; Leonard, Peter (cond)
- Opus One 28; 33s; rel 1976; cip

Morning Music
[9745] Louisville Orchestra; Mester, Jorge (cond)
- LS-73-5; 33s (Louisville Orchestra First Edition Records 1973 No 5); rel 1974; cip

One Thousand Paper Cranes (1966)
[9746] Silverman, Stanley (gtr); Ghent, Natasha (vla); Thomas, Andrew (hpschd)
- Opus One 9; 33s; rel 1972; cip

WIGGLESWORTH, Frank (1918-)
Lake Music (1947)
[9747] Baron, Samuel (fl)
- CRI-212; 33m/s; rel 1966/?; cip

[9748] LeRoy, Rene (fl)
- New Music Quarterly Recordings 1000A-B; 78; rel 1949

Symphony No 1 (1952)
[9749] Vienna Orchestra; Adler, F. Charles (cond)
- CRI-110; 33m/s; rel 1957/?; cip

WILDER, Alec (1907-80)
Air for Bassoon
[9750] Goltzer, Albert (bsn); Columbia String Orchestra; Sinatra, Frank (cond)
- Columbia ML-4271; 33m; rel 1950; del 1956
- Columbia CL-884; 33m; rel 1956; del 1959
- Odyssey 32-16-0262; 33s; rel 1968; del 1971

Air for English Horn
[9751] Miller, Mitchell (E hn); Columbia String Orchestra; Sinatra, Frank (cond)
- Columbia ML-4271; 33m; rel 1950; del 1956
- Columbia CL-884; 33m; rel 1956; del 1959
- Odyssey 32-16-0262; 33s; rel 1968; del 1971

Air for Flute
[9752] Baker, Julius (fl); Columbia String Orchestra; Sinatra, Frank (cond)
- Columbia ML-4271; 33m; rel 1950; del 1956
- Columbia CL-884; 33m; rel 1956; del 1959
- Odyssey 32-16-0262; 33s; rel 1968; del 1971

[9753] Pellerite, James (fl); Robert, Walter (pf)
- Coronet M-1291/S-1291; 33m/s; rel 1969/?; cip

Air for Oboe
[9754] Miller, Mitchell (ob); Columbia String Orchestra; Sinatra, Frank (cond)
- Columbia ML-4271; 33m; rel 1950; del 1956
- Columbia CL-884; 33m; rel 1956; del 1959
- Odyssey 32-16-0262; 33s; rel 1968; del 1971

Brassinity
[9755] Tidewater Brass Quintet
- Golden Crest CRSQ-4156; 33q; rel 1977; cip

Carl Sandburg Suite (1960)
[9756] orchestra; Ehret, Walter (cond)
- Golden Crest CR-4026/CRS-4026; 33m/s; rel 1961; del 1971

Chick Lorimer
[9757] Bolin, Shannon (voice); Kaye, Milton (pf)
- Golden Crest RE-7079; 33s; rel 1978

Children's Plea for Peace (1969)
[9758] Eastman Symphonic Wind Ensemble; children's chorus
- Turnabout TVS-34413; 33s; rel 1971; del 1974

(Four) Children's Songs
[9759] Bolin, Shannon (voice); Kaye, Milton (pf)
- Golden Crest RE-7079; 33s; rel 1978

Children's Suite (Effie the Elephant)
[9760] Bobo, Roger (tu); Grierson, Ralph (pf)
- Crystal S-125; 33s; rel 1969; cip

Child's Introduction to the Orchestra, A (1954)
[9761] Sandpiper Chorus; Golden Symphony Orchestra; Miller, Mitch (cond)
- Golden LP-1; 33m; rel 1962

Coleen, The
[9762] Bolin, Shannon (voice); Kaye, Milton (pf)
- Golden Crest RE-7079; 33s; rel 1978

Did You Ever Cross Over to Snedon's
[9763] Bolin, Shannon (voice); Kaye, Milton (pf)
- Golden Crest RE-7079; 33s; rel 1978

(Twenty-Two) Duets for French Horns: Nos 3, 15, 17, and 19
[9764] Smith, Calvin (hn); Zsembery, William (hn)
- Crystal S-371; 33s; rel 1976; cip

Effie Suite
[9765] Phillips, Harvey (tu); Harris, Arthur (pf)
- Golden Crest RE-7054; 33s; rel 1973*

Ethel Ayer Suite
[9766] Phillips, Harvey (tu); Spinney, Bradley (pf); Leighton, Bernard (perc)
- Golden Crest RE-7054; 33s; rel 1973*

Jesse Suite
[9767] Phillips, Harvey (tu); Spinney, Bradley (pf); Leighton, Bernard (perc)
- Golden Crest RE-7054; 33s; rel 1973*

Little Harvey Suite
[9768] Phillips, Harvey (tu); Spinney, Bradley (pf); Leighton, Bernard (perc)
- Golden Crest RE-7054; 33s; rel 1973*

Little Love Song, A
[9769] Bolin, Shannon (voice); Kaye, Milton (pf)
- Golden Crest RE-7079; 33s; rel 1978

Margaret
[9770] Bolin, Shannon (voice); Kaye, Milton (pf)
- Golden Crest RE-7079; 33s; rel 1978

(Twelve) Mosaics: Pattern in Color
[9771] Fuszek, Rita (pf)
- Educo 3108; 33

Names from the War
[9772] Garroway, Dave (nar); Walter Ehret Chorale; New York Woodwind Quintet (augmented); New York Brass Quintet (augmented)
- Golden·Crest CR-4026/CRS-4026; 33m/s; rel 1961; del 1971

Neurotic Goldfish, The (arr for 2 pfs)
[9773] Whittemore, Arthur (pf); Lowe, Jack (pf)
- Victor 10-1360; 78; 10"

Nonet for Brass (1969)
[9774] Horn Club of Los Angeles; Schuller, Gunther (cond)
- Angel S-36036; 33s; rel 1970; cip

Pied Beauty
[9775] Bolin, Shannon (voice); Kaye, Milton (pf)
- Golden Crest RE-7079; 33s; rel 1978

Plowman, The
[9776] Bolin, Shannon (voice); Kaye, Milton (pf)
- Golden Crest RE-7079; 33s; rel 1978

Quintet, Brass, No 1 (1959)
[9777] Los Angeles Brass Quintet
- Crystal M-102/S-102; 33m/s; rel 1967; cip

Quintet, Brass, No 4 (1973)
[9778] Tidewater Brass Quintet
- Golden Crest CRSQ-4156; 33q; rel 1977; cip

Quintet, Brass, No 5 (1975)
[9779] Tidewater Brass Quintet
- Golden Crest CRSQ-4156; 33q; rel 1977; cip

Quintet, Brass, No 6 (1977)
[9780] Tidewater Brass Quintet
- Golden Crest CRSQ-4174; 33q; rel 1978; cip

Quintet, Brass, No 7
[9781] Tidewater Brass Quintet
- Golden Crest CRSQ-4179; 33q

Quintet, Winds
[9782] New York Woodwind Quintet
- Philharmonia 110; 33m; rel 1955; del 1959

Quintet, Winds, No 1: Up Tempo
[9783] New York Woodwind Quintet
- Everest LPBR-6092/SDBR-3092; 33m/s; rel 1963; del 1978

Quintet, Winds, No 2 (1956)
[9784] New York Woodwind Quintet
- Golden Crest CR-3019; 33m; rel 1957; del 1961
- Golden Crest CR-4028/CRS-4028; 33m/s; rel 1961/1979; cip

Quintet, Winds, No 3
[9785] New York Woodwind Quintet
- Concert-Disc M-1223/CS-223; 33m/s; rel 1961; cip

Quintet, Winds, No 4
[9786] New York Woodwind Quintet
- Concert-Disc M-1223/CS-223; 33m/s; rel 1961; cip

Quintet, Winds, No 6 (1960)
[9787] New York Woodwind Quintet
- Concert-Disc M-1223/CS-223; 33m/s; rel 1961; cip

River Run
[9788] Bolin, Shannon (voice); Kaye, Milton (pf)
- Golden Crest RE-7079; 33s; rel 1978

Rose on the Wind, The
[9789] Bolin, Shannon (voice); Kaye, Milton (pf)
- Golden Crest RE-7079; 33s; rel 1978

Slow Dance
[9790] Columbia String Orchestra; Sinatra, Frank (cond)
- Columbia ML-4271; 33m; rel 1950; del 1956
- Columbia CL-884; 33m; rel 1956; del 1959
- Odyssey 32-16-0262; 33s; rel 1968; del 1971

Small Suite, Flute and Piano (The Judy Holliday Suite)
[9791] Nanzetta, Virginia (fl); Kaye, Milton (pf)
- Golden Crest RE-7065; 33s; rel 1976

Sonata, Bass Trombone and Piano (1968)
[9792] Knaub, Donald (b tbn); Snyder, Barry (pf)
- Golden Crest RE-7040; 33s; rel 1971; cip

Sonata, Bassoon and Piano, No 2 (1968)
[9793] Lottridge, Richard (bsn); Chilton, Carroll (pf)
- Golden Crest RE-7055; 33s; rel 1974; cip

Sonata, Clarinet and Piano (1963)
[9794] Weiss, Mitchell (cl); Carno, Zita (pf)
- Sound Master SMP-1003; 33s; rel 1973*

Sonata, Contrabass and Piano (1961)
[9795] Karr, Gary (cb); Leighton, Bernard (pf)
- Golden Crest RE-7031; 33m/s; rel 1969/1979; cip

Sonata, English Horn and Piano
[9796] Stenberg, Patricia (E hn); Wolf, Gary (pf)
- Golden Crest RE-7039; 33s; rel 1970; cip

Sonata, Flute and Piano, No 2 (1962)
[9797] Nanzetta, Virginia (fl); Kaye, Milton (pf)
- Golden Crest RE-7065; 33s; rel 1976

Sonata, Flute and Piano (1965)
[9798] Pellerite, James (fl); Webb, Charles (pf)
- Coronet S-1713; 33s; rel 1972; cip

Sonata, Flute, Piccolo, and Alto Flute
[9799] Hammond, Don (fl)
- Golden Crest RE-7005; 33m/s; rel 1961/1979; cip

Sonata, Horn and Piano, No 1 (1954)
[9800] Barrows, John (hn); Kaye, Milton (pf)
- Golden Crest RE-7002; 33m/s; rel 1960/1979; cip

[9801] no performers given
- Coronet LPS-3039; 33s; rel 1977; cip

Sonata, Horn and Piano, No 2 (1957)
[9802] Barrows, John (hn); Kaye, Milton (pf)
- Golden Crest RE-7002; 33m/s; rel 1960/1979; cip

Sonata, Horn and Piano, No 3 (1965)
[9803] Barrows, John (hn); Barrows, Tait Sanford (pf)
- Golden Crest RE-7034; 33s; rel 1970; cip

Sonata, Horn, Tuba, and Piano
[9804] Barrows, John (hn); Phillips,
Harvey (tu); Sanford, Frances (pf)
or Leighton, Bernard (pf)
- Golden Crest RE-7018; 33m/s;
rel 1965/1979; cip

Sonata, Trombone and Piano
[9805] Swallow, John (tbn); Wingreen,
Harriet (pf)
- Golden Crest RE-7015; 33m/s;
rel 1965/1979; cip

Sonata, Trumpet and Piano (1963)
[9806] Wilder, Joe (tpt); Kaye, Milton (pf)
or Wingreen, Harriet (pf)
- Golden Crest RE-7007; 33m/s;
rel 1961/1979; cip

Sonata, Tuba and Piano
[9807] Phillips, Harvey (tu); Kaye, Milton
(pf)
- Golden Crest RE-7006; 33m/s;
rel 1961/1979; cip

Sonata, Violoncello and Piano
[9808] Soyer, David (vcl); Wingreen,
Harriet (pf)
- Golden Crest RE-7009; 33m/s;
rel 1962/1979; cip

Song for a Friend, A
[9809] Levy, Robert (tpt); Levy, Amy Lou
(pf)
- Golden Crest RE-7045; 33q; rel
1972; cip

Song for Carol
[9810] Phillips, Harvey (tu); Spinney,
Bradley (pf); Leighton, Bernard
(perc)
- Golden Crest RE-7054; 33s; rel
1973*

Songs for Patricia
[9811] Bolin, Shannon (voice); Kaye,
Milton (pf)
- Golden Crest RE-7079; 33s; rel
1978

Suite, Brass Quintet (1959)
[9812] New York Brass Quintet
- Golden Crest
CR-4017/CRS-4017; 33m/s; rel
1960/1961; cip

Suite, Clarinet, Bassoon, and Piano
[9813] Academy Trio
- Golden Crest CRS-4115; 33s; rel
1975; cip

**Suite, Contrabass and Guitar
(1968)**
[9814] Karr, Gary (cb); Hand, Frederic
(gtr)
- Golden Crest RE-7031; 33m/s;
rel 1969/1979; cip

**Suite, Contrabass and Piano
(1965)**
[9815] Karr, Gary (cb); Leighton, Bernard
(pf)
- Golden Crest RE-7031; 33m/s;
rel 1969/1979; cip

Suite, Flute
[9816] Nanzetta, Virginia (fl)
- Golden Crest RE-7065; 33s; rel
1976

Suite, Flute, Clarinet, and Piano
[9817] Weiss, Janet (fl); Weiss, Mitchell
(cl); Carno, Zita (pf)
- Sound Master SMP-1003; 33s;
rel 1973*

Suite, Horn and Piano
[9818] Barrows, John (hn); Kaye, Milton
(pf)
- Golden Crest RE-7002; 33m/s;
rel 1960/1979; cip

**Suite, Horn, Tuba, and Piano, No 2
(1972)**
[9819] Barrows, John (hn); Phillips,
Harvey (tu); Kaye, Milton (pf)
- Golden Crest CRSQ-4147; 33q;
rel 1979; cip

Suite, Piano
[9820] Snyder, Barry (pf)
- Golden Crest RE-7058; 33s; rel
1975; cip

Suite, Trumpet and Piano (1969)
[9821] Levy, Robert (tpt); Levy, Amy Lou
(pf)
- Golden Crest RE-7045; 33q; rel
1972; cip

Suite, Winds (1956)
[9822] New York Woodwind Quintet
- Golden Crest CR-3019; 33m; rel
1957; del 1961
- Golden Crest
CR-4028/CRS-4028; 33m/s; rel
1961/1979; cip

Theme and Variations
[9823] Columbia String Orchestra; Sinatra,
Frank (cond)
- Columbia ML-4271; 33m; rel
1950; del 1956
- Columbia CL-884; 33m; rel
1956; del 1959
- Odyssey 32-16-0262; 33s; rel
1968; del 1971

Thomas Suite
[9824] Phillips, Harvey (tu); Spinney,
Bradley (pf); Leighton, Bernard
(perc)
- Golden Crest RE-7054; 33s; rel
1973*

Tuba Encore Piece
[9825] Bobo, Roger (tu); Grierson, Ralph
(pf)
- Crystal S-392; 33s; rel 1978; cip

While We're Young
[9826] Bolin, Shannon (voice); Kaye,
Milton (pf)
- Golden Crest RE-7079; 33s; rel
1978

**WILDING-WHITE, Raymond
(1922-)**
Paraphernalia (1959)
[9827] Hauptman, Margaret (sop); Anop,
Eleanor Pudil (al); Bell, Marshall
(bar); Kulas Chamber Ensemble;
Wilding-White, Raymond (cond)
- CRI-182; 33m/s; rel 1964; cip

WILKINSON, Scott (1922-)
This is the American Earth (1976)
[9828] Hoffman, Irwin (nar); University of
New Mexico Concert Choir
(members of); University of New
Mexico Instrumental Ensemble;
Clark, John M. (cond)
- Opus One 41; 33s

WILLIAMS, Clifton (1923-)
**Concertino, Percussion and Band
(1959)**
[9829] North Texas State University
Symphonic Band; McAdow,
Maurice (cond)
- Austin 6164; 33m; rel 1963; del
1971

Dedicatory Overture
[9830] University of Maryland Concert
Band; Ostling, Acton, Jr. (cond)
- Coronet 955; 33m; rel 1969; del
1978

Fanfare and Allegro (1956)
[9831] Chicago Symphonic Band
- Summy 2; 33m/s; rel 1958; del
1966
[9832] Eastman Symphonic Wind
Ensemble; Fennell, Frederick
(cond)
- Mercury MG-50220/SR-90220;
33m/s; rel 1960; del 1972
- Mercury SRI-75094; 33s; rel
1978; cip

Festival (1961)
[9833] Ohio State University Concert
Band; McGinnis, Donald E. (cond)
- Coronet S-1502; 33s; rel 1969;
del 1978

Sinfonians, The
[9834] Cornell University Symphonic Band;
Stith, Marice (cond)
- Cornell CUWE-9; 33s; rel 1971;
cip

Sinfonians, The (cont'd)
[9835] University of Texas Band
- Austin 6232; 33m; rel 1963; del 1971

Symphonic Suite, Band (1957)
[9836] Oklahoma City University Symphony Band
- Summy 3; 33m/s; rel 1958; del 1966

WILLIAMS, David McKay (1887-)

In the Year That King Uzziah Died
[9837] First Presbyterian Church (Kilgore, TX) Choir; Austin College Choir; Perry, Roy (org); Bedford, Robert W. (cond)
- Aeolian-Skinner AS-10; 33m; rel 1956; del 1958

King's Highway, The
[9838] St. Bartholomew's Episcopal Church (New York) Choir; Friedell, Harold (org) (cond)
- Grayco LPM-101; 33m; 10"; rel 1954

WILLIAMS, Jan (1946-)

Dream Lesson
[9839] Williams, Jan (perc); tape
- Turnabout TVS-34514; 33s; rel 1973; cip

WILLIAMS, John T. (1932-)

Sinfonietta
[9840] Eastman Symphonic Wind Ensemble; Hunsberger, Donald (cond)
- Deutsche Grammophon 2530.063; 33s; rel 1971; del 1975

WILLINGHAM, Jerry*

T'Chu
[9841] Bennett, Sabrina (fl); Huffman, Kat (bsn); Sleeper, Tom (tbn); Solomon, Jeff (hn); Stafford, LeAnn (mrmb)
- Irida 0026; 33s; rel 197?

WILSON, Donald (1937-)

Dedication (1960)
[9842] Rome Chamber Orchestra; Flagello, Nicolas (cond)
- Peters Internationale PLE-059; 33s; rel 1978; cip

WILSON, Eugene*

Light Fantastic Too, The (1977)
[9843] Blackburn, Fiona (sop); Martin, Jane (fl); Rogers, Robert (pf); Moore, Kenneth (perc)
- Opus One 46; 33s; rel 1979; cip

WILSON, Galen (1926-)

Applications
[9844] Electronic music
- Capra 1201; 33s; rel 1969; cip

WILSON, George B. (1927-)

Concatenations (1969)
[9845] Illinois Contemporary Chamber Players; London, Edwin (cond)
- CRI-271; 33s; rel 1971; cip

Exigencies (1968)
[9846] Electronic music
- CRI-271; 33s; rel 1971; cip

WILSON, Harry R. (1901-68)

Finger of God, The
[9847] Columbia University Teachers College Concert Choir; Ohl, Dorothy (org); Wilson, Harry R. (cond)
- Music Library MLR-7071; 33m; rel 1956; del 1974

Thing of Beauty, A
[9848] Columbia University Teachers College Concert Choir; Ohl, Dorothy (org); Wilson, Harry R. (cond)
- Music Library MLR-7071; 33m; rel 1956; del 1974

WILSON, Olly (1937-)

Akwan (1972)
[9849] Bunger, Richard (pf); Baltimore Symphony Orchestra; Freeman, Paul (cond)
- Columbia M-33434; 33s; rel 1975; del 1979

Cetus (1967)
[9850] Electronic music
- Turnabout TVS-34301; 33s; rel 1969; del 1975

Echoes (1974)
[9851] Rehfeldt, Phillip (cl); tape
- CRI-367; 33s; rel 1977; cip

Piece for Four (1966)
[9852] Willoughby, Robert (fl); Young, Gene (tpt); Schwartz, Joseph (pf); Turetzky, Bertram (cb)
- CRI-264; 33s; rel 1971; cip

Piece for Piano and Electronic Sound (1971)
[9853] Hinderas, Natalie (pf); tape
- Desto DC-7102-03; 33s; 2 discs; rel 1970; cip

Sometimes (1976)
[9854] Brown, William (ten); tape
- CRI-370; 33s; rel 1977; cip

WILSON, Richard (1941-)

Concert Piece, Violin and Piano (1967)
[9855] Schulte, Rolf (vln); Oppens, Ursula (pf)
- CRI-315; 33s; rel 1974; cip

Music for Solo Flute (1972)
[9856] Sollberger, Harvey (fl)
- CRI-315; 33s; rel 1974; cip

Music for Violin and Violoncello (1969)
[9857] Matsuda, Yoko (vln); Sherry, Fred (vcl)
- CRI-271; 33s; rel 1971; cip

WINHAM, Godfrey

NP (Two Pieces for Computer-Synthesized Sound)
[9858] Electronic music
- CRI-393; 33s; rel 1979; cip

WINSOR, Philip (1938-)

Melted Ears (1967)
[9859] Albright, William (pf); Warburton, Thomas (pf)
- Advance FGR-14S; 33s; rel 1972; cip

WIRTH, Carl A. (1912-)

Diversions in Denim
[9860] Fredonia Saxophone Ensemble; Wyman, Lawrence (cond)
- Mark MES-37575; 33s; rel 1972*

Portals
[9861] Rascher Saxophone Ensemble
- Coronet LPS-3022; 33s; rel 1975; cip

WISE, James W.

Gather Ye Rosebuds (Songs to Study English 101 By)
[9862] Welch, Mitzie (voice); Hoh, Richard (voice); orchestra
- Golden Crest CR-31010; 33m; rel 1964

WITKIN, Beatrice (1916-)

Breath and Sounds (1970-71)
[9863] Hanks, Thompson (tu); tape
- Opus One 12; 33s; rel 1972; cip

Chiaroscuro (1968)
[9864] Sylvester, Robert (vcl); Carno, Zita (pf)
- Opus One 10; 33s; rel 1972; cip

Contour (1964)
[9865] Carno, Zita (pf)
- Opus One 10; 33s; rel 1972; cip

Duo, Violin and Piano (1960-61)
[9866] Simon, Louis F. (vln); Carno, Zita
(pf)
- Opus One 10; 33s; rel 1972; cip

Interludes (1960)
[9867] Dunkel, Paul (fl)
- Opus One 12; 33s; rel 1972; cip

Parameters (1964)
[9868] Dunkel, Paul (fl) (pic) (al fl);
Blustine, Allen (cl) (b cl); Ajemian,
Anahid (vln); Sylvester, Robert
(vcl); Carno, Zita (pf); Brehm,
Alvin (cond)
- Opus One 12; 33s; rel 1972; cip

Prose Poem (1963-64)
[9869] Kraft, Jean (al); Silver, Joseph
(nar); Tillotson, Brooks (hn);
Sylvester, Robert (vcl);
DesRoches, Raymond (perc);
Brehm, Alvin (cond)
- Opus One 10; 33s; rel 1972; cip

Triads and Things (1968)
[9870] New York Brass Society; Thomas,
Andrew (cond)
- Opus One 12; 33s; rel 1972; cip

WOLFE, Jacques (1896-1973)
British Children's Prayer
[9871] McCormack, John (ten); Moore,
Gerald (pf)
- Gramophone DA-1817; 78; 10'';
rel pre-1952

De Glory Road
[9872] Tibbett, Lawrence (bar); Wille,
Stewart (pf)
- Victor 7486; 78

Gwine to Hebb'n
[9873] Symonette, Randolph (b bar);
Harnley, Lesley (pf)
- Colosseum CLPS-1008; 33m; rel
1951; del 1958

Sailormen
[9874] Eddy, Nelson (bar); orchestra;
Armbruster, Robert (cond)
- Columbia ML-2091; 33m; 10'';
rel 1950; del 1956

WOLFE, Stanley (1924-)
(Three) Children's Profiles (1955)
[9875] Richter, Marga (pf)
- MGM E-3147; 33m; rel 1955;
del 1959

WOLFF, Christian (1934-)
Accompaniments (1972)
[9876] Rzewski, Frederic (pf) (perc)
(voice)
Rec 3/15/76
- CRI-357; 33s; rel 1976; cip

Duet II, Horn and Piano (1961)
[9877] Hillyer, Howard (hn); Tudor, David
(pf)
- Time 58009/S-8009; 33m/s; rel
1963; del 1970
- Mainstream MS-5015; 33s; rel
1970; del 1979

Duo for Violinist and Pianist (1961)
[9878] Raimondi, Matthew (vln); Tudor,
David (pf)
- Time 58009/S-8009; 33m/s; rel
1963; del 1970
- Mainstream MS-5015; 33s; rel
1970; del 1979

**For One, Two, or Three People and
a Conductor (1964)**
[9879] Tudor, David (org)
- Odyssey
32-16-0157/32-16-0158;
33m/s; rel 1967; del 1978

Lines (1972)
[9880] Rubin, Nathan (vln); Halpin,
Thomas (vln); Ellis, Nancy (vla);
Judiyaba (vcl)
Rec 3/73
- CRI-357; 33s; rel 1976; cip

Summer (1961)
[9881] Concord String Quartet
- Vox SVBX-5306; 33s; 3 discs; rel
1973; cip

[9882] Quartett Societa Cameristica
Italiana
Rec 10/68 and 11/69
- Wergo WER-60-053; 33s (Les
Grands interpretes de la musique
moderne); rel 1977*

[9883] Raimondi, Matthew (vln);
Kobayashi, Kenji (vln); Trampler,
Walter (vla); Soyer, David (vcl)
- Time 58009/S-8009; 33m/s; rel
1963; del 1970
- Mainstream MS-5015; 33s; rel
1970; del 1979

WOLFF, Henry and HENNINGS,
Nancy
Tibetan Bells
[9884] Wolff, Henry (perc); Hennings,
Nancy (perc); Gladstone, Drew
(perc); tape
- Island SMAS-9319; 33s; rel
1972

WOLPE, Stefan (1902-72)
Chamber Piece No 1 (1964)
[9885] Contemporary Chamber Ensemble;
Weisberg, Arthur (cond)
- Nonesuch H-71220; 33s; rel
1969; cip

Chamber Piece No 2 (1965-66)
[9886] Parnassus; Korf, Anthony (cond)
- New World NW-306; 33s; rel
1980

Form (1959)
[9887] Chamberlain, Anne (pf)
- Ars Nova/Ars Antiqua AN-1007;
33s; rel 1971; del 1974

[9888] Miller, Robert (pf)
- CRI-306; 33s; rel 1974; cip

[9889] Sherman, Russell (pf)
- Acoustic Research AR-0654.087;
33s; rel 1971
- New World NW-308; 33s; rel
1980

**Form IV (Broken Sequences)
(1969)**
[9890] Miller, Robert (pf)
- CRI-306; 33s; rel 1974; cip

Frieden heisst Sieg
[9891] Busch, E. (bar); instrumental
ensemble
- Eterna (East German) 10-99; 78;
rel pre-1956

In Two Parts (1962)
[9892] Bradbury, Colin (cl); Mason, David
(tpt); Datyner, Henry (vln);
Tunnell, Charles (vcl); Jefferies,
Michael (hp); Wolpe, Katharina
(pf); Prausnitz, Frederik (cond)
- Argo ZRG-757; 33s; rel 1976;
cip

Pastorale (1939)
[9893] Chamberlain, Anne (pf)
- Ars Nova/Ars Antiqua AN-1007;
33s; rel 1971; del 1974

**Piece for Trumpet and Seven
Instruments (1971)**
[9894] Guarneri, Mario (tpt); Crystal
Chamber Orchestra; Kraft,
William (cond)
- Crystal S-352; 33s; rel 1978; cip

**Piece for Two Instrumental Units
(1962-63)**
[9895] Dunkel, Paul (fl); Lucarelli, Bert
(ob); Sylvester, Robert (vcl);
Deak, Jon (cb); Heldrich, Claire
(perc); Thomas, Andrew (pf);
Gottlieb, Linda (vln); Gilbert,
David (cond)
- Opus One 9; 33s; rel 1972; cip

**Piece in Two Parts for Flute and
Piano (1960)**
[9896] Baron, Samuel (fl); Sanders,
Samuel (pf)
- Desto DC-7104; 33s; rel 1972;
cip

**Piece in Two Parts for Violin Alone
(1964)**
[9897] Harbison, Rosemary (vln)
- Acoustic Research AR-0654.087;
33s; rel 1971
- New World NW-308; 33s; rel
1980

Presto agitato
[9898] Chamberlain, Anne (pf)
  - Ars Nova/Ars Antiqua AN-1007;
    33s; rel 1971; del 1974

Quartet, Strings (1968-69)
[9899] Concord String Quartet
  - Vox SVBX-5306; 33s; 3 discs; rel
    1973; cip

Quartet, Tenor Saxophone, Trumpet, Percussion, and Piano (1950)
[9900] Cohn, Al (ten sax); Nagel, Robert
    (tpt); Howard, Al (perc); Maxin,
    Jacob (pf); Baron, Samuel (cond)
    Rec 9/54
  - Esoteric ES-530; 33m; rel 1954;
    del 1964
  - Counterpoint/Esoteric
    CPT-530/CPST-5530; 33m/s;
    rel 1964/1966; cip

[9901] Contemporary Chamber Ensemble;
    Weisberg, Arthur (cond)
  - Nonesuch H-71302; 33s; rel
    1974; cip

Second Piece for Violin Alone (1966)
[9902] Zukofsky, Paul (vln)
  - Desto DC-6435-37; 33s; 3 discs;
    rel 1975; cip

Solo Piece, Trumpet (1966)
[9903] Levy, Robert (tpt)
  - Golden Crest RE-7045; 33q; rel
    1972; cip

[9904] Schwarz, Gerard (tpt)
  - Desto DC-7133; 33s; rel 1973;
    cip

Sonata, Violin and Piano (1949)
[9905] Magnes, Frances (vln); Tudor,
    David (pf)
    Rec 9/54
  - Esoteric ES-530; 33m; rel 1954;
    del 1964
  - Counterpoint/Esoteric
    CPT-530/CPST-5530; 33m/s;
    rel 1964/1966; cip

(Ten) Songs from the Hebrew (1938)
[9906] Carmen, Arline (al); Lishner, Leon
    (bar); Tudor, David (pf)
  - Columbia ML-5179; 33m; rel
    1957; del 1968
  - Columbia CML-5179; 33m; rel
    1968; del 1974
  - Columbia AML-5179; 33m; rel
    1974; del 1976

(Four) Studies on Basic Rows (1935-36): Passacaglia
[9907] Tudor, David (pf)
    Rec 9/54
  - Esoteric ES-530; 33m; rel 1954;
    del 1964
  - Counterpoint/Esoteric
    CPT-530/CPST-5530; 33m/s;
    rel 1964/1966; cip

Trio in Two Parts, Flute, Violoncello, and Piano (1964)
[9908] Sollberger, Harvey (fl); Krosnick,
    Joel (vcl); Wuorinen, Charles (pf)
  - CRI-233; 33s; rel 1969; cip

WOOD, Joseph Roberts (1915-)
Poem (1950)
[9909] Asahi Orchestra of Tokyo; Korn,
    Richard (cond)
  - CRI-134; 33m/s; rel 1960/?; cip

WOOD, William (1935-)
Sonata, Violin and Piano (1973)
[9910] Felberg, Leonard (vln); Robert,
    George (pf)
  - Opus One 30; 33s; rel 1977; cip

Trios, Winds (1975)
[9911] Randall, Darrel (ob) (E hn); Bowen,
    Frank (fl) (pic); Williams, Floyd
    (cl)
  - Opus One 29; 33s; rel 1976; cip

Vortrag (1972)
[9912] Randall, Darrel (ob); Angel, Rita
    (pf)
  - Opus One 37; 33s; rel 1978; cip

WOOLLEN, Russell (1923-)
Lento (1970)
[9913] Stockton, Ann Mason (hp)
  - Crystal S-107; 33s; rel 1973; cip

Missa domus aurea (Op 40) (1957): Motectus ad libitum ad offertorium
[9914] Mid-America Chorale; Dexter, John
    (cond)
  - CRI-191; 33m/s; rel 1964/?; cip

Quartet, Flute and Strings (1953)
[9915] National Gallery Symphony
    Orchestra (members of)
  - Transition 15; 33m; rel 1956;
    del 1958

WORK, John Wesley, Jr. (1901-67)
Scuppernong Suite
[9916] Hinderas, Natalie (pf)
  - Desto DC-7102-03; 33s; 2 discs;
    rel 1970; cip

WORK, Julian (1910-)
Autumn Walk
[9917] Eastman Symphonic Wind
    Ensemble; Fennell, Frederick
    (cond)
  - Mercury MG-50220/SR-90220;
    33m/s; rel 1960; del 1972

WORLEY, John
Oneonta Quartet: Scherzo
[9918] Rascher Saxophone Ensemble
  - Coronet LPS-3022; 33s; rel
    1975; cip

WRIGHT, Maurice (1949-)
Electronic Composition (1973)
[9919] Electronic music
  - Odyssey Y-34139; 33s; rel
    1976; cip

WRIGHT, Searle (1918-)
Carol-Prelude on Greensleeves
[9920] MacDonald, Robert (org)
  - Mirrosonic CS-7232; 33s; rel
    197?

[9921] Mason, Marilyn (org)
  - Aeolian-Skinner AS-7; 33m; rel
    1956; del 1958
  - Washington WAS-7; 33m; rel
    1958; del 1962

[9922] Obetz, John (org)
  - Celebre 8006; 33s; rel 197?

[9923] Whitehead, William (org)
  - Cameo C-4009/SC-4009;
    33m/s; rel 1962

[9924] Zamkochian, Berj (org)
  - Allen Organ Co GRT-1162; 33m;
    rel 1963
  - Columbia
    XTV-88765-66/XSV-88767-68
    (matrix no); 33m/s; rel 1963?

Green Blade Riseth, The
[9925] St. Luke's Episcopal Church (San
    Francisco) Choir; Whitley, Bob
    (org)
  - Aeolian-Skinner AS-321; 33s; rel
    1966

Introduction, Passacaglia, and Fugue
[9926] Swann, Frederick (org)
  - Mirrosonic CS-7230; 33s; rel
    1972

Prelude on Brother James's Air
[9927] Becker, C. Warren (org)
  - Chapel LP-5-134/ST-134;
    33m/s; rel 1968

[9928] Curtis, Stanley (org)
  - Apollo Sound AS-1004; 33s; rel
    1968

[9929] Hancock, Gerre (org)
  - Baldwin S-LP-101; 33s; rel
    1966?

[9930] Mason, Marilyn (org)
  - Aeolian-Skinner AS-7; 33m; rel
    1956; del 1958
  - Washington WAS-7; 33m; rel
    1958; del 1962

[9931] Obetz, John (org)
  - Celebre 8004; 33s; rel 197?

[9932] Whitehead, William (org)
  - Cameo C-4009/SC-4009;
    33m/s; rel 1962

[9933] Zamkochian, Berj (org)
  - Allen Organ Co GRT-1162; 33m;
    rel 1963

WUORINEN, Charles (1938-)

Bearbeitungen ueber das Glogauer Liederbuch (1962)
[9934] Speculum Musicae (members of)
- Nonesuch H-71319; 33s; rel 1976; cip

Chamber Concerto, Flute and Ten Instruments (1964)
[9935] Sollberger, Harvey (fl); Group for Contemporary Music at Columbia University; Wuorinen, Charles (cond)
- CRI-230; 33s; rel 1968; cip

Chamber Concerto, Violoncello and Ten Instruments (1963)
[9936] Sherry, Fred (vcl); Group for Contemporary Music at Columbia University; Wuorinen, Charles (cond)
- Nonesuch H-71263; 33s; rel 1972; cip

Composition, Oboe and Piano (1965)
[9937] Ostryniec, James (ob); Wuorinen, Charles (pf)
Rec 6/17/77
- Orion ORS-78288; 33s; rel 1978; cip

Concerto, Piano and Orchestra (1966)
[9938] Wuorinen, Charles (pf); Royal Philharmonic Orchestra; Dixon, James (cond)
- CRI-239; 33s; rel 1969; cip

Duo, Violin and Piano (1967)
[9939] Zukofsky, Paul (vln); Wuorinen, Charles (pf)
- Acoustic Research AR-0654.086; 33s; rel 1971

Grand Bamboula (1971)
[9940] Light Fantastic Players; Shulman, Daniel (cond)
- Nonesuch H-71319; 33s; rel 1976; cip

Janissary Music (1967)
[9941] DesRoches, Raymond (perc)
- CRI-231; 33s; rel 1968; cip

Long and the Short, The (1970)
[9942] Zukofsky, Paul (vln)
- Mainstream MS-5016; 33s; rel 1974*

Making Ends Meet (1967)
[9943] Wentworth, Jean (pf); Wentworth, Kenneth (pf)
- Desto DC-7131; 33s; rel 1973; cip

Percussion Symphony (1976)
[9944] New Jersey Percussion Ensemble; Wuorinen, Charles (cond)
Rec 3/78
- Nonesuch H-71353; 33s; rel 1978; cip

Prayer of Jonah, The (1962)
[9945] King's Chapel Choir, Boston; Cambridge Festival Strings; Pinkham, Daniel (cond)
Rec 1963
- Cambridge CRM-416/CRS-1416; 33m/s; rel 1964; del 1971

Prelude and Fugue (1956)
[9946] Percussion Ensemble; Kraus, Paul (cond)
- Golden Crest CR-4004/CRS-4004; 33m/s; rel 1957/1979; cip

Quartet, Strings (1971)
[9947] Fine Arts Quartet
- Turnabout TVS-34515; 33s; rel 1973; del 1978

Ringing Changes (1971)
[9948] New Jersey Percussion Ensemble; Wuorinen, Charles (cond)
- Nonesuch H-71263; 33s; rel 1972; cip

Sonata, Piano (1969)
[9949] Miller, Robert (pf)
- CRI-306; 33s; rel 1974; cip

Speculum speculi (1973)
[9950] Speculum Musicae; Sherry, Fred (cond)
Rec 2/74
- Nonesuch H-71300; 33s; rel 1974; cip

Symphony III (1959)
[9951] Japan Philharmonic Symphony Orchestra; Watanabe, Akeo (cond)
- CRI-149; 33m/s; rel 1962/?; cip

Time's Encomium (1969)
[9952] Electronic music
- Nonesuch H-71225; 33s; rel 1969; cip

Trio, Strings (1969)
[9953] Speculum Musicae (members of)
- Nonesuch H-71319; 33s; rel 1976; cip

Two-Part Symphony (1977-78)
[9954] American Composers Orchestra; Davies, Dennis Russell (cond)
- CRI-410; 33s; rel 1980; cip

Variations, Bassoon, Harp, and Timpani (1972)
[9955] MacCourt, Donald (bsn); Jolles, Susan (hp); Gottlieb, Gordon (timp)
- New World NW-209; 33s; rel 1977

Variations, Flute, I (1964)
[9956] Sollberger, Harvey (fl)
- Nonesuch HB-73028; 33s; 2 discs; rel 1975; cip

Variations, Flute, II (1970)
[9957] Sollberger, Harvey (fl)
- Nonesuch HB-73028; 33s; 2 discs; rel 1975; cip

Variations, Piano (1965)
[9958] Burge, David (pf)
- Advance FGR-3; 33m; rel 1967; cip

Winds, The (1977)
[9959] Parnassus; Korf, Anthony (cond)
- New World NW-306; 33s; rel 1980

WURTZLER, Aristid von (1925-)

Capriccio
[9960] New York Harp Ensemble; Wurtzler, Aristid von (cond)
- Musical Heritage Society MHS-3890; 33s

Chordophonic
[9961] New York Harp Ensemble; Wurtzler, Aristid von (cond)
- Musical Heritage Society MHS-3307; 33s; rel 1975

Concert Improvisation
[9962] Wurtzler, Aristid von (hp); Festival Orchestra; Valante, Harrison R. (cond)
- Musical Heritage Society MHS-3370; 33s; rel 1976

Impressions
[9963] New York Harp Ensemble; tape; Wurtzler, Aristid von (cond)
- Musical Heritage Society MHS-3307; 33s; rel 1975

Meditation
[9964] New York Harp Ensemble; Wurtzler, Aristid von (cond)
- Musical Heritage Society MHS-3483; 33s

Modern Sketches
[9965] Wurtzler, Aristid von (hp); Festival Orchestra; Valante, Harrison R. (cond)
- Musical Heritage Society MHS-3370; 33s; rel 1976

Prelude No 3 (Op 50)
[9966] New York Harp Ensemble;
Wurtzler, Aristid von (cond)
- Musical Heritage Society
MHS-3890; 33s

Space Odyssey
[9967] New York Harp Ensemble;
Wurtzler, Aristid von (cond)
- Musical Heritage Society
MHS-1844; 33s; rel 1974

Variations on a Theme by Corelli
[9968] New York Harp Ensemble;
Wurtzler, Aristid von (cond)
- Musical Heritage Society
MHS-3890; 33s

WYKES, Robert Arthur (1926-)

(Four) American Indian Lyrics (1957)
[9969] Washington University Choir
- Washington University 1009;
33m; rel 1960; del 1973

Concerto, Eleven Instruments (1956)
[9970] Washington University Chamber
Orchestra; Jardine, Leigh (cond)
- Washington University 1009;
33m; rel 1960; del 1973

Sonata, Flute and Piano (1955)
[9971] Tipton, Albert (fl); Norris, Mary (pf)
- Washington University 1009;
33m; rel 1960; del 1973

(Four) Studies, Piano (1958)
[9972] Shatzkamer, William (pf)
- Washington University 1009;
33m; rel 1960; del 1973

WYLIE, Ruth Shaw (1916-)

Psychogram (1968)
[9973] Cantanese, Rosemary (pf)
- CRI-353; 33s; rel 1976; cip

WYNER, Yehudi (1929-)

Concert Duo, Violin and Piano (1955-57)
[9974] Raimondi, Matthew (vln); Wyner,
Yehudi (pf)
- CRI-161; 33m/s; rel 1963/?; cip

Intermedio (1974)
[9975] Wyner, Susan Davenny (sop);
string orchestra; Wyner, Yehudi
(cond)
- CRI-352; 33s; rel 1976; cip

Serenade, Seven Instruments (1958)
[9976] Baker, Julius (fl); Froelich, Ralph
(hn); Nagel, Robert (tpt); Brown,
Keith (tbn); Zaratzian, Harry (vla);
McCracken, Charles (vcl); Wyner,
Yehudi (pf); Torkanowsky, Werner
(cond)
- CRI-141; 33m; rel 1961; cip

(Three) Short Fantasies (1963-71)
[9977] Miller, Robert (pf)
- CRI-306; 33s; rel 1974; cip

WYTON, Alec (1921-)

Fanfare
[9978] Wyton, Alec (org)
- Word W-4015/WST-9002;
33m/s; rel 1959; del 1976

Fantasie-Improvisation on Azmon
[9979] Keiser, Marilyn (org)
Rec 3/23/68
- Wicks Organ Co 832W-0782-1-2
(matrix no); 33s; 2 discs; rel
1969

In Praise of Merbecke
[9980] Wyton, Alec (org)
- Word W-4015/WST-9002;
33m/s; rel 1959; del 1976

Resurrection Suite: This Joyful Eastertide
[9981] Keiser, Marilyn (org)
Rec 3/23/68
- Wicks Organ Co 832W-0782-1-2
(matrix no); 33s; 2 discs; rel
1969

YANNATOS, James (1929-)

Cycles (1974)
[9982] Contemporary Music Ensemble of
Boston
- Afka SK-4628; 33s; rel 1978;
cip

Minicycle I (Moods) (1969)
[9983] Heller, Joan (sop); Yannatos,
James (pf)
- Afka SK-4628; 33s; rel 1978;
cip

Prieres dans l'arche (1965)
[9984] Shelton, Lucy (sop); Yannatos
Ensemble; Yannatos, James
(cond)
- Afka SK-4628; 33s; rel 1978;
cip

Sonata, Clarinet and Piano (1962)
[9985] Hill, Thomas (cl); Berman,
Lawrence (pf)
- Afka SK-4628; 33s; rel 1978;
cip

YARDEN, Elie (1923-)

Divertimento (1963)
[9986] University of Chicago
Contemporary Chamber Players;
Shapey, Ralph (cond)
- CRI-302; 33s; rel 1973; cip

YARDUMIAN, Richard (1917-)

Armenian Suite (1937)
[9987] Bournemouth Symphony Orchestra;
Brusilow, Anshel (cond)
- HNH Records HNH-4043; 33s;
rel 1978; del 1980

Armenian Suite (1937) *(cont'd)*
[9988] Philadelphia Orchestra; Ormandy,
Eugene (cond)
- Columbia ML-4991; 33m; rel
1955; del 1962

Armenian Suite (arr for 2 pfs by John Ogdon)
[9989] Ogdon, John (pf); Lucas, Brenda
(pf)
- EMI/His Master's Voice
BOX-86801-05 (in set SLS-868);
33s; 5 discs; rel 1974

Cantus animae et cordis (1955)
[9990] Bournemouth Symphony Orchestra;
Brusilow, Anshel (cond)
- HNH Records HNH-4043; 33s;
rel 1978; del 1980
[9991] Philadelphia Orchestra; Ormandy,
Eugene (cond)
- Columbia ML-5629/MS-6229;
33m/s; rel 1961; del 1965

Chorale Prelude on Veni, sancte spiritus (1959)
[9992] Philadelphia Orchestra; Ormandy,
Eugene (cond)
- Columbia ML-5629/MS-6229;
33m/s; rel 1961; del 1965
- Columbia ML-6259/MS-6859;
33m/s; rel 1966; del 1970

Chromatic Sonata (1946)
[9993] Ogdon, John (pf)
- EMI/His Master's Voice
BOX-86801-05 (in set SLS-868);
33s; 5 discs; rel 1974

Concerto, Violin and Orchestra (1949)
[9994] Brusilow, Anshel (vln); Philadelphia
Orchestra; Ormandy, Eugene
(cond)
- Columbia ML-4991; 33m; rel
1955; del 1962
- Columbia ML-5862/MS-6462;
33m/s; rel 1963; del 1965

Danse (1942)
[9995] Ogdon, John (pf)
- EMI/His Master's Voice
BOX-86801-05 (in set SLS-868);
33s; 5 discs; rel 1974

Desolate City (1943-44): Desolation
[9996] Philadelphia Orchestra; Ormandy,
Eugene (cond)
- Columbia ML-4991; 33m; rel
1955; del 1962

Mass on Come, Creator Spirit (1966)
[9997] Chookasian, Lili (m sop); Fordham University Glee Club (members of); Thomas More College Women's Chorale (members of); Chamber Symphony of Philadelphia Chorale; Chamber Symphony of Philadelphia; Brusilow, Anshel (cond)
- RCA LM-2979/LSC-2979; 33m/s; rel 1967; del 1971

Passacaglia, Recitative, and Fugue (1957)
[9998] Ogdon, John (pf); Bournemouth Symphony Orchestra; Berglund, Paavo (cond)
- EMI/His Master's Voice ASD-3367; 33q; rel 1977

[9999] Ogdon, John (pf); Royal Philharmonic Orchestra; Buketoff, Igor (cond)
- RCA LSC-3243; 33s; rel 1971; del 1976

[10000] Pennink, John (pf); Philadelphia Orchestra; Ormandy, Eugene (cond)
- Columbia ML-5629/MS-6229; 33m/s; rel 1961; del 1965

Prelude and Chorale (1944)
[10001] Ogdon, John (pf)
- EMI/His Master's Voice BOX-86801-05 (in set SLS-868); 33s; 5 discs; rel 1974

(Three) Preludes, Piano (1936-44)
[10002] Ogdon, John (pf)
- EMI/His Master's Voice BOX-86801-05 (in set SLS-868); 33s; 5 discs; rel 1974

Psalm 130 (1947)
[10003] Zulick, Howell (ten); Philadelphia Orchestra; Ormandy, Eugene (cond)
- Columbia ML-4991; 33m; rel 1955; del 1962

Symphony No 1 (1961)
[10004] Bournemouth Symphony Orchestra; Brusilow, Anshel (cond)
- HNH Records HNH-4043; 33s; rel 1978; del 1980

[10005] Philadelphia Orchestra; Ormandy, Eugene (cond)
- Columbia ML-5862/MS-6462; 33m/s; rel 1963; del 1965
- Columbia ML-6259/MS-6859; 33m/s; rel 1966; del 1970

Symphony No 2 (Psalms) (1964)
[10006] Chookasian, Lili (al); Philadelphia Orchestra; Ormandy, Eugene (cond)
- Columbia ML-6259/MS-6859; 33m/s; rel 1966; del 1970

YLVISAKER, John (1937-)
Mass for the Secular City
[10007] no performers given
- Avant Garde AVM-102-04/AVS-102-04; 33m/s; 3 discs; rel 1967

YON, Pietro Alessandro (1886-1943)
Gesu bambino (1917)
[10008] Courboin, Charles (org)
- Victor 15824; 78; rel 1940

[10009] Fox, Virgil (org)
- RCA LM-1845; 33m; rel 1954
- Capitol P-8531/SP-8531; 33m/s; rel 1960

[10010] MacDonald, Robert (org)
- Mirrosonic CS-7232; 33s; rel 197?

L'Organo primitivo
[10011] Bayco, Frederic (org)
- Capitol SP-8681; 33s; rel 1968; del 1970

[10012] Bielby, Jonathan (org)
- Vista VPS-1034; 33s; rel 1976

[10013] Ellsasser, Richard (org)
- MGM E-3031; 33m; rel 1953; del 1959

[10014] Farnam, Lynnwood (org)
- Ultra Fidelity UF-3; 33m; rel 1959

[10015] Fry, Edward (org)
- Ace of Diamonds (Decca) SDD-R-404; 33s; rel 1973

[10016] Prince-Joseph, Bruce (org)
- Hi-Fi R-720/S-720; 33m/s; rel 1959; del 1967
- Everest LPBR-6156/SDBR-3156; 33m/s; rel 1967; cip

Minuetto antico e musetta
[10017] Farnam, Lynnwood (org)
- Ultra Fidelity UF-2; 33m; rel 1959

YOUNG, Gordon (1919-)
Prelude and Fugato on Crusader's Hymn
[10018] Young, Gordon (org)
- Grosse Pointe 235612; 33m; rel 1957

YOUNG, Jane Corner (1916-)
Dramatic Soliloquy (1961)
[10019] Loesser, Arthur (pf)
- CRI-183; 33m/s; rel 1964/?; cip

We People (1967)
[10020] Braun, Phylis (sop); Downs, Warren (vcl); Young, Jane Corner (pf)
- Advent USR-5005; 33s; rel 1973; cip

YTTREHUS, Rolv (1926-)
Music for Viola, Winds, and Percussion (1961)
[10021] no performers given
- Capra 1202; 33s; rel 1971; del 1973

Sextet (1969-70, rev 1974)
[10022] Anderson, Ronald (tpt); Benjamin, Barry (hn); Kornacher, Thomas (vln); Walter, David (cb); Tower, Joan (pf); Heldrich, Claire (perc); Guigi, Efrain (cond)
- CRI-321; 33s; rel 1974; cip

ZABRACK, Harold (1929-)
Dialogue
[10023] Zabrack, Harold (pf)
- Educo 3095; 33

Elegie for Left Hand Alone
[10024] Zabrack, Harold (pf)
- Educo 3095; 33

Introspection
[10025] Zabrack, Harold (pf)
- Educo 3095; 33

Landscape
[10026] Zabrack, Harold (pf)
- Educo 3095; 33

Scherzo (Hommage a Prokofieff)
[10027] Zabrack, Harold (pf)
- Educo 3095; 33

Sonata, Piano, No 1 (1964)
[10028] Zabrack, Harold (pf)
- Educo 3095; 33

ZADOR, Jeno (Eugene) (1894-1977)
Christopher Columbus (1939)
[10029] Barrymore, Lionel (nar); Long Island Concert Choir; American Symphony Orchestra; Halasz, Laszlo (cond)
- Orion ORS-76251; 33s; rel 1977; cip

(Five) Contrasts (1965)
[10030] Budapest Radio Symphony Orchestra; Ferencsik, Janos (cond)
- Orion ORS-7279; 33s; rel 1972; cip

Csardas Rhapsody (1939)
[10031] Hollywood Pops Symphony Orchestra; Forester, David (cond)
- Fantasy 9001; 33m; rel 1958; del 1970

Dance
[10032] Frankenland State Symphony Orchestra; Kloss, Erich (cond)
- Belvedere 7099; 33m; rel 1959; del 1968

Dance *(cont'd)*
- Music Library MLR-7099; 33m;
  rel 1968; del 1974

Divertimento, Strings (1955)
[10033]Frankenland State Symphony
  Orchestra; Kloss, Erich (cond)
- Belvedere 7099; 33m; rel 1959;
  del 1968
- Music Library MLR-7099; 33m;
  rel 1968; del 1974
- Orion ORS-7279; 33s; rel 1972;
  cip

**Duo Fantasy (1973) (arr for 2 vcls
and pf)**
[10034]Rejto, Gabor (vcl); Rejto, Peter
  (vcl); Rejto, Alice (pf)
- Orion ORS-7282; 33s; rel 1972;
  cip

Hungarian Caprice (1935)
[10035]Fitch, Ray (tarogato); Minneapolis
  Symphony Orchestra; Ormandy,
  Eugene (cond)
- Victor 14031; 78; rel pre-1943

[10036]Frankenland State Symphony
  Orchestra; Kloss, Erich (cond)
- Belvedere 7099; 33m; rel 1959;
  del 1968
- Music Library MLR-7099; 33m;
  rel 1968; del 1974
- Orion ORS-7279; 33s; rel 1972;
  cip

Lonely Wayfarer
[10037]Women's Lyric Club
- Music Library MLR-7095; 33m;
  rel 1960; del 1974

Quintet, Brass (1973)
[10038]Modern Brass Quintet
- Orion ORS-74140; 33s; rel
  1974; cip

Quintet, Winds (1972)
[10039]Los Angeles Wind Quintet
- Orion ORS-73126; 33s; rel
  1973; cip

(Three) Rondells
[10040]Women's Lyric Club
- Music Library MLR-7095; 33m;
  rel 1960; del 1974

Studies, Orchestra (1970)
[10041]Westphalian Symphony Orchestra;
  Freeman, Paul (cond)
- Orion ORS-74140; 33s; rel
  1974; cip

**Variations on a Hungarian Folksong
(1927)**
[10042]Frankenland State Symphony
  Orchestra; Schoenherr, Wilhelm
  (cond)
- Belvedere 7099; 33m; rel 1959;
  del 1968
- Music Library MLR-7099; 33m;
  rel 1968; del 1974

**Variations on a Hungarian Folksong
(1927)** *(cont'd)*
- Orion ORS-7279; 33s; rel 1972;
  cip

ZAIMONT, Judith Lang (1945-)
(Three) Ayres
[10043]Gregg Smith Singers; Smith, Gregg
  (cond)
- Golden Crest ATH-5051; 33s; rel
  1978; cip

Calendar Set, A (1972-78)
[10044]Steigerwalt, Gary (pf)
- Leonarda LPI-101; 33s; rel 1980

**Chansons nobles et sentimentales
(1974)**
[10045]Bressler, Charles (pf); Zaimont,
  Judith Lang (pf)
- Leonarda LPI-101; 33s; rel 1980

Greyed Sonnets
[10046]Gregg Smith Singers; Smith, Gregg
  (cond)
- Golden Crest ATH-5051; 33s; rel
  1978; cip

Nocturne (La fin de siecle) (1978)
[10047]Zaimont, Judith Lang (pf)
- Leonarda LPI-101; 33s; rel 1980

Songs of Innocence
[10048]Gregg Smith Singers; Smith, Gregg
  (cond)
- Golden Crest ATH-5051; 33s; rel
  1978; ctp

Sunny Airs and Sober
[10049]Gregg Smith Singers; Smith, Gregg
  (cond)
- Golden Crest ATH-5051; 33s; rel
  1978; cip

ZAJDA, Edward M.*
In March for Ann
[10050]Electronic music
- Ars Nova/Ars Antiqua AN-1006;
  33s; rel 1970; del 1973

Magnificent Desolation
[10051]Electronic music
- Ars Nova/Ars Antiqua AN-1006;
  33s; rel 1970; del 1973

Points
[10052]Electronic music
- Ars Nova/Ars Antiqua AN-1006;
  33s; rel 1970; del 1973

Study No 3
[10053]Electronic music
- Ars Nova/Ars Antiqua AN-1006;
  33s; rel 1970; del 1973

Study No 10 (1965-66)
[10054]Electronic music
- Ars Nova/Ars Antiqua AN-1006;
  33s; rel 1970; del 1973

ZAMECNIK, J. S. (1872-1953)
Indian Dawn
[10055]Alda, Frances (sop); orchestra
- Victor 1094; 78; 10"; rel 1925

ZAMKOCHIAN, Berj
Armenian Organ Mass
[10056]Zamkochian, Berj (org)
- Gregorian Institute of America
  M/S-135; 33s; rel 197?

ZANINELLI, Luigi (1932-)
Dance Variations
[10057]American Woodwind Quintet
- Golden Crest
  CR-4075/CRS-4075; 33m/s; rel
  1966/1967; cip

(Three) Infinitives (1975)
[10058]Waldoff, Stanley (pf)
- Musical Heritage Society
  MHS-3808; 33s; rel 1978

ZATMAN, Andrew (1945-)
**(Twenty-Four) Preludes, Piano
(1965)**
[10059]Zatman, Andrew (pf)
- Orion ORS-6909; 33s; rel 1969;
  cip

Sonata, Piano, No 2 (1967)
[10060]Zatman, Andrew (pf)
- Orion ORS-6909; 33s; rel 1969;
  cip

ZECHIEL, Ernest*
**(Six) Chorale Preludes: Rest Thou
Contented and Be Silent**
[10061]Ash, Harold (org)
- McIntosh Music MC-1005; 33m;
  rel 1956; del 1958

ZEISL, Eric (1905-59)
(Sechs) Kinderlieder (1933)
[10062]Beems, Patricia (sop); Zeisl, Eric
  (pf)
- SPA-5; 33m; rel 1952; del 1970

**(Thirteen) Pieces for Barbara
(1944)**
[10063]Zeisl, Eric (pf)
- SPA-5; 33m; rel 1952; del 1970

Sonata, Viola and Piano (1950-51)
[10064]Reher, Sven (vla); Schlatter, Eda
  (pf)
- SPA-10; 33m; rel 1952; del
  1970

Sonata, Violin and Piano (Brandeis) (1949-50)
[10065]Baker, Israel (vln); Menuhin, Yaltah (pf)
- SPA-10; 33m; rel 1952; del 1970

ZEMACHSON, Arnold
Chorale and Fugue, D Minor (Op 4)
[10066]Minneapolis Symphony Orchestra; Ormandy, Eugene (cond)
- Victor 8924-25; 78; 2 discs; rel pre-1936

ZIFFRIN, Marilyn J. (1926-)
(Four) Pieces, Tuba (1973)
[10067]Cummings, Barton (tu)
- Crystal S-391; 33s; rel 1978; cip

ZIMBALIST, Efrem (1889-)
Coq d'Or Phantasy
[10068]Besrodni, Igor (vln); piano
- USSR/State Music Trust 17221-22; 78; rel pre-1953

Improvisation
[10069]Zimbalist, Efrem (vln)
- Victor 1054; 78; 10''; rel 1912-24

Improvisation on a Japanese Tune
[10070]Zimbalist, Efrem (vln); Bay, Emanuel (pf)
- Columbia (Japanese) J-5113; 78; rel pre-1952
- Columbia 2110D; 78

Quartet, Strings, E Minor (1932)
[10071]Gordon String Quartet
- Schirmer 2521-24 (in set 6); 78; 4 discs; rel pre-1942

Sarasateana
[10072]Primrose, William (vla); Stimer, David (pf)
- Victor 10-1441-42 (in set MO-1242); 78; 2-10''; rel pre-1952

(Three) Slavonic Dances (1911): (No 1) Russian Dance
[10073]Zimbalist, Efrem (vln); piano
- Victor 64955; 78; 10''; rel 1912-24
- Victor 889; 78; 10''; rel 1912-24

(Three) Slavonic Dances: (No 2) Hebrew Melody and Dance
[10074]Zimbalist, Efrem (vln); Chotzinoff, Samuel (pf)
- Gramophone 4-7987 (in set DA-405); 78; rel 1912-24
- Victor 64455; 78; 10''; rel 1912-24
- Victor 887; 78; 10''; rel 1912-24
- Discopaedia MB-1008; 33m; rel 197?

(Three) Slavonic Dances: (No 3) Polish Dance
[10075]Zimbalist, Efrem (vln); orchestra
- Gramophone 4-7992 (in set DA-407); 78; rel 1912-24
- Victor 64562; 78; 10''; rel 1912-24
- Victor 889; 78; 10''; rel 1912-24
- Discopaedia MB-1008; 33m; rel 197?

Sonata, Violin and Piano, G Minor
[10076]Frank, Philip (vln); Frank, Bernard (pf)
- Umbrella UMB-DD3; 33s; rel 1980; cip

[10077]Malan, Roy (vln); Thompson, Marilyn (pf)
- Genesis GS-1070; 33s; rel 1977; cip

Suite dans la forme ancienne: (No 2) Sicilienne and (No 3) Minuet
[10078]Zimbalist, Efrem (vln); Chotzinoff, Samuel (pf)
- Gramophone DB-586; 78; rel 1912-24
- Victor 74280; 78; rel 1912-24
- Victor 6369; 78; rel 1912-24
- Discopaedia MB-1008; 33m; rel 197?

ZIMBALIST, Efrem, Jr. (1923-)
Sonata, Violin and Piano
[10079]Frank, Philip (vln); Frank, Bernard (pf)
- Umbrella UMB-DD3; 33s; rel 1980; cip

[10080]Malan, Roy (vln); Sutherland (pf)
- Genesis GS-1070; 33s; rel 1977; cip

ZINOS, Fredrick (1942-)
Elegy
[10081]Cummings, Barton (tu); Moore, Mary J. (pf)
- Crystal S-391; 33s; rel 1978; cip

ZONN, Paul (1938-)
Chroma (1967)
[10082]Zonn, Wilma (ob); Maddox, Arthur (pf)
- CRI-299; 33s; rel 1973; cip

Divertimento No 1
[10083]Perantoni, Daniel (tu); contrabass; percussion
- Ubres SN-101; 33s; rel 1976; cip

Gemini-Fantasy
[10084]University of Illinois Contemporary Chamber Players; London, Edwin (cond)
- CRI-405; 33s; rel 1979; cip

Liberata I (1967)
[10085]Zonn, Paul (cl); Zonn, Wilma (ob); University of Illinois Contemporary Chamber Players (members of)
- Ubres CS-301; 33s; rel 1976; cip

ZUCKERMAN, Mark (1948-)
Paraphrases (1971)
[10086]Winn, James (fl)
Rec 9/11/73
- CRI-342; 33s; rel 1975; cip

ZUPKO, Ramon (1932-)
Fixations (1974)
[10087]Elan, Nancy (vln); Bogatin, Barbara (vcl); Thomas, Andrew (pf); tape; Sollberger, Harvey (cond)
Rec 3/77
- CRI-375; 33s; rel 1978; cip

Fluxus I (1977)
[10088]Electronic music
- CRI-375; 33s; rel 1978; cip

Fluxus II (1978)
[10089]Stokman, Abraham (pf)
- CRI-425; 33s; rel 1980

Masques (1973)
[10090]Rappeport, Phyllis (pf); Western Brass Quintet
- CRI-425; 33s; rel 1980

Nocturnes (1977)
[10091]Stokman, Abraham (pf); Stokman, Arlene (pf)
- CRI-425; 33s; rel 1980

ZUR, Menachem (1942-)
Chants (1974)
[10092]Electronic music
- Odyssey Y-34139; 33s; rel 1976; cip

INDEXES

Index to Performing Groups

Index to Performing Groups

6650, 7111, 7122, 7184,
7858, 8027, 8443, 8864,
8881, 8937, 8954, 9228,
9241, 9312-13, 9316,
9318, 9321, 9551, 9643,
9938, 9999
**Rozhdestvensky
Orchestra** ... 5521
RTE String Quartet ...
5781
**Russ Case and his
Chorus** ... 4842
**Russ Case and his
Orchestra** ... 4842,
7585
**Saidenberg Chamber
Orchestra** ... 4292
**Saidenberg Chamber
Players** ... 6020
**Saidenberg Symphony
Orchestra** ... 310
**Sam Houston State
University Concert Band**
... 8914
**Sam Houston State
University Symphonic
Band and Wind
Ensemble** ... 9359,
9363-64, 9366-68
San Antonio Symphony ..
... 2236
**San Antonio Symphony
Mastersingers** ... 2239,
9086
San Diego Music Chorale
... 9635
**San Diego Symphony
Orchestra** ... 9635
Sandpiper Chorus ...
9761
**San Francisco Chamber
Ensemble** ... 4379
**San Francisco
Conservatory New
Music Ensemble** ...
1429, 6800, 8085
**San Francisco
Contemporary Music
Players** ... 2832, 8087
**San Francisco Schola
Cantorum** ... 233
**San Francisco State
College A Cappella
Choir** ... 7012, 8131,
9595
**San Francisco Symphony
Orchestra** ... 787, 2491,
3532, 4082, 4437, 5244,
5843, 8110-11
**San Jose State College A
Cappella Chamber
Chorus** ... 2019
**San Jose State College A
Cappella Choir** ... 9115
**Santa Cruz Chamber
Symphony** ... 1911
Santa Fe Opera ... 9181
Sauter-Finegan Orchestra
... 3578
Savoy Hotel Orpheans ...
3619
Schoenfeld Trio ... 4373
Schola Cantorum ... 1414
Schuetz Choir of London .
... 5284

Schulman Quartet ...
3295
**Scripps Gamelan of the
University of California** .
... 3107
Seattle Chamber Singers .
... 383, 680, 1712,
2062, 2067, 3641, 3671,
5502, 7241
Seattle Quartet ... 9513
**Seattle Symphony
Orchestra** ... 1055,
4154, 8949
Sequoia Quartet ... 8165
Serenus Quartet ... 7627
Sevan Philharmonic ...
5114
Severance String Quartet
... 2805
**Shanghai Municipal
Orchestra** ... 193, 195
Shepherd Quartet ...
1895-96
Shuman Brass Choir ...
8800
Sidney Bechet Quintet ...
3736
Siegel-Schwall Band ...
8110
Silvermine String Quartet
... 2977
**Singing City Choir of
Philadelphia** ... 1190,
6381, 9087, 9116, 9685
Sinnhoffer Quartet ...
6348-49
**Slovak Philharmonic
Orchestra** ... 3533,
3804
**Smith College Chamber
Singers** ... 6307, 6309
Solisti di Zagreb, I ...
301, 1606
**Sonic Arts Symphonic
Percussion Consortium** .
... 1818-21
**Sonic Boom Percussion
Ensemble** ... 1817,
1822, 4542, 5728
**Soni Ventorum Wind
Quintet** ... 4016, 4044,
6816, 7376
**Southern Baptist
Theological Seminary
Choir** ... 373, 3358,
4697
**Southern Illinois String
Quartet** ... 223
South High Girls Chorus .
... 7805
**South Hills High School
Chorus** ... 6321, 7276
**Southwestern State
University (Weatherford,
OK) Wind Symphony** ...
8673-78
Speculum Musicae ...
1542, 2388, 4595, 4779,
6230, 6559, 7296, 8082,
8126, 9934, 9950, 9953
**Speculum Musicae String
Quartet** ... 7650
**Springfield Symphony
Orchestra** ... 3423,
8235, 8783, 8826, 8913,
9226

St. Louis Quartet ...
2509, 7743
**St. Louis Symphony
Orchestra** ... 749, 841,
2125, 3531, 3549, 3572,
3591, 3601, 3609, 3837,
3887
St. Olaf Choir ... 653,
663
**St. Paul Chamber
Orchestra** ... 1093,
1097, 1933, 3146, 4469,
4615, 4943, 5397, 7651,
8905, 9224
Stanford University Choir
... 9088
**Stanford University
Chorus** ... 9094, 9185
**Stanley Quartet of the
University of Michigan** ..
... 3203-04, 7452
Stanyan Strings ... 6459
**State University of New
York at Potsdam
Orchestra** ... 2624
Steinerius Duo ... 4045,
4047
**Steve Reich and his
Ensemble** ... 7617,
7620-22
**Stewart-Williams
Company** ... 3633
**Stockholm Radio
Symphony Orchestra** ...
5206
**Stockholm Symphony
Orchestra** ... 443
Stradivari Quartet ...
378, 4899, 4905
**String Orchestra of New
York** ... 7202
**Stuttgart Chamber
Orchestra** ... 302, 7615
Stuttgart Philharmonia ...
3051-52, 5969, 6944
Stuttgart Radio Orchestra
... 9576
Stuyvesant Sinfonietta ...
8553
Stuyvesant String Quartet
... 999, 1004
**Susquehanna University
Symphonic Band** ...
2030
**Sydney Civic Symphony
Strings** ... 4202
Symphonie de Madrid ...
6455
Symphony Artists Band ..
... 8801
Symphony of the Air ...
343, 361, 391, 393, 433,
770, 893, 1021, 1965,
3845, 4602, 6673, 9190,
9202
**Symphony of the Air
Pops Orchestra** ...
3541, 3581, 3697, 3855
Symphony String Quartet
... 8818
**Syracuse Music Festival
Chorus** ... 4958
**Syracuse Symphony
Orchestra** ... 1272
**Syracuse University Glee
Club** ... 7114

**Tanglewood Festival
Chorus** ... 1545, 2018,
2809, 5406, 5408, 5410,
5494, 8446
**Teatro La Fenice
Orchestra** ... 5710
**Teatro Verdi di Trieste
Orchestra** ... 6684
**Temple Bnai Jeshurun
(New York) Chorus** ...
2978
**Temple on the Heights
(Cleveland) Choir** ...
2978
**Temple University
Concert Choir** ... 5866
Temple University Trio ...
7243, 7410, 7710
**Tennessee Tech Chamber
Orchestra** ... 9357
**Tennessee Tech
Symphonic Band** ...
9360, 9365
**Tennessee Tech
Symphonic Wind
Ensemble** ... 3010-11,
3015, 3017-21
**Tennessee Tech Tuba
Ensemble** ... 482, 541,
5231, 7970, 8938
Texas Boys Choir ...
2007, 8679-81
Texas Tech Concert Band
... 724, 2400
Thames Chamber Choir ..
... 4891
Tidewater Brass Quintet .
... 95, 3135, 5178,
9358, 9755, 9778-81
Tipton Trio ... 7945
Tokyo String Ensemble ..
... 303
Tommy Dorsey Orchestra
... 2574
Topsy Turvy Moon ...
6750
**Toronto Symphony
Orchestra** ... 2967
Trio a Cordes de Paris ...
2111
Trio della Casa Serena ...
7738
Trio Pro Viva ... 2481,
4963, 5748, 6799, 9239
**Tristan Fry Percussion
Ensemble** ... 5012,
5069, 8382
Turin Radio Orchestra ...
6685
TVR Symphony Orchestra
... 3598, 3818, 3884
**U.S. Air Force Academy
Band** ... 4626
U.S. Air Force Band ...
4058
U.S. Army Band ... 3152
U.S. Marine Band ... 316,
3087, 4025
**U.S. Military Academy
Band** ... 317, 4671,
8885
**U.S. Military Academy
Chapel Choir** ... 9104,
9143
**U.S. Military Academy
Glee Club** ... 4603,

6527, 7591, 9142
UCLA Brass Ensemble ...
4623, 4632, 4665
UCLA Bruin Band ... 608
UCLA Chamber Ensemble
... 173, 495
UCLA Wind Ensemble ...
4625, 4670, 6107
**United States
International Orchestra** .
... 2244, 6033-34
University Circle Singers .
... 2996
University-Civic Chorale ..
... 9467, 9490
**University of Arizona
Symphony** ... 6863
**University of British
Columbia Chamber
Singers** ... 1764
**University of Buffalo
Percussion Ensemble** ...
3354
**University of California
Chamber Singers
Associated Students** ...
7465
**University of Chicago
Contemporary Chamber
Players** ... 5856, 7176,
7552, 8206, 8412, 8467-
70, 8474, 9232, 9663,
9697, 9986
**University of Connecticut
Concert Choir** ... 6308
**University of Georgia
Instrumentalists** ...
3462-63, 3466, 3468-69,
3471, 3473, 3478, 3482,
3488-89, 3491-93
**University of Georgia
String Quartet** ... 3483,
3494
**University of Georgia
Vocalists** ... 3459, 3462-
63, 3466, 3468-69, 3471,
3478, 3482, 3488, 3491
University of Illinois Choir
... 7281
**University of Illinois
Composition String
Quartet** ... 4931-32
**University of Illinois
Concert Choir** ... 6312
**University of Illinois
Contemporary Chamber
Ensemble** ... 6310
**University of Illinois
Contemporary Chamber
Players** ... 3393, 3430,
4931, 5635, 6311, 6314,
10084-85
**University of Illinois
Ensemble** ... 7145-46,
7151
**University of Illinois
Faculty Brass Quintet** ...
7486
**University of Illinois
Percussion Ensemble** ...
1857, 1865, 4942, 5633,
5736, 5924, 6448, 6450,
9487
**University of Illinois
Symphonic Band** ...
4163, 4173, 4186, 4190,

Index to Performing Groups

World Symphony
  Orchestra . . . 2000,
  6158
World Youth Symphony
  Orchestra . . . 5103
WQXR Strings . . . 4010
Yaddo Chamber
  Orchestra . . . 2408,
  3197, 6911, 9410
Yaddo Orchestra . . .
  1213, 2406, 2419, 2675,
  2758, 2775-76, 2878,
  3033, 3212, 3329, 3461,
  6213, 6412, 7436
Yaddo String Quartet . . .
  620, 1091, 3202, 6404,
  7455, 9682
Yaddo Woodwind Quartet
  . . . 8747
Yaddo Woodwind Quintet
  . . . 478, 5573
Yale Divinity School Choir
  . . . 8809, 9153
Yale Quartet . . . 7453
Yale Theater Orchestra . .
  . . . 5289, 5294, 5304,
  5317, 5322, 5333, 5369-
  70, 5382, 5391, 5400,
  5418, 5435, 5485
Yale University Band . . .
  1988, 2401, 2641, 7440,
  8261
Yale Woodwind Quartet . .
  . . . 2770
Yale Woodwind Quintet . .
  . . . 5893
Yannatos Ensemble . . .
  9984
Yonsei University Chorus
  . . . 9534
York Wind Quintet . . .
  1082
Zurich Baroque Strings . .
  . . . 304
Zurich Radio Orchestra . .
  . . . 494, 962, 1550,
  3925, 6726, 7343, 8355
Zurich String Quartet . . .
  9276

Index to Conductors

Index to Conductors

Index to Conductors

Index to Vocalists and Narrators

Index to Vocalists and Narrators

Index to Vocalists and Narrators

Index to Instrumentalists

Bennett, Harold (fl) ... 5083

Bennett, Robert Russell (pf) ... 580

Bennett, Sabrina (fl) ... 9841

Benno, Norman (ob) ... 8915

Benoist, Andre (pf) ... 4638, 8774-75

Benoit, Regis (pf) ... 1488, 1515, 3307, 4275, 4302, 4309, 9372, 9374-75

Benton, T. P. (fl) ... 7818-19

Benton, Tom (harmonica) ... 7818-19

Benvenuti, Joseph (pf) ... 3048

Benvenuti, Mario (vln) ... 1638

Berberich, Frank ... 7152

Berfield, David (pf) ... 2100, 2438, 2974

Berg, Bruce (vln) ... 6813, 6982

Berg, Christopher (pf) ... 627-33, 3074

Berger, Arthur (pf) ... 637

Berger, Karl (vib) ... 8121-23, 8127

Berger, Melvin (vla) ... 8791

Berkeley, Harold (vln) ... 1042

Berkeley, Marion (pf) ... 1042

Berkofsky, Martin (pf) ... 5047

Berkowitz, Ralph (pf) ... 406, 902, 9284

Berlinski, Herman (org) 687, 689-91, 693-94, 898, 3407, 9668

Berman, Lawrence (pf) 9985

Bernard, Claire (vln) ... 320

Bernsohn, Lorin (vcl) ... 1564

Bernstein, Leonard (pf) 711-15, 774, 874, 2179, 2684, 3787

Bernstein, Seymour (pf) 43

Berres, George (vln) ... 8861, 8863, 8878

Berry, Wallace (pf) ... 792

Berthelier, M. (pf) ... 3782

Besrodni, Igor (vln) ... 908, 3770, 9329, 10068

Beths, Vera (vln) ... 113, 115

Beversdorf, Thomas (hn) ... 800

Bialkin, Maurice (vcl) ... 46, 2508, 9240

Bianca, Sondra (pf) ... 3552-53, 3596, 3738, 3788, 3882, 4461, 4510, 9288

Bichel, Kenneth (kbds) 6774

Bick, Donald (perc) ... 6845

Bielby, Jonathan (org) ... 6064, 10012

Biggs, E. Power (org) ... 445, 2206, 5527, 5657, 7326, 7377, 8762

Bigler (tpt) ... 4619

Billing, C. (pf) ... 5757

Bilson, Malcolm (pf) ... 5747, 8843

Biltcliffe, Edwin (pf) ... 238, 372, 672, 1723, 1730, 1979, 2281, 2674, 2677, 3172, 3183, 3262, 3267, 4303, 4429, 6054, 6329, 6339, 6792, 7211, 7335, 7876, 7948, 9219, 9590, 9650

Binz, G. (pf) ... 3789

Birdwell, Edward (hn) ... 4231

Biret, Idil (pf) ... 6744

Bitetti, Ernesto (gtr) ... 1592, 1594, 1604, 1636

Bitter, Marguerite (pf) ... 1325

Black, Archie (pf) ... 1642

Black, Frank (pf) ... 2540, 8785

Black, Patricia (pf) ... 2262, 5197

Black, Robert (pf) ... 8463, 8466

Black, Robert (sax) ... 2262, 5197

Blackshere, Lawrence (perc) ... 3102

Black, Stanley (pf) ... 3790

Blackwell, Virgil (cl) ... 1811, 3044, 7700

Blackwood, Easley (hpschd) ... 853

Blackwood, Easley (pf) 854, 7174

Blades, James (perc) ... 3065

Blanchot, Maurice (pf) ... 930

Blatt, Josef (pf) ... 5802

Blee, Eugene (tpt) ... 6905

Blitzstein, Marc (pf) ... 869, 871, 873, 876-77, 879, 883-84, 887-88

Bloch, Ernest (pf) ... 965

Bloch, Joseph (pf) ... 2381, 2383, 6641, 6646, 6762

Bloch, Kalman (cl) ... 9684

Bloch, Robert (vln) ... 3102

Bloom, Arthur (cl) ... 2808, 3132, 3919, 5242, 6565, 7090, 7272, 9629

Bloom, Robert (ob) ... 5622, 7453

Blustine, Allen (cl) ... 2551, 3142, 7418, 7421, 7570, 8238, 8345, 8723, 8896, 9294

Blustine, Allen (cl) (b cl) 9868

Boardman, Roger (pf) ... 3895

Bobo, Roger (tu) ... 5913, 6098, 7647, 8782, 8855, 9017, 9760, 9825

Bodenhorn, Aaron (vcl) 2771, 5761, 5962, 6410, 9547

Boehm-Kooper, Mary Louise (pf) ... 521, 531, 2689, 3304, 5242, 6581, 7090, 7848

Boehn, Ole (vln) ... 6124

Bogas, Roy (pf) ... 989, 5253, 5472

Bogatin, Barbara (vcl) ... 10087

Bogin, Abba (pf) ... 274, 8989

Bogin, Harold (pf) ... 964, 983

Bohm, Jerome (pf) ... 4305

Bolcom, William (pf) ... 42, 1094, 1096, 1098, 3659, 3739, 8618, 9154

Boldt, Frina Arschanska (pf) ... 4925

Boldt, Kenwyn (pf) ... 4926

Bolotowsky, Andrew (b fl) ... 5698

Bolotowsky, Andrew (fl) 1650, 2703

Bolter, Norman (tbn) ... 1249

Bondi, Eugene (vcl) ... 249

Bonnet, Joseph (org) ... 827

Bonny, Francis (tpt) ... 5047

Booth, Alan (pf) ... 8991

Borden, David (syn) (elec pf) ... 1104, 2803-04

Borodkin, Samuel (perc) 9732

Bossart, Eugene (pf) ... 6506, 6535

Bossert, James (org) ... 172

Bothwell (perc) ... 4619

Bouchett, Richard (org) 8732

Boukoff, Yury (pf) ... 6672

Bourdin, Roger (fl) ... 9447

Bowen, Frank (fl) (pic) 8236, 9911

Bowers (perc) ... 4619

Bowles, Paul (pf) ... 1120, 1126

Bowman, Brian (euph) ... 9, 1089, 7973

Boyar, Neal (perc) ... 5047

Boyer, Paul (fl) ... 5829

Boyes, Shibley (pf) ... 1489, 1518, 6299

Boykan, Constance (fl) 1111

Boykan, Martin (pf) ... 1109

Boynet, Emma (pf) ... 6296

Bradbury, Colin (cl) ... 9892

Brafman, Allan ... 6060

Brahn, Helene (pf) ... 979, 1071

Brandwynne, Lois (pf) ... 5250

Brant, Henry (org) ... 1163-64, 1171

Brant, Henry (perc) ... 1162

Brant, Henry (pf) ... 8081

Brant, Henry (ten instruments) ... 1166

Braunlich, Helmut (vln) 6848, 6918

Braxton, Anthony (cl) ... 8123, 8127

Braxton, Anthony (sax) (fl) or (cl) ... 1176

Brehm, Alvin (cb) ... 2817, 5436, 7272, 8248, 8281-82, 8723

Breidenthal, David (bsn) 1773

Brengola, Riccardo (vln) 1638

Brennand, Charles (vcl) 704, 706-07

Brenner, Englebert (E hn) ... 46

Bress, Hyman (vln) ... 889, 906, 909, 943, 963, 1043, 1062, 1069, 8438

Bressler, Charles (pf) ... 10045

Brevig, Per (tbn) ... 2735, 7967, 7975, 8792

Brewer, Edward (hpschd) ... 163

Brewster, Steve (cb) ... 798

Brey, Carter (vcl) ... 9380

Bricard, Nancy (pf) ... 8838

Brice, Jonathan (pf) ... 661, 1486

Brieff, Anabel (fl) ... 1564

Brill, Samuel (vcl) ... 3384

Brings, Allen (pf) ... 4800, 6798, 7425

Brink, Robert (vln) ... 504, 2338, 5022, 7318, 7320

Briscuso, Joseph (al sax) ... 6897

Britten, Benjamin (pf) ... 2055, 6487

Brittenham, Robert (org) ... 1193

Britt, Horace (vcl) ... 7682

Brodie, Paul (sax) ... 2428, 3781, 5800

Brostoff, Arnold (vln) ... 6041

Brouwer, Leo (gtr) ... 6998

Brown (pf) ... 2246, 5918, 6267, 7857, 9507

Brown (vcl) ... 5181

Brown, Alfred (vla) ... 8248, 8281-82

Brown, Eddy (vln) ... 7471, 8899

Browning, John (pf) ... 318, 394, 2474

Brown, Keith (tbn) ... 8840, 9976

Brown, Lawrence (pf) ... 882, 1883, 5623, 7810

Brown, Lucy (pf) ... 2982-83

Brown, Marion (various instruments) ... 1214

Brown, Robert (pf) ... 8241

Brubeck, Dave (pf) ... 1234-35

Bruce, Neely (hpschd) ... 1442

Bruce, Neely (pf) ... 4928

Brunell, David (pf) ... 1462, 1464, 1466

Bryan, Keith (fl) ... 791, 1267, 1897, 1983, 7389, 9426

Bryant, Allan (gtr) ... 1241-44

Bryce, Jackson (bsn) ... 7657

Brymer, Jack (cl) ... 8560

Buccheri, Elizabeth (pf) 5697

Buchla, Donald (pf) ... 7959

Budnevich, Ruth (pf) ... 777

Buffington, James (hn) 203, 8089, 8278, 8453

Bunger, L. (pf) ... 5412

Bunger, Richard (pf) ... 129, 1387, 1419, 1798, 5412, 6096, 8942, 9849

Bunke, Jerome (cl) ... 772, 1833

Bunker, Larry (perc) ... 6095, 8093

Buratto, Alan (pf) ... 2009, 8681

Burge, David (perc) ... 2459

Burge, David (pf) ... 1257, 1259, 1713, 2455, 2463, 2488, 2874, 4556, 5169, 6468, 6569, 7821, 9958

Burge, Lois Svard (pf) ... 3388, 5229

Burnett, Frances (pf) ... 403, 3271

Burnham, Edward (perc) 3348

Burns, Ralph (pf) ... 3723

Burton, Barbara (perc) 4527

Burton, Catherine (pf) ... 3908, 4255

Burton, Eldin (pf) ... 1263-65, 1269-70

Burton, John (vcl) ... 501

Glasier, Jonathan (new harmonic canon I) ... 7137

Glazer, David (cl) ... 506, 1130, 1533, 1535, 3435, 7750, 8793, 9598

Glazer, Frank (pf) ... 1011, 2215, 2630, 3743, 5330, 5346, 5357-59, 5411, 5439, 5455, 5458, 5462, 5467, 5474, 5518, 7674, 7929, 8457, 8805

Gleghorn, Arthur (fl) ... 9452

Glenn, Carroll (vln) ... 2190, 2227, 4687, 5241

Glick, Jacob (vla) ... 1163, 5557, 6763

Glickman, Loren (bsn) ... 274, 1536, 6696

Glotzbach, Robert (pf) ... 1090, 4724, 7500, 9530-33

Glover, Stephen (pf) ... 3990

Goberman, John (vcl) ... 863

Gobet, F. (pf) ... 2492

Godowsky, Leopold (pf) 3986

Goebels, Franzpeter (hpschd) ... 6956

Goehr, Walter (org) ... 6553

Gold, Arthur (pf) ... 428, 1121, 1129, 1132, 1136, 1141, 4516, 7723, 7745, 7752, 7755-56, 9218

Gold, Diane (fl) ... 539, 3296, 4983

Gold, Edward (pf) ... 818

Goldman (vln) ... 2246, 5918, 6267, 7857, 9507

Goldsand, Robert (pf) ... 3763

Goldstein, B. (vln) ... 1047

Goldstein, Malcolm (vln) 3426

Goldstein, Mark (perc) 2252

Goldstein, William (cl) ... 8237

Goliav, Yoan (cb) ... 5880, 5883

Goltzer, Albert (bsn) ... 9750

Goltzer, Albert (ob) ... 9058

Goltzer, Harold (bsn) ... 273

Golub, Elliot (vln) ... 3894

Gomberg, Harold (ob) ... 6295, 8334

Gomberg, Ralph (ob) ... 1565, 3059

Gomez, Vincente (gtr) ... 4039-40

Gonzalez, Jose Luis (gtr) ... 1660

Goodman, Benny (cl) ... 767, 1959-60, 4084

Goodman, Bernard (vln) 1274

Goodman, Lillian Rehberg (vcl) ... 964, 983

Goodman, Saul (perc) ... 3063, 5127, 6225

Goossens, Leon (ob) ... 9056-57

Goossens, Sidonie (hp) 8157

Gordon, Anita (pf) ... 7390

Gordon, Jacques (vla) ... 6296

Gordon, Jacques (vln) ... 2096, 6282, 6291-92

Gordon, Kenneth (vln) ... 5940

Gorodner, Aaron (cl) ... 4628, 5760

Gosa, Vickie Sylvester (vln) ... 249

Goslee, George (bsn) ... 4049

Gottlieb, Gordon (perc) 432, 509, 1086, 2807, 3917, 5850, 8583, 9955

Gottlieb, Linda (vln) ... 9895

Gottlieb, Victor (vcl) ... 2520, 8709, 8711

Gould, Mark (tpt) ... 2735

Gould, Morton (pf) ... 3556, 3660, 3744, 3800, 4051, 4065, 4071, 4076, 4085, 4096-98, 4125, 4128, 4151

Goupil, Auguste (perc) 4155

Gowen, Bradford (pf) ... 6, 16, 2286, 3045, 4046, 5726, 7178

Gozesky, Betty (pf) ... 6128

Graffman, Gary (pf) ... 3801, 6138

Graf, Peter-Lukas (fl) ... 9453

Graham, John (vla) ... 490, 2335, 5168, 5449

Grainger, Percy (pf) ... 2666, 4172, 4185, 4199, 4208, 4212, 4466

Granat, Endre (vln) ... 1459, 4736, 4744, 4751, 7997, 8010, 8016, 8022, 8032, 8037

Grandjany, Marcel (hp) 4219, 4221-24, 4227

Granger, Milton (pf) ... 595, 599, 2519, 2729, 2827, 4718, 5198, 5695

Gratovich, Eugene (vln) 1515, 3307

Graudan, Joanna (pf) ... 6319

Graudan, Nikolai (vcl) ... 6319

Graves, Mel (cb) ... 9370

Gray, Gary (cl) ... 2505, 6093, 6190

Gray, George (perc) ... 8875

Grayson, Richard (org) 4424

Grayson, Richard (pf) ... 4239-40, 5243, 5469, 7956, 7965, 9311

Grayson, Richard (syn) 4238, 4241, 4243

Greco, Lucille A. (vcl) ... 405

Green, Barry (cb) ... 6711, 7514, 8166

Greenberg, Lloyd (cl) ... 3926-27, 9073

Green, Edward (pf) ... 1527

Greene, Lucy (pf) ... 7074-75

Greenhoe, David (tpt) ... 5812

Greenhouse, Bernard (vcl) ... 241, 639, 1572, 4828, 5083, 6176, 9656

Green, Ray (cel) ... 4802

Green, Ray (pf) ... 4248, 4252-53

Greenslade, Hubert (pf) 5940

Gref, Ann (pf) ... 8236

Gref, Ann (vln) ... 7794

Gref, Warren (hn) ... 8236

Gregory, Liz (fl) ... 4732

Grey, Geoffrey (vln) ... 6131

Grier, Francis (pf) ... 949

Grierson, Ralph (elec org) ... 7618

Grierson, Ralph (elec pf) ... 5923

Grierson, Ralph (pf) ... 1253, 1362, 1460, 3545, 3767, 4806, 6165, 7856, 8782, 8832, 8941, 9017, 9760, 9825

Grieves, Wallace (vln) ... 1343, 1507

Griffis, Elliot (pf) ... 4364, 4366-70, 4372, 4374-76

Grignet, Patricia (E hn) 1687

Grimes, John (timp) ... 7328

Gromko, William (vla) ... 1057

Groot, Cor de (pf) ... 4099

Grossman, Arthur (bsn) 32, 1585, 3892, 4043, 7068, 7180, 7226, 8712

Gross, Robert (vln) ... 4422, 4424-25, 5186, 5243, 5469, 7956, 7965, 8439, 8998

Grosz, Edith (pf) ... 9314

Grove, Roger (pf) ... 3275, 6860

Gruber, Emanuel (vcl) ... 7853

Gruen, John (pf) ... 4427-28, 4430, 4432-34, 4436

Gruen, Rudolph (pf) ... 4327

Grumlikova, Nora (vln) 941, 1065

Gruntz, George (hpschd) ... 1203

Gualda, Sylvio (timp) ... 1549

Guarneri, Mario (tpt) ... 1523, 9894

Gueneux, Georges (fl) ... 8114

Guinaldo, Norberto (org) ... 4449-57

Gulli, Franco (vln) ... 1063

Guralnik, Robert (pf) ... 396, 5887, 5891-92, 7734, 7739

Gurt, Joseph (pf) ... 488, 3207, 5238

Gusak, Marina (pf) ... 931

Gustetto, Martha (pf) ... 7562-63, 7566

Guy, Larry (cl) ... 3141

Guzelimian, Armen (pf) 6182, 6187, 9250, 9265

Gwin, Daniel (cb) ... 8241

Gzhashvili, Gleb (pf) ... 7718

Haas, Werner (pf) ... 3557, 3605, 3802

Haendel, Ida (vln) ... 891, 915, 2146, 5941-42

Haerle, Dan (pf) ... 246

Haffner, Barbara (vcl) ... 6801

Hagen, David (pf) ... 2461

Haines, David (pf) ... 3803

Hakes, Michael (perc) ... 8166

Hala, Josef (pf) ... 3804

Hale, Alana (tpt) ... 8911

Hall, James (elec gtr) ... 3008

Hall, James (gtr) ... 4531, 8248, 8281-82

Hall, Keith (b cl) ... 8911

Halpin, Thomas (vln) ... 9880

Hambro, Leonid (pf) ... 773, 2164, 2175, 2192, 2639, 3878, 4315, 4342, 7633

Hamilton, Robert (pf) ... 6469, 6475

Hamme, A. (org) ... 3071

Hammond, Don (al fl) ... 3111

Hammond, Don (fl) ... 1199, 9799

Hampton, Bonnie (vcl) ... 3102, 7063, 7066, 8693

Hancock, Gerre (org) ... 1234, 4541, 9929

Hand, Frederic (gtr) ... 9814

Handy, D. Antoinette (fl) 2513-14, 5717, 6077, 8683

Haney, Lewis (tbn) ... 6271

Hanks, Thompson (tu) ... 9863

Hanks, Toby (tu) ... 7604, 8852

Hanson, Raymond (pf) ... 3381

Harbison, Helen (vcl) ... 4593

Harbison, Rosemary (vln) ... 9897

Harbold, Lynn (perc) ... 3348

Harding Sisters (org) (pf) ... 6247

Hardy, Gary (tpt) ... 8911

Harmon, Thomas (org) 452, 3072, 4623, 4632, 4665, 5722, 7102, 8751

Harnley, Lesley (pf) ... 2056, 6437, 9041, 9873

Harper, Claire (vln) ... 6410

Harper, Nelson (pf) ... 890, 899, 1051

Harrington, Grace (pf) ... 8397

Harris, Alan (vcl) ... 5330, 5346, 5358-59, 5439, 5518

Harris, Arthur (pf) ... 9765

Harris, Charles (org) ... 7898

Harris, Herbert (perc) ... 509

Harris, Johana (pf) ... 1012, 4620, 4626, 4629, 4633, 4637, 4643-47, 4649-50, 5727, 7383

Harrison, B. (vcl) ... 4217

Harth, Sidney (vln) ... 265, 916-17, 2961, 3087-88, 7714

Harth, Teresa (vln) ... 3087-88

Hartsuiker, Ton (pf) ... 1204

Harvey, Keith (vcl) ... 6458

Haskell, Mike (tbn) ... 8911

Haskell, MiKe (tbn) ... 8911

Hassard, Donald (pf) ... 167, 1134, 1142, 1722, 1727, 2840, 2842, 2847

Hasty, Stanley (cl) ... 5357

Hatto, Joyce (pf) ... 3805

Haubiel, Charles (pf) ... 4752, 9345

Hautzig, Walter (pf) ... 2012

Hawkins, Coleman (ten sax) ... 8259

Hawk, Marcellene (pf) ... 9734

Hayami, Kazuko (pf) ... 5988-89, 9557

Hayashi, Hidemitsu (pf) 772

Hayes, Bryant (cl) ... 1679

Hays, Doris (pf) ... 2256,

Johnson, David (perc) ... 7154

Johnson, David N. (org) ...5609-11, 5613-14, 5617-18

Johnson, Maxine (vla) ... 6112

Johnson, Roy Hamlin (pf) ...7470

Johnson, Tommy (tu) ... 8215

Johnston, Ben ...7135, 7140

Johnston, Ben (perc) ... 7138, 7138

Johnston, Betty ...7135, 7140

Jolles, Susan (hp) ... 863, 9955

Jolley, David (hn) ... 8723, 9073

Jonas, Maryla (pf) ... 9166

Jones, D. Hugh (org) ... 9102

Jones, Harold (fl) ... 6852, 8991

Jones, James (hn) ... 4230

Jones, Joyce (org) ... 822, 966, 2948

Jones, Karon (vln) ... 7565

Jones, Linda (pf) ... 9064

Jones, Norman (vcl) ... 6131

Jones, Thomas (perc) ... 7125

Joseph, Charles (vln) ... 3390, 5759

Josi, Renato (hpschd) ... 8370

Josi, Renato (pf) ... 5034, 8370

Joste, Martine (pf) ... 6743

Josten, Werner (pf) ... 5662-68, 5671, 5673-74, 5677, 5680-82

Judd, Terence (pf) ... 398

Judiyaba (vcl) ...9880

Jurriaanse, Govert (fl) ... 1204, 1210

Kagen, Sergius (pf) ... 6907

Kahn, Erich Itor (pf) ... 404, 5685-87

Kahn, Sue Ann (fl) ... 582

Kalir, Lilian (pf) ... 4909

Kalisch, Joan (vla) ... 8121-22

Kalish, Gilbert (pf) ... 221, 490, 534, 638, 644, 864, 1375, 1385, 1528, 1531, 2457, 2462, 3130, 3308, 4614, 5267, 5270, 5278, 5291, 5295, 5318, 5338, 5348, 5350-51, 5362, 5367, 5379, 5401, 5431, 5449, 5456, 5459, 5463, 5468, 5475, 5505-06, 5643, 5964, 5978, 6179, 6565, 6655, 6844,

7397, 7704, 7750, 7825, 8271, 8415, 8465, 8723

Kane, Artie (pf) ... 3545, 3767

Kane, Walter (sax) ... 84

Kann, Hans (pf) ... 3987-88, 3991, 3993, 4003

Kaplan, Leigh (pf) ... 4803-04

Kaplan, Lewis (vln) ... 3926-27, 7415, 7423

Kaplan, Melvin (E hn) ... 5050

Kaplan, Melvin (ob) ... 163, 1239, 4740, 7483, 8549

Kaplan, Phillip (fl) ... 5127

Kaplan, Sol (pf) ... 5694

Karis, Aleck (pf) ...7295

Karlas, Despy (pf) ... 3474, 3483

Karlsen, Rolf (org) ... 8737

Karman, Ivor (vln) ... 2228

Karp, Howard (pf) ... 8557, 8846

Karpienia, Joseph (gtr) ... 1650, 2703, 5698

Karpilovsky, Murray (cl) 7476

Karr, Gary (cb) ... 972, 5879, 5884, 9795, 9814-15

Kashkashian, Kim (vla) 1086

Katchen, Julius (pf) ... 3558, 3808-09, 7934

Kates, Stephen (vcl) ... 3, 3334, 6218

Katims, Milton (vla) ... 1055, 6295

Katz, Erich (rec) ... 5699-701

Katz, Martin (pf) ... 2792, 5297, 5432, 5442

Kauffungen, Eva (hp) ... 8116-17

Kaufman, Annette (pf) ... 581, 587, 2099, 2147, 4790, 6389, 8860, 8863, 8867, 8870, 8872, 8879, 8893, 9330

Kaufman, Louis (vln) ... 322, 577, 580-81, 587-88, 1049, 2098-99, 2147, 2191, 4790, 6389, 7459, ...3728, 3878, 8860-61, 8863, 8867, 8870, 8872, 8878-79, 8893, 9282, 9330

Kaufman, Pearl (pf) ... 8708-09

Kavafian, Ani (vln) ... 5482

Kavalovski, Charles (hn) 4770, 6953

Kaye, Milton (pf) ... 579, 3443, 3999, 4005, 4870, 6549, 9718, 9757, 9759, 9762-63, 9769-70, 9775-76, 9788-89, 9791, 9797, 9800, 9802, 9806-07, 9811, 9818-19, 9826

Kayser, Jan Henrik (pf) 544

Keany, Helen (hpschd) 8629

Keene, Constance I. (pf) 1752-53

Keiser, Marilyn (org) ... 9979, 9981

Kelberine, Alexander (pf) ...6420

Kellaway, Roger (elec org) ...7618

Keller, Jeffrey (tbn) ... 4229, 4232

Kell, Reginald (cl) ... 1121, 1226, 6850-51, 6855, 9053

Kempter, Dorothy (vcl) 7785, 9027

Kennedy, Joseph (vln) ... 6077

Kennedy, Nigel (vln) ... 920

Kepalaite, Aldona (pf) ... 6723

Kerekjarto, Duci de (vln) ... 3086, 3089-90

Kessler, Jerome (vcl) ... 8660

Ketchum, Janet (fl) ... 484, 3225, 9716

Ketoff, Paolo (reverberation plate) ... 2890

Ketoff, Paolo (vibrator) 2890

Keys, Karen (pf) ... 791, 1267, 1897, 1983, 6039, 7389, 9426

Kid, Russell (tpt) ... 1455, 7427

Kiecki, H. (cl) ...21

Kies, Christopher (hpschd) ...1567

Kiessling, H. (vln) ... 3810

Kilby, Muriel (pf) ... 1266

Killmer, Richard E. (ob) 6614

Kimball, Gene (electronics) ... 5935

Kim, Earl (pf) ... 5769

Kincaid, William (fl) ... 4293, 4571, 5739, 5742

King, Gibner (pf) ... 2915, 6192, 6436

Kingsley, Gershon (pf) ... 870

Kingsley, Gershon (syn) 3728, 3878

King, Terry (vcl) ... 2280, 2292, 2305, 8861, 8863, 8878

Kin, Seow Yit (pf) ... 920

Kipnis, Igor (hpschd) ... 7835

Kirchner, Leon (pf) ... 5782, 5793, 5795

Kirkbride, Jerry (cl) ... 1936

Kirkpatrick, Gary (pf) ... 31

Kirkpatrick, John (pf) ... 2360, 5282, 5308, 5320, 5349, 5365, 5381, 5383, 5386, 5388, 5392, 5394, 5402-03, 5419, 5422, 5427-28, 5430, 5440,

5444, 5497, 5504, 5549, 5554, 5556, 5619, 7092, 8061-62

Kirkpatrick, Ralph (hpschd) ... 1530, 3212, 6351, 7396

Kirsch, Florence (pf) ... 1081

Kirstein, Jeanne (pf) ... 1352, 1363, 1378, 1382, 1388-91, 1397, 1416-17, 1422

Kissling, Elizabeth (vla) 3085

Kitzinger, Fritz (pf) ... 1058

Klauss, Walter (org) ... 5299, 5409, 7417

Kling, Paul (vln) ... 852

Kling, Taka (hp) ... 4218

Klucevsek, Guy (acc) ... 3339

Knaack, Donald (perc) ... 1420

Knardahl, Eva (pf) ... 2182

Knaub, Donald (b tbn) ... 8, 8845, 9792

Kneeream, Ralph (org) 6330

Knepper, Jimmy (tbn) ... 203, 8089, 8278, 8453

Kneubuhl, John (gtr) ... 235, 4607, 5809, 7022-24, 8921

Knitzer, Jack (bsn) ... 8319

Knor, Stanislav (pf) ... 3559

Knudson, Thurston (perc) ...4155

Knuth, Penelope (vla) ... 8827

Kobayashi, Kenji (vln) ... 9883

Kobialka, Daniel (vln) ... 505, 1160, 1162, 1768, 3380, 3969, 4683, 5784, 6556, 7832, 9014

Kobialka, Jan (vcl) ... 7832

Kobialka, Machiko (tack pf) ...4683

Koch, Frederick (pf) ... 4007, 5836

Koehler, David (cb) ... 572

Koene, Francis (vln) ... 942

Koff, Howard (vcl) ... 3357

Koff, Robert (vln) ... 8455

Kogan, Leonid (vln) ... 921

Kohler, Jean (pf) ... 5826, 6377, 9378

Kohon, Harold (vln) ... 8504, 9343

Kok, Alexander (vcl) ... 8245

Kolar, Jaroslav (pf) ... 941

Kolberg, Hugo (vln) ... 7358

Kontarsky, Aloys (pf) ... 1201, 5450

Kooper, Kees (vln) ... 531, 922, 2689, 5242, 7090, 7848, 9207

Koor (perc) ...6696

Korman, Fred (ob) (E hn) ...2997

Kornacher, Thomas (vln) ...10022

Korn, Barbara (pf) ... 197, 7391

Korn, Richard (cl) ... 4049, 5761

Korte, Elizabeth (pf) ... 5865

Kosakoff, Reuven (pf) ... 2980, 2984

Kosinski, William (E hn) 6289

Kotik, Petr (fl) ... 5873-74

Kotowska, Adela (pf) ... 891

Kougell, Alexander (vcl) 1239, 1563, 4740, 5900, 5907, 7483, 7711, 7908

Koussevitzky, Serge (cb) ...5876, 5881, 5885

Kout, Trix (fl) ...4780

Koutzen, Boris (vln) ... 5889

Koutzen, George (vcl) ... 3227

Kowalsky, Jeffrey (perc) 4921

Kraber, Karl (fl) ... 1936, 3425, 3920

Kraft, William (perc) ... 5910

Krainis, Bernard (rec) ... 2788, 6716

Kramer, Jonathan (mixer) ...5935

Kramer, Selma (pf) ... 4735, 4743

Krasner, Louis (vln) ... 7395

Kraus, Philip (perc) ... 1199, 3111

Kreger, James (vcl) ... 1838

Kreiselman, Jack (cl) ... 3895, 3939

Kreisler, Fritz (vln) ... 1295, 1322, 1333, 2572-73, 5624, 5930, 6150

Kremer, Gidon (vln) ... 769

Kremer, Rudolf (org) ... 5938

Krigbaum, Charles (org) 2759, 2764-65

Kroll, William (vln) ... 2975, 7711, 9371

Kronold, Hans (vcl) ... 1112

Krosnick, Joel (amplf vcl) ...5697

Krosnick, Joel (vcl) ... 1573, 2549, 8829, 9908

Kubalek, Antonin (pf) ... 3781

Kubera, Joseph (pf) ... 4993

Index to Instrumentalists

McDonald, Lawrence (cl)
... 6300, 6303
MacDonald, Robert (org)
... 7525, 9920, 10010
McDonald, Susann (hp) ..
... 1601, 5067, 5096,
7247, 8137, 8156, 9546,
9615
McDunn, Mark (tbn) ...
6957
McFarland, Glenn (gtr) ..
... 3320-21, 3324
McGee, Gary (cl) ...
5851
McGill, Helen (ondes
martenot) ... 4539
McGinnis, Donald E. (fl)
(cl) ... 502
McGinnis, Robert (cl) ...
4996
MacGowan, William (org)
... 9543
McGuire, Harvey (E hn) .
... 6888
Machula, Tibor de (vcl) ..
... 1017
McInnes, Donald (vla) ...
668, 8292, 9355-56
MacInnes, James (pf) ...
3333, 3364
Mack, Ellen (pf) ... 4037
MacKenzie, Arthur (pf) ..
... 4991
Mack, John (ob) ... 6297
McKusik, Hal (sax) ...
203, 8089, 8278, 8453
McLean, Barton (syn) ...
6470, 6472
Maclean, Q. (pf) ... 3876
McManus, Dorothy (pf) ..
... 4039-40
McPhee, Colin (pf) ...
6487
McVey, David (org) ...
8771
Maddox, Arthur (pf) ...
10082
Madeleine, J. (pf) ...
3997
Madini-Moretti (pf) ...
7744
Magnes, Frances (vln) ...
8398, 9905
Magnetti, Ermelinda (pf) .
... 1630
Magnin, Alexandre (fl) ...
8114, 8117
Magnusson, Gisli (pf) ...
1826
Magyar, Thomas (vln) ...
924
Maier, Guy (pf) ... 4907
Mainous, Jean Harris
(kbds) ... 190
Mainous, Jean Harris (pf)
... 6376
Majeske, Daniel (vln) ...
8475, 8477, 8483, 8485-
87, 8490-91, 8493,
8496-97, 8500-01
Makarov, Abram (pf) ...
908, 3770, 9329
Makas, Anthony (pf) ...
639, 1572, 2960, 2964,
2966, 2968, 2970-71,
7388, 7625

Malan, Roy (vln) ...
10077, 10080
Malfitano, Joseph (vln) ..
... 5035
Malno, Kras (vla) ...
7370
Malone, Eileen (hp) ...
4566, 4573
Mamlock, Theodore (vln)
... 900, 1715
Mancinelli, Aldo (pf) ...
4278, 4317, 4344, 4355
Mandel, Alan (pf) ... 35,
2384, 4312, 5345, 6133,
6137, 7094, 7827, 8063,
8562-65, 8567, 8570,
8572, 8574, 8576-77,
8585-86, 8588-90, 8593,
8595, 8599, 8794, 8804,
9193
Mandel, Nancy (vln) ...
8586, 8589-90
Mangold, Marilyn (pf) ...
1912
Manley, Gordon (pf) ...
8869, 8887, 8891
Mann, Bob (gtr) ... 6977
Mannes (perc) ... 8093
Mann, Robert (vln) ...
5972
Manoogian, Vartan (vln) .
... 9589
Mansbacher, Thomas
(vcl) ... 7064
Manucci, Livio (vcl) ...
4752, 9345
Manz, Paul (org) ... 6544
Maoyani, Ruth (hp) ...
7246
Marcellus, John (b tbn) ..
... 6698
Marchand, Andreas (pf) .
... 6568
Marchetti, Walter (pf) ...
1379
Marchetti, Walter (radio)
... 1395
Marconi, Don (perc) ...
3969
Marcus, Jonathan (gtr) ..
... 3348
Mardirosian, Haig (org) ..
... 6546
Margolis, Sanford (elec
pf) ... 6302
Mariano, Joseph (fl) ...
311, 4294, 4573, 5740,
7865
Marias, Juan (gtr) ...
6455
Mariotti, Arno (ob) ...
2758, 3299
Markov, Albert (vln) ...
6549
Mark, Peter (vla) ... 126,
1900
Marks, Alan (pf) ... 8435
Marlowe, Sylvia (hpschd)
... 635, 641, 1563,
4507, 5083, 6177, 6488,
7720, 7735-37, 7751,
7908, 8458, 9194, 9211,
9656
Marquart, Vincent (tpt) ..
... 8911

Marshall, Elizabeth (pf) ..
... 264, 3229, 3233-34,
3244, 3246, 7749
Marshall, Frank (pf) ...
6550
Marsh, Douglas (vcl) ...
474
Marsh, Peter (vln) ...
206
Marson, John (hp) ...
5871
Martin, Charlotte (pf) ...
1954, 2295, 2310, 2959,
2969, 3395, 4371, 4543,
4553, 4555, 6784-85,
7340-41, 7443, 8424,
9046, 9106, 9130, 9731
Martin, James (fl) ...
1903
Martin, Jane (fl) ... 9843
Martin, Robert L. (vcl) ...
2558, 2560
Marvel, Robert (pf) ...
6575
Marvin, Frederick (pf) ...
109
Marx, Josef (ob) ...
1139, 1564, 2319, 6558,
7420
Mascellini, Guido (vcl) ...
1186
Mason, Berkeley (org) ...
6153
Mason, David (tpt) ...
9892
Mason, Marilyn (org) ...
40, 821, 978, 1881,
1991, 2378, 2434, 6271,
6277, 8408, 8411, 8730,
8738, 8745, 9221, 9921,
9930
Masselos, William (pf) ...
961, 1130, 1139, 1360-
61, 2003, 2219, 2279,
3913, 4345, 4798, 4999,
5025, 5038, 5046, 5048,
5072, 5075, 5972, 6625,
6630, 7181, 7665, 8044-
45, 8048, 8952, 8971,
9315, 9643, 9646, 9648,
9652
Mastics, Marianne
Matousek (pf) ... 8510-
11, 8513, 8517-18,
8520-21, 8525, 8527-30,
8534-36, 8539
Mastromatteo, Anamaria
(vcl) ... 1186
Masuzzo, Dennis (cb) ...
2252
Mather, Betty Bang (fl) ..
... 4898, 5597
Mather, Bruce (harm) ...
1095
Mather, Bruce (pf) ...
1095
Matsuda, Yoko (vln) ...
27, 9857
Matthews, Thomas (org) .
... 1848, 6593
Mauldin, Bonnie (cl) ...
6599
Mauldin, Michael (pf) ...
6598-99
Maund, Peter (perc) ...
3103

Maury, Lowndes (pf) ...
2195, 6601
Maximilien, Wanda (pf) ..
... 6758-59, 6761
Maximoff, Richard (vla) ..
... 531, 5242
Maxin, Jacob (pf) ...
5888, 5892, 5951, 5956,
9900
Mayer, Anne (pf) ...
7655
May, Ernest (org) ...
5076
Mayes, Samuel (vcl) ...
7406, 9721
May, Michael (pf) ...
6069
Maynard, Judson (org) ..
... 9401
Mayorga, Lincoln (pf) ...
3750, 8093
Mazzeo, Rosario (cl) ...
807
Meale, Arthur (org) ...
6148, 6155
Mear, Sidney (tpt) ...
311
Mehta, Dady (pf) ... 794-
95, 5239
Melnick, Bertha (pf) ...
273, 6802
Menasce, Jacques de
(pf) ... 6639, 6643
Menhennick, Ray (vla) ...
9282
Menuhin, Yaltah (pf) ...
114, 764, 10065
Menuhin, Yehudi (vln) ...
892, 925, 944, 1064,
1066, 2194
Merlet, Michel (hpschd) .
... 6743
Mersson, Boris (pf) ...
8113, 8119
Merz, Albert (perc) ...
6698, 6845
Metzler, Richard (asst pf)
... 5511
Michel, Catherine (hp) ...
1602
Michelin, Bernard (vcl) ..
... 276
Middleton, Peter (fl) ...
1793, 7154
Mikulak, Marcia (pf) ...
8051-53
Millard, Janet (fl) ...
5181, 7270
Miller, Ken (vcl) ... 5225
Miller, Leroy (pf) ... 990,
1036
Miller, Max (org) ...
2611, 7120
Miller, Mitchell (E hn) ...
9751
Miller, Mitchell (ob) ...
310, 1121, 7735, 9754
Miller, Robert (pf) ...
155, 217, 220
Miller, Robert (Pf) ...
643
Miller, Robert (pf) ...
1411, 2260, 2276, 2326,
2456, 2549, 2564, 3050,
3057, 3387, 3389, 4596,
5637, 6073, 6162, 7043,

7192, 7421, 8780, 9888,
9890, 9949, 9977
Miller, Robert (pf)
(hpschd) ... 8781
Miller, Todd ... 7152
Mills, Fred (tpt) ... 9213
Mills, John (gtr) ... 1633
Mills, Linda (pic) ... 8911
Milne, Hamish (pf) ...
981
Milstein, Nathan (vln) ...
926-27
Minger, Frederick (pf) ...
6892-93, 6895-98
Minor, Brian (sax) ...
8825
Miquelle, Georges (vcl) ..
... 1018, 4829
Mitchell, Danlee (new
kithara I) ... 7137
Mitchell, Evelyn (pf) ...
7345-46
Mitchell, Ian Douglas
(gtr) ... 6755
Mitchell, Marjorie (pf) ...
399, 956, 1484, 7354,
9576
Mitnik, Andrei (pf) ...
921
Mitropoulos, Dimitri (pf) .
... 6295
Mittman, Leopold (pf) ...
407, 927
Mocsany, Edith (pf) ...
2229
Moe, Lawrence (org) ...
2660, 3103, 3107
Moiseiwitsch, Benno (pf)
... 1749
Molfese, Nicholas (cb) ...
8352
Molin, Miriam (pf) ...
8386
Moll, David (vln) ...
8823-24
Molnar, Ferenc (vla) ...
5843-44
Monasevitch, Grischa
(vln) ... 9282
Monroe, Ervin (fl) ...
6771
Montague, Gramiston
(pf) ... 7576, 7580
Monteux, Claude (fl) ...
9656
Montgomery, David (pf) ...
... 228, 1477, 3286,
5533
Moore (pf) ... 2510
Moore, Arthur (tbn) ...
1210
Moore, David (vcl) ...
2561, 2657, 3139, 5970,
7254, 8238, 8240, 9236
Moore, Douglas (pf) ...
6777
Moore, Douglas (vcl) ...
3283, 3301, 3305-06,
3309
Moore, Gerald (pf) ...
915, 928, 2146, 4496,
4502, 5942, 6584, 9056-
57, 9062, 9871
Moore, Kenneth (perc) ...
... 1763, 9843

Index to Instrumentalists

4763, 5741, 7866, 9456,
9753, 9798
Pelletier, Wilfred (pf) ...
1496, 4494, 5932
Pelta, Henriette (pf) ...
6703, 6707-08
Peltzer, Dwight (pf) ...
797, 1085, 1183-84,
2500-02, 2504, 2507-08,
5906, 5908-09, 7422,
8050, 8083-84, 8086,
8088, 9234, 9240, 9624,
9741
Pence, Homer (bsn) ...
5814
Pence, Judith (ob) ...
5813-14
Pennario, Leonard (pf) ..
... 3567, 3594, 3600,
3710, 3752, 3822-23,
3858, 3885, 7164, 7997,
8016, 8021, 8032
Pennink, John (pf) ...
10000
Perantoni, Daniel (tu) ...
4477, 8557, 8846,
10083
Peress, Maurice (hpschd)
... 2238
Perkins, Barbara (vln) ...
2498
Perkins, K. (pf) ... 3824
Perle, George (pf) ...
7191
Perras, John (fl) ... 73,
3061
Perry, John (pf) ... 5861,
7398
Perry, Roy (org) ... 8620,
9837
Persantoni, Daniel (tu) ...
7489, 7491
Persichetti, Dorothea (pf)
... 7203
Persichetti, Vincent (pf) .
... 7203
Persichilli, Angelo (al fl) .
... 2916
Persichilli, Angelo (fl) ...
2916
Persichilli, Angelo (pic) ...
... 2916
Persinger, A. (pf) ... 925
Persson, Fred (pf) ...
4269
Persson, Mats (pf) ...
1403
Peschke, Werner (fl) ...
9409
Peters, Lynn (cb) ... 33,
8449
Peters, Mitchell (perc) ...
1451, 1454, 1460, 5126,
5914
Peterson, Alfred (cl) ...
4249
Peterson, Oscar (clav) ...
3721
Peterson, Wayne (pf) ...
7270
Pezzullo, Louis (tbn) ...
2498
Phelps, Ruth Barrett
(org) ... 2568, 3093,
7527

Phillips, Barre (cb) ...
7274, 8243, 8245
Phillips, Burrill (pf) ...
7287
Phillips, Edna (hp) ...
6422, 9721
Phillips, Harvey (tu) ...
251, 602-03, 4143, 4728,
4771, 7250, 7968, 9765-
68, 9804, 9807, 9810,
9819, 9824
Phillips, Karen (vla) ...
508, 1364, 3127, 3132,
3914
Phillips, Larry (org) ...
7323, 7328, 7337
Phillips, Robert (pf) ...
4176, 5854
Piatigorsky, Gregor (vcl) .
... 406, 970, 1025,
3335, 8024, 9258
Picker, Tobias (pf) ...
7294
Pick, Richard (gtr) ...
7292-93
Pierce, Joshua (pf) ...
1349, 1353, 1373, 1386,
1396, 1400, 1408, 1418
Pierce, Raylene (pf) ...
7006
Pierlot, P. (pf) ... 7279
Pietsch, K. P. (pf) ...
6355
Pignotti, Alfio (vln) ...
795, 5239
Pines, Doris (pf) ...
3985, 3989, 3992, 4004
Pinkham, Daniel (hpschd)
... 504, 5022, 7318,
7321, 7330
Pinkham, Daniel (org) ...
7331
Pinkham, Daniel (pf) ...
2338
Pino, David (cl) ... 3039,
7716
Pintavalle, John (vln) ...
2229
Piper, Jeffrey (tpt) ...
8241
Pippin, Donald ... 7135,
7140
Piston, Walter (pf) ...
7395, 7399
Pitot, Genevieve (pf) ...
5323
Pittaway, Rudolph (pf) ...
7413
Pittel, Harvey (sax) ...
2431, 4760, 5689, 7849,
8832
Pittel, Harvey (sop sax) ..
... 7856
Pizarro, David (org) ...
1849, 1851, 3105
Planes, Alain (pf) ... 250
Plank, Max (al sax) ...
5234
Plasko, George M. F. (cl)
... 5225
Pleasants, Virginia
(hpschd) ... 277, 7437
Pleshakov, Vladimir (pf) .
... 1967, 1973, 5275,
5280, 5305-06, 5309,
5331, 5339-40, 5352,

5360-61, 5384, 5389,
5405, 5416, 5424, 5426,
5507-08, 5541, 5545,
5548, 6186, 8115, 8118
Plog, Anthony (tpt) ...
1452, 1455, 5078, 5098,
6035, 7214, 7426-27,
7429, 7646, 8725-26
Plumacher, Theo (vla) ...
5450
Plummer, Stanley (vln) ..
... 2858, 6095, 6103,
6109, 6112, 6189
Podis, Eunice (pf) ...
6297
Polin, Claire (fl) ... 2362,
7432
Polisi, Joseph (bsn) ...
6597, 7015
Polivnick, Paul (vla) ...
6185
Pollack, Daniel (pf) ...
400
Pollikoff, Max (vln) ...
3008, 6333, 6354, 9002
Pollock, Robert (pf) ...
7434
Pommers, Leon (pf) ...
2973
Ponce, Walter (pf) ...
7423
Ponse, Luctor (pf) ...
8387
Pontier, Pierre (pf) ...
2429
Ponti, Michael (pf) ...
5261, 5268, 5272, 5276,
5290, 5292, 5307, 5314,
5319, 5321, 5341, 5344,
5483, 5512, 5520, 5547,
5550-51
Pope, George (fl) (pic) ..
... 8241
Poper, Roy (tpt) ... 1523
Popiel, Peter J. (tu) ...
597, 4726, 4731
Porter, Lois (vln) ... 474,
2419, 2854, 6410, 6727
Porter, Quincy (vla) ...
2771, 6410, 7460
Posta, Frantisek (cb) ...
5877
Post, Nora (ob) ... 8667,
8669
Potter, Harrison (pf) ...
1037, 4346
Potter, Louis J. (vcl) ...
7611
Potter, Martha (vln) ...
5769
Pottle, Ralph (hn) ...
3055
Poulenc, Francis (pf) ...
360
Poulet, Gerard (pf) ...
930
Powell, John (pf) ...
7469, 7471, 7473-74
Powell, Maud (vln) ...
1334, 4868
Powell, Roger (syn) (pf) .
... 7495
Power, Andrew J. (perc) .
... 8107, 8185
Pozzi, Pina (pf) ... 1049
Prado, Robert ... 6060

Prager, Nathan (tpt) ...
6271
Preble, Elinor (fl) ...
8629
Pressler, Menahem (pf) .
... 241, 958, 4323,
6176, 7671, 8797
Press, Myron (pf) ...
505, 1768, 5784
Preston, Victor (cb) ...
2498
Preucil, William (vla) ...
3981, 3984
Preves, Milton (vla) ...
979, 1071
Previn, Andre (pf) ...
339, 3568-69, 3825-26,
6227-29, 8701, 9279
Price, Erwin L. (tbn) ...
3435
Price, Herbert (tu) ...
1790
Price, Paul (perc) ...
1181, 8464
Price, Wilbur (pf) ...
6303
Priebe, Cheryl (ob) ...
1567
Priest, Anita (org) ...
3357
Priest, Glen (pf) ... 2596,
2621-22, 2632
Priest, Maxine (pf) ...
3005, 7038
Primrose, William (vla) ...
980, 1058-59, 1072,
4646, 10072
Prince, Howard (tbn) ...
1077
Prince-Joseph, Bruce
(org) ... 2949, 6972,
7508, 9638, 10016
Pritchard, Robert (pf) ...
7509-10
Prosser, Carol (org) ...
6511
Proto, Frank (cb) ...
7513, 7515-17
Provost, Richard (gtr) ...
565
Puffer, Ted (pf) ... 5655
Pulis, Gordon (tbn) ...
6271
Purswell, Patrick (fl) ...
3438, 5634, 7519
Purves, Del (pf) ... 2631,
4347
Purvis, Richard (org) ...
2955, 7520-23, 7526,
7528, 7531, 7534, 7537-
38, 7540, 7543, 7545,
7547-48, 7551
Pyle, Ralph (hn) ... 6100
Quan, Linda (vln) ... 163,
3389, 5168, 7166, 7295,
7418
Quillian, James (pf) ...
4270
Quincy, Samuel (pf) ...
414
Rabbai, Joseph (cl) ...
2238, 2547, 7877, 8792
Rabin, Michael (vln) ...
2972-73, 5945
Rabushka (vln) ... 3125,
3129

Race, William (pf) ...
5791
Radluker, Guenther (pf) .
... 8558
Ragatz, Oswald (org) ...
5599
Raimondi, Matthew (vln) .
... 155, 506, 862, 1200,
3111-12, 3114, 3125-26,
3129, 6092, 6163, 6842,
8464, 9878, 9883, 9974
Raleigh, Stuart W. (pf) ...
111, 3455, 7872, 8461
Ramey, Phillip (pf) ...
1471-72
Ramos, Manuel Lopez
(gtr) ... 1637, 1645
Rampal, Jean-Pierre (fl) .
... 8990
Ramsay, H. (org) ...
3877
Ramsbottom, Gene (cl) ..
... 1763
Ranck, John (pf) ...
4279, 4313, 6819, 9696
Randall, Darrel (E hn) ...
8236, 8241
Randall, Darrel (ob) ...
7774, 7788-89, 7794-95,
9912
Randall, Darrel (ob) (E
hn) ... 9911
Raney, Tom (perc) ...
7618, 7641
Ranger, Louis (cor) ...
1522
Ranger, Louis (tpt) ...
1521, 2735
Ransom, Anne (hp) ...
7657
Ranta, Michael ... 7131,
7143, 7152
Rantucci, Oswald (mand)
... 3348
Raph, Alan (tbn) ... 503,
766
Raphling, Sam (pf) ...
7575, 7577-79, 7581
Rapier, Leon (tpt) ...
996, 5009
Rapier, Wayne (ob) ...
7398
Rappaport, Jerome (pf) ...
... 991
Rappeport, Phyllis (pf) ...
4920, 10090
Rascher, Sigurd (sax) ...
1158, 2432, 3780, 4766,
6160
Rath, Richard (ob) ...
660, 6960
Rattay, Howard (vln) ...
1113
Raucea, Dario (pf) ...
1615
Ravenna, Giorgio (vcl) ...
1186
Raver, Leonard (org) ...
7921, 8065
Ravina, Oscar (vln) ...
7718
Rawicz, M. (pf) ... 3865
Rawsthorne, Noel (org) ...
... 2908
Rayfield, Robert (org) ...
824

Index to Instrumentalists

Scavarda, Donald (pf) ... 8190

Schaberg, Roy (hn) ... 15

Schaefer, Theodore (org) ... 8731, 8734

Schaefer, Theodore (pf) ... 5137, 5139, 5141-43, 5146, 5149, 5157-58

Schaller, L. (b cl) ... 1121

Schapiro, Maxim (pf) ... 9161

Schecter, Peggy (fl) ... 8243

Schein, Ann (pf) ... 838, 2193, 5470, 7901, 7915

Schell, Linda ... 7131, 7143, 7152

Schickele, Peter (pf) ... 8195

Schick, George (pf) ... 950

Schietroma, Robert (perc) ... 190

Schioler, Victor (pf) ... 3833

Schlatter, Eda (pf) ... 10064

Schlomovitz, Phyllis (hp) ... 2362, 7432

Schmidt, Willy (fl) ... 9409

Schmitt, Homer (vln) ... 3171

Schneider, Alexander (vln) ... 7396, 9658

Schneider, Edwin (pf) ... 1746, 2870, 5933

Schnier, Harold (vcl) ... 1599

Schoenbach, Sol (bsn) ... 1586, 3037, 7278

Schoenfeld, Alice (vln) ... 9257, 9540, 9546

Schoenfeld, Eleanore (pf) ... 9546

Schoenfeld, Eleanore (vcl) ... 9257, 9540

Schoenfield, Paul (pf) ... 1716, 8227, 8807

Schoettler, Frederic (pf) ... 7676, 7684, 7693

Schonbach, Sanford (vla) ... 4645, 5846

Schonbeck, Gunnar (cl) ... 1447

Schreiner, Alexander (org) ... 654, 1738, 1814, 2254, 2727, 4559, 4568, 5220, 6116, 6275, 6594, 7806, 8231, 8555-56, 9100, 9123, 9539

Schrock, Sheryl (fl) ... 2234

Schuldmann, Sanda (pf) ... 402, 2695

Schulkoski, Robyn (perc) ... 6598, 8236, 8241

Schulman, Harry (ob) ... 5083

Schulte, Rolf (vln) ... 2335, 5170, 7043, 7421, 9855

Schuster, Earl (ob) ... 6405

Schutt, Kenneth (fl) ... 8105

Schuyler, D. (pf) ... 3582, 3765

Schwartz, David (vla) ... 7482

Schwartz, Elliott (pf) ... 8345

Schwartz, Elliott (various instruments) ... 1214

Schwartz, Joseph (pf) ... 9852

Schwartz, Nathan (pf) ... 112, 116-18, 484, 1836, 2493, 2931, 7063, 7066

Schwarz, Gerard (cor) ... 8618, 9154

Schwarz, Gerard (flhn) ... 1522

Schwarz, Gerard (tpt) ... 1159, 1521, 2737-38, 4231, 4789, 5086, 6835, 8792, 9739, 9904

Schwegler, Willy (fl) ... 5450

Scime, Roger (pf) ... 3581, 3855

Scott, Janet (fl) ... 7346

Scott, Leslie (cl) ... 7345

Scribner, William (bsn) ... 6775

Sebastian, John (harmonica) ... 3543, 4463, 5034, 8370-71

Segall, Bernardo (pf) ... 7854

Segal, Peter (gtr) ... 3225, 9716

Segovia, Andres (gtr) ... 1595, 1607, 1632, 1635, 1638, 1646, 1659, 1661, 4608

Seguirini, N. (pf) ... 3834

Seidel, Toscha (vln) ... 1261, 6822

Seifert, Zbigniew (vln) ... 6797, 9299-301

Seiger, Joseph (pf) ... 911, 1714, 2947, 5676, 6712, 7193

Sektberg, Willard (pf) ... 3907, 4301

Selkina, E. (pf) ... 1047

Sellers, Michael (pf) ... 7051, 7054-55, 7057-58, 7062, 7067, 8046, 8049

Sellick, Phyllis (pf) ... 1478

Selmi, Giusseppe (vcl) ... 1186

Seltzer, Cheryl (pf) ... 5849, 5853

Semprini, A. (pf) ... 2165, 3835

Senofsky, Berl (vln) ... 4037

Senofsky, Ellen Mack (pf) ... 6218

Seplow, Kathy (vln) ... 3426

Sepsenwol, Noah (vla) ... 6711

Serbage, Midhat (vln) ... 79

Serkin, Peter (pf) ... 572

Seyfried, Karl-Hermann (fl) ... 9409

Shaffer, Elaine (fl) ... 1985

Shansky, Marjorie (al fl) ... 6847

Shansky, Marjorie (fl) ... 2499

Shapero, Harold (pf) ... 8460

Shapiro, Eudice (vln) ... 902, 2520, 4645, 4650, 4688, 5126, 5793, 5846, 6263, 8708-09, 8847, 9284

Shapiro, Harvey (vcl) ... 5889

Shapiro, Jack (vln) ... 3912

Shapiro, Susanne (hpschd) ... 3896

Sharon, Linda (vln) ... 2958

Sharp, Maurice (fl) ... 3297, 4295, 4574

Sharrow, Leonard (bsn) ... 3038, 6371, 7069, 8319, 9687

Shatzkamer, William (pf) ... 9972

Shaughnessy, Robert (gtr) ... 8504

Shaulis, Zola (pf) ... 340, 1041, 4442

Shaw, Artie (cl) ... 8552, 8554

Shearer, Grieg (fl) ... 8342

Shechter, Myriam (pf) ... 2428

Shefter, Bert (pf) ... 3836

Sheldon, Paul (cl) ... 2393

Shelhorn, Donald (pf) ... 9734

Sheridan, Frank (pf) ... 2975

Sherman, Russell (pf) ... 3113, 3123-24, 9889

Sherry, Fred (vcl) ... 531, 1566, 1669, 1776, 2689, 3914, 3919, 5242, 6365, 6540, 7418, 7421, 7848, 8719, 9857, 9936

Shields, Roger (pf) ... 97, 370, 401, 1500, 2220, 2257, 2261, 2287, 2367, 3754, 4319, 4648, 4921, 4927-28, 4930, 5454, 5477, 5480, 7371, 7691, 8063, 8420, 9165, 9210

Shifrin, David A. (cl) ... 3030

Shipps, Stephen (vln) ... 249

Shirey, Richard (pf) ... 6884-86

Shkolnik, Sheldon (pf) ... 6041

Shostac, David (fl) ... 5868

Shrader, David (perc) ... 2454

Shugerman, Ruth (pf) ... 8912

Shulman, Daniel (pf) ... 6820

Shulman, Harry (ob) ... 6696, 9642, 9656

Shuman, Davis (tbn) ... 4010, 4012, 8388

Siddell, Bill (pf) ... 1343, 1507, 7112

Sidoti, Genevieve (pf) ... 5746, 8841

Siegel, Clara (pf) ... 8824

Siegel, Corky (harmonica) ... 8111

Siegel, Corky (pf) ... 8111

Siegel, Jeffrey (pf) ... 972, 3572, 3601, 3837, 3887, 5884

Siegel, Samuel (vln) ... 245

Siegmeister, Elie (pf) ... 8584, 8594

Sifler, Paul J. (org) ... 8602-10, 8613

Sifler, Paul J. (pf) ... 8612, 8614

Sigurdson, Gary (fl) ... 3226, 3230

Siki, Bela (pf) ... 8949, 9355-56

Silberberg, Robert (fl) ... 2419

Silberstein, Jascha (vcl) ... 9437

Silfies, George (pf) ... 969, 5947

Silpigni, Constance (vla) ... 5813, 5829

Silpigni, Constance (vln) ... 5812, 5816

Silpigni, Salvatore (vcl) ... 5816, 5829

Silva, Luigi (vcl) ... 9158

Silver, Eric (pf) ... 3573, 3838

Silverman, Barry (perc) ... 5926, 7314

Silverman, Robert (pf) ... 2082, 2086, 2168, 2184

Silverman, Stanley (gtr) ... 7570, 8159, 9746

Silverstein, Joseph (vln) ... 534, 2230, 3308

Simenauer, Peter (cl) ... 9213

Simmons, Peter (bsn) ... 9022

Simms, John (pf) ... 1045, 1052, 4898, 5597, 7457

Simonetti, Gianni-Emilio (pf) ... 1372, 1379

Simonetti, Gianni-Emilio (radio) ... 1395

Simon, Louis F. (vln) ... 9866

Simonsen, Irene (fl) ... 8188

Simons, Netty (pf) ... 8624

Simpson, Loyd (pf) ... 520, 6994

Singer, Gregory (pf) ... 193

Singer, Joan (pf) ... 1956, 1980, 2005, 2013, 2051, 2083, 2087, 2169, 2173, 2185, 2221

Sinta, Donald (sax) ... 486, 596, 598, 600, 613, 2433, 2517, 4708, 4712, 4767

Siwek, Roman (tbn) ... 7127

Siwe, Thomas (perc) ... 4920, 5697

Skernick, Abraham (vla) ... 2958, 6297, 7989

Skidmore, Dorothy (fl) ... 7125

Skipworth, George (pf) ... 993, 2818-19, 8365-66

Skowronek, Felix (fl) ... 2454, 3892, 4043, 8712

Slater, Vivien (pf) ... 6813, 8512, 8514-15, 8519, 8524, 8526, 8532

Slatkin, Felix (vln) ... 5694

Sleeper, Tom (tbn) ... 9841

Slonimsky, Nicolas (pf) ... 8651-55, 8657, 8659-63

Smadja, Germaine (pf) ... 2625

Small, Hubert (fl) ... 6232, 6252-53

Smellie, Mary (pf) ... 485

Smeyers, David (cl) ... 857

Smith, Andre (tbn) ... 2806

Smith, Brooks (pf) ... 586, 918, 1053, 1619, 1622, 3735, 3772, 5944, 8551, 9053

Smith, Calvin (hn) ... 4727, 4759, 6203, 6954, 8217, 8255, 9764

Smith, Carleton Sprague (fl) ... 2360

Smith, Cyril (pf) ... 1478

Smith, Henry Charles (tbn) ... 2572, 4725

Smith, J. R. (tu) ... 5240

Smith, Jane (syn-ket) ... 2890

Smith, Jon ... 6060

Smith, Lovie (vib) ... 8911

Smith, Mark Sutton (pf) ... 1527

Smith, Martin (hn) ... 2735

Smith, Melville (org) ... 585, 7463, 8409, 8516

Smith, Norman (tpt) ... 2738

Smith, Richard B. (org) ... 8694

Smith, Robert D. (tbn) ... 8349

Smith, Rollin (org) ... 455, 1696, 1992, 3287, 3909, 5265, 5579, 5581-83, 5585, 7100, 8740,

Terrasse, Andre (pf) ... 7439

Terry, William (pf) ... 6077

Thalben-Ball, George (org) ... 1878, 2435, 9322

Thaviu, Samuel (vln) ... 4620, 7370

Therese, F. (pf) ... 3997

Thimmig (cb cl) ... 6566

Thomas, Andrew (hpschd) ... 8233, 9746

Thomas, Andrew (kbds) ... 9236

Thomas, Andrew (pf) ... 2657, 5907, 5970, 9067, 9072, 9520, 9523, 9895, 10087

Thomas, Duane (harmonic canon II) ... 7137

Thomas, Ladd (org) ... 5098

Thomas, Michael Tilson (elec org) ... 7618

Thomas, Michael Tilson (pf) ... 1362, 8080

Thomas, Milton (vla) ... 706, 1788, 2521, 6094, 6103, 6106, 8016

Thomas, Ronald (vln) ... 325

Thompson, Marcus (vla) ... 1073, 6775, 8923, 9508

Thompson, Marilyn (pf) ... 803, 10077

Thompson, Randall (pf) ... 9140

Thompson, Robert (org) ... 7338

Thomson, M. ... 3640

Thomson, Virgil (pf) ... 9156, 9196

Thorne, Francis (pf) ... 9230-31

Thrailkill, Gene (drs) ... 8346

Thumm, Francis (chromelodeon) ... 7137

Tichman, Herbert (cl) ... 777

Tieu, Teresia (hp) ... 1210

Tilbury, John (pf) ... 1410

Tillius, Carl (pf) ... 3994

Tillotson, Brooks (hn) ... 532, 2272, 9869

Timmons, Tim (al sax) ... 2518, 5196

Tinterow, Bernard (vln) ... 2771

Tipei, Sever (pf) ... 3898-99

Tipo, Maria (pf) ... 992

Tipton, Albert (fl) ... 9971

Titus, Parvin (org) ... 6451, 9603

Toch, Ernst (pf) ... 9254, 9280-81

Todd, J. D. (pf) ... 3891

Tollefson, Arthur (pf) ... 9160, 9162, 9192

Tolomeo, Michael (vla) ... 3912

Tomfohrde, Betty Ruth (pf) ... 409, 415, 422, 427, 1742, 2841, 4307, 4500, 4976

Toperczer, Peter (pf) ... 2090

Torello, Anton (cb) ... 9721

Torre, Rey de la (gtr) ... 6126, 6999

Toszeghi, Andras von (vla) ... 981

Totenberg, Roman (vln) ... 946

Toth, Andor (vcl) ... 803

Tower, Joan (pf) ... 9296, 10022

Towlen, Gary (pf) ... 2634, 3757

Traber, William (mrmb) ... 4802

Trampler, Walter (vla) ... 210, 493, 3125, 3129, 3435, 3958, 5250, 7074, 7188, 7664, 8455, 9655, 9883

Travers, Patricia (vln) ... 2642, 8414

Travis, Roy (syn) ... 9319

Treger, Charles (vln) ... 491

Trenkner, Evelinde (pf) ... 1570, 1967, 1973

Trice, Jerry (tu) ... 845

Troob, Jolie (fl) ... 1567

Trovillo, George (pf) ... 1617, 1629, 1641, 1740, 1744, 3666, 4978, 6908, 7017, 8183, 8505

Troxler, Rebecka (fl) ... 9022

Trucco, Victor (pf) ... 1448

True, Nelita (pf) ... 596, 600, 611, 2433, 2629, 4712, 4767

Tryon, Jesse (vln) ... 1263, 1270

Trythall, Richard (pf) ... 9348

Tsutsumi, Tsuyoshi (vcl) ... 1868

Tucker, Gregory (pf) ... 245, 1835, 2679, 6395, 9327, 9351-52

Tudor, David ... 1432-33, 1443

Tudor, David (bandoneon) ... 6881

Tudor, David (cartridge) ... 1354

Tudor, David (elec car) ... 1380

Tudor, David (hpschd) ... 1442

Tudor, David (org) ... 9879

Tudor, David (pf) ... 1197, 1199-200, 1202, 1357, 1384, 1427, 3111-14, 3117, 3123-24, 3126,

3132, 3780, 6160, 9877-78, 9905-07

Tung, Mimi (pf) ... 7785

Tunnell, Charles (vcl) ... 9892

Turetzky, Bertram (cb) ... 1421, 1783-84, 1794, 2497, 2714, 2985, 2991, 2995, 2997, 3000, 3009, 3026, 3108, 3438, 5631, 5634, 5683, 6220, 6306, 6558, 6833, 7040, 7046, 7183, 7291, 7416, 8237, 8623, 8627, 9006, 9014, 9370, 9735, 9852

Turetzky, Nancy (fl) ... 2714, 3000, 3009, 3108, 3438, 7046, 8623, 9014

Turetzky, Nancy (fl) (al fl) (pic) ... 2997, 7416

Turetzky, Nancy (pic) ... 6833

Turetzky, Nancy (timp) ... 3009

Turner, Jim (musical saw) ... 1258, 7171

Turner-Jones, Terry (pf) ... 4765

Tursi, Francis (vla) ... 463, 465, 5330, 5346, 5358-59, 5439, 5743, 6298

Uitti, Frances (vcl) ... 2916, 4788

Ulyate, William (b cl) ... 1599

Underwood, Dale (sax) ... 487, 2409, 4711, 4713, 4768, 6062

Underwood, Keith (fl) ... 846

Upper, Henry (pf) ... 802

Vaggione, Horatio ... 1428

Vallecillo-Gray, Irma (pf) ... 2858, 6093, 6183, 6190, 9313

Vallribera, P. (pf) ... 923

Vamos, Almita (vln) ... 6200

Vamos, Roland (vln) ... 6200

Van Appledorn, Mary Jean (pf) ... 9399-400

Van Bronkhorst, Warren (vln) ... 7286

Van Driesten, Roelof (vln) ... 1204

Van Ijzer (pf) ... 942

Van, Jeffrey (gtr) ... 164

Van Tyn, Robert (ob) ... 7657

Van Vactor, David (fl) ... 3032, 5962, 7455, 9419

Van Valkenberg, James (vla) ... 249

Van Veelen, Paul (org) ... 9431

Vardi, Emanuel (vla) ... 1867, 4079, 5121, 8389, 8391, 8397

Vardi, Emanuel (vln) ... 8390

Vardi, Pauline (pf) ... 8391

Varga, Laszlo (vcl) ... 1031, 5967, 5971, 8257

Vaughn, Ron (perc) ... 8827

Vecchi, Guido (vcl) ... 5566

Vechtomov, Sasha (vcl) ... 939

Vechtomov, Vladimir (gtr) ... 939

Veeh, Alvin (tbn) ... 8225

Velasco, E. (org) ... 6246

Verbit, Martha Anne (pf) ... 7052-53, 7060, 7065

Verdery, Benjamin (gtr) ... 6984

Veri, Frances (pf) ... 3592, 3604, 3867, 3889

Villa, Joseph (pf) ... 309

Violette, Andrew (perc) ... 9521

Violette, Andrew (pf) ... 2391, 7165, 7875, 9067, 9342, 9520, 9522-23

Vischer, Antoinette (hpschd) ... 1203, 1442

Viscuglia, Felix (cl) ... 8629

Vito, Edward (hp) ... 2599, 3722, 3874, 4228, 6580, 8145, 9524-25

Vito, J. (hp) ... 3722, 3874

Voight, John (cb) ... 9527-28

Vokolek, Pamela (hp) ... 2454

Von Kurtz, Johann (pf) ... 3843

Von Moltke, Veronica Jochum (pf) ... 4618, 7456

Votapek, Ralph (pf) ... 1643, 2240, 3888

Vronsky, Vitya (pf) ... 224-25, 1974

Vrotney, Richard (bsn) ... 532, 2272

Wackshal, Seymour (vln) ... 82

Wade, Archie (fl) ... 8915

Wadsworth, Charles (pf) ... 2065

Wagenaar, Bernard (pf) ... 9536, 9538

Wagner, Josef (pf) ... 5760

Wagner, Richard (cl) ... 5255, 5601

Wagnitz, Ralph (hn) ... 4229, 4232

Walcott, Collin (glass harmonica) ... 6769

Walcott, Collin (perc) ... 509

Waldman, Cathy (pf) ... 8164

Waldman, Yuval (vln) ... 8164

Waldoff, Stanley (pf) ... 342, 533, 2475, 3766, 3995, 4132, 10058

Walevksa, Christine (vcl) ... 1032

Walford, David (tpt) ... 4229

Walker, Frances (pf) ... 6301, 8886

Walker, George (pf) ... 9559-60, 9562-64

Wallfisch, Ernst (vla) ... 982, 1054, 1060, 1074, 6313, 7170

Wallfisch, Lory (pf) ... 982, 1060, 1074, 6313

Wallowitch, John ... 9569

Walmer, Max (pf) ... 2250-51, 7624, 7629

Walta, Jaring (vln) ... 1204, 1210

Walter, David (cb) ... 9657, 10022

Wanausek, Camille (fl) ... 4296

Wanger, Fredrik (pf) ... 8148

Wann, Lois (ob) ... 2771, 5699-701

Warburton, Thomas (pf) ... 9859

Ward, Mark (vcl) ... 9574

Ward-Steinman, David (pf) ... 9598-600

Ware, John (tpt) ... 43, 6271

Warfield, Gerald (pf) ... 9602

Warkentin, Wanda (vcl) ... 3085

Warner, Melvin (cl) ... 8707

Warner, W. Ring (cb) ... 2454

Watanabe, Miwako (vln) ... 6185

Watkins, David (hp) ... 9616

Watson, Kenneth (perc) ... 1774, 1788, 1790, 6095, 9618

Watters, Clarence (org) ... 9619

Watters, Mark (bar sax) ... 6266, 7158

Watts, Andre (pf) ... 3758, 3860

Weaver, John (org) ... 9636

Webb, Charles (fl) ... 1268

Webb, Charles (pf) ... 799-800, 3415, 4763, 9798

Webb, Frances Mitchum (pf) ... 3039

Weber, David (cl) ... 273-74

Webster, Beveridge (pf) ... 1571, 2223, 3204, 7645, 8337, 8436, 9020-21

Webster, Michael (cl) ... 6564, 7645, 9020, 9660

Weckler, Ellen (pf) ... 486

Weeks, Douglas (pf) (cel) ... 8827

Wehlan, John (vln) ... 6579

Index to Instrumentalists

Errata

(Because of computer problems, the following names did not appear in the four performer indexes.)

The Institute for Studies in American Music at Brooklyn College, City University of New York, is a division of the college's Conservatory of Music. It was established in 1971. The Institute contributes to American-music studies in several ways. It publishes a series of monographs, a periodical newsletter, and special publications of various kinds. It serves as an information center and sponsors conferences and symposia dealing with all areas of American music including art music, popular music, and the music of oral tradition. The Institute also encourages and supports research by offering fellowships to distinguished scholars and, for assistance in funded projects, to junior scholars as well. The Institute supervises the series of music editions *Recent Researches in American Music* (published by A-R Editions, Inc.). I.S.A.M. activities also include presentation of concerts and lectures at Brooklyn College, for students, faculty, and the public.

The Koussevitzky Music Foundation, Inc. was founded in 1942 by the late Dr. Serge Koussevitzky. The Foundation and its sister foundation, The Serge Koussevitzky Music Foundation in the Library of Congress, grant commissions for the composition of new music to composers of demonstrated merit. The list of works commissioned by the Foundation includes many of the major works of twentieth-century American music.

Ward